W9-DGD-008

Handbook of
CONTEMPORARY FAMILIES

Considering the Past,
Contemplating the Future

Handbook of
CONTEMPORARY FAMILIES

Considering the Past, Contemplating the Future

Edited by
Marilyn Coleman
University of Missouri, Columbia

Lawrence H. Ganong
University of Missouri, Columbia

DISCARD
PROPERTY OF WLU
SOCIAL WORK LIBRARY

SAGE Publications
International Educational and Professional Publisher
Thousand Oaks ■ London ■ New Delhi

Copyright © 2004 by Sage Publications, Inc.

All rights reserved. No part of this book may be reproduced or utilized in any form or by any means, electronic or mechanical, including photocopying, recording, or by any information storage and retrieval system, without permission in writing from the publisher.

For information:

Sage Publications, Inc.
2455 Teller Road
Thousand Oaks, California 91320
E-mail: order@sagepub.com

Sage Publications Ltd.
6, Bonhill Street
London EC2A 4PU
United Kingdom

Sage Publications India Pvt. Ltd.
B-42, Panchsheel Enclave
Post Box 4109
New Delhi 110 017 India

Printed in the United States of America

Library of Congress Cataloging-in-Publication Data

Handbook of contemporary families : considering the past, contemplating the future / editors Marilyn Coleman, Lawrence H. Ganong.
        p. cm.
Includes bibliographical references and index.
ISBN 0-7619-2713-1 (cloth)
    1. Family—United States. 2. Pluralism (Social sciences)—United States. I. Coleman, Marilyn. II. Ganong, Lawrence H.
HQ536.H3185 2004
305.85'0973—dc222

                                                2003015932

03   04   05   06   07   10   9   8   7   6   5   4   3   2   1

Acquiring Editor:	Jim Brace-Thompson
Editorial Assistant:	Karen Ehrmann
Production Editor:	Sanford Robinson
Copy Editor:	Elisabeth Magnus
Typesetter:	C&M Digitals (P) Ltd.
Indexer:	Jean Casalegno
Cover Designer:	Michelle Lee Kenny

Contents

Introduction   ix

PART I: CONSIDERING THE PAST,
CONTEMPLATING THE FUTURE   1

1. Household Diversity: The Starting Point for
    Healthy Families in the New Century   3
    JOHN SCANZONI

2. Alternate Lifestyles Today: Off the Family Studies Screen   23
    ROGER H. RUBIN

3. The Social and Cultural Construction of
    American Childhood   36
    STEVEN MINTZ

PART II: CONTEMPORARY COUPLES   55

4. Cohabitation and Family Change   57
    JUDITH A. SELTZER

5. Variations in Marriage Over Time: An Ecological/
    Exchange Perspective   79
    RONALD M. SABATELLI
    KAREN RIPOLL

6. Gay Men and Lesbians: The Family Context   96
    LAWRENCE A. KURDEK

7. Ambiguous Constructions: Development
    of a Childless or Child-Free Life Course   116
    RICHARD BULCROFT
    JAY TEACHMAN

8. Intimate Relationships in Later Life: Current Realities, Future Prospects 136

TERESA M. COONEY

KATHLEEN DUNNE

PART III: GENDER ISSUES IN CONTEMPORARY FAMILIES 153

9. Jobs, Marriage, and Parenting: Working It Out in Dual-Earner Families 155

MAUREEN PERRY-JENKINS

ELIZABETH TURNER

10. Gendered Family Relations: The More Things Change, the More They Stay the Same 174

LORI A. MCGRAW

ALEXIS J. WALKER

11. Feminist Visions for Transforming Families: Desire and Equality Then and Now 192

KATHERINE R. ALLEN

PART IV: RAISING CHILDREN IN CONTEMPORARY FAMILIES 207

12. Encountering Oppositions: A Review of Scholarship About Motherhood 209

SUSAN WALZER

13. Fathering: Paradoxes, Contradictions, and Dilemmas 224

SCOTT COLTRANE

14. Pathogenic-Conflict Families and Children: What We Know, What We Need to Know 244

W. GLENN CLINGEMPEEL

EULALEE BRAND-CLINGEMPEEL

PART V: CHANGING FAMILY STRUCTURES 263

15. Divorce in Social and Historical Context: Changing Scientific Perspectives on Children and Marital Dissolution 265

PAUL R. AMATO

16. **Single-Parent Families: Risks, Resilience, and Change** 282

MICHELE T. MARTIN

ROBERT E. EMERY

TARA S. PERIS

17. **Britain's Changing Families** 302

GRAHAM ALLAN

SHEILA HAWKER

GRAHAM CROW

18. **Stepfamilies: Changes and Challenges** 317

KAY PASLEY

BRAD S. MOOREFIELD

PART VI: RACE AND ETHNICITY IN CONTEMPORARY FAMILIES 331

19. **Continuing Research on Latino Families: El Pasado y el Futuro** 333

LINDA CITLALI HALGUNSETH

20. **Diversity in African American Families: Trends and Projections** 352

M. BELINDA TUCKER

SASKIA K. SUBRAMANIAN

ANGELA D. JAMES

21. **Asian American Families: Diverse History, Contemporary Trends, and the Future** 369

MASAKO ISHII-KUNTZ

22. **A "Seven-Generation" Approach to American Indian Families** 385

WALTER T. KAWAMOTO

TAMARA C. CHESHIRE

23. **Muslim Families in the United States** 394

BAHIRA SHERIF-TRASK

PART VII: FAMILIES IN SOCIETY 409

24. **Families and Religious Beliefs, Practices, and Communities: Linkages in a Diverse and Dynamic Cultural Context** 411

DAVID C. DOLLAHITE

LOREN D. MARKS

MICHAEL A. GOODMAN

25. Family Law for Changing Families in the New Millenium   432
   MARY ANN MASON
   MARK A. FINE
   SARAH CARNOCHAN

26. Building Enduring Family Policies
   in the 21st Century: The Past as Prologue?   451
   KAREN BOGENSCHNEIDER
   TOM CORBETT

27. The Disturbing Paradox of Poverty in American
   Families: What We Have Learned Over the Past Four Decades   469
   MARK R. RANK

PART VIII: TECHNOLOGY AND CONTEMPORARY
FAMILIES   491

28. Brave New Families: Modern Health
   Technologies and Family Creation   493
   DIANNE M. BARTELS

29. Understanding the Effects of the Internet on Family Life   506
   ROBERT HUGHES, JR.
   JASON D. HANS

PART IX: WORKING WITH CONTEMPORARY
FAMILIES   521

30. Family Therapy's Response to Family
   Diversity: Looking Back, Looking Forward   523
   LEIGH A. LESLIE
   GOLDIE MORTON

31. Contemporary Family Life Education:
   Thirty Years of Challenge and Progress   538
   DEBORAH B. GENTRY

Author Index   555

Subject Index   583

About the Editors   611

About the Contributors   613

Introduction

Whenever the calendar marks a significant change, such as a new year, a new decade, or, more notably, a new century or millennium, scholars and other social commentators take stock of the recent past. Such calendar changes also sometimes lead scholars to prognosticate about what the future is likely to bring. The new century (and new millennium) were marked early on by the shocking terrorist events of September 11, 2001. Shortly after this event, newspapers, magazines, and broadcast media were filled with speculations about how life, including family life, might change. Early news stories suggesting that people had canceled their plans to divorce and that the rate of marriage had skyrocketed because of the events of September 11 were eventually shown to be false. However, other claims continue to be made about the effects of world unrest and fears regarding terrorism on relationships and families. To know what is changing, we need to know where we have been. As we face challenges wrought by monumental events that have changed our perception of the world, there is a need for clear-eyed, scholarly examinations of what has happened to families in the past and for some data-based speculations about what is likely to happen in the future.

In this book, a multidisciplinary group of authors explore what has happened to families in roughly the last 30 years and speculate about future trends. In addition, they critique the approaches used to study relationships and families and suggest new approaches. In particular, the authors were asked to address several issues: What has happened to marriage and families? What is the current state of families? What do we know, and what do we need to know? Did family scholarship in the past help professionals and families adapt to the rapid changes that were occurring, and will current scholarship help families with the rapid changes that are occurring now? How effective are extant theories and research methods in helping us learn about and understand families in their diversity? Can we predict what family members will encounter in the next few decades? Where is family scholarship headed? Where are families headed?

This volume, in part, is a revisitation of issues examined in two earlier books that were products of annual meetings of the Groves Conference on Marriage and the Family (Macklin & Rubin, 1983; Sussman, 1972). The Groves Conference, formed in 1934, is a multidisciplinary organization of researchers, scholars, and practitioners that meets each year to discuss developments in theory and research on marriages and families. In 1971, Groves met to consider alternative lifestyles and changes that were occurring in families. From that meeting, Marvin Sussman (1972) edited *Non-Traditional Family Forms in the 1970's*. Ten years later, Groves devoted its annual meeting to contemplating what had happened in the prior decade and what had been learned. A result of that conference was a book edited by Eleanor Macklin and Roger Rubin (1983), *Contemporary Families and Alternative Lifestyles: Handbook on Research and Theory.*

In 2000, we co-chaired the Groves Conference annual meeting, where the focus again was on examining the state of American families and what is known about them. At this conference, scholars, researchers, and practitioners examined the scholarship on families that had emerged since the seminal 1971 conference. Highlights of this meeting for us were two back-to-back panel presentations, one of distinguished senior family scholars (Catherine Chilman, Margaret Feldman, Harriette McAdoo, Roger Rubin, and Marvin Sussman), and the other of doctoral students and new professionals. In the first panel, participants presented their views of how relationships and families, and methods of studying them, had changed over their careers. The young professionals speculated about how marriages and families, and family scholarship in general, would change during their careers. The information shared by the panelists influenced our thoughts regarding the framework of this book.

We had decided to revisit the earlier Groves Conference themes in part because we had observed that recent generations of graduate students and new professionals had little awareness of what had occurred in families and family study before, at best, the last decade (and that their knowledge tended to be based on whether they had read the most recent decade review issue of the *Journal of Marriage and Family*). These panel presentations confirmed our observations. For instance, the students and new professionals were amazed that alternative lifestyles such as group sex and swinging had ever been seriously investigated. They were astonished that establishments such as Plato's Retreat, the notorious Upper West Side New York City sex club (now identified by a small plaque near the door of the current business establishment) ever existed. Although they were somewhat knowledgeable about virtual sex encounters on the Internet, the young professionals and graduate students were unaware that real sex was widely available to heterosexual married and unmarried individuals interested in experimenting with multiple partners and that such relationships had been studied. Also, even though several of these young professionals described themselves as feminists, they nonetheless were surprised by the personal and professional challenges that the distinguished female scholars on the panel had faced.

As an outcome of that Groves meeting, we edited a collection of 12 articles that appeared in the *Journal of Family Issues* (September and October 2001). We thought we were done with this project, but as a result of feedback from readers of those articles, we began to consider the possibility of adding a third book to the earlier volumes of scholarly stocktaking (i.e., Macklin & Rubin, 1983; Sussman, 1972). We decided to undertake a more comprehensive update than we had been able to do in 12 journal articles, and this book is that larger review.

CHANGES IN FAMILY SCHOLARSHIP

Looking back on the earlier speculations (Macklin & Rubin, 1983; Sussman, 1972) regarding families and relationships from the safe perspective of some 20 or 30 years later, we are amused at the naiveté of some comments, amazed at the accuracy of others, bemused that some issues are still debated, and chagrined that other topics have yet to be thoroughly investigated. Rather than being set free to establish new forms of families and new ways of thinking about relationships, as many of the authors predicted in the early 1970s, the United States entered a time of neoconservatism that many would describe as reactionary and that was unanticipated by most of the Groves Conference members attending those early '70s meetings. As John Scanzoni relates in the opening chapter of this book, only Margaret Mead anticipated that the changes in families in the 1960s and early 1970s would cause an extreme backlash and negative reactions.

Changes in how individuals and family members think and live have made some language outdated and some family topics irrelevant. For example, few scholars or practitioners use the almost quaint-sounding term *alternative lifestyles* when referring to the diverse array of families and relationships in which people live. Scholars of the time would surely have been stunned had they anticipated the rapid and near-universal ending of alternative-lifestyle study (though as Rubin's chapter proposes, it was the *study* of the behaviors and not the behaviors themselves that stopped). It also is likely that scholars in 1972 would not have guessed that the term *alternative lifestyles* would segue into *family diversity* and that lifestyle choices such as group marriage, swinging, and communal living would be replaced as topics of study by other stigmatized and understudied phenomena that had long been a part of the landscape–stepfamilies, families of color, and gay/lesbian families. Topics that were treated as novel and important in 1983, such as dual-worker couples, now are considered normal in most senses of the word.

Some areas of family studies are nearly extinct, not so much because of behavior changes in families as because of the conservative direction U.S. society has taken in recent decades. For instance, although there is evidence that swinging is as popular as ever, studies of such groups have all but disappeared from mainstream journals. Other areas of study considered cutting edge 30 years ago (i.e., divorce, remarriage, and gay/lesbian marriages) continue to be popular but often become bogged down in a quagmire of controversy. The effect of the Internet on families is a rapidly evolving area of study, as are many areas of family-related health technology, and these areas also are likely to become mired in controversy. This book is an attempt to comprehensively view the major issues related to family in its many diverse forms over the previous several decades and to provide some insight into what to expect in the future. It is an attempt to both consider the past and contemplate the future.

The chapters in this book are thoughtful and scholarly examinations of previous work, and the authors have provided a basis for future study as well. Whether their anticipations about families in the near future will prove any more accurate than those of scholars in the early '70s remain to be seen. Exploring these issues, however, provides an enlightening review for mature scholars and presents a dynamic history, perhaps for the first time, to new professionals.

PLAN OF THIS BOOK

Presenting a comprehensive view of contemporary families is an onerous task. Although this book includes 31 chapters, you will immediately identify areas of omission. We tried to be comprehensive, but we wanted to choose topics that could be connected, at least in some ways, to the reviews of contemporary families from the '70s and '80s, so that readers could more easily make connections to how and why family scholarship has evolved over time.

The first part of this book contains chapters that present overviews of family scholarship. In Parts II and III, authors examine a variety of contemporary couples (cohabiting, married, gay and lesbian, childless or child-free, and later-life couples) and gender issues in families. Part IV, on raising children in contemporary families, includes chapters on mothering, fathering, and pathogenic parenting processes; it is followed by examinations of changing family structures (Part V) and race and ethnicity in families (Part VI). In Part VII, "Families in Society," we have included chapters that examine religion, law, policy, and poverty among families. The chapters in Part VIII, on technology and families, could have been included in Part VII as well, because health care technology and the Internet are certainly part of the societal context for contemporary families. Finally, Part IX includes two chapters on practice with families, one on family therapy and one on family life education.

Family scholars of 30 years ago seemed unafraid to project what the future held for families, or perhaps they were more confident in what they knew about families than we are today. Within the last 20 years, we have expanded and legitimated qualitative approaches to the study of families, new statistical tools such as Lisrel have allowed researchers to employ increasingly sophisticated designs to examine family processes, and more large nationally representative data sets (often mentioned by the authors in this book) are available. Scholars today also collaborate electronically over thousands of miles (or kilometers), and the Web allows us to broaden our research capabilities and retrieve information without leaving our homes. (The Internet may even become an important source of relationship formation, as suggested in Chapter 29.) Additionally, information has increased exponentially in many fields over the last 30 years. To use our own area of study as an example, only 11 empirical studies of stepfamilies had been conducted in the United States by as late as 1979. Twenty years later, that number had multiplied to well over 1,200. The explosion of information has been accompanied by increasingly diverse interpretations of the data. For example, ferocious controversies have erupted between divorce scholars who interpret the effects of divorce (see Hetherington & Kelly, 2002; Wallerstein & Blakeslee, 1989). It is no wonder that family scholars are more careful about speculating or taking a stand, perhaps because they are more aware of the limits of what they know and what they need to know. Or is it because they get almost instant feedback via e-mail from those who disagree with them? Media coverage can be daunting to scholars whose speculations may be out of step with the current political climate.

It is easier to understand why scholars often fail to provide much history behind what they are presenting. Journal editors are interested in reporting what is new, and journal space is scarce. However, especially for new scholars, a better grounding of current knowledge in history can be helpful. Scholars are not exempt from the influence of the culture and the times in which they live, as John Scanzoni and Paul Amato cogently point out in Chapters 1 and 15 of this book.

Finally, edited books don't come together without the assistance of a large cadre of helpers. First of all, we want to thank the authors of the provocative chapters presented here. We believe that they have individually and collectively made important contributions to the field. Another important group, the reviewers, was wonderfully cooperative when asked for nearly instant turnaround on the manuscripts. Their feedback was quick, thorough, and extremely helpful. In some cases, the reviewer's comments resulted in massive refocusing of a chapter. The authors and reviewers represent contemporary family life nearly as comprehensively as the chapters reflect. They include multiple ethnic and racial groups, gay and lesbian individuals, scholars of various religious persuasions, males and females in nearly equal number, the old and young, single, married, divorced, and remarried, and some of the graduate student coauthors might even consider themselves in the poverty category. During the development of this book, authors and reviewers experienced numerous family transitions, including serious illnesses, the death of family members, divorce, marriage, and birth. These authors and reviewers were living contemporary family lifestyles and experiencing many of the issues presented in this book even as they wrote about them. We are indebted to all of them.

REFERENCES

Hetherington, E. M., & Kelly, J. (2002). *For better or for worse: Divorce reconsidered*. New York: Norton.

Macklin, E., & Rubin, R. (1983). *Contemporary families and alternative lifestyles: Handbook on research and theory*. Beverly Hills, CA: Sage.

Sussman, M. (1982). *Non-traditional family forms in the 1970's*. Minneapolis, MN: National Council on Family Relations.

Wallerstein, J., & Blakeslee, S. (1989). *Second chances: Men, women and children after a decade of divorce—Who wins, who loses, and why*. New York: Ticknor & Fields.

Part I

CONSIDERING THE PAST, CONTEMPLATING THE FUTURE

Household Diversity
The Starting Point for Healthy Families in the New Century

JOHN SCANZONI

Despite its many virtues, the rise in the West of the individualistic, nuclear, child-oriented family that is the sole legitimate context for sexual bonding and a primary context for affective bonding is not an unmixed blessing. It is no more permanent a phenomenon than were the economic ties of property and interest that united families in the past, even if it exemplifies the rough general direction in which Western society has been moving over the last 300 years (Stone, 1979, p. 427).

Today's quest for household diversity represents an unfolding stage in the progression of Western thinking about sexuality, gender, relationships, households, marriages, children, and families. It is the current manifestation of a metamorphosis that, although accelerated in the late 1960s, had been occurring for at least two centuries. During the era after World War II, the accepted wisdom was that the isolated nuclear family style of that period was the culmination of a long journey: the end point of changes in families that had been occurring for several hundred years. Accordingly, that style was commonly regarded as the standard—the ultimate gauge against which all other forms of families were measured and, invariably, found wanting. "The normal American family" was how Parsons (1965) characterized it.

The standard family had two linked aspects: the internal structure of the household and the household's relation to its external context. In terms of internal structure, the household consisted of a heterosexual, and parenting, couple, only ever married to each other. The man's principal roles were good provider and instrumental task leader, and the woman's were good wife/mother and expressive guide. Externally, the household was structurally isolated—that is, independent from the day-to-day control and ultimate authority of its blood kin. Its autonomy was indicated by a high degree of privacy. And because its boundaries were deemed sacrosanct, happenings within the household were concealed from the prying eyes of outsiders. Nonetheless, despite the hegemony of the standard, citizens were (and are) experimenting with a variety of ways to reconfigure the internal structure of the household. By comparison, revising its external structure remains a low priority.

In this chapter, I trace the progression of internal changes over the past 40 years and examine the changes both from the vantage point of the citizens doing them and from the reactions and advocacy of professionals studying them. I suggest that notwithstanding their growing pervasiveness, the behavioral variations remain perceived (in the United States) as temporary options that are less significant than today's (neo)standard ("neo" in the sense that it is now common for wives and mothers to be engaged in paid labor). As a result, in most research on families, *diversity* does not yet convey the essential meaning that it does in the realm of plant/animal ecology, from which the label was borrowed in the first place. I argue, however, that diversity of families ought to convey that same essential meaning. To facilitate this approach to diversity, I suggest a model that modifies the household's external structure by connecting the household more closely with its neighborhood. The model seeks to combine the freedoms now characteristic of internal household patterns with linkages to a neighborhood, linkages characterized by the notion of social capital. The chapter contrasts the remarkably tenacious functionalist perspective on families with a constructionist perspective that synthesizes core insights from several approaches, notably symbolic interaction.

ALTERNATE FAMILIES

In his preface to the book arising from the first (1971) Groves Conference on "variant family forms" and "experimental marriage styles," Sussman (1972) observed that such topics were rapidly becoming the "salient investigative issue of the 1970s" (p. 3). The conference theme was a response to newly emerging behaviors that departed from the standard script in realms such as sexuality, marriage, divorce, cohabitation, and women's employment. Very few professionals (e.g., researchers, clinicians) had publicly called for changes in those and related spheres before their actual emergence. However, as citizens themselves began to depart from the script, and as the media publicized those behaviors, some professionals assumed an advocacy role and justified it on the bases of freedom and justice. Those twin themes lay, after all, at the core of both the 1960s civil rights and women's liberation movements. Hence, advocating shifts in gender relations and in families was viewed as the moral equivalent of advocating freedom and justice in racial and ethnic relations.

Given that proponents of the status quo have now overrun the high moral ground in the policy debate over families (e.g., Popenoe, 1996), it seems unimaginable that in the 1970s advocates for change once occupied that same position of moral advantage (Steiner, 1981). The eager anticipation felt by some professionals of that era is today virtually impossible to convey. They were sublimely confident that families were on the cusp of a genuinely new era, moving toward a bright future that contrasted sharply to what they viewed as a bleak past. Otto (1970a), for example, asserted that "[a]fter five hundred thousand years of human history, man is now at a point where he can create marriage and family possibilities uniquely suited to his time, place, and situation" (p. 9). Reflecting back on that era, the 1971 Groves Conference chair Catherine Chilman (1983) mused, "What adventurers we, and others like us, thought we were! So enlightened, brave, honest, sincere, possessors of a higher morality" (pp. 15–16). The grand hopes of many professionals that families of the future would be better were set against a landscape strewn with disappointments over the standard family of the post–World War II era.

Some professionals had in fact expressed their disappointments even before it became fashionable to do so. Mead's critique of the standard family appeared in an anthology aimed at forecasting a wide range of social trends stretching ahead to the year 2000. Her assessment that the postwar family was "a massive failure" (1967, p. 871) was stark indeed. Consequently, she advocated family change so that as many citizens as possible "would be free to function, for the first time in history, as individuals" (p. 872). Specifically, Mead argued that by squelching women's creative potential, the standard family deprived society of their contributions: "We are so urgently in need of every form of creative imagination to meet the challenges already before us" (p. 875). As far as she was concerned, family change resulting in greater personal freedom would lead to "better ways of drawing on feminine constructive creativity in social inventions" (p. 875). Her suggestions for changes centered on creating what anthropologists called fictive kin clusters of interdependent households "such as are formed in kinship societies [and] in large extended families" (Mead, 1967, p. 873).

As far as I can tell, Mead was alone in anticipating that changes in families would cause severe negative reactions: "Radically new styles of [family] behavior may engender counter-revolutions that may be ideological or religious in character" (p. 874). She predicted that women would be the prime targets of the counterrevolution, which would be framed in terms of the overriding need for social order. To help mute that reaction, she argued that family changes must be carried out in a "socially responsible" manner that addressed the particular vulnerabilities of women, men, and children alike.

Before Mead and close to the zenith of the standard family type, Nisbet (1953) delivered his own critique of the standard family. Whereas Mead proposed alterations in both the internal and external structure of the household, Nisbet focused chiefly on the latter. His central complaint was that the family in isolation was "too small" a structure to do everything society expected it to do: "[The] family is a major problem in our culture simply because we are attempting to make it perform psychological and symbolic functions with a structure that has become fragile and an institutional importance that is almost totally unrelated to the economic and political realities of our society" (p. 62). Like Mead, he argued that the interests of women, men, and children would be optimally achieved by experimenting with fictive kin, "groups and associations lying intermediate to the individual and the larger values and purposes of his society" (p. 73). Nisbet was as radical as any of the subsequent 1970s advocates for family change in his assertion that "[t]here is no single type of family, anymore than there is a single type of religion, that is essential to personal security and collective prosperity" (p. 70).

Nisbet and Mead were visionaries, contending that change ought to occur. But after it became clear that change was emerging, many 1970s professionals sought to account for it and to advocate its continuation. They reasoned that citizens' previous acquiescence to the norm of the standard family had obscured a flaw in that arrangement, namely that the standard family constricted the freedom of women, men, and children. "To what extent does the American family structure contribute to the optimum . . . [d]evelopment, actualization, and fulfillment of [its members'] human potential?" asked Otto (1970a, pp. 4–5), to which a chorus of professionals replied, "Not much" (Otto, 1970b). As a result, they perceived the emergence of new kinds of family behaviors as healthy and called for further "innovation, experimentation and change" (Otto, 1970a, p. 9). Sussman and Cogswell (1972) struck a similar note when they observed that "[t]he underlying theme of [articles from the first Groves Conference] is that individuals today are searching to find themselves" (p. 13).

Significantly, Sussman and Cogswell (1972) elaborated their argument by raising the issue that has since become pivotal to defenders of the status quo (e.g., Popenoe, 1996). They claimed that "[t]he focus on parental roles . . . has resulted in an unhealthy neglect of the interaction, needs, and dynamic processes of the marital dyad. Marital roles are considered secondary to parental ones. . . . The ideology of the new[ly emerging family] forms holds that adults must live for themselves and not only for their children" (pp. 7–8). Likewise, noted Olson (1972), "[I]ndividuals are seeking a relationship that will provide growth for them as individuals and as a couple. . . . There is a search for an authentic and mutually actualizing relationship [, . . .] [one in which the] growth and development of both partners is facilitated to a greater extent than it could be for either of these individuals outside the relationship" (p. 22). If there was a single complaint about the standard family around which all its critics could rally, it was that it inhibited the possibility for women and men to be mutual confidantes, capable of peering into and touching each other's innermost being. The dearth of the "soul mate" phenomenon in both middle-class (Seeley, Sim, & Loosley, 1956) and working-class (Rainwater, Coleman, & Handel, 1959) marriages of the 1950s had been empirically documented. Olson observed that the youth of his day sought to upgrade Burgess's companionate couple to include far more than mere shared leisure time activities. Youth's demand, galvanized by both the feminist and the human development movements, was that one's dyadic-love partner must also give and receive emotional intimacy.

Having matured in the nuclear family's "Golden Age," these youth were painfully aware of and deeply frustrated by perhaps its most ubiquitous characteristic: "Marriage as a relationship . . . is less often cherished than simply tolerated and endured" (Olson, 1972, p. 22). Zablocki's (1980, p. 346) respondents were merciless critics of postwar marriage patterns, making such comments as "Marriage is institutionalized neurosis"; "Marriage is a trap, an artificial commitment toward a limited life-style"; "It's an unnecessary bondage that limits people's creative, intellectual, and community growth"; and "I don't think much of my parents' marriage." These youth, as well as some mature citizens, were growing increasingly restive over the "quiet desperation" (Goode, 1963) that characterized all too many standard marriages. It is safe to say that more than anything else, the quest for mutual emotional intimacy and the linked pursuit of gender equity were the two most fundamental reasons for the varieties of family experimentation begun at that time (Marciano, 1975, p. 408).

To place those yearnings in perspective, we must discriminate between the advocates' agendas and what was in the hearts and minds of most citizens. There is little indication that the latter were self-consciously seeking to invent new ways of doing families. Instead, their manifest intent corresponded to that of 19th-century citizens divesting themselves of the ancient bonds of kin control and authority. Back then, and again in the 1960s and 1970s, most citizens sought merely the modest objective of making life better for themselves and their children, as they perceived or constructed it. Nonetheless, at both junctures in history, "few grasped the full implications" of what they were doing (Dizard & Gadlin, 1990, p. 14). Despite their limited aim, citizens were and are inadvertently constructing very different ways of doing families. Two centuries ago, people were shaping both the external and internal features of the nuclear family style that eventually came to predominate. In recent decades, growing numbers of citizens are finding that style to be as unworkable as the extended family style it replaced. And like their 19th-century counterparts, today's citizens are in a transitional period in which prevailing cultural norms reinforce yesterday's family pattern, whereas their own behavioral struggles indicate movement toward something different.

THE CLASH OF COMPETING THEORIES

By the 1970s, functionalist theory was abandoned by virtually every specialty in sociology. In studies of families, it was no longer fashionable to use functionalist jargon overtly in journals or books. Nonetheless, functionalism has never been totally expunged from studies of families. Despite the range of theories that ostensibly replaced it (Doherty, 1999; Vargus, 1999), the ghost of functionalism will not go away no matter how much we wish it to (e.g., Popenoe, 1996). Put in its simplest form, a functionalist model assumes that a society's wellspring is its culture—its beliefs, values, and norms (Kingsbury & Scanzoni, 1993). If the culture is sound, then persons, families, and society are healthy; but if the culture is not sound, then all is in jeopardy. For functionalists then and now, the standard family script is thought to be inextricable from sound culture. Hence, when the 1972 Congress passed the Equal Rights Amendment (ERA), the lawyer Phyllis Schlafly led her successful charge to defeat it, arguing that it "would take away the marvelous legal rights of a woman to be a full-time wife and mother in the house supported by her husband"

(quoted in Blumenthal, 1996, p. 32). In their analysis, Matthews and DeHart (1990) concluded that the fundamental cause for the ERA's defeat was its perceived affront to cultural norms regarding gender: "Proponents [of the ERA] were comfortable with malleable gender roles; opponents [secular and religious] felt such malleability to be threatening. Cultural patterns, the latter believed, were part of the 'givens' of life" (p. 223).

On the other side, the sorts of changes advocated by the 1960s and 1970s professionals were informed (often implicitly) by what was then called process theory, an approach that subsumed the central tenets of a variety of perspectives including (but not limited to) symbolic interaction, exchange, and conflict (Buckley, 1967). Giddens (1984) elaborated that tradition and called it *structuration theory*. Alexander (1988) developed it still further and labeled it *new action theory*. Maines (2000) and Glassner (2000) built on it as well but used the label *constructionist* in a broad sense to embrace a number of contemporary perspectives that hold several (but by no means all) assumptions in common. One is that they reject culture as the ultimate source of social patterns. Hence, they repudiate the functionalist inclination to reify patterns such as the family. Instead, they argue that families (like any other social patterns) are produced and created by the actions of persons operating within the social structure and cultural milieu that surrounds them (Maines, 2000).

The surrounding environment may motivate persons to conform willingly to its opportunities, may enable them to innovate, may force them to comply to its demands unwillingly, or may constrain them by shutting out alternative options. If it enables them to innovate, the new social patterns that persons create are themselves subject to alterations because of shifts in their surrounding context, changes in the persons' objectives, or both. The essential dynamic of a constructionist model is best illustrated by a contrast with what Selznick (1961) described as a major flaw of Parsons's functionalist approach: "In Parsons' writing there is no true embrace of the idea that structure is being continuously opened up and reconstructed by the problem-solving behavior of individuals responding to concrete situations" (p. 934).

Many theorists in the constructionist tradition wish to convey an insight that was central to the work of a number of early-20th-century sociologists, principally Simmel (Levine, Carter, & Miller, 1976): that although social patterns might seem fixed (or reified) if viewed as a snapshot, the reality is that they are continually changing at a pace ranging from barely perceptible to very rapid. Hence, one aim of social scientists is to capture that motion picture–like action. In doing so, they challenge the functionalist view that family change is determined by economic and demographic forces in the face of which individuals can do little but submit (e.g., Taubin & Mudd, 1983). To be sure, such forces represent external risks that may sometimes engulf individuals (Giddens, 1994). Nevertheless, from a constructionist perspective, individuals can and do make choices that may place them at some risk (i.e., may engage in what Giddens called manufactured risk), thus rendering the notions of choice and personal control not so meaningless after all.

Another discarded bias of functionalism is that the standard family style predominating in the 1950s represented the summit of social evolution in the same manner that "American society has reached the maximum level of industrialization" (Pitts, 1964, p. 88). Parsons (1955) used the term *differentiation* to describe the centuries-long process of extricating the nuclear unit from the extended family. Unfortunately, he could not imagine that the post–World War II family style might not be the end of the line. In no

way did he anticipate that there might be life after the standard script. For functionalists of that era, the notion of a possible transition from industrial to postindustrial societies and the notion of a possible accompanying transition from industrial to postindustrial families seemed equally preposterous.

Finally, constructionist models reject the functionalist obsession with deviance. Cuber (1970) argued that even before the ferment of the late 1960s and 1970s any new modes of organizing families were invariably designated as deviant. Innovation was unthinkable because of the prevailing functionalist view that the standard family script was immutable. Failure to conform to it could only be construed as deviance. Deviant behavior is defined as "'aberrant' (and negatively evaluated, overtly or implicitly)" (Marciano, 1975, p. 407). Hence, the behavior is perceived as substandard, inferior, distasteful, and irresponsible, even abnormal (Marciano, 1975).

Cuber (1970) noted that once a certain behavior pattern was designated as aberrant, the designator offered ways to correct or counteract such behaviors, suggesting that these were mere transgressions of the verities, not that they might herald the shape of "better things to come." Correcting behaviors reflected the dominant functionalist bias of that era. Heralding better things indicated the views of process theorists, who were then in the minority. In short, the deviance-labeling process was firmly in place before the upheavals of the 1970s. The notion that one might set about to modify existing family behaviors was met by stiff resistance in the form of deviance labeling, followed by unctuous homilies on how to maintain the status quo. Cuber added that any professional who dared to recommend ways to "replace the current marriage-family-kinship system is suspect among many of his peers . . . for his downright subversive intentions" (p. 12).

At that time, African Americans were the favored targets of deviance labeling: "Many statistical studies which compare Negroes and whites fall into the almost inevitable position of characterizing the Negro [family] as deviant" (Billingsley, 1968, p. 200). Billingsley's response to functionalist critics using that label and offering homilies was that although family patterns among blacks were indeed distinctive, it was utterly inappropriate to view them as deviant, aberrant, and irresponsible. Cazenave (1980) held that the deviance label, as applied to poor black lone mothers, was inappropriate and mean-spirited. Ironically, what few observers at the time foresaw was that many of the patterns that were then distinctive among blacks would eventually surface in white society.

Following Marciano (1975), Buunk and van Driel (1989) asserted that the word *deviant* should be banished from the literature. Their preferred label was *variant*—"a neutral term instead of 'deviant' or 'alternative'" (p. 19). They applied "variant" to any sort of household composition that differed from the standard family. Most importantly, Buunk and van Driel reasoned that the professional should construct household patterns in the same manner as the persons who were actually living them. They noted, for example, that persons living in a household different from the standard family would readily perceive their own behaviors as variant. But because the persons would not perceive the patterns as deviant, the professional should follow suit. In effect, Buunk and van Driel rejected functionalist reasoning that household behaviors should be measured according to an external standard, regardless of how the persons engaging in them might feel. Apart from Gupta and Cox (1987), and Jurich and Hastings (1983), the deviance tag nearly disappeared from literature on families in the 1980s. In its place, Buunk and van Driel's type of reasoning gradually gained a large number of adherents among professionals (Chilman, Nunnally, & Cox, 1988), and the deviance

label gradually became a politically incorrect embarrassment.

THE UNEASY EMBRACE OF ALTERNATE FAMILIES

Nonetheless, by the 1980s, professionals who had previously embraced household variety slowly became anxious and perplexed over some of its unforeseen consequences, aftereffects having to do with the management of freedom. Like many other citizens, professionals were to some degree swayed by the counterrevolution being mounted by the New Right (Scanzoni, 1989, 1991). Recall Mead's (1967) warning that if freedom was not exercised in a "socially responsible" manner, "intense efforts might be made to nullify the effect of innovations in life styles" (p. 874). Chilman (1983) reflected the uneasiness of professionals who some years earlier had vigorously endorsed experiments with families. She cited the complaints of the Right that "more and more families were involved in a series of disasters . . . [that] included rising rates of divorce and separation, nonmarital births and abortion" (p. 18). Although the Right seldom used the label *deviant*, they nonetheless successfully conveyed that the emerging phenomenon of household variety was aberrant, distasteful, and irresponsible. In effect, they shrewdly conveyed the impression of its deviance without ever making the tag itself a matter of contention.

Although Chilman (1983) by no means approved of the Right's call to resurrect the standard family, she felt that the 1970s quest for individualism, freedom, and self-fulfillment might have moved too far too fast: "Most of us need some normative . . . support. Left totally on our own, we tend to lose control" (p. 19). The Right's fundamental accusation was that feminists and advocates for alternate families had "separated liberation from obligation" (Matthews & DeHart, 1990, p. 152). Chilman responded by endorsing variety—citizens, she said, would never relinquish their "arduously achieved freedoms"—but she underscored her discomfiture by wondering whether citizens would be clever enough to reinvent responsibility in order "to turn back the dangerous forces of today's reactionary politics" (p. 24).

Inspired by Chilman, the several contributors to the Macklin and Rubin (1983) anthology (drawn from the 1981 Groves Conference on variant families) imbued their work with the sense that the citizens creating variant families sought to be socially responsible. But the contributors consistently observed even when citizens strove to behave responsibly, the larger society failed to support their efforts to create innovative patterns of commitment. A decade earlier, Cogswell and Sussman (1972) had also observed that citizens trying to effect changes in families got no social support, either tangible or intangible. Recently, Acock and Demo (1994) reported that the current situation is pretty much the same—there remains a huge chasm between citizens' innovations and supportive public policy.

To explain that chasm, one need look no further than the persistent notion that despite all the variants, the reified standard family style is still the best and that it sets forth clear ideals for which citizens should strive (Popenoe, 1996). Given these cultural ideals, there is no political support for policies or programs aimed at supporting variants (Skolnick, 1998). To the contrary, even the 1996 Welfare Reform Act (which, ironically, lent tacit government sanction to the feminist belief that a woman should be able to support herself and any children apart from a man) declared in its preamble that the married two-parent family is the "foundation of a successful society" and "an essential institution . . . which promotes the interests of children" (quoted in Clawson, 1997, p. vii).

Further, in 2002, while Congress was debating changes in the Welfare Reform Act, President Bush and his spokespersons frequently declared publicly that the law should be modified to more strongly encourage marriage (Goldstein, 2002). Those officials reasoned that the best way for a mother to avoid poverty was to be married.

Thompson and Gongla (1983) showed why the failure of public policy to support variant families is so insidious. They argued that lone parenthood was viewed as a "temporary condition. . . . The conventional wisdom is that . . . [it] will 'go away' when the single-parent (re)marries. . . . Single-parent families are [thus] not recognized as 'real' families" (p. 112). *Real* or *genuine* means the two-parent household of the standard script. Because no variant was or is perceived as genuine, policy makers are justified in ignoring the lone-parent household: They are under no compulsion to devise programs aimed explicitly at enhancing its viability. Unfortunately, the absence of intangible and tangible reinforcement has exacerbated the alleged weaknesses of lone-parent households, in turn strengthening the perception that these households are not "real" families. Currently, the United States, in contrast to, say, the Scandinavian societies, has no policy that reinforces the notion of the lone-parent household as a desirable, ongoing status. Instead, in the United States the de facto policy is that the best strategy to solve this social problem is to insist on marriage (Council on Families in America, 1995; Popenoe, 1996; Waite & Gallagher, 1999).

Reasoning from a constructionist perspective, Thompson and Gongla (1983) argued that when a "society tacitly defines a group as being outside the mainstream, members of that group will fare badly" (p. 112). Because society strongly believes that "two parents are better than one," it is virtually inevitable that lone-parent families will falter when compared with dual-parent households.

Mainstream implies that there are tributaries of lesser importance. That remains the principal distinction between the reified standard family and variant families.

A NEW STANDARD FAMILY

Ignoring the angst of Chilman and others, some professionals today reject constructionist thinking and have instead embraced functionalist models. They perceive household variety both as cause for solemn hand-wringing and as reason to intone the ancient mantra, "In many ways, 'things are not as good as they were when I was growing up'" (Popenoe, 1996, p. 254). Rather than "herald[ing variety as] the shape of better things to come" (Cuber, 1970, p. 11), their fear is that the "endless negotiation [required to maintain variety] is no way to run a family or a culture" (Popenoe, 1996, p. 247). The basic flaw in Popenoe's reasoning arises from his preoccupation with a cultural script (see Stacey, 1999, for an incisive critique of his work in general). Given that the script for the old (and reified) standard family is now ignored, his intention is to rewrite the script for a new (but just as reified) standard family. But like Parsons he mistakenly presumes that economic, political, and technological forces stand still long enough for anyone to write a family script to fit them.

Although Popenoe (1996) borrowed the metaphor of the cultural script from the conventional theater, the situation confronting us today is rather like improvisational theater: Neither the behaviors of the players nor the interventions of the patrons can be reliably predicted. Maximum enrichment of players and patrons rests on their shared skills in navigating an uncertain course. Those skills include the ability to think critically and creatively and to engage in imaginative problem solving and negotiation. Furthermore, those same skills are the sine qua non for effective and rewarding participation in all realms of postindustrial society, including the household. The increasingly dynamic nature of adult dyadic-love relationships—marriage, cohabitation (straight, gay/lesbian), and boyfriend-girlfriend—as well as of parent-child relationships requires that we analyze them using some sort of constructionist model (Cowan & Cowan, 1998). The element that Popenoe (1996) dismissed, negotiation, lies at the core of today's relationships and households (Scanzoni, 1983; Scanzoni & Godwin, 1990; Scanzoni, Polonko, Teachman, & Thompson, 1989; Scanzoni & Szinovacz, 1980).

To shore up his faith in the efficacy of a fixed cultural script, Popenoe employed the same contrivance as Parsons when justifying the rationale for his cultural givens. Parsons claimed a powerful congruence between his model of the standard family and "the psychological and biological characteristics of the human species" (Pitts, 1964, p. 57). Popenoe (1996) similarly offered a new functionalist model that he said "represents a 'best fit' with biosocial reality" (p. 248). His new standard family would retain "relatively traditional gender roles, but only at the stage of marriage when children are young" (p. 254). His cultural givens were "based on the requirements of optimal child development, [and] on the biological differences between men and women" (p. 254). He aimed to replace the prior uniformity with a different uniformity. The new standard is somewhat less onerous—but ultimately just as oppressive.

Popenoe drew quite selectively from the biological literature to support his case. He interpreted the research findings to mean, among other things, that children's well-being, as well as their later well-being in adulthood, is strongly influenced by the full-time presence of their mother, especially during their earliest years. He and other neo-functionalists appear to have been seduced by what Skolnick (1998) called the "new biologism, a growing sense that the true essence of a person is rooted in the primordial differences of gender, race, ethnicity, genes" (p. 240). Kagan (1999) coined the term *infant determinism* to highlight faulty reasoning such as Popenoe's. On the basis of Bruer's (1999) review of the literature, we may conclude that Popenoe's ideas belong to the now discredited myth of the first 3 years. In the light of new childhood development research, Popenoe's insistence on the ubiquitous presence of the mother during the child's early years is naive: "Psychological development is coming to be understood as not so much a direct outcome of early events as a complex, transactional process, involving a changing child, a changing environment, and an ongoing series of life events and transitions" (Skolnick, 1998, p. 249). Developmentalists are increasingly skeptical of the notion that early experiences govern children invariably for ill or for good throughout their entire life. Although obviously important, these are but one group of a series of complex lifelong encounters between the individual's genetic makeup, personality, and social context (Corsaro, 1997; Harris, 1998).

Popenoe (1996) sought to make a case for his new script not only on the basis of biology but also on the basis of the alleged sufferings of children growing up in family variants. But thoughtful scholars examining the same data are much more tentative regarding the implications of variants: "We really don't know whether children are worse off today than they were at mid-century, or especially 25 years ago, or just how much children's development has been compromised by changes in the family. . . . A recent [federal] publication . . . shows that in many important respects children's circumstances have been improving over the last decade or so despite the fact that the nuclear family has been in decline" (Furstenberg, 1999, p. 16).

Similarly, on the basis of their analyses of data from the National Survey of Families and Households, Acock and Demo (1994) reported that, when comparing varieties of households, they found no empirical support for the thesis that the neostandard family is "the optimal environment for marital happiness and for rearing healthy, adjusted children" (p. 231).

The ultimate defect in the strategy of using social science data to compare the neostandard family with "others" and then to conclude that the latter are falling short is glaringly apparent when we recall Thompson and Gongla's (1983) reasoning regarding the lone-parent household. Despite the growing pervasiveness of behavioral variations, there seems little doubt that most U.S. citizens still believe that the (neo) standard model is preeminent and thus more desirable than any other household arrangement (Furstenberg, 1999; Sugarman, 1998). How valid can it be to compare Households A and B to determine their relative efficacy in child rearing when their social, cultural, and political context invariably favors A? See, for instance, Waite and Gallagher's (1999) flawed attempt to prove the superiority of marriage.

Citizens grow up learning that although they should be tolerant of household variants, only one form of family is the culturally affirmed and socially supported ideal. Consider, for example, the huge sculpture of a family group (father, mother, boy, girl) "placed on a busy street corner in Philadelphia." "Because the bronze will endure," said a local art critic, it "stands as a moral statement, a celebration of the family'" (quoted in Taubin & Mudd, 1983, p. 258). However, according to Taubin and Mudd, the critic noted a "'disquieting element' in this 'conservative message'" (p. 258). The message is that there is indeed a standard family to be celebrated and that variant families are not to be praised: Uniformity, not variety, is extolled. Even the maligned

Hollywood media leave little doubt that uniformity is the approved ideal persons should eventually strive for. The fact that most citizens firmly believe that the neostandard model is more desirable, even when they fall short of it, must surely have consequences. The dissonance between their efforts at household innovation and the lack of social approval and support for their efforts is likely to rouse feelings of self-doubt, inadequacy, shame, and guilt. Their ambivalence, in turn, is bound to hamper their attempts at creative experimentation and to check their struggles for effective innovation.

DIVERSITY: THE STARTING POINT FOR HEALTHY FAMILIES

Accordingly, if our goal is to develop public policy that buttresses citizens' efforts at experimentation and innovation, we must reconstruct the meaning of household diversity, reconsider the relative social worth (status, prestige) assigned to practicing diversity, and consider the possibility that household diversity is ultimately more desirable than household uniformity. After almost five decades, the term *diversity* still draws our attention to the household's internal composition and continues to trigger the sense that compositional variety of any type (though now widely tolerated) possesses less social worth (status, prestige) than the neostandard family and is less healthy (for children, adults, and society).

On the other hand, by noting that the theme of the 1973 Groves Conference on variant families was "Letting Many Flowers Bloom," Macklin and Rubin (1983) suggested quite a different attitude toward diversity. Rather than merely tolerating it, they appeared to be following the lead of plant and animal ecologists by celebrating it. In ecology, diversity means not only that a variety of species ("many flowers") flourish,

among which none is considered to be the "best," but also that each species belongs to an ecosystem, a community of interconnected living things. Because the health of each species is inextricable from that of the others in the ecosystem, variety indicates, and cannot exist without, interdependence, or symbiosis. Each species makes its own distinctive contribution to its peers, and each must give as well as receive in order to thrive. Thus, the healthier A's peers are, the healthier A is likely to be. These exchanges, however, are seldom, if ever, simply between two species. In certain instances, Species A might contribute to B, B might benefit C, and so on, until A eventually gets its required inputs. Such complex interdependence is foundational to the health of each species. The flip side is that the health of each species is the basis for a thriving symbiosis.

Because ecologists believe that the health of an ecosystem is inseparable from the health of each species, they argue that public policy should endorse both variety and interdependence. Hence, in a similar vein, is it too outrageous to suggest that public policy for families might in certain respects adapt an ecological approach? Can we glean a useful insight from the ecologists' recognition of a vital connection between the interdependence of all distinctive living things within a system and the health of each?

Such a policy would be based on the premise that household diversity might be more desirable than household uniformity. Household diversity here would encompass the ecological concepts of both variety and interdependence. In terms of variety, policy would be guided by the assumption that it would be healthier to have households of dissimilar compositions than households uniformly patterned on the neostandard model and that society would be better off developing a culture of household variety than anxiously holding onto what some (Council on Families in America, 1995) call a marriage culture. In terms of interdependence, the assumption would be that it is healthier to develop a network of connectedness among households of varying compositions than to retain the current levels of household non-connectedness. Consequently, household health and network health would be seen as closely aligned.

This approach to diversity would require that we define both types of health and describe the characteristics of household connectedness, or interdependence. It would also be helpful to identify the distinctive contributions that households of varying compositions might be able to make to each other.

Several observers have already begun to grapple with the prickly issues involved in trying to get citizens to engage with each other outside the boundaries of their own households. Dizard and Gadlin (1990), for instance, observed that if it is credible to speak of a "crisis of the family [it] is less about the trials and tribulations of individual families, or even the form the family takes, than it is about the steadily shrinking range of social contexts that call forth our capacities to cooperate, love, and make sacrifices for one another" (p. 8).

In an anthology dedicated to developing new policies for families, Heclo (1995) remarked that middle-class citizens throughout Western societies are now asking, "Why should we care for each other? Why should I not just live as I like?" (p. 686). He concluded that the "emerging debate [about families] is not simply about a policy problem. . . . [It is instead] about a moral problem" (p. 687). The puzzle is, "What is the right thing we should want to be?" (p. 686). The answer might be forthcoming, he added, if we could somehow recreate "'[a] sense . . . [t]hat we need one another . . . [to engage in] a giving and receiving activity which is appropriate to what I am as a human being'" (p. 686).

Both sources implicitly endorse the dual aspects of diversity cited above. Both have come to terms with the reality that household variety is a social given. Not only is it here to stay, but its incidence is likely to increase, and the appropriate response is not to try to squeeze households into the neostandard form. Further, both sources indicate the need to develop some sort of symbiosis across a range of household forms so that both they and society might benefit.

Accordingly, let us assume that we are debating the guidelines for public policy aimed at cultivating household diversity. The predominant cultural message now presumes that the health of adults, children, and society flows from homogeneity—conformity to the self-contained, stably married household. But if uniformity reigned in a biological ecosystem, it would not be long before that dull sameness led to the system's decline. The social fact is that for several decades household uniformity has steadily dropped in the face of expanding household variety. The policy we are debating accepts that continuing expansion of this variety is a permanent feature of Western society. Further, it suggests that household innovations are healthy because they reflect the freedom of persons to explore who they are and to be fulfilled while also contributing to others.

Although personal freedom, growth, independence, and exploration were burning issues in the 1960s and 1970s, they have more recently come to seem quaint in the context of the counterrevolution that Mead (1967) anticipated. Nonetheless, the quest for individual freedom lies at the core of Western society, and the continuing drift toward household variety suggests that, at the behavioral level, individualism is by no means dormant.

Hence, a policy of household diversity would celebrate innovation and variety because that is a prime indicator of personal health. By no stretch of the imagination, however, does diversity begin and end with freedom and exploration. That assumption, noted Mead (1967), was one of the serious mistakes of earlier activists. The health of the household and its members is also indicated through its symbiotic connections with other households.

Consequently, let us assume that we have the task of proposing research to cast some empirical light on household diversity: what its characteristics are and how it might operate. Our broad objective is to target urban neighborhoods currently characterized by a good deal of household variety. The households range in composition from the neostandard to the several forms described throughout this book. At the same time, the neighborhood households exhibit typical levels of social nonconnectedness. Next, let us say that a more specific aim is to focus on a particular neighborhood and to identify households of varying compositions that might have an interest in cultivating a certain degree of household connectedness. Any such linkages would serve to affirm their compositional differences and to facilitate their cross-household contributions.

To achieve our specific aim, let us say that the researchers adopt an action research methodology (Greenwood & Levin, 1998; Hasell & Scanzoni, 2000). Among other things, researchers in this tradition believe that we achieve a scientific understanding of social reality more fully by attempting to change it than by merely describing it. In this instance, the strategy is to carry out a field experiment to see if a team of action researchers (friendly outsiders) and neighborhood householders (insiders) might together be able to construct a certain level of social connectedness across households of varying composition, including the neostandard.

Neostandard households in the neighborhood are attuned to the prevailing cultural message that they are at the top of the household totem pole in terms of social worth, honor, status, and prestige. Because their elevated position leads them to ask what they could gain by altering the status quo, they may feel less inclined to participate in our field experiment.

On the other hand, households whose compositions differ from the neostandard receive numerous cultural signals that they are lower down on the totem pole. Today's cultural messages tell them that to move upward in the household status hierarchy, they must take all appropriate steps to conform to the neostandard. Cohabiting couples, for example, continually receive not-so-subtle messages from kin, friends, and media that they should marry or split. Network participation, however, unlocks an innovative option. By increasing their range of choices, the network relieves the unremitting pressure to conform to the neostandard. The network celebrates differences by asserting that each type of household, just as it stands, has something worthwhile to contribute. Hence, because the network lends symbolic affirmation and social legitimation to variety, nonconforming households may feel more inclined to participate.

Although that type of social legitimation is by itself a keen incentive for nonconforming households to participate in our field experiment, both they and especially neostandard households will surely require more. Whether households participate will ultimately depend on the nature of the proposed linkages. Consequently, to clarify what such linkages might be and how they might benefit participants, it may be useful for researchers to appropriate and adapt the broad construct of social capital (Coleman, 1990).

That construct appears extremely useful for illuminating the complexity of connectedness among households of varying compositions (Scanzoni, 2000, 2001a, 2001b). We begin with the assumption that the presence of a well-functioning social capital network is both beneficial and healthy. The promise of benefits and health is a mechanism to attract households, both neostandard and nonconforming, to experiment with the network. Households will stay with the experiment as long as they believe it is fulfilling its promise but will drop out if they lose faith. Hence, a principal goal of our team of action researchers and householders will be to try to cultivate a healthy social capital network across households. Although the definition and description of such a network can be ambiguous (Edwards & Foley, 1997; Lin, Cook, & Burt, 2001; Portes, 1998), it generally incorporates the following dimensions:

- A social capital network relies on the giving of contributions and the getting of inputs among members of a group of delimited size, sometimes known as a primary group (Scanzoni & Marsiglio, 1993). Reluctance to take from the group tends to chip away at it as much as a failure to give.

- Those ongoing exchanges are not constructed as mutual (i.e., two-way between A and B). The usual idea of payback to a particular person for a favor does not play much of a role in those sorts of exchanges. Nor are the exchanges restricted to certain relationships, as, for instance, between two persons who have agreed to be sexually monogamous.

- Instead, the exchanges are constructed principally as generalized reciprocity—A to B, to C, and so on (Ekeh, 1974; Levi-Strauss, 1957). The basis of generalized reciprocity is that one contributes to one's group by giving to another member. For example, by making an input to Ed, Sharon contributes to their group through Ed. Although Ed benefits, Ed is not first and foremost in Sharon's debt. Instead, Ed is mainly indebted to their group.

- Because there is no quid pro quo accounting scheme, one can neither fully repay the group nor be certain that one has ever been fully repaid. In effect, one's giving and getting tend to be open-ended. As a result, argued Coleman (1990), the giving and getting take on the character of a moral obligation to continue one's participation in the group. Said another way, because one cannot be certain either that one owes or that one is owed, the right thing is simply to continue giving and receiving.

- More specifically, one is obliged to demonstrate via receiving and giving that one is indeed a trustworthy group member. The significance of trustworthiness underscores that the absence of a tit-for-tat schema in no way implies that one is not accountable to the group. There is hardly anything more important to a group member than being perceived as trustworthy, as someone who can be relied on to give and to receive.

- Persons demonstrating that they are trustworthy are accorded status, esteem, and prestige from their group and, as a result, gain influence within it.

- Failure to be trustworthy stigmatizes one as a free rider, and that incurs the risk of being placed, to one degree or another, outside the group's ongoing exchanges (Rivers & Scanzoni, 1997; Wilson & Pahl, 1988).

- When group members perceive that they and their peers are uniformly trustworthy, they develop a sense of solidarity, or esprit de corps. They perceive themselves as a "we-group," and this sense of "we-ness" is a prime constituent of the social glue holding a primary group together (Faris, 1957). Without reifying it, members construct their group as an entity that is perceived as lying beyond themselves and their interactions. In any case, they grasp that it is in the best interest of all members to ensure its continued solidarity.

- A major threat to the group's feeling of solidarity is a complaint by one or more members that they are being treated unfairly and that they are not receiving the group inputs they should. In response, persons with influence in the group must take steps to alleviate, either through implicit problem solving or by explicit negotiation, the members' sense of inequity.

- Both adults and children/youth participate in both the giving and the getting aspects of their network's ongoing exchanges. Coleman (1990) argued that one of the major deficiencies of today's nonconnected household style is its inability to supply a structural mechanism within which children/youth feel obliged to make contributions to persons and entities beyond themselves and their immediate household.

- The primary group's generalized reciprocity can be recognized across at least three realms.

  1. Services—child care, transportation, household chores, and so on.

  2. Intangible inputs such as providing support and encouragement in times of distress; celebrating in times of joy; or being a sounding board during periods of transitions in household composition, when problems arise with partner and/or children, or when insights are needed into educational and occupational choices. This category would also include unique intangible inputs stemming from compositional variety. Adults and children/youth from varying household forms are likely to have a great deal to share with one another about their experiences either of being different or of conforming. As a result, persons in particular kinds of households might gain insights into the difficulties as well as the gratifications of other kinds of household arrangements. Adults and children in the network would thus acquire an appreciation of why and how others live as they do and an awareness of ways to affirm and assist them in doing so.

  3. Tangible inputs, such as the borrowing of household goods, tools, and other items and the passing on of clothing items. Occasionally there might even perhaps be limited financial assistance.

The three realms of generalized reciprocity show why the term *fictive kin* could be applied to this type of primary group (Rivers & Scanzoni, 1997). Stoller's (1970) preferred label is *intimate network*.

The literature (Coleman, 1990; Putnam, 2000) suggests that a neighborhood with a social capital network of this sort will be healthier than a neighborhood without it. Social health is indicated by the presence of these interrelated components, and a social capital network marked by these components would be judged as robust. Still more broadly in terms of social health, it can be argued that households that participate in the cultivation of a social capital network are contributing to the weaving and/or repairing of the social fabric, or to the construction of what Bell (1990) called the public household. If our action research team of professionals and householders is able to cultivate social health in this manner, we may say that they have carried out a successful field experiment.

Further, our action research team will probably find that network health and the emotional health of the adults and children/youth in its households are correlated. The literature (Friedman & Lackey, 1991) suggests that psychological well-being is correlated positively with a sense of control over the circumstances of one's life. A sense of control can be viewed as a proxy for a feeling of empowerment that Giddens (1994, p. 15) defined as people's sense that they can "make things happen rather than have things happen to them" (p. 15).

Thus defined, our action research team will explore the ways in which network participation might enable persons to feel empowered. We expect that one of the consequences of participation in a social capital network will be that it enables persons in a variety of household types to make things happen, things they might not otherwise have been able to do. Empowerment of that sort becomes an additional component of the emotional health of those persons.

For example, let us assume that the social capital network includes at least one lone-parent household and that the network supplies both symbolic and actual support for her household. That support both enables her to achieve and maintain economic self-sufficiency and meets her children's interest in having adult attention. As a result, she and her children feel more empowered than comparable non-networked lone mothers and their children. Due to their empowerment, she and her children can be expected to score higher than comparable non-networked mothers and children on measures of emotional well-being.

To take another example, will wives in neostandard households belonging to a social capital network feel more empowered, and thus emotionally healthier, than wives lacking such a network? Specifically, will networked wives discover that their participation provides them with a degree of informal support from group members (unavailable to non-networked wives) in their ongoing negotiations with their husbands? Will they, as a consequence, be able to negotiate more effectively with their husbands than economically comparable non-networked wives (Scanzoni & Godwin, 1990)? As a result, will networked wives feel emotionally healthier than economically comparable non-networked wives?

Our action research team would explore other potential linkages among participants in a robust social capital network marked by household variety, personal empowerment, and the emotional health of adults and children/youth. Such investigation would contribute to a hoped-for public debate over the wisdom of continuing to pursue social policy aimed ultimately at family uniformity. The debate would consider whether, given what is being learned about empowerment and health, it might not make more sense to think instead about social policy aimed at household diversity.

CONCLUSION

Before the 1960s, the 20th-century family was characterized by internal uniformity and external nonconnectedness. But since that time, households have become increasingly marked by a great deal of internal variety, although external nonconnectedness has persisted. Given the trend toward growing internal variety, will the 21st century witness a gradual change away from external nonconnectedness? If so, what is the likelihood of devising public policy whose broad objective is to implement household diversity in both of its dual senses?

A diversity approach requires that we come to terms with the social fact that varieties of households exist and that their incidence will almost certainly increase in the new century. Variety is not viewed as a problem to be solved by putting pressure on households to conform to the neostandard model. Instead, it is celebrated as an indicator of freedom. But because responsibility is the flip side of freedom, variety is likely to thrive in a social context marked by a degree of household interdependence achieved through a social capital network.

To be sure, not all adults now experiencing household variety have chosen it. They may feel that circumstances beyond their control have constrained them and that they would much rather live, for instance, in a neostandard household. This issue is particularly salient for poor mothers with children but no resident male. Hence, a policy of household diversity would need to operate in tandem with policies that provide a sound education and meaningful occupational opportunities for all citizens of all ages. It has been recognized at least since the mid–19th century that a woman who is not economically autonomous (self-sufficient) cannot truly be a free person.

That said, the benefits (tangible and intangible) to a lone mother (whether poor or not) of participating in a social capital network would seem to be considerable both for her and her children. At the very least, network participation provides a viable alternative to the political nostrum that marriage is a cure for poverty. Network participation also relieves the pressure to marry merely to gain an adult male role model for one's children. It enables a woman or man (poor or not, with children or not) to avoid being swept into an ill-advised marriage (or any relationship) for any reason. By the same token, the network might also enable a person to make the difficult transition out of a relationship (including marriage) that was no longer desired. Furthermore, the network might serve as a resource for couples (including married couples) wanting to sustain their relationship during times of conflict and/or stress.

Finally, a policy of household diversity resting on interdependence as well as variety might eventually dislodge the Right from the high moral ground it has recently come to occupy regarding families. Those on the Right reason that the most ethical, virtuous, and righteous thing a person can do is to commit him- or herself to a heterosexual marriage that produces children and remains stable. But by no means is household uniformity the cure-all they make it out to be. Hence, what if the 1960s and 1970s critics of uniformity were on to something after all? What if diversity is not only more honest than uniformity but also healthier? At the very least, such an approach obliges the defenders of uniformity to explain why diversity is not a more compelling option for the new century.

REFERENCES

Acock, A., & Demo, D. (1994). *Family diversity and well being*. Thousand Oaks, CA: Sage.

Alexander, J. C. (1988). The new theoretical movement. In N. Smelser (Ed.), *Handbook of sociology* (pp. 77–102). Newbury Park, CA: Sage.

Bell, D. (1990). Resolving the contradictions of modernity and modernism, part II. *Society, 27*, 66–75.

Billingsley, A. (1968). *Black families in white America*. Englewood Cliffs, NJ: Prentice Hall.

Blumenthal, S. (1996, August 30). A doll's house. *New Yorker*, pp. 30–33.

Bruer, J. (1999). *The myth of the first three years*. New York: Free Press.

Buckley, W. (1967). *Sociology and modern systems theory*. Englewood Cliffs, NJ: Prentice Hall.

Buunk, B., & van Driel, B. (1989). Marriage, family, and variant lifestyles. In B. Buunk & B. van Driel (Eds.), *Variant lifestyles and relationships* (pp. 9–21). Newbury Park, CA: Sage.

Cazenave, N. A. (1980). Alternate intimacy, marriage, and family lifestyles among low-income black Americans. *Alternate Lifestyles, 4*, 425–444.

Chilman, C. (1983). The 1970s and American families. In E. Macklin & R. Rubin (Eds.), *Contemporary families and alternative lifestyles* (pp. 15–26). Beverly Hills, CA: Sage.

Chilman, C., Nunnally, E., & Cox, F. (Eds.). (1988). *Variant family forms*. Newbury Park, CA: Sage.

Clawson, D. (1997). War on the poor. *Contemporary Sociology, 26*, vii.

Cogswell, B., & Sussman, M. (1972). Changing family and marriage forms: Complications for human services systems. In M. Sussman (Ed.), *Nontraditional family forms in the 1970s* (pp. 137–148). Minneapolis, MN: National Council on Family Relations.

Coleman, J. S. (1990). *Foundations of social theory*. Cambridge, MA: Harvard University Press.

Corsaro, W. A. (1997). *The sociology of childhood*. Thousand Oaks, CA: Pine Forge.

Council on Families in America. (1995). *Marriage in America*. New York: Institute for American Values.

Cowan, P., & Cowan, C. (1998). New families: Modern couples as new pioneers. In M. Mason, A. Skolnick, & S. Sugarman (Eds.), *All our families* (pp. 169–192). New York: Oxford University Press.

Cuber, J. D. (1970). Alternate models from the perspective of sociology. In H. Otto (Ed.), *The family in search of a future* (pp. 11–24). New York: Appleton-Century-Crofts.

Dizard, J. E., & Gadlin, H. (1990). *The minimal family*. Amherst: University of Massachusetts Press.

Doherty, W. (1999). Postmodernism and family theory. In M. Sussman, S. Steinmetz, & G. Peterson (Eds.), *Handbook of marriage and the family* (2nd ed.) (pp. 205–218). New York: Plenum.

Edwards, B., & Foley, M. W. (Eds.). (1997). Social capital, civil society, and contemporary democracy [Special issue]. *American Behavioral Scientist, 40.*

Ekeh, P. (1974). *Social exchange theory*. Cambridge, MA: Harvard University Press.

Faris, E. (1957). The primary group: Essence and accident. In L. A. Coser & B. Rosenberg (Eds.), *Sociological theory* (pp. 298–303). New York: Macmillan.

Friedman, M., & Lackey, G. (1991). *The psychology of human control*. New York: Praeger.

Furstenberg, F. (1999). Children and family change: Discourse between social scientists and the media. *Contemporary Sociology, 28,* 10–17.

Giddens, A. (1984). *The constitution of society*. Berkeley: University of California Press.

Giddens, A. (1994). *Beyond left and right*. Stanford, CA: Stanford University Press.

Glassner, B. (2000). Where meanings get constructed. *Contemporary Sociology, 29,* 590–594.

Goldstein, A. (2002, April 1). Tying marriage vows to welfare reform: White House push for state strategies to promote family ignites dispute. *Washington Post,* p. A01.

Goode, W. J. (1963). *World revolution and family patterns*. New York: Free Press.

Greenwood, D. J., & Morten, L. (1998). *Introduction to action research: Social research for social change*. Thousand Oaks, CA: Sage.

Gupta, G., & Cox, S. (Eds.). (1987). *Deviance and disruption in the American family*. Lexington, MA: Ginn.

Harris, J. (1998). *The nurture assumption*. New York: Free Press.

Hasell, M. J., & Scanzoni, J. (2000). Cohousing in HUD housing: Prospects and problems. *Journal of Architectural and Planning Research, 17,* 133–145.

Heclo, H. (1995). The social question. In K. McFate, R. Lawson, & W. J. Wilson (Eds.), *Poverty, inequality, and the future of social policy* (pp. 665–692). New York: Russell Sage.

Jurich, A., & Hastings, C. (1983). Teaching about alternative family forms and lifestyles. In E. Macklin & R. Rubin (Eds.), *Contemporary families and alternative lifestyles* (pp. 362–378). Beverly Hills, CA: Sage.

Kagan, J. (1999). *Three seductive ideas*. New York: Oxford University Press.

Kingsbury, N., & Scanzoni, J. (1993). Structural-functionalism. In P. Boss, W. Doherty, R. LaRossa, W. Schumm, & S. Steinmetz (Eds.), *Sourcebook of family theories and methods* (pp. 195–217). New York: Plenum.

Levi-Strauss, C. (1957). The principle of reciprocity. In L. Coser & B. Rosenberg (Eds.), *Sociological theory* (pp. 84–94). New York: Macmillan.

Levine, D., Carter, E. B., & Miller, E. (1976). Simmel's influence on American sociology. *American Journal of Sociology, 81,* 813–845.

Lin, N., Cook, K., & Burt, R. (Eds.). (2001). *Social capital.* New York: Aldine de Gruyter.

Macklin, E., & Rubin, R. (Eds.). (1983). *Contemporary families and alternative lifestyles.* Beverly Hills, CA: Sage.

Maines, D. (2000). The social construction of meaning. *Contemporary Sociology, 29,* 577–584.

Marciano, T. D. (1975). Variant family forms in a world perspective. *Family Coordinator, 24,* 407–420.

Matthews, D., & DeHart, J. (1990). *Sex, gender, and the politics of ERA.* New York: Oxford University Press.

Mead, M. (1967). The life cycle and its variations: The division of roles. *Daedalus, 96,* 871–875.

Nisbet, R. A. (1953). *The quest for community.* New York: Oxford University Press.

Olson, D. (1972). Marriage of the future: Revolutionary or evolutionary change? In M. Sussman (Ed.), *Non-traditional family forms in the 1970s* (pp. 15–26). Minneapolis, MN: National Council on Family Relations.

Otto, H. (1970a). Introduction. In H. Otto (Ed.), *The family in search of a future* (pp. 1–10). New York: Appleton-Century-Crofts.

Otto, H. (1970b). The new marriage: Marriage as a framework for developing personal potential. In H. Otto (Ed.), *The family in search of a future* (pp. 111–118). New York: Appleton-Century-Crofts.

Parsons, T. (1955). The American family: Its relations to personality and to the social structure. In T. Parsons & R. Bales (Eds.), *Family, socialization and interaction process* (pp. 3–33). New York: Free Press.

Parsons, T. (1965). The normal American family. In S. Farber, P. Mustacchi, & R. H. L. Wilson (Eds.), *Man and civilization* (pp. 31–50). New York: McGraw-Hill.

Pitts, J. R. (1964). The structural-functional approach. In H. T. Christensen (Ed.), *Handbook of marriage and the family* (pp. 51–124). Chicago: Rand McNally.

Popenoe, D. (1996). Modern marriage: Revising the cultural script. In D. Popenoe, J. Elshtain, & D. Blankenhorn (Eds.), *Promises to keep* (pp. 247–270). Lanham, MD: Rowman & Littlefield.

Portes, A. (1998). Social capital: Its origins and applications in modern sociology. *Annual Review of Sociology, 24,* 1–24.

Putnam, R. (2000). *Bowling alone.* New York: Simon & Schuster.

Rainwater, L., Coleman, R., & Handel, G. (1959). *Workingman's wife.* New York: Oceana.

Rivers, R. M., & Scanzoni, J. (1997). Social families among African-Americans: Policy implications for children. In H. McAdoo (Ed.), *Black families* (pp. 333–348). Newbury Park, CA: Sage.

Scanzoni, J. (1983). *Shaping tomorrow's family: Theory and policy for the 21st century.* Newbury Park, CA: Sage.

Scanzoni, J. (1989). Alternative images for public policy: Family structure versus families struggling. *Policy Studies Review, 8,* 599–609.

Scanzoni, J. (1991). Balancing the policy interests of children and adults. In E. Anderson & R. C. Hula (Eds.), *The reconstruction of family policy* (pp. 11–22). New York: Greenwood.

Scanzoni, J. (2000). *Designing families.* Thousand Oaks, CA: Pine Forge.

Scanzoni, J. (2001a). From the normal family to alternate families: The quest for diversity with interdependence. *Journal of Family Issues, 22,* 688–710.

Scanzoni, J. (2001b). Reconnecting household and community: An alternative strategy for theory and policy. *Journal of Family Issues, 22,* 243–264.

Scanzoni, J., & Godwin, D. (1990). Negotiation effectiveness and acceptable outcomes. *Social Psychology Quarterly, 53,* 239–251.

Scanzoni, J., & Marsiglio, W. (1993). New action theory and contemporary families. *Journal of Family Issues, 14,* 105–132.

Scanzoni, J., Polonko, K., Teachman, J., & Thompson, L. (1989). *The sexual bond: Rethinking families and close relationships.* Newbury Park, CA: Sage.

Scanzoni, J., & Szinovacz, M. (1980). *Family decision-making.* Newbury Park, CA: Sage.

Seeley, J. R., Sim, R.A., & Loosley, E. (1956). *Crestwood Heights.* New York: Basic Books.

Selznick, P. (1961). Review article: The social theories of Talcott Parsons. *American Sociological Review, 26,* 930–952.

Skolnick, A. (1998). Solomon's children: The new biologism, psychological parenthood, attachment theory, and the best interests standard. In M. A. Mason, A. Skolnick, & S. D. Sugarman (Eds.), *All our families* (pp. 236–255). New York: Oxford University Press.

Stacey, J. (1999). Virtual truth with a vengeance. *Contemporary Sociology, 28,* 18–22.

Steiner, G. (1981). *The futility of family policy.* Washington, DC: Brookings Institute.

Stoller, F. H. (1970). The intimate network of families as a new structure. In H. Otto (Ed.), *The family in search of a future* (pp. 145–160). New York: Appleton-Century-Crofts.

Stone, L. (1979). *The family, sex, and marriage in England 1500–1800* (abridged ed.). New York: Harper & Row.

Sugarman, S. D. (1998). Single-parent families. In M. A. Mason, A. Skolnick, & S. D. Sugarman, (Eds.), *All our families* (pp. 13–38). New York: Oxford University Press.

Sussman, M. (1972). Preface. In M. Sussman (Ed.), *Non-traditional family forms in the 1970s* (pp. 3–4). Minneapolis, MN: National Council on Family Relations.

Sussman, M., & Cogswell, B. (1972). The meaning of variant and experimental marriage styles and family forms. In M. Sussman (Ed.), *Non-traditional family forms in the 1970s* (pp. 7–14). Minneapolis, MN: National Council on Family Relations.

Taubin, S., & Mudd, E. (1983). Contemporary traditional families: The undefined majority. In E. Macklin & R. Rubin (Eds.), *Contemporary families and alternative lifestyles* (pp. 256–270). Beverly Hills, CA: Sage.

Thompson, E. H., & Gongla, P. (1983). Single parent families: In the mainstream of American society. In E. Macklin & R. Rubin (Eds.), *Contemporary families and alternative lifestyles* (pp. 97–124). Beverly Hills, CA: Sage.

Vargus, B. (1999). Classical social theory and family studies: The triumph of reactionary thought in contemporary family studies. In M. Sussman, S. Steinmetz, & G. Peterson (Eds.), *Handbook of marriage and the family* (2nd ed., pp. 190–204). New York: Plenum.

Waite, L., & Gallagher, M. (1999). *The case for marriage.* New York: Doubleday.

Wilson, P., & Pahl, R. (1988). The changing sociological construct of family. *Sociological Review, 36,* 233–272.

Zablocki, B. (1980). *Alienation and charisma.* New York: Free Press.

CHAPTER 2

Alternative Lifestyles Today
Off the Family Studies Screen

ROGER H. RUBIN

A review of recent compendia on American families (Demo, Allen, & Fine, 2000; Rouse, 2002; Sussman, Steinmetz, & Peterson, 1999) suggests that currently the field of family studies barely recognizes several alternative lifestyles. Specifically, I refer to swinging or comarital sex; the consenting of married couples to sexually exchange partners (Buunk & van Driel, 1989); group marriages; and communes. They are "off the screen," thus maintaining their virtual invisibility in texts, family life education, research, theory, policy, and clinical work. The genesis of interest in alternative lifestyles occurred in the late 1960s and early 1970s. This was a period of intense reexamination of interpersonal relationships, marriage, and family life. The social turmoil of the Vietnam War and movements demanding civil rights, black power, women's liberation, and gay recognition served as catalysts for the public

emergence of what became popularly known as alternative lifestyles. This national exploration was further fueled by rising divorce rates and a sexual revolution among women, raising challenging questions about the meaning of marriage, family life, gender roles, and sexuality.

The term *alternative lifestyles* included a variety of nontraditional family forms and personal living arrangements, including singlehood, nonmarital heterosexual cohabitation, single-parent families, stepfamilies, dual-career/work families, gay and lesbian relationships, open marriages and multiple relationships, and communes. Although many of these lifestyles became mainstream topics for family studies, those on the fringes have been largely ignored over the past two decades.

The reasons for the scholarly neglect of these lifestyles are numerous. The appearance of AIDS may have led to the assumption that

AUTHOR'S NOTE: Thanks to Steven Boggs, Mariana Falconier, and Andrew Smith for their assistance.

these lifestyles had disappeared. A lack of research funding and limited academic rewards for examining personal and family choices that are often viewed as being at odds with achieving status, acceptance, and success in contemporary society may be another explanation. Also, mass media attention shifted to lifestyles that seemed to be rapidly becoming a part of the American family scene, such as cohabitation, single parenthood, stepfamilies, and dual-partner working families. Homosexuality also became somewhat more tolerated, and public debate about homosexuality became commonplace, ranging from military policies to issues regarding civil unions and same-sex marriage.

This chapter turns its attention to the periphery of the alternative-lifestyle discussion. An examination of what occurred in the past two decades leads me to conclude that much can be learned about contemporary family life by examining the extremes. The continued practice of these behaviors suggests that they fulfill ongoing purposes and functions that defy the disdain often directed at them by religious and social institutions as well as by clinicians, educators, researchers, and policy makers.

THE STUDY OF ALTERNATIVE LIFESTYLES

Within academic circles, the study of alternative lifestyles is linked to several significant events. The 1971 Groves Conference on Marriage and the Family, with its annual meeting theme, "The Future of Marriage and Parenthood," was perhaps the first organized attempt by family scholars to begin cataloging the sweeping changes surrounding late-20th-century American family life. The need was apparent to 1971 attendee Robert Whitehurst, who pointed out that we did not have good terminology and that there existed a

shortage of data on almost everything related to alternative lifestyles. Discussions included whether "the family" had a viable future, what future parenthood would look like, and perhaps most significantly an attempt to identify new interpersonal lifestyles. Lifestyle seminars included such topics as male and female homosexuality, college student cohabitation, the affiliative family, androgyny, mate swapping, group marriage, and communal living.

Intellectual debate was capped by presentations from some of the foremost family scholars of the time. Jessie Bernard distinguished marriage from lifestyle by emphasizing the specific socially framed parameters of marriage versus the greater freedom of establishing any form of household arrangement in a lifestyle. Rustom Roy elaborated on the book that he had written with his wife Della, *Honest Sex: A Revolutionary New Sex Guide for the Now Generation of Christians* (1968). In that book, Roy and Roy argued that traditional monogamy was obsolete and that loving one's neighbors should be taken literally because traditional monogamy isolates individuals and families and does not facilitate the development of meaningful personal relationships. Not only did they challenge so-called biblical rules and treat the idea of one exclusive sex partner as an absurdity when universally applied, but they even urged the legalization of bigamy.

Duane Denfield and Michael Gordon, who had coined the expression "the family that swings together, clings together" in a 1970 article, described the more positive aspects of mate swapping while recognizing that studies of dropouts from swinging had not yet been conducted. The limited ability of architects to understand social and behavioral research and design living spaces conducive to communal lifestyles was criticized by George Trieschman, who condemned the lack of a humanistic architecture. Robert Ryder commented that the term *commune* was almost meaningless, as the variety of communal arrangements made them almost impossible to operationally define. Ryder raised the concern that communes and marriage might suffer from the same idealization, the belief that there was an institutional guarantee of success and happiness. He argued that communes require energy, resources such as money, and charismatic leaders to maintain them; those based primarily on loving will not last. Ethel Vatter and Sylvia Clavan raised awareness regarding the importance of older people in communes and of older single women adopting families to exchange emotional and material resources. Androgyny was introduced into the Groves discussion by Joy and Howard Osofsky, who defined it as a lifestyle with no sexual differentiation in roles. A plea for longitudinal studies of families came from Margaret Feldman.

Finally, among the issues and questions raised regarding this new area of research was a concern about American society's responses to alternative lifestyles. Would there be a reactionary crackdown from legal and government sources, outright condemnation from religious authorities, and a consensus among unsympathetic counselors, therapists, and human service professionals that the practitioners of alternative lifestyles were ill? Eleanor Macklin, Catherine Chilman, David Olson, Marvin Sussman, Carlfred Broderick, Harold Feldman, Gladys Groves, Robert Harper, Lester Kirkendall, David and Vera Mace, Marie Peters, Gerhard Neubeck, James Ramey, Nena O'Neill, Rose Somerville, Roger Rubin, and many other attendees at this pioneering conference would make contributions over the next 30 years examining the shifting parameters of American family life.

The 1972 Groves conference, "Societal Planning for Family Pluralism," continued the earlier developments in legitimizing the study of the alternative-lifestyle movement.

Another participant, James Ramey, whose articles on group marriages and communes had appeared in such publications as *Journal of Sex Research*, extolled the practical advantages of communal living, particularly in pooling resources. For example, fewer automobiles are needed when others can transport you; housing facilities may be of better quality than individuals and separate families could afford; caregiving for children, the disabled, and other dependents increases with more adults present; children have additional adult role models; and collaborative financial investment strategies improve economic circumstances. Ramey described one commune composed of professionals with $51 million in assets that labeled itself an investment club. Their large housing complex provided day care and a communal dining area. On the downside, Ramey reported the fragility of group ventures that sometimes faltered under the effect of career and personal problems that were due to demands from the broader society.

The efficacy of group experiences for adults and children was questioned by other conference participants, including Nena and George O'Neill, coauthors of the best-selling book *Open Marriage* (1972). They expressed concern about rearing children age 5 and younger in group situations. They even criticized their own ideas by saying that the major weakness in opening the boundaries of permanent monogamous relationships was the inability of individuals to analyze and understand their own relationships. People carried role expectations, especially based on their parents' marriages, into their own marriages, and these expectations were difficult to expel. In an open marriage, marriage should always be the primary relationship, and if extramarital sex did occur, it should be viewed as something feeding into the relationship and not threatening it. In other words, extramarital sex was acceptable only when it filtered back positively into the marriage.

Finally, the conference workshops produced a number of predictions regarding the future course of American family life. Most of these were based on a perceived need for increased intimacy as mass culture grew and became more impersonal.

As the 1970s progressed, practitioners, researchers, and other scholars continued to meet and pursue an agenda of lively debate and discourse over the future of American family life. Among these meetings was "Adventures in Loving: A Conference on Alternative Lifestyles," held at the University of Maryland in 1975. Once again, leading authorities on alternative lifestyles, academic experts, writers, and others were brought together. Among the participants was Robert Rimmer, author of the best-selling novels *The Harrad Experiment* (1966) and *Proposition 31* (1968). *The Harrad Experiment* described coeducational housing at a New England university, an arrangement unheard of at the time. *Proposition 31* took its name from a California legislative proposal to legalize group marriages. The popularity of these two fictionalized accounts of alternative lifestyles brought new awareness of these possibilities to a wide public that academic treatises could never reach.

The 1975 conference also featured Larry and Joan Constantine, who had traveled the country interviewing people for their seminal book *Group Marriage* (1973). They concluded that opening boundaries in relationships and increasing people's options was at the crux of the movement toward group marriages and multiple relationships. Another conference participant, James Ramey, founder and director of the Center for the Study of Innovative Lifestyles, described an open marriage as one in which two people were primarily involved with each other although emotional and sexual relationships existed outside the primary relationship. Citing the increasing divorce rates, Ramey saw the exploration of alternative

models as a significant step in determining what might bring intellectual, emotional, social, familial, sexual, and career fulfillment. Additional topics explored were monogamy and beyond, relationship choices, multiple commitments, freedom and responsibility, communes, and swinging.

These were highly controversial topics, often leading to public scrutiny and at times denunciation. After receiving complaints by individuals from the nonuniversity community, the University of Maryland's president had to defend the use of campus facilities for the conference. I was one of the conference organizers, and such criticisms were no surprise to me. In 1974, a U.S. congressman from Maryland, at the behest of several constituents, questioned the appropriateness of three invited speakers, participants in a triadic marriage, to my course "Family Relationships." The speakers were university graduates, and two were married to one another (Rubin, 1978). The congressman's telegram to the university administration stated, "The thin line between making a class interesting and pandering villainousness may have been crossed. Certainly that is the view of some of those that have been exposed to this. The instructor, Dr. Roger Rubin, enjoys great vogue of popularity, but so do the perverters [sic] of X-rated movies. While some may tolerate and even be amused by such panty raids [sic] and nude runs I do not think that the same tolerance should be extended to courses of instruction and hope that this is not the case in the present instance" (personal communication, February 28, 1974).

In a follow-up letter to the dean of the College of Human Ecology, the congressman stated, "I really hoped for assurances that this course had not become a circus sideshow of disturbed persons on one side and student voyeurs on the other" (personal communication, March 22, 1974). Despite such pressures, interest in alternative lifestyles continued, and by today's mass media standards, such criticism seems quaint. However, this kind of pressure helps explain the future cautiousness and the lack of interest and boldness in the academic study of alternative lifestyles.

Not until 1981 did alternative lifestyles again become the dominant theme of a Groves conference. The meeting, titled "The Pursuit of Happiness: Progress and Prospects," was the basis for the publication *Contemporary Families and Alternative Lifestyles: Handbook on Research and Theory* (Macklin & Rubin, 1983). The conference again brought together some of the leading scholars associated with the study of alternative lifestyles, including the Constantines, Judith Fischer, Nena O'Neill, James Ramey, Robert Whitehurst, Robert Francoeur, Bram Buunk, and Roger Libby. Topics explored included singlehood, nonmarital cohabitation, open and multiple relationships, same-sex intimate relationships, alternative lifestyles in minority ethnic communities, affiliated families and communities, and children and the elderly in alternative lifestyles. Also discussed were the traditional nuclear family, remarriage and stepfamilies, single-parent families, and dual-career/-worker marriages. Issues surrounding religious reactions to alternative lifestyles as well as implications for teaching, the law, clinical work, and international perspectives were included. Although we did not know it, this would be the last major family studies conference on alternative lifestyles until 2000. That year, the Groves Conference's theme, "Considering the Past and Contemplating the Future: Family Diversity in the New Millenium," reconnected with the Groves meetings of 1971, 1972, and 1981 and the 1975 University of Maryland conference. For the family field, it attempted to reestablish the importance of studying that with which we may be least comfortable.

SWINGING, GROUP MARRIAGES, AND COMMUNES

Of the many alternative lifestyles that captured the interest of family researchers beginning in the 1960s, swinging, group marriages, and some communal arrangements gained the least semblance of public tolerance or acceptance over the next few decades. Perhaps the primary reason was that they shared the theme of nonexclusivity in sexual partnerships. Such unorthodoxy challenges existing religious, legal, and social rules.

Swinging became the generic term for the sexual exchange of marital partners with other like-minded participants. Among swingers, sex is the defining attraction. Otherwise, they maintain their couple autonomy. Group marriages go beyond swinging by including economic, emotional, housing, and child care relationships. They range from a minimum of three participants, two of whom have to be legally married, to increasing numbers of couples and singles who form complex family networks. These arrangements differ from traditional polygamous marriage so common to many societies in that they are not legally or socially sanctioned and do not claim mainstream religious support. The fact they sometimes include unmarried people makes them unusual. Members understand that sexual accessibility is expected although not necessarily directed toward every adult. Sometimes group marriages will merge into larger communal arrangements that take on idealistic principles promoting innovative methods for human cooperation.

As early as 1964, Breedlove and Breedlove (1964) studied hundreds of swinging couples, conveying an image of respectable citizens who deviated only in this respect. Their estimate of indulging couples was in the millions. However, not until Gilbert Bartell's book *Group Sex: An Eyewitness Report on the American Way of Swinging* (1971) was broader academic interest stimulated in a topic that had barely been studied previously. Like the Breedloves, Bartell concluded that swingers were overwhelmingly white, middle class, age 30-something, parents, religiously identified, politically conservative, and secretive about their activities and that they included teachers, salesmen, and housewives. Except for religious participation/identification, Jenks (1998) drew a similar profile three decades later. In other words, apparently the more privileged, stable, and ordinary citizen was most likely to swing! This defied conventional wisdom and raised doubts about the facade of American marital life. Bartell's research would be eclipsed a year later with the publication of *Open Marriage* (O'Neill & O'Neill, 1972). The term *open marriage,* through the efforts of the mass media, would become synonymous with acceptable extramarital sexual relationships, a great disservice to the original intent of its anthropologist authors. The purpose of their inquiry was to broaden the view of gender roles in intimate male-female relationships. The O'Neills concluded that rigid, prescribed, gender-based scripts were destructive to the long-term growth and healthy evolution of relationships. They proposed an arrangement in which mutual trust permitted an opening of the marital relationship to new opportunities for personal fulfillment, including those afforded by opposite-sex members to whom the partners were not committed. This was a proposed alternative to the stagnation, unrealistic self-sacrifice, frustration, and anger that the O'Neills interpreted as a major factor in rising divorce rates. Although their book was more about a married person's going to the opera with an opposite-sex friend than about extramarital sex, the popular culture's increasing interest in all things sexual identified the O'Neills' treatise as justification for extramarital sexual activity.

By the early 1970s, an increasing number of books on alternative lifestyles, incorporating material on swinging, group marriages, and communes, became available. Otto's edited book *The Family in Search of a Future* (1970) was partially based on a symposium held at the 1967 annual meeting of the American Psychological Association. Prominent behavioral and social scientists contributed, including Albert Ellis (1970), who wrote about group marriage, claiming that it had a long history in human experience. He argued that mate swapping had become the primary example of group marriage in American society, and he predicted that group sex but not group marriage would increase. Perhaps the most widely discussed of the articles was Victor Kassel's (1970) examination of polygyny after age 60. His position was that multiple marriages, especially between a man and several women, would solve many of the social problems of the elderly.

The writings of Bartell and the Roys gained further exposure in compendia such as Hart's *Marriage: For and Against* (1972), which recognized that many well-respected social scientists were now seriously considering new marriage forms, including group marriage and group sex. The book *Intimate Life Styles,* edited by DeLora and DeLora (1972), offered a predominantly college audience direct access to Bartell's (1971) study of group sex among midwestern Americans and Denfield and Gordon's (1970) classic study on the sociology of mate swapping. It was also one of the first readers to include the works of the Roys (Roy & Roy, 1968) on the need to alter the monogamy paradigm and the pioneering research of the Constantines (Constantine & Constantine, 1973) on multilateral marriage (group marriage). The popularity of writings on communal lifestyles was further evidenced in *The Future of the Family,* edited by Louise Kapp Howe (1972). This book attested to the importance of the study of communal life in the family studies field. The academic recognition of controversial lifestyle topics was endorsed again by the publication of a special issue of the *Family Coordinator* (now called *Family Relations*) (Sussman, 1972). Several of the articles originated in the 1971 Groves Conference on Marriage and the Family.

Renovating Marriage, edited by Libby and Whitehurst (1973), offered studies generally reconfirming the white, middle-class image of swinging and provided an extensive literature review dating back to one of the earliest studies on wife swapping by Wilson and Myers (1965). A more personal view of expanding the dimensions of the marital bond was found in *The New Intimacy: Open-Ended Marriage and Alternative Lifestyles* (Mazur, 1973). Inspired by the work of the Constantines, Libby, Rimmer, and others, Mazur offered his views and guidelines for living an unconventional marriage and documented his thesis with the research and thinking of the time. One reader almost totally devoted to swinging, group marriages, and communes was *Beyond Monogamy* (Smith & Smith, 1974). On the opening page, the Smiths quoted the words of Judge Ben Lindsey in his seminal book *The Companionate Marriage* that "the couples who mutually agree that adultery is all right are a strange and interesting phenomenon in American life today . . . that it is surely indicative that something extraordinary is happening to one of the most firmly established of our customs" (p. v). Another example of the fascination in the 1970s with reconstructing marriage was Casler's book *Is Marriage Necessary?* (1974). Casler promoted the idea that much of what people believed about marriage was a myth and that marriage was a potential entrapment for the human psyche. Among the most thoughtful contributors to the 1970s examination of marriage were Anna and Robert Francoeur,

who explored sex and marriage within a religious, ethical, biological, evolutionary, and historical context. Their book *Hot and Cool Sex* (Francoeur & Francoeur, 1974) maintained that societal change had created new ways for men and women to relate sexually. Ultimately, this meant that the hot sex of traditional closed marriage would increasingly be replaced by the cool sex afforded in more open relationships as multilateral opportunities and intimacies increased between the sexes.

The search for alternatives to marriage continued with Duberman's *Marriage and Its Alternatives* (1974), in which the author noted a change in attitude among some experts regarding adultery. Citing the works of David Olson, Larry and Joan Constantine, Ethel Alpenfels, and Rustum and Della Roy among others, Duberman concluded that they believed personal satisfaction had become today's primary relationship goal and that expanded family parameters, sometimes including sexual variety, were the key to success greater than that provided in dyadic relationships. In 1976, Ramey published *Intimate Friendships*, a description of the dramatic changes he had observed in American society. He said the building block of the society was now the individual, who selected at various times over the life cycle to live in different but equally viable and acceptable personal relationships, and that intimate friendships were possible in all kinds of relationships.

The dialogue on sex and intimacy continued in *Marriage and Alternatives: Exploring Intimate Relationships,* edited by Libby and Whitehurst (1977). This book continued to challenge the assumption of sexual exclusivity within marriage. Brian Gilmartin's chapter contributed the most extensive study of swinging completed at the time. Most important was his use for the first time of a control group to compare socialization variables such as early relationships with parents and kin, early interest in the opposite sex, and political and religious affiliations. Gilmartin concluded that if partners have a shared perception of their sexual behavior, no harm will be done to their marriage solely on account of their swinging.

Murstein (1978), an eminent psychologist and social historian of romance, dating, and courtship, reported on swinging, group marriages, and communes in his edited book *Exploring Intimate Life Styles*. He observed that the depersonalization and avoidance of emotional involvement among swingers relegated swinging to temporary status in the lives of its practitioners. However, Murstein also concluded that its appeal as a solution to specific needs such as autonomy and high sexual drive would sustain its presence in the culture.

By 1982, the study of swingers, group marriages, and communes was fading. A 1982 special issue of *Marriage and Family Review,* "Alternatives to Traditional Family Living," edited by Gross and Sussman, did not contain a single reference to swinging or American communal life. Fortunately, the sociologist Richard Jenks, who published multiple articles on swinging in the mid-1980s, stands out as an exception to scholarly indifference. Jenks (1985a) reported that swingers and non-swingers differed only in the practice of swinging and not on a variety of more general attitudes and practices. Jenks (1985b) further reported that swingers' liberal attitudes were primarily related to sexual issues and that swingers were more conventional in other social areas. As he attempted to develop a social psychological model of swinging from his research, Jenks (1985c) once again found that swingers were less marginal to the community than predicted. His more recent literature review on swinging (Jenks, 1998) serves as a primary source on the topic and a culmination of his earlier work.

Whatever other professional literature exists on swinging was reported almost exclusively in the 1980s. Biblarz and Biblarz (1980) questioned the theoretical and research methodology employed in previous studies, claiming researcher bias and poor empirical techniques. Peabody (1982) examined the psychotherapeutic implications of swinging, open marriage, and group marriages, and Whitehurst (1983) predicted that vast social changes in society would foster increasing opportunities for the growth of choices and pluralism in lifestyles. Bisexuality among swinging married women, reported by Dixon (1984), added a new dimension to the study of the consequences of mate swapping. Differences in personality variables among swingers, ex-swingers, and control group members were found by Murstein, Case, and Gunn (1985). Further personality concerns about swingers were raised when the Minnesota Multiphasic Personality Inventory was applied by Duckworth and Levitt (1985). Their findings suggested serious emotional disturbances, substance abuse, and major sexual problems among a significant number of swingers.

In the 1990s, one must turn to the popular press for information on swinging. Among the publications reporting on swinging and group sex were *New York, New York* (Gross, 1992), *Gentlemen's Quarterly* (Newman, 1993), *New York Times Magazine* (Roth & Heard, 1997), *Rolling Stone* ("Hot Sport," 1998), *Mademoiselle* (Chen, 1998), *Esquire* (Richardson, 1999), and *Glamour* (Bried, 1999). A *New York Times Magazine* article on swinging (Rayner, 2000) included an interview of Robert McGinley, president of the North American Swing Club Association, who reported that the group had increased from 150 to 310 affiliates in the past 5 years. McGinley claimed that swinging had become highly organized and institutionalized. He asserted that it strengthened marriage and had received a bad reputation from the press during the 1960s and 1970s. According to

Gould and Zabol (1998), there are about 3 million married, middle-aged, middle-class swingers, or lifestyle practitioners, as they are now called. This is an increase of almost 1 million since 1990.

In the semantics of group sex, a new term, *polyamory,* is evidence of a behavior's renewed visibility. Polyamorists are more committed to emotional fulfillment and family building than recreational swingers. Larsen (1998) stated that as "an outgrowth of both the group marriage and communal living movements of the 60s and 70s, the still-young polyamory movement espouses the value of committed, loving, relationships with more than one partner" (p. 20). Through its Web site, the Polyamory Society promotes the impression that middle-class professionals, artists, academics, and the computer literate are solidly representative of its members.

The MTV program *Sex in the 90's: It's a Group Thing* (aired in November 1998, cited in Cloud, 1999) provided public exposure to polyamory. According to *Time* magazine (Cloud, 1999), perhaps 250 polyamory support groups exist, the majority available through the Internet. According to Larsen (1998), increasing numbers of young adults are trying out polyamory as an alternative to their parents' failed monogamous marriages. Anapol, a leading proponent, wrote extensively about it in her book *Polyamory: The New Love Without Limits: Secrets of Sustainable Intimate Relationships* (1997).

Advances in communication appear to be contributing to the increase in swinging. In the 1970s, 75% of the swingers found each other through a growing literature, especially swingers' magazines (Gilmartin, 1977). Today, the Internet may have replaced magazines in linking potential participants.

Regenerating scholarly study of these alternatives to monogamy may fall to new organizations. The Institute for 21st Century Relationships was founded in 2000 to support consenting adult choices in lifestyle selection. To stimulate a research agenda, the institute plans to hold an annual conference on alternative relationships (including a professionals' symposium), publish a semiannual periodical titled *Journal of Alternative Relationships,* and provide research incentives. Robert Francoeur, Rustom Roy, and Lawrence Casler are advisory board members.

An exception to the decline in the study of communes is the recent comprehensive publication of *Families and Communes: An Examination of Nontraditional Lifestyles* (Smith 1999), which drew many conclusions from the *Communities Directory: A Guide to Cooperative Living* (Fellowship for Intentional Community, 1995), a major resource identifying contemporary communal arrangements. Smith estimated that there are currently 3,000 to 4,000 communes: "These numbers indicate that there probably are close to as many people living communally today as there were in any given year during the period from 1965 to 1975" (p. 107). Although aware of the inherent difficulty in defining a commune, Smith maintained that the value of studying them lay in the comparison and contrast with the nuclear family. He rejected the idea of Kanter (1973) and others that ultimately communal life and families were incompatible. Rather, Smith saw both lifestyles as a search for human connection in a world increasingly devoid of meaningful intimacy.

Communes today remain both urban and rural, and about one third of them are religious or spiritual. Others represent a diverse range of interests, including ecological and environmental, health, personal morality, lesbian feminist, peace and human rights, and collective co-ownership. Only 4% focus primarily on family life, but families in various forms remain active and viable in most communal settings. Berry (1992) wrote that contemporary communes do not reject many of the dominant society's values, as was truer in the 1960s and 1970s. Rather, they supplement these values with their own idiosyncratic components for self-development.

FAMILY PROFESSIONALS AND THE FUTURE OF ALTERNATIVE LIFESTYLES

What is one to conclude from the paucity over the past 20 years of academic interest in conducting research and theorizing about swinging, group marriages, and communes? Given that Murdock (1949) reported that only 43 of 238 human societies considered monogamy the ideal, the aversion to studying multiple marital relationships seems at odds with reality. However, an examination of three currently popular marriage and family textbooks (Cherlin, 1999; Davidson & Moore, 1996; Olson & DeFrain, 2003) found virtually no mention of these alternative lifestyles. None of these sources indexed the words *swinging, group marriages,* or *communes.* It is like a family secret. Everyone is aware of it, but no one acknowledges it.

The present denial in family studies of the existence of sexual mate sharing among married couples limits the debate regarding the parameters of contemporary marriage. The evolution of this denial is illustrated by changes in the journal *Alternative Life Styles: Changing Patterns in Marriage, Family, and Intimacy,* founded in 1978 by Libby. In 1985, the journal became *Lifestyles: A Journal of Changing Patterns.* By 1988, it had been renamed *Lifestyles: Family and Economic Issues,* only to be further transformed in 1992 into the *Journal of Family and Economic Issues,* a journal having absolutely nothing to do with alternative lifestyles.

Perhaps also in denial are marriage and family therapists who are not clamoring for information on alternative lifestyles. Why not? Are they not seeing clients who sexually share partners? Do therapists not look for such behavior? Stayton (1985) stated that marital and family therapy training is based on the traditional monogamous nuclear family model and thus inadequately prepares clinicians for dealing with alternative lifestyles such as swinging, group sex, group marriage, and communes.

Health professionals should be knowledgeable about alternative lifestyles, given AIDS and other sexually transmitted diseases. Tevlin (1996) reported that swingers do not consistently practice safe sex. And according to Gould and Zabol (1998), at New Horizon, the world's second largest swing club, condoms, although readily available, may not always be used. However, Larsen (1998) reported that some polyamorists practice "safe sex circles" in which only those who have tested negatively for sexually transmitted diseases participate (she claimed lower disease rates for this group than for those who secretively cheat on their spouses). However, the fear of disease has apparently not inhibited the recent growth of swinging.

Swinging, group marriages, and communes may remain on the periphery of study and tolerance because they threaten the cultural image of what marriage is supposed to be. Other forms of alternative lifestyles do not attribute the basis for their existence to the concept of multiple sexual partners. However, this avoidance may no longer be possible. The current debate on same-sex marriage has set the stage for broader discussion over which relationships should be legally recognized. Some ask if legalized polygamy will be the next step after gay marriage, noting that religious, social, and biological arguments for and against such marriages can be brought forth just as they are concerning homosexual couples. According to *Newsweek* magazine, between 20,000 and 50,000 people in Mormon splinter groups already live in polygamous families (Murr, 2000). All of this is ammunition for the culture war over the family. Liberals and conservatives argue over whether all lifestyles should be accorded equal status and recognition. Are some superior to others or just different? Recently, Waite and Gallagher (2000) strongly implied that monogamous marriage is the preferred option, leading to better emotional and physical health. Alternative-lifestyle advocates argue that providing options strengthens marital relationships.

Smith (1999) stated that "studying alternative families can give us insights into our own families and the status quo" (p. 134). The recognition of this provides the intellectual justification for continuing study on the least popular of the alternative lifestyles—swinging, group marriages, and communes.

REFERENCES

Anapol, D. (1997). *Polyamory: The new love without limits: Secrets of sustainable intimate relationships*. San Rafael, CA: IntiNet Resource Center.

Bartell, G. (1971). *Group sex: An eyewitness report on the American way of swinging*. New York: Wyden.

Berry, B. J. L. (1992). *America's utopian experiments: Communal havens from longwave crises*. Hanover, NH: University Press of New England.

Biblarz, A., & Biblarz, D. N. (1980). Alternative sociology for alternative life styles: A methodological critique of studies of swinging. *Social Behavior and Personality, 8*, 137–144.

Breedlove, W., & Breedlove, J. (1964). *Swapclubs*. Los Angeles: Sherbourne.

Bried, E. (1999, November). The Kink-o-meter. *Glamour, 97*, 82.

Buunk, B., & van Driel, B. (1989). *Variant lifestyles and relationships*. Newbury Park, CA: Sage.

Casler, L. (1974). *Is marriage necessary?* New York: Popular Library.

Chen, D. (1998, November). What goes on at a swinger's club? *Mademoiselle, 104*, 167–170.

Cherlin, A. J. (1999). *Public and private families* (2nd ed.). New York: McGraw-Hill.

Cloud, J. (1999, November 15). Henry & Mary & Janet &.... *Time, 155*, 90–91.

Constantine, L., & Constantine, J. M. (1973). *Group marriage*. New York: Collier.

Davidson, K. J., & Moore, N. B. (1996). *Marriage and family*. Boston: Allyn & Bacon.

DeLora, J. S., & DeLora, J. R. (Eds.). (1972). *Intimate life styles*. Pacific Palisades, CA: Goodyear.

Demo, D., Allen, K., & Fine, M. (Eds.). (2000). *Handbook of family diversity*. New York: Oxford University Press.

Denfield, D., & Gordon, M. (1970). The sociology of mate swapping: Or the family that swings together clings together. *Journal of Sex Research, 6*, 85–100.

Dixon, J. K. (1984). The commencement of bisexual activity in swinging married women over age thirty. *Journal of Sex Research, 20*, 71–90.

Duberman, L. (1974). *Marriage and its alternatives*. New York: Praeger.

Duckworth, J., & Levitt, E. E. (1985). Personality analysis of a swingers club. *Lifestyles, 8*, 35–45.

Ellis, A. (1970). Group marriage: A possible alternative? In H. A. Otto (Ed.), *The family in search of a future* (pp. 85–97). Norwalk, CT: Appleton-Century-Crofts.

Fellowship for Intentional Community. (1995). *Communities directory: A guide to cooperative living*. Langley, WA: Author.

Francoeur, A. K., & Francoeur, R. T. (1974). *Hot and cool sex.* New York: Harcourt Brace Jovanovich.

Gilmartin, B. (1977). Swinging: Who gets involved and how? In R. W. Libby & R. N. Whitehurst (Eds.), *Marriage and alternatives* (pp. 161–185). Glenview, IL: Scott, Foresman.

Gould, T., & Zabol, M. (1998). The other swing revival. *Saturday Night, 113,* 48–58.

Gross, H., & Sussman, M. B. (Eds.). (1982). Alternatives to traditional family living [Special issue]. *Marriage and Family Review, 5*(2).

Gross, M. (1992, June 8). Sex in the 90s. *New York, New York, 25,* 34–43.

Hart, H. H. (Ed.). (1972). *Marriage: For and against.* New York: Hart.

Hot sport. (1998, August 20). *Rolling Stone, 793,* 82.

Howe, L. K. (Ed.). (1972). *The future of the family.* New York: Touchstone.

Jenks, R. J. (1985a). A comparative study of swingers and nonswingers: Attitudes and beliefs. *Lifestyles, 7,* 5–20.

Jenks, R. J. (1985b). Swinging: A replication and test of a theory. *Journal of Sex Research, 21,* 199–205.

Jenks, R. J. (1985c). Swinging: A test of two theories and a proposed new model. *Archives of Sexual Behavior, 14,* 517–527.

Jenks, R. J. (1998). Swinging: A review of the literature. *Archives of Sexual Behavior, 27,* 507–521.

Kanter, R. M. (Ed.). (1973). *Communes: Creating and managing the collective life.* New York: Harper & Row.

Kassel, V. (1970). Polygyny after sixty. In H. A. Otto (Ed.), *The family in search of a future* (pp. 137–143). Norwalk, CT: Appleton-Century-Crofts.

Larsen, E. (1998, November/December). Poly sex for beginners. *Utne Reader, 90,* 20–21.

Libby, R. W., & Whitehurst, R. N. (Eds.). (1973). *Renovating marriage.* Danville, CA: Consensus.

Libby, R. W., & Whitehurst, R. N. (Eds.). (1977). *Marriage and alternatives: Exploring intimate relationships.* Glenview, IL: Scott, Foresman.

Macklin, E. D., & Rubin, R. H. (Eds.). (1983). *Contemporary families and alternative lifestyles: Handbook on research and theory.* Beverly Hills, CA: Sage.

Mazur, R. (1973). *The new intimacy: Open-ended marriage and alternative lifestyles.* Boston: Beacon.

Murdock, G. P. (1949). *Social structure.* New York: Macmillan.

Murr, A. (2000, November 13). Strange days in Utah. *Newsweek, 136,* 74.

Murstein, B. (Ed.). (1978). *Exploring intimate life styles.* New York: Springer.

Murstein, B., Case, D., & Gunn, S. P. (1985). Personality correlates of ex-swingers. *Lifestyles, 8,* 21–34.

Newman, J. (1993, October). Strange bedfellows. *GQ: Gentlemen's Quarterly, 63,* 161–167.

O'Neill, N., & O'Neill, G. (1972). *Open marriage.* New York: M. Evans.

Olson, D. H., & DeFrain, J. (2003). *Marriages and families* (4th ed.). Boston: McGraw-Hill.

Otto, H. A. (Ed.). (1970). *The family in search of a future.* Norwalk, CT: Appleton-Century-Crofts.

Peabody, S. A. (1982). Alternative life styles to monogamous marriage: Variants of normal behavior in psychotherapy clients. *Family Relations, 31,* 425–434.

Ramey, J. (1976). *Intimate friendships.* Englewood Cliffs, NJ: Prentice Hall.

Rayner, R. (2000, April 9). Back in the swing. *New York Times Magazine, 149,* 42–43.

Richardson, J. H. (1999, May). Scenes from a (group) marriage. *Esquire, 131,* 112–120.

Rimmer, R. H. (1966). *The Harrad experiment.* New York: Bantam.

Rimmer, R. H. (1968). *Proposition 31*. New York: Signet.

Roth, M., & Heard, A. (1997, February 16). They call it polyluv. *New York Times Magazine, 146,* 12.

Rouse, L. (2002). *Marital and sexual lifestyles in the United States.* New York: Haworth.

Roy, R., & Roy, D. (1968). *Honest sex: A revolutionary new sex guide for the now generation of Christians.* New York: Signet.

Rubin, R. H. (1978). A triadic relationship. In B. Murstein (Ed.), *Exploring intimate life styles* (pp. 147–162). New York: Springer.

Smith, J. R., & Smith, L. G. (Eds.). (1974). *Beyond monogamy.* Baltimore: Johns Hopkins University Press.

Smith, W. L. (1999). *Families and communes: An examination of nontraditional lifestyles.* Thousand Oaks, CA: Sage.

Stayton, W. R. (1985). Alternative lifestyles: Marital options. In D. C. Goldberg (Ed.), *Contemporary marriage: Special issues in couples therapy* (pp. 241–260). Belmont, CA: Dorsey.

Sussman, M. (Ed.). (1972). *Non-traditional family forms in the 1970s.* Minneapolis, MN: National Council on Family Relations.

Sussman, M., Steinmetz, S., & Peterson, G. (Eds.). (1999). *Handbook of marriage and the family* (2nd ed.). New York: Plenum.

Tevlin, J. (1996, March 13). The swing set. *Twin Cities Reader, 22,* 12–17.

Waite, L. J., & Gallagher, M. (2000). *The case for marriage.* New York: Doubleday.

Whitehurst, R. (1983). Sexual behavior in and out of marriage. *Marriage and Family Review, 6,* 115–124.

Wilson, T. J. B., & Myers, E. (1965). *Wife swapping: A complete 8 year survey of morals in North America.* New York: Volitant.

CHAPTER 3

The Social and Cultural Construction of American Childhood

STEVEN MINTZ

Childhood is not an unchanging, biological stage of life, and children are not just "grow'd," like Topsy in Harriet Beecher Stowe's *Uncle Tom's Cabin*. Rather, childhood is a social and cultural construct. Every aspect of childhood—including children's relationships with their parents and peers, their proportion of the population, and their paths through childhood to adulthood—has changed dramatically over the past four centuries. Methods of child rearing, the duration of schooling, the nature of children's play, young people's participation in work, and the points of demarcation between childhood, adolescence, and adulthood are products of culture, class, and historical era (Heywood, 2001; Illick, 2002).

Childhood in the past was experienced and conceived of in quite a different way than today. Just two centuries ago, there was far less age segregation than there is today and much less concern with organizing experience by chronological age. There was also far less sentimentalizing of children as special beings who were more innocent and vulnerable than adults. This does not mean that adults failed to recognize childhood as a stage of life with its own special needs and characteristics. Nor does it imply that parents were unconcerned about their children and failed to love them and mourn their deaths. Rather, it means that the experience of young people was organized and valued very differently than it is today.

Language itself illustrates shifts in the construction of childhood. Two hundred years ago, the words used to describe childhood were far less precise than those we use today. The word *infancy* referred not to the months after birth but to the period in which children were under their mother's control, typically from birth to age 5 or 6. The word *childhood* might refer to someone as young as 5 or 6 or as old as the late teens or early 20s. The word was vague because chronological age was less important than physical strength, size, and maturity. Instead of using our term *adolescence* or *teenager*, Americans two centuries ago used a broader and more expansive term, *youth*, which stretched from the preteen years until the early or mid-20s. The vagueness of this term reflected the amorphousness of the life stages. A young person did not achieve full adult status until marriage and establishment of an independent farm or entrance into a full-time trade or profession. Full adulthood might be attained as early as the mid- or late teens but usually did not occur until the late 20s or early 30s (Chudacoff, 1989; Kett, 1977).

How, then, has childhood changed over the past 400 years? The transformations might be grouped into four broad categories. The first involves shifts in the timing, sequence, and stages of growing up. Over the past four centuries, the stages of childhood have grown much more precise, uniform, and prescriptive. Demography is a second force for change. A sharp reduction in the birthrate has more rigidly divided families into distinct generations and allowed parents to lavish more time, attention, and resources on each child. A third major shift involves the separation of children from work, the equation of childhood with schooling, and the increasing integration of the young into a consumer society. The fourth category is attitudinal. Adult conceptions of childhood have shifted profoundly over time, from the 17th-century Puritan image of children as depraved beings who needed to be restrained, to the Enlightened notion of children as blank slates who could be shaped by environmental influences, to the Romantic conception of children as creatures with innocent souls and redeemable, docile wills, to the Darwinian emphasis on highly differentiated stages of children's cognitive, physiological, and emotional development, to the Freudian conception of children as seething cauldrons of instinctual drives, to contemporary notions that emphasize children's competence and capacity for early learning.

CARICATURE AND HISTORY

Our images of childhood in the past tend to be colored by caricature and stereotype. According to one popular narrative, the history of childhood is essentially a story of progress: a movement away from ignorance, cruelty, superstition, and authoritarianism to enlightenment and heightened concern. From a world in which children were treated as little adults, grown-ups only gradually came to recognize children as having special needs and a unique nature. In this Whiggish narrative, the New England Puritans play a pivotal role. These zealous Calvinist Protestants serve as the retrograde symbols of a less enlightened past.

The Puritans are easily caricatured as an emotionally cold and humorless people who regarded even newborn infants as embodiments of sin, who terrorized the young with threats of damnation and hellfire, and who believed that the chief task of parenthood was to break children's sinful will. Yet if we are to truly understand the changes that have occurred in young people's lives, it is essential to move beyond the misleading stereotype of stern Puritan patriarchs bent on crushing children's will through fear of damnation. The fact is that the Puritans were among the very first people in the Western world to seriously and systematically reflect on the nature of childhood. Surviving evidence suggests that many Puritan parents cherished their children, expressed deep concern for their salvation, and were convinced that the prospects of their movement ultimately depended on winning the rising generation's minds and souls.

The Puritans did, however, conceive of children very differently than we do today. They regarded young children as "incomplete adults" who were dangerously unformed, even animalistic, in their inability to speak and their impulse to crawl and who needed to be transformed as rapidly as possible into speaking, standing human beings. This conception of childhood shaped Puritan child-rearing practices. Instead of allowing infants to crawl on the floor, they placed them in "walking-stools" or "go-carts"—similar to modern-day "walkers." They placed even very young girls in corsets to make them appear more adultlike, and for the same reason they sometimes placed a rod along the spine of children of both sexes to ensure an erect posture (Calvert, 1992).

Though Puritan parents and ministers expressed concern about sin, their primary stress was not on repressing immorality but rather on instilling piety within children and promoting their spiritual conversion. Surviving evidence suggests that Puritan American parents were in closer and more constant contact with their children and interacted more often and more deeply with them than their counterparts in Europe. When the Puritans did seek to combat child-ish and youthful sins, they relied less on physical punishment than on communal oversight, education, work, and an unusually intense family life. Instead of emphasizing physical punishment and external con-straints, Puritan parents stressed internalized restraints as they sought to instill within their children feelings of unworthiness and of vul-nerability to divine judgment. Within their home, Puritan children were taught the necessity of recognizing their sinfulness and striving for repentance and salvation (Demos, 1970; Morgan, 1966).

Until surprisingly recently, it was taken for granted that 17th-century New England did not recognize a stage of development compa-rable to modern adolescence and lacked any-thing remotely resembling a modern youth culture. We now know that this view is wrong. Contrary to the older notion that the ready availability of land and a shortage of labor accelerated the passage to adulthood, it is clear that childhood in New England, as in old England, was followed by a protracted transitional period of "semidependence" called youth. Not wholly dependent on their parents for economic support, yet not in a position to set up an independent household, young people moved in and out of their parental home and participated in a distinc-tive culture of their own. As early as age 7 or 8 (but usually in their early teens), many young people lived and worked in other people's homes as servants or apprentices.

DIVERSITY IN COLONIAL AMERICA

Diversity from one region to another was a hallmark of life in colonial America. New England was extremely healthy and stable; Maryland and Virginia were deadly and chaotic. New England was settled primarily by families, the Chesapeake region predomi-nantly by single young males in their teens and 20s.

In 17th-century New England, a healthful environment and a balanced sex ratio encouraged the establishment of households that were more stable and patriarchal than in England itself. Plentiful land allowed early New Englanders to maintain inheritance pat-terns that kept children close to home. The church and community strongly reinforced paternal authority, and fathers intervened in their offspring's lives even after their off-spring had reached adulthood—for example, by having legal authority to consent, or deny consent, to marriages.

In the colonial Chesapeake, in contrast, a high mortality rate and a sharply skewed sex ratio inhibited the formation of stable families until the late 17th or 18th centuries. Stepparents, stepchildren, stepsiblings, and orphans were common, and parents rarely lived to see their grandchildren. The defining experience in the lives of immigrant youth in the 17th-century Chesapeake region was the institution of indentured servitude.

Approximately three quarters of English migrants to the Chesapeake arrived as indentured servants, agreeing to labor for a term of service—usually 4 to 7 years—in exchange for passage and room and board. Before 1660, approximately 50,000 English immigrants arrived in Virginia. Most were young, single, and male, usually in their late teens or early 20s. More than half of all indentured servants died before their term of service expired. In England, service was often described as a familylike relationship in which servants were likened to children. In the Chesapeake, in contrast, servants were treated more like chattel property who were at risk of physical abuse and disease (Mintz & Kellogg, 1988).

In the Middle Colonies of New York, New Jersey, Pennsylvania, and Delaware, and particularly among the Quakers, conceptions of family and childhood first arose that anticipated those characteristic of the 19th and 20th centuries. Unlike New England and Chesapeake households, which often sheltered servants, apprentices, laborers, and other dependents within their walls and which often lived in close proximity to extended relatives, the Middle Colonies tended to have private families, consisting exclusively of a father, mother, and children bound together by ties of affection. Not essentially a unit of production or a vehicle for transmitting property and craft skills, the private family was regarded as an instrument for educating children and forming their character. Quaker parents, in particular, emphasized equality over hierarchy, gentle guidance over strict discipline, and relatively early autonomy for children (Levy, 1988).

Far from being a static or slowly changing era, the colonial period was a time of dynamic and far-reaching changes. Even before the American Revolution, the progression of young people toward adulthood had grown increasingly problematic. In the face of rapid population growth, there was no longer sufficient land to sustain the older distribution of social roles within local communities. Economic, demographic, and other social changes weakened parental and communal control over the young—a development manifest in a dramatic increase in rates of illegitimacy and in pregnancies contracted before marriage. The rate of premarital pregnancies (involving brides who bore children in less than 8 months after marriage) rose from under 10% of first births at the end of the 17th century to about 40%. At the same time, the older system of indentured servitude declined. By the end of the century, apprenticeship, instead of being a system of training in a craft skill, was becoming a source of cheap labor. Choice of a vocation was becoming more problematic, and the teen years were becoming a period of increasing uncertainty (Greven, 1970; Rorabaugh, 1986).

THE LATE-18TH- AND EARLY-19TH-CENTURY PARADOX: THE SENTIMENTALIZATION AND REGIMENTATION OF CHILDHOOD

The Enlightenment and the Romantic movement produced two new conceptions of childhood and youth that were to have vast repercussions for the future. From the Romantic movement came a conception of the child as a symbol of organic wholeness and spiritual vision, a creature purer and more sensitive and intuitive than any adult. From the Enlightenment came a celebration of youth as a symbol of innovation and social change, an image captured in Eugene Delacroix's painting *Liberty Leading the People,* where liberty is personified as a young male (Coveney, 1967; Gillis, 1974). The 19th-century urban middle class would simplify and popularize these notions, depicting the child in terms of asexual innocence, sinless purity, and vulnerability and as a symbol of the future. This attitude could be seen in the practice of dressing young girls and boys in identical asexual smocks or gowns and leaving young boys with long curls. It was also evident in a mounting effort to shelter young people from the contamination of the adult world (Calvert, 1992; Ryan, 1981).

But the urban middle class also embraced a somewhat contradictory set of values. If childhood was to be a carefree period of play, it was also to serve as training ground for adulthood. By the early 19th century, the process of socialization had grown problematic in new ways. Unable to transmit their status position directly to their children by bequeathing them family lands, middle-class parents adopted a variety of new strategies to assist their children. They sharply reduced their birthrates, which fell from an average of 7 to 10 children in 1800 to 5 in 1850 and just 3 in 1900. Reduced birthrates, accomplished through a mixture of abstinence and coitus interruptus, supplemented by abortion, allowed parents to devote more attention and resources to each child's upbringing. Meanwhile, industrialization and urbanization took the urban middle-class father from the home, leaving the mother in charge—and that situation led to new child-rearing techniques. There was a greater emphasis on the maternal role in shaping children's moral character and on the manipulation of guilt and withdrawal of affection rather than physical coercion. At the same time, young people's residence in the parental home became more prolonged and continuous, usually lasting until their late teens or early 20s. Perhaps the most important development was the emergence, beginning in Massachusetts in the 1830s, of a new system of public schooling emphasizing age-graded classes, longer school terms, and a uniform curriculum (Cott, 1977; Reinier, 1996).

THE PERSISTENT IMPORTANCE OF CLASS, ETHNICITY, GENDER, AND REGION

During the 19th century, there was no single, common pattern of childhood. Rather, there were a multiplicity of childhoods, differentiated by class, ethnicity, gender, and geographical location. Indeed, at no point in American history was childhood more diverse than in the mid– and late 19th century. Gender, ethnicity, race, region, and, above all, social class helped determine the length of childhood, the duration of schooling, the age of entry into work, even the kinds of play that children took part in, the toys they acquired, and the books they read (Clement, 1997).

The children of the urban middle class, prosperous commercial farmers, and southern planters enjoyed increasingly long childhoods, free from major household or work responsibilities until their late teens or 20s, whereas the offspring of urban workers, frontier farmers, and blacks, both slave and free, had briefer childhoods and became involved in work inside or outside the home before they reached their teens. Many urban working-class children contributed to the family economy by scavenging in the streets, vacant lots, or back alleys, collecting coal, wood, and other items that could be used at home or sold. Others took part in the street trades, selling gum, peanuts, and crackers. In industrial towns, young people under the age of 15 contributed on average about 20% of their family's income. In mining areas, boys as young as 10 or 12 worked as breakers, separating coal from pieces of slate and wood, before becoming miners in their mid- or late teens. On farms, children as young as 5 or 6 might pull weeds or chase birds and cattle away from crops. By the time they reached the age of 8, many tended livestock, and as they grew older they milked cows, churned butter, fed chickens, collected eggs, hauled water, scrubbed laundry, and harvested crops. A blurring of gender roles among children and youth was especially common on frontier farms (Clement, 1997; Nasaw, 1985; Stansell, 1986).

Schooling varied as widely, as did work routines. In the rural North, the Midwest, and the Far West, most mid- and late-19th-century students attended one-room schools for 3 to 6 months a year. In contrast, city children attended age-graded classes taught by professional teachers 9 months a year. In both rural and urban areas, girls tended to receive more schooling than boys (Clement, 1997).

CHILD PROTECTION

As early as the 1820s, middle-class reformers were shocked by the sight of gangs of youths prowling the streets, young girls selling matchbooks on street corners, and teenage prostitutes plying their trade in front of hotels or on theaters' third floor. Concerned about the "deviant" family life of the immigrant and native-born working classes, reformers adopted a variety of strategies to address problems of gangs, juvenile delinquency, and child abuse, neglect, and poverty in the nation's rapidly growing cities. Child savers, as these youth workers and reformers were known, were determined to save children from the moral and physical dangers of city streets, poverty, and parental ignorance and abuse.

During the 19th century, reformers' interest in improving the well-being of American children led them to create age-specific programs and institutions for delinquent, disabled, and dependent young people, from public schools, orphan asylums, and foundling homes to YMCAs, children's hospitals, and reform schools. Child savers tended to believe that moral training would alleviate many of the problems associated with urbanization, industrialization, and immigration. The number of institutions that the child savers created is astounding. By 1900, a directory of public and private charities for young people and their families was 620 pages long. Meanwhile, African Americans, Irish and Italian Catholics, eastern European Jews, and other ethnic groups established their own child-saving institutions and agencies, rooted in their own needs and attitudes toward childhood, poverty, and relief. African Americans devised an informal system of adoption that was later institutionalized within the black community itself. Concern with children was a trans-Atlantic phenomenon. Indeed, the inspiration for such innovations as tax-supported public schools and kindergartens (the first of which appeared in St. Louis in 1873), and for such reform movements as raising age-of-consent laws, came from abroad. Britain enacted at least 79 statutes on the subject of child welfare and education between 1870 and 1908 (Ashby, 1997).

Child saving—a phrase initially associated with Elbridge Gerry's New York Society for the Prevention of Cruelty to Children, which was founded in 1874—evolved through a series of overlapping phases. The first phase, which we might term "child rescue," began during the 1790s and involved the establishment by private philanthropists of congregate institutions for poor, dependent, and delinquent children, ranging from Sunday schools and orphan asylums to houses of refuge and reform schools. Instead of assisting poor children in their own homes or relying on a system of indentures to handle problems of delinquency, dependency, and poverty, reformers generally viewed congregate institutions as the most effective and cost-efficient way to address problems that were more visible in an urban setting. These institutions sought to instill "middle class values and lower class skills" (Platt, 1977, p. 176) by internalizing the values of order and self-discipline, while instructing male inmates in manual skills and simple crafts and female inmates in knitting, sewing, and housework (Ashby, 1997; Holloran, 1989).

The child-saving agencies, which were generally staffed by untrained, underpaid caretakers or political appointees, tended to blur the distinction between dependent children, delinquents, and potential delinquents. These institutions, which served both as schools and as prisons, adopted expansive definitions of delinquency, including acts that would not be crimes if committed by adults, such as truancy, incorrigibility, disobedience, and running away. Definitions of deviance were significantly influenced by gender. Females, but not males, were institutionalized for sexual promiscuity. Fixated on urban problems, the institutions tended to neglect rural children, who were frequently confined with adults in county poorhouses. Even when institutions were built in rural areas, the inmates were overwhelming urban in origin. It is important, however, to recognize that these new institutions were not simply imposed upon the poor. Parents in poverty often used these institutions for their own purposes. In times of crisis, orphan asylums served as temporary boardinghouses (Ashby, 1997; Brenzel, 1983; Schneider, 1992).

This first phase of child saving set important precedents for the future. It established two crucial legal principles—"the best interests of the child," an expansive concept that gave judges broad discretion to make decisions regarding children's custody, and *parens patriae*, the legal doctrine that gives the government authority to serve as a child's guardian. The doctrine of *parens patriae* had two sides. On the one hand, it held that the state had the legal authority to intervene in cases where families had failed, and it therefore mandated public intervention to rectify parental failure, abuse, or neglect. On the other hand, the doctrine implied that the state should intervene only in the most extreme instances of abuse or neglect. This meant that in the interest of respecting family privacy, public authorities would ignore all but the most severe problems (Sutton, 1988).

By the 1850s, a reaction against congregate institutions had begun to set in as the prisonlike character of asylums and orphanages became increasingly self-evident. A number of reformers responded by creating smaller, more familylike "cottages," while the new children's aid societies inaugurated a program of orphan trains, fostering out poor city children to farm families in the Midwest and later in the Far West. By 1929, the aid societies had transported over 200,000 children and adolescents from eastern cities. Driven by a mixture of charitable and economic motives, the aid societies hoped to remove poor children from pernicious urban influences and supply workers for labor-short rural areas. Despite efforts to find alternatives to the institutional care of dependent and delinquent children, congregate institutions continued to dominate the care of destitute, delinquent, dependent, and disabled children well into the 20th century. Many working-class and immigrant parents were simply unable to maintain their children during periods of crisis. In addition, it proved impossible to place many infants or sick or disabled children in foster homes. In some cases, children voluntarily returned to institutions after harrowing experiences in foster homes (Ashby, 1997; Holt, 1992; O'Connor, 2001).

A second phase of reform, which we might call "child protection," was sparked by the "discovery" of child abuse in the 1870s, when doctors, crusading journalists, humanitarian reformers, and urban elites began to turn their attention to the problems of children of the immigrant poor. Patterned after reformers' earlier interest in cruelty toward animals, these campaigns sought to rescue innocent children who had been mistreated or abandoned. Concern with child abuse led to investigation of other forms of abuse, such as the phenomenon of "baby farming," the practice of sending unwanted infants off to boarding homes where they were badly neglected or simply allowed to die. Other abuses that aroused the concern of child protectors were claims that children being murdered for insurance money and that young girls were being sold into the white slave trade, prostitution. As early as the 1870s, child protectors campaigned to move children out of poorhouses (which often meant separating children from their parents). In subsequent years, reformers called for regulating or abolishing baby farming, raising the age of consent for sexual relations, and establishing day nurseries for working mothers. Societies for the Prevention of Cruelty to Children played a crucial role in the expansion of state power to regulate families. Even though they were private agencies, they were granted authority to search homes to investigate suspected cases of abuse and to remove children from their parents. The "Cruelty" was often accused of breaking up poor families on flimsy grounds, but one of the most striking findings of recent scholarship is that much of the demand for state intervention came from family members themselves. Initially led by gentleman amateurs, the child protection organizations gradually came under the administration of professional middle-class female social workers (Gordon, 1988; Pleck, 1987).

The third and most far-reaching phase in the history of child welfare is associated with the Progressive Era. Beginning in the 1890s, professional charity and settlement house workers, educators, penologists, and sociologists called for expanded state responsibility and professional administration to assist dependent and delinquent children. They championed campaigns against child labor, compulsory education laws, juvenile courts, kindergartens, the playground movement, and public health measures to reduce child mortality. They sought to keep poor children with their parents and out of massive, regimented, ineffective institutions, off crowded and perilous streets, and away from exploitative and dangerous sweatshops, mines, and factories (Macleod, 1998; Tiffin, 1982).

An especially important constituency for child welfare initiatives came from activist women organized into clubs and federations throughout the country. Among the first women to attend college, these clubwomen organized at the grassroots level and succeeded in winning laws limiting work hours for women; establishing a federal Children's Bureau; and enacting laws, subsequently overturned by the courts, abolishing child labor. Less suspicious of government corruption than easterners, midwesterners, such as Nebraska-born Grace and Edith Abbott, Homer Folks from Michigan, and Edwin Witte of Wisconsin, took the lead in pressing for a federal role in child welfare. The 1909 White House Conference on Children and establishment of the U.S. Children's Bureau in 1912 demonstrated that child welfare had become a national concern.

Some of the Progressive Era's greatest successes involved children's health, aided by the discovery of the germ theory of disease and the pasteurization of milk. In New York City, the infant death rate fell from 144 per 1,000 in 1908 to less than 50 per 1,000 by 1939. Deaths from infectious disease also dropped sharply. In New York, the mortality rate from tuberculosis dropped 61% between 1907 and 1917 (Lindenmeyer, 1997; Prescott, 1998).

Another significant advance involved enactment of mother's pensions, which allowed impoverished mothers to care for children in their own homes. Illinois adopted the first mothers' pension law in 1911; 8 years later, 39 states and Alaska and Hawaii had enacted similar laws. However, the mother's pension laws discriminated against mothers of color and provided benefits only to women deemed respectable. Benefits were so inadequate that most recipients had to supplement benefits with wage labor. The Social Security Act of 1935 added federal funds to the state programs. But the programs remained stingy and stigmatizing, as aid was means tested and morals tested. Recipients of aid were required to prove that they were completely impoverished; they were also subject to surprise visits to ensure their respectability. A short-lived achievement was enactment of the Sheppard-Towner Act, which disseminated information about pre- and postnatal care for mothers and infants and provided home visits for mothers mainly in rural areas. This latter triumph was reversed by the end of the 1920s by opposition from the medical profession and the Public Health Service, which resented encroachment into their domains. Child labor was finally abolished by the 1937 Fair Labor Standards Act (Lindenmeyer, 1997; Tiffin, 1982).

One of the most lasting achievements of the Progressive Era child savers was the creation of the modern juvenile justice system. A loss of confidence in the ability of reform schools to rehabilitate youthful offenders, combined with a Progressive faith in the ability of professionals to assist young people, inspired the creation of juvenile courts and the probation system. In the new juvenile justice system, youthful offenders were treated as delinquents rather than as criminals; proceedings took place in private, without a jury or a transcript; and a juvenile court judge had the discretion to commit delinquents to an institution or to probation for the remainder of their childhood and adolescence. What was most distinctive about the juvenile court was its emphasis on probation and family-centered treatment. The alleged purpose of the juvenile court was to protect and rehabilitate youthful offenders, not to punish

them. But because these were not viewed as adversarial proceedings, due process protections did not apply. In addition, young people could be brought before juvenile courts for status offenses that would not be crimes for adults. In most jurisdictions, juvenile offenders were not entitled to receive prior notice of charges against them, to be protected against self-incrimination, to cross-examine witnesses, or to have an attorney defend them (Getis, 2000).

Following World War I, emphasis on child saving declined. Attention was directed away from the economic threats to children's welfare and focused instead on individual psychology. Child guidance clinics sought to address the problems of maladjusted, rebellious, and predelinquent children. The declining emphasis on children's welfare reflected a variety of factors: the waning influence of the women's movement; social workers' embrace of psychoanalytic theories that emphasized individual adjustment; and the Great Depression and World War II, which diverted public attention away from children's issues. One positive effect of this shift in focus was that it challenged an earlier overemphasis on eugenics and encouraged a recognition of the importance of the environmental factors influencing children's development. Institutions like the Iowa Child Welfare Research Station, the world's first institute to conduct scientific research on children's development, and rival centers at Berkeley, Minnesota, and Yale demonstrated the decisive importance of a child's experiences during the first years of life, helping to pave the way for early childhood education programs such as Head Start (Cravens, 1993; Jones, 1999).

Child saving raises difficult issues of evaluation. The child savers have been accused of class bias, discrimination against single mothers, imposition of middle-class values on the poor, and confusion of delinquency and neglect with survival strategies adopted by the poor. There can be no doubt that many of the policies adopted by the child savers broke up families and criminalized behavior that had not been regarded as illegal in the past. Meanwhile, there was a marked disjuncture between the reformers' heady aspirations and their actual achievements. Hobbled by legislative stinginess, many of their reforms had negligible effects (Hawes, 1991).

UNIVERSALIZING MIDDLE-CLASS CHILDHOOD

A revolution in the lives of young people began toward the end of the 19th century. Among this revolution's defining characteristics were the development of more elaborate notions of the stages of childhood development, prolonged education, delayed entry into the workforce, and the increasing segregation of young people in adult-sponsored, adult-organized institutions—ranging from junior high and high schools to the Boy and Girl Scouts (Macleod, 1983, 1998). Partly the result of demographic and economic developments, which reduced the demand for child labor and greatly decreased the proportion of children in the general population—from half the population in the mid-19th century to a third by 1900—these changes also reflected the *imposition* by adults of new structures on young people's lives as well as a new conception of children's proper chronological development (Kett, 1977).

Before the Civil War, young people moved sporadically in and out of their parental home, schools, and jobs—an irregular, episodic pattern that the historian Joseph F. Kett (1977) termed "semidependence." A young person might take on work responsibilities, within or outside the home, as young as age 8 or 9 and enter an apprenticeship around age 12 or 14, returning home periodically for briefer or longer periods. The teen years were a period of uncertain status and anxiety marked by a jarring mixture of freedom and subordination. During the second half of the 19th century, there were heightened efforts to replace unstructured contacts with adults with age-segregated institutions. Lying behind this development was a belief that young people would benefit from growing up with others their own age; that youth should be devoted to education, play, and character-building activities; and that maturation should take place gradually, inside a loving home and segregated from adult affairs. Urbanization also contributed to this development, as more same-aged children congregated in cities. Universalizing the middle-class pattern of childhood was the product of protracted struggle. Not until the 1930s was child labor finally outlawed (by the Fair Labor Standards Act of 1937), and not until the 1950s did high school attendance become a universal experience (Kett, 1977; Macleod, 1983; Storrs, 2000; Trattner, 1970).

The impact of this revolution in young people's lives remains in dispute. On the positive side, it greatly expanded educational opportunities and reduced the exploitation of children in factories, mines, and street trades. But this revolution also entailed certain costs. The adult-organized institutions and organizations that were developed around the turn of the 20th century promoted norms of conformity and anti-intellectualism and made it more difficult for young people to assert their growing maturity and competence outside the realm of sports. More uniform and standardized age norms also made it more difficult for those who could not adapt to a more structured sequence of growing up. Ironically, the creation of adult-organized institutions allowed young people to create new kinds of youth cultures that were at least partially free of adult control and supervision (Graebner, 1990; Kett, 1977).

In the wake of the Darwinian revolution, educators, psychologists, church workers, youth workers, and parents themselves began to pay increasing attention to the stages of children's physiological and psychological development and to develop new institutions that were supposed to meet the needs of young people of distinct ages. Before the Civil War, and especially before the 1840s, chronological age was only loosely connected to young people's experience. Physical size and maturity were more important than a young person's actual age. Schools, workplaces, young men's organizations (such as volunteer military and fire companies and literary or debating societies), and even colleges contained young people of widely varying ages. But beginning with the establishment of age-graded school classrooms in the 1840s and 1850s, age consciousness intensified. During the mid- and late 19th century, there was a growing concern with the proper chronological development of young people and a growing abhorrence of "precocity." One of the first signs of this shift in attitude took place in the 1830s and 1840s, when children as young as 3, 4, 5, and even 6 were expelled from public schools—a development partially reversed in the late 1880s with the first public funding of kindergartens (Chudacoff, 1989; Kett, 1977).

A key contributor to the heightened sensitivity to age was the educational psychologist G. Stanley Hall. His survey of children entering Boston schools in 1880 inspired the "child study" movement, which encouraged teachers and parents to collect information about the stages of child development. The years surrounding puberty were singled out for special attention. The publication in 1904 of Hall's two-volume work *Adolescence* would give reformers, educators, and parents not only a label but also an explanation for the unique character of this age group. Hall argued that children recapitulated the stages of evolution of the human race, from presavagery to civilization. To become happy, well-adjusted adults, children had to successfully pass through each of these stages. Adolescence, between 13 and 18 years of age, was particularly crucial. "The dawn of puberty," Hall wrote, "is soon followed by a stormy period when there is a peculiar proneness to be either very good or very bad." A period of awkwardness and vulnerability, adolescence was a time not only of sexual maturation but also of turbulent moral and psychological change (Kett, 1977; Ross, 1972).

Even before Hall popularized the term *adolescence,* religious, health, and educational concerns had led reformers to focus on the years surrounding puberty. Fearful that the early teen years saw a falling away from religious faith, a new emphasis was placed on religious rituals that coincided with the onset of puberty, such as confirmation and the Jewish bar mitzvah. Adult-sponsored organizations emphasizing "muscular Christianity," such as Christian Endeavor, the Epworth League, and the YMCA, were founded or expanded to meet young people's health and religious needs (Macleod, 1983; Putney, 2001).

By the end of the 19th century, anxieties about the teen years had further intensified. The term *adolescence* was no longer merely descriptive; it had become prescriptive. Worries about precocious sexual activities among girls led reformers, beginning in the 1880s, to lobby to raise age-of-consent laws and to stringently enforce statutory rape laws. Concern that young people would be contaminated by exposure to commercial entertainments at night led to adoption, in many cities, of curfews. Fear that if young men entered the workforce too soon, without adequate schooling, they would find themselves stuck in dead-end jobs stimulated demand for child labor legislation—a demand that received support from labor unions concerned about the substitution of teen laborers for adult workers (Kett, 1977; Macleod, 1998; Odem, 1995).

In 19th-century working-class and farm families, children were valuable contributors to the family economy, whereas urban middle-class children were increasingly sheltered from the world of work. Beginning in the late 19th century, social reformers demanded that the protections for middle-class children apply to working-class and immigrant children as well. All children, regardless of their family's circumstances, had a right to an education and a safe and protected childhood. Children were transformed from objects of utility into objects of sentiment (Zelizer, 1994). Bitter political and legal battles erupted over what a childhood should be. Whereas many poor and immigrant parents clung to the notion that children should be economically useful, middle-class child savers saw this as exploitation of children. The organized working class had long been opposed to child labor, but certain employers, especially southern mill owners, fostered the view that work was good for children (Macleod, 1998).

During the 20th century, the process of growing up gradually grew more uniform. All young people, irrespective of class, ethnicity, gender, and region, were expected to pass through the same institutions and experiences at roughly the same age. Perhaps the most important development was the transformation of the high school from an institution for college preparation for the few to one preparing all young people for life (Chudacoff, 1989; Macleod, 1998).

CHILDREN AS ACTIVE AGENTS

Children are not passive recipients of the broader culture. They are adaptive within the limits of the environment in which they find themselves. Sometimes young people have exhibited a collective power that is remarkable. In 1899, newsboys in New York formed a union and staged a largely successful strike against William Randolph Hearst and Joseph Pulitzer (Nasaw, 1985).

In the late 19th century, the children of the "New Immigrants" from eastern and southern Europe often served as crucial cultural intermediaries. Age relationships within families were often inverted, as young people, who often picked up English and American customs more easily than their parents, helped negotiate relationships between their families and landlords, employers, and government bureaucrats (Berrol, 1995).

In the 20th century, young people repeatedly served as a cultural avant-garde, playing a pivotal role in the process of cultural change. The development of dating, which began to appear in the 1910s, illustrates the ability of young people to create a culture apart from that imposed by adults. Around the same time, working-class children and youth quickly embraced the expanding world of commercial entertainment of penny arcades, movies, and amusement parks, soon making up a large share of the audience for commercial amusements. At least since the 1920s, the teen years have often been a period of intercultural mixing, as young people have absorbed and revised clothing and musical styles from groups across ethnic and class lines (Peiss, 1986).

Finally, throughout the 20th century young people played political roles that have often been forgotten or marginalized. During the late 1950s and 1960s, young people stood at the forefront of efforts to integrate public schools and to protest the Vietnam War. Though we generally associate the student protests of the 1960s with college students, there were massive demonstrations, involving tens of thousands of high school students, demanding more equitable funding of public education, bilingual education, a more relevant curriculum, and smaller classes.

CHILDREN'S RIGHTS

During the turbulent 1960s and early 1970s, several influential social critics—such as Edgar Z. Friedenberg, Paul Goodman, Jules Henry, and Kenneth Keniston—argued that postwar society's methods of child rearing and socialization interfered with young people's central developmental tasks. The postwar young grew up in a world of contradictions. Middle-class society valued independence but made the young dependent on adults to fulfill their needs; it stressed achievement but gave the young few avenues in which to achieve. By adhering to a romantic view of childhood innocence, middle-class society denied young people their freedom and their rights. American society had segregated children into a separate category and failed to recognize their growing competence and maturity; in its concern for protecting childhood innocence, it had limited the responsibilities given to young people and punished them severely when they fell from that state of innocence (Holt, 1975).

The concept of children's rights was one of the most significant outgrowths of the liberation struggles of the 1960s. It was also a product of a significant demographic development, the postwar baby boom, which dramatically altered the ratio of adults to children, shifting cultural influence to the young. The phrase *children's rights* was not new. As early as 1905, the Progressive Era reformer Florence Kelley asserted that a right to childhood existed. During the late 1940s, a number of books invoking the phrase appeared. But in general, the phrase involved enumerating children's needs, such as a right to an education, a right to play, and a right to be loved and cared for. These early defenses of children's rights emphasized children's vulnerable status and their need for a nurturing environment and wanted to permit the state to assume a broader role in intervening in families in cases of need (Hawes, 1991).

Advocates of children's rights during the 1960s and 1970s had a different goal in mind. They wanted to award minors many of the same legal rights as adults, including the right to make certain medical or educational decisions on their own and a right to have their voice heard in decisions over adoption, custody, divorce, termination of parental rights, or child abuse. The Supreme Court rulings in the 1969 *Tinker* case, which guaranteed students the right to free speech and expression, and the 1967 case *In re Gault,* which granted young people certain procedural rights in juvenile court proceedings, marked the beginning of a legal revolution in the rights of children. A major arena of legal conflict involved the explosive issue of teenage sexuality. The most controversial issue was whether minors would be able to obtain contraceptives or abortions without parental consent. In a 1977 case, *Carey v. Population Services International* (1977), the Supreme Court invalidated a New York law that prohibited the sale of condoms to adolescents under 16, concluding that the "right to privacy in connection with decisions affecting procreation extends to minors as well as adults." The Court held that the state interest in discouraging adolescents' sexual activity was not furthered by withholding from them the means to protect themselves.

In subsequent cases, courts struck down state laws requiring parental notice or consent if their children sought contraceptives. In *Planned Parenthood Association v. Matheson* (D. Utah 1983), for example, a federal district court recognized that teenagers' "decisions whether to accomplish or prevent conception are among the most private and sensitive" and concluded that "the state may not impose a blanket parental notification requirement on minors seeking to exercise their constitutionally protected right to decide whether to bear or beget a child by using contraceptives." The two most important sources of federal family planning funds in the nation—Title X of the Public Health Service Act of 1970 and Medicaid (Title XIX of the Social Security Act of 1965)—require the confidential provision of contraceptive services to eligible recipients, regardless of their age or marital status. By 1995, condom availability programs were operating in at least 431 public schools.

Schools became a central battlefield in the children's rights controversies. In the majority opinion in the *Tinker* case, Associate Justice Abe Fortas wrote that schools were special places and that civil liberties had to be balanced against "the need for affirming the comprehensive authority of the states and of school officials, to prescribe and control conduct." In subsequent cases, the court has sought to define this balance. In the 1975 case of *Goss v. Lopez,* the Court granted students the right to due process when they were threatened with a suspension of more than 10 days and declared that a punishment cannot be more serious than the misconduct. But the Court, fearful of undercutting principals' and teachers' authority, announced that schools needed to provide only informal hearings, not elaborate judicial procedures. And students, the Court went on to say, did not have a right to a hearing for a minor punishment such as a detention or if they posed a danger to other students or school property. In other cases, the justices ruled that school officials could search student lockers, but only when they had grounds for believing that a specific locker contained dangerous or illegal items. It permitted administrators to impose random drug tests, but only on students engaging in extracurricular activities. It allowed school authorities to censor school newspapers only when these were sponsored by the school itself (*Board of*

Education of Independent School District No. 92 of Pottawatomie County v. Earls, 2002; *Hazelwood School Dist. v. Kuhlmeier,* 1988; *United States v. Sokolow,* 1988).

Gender equity for girls and young women offered yet another front in the battle for children's rights. The basic legal tool for attaining gender equity was Title IX of the Educational Amendments of 1972, which prohibited sex discrimination in any educational program or activity. It required schools to grant female students equal academic and athletic opportunities. Academic opportunity was the initial concern, but athletics quickly became the most visible field of contention. In 1971, 3.7 million boys and just 294,015 girls participated in high school sports. By 2000, boys' participation had risen to 3.9 million and girls' to 2.7 million, a nearly tenfold increase.

Since the mid-1970s, utopian visions of children's liberation have been displaced by a preoccupation with child abuse and protection—and with punishing juveniles who commit serious crimes as adults. A series of "moral panics" over children's well-being fueled this cultural shift. Over the past three decades, American society experienced a series of highly publicized panics over teen pregnancy; stranger abduction of children; ritual sexual abuse in day care centers; youthful smoking, drinking, and illicit drug use; and youth gangs, juvenile predators; and school shootings (Jenkins, 1998).

Panics about children's well-being are nothing new. During World War II, there was an obsession with latchkey children and fear about a purported explosion in juvenile delinquency. After the war, there were panics over youth gangs and, most remarkably, over the supposedly deleterious effects of comic books. But there seems little doubt that the panics that have spread since 1970 have been more widely publicized and have had a greater impact on public perception and policy. In retrospect, it seems clear that the waves of public hysteria over these problems were truly "moral panics" in a sociological sense. That is, they were highly exaggerated. They were inextricably linked to anxieties over profound changes in adults' lives—especially the increase in married women's participation in the workforce and family instability, shifts in sexual mores, and the growing prevalence of drug use. By virtually every statistical measure, young people are better off today than in any previous generation. They are better educated. The gains are especially pronounced among girls, ethnic minorities, and children with disabilities. Yet even as their condition has improved, public anxiety has increased. There is little doubt that public concern simply represents the latest example of American nostalgia for a mythical golden age (Gilbert, 1986; Males, 1996, 1999).

A RETURN TO LITTLE ADULTHOOD

What is a contemporary child? Few would describe a child in Victorian terms, as an innocent, asexual creature with a nature fundamentally different from that of adults. Nor would many define a child as some children's rights advocates did in the late 1960s or early 1970s, as a rights-bearing individual who should have precisely the same privileges and freedoms as adults. Our society still regards children as special beings with distinct needs, but more than ever before we also see children in other ways: as individuals who are capable of learning at an early age, as more precocious, knowledgeable, and independent than any recent generation, and as independent consumers to be sold to.

We live in a time of profound uncertainty about what constitutes a child. Contemporary society has blurred the distinctions between childhood, adolescence, and adulthood, dressing children in adult-style clothes,

ascribing to them adult thoughts, and treating them like grown-ups in miniature. We no longer have a consensus about the proper dividing line between childhood, adolescence, and adulthood. There is great division within our society about when a young person is old enough to have sex or smoke or drink or do paid work or take full responsibility for criminal behavior.

It is a common lament that children today are growing up too fast and that our culture is depriving them of the carefree childhood they deserve. Children today watch television shows and movies saturated with sexual innuendo and violence. Many of their play activities are organized by adults or are highly individualized and technologically mediated by computers and video games; as a result they have less opportunity for unstructured group play. Meanwhile, they engage in sex at a younger age, spend less time with adults, and are heavily influenced by peers and by a commercial culture. Of course, we have not returned to the premodern world of childhood. We have something that is very new. Though young people are no longer the binary opposite of adults, and have become independent consumers and avid patrons of mass culture, they remain segregated in age-graded school and dependents in their parental homes, and they are regarded as having a nature different from that of grown-ups.

There is a widespread view that young people are caught between two conflicting trends: a riskier, more toxic social environment and less parental support. But there is no consensus about what, if anything, to do about this. The dominant strategy has been to try to preserve childhood as a time of innocence through public policy. By installing V-chips in television sets, imposing curfews and school dress codes, and using restrictions on drivers' licenses to enforce prohibitions on teen smoking and drinking, adult society seeks to empower parents and to reassert childhood as a protected state. Such policies as random drug tests for students in extra-curricular activities, abstinence-only sex education programs, and more stringent enforcement of statutory rape laws represent attempts to counteract the impact of permissive culture on young people's lives.

But if there is any lesson that the history of childhood can teach us, it is the error of thinking that we can radically separate the lives of children from those of adults. Young people's behavior tends to mimic that of their parents and the adults who surround them. The best predictor of whether a young person will smoke, take drugs, or engage in violent activity is his or her parents' behavior. Restrictions on young people's behavior have often proven to be ineffective or counterproductive.

Nostalgia provides no substitute for effective public policies that address the real problems of poverty, family instability, health care, and education that many young people confront. We could not return to the 1950s even if we really wanted to. A century ago, a small group of "child savers" awakened their society to problems of child poverty, abuse, and neglect, ill health, and inadequate schooling that were far greater and far less tractable than any of the problems that we now confront. It is easy to condemn these earlier reformers for their paternalism and interest in social control, but for all their biases and limitations, they demonstrated a creativity and energy that we can only admire. The challenge of our time is to duplicate their passion and their achievements while overcoming their limitations.

REFERENCES

Ashby, L. (1997). *Endangered children: Dependency, neglect, and abuse in American history*. New York: Twayne.

Berrol, S. C. (1995). *Growing up American: Immigrant children in America, then and now*. New York: Twayne.

Board of Education of Independent School District No. 92 of Pottawatomie County v. Earls (2002), No. 01-332.

Brenzel, B. M. (1983). *Daughters of the state: A social portrait of the first reform school for girls in North America, 1856–1905*. Cambridge, MA: MIT Press.

Calvert, K. L. F. (1992). *Children in the house: The material culture of early childhood, 1600–1900*. Boston: Northeastern University Press.

Carey v. Population Services International, 431 U.S. 678 (1977).

Chudacoff, H. P. (1989). *How old are you? Age consciousness in American culture*. Princeton, NJ: Princeton University Press.

Clement, P. (1997). *Growing pains: Children in the Industrial Age, 1850–1890*. New York: Twayne.

Cott, N. F. (1977). *The bonds of womanhood: "Woman's sphere" in New England, 1780–1835*. New Haven, CT: Yale University Press.

Coveney, P. (1967). *The image of childhood: The individual and society: A study of the theme in English literature*. Baltimore: Penguin.

Cravens, H. (1993). *Before Head Start: The Iowa Station and America's children*. Chapel Hill: University of North Carolina Press.

Demos, J. (1970). *A little commonwealth: Family life in Plymouth Colony*. New York: Oxford University Press.

Getis, V. (2000). *Juvenile court and the progressives*. Urbana: University of Illinois Press.

Gilbert, J. B. (1986). *A cycle of outrage: America's reaction to the juvenile delinquent in the 1950s.* New York: Oxford University Press.

Gillis, J. R. (1974). *Youth and history: Tradition and change in European age relations, 1770–present.* New York: Academic Press.

Gordon, L. (1988). *Heroes of their own lives: The politics and history of family violence, Boston, 1880–1960.* New York: Viking.

Goss v. Lopez. 419 U.S. 565 (1975).

Graebner, W. (1990). *Coming of age in Buffalo: Youth and authority in the postwar era.* Philadelphia: Temple University Press.

Greven, P. J. (1970). *Four generations: Population, land, and family in colonial Andover, Massachusetts.* Ithaca, NY: Cornell University Press.

Hawes, J. M. (1991). *The children's rights movement: A history of advocacy and protection.* Boston: Twayne.

Hazelwood School Dist. v. Kuhlmeier, 484 U.S. 260 (1988).

Heywood, C. (2001). *A history of childhood: Children and childhood in the West from medieval to modern times.* Cambridge, UK: Polity.

Holloran, P. C. (1989). *Boston's wayward children: Social services for homeless children, 1830–1930.* Cranbury, NJ: Associated University Presses.

Holt, J. C. (1975). *Escape from childhood: The needs and rights of children.* Harmondsworth, NY: Penguin.

Holt, M. I. (1992). *The orphan trains: Placing out in America.* Lincoln: University of Nebraska Press.

Illick, J. (2002). *American childhoods.* Philadelphia: University of Pennsylvania Press.

In re Gault, 387 U.S. 1 (1967).

Jenkins, P. (1998). *Moral panic: Changing concepts of the child molester in modern America.* New Haven, CT: Yale University Press.

Jones, K. W. (1999). *Taming the troublesome child: American families, child guidance, and the limits of psychiatric authority.* Cambridge, MA: Harvard University Press.

Kett, J. F. (1977). *Rites of passage: Adolescence in America, 1790 to the present.* New York: Basic Books.

Levy, B. (1988). *Quakers and the American family: British settlement in the Delaware Valley, 1650–1765.* New York: Oxford University Press.

Lindenmeyer, K. (1997). *A right to childhood: The U.S. Children's Bureau and child welfare, 1912–46.* Urbana: University of Illinois Press.

Macleod, D. I. (1983). *Building character in the American boy: The Boy Scouts, YMCA, and their forerunners, 1870–1920.* Madison: University of Wisconsin Press.

Macleod, D. I. (1998). *The Age of the Child: Children in America, 1890–1912.* New York: Twayne.

Males, M. A. (1996). *The scapegoat generation: America's war on adolescents.* Monroe, ME: Common Courage Press.

Males, M. A. (1999). *Framing youth: Ten myths about the next generation.* Monroe, ME: Common Courage Press.

Mintz, S., & Kellogg, S. (1988). *Domestic revolutions: A social history of American family life.* New York: Free Press.

Morgan, E. S. (1966). *The Puritan family: Religion and domestic relations in seventeenth-century New England.* New York: Harper & Row.

Nasaw, D. (1985). *Children of the city: At work and at play.* Garden City, NY: Anchor Press/Doubleday.

O'Connor, S. (2001). *Orphan trains: The story of Charles Loring Brace and the children he saved and failed.* Boston: Houghton Mifflin.

Odem, M. E. (1995). *Delinquent daughters: Protecting and policing adolescent female sexuality in the United States, 1885–1920.* Chapel Hill: University of North Carolina Press.

Peiss, K. L. (1986). *Cheap amusements: Working women and leisure in turn-of-the-century New York*. Philadelphia: Temple University Press.

Planned Parenthood Association v. Matheson, 582 F. Supp. 1001, 1007-09 (D. Utah 1983).

Platt, A. M. (1977). *The child savers: The invention of delinquency*. Chicago: University of Chicago Press.

Pleck, E. H. (1987). *Domestic tyranny: The making of social policy against family violence from colonial times to the present*. New York: Oxford University Press.

Prescott, H. M. (1998). *A doctor of their own: The history of adolescent medicine*. Cambridge, MA: Harvard University Press.

Putney, C. (2001). *Muscular Christianity: Manhood and sports in Protestant America, 1880–1920*. Cambridge, MA: Harvard University Press.

Reinier, J. S. (1996). *From virtue to character: American childhood, 1775–1850*. New York: Twayne.

Rorabaugh, W. J. (1986). *The craft apprentice: From Franklin to the Machine Age in America*. New York: Oxford University Press.

Ross, D. (1972). *G. Stanley Hall: The psychologist as prophet*. Chicago: University of Chicago Press.

Ryan, M. P. (1981). *Cradle of the middle class: The family in Oneida County, New York, 1790–1865*. New York: Cambridge University Press.

Schneider, E. C. (1992). *In the web of class: Delinquents and reformers in Boston, 1810s–1930s*. New York: New York University Press.

Stansell, C. (1986). *City of women: Sex and class in New York, 1789–1860*. New York: Knopf.

Storrs, L. R. Y. (2000). *Civilizing capitalism: The National Consumers' League, women's activism, and labor standards in the New Deal era*. Chapel Hill: University of North Carolina Press.

Sutton, J. (1988). *Stubborn children: Controlling delinquency in the United States, 1640–1981*. Berkeley: University of California Press.

Tiffin, S. (1982). *In whose best interest? Child welfare reform in the Progressive Era*. Westport, CT: Greenwood.

Tinker v. Des Moines School Dist., 393 U.S. 503 (1969).

Title IX, Educational Amendments of 1972, 20 U.S.C. 1681–1688.

Title X, Public Health Service Act of 1970, Pub. L. No. 91-572.

Title XIX, Social Security Act of 1965, Pub. L. No. 89-97.

Trattner, W. I. (1970). *Crusade for the children: A history of the National Child Labor Committee and child labor reform in America*. Chicago: Quadrangle.

United States v. Sokolow, 490 U.S. 1 (1988).

Zelizer, V. A. R. (1994). *Pricing the priceless child: The changing social value of children*. Princeton, NJ: Princeton University Press.

Part II

CONTEMPORARY COUPLES

CHAPTER 4

Cohabitation and Family Change

JUDITH A. SELTZER

Increasingly delayed marriage (Goldstein & Kenney, 2001), greater approval of sex before marriage (Thornton & Young-DeMarco, 2001), and high rates of marital instability (Goldstein, 1999) pave the way for unmarried couples in the United States, including those who do not plan to marry, to live together. For the past three decades, cohabitation rates have risen dramatically among all demographic groups, including parents. Growth in the numbers of adults who have ever cohabited has shifted researchers' conception of cohabitation as an appropriate topic in reviews on nontraditional family forms (Macklin, 1980; Sussman, 1972) to one that highlights the widespread acceptance of cohabitation whether or not the couple plans to marry (Thornton & Young-DeMarco, 2001).

Despite greater acceptance of cohabitation, the public and researchers still disagree about whether cohabiting unions harm individuals and threaten the larger social order. Couples who live together before marriage have higher divorce rates than those who do not live together before marriage (Bumpass & Lu, 2000; Lillard, Brien, & Waite, 1995). Children born to cohabiting couples have unstable family lives compared to children born to married parents (Manning, Smock, & Majumdar, 2002). The relative importance researchers assign to cohabitation itself and to the characteristics of those who choose to cohabit or bear children in cohabiting unions (e.g., those with more liberal attitudes or who are less religious) is at the core of the debate about whether cohabitation is harmful. Both the experience of

AUTHOR'S NOTE: This work benefited from resources provided by the University of California, Los Angeles, California Center for Population Research, which receives support from Grant No. R24-HD041022 from the National Institute of Child Health and Human Development. I am grateful to Marilyn Coleman and the anonymous reviewers for helpful suggestions on a previous version of this chapter.

cohabitation and selection into cohabiting unions contribute to marital instability among cohabitors who divorce (Axinn & Thornton, 1992; see Seltzer, 2000b, for a review of this evidence).

A major theme since the 1970s in research on cohabitation is whether cohabitation is a stage in courtship that leads to marriage or an alternative to marriage. This theme still motivates most contemporary research on cohabitation in the United States. Because cohabitation and marriage are similar, at least superficially, in their status as heterosexual, co-resident unions, many studies compare the two relationships. The comparisons demonstrate the tensions between treating unions as private relationships governed only by the feelings of the two couple members and treating the unions as public phenomena governed by informal social rules and administrative and legal rules about the rights and responsibilities of couple members. Marriage is a well-developed, albeit changing, social institution in the United States, whereas cohabitation, at best, is an incomplete institution (Blumstein & Schwartz, 1983; Nock, 1995). Because cohabiting unions have become more common over the past 30 years, they are a more routine component of social life in the United States in much the same way as remarriage after divorce became more routine in the 1970s (Cherlin, 1978).

Emphasis on the changing institutionalization of cohabitation points to a weakness in debates that frame cohabitation in terms of dichotomies: that is, as either a courtship stage or an alternative to marriage. This type of debate ignores the diversity of cohabiting experiences for individuals and for the U.S. population. The meaning of a cohabiting union may change over time for the cohabiting individuals. What begins as a convenient living arrangement or strategy in the dating game may become a more serious relationship that leads to marriage or plans for marriage (Sassler & Jobe, 2002). Alternatively, those who live together as a step on the way to marriage may change their minds about whether the other person would make a good spouse. Three quarters of cohabiting women expect to marry their partners (Manning & Smock, 2002), but only about a third of all cohabitors marry within 3 years (Bumpass, 1995). Of course, the decision to marry involves two people. About one fifth of cohabiting partners disagree with each other about whether they plan to marry (Bumpass, Sweet, & Cherlin, 1991). Men's preferences may matter more than women's (Brown, 2000), a finding to which I return later.

The meaning of cohabitation also may change over historical time at the population level as it is adopted by a wider variety of people who differ in their reasons for living together (see Manting, 1996, on the changing meaning of cohabitation in the Netherlands). Shifts in the meaning of cohabitation at the population level occur because of changes in the composition of cohabiting couples: that is, the relative mix of couples who cohabit as a step on the way to marriage and those who do not intend to marry when they begin living together. Even when one group dominates the population of cohabitors, substantial variation in types of cohabiting unions remains (Casper & Sayer, 2002). The primary challenge of describing the meaning of cohabitation in the United States over the past 30 years is characterizing a moving target. The meaning of cohabitation continues to shift over time as it becomes more acceptable in a wider range of circumstances. The changing social context further alters the meaning of cohabitation.

The quality and quantity of social science data on who cohabits and the meaning of cohabitation have improved dramatically since 1970. As cohabitation has become more common, researchers have included more questions about cohabitation on demographic surveys and in interviews about family life. The repeated finding in population surveys that cohabitation is more common among those with fewer economic and educational resources has fostered new research on couple relationships that examines the reasons for this difference instead of focusing on relationships between college students who cohabit (Macklin, 1980). Attempts to understand the meaning of cohabitation in the kinship system use both quantitative and qualitative evidence. At its best, knowledge gained from one style of research informs the collection and analysis of other types of data on cohabitation. Improvements in the quality of data about cohabitation in the United States parallel improvements in European countries (Kiernan, 2002), thereby permitting comparisons of cohabitation and its effects across social contexts that differ in their economic and social supports for cohabiting couples.

This chapter describes changes in U.S. cohabitation since 1970. It emphasizes what social scientists know, how they know it, and what they still do not know but should try to learn in the coming decades. I treat cohabitation as a dyadic union between unmarried heterosexual adults who co-reside. New information about gay and lesbian couples who live together (Black, Gates, Sanders, & Taylor, 2000) and changes in policies that define the rights of homosexual partners make this an important area for new research but one that is beyond the scope of this chapter. My chapter builds on other recent reviews and collections of papers on cohabitation (Booth & Crouter, 2002; Casper & Bianchi, 2002; Seltzer, 2000b; Smock, 2000; Smock & Manning, 2001; Waite, Bachrach, Hindin, Thomson, & Thornton, 2000).

FACTS ABOUT COHABITATION

Demography of Cohabitation

In 1970, approximately 523,000 households were maintained by unmarried couples (U.S. Bureau of the Census, 1998). By 2000, the number had increased to 4.9 million (Simmons & O'Neill, 2001). I use 1970 as the comparison point because this handbook examines change over the past 30-some years. However, census data also show that the start of the dramatic rise in the rate of increase in cohabiting couples in the United States was around 1970 (Glick & Spanier, 1980). This cross-sectional evidence understates the number of adults who have ever cohabited because cohabiting unions typically do not last long. For instance, by 1995 nearly 40% of women 20 to 24 years old had ever cohabited, but only 11% were currently in cohabiting unions (Bramlett & Mosher, 2002, Tables B and C). Estimates of whether a person has ever cohabited also show that cohabitation has become increasingly common (Bumpass & Lu, 2000). By the mid-1990s, over half of all first unions (marriages and cohabitations combined) were cohabiting unions (Bumpass & Lu, 2000).

Young persons are more likely to be cohabiting than older persons (Bumpass & Sweet, 1989, Table 1), a pattern consistent with interpretations of cohabitation as a stage in the courtship process. However, older persons have also become more likely to cohabit in recent decades (Waite, 1995). The rapid rise in rates of cohabitation for newer cohorts means that age differences in whether individuals have ever cohabited are likely to diminish over time as older adults who came of age when cohabitation was less acceptable than it is today are replaced by those who came of age when cohabitation was more acceptable (Bumpass & Sweet, 1989, 1995; Oropesa, 1996). Cohabiting unions are more common among those who have been married previously than among the never married (Bumpass & Lu, 2000, Table 1). The prevalence of cohabiting unions among the previously married is especially important because much early research on why unmarried couples live together focuses on those who have never been married.

Patterns of marriage and divorce differ substantially by race and ethnicity (Cherlin, 1992), so it is not surprising that there are race-ethnic differences in cohabitation as well. In 1995, just over half of non-Hispanic black women had married by age 30 compared to more than three quarters of Hispanic women and non-Hispanic whites and Asians (Bramlett & Mosher, 2002, Figure 2, Table 1). In addition, rates of marital separation and divorce are much higher for black than white women, a continuation of a long-term trend in the United States (Bramlett & Mosher, 2002, Table D; Sweeney & Phillips, 2002). Compared to whites, black women are more likely to cohabit than to marry as their first union (Raley, 2000). In fact, when both cohabiting unions and marriages are taken into account, the race gap in union formation is reduced by about half (Raley, 1996). Black women are less likely to formalize their first cohabiting unions by marriage than are white women. Rates of marriage for Hispanic women in their first cohabiting union are between those of black and white women (Bramlett & Mosher, 2002). Cohabitation rates have increased in recent decades for blacks, Hispanics, and non-Hispanic whites, but the pace of increase has been greater among whites than for the other groups (Bumpass & Lu, 2000, Table 2).

Persons with less education and more uncertain economic prospects are more likely to cohabit than to marry, perhaps because the institution of marriage is defined by long-term economic responsibilities (Bumpass & Lu, 2000; Clarkberg, 1999; Willis & Michael, 1994; Xie, Raymo,

Goyette, & Thornton, 2003). Economic resources also affect whether cohabitors plan to marry their partners (Bumpass et al., 1991) and whether they are able to fulfill these plans (Smock & Manning, 1997). Although much of the academic literature in the 1980s and 1990s argued that women's economic opportunities were a primary source of historical change in couple relationships (see Oppenheimer, 1997, for a review), men's economic resources and career prospects are more important determinants of whether a cohabiting couple will marry than women's (Smock & Manning, 1997). The importance of men's economic prospects for marriage is consistent with historical and more contemporary evidence about the economic requirements for marriage in Western kinship systems (Hajnal, 1965; Oppenheimer, Kalmijn, & Lim, 1997). Although the educational differential in cohabitation has persisted since the 1970s, cohabitation rates have increased for all education and income groups (Bumpass & Lu, 2000; Glick & Norton, 1979). Economic characteristics explain some but not all of the race-ethnic differences in cohabitation and marriage (Raley, 1996). Cultural differences also play an important role in accounting for race-ethnic variation in union formation. For instance, Puerto Rican women's attitudes and behavior demonstrate greater acceptance of cohabitation and of childbearing in cohabiting unions compared to those of non-Hispanic whites (Manning, 2001; Oropesa, 1996).

Cohabiting partners are very similar to each other on race-ethnicity and education but not as similar as spouses are to each other (Blackwell & Lichter, 2000; Casper & Bianchi, 2002). Compared to spouses, cohabiting partners are also more likely to differ on religion (Schoen & Weinick, 1993). Women in cohabiting unions are more likely to be a couple of years older than their partners than wives are to be older than their husbands

(Casper & Bianchi, 2002). The greater heterogamy or differences between partners in cohabiting unions may occur because those who cohabit have more liberal attitudes about a variety of aspects of family life, including who is an appropriate partner. Alternatively, cohabiting unions require less commitment than marriages, so partners may be willing to experiment more with relationships they might be unwilling to formalize.

Relationship Stability, Marriage, and Childbearing: Facts About Change in What Cohabitation Means

Three demographic trends suggest that the meaning of cohabitation is shifting. First, although more than half of marriages today are preceded by cohabitation (Bumpass & Lu, 2000), cohabiting unions are less likely to be a prelude to marriage now than in the recent past (Bumpass, 1995, 1998). Second, cohabiting couples are more likely to be parents either because they have had a child together or because they live with children from previous relationships (Casper & Bianchi, 2002; Raley, 2001). Finally, single women who become pregnant are almost as likely to cohabit as to marry the child's father by the time the child is born (Raley, 2001).

Cohabitation and Marriage

Cohabiting unions do not last long before the couple marries or ends the relationship. About half of cohabiting unions end in a year or less, and only 1 in 10 lasts at least 5 years. Cohabiting relationships became less stable between the mid-1970s and the early 1990s, mainly because of a decline in the percentage of couples who married their cohabiting partner. Among first cohabiting unions formed between 1975 and 1984, 60% of the couples eventually married compared to 53% of those in first cohabiting unions formed in 1990–94 (Bumpass & Lu, 2000;

Bumpass & Sweet, 1989). Recent cohorts are also more likely to live with at least one partner other than their eventual spouse compared to those of the early 1980s (Bumpass & Lu, 2000, Table 3). Cohabiting is one way to learn more about a potential spouse's characteristics. As it becomes more difficult to identify an appropriate potential spouse, individuals may have several cohabiting unions with different partners as a way to sort partners. Oppenheimer's (1988) theory of marital search suggests a lengthening of the search process because it takes longer for both men and women to complete their schooling and establish themselves in careers than it did 30 or 40 years ago. Even if the increase in the number of partners is part of the search process, the wider experience of cohabiting unions that do not end in marriage reduces the stigma associated with cohabitation as a union that might not lead to marriage. Reduction in stigma, in turn, fosters a rise in cohabiting unions in which partners do not anticipate marriage. Decline in the percentage of cohabiting couples who eventually marry is consistent with the interpretation of change in the meaning of cohabitation as a stage on the way to first marriage.

Cohabitation and Childbearing

Cohabitation is also becoming a more common setting for rearing and even bearing children. In 1978, almost 28% of cohabiting couples lived with one or both partners' children, but by 1998 this percentage had increased to 37% (Casper & Bianchi, 2002, Table 2.1). Another way to consider the extent to which cohabiting unions are a setting for child rearing is by examining whether children have ever lived with their mother and her cohabiting partner. Two out of every five children will live in a cohabiting family at some point during childhood on the basis of estimates for the 1990s (Bumpass &

Lu, 2000). In addition to raising children from previous relationships, a small but growing percentage of cohabiting couples are having biological children together. Between the early 1980s and 1990s, the percentage of cohabiting couples who had a child together increased from 12% to 15% (Bumpass & Lu, 2000). Even without this increase in fertility rates among cohabitors, the increasing number of cohabiting couples has contributed to the rise in the number of children born in cohabiting unions (Raley, 2001).

Childbearing outside marriage increased dramatically in the second part of the 20th century. Just in the past 30 years, the birthrate for unmarried women increased by 70%, from 26.4 to 45.0 (Martin et al., 2002). Most unmarried women who bear a child are single (Raley, 2001); however, the nature of non-marital childbearing has changed over time so that increasing percentages of children born outside marriage are born to cohabiting parents. In fact, most of the recent increase in childbearing outside marriage is due to the increase in births to cohabitors (Bumpass & Lu, 2000). That the rates have increased as well as the number of cohabitors having children suggests a change in cohabiting behavior. Having a child reflects substantial commitment to the relationship and to joint responsibilities, even in an era when many adults become single parents. The increase in child rearing in cohabitation points to cohabitation as something other than a precursor to first marriage for a growing percentage of the population. That is, cohabitation may be an alternative to marriage for some subgroups, or at least a suitable context for raising children whether or not marriage will follow. Edin's (2002) finding that low-income parents think marriage is unnecessary for couples raising children together is consistent with this interpretation. Future research should also examine attitudes about marriage and parenthood for those without children and in different socioeconomic groups.

Another sign that cohabiting relationships are a more acceptable setting for child rearing is that by the mid-1990s single women who became pregnant were more likely to move in with the child's father than had been true a decade earlier (Raley, 2001, Table 3). In earlier cohorts, pregnant single women were likely to marry to legitimate their child's birth, but by the early 1990s about the same percentage began to cohabit as marry by the time their child was born. Because childhood experiences affect children's attitudes and behavior in adulthood, children raised by cohabiting parents will be even more likely to cohabit than children who never live with cohabiting parents. This implies further increases in U.S. cohabitation rates.

Change in the meaning of cohabitation is interdependent with other changes in U.S. families. Men's and women's obligations in marriage are shifting to an arrangement in which both spouses help fulfill their family's economic needs (see Chapter 10 of this book). More young adults think that both mothers and fathers should do housework and look after children. Divorce is more acceptable, and childbearing outside marriage no longer carries the severe stigma for mother or child that it once did (Thornton & Young-DeMarco, 2001). Both economic and cultural factors contribute to these broad changes (Bumpass, 1990; Lesthaeghe, 1995; Smock & Gupta, 2002). Whatever the initial sources of change, since cohabitation became widespread, the change in behavior has had a momentum of its own.

How Cohabiting Couples Live

Maintaining a household requires that someone accomplish basic tasks. Money must come into the household, usually through earnings from employment. Someone must spend the money to pay rent and provide food, heat, and other basic necessities. Someone must cook and clean. If children live there, someone must supervise and care for them. Who does these different tasks depends on social rules about the appropriate work for men and women, adults and children. The division of labor also depends on personal negotiations between household members. The demographic facts about cohabitation are better known than the facts about how cohabitors manage their lives. This section provides a broad interpretation of existing evidence, but knowledge of the facts about cohabitors' lives would benefit from more research.

Young women and men with liberal attitudes about gender roles are more likely to cohabit than to marry (Clarkberg, Stolzenberg, & Waite, 1995). Their behavior is consistent with these attitudes. Both partners in cohabiting couples are more likely to work for pay than partners in married couples (Casper & Bianchi, 2002, Table 2.2). Cohabiting couples also divide housework somewhat more equally than do married couples, with cohabiting women doing less housework than married women (Brines & Joyner, 1999; Nock, 1995; Shelton & John, 1993; South & Spitze, 1994). Women, however, do much more housework than men do in both types of couples. When men begin cohabiting, they reduce the time they spend on housework compared to when they were single. The same is true for men who marry (Gupta, 1999). Differences in women's and men's preferences, their earning potential, and expectations about gender differences in household responsibilities contribute to the greater amount of housework women do.

Unfortunately, there are no data on trends in men's and women's relative contributions to housework in cohabiting relationships. Compared to married couples, cohabiting couples in recent cohorts are likely to divide work more evenly than in the past, at least among those without children. This is because fewer cohabiting unions today lead to marriage, where behavior is guided by the implicit long-term contract about the exchange of women's unpaid housework for their male partner's earnings. In addition, increases in cohabitation among more highly educated women may be a bargaining strategy that women use to test their partners' willingness to share housework before marriage. Wage rates for highly educated women have increased relative to men's in recent cohorts, providing women with somewhat more bargaining power than in earlier cohorts (Cherlin, 2000).

Married couples are much more likely to pool their incomes than cohabiting couples (Bauman, 1999; Blumstein & Schwartz, 1983; Kenney, 2002; Landale, 2002). Income pooling may signal commitment to the relationship, but it may also enhance union stability by reducing conflict about how money is spent and other transaction costs (Seltzer, 2002; Treas, 1993). Cohabitors with children are more likely to pool their incomes, perhaps as a way to recognize the shared responsibilities for children's needs (Winkler, 1997). Compared to married parents, cohabiting parents spend less money and a smaller share of their incomes on health care and educational expenses (DeLeire & Kalil, 2002). However, compared to those who live with a single parent, children whose parents cohabit may still benefit from the cohabiting partner's income through public goods, such as improved housing and other shared resources (Citro & Michael, 1995; Moffitt, Revelle, & Winkler, 1998). Taking account of cohabiting parents' incomes would have reduced by nearly 30% the proportion of children in cohabiting-couple families who were in poverty in 1990 (Manning & Lichter, 1996). Children whose parent or parents are cohabiting suffer economic disadvantages compared to those whose parents marry, largely because those who cohabit have less schooling and lower earnings than those who marry (see the above discussion in "Demography of Cohabitation"; also Manning & Lichter, 1996; Morrison & Ritualo, 2000).

How much cohabiting partners contribute to children's material needs may depend on whether the children are the biological children of both partners or from one partner's previous relationship. For instance, Case, Lin, and McLanahan (1999) showed that households in which men are helping to raise their partners' children from a previous union spend less on food than households in which married parents and children live. Income pooling and money management among cohabitors is an important topic for future research (Bumpass & Sweet, 2001; Seltzer, 2002). New studies should compare cohabiting parents to couples without children because the former already demonstrate a higher level of commitment to the union by having a child together.

Cohabitation and Children's Welfare

Until recently, children who lived with cohabiting parents were treated by researchers as though they were living with a single parent. This assumption understates children's access to economic resources. It probably also understates the time and attention children receive from adults, especially when the cohabiting partners are the children's biological parents. A recent study of new parents found that mothers and their infants born outside marriage get more support from the child's biological father when the parents are living together than when the parents are romantically involved with each other but live in separate households (Carlson & McLanahan, 2002). The same study showed that compared to married biological fathers, cohabiting fathers interacted with their young children in similar ways (Carlson & McLanahan, 2001). Time-use data also show that biological fathers spend about the same amount of time engaged with their children whether they are cohabiting or married to the children's mother. However, once other differences between cohabiting and married families are taken into account, cohabiting biological fathers spend less time in activities with their children than married biological fathers do (Hofferth & Anderson, 2003). Social scientists are just beginning to study how cohabiting fathers participate in child rearing when their relationship with the children's mother ends (Cooksey & Craig, 1998; Landale & Oropesa, 2001; Manning, 2002; Seltzer, 2000a).

Marriage has little effect on the types of child-rearing activities men pursue with their partner's children (i.e., children who are not the men's biological children). Married stepfathers, however, spend more time in children's organized activities, such as school, religious, and community activities, than do male cohabiting partners (Brown, 2002; Thomson, McLanahan, & Curtin, 1992). Marriage to the child's mother may legitimate the stepfather's participation in the child's public life because schools and other public settings have administrative structures that recognize the social authority over children that comes with marriage to the child's mother. Rules about adults' responsibilities for their cohabiting partner's children are less clearly defined. This may create institutional barriers to cohabiting fathers' participation as well as increase their reluctance to participate.

Cohabitation, like remarriage, also may affect how mothers interact with their children. A second adult can reinforce the mother's authority, provide her with emotional support, and help supervise the children. Single mothers who remarry or begin a cohabiting relationship do not discipline their children as harshly as mothers who do not acquire a new partner, but there are no differences between mothers who cohabit and those who remarry (Thomson, Mosley, Hanson, & McLanahan, 2001). Evidence on whether cohabitation improves supervision is mixed (Thomson et al., 2001).

Evaluating the effects of cohabitation on children's well-being requires distinguishing between children who live with their unmarried biological parents and those who live with biological parents and cohabiting partners (informal stepfamilies). Biological parents usually invest more in their children than do stepparents (for a review, see Anderson, Kaplan, & Lancaster, 2001). Many children who live with a parent and a cohabiting partner have experienced the disruption of their biological parents' union, an experience that also affects children's welfare. Because the rise in the numbers of cohabitors who bear children is relatively recent, few studies have a large enough sample to support a comparison between the well-being of children who live with cohabiting biological parents and that of children whose biological parents are married. These comparisons are more feasible in studies of younger children than in studies of teenagers because so few cohabitors stay together for more than a few years.

The lack of precision due to small sample sizes can be addressed, in part, by looking for consistent findings across studies. It is sometimes difficult, however, to reconcile inconsistent findings across studies because the studies differ in whether they control for other factors, such as income, that affect both cohabitation and child well-being. For instance, data from the 1997 National Survey of America's Families (NSAF) show that among teenagers living with both biological parents, teens whose parents are married are much less likely to have behavioral or emotional problems than teens whose parents are cohabiting (Brown, 2002).[1] In contrast, data from the National Survey of Families and Households (NSFH) conducted 10 years earlier suggest that children who live with both biological parents look very similar on a range of child well-being

measures, regardless of whether their parents are married to each other (Hanson, McLanahan, & Thomson, 1997).[2] The greater difference between teenagers in families with married and unmarried biological parents in Brown's study might be due to the absence of statistical controls for family characteristics that explain both cohabitation and teens' well-being.

Whether cohabitation is good or bad for children also depends on what alternative the children have to living in a cohabiting-couple family. For many children, the alternative is living with a single mother. For others, it is living with a biological parent and the parent's new spouse (formal stepfamily). Compared to children living with a single mother, those who live with their mother and her cohabiting partner (not the child's father) have more behavioral problems, worse school performance, and higher rates of delinquency (Manning & Lamb, 2002; Nelson, Clark, & Acs, 2001; Thomson, Hanson, & McLanahan, 1994). Whether these differences between children in single-mother and cohabiting families persist once differences by family type in economic resources and child-rearing practices are taken into account varies across studies. Nelson et al. (2001) and Thomson et al. (1994) found disadvantages for children in cohabiting families when they controlled for other family characteristics in the NSAF and NSFH, respectively. Manning and Lamb (2002), using the National Longitudinal Study of Adolescent Health (Bearman, Jones, & Udry, 1997),[3] found that teenagers in single-mother and cohabiting families were very similar on a wide range of outcomes once other family characteristics were taken into account. Finally, there is some evidence that teenagers who live with a mother and her cohabiting partner do not fare as well as teens living with a mother and stepfather on behavioral problems, including delinquency and academic achievement (Manning &

Lamb, 2002; Nelson et al., 2001). Thomson et al. (1994) reported a similar finding for an earlier cohort.

Research on the effects of cohabitation on children's well-being is still quite sparse. Much of it relies on cross-sectional evidence in which causal associations are ambiguous. In particular, many studies do not take account of preexisting differences between those who cohabit and those who do not that might explain an association between cohabitation and children's welfare. Longitudinal studies, including those that use retrospective reports of childhood living arrangements, are hampered by small numbers of cases. Small samples and incomplete histories of parents' unions limit the dimensions of cohabitation that can be taken into account—for instance, whether the cohabiting union is between the children's biological parents or a parent and nonparent, the duration of the union, and the number of formal and informal unions the child has experienced. Duration and stability of parents' unions are especially important for assessing the effects of cohabitation on children because children benefit from stable living arrangements (Hao & Xie, 2002).

Restricting cohabitation histories to information obtained from household composition observed annually or to only marriagelike relationships also severely hampers research on the effects of cohabitation on children. For instance, the relationship history in the National Longitudinal Study of Adolescent Health (Add Health) questionnaire asks parents to report about current and previous relationships that were the same as marriage even if the partners were not formally married. This restriction to marriagelike relationships probably reduces reports about short-term relationships in which the partners were not very committed to each other. These relationships may increase disruption in children's lives at the same time that they provide a model of casual unions. Annual observations also miss

short-term unions, a serious problem given that about half of cohabiting unions end in a year or less (Bumpass & Lu, 2000). As increasing numbers of cohabiting couples live together without planning marriage or behaving as if their unions are long-term alliances, collecting data on only marriage-like cohabiting unions will underestimate children's exposure to cohabitation and its effects on their welfare.

Many of the weaknesses in past research arise because of the low incidence of cohabitation involving children for many of the cohorts represented in commonly used data sources, such as the 1987–88 NSFH panel and the 1979 National Longitudinal Survey of Youth (Zagorsky & White, 1999).[4] The cohorts represented by these studies may also differ in the effects of cohabitation on children because the meaning of cohabitation has changed over time as it has become more common and as childbearing in cohabiting unions has been less stigmatized. Other studies, such as McLanahan, Garfinkel, Brooks-Gunn, and Tienda's Fragile Families and Child Wellbeing Study[5] and Add Health, will become more useful as additional waves of data are released. Because race-ethnic groups may differ in the acceptability of having children in cohabiting unions and because the effects of cohabitation on some child outcomes vary by race-ethnicity (Dunifon & Kowaleski-Jones, 2002), it is important for new research to examine the effects of cohabitation on children within race-ethnic groups whenever possible (see Manning, 2002, for a more complete discussion of this and related issues).

Cohabitation and Family Ties

Whether a couple decides to cohabit is a personal decision, but the partners make this decision in the context of the broader social environment, including their network of family and friends. Couples who are considering living together take into account whether their parents and friends will think they are making a good decision (Liefbroer & de Jong Gierveld, 1993). Young women whose mothers approve of cohabitation are more likely to cohabit than marry (Axinn & Thornton, 1993, Table 1). If parents disapprove, cohabitation may strain their relationships with adult children. Parents whose adult children are married say they are closer to their children than parents whose children are cohabiting (Aquilino, 1997). Cohabitors also report less positive relationships with their parents than married persons (Nock, 1995). However, cohabiting couples are more integrated into their parents' social and leisure activities than are unmarried adult children (Aquilino, 1997). An indication of similarity between cohabiting and married couples' integration in their kin networks is that partners in each type of couple are about equally likely to have been introduced to each other by family members (Laumann, Gagnon, Michael, & Michaels, 1994). Moreover, the cohabiting experiences of young adult children increase mothers' acceptance of cohabiting unions (Axinn & Thornton, 1993). These findings suggest the importance of examining the causes and effects of cohabitation on couples' broader social networks instead of focusing solely on the couple or the couple's children.

IMPROVEMENTS IN DATA

Counting Cohabitors

Two innovations have revolutionized knowledge about cohabitation: (a) the creation of demographic time series that chart the growth in cohabitation and its spread across socioeconomic and demographic groups and (b) the inclusion of cohabiting

couples in studies of family life and household organization. The U.S. Bureau of the Census did not identify unmarried partners with a relationship code on the household roster until the 1990 census. However, since the 1970s, researchers have used the creative strategy of identifying likely cohabiting partners in decennial and Current Population Survey data, a strategy first developed by Paul Glick and his colleagues (e.g., Glick & Norton, 1979). Cohabitors were identified as persons of the opposite sex sharing living quarters (POSSLQ). Other researchers have modified the procedures for identifying cohabitors to improve counts of couples who live in households with more than two adults (Sweet, 1979), including a recent study that includes a comparison between a revised POSSLQ measure and explicit survey reports about who is cohabiting (Casper & Cohen, 2000). The early POSSLQ measures appear to underestimate the numbers and rate of growth in cohabiting couples in the United States compared to more recent adjustments to the POSSLQ measure to include households in which couples live with children older than 15 years. The adjusted measure captures a higher percentage of cohabitors who identify themselves as partners and misses fewer self-identified partners than the unadjusted POSSLQ measure (Casper & Cohen, 2000).

The development of retrospective cohabitation histories in surveys about family-related topics complemented the data on cross-sectional trends available from census sources. The 1987–88 NSFH identified cohabitors on the household roster and asked all respondents, male and female, if they had ever lived with someone, the dates each cohabitation began and ended, and a full marriage history, including whether the cohabiting partners married each other. Asking questions on the start and end dates of cohabiting unions continued the principle in several decades of demographic research that treated the end of marriage as when the couple stopped living together rather than the date spouses were legally divorced (e.g., see Bumpass, 1984). The detailed retrospective reports from the NSFH are the data used in much of my summary of the facts of cohabitation. Several other surveys include cohabitation histories, such as the 1995 National Survey of Family Growth (NSFG) (Kelly, Mosher, Duffer, & Kinsey, 1997).[6] The NSFG is particularly valuable for studying change over time in cohabitation because since 1982 it has included some cohabitation information and because the NSFG is repeated periodically, although not at regular intervals. The 2002 survey data will provide important new information about the cohabitation experiences of recent cohorts by including cohabitation histories for men as well as women. Including men in the study is a valuable addition in light of the importance of men's economic characteristics and attitudes for cohabitation and marriage decisions.

It is now much more routine for surveys, including those about topics other than family relationships, to ask if respondents are cohabiting. Without the innovative use of census and survey data to describe the changes in cohabitation over the past several decades, social scientists would know very little about who cohabits and the association between cohabitation and important social and economic characteristics. Future researchers will not be able to answer the most basic factual questions about cohabitation or address theoretical debates on the meaning of cohabitation unless they make systematic efforts to collect data at routine, periodic intervals on individuals' history of cohabiting relationships. Large samples are necessary to describe reliably differences among subgroups. The need to collect data routinely is particularly important at this historical juncture because many standard sources of data on marriage, divorce, and

other family relationships have deteriorated during the 1990s. For instance, vital statistics on marriage and divorce were not compiled at the national level after 1995. The age-at-first-marriage question was deleted from the decennial census in 1990, and the U.S. Bureau of the Census's Current Population Survey omitted the marriage history from the June 2000 survey, ending a time series that has provided invaluable data on trends in children's experiences in single-parent and stepfamily households. (See the U.S. Forum on Child and Family Statistics, 1996, for a recent report about measures of marriage and cohabitation in federal data sources.)

Gathering the Facts About Cohabitors' Lives

Perhaps because demographic data showed that commonly accepted myths about cohabitation were false (e.g., the myth that cohabitation was more common among college students than among those with less education), researchers began to broaden their investigations to examine other aspects of cohabitors' lives beyond the demographic contours. Among the richest accounts of how cohabiting couples manage their lives is Blumstein and Schwartz's (1983) *American Couples* study, which compares cohabiting couples to three other types of couples: married heterosexual couples, gay couples, and lesbian couples. The comparison provides variation on the degree of institutionalization and gender, both of which provide social guidelines for how partners divide work. By including information about the quality of couples' relationships, the study also speaks to how individual couples negotiate their roles within the relationship in the context of institutional constraints. Despite these strengths, the study has some weaknesses, including the volunteer sample and largely cross-sectional design. Studies using national surveys and probability samples complement the *American Couples* study, but because most of the surveys address multiple topics, they do not provide the same rich account of couples' lives. The NSFH comes closest to the *American Couples* study because it has broad coverage of household life, asks the same questions of cohabiting and married couples, and includes reports about family relationships from multiple perspectives, including partners and spouses as well as children (Sweet & Bumpass, 1996; Sweet, Bumpass, & Call, 1988).

The NSFH and several other commonly used surveys for studying cohabitation, such as the National Longitudinal Survey of the High School Class of 1972 (U.S. Dept. of Education, 1999)[7] and Thornton, Freedman, and Axinn's Intergenerational Panel Study of Parents and Children, begun with children born in the early 1960s,[8] provide valuable insight into the meaning of cohabitation for the cohorts represented by the samples. Data from these studies are much less appropriate for questions about what cohabitation means today, now that it is a considerably more common experience and is acceptable under a wider range of circumstances than when respondents in these earlier studies were making decisions about cohabitation. To describe family change requires repeated surveys. These are expensive projects to mount, but it may be possible to combine small extensions to surveys already planned as periodic surveys—for instance, the Survey of Income and Program Participation (SIPP)[9] and the NSFG—with new, more complete surveys at much longer periodic intervals. Efforts to evaluate how well cohabitors are identified in the SIPP lay the groundwork for more researchers to use these data to study cohabitation (Baughman, Dickert-Conlin, & Houser, 2002).

Whether members of a couple think of themselves as living together may differ from whether researchers or even friends define them as a cohabiting couple. For instance, a couple may spend every night together and have most of their possessions in one place but not describe themselves as cohabiting (Sassler & Jobe, 2002). How questions about cohabiting relationships are worded and the context in which questions are posed affect estimates of levels and trends (Casper & Cohen, 2000). Change over historical time or differences across social settings in the stigma associated with cohabitation may bias estimates of cohabitation rates derived from explicit reports about cohabitation. Social scientists know little about how respondents understand questions about cohabitation. Comparisons among estimates from different surveys provide some insight into whether estimates of incidence and duration are robust to changes in question wording and sequence, but new studies of cohabitation would benefit from careful instrument development.

A challenge to developing good measures of cohabitation is that each partner may view the relationship differently. Just as marriage has a "his and hers" dimension, men and women who cohabit may differ in whether and when they define themselves as living together (e.g., when they moved their clothes to the same place; when they stopped paying rents in two places; when they spent most, but not all, nights together). Both partners' reports are important because the decision to cohabit, how the couple manages daily life together, and the stability of the relationship depend on both partners' preferences. Unfortunately, the quality of men's reports about family events and the timing of these events is not as good as that of women's reports (Auriat, 1993; Rendall, Clarke, Peters, Ranjit, & Verropoulou, 1999). Because cohabiting unions are typically short, much of what we know about their timing comes from retrospective reports. It is crucial for new studies to investigate how to improve the quality of reports from both women and men, but especially from men.

Couple data are very valuable for examining the competing interests of cohabiting partners and the quality of their relationship with each other. Although it is difficult to obtain high response rates in surveys of individuals, response rates for couple samples are even lower. Couples in which both partners participate in the study differ from those in which only one participates (Sassler & McNally, 2002). New work should explore how to improve survey participation of both partners and the conditions under which reports from one partner are sufficient.

Cohabiting relationships are important from an academic and social policy perspective because cohabitors share some resources and obligations. Yet it is not necessary to live together full time to share resources and obligations. Couples in serious dating relationships are also likely to share resources. Some couples who are even more committed to each other than many cohabitors may live apart, a relationship sometimes called "living apart together" (Leridon & Villeneuve-Gokalp, 1989; Liefbroer & de Jong Gierveld, 1993). As cohabiting relationships become more varied in the degree of commitment between partners, this increases the conceptual ambiguity of examining only couples who live together instead of broadening the focus of research to include those who are dating and other couples who live apart.

Methods of Studying Cohabitation

In addition to the advances in the quality of cohabitation data available, there have been several methodological advances. Statistical techniques for estimating rates of cohabitation and the duration of relationships from partial or censored histories are more widely used now than 30 years ago. These event history techniques allow researchers to examine the associations between background characteristics and rates of cohabitation, taking account of other individual or family characteristics that may vary over an individual's life (e.g., educational attainment, full-time employment). Over the past three decades, estimation procedures also have been developed to take into account that individuals decide about their relationships in a context that includes choices and expectations about what the future might bring (Lillard, 1993; Lillard et al., 1995). These methods recognize that whether a person cohabits or has a child outside marriage may depend on factors that also predict whether the person will marry (Brien, Lillard, & Waite, 1999).

Recently investigators have begun to work harder to combine qualitative and quantitative data to learn more about cohabitation. Researchers use several strategies for combining these styles of data. Some use open-ended, in-depth interviews to examine the attitudes, perceptions, and plans of recent cohabitors to explore questions unanswered so far by quantitative studies (Smock & Manning, 2001; see also the Cohabitation and Marriage Study that these authors are conducting, Manning and Smock, 2003). Others collect ethnographic and in-depth interview data as components of multi-method projects, including formal surveys. Examples of such studies include McLanahan et al.'s Fragile Families and Child Wellbeing Study and Cherlin et al.'s Welfare, Children and Families Study, conducted in three cities.[10] A benefit of combining strategies is that investigators can modify survey questions or use open-ended interviews to explore puzzling findings and develop a more complete understanding of the actors' own explanations for their behavior.

It is tempting to pursue new research that focuses exclusively on actors' feelings and interpretations of their behavior, but this ignores the importance of the social environment in which adults decide about cohabitation and other couple or family relationships. Whether others approve of cohabitation and the conditions under which it is appropriate also affect adults' decisions about cohabitation. Individuals can report their perceptions of others' attitudes, but this cannot substitute for public opinion data from representative, probability samples. Public opinion data from repeated cross-sectional studies have helped describe the changing normative environment that contributed to the rise in cohabitation (Thornton & Young-DeMarco, 2001). These data are still valuable for describing the trajectory of future changes. Researchers should also collect data about attitudes using new questions about cohabitation and obligations between members of a couple and how these relate to other obligations—for instance, between spouses and between parents and children.

COHABITATION AND THE FUTURE

It is always dangerous to predict the future, particularly when the prediction is about a phenomenon as rapidly changing as cohabitation is in the United States today. Since 1970, cohabitation has become much more prevalent among diverse demographic and social groups. Recent data suggest that these trends will continue. Cohabitation is here to stay. The meaning of cohabitation and its place in the U.S. kinship system continues to change, making it difficult to characterize. Debates that describe cohabitation dichotomously—as either a courtship stage or an alternative to marriage—miss the heterogeneity of cohabitation and ignore the changing composition of cohabitors over time.

Differences in the meaning of cohabitation for those who are educated and have sufficient, secure incomes and those who are less well educated and more economically vulnerable will be important for future studies of couple and family relationships. This is especially true because recent trends suggest an increasing bifurcation in family experience.

Cohabitation is sometimes called the poor man's marriage. When men have limited economic resources, they and their potential wives postpone marriage until they can afford the material goods and economic stability they believe that marriage requires. Couples may live together while they wait to attain these economic goals. Some equate marriage with success (Edin, 2002). Many never achieve their goals because of the declining wages and job opportunities for men who lack college educations. Some who are waiting to marry have children while they are cohabiting. Unmarried parents discuss the decision to marry and the economic requirements for marriage separately from their reasons for having children (Edin, 2002). They do not believe that they must marry to raise children. Cohort comparisons show that women who bear a child outside marriage are increasingly likely to bear all of their children outside marriage (Hoffman & Foster, 1997). Other evidence of an increasing division between the advantaged and less advantaged comes from marriage studies that show that college-educated women are more likely to marry than those with less schooling (Goldstein & Kenney, 2001), that husbands' education reduces the chance of divorce (Teachman, 2002), and that there is growing similarity between husbands' and wives' educations (Mare, 1991).

Children depend on their parents' resources. Increasing disparity between the family circumstances of children whose parents are highly educated and have reasonably secure economic futures and those whose parents are less secure exacerbates the disadvantages children experience when they are born outside marriage. Cohabitation may alleviate some of these disadvantages but expose children to other threats, such as multiple transitions in family structure as the biological parents end their relationship and start new ones. How these children grow up and the relationships they form or consider appropriate to form will determine the future of cohabitation and its place in the kinship system.

Finally, debates about cohabitation emphasize the experience of young adults and implications of cohabitation for children. This ignores that cohort replacement will increase cohabitation among older persons. Older persons who cohabit may be less able or willing to share their household with an unmarried daughter and her child or to transfer money to adult children. Older cohabitors may also need less help from adult children. As the U.S. population ages, it will become even more important to examine the meaning of cohabitation during old age and its implications for the distribution of resources within and between generations.

NOTES

1. For public use data files of the NSAF, see the Web site of the Urban Institute: www.urban.org/Content/Research/NewFederalism/NSAF/Overview/NSAFOverview.htm.

2. For description of the sample and overviews of the content of the NSFH, see the Web site of the Social Science Computing Cooperative at www.ssc.wisc.edu/nsfh/.

3. For data sets, methodology, and data details, see the Web site of the Carolina Population Center at www.cpc.unc.edu/addhealth.

4. For data files and description of the NLSY, see the U.S. Department of Labor's Bureau of Labor Statistics Web site at www.bls.gov/nls/nlsy79.htm.

5. For study design and data files of the Fragile Families and Child Wellbeing Study, see the Web site of the Center for Research on Child Wellbeing at http://crcw.princeton.edu/fragilefamilies.

6. For description and data of the NSFG, see the Web site of the National Center for Health Statistics at www.cdc.gov/nchs/nsfg.htm.

7. For an overview of this survey and access to its data, see the National Center for Education Statistics Web site at http://nces.ed.gov/surveys/nls72/.

8. For data and description of the Intergenerational Panel Study, see the Sociometrics Web site at www.socio.com/srch/summary/afda2/fam37-47.htm.

9. For data and description of the SIPP, see the U.S. Census Bureau's Web site at http://www.sipp.census.gov/sipp/.

10. For some results of this study, see the Johns Hopkins University Web site at www.jhu.edu/~welfare.

REFERENCES

Anderson, K. G., Kaplan, H., & Lancaster, J. B. (2001, September). *Men's financial expenditures on genetic children and stepchildren from current and former relationships* (Population Studies Center Rep. No. 01-484). Ann Arbor: University of Michigan, Institute for Social Research.

Aquilino, W. S. (1997). From adolescent to young adult: A prospective study of parent-child relations during the transition to adulthood. *Journal of Marriage and the Family, 59,* 670–686.

Auriat, N. (1993). "My wife knows best": A comparison of event dating accuracy between the wife, the husband, the couple, and the Belgium Population Register. *Public Opinion Quarterly, 57,* 165–190.

Axinn, W. G., & Thornton, A. (1992). The relationship between cohabitation and divorce: Selectivity or causal influence? *Demography, 29,* 357–374.

Axinn, W. G., & Thornton, A. (1993). Mothers, children, and cohabitation: The intergenerational effects of attitudes and behavior. American Sociological Review, 58, 233–246.

Baughman, R., Dickert-Conlin, S., & Houser, S. (2002). How well can we track cohabitation using the SIPP? A consideration of direct and inferred measures. *Demography, 39,* 455–465.

Bauman, K. J. (1999). Shifting family definitions: The effect of cohabitation and other nonfamily household relationships on measures of poverty. *Demography, 36,* 315–325.

Bearman, P. S., Jones, J., & Udry, J. R. (1997). The National Longitudinal Study of Adolescent Health: Research design. Retrieved July 1, 2003, from the Web site of the Carolina Population Center: www.cpc.unc.edu/addhealth.

Black, D., Gates, G., Sanders, S., & Taylor, L. (2000). Demographics of the gay and lesbian population in the United States: Evidence from available systematic data sources. *Demography, 37,* 139–154.

Blackwell, D. L., & Lichter, D. T. (2000). Mate selection among married and cohabiting couples. *Journal of Family Issues, 21,* 275–302.

Blumstein, P., & Schwartz, P. (1983). *American couples.* New York: William Morrow.

Booth, A., & Crouter, A. C. (Eds.). (2002). *Just living together.* Mahwah, NJ: Lawrence Erlbaum.

Bramlett, M. D., & Mosher, W. D. (2002). *Cohabitation, marriage, divorce, and remarriage in the United States* (Vital and Health Statistics, 23[22], DHHS Pub. No. [PHS] 2002-1998). Washington, DC: Government Printing Office. Retrieved April 6, 2003, from www.cdc.gov/nchs/data/series/sr_23/sr23_022.pdf

Brien, M. J., Lillard, L. A., & Waite, L. J. (1999). Interrelated family-building behaviors: Cohabitation, marriage, and nonmarital conception. *Demography, 36,* 535–551.

Brines, J., & Joyner, K. (1999). The ties that bind: Principles of cohesion in cohabitation and marriage. *American Sociological Review, 64,* 333–355.

Brown, S. L. (2000). Union transitions among cohabitors: The significance of relationship assessments and expectations. *Journal of Marriage and the Family, 62,* 833–846.

Brown, S. L. (2002). Child well-being in cohabiting families. In A. Booth & A. C. Crouter (Eds.), *Just living together* (pp. 173–187). Mahwah, NJ: Lawrence Erlbaum.

Bumpass, L. L. (1984). Children and marital disruption: A replication and update. *Demography, 21,* 71–82.

Bumpass, L. L. (1990). What's happening to the family? Interactions between demographic and institutional change. *Demography, 27,* 483–498.

Bumpass, L. L. (1995). *The declining significance of marriage: Changing family life in the United States* (National Survey of Families and Households Working Paper No. 66). Madison: University of Wisconsin, Center for Demography and Ecology.

Bumpass, L. L. (1998). The changing significance of marriage in the United States. In K. O. Mason, N. O. Tsuya, & M. K. Choe (Eds.), *The changing family in comparative perspective* (pp. 63–79). Honolulu: East-West Center.

Bumpass, L. L., & Lu, H.-H. (2000). Trends in cohabitation and implications for children's family contexts in the United States. *Population Studies, 54,* 29–41.

Bumpass, L. L., & Sweet, J. A. (1989). National estimates of cohabitation. *Demography, 26,* 615–625.

Bumpass, L. L., & Sweet, J. A. (1995). *Cohabitation, marriage, and nonmarital childbearing and union stability: Preliminary findings from NSFH2* (National Survey of Families and Households Working Paper No. 65). Madison: University of Wisconsin, Center for Demography and Ecology.

Bumpass, L. L., & Sweet, J. A. (2001). Marriage, divorce, and intergenerational relationships. In A. Thornton (Ed.), *The well-being of children and families* (pp. 295–313). Ann Arbor: University of Michigan Press.

Bumpass, L. L., Sweet, J. A., & Cherlin, A. J. (1991). The role of cohabitation in declining rates of marriage. *Journal of Marriage and the Family, 53,* 913–927.

Carlson, M., & McLanahan, S. (2001, November). *Shared parenting in fragile families* (Working Paper 01-16-FF). Princeton, NJ: Princeton University, Center for Research on Child Wellbeing.

Carlson, M. J., & McLanahan, S. S. (2002, November). *Early father involvement in fragile families* (Working Paper 01-08-FF). Princeton, NJ: Princeton University, Center for Research on Child Wellbeing.

Case, A., Lin, I.-L., & McLanahan, S. (1999). Household resource allocation in stepfamilies: Darwin reflects on the plight of Cinderella. *American Economic Review, 89,* 234–238.

Casper, L. M., & Bianchi, S. M. (2002). Cohabitation. In *Trends in the American family* (pp. 39–68). Thousand Oaks, CA: Sage.

Casper, L. M., & Cohen, P. H. (2000). How does POSSLQ measure up? Historical estimates of cohabitation. *Demography, 37,* 237–245.

Casper, L. M., & Sayer, L. C. (2002). *Cohabitation transitions: Different purposes and goals, different paths.* Revised version of paper presented at the annual meeting of the Population Association of American, Los Angeles, March 2000.

Cherlin, A. J. (1978). Remarriage as an incomplete institution. *American Journal of Sociology, 84,* 634–650.

Cherlin, A. J. (1992). *Marriage, divorce, remarriage.* Cambridge, MA: Harvard University Press.

Cherlin, A. J. (2000). Toward a new home socioeconomics of union formation. In L. J. Waite, C. Bachrach, M. Hindin, E. Thomson, & A. Thornton (Eds.), *The ties that bind* (pp. 126–144). New York: Aldine de Gruyter.

Citro, C. F., & Michael, R. T. (1995). *Measuring poverty.* Washington, DC: National Academy Press.

Clarkberg, M. (1999). The price of partnering: The role of economic well-being in young adults' first union experiences. *Social Forces, 77,* 945–968.

Clarkberg, M., Stolzenberg, R. M., & Waite, L. J. (1995). Attitudes, values, and entrance into cohabitational versus marital unions. *Social Forces, 74,* 609–634.

Cooksey, E. C., & Craig, P. H. (1998). Parenting from a distance: The effects of paternal characteristics on contact between nonresidential fathers and their children. *Demography, 35,* 187–200.

DeLeire, T., & Kalil, A. (2002, April). *How do cohabiting couples with children spend their money?* (Working Paper No. 290). Chicago: Northwestern University and University of Chicago, Joint Centers for Poverty Research.

Dunifon, R., & Kowaleski-Jones, L. (2002). Who's in the house? Race differences in cohabitation, single parenthood, and child development. *Child Development, 73,* 1249–1264.

Edin, K. (2002, May 21). Interview for *Frontline.* Retrieved on April 6, 2002, from www.pbs.org/wgbh/pages/frontline/shows/marriage/interviews/edin.html

Glick, P. C., & Norton, A. J. (1977/1979). Marrying, divorcing, and living together in the U.S. today. *Population Bulletin 32*(5). Washington, DC: Population Reference Bureau.

Glick, P. C., & Spanier, G. B. (1980). Married and unmarried cohabitation in the United States. *Journal of Marriage and the Family, 42,* 19–30.

Goldstein, J. R. (1999). The leveling of divorce in the United States. *Demography, 36,* 409–414.

Goldstein, J. R., & Kenney, C. T. (2001). Marriage delayed or marriage forgone? New cohort forecasts of first marriage for U.S. women. *American Sociological Review, 66,* 506–519.

Gupta, S. (1999). The effects of transitions in marital status on men's performance of housework. *Journal of Marriage and the Family, 61,* 700–711.

Hajnal, J. (1965). European marriage patterns in perspective. In D. V. Glass & D. E. C. Eversley (Eds.), *Population in History* (pp. 101–138). Chicago: Aldine.

Hanson, T. L., McLanahan, S., & Thomson, E. (1997). Economic resources, parental practices, and children's well-being. In G. J. Duncan & J. Brooks-Gunn (Eds.), *Consequences of growing up poor* (pp. 190–238). New York: Russell Sage.

Hao, L., & Xie, G. (2002). The complexity and endogeneity of family structure in explaining children's misbehavior. *Social Science Research, 31,* 1–28.

Hofferth, S. L., & Anderson, K. G. (2003). Are all dads equal? Biology versus marriage as a basis or parental investment. *Journal of Marriage and Family, 65,* 213–232.

Hoffman, S. D., & Foster, E. M. (1997). Nonmarital births and single mothers: Cohort trends in the dynamics of nonmarital childbearing. *History of the Family, 2,* 255–275.

Kelly, J. E., Mosher, W. D., Duffer, A. P., & Kinsey, S. H. (1997). *Plan and operation of the 1995 National Survey of Family Growth* (Vital and Health Statistics, Series 1, No. 36). Washington, DC: National Center for Health Statistics.

Kenney, C. T. (2002). *Household economies: Money management and resource allocation among married and cohabiting parents.* Unpublished doctoral dissertation, Princeton University, Princeton, NJ.

Kiernan, K. (2002). Cohabitation in western Europe: Trends, issues, and implications. In A. Booth & A. C. Crouter (Eds.), *Just living together* (pp. 3–31). Mahwah, NJ: Lawrence Erlbaum.

Landale, N. S. (2002). Contemporary cohabitation: Food for thought. In A. Booth & A. C. Crouter (Eds.), *Just living together* (pp. 33–40). Mahwah, NJ: Lawrence Erlbaum.

Landale, N. S., & Oropesa, R. S. (2001). Father involvement in the lives of mainland Puerto Rican children: Contributions of nonresident, cohabiting and married fathers. *Social Forces, 79,* 945–968.

Laumann, E. O., Gagnon, J. H., Michael, R. T., & Michaels, S. (1994). *The social organization of sexuality.* Chicago: University of Chicago Press.

Leridon, H., & Villeneuve-Gokalp, C. (1989). The new couples: Number, characteristics and attitudes. *Population, 44,* 203–235.

Lesthaeghe, R. (1995). The second demographic transition in Western countries: An interpretation. In K. O. Mason & A.-M. Jensen (Eds.), *Gender and family change in industrialized countries* (pp. 17–82). Oxford, UK: Clarendon.

Liefbroer, A. C., & de Jong Gierveld, J. (1993). The impact of rational considerations and perceived opinions on young adults' union formation intentions. *Journal of Family Issues, 14,* 213–235.

Lillard, L. A. (1993). Simultaneous equations for hazards: Marriage duration and fertility timing. *Journal of Econometrics, 57,* 189–217.

Lillard, L. A., Brien, M. J., & Waite, L. J. (1995). Premarital cohabitation and subsequent marital dissolution: A matter of self-selection. *Demography, 32,* 437–457.

Macklin, E. D. (1980). Nontraditional family forms: A decade of research. *Journal of Marriage and the Family, 42,* 905–922.

Manning, W. D. (2001). Childbearing in cohabiting unions: Racial and ethnic differences. *Family Planning Perspectives, 33,* 217–223.

Manning, W. D. (2002). The implications of cohabitation for children's well-being. In A. Booth & A. C. Crouter (Eds.), *Just living together* (pp. 121–152). Mahwah, NJ: Lawrence Erlbaum.

Manning, W. D., & Lamb, K. (2002). *Parental cohabitation and adolescent well-being* (Working Paper No. 02-04). Bowling Green, OH: Bowling Green State University, Center for Family and Demographic Research.

Manning, W. D., & Lichter, D. T. (1996). Parental cohabitation and children's economic well-being. *Journal of Marriage and the Family, 58,* 998–1010.

Manning, W. D., & Smock, P. J. (2002). First comes cohabitation and then comes marriage? *Journal of Family Issues, 23,* 1065–1087.

Manning, W. D., & Smock, P. J. (2003). *The formation of cohabiting unions: New perspectives from qualitative data.* Paper presented at the annual meeting of the Population Association of America, Minneapolis, MN.

Manning, W. D., Smock, P. J., & Majumdar, D. (2002). *The relative stability of cohabiting and marital unions for children* (Working Paper No. 02-18). Bowling Green, OH: Bowling Green State University, Center for Family and Demographic Research.

Manting, D. (1996). The changing meaning of cohabitation and marriage. *European Sociological Review, 12,* 53–65.

Mare, R. D. (1991). Five decades of educational assortative mating. *American Sociological Review, 56,* 15–32.

Martin, J. A., Hamilton, B. E., Ventura, S. J., Menacker, F., Park, M. M., & Sutton, P. D. (2002). *Births: Final data for 2001 (*National Vital Statistics Reports 51[2].) Hyattsville, MD: National Center for Health Statistics.

Moffitt, R. M., Revelle, R., & Winkler, A. E. (1998). Beyond single mothers: Cohabitation and marriage in the AFDC program. *Demography, 35,* 259–278.

Morrison, D. R., & Ritualo, A. (2000). Routes to children's economic recovery after divorce: Are cohabitation and remarriage equivalent? *American Sociological Review, 65,* 560–580.

Nelson, S., Clark, R. L., & Acs, G. (2001). Beyond the two-parent family: How teenagers fare in cohabiting couple and blended families (Series B, No. B-31). Report for the National Survey of America's Families. Retrieved July 1, 2003, from the Web site of the Urban Institute: www.urban.org/UploadedPDF/ anf_b31.pdf.

Nock, S. L. (1995). A comparison of marriages and cohabiting relationships. *Journal of Family Issues, 16,* 53–76.

Oppenheimer, V. K. (1988). A theory of marriage timing. *American Journal of Sociology, 94,* 563–591.

Oppenheimer, V. K. (1997). Women's employment and the gain to marriage: The specialization and trading model. *Annual Review of Sociology, 23,* 431–453.

Oppenheimer, V. K., Kalmijn, M., & Lim, N. (1997). Men's career development and marriage timing during a period of rising inequality. *Demography, 34,* 311–330.

Oropesa, R. S. (1996). Normative beliefs about marriage and cohabitation: A comparison of non-Latino whites, Mexican Americans, and Puerto Ricans. *Journal of Marriage and the Family, 58,* 49–62.

Raley, R. K. (1996). A shortage of marriageable men? A note on the role of cohabitation in black-white differences in marriage rates. *American Sociological Review, 61,* 973–983.

Raley, R. K. (2000). Recent trends and differentials in marriage and cohabitation. In L. J. Waite, C. Bachrach, M. Hindin, E. Thomson, & A. Thornton (Eds.), *The ties that bind* (pp. 19–39). New York: Aldine de Gruyter.

Raley, R. K. (2001). Increasing fertility in cohabiting unions: Evidence for a second demographic transition in the United States? *Demography, 38,* 59–66.

Rendall, M. S., Clarke, L., Peters, H. E., Ranjit, N., & Verropoulou, G. (1999). Incomplete reporting of men's fertility in the United States and Britain: A research note. *Demography, 36,* 135–144.

Sassler, S., & Jobe, T. (2002, May). *To live together . . . as man and wife? The process of entering into cohabiting unions.* Paper presented at the annual meeting of the Population Association of America, Atlanta, GA.

Sassler, S., & McNally, J. (2002). *Cohabiting couples' economic circumstances and union transitions: A re-examination accounting for selective data loss.* Revised version of paper presented at the annual meeting of the Population Association of America, Los Angeles, March 2000.

Schoen, R., & Weinick, R. M. (1993). Partner choice in marriages and cohabitations. *Journal of Marriage and the Family, 55,* 408–414.

Seltzer, J. A. (2000a). Child support and child access: Experiences of divorced and nonmarital families. In J. T. Oldham & M. S. Melli (Eds.), *Child support: The next frontier* (pp. 69–87). Ann Arbor: University of Michigan Press.

Seltzer, J. A. (2000b). Families formed outside of marriage. *Journal of Marriage and the Family, 62,* 1247–1268.

Seltzer, J. A. (2002, July). *Income pooling and individual and family mobility.* Paper presented at the World Congress of Sociology, Brisbane, Australia.

Shelton, B. A., & John, D. (1993). Does marital status make a difference? *Journal of Family Issues, 14,* 401–420.

Simmons, T., & O'Neill, G. (2001). Households and families: 2000 (Census 2000 Brief C2KBR/01-8). Washington, DC: U. S. Bureau of the Census. Retrieved April 6, 2003, from www.census.gov/prod/2001pubs/c2kbr01-8.pdf.

Smock, P. J. (2000). Cohabitation in the United States: An appraisal of research themes, findings, and implications. *Annual Review of Sociology, 26,* 1–20.

Smock, P. J., & Gupta, S. (2002). Cohabitation in contemporary North America . In A. Booth & A. C. Crouter (Eds.), *Just living together* (pp. 53–84). Mahwah, NJ: Lawrence Erlbaum.

Smock, P. J., & Manning, W. D. (1997). Cohabiting partner's economic circumstances and marriage. *Demography, 34,* 331–341.

Smock, P. J., & Manning, W. D. (2001). *A case for qualitative methods in U. S. family demography: Understanding the meaning of unmarried cohabitation* (Working Paper No. 01-07). Bowling Green, OH: Bowling Green State University, Center for Family and Demographic Research.

South, S. J., & Spitze, G. (1994). Housework in marital and nonmarital households. *American Sociological Review, 59,* 327–347.

Sussman, M. B. (Ed.). (1972). *Non-traditional family forms in the 1970's.* Minneapolis, MN: National Council on Family Relations.

Sweeney, M. M., & Phillips, J. A. (2002). *Understanding racial differences in marital disruption: Recent trends and explanations.* Revised version of paper presented at the annual meetings of the Population Association of America, Washington, DC, March 2001.

Sweet, J. A. (1979). *Estimates of levels, trends, and characteristics of the "living together" population from the Current Population Survey* (Working Paper No. 79-49). Madison: University of Wisconsin, Center for Demography and Ecology.

Sweet, J. A., & Bumpass, L. L. (1996). *The National Survey of Families and Households—Waves 1 and 2: Data description and documentation.* Madison: University of Wisconsin, Center for Demography and Ecology.

Sweet, J., Bumpass, L., & Call, V. (1988). *The design and content of the National Survey of Families and Households* (NSFH Working Paper 1). Madison: University of Wisconsin, Center for Demography and Ecology.

Teachman, J. D. (2002). Stability across cohorts in divorce risk factors. *Demography, 39,* 331–351.

Thomson, E., Hanson, T. L., & McLanahan, S. S. (1994). Family structure and child well-being: Economic resources vs. parental behaviors. *Social Forces, 73,* 221–242.

Thomson, E., McLanahan, S. S., & Curtin, R. B. (1992). Family structure, gender, and parental socialization. *Journal of Marriage and the Family, 54,* 368–378.

Thomson, E., Mosley, J., Hanson, T. L., & McLanahan, S. S. (2001). Remarriage, cohabitation, and changes in mothering behavior. *Journal of Marriage and Family, 63,* 370–380.

Thornton, A., & Young-DeMarco, L. (2001). Four decades of trends in attitudes toward family issues in the United States: The 1960s through the 1990s. *Journal of Marriage and Family, 63,* 1009–1037.

Treas, J. (1993). Money in the bank: Transaction costs and the economic organization of marriage. *American Sociological Review, 58,* 723–734.

U.S. Bureau of the Census. (1998). *Population profile of the United States: 1997* (Current Population Reports Series P23-194). Washington, DC: Government Printing Office. Retrieved April 6, 2003, from www.census.gov/prod/3/98pubs/p23-194.pdf.

U.S. Department of Education, Center for Education Statistics. (1999). *National Study of the Class of 1972* [Computer file]. ICPSR version. Chicago: National Opinion Research Center [Producer]. Ann Arbor, MI: Inter-University Consortium for Political and Social Research [Distributor].

U.S. Forum on Child and Family Statistics. (1996). Measuring the formation and dissolution of marital and cohabiting unions in federal surveys. Retrieved June 20, 2003, from www.childstats.gov/DataColl/union.asp.

Waite, L. J. (1995). Does marriage matter? *Demography, 32,* 483–507.

Waite, L. J., Bachrach, C., Hindin, M., Thomson, E., & Thornton, A. (Eds.). (2000). *The ties that bind.* New York: Aldine de Gruyter.

Willis, R. J., & Michael, R. T. (1994). Innovation in family formation: Evidence on cohabitation in the United States. In J. Ermisch & N. Ogawa (Eds.), *The family, the market and the state in ageing societies* (pp. 9–45). Oxford, UK: Clarendon.

Winkler, A. E. (1997). Economic decision-making by cohabitors: Findings regarding income pooling. *Applied Economics, 29,* 1079–1090.

Xie, Y., Raymo, J., Goyette, K., & Thornton, A. (2003). Economic potential and entry into marriage and cohabitation. *Demography, 40,* 351–367.

Zagorsky, J. L., & White, L. (Eds.). (1999). *NLSY79 user's guide: A guide to the 1979–1998 National Longitudinal Survey of Youth Data.* Columbus: Ohio State University, Center for Human Resource Research.

CHAPTER 5

Variations in Marriage Over Time
An Ecological/Exchange Perspective

RONALD M. SABATELLI AND KAREN RIPOLL

W e have been given the task of addressing the recent past (the last 30 years) and the near future of marriage—and in particular we have been asked to reflect on the degree to which family social scientists have succeeded at capturing the shifts that have occurred in marriage over this time period. During the 1960s, '70s, and '80s, family scholarship reflected an awareness that marriage was being transformed by the sexual revolution, the feminist movement, and the widespread shifts in women's roles that were occurring in the society. We were aware that the times were changing, that marriage was "under siege," that an ever-increasing number of children were growing up in disrupted and/or single-parent households.

At the same time, though rates of divorce were increasing and stabilizing at historically high levels during the past 30 years, rates of remarriage remained relatively high (Bramlett & Mosher, 2001). This resulted in an ever-increasing number of children experiencing life in married, single-parent, and then stepfamily households (Cherlin, 1992). During this time period, as well, there were notable increases in the number of children born to single mothers and the number of couples cohabiting instead of marrying (Bumpass & Sweet, 1989). In other words, a number of interrelated changes occurred in the structures of marriages and families over the past 30 years. All of these trends may very well represent shifts in the underlying functions of marriage within society. They may represent, as well, a shift in the centrality of marriage as the pivotal subsystem within the family system.

As we thought about how to write about the last 30 years of marriage, we were challenged to work out a way of understanding the broad trends that have occurred within marriages over time while remaining sensitive to the variability in the ways that marriages are structured and experienced within cohorts in any one historical period. In other words, generalizing about marriages is hard. Although they *may* vary over historical time, they *definitely* vary within cohorts. Thus, we needed to find a way to write about marital differences *between cohorts* that also accounted for variations in how marriages are structured and experienced *within cohorts*.

THE ECOLOGICAL/ EXCHANGE FRAMEWORK

We turned to principles from ecological and social exchange theories (see Figure 5.1) to account for between- and within-cohort variations regarding marital structures and experiences. Through an integration of ecological and social exchange perspectives, we have been able to highlight both macro-level and micro-level factors that have interacted to shape the trends and trajectories of marriages over the past 30 years. The framework provides us with a context, as well, to discuss whether family scholarship has kept pace with these trends and to examine future marital trends and concerns.

SOCIAL EXCHANGE THEORY

We begin by presenting a brief overview of social exchange theory. Social exchange is not a single theory. Rather, it consists of a number of different exchange perspectives that share a set of core assumptions and key concepts; each perspective has contributed to the development of the exchange framework.

The exchange framework is built upon the combination of central tenets of behaviorism and elementary economics where human behavior is envisaged as a function of its payoff (Sabatelli & Shehan, 1993). According to the central tenets of the exchange framework, people seek through their interactions with others to maximize their rewards and minimize their costs. That is, the degree to which people are attracted to a relationship is based on the balance of rewards and costs available to them from the relationship and on the rewards and costs available from competing alternatives.

How the marital exchange system is experienced by each partner and how the relationship system is structured (see Figure 5.2) are influenced by (a) the levels of attraction and dependence experienced by each partner and (b) the levels of attraction and dependence experienced between partners. Individuals feel attracted to partners when the relationships are highly rewarding and the rewards compare favorably to those available in alternatives. How the rewards available in a relationship measure up to rewards available in alternatives determines the degree to which individuals are dependent on an existing relationship (Thibaut & Kelley, 1959). Furthermore, reciprocal or symmetrical patterns of attraction and dependence, characterized as interdependence, give rise to feelings of trust and commitment and foster relationship stability (McDonald, 1981; Sabatelli, 1999).

The fact that marriages generally have become more unstable than in the past (see Chapter 15 of this book) implies that in some fundamental way they have become less attractive and satisfying and that contemporary married individuals experience less dependence on their marriages compared to past cohorts. It is important, therefore, to develop a better theoretical understanding of the factors mediating these two key dimensions of the marital exchange system.

The Attractiveness of the Marriage Relationship

According to social exchange perspectives, rewards are defined as the "pleasures, satisfactions, and gratifications the person enjoys" (Thibaut & Kelley, 1959, p. 12). Rewards are physical, social, and psychological effects that a person likes to obtain from

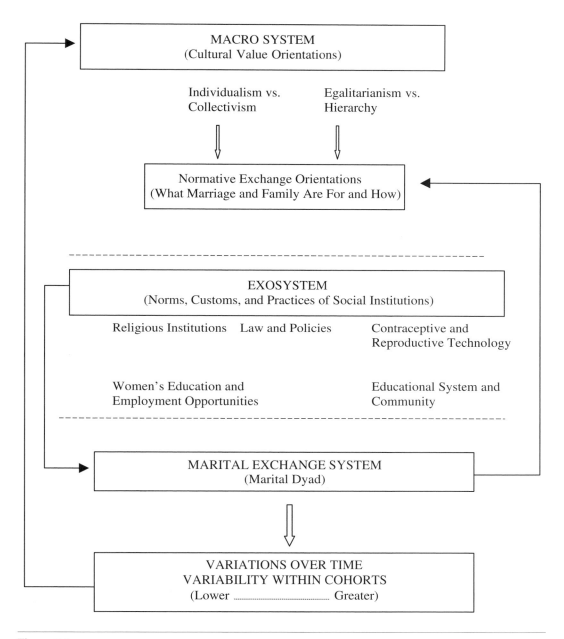

Figure 5.1

participating in a relationship (Nye, 1979). On the other hand, costs are any negative experiences due to things the person dislikes (punishments) or rewards forgone from being involved in a relationship (Nye, 1979; Sabatelli, 1999). Resources are any material or symbolic commodities that can be exchanged within interpersonal relationships (Foa & Foa, 1974) and that give a person the capacity to reward another (Emerson, 1976).

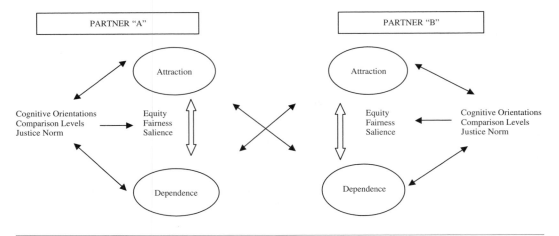

Figure 5.2

Although higher outcomes bring higher satisfaction in general, social exchange perspectives also consider the influence of individuals' expectations on how relationships are evaluated and experienced. What constitutes a satisfying relationship is different from person to person because each person has different standards and expectations for evaluating relationship outcomes. The concepts of *cognitive orientations* (Burns, 1973; McDonald, 1981) and *comparison level,* or CL (Thibaut & Kelley, 1959), refer to people's subjective standards and expectations that influence how they structure and evaluate their relationships. These cognitive orientations and subjective expectations are influenced by societal norms, experiences from previous relationships, and knowledge from observations of other people's relationships (Sabatelli, 1999; Sabatelli & Shehan, 1993). They represent each individual's views of how marital exchanges should be set up or structured (Burns, 1973; McDonald, 1981). They represent, as well, individuals' views of what is important to them in a relationship and what is realistically available to them from a relationship (Nye, 1979; Sabatelli, 1999; Thibaut & Kelley, 1959). Relationship satisfaction results when the outcomes derived from the relationship meet or exceed these cognitive expectations (Sabatelli, 1984).

Consequently, to understand changes that have occurred in marriages over the past 30 years, we need to consider whether there have been changes in the rewards and costs available to men and women from marriage. We are compelled as well to consider whether individuals' expectations of their relationships have changed in response to changes in cultural and social conditions.

Dependence on the Marriage Relationship

Dependence is defined as the degree to which people believe that they are subject to or reliant on the other for relationship rewards. Thibaut and Kelley (1959) developed the concept of *comparison level of alternatives* (*CLalt*), defined as the lowest level of outcomes a person will accept from a relationship in light of available alternatives, to account for relational dependence. When the outcomes available in an alternative relationship exceed those available in a person's current relationship, the person experiences a low level of dependence on the relationship.

Conversely, when the outcomes available from within a relationship exceed those available in alternatives, dependence on the relationship is high.

Power and decision-making dynamics are influenced in large part by the balance of dependence within a relationship (Blau, 1964; Cook & Emerson, 1978). Simply put, power and dependence are inversely related. Dependence is the primary mediator of stability. In this regard, a person who believes that a better alternative exists is more likely to leave a relationship than a person who believes that no better relationship exists. Thus, staying in or leaving a relationship is not simply a matter of how rewarding that relationship is. Relationships that are rewarding are more likely to be stable because a high level of rewards reduces expectations about the likelihood of a better alternative existing. Unsatisfactory relationships, in turn, may remain stable for lack of better alternatives (i.e., because of the high level of dependence on the relationship). These relationships were termed *nonvoluntary relationships* by Thibaut and Kelley (1959).

Relationship stability is further mediated by *barriers* that increase the costs of dissolution (Levinger, 1974, 1982). Levinger posited the existence of two types of barriers—internal and external—that discourage an individual from leaving a relationship by fostering dependence even if attraction is negative. Internal barriers are the feelings of obligation and indebtedness to the partner that contribute to dependence by increasing the psychological costs of terminating the relationship. Within marital and family relationships, internal constraints might involve the moral belief that marriage is forever or that children should be reared in a home with both parents present. External barriers are primarily group affiliations, community pressures, legal pressures, and material-economic considerations that foster dependence by increasing the social and/or economic costs of terminating the relationship.

THE HISTORICAL AND CULTURAL CONTEXT OF THE EXCHANGE RELATIONSHIP

Most of the key figures in the development of American social exchange theory, including Homans (1961), Blau (1964), and Thibaut and Kelley (1959), had strong individualistic orientations (Sabatelli & Shehan, 1993). These theorists viewed the exchange relationship as being shaped by the individuals' drives to maximize rewards and minimize costs. However, when family scholars adopted the social exchange framework to the study of marriage, some of them called attention to the limitations of these individualistic exchange models. The major point advanced by these marital exchange theorists was that individualistic notions alone cannot explain the complex exchange patterns observed within marriages. For example, McDonald (1981) pointed out how successful marital relationships require partners to move from a focus on immediate rewards and develop a long-term exchange orientation. Scanzoni (1972) noted that individualistic principles fail to account for the asymmetrical patterns of rewards and power found in many marriages. Furthermore, Rodman (1972) called attention to the widespread cultural differences in how marriages are structured.

In addition to each partner's desire to maximize rewards and minimize costs, marital relationships are shaped by the marital exchange customs promoted within a society at any one moment in time. These cultural customs reflect the prevailing views of relationships grounded in social discourse of the times. This discourse, of course, is influenced by broader cultural, economic, and political conditions.

Furthermore, cultural and societal factors affect the resources men and women bring to marital exchanges, thereby influencing patterns of power and dependence. The balance of resources within a marital relationship is a reflection of the broader cultural climate that influences the distribution of resources and alternatives available to men and women in marital relationships. To understand trends in marriage over time, we need to be aware of the ways in which cultural and societal factors influence the exchanges in marriages.

ECOLOGICAL SYSTEMS AND THE EXCHANGE RELATIONSHIP

Ecologically oriented life span developmental theorists account for patterns of development by focusing on how historical, cultural, and environmental conditions dynamically and nonrecursively interact with one another to create a unique ecological niche for individuals (Super & Harkness, 1999). Marriages exist in an ecological niche that has a powerful effect on the variability in how relationships are structured and experienced over time and within a historical period. In the ecological/exchange framework depicted in Figure 5.1, we call attention to the broader historically grounded contextual factors that can influence the patterns of attraction and dependence found in marital relationships.

The Macrosystem and the Structure and Experience of Marriage

Individual developmental trends and patterns of behavior are tied indirectly to the cultural value orientations of the broader macrosystem (Bronfenbrenner, 1988). Cultural value orientations give individuals in a given society particular ways of viewing the world as well as expectations regarding behavior in a variety of social settings (Duck,

1994). They help to shape the ways in which marriages are structured, organized, and experienced.

Several researchers have developed schemes for classifying and describing macro-level cultural value orientations (Hofstede, 1994; Schwartz, 1997; Trompenaars, 1993). Triandis (1995) observed considerable overlap among these different classification schemes and created an integrated classification scheme built around the existence of two central cultural value dimensions: individualism versus collectivism and hierarchy versus egalitarianism. Individualism was defined as "the subordination of the goals of the collectivities to individual goals, and a sense of independence and lack of concern for others" (Hui & Triandis, 1986, p. 245). Collectivism, on the other hand, was defined as "a sense of harmony, interdependence, and concern for others" that reflects "the subordination of individual goals to the goals of a collective" (pp. 244–245). Hierarchy reflects the legitimacy of fixed rules and resources, whereas egalitarianism emphasizes freedom and equality (Schwartz, 1997). Castillo (1997) described the hierarchy-egalitarianism dimension as the degree of dominance hierarchies based on gender, class, race, age, ethnicity, or any combination of these characteristics.

In the United States, there is clearly more of a cultural emphasis on individualism than collectivism. It is less clear, however, whether the cultural value orientations found within the United States reflect egalitarian or hierarchical ideals. Castillo (1997), for example, sees the United States as a hierarchical society based on a well-developed class hierarchy rooted in free market capitalism and strong racial and ethnic hierarchies. However, when marital relationships are the unit of analysis, we believe that hierarchy based on gender (rather than on class, race, and ethnicity) should be the primary standard for determining whether a given culture is hierarchical or egalitarian. In this regard, there is no doubt that over most of its history the United States was dominated by relatively hierarchical patterns because of the ways in which patriarchy and female subordination were legitimized. However, over the last 30 years, these gender patterns have shifted, providing considerable insight into how the experience and structure of marriage have changed.

Macro-Level Values and Normative Exchange Orientations

Social exchange theorists tie the exchange relationship to cultural value orientations through the concept of normative exchange orientations. Normative orientations represent the "sources of consensus of expectations" as applied to marriagelike relationships (McDonald, 1981). These norms are embedded in culturally and legally prescribed role expectations that arise from the broader societal context within which relationships exist. These normative expectations reflect the expectations that men and women bring to their intimate exchanges.

In American society, the heavy historical emphasis on individualism and an emerging and greater emphasis on egalitarianism over the past 30 years influence the prevailing normative expectations that men and women bring to their marriages. As relationships are judged on the basis of the degree to which partners' experiences fulfill expectations (Sabatelli, 1984), these normative expectations become a focal point in the analysis of both how relationships are structured and how they are experienced over time.

Trends in how marriages are experienced and structured and the variability of marriages at any one time reflect, on some level, broader cultural value orientations. Clearly, Americans believe in individual choice and freedom when it comes to marriage. Individuals feel they should be free to choose

their marital partners, and they expect their marriages to be special relationships dominated by high levels of rewards, intimacy, and sexual exclusivity. Individuals like for their relationships to be stable over time, but there is clearly an expectation that marriages need to be highly gratifying to remain stable (Goodwin, 1999).

In addition, the last 30 years have seen shifts in the hierarchy-versus-egalitarianism dimension of cultural value orientations. There appears to be a greater emphasis on justice within U.S. marriages today than in the past. The importance of justice, as reflected in individuals' expectations of fairness and equity within their relationships, appears to be linked to both individualism and shifts in egalitarianism in society. Although partners try to maximize their joint outcomes as a unit, it is very much a part of the cultural landscape for partners to evaluate whether relationship outcomes are fairly distributed between them. The processes of negotiating roles and division of power are also largely based on the norms of fairness and equity. Shared activities and togetherness as equal partners are ideal images of marriage in American society (Ingersoll-Dayton, Campbell, Kurokawa, & Saito, 1996).

The Exosystem and the Structure and Experience of Marriage

Within the ecological/exchange framework, the exchange relationship is further structured by the norms, conventions, and practices of social institutions. We cannot, in other words, divorce the trends in marriages over time and the patterns of exchange characterizing marriages within cohorts from the social institutions contributing to the ecological niche of married couples. These social institutions are what Bronfenbrenner (1979) defined as the exosystem.

Macro-level value orientations filter into prevailing social and family policies found in a society and are reflected in the prevailing practices found in the social institutions. The practices and norms of these social institutions regulate individuals' access to resources that they bring to their marriages. Whether individuals are dependent on their relationships, the alternatives they have available, and the barriers to and costs associated with terminating a marriage are all influenced by the customs of social institutions.

Over the past 30 years, numerous changes in the exosystem have had a direct bearing on how marital roles and relationships are structured. For example, education and employment opportunities for women have changed markedly. As a result, married women with children have increasingly worked for wages outside their homes and gained greater access to economic resources. In the past, women's access to educational and economic opportunities was blocked, resulting in men's having more money, social and political power, and control over their fate than women did. This economic dependence of women resulted in women's relative dependence on men, and women were expected to place responsibilities to their families ahead of responsibilities to themselves.

There also have been shifts in laws and policies that influence and reflect the changing climate of family life in America. Divorce laws have changed markedly over the last 30 years. In addition, abortion laws have changed, making it relatively easier for women to exercise choice over parenthood. The ability to control fertility and childbearing decisions has been further influenced by changes in contraceptive and reproductive technologies (see Chapter 28 of this book).

The ecological/exchange model calls attention to the ways in which norms, customs, and practices of social institutions shift over time and how these shifts influence the ways in which exchange relationships are structured. The dependence and reliance of women on marriage has progressively changed over the past 30 years in response to changes in social, political, judicial, economic, and medical institutions. Educational and economic opportunities have expanded for women, and policies and laws protect the rights of women in ways that are different than in the past. These changes affect both the expectations of and dependence on the marriages that women experience. The micro-level patterns and dynamics found within marital exchange relationships cannot be divorced from macro-level value orientations and prevailing practices in societal institutions. We turn our attention now to the trends in marriages over the last 30 years as viewed from an ecological/exchange perspective.

HOW HAVE MARRIAGES CHANGED?

Within the past 30 years, two distinct societal trends were observed with respect to marriage: namely, divorce replaced death as the most common end point of a marriage, and rates of divorce dramatically increased (see Chapter 15 of this book; also, for trends in Europe, see Chapter 17 of this book). In 1900, two thirds of marriages ended as a result of spousal death within 40 years; by 1976, that figure had gone down to just over one third (Uhlenberg, 1980). By the end of the 20th century, divorce had replaced death as the most common end point of most marriages.

In the United States, the proportion of marriages begun each year that ended in divorce steadily increased from less than 10% in 1867 to over 55% for 1985 (Cherlin, 1992). Recent data suggest that since the mid-1980s the divorce rate in the United States has decreased slightly (Bramlett & Mosher, 2001). Even so, demographers expect that 25% of contemporary marriages will dissolve by their seventh year and approximately half will end before their

20th year as a result of divorce (Bramlett & Mosher, 2001; Peck, 1999; Pinsoff, 2002). Not surprisingly, these shifts in divorce rates have generated social and political discourse on the problems of divorce. With few exceptions (Ahrons, 1994; Goldsmith, 1982), divorce has been defined as an undesirable end to marriage. Many studies have been devoted to the documentation of the deleterious short- and long-term effects of divorce on children and adults, and divorce has been viewed as a social disorder whose frequency approaches epidemic proportions and urgently needs to be reduced (Gallagher, 1996; Popenoe, 1996). The ending of marriages presumably threatens social order, disrupts kinship ties, creates economic instability, and potentially disrupts the lives of children. There is a lot at stake, in other words, when marriages fail to function as the pivotal and key subsystem within the family system.

HOW TO ACCOUNT
FOR THE RISE IN DIVORCE RATES

We think it is naively and nostalgically assumed, even by many family social scientists, that marriages of the past lasted because of the intrinsic happiness experienced by those within them. Though there are no data to support our view, we think that marriages in the past were probably no happier than marriages today. William Lederer and Don Jackson (1968) had this to say about the quality of marital relationships in the 1960s:

> More often than spouses care to admit, marriage results in years of dislike and mutual destruction, rather than love and mutual growth. In interviews with hundreds of average marital pairs we learned that approximately 80% of the couples had seriously considered divorce at one time or another, and many of them still think about

it frequently. Often, only the existence of children, the restrictions of poverty, the edicts of religion, or a lack of courage blocks the decision to get divorced. (pp. 15–16)

In other words, marriages have been ailing for some time. What has changed, however, is the willingness and ability of contemporary couples to terminate unhappy relationships. That is, the divorce trends over the past 30 years, when examined from an ecological/exchange perspective, suggest that the degree to which men and women are dependent on their marriages has changed and that these changes are the results of broader cultural and societal transformations.

The research of Michael (1988), an economist, pinpointed ecological factors influencing the divorce trends observed in the United States over the past 30 years. Michael systematically examined the contributions of various factors to the doubling of the divorce rate between 1960 and 1980. He ruled out U.S.-specific phenomena because of the comparable rise in the divorce rate in western Europe. His analyses led him to dismiss arguments attributing the rise in divorces to the increased aging of the population, to increasing rates of second and third marriages, and to geographical locations. Furthermore, he dismissed the easing of divorce laws in the United States as a cause of increased divorce rates: "Many states exhibited rising divorce rates several years before a change in the law occurred" (p. 369). From a complex regression analysis, two variables emerged in Michael's study to account most consistently for the rise of the divorce rate: the diffusion of contraceptive technology and the impact of this technology on fertility rates in the United States and shifts in women's income. He unequivocally concluded, "The rise in women's income is a dominant force affecting the divorce rate" (p. 392). Interestingly, the rise in women's income in the 20 years examined by Michael was paralleled by rises in men's income, a variable that has been consistently associated with a diminished likelihood of divorce.

What is striking about these two variables, from an ecological/exchange perspective, is that they greatly increased women's choices, or, conversely, reduced women's dependence on marriage. On the one hand, women's greater economic opportunities and choices reduced their economic dependence on men/marriage and provided them with opportunities to support themselves. A significant barrier to the termination of relationships was reduced when women began gaining greater economic assets. The willingness to end an unhappy marriage is higher when the social and economic costs of leaving are reduced. On the other hand, smaller family sizes and control over conception further reduce the barriers to leaving a marriage.

We need to be careful in assuming that all of the changes in divorce rates are due to changes in the dependence that women experience on marriage. The changing economic conditions of women also changed one of the barriers that men historically experienced to ending their unhappy marriages. Although men have had more economic resources than women, we speculate that the social costs of divorcing as well as the economic loss of assets were barriers that held men in marriages more in the past than today. The increases in both women and men's income have made it more economically feasible for men to divorce when they are in distressed relationships. Changes in the divorce laws have reduced the economic burdens experienced by men when they initiate a divorce. To understand changes in divorce rates, we must examine the factors that foster dependence even when relationships are unsatisfactory. The ecological/exchange framework focuses attention on the interaction of social/political/cultural changes that have

lessened the dependence of both men and women on their marriages.

CHANGING MARITAL EXPECTATIONS WITH RESPECT TO JUSTICE AND POWER

Although we think that the proportion of distressed marriages 30 years ago was probably no different than now, it is interesting to speculate on whether the reasons for the distress have changed. Shifts in cultural value orientations toward egalitarian ideals combined with changes in social and economic policies have more than likely resulted in changes in the cognitive expectations that individuals, and particularly women, bring to their marriages. In this regard, we believe that it is more likely today than in the past for tensions within marriages to revolve around issues of justice, equity, and fairness. Probably women today are less likely than women in the past to tolerate oppressive conditions within their marriages.

Furthermore, as broader societal shifts have increased the resources and alternatives available to women, it is probably more true today than in the past that power is expected to be shared within a marriage. The ability of people to exercise authority over themselves and act with power in a relationship is determined by the degree to which they can minimize their dependence on the other for rewards. The social context affects the degree of power a person possesses by assigning differential values to resources. In general, persons who possess a large number of valued resources have more power because they are able to violate the norms of reciprocity and fairness without experiencing negative sanctions (Blau, 1964; Homans, 1961).

Thus, differences in power originate from imbalances in resources, and the ability to provide rewards within relationships and power differentials create the potential for conflict. The more dependent a spouse is on a marriage, because the partner either provides greater resources or has better alternatives, the less power he or she will have in the relationship. This is because the less dependent partner has the ability to control the fate and/or behavior of the more dependent spouse. This can occur when one person controls highly desired outcomes and no other source of reward is available to the more dependent spouse (Thibaut & Kelley, 1959). There is no doubt that women have gained resources and in general exercise greater control over their fate. To us, this means that perceived injustices are more likely to be contested within marital relationships than ever before. It also means that efforts on the part of one partner to exercise authority or control over the other are more likely today than ever before to be experienced as nonlegitimate.

We hasten here to point out that we are talking here primarily about differences between cohorts. A tremendous amount of variation still exists in how marriages are structured, given the differences between partners in their levels of attraction to and dependence on their relationships. There is no doubt that a certain proportion of contemporary couples reside within exchange systems characterized by an asymmetrical distribution of resources and asymmetrical patterns of dependence. Within these relationships, power and authority are more likely to reside in one spouse, and more dependent partners, if unhappy with their relationships, are nonetheless likely to stay married rather than seek a divorce.

What the ecological/exchange perspective implies is that historically relationships were likely to be stable because husbands were more benefited than wives and wives were more dependent than husbands. This resulted in stable relationships where the distribution of power favored men over women. As relationships have become more symmetrical with respect to resources and alternatives, marriages have become, probably, more contentious (not necessarily less happy) around issues of justice and power. The irony here is that although these equally dependent relationships may hold a greater potential for intimacy, they are probably more volatile and unstable when experienced as inequitable or unjust.

RACIAL AND CLASS VARIATIONS IN THE EXPERIENCE AND STRUCTURE OF MARRIAGE

By and large, it comes as no surprise that most of the research and theorizing today about marriages focuses on middle- and upper-income white couples. The ecological/exchange framework provides insights into how marriages are structured and experienced in minority and poor populations of married couples. We illustrate the utility of this perspective by focusing particularly on trends and issues in African American marriages.

In general, trends in divorce rates of African Americans have been similar to, although somewhat higher than, those of white Americans (Pinsoff, 2002; Tucker & Mitchell-Kernan, 1995; see also Chapter 20 of this book). The greatest change, however, in the African American community over the past 30 years has been in the marriage rate. As of 1992, "[F]ewer than three of four black women overall can expect to marry compared to nine of 10 white women" (Tucker & Mitchell-Kernan, 1995, p. 12). Mostly this has been attributed to changes in the demographic sex ratio and male employment (or underemployment). Simply stated, in the last 20 years, in the African American community, there have not been enough men for the available women, and many of the men who have been available as potential marriage partners have been unattractive as providers because of unemployment or relative (to female) underemployment (Patterson, 1998).

From the perspective of the ecological/ exchange framework, the experience and structure of African American marriages are intrinsically tied to contextual factors (Pinderhughes, 2002). In the United States, educational, judicial, and political institutions have restricted selected groups, like African Americans, from access to various forms of resources and have thus maintained social inequality and oppression. This has directly affected the availability of marriageable partners in low-socioeconomic groups and has led women to consider alternatives such as cohabiting or remaining single. Low-income mothers believe they cannot attain the respectability marriage can provide if they marry someone who has an unstable work history, is involved in criminal activity, or has uncertain employment prospects (Jayakody & Cabrera, 2002).

Yet it can be argued that the same practices and norms of social institutions that have restricted men's economic power in ethnic and class minorities have indirectly shaped women's expectations about marriage. Among African Americans, unlike white Euro-Americans, women's autonomy has a long history. In the 1950s and 1960s, when the labor force participation of white mothers was still low, employment of mothers had long been the norm for African American women. Most working-class African American mothers interviewed about their choice of independent motherhood claimed that expectations of economic independence in their upbringing contributed to their view of marriage as nonimperative and noneconomic (Blum & Deussen, 1996). Thus, the experience of African Americans and other ethnic and socioeconomic groups clearly demonstrates the complex interaction between practices and norms in social institutions and their effects on the ways men and women structure dyadic intimate relationships.

Ecological factors account for the fact that the strong ties generally heralded in African American families are not between spouses or lovers but between blood and adopted kin. This crisis in heterosexual relationships is thought to have resulted, in part, from the ways in which stereotypes structure the expectations that African American men and women bring to their relationships (Pinderhughes, 2002). Stereotypes of men as irresponsible, undependable, abusive, and exploitative, or of women as evil, domineering, and suspicious, according to Pinderhughes, enter into the expectations that each partner has of the other and become the source of marital problems. When these stereotypes are internalized and incorporated into the expectations of self or spouse, relationship conflicts result (Black, 1999; Boyd-Franklin & Franklin, 1999).

Tensions around power and authority increase stress in African American marriages (Hatchett, Veroff, & Douvan, 1995). Higher educational levels, increased income, and more power in the home for women compound the dissonance that men especially experience because of the larger society's expectation that men will have more power. Furthermore, according to Pinderhughes (2002), the current value placed on egalitarianism in husband-wife roles does not diminish the gender/power issue for African Americans; rather, it can compound it for men who are sensitive to threats to their manhood. African American men are more likely than African American women, white men, or white women to place a high value on the traditional sex-role power distribution and male authority. A wife's demand for flexibility—which is needed for adaptive functioning in dual-earner families—may compromise a husband's feelings of masculinity if he feels powerless in other contexts. Tucker and Mitchell-Kernan (1995) warned that this issue may put African American marriages at risk.

Marital instability, tension, and conflict can also be fueled by economic anxiety or provider role anxiety: that is, concern about the ability to provide for one's family (Hatchett et al., 1995). For men of color, success in the provider role is of major psychological significance (McLloyd, Cauce, Tacheuchi, & Wilson, 2000). Provider role anxiety is heightened if men have to struggle against the persistent stereotypes of themselves as unreliable family men and providers. Broader cultural, educational, and economic policies restricting the access of minority males to economic opportunities are the ecological basis for these provider role anxieties.

In sum, an ecological/exchange perspective on contemporary marriages points to the ways in which marriages in different racial and economic groups are structured by cultural and social factors. Although access to educational and economic opportunities has changed the experiences of women generally, the inaccessibility of these opportunities for African American and other minority males in particular results in the evolution of different exchange patterns in minority populations. By and large, the ecological niche of minority marriages fails to nurture and support a conventional marriage and family structure.

LOOKING TO THE FUTURE BY EXAMINING THE PAST

Were social scientists paying attention to these trends? Of course they were. Divorce rates are hard not to notice, so the state of American marriage over the last 30 years has been a source of concern for family social scientists.

At the same time, we think that family social scientists have not fully grasped why marriages were changing and divorce rates were increasing because those who study marriages on a micro level have tended to work independently of those who analyze marital trends from macro perspectives. But to understand the complexity of marriage, one must examine both macro-level and micro-level factors as they contribute to how relationships are experienced and structured. Such an interdisciplinary and integrated perspective provides insights into the reasons behind observed trends, broadens perspectives on sources of stress and supports for marriages, and informs discourses on future trends and on interventions.

As a case in point, we know more today than ever before about how conflicts are managed and mismanaged within marriage, thanks to the work of Gottman and colleagues (Gottman, 1993; Gottman & Notarius, 2002). They persuasively argue that the mismanagement of conflicts, characterized by cascading negativity, leads to high levels of marital distress. They also contend that divorce follows from the distress experienced within relationships when negativity and conflict spiral out of control.

Gottman and colleagues argue that couples divorce because of the mismanagement of conflict and cascading negativity. We believe that these factors contribute to marital distress and divorce, but we also believe it would be misleading to attribute the trends in divorce over the last 30 years entirely to cascading negativity and conflict mismanagement. In the past, when couples mismanaged conflicts (and we believe that conflict was just as likely to be mismanaged in the past as it is today), marriages were likely to remain intact because the barriers to and costs of dissolving a relationship and the alternatives available to both men and women were different in the past than they are now.

The ecological/exchange framework compels us to develop a keener awareness of what is going on outside marriages if our goal is to understand what is going on inside contemporary marriages. The marital exchange system is a system within a network of systems that all have a bearing on how relationships are experienced and structured. The trends noted in divorce, for example, cannot be separated from concurrent shifts in educational, economic, medical, and political policies.

With respect to broader contextual shifts, readers will note that many of the marital changes we have written about are framed as being driven by women. From an ecological/exchange perspective, the significance of feminism and its impact on the shifts in macro-level values, normative expectations regarding marriage, and exosystem policies and practices cannot be discounted. Feminists highlight the ways in which women are disadvantaged by the structure of heterosexual marriage. "Women have pressed for change because women have borne the weight of the inequities woven into the very fabric of heterosexual marriage. Shifting the burdens of marriage into something more closely resembling parity is what feminism is about and that task is far from accomplished" (Rampage, 2002, p. 264).

Hence, a new paradigm of marriage has been evolving—a shift driven in large part by feminist discourse. This paradigm shift places a heavy emphasis on equity, fairness, and justice within marriage, an emphasis that we think will continue in the near future. And because women and men are more likely to be truly interdependent partners in the future than they have been in the past, there is both greater potential for intimacy within relationships and a higher likelihood that relationships will remain volatile and unstable.

The ecological/exchange perspective also illuminates possible solutions to societal problems posed by distress and disruption characterizing contemporary marriages. It suggests that attempts to stabilize marriages and reinvigorate the marital exchange system must either promote the rewarding qualities of marriage or increase the barriers to and costs of dissolving a marriage. To a large extent, promoting marriage or preventing divorce has become part of the national political agenda (Parke & Ooms, 2002, pp. 1–8). Indeed, a few of the most controversial new policies, such as covenant marriage laws and marriage bonuses paid to welfare recipients, have received widespread publicity. Little attention has been paid, however, to other strategies to strengthen marriage and reduce divorce that states and communities have enacted, many of which arouse less controversy (Parke & Ooms, 2002).

For example, several states have declared reducing divorce and strengthening marriage as public goals. In 1999, the governor of Oklahoma announced a goal to reduce the state divorce rate by one third within 10 years and hosted a statewide conference to solicit ideas for how to accomplish the goal. Couples applying for marriage licenses in Arizona and Florida are given marriage handbooks that provide information on how to build strong marriages, the effects of divorce, and available community resources. In Utah, couples are given an educational videotape. Reduction of marriage license fees for couples who attend a 4-hour premarital education course is one of the components of the 1998 Florida Marriage Preparation and Preservation Act. Maryland and Minnesota have enacted similar marriage license fee reduction laws, with Minnesota requiring couples to take a 12-hour course including conflict management and communication skills.

The broad point here is that for marriages to become more stable in the future, family social scientists can direct energies toward either improving the quality of marriages or increasing the barriers to and costs of dissolving marriages. We have no doubt that marriages that are unhappy will remain unstable and that efforts to stabilize marriage by creating barriers and deterrents to getting out are destined to fail. From a normative perspective, intimacy is what people expect from marriages, and they are less likely than ever before to tolerate an empty shell of a relationship. Therefore, it is important that family social scientists consider ways of strengthening the intimate and cooperative bond experienced by marital pairs. Stronger marriages in the future will not result from making it harder to get out of a bad marriage. It is time to think critically about how to mobilize resources on both macro and micro levels to create stronger and more rewarding marriages.

REFERENCES

Ahrons, C. (1994). *The good divorce.* New York: Harper Collins.

Black, L. W. (1999). Therapy with African Americans. In P. Papp (Ed.), *Couples on the fault line* (pp. 205–221). New York: Guilford.

Blau, P. (1964). *Exchange and power in social life.* New York: John Wiley.

Blum, L. M., & Deussen, T. (1996). Negotiating independent motherhood: Working-class African American women talk about marriage and motherhood. *Gender and Society, 10,* 199–211.

Boyd-Franklin, N., & Franklin, A. J. (1999). African American couples in therapy. In M. McGoldrick (Ed.), *Re-visioning family therapy* (pp. 268–281). New York: Guilford.

Bramlett, M. D., & Mosher, W. D. (2001). *First marriage dissolution, divorce and remarriage in the United States* (Advance Data from Vital and Health Statistics, No. 323). Hyattsville, MD: National Center for Health Statistics.

Bronfenbrenner, U. (1979). *The ecology of human development.* Cambridge, MA: Harvard University Press.

Bronfenbrenner, U. (1988). Interacting systems in human development. Research paradigms: Present and future. In N. Bolger, A. Caspi, G. Downey, & M. Moorehouse (Eds.), *Persons in context: Developmental processes* (pp. 25–49). New York: Cambridge University Press.

Bumpass, L., & Sweet, J. (1989). *National estimates of cohabitation: Cohort levels and union stability* (National Survey of Families and Households Working Paper No. 2). Madison: University of Wisconsin, Madison, Center for Demography and Ecology.

Burns, T. (1973). A structural theory of social exchange. *Acta Sociologica, 16,* 188–208.

Castillo, R. J. (1997). *Culture and mental illness.* Pacific Grove, CA: Brooks/Cole.

Cherlin, A. J. (1992). *Marriage, divorce and remarriage.* Cambridge, MA: Harvard University Press.

Cook, K., & Emerson, R. (1978). Power, equity and commitment in exchange networks. *American Sociological Review, 43,* 721–739.

Duck, S. W. (1994). *Meaningful relationships.* Thousand Oaks, CA: Sage.

Emerson, R. (1976). Social exchange theory. In A. Inkeles, J. Coleman, & N. Smelser (Eds.), *Annual review of sociology* (Vol. 2, pp. 335–362). Palo Alto, CA: Annual Reviews.

Foa, U. G., & Foa, E. B. (1974). *Social structures of the mind.* Springfield, IL: C C Thomas.

Gallagher, M. (1996). *The abolition of marriage.* Washington, DC: Regnery.

Goldsmith, J. (1982). The postdivorce family system. In F. Walsh (Ed.), *Normal family processes* (pp. 297–330). New York: Guilford.

Goodwin, R. (1999). *Personal relationships across cultures.* London: Routledge.

Gottman, J. M. (1993). A theory of marital dissolution and stability. *Journal of Family Psychology, 7,* 57–75.

Gottman, J. M., & Notarius, C. I. (2002). Marital research in the 20th century and a research agenda for the 21st century. *Family Process, 41,* 159–198.

Hatchett, S., Veroff, J., & Douvan, E. (1995). Marital stability and marriage among black and white couples in early marriage. In M. Tucker & C. Mitchell-Kernan (Eds.), *The decline in marriage among African Americans* (pp. 177–211). New York: Russell Sage Foundation.

Hofstede, G. (1994). *Cultures and organizations.* London: Harper-Collins.

Homans, G. C. (1961). *Social behavior.* New York: Harcourt, Brace & World.

Hui, C. H., & Triandis, H. C. (1986). Individualism-collectivism: A study of cross-cultural researchers. *Journal of Cross-Cultural Psychology, 17,* 225–248.

Ingersoll-Dayton, B., Campbell, R., Kurokawa, Y., & Saito, M. (1996). Separateness and togetherness: Interdependence over the life course in Japanese and American marriages. *Journal of Social and Personal Relationships, 13,* 385–398.

Jayakody, R., & Cabrera, N. (2002). What are the choices for low-income families? Cohabitation, marriage, and remaining single. In A. Booth & A. C. Crouter (Eds.), *Just living together* (pp. 85–95). Mahwah, NJ: Lawrence Erlbaum.

Lederer, W. J., & Jackson, D. D. (1968). *The mirages of marriage.* New York: Norton.

Levinger, G. (1974). A three-level approach to attraction: Toward an understanding of pair relatedness. In T. Huston (Ed.), *Foundations of interpersonal attraction* (pp. 49–67). New York: Academic Press.

Levinger, G. (1982). A social exchange view on the dissolution of pair relationships. In F. I. New (Ed.), *Family relationships* (pp. 97–122). Beverly Hills, CA: Sage.

McDonald, G. W. (1981). Structural exchange and marital interaction. *Journal of Marriage and the Family, 43,* 825–839.

McLloyd, V., Cauce, A., Tacheuchi, D., & Wilson, L. (2000). Marital processes and parental socialization in families of color: A decade review of research. *Journal of Marriage and the Family, 62,* 1–27.

Michael, R. T. (1988). Why did the U.S. divorce rate double within a decade? *Research in Population Economics, 6,* 367–399.

Nye, F. I. (1979). Choice, exchange and the family. In W. Burr, R. Hill, F. I. Nye, & I. Reiss (Eds.), *Contemporary theories about the family* (Vol. 2, pp. 1–41). New York: Free Press.

Parke, M., & Ooms, T. (2002). *More than a dating service? State activities designed to strengthen and promote marriage* (Center for Law and Social Policy, Brief No. 2). Washington, DC: Center for Law and Social Policy.

Patterson, O. (1998). *Rituals of blood.* New York: Basic Books.

Peck, K. (1999). The fifty percent divorce rate: Deconstructing a myth. *Journal of Sociology and Social Welfare, 20,* 135–144.

Pinderhughes, E. B. (2002). African American marriage in the 20th century. *Family Process, 41,* 269–292.

Pinsoff, W. M. (2002). The death of "Till death us do part": The transformation of pair-bonding in the 20th century. *Family Process, 41,* 135–158.

Popenoe, D. (1996). *Life without father.* New York: Free Press.

Rampage, C. (2002). Marriage in the 20th century: A feminist perspective. *Family Process, 41,* 261–268.

Rodman, H. (1972). Marital power and the theory of resources in cultural context. *Journal of Comparative Studies, 3,* 50–69.

Sabatelli, R. M. (1984). The Marital Comparison Level Index: A measure for assessing outcomes relative to expectations. *Journal of Marriage and the Family, 46,* 651–662.

Sabatelli, R. M. (1999). Marital commitment and family life transitions: A social exchange perspective on the construction and deconstruction of intimate relationships. In J. M. Adams & W. H. Jones (Eds.), *Handbook of interpersonal commitment and relationship stability*. New York: Kluwer Academic/Plenum.

Sabatelli, R. M., & Shehan, C. L. (1993). Exchange and resource theories. In P. G. Boss, W. J. Doherty, R. LaRossa, W. R. Schumm, & S. K. Steinmetz (Eds.), *Sourcebook of family theories and methods* (pp. 385–411). New York: Plenum.

Scanzoni, J. (1972). *Sexual bargaining*. Englewood Cliffs, NJ: Prentice Hall.

Schwartz, S. (1997). Values and culture. In D. Munro, S. Carr, & J. Schumaker (Eds.), *Motivation and culture* (pp. 69–84). New York: Routledge.

Super, C. M., & Harkness, S. (1999). The environment as culture in developmental research. In S. L. Friedman & T. D. Wachs (Eds.), *Measuring environment across the life span* (pp. 279–323). Washington, DC: American Psychological Association.

Thibaut, J., & Kelley, H. (1959). *The social psychology of groups*. New York: John Wiley.

Triandis, H. C. (1995). *Individualism and collectivism*. Boulder, CO: Westview.

Trompenaars, F. (1993). *Riding the waves of culture*. London: Nicholas Brealey.

Tucker, M., & Mitchell-Kernan, C. (1995). Trends in African American family formation: A theoretical and statistical overview. In M. Tucker & C. Mitchell-Kernan (Eds.), *The decline in marriage among African Americans* (pp. 3–27). New York: Russell Sage Foundation.

Uhlenberg, P. (1980). Death and the family. *Journal of Family History, 5*, 313–320.

CHAPTER 6

Gay Men and Lesbians
The Family Context

LAWRENCE A. KURDEK

Because of the stigma associated with being identified as gay or lesbian, there are no reliable data on the number of gay and lesbian Americans. Further, whatever prevalence data are available vary according to whether "homosexuality" is defined in terms of behavior, attraction, or identification. Perhaps the most reliable data come from Laumann, Gagnon, Michael, and Michaels's (1994) National Health and Social Life Survey of 3,432 Americans who were interviewed face to face in 1992 on the basis of probability sampling. Laumann et al. found that 4.9% of men and 4.1% of women reported same-gender sex partners since the age of 18, 6.2% of men and 4.4% of women reported some attraction to same-sex persons, and 2.8% of men and 1.4% of women reported identifying with a label denoting same-gender sexuality. Hewitt (1998) reports similar prevalence rates from other surveys. Even though these estimates are well below the 10% figure usually associated with the Kinsey data (Kinsey, Wardell, & Martin, 1948; Kinsey, Wardell, Martin, & Gebhard,

1953) and were obtained from data collected in 1992, it is clear that a sizable number of Americans—and their family members—deal with issues regarding being gay or lesbian.

Although there is currently active scholarly interest in the multidimensional character and assessment of homosexuality (e.g., Peplau, 2001), the developmental process of constructing a gay or lesbian identity (e.g., Dube, 2000), attitudes and prejudice toward gay men and lesbians (e.g., Chen & Kenrick, 2002), the effects of HIV-positive status on relationships (e.g., Hatala, Baack, & Parmenter, 1998), validation of existing measures (e.g., Greenfield & Thelen, 1997) or findings (e.g., Buunk & Dijkstra, 2001) with gay and lesbian samples, and use of data from gay and lesbian individuals to test hypotheses derived from theories of evolutionary psychology (e.g., Buunk & Dijkstra, 2001), the focus of this chapter is on the intersection between the study of families and the study of gay men and lesbians. In keeping with this theme and the space limitations of this volume, I review selectively what is known and what needs to be known in two content areas pertinent to this general area of study. The first deals with gay and lesbian adolescents and the second with gay and lesbian couples.

GAY AND LESBIAN ADOLESCENTS AND THEIR FAMILIES

What Is Known

Perhaps the first time family members directly confront issues relevant to homosexuality is when another family member freely discloses his or her identity as a gay man or lesbian or has such an identity discovered. The best-studied scenario is one in which an adolescent's sexual orientation is made known to his or her family members. Although adolescence is a developmental period during which many aspects of one's identity are in flux (Graber & Archibald, 2001), an increasing number of adolescents are claiming a gay or lesbian identity (Savin-Williams, 1998). This cohort effect may be due to general social-cultural changes in which attitudes toward homosexuality have become relatively less negative. Nonetheless, it is sobering to note that data from the 1998 General Social Survey indicate that more than 50% of the 25,668 respondents thought that sexual relations between two adults of the same sex are always wrong (Butler, 2000) and that data from a randomly selected nationally representative sample collected in the year 2000 indicate that 38% of the 2,283 respondents completely agreed that homosexual behavior is morally wrong (Kaiser Family Foundation, 2001).

As one might expect from problems in determining the number of gay and lesbian adults, there are also no conclusive data on the number of gay and lesbian adolescents. Remafedi, Resnick, Blum, and Harris (1992) found in a survey of 34,706

Minnesota students from Grades 7 through 12 (49.8% male and 50.2% female) that 0.7% of the males and 0.2% of the females described themselves as mostly or totally homosexual and that 0.8% of the males and 0.9% of the females described themselves as bisexual. In a national study of 12- to 19-year-old high school students (5,758 males and 6,182 females), Russell, Seif, and Truong (2001) found that 0.7% of the males and 1.5% of the females indicated exclusive same-sex attraction and that 6.5% of the males and 3.7% of the females indicated bisexual attractions. Because the sexual identity of young adolescents is unlikely to be stable (Diamond, 2000), it is unclear how many of these adolescents will retain a gay or lesbian identity into adulthood.

The "coming out" process of adolescents has been of interest to family scholars because it poses issues for parent-child relationships, because gay and lesbian youth are at risk for negative consequences associated with the verbal and physical abuse they are likely to receive, and because heterosexual family members confront their own issues regarding identifying themselves as being related to a gay or lesbian individual. With regard to parent-child relationships, although relevant data are not extensive (see Rotheram-Borus & Langabeer, 2001, and Savin-Williams, 2001b, for reviews), the initial reactions that parents have to their child's disclosing a gay or lesbian identity are quite diverse—including disbelief, denial, shock, anger, and lack of surprise—but are typically neither extremely positive (immediate acceptance) nor extremely negative (dismissal from the home or physical abuse). There is also evidence (Maguen, Floyd, Bakeman, & Armistead, 2002; Savin-Williams, 2001b) that gay and lesbian adolescents are more likely to disclose their sexual orientation to friends than to parents, that if adolescents do disclose their orientation to a family member it is more likely to be to mothers than to fathers, and that mothers react more positively than fathers do.

Regarding the at-risk status of gay and lesbian youth, Rivers and D'Augelli (2001) noted that gay and lesbian adolescents deal with unique stressors in addition to those experienced by adolescents in general. These include feeling different, perceiving little family support, and viewing HIV and AIDS as gay diseases. Among the most unfortunate consequences of these stressors is the likelihood that gay and lesbian adolescents will be the targets of verbal abuse (Thurlow, 2001) and physical abuse (Rivers & D'Augelli, 2001; Savin-Williams, 1994). Such abuse, in turn, may lead gay and lesbian youth to be at risk for school problems, running away, substance abuse, prostitution, and attempts at suicide (Russell et al., 2001; Savin-Williams, 2001c).

Finally, although *coming out* is usually used to describe the process of one's coming to terms with one's *own* gay or lesbian sexual identity, it is increasingly also being used to describe public acknowledgment of being related to a gay or lesbian individual. Crosbie-Burnett, Foster, Murray, and Bowen (1996) developed a social-cognitive behavioral model to integrate the multiple aspects of how families adjust to the news of having a gay/lesbian family member. This model describes the coming out process with regard to subsystems in a family that include a mother, a father, a gay/lesbian child, and a heterosexual child (e.g., the gay child–mother/father subsystems, the heterosexual child–mother/father subsystems, the marital subsystem, and the sibling subsystem) and links the family of origin to the extended family (such as cousins, aunts, uncles, and grandparents), the community (such as school and church), and other social contexts (such as the workplace).

What Needs to Be Known

Because empirical research on gay and lesbian adolescents is relatively new, many specific topics need further study (see Savin-Williams, 2001b, for a detailed research agenda). Three are highlighted here.

The Antecedents of a Gay or Lesbian Identity

The fact that many adolescents claim a gay, lesbian, or bisexual identity indicates that the factors determining sexual orientation are likely to operate fairly early in development. Further, whatever factors are responsible for sexual orientation are also likely to be complex. For example, although there is evidence that prenatal estrogen contributes to the development of a homosexual orientation in women (Meyer-Bahlburg et al., 1995), that gay adolescents have a greater than average number of male siblings and a later than average birth order than nongay counterparts (Blanchard, Zucker, Bradley, & Hume, 1995), and that childhood cross-sex-typed behavior is predictive of adult homosexual orientation for both men and women (Bailey & Zucker, 1995), the relevant effects are not large and, consequently, argue against any single factor determining sexual orientation. Simply put, some children or adolescents with *all* of the relevant characteristics just listed will not develop into adults who claim a gay, lesbian, or bisexual orientation. Further, some individuals may recognize same-sex attractions but not engage in same-sex behaviors, and some individuals may engage in same-sex behaviors but not incorporate that dimension into their sexual identity (Savin-Williams, 2001a). Following the lead of scholars such as Horowitz and Newcomb (2001) and Peplau (2001), one avenue for future research is to adopt the perspective that human sexuality is fluid, malleable, and dependent on context. This perspective would be a useful conceptual basis for prospective studies attempting to describe the complex pathways by which sexual attractions, behaviors, and identities are shaped.

The Ecology of the Coming out Process

Despite the comprehensive nature of Crosbie-Burnett et al.'s (1996) model, surprisingly few researchers have used it to guide the study of how a family member's coming out affects other family members and the social contexts within which the family is embedded (however, see Oswald, 2000). The Crosbie Burnett et al. model provides a rich framework for future studies examining how the identification of a gay or lesbian family member leads other family members to revise schemas about both themselves (e.g., I am the father of a gay son and may not be a grandparent) and the gay/lesbian person (e.g., My son will not get married and probably will not raise children) as well as how issues within the family (such as the secret of having a gay or lesbian member; see Vangelisti & Caughlin, 1997) spill over to the wider social context. The Crosbie-Burnett model can also be extended to include the study of older individuals who experience the coming out process after adolescence (e.g., women who explore lesbian identities after having been married; Morris, Balsam, & Rothblum, 2002).

Resilience in Gay and Lesbian Youth

Although much of the work done with adolescents has addressed the ways in which gay and lesbian youth are at risk for a variety of problems, there has also been a call (e.g., Oswald, 2002; Savin-Williams, 2001c) for future researchers to examine how gay and lesbian youth, despite the psychological and social stressors they experience, manage to negotiate the developmental tasks of

adolescence and young adulthood and achieve a stable identity in adulthood. Although personality factors (such as psychological hardiness) may be important, coping mechanisms and social support are also likely to be highly relevant.

GAY AND LESBIAN COHABITING COUPLES

What We Know

Estimating the number of American gay and lesbian couples is even more problematic than estimating the number of gay/lesbian individuals because presenting oneself publicly as part of a gay or lesbian couple may open the door for discrimination, abuse, and even violence (Bryant & Demian, 1994; Kaiser Family Foundation, 2001). Thus, current estimates regarding the number of gay and lesbian couples are likely to be underestimates of the actual number. Still, on the basis of data from the 2000 U.S. Census (U.S. Bureau of the Census, 2002), 301,026 households were headed by a male householder and a male partner, and 293,365 households were headed by a female householder and a female partner. Contrary to popular myths (Herek, 1991) that lesbians and gay men are not capable of forming durable cohabiting relationships, surveys indicate that between 45% and 80% of lesbians and between 40% and 60% of gay men are currently involved in a romantic relationship (Bradford, Ryan, & Rothblum, 1994; Falkner & Garber, 2002; Morris et al., 2002). More importantly, several authors (Blumstein & Schwartz, 1983; Bryant & Demian, 1994; Falkner & Garber, 2002; Kurdek, 2003; "*The Advocate* Sex Poll," 2002) report that between 8% and 21% of lesbian couples and between 18% and 28% of gay couples have lived together 10 or more years. Clearly, despite a general social climate of prejudice against gay men and lesbians, being part of a couple is integral to the lives of many lesbians and gay men.

The limited information we have regarding lesbian and gay couples can be used to answer four general questions: (a) What is the ethnography of gay and lesbian relationships? (b) Do gay and lesbian couples differ from heterosexual couples? (c) Do gay and lesbian couples differ from each other? and (d) How does the experience of parenting affect couple-level functioning? Each of these questions is addressed in turn.

A General Ethnography of Lesbian and Gay Couples: What Are Gay and Lesbian Couples Like?

Because of the social stigma surrounding homosexuality, lesbians and gay men receive little—if any—information regarding lesbian and gay couples in the course of their socialization. As a result, lesbian and gay close relationships develop without consensual norms (Laird, 1993). It should be underscored at the outset that most of the available descriptive data on lesbian and gay couples come from relatively young, white, and well-educated volunteer respondents. Thus, the "typical couple" profiles presented below probably apply to only a select group of lesbian and gay couples. The most detailed descriptive account of lesbian and gay couples comes from Bryant and Demian's (1994) national survey of 1,749 individuals who represented 706 lesbian couples and 560 gay couples. Selected findings of the study are presented by survey topic. Unless indicated otherwise, the data come from the Bryant and Demian survey.

Previous Relationships. Do members of gay and lesbian couples have extensive previous experience with heterosexual relationships? Many of the gay and lesbian respondents (38% and 32%, respectively)

indicated that their current relationship was their first major lesbian/gay relationship. Lesbians were more likely than gay men to have been involved in a heterosexual marriage (27% vs. 19%, respectively). Consistent with the latter finding, Blumstein and Schwartz (1983) reported that 22% of their lesbian respondents and 15% of their gay respondents had been previously married, and Morris et al. (2002) reported that 25% of their sample of lesbian women had been married. However, it is unclear how previous experiences with heterosexual relationships and marriage affect the development of gay and lesbian couples.

Name Used to Identify Partner. Given that gay and lesbian relationships are not socially legitimized, one might expect that there would be little consensus on how members of these couples refer to each other. Most gay men (40%) called their partner "lover," whereas most lesbians (35%) referred to their partner as "partner" or "life partner." McWhirter and Mattison (1984) also reported that most members of gay couples referred to each other as "lover." It appears that no studies have addressed how the simple act of naming one's partner affects relationship functioning, although heterosexual couples typically go through a stagelike sequence of changing the way they refer to their partner as the relationship progresses (e.g., "date" to "boyfriend/girlfriend" to "fiancé/fiancée" to "husband/wife").

How Partner Was Met. Because one's sexual identity is often kept a secret and is not readily detected, how do possible partners meet each other? Lesbians were most likely to have met their partner through friends (28%), at work (21%), or at a social event (16%). Gay men were most likely to have met their partner at a bar (22%), through friends (19%), or at a social event (13%). McWhirter and Mattison (1984) also mentioned that the first contact between members of a gay couple was likely to occur in a gay establishment.

Relationship Rituals. Because gay and lesbian couples cannot legally get married in the United States, they do not have readily accessible strategies for formalizing their relationships. Nonetheless, 57% of the lesbians and 36% of the gay men reported that they wore a ring or some other symbol to represent their relationship. Nineteen percent of the lesbians and 11% of the gay men had held some type of commitment ceremony. The current trend toward reporting the union of same-sex couples in "marriage" announcements suggests that gay and lesbian couples may be receiving stronger social validation now than in the past, though not without controversy.

Residence. Cohabitation may be a significant event in the course of any relationship because it marks a milestone in the extent to which each partner identifies with the relationship. Most of the couples (82% male, 75% female) had lived together during the previous year of the relationship. Thirty-six percent of the male couples and 32% of the female couples jointly owned their residence, whereas 27% and 33%, respectively, jointly rented or leased their residence. Housing discrimination was reported by 15% of the renters and 9% of the homeowners. McWhirter and Mattison (1984) reported that most of the male couples they studied moved in together after about 1 month of acquaintance.

Finances. Although living together can certainly be seen as a public statement of being a couple, how partners arrange finances can also be seen as a statement of the extent to which the partners are invested in the longevity of the relationship. Eighty-two percent of the gay male couples and

75% of the lesbian couples shared all or part of their incomes. Both Blumstein and Schwartz (1983) and McWhirter and Mattison (1984) reported that the probability of a couple's pooling finances increased with the length of time living together.

Division of Household Labor. One clear indication that members of gay and lesbian couples construct their own relationships is that, unlike members of heterosexual couples who may use gender as a way of determining who does what household tasks, members of gay and lesbian couples begin their relationships with no preset ideas of how household labor will be divided. In their study of gay couples, McWhirter and Mattison (1984) noted that the handling of household chores varied by stage of the relationship. In the first year of the relationship, partners shared almost all chores. Later, however, routines got established as chores were assigned primarily on the basis of each partner's skill and work schedule. In instances where each partner was skilled, partners willingly unlearned previous skills to create complementarity and a sense of balance in the relationship. Blumstein and Schwartz (1983) and Kurdek (1993) noted that lesbian couples at any stage of the relationship were particularly likely to divide household labor equally. Blumstein and Schwartz speculate that lesbians may avoid task specialization in the area of household work because of the low status traditionally associated with the women who do it. This speculation is consistent with other reports that lesbian couples are more likely than either gay or heterosexual couples to follow an ethic of equality (Chan, Brooks, Raboy, & Patterson, 1998; Clunis & Green, 1988; Peplau & Cochran, 1990).

Conflict. One consequence of the interdependence experienced by relationship partners is that conflict is almost certain to arise.

Most of the lesbian and gay male respondents (28% and 26%, respectively) reported two small arguments per month. The percentage of lesbians reporting verbal abuse and physical abuse from their partners was 17% and 3%, respectively. Corresponding values for gay men were 15% and 3%. With regard to the content of conflict, Kurdek (1994a) found that managing finances, driving style, affection/sex, being overly critical, and household tasks were troublesome areas for both gay and lesbian couples.

Social Support. Given the stigma associated with being gay or lesbian, traditional sources of support for members of a couple (such as parents) may not exist. Indeed, both gay men and lesbians indicated that the major source of social support for their relationships came from other gay/lesbian friends, followed in order by siblings, mother, and father. Most gay men (43%) and most lesbians (47%) were also most likely to turn to friends for help with their relationships. Similar findings were reported by Kurdek (1988).

Legal Arrangements. Because gay and lesbian couples enjoy no "default" legal privileges, members of these couples often protect their relationships in a proactive manner. Thirty-two percent of the lesbian respondents and 39% of the gay male respondents had executed a will, and 28% of the lesbian respondents and 27% of the gay respondents had made arrangements for power of attorney.

Stages of Relationship Development. In recognition of the fact that gay and lesbian couples, just like heterosexual couples, undergo rather systematic changes in their relationships, McWhirter and Mattison (1984) have described the development of gay couples, and Clunis and Green (1988) have described the development of lesbian

couples. McWhirter and Mattison derived their stage model from a cross-sectional study of 156 predominantly white, well educated male couples. Clunis and Green modified and expanded the McWhirter and Mattison stages on the basis of their experiences as therapists. Both sets of authors noted that not all couples fit the stage model, and neither set tested their model with longitudinal data.

McWhirter and Mattison proposed that gay male couples develop in a six-stage sequence. The Blending Stage occurs in the first year and is characterized by merging, limerance (e.g., intense preoccupation with and longing for the partner), shared activity, and high sexual activity. Years 2 and 3 (Nesting) are marked by homemaking, finding compatibility, the decline of limerance, and ambivalence about the relationship. Recognizing individual needs, expressing dissatisfactions, dealing with conflict, and establishing traditions occur during the Maintaining Stage (Years 4 and 5). The Building Stage happens during Years 6 through 10 and includes collaborating, increasing individual productivity, establishing independence and individual habits, and acknowledging the dependability of partners. Years 11 through 20 are described as a Releasing Stage that involves trusting, merging of money and possessions, midlife evaluations of priorities, and taking each other for granted. The last stage, Renewing, occurs after 20 or more years of cohabitation and is characterized by achieving financial and emotional security; shifting perspectives regarding time, health, and loss; restoring romance in the partnership; and remembering events in the relationship history.

Unlike McWhirter and Mattison (1984), Clunis and Green (1988) begin the description of their developmental stage model with a Prerelationship Stage, which refers to the time during which partners decide whether to invest time and energy in getting to know each other better. This is followed by a Romance Stage that has many of the characteristics of McWhirter and Mattison's Blending Stage and then a Conflict Stage that is similar to McWhirter and Mattison's Maintaining Stage. With the Acceptance Stage comes a sense of stability and an awareness of the faults and shortcomings of each partner. This is followed by the Commitment Stage, in which partners work on balancing opposing needs while accepting each other as trustworthy. In the Collaboration Stage, the couple works to create something together (e.g., a baby, a business venture) in the world outside the relationship that enhances the relationship.

In a test of the McWhirter and Mattison's (1984) stage model, Kurdek and Schmitt (1986) used cross-sectional data to examine differences in multiple assessments of relationship quality for gay, lesbian, and heterosexual couples from the first three stages of the model (Blending, Nesting, and Maintaining). Regardless of type of couple, findings were consistent with McWhirter and Mattison's prediction that the second and third years of the relationship were likely to involve stress and disillusionment. Relative to Blending couples and Maintaining couples, Nesting couples reported the lowest satisfaction with affection and sex, the lowest amount of shared activity, and the most frequent number of dysfunctional beliefs regarding sexual perfection.

Sexual Behavior. Although the defining feature of a gay or lesbian relationship is some type of sexual behavior with another member of one's own sex, the extant literature on the sexual behavior of gay and lesbian couples is surprisingly sparse. Blumstein and Schwartz (1983) and McWhirter and Mattison (1984) found no evidence that lesbian partners and gay partners regularly assume "active" and "passive" roles in sexual interactions. However, there is limited

evidence regarding the specific types of sexual activity engaged in by gay and lesbian couples. McWhirter and Mattison reported that over 90% of the gay couples they interviewed engaged in kissing and hugging, body rubbing and kissing, tongue kissing, fellatio, being fellated, mutual fellatio, and mutual masturbation. Seventy-one percent of the respondents reported engaging in anal intercourse, and 41% reported engaging in analingus. Eighty-three percent of the respondents reported they were satisfied with their sexual relationship, and 91% reported that their level of satisfaction had increased since the beginning of the relationship. Of the 81 respondents who reported sexual problems, the most common (43%) was erectile failure.

Loulan (1987) reported the results from survey data gathered from 1,566 lesbians, 62% of whom were coupled. At least 80% of the respondents reported that they did the following activities to their partners: touching breasts, kissing breasts, licking breasts, and putting fingers in vagina. Seventy-one percent of the respondents reported that they performed oral sex on their partner; 56% said they put their tongue in their partner's vagina; and 55% said they masturbated their partner. Diamant, Lever, and Schuster (2000) reported similar findings regarding sexual activities in their sample of 6,935 lesbians.

Do Gay/Lesbian Couples Differ From Heterosexual Couples?

Despite an increased scientific interest in gay and lesbian couples (e.g., see review by Peplau & Spaulding, 2000), systematic comparisons of members of both gay and lesbian couples to members of heterosexual couples (as well as comparisons of members of gay couples to members of lesbian couples) have been characterized by several methodological problems. These include studying only one partner from the couple (e.g., Peplau, Cochran, & Mays, 1997); averaging individual scores from both partners (e.g., Schreurs & Buunk, 1996); using measures with unknown psychometric properties (e.g., Blumstein & Schwartz, 1983); performing qualitative analyses of in-depth interviews that—although providing a rich description of the lives of some gay men and lesbians—make it difficult to determine the size and generality of any effects (e.g., Carrington, 1999); comparing couples without first ensuring that the members of these couples were equivalent on demographic characteristics such as age, education, income, and length of relationship (e.g., Haas & Stafford, 1998); treating members of the couples as independent units of analysis (e.g., Mackey, Diemer, & O'Brien, 2000); and recognizing the interdependence of scores derived from the same couple but performing statistical analyses that did not take this interdependence into account (e.g., Gaines & Henderson, 2002).

Kurdek (2001) addressed these methodological limitations by collecting longitudinal data from both members of gay, lesbian, and heterosexual married couples with psychometrically sound measures, providing estimates of effect sizes, using demographic variables (e.g., age, education, income, and months living together) as control variables, and employing statistical analyses (multilevel modeling; see Kenny, Mannetti, Pierro, Livi, & Kashy, 2002) that took partner interdependence into account. Because children are known to affect marital functioning (e.g., Erel & Burman, 1995) and because the gay and lesbian couples studied did not have children, members of both gay and lesbian couples were compared to members of married couples without children on sets of individual differences, relationship-related attitude, conflict resolution, and social support variables known to be linked to relationship quality (Huston, 2000; Karney & Bradbury,

1995) as well as on global appraisals of the relationship.

Overall, few differences between members of gay/lesbian couples and members of nonparent couples were found, and most of these effects were small. Nonetheless, some specific differences were notable. With regard to individual-differences variables, only 9 of the 36 effects (25%) were significant. Relative to members of married couples, members of both gay and lesbian couples had higher private self-consciousness (focus on their own thoughts and feelings, perhaps due to their stigmatized status), were more comfortable with closeness (perhaps because many were in long-term relationships without much institutional or social support), and were higher in openness (proclivity toward variety, intellectual curiosity, and aesthetic sensitivity, perhaps due to a propensity to explore an alternative lifestyle). With regard to relationship-related attitudes, only 6 of the 22 effects (27%) were significant, with members of both gay and lesbian couples reporting more autonomy than members of married couples (perhaps reflecting high levels of agency and instrumentality for economically advantaged gay and lesbian partners) and—in the one of the strongest effects in the study—with members of lesbian couples reporting higher levels of equality than members of married couples (perhaps due to lesbians having encountered inequities more frequently in their past relationships).

Although members of the three types of couples were relatively equivalent on the set of conflict resolution variables (only 1 of the 16 effects [6%] was significant), consistent effects were obtained for the set of social support variables (for which 6 of the 10 effects [60%] were significant), with members of gay and lesbian couples reporting less support from family members than members of married couples (probably due to the stigma of being gay or lesbian) and members of lesbian partners reporting more support from friends than members of married couples (perhaps due to lesbians' living within close geographical proximity to other lesbians). Finally, with regard to global appraisals of the relationship, only two of the eight effects (25%) were significant, with members of lesbian couples reporting higher satisfaction than members of married couples (perhaps the result of two "doses" of women's relationship-enhancing socialization experiences) and members of gay couples reporting less commitment than members of married couples (perhaps the result of two "doses" of men's self-enhancing socialization experiences).

In sum, although some significant effects were obtained and interpretable, the bulk of the evidence clearly indicated that members of gay/lesbian couples were more similar to than different from members of married couples without children, with only 24 of the total of 92 effects (26%) being significant. Additional evidence of the general similarity among members of gay/lesbian couples to members of heterosexual couples comes from reports of no differences between members of gay/lesbian couples and members of married couples in the areas of conflict and conflict resolution styles (Kurdek, 1994a, 1994b), the rate of change in relationship satisfaction (Kurdek, 1998), and adjustment to relationship dissolution (Kurdek, 1997a) as well as in the predictors of relationship quality (Kurdek, 1997a, 1997b, 1997c, 2000), change in relationship quality (Kurdek, 1998), and dissolution (Kurdek, 1998). However, it should be noted that these findings are not independent of each other because they are based on the same longitudinal samples.

Do Gay and Lesbian Couples Differ From Each Other?

Using almost the same sets of variables as those used in comparing members of

gay/lesbian couples to members of married couples, Kurdek (2003) compared members of gay couples to members of lesbian couples at multiple points over time. Again, demographic variables were used as control variables, comparisons used statistical analyses that took partner interdependence into account, and effect sizes were calculated. Overall, even fewer differences were found between members of gay couples and members of lesbian couples than were found between members of gay/lesbian couples and members of nonparent, married couples, and what differences were found were mostly small.

Only 1 of the 22 effects (4%) for the set of individual differences variables was significant, and no effects were found for the sets of eight conflict resolution variables and the set of five social support variables. However, three of the eight effects (37%) for the set of relationship-related attitude variables were significant, with members of lesbian couples reporting stronger liking, trust, and equality than members of gay couples. These differences are consistent with the view that lesbians create relationships in which women's relationship-enhancing influences are activated and potentiated (Ferree, 1990) and that lesbian partners—as women—are likely to redress the imbalances in power and influence that they are likely to have experienced in their relationship histories (Fox & Murry, 2000). As additional evidence of the general similarity between members of gay couples and members of lesbian couples, no differences between members of these two types of couples have been found in level of similarity between members within the couple (assortative mating or homogamy; Kurdek, 2003), areas of conflict and conflict resolution styles (Kurdek, 1994a, 1994b), the rate of change in relationship quality (Kurdek, 1996, 2003), the predictors of relationship quality (Kurdek, 1996, 2003), the prevalence of dissolution (19% for gay couples and 23%

for lesbian couples, Kurdek, 2003), and adjustment to relationship dissolution (Kurdek, 1997a). However, it should be noted that these findings are not independent of each other because they are based on the same longitudinal samples.

How Does Parenting Affect Couple-Level Functioning?

Consistent with the questionable reliability of other prevalence data already presented, there are no reliable data on the number of children living part time or full time with gay and lesbian couples. In the Bryant and Demian (1994) sample, 21% of the lesbians and 9% of the gay men reported "caring" for children, although it was not clear whether these children resided with the couple (20% of Morris et al.'s 2002 lesbian sample also had children). These children were offspring from a previous marriage for 74% of the lesbians and for 79% of the gay men. Thirteen percent of the lesbians were impregnated through donor insemination. Ten percent of the lesbians and 4% of the gay men planned to have children. Blumstein and Schwartz (1983) reported that 7% of their lesbian couples had children living with them more than 6 months per year. Unfortunately, gay couples were not asked about children. Eleven percent of the respondents from the Kaiser Family Foundation (2001) study reported having children under age 18 living in the household, but separate numbers were not given for gay and lesbian respondents.

Much of the work with regard to gay and lesbian parents has focused on the adjustment of children growing up with gay or lesbian parents, and the relevant studies have almost exclusively involved lesbian mothers (see reviews by Patterson, 2000, and Stacey & Biblarz, 2001). Two kinds of families have been studied: one in which children were born before the mother began a relationship

with another woman (e.g., in the context of marriage which was ended through divorce) and the other in which children were born during that relationship (usually by means of donor insemination).

From a parenting transition perspective (Capaldi & Patterson, 1991), the first kind of family has much in common with families in which children experience both parental divorce and the remarriage of at least one parent. However, few studies (e.g., Lynch, 2000) have compared children in the two forms of "remarried" families. Instead, most studies involve comparing children of custodial lesbian mothers to children of custodial heterosexual mothers. In her review of these studies, Patterson (2000) noted that the majority of studies have found no differences between children with the two types of mothers on measures of sexual identity, personal development, and social relationships. Stacey and Biblarz (2001), however, pointed to a pattern in some of these studies (e.g., Green, Mandel, Hotvedt, Gray, & Smith, 1986) that shows that children living with lesbian mothers are likely to internalize nontraditional gender roles. Patterson also noted that few studies have revealed differences in the adjustment of the two types of mothers.

The second kind of family has been of particular interest because children in these families cannot be expected to suffer any of the negative consequences (e.g., Capaldi & Patterson, 1991) associated with marital conflict, divorce, repartnering, and, possibly, the mother's coming out process. Stacey and Biblarz (2001) noted, however, that because donor insemination is an expensive process, it may be available to only economically privileged couples. Consequently, the generalizability of relevant findings can be questioned. Nonetheless, as with findings for the first kind of family, those for this type of family show no adverse effects associated with living with a lesbian couple. In fact, there is some evidence that the lesbian co-parent (i.e., the member of the couple who does not give birth) is more skilled and invested in parenting than fathers typically are (e.g., Brewaeys, Ponjaert, Van Hall, & Golombok, 1997). To the extent that lesbian couples represent a "double dose" of female-linked socialization experiences and expectations, this pattern of enhanced parenting for lesbian couples is similar to the pattern of enhanced relationship quality for lesbian couples reported earlier.

What We Need to Know

Although there are many gaps in our knowledge of lesbian and gay couples, only eight will be highlighted.

Recruiting Nationally Representative Samples

One major advance in the study of gay and lesbian couples is the recruitment of fairly large samples of gay and lesbian individuals, some of whom are in relationships. The most common strategies used in recruitment have been to distribute questionnaires to visitors to gay and lesbian bookstores, community centers, and political/social groups (e.g., Morris et al., 2002); to send questionnaires to individuals on mailing lists for gay/lesbian political, social, and health care organizations (e.g., Peplau et al., 1997); to request participants from notices placed in gay/lesbian periodicals (e.g., Diamant et al., 2000) or gay/lesbian online sites (Falkner & Garber, 2002); and to use snowball sampling from friendship networks (e.g., Kurdek, 2003). Although these recruitment strategies result in national samples, they are unlikely to be representative samples. However, because many members of the larger gay/lesbian population are hidden and because information about sexual orientation is not obtained in government-sponsored surveys, it is extremely difficult to assess whether any sample of gay and lesbian persons is representative. This dilemma might be addressed if census forms make it easier for same-sex couples to identify themselves, if antigay/lesbian sentiments continue their gradual decline, and if innovative sampling strategies (e.g., the adaptive sampling approach described by Blair, 1999) continue to be devised.

Roles, Scripts, and Structure

In the absence of conventional partner roles (such as husband and wife), it is unclear how members of lesbian and gay couples create predictability in their relationships (Klinkenberg & Rose, 1994). Do they seek out "established" couples for advice? Do they construct roles on a trial-and-error basis or on the basis of which tasks need to be performed (McWhirter & Mattison, 1984)? One way to obtain information on these issues would be to conduct a longitudinal study of lesbian and gay couples that starts when partners first begin dating and to document how roles in the relationship get established and change over time. As a beginning step in this direction, Klinkenberg and Rose (1994) showed that gay and lesbian individuals followed well-defined scripts for their first dates. The scripts for gay men tended to include sexual behavior more frequently than those of lesbians, whereas the scripts of lesbians included intimacy and sharing of emotions more frequently than those of gay men. Relative to the scripts for heterosexual women, those for lesbians did not include telling parents about the date and monitoring the date with regard to safety concerns.

The Construction of Commitment

Work with heterosexual couples has indicated that partners employ several psychological strategies to enhance commitment to maintaining their relationships. These include a tendency to accommodate and to forgive rather than to retaliate in response to a partner's transgression, to sacrifice desirable activities when the partner does not want to engage in these activities, to derogate tempting alternatives to the relationship, and to produce relationship-enhancing illusions (e.g., Finkel, Rusbult, Kumashiro, & Hannon, 2002). Given the striking similarities found in the functioning of gay/lesbian and heterosexual couples summarized above, there is no reason to expect that these strategies would not also be important for gay and lesbian couples. However, because commitment can also be enhanced by forces outside the relationship ("constraint commitment"; Kurdek, 2000), it would be of interest to see if relationship outcomes for gay and lesbian couples are affected by the degree to which members of social systems that include one or both partners of the couple explicitly support the relationship (Oswald, 2002). These systems might include families of origin, friends, co-workers, neighbors, and members of the immediate heterosexual and lesbian/gay community. Because gay and lesbian partners experience little institutionalized external support for their relationships, it would also be of interest to see if the link between psychological maintenance strategies and commitment is moderated by the degree of perceived external constraints to leaving the relationship. It is possible that this link is especially strong when few external constraints are perceived.

Relationship Tensions

Because resolving conflict constructively is critical to relationship satisfaction and relationship stability (Karney & Bradbury, 1995), it would be useful to examine dyadic processes in conflict resolution for gay and lesbian couples using methods other than self-report ones (Kurdek, 1994b). Kollock,

Blumstein, and Schwartz (1985) audiotaped conversations of members from gay, lesbian, and heterosexual couples in which members were to arrive at a joint decision. They found that regardless of type of couple, the partner with the greater power (the one who had more influence in daily decisions) was more likely to interrupt the speech of the less powerful partner. In what appears to be the only published study using videotaped observations of conflict interaction, Gottman et al. (in press) found that initiators of conflict discussion from gay and lesbian couples were less belligerent and less domineering than those from married couples, that gay and lesbian partners were more positive in how they received conflict-related information than married partners, that gay partners had trouble repairing conflict when their partners become too negative, and that lesbian partners were more expressive of both positive and negative affect than gay partners. These intriguing findings need to be replicated and extended. Also in need of empirical support is Patterson and Schwartz's (1994) speculation that gay and lesbian couples are more likely than heterosexual couples to control consciously the level of conflict in their interactions in order to ensure the survival of their relationships.

Sexual Behavior

Sexual behavior in gay and lesbian couples has not been widely studied. The limited data on this topic are of note because of all of the areas of couplehood studied by Blumstein and Schwartz (1983), the largest differences between lesbian and gay couples occurred in this area. Blumstein and Schwartz found that gay couples were more sexually active than lesbian couples in the early years of the relationship. After 10 years together, however, gay couples had sex less frequently and often devised explicit arrangements for sexual activity outside the relationship. Gay couples' acceptance of sexual nonexclusivity is one of the most distinctive features of their relationships ("*The Advocate* Sex Poll," 2002), yet we know little regarding how nonexclusivity affects the relationships of gay men in light of the HIV/AIDS epidemic (Hatala et al., 1998).

Parenting

Because lesbian couples have only recently chosen donor insemination as a strategy for becoming parents, most of the children studied in these families are fairly young. Longitudinal studies that track the development of these children through adolescence and young adulthood would be of interest because of speculation (e.g., Patterson, 1992) that adolescents—who are negotiating their own sexual identities and are prone to the positive and negative effects of peer contact—may have some difficulty openly acknowledging that they have a lesbian parent. Given that some lesbian couples are likely to separate (Kurdek, 2003), information is also needed on how children are affected by the conflict that is likely to precede the separation, how children adjust to the separation, and how children are affected by the possible repartnering of both the birth mother and the lesbian co-parent. To the extent that gay and lesbian couples have been used to test tenets of evolutionary psychological theories (Buunk & Dijkstra, 2001), "divorcing" lesbian couples are of particular interest with regard to child custody and visitation issues because a couple with two women—which represents a possible double dose of evolutionarily based parenting investment—may have stronger competing claims about parenting issues than a couple with a man and woman. Finally, although the number of gay couples raising children full time is small, a larger number of gay couples may include one partner who has children from a previous marriage. These children are likely to live primarily with their mothers but may have regular contact with their gay fathers and their father's partner. We know little about how these families function and change with the development of the child involved and how these children come to understand the nature of their father's relationship.

Diversity Within Diversity

To date, the study of lesbian and gay couples has primarily attended to the type-of-couple variable as a moderator variable (e.g., is the link between Relationship Process X and Relationship Outcome Y as strong for lesbian and gay couples as for heterosexual couples?). Although these studies are important for documenting the robustness of relationship process across diverse types of couples, they necessarily involve treating each type of couple as a homogeneous group. This is unfortunate in light of evidence that the initiation, development, and dissolution of relationships are affected by the personal-social-cultural-historical context within which members of a couple develop (Huston, 2000). But how does one identify what kinds of diversity are important within each type of couple? For gay and lesbian couples, there is evidence (see Friend, 1991; Greene, 1997) that older lesbians and gay men as well as lesbians and gay men of color are likely to experience rejection and forms of discrimination from other gay men and lesbians as well as from the heterosexual majority. In addition, geographical location is likely to affect relationship development inasmuch as some areas of the country are more repressive or more liberal than others. For instance, large cities are more likely than small towns or rural areas to have lesbian and gay organizations and establishments in which lesbians and gay men can meet prospective partners and take advantage of available support programs and local ordinances protecting gay and lesbian individuals. It remains for future researchers to determine the extent to which these factors affect the development of gay and lesbian relationships.

Methodologies and Theories

Although the past decade has seen an enormous increase in scientific information about gay and lesbian couples, future work would benefit from new methodologies. At the descriptive level, much could be learned from diary-type data that would provide information about change in relationship functioning over time at the micro level (see Huston, 2000). At the statistical level, the issue of nonindependence in partners' scores is no longer a problem with the advent of hierarchical linear modeling (e.g., Kenny et al., 2002; Kurdek, 2000) and the extension of work with the intraclass correlation coefficient (Gonzalez & Griffin, 2001).

Although there are several well-done reviews of the literature on gay and lesbian couples (e.g., Peplau & Spalding, 2000), overall, the level of theoretical analysis in this area is not very advanced (see, however, Peplau, 2001). One might argue that theoretical advances need to wait until descriptive data are available from samples of gay and lesbian couples that are not predominantly white and privileged. Still, conceptual work at two levels seems promising and complementary. At the first level, specific content-based models of couples with particular characteristics (e.g., gay couples, lesbian couples, gay/lesbian couples of color, aging gay/lesbian couples) can systematically describe how diverse couples flesh out the content of their relationships. Diary-type data and qualitative interviews (e.g., Carrington, 1999) may be especially useful in this regard. At the second, more abstract level, the development of general function-based theories of close relationships (such as interdependence theory; see Finkel et al., 2002) would be enhanced if data from gay and lesbian couples were routinely used to test such theories. Large-scale data collections and the use of sophisticated data analytic techniques (such as hierarchical linear modeling) to test for the robustness of findings across diverse types of couples would be especially useful in this regard. Despite the tremendous diversity in how two people create the form of their relationship, there is likely to be equally impressive uniformity in the structure of how *any* couple begins, endures, and dissolves.

REFERENCES

Bailey, J. M., & Zucker, K. J. (1995). Childhood sex-type behavior and sexual orientation: A conceptual analysis and quantitative review. *Developmental Psychology, 31,* 43–55.

Blair, J. (1999). A probability sample of gay urban males: The use of two-phase adaptive sampling. *Journal of Sex Research, 36,* 39–44.

Blanchard, R., Zucker, K. J., Bradley, S. J., & Hume, C. S. (1995). Birth order and sibling sex ratio in homosexual male adolescents and probably prehomosexual feminine boys. *Developmental Psychology, 31,* 22–30.

Blumstein, P., & Schwartz, P. (1983). *American couples: Money, work, sex.* New York: William Morrow.

Bradford, J., Ryan, C., & Rothblum, E. D. (1994). National lesbian health care survey: Implications for mental health care. *Journal of Consulting and Clinical Psychology, 62,* 228–242.

Brewaeys, A., Ponjaert, I., Van Hall, E. V., & Golombok, S. (1997). Donor insemination: Child development and family functioning in lesbian mother families. *Human Reproduction, 12,* 1349–1359.

Bryant, A. S., & Demian. (1994). Relationship characteristics of gay and lesbian couples: Findings from a national survey. *Journal of Gay and Lesbian Social Services, 1,* 101–117.

Butler, A. C. (2000). Trends in same-gender sexual partnering, 1988–1998. *Journal of Sex Research, 37,* 333–343.

Buunk, B. P., & Dijkstra, P. (2001). Evidence from a homosexual sample for a sex-specific rival-oriented mechanism: Jealousy as a function of a rival's physical attractiveness and dominance. *Personal Relationships, 8,* 391–406.

Capaldi, D. M., & Patterson, G. R. (1991). Relation of parental transitions to boys' adjustment problems: I. A linear hypothesis. II. Mothers at risk for transitions and unskilled parenting. *Child Development, 60,* 1437–1452.

Carrington, C. (1999). *No place like home: Relationships and family life among lesbians and gay men.* Chicago: University of Chicago Press.

Chan, R. W., Brooks, R. C., Raboy, B., & Patterson, C. J. (1998). Division of labor among lesbian and heterosexual parents: Associations with children's adjustment. *Journal of Family Psychology, 12,* 402–419.

Chen, F. F., & Kenrick, D. T. (2002). Repulsion or attraction? Group membership and assumed attitude similarity. *Journal of Personality and Social Psychology, 83,* 111–125.

Clunis, D. M., & Green, G. D. (1988). *Lesbian couples.* Seattle, WA: Seal.

Crosbie-Burnett, M., Foster, T. L., Murray, C. I., & Bowen, G. L. (1996). Gays' and lesbians' families-of-origin: A social-cognitive-behavioral model of adjustment. *Family Relations, 45,* 397–403.

Diamant, A. L., Lever, J., & Schuster, M. A. (2000). Lesbians' sexual activities and efforts to reduce risk for sexually transmitted diseases. *Journal of the Gay and Lesbian Medical Association, 4,* 41–48.

Diamond, L. M. (2000). Sexual identity, attractions, and behavior among young sexual-minority women over a 2-year period. *Developmental Psychology, 36,* 241–250.

Dube, E. M. (2000). The role of sexual behavior in the identification process of gay and bisexual males. *Journal of Sex Research, 37,* 123–132.

Erel, O., & Burman, B. (1995). Interrelatedness of marital relations and parent-child relations: A meta-analytic review. *Psychological Bulletin, 118,* 108–132.

Falkner, A., & Garber, J. (2002). *2001 gay/lesbian consumer online census.* Syracuse, NY: Syracuse University, OpusComm Group, and GSociety.

Ferree, M. M. (1990). Beyond separate spheres: Feminism and family research. *Journal of Marriage and the Family, 52,* 866–884.

Finkel, E. J., Rusbult, C. E., Kumashiro, M., & Hannon, P. A. (2002). Dealing with betrayal in close relationships: Does commitment promote forgiveness? *Journal of Personality and Social Psychology, 82,* 956–974.

Fox, G. L., & Murry, V. M. (2000). Gender and families: Feminist perspectives and family research. *Journal of Marriage and the Family, 62,* 1160–1172.

Friend, R. A. (1991). Older lesbian and gay people: A theory of successful aging. *Journal of Homosexuality, 23,* 99–118.

Gaines, S. O., & Henderson, M. C. (2002). Impact of attachment style on responses to accommodative dilemma among same-sex couples. *Personal Relationships, 9,* 89–93.

Gonzalez, R., & Griffin, D. (2001). A statistical framework for modeling homogeneity and interdependence in groups. In G. J. O. Fletcher & M. S. Clark (Eds.), *Blackwell handbook of social psychology: Interpersonal processes* (pp. 505–534). Malden, MA: Blackwell.

Gottman, J. M., Levenson, R. W., Swanson, C., Swanson, K., Tyson, R., & Yoshimoto, D. (In press). Observing gay, lesbian, and heterosexual couples' relationships: Mathematical modeling of conflict interaction. *Journal of Homosexuality*.

Graber, J. A., & Archibald, A. A. (2001). Psychosocial change at puberty and beyond: Understanding adolescent sexuality and sexual orientation. In A. R. D'Augelli & C. J. Patterson (Eds.), *Lesbian, gay, and bisexual identities and youth: Psychological perspectives* (pp. 3–26). New York: Oxford University Press.

Green, R., Mandel, J. B., Hotvedt, M. E., Gray, J., & Smith, L. (1986). Lesbian mothers and their children: A comparison with solo parent heterosexual mothers and their children. *Archives of Sexual Behavior, 15*, 167–184.

Greene, B. (Ed.). (1997). *Ethnic and cultural diversity among lesbians and gay men.* Thousand Oaks, CA: Sage.

Greenfield, S., & Thelen, M. (1997). Validation of the Fear of Intimacy Scale with a lesbian and gay male population. *Journal of Social and Personal Relationships, 14*, 707–716.

Haas, S. M., & Stafford, L. (1998). An initial examination of maintenance behaviors in gay and lesbian relationships. *Journal of Social and Personal Relationships, 15*, 846–855.

Hatala, M. N., Baack, D. W., & Parmenter, R. (1998). Dating with HIV: A content analysis of gay male HIV-positive and HIV-negative personal advertisements. *Journal of Social and Personal Relationships, 514*, 168–276.

Herek, G. M. (1991). Myths about sexual orientation: A lawyer's guide to social science research. *Law and Sexuality, 1*, 133–172.

Hewitt, C. (1998). Homosexual demography: Implications for the spread of AIDS. *Journal of Sex Research, 35*, 390–396.

Horowitz, J. L., & Newcomb, M. D. (2001). A multidimensional approach to homosexual identity. *Journal of Homosexuality, 42*, 1–19.

Huston, T. L. (2000). The social ecology of marriage and other intimate unions. *Journal of Marriage and the Family, 62*, 298–320.

Kaiser Family Foundation. (2001, November). Inside-OUT: A report of the experiences of lesbians, gays and bisexuals in America and the public's views on issues and policies related to sexual orientation. Retrieved October 27, 2002, from www.kff.org/content/2001/3193/LGBChartpack.pdf

Karney, B. R., & Bradbury, T. N. (1995). The longitudinal course of marital quality and stability: A review of theory, method, and research. *Psychological Bulletin, 118*, 3–34.

Kenny, D. A., Mannetti, L., Pierro, A., Livi, S., & Kashy, D. A. (2002). The statistical analysis of data from small groups. *Journal of Personality and Social Psychology, 83*, 126–137.

Kinsey, A. C., Wardell, B. P., & Martin, C. E. (1948). *Sexual behavior in the human male.* Philadelphia: J. B. Saunders.

Kinsey, A. C., Wardell, B. P., Martin, C. E., & Gebhard, P. H. (1953). *Sexual behavior in the human female.* Philadelphia: J. B. Saunders.

Klinkenberg, D., & Rose, S. (1994). Dating scripts of gay men and lesbians. *Journal of Homosexuality, 26*, 23–35.

Kollock, P., Blumstein, P., & Schwartz, P. (1985). Sex and power in interaction: Conversational privileges and duties. *American Sociological Review, 50*, 34–36.

Kurdek, L. A. (1988). Perceived social support in gays and lesbians in cohabiting relationships. *Journal of Personality and Social Psychology, 54*, 504–509.

Kurdek, L. A. (1993). The allocation of household labor in gay, lesbian, and heterosexual couples. *Journal of Social Issues, 49*, 127–139.

Kurdek, L. A. (1994a). Areas of conflict for gay, lesbian, and heterosexual couples: What couples argue about influences relationship satisfaction. *Journal of Marriage and the Family, 56*, 923–934.

Kurdek, L. A. (1994b). Conflict resolution styles in gay, lesbian, and heterosexual nonparent, and heterosexual parent couples. *Journal of Marriage and the Family, 56*, 705–722.

Kurdek, L. A. (1996). The deterioration of relationship quality or gay and lesbian cohabiting couples: A five-year prospective longitudinal study. *Personal Relationships, 3*, 417–442.

Kurdek, L. A. (1997a). Adjustment to relationship dissolution in gay, lesbian, and heterosexual partners. *Personal Relationships, 4*, 145–161.

Kurdek, L. A. (1997b). The link between facets of neuroticism and dimensions of relationship commitment: Evidence from gay, lesbian, and heterosexual couples. *Journal of Family Psychology, 11*, 503–514.

Kurdek, L. A. (1997c). Relation between neuroticism and dimensions of relationship commitment: Evidence from gay, lesbian, and heterosexual couples. *Journal of Family Psychology, 11*, 109–124.

Kurdek, L. A. (1998). Relationship outcomes and their predictors: Longitudinal evidence from heterosexual married, gay cohabiting, and lesbian cohabiting couples. *Journal of Marriage and the Family, 60*, 553–568.

Kurdek, L. A. (2000). Attractions and constraints as determinants of relationship commitment: Longitudinal evidence from gay, lesbian, and heterosexual couples. *Personal Relationships, 7*, 245–262.

Kurdek, L. A. (2001). Differences between heterosexual-nonparent couples and gay, lesbian, and heterosexual parent couples. *Journal of Family Issues, 22*, 727–754.

Kurdek, L. A. (2003). Differences between gay and lesbian cohabiting couples. *Journal of Social Personal Relationships, 20*, 411–436.

Kurdek, L. A., & Schmitt, J. P. (1986). Early development of relationship quality in heterosexual married, heterosexual cohabiting, gay, and lesbian couples. *Developmental Psychology, 22*, 305–309.

Laird, J. (1993). Lesbian and gay families. In F. Walsh (Ed.), *Normal family processes* (pp. 282–328). New York: Guilford.

Laumann, E. O., Gagnon, J. H., Michael, R. T., & Michaels, S. (1994). *The social organization of sexuality: Sexual practices in the United States.* Chicago: University of Chicago Press.

Loulan, J. (1987). *Lesbian passion: Loving ourselves and each other.* San Francisco: Spinster.

Lynch, J. M. (2000). Considerations of family structure and gender composition: The lesbian and gay stepfamily. *Journal of Homosexuality, 40*, 81–95.

Mackey, R. A., Diemer, M. A., & O'Brien, B. A. (2000). Psychological intimacy in the lasting relationships of heterosexual and same-gender couples. *Sex Roles, 43*, 201–227.

Maguen, S., Floyd, F. J., Bakeman, R., & Armistead, L. (2002). Developmental milestones and disclosure of sexual orientation among gay, lesbian, and bisexual youths. *Journal of Applied Developmental Psychology, 23*, 219–233.

McWhirter, D. P., & Mattison, A. M. (1984). *The male couple: How relationships develop.* Englewood Cliffs, NJ: Prentice Hall.

Meyer-Bahlburg, H. F. L., Ehrhardt, A. A., Rosen, L. R., Gruen, R. S., Veridiano, N. P., Vann, F. H., & Neuwalder, H. F. (1995). Prenatal estrogens and the development of sexual orientation. *Developmental Psychology, 31*, 12–21.

Morris, J. F., Balsam, K. F., & Rothblum, E. D. (2002). Lesbian and bisexual mothers and nonmothers: Demographics and the coming-out process. *Developmental Psychology, 16*, 144-156.

Oswald, R. F. (2000). Family and friendship relationships after young women come out as bisexual or lesbian. *Journal of Homosexuality, 38,* 65–83.

Oswald, R. F. (2002). Resilience within the family networks of lesbians and gay men: Intentionality and redefinition. *Journal of Marriage and Family, 64,* 374–394.

Patterson, C. J. (1992). Children of lesbian and gay parents. *Child Development, 63,* 1025–1042.

Patterson, C. J. (2000). Family relationships of lesbians and gay men. *Journal of Marriage and the Family, 62,* 1052–1069.

Patterson, C. J., & Schwartz, P. (1994). The social construction of conflict in intimate same-sex couples. In D. Cahn (Ed.), *Conflict in personal relationships* (pp. 3–26). Hillsdale, NJ: Lawrence Erlbaum.

Peplau, L. A. (2001). Rethinking women's sexual orientation: An interdisciplinary, relationship-oriented approach. *Personal Relationships, 8,* 1–19.

Peplau, L. A., & Cochran, S. D. (1990). A relational perspective on homosexuality. In D. P. McWhirter, S. A. Sanders, & J. M. Reinisch (Eds.), *Homosexuality/ heterosexuality: Concepts of sexual orientation* (pp. 321–349). New York: Oxford University Press.

Peplau, L. A., Cochran, S. D., & Mays, V. M. (1997). A national survey of the intimate relationships of African American lesbians and gay men. In B. Greene (Ed.), *Ethnic and cultural diversity among lesbians and gay men* (pp. 11–38). Thousand Oaks, CA: Sage.

Peplau, L. A., & Spalding, L. R. (2000). The close relationships of lesbians, gay men, and bisexuals. In C. Hendrick & S. S. Hendrick (Eds.), *Close relationships: A sourcebook* (pp. 111–123). Thousand Oaks, CA: Sage.

Remafedi, G., Resnick, M., Blum, R., & Harris, L. (1992). Demography of sexual orientation in adolescents. *Pediatrics, 89,* 714–721.

Rivers, I., & D'Augelli, A. R. (2001). The victimization of lesbian, gay, and bisexual youths. In A. R. D'Augelli & C. J. Patterson (Eds.), *Lesbian, gay, and bisexual identities and youths* (pp. 199–223). New York: Oxford University Press.

Rotheram-Borus, M. J., & Langabeer, K. A. (2001). Developmental trajectories of gay, lesbian, and bisexual youths. In A. R. D'Augelli & C. J. Patterson (Eds.), *Lesbian, gay, and bisexual identities and youths* (pp. 97–128). New York: Oxford University Press.

Russell, S. T., Seif, H., & Truong, N. L. (2001). School outcomes of sexual minority youth in the United States: Evidence from a national study. *Journal of Adolescence, 24,* 111–127.

Savin-Williams, R. C. (1994). Verbal and physical abuse as stressors in the lives of lesbian, gay male, and bisexual youths: Associations with school problems, running away, substance abuse, prostitution, and suicide. *Journal of Consulting and Clinical Psychology, 62,* 261–269.

Savin-Williams, R. C. (1998). The disclosure to families of same-sex attractions by lesbian, gay, and bisexual youths. *Journal of Research on Adolescence, 8,* 49–68.

Savin-Williams, R. C. (2001a). A critique of research on sexual-minority youths. *Journal of Adolescence, 24,* 5–13.

Savin-Williams, R. C. (2001b). *Mom, Dad: I'm gay.* Washington, DC: American Psychological Association.

Savin-Williams, R. C. (2001c). Suicide attempts among sexual-minority youths: Population and measurement issues. *Journal of Consulting and Clinical Psychology, 69,* 983–991.

Schreurs, K. M. G., & Buunk, B. P. (1996). Closeness, autonomy, equity, and relationship satisfaction in lesbian couples. *Psychology of Women Quarterly, 20,* 577–592.

Stacey, J., & Biblarz, T. J. (2001). (How) does the sexual orientation of parents matter? *American Sociological Review, 66,* 159–183.

The Advocate sex poll. (2002, August 20). *Advocate,* pp. 38–43.

Thurlow, C. (2001). Naming the "outsider within": Homophobic pejoratives and the verbal abuse of lesbian, gay, and bisexual high-school students. *Journal of Adolescence, 24,* 25–38.

U.S. Bureau of the Census. (2002). *Summary File 1: 2000 Census of Population and Housing.* Washington, DC: Author.

Vangelisti, A. L., & Caughlin, J. P. (1997). Revealing family secrets: The influence of topic, function, and relationships. *Journal of Social and Personal Relationships, 14,* 679–706.

CHAPTER 7

Ambiguous Constructions
Development of a Childless or Child-Free Life Course

RICHARD BULCROFT AND JAY TEACHMAN

Research and theory on childlessness date back to the 1930s. For the most part, early studies of childlessness treated the phenomenon as a deviance or abnormality, with the childless characterized as self-centered and infantile (Popenoe, 1936, 1954). Later, the focus shifted to a concern about the potentially negative demographic consequences of a move toward childlessness. In an attempt to predict whether childlessness would increase and threaten population replacement, researchers examined the motivations that men and women expressed for childlessness, giving special attention to the economic motivations for having children in a modern society (Blake, 1968; Blake & Davis, 1963; Easterlin, 1966; Hoffman & Hoffman, 1973). In the 1970s and early 1980s, however, studies of childlessness were increasingly conducted within the context of "alternative lifestyles," with an emphasis

placed on how men and women could construct marriages outside traditional norms. A product of the second wave of feminism, this primarily qualitative research attempted to demonstrate the viability of "child-free" families (Nason & Poloma, 1976; Veevers, 1973, 1975, 1980). Since 1990, however, considerable effort has been made to obtain quantitative data based on representative studies of childlessness as well as to further expand our understanding of those who live a life without parenting. In this chapter, we will use Houseknecht's (1987) review of the literature before 1987 as a starting point. Also, although there is a considerable literature on infertility and childlessness due to subfecundity, we will focus on those who do not have children for reasons other than reproductive incapacity. As we note later, however, this distinction is not always clear, and some issues confront all the childless regardless of cause.

DEFINING CHILDLESSNESS

What is childlessness? Childlessness is most directly defined as the absence of children, either by intention (voluntary) or by circumstance (involuntary). However, trying to classify individuals and couples into types of childlessness is problematic. First, most researchers and theorists have conceptualized childlessness as an individual phenomenon, focusing most frequently on women. However, focusing only on women at the individual level of analysis obscures the issue of male childlessness as well as the dyadic processes involved in decisions to remain childless (Thomson, 1997).

Second, the distinction between childlessness by choice versus circumstance is blurred by the biological facts of infertility and subfecundity. Infertility is not always a definitive diagnosis. For most fertile couples, conception occurs within a year of trying, but for some it may take several years and significant interventions. Does a lack of motivation to continue trying or to undergo expensive and invasive treatments indicate biology or choice as a reason for childlessness (see Letherby, 1999)? Subfecundity occurs when couples delay childbearing to a point where conception becomes less probable. Are these couples childless by biological circumstance or by choice, especially when they delay with the knowledge that in doing so they may reduce their chances of having a child?

Third, even though we may be able to estimate infertility rates, other circumstances may bring about unintended childlessness. Therefore, there is a need to assess childbearing intentions as well as childbearing outcomes in studies of childlessness. Some authors (e.g., Houseknecht, 1987; Jacobson, Heaton, & Taylor, 1988) have argued that to be classified as voluntarily childless a person must both intend not to have a child and then fulfill that intention over his or her life course. However, classifying young adults in the early years of their childbearing capacity is problematic; as individuals age and make choices leading to the delay of childbearing, they frequently revise their expectations to fit their realities. In contrast, Rovi (1994) argued that it is the expression of childlessness intentions alone that is of significance; the intentions of individuals and couples to remain childless define their lifestyles regardless of future childbearing outcomes.

Fourth, when childlessness intentions are used to classify couples, one must determine the level of commitment to those intentions. Houseknecht (1987) distinguished between permanent and temporary childlessness; however, making such a distinction requires that the researcher wait until the individual exceeds childbearing age. Perhaps a more useful distinction is between early articulators and postponers (Houseknecht, 1987; Veevers, 1980) or active and passive deciders (Gillespie, 1999). As Veevers noted, early articulators appear to represent a unique group of individuals who formed commitments to childlessness in adolescence. Thus, factors affecting their choice and their experience of childlessness should be different from those of postponers.

DEMOGRAPHICS OF CHILDLESSNESS

What is the prevalence of childlessness in U.S. society, and how has it changed over time? One way to answer these questions is to assess childbearing outcomes for women who are at the end of their childbearing ages (40–44). In 2000, 19% of women were childless, doubling the 1980 percentage for this same age group of women (Bacu & O'Connel, 2000). Although this was a significant increase, the percentage of women in this age group who remained childless was similar or higher in previous historical periods. For example, Morgan (1991) reported rates of childlessness ranging from 15% in 1880 to 22% in 1940. He also found significant variation in childlessness around the end of the 19th century, with childlessness being highest in the Northeast (over 30%) and lowest in the South and Midwest (less than 10%).

There are two problems with using total fertility at age 40 as a measure of childlessness. First, it may not reflect childlessness rates for younger adults of childbearing age. Second, it does not inform as to whether the decision to remain childless was intentional or voluntary. Were the childless in 1910 childless by choice or by circumstance? Recent rates of infertility are estimated to be about 5% for those between ages 15 and 24 and 15% for all women at any given time, with 75% of infertile women capable of achieving a pregnancy through medical intervention (Mosher & Pratt, 1990). Are these rates comparable to past rates? It is impossible to know for certain, but Morgan (1991) has determined that most childlessness at the start of the 20th century (especially in the Northeast) was not due to sterility, poor health, or disease. Nevertheless, we do not have data on childbearing intentions to help us interpret the past. Such measures do exist today, however, and can yield important insights into childlessness trends in the future.

Two methods have been developed for projecting childlessness rates for the future. The cohort approach (the Coale-McNeil model) used by Bloom and Trussell (1984) bases projections on how rates of childlessness at an early age predict later permanent childlessness for previous cohorts of women who have completed their fertility. The period approach uses current age-specific childlessness rates and then "ages" current cohorts of women through those rates to determine their likelihood of ever having a first birth. Although both approaches have potential drawbacks, Morgan and Chen (1992) showed that the period approach

yields more accurate projections. Using this approach, they projected a childlessness rate of approximately 20% for white women and 4% for nonwhite women born in 1962.

Do these projected rates of childlessness reflect trends in the intentions to remain childless? Rovi (1994) found a general trend among married women of childbearing age between 1972 and 1988 for an increase in expressed desires to remain child-free (2.6% in 1972 vs. 6.4% in 1988) and to postpone parenthood (6.6% in 1972 vs. 16.3% in 1988). Thornton and Young-DeMarco (2001) also found little attitudinal support for a child-free life in their analysis of several large data sets. Areas where attitudinal change has been most significant include decreases in the perception that persons "ought to have children," decreases in the perception that children interfere with personal life, and increases in the perception that fatherhood is fulfilling. These changes suggest an increase in the significance of parenting to couples, with a decreasing sense of obligation to reproduce. The needs and happiness of the parents as well as potential children have become paramount.

THEORIES OF CHILDLESSNESS

Why do individuals and couples choose to remain childless or child-free? Theories of childlessness can be broadly categorized as (a) biological/evolutionary, (b) cultural, (c) rational choice and exchange, (d) family or life course development, and (e) feminist.

Biological/Evolutionary Perspective

A single evolutionary theory of childlessness has not been clearly articulated, but several hypotheses have been proposed and tested on the basis of broad evolutionary principles. The earliest of these hypotheses was posed by Popenoe (1936), who argued that there *c advantage* to childlessness, as ~~higher~~ higher rates among women who ~~suitable for marriage (divorcees)~~ ~~d (b)~~ not have strong family orienta- ~~ns (~~ who do not remarry). Early ~~arent-child attachment also stim-~~ ~~ing about childlessness from an~~ ~~perspective.~~ Bardwick (1974) ~~maternal predispositions to form~~ would create psychological need among women to bear children. Thus, childlessness was viewed as an abnormal condition that could create significant psychological distress. More recent theorizing from an evolutionary perspective has focused on how ecological conditions may suppress the need for childbearing and how this effect is adaptive. This *reproduction suppression* model identifies psychosocial stress as a mediating mechanism linking nonoptimal environmental conditions to decreased fertility and desire for childbearing (Wasser & Isenberg, 1986). Preliminary research by Edelmann and Golombok (1989) and Wasser (1994) suggests that stress is a factor in infertility, delayed childbearing, and voluntary childlessness.

Two variables that could be linked more directly to a biological/evolutionary perspective are age and gender. Although age reduces the ability of women to realize childbearing intentions due to reduced fecundity (Krishnan, 1993; Myers, 1997), Schlesinger and Schlesinger (1989) argued that age increases the desire to have children among the childless because childbearing is a biological imperative. Research on the effects of age on birth intentions has been mixed, however. One study of women aged 18 to 30 showed increased intentions to have children with age (Taris, 1998). However, studies that have included wider (and older) ranges of age have found positive relationships between age and intentional childlessness (Heaton, Jacobson, & Holland, 1999; Jacobson et al., 1988; Ory, 1978; Rovi, 1994; Seccombe, 1991).

With respect to gender, parental investment theory (Buss, 1999; Geary, 1998) would predict that women are less likely to desire childlessness than men and are more concerned about caregiving issues in deciding when or whether to have a child. Accordingly, men will value childbearing less and be more focused on economic concerns. Contrary to these predictions, however, researchers have found that men are more pronatalistic in their assessments of the value of children (Seccombe, 1991; Taris, 1998), although they express more economic concerns. Women are more concerned about age, stress, worry, and later caregiving in their musings over childbearing.

Cultural Norms Perspective

Cultural theories propose that childlessness is a function of normative pressures and socialization experiences that shape fertility preferences either specifically or more generally. Gillespie (1999) identified two processes leading to a weakening of pronatalistic norms linked to the development of a modern capitalistic economy. The first involves individuals making rational choices in an economic context that has increasingly made nonfamily career options open to women. The second process involves a more fundamental shift in the social definition of marriage and family life from one that emphasizes traditional ties that bind to one that emphasizes choice and companionship, goals that may also be less consistent with childbearing. A third process, identified by Nock (1987), involves a shift toward a worldview premised on a belief in gender equality (Luker, 1986) that excludes motherhood as an important identity for women. Trends toward greater childlessness in more modern societies support the cultural explanation, as does contemporary research on childlessness across cultural subgroups.

One variable that reflects the impact of culture on childlessness in the United States is race. U.S. census and other survey data have shown that whites are significantly more likely to choose childlessness (Jacobson et al., 1988; Rovi, 1994), be childless (Chen & Morgan, 1991), and delay childbearing (Bloom & Trussell, 1984; Myers, 1997). Some of these effects, however, appear to be related to socioeconomic status (Jacobson & Heaton, 1991). As Heaton et al. (1999) showed, blacks are more likely than whites to intend to bear children and fulfill their childbearing intentions, less likely to postpone intended childbearing, less likely to switch to a childless intent, and less likely to fulfill childlessness intentions. These findings suggest that compared to white women, black women form their childbearing intentions earlier in life and have greater opportunities and/or pressures to fulfill childbearing intentions or to have a child in spite of intentions. One possible explanation for these effects is a strong pronatalistic value in the African American culture derived from a matrifocal cultural heritage or, as May (1995) suggested, from the experiences of slavery.

Religion and religiosity represent another cultural force in decisions to remain childless. Although broad religious groups (e.g., Catholics vs. Protestants vs. Jews) do not differ significantly in childlessness, those without any religious affiliation are more likely to be childless (Houseknecht, 1987; Jacobson et al., 1988; Jacobson & Heaton, 1991; Krishnan, 1993; Poston, 1990; Rovi, 1994). These findings are consistent with the reduced significance of religious denomination and the more consistent effects of religiosity as a determinant of family outcomes noted by Dollahite and colleagues (see Chapter 24 of this book).

Third, region and residence should predict childlessness to the extent that these variables are related to norms governing childbearing behavior. In regions of the country where profamily norms are expected to be weaker (e.g., the western United States), women are more likely to be childless (Jacobson et al., 1988). In areas of greater modernity and lower social solidarity (e.g., urban environments), women are more likely to intend to remain child-free or postpone childbearing (Rovi, 1994). Urban residence, however, is not related to actual childlessness (Jacobson et al., 1988), perhaps due to the greater concentration of African Americans and greater likelihood of nonmarital childbearing in urban areas.

Finally, research on gender role ideology provides the most direct evidence of a link between culture and childlessness. Research has consistently found a negative relationship between childlessness and women's traditional family values and gender role beliefs (Houseknecht, 1987; Jacobson & Heaton, 1991; Kaufman, 2000). The shift away from traditional gender roles, however, has contradictory effects on men and women, with nontraditional men desiring children more than traditional men (Kaufman, 2000).

Rational Choice and Exchange Perspective

In rational choice theory, children are evaluated as having direct costs and benefits (e.g., time and money investments, energy demands, caregiving in later life), indirect costs and benefits (e.g., social sanctions, stigma, increased marital stability), and opportunity costs (e.g., forgone leisure time, employment, or occupational advancement). Accordingly, individuals (or couples) will choose to remain childless when (a) the costs of children are high relative to their rewards; (b) the benefits of a childless lifestyle are high relative to the costs of such a lifestyle; and/or (c) alternatives to childbearing are available and the opportunity costs of childbearing are high.

Rational choice theories differ from exchange theories in their concern for explaining aggregate fertility behavior and their corresponding emphasis on values of childbearing that have universal and fungible characteristics. They seek predictors of childbearing that have immanent value (Myers, 1997): that is, predictors that do not vary from one individual to another on the basis of subjective values but instead have predictive power by virtue of their ability to make the achievement of other subjective values possible. One such predictor could be wealth, but attempts to explain societal change in fertility on the basis of changes in wealth alone have largely failed. Another is the underlying value of children for reducing life course uncertainty (Friedman, Hechter, & Kanazawa, 1994), although this aspect of fertility has been challenged on theoretical, conceptual, and empirical grounds (Lehrer, Grossbard-Schechtman, & Leasure, 1996; Myers, 1997). More recently, Schoen, Young, Nathanson, Fields, and Astone (1997) have argued that aggregate change in fertility can be explained by variation in the value of children for creating and maintaining social bonds essential to survival. Thus, childlessness remains low even in modern societies because it retains this immanent value.

At the micro level, work and occupational status, career orientation, education, and income have been predicted to increase the opportunity costs of children and thereby to increase childlessness. These variables have been found to consistently predict childlessness and childlessness intentions in both qualitative studies (Houseknecht, 1987) and quantitative studies (Heaton et al., 1999; Hodge & Ogawa, 1991; Jacobson et al., 1988; Jacobson & Heaton, 1991; Kiernan, 1989; Krishnan, 1993; Myers, 1997; Rovi, 1994). There have been important exceptions in this research (Seccombe, 1991), however, and some results suggest that women's income and education may not undermine

the desire for children as much as they create both opportunities and new conditions for fulfilling fertility intentions (Heaton et al., 1999).

Life Course Perspective

The life course perspective sees childlessness as a function of individuals' reactions to circumstance and social expectations. At the most basic level, this perspective holds that the desire for children will change with age and marital status due to societal norms linked to these life changes. As has been noted, however, this perspective goes beyond simple age norms and considers the impact of time, developmental readiness, and past life events on future trajectories (Nichols & Pace-Nichols, 2000; White & Klein, 2002).

Determinants of childlessness can be found in early life course experiences in the family, such as parental socioeconomic status and birth order. Higher parental socioeconomic status has been found to be related to less coercive parenting styles with moderate to high levels of parental warmth, greater independence training, and a greater emphasis on achievement: all predictors of childlessness (Houseknecht, 1987). These parenting styles are likely to foster greater independence and autonomy in children and the early development of an achievement identity versus a mothering identity, also found to predict childlessness (Houseknecht, 1987). Results from research on the effects of parental socioeconomic status, however, have been mixed. Although some researchers have found that higher parental status is more strongly correlated with delayed childbearing and childlessness (Blossfeld & Jaenichen, 1992; McLaughlin & Micklin, 1983), others have found no relationship (Jacobson et al., 1988). Birth order has shown more consistent effects (Houseknecht, 1987), with the presence of siblings increasing the likelihood of later childbearing (Rovi,

1994). Finally, disruption of the early life course (e.g., by parental divorce) also increases the likelihood of childlessness (Goldscheider & Waite, 1991) and negatively affects young adults' attitudes toward parenthood (Axinn & Thornton, 1996).

In addition to the effects of early life course experiences on childlessness, this perspective highlights the influence of development norms on childlessness. Two family development norms in our society are that marriage should precede parenthood and that parenthood should occur early in marriage (White, 1991). Although marriage reduces the likelihood of childlessness (Jacobson et al., 1988; Jacobson & Heaton, 1991), results from Heaton et al. (1999) suggest that both marriage and cohabitation act as catalysts to establish initial childbearing or childlessness intentions rather than elicit such intentions. Research supports the prediction that being off-time in one's family life course increases childlessness. Couples in their second marriage are less likely than those in first marriages to have a child in the near future (Myers, 1997), and childlessness is more likely among those who are older at the time of marriage (Hodge & Ogawa, 1991; Kiernan, 1989; Krishnan, 1993). Duration of marriage also puts couples at risk of childlessness (Hodge & Ogawa, 1991; Myers, 1997; Tomes, 1985), although in the early years of marriage duration is positively related to the perceived profitability of having children (Taris, 1998).

Finally, current family life conditions can influence childbearing/childlessness intentions. The likelihood of childlessness increases with egalitarian role relationships and wife income contributions. Childlessness decreases with marital role differentiation, traditional gender roles, and husband decision making (Myers, 1997; Walter, 1986). In addition, Taris (1998) found that a positive evaluation of one's current state of childlessness decreases the perceived profitability of having a child as well as the intention to have a child. Nationally representative longitudinal studies in the United States, however, have shown a negative relationship between marital satisfaction/stability and childlessness (Lillard & Waite, 1993; Myers, 1997).

Feminist Perspectives

Feminist approaches (Ferguson, 1989; Gillespie, 2000, 2001; Hird & Abshoff, 2000; May, 1995; Morell, 1994, 2000; Phoenix & Woollett, 1991) have been less concerned about the determinants of childlessness, focusing instead on gendered cultural narratives that shape perceptions and experiences of childbearing and childlessness. It is argued that one means by which cultural and symbolic forms shape and reinforce gender inequalities is through the fostering of a gender identity linked to motherhood. In one of the most influential studies of childlessness from this perspective, Veevers (1980) linked childlessness with the extent to which women reject the "mystique" of motherhood. A decade later, Gillespie (1999) further articulated this linkage:

> Motherhood as fixed, unchanging, natural, fulfilling and central to feminine identity is a deeply embedded concept in Western culture.... [N]urturance of children has historically been seen to be what women do, and mothers have been seen to be what women are, constituting the central core of the self or feminine identity....Women's natural instincts as well as their bodies are seen to be ideally suited to reproduction, and failing to fulfill this bodily imperative can denote a deficiency or be seen as "unnatural." (p. 44)

For a review of how the emphasis on motherhood has changed historically and the diversity of contemporary views of motherhood, see Chapter 12 of this book.

From this perspective, the term *childless* conveys a meaning of absence that goes beyond the objective condition and implies a deficiency that characterizes women primarily and exerts a pressure on women to bear children. During the second wave of feminism, a movement was made away from this term and toward the term *child-free* in an effort to neutralize the negative connotations of not having children. In more recent decades, however, feminism has moved to a position that once again emphasizes the centrality of motherhood as a defining experience that distinguishes women from men and therefore is a central element in women's identity (Hird & Abshoff, 2000). This maternal feminism (Bulbeck, 1998, as cited in Morell, 2000) seeks to empower women in and through their childbearing capacities rather than to reject or deny an element to their existence that has long been devalued. As Morell (2000) noted, this movement has given voice to women's experiences and perspectives but has also overshadowed the voices of women without children. This renewed emphasis on childbearing has been termed the new pronatalism, and it exerts as strong a cultural force on women's lives as the old, with the added component of racial and class-based differences in those expectations (May, 1995).

RATIONALES FOR AND INTERPRETATIONS OF CHILDLESSNESS

Researchers have attempted to understand the causes of childlessness by assessing individuals' expressed motivations for their childlessness. Although these data may reflect true motivations, it is equally likely that they are constructions or rationales based on dominant cultural narratives and attempts by the childless to deflect negative stereotypes by explaining their choices

within socially accepted frames or value systems (Gillespie, 1999; Morell, 2000). According to Houseknecht (1987), reasons given to researchers will be presented within "an acceptable vocabulary of motives previously established by the historical epoch and the social structures in which one lives" (p. 376). In her review of the research, she found the following rank order of reasons given for remaining childless: (a) freedom and self-fulfillment; (b) marital quality; (c) career and monetary considerations; (d) concern for population growth (women) and dislike for children (men); (e) early socialization experiences and doubts about ability to parent (women); (f) concern about childbirth and recovery (women); and (g) concern about raising children under unstable or negative world conditions (women).

More recent research by Gillespie (1999) confirms Houseknecht's (1987) conclusions but qualifies them by the type of childlessness. Most of the childless women in her qualitative study had made *active* choices, usually early in life, and the basis for their decision was often the rejection of motherhood as a life course option. In some cases, these women had had previous experiences (e.g., witnessing the breakup of a close relative's marriage after having a child; experiencing an unplanned pregnancy terminated through abortion) that either shifted their values or directed their identity formation processes in a different direction than the prevailing norms. The *passive* deciders showed low commitment to motherhood and greater openness to alternative identities from the very beginning. Their reasons were often couched within the framework of life decisions premised on ongoing assessments of values, inclinations, abilities, and life circumstances.

For both the active and passive deciders, Gillespie (1999) found that the "pull of childlessness often co-existed with a push away from motherhood" (p. 44). For many of these childless women, children were not appealing, and motherhood was perceived to be "uninteresting, dreary and too hard" (p. 45), even though the women were often involved in other caregiving activities.

Other reasons for childlessness reported by individuals over the age of 55 (Connidis & McMullin, 1996) included responsibilities for parents and others in their family of orientation, difficulties in establishing themselves to support a family, fate, self-actualization, altruism, yielding to the preferences or situations of one's spouse, practical concerns (e.g., finances, mobility), sexual orientation, and poor well-being. Several individuals reported childhoods in which they experienced alcoholism, violence, being orphaned, or having parenting responsibilities thrust upon them as children. Interestingly, among the ever-married, the most common reasons for childlessness given were physiological factors and age, although 80% said that their decision was a choice rather than due to circumstances.

Men's reasons for childlessness were more likely than women's to reflect instrumental concerns having to do with career and work focus, traveling and adventure, lack of neighborhood supports, and negative early childhood experiences (poverty and abuse) (Lunneborg, 1999). Men saw freedom to work as a more important reason to remain childless than did women, and their emphasis on work, travel, and so on seemed tied to concerns about fulfilling developmental goals and maintaining responsible control over their lives. These men seemed to have developed an early concern for fulfilling male role expectations in the areas of financial responsibility, and they could articulate clear work and career patterns from an early age. Men in Lunneborg's study expressed little concern for their relationships as a factor in their desire for childlessness, and they tended to acquiesce to their spouse's desires or find a spouse who shared their desire for childlessness.

They did not express a fear of mistakes or later disappointments in child outcomes, although more than half said that they found children distressing and out of control. They also expressed difficulty with being responsible for another person as much as they would have to be for a child.

Decision-Making Processes

Few studies have examined the process individuals go through in making their decision to remain childless. Although dated, Veevers (1980) provides the most systematic analysis of this process. The sequence that characterized most of her couples was one that started with a decision to postpone childbearing for a definite period of time while the couple tended to other life course transitions and tasks. This initial decision established the effective use of birth control and established an inertia level requiring greater conviction to decide to have a child. Following the initial period of postponement, a second decision was made to indefinitely postpone childbearing due to the discovery of unanticipated rewards from childlessness or to the existence of new contingencies in their relationship or in their social situation that made childbearing less certain. Some couples noted an increased awareness of the demands of child rearing and revised their estimation of what was necessary to have in place before childbearing so as to optimize child outcomes and parenting experiences. Couples also often experienced a third stage in their decision making: the delineation of the pros and cons of parenthood. During this delineation, no firm decision was made regarding childlessness. Couples still felt they were capable of having children (with most being aware of the effects of age on fecundity), and husbands frequently took the role of devil's advocate in an effort to help their wives make a final decision regarding having children. Finally, as a result of this weighing of pros and cons and a consideration of their life situations, couples came to accept their condition as a permanent one based on their choice.

Although Veevers (1980) and Lunneborg (1999) noted the role of spouses as devil's advocates in the decision-making process, little is known about how men and women negotiate and make joint decisions or passive decisions about having children. Some studies have shown that when disagreements occur, the likelihood of childlessness falls somewhere between joint intenders and joint nonintenders (Thomson, McDonald, & Bumpass, 1990), although other studies have shown that disagreements increase contraception use (Thomson, 1989) and inhibit pregnancy-seeking behaviors (Miller & Pasta, 1996). With respect to whose desires or intentions are more significant among disagreeing couples, the evidence is less clear. One possible outcome is that the more powerful partner makes the final decision. Alternatively, the husband may acquiesce to his wife because she will be more responsible for care of the child after it is born (what Thomson, 1997, calls the "sphere-of-influence argument"; p. 343).

EXPERIENCES OF CHILDLESSNESS

Living without children, whether intentionally or not, creates challenges that must be confronted. Childlessness is stigmatized (Miall, 1994), and as a result, childless individuals must either cope with stigma or construct symbolic communities that support their chosen identities without children.

Stigmatization

Before 1990, research had documented widespread stigmatization of the childless (Ganong, Coleman, & Mapes, 1990;

Houseknecht, 1987). Public perceptions of the childless emphasized their psychological deficiency, immorality, and disadvantage. Although most of this research focused on women, some included men and found them to be equally stigmatized. In their meta-analysis of the research before 1990, however, Ganong et al. (1990) did not find that the involuntarily childless received the same degree of stigmatization.

Since these two reviews, studies have shown that people still have biases about voluntarily childless individuals. More recent studies have shown that both women and men are assigned more negative traits when they do not have children and that the assigned traits may vary by gender. For example, childless women today are perceived to have "agency" (LaMastro, 2001) but are also seen as less driven, less caring, less emotionally healthy, low in warmth, and possessing more negative emotional traits (LaMastro, 2001; Lampman & Dowling-Guyer, 1995). They are also rated as living lives that are less rewarding, less fulfilling, more unhappy in later life, and more instrumental (Mueller & Yoder, 1997, 1999). Childless men are rated as significantly less driven, less agentic, and lower in warmth and caring (Lampman & Dowling-Guyer, 1995; LaMastro, 2001).

Coping With Stigma and Transforming Identities

Given widespread negative societal reactions to the childless, how do the involuntarily childless cope with stigmatization, and how do the voluntarily childless come to choose a stigmatized lifestyle? Ireland (1993) identified three types of childless women and their coping styles: traditional, transitional, and transformative child-free. The traditional childless (i.e., the infertile) needed to mourn the loss of a significant identity (motherhood) before they could cope effectively. Traditional childless women attempted to sustain the illusion that they could conceive but that circumstances had prevented it. This illusion was critical to their ability to maintain a definition of self as feminine that was linked to their biological capacities in reproduction. They could not sustain this illusion indefinitely, however, and at some point they had to uncouple motherhood from their definition of femininity. One method for doing so was to alter their definition of the situation from "I can't have a child" to "I didn't want to have children." To do so, however, required a high degree of flexibility on the part of both the woman and her spouse and was facilitated by feminist ideologies and discourses that provided alternative models of femininity. Other important strategies for coping included increased investments in careers, increased investments in and reconceptualizations of marriage (e.g., egalitarianism), the restructuring of friendship networks, and/or the assumption of alternative family or child care roles.

In contrast, the transitional child-free and childless were not initially committed to motherhood as central to their feminine identity but were open to the possibility. They were mostly ambivalent about having children and were often willing to leave the outcome to chance or their partners. Early in their adult life course, they experienced little pressure to have children, but with age and time those pressures increased, many times resulting in feelings of deviance. The coping strategies that these women employed included avoidance of marital commitments that increased pressures to have children, focus on creative expression at work, and the creative merging of traditional male and female traits into a synthesis that disassociated femininity from motherhood and incorporated many of the traits of motherhood into other roles.

Finally, transformative child-free women were the least likely to feel the pressures of social stigma. These women rejected the "motherhood mystique" early in life and developed gender identities that incorporated a high degree of autonomy and independence. They had high levels of self-esteem and self-confidence and found it easier to deflect negative societal reactions and resist pressures, although they still expressed a need for continued affirmation of their nonmother identities through the construction of sympathetic networks and identification with feminist ideology. These women were strongly committed to childlessness early in life and tended to seek out intimate partners and friends who shared their values and could be "sojourners" with them through life.

CONSEQUENCES OF CHILDLESSNESS

How does childlessness affect couples and individuals throughout the life course? Two areas of concern have been the effects of childlessness on marriage and the long-term effects of childlessness on the quality of life on old age.

Effects on Marriage

There are no specific studies of how voluntarily childless couples construct alternative marital lifestyles, although there is significant research showing that children have a negative impact on marital quality and satisfaction (Callan, 1986; Crohan, 1996; Glenn & McLanahan, 1982; Lawson, 1988; Lupri & Frideres, 1981; Olson et al., 1983; Shapiro, Gottman, & Carrer, 2000; Somers, 1993) and have a positive effect on marital stability (Andersson, 1995, 1997; Waite & Lillard, 1991; Wineberg, 1990). When divorce does occur, however, the childless experience fewer problems and lower levels of stress (Barnet, 1990). On the other hand, more specific studies have been done on how coping with infertility affects marriage and marital interaction processes.

The few studies of the effects of involuntary childlessness on marriage show mixed results. Many of these couples make adjustments and manage highly rewarding marriages; others experience more negative effects (Chandra et al., 1991; Monach, 1993; Ulbrich, Coyle, & Llabre, 1990). For example, the stress and invasiveness of fertility treatments can have negative effects on marital adjustment and satisfaction (Ulbrich et al., 1990). In general, however, infertile couples display changes in sexual activity and marital satisfaction over time that are similar to those of fertile couples (Slade, Raval, Buck, & Lieberman, 1992). An important aspect of the marital life course of involuntarily childless couples is how they manage and experience time in their relationship. Martin-Mathews and Mathews (2001) discussed the importance of three types of timetables in the developmental life course of infertile couples: family and societal timetables, body timetables, and treatment timetables. All three timetables shape the experiences of these childless couples and thereby shape a life course without children.

Later-Life Consequences

Often, reactions of others to the childless are couched in cautionary tales about the long-term negative consequences of their choice not to have children. However, these negative cautions are more perceived than real. In one study, older couples that remained childless by choice were more likely to perceive advantages than disadvantages in not having children. Perceived advantages were fewer worries and problems, less financial stress, and greater freedoms. Among the perceived disadvantages were lack of companionship, greater loneliness, missed experiences and completeness, and lack of support and care. These latter perceptions, however, did not reflect their more positive life evaluations (Connidis & McMullin, 1999).

Related to these perceptions is the potential for experiencing regrets in later life that could negatively affect well-being. As Morell (2000) noted, cultural narratives of regret derive from pronatalist ideologies and frame women's experiences such that normal life reflections on paths not taken are exaggerated. Women have expressed regrets about not meeting the societal expectations for one's life course and specifically feminine identity, about how not having children left them lacking a sense of continuity of self and family after death, and about feelings of marginalization stemming from nonparticipation in a world structured around pronatalism (Alexander, Rubinstein, Goodman, & Luborsky, 1992). It is important to keep in mind, however, that no link has been established between these regrets and psychological well-being.

Although regrets are a potential negative influence on well-being, most predictions of lower well-being in later life are premised on the assumption that childlessness reduces the availability of social relationships that serve as sources of social exchange and support in later life (Connidis & McMullin, 1994; Wu & Pollard, 1998). Research supports neither a task-specific (Litwak, 1985) nor a compensatory/substitution model (Cantor, 1979) of later-life support networks, models that emphasize the priority of parent-child ties over others. There is support for a functional-specificity model. Simons (1983–84), however, predicts that childless individuals will develop specialized support networks not linked to particular types of relationships. Childless individuals apparently replace missing children in their support networks with people other than relatives

(Johnson & Troll, 1992; Wu & Pollard, 1998). They also are less likely to rely upon spouses and more likely to rely on siblings and formal or paid supports for daily living (Campbell, Connidis, & Davies, 1999; Choi, 1994; Connidis & McMullin, 1994). In the end, elderly childless individuals are no different from those with children in reporting sufficient supports across a variety of specific instrumental and expressive needs (Connidis & McMullin, 1994), and their lower reliance on close family members does not seem to affect their quality of life. Although some research has shown lower levels of affective balance and life satisfaction (Connidis & McMullin, 1993; McMullin & Marshall, 1996) and higher rates of institutionalization (Freedman, 1996; Rowland, 1998) and loneliness (Zhang & Hayward, 2001) in later life among the childless, these effects are not consistent (see Koropeckyj-Cox, 1998) and are limited to the involuntarily childless and to unmarried childless men. On the positive side, the childless elderly report lower levels of stress, perhaps due to reduced caregiving responsibilities (i.e., the cost of caring) associated with close family ties (McMullin & Marshall, 1996).

Finally, there are important differences in the effects of childlessness in later life on well-being based on gender, marital status, and race. Elderly childless men compared to childless women are less outgoing, are less likely to be involved in voluntary organizations, have less significant relationships with neighbors, and have fewer close friends that they can rely upon. However, they do not differ in terms of relationships with siblings, nieces, and nephews (Wenger, 2001). Childlessness enhances relationships with siblings, nieces, and nephews more for never-married than married women and has a more negative effect on the development of close friendships for never-married than married men (Wenger, 2001). The early development among African Americans of lifelong ties with nieces and nephews suggests that the greater boundary flexibility of African American families and the practice of "child swapping" may facilitate the development of functional ties for African American elderly who are childless (Johnson & Barer, 1995). They are also more likely to maintain more active friendship ties.

CONCLUSION

What do we know about childlessness and the lifestyles of couples without children? First, there is evidence to support the influence of biological/genetic forces, rational choice, cultural norms, and life course events and trajectories on the likelihood of not having and not desiring children. What is less clear is the relative importance of these forces and the extent to which our knowledge of the determinants of childhood is limited by our own biases and culturally specific perspectives. Second, studies of the reasons and rationales given by those without children may or may not represent true causes but do reflect dominant cultural values of individualism, freedom, and personal development as well as cultural narratives that frame the experience of childlessness in the light of an emerging new pronatalism. Third, the negative consequences of childlessness as a function of social stigma have been well documented, as have the strategies used by those without children (by choice or circumstances) to resist or deflect stigmatization. The impact of dealing with infertility and the treatment options that couples face in relationships has also been explored, although not in depth here, as have the later-life consequences of a life course without children. With the exception of the potential negative effects of invasive infertility treatments on marital relationships, the evidence does not support a view of the childless as unhappy, unfulfilled, or at risk in middle or later life.

What is less clearly understood, however, is how those without children construct a normal life course, how their interactions differ over time, and what factors affect the happiness and stability of such relationships.

A significant contribution has been made to this research by feminist poststructuralist theorists. It could be argued that the study of predictors of childlessness in itself reflects and reinforces dominant pronatalistic norms to the extent that researchers search for individual-level variables to explain what is often framed as non-normative behavior. This is particularly true of studies that focus on negative childhood experiences. As feminists in the 1970s and 1980s noted, the terminology used in research contributes to a deviant view of those (especially women) who go through life without having children. Since that time, however, rather than explore the unique qualities of a child-free marriage or family life course, we have worked to draw clearer distinctions between involuntary childlessness (seen as justifiable) and volitional childlessness (seen as questionable or risky), even though such distinctions may be artificial and ambiguous. There is a growing concern, perhaps tied to the emergence of a new pronatalism, about identifying and helping the involuntarily childless to achieve the goal of having children. The result of this concern, however, may be the reinforcement of the desirability of the goal itself and a failure to gain a fuller understanding of the development of a normal marital and family life without children.

But what about the future of research and theory in this area and the future of marriage and family life without children? With respect to research and theory, trends in two directions are likely to continue. First, it is likely that increasing attention will be given to the struggles faced by those who are infertile or involuntarily childless. Our modern technological society has greatly reduced the number of men and women who cannot attain parental status, but it has done so at significant cost. In the future, research on childlessness is likely to explore in greater detail how individuals and couples manage the needed interventions to have children and how those interventions affect the quality and stability of relationships. This attention to the involuntarily childless is likely to increasingly marginalize the voluntarily childless. Second, with the growth of a new pronatalism, feminist scholarship in this area is also likely to grow as researchers further explore strategies of individual resistance and social change. Where should we venture as researchers and theorists? One question in need of future research and theory is how individuals and couples construct their marital and family life course without children over time and what factors affect the health and durability of such relationships.

With respect to the future of childlessness and child-free marriages, the trends are less clear. There seems to be little question that advances in reproductive technologies will make most childlessness an issue of volition or commitment to childbearing. As Beck (1992) and Beck and Beck-Gernsheim (1995) have noted, the growth and application of technology to solve problems in a modern society often make public problems private. Increasingly, those who do not have children will find that they bear the bulk of the responsibility for not doing so. Without changes in cultural norms, this could have increasingly negative consequences. Will women (and men) choose, then, to have children (even if it means significant personal and financial costs) rather than face these consequences? This question is difficult to answer. On the one hand, we have noted the emergence and power of a new pronatalism in society. The endorsement of this norm is likely to reduce intentions and desires to live a child-free lifestyle. A downward trend in childlessness is also expected on the basis of improvements in reproductive technologies, the emergence of new identities for men that incorporate active parenting roles, and the increasing need in a modern society to find personal authenticity and meaning and construct personal biography through marital and family life events. On the other hand, modernity reinforces norms of individualism and self-fulfillment, often in the context of public selves. As we pursue status in society through our achievements, more men and women will increasingly delay marriage and childbearing, perhaps to a point where we rationally calculate the potential rewards and costs and decide to live a life without children.

REFERENCES

Alexander, B. B., Rubinstein, R. L., Goodman, M., & Luborsky, M. (1992). A path not taken: A cultural analysis of regrets and childlessness in the lives of older women. *Gerontologist, 32,* 618–626.

Andersson, G. (1995). Divorce risk trends in Sweden 1971–1993. *European Journal of Population, 11,* 293–311.

Andersson, G. (1997). The impact of children on divorce risks of Swedish women. *European Journal of Population, 13,* 109–145.

Axinn, W., & Thornton, A. (1996). The influence of parents' marital dissolutions on children's attitudes toward family formation. *Demography, 33,* 66–81.

Bacu, A., & O'Connel, M. (2000). *Fertility of American women* (Current Population Reports, P20-543RV). Washington, DC: U.S. Bureau of the Census.

Bardwick, J. M. (1974). Evolution and parenting. *Journal of Social Issues, 30,* 39–62.

Barnet, H. S. (1990). Divorce stress and adjustment model: Locus of control and demographic predictors. *Journal of Divorce, 13,* 93–109.

Beck, U. (1992). *Risk society: Towards a new modernity.* Newbury Park, CA: Sage.

Beck, U., & Beck-Gernsheim, E. (1995). *The normal chaos of love.* Cambridge, UK: Polity.

Blake, J. (1968). Are babies consumer durables? *Population Studies, 22,* 5–25.

Blake, J., & Davis, K. (1963). Population and public opinion: The need for basic research. *American Behavioral Scientist, 5,* 24–29.

Bloom, D. E., & Trussell, J. (1984). What are the determinants of delayed childbearing and permanent childlessness in the United States? *Demography, 21,* 591–611.

Blossfeld, H.-P., & Jaenichen, U. (1992). Educational expansion and changes in women's entry into marriage and motherhood in the Federal Republic of Germany. *Journal of Marriage and the Family, 54,* 302–315.

Bulbeck, C. (1998). *Re-orienting western feminisms: Women's diversity in a postcolonial world.* New York: Cambridge University Press.

Buss, D. M. (1999). *Evolutionary psychology: The new science of the mind.* Boston: Allyn & Bacon.

Callan, V. J. (1986). Single women, voluntary childlessness, and perceptions about life and marriage. *Journal of Biosocial Science, 18,* 479–487.

Campbell, L. D., Connidis, I. A., & Davies, L. (1999). Sibling ties in later life: A social network analysis. *Journal of Family Issues, 20,* 114–148.

Cantor, M. H. (1979). Neighbors and friends: An overlooked resource in the informal support system. *Research on Aging, 1,* 434–463.

Chandra, P. S., Chaturvedi, S. K., Isaac, M. K., Chetra, H., Sudarshan, C. Y., & Beena, M. B. (1991). Marital life among infertile spouses: The wife's perspective and its implications in therapy. *Family Therapy, 18,* 145–154.

Chen, R., & Morgan, S. P. (1991). Recent trends in the timing of first births in the United States. *Demography, 28,* 513–531.

Choi, N. G. (1994). Patterns and determinants of social service utilization: Comparison of the childless elderly and elderly parents living with or apart from their children. *Gerontologist, 34,* 353–362.

Connidis, I. A., & McMullin, J. A. (1993). To have or have not: Parent status and the subjective well-being of older men and women. *Gerontologist, 33,* 630–636.

Connidis, I. A., & McMullin, J. A. (1994). Social support in older age: Assessing the impact of marital and parent status. *Canadian Journal on Aging, 13,* 510–527.

Connidis, I. A., & McMullin, J. A. (1996). Reasons for and perceptions of childlessness among older persons: Exploring the impact of marital status and gender. *Journal of Aging Studies, 10,* 205–222.

Connidis, I. A., & McMullin, J. A. (1999). Permanent childlessness: Perceived advantages and disadvantages among older persons. *Canadian Journal on Aging, 18,* 447–465.

Crohan, S. E. (1996). Marital quality and conflict across the transition to parenthood in African American and white couples. *Journal of Marriage and the Family, 58,* 933–944.

Easterlin, R. A. (1966). On the relation of economic factors to recent and projected fertility changes. *Demography, 3,* 131–153.

Edelmann, R. J., & Golombok, S. (1989). Stress and reproductive failure. *Journal of Reproductive and Infant Psychology, 7,* 79–86.

Ferguson, A. (1989). *Blood at the root: Motherhood, sexuality, and male dominance.* London: Pandora.

Freedman, V. A. (1996). Family structure and the risk of nursing home admission. *Journal of Gerontology, 51B,* S61–S69.

Friedman, D., Hechter, M., & Kanazawa, S. (1994). A theory of the value of children. *Demography, 31,* 375–400.

Ganong, L. H., Coleman, M., & Mapes, D. (1990). A meta-analytic review of family structure stereotypes. *Journal of Marriage and the Family, 52,* 287–297.

Geary, D. C. (1998). *Male, female: The evolution of human sex differences.* Washington, DC: American Psychological Association.

Gillespie, R. (1999). Voluntary childlessness in the United Kingdom. *Reproductive Health Matters, 7,* 43–53.

Gillespie, R. (2000). When no means no: Disbelief and deviance as discourses of voluntary childlessness. *Women's Studies International Forum, 23,* 223–234.

Gillespie, R. (2001). Contextualizing voluntary childlessness within a postmodern model of reproduction: Implications for health and social needs. *Critical Social Policy, 21,* 139–159.

Glenn, N. D., & McLanahan, S. (1982). Children and marital happiness: A further specification of the relationship. *Journal of Marriage and the Family, 44,* 63–72.

Goldscheider, F., & Waite, L. (1991). *New families, no families? The transformation of the American home.* Berkeley: University of California Press.

Heaton, T., Jacobson, C. K., & Holland, K. (1999). Persistence and change in decisions to remain childless. *Journal of Marriage and the Family, 61,* 531–539.

Hird, M., & Abshoff, K. (2000). Women without children: A contradiction in terms? *Journal of Comparative Family Studies, 31,* 347–366.

Hodge, R. W., & Ogawa, N. (1991). *Fertility change in contemporary Japan.* Chicago: University of Chicago Press.

Hoffman, L. W., & Hoffman, M. L. (1973). The value of children to parents. In J. T. Fawcett (Ed.), *Psychological perspectives on population* (pp. 19–76). New York: Basic Books.

Houseknecht, S. K. (1987). Voluntary childlessness. In M. P. Sussman & S. K. Steinmetz (Eds.), *Handbook of marriage and the family* (pp. 369–395). New York: Plenum.

Ireland, M. S. (1993). *Reconceiving women: Separating motherhood from female identity.* New York: Guilford.

Jacobson, C. K., & Heaton, T. B. (1991). Voluntary childlessness among American men and women in the late 1980s. *Social Biology, 38,* 79–93.

Jacobson, C. K., Heaton, T. B., & Taylor, K. M. (1988). Childlessness among American women. *Social Biology, 35,* 186–197.

Johnson, C. L., & Barer, B. M. (1995). Childlessness and kinship organization: Comparisons of very old whites and blacks. *Journal of Cross-Cultural Gerontology, 10,* 289–306.

Johnson, C. L., & Troll, L. (1992). Family functioning in late late life. *Journal of Gerontology, 47,* S66–S72.

Kaufman, G. (2000). Do gender role attitudes matter? Family formation and dissolution among traditional and egalitarian men and women. *Journal of Family Issues, 21,* 128–144.

Kiernan, K. E. (1989). Who remains childless? *Journal of Biosocial Science, 21,* 387–398.

Koropeckyj-Cox, T. (1998). Loneliness and depression in middle and old age: Are the childless more vulnerable? *Journal of Gerontology, 53B,* S303–S312.

Krishnan, V. (1993). Religious homogamy and voluntary childlessness in Canada. *Sociological Perspectives, 36,* 83–93.

LaMastro, V. (2001). Childless by choice? Attributions and attitudes concerning family size. *Social Behavior and Personality, 29,* 231–244.

Lampman, C., & Dowling-Guyer, S. (1995). Attitudes toward voluntary and involuntary childlessness. *Basic and Applied Social Psychology, 17,* 213–222.

Lawson, D. M. (1988). Love attitude and marital adjustment in the family life cycle. *Sociological Spectrum, 8,* 391–406.

Lehrer, E., Grossbard-Schechtman, S., & Leasure, J. W. (1996). Comment on "A theory of the value of children." *Demography, 33,* 133–138.

Letherby, G. (1999). Other than mother and mothers as others: The experience of motherhood and non-motherhood in relation to infertility and involuntary childlessness. *Women's Studies International Forum, 22,* 359–372.

Liliard, L. A., & Waite, L. J. (1993). A joint model of marital childbearing and marital disruption. *Demography, 30,* 653–681.

Litwak, E. (1985). *Helping the elderly: The complementary roles of informal networks and formal systems.* New York: Guilford.

Luker, K. (1986). *Abortion and the politics of motherhood.* Berkeley: University of California Press.

Lunneborg, P. (1999). *Chosen lives of childfree men.* Westport, CT: Bergin & Garvey.

Lupri, E., & Frideres, J. (1981). The quality of marriage and the passage of time: Marital satisfaction over the family life cycle. *Canadian Journal of Sociology, 6,* 283–305.

Martin-Mathews, A., & Mathews, R. (2001). Living in time: Multiple timetables in couples' experiences of infertility and its treatment. In K. J. Daly (Ed.), *Minding the time in family experience: Emerging perspectives and issues* (pp. 111–134). Oxford, UK: Elsevier Science.

May, E. (1995). *Barren in the promised land: Childless Americans and the pursuit of happiness.* New York: Basic Books.

McLaughlin, S. D., & Micklin, M. (1983). The timing of the first birth and changes in personal efficacy. *Journal of Marriage and the Family, 45,* 47–55.

McMullin, J., & Marshall, V. W. (1996). Family, friends, stress, and well-being: Does childlessness make a difference? *Canadian Journal on Aging, 15,* 355–373.

Miall, C. E. (1994). Community constructs of involuntary childlessness: Sympathy, stigma, and social support. *Canadian Review of Sociology and Anthropology, 31,* 392–421.

Miller, W. B., & Pasta, D. J. (1996). Couple disagreement: Effects on formation and implementation of fertility decisions. *Personal Relationships, 3,* 307–336.

Monach, J. H. (1993). *Childless: No choice. The experience of involuntary childlessness.* London: Routledge.

Morell, C. (1994). *Unwomanly conduct: The challenges of intentional childlessness.* New York: Routledge.

Morell, C. (2000). Saying no: Women's experiences with reproductive refusal. *Feminism and Psychology, 10,* 313–322.

Morgan, S. (1991). Late nineteenth- and early twentieth century childlessness. *American Journal of Sociology, 97,* 779–807.

Morgan, S. P., & Chen, R. (1992). Predicting childlessness for recent cohorts of American women. *International Journal of Forecasting, 8,* 477–493.

Mosher, W., & Pratt, W. (1990). *Fecundity and infertility in the U.S., 1965–1988.* (Advance Data, No. 192). Washington, DC: National Center for Health Statistics.

Mueller, K. A., & Yoder, J. D. (1997). Gendered norms for family size, employment, and occupation: Are there personal costs for violating them. *Sex Roles, 36,* 207–220.

Mueller, K. A., & Yoder, J. D. (1999). Stigmatization of non-normative family size status. *Sex Roles, 41,* 901–919.

Myers, S. (1997). Marital uncertainty and childbearing. *Social Forces, 75,* 1271–1289.

Nason, E. M., & Poloma, M. M. (1976). *Voluntary childless couples: The emergence of a variant lifestyle.* Beverly Hills, CA: Sage.

Nichols, W. C., & Pace-Nichols, M. A. (2000). Family development and family therapy. In W. C. Nichols, M. A. Pace-Nichols, D. S. Becvar, & A. Y. Napier (Eds.), *Handbook of family development and intervention* (pp. 3–22). New York: John Wiley.

Nock, S. L. (1987). The symbolic meaning of childbearing. *Journal of Family Issues, 8,* 373–393.

Olson, D., McCubbin, H., Barnes, H., Larsen, A., Muxen, M., & Wilson, M. (1983). *Families: What makes them work.* Beverly Hills, CA: Sage.

Ory, M. G. (1978). The decision to parent or not: Normative and structural components. *Journal of Marriage and the Family, 40,* 531–539.

Phoenix, A., & Woollett, A. (1991). Motherhood: Social construction, politics and psychology. In A. Phoenix, A. Woollett, & E. Lloyd (Eds.), *Motherhood: Meanings, practices and ideologies* (pp. 13–27). Newbury Park, CA: Sage.

Popenoe, P. (1936). Motivation of childless marriages. *Journal of Heredity, 27,* 467–472.

Popenoe, P. (1954). The childless marriage: Sexual and marital maladjustments. *Fertility and Sterility, 5,* 168–172.

Poston, D. L. (1990). Voluntary and involuntary childlessness among Catholic and non-Catholic women: Are the patterns converging? *Social Biology, 37,* 251–265.

Rovi, S. (1994). Taking "no" for an answer: Using negative reproductive intentions to study the childless/childfree. *Population Research and Policy Review, 13,* 343–365.

Rowland, D. (1998). Consequences of childlessness in later life. *Australasian Journal on Ageing, 17,* 24–28.

Schlesinger, B., & Schlesinger, R. (1989). Postponed parenthood: Trends and issues. *Journal of Comparative Family Studies, 20,* 355–363.

Schoen, R., Young, Y. J., Nathanson, C. A., Fields, J., & Astone, N. M. (1997). Why do Americans want children? *Population and Development Review, 23,* 333–358.

Seccombe, K. (1991). Assessing the costs and benefits of children: Gender comparisons among childfree husbands and wives. *Journal of Marriage and the Family, 53,* 191–202.

Shapiro, A. F., Gottman, J. M., & Carrer, S. (2000). The baby and the marriage: Identifying factors that buffer against decline in marital satisfaction after the first baby arrives. *Journal of Family Psychology, 14,* 59–70.

Simons, R. L. (1983–84). Specificity and substitution. in the social networks of the elderly. *International Journal of Aging and Human Development, 18,* 121–139.

Slade, P., Raval, H., Buck, P., & Lieberman, B. E. (1992). A 3-year follow-up of emotional, marital and sexual functioning in couples who were infertile. *Journal of Reproductive and Infant Psychology, 10,* 233–243.

Somers, M. D. (1993). A comparison of voluntary childfree adults and parents. *Journal of Marriage and the Family, 55,* 643–650.

Taris, T. (1998). Fertility in the Netherlands as an expected value process and development readiness. *Journal of Psychology, 132,* 61–77.

Thomson, E. (1989). Dyadic models of contraceptive choice, 1957 and 1975. In D. Brinberg & J. Jaccard (Eds.), *Dyadic decision making* (pp. 268–285). New York: Springer-Verlag.

Thomson, E. (1997). Couple childbearing desires, intentions, and births. *Demography, 34,* 343–354.

Thomson, E., McDonald, E., & Bumpass, L. L. (1990). Fertility desires and fertility: His, hers, and theirs. *Demography, 27,* 579–588.

Thornton, A., & Young-DeMarco, L. (2001). Four decades of trends in attitudes toward family issues in the United States: The 1960s through the 1990s. *Journal of Marriage and Family, 63,* 1009–1037.

Tomes, N. (1985). Childlessness in Canada 1971: A further analysis. *Canadian Journal of Sociology, 10,* 37–68.

Ulbrich, P. M., Coyle, A. T., & Llabre, M. M. (1990). Involuntary childlessness and marital adjustment: His and hers. *Journal of Sex and Marital Therapy, 16,* 147–158.

Veevers, J. E. (1973). Voluntary childless wives: An exploratory study. *Sociology and Social Research, 57,* 356–366.

Veevers, J. E. (1975). The moral careers of voluntary childless wives: Notes on the defense of a variant world view. *Family Coordinator, 24,* 473–487.

Veevers, J. E. (1980). *Childless by choice.* Toronto, Ontario: Butterworth.

Waite, L. J., & Lillard, L. A. (1991). Children and marital disruption. *American Journal of Sociology, 96,* 930–953.

Walter, C. A. (1986). *The timing of motherhood.* Lexington, MA: D. C. Heath.

Wasser, S. K. (1994). Psychosocial stress and infertility. Cause or effect? *Human Nature, 5,* 293–306.

Wasser, S. K., & Isenberg, D. Y. (1986). Reproductive failure among women: Pathology or adaptation? *Journal of Psychosomatic Obstetrics and Gynaecology, 5,* 153–175.

Wenger, G. (2001). Ageing without children: Rural Wales. *Journal of Cross-Cultural Gerontology, 16,* 79–109.

White, J. M. (1991). *Dynamics of family development: The theory of family development*. New York: Guilford.

White, J. M., & Klein, D. M. (2002). *Family theories* (2nd ed.). Thousand Oaks, CA: Sage.

Wineberg, H. (1990). Delayed childbearing, childlessness and marital disruption. *Journal of Comparative Family Studies, 21*, 99–110.

Wu, Z., & Pollard, M. S. (1998). Social support among unmarried childless elderly persons. *Journal of Gerontology, 53B*, S324–S335.

Zhang, Z., & Hayward, M. D. (2001). Childlessness and the psychological well-being of older persons. *Journal of Gerontology, 56B*, S311–S320.

CHAPTER 8

Intimate Relationships in Later Life
Current Realities, Future Prospects

Teresa M. Cooney and Kathleen Dunne

This chapter addresses current research and theorizing regarding the intimate relationships of adults in mid- to late life. Within the literature on intimate and close relationships, this period of the life span has received limited attention. As is the case with research and theory on adulthood and aging more generally, scholarship pertaining to intimate relationships and aging has a relatively short history compared to scholarship focused on earlier periods of the life span.

A BIT OF HISTORY

Before the 1940s, attention to the study of adult development and gerontology was largely nonexistent in the United States. The late Bernice Neugarten (1988) claimed that her course at the University of Chicago entitled "Maturity and Old Age," which originated in the late 1940s, was probably the first of its kind to be taught at an American university. Around this same time, researchers

were beginning to consider aging issues. The Social Science Research Council formed a subcommittee on Social Adjustment in Old Age in 1943, and during the 1940s University of Chicago researchers Ernest Burgess, Robert Havighurst, and Ethel Shanas initiated several studies focused on adult adjustment (Neugarten, 1988). The 1950s saw the initiation of Duke University's longitudinal studies of aging and Neugarten and Havighurst's oft-cited Kansas City Studies of Adult Life. By 1968, when Neugarten published her influential reader *Middle Age and Aging*, an extensive array of theoretical and empirical work on mid- and late adulthood was underway.

Despite advances in the field of adulthood and aging by the late 1960s, there was still limited understanding of the importance and meaning of intimacy and couple relationships for older individuals. Because those who survived to old age were typically single and often widowed, scholars appear to have easily dismissed the need to understand couple relationships at this point in the life span. Also, despite the work of Alfred Kinsey and colleagues (Kinsey, Pomeroy, & Martin, 1948, 1953) and Masters and Johnson (1982), the prevailing public attitude was that older adults, who were beyond their reproductive years, were incapable of and uninterested in sexual expression and involvement. Indeed, older persons' participation in nonmarital intimate relationships and/or sexual activity (either within or outside marriage) was the butt of many jokes and generally elicited negative stereotypes ("dirty old man!"). Not surprisingly, until the late 1970s and early 1980s (see, e.g., Starr & Weiner, 1981), little empirical attention was devoted to sexuality in the second half of life. Moreover, the study of older adults' participation in such close relationships as marital and cohabiting unions and dating relationships, where sexual and nonsexual intimacy might occur, was also extremely limited.

The last 20 years have produced incredible growth in the literature on close, intimate relationships, as well as relationship transitions, in mid- to later life. In this chapter, we explore what is known about various close, intimate relationships among older adults and consider how transitions in relationship status affect late-life adjustment and well-being. In addition, we consider some of the sociodemographic changes in recent decades that are likely to shape future relationship patterns for older adults. We speculate about how patterns of intimate relationships in late life will possibly differ for today's cohorts of older adults and those who will reach this life stage in the next 20 to 30 years.

THE IMPORTANCE OF HISTORICAL CONTEXT

The life course is heavily influenced by sociohistorical context. Therefore, the role options individuals have, the norms that guide their life choices and behaviors, and the institutional supports available as they attempt to carry out their roles vary for persons of different birth cohorts. As a result, life experiences of persons from different cohorts are likely to vary widely, as is their adjustment to various roles at different points in the life cycle. As noted, our focus in this chapter is individuals' marital and intimate relationship experiences. Thus, it is useful to briefly review some of the major social changes and demographic shifts of the 20th century that are likely to have influenced marital and intimate relationships the most.

One dramatic change in the last 100 years is the reduction in mortality and the increase in life expectancy. Since 1900, life expectancy at birth rose by almost 50%, from 47.3 to 75.5 years (Treas, 1995). Another shift has been the increase in educational attainment for both men and women. Although about one in three persons aged 75 and older in 1990 had less than a high school education, this is true of less than 5% of the population aged 20 to 44 today. In 1990, fewer than 10% of older persons had college degrees, whereas now about one in four persons aged 25 to 44 has finished college (Spain & Bianchi, 1996). Women's labor force involvement also has changed; women born between 1946 and 1955 were twice as likely and women born between 1956 and 1965 were three times as likely as women of their mothers' cohorts to be working from ages 25 to 34.

In addition to demographic transformations, life course theorists argue that American society has changed in other ways that influence life course development. Examples include heightened emphasis on individualism and the creation of more public supports to assist families in responding to financial hardships. Consequently, individuals today, compared to those living

50 to 100 years ago, are more likely to make life choices and pursue individual goals at their own discretion, with less need to coordinate their actions with the larger family collective. Some argue that the life course has become less standardized and regimented; greater flexibility in the timing and ordering of education, work, and family roles provides adults today with increasingly diverse relationship experiences and options for shaping their lives (Buchmann, 1989).

INCREASING HETEROGENEITY IN MARITAL STATUSES

Whether a person's later years are shared with a spouse or spent alone is largely determined by sex, and this won't change in the 21st century. Census data reveal that, among adults aged 65 and over today, three of four men are married, compared to just over half of women (U.S. Bureau of the Census, 1999). Wade (1989) projected that the proportion of married older men will drop to 69% by 2040; the figure for women will remain around 42%. The decline in marriage for men will result primarily from a doubling of the percentage of older never-married men. For older women, change will primarily involve a reduction in the proportion widowed and an increase in the proportion divorced. Therefore, the 21st century will be characterized by greater heterogeneity in marital statuses for the older population. Smaller percentages of older adults will be married than is true today; more elders, especially men, will never have been legally married; and, among the formerly married, marital disruption will be almost as likely to have resulted from divorce as from death of a spouse, especially for women.

The potential for being married in later life increased substantially over the 20th century due to reductions in mortality. Of couples marrying at age 25 in 1900, only 19%

could expect to stay continuously married to age 70 (Uhlenberg, 1990). By 1990, reduced mortality meant that 54% of those marrying at age 25 could anticipate such a lengthy union. However, the proportion of the life span devoted to marriage has actually declined because of concomitant increases in age at marriage and divorce rates. Marriage now occupies about 45% of men's life span and 41% of women's, down from over 50% for both in 1970 (Schoen & Weinick, 1993). Continuance of these trends suggests that fewer people will be in long-term marriages in old age in the future.

Long-Term Marriage

Long-term marriages are characterized by both continuity and discontinuity. Feelings of relative happiness or unhappiness in marriage show high continuity over time (Alford-Cooper, 1998; Brubaker, 1985). That is, the same things that make a given couple happy or unhappy early in marriage tend to make them happy or unhappy later in marriage, and couples having happier early marital experiences tend to have happier experiences later. Continuity also is evident in the division of household duties. The division of labor after retirement is generally similar to the way it was before retirement, with wives doing more of the traditional feminine chores, even when both spouses have retired (Lee & Shehan, 1989).

Discontinuities also occur in long-term marriages. For example, marital satisfaction in long-term marriages decreases from the early to the middle years, during child rearing, and then increases in later life, when children have usually left home and couples have more time together (Goodman, 1999). Thus, most people in long-term marriages report being happy with their marriages (Alford-Cooper, 1998).

Another possible discontinuity in long-term marriage is found in how individuals characterize their relationships. Couples married many years report more pleasure, less conflict and negativity, more affection and intimacy, and fewer marital problems than do couples who have been married fewer years (Carstensen, Gottman, & Levenson, 1995). These differences may exist because of the reduced stress and added time spouses in long-term marriages tend to have after retirement and the departure of children. Those in long-term marriages also may be more grateful for the relationships they have because many their age are widowed (Goodman, 1999).

How other life transitions affect marriage is important to consider. Retirement often results in long-term married spouses being home together for the first time. This requires a "reconsideration of how time is spent, of priority given to activities, and of territorial issues" between spouses (Scott, 1997, p. 371). In a study of couples married at least 50 years, those who were happier and more satisfied with marriage were less likely to report that partners got in each other's way after retirement; overall, 43% claimed that their marriage improved, 53% reported it was about the same, and 4% claimed that their relationship declined (Alford-Cooper, 1998).

A more complete picture of the effects of retirement on long-term marriage experiences is gained by distinguishing among patterns of retirement. Brubaker (1985) proposed four types of retirement based on the work and retirement patterning of both the husband and wife in a couple. Although few researchers make such distinctions, those that have report that the effects of retirement on long-term marriage differ across couples' retirement styles. One study found that 10% of never-employed wives complained about loss of autonomy after their husbands retired and indicated a decline in marital happiness. In contrast, 33% in dual-earning families reported increased happiness after both spouses retired (Tryban, 1985). Perhaps

dual-earner wives have more control over the timing of retirement in their lives than do traditional wives, which contributes to their happiness. Another study found that husbands' retirement had a negative effect on their marital satisfaction and on the marital satisfaction of working wives until the wives retired (Lee & Shehan, 1989). Further research that attends to different retirement patterns among couples is needed to fully understand this issue.

Both positive and negative changes for the future of long-term marriage can be conjectured. Although we can expect a smaller proportion of older adults to be in long-term marriages in the future, due to later ages at marriage and higher divorce rates, couples that are married after several decades may be more satisfied with their marriages than older couples today. Long-term marriage partners in the future are more likely to have remained married out of choice, which may not be the case for older couples today, whose marital lives were largely spent in a period that was less accepting of divorce. The greater economic dependence of wives on husbands in the past also may have trapped some unhappily married women in dissatisfying marriages out of economic necessity. This type of situation should be less common in the future.

Long-term married couples in the future also will be faced with tougher decisions regarding the coordination of the husband and wife's retirement, as older couples will increasingly consist of two continuously employed partners. Moreover, many more of the wives will have established careers rather than sporadically assuming different short-term jobs. How greater commitment and investment to career may affect the retirement decisions of married women, relative to their husbands' decisions, is unknown. Perhaps they will be less willing to follow the retirement timing choices of their husbands. When their older and possibly less healthy husbands are ready to retire, these women may resist because of their own career interests and attachments.

Finally, qualitative aspects of retirement in long-term marriages may change. Given the lower mortality rates and earlier retirement ages of recent decades, couples will have an opportunity for increasingly long periods of postretirement time together. For happily married couples, the expansion of years when they are free of work and child-rearing responsibilities will mean they can devote more time to each other. For the less happily married, longer retirements may be less bearable once other life roles and demands no longer exist.

Remarriage

Little is known about remarriages in later life, either those occurring in old age or those formed earlier and continuing over long durations. The few studies that have been done examine postbereavement remarriage. Remarried widows aged 40 and older reported fewer concerns than widows who had not remarried in one study, although those who had only considered remarriage reported more worries than other nonremarried women (Gentry & Shulman, 1988). These worries were age related, as it was the oldest women who had not considered remarriage. For some widows, feeling disloyal and other unpleasant reactions are experienced when they consider remarrying, especially if children and others object. Adult children's concerns about parental remarriage often center on inheritance (Bulcroft & O'Connor, 1986).

Other longitudinal research from persons aged 50 and older indicates that remarriage leads to positive outcomes for bereaved persons. Although remarried adults did not differ initially from the continually widowed, after 5 years they reported higher self-esteem, more life and friendship satisfaction, and less

stress (Burks, Lund, Gregg, & Bluhm, 1988). Older persons may benefit from remarriage because of the relatively high-quality remarriages they establish. One of the few studies to consider the quality of remarriages for older adults found high marital satisfaction, especially for men, when compared to remarried, middle-aged persons (Bograd & Spilka, 1996). They also may have felt more secure about their remarriages, as most had been in long-term first marriages that ended by spousal death, whereas the middle-aged remarrieds had mostly experienced divorce.

Remarriage in later life appears to be a positive experience for older adults today and is likely to be more common for older adults in the future, although how remarriage quality will change is unclear. There may be less resistance to remarriage among older adults and their families in the 21st century if people adjust to marital patterns that involve more remarriages, especially after divorce. Offspring with divorced parents may be less concerned about inheritance and parental loyalties and thus more supportive of parental remarriage. Step relationships formed from these remarriages will be important to study, especially regarding issues such as caregiving and support.

Nonmarital Living Situations

A larger proportion of older adults in the future are expected to be single or formerly married than today. Currently, widowed men outnumber the divorced by more than two to one in old age, and they surpass the never-married by three to one. By 2040, an estimated 12.9% of older men will be widowed, 10.4% never married, and 7.4% divorced. For older women, the proportion of both the never married (7.3%) and the divorced (13.2%) is expected to climb in the next 40 years, accompanied by a drop in widowhood to 37% (Wade, 1989). Such changes underscore the need for greater attention to the differences in life situations and well-being for unmarried persons.

Studies of older adults often combine all unmarried persons into one group and compare them to married individuals. Whether scholars assume the common role-loss approach (Hatch, 2000) or frame widowhood and divorce as support-disrupting events, they typically focus on problems of older adults as a result of these transitions. Little consideration is given to potentially positive adaptations or benefits of marital disruption.

Gender has been a central focus in the study of adjustment to widowhood and divorce. Gender socialization theory, with its focus on differential training for and experience in males' and females' social roles, has been used to explain differences in marital disruption for men and women (Hatch, 2000). For example, death of a spouse usually threatens women's financial security, whereas for men it generally creates problems in social and emotional adjustment. Gender socialization theory has been used to argue that women are more distressed than men after marital disruptions because spousal roles are more salient for women's than men's identities (Carey, 1979) and their social status is derived from marriage (Kimmel, 1990).

Widowhood

Fewer older persons will be widowed in the future, and the mean length of widowhood will decline because of later entry into marriage (Schoen & Weinick, 1993). However, widowhood will still be a common experience of later life.

Economic changes and strain for widows have been widely studied. Both sexes deal with economic loss when a spouse dies. Widows often lose the contributions of the main provider, and widowers face financial setbacks due to inadequate planning for their wives' deaths (Smith & Zick, 1986). Many older couples have more life insurance for the man than for the wife. Thus, if the wife dies first, her husband may face reduced monthly income plus burial and funeral costs. However, the magnitude of financial loss after spousal death is greater for women than men, as is the risk of poverty (Burkhauser, Butler, & Holden, 1991). Greater economic risk for women is partly due to the longer time they are widowed, a result of sex differences in mortality and remarriage.

Social and emotional support also is threatened by spousal death. Gender socialization theory posits that social disruption will be greater for men than women; because wives are men's main confidants, widowhood results in fewer emotional outlets for men (Babchuck, 1978). Widows have the most friends, formerly married men have the fewest, and men's contacts with friends dissipate more than women's when their spouse dies (Hatch & Bulcroft, 1992).

Early research portrayed widowers as seriously disadvantaged compared to widows in their relationships with grown children (Berardo, 1970). Yet more recent data indicate that children may only slightly favor mothers over fathers (Lee, Willetts, & Seccombe, 1998). Widows receive more aid after a spouse's death than they give (Heinemann, 1983). Contact with children also increases after widowhood (Gibbs, 1985), with offspring serving as primary sources of instrumental support to widows. Indeed, the maintenance of ties to adult offspring after spousal death is predictive of longer survival (Silverstein & Bengtson, 1991).

Gender differences in social and family connections after widowhood may be explained by gender socialization theory. Females are raised to attend to emotions and relationships, so they often become the managers of social and kin relationships (Di Leonardo, 1987) and child rearing. These experiences pay relational dividends for women by fostering connections that provide assistance back to them when needs arise. Men's reliance on women for these tasks may contribute to their reduced social interaction and isolation following widowhood.

The social context of widowhood also shapes different experiences for men and women. Because there are more widows than widowers, integration into the social world may be more difficult for widowers. Living near peers of similar status has social benefits; widows participate in community activities and interact with friends at higher rates when residing in places with a greater ratio of widows to married couples (Hong & Duff, 1994). Compared to nonbereaved peers, widowed persons report greater distress and depression, with widowers appearing most depressed (Lee et al., 1998; Umberson, Wortman, & Kessler, 1992). In most samples, widowhood tends to be more recent for men than for women, possibly accounting for this difference. Further, men exhibit less psychological recovery than women do (Lee et al., 1998). More health problems (Lee et al., 1998), lack of extensive social involvement, and resistance to help seeking (McMullen & Gross, 1983) are more typical of widowers than widows as well.

Perhaps the ultimate concern centering on widowhood, especially for men, is an increased risk of health problems and mortality compared to married individuals (Hu & Goldman, 1990). The buffering effects of marriage on health for men are attributed to their wives' roles as "health brokers" (O'Bryant & Hansson, 1995, p. 445) and to the suppression effect that marriage has on men's risk-taking behavior (e.g., excessive drinking). Financial stress mediates depression for women, but economic pressures are less predictive of depression for men than are domestic demands (Umberson et al., 1992).

Some research suggests that widowhood can foster positive life changes and adaptive behavior. The health of some widows, for example, has improved with this transition (Murrell, Himmelfarb, & Phifer, 1995), perhaps because they are relieved of spousal caregiving, which so many women face when their husband's health fails. Some widows also report enhanced efficacy (Arbuckle & deVries, 1995) and self-confidence (Umberson et al., 1992), maybe due to more opportunities for autonomy and learning new skills (Lund, Caserta, Dimond, & Shaffer, 1989).

Divorce and Aging

For adults entering late adulthood in the first decades of the 21st century, divorce will have a more salient role in their lives than it has for current elderly. Many will have divorced relatively early in marriage and remarried before late life. A growing number, especially women, will divorce and stay single into late life (Bumpass, Sweet, & Martin, 1990). Finally, it is projected that among more recent cohorts, a greater share of persons will divorce during and after midlife (Uhlenberg, Cooney, & Boyd, 1990).

Economic setbacks associated with divorce are immediately apparent and continue over the long term. Among adults aged 50 to 73 who were married at least 15 years, men had a 61% decline in income and women reported a 66% loss (Gander, 1991). More attention has been paid to the economic plight of divorced women than men. In a comparison of divorced and widowed women aged 40 and older, the most serious financial problems were found for women who had been divorced at least 5 years (Uhlenberg et al., 1990). Divorced women were economically disadvantaged, despite their having higher employment rates than widowed and married peers. Economic recovery from divorce is unlikely for women unless they remarry (Hoffman & Duncan, 1988).

In late life, financial security rests on assets and savings as well as current earnings. Divorce is likely to disrupt saving and asset accumulation that couples often do in preparation for old age (Fethke, 1989). There may be a disincentive for couples to save if they anticipate divorce and the likelihood of dividing assets. Older couples that save and invest still may lose wealth by dividing assets such as home equity and losing benefits from insurance policies and pensions. Finally, costs imposed by divorce (e.g., legal fees, costs of living apart) may slow the reaccumulation of wealth. Thus, because of high divorce rates, Fethke (1989) asserted, "In future years, then, there may be a new class of elderly poor, those who have experienced the breakup of their marriage" (p. S127). Fethke's arguments have not been empirically studied.

Divorce also has negative psychological and emotional effects in later life, especially for men. Divorced women report less satisfaction with family life and life in general than married women, although they do not differ from widows (Hyman, 1983). Divorced men report less friendship satisfaction than married and widowed men and less family and life satisfaction than married men (Hyman, 1983). Similarly, among persons divorcing before and after age 50, divorced women were more satisfied with their recent life changes than were men, regardless of age (Hammond & Muller, 1992). Similar gender contrasts were revealed in a recent study of personality change in midlife (Costa, Herbst, McCrae, & Siegler, 2000). Compared to persons who remained married over the 10-year study period, women who divorced felt greater self-empowerment, and men who divorced revealed increased depression and reduced achievement motivation. These findings suggest different costs and rewards to marriage for men and women.

Postdivorce emotional adjustment appears to be mediated by social support. Having a confidant reduces depression (Miller, Smerglia, Gaudet, & Kitson, 1998). Network support is critical too, as greater well-being and a positive self-concept are more characteristic of persons who have stable social networks from pre- to postdivorce (Daniels-Mohring & Berger, 1984). Differences in the availability and use of social support by men and women probably explain some of these gendered outcomes. Indeed, regardless of age at divorce, women are more likely than men to depend on others for emotional support during the divorce process (Hammond & Muller, 1992).

Family support to older adults is seriously affected by divorce. Whether couples dissolved a long-term marriage or ended a shorter marriage years ago when children were young, divorce influences their potential support from offspring. Adult offspring whose parents divorce later in life report less contact with both parents, especially fathers, than do offspring with married parents (Cooney, 1994). Older fathers with a history of divorce are less likely to get support from their adult offspring than are married fathers (Cooney & Uhlenberg, 1990). Women divorcing from long-term (*M* = 28 years) marriages are more likely than men to consider their children as supports (Wright & Maxwell, 1991). Compared to fathers, older mothers receive more advice, services, and financial and emotional support from children. Support from offspring after divorce is especially valuable for middle-aged and older persons because their parents are unlikely to help due to age. Divorces that occurred in the distant past are related to less intergenerational contact in later life (Bulcroft & Bulcroft, 1991b; Cooney & Uhlenberg, 1990). Affective relations also are affected. Adult children of divorced parents felt less loved and listened to by their fathers than did adults with married parents (Webster & Herzog, 1995).

Support issues become increasingly salient when older parents are in poor health, and poorer health status is associated with divorce. Using data from 1950 on for 16 developed nations, Hu and Goldman (1990) documented an association between nonmarital status, in general, and heightened mortality rates for adults. When age is controlled for, being unmarried is a greater mortality threat for men than for women. Divorced men have the highest mortality rates relative to married men (2.5 times greater in the United States).

Few studies of divorce attend to the positive life changes it may present for individuals. Some positive personality changes may accompany divorce (Costa et al., 2000); limited data suggest that experiencing divorce in adulthood may contribute to developing coping skills important to adjustment in late life. O'Bryant and Straw (1991) found that recent widows and previously divorced women demonstrate more self-sufficiency than continuously married women and exhibit better adjustment to widowhood after age 60 than do never-divorced widows. Experiencing marital transitions across the early life course may therefore benefit future cohorts in their adaptation to late life.

The social and economic contexts of older adults who are widowed or divorced in the future may be quite different from those documented over the past 20 years. The continuous involvement of women in paid labor through adulthood, a pattern more characteristic of baby boomers than of cohorts before them, may affect both the economic and social well-being of the divorced. Specifically, the economic status of future divorced women may improve markedly relative to both widowers and their same-sex counterparts today due to their employment patterns. Indeed, Smith and Zick (1986) reported that work history is a stronger predictor than gender of economic stability in widowhood. In studying economic changes over a 5-year period spanning pre- to post-widowhood for both sexes, they found that a continuous work history reduced chances of poverty. Compared to persons with 16 to 34 years in the labor force, those working less than 4 years had a 10-fold greater risk of poverty. Women's labor force participation across adulthood has reduced their economic dependency within marriage over the past several decades (Sorensen & McLanahan, 1987). As a result, the loss of income by older women when they lose a spouse will be less severe than it is today. As more women establish continuous work histories and move into higher-level jobs, their access to benefits and pensions will increase. Between 1990 and 2030, the percentage of older unmarried women with pension income is expected to triple from about 26% to 73% (Zedlewski, Barnes, Burt, McBride, & Meyer, 1990). Reduced adherence to gender-segregated work-family roles among young and middle-aged women today suggests that widows and divorcees in the 21st century will be better situated financially than those today.

Women's greater involvement in paid work may affect men's aging as well, as it has somewhat altered men's roles in the home in the last 30 years. Men contribute more to domestic chores than they did a few decades ago (Schor, 1992). Such role changes may better equip them to deal with domestic chores when they become widowed or divorced. Increased domestic proficiency may reduce stress for older divorced men, just as improved economics will benefit older women's emotional health (Umberson et al., 1992). Being able to better manage domestic tasks may contribute to reduced health problems for older, formerly married men.

Changing social situations also may facilitate the adjustment of divorced persons. Given projections in the growth of never-married and formerly married populations, especially for men, and increasing social acceptance of singlehood and divorce, how older adults feel about being unmarried and their range of social options may change. Growing numbers of unmarried peers may give older men a more comfortable social environment with more extensive male support systems and more formal services.

Finally, in the future, reductions may occur in the health risks associated with being unmarried for men. Hu and Goldman (1990) reported that as countries experience growth in particular nonmarital statuses over time, the relative mortality ratio associated with that particular status declines. The relatively poor health of formerly married and single men may therefore be less of a problem in the future as their numbers increase in the older population.

Never-Married Older Adults

Research has neglected never-married older adults, who make up about 8% of the older population. In the next 40 years, the proportion of never-married men older than 65 is expected to more than double (Wade, 1989).

Never-married elders are heterogeneous in their motivations for remaining single, living situations over time, relationships, and adjustment in later life (Allen, 1989; Rubinstein, 1987). This heterogeneity presents challenges for researchers.

Most empirical evidence suggests that never-married persons are not socially isolated and report high life satisfaction compared to ever-married peers (Stull & Scarisbrick-Hauser, 1989). Although they may report more frequent bouts of loneliness (Rubinstein, 1987), and somewhat lower levels of happiness than married persons (Stull & Scarisbrick-Hauser, 1989), the never-married appear better adjusted than widowed and divorced persons (Rubinstein, 1987; Stull & Scarisbrick-Hauser, 1989).

Although never-married persons may have relatively low levels of family contacts and support in later life, because most have no children (Choi, 1996), they tend to report

extensive friendship ties that compare favorably to those of ever-married persons (Babchuck, 1978; Choi, 1996; Stull & Scarisbrick-Hauser, 1989). Their social lives include more salient relationships with siblings; in late life, they are more likely than divorced persons to reside with relatives, especially siblings (Choi, 1996; Stull & Scarisbrick-Hauser, 1989). Such arrangements shelter older never-married persons from some of the drawbacks of living alone, like a greater risk of institutionalization (Stull & Scarisbrick-Hauser, 1989). Although co-resident siblings or friends may give older never-married persons support and companionship, their age similarity places them at risk for experiencing functional limitations at about the same time. Thus, the substitution value of friends and siblings for offspring may weaken over time.

Gender differences in the life experiences of single older adults have not been widely studied but are important to address given the projected increases in singlehood for men. Singlehood may be easier to adjust to for men than for women because society places fewer social prohibitions on single men. For example, it is more acceptable for men than women to participate in public nightlife alone, and men have a larger field of eligible partners for dating than do women. However, the larger number of older, single women may provide a wider support system for never-married women than it does for men. Hong and Duff's (1994) research on widows points to the importance of this factor for socialization purposes.

Issues likely to influence the social and psychological adjustment of older never-married persons that should bear investigation are their relational careers and transitions across adulthood. Although they are not at risk for losing a spouse, they still will encounter important relationship losses and transitions if they have significant attachments to others, such as parents, siblings, and special friends (Rubinstein, 1987). In the future, some may have had long-term cohabiting relationships. Whether these ties assume a unique character when one is unmarried and how the loss of these relationships is handled by older never-married persons are unknown.

Questions about the positive adaptation and developmental strengths gained from never marrying require attention as well. Regardless of whether lifetime singlehood was chosen or was the result of factors beyond control (e.g., limited marriage market, family demands, poor health), individuals who do not marry are likely to adapt to the situation and establish strengths as single persons (e.g., self-sufficiency, reliable networks). Their lives may therefore be characterized by greater continuity (e.g., in terms of relationships, work histories) than those of married persons (Choi, 1996; Stull & Scarisbrick-Hauser, 1989), which could contribute to fewer adaptation problems in late life. The higher educational attainment, more continuous work history, and greater access to pensions of single women illustrate this. Such assets give single women a financial advantage over formerly married women in late life (Choi, 1996), with possible effects on housing and lifestyle choices, health and use of health care, and life satisfaction.

How singlehood is experienced and its meaning in later life may change in the 21st century. Although single women are generally better off financially than formerly married persons (Choi, 1996), women's increasingly higher education and better jobs should mean greater financial security in later life for future cohorts of single women compared to single women today. Nonfamilial support networks are likely to be larger, as more women in the future will be either never married or formerly married. Family support systems may be more extensive as well, as baby boomers entering old age in the 21st century will have more

siblings, and more singles will have children than earlier cohorts as a result of increases in nonmarital childbearing in the last 50 years. Rates of nonmarital childbearing for women ages 25 to 34 today are three times greater than they were at comparable ages for women who are now ages 75 to 84 (Spain & Bianchi, 1996). These possible variations in support systems could affect emotional and material well-being for never-married elders in the future.

Finally, it is important to consider that the meaning of being never married may also change in the future. Studies suggest that many elders today who never married did so by default, in response to family demands and missed opportunities (Allen, 1989). More single persons today, however, are likely to say that they *chose* this status, and social acceptance of this choice is probably greater today as well. Thus, the experience of being single may be even more positive for older adults in the future than today because they will face less social stigma and may feel a greater sense of control over how their lives have taken shape.

Gay Men and Lesbians in the Aging Population

The few systematic, representative studies regarding issues of aging among older gay and lesbian adults (Boxer, 1997) focus mostly on social support and adjustment. These studies challenge the stereotype of older gay males and lesbians as lonely, depressed, and devoid of close contacts (Friend, 1990). The support received by older homosexuals is comparable to that of heterosexuals, although the composition of their support groups differ (Berger & Kelly, 1986). Older gays and lesbians receive more support from their families of choice (Dorfman et al., 1995), which are composed of selected relatives, close friends, and current and/or former lovers (Boxer, 1997).

Older gay males and lesbians report levels of adjustment and morale similar to those reported by older heterosexuals (Cohler, Galatzer-Levy, & Hostetler, 2000). Homosexuals also cite similar concerns regarding growing older, such as potential health and financial problems and loneliness (Quam & Whitford, 1992). The adjustment of elderly gay males and lesbians probably has been shaped by the sociohistorical context in which they came of age. The heterosexism and homophobia that existed during most of their adulthoods and the lack of role models probably have affected them. Many older gays and lesbians concealed their sexual orientation in order to conform, fearing losses of job, family, and friends (Berger & Kelly, 1986; Friend, 1990), and some may even have married to hide their homosexuality.

Although aging gay men and lesbians today appear generally well adjusted, adjustment of gays and lesbians in the 21st century raises several possibilities. Because cohorts are moving through adulthood in a societal context that is more accepting of homosexuality and that presents fewer obstacles to maintaining a gay or lesbian identity, adjustment may be better for future cohorts of older gays and lesbians. Fewer persons may feel forced to conceal their sexual orientation and live their lives closeted from family, friends, and coworkers. Participation in public commitment ceremonies and recognized unions and, for some, access to same-sex partner benefits are experiences unavailable to earlier cohorts that may ultimately affect late-life well-being (Hostetler & Cohler, 1997). Along with new opportunities, however, current cohorts of gay and lesbian adults are faced with new challenges that older counterparts may have largely avoided, such as AIDS. The spread of AIDS may have led to different lifestyle choices and approaches to partnering and may even have affected social support. Middle-aged gay males have had fewer sexual partners than

older gay males (Deenen, Gijs, & van Naerssen, 1994), and members of younger cohorts may have lost more friends and partners to AIDS compared to today's elders, so they may experience less social support as they grow older (Boxer, 1997).

Dating and Nonmarital Cohabitation

Although the phenomenon is generally ignored by researchers, many unattached older adults are involved in intimate nonmarital relationships. This may be true for men especially, who date more in midlife and continue to date longer than women (Bulcroft & Bulcroft, 1991a).

Companionship is the main incentive for older men and women who date. Yet when asked about the rewards they derive from dating, men are more likely than women to note payoffs in intimacy and emotional support, and women are more likely to identify status rewards (Bulcroft & O'Connor, 1986). Such differences may reflect the unique gender socialization of today's older cohorts, with men placing greater stock in women to fulfill their emotional needs (Babchuck, 1978) and women turning to men for instrumental support and social standing. In the future, what older men and women value about dating may be less distinct as their societal roles become less differentiated. In addition, older adults may date more in the future because fewer of them will have experienced one long-term marriage across adulthood. The greater diversity of relationship and marital experiences in adulthood may help older persons feel more comfortable with dating. Similarly, future elderly may be less likely than older persons today to have had only one sexual partner in their lifetime, as a result of higher incidences of premarital sex, cohabitation, and divorce. Thus, older adults in the future may be more open to and comfortable with forming intimate sexual relationships. Increased recognition within society that older adults have sexual interests and can be sexually active also may contribute to such changes.

Nonmarital cohabitation also may become a more common outlet for achieving intimacy among older adults in the future, given that its prevalence in the general population has sky-rocketed in the past 30 years. Unfortunately, empirical evidence on cohabitation among older adults is limited. Using data from the 1960 and 1990 U.S. censuses, Chevan (1996) estimated that in 1990 there were 407,000 cohabitors aged 60 or older (about 2.4% of unmarried elders), compared to just 9,600 in 1960. However, estimates of cohabitation in later life require more validation. The figures cited here are offered to demonstrate growth in the phenomenon of later-life cohabitation rather than to serve as valid estimates.

We have no research base on cohabiting unions in later life. Quite possibly, cohabiting in later life may be preferable to marriage for some older adults (and their families), especially if the elders have been married before and if offspring believe their own inheritance is safer if an elderly parent cohabits rather than remarries.

Despite relatively low rates of cohabitation for older adults today, chances are good that these numbers will climb in the future. Not only does the baby boom cohort have a history of cohabiting across adulthood, but rates also are notably high (11% currently cohabiting) for persons born 1931 to 1950, who were ages 40 to 59 in 1990 (Chevan, 1996). Cohabitation rates also are significantly higher among persons who have been previously married (Bumpass, Sweet, & Cherlin, 1991).

FUTURE RESEARCH ON
LATER-LIFE RELATIONSHIPS

We contend that relationship experiences and options for older adults will be increasingly diverse in the future. Furthermore, the aged population in the United States will become considerably more heterogeneous in terms of racial and ethnic makeup. These changes demand that research on later-life intimacy and relationships move beyond examination of primarily white samples to attend more carefully to between-group variations. This wider focus should address how various later-life relationship experiences may differ on the basis of sociodemographic characteristics, as well as on the basis of earlier life experiences and events, as discussed in this chapter.

In studying older adults in partnered relationships, a few other conceptual and methodological shifts are called for. One development that has characterized research on younger couples is increased use of methods other than, or in addition to, self-reports. Observational methods, for example, are becoming increasingly popular in studies of couple dynamics. Yet they have not been used in work on older couples. More attention also should be directed to studying dyads in later life, attending to the coordination of linked lives, as life course scholars suggest. This need is evident in studying couples' retirement decisions and also applies to how couples coordinate the potential physical care needs of both spouses.

Whether older adults are partnered or alone, greater understanding of their well-being will also come from considering their relationship careers across adulthood rather than focusing only on their current status. Considering not only the duration of particular statuses but also their sequencing (e.g., divorce or widowhood before remarriage) will surely lend insight into individuals' adjustment to various transitions as well as their later-life well-being.

Although many critical variables can be assessed with retrospective methods, more longitudinal studies are needed. Such designs lend themselves to assessing continuity and discontinuity over time (e.g., interaction patterns in long-term marriages, adjustment to divorce), as well as providing data to evaluate selection effects. This is important as researchers study the direction of effects between economic disadvantage and divorce, for example, and make policy and intervention suggestions.

In sum, the 21st century will present a wider variety of relationship situations for older adults as a result of sociohistorical changes in recent decades. In an effort to conduct meaningful and relevant work, we must expand our thinking to include the new issues that emerge as a result of these changes. Similarly, our methods will have to change to sensitively accommodate the increasingly heterogeneous population of older adults and their varied life experiences.

REFERENCES

Alford-Cooper, F. (1998). *For keeps: Marriages that last a lifetime.* Armonk, NY: Sharpe.

Allen, K. (1989). *Single women/family ties.* Newbury Park, CA: Sage.

Arbuckle, N. W., & deVries, B. (1995). The long-term effects of later life spousal and parental bereavement on personal functioning. *Gerontologist, 35,* 637–647.

Babchuck, N. (1978). Aging and primary relations. *International Journal of Aging and Human Development, 9,* 137–151.

Berardo, F. (1970). Survivorship and social isolation: The case of the aged widower. *Family Coordinator, 19,* 11–15.

Berger, R. M., & Kelly, J. J. (1986). Working with homosexuals of the older population. *Social Casework, 67,* 203–210.

Bograd, R., & Spilka, B. (1996). Self-disclosure and marital satisfaction in mid-life and late-life remarriages. *International Journal of Aging and Human Development, 42,* 161–172.

Boxer, A. M. (1997). Gay, lesbian, and bisexual aging into the twenty-first century: An overview and introduction. *Journal of Gay, Lesbian, and Bisexual Identity, 2*(3/4), 187–197.

Brubaker, T. (1985). *Later life families.* Newbury Park, CA: Sage.

Buchmann, M. (1989). *The script of life in modern society.* Chicago: University of Chicago Press.

Bulcroft, R. A., & Bulcroft, K. A. (1991a). The nature and functions of dating in later life. *Research on Aging, 13,* 244–260.

Bulcroft, K. A., & Bulcroft, R. A. (1991b). The timing of divorce: Effects on parent-child relationships in later life. *Research on Aging, 13,* 226–243.

Bulcroft, K., & O'Connor, M. (1986). The importance of dating relationships on quality of life for older persons. *Family Relations, 35,* 397–401.

Bumpass, L., Sweet, J., & Cherlin, A. (1991). The role of cohabitation in declining rates of marriage. *Journal of Marriage and the Family, 53,* 913–927.

Bumpass, L., Sweet, J., & Martin, T. C. (1990). Changing patterns of remarriage. *Journal of Marriage and the Family, 52,* 747–756.

Burkhauser, R. V., Butler, J. S., & Holden, K. C. (1991). How the death of a spouse affects economic well-being after retirement: A hazard model approach. *Social Science Quarterly, 72,* 504–519.

Burks, V., Lund, D. A., Gregg, C. H., & Bluhm, H. P. (1988). Bereavement and remarriage for older adults. *Death Studies, 12,* 51–60.

Carey, R. G. (1979). Weathering widowhood: Problems and adjustment of the widowed during the first year. *Omega: The Journal of Death and Dying, 10,* 163–174.

Carstensen, L. L., Gottman, J. M., & Levenson, R. W. (1995). Emotional behavior in long-term marriage. *Psychology and Aging, 10,* 140–149.

Chevan, A. (1996). As cheaply as one: Cohabitation in the older population. *Journal of Marriage and the Family, 58,* 656–667.

Choi, N. K. (1996). The never-married divorced elderly: Comparison of economic and health status, social support, and living arrangement. *Journal of Gerontological Social Work, 26(1/2),* 3–25.

Cohler, B. J., Galatzer-Levy, R., & Hostetler, A. J. (2000). Gay and lesbian lives across the adult years. In B. J. Cohler & R. Galatzer-Levy (Eds.), *The course of gay and lesbian lives: Social and psychoanalytic perspectives* (pp. 193–251). Chicago: University of Chicago Press.

Cooney, T. M. (1994). Young adults' relations with parents: The influence of recent parental divorce. *Journal of Marriage and the Family, 56,* 45–56.

Cooney, T. M., & Uhlenberg, P. (1990). The role of divorce in men's relations with their adult children after mid-life. *Journal of Marriage and the Family, 52,* 677–688.

Costa, P. T., Herbst, J. H., McCrae, R. R., & Siegler, I. C. (2000). Personality at midlife: Stability, intrinsic maturation, and response to life events. *Assessment, 7,* 365–378.

Daniels-Mohring, D., & Berger, M. (1984). Social network changes and the adjustment to divorce. *Journal of Divorce, 8(1),* 17–32.

Deenen, A., Gijs, L., & van Naerssen., L. X. (1994). Thirty-five years of research into gay relationships. *Journal of Psychology and Human Sexuality, 7(4),* 19–39.

Di Leonardo, M. (1987). The female world of cards and holidays: Women, families, and the work of kinship. *Journal of Women in Culture and Society, 12,* 440–453.

Dorfman, R., Walters, K., Burke, P., Hardin, L., Karanik, T., Raphael, J., & Silverstein, E. (1995). Old, sad and alone: The myth of the aging homosexual. *Journal of Gerontological Social Work, 24,* 29–44.

Fethke, C. (1989). Life-cycle models of savings and the effect of timing of divorce on economic well-being. *Journal of Gerontology, 55,* S121–S128.

Friend, R. A. (1990). Older lesbian and gay people: A theory of successful aging. *Journal of Homosexuality, 23,* 99–118.

Gander, A. M. (1991). Economics and well-being of older divorced persons. *Journal of Women and Aging, 3,* 37–57.

Gentry, M., & Shulman, A. D. (1988). Remarriage as a coping response for widowhood. *Psychology and Aging, 3,* 191–196.

Gibbs, J. (1985). Family relations of the older widow: Their location and importance for her social life. In W. Peterson & J. Quadagno (Eds.), *Social bonds in later life* (pp. 91–114). Beverly Hills, CA: Sage.

Goodman, C. (1999). Intimacy and autonomy in long term marriage. *Journal of Gerontological Social Work, 32,* 83–97.

Hammond, R. J., & Muller, G. O. (1992). The late-life divorced: Another look. *Journal of Divorce and Remarriage, 17,* 135–150.

Hatch, L. R. (2000). *Beyond gender differences.* Amityville, NY: Baywood.

Hatch, L. R., & Bulcroft, K. (1992). Contact with friends in later life: Disentangling the effects of gender and marital status. *Journal of Marriage and the Family, 54,* 222–232.

Heinemann, G. D. (1983). Family involvement and support for widowed persons. In T. H. Brubaker (Ed.), *Family relationships in late life* (pp. 127–148). Beverly Hills, CA: Sage.

Hoffman, S. D., & Duncan, G. J. (1988). What are the economic consequences of divorce? *Demography, 25*, 641–645.

Hong, L. K., & Duff, R. W. (1994). Widows in retirement communities: The social context of subjective well-being. *Gerontologist, 34*, 347–352.

Hostetler, A. J., & Cohler, B. J. (1997). Partnership, singlehood, and the lesbian, and gay Life course: A study in Chicago. *Journal of Gay, Lesbian, and Bisexual Identity, 2*, 199–230.

Hu, Y., & Goldman, N. (1990). Mortality differentials by marital status: An international comparison. *Demography, 27*, 233–250.

Hyman, H. H. (1983). *Of time and widowhood.* Durham, NC: Duke University Press.

Kimmel, D. C. (1990). *Adulthood and aging.* New York: John Wiley.

Kinsey, A., Pomeroy, W., & Martin, C. (1948). *Sexual behavior in the human male.* Philadelphia: W. B. Saunders.

Kinsey, A., Pomeroy, W., & Martin, C. (1953). *Sexual behavior in the human female.* Philadelphia: W. B. Saunders.

Lee, G. R., & Shehan, C. L. (1989). Retirement and marital satisfaction. *Journal of Gerontology, 44*, S226–S230.

Lee, G. R., Willetts, M. C., & Seccombe, K. (1998). Widowhood and depression. *Research on Aging, 20*, 611–630.

Lund, D. A., Caserta, M. S., Dimond, M. F., & Shaffer, S. K. (1989). Competencies, tasks of daily living, and adjustments to spousal bereavement in later life. In D. Lund (Ed.), *Older bereaved spouses: Research with practical applications* (pp. 135–152). New York: Hemisphere.

Masters, W., & Johnson, V. (1982). *Human sexuality.* Boston: Little, Brown.

McMullen, P. A., & Gross, A. E. (1983). Sex differences, sex roles, and health-related help-seeking. In J. D. Fisher, A. Nadler, & B. M. Depaulo (Eds.), *New directions in helping* (Vol. 2). New York: Academic Press.

Miller, N. B., Smerglia, V. L., Gaudet, D. S., & Kitson, G. C. (1998). Stressful life events, social support, and the distress of widowed and divorced women. *Journal of Family Issues, 19*, 181–203.

Murrell, S. A., Himmelfarb, S., & Phifer, J. F. (1995). Effects of bereavement/loss and pre-event status on subsequent physical health in older adults. In J. Hendricks (Ed.), *Health and health care utilization in later life* (pp. 159–177). Amityville, NY: Baywood.

Neugarten, B. L. (1968). *Middle age and aging.* Chicago: University of Chicago Press.

Neugarten, B. L. (1988). The aging society and my academic life. In M. W. Riley (Ed.), *Sociological lives* (pp. 91–106). Newbury Park, CA: Sage.

O'Bryant, S., & Hansson, R. (1995). Widowhood. In R. Blieszner & V. H. Bedford (Eds.), *Handbook of aging and the family* (pp. 440–458). Westport, CT: Greenwood.

O'Bryant, S. L., & Straw, L. B. (1991). Relationship of previous divorce and previous widowhood to older women's adjustment to recent widowhood. *Journal of Divorce and Remarriage, 15*, 46–67.

Quam, J. K., & Whitford, G. S. (1992). Adaptation and age-related expectations of older gay and lesbian adults. *Gerontologist, 32*, 367–374.

Rubinstein, R. L. (1987). Never married elderly as a social type: Re-evaluating some images. *Gerontologist, 27*, 108–113.

Schoen, R., & Weinick, R. M. (1993). The slowing metabolism of marriage: Figures from 1988 U.S. marital status life tables. *Demography, 30*, 737–746.

Schor, J. B. (1992). *The overworked American.* New York: Basic Books.

Scott, J. P. (1997). Family relationships of midlife and older women. In J. M. Coyle (Ed.), *Handbook on women and aging* (pp. 367–384). Westport, CT: Greenwood.

Silverstein, M., & Bengtson, V. (1991). Do close parent-child relations reduce the mortality risk of older parents? *Journal of Health and Social Behavior, 32,* 382–395.

Smith, K. R., & Zick, C. D. (1986). The incidence of poverty among the recently widowed: Mediating factors in the life course. *Journal of Marriage and the Family, 48,* 619–630.

Sorensen, A., & McLanahan, S. (1987). Married women's economic dependency, 1940–1980. *American Journal of Sociology, 93,* 659–687.

Spain, D., & Bianchi, S. M. (1996). *Balancing act.* New York: Russell Sage Foundation.

Starr, B., & Weiner, M. (1981). *The Starr-Weiner report on sex and sexuality in the mature years.* New York: McGraw-Hill.

Stull, D. E., & Scarisbrick-Hauser, A. (1989). Never-married elderly: A reassessment with implications for long-term care policy. *Research on Aging, 11,* 124–139.

Treas, J. (1995). Older Americans in the 1990s and beyond. *Population Bulletin, 50,* 1–47.

Tryban, G. M. (1985). Effects of work and retirement within long-term marital relationships. *Lifestyles, 7,* 207–223.

Uhlenberg, P. (1990, October). *Implications of increasing divorce for the elderly.* Paper presented at the United Nations International Conference on Aging Populations in the Context of the Family, Kitakyushu, Japan.

Uhlenberg, P., Cooney, T., & Boyd, R. (1990). Divorce for women after midlife. *Journal of Gerontology, 45,* S3–S11.

Umberson, D., Wortman, C. B., & Kessler, R. C. (1992). Widowhood and depression: Explaining long-term gender differences in vulnerability. *Journal of Health and Social Behavior, 33,* 10–24.

U.S. Bureau of the Census. (1999). *Statistical abstract of the United States: 1999.* Washington, DC: Author.

Wade, A. (1989). *Social Security area population projections, 1989* (Actuarial Study No. 105). Washington, DC: Government Printing Office.

Webster, P. S., & Herzog, A. R. (1995). Effects of parental divorce and memories of family problems on relationships between adult children and their parents. *Journal of Gerontology: Social Sciences, 50,* S24–S34.

Wright, C. L., & Maxwell, J. W. (1991). Social support during adjustment to later-life divorce: How adult children help parents. *Journal of Divorce and Remarriage, 15,* 21–48.

Zedlewski, S. R., Barnes, R. O., Burt, M. R., McBride, T. D., & Meyer, J. A. (1990). *The needs of the elderly in the 21st century.* Washington, DC: Urban Institute Press.

Part III

GENDER ISSUES
IN CONTEMPORARY
FAMILIES

Jobs, Marriage, and Parenting
Working It Out in Dual-Earner Families

MAUREEN PERRY-JENKINS AND ELIZABETH TURNER

"Each marriage bears the footprints of economic and cultural trends which originate far outside the marriage" (Hochschild, 1989, p. 11). Dual-earner marriages, in particular, have emerged from, and borne the costs and benefits of, the dramatic social and economic changes that have occurred over the past half-century. In particular, one of the most striking and consistent demographic changes over the past 30 years has been the steady and linear upward trend in women's labor force participation (Cohen & Bianchi, 1999). From a historical perspective, the structures and functions of families in the United States are far different today than they were at the beginning of the 20th century. In 1920, 75% of working households were composed of single-earner, married couples, and dual-earner, married households made up only approximately 9% of working families. In less than a century, those statistics have shifted dramatically. The latest data from the Bureau of Labor Statistics (2001) indicate that 63.2% of all married couples with children under 18 are dual earners, and 55.9% of all married couples with children under 6 are dual earners, whereas families in which only the husband works constitute only 19.4% of all married-couple families.

As dual-earner families became the normative household type over the 20th century, the question of how families cope with and negotiate new work and family role responsibilities became the topic of much research and scholarly debate. Although some family scholars suggest that we are currently in a stalled revolution where we lack new models and social arrangements to support the dual-earner lifestyle (Hochschild, 1989), others point to families who are successfully creating and managing their dual-earner arrangements (Deutsch, 1999). Scholars from a variety of disciplines, incorporating multiple theoretical perspectives and using a wide range of methodological approaches, have focused much attention on dual-earner families. Perhaps the most important revelation to emerge from this effort is that there appears to be no one, uniform experience for couples attempting to "have it all," namely, jobs, a relationship, and children. The first goal of this chapter is to review the theoretical approaches that have been used to study dual-earner families and to provide a summary of the key findings linking work and family life in dual-earner households. Building on this knowledge base, the second goal of this chapter is to point to new directions where research on dual-earner families could go in our efforts to better understand how social contexts differentially shape the work and family processes that occur within dual-earner families.

THEORETICAL APPROACHES TO THE STUDY OF DUAL-EARNER FAMILIES

The study of dual-earner families arose in direct response to women's dramatic increase in labor force participation. In a review of the work-family literature in the 1990s, Perry-Jenkins, Repetti, and Crouter (2000) highlighted four broad conceptual approaches that have guided this field of study. The first approach, one that informed much of the early research on dual-earner families, comes primarily from developmental psychology and is most accurately referred to as the *maternal employment* literature. In over six decades of research, scholars have examined the effects of maternal employment on children's development. Although this approach is rich in its attention to developmental outcomes for adults and children, its conceptualization of work is limited. In this early work, maternal and child outcomes were often compared in

single-earner versus dual-earner households, with the overwhelming conclusion being that women's employment alone is unrelated to either positive or negative developmental outcomes for children (Harvey, 1999). From an ecological perspective, this practice of comparing different groups of individuals, such as dual- and single-earner couples, on some psychological or relational outcome is referred to as the *social address model* (Bronfenbrenner & Crouter, 1983). As Bronfenbrenner and Crouter noted, social address approaches, which focus only on group comparisons, provide no insight into the processes that link work and family. Thus, the conclusion that mothers' work hours are unrelated to children's developmental outcomes does not mean that employment is unimportant or unrelated to family life; rather, it means that conditions of work, such as schedules, satisfaction, autonomy, support, and complexity, are more significant indicators of individual and family outcomes than the simple fact of work.

It should be noted that, historically, the maternal employment literature primarily examined the effects of *mothers'* work hours on children's social, emotional, and cognitive development, although the majority of working mothers being studied at the time lived in dual-earner households with employed spouses. This early work rested on the assumption that it was women's employment and men's *unemployment* that were the causes of most concern for children's development. As the field developed, fathers' employment began to receive greater attention in this literature (Marsiglio, Amato, & Day, 2000), and more attention was paid to issues of the temporal patterns of parents' employment, such as shift work and seasonal work, that could, in turn, affect the temporal rhythms of family life (Perry-Jenkins et al., 2000).

The second theoretical approach that has been used to explore the effects of employment on family life stems from sociology and focuses much greater attention on characteristics of employment; it is referred to as the *work socialization perspective*. Specifically, scholars in this tradition examine how conditions of employment, such as autonomy and job complexity, socialize workers' values, which, in turn, spill over into family life (Kohn, 1995; Kohn & Schooler, 1982). Findings have revealed, for example, that mothers who take on jobs low in complexity show decrements over time in the quality of home environments they provide their children (Menaghan & Parcel, 1995), whereas increases in mothers' job complexity have been linked to enhanced reading scores for children (Parcel & Menaghan, 1994b).

A third approach to the study of work-family connections is the *occupational stress* literature, with roots in both clinical and health psychology, which explores how short- and long-term stresses at work are related to employee well-being and family relationships. One of the most important findings to emerge from this line of research points to the role of individuals' assessments and internal responses to workplace stressors as an important mediator linking workplace conditions to mental health (Perry-Jenkins et al., 2000). Especially relevant for dual-earner families are studies that explore crossover effects, whereby the work experiences of one spouse affect the well-being of his or her partner.

Finally, the *multiple-roles* literature, which stems from both social psychology and sociology, focuses on how individuals manage the roles of parent, spouse, and worker and the consequences of this balance for health and family relationships. Although debate has arisen as to whether multiple roles compromise or enhance mental health and family relationships, it appears that an important third factor to consider is workers' perceptions of the quality of each role. Moreover, the multiple-roles literature has

addressed the interactive nature of roles whereby a positive marital relationship may serve as a buffer against stressful and negative work experiences (Barnett, Marshall, & Pleck, 1992; Repetti, 1992).

All of these traditions have examined the effects of work on family life, and in a few cases family effects on work, and each approach has its own strengths and weaknesses. When findings from these different research traditions are examined in their totality, it is clear that much has been learned about how work shapes the lives of workers and their families. What has been missing, however, from much of the theoretical literature on the work-family interface is attention to the role of sociocultural contexts as they shape work-family processes. From an ecological perspective, Bronfenbrenner (1986) proposed that we must carefully attend not only to aspects of social context, such as race, class, gender, and family structure, but to the idea that family processes may differ across contexts and ultimately hold different consequences for human development. In the dual-earner literature, there is still a paucity of studies that explore how aspects of race and ethnicity, social class, and gender (e.g., same-sex households) may affect the type of work-family processes that occur within families. Thus, in the following review of research on dual-earner families, it will be important to keep a critical eye on what we have learned thus far and the extent to which our research has been sensitive to the ways in which race/ethnicity, social class, and gender may moderate relationships between work experiences, workers' well-being, and their family relationships.

REVIEW OF KEY RESEARCH FINDINGS

The question of how the dual-earner lifestyle shapes the lives of individual family members and their relationships has been the focus of much empirical research. Scholars have explored the relationships among spouses' employment and individuals' mental health, their marital relationships, parent-child relationships, and children's development. The following review will highlight the key findings in each of these areas.

Women's and Men's Mental Health in Dual-Earner Families

An implicit assumption guiding the early research on women's employment was that managing two jobs while maintaining a marriage and family life takes both a psychological and a physical toll on the adults involved in this endeavor. Contrary to expectation, however, there is little empirical evidence of any direct negative effects of paid employment on women's or men's mental health (Steil, 1997). Married men, whether their wife is employed or unemployed, report significantly lower levels of psychopathology than unmarried men (Steil, 1997). For wives, in general, employment appears to enhance their psychological well-being, even across race (Guarnaccia, Angel, & Worobey, 1991) and social class (Ferree, 1976; Scarr, Phillips, & McCartney, 1989). Two competing hypotheses have been advanced linking multiple roles (e.g., worker, spouse, parent) to psychological well-being (Hyde, DeLamater, & Hewitt, 1998). The scarcity hypothesis holds that there is only limited time to fulfill the responsibilities of multiple roles and that as the demands for time become too high in dual-earner households, inter-role conflict will occur. This conflict will, in turn, lead to negative mental health outcomes for both spouses (Baruch, Biener, & Barnett, 1987; Voydanoff, 1987), especially for women working full time (Rogers, 1996). In contrast, the enhancement hypothesis posits that holding multiple roles enhances psychological functioning (Baruch et al., 1987).

Theorists holding this view posit that success in one role can buffer disappointment or failure in another, that the diversity of experiences across roles enhances one's perspective on life, and, finally, that the economic contribution of two workers decreases financial strain. To date, the empirical findings, at least in terms of mental health outcomes, support the enhancement hypothesis. Specifically, a number of studies have found that women who are employed or who increase their labor force participation report lower distress than their unemployed counterparts (Glass & Fujimoto, 1994; Wethington & Kessler, 1989).

Research indicates, however, that the positive effects of employment accrue differentially on the basis of a number of occupational conditions. Specifically, time demands, flexibility, pressure, lack of control, and unsupportive supervisors and/or co-workers can all shape employees' experiences of their jobs and their well-being. Not surprisingly, these conditions vary by social class, suggesting that those employed in hourly, unskilled, or service occupations are most at risk for bearing the negative effects of employment. Research indicates, however, that how job characteristics are interpreted and experienced by the worker is a key mediator variable linking work conditions to mental health.

For example, the chronic stress transfer literature indicates that it is not objective job characteristics that are related to worker well-being but rather feelings of job stress that have been related to self-reports of depression, which, in turn, have been linked to poorer marital relations (Barling & MacEwen, 1992; Sears & Galambos, 1992). Moreover, a number of studies have found that employees who experience more work-family overload also report greater emotional distress (Gerstel & Gallagher, 1993; Guelzow, Bird, & Koball, 1991; Paden & Buehler, 1995). Some research with dual-earner couples has attempted to examine crossover effects where one partner's job experiences are related to the other partner's mental health. For example, some studies have linked overload and pressure at work reported by one spouse to feelings of overload and depression reported by his or her partner (Crouter, Bumpus, Maguire, & McHale, 1999; Wortman, Biernat, & Lang, 1991), whereas others have not detected any crossover effects (Sears & Galambos, 1992). Future research is needed to understand for whom and under what conditions one spouse's job has the greatest impact on his or her partner's mental health.

An implicit assumption in much of the dual-earner literature is that the cumulative, long-term effects of the dual-earner lifestyle will eventually compromise the quality of spouses' mental health and family relationships. Few studies, however, have explicitly examined these relationships longitudinally. In an exception, Barnett, Raudenbush, Brennan, Pleck, and Marshall (1995) examined how changes in job quality and marital experiences were related to change in psychological distress in a sample of white, middle-class dual-earner couples. Findings revealed that for both husbands and wives, when job quality decreased, distress increased. The relation between marital change and distress differed by gender, revealing that if the marital relationship deteriorated over time, women were likely to experience greater psychological distress than men. These findings are important for two reasons. First, the researchers move past static, cross-sectional models to explore the inherently dynamic nature of work and family life. Second, the use of hierarchical linear modeling, with its capacity to explore the dependency between spouses' reports, reflects the fact that when individuals live together one spouse's sense of distress or marital harmony influences the other spouse's. Future research must continue to explore this important and inherent dependency in couple's lives.

Dual-Earner Lifestyle and the Marital Relationship

The implications of the dual-earner lifestyle for couples' marital relations have received the most attention in the work-family literature. Rogers (1996) tested the scarcity and enhancement hypotheses described above in explaining marital happiness and conflict. Findings supporting the scarcity hypothesis revealed that full-time employed mothers with high family demands (i.e., more children) reported less marital happiness and more marital conflict. For mother-stepfather families, however, as family demands increased, mothers' full-time employment was associated with greater marital happiness and lower marital conflict. In a more recent study, the reciprocal effects of income and marital quality were examined (Rogers, 1999). It was found that increases in marital discord were associated with increases in wives' income, specifically by increasing the likelihood that nonemployed wives would enter the labor force.

In a rare look at the sex lives of dual-earner couples, Hyde et al. (1998) examined sexual satisfaction, frequency of intercourse, and decreased sexual desire for a sample of dual- and single-earner couples across the transition to parenthood. The authors reported no support for the scarcity hypothesis because sexual satisfaction and activity did not suffer in dual-earner families. Their findings did reveal that role quality, especially job role quality, was related to sexual satisfaction. Though some support has emerged for a direct link between work and marital quality, a more fruitful line of analysis has examined processes whereby work conditions are related to perceptions of job quality or mental health that, in turn, affect the marriage.

In fact, the literature that has explored linkages between work and marriage has uncovered few strong and consistent direct links between work status and marital outcomes (Hyde et al., 1998); rather, it appears that the variable of spouses' perceptions of the quality of their roles is the important mediator linking work roles to marital quality. Thus, the division of unpaid work in the home, or the home-caretaker role, becomes a major point of contention among many dual-earner couples. Hochschild (1989) highlighted how women's movement into the workforce has challenged couples to examine assumptions regarding the division of unpaid work in the home, specifically household chores and child care. Although the majority of dual-earner couples believe in the ideology of fairness in sharing paid and unpaid work, in the reality of day-to-day life, equality in family work is not the norm (Coltrane, 2000; see also Chapter 10 of this book).

Although questions concerning how women's employment in dual-earner families is related to the division of household and child care tasks and, in turn, shapes perceptions of marriage have been addressed by many researchers (Coltrane, 2000; Spitze, 1988), the answers remain ambiguous. Women continue to perform the lion's share of family work, though men's participation has increased slightly over the past few decades (Coltrane, 2000; see also Chapter 10 of this book). The division of unpaid labor in dual-earner families has been linked to partners' mental health and marital relationships. Specifically, the more housework is shared, the less depression wives report (Ross, Mirowsky, & Huber, 1983) and the higher marital quality and well-being wives report (Barnett & Baruch, 1987). These same relationships examined for husbands reveal less clear results. Researchers have found that shared housework is unrelated to men's depression (Ross et al., 1983) but is positively related to enhanced well-being (Pleck, 1985).

Although the aforementioned relationships between the division of unpaid labor and spouses' mental health and marital relationships have been found, the findings, though significant, are often not strong or consistent. One of the most surprising findings in the division-of-labor literature is that although women, on average, consistently perform more household chores than men, only a minority of women view this unequal division of labor as unfair (Thompson & Walker, 1989). This finding even holds up cross-culturally, where Zuo and Bian (2001) found that for a sample of dual-earner Chinese couples, the actual division of labor was largely unrelated to perceptions of fairness in the relationship. These studies have led family scholars to propose that beliefs about the fairness of household labor may be as, or even more, critical in relation to marital quality than the relative or absolute amounts of household chores completed (Blair & Johnson, 1992; Thompson, 1991; Wilkie, Ferree, & Ratcliff, 1998). In testing this hypothesis, Wilkie et al. (1998) found that the division of labor affects marital satisfaction mainly through perceptions of fairness. Similarly, Blair (1993) reported that the strongest predictor of both husbands' and wives' perceptions of marital conflict was *wives'* assessment of unfairness in the marriage. Perry-Jenkins and Folk (1994) found that for middle-class dual-earner couples, the variable of perceptions of fairness regarding the division of labor was a key mediator linking reported division of labor to marital conflict, with higher perceptions of fairness being linked to lower reports of marital conflict. In contrast, this relationship did not emerge for working-class dual-earner couples. Thus, the research to date points to the importance of not only the division of labor but also perceptions of its fairness as important indicators of marital quality in dual-earner families. However, Perry-Jenkins and Folk's (1994) findings raise the question of how social contexts, such as race, ethnicity, and social class, moderate these relationships.

With regard to gender role ideology, research has found that African Americans and Mexican Americans have more positive attitudes toward working wives than European Americans but are also more likely to endorse the idea that the man should be the main breadwinner (Blee & Tickamyer, 1995; Kamo & Cohen, 1998). When it comes to gendered behaviors, a number of studies have found that, compared to European American men, African American men perform more child care and household tasks; however, African American women still perform the majority of family work (McLoyd, 1993). In addition, African American husbands or partners are more likely than their white counterparts to view the division of labor as unfair to their wives or partners (John, Shelton, & Luschen, 1995). In a related study, Shelton and John (1993) found that Hispanic men perform more female-typed tasks than European American men.

The question of how these different values and belief systems within different racial groups may lead to unique patterns of relationships among work hours, work conditions, and marital relations is an important new direction for research. Because research indicates that the meaning and interpretation that spouses give to their paid and unpaid work ultimately hold consequences for mental health and marital relations and because this meaning appears to vary by race, class, and gender, it is unlikely that our current findings based primarily on white, middle-class families will extrapolate to families of different races and social classes.

Dual-Earner Lifestyle, Parent-Child Relationships, and Child Development

The approach one uses to understand work-family connections affects what facets of this relationship are focused on (Crouter & McHale, 1993). Researchers focusing primarily on the workplace have explored (a) work as a socializer of values that are transmitted to children; (b) work as a setting that provides opportunities (e.g., learning new skills) or constraints (e.g. time inflexibility) that can positively or negatively affect one's ability to parent; and (c) the workplace as a place that shapes the emotional states of workers, moods that may then be brought home to affect the quantity and quality of parent-child interactions.

The work socialization perspective, grounded in the sociology of work and occupations, rests on the basic assumption that occupational conditions, such as autonomy and complexity, shape the beliefs and values of workers, which in turn influence parenting styles and child outcomes. For example, Parcel and Menaghan (1993) found that higher levels of occupational complexity for fathers served as a protective factor against later child behavior problems. In a related study, Cooksey, Menaghan, and Jekielek (1997) found that when they controlled for family structure, maternal employment characteristics such as more autonomy, working with people, and problem solving predicted decreases in child behavior problems. The actual processes whereby work conditions shape parental values and ensuing parental behavior style, though they can be inferred from Parcel and Menaghan's (1994b) work, need more direct empirical investigation. Thus, although a few studies have linked work conditions to parental behaviors and, in turn, to child outcomes, a process that supports the work socialization perspective (Greenberger, O'Neil, & Nagel, 1994; Grimm-Thomas & Perry-Jenkins, 1994; Whitbeck et al., 1997), we need more longitudinal and quasi-experimental studies that can more effectively tease apart causality issues. In addition, greater attention must be paid to selection effects that lead certain types of parents to choose particular occupations and the extent to which child characteristics affect the types of jobs parents choose.

Research on work as a setting that provides opportunities and/or constraints has shown that skills acquired at work, such as problem solving and group decision making, can be translated into more democratic or authoritative parenting styles at home (Crouter, 1984). Finally, at an even more proximal level, researchers have begun to elucidate processes whereby day-to-day variation in work-induced moods affects subsequent parent-child interactions at home. Repetti and Wood (1997), for example, found that employed parents tend to withdraw from family interactions following a high-stress workday. Specifically, mothers were more withdrawn from their preschoolers on days when they experienced greater workloads or interpersonal stress at work. All these findings suggest that, ranging from macro levels (i.e., worldviews and values) to more micro, proximal levels (i.e., work-induced moods), experiences of work can affect everything from parental values, to parenting styles, to patterns of parent-child interactions.

Crouter and McHale (1993) pointed out that research on the work-family relationship that focuses primarily on the family as its point of entry has attended to quite different processes linking parental work to child outcomes. This approach has paid less attention to conditions of work and focused more on the fact that employed parents may face unique challenges such as finding time to share activities with children, to monitor children's activities, and to maintain close, satisfying parent-child relations. Thus, the issue of how much and when parents work has been the focus of much research over the past decade (Hochschild, 1997; Perry-Jenkins et al., 2000; Schor, 1991) because the amount of time parents work and when they work affect parents' ability to be involved in

child-oriented activities and/or their ability to monitor children's daily activities (Crouter, MacDermid, McHale, & Perry-Jenkins, 1990; Macoby & Martin, 1983). At least one pair of researchers suggest that paternal monitoring of children differs across cultural groups: Toth and Xu (1999) found that African American and Latino fathers reported supervising their children's activities more than European American fathers and that Latino fathers spent more time in shared activities with their children than European American fathers. These findings highlight the importance of culture as a critical variable that may moderate work-parenting relationships.

The question of whether the sheer amount of time parents work is related to child outcomes has been raised as an important issue, especially given the increased time that employed men and women are spending on the job (Crouter, Bumpus, Head, & McHale, 2001; Schor, 1991). Parcel and Menaghan (1994a) found that working more than 40 hours per week is related to more negative child outcomes; however, occupational complexity interacts with maternal work hours by decreasing the negative effects of long work hours. In one of the rare studies to look beyond outcomes for young children, Crouter and colleagues found that the combination of fathers' long work hours and high overload was consistently associated with less positive father-adolescent relations.

Beyond the number of work hours, Presser's (1994, 1999) research on shift work highlights how temporal patterning of work hours in dual-earner families has important implications for family life. Her research suggests that the less husbands' and wives' work hours overlap, the more family work and child care men perform. Shift work may affect parents' ability to interact with their children and supervise their activities (Presser, 2000), although Presser found this pattern of relationships to be complex and a function of the shift the parent worked, the gender of the parent, the type of parent-child activity assessed, and the developmental stage of the child. For instance, parents of a preschooler working evening or night shifts could have more time with their child than those working day shifts. In contrast, working an evening shift would provide parents of school-aged children with few or no overlapping hours at home with their children during their workweek. If we identify parent-child interaction as an important mediator variable, our next step is to explore how parent-child interactions may mediate the link between nonstandard work schedules and children's developmental outcomes in multiple areas, such as social, emotional, and cognitive dimensions of development.

Thus far, our discussion has focused on the direct and indirect influences of parental work on children's development. But just as important to children's development are the issues of where and how children are spending their time when parents are at work. In a recent Urban Institute report, 41% of children under 5 spend 35 or more hours in nonparental care, and an additional 25% spend between 15 and 34 hours in nonparental care (Capizzano & Adams, 2000). Thus, one of the most important factors affecting children's development is the quality of nonparental care that children receive. Findings from the Early Child Care Research Network of the National Institute of Child Health and Human Development [NICHD] revealed few simple effects of nonmaternal care in the first year of life. However, results did indicate more complex relationships: Poor-quality care, unstable care, and more than minimal hours of care coupled with insensitive mothering were related to poorer child outcomes and less secure mother-infant attachments (NICHD, 1997a, 1997b).

Care and supervision issues remain important issues for school-aged children and adolescents. In a recent study using nationally representative data from the Panel Study of Income Dynamics, it was found that 73% of children ages 5 to 12 go straight home from school (with only 14% of those children being alone), 11% go to child care, 8% stay at school, and 8% go somewhere else (Hofferth & Sandberg, 2001). The question of how after-school time is spent and its relation to children's development has not received a great deal of attention. For lower-income, but not middle-income, children, unsupervised after-school time was related to more externalizing behaviors (e.g., yelling, hitting), whereas attending an after-school program was related to fewer internalizing behaviors (e.g., introversion) (Marshall et al., 1997). Adolescents performed better academically when engaged in supervised after-school activities than when unsupervised (Muller, 1995). Clearly, these studies point to the importance of including child care factors into the study of work and family issues for dual-earner families.

CONTEMPLATING THE FUTURE OF DUAL-EARNER FAMILIES

How dual-earner families will change and cope with work-family challenges over the next few decades is an intriguing question that scholars and researchers must address with strong theoretical models and new methodologies. In this last section, we propose new directions for research that will more fully capture the complexity and realities of life in dual-earner households.

The Sociocultural Context of Dual-Earner Families

An ecological perspective emphasizes the importance of extrafamilial contexts as they influence family and individual functioning (Bronfenbrenner, 1986). To date, the predominant focus in both the broad work-family literature and dual-earner research in particular has been on white, middle-class, two-parent families, a trend that has sharply restricted an understanding of how work-family relationships differ across social class, racial, and ethnic lines. A more ecologically valid approach to studying dual-earner families would place greater emphasis on the diversity of contexts that can shape parents' experiences.

Family scholars have emphasized that experiences of dual-career families are not generalizable to dual-earner families due to differences in the nature of the problems confronted by these two types of families, their resources, and the solutions they devise to deal with their problems (Mortimer & London, 1984; Rubin, 1976, 1994). Nevertheless, only a handful of studies have examined the implications of women's employment in working-class families. In her classic study, Komarovsky (1962) demonstrated how values about work and family life—providing and mothering—were quite clearly delineated in the working-class families of the 1960s. More recently, a number of studies have refuted the idea that working-class families divide household tasks strictly along gender lines and that employed women in the working class are employed only for financial reasons (Ferree, 1987; Rubin, 1994; Ybarra, 1982). Ybarra (1982) found that in working-class, Latino families, wives' employment was correlated with more egalitarian family roles. In addition, it was found that the majority of these working-class women *preferred* to be employed. Thompson and Walker (1989) suggested that the realities of class lead working-class families to more equitably divide up paid and unpaid work. Perry-Jenkins and Folk (1994) found different processes linking division of labor, perceptions of its fairness, and marital quality for working-class versus middle-class couples. Thus, we must move beyond our tendency

to control for variability in social class indicators, such as education, income, and occupational prestige, and explore how these aspects of families' lives moderate the ways in which work and family are connected.

Research on gender and race effects on occupational characteristics suggests that both factors differentially influence occupational attainment and earnings. With respect to earnings, gender effects are more discernible than race effects: Women earn less than men, although black men earn less than white men. In contrast, occupational prestige is influenced by both race and gender, with 13% of white women in high-prestige jobs and only 10% of black women and 9% of black men in high-prestige jobs (Xu & Leffler, 1996). These differences in income and job prestige, which arise as a function of race and gender, are likely to influence how well dual-earner families are able to cope with work-family stressors. Moreover, the literature on working-class occupations suggests that workers in lower-level jobs have less autonomy and control on the job, as well as fewer supportive workplace policies—again, conditions that hold consequences for workers' ability to manage work and family life. In short, gender, race, and class matter, and "they matter because they structure interactions, opportunities, consciousness, ideology and the forms of resistance that characterize American life" (Anderson, 1996, p. ix). It is expected that as we look more carefully within the contexts of race and class, as well as family structure, we will be able to outline common and unique factors both at work and at home that affect how parents and children in these different contexts fare in terms of their mental health and family relationships.

Research on work and family issues in African American families is rare. In a study that explored work and family roles in black families, Broman (1991) found that involvement in multiple roles had differential effects on black women and men. Specifically, employed wives reported the lowest levels of family life satisfaction, whereas married, employed men reported the highest family satisfaction. In addition, couples' organization of work and family role responsibilities was related to assessments of family life satisfaction but not to psychological well-being outcomes. Broman suggested that the usefulness of social role theory may be domain specific for blacks: useful in understanding family life satisfaction but not mental health. He and McLoyd (1993) argued further that the different historical experiences of blacks and whites in the United States have implications not only for racial differences in work and family role configurations but for different associations between role patterns and family and individual outcomes for blacks and whites.

The few studies of Latino families reveal work-family relationships similar to those often described in European American dual-earner families. Specifically, Chicano men endorse the idea that wives' income is needed to support families' standard of living, and Chicano women report less depression when husbands are involved in family work (Saenz, Goudy, & Lorenz, 1989; Williams, 1988).

Some of the most important advances over the past decade are the new conceptual frameworks that urge us to place families in context and to take into account that ethnicity and race do not exist in isolation from class and gender hierarchies. A major challenge for the new century is translation of these sophisticated and nuanced models into sound empirical research (McLoyd, Cauce, Takeuchi, & Wilson, 2000, p. 1087).

Future work should take on the challenge presented by McLoyd and her colleagues by examining how race, gender, and family structure intersect within dual-earner families to influence the well-being and family relationships of women and men as they negotiate work and family responsibilities.

Work-Family Processes in Context

Although an ecological perspective suggests that broader social systems directly and indirectly influence adult and child development, there is a basic need to determine how distal factors (i.e., class, race, family structure) influence development through proximal processes (Bronfenbrenner, 1986; O'Connor & Rutter, 1996). As O'Connor and Rutter (1996) pointed out, "[T]he link between culture and proximal processes must go beyond demonstrating group mean differences to include information on how key features are perceived differently in different groups. . . . It is equally necessary to consider variability within cultural groups" (p. 787). For example, the occupational stress literature documents ways in which pressure and stress at work can affect a worker's mood, which in turn can lead to social withdrawal and/or conflict at home. Future research that is attentive to process issues needs to integrate the short- and long-term stress transmission processes with attention to ways in which job pressures may be reduced in situations of job control and autonomy. Finally, some of the most important findings over the past decade point to the importance of interaction effects in work-family models. For example, Parcel and Menaghan's (1994a, 1994b) work highlights ways in which occupational complexity combined with specific family circumstances (e.g., structure, class) affects home environments and parenting styles.

Methodological Issues

Although the dual-earner literature has clearly moved past the social address approach to explore within-family processes that link work and family life, a few scholars have begun to explicitly and systematically explore the heterogeneity of dual-earner families (Crouter & Manke, 1997; Kinnunen & Mauno, 2001). Crouter and Manke (1997) proposed that categorizing dual-earner couples on the basis of mothers' work hours (e.g., part time, full time, homemaker) or men's occupational prestige (e.g., dual earner vs. dual career) oversimplifies the dual-earner experience and ignores covariations that occur around multiple work characteristics. To address this shortcoming, they used cluster analysis to typologize dual-earner families on four dimensions: hours, prestige, role overload, and job involvement. Three groups emerged: (a) high-status dual earners, (b) low-stress dual earners, and (c) main-secondary provider families. These types, based on characteristics of both parents' jobs, were then related to other aspects of family life such as parental monitoring and marital quality. Parents in the low-stress group were better monitors than parents in the other two groups, and these parents also reported more marital satisfaction than the high-status group. In a partial replication of this work, Kinnunen and Mauno also explored dual-earner typologies and obtained some similar but unique findings related to job exhaustion, which was most significantly linked to negative family outcomes. We highlight these studies because they look beyond the social address of dual-earner couples to examine within-group variability and pay attention to the dyadic level of analysis by combining data from both parents' work situations. Spouses and children in dual-earner families must deal with the effects of two jobs and their intersection, yet our analyses often ignore this interdependence.

Once we begin to examine how dual-earner families differ as a function of race, ethnicity, social class, and life stage, it becomes apparent that exactly what we mean by the very terms *work* and *family* should be examined. As Thorne (2001) pointed out, "[F]ruitful topics will illuminate social processes that don't necessarily stop at the pre-specified boundaries of work and family" (p. 374). Work often extends into family life as computers, beepers, and cell phones come into our homes, and our jobs can include multiple family members (see Chapter 29 of this book). Family boundaries usually extend far beyond the oft-used definition of family found in our research that is limited to "mother, father, and target child." We would greatly benefit from research that starts to give the terms *work* and *family* social and cultural relevance for the individuals that live in dual-earner families.

Although conceptual models often accentuate the dynamic nature of both work and family experiences, empirical research is much less sensitive to within- and between-individual change over time. Distress is relational for dual-earner couples (Barnett, Marshall, Raudenbush, & Brennan, 1993), in that change over time in one partner's psychological distress is related to change in the other partner's distress. Models must take this level of dependency into account.

Hierarchical linear modeling (HLM) provides a unique conceptual orientation and analytical technique for the study of psychological and relationship change over time. HLM is uniquely suited to explore change over time in individuals' and couples' work and family experiences and makes it possible to identify significant predictors of differences in individuals' variation in job stress or marital love over time. Predictors of change in mental health or family relationships may be due to more structural and time-invariant variables, such as family size, parental age, and child temperament, or predictors that may change concurrently with the dependent variables, such as job autonomy, role overload, and workplace support (time-variant variables). For example, Barnett et al. (1995) explored how changes in job experiences are related to change in psychological distress for both partners in dual-earner marriages. To address the dependence of data for married couples, the longitudinal model for individuals was combined with a cross-sectional model for matched pairs (Barnett et al., 1995; Maguire, 1999). Future research on dual-earner couples will benefit greatly from this analytic strategy, which makes it possible to look past averages and independent reports and explore issues of change and dependence among family members.

Another way to conceptualize change over time from a more macro perspective is to examine challenges faced by dual-earner families from a life course perspective. The predominant focus in the dual-earner literature has been on families with young children. We know little about how work-family issues may differ for families with adolescents, for empty nesters, or for families with young adults who return home. Thus, although our research has focused on those families whose resources are most tightly stretched, dual-earners with young children, we neglect to emphasize that this is a relatively short period in a family's life course (although for those living through it, it may feel like an eternity). A life course perspective challenges us to examine how work-family strategies and relationships change over time and, in part, as a function of historical, social, and family factors.

Work-Family Policy

A sentiment that underlies much of the dual-earner literature, as well as societal reactions to this lifestyle, is sadness over the loss of an unhurried, simpler, happier time for families, even though our historical data suggest that those simpler, happier times exist only as myths (Coontz, 1992). In fact, empirical data actually suggest that dual-earner families fare quite well on mental health, marital, and child indicators, yet societal ambivalence regarding maternal employment, and consequently dual-earner families, still exists (Pleck, 1992). As Pleck suggests, this ambivalence is reflected in our lack of social policies to support working families.

In fact, to date, research on work and family has rarely been translated into policies at work, state, or federal levels, with the possible exception of the Family and Medical Leave Act (FMLA). FMLA legislation, which provides for 12 weeks of unpaid leave for parental responsibilities, was passed in 1993; however, it is sorely inadequate. It excludes 95% of employers and 50% of employees (because it applies only to workplaces with 50 or more employees), and as unpaid leave it offers little support to low-income families who cannot afford unpaid time off (Gerstel & McGonagle, 1999). On a brighter note, California has become the first state to pass legislation to provide partial pay for parental leave for working parents.

Looking beyond social policy, another potential site for change is the workplace (MacDermid & Targ, 1995). The research evidence is clear: Jobs that have some degree of autonomy, control, flexibility, and support are good for workers, their mental health, and their family relationships. Some companies have been extremely creative in making what appears to be monotonous, highly controlled work into participative and engaging work (Crouter, 1984; Lambert, 1999). When this happens, benefits to the worker accrue as well as benefits to the employer in terms of less turnover, fewer sick days, and greater productivity.

It is our belief that, given current knowledge about workplace policies and conditions that have been associated with the well-being of workers and their families, a fruitful direction for the next decade would be to develop experimental or quasi-experimental studies that begin to pinpoint how changes in workplace polices (i.e., flexible schedules) or changes in work conditions (i.e., increases in autonomy, supervisor supports) affect workers' mental health and family relationships. A confound in our non-experimental designs is selection effects, non-random effects that cloud our understanding of work-family processes because certain types of individuals choose particular types of employment. Carefully designed studies with control and experimental groups will not only highlight those factors that enhance family life but allow us to get a handle on selection effects.

Finally, at the level of the family, some research points to the effective strategies that couples have developed to better manage their work and family lives. In their qualitative study of 100 individuals in dual-earner families, Becker and Moen (1999) identified three separate strategies that couples used to cope with work and family demands. The first strategy was *placing limits* on the number of hours they worked and reducing expectations for career advancement. There were gender differences in this strategic approach, with two thirds of women and only one third of men using this technique. The second approach, *trading off*, reflected a value couples shared about egalitarianism. This was a life course strategy where partners would take turns, over their lives, giving priority first to one partner's career and then the other's. Finally, many couples coped by having *one-job, one-career* families. In 40% of the families interviewed, one person had what both spouses perceived as a job while the other had a career. This strategy was gendered, with over two thirds of the couples falling into the wife-job/husband-career category.

Deutsch (1999) documented similar strategies used by equal-sharing dual-earner couples. In her study, 150 couples were identified as *equal sharers*, couples in which both partners reported that family work was divided equally between parents. Deutsch's data highlight the importance of a life course perspective in examining work-family issues because approximately half of her equal-sharing couples reported a period of inequality when their children were very young (under 3 years of age) (F. Deutsch, personal communication,

November 7, 2002). Although this time was often characterized by high levels of paternal involvement, mothers performed significantly more of the family work. However, once children entered more formal care arrangements (e.g., preschool or kindergarten), couples quickly transitioned into an equal-sharing mode. Deutsch also noted that another common approach taken by equal sharers was a *cutting-back* strategy, which looked different in her middle-class versus working-class dual-earner couples. Middle-class career couples limited both work hours and opportunities for career advancement as a way to successfully combine work and family life, thus at times limiting their potential for career success. For working-class couples, equal sharers were more likely to have two spouses who worked full time, so that husbands did not need to work two or three jobs to make ends meet. This allowed both parents an equal opportunity to share in family life. Often these couples relied on shift work and alternating work schedules not only to avoid the costs of child care but to give both parents equal opportunity to raise their children.

Both of these qualitative studies provide important insights into the strategies couples use to reduce work and family conflict. They are important because they move us beyond the question of "How does work affect family?" to "How do individuals and couples shape their work and family lives successfully?" The next steps should include attention to how these strategies might work for families of different races and ethnicities, for workers with different job arrangements such as shift workers, and for seasonal and contingent workers. In addition, we would benefit from more information about family relations and supports that extend beyond the nuclear parent-child family to examine broader family networks that include the role of kin and fictive kin in supporting working parents.

Imagining what the future holds for dual-earner families is an interesting exercise. The growing use of technology means work can happen at any place and at any time. These technological changes create greater flexibility for workers along with greater demands to work around the clock. The projected shortage of workers over the next three decades is expected to lead to increases in benefits that attract skilled workers (Judy & D'Amico, 1997), but the fate of low-income, unskilled workers may be at risk. Future research on dual-earner families must continue to focus on processes that link employment conditions to family life, with greater attention to the bidirectional nature of these relationships and greater sensitivity to the ways in which race, class, and gender moderate these relationships. Finally, as we began this chapter, we noted that all marriages bear the imprints of economic and cultural trends. To understand the dynamic nature of dual-earner marriages, our lens must continually change focus to include broader macro-level social and economic events that ultimately affect our vision of micro-level relationships and processes in families.

REFERENCES

Anderson, M. L. (1996). Foreword. In E. N-L. Chow, D. Y. Wilkinson, & M. B. Baca Zinn (Eds.), *Race, class, and gender*. Thousand Oaks, CA: Sage.

Barling, J., & MacEwen, K. E. (1992). Linking work experiences to facets of marital functioning. *Journal of Organizational Behavior, 13,* 573–583.

Barnett, R., & Baruch, G. (1987). Mothers' participation in childcare: Patterns and consequences. In F. Crosby (Ed.), *Spouse, parent, and worker* (pp. 91–108). New Haven, CT: Yale University Press.

Barnett, R. C., Marshall, N. L., & Pleck, J. (1992). Men's multiple roles and their relationship to men's psychological distress. *Journal of Marriage and the Family, 54,* 358–367.

Barnett, R. C., Marshall, N. L., Raudenbush, S., & Brennan, R. T. (1993). Gender and the relationship between job experiences and psychological distress: A study of dual-earner couples. *Journal of Personality and Social Psychology, 64,* 794–806.

Barnett, R. C., Raudenbush, S. W., Brennan, R. T., Pleck, J. H., & Marshall, N. L. (1995). Change in job and marital experiences and change in psychological distress: A longitudinal study of dual-earner couples. *Journal of Personality and Social Psychology, 69,* 839–850.

Baruch, G. K., Biener, L., & Barnett, R. C. (1987). Women and gender in research on work and family stress. *American Psychologist, 42,* 130–136.

Becker, P. E., & Moen, P. (1999). Scaling back: Dual-earner couples' work-family strategies. *Journal of Marriage and the Family, 61,* 995–1007.

Blair, S. L. (1993). Employment, family, and perceptions of marital quality among husbands and wives. *Journal of Family Issues, 14,* 189–212.

Blair, S. L., & Johnson, M. P. (1992). Wives' perceptions of fairness of the division of household labor: The intersection of housework and ideology. *Journal of Marriage and the Family, 54,* 570–581.

Blee, K., & Tickamyer, A. (1995). Racial differences in men's attitudes about women's gender roles. *Journal of Marriage and the Family, 57,* 21–30.

Broman, C. L. (1991). Gender, work-family roles, and psychological well-being of blacks. *Journal of Marriage of Family, 53,* 509–520.

Bronfenbrenner, U. (1986). Ecology of the family as a context for human development: Research perspectives. *Developmental Psychology, 22,* 723–742.

Bronfenbrenner, U., & Crouter, A. C. (1983). The evolution of environmental models in developmental research. In P. Mussen (Ed.), *Handbook of child psychology* (pp. 358–414). New York: John Wiley.

Capizzano, J., & Adams, G. (2000). *The hours that children under five spend in child care: Variation across states* (National Survey of America's Families, Series B, No. B-8). Washington, DC: Urban Institute.

Cohen, P. N., & Bianchi, S. M. (1999, December). Marriage, children, and women's employment: What do we know? *Monthly Labor Review,* pp. 22–31.

Coltrane, S. (2000). Research on household labor: Modeling and measuring the social embeddedness of routine family work. *Journal of Marriage and the Family, 62,* 1208–1233.

Cooksey, E. C., Menaghan, E. G., & Jekielek, S. M. (1997). Life course effects of work and family circumstances on children. *Social Forces, 76,* 637–667.

Coontz, S. (1992). *The way we never were.* New York: Basic Books.

Crouter, A. C. (1984). Participative work as an influence on human development. *Journal of Applied Developmental Psychology, 5,* 71–90.

Crouter, A. C., Bumpus, M. F., Head, M. R., & McHale, S. M. (2001). Implications of overwork and overload for the quality of men's relationships. *Journal of Marriage and Family, 63,* 404–416.

Crouter, A. C., Bumpus, M. F., Maguire, M. C., & McHale, S. M. (1999). Linking parents' work pressure and adolescents' well-being: Insights into dynamics in dual-earner families. *Developmental Psychology, 35,* 1453–1461.

Crouter, A. C., MacDermid, S. M., McHale, S. M., & Perry-Jenkins, M. (1990). Parental monitoring and perceptions of children's school performance and conduct in dual-earner and single-earner families. *Developmental Psychology, 26,* 649–657.

Crouter, A. C., & Manke, B. (1997). Development of a typology of dual-earner families: A window into differences between and within families in relationships, roles and activities. *Journal of Family Psychology, 11,* 62–75.

Crouter, A. C., & McHale, S. M. (1993). The long arm of the job: Influences of parental work on childrearing. In T. Luster & L. Okagaki (Eds.), *Parenting: An ecological perspective* (pp. 179–202). New York: Lawrence Erlbaum.

Deutsch, F. (1999). *Halving it all.* Boston: Harvard University Press.

Ferree, M. M. (1976). Working class jobs: Housework and paid work as sources of satisfaction. *Social Problems, 22,* 431–441.

Ferree, M. M. (1987). Family and jobs for working-class women: Gender and class systems seen from below. In N. Gerstel & H. E. Gros (Eds.), *Families and work.* Philadelphia: Temple University Press.

Gerstel, N., & Gallagher, S. K. (1993). Kinkeeping and distress: Gender, recipients of care, and work-family conflict. *Journal of Marriage and the Family, 55,* 598–608.

Gerstel, N., & McGonagle, K. (1999). Job leaves and the limits of the Family and Medical Leave Act: The effects of gender, race, and family. *Journal of Work and Occupations, 26,* 510–534.

Glass, J., & Fujimoto, T. (1994). Housework, paid work, and depression in husbands and wives. *Journal of Health and Social Behavior, 35,* 179–194.

Greenberger, E., O'Neil, R., & Nagel, S. K. (1994). Linking workplace and homeplace: Relations between the nature of adults' work and their parenting behaviors. *Developmental Psychology, 30,* 990–1002.

Grimm-Thomas, K., & Perry-Jenkins, M. (1994). All in a day's work: Job experiences, self-esteem, and fathering in working-class families. *Family Relations, 43,* 174–181.

Guarnaccia, P. J., Angel, R., & Worobey, J. L. (1991). The impact of marital status and employment status on depressive affect for Hispanic Americans. *Journal of Community Psychology, 19,* 136–149.

Guelzow, M., Bird, G., & Koball, E. (1991). An exploratory path analysis of the stress process for dual-career men and women. *Journal of Marriage and the Family, 53,* 151–164.

Harvey, E. (1999). Short-term and long-term effects of parental employment on children of the National Longitudinal Survey of Youth. *Developmental Psychology, 35,* 445–459.

Hochschild, A. R. (1989). *The second shift.* New York: Avon.

Hochschild, A. R. (1997). *The time bind.* New York: Henry Holt.

Hofferth, S. L., & Sandberg, J. F. (2001). How American children spend their time. *Journal of Marriage and Family, 63,* 295–308.

Hyde, J. S., DeLamater, J. D., & Hewitt, E. C. (1998). Sexuality and the dual-earner couple multiple roles and sexual functioning. *Journal of Family Psychology, 12,* 354–368.

John, D., Shelton, B. A., & Luschen, K. (1995). Race, ethnicity, gender, and perceptions of fairness. *Journal of Family Issues, 16,* 357–379.

Judy, R. W., & D'Amico, C. (1997). *Workforce 2020.* Indianapolis, IN: Hudson Institute.

Kamo, Y., & Cohen, E. L. (1998). Division of household work between partners: A comparison of black and white couples. *Journal of Comparative Family Studies, 29,* 131–145.

Kinnunen, U., & Mauno, S. (2001). Dual-earner families in Finland: Differences between and within families in relation to work and family experiences. *Community, Work and Family, 4,* 87–107.

Kohn, M. L. (1995). Social structure and personality through time and space. In P. Moen, G. H. Elder, Jr., & K. Luscher (Eds.), *Examining lives in context* (pp. 141–168). Washington, DC: American Psychological Association.

Kohn, M. L., & Schooler, C. (1982). Job conditions and personality: A longitudinal assessment of their reciprocal effects. *American Journal of Sociology, 87,* 1257–1286.

Komarovsky, M. (1962). *Blue-collar marriage.* New York: Vintage.

Lambert, S. J. (1999). Lower-wage workers and the new realities of work and family. *Annals of the American Academy of Political and Social Science, 562,* 174–190.

MacDermid, S. M., & Targ, D. B. (1995). A call for greater attention to the role of employers in developing, transforming, and implementing family policies. *Journal of Family and Economic Issues, 16,* 145–167.

Macoby, E., & Martin, J. (1983). Socialization in the context of the family: Parent-child interaction. In P. H. Mussen (Ed.), *Handbook of child psychology* (Vol. 4, pp. 1–101). New York: John Wiley.

Maguire, M. C. (1999). Treating the dyad as the unit of analysis: A primer on three analytic approaches. *Journal of Marriage and the Family, 61,* 213–223.

Marshall, N. L., Coll, C. G., Marx, F., McCartney, K., Keefe, N., & Ruh, J. (1997). After-school time and children's behavioral adjustment. *Merrill-Palmer Quarterly, 43,* 497–514.

Marsiglio, W., Amato, P., & Day, R. D. (2000). Scholarship on fatherhood in the 1990s and beyond. *Journal of Marriage and the Family, 62,* 1173–1191.

McLoyd, V. C. (1993). Employment among African-American mothers in dual-earner families: Antecedents and consequences for family life and child development. In J. Frankel (Ed.), *The employed mother in the family context.* New York: Springer.

McLoyd, V. C., Cauce, A. M., Takeuchi, D., & Wilson, L. (2000). Marital processes and parental socialization in families of color: A decade review of research. *Journal of Marriage and the Family, 62,* 1070–1093.

Menaghan, E. G., & Parcel, T. L. (1995). Social sources of change in children's home environment: The effects of parental occupational experiences and family conditions. *Journal of Marriage and the Family, 57,* 69–84.

Mortimer, J. T., & London, J. (1984). The varying linkages of work and family. In P. Voydanoff (Ed.), *Work and family* (pp. 20–35). Palo Alto, CA: Mayfield.

Muller, C. (1995). Maternal employment, parent involvement, and mathematics achievement among adolescents. *Journal of Marriage and the Family, 57,* 85–100.

National Institute of Child Health and Human Development Early Child Care Research Network. (1997a). The effects of infant child care on infant-mother attachment security: Results of the NICHD Study of Early Child Care. *Child Development, 68,* 860–879.

National Institute of Child Health and Human Development Early Child Care Research Network. (1997b). Familial factors associated with the characteristics of nonmaternal care for infants. *Journal of Marriage and the Family, 59,* 389–408.

O'Connor, T. G., & Rutter, M. (1996). Risk mechanisms in development: Some conceptual and methodological considerations. *Developmental Psychology, 32,* 787–795.

Paden, S. L., & Buehler, C. (1995). Coping with the dual-income lifestyle. *Journal of Marriage and the Family, 57,* 101–110.

Parcel, T. L., & Menaghan, E. G. (1993). Family social capital and children's behavior problems. *Social Psychology Quarterly, 56,* 120–135.

Parcel, T. L., & Menaghan, E. G. (1994a). Early parental work, family social capital, and early childhood outcomes. *American Journal of Sociology, 99,* 972–1009.

Parcel, T. L., & Menaghan, E. G. (1994b). *Parents' jobs and children's lives.* New York: Aldine de Gruyter.

Perry-Jenkins, M., & Folk, K. (1994). Class, couples and conflict: Effects of the division of labor on assessments of marriage in dual-earner families. *Journal of Marriage and the Family, 56,* 165–180.

Perry-Jenkins, M., Repetti, R., & Crouter, A. C. (2000). Work and family in the 1990s. *Journal of Marriage and the Family, 62,* 27–63.

Pleck, J. H. (1985). *Working wives, working husbands.* Beverly Hills, CA: Sage.

Pleck, J. H. (1992). Work-family policies in the United States. In H. Kahne & J. Z. Giele (Eds.), *Women's work and women's lives* (pp. 248–276). San Francisco: Westview.

Presser, H. B. (1994). Employment schedules among dual-earner spouses and the division of household labor by gender. *American Sociological Review, 59,* 348–364.

Presser, H. B. (1999). Toward a 24-hour economy. *Science, 284,* 1778–1779.

Presser, H. B. (2000). Work schedules and marital instability. *Journal of Marriage and the Family, 62,* 93–110.

Repetti, R. L. (1992). Social withdrawal as a short term coping response to daily stressors. In H. S. Friedman (Ed.), *Hostility, coping, and health* (pp. 151–165). Washington, DC: American Psychological Association.

Repetti, R. L., & Wood, J. (1997). Effects of daily stress at work on mothers' interactions with preschoolers. *Journal of Family Psychology, 11,* 90–108.

Rogers, S. J. (1996). Mothers' work hours and marital quality: Variations by family structure and family size. *Journal of Marriage and the Family, 58,* 606–617.

Rogers, S. J. (1999). Wives' income and marital quality: Are there reciprocal effects. *Journal of Marriage and the Family, 61,* 123–132.

Ross, C. E., Mirowsky, J., & Huber, J. (1983). Dividing work, sharing work, and in-between: Marriage patterns and depression. *American Sociological Review, 48,* 809–823.

Rubin, L. B. (1976). *Worlds of pain.* New York: Basic Books.

Rubin, L. B. (1994). *Families on the fault line.* New York: HarperCollins.

Saenz, R., Goudy, W., & Lorenz, F. O. (1989). The effects of employment and marital relations on depression among Mexican American women. *Journal of Marriage and the Family, 58,* 239–251.

Scarr, S., Phillips, D., & McCartney, K. (1989). Working mothers and their families. *American Psychologist, 44,* 1402–1409.

Schor, J. (1991). *The overworked American.* New York: Basic Books.

Sears, H. A., & Galambos, N. L. (1992). Women's work conditions and marital adjustment in two-earner couples: A structural model. *Journal of Marriage and the Family, 54,* 789–797.

Shelton, B. A., & John, D. (1993). Ethnicity, race, and difference: A comparison of white, black and Hispanic men's household labor time. In J. Hood (Ed.), *Men, work and family* (pp. 131–149). Newbury Park, CA: Sage.

Spitze, G. (1988). Women's employment and family relations: A review. *Journal of Marriage and the Family, 50,* 595–618.

Steil, J. M. (1997). *Marital equality.* Thousand Oaks, CA: Sage.

Thompson, L. (1991). Family work: Women's sense of fairness. *Journal of Family Issues, 12,* 181–196.

Thompson, L., & Walker, A. J. (1989). Gender in families: Women and men in marriage, work and parenthood. *Journal of Marriage and the Family, 51,* 845–871.

Thorne, B. (2001). Pick-up time at Oakdale Elementary School. In R. Hertz & N. L. Marshall (Eds.), *Working families* (pp. 354–376). Berkeley: University of California Press.

Toth, J. F., & Xu, X. (1999). Ethnic and cultural diversity in fathers' involvement: A racial/ethnic comparison of African Americans, Hispanic, and white fathers. *Youth and Society, 31,* 76–99.

U.S. Bureau of Labor Statistics. (2001). *Employment characteristics of families in 2001* (Current Population Survey). Washington, DC: Government Printing Office.

Voydanoff, P. (1987). *Work and family life.* Newbury Park, CA: Sage.

Wethington, E., & Kessler, R. (1989). Employment, parental responsibility, and psychological distress. *Journal of Family Issues, 10,* 527–546.

Whitbeck, L. B., Simons, R. L., Conger, R. D., Wickrama, K. A. S., Ackley, K. A., & Elder G. H., Jr. (1997). The effects of parents' working conditions and family economic hardship on parenting behaviors and children's self-efficacy. *Social Psychology Quarterly, 60,* 291–303.

Wilkie, J. R., Ferree, M. M., & Ratcliff, K. S. (1998). Gender and fairness: Marital satisfaction in two-earner families. *Journal of Marriage and the Family, 60,* 577–594.

Williams, N. (1988). Role making among married Mexican American women: Issues of class and ethnicity. *Journal of Applied Behavioral Science, 24,* 203–217.

Wortman, C., Biernat, M., & Lang, E. (1991). Coping with role overload. In M. Frankenhaeuser, U. Lundberg, & M. Chesney (Eds.), *Women, work, and health: Stress and opportunities* (pp. 85–110). New York: Plenum.

Xu, W., & Leffler, A. (1996). Gender and race effects on occupational prestige, segregation, and earnings. In E. N-L. Chow, D. Y. Wilkinson, & M. B. Baca Zinn (Eds.), *Race, class, and gender.* Thousand Oaks, CA: Sage.

Ybarra, L. (1982). When wives work: The impact on the Chicano family. *Journal of Marriage and the Family, 44,* 169–178.

Zuo, J., & Bian, Y. (2001). Gendered resources, division of housework, and perceived fairness: A case of urban China. *Journal of Marriage and Family, 63,* 1122–1333.

CHAPTER 10

Gendered Family Relations

The More Things Change, the More They Stay the Same

LORI A. MCGRAW AND ALEXIS J. WALKER

O ver the past 30 years, tremendous change has occurred in the ways that North Americans structure family life. In many ways, what was commonly expected of women and men in the early 1970s is not the same as what is expected of them today. Perhaps the most significant change has occurred in how women arrange their paid and unpaid work. Though working-class and minority women in the United States have almost always combined the unpaid work of child care and housework with low-wage jobs, middle-class women are increasingly working for pay not only before marriage and the arrival of children but also when their children are young (Cohen & Bianchi, 1999). In these times, unlike times past, most women and men agree that women should have opportunities to participate in higher education and paid employment.

This change in women's paid labor force participation has been accompanied by a decline in their participation in unpaid family work. Compared to 30 years ago, women spend significantly less time engaged in housework and child care. Consequently, present-day children are much more likely to spend time in nonparental care than they were in the 1970s (Glass & Estes, 1997). Interestingly, men have increased only slightly their participation in housework and child care during this same period—despite popular depictions of men as much more involved in family work now than in the past. In other words, gender arrangements in families have changed, but they also have remained the same. In this chapter, we examine both change and stability in paid and unpaid labor to provide an elaboration on how gender is constructed both in families and in the larger social and economic structure of the United States.

As noted above, gendered relations within families can be characterized as exhibiting both change and continuity. It is also true, however, that women's lives have changed more dramatically than men's lives, and this disjuncture has created tension resulting in disagreements about the appropriate roles for women and, to a lesser extent, for men. The disagreement about gendered relations within families has come to be known as the *family values* debate. Though the debate has been characterized as a problem with family values, the fundamental issue is really about changes in women's work over the past 30 years.

The argument against change in women's family roles and responsibilities is most prominently articulated by David Popenoe (1993), who suggested that "families have lost functions, power, and authority, that familism as a cultural value has diminished, and that people have become less willing to invest time, money, and energy in family life, turning instead to investments in themselves" (p. 527). He claimed that the family as an institution is in a state of decline and that it would be strengthened if more families had one full-time wage earner and a second adult who accepted responsibility for caring for that wage earner, their children, and any other dependent family members. Those in agreement with Popenoe suggest that divorce should be made more difficult to obtain in order to discourage further family decline. Although the language Popenoe used was gender neutral, he focused on the problematic nature of maternal employment. His hidden message was that *women* have become less willing to invest time, money, and energy in family life, turning instead to investments in themselves. Problematically, the implementation of a single-wage-earner-with-a-caregiving-partner policy leaves one partner of an intact couple economically vulnerable and leaves out the multitude of families that do not consist of two adults.

Conversely, opponents of the *family decline* position emphasize that women have the right to pursue individual freedom and

power via education and employment and that this pursuit can be family friendly. Perhaps the most prominent proponent of the alternative view is Judith Stacey (1993). Stacey suggested that social scientists should focus on

> restructuring work schedules and benefit policies to accommodate familial responsibilities, redistributing work opportunities to reduce unemployment rates that destroy spirits and families, enacting comparable worth standards of pay equity to enable women as well as men to earn a family wage, and providing universal health, prenatal, and child care (p. 547)

rather than on berating mothers who work in the paid labor force and who are raising children in single-parent, divorced, or blended families. She also argued that "under present conditions of political, economic, social, and sexual inequality, truly egalitarian marriage is not possible for the majority" (p. 547). She suggested that social inequality in marriage combined with women's slight increase in financial power rather than women's selfishness is the primary contributor to marital instability. Opponents of the family decline position suggest that instead of making divorce more difficult to obtain, improving the quality of marriages—via the encouragement of loving, democratically structured relationships—would help dissuade heterosexual couples from divorce.

Though these relatively polarized positions highlight the social tensions within our society, they also detract from substantive efforts to answer the following questions: (a) How should paid and unpaid work be organized? (b) Who should be responsible for engaging in both types of work? (c) What value should we place on "men's" and "women's" work? and (d) What role should society play in resolving these questions?

We do not have the answers to all of these questions; however, in this chapter we explore more deeply the connections among gender, work, and family, illustrating how changes in women's paid work participation have transformed the organization of families and the relationships within them. We also explore men's slight increase in family work and the resistance of the marketplace to accommodating to the needs of family life, particularly families with members who have high needs for care. (For a discussion on adult psychological well-being, marital outcomes, parent-child relations, and child outcomes among dual-earner families, see Chapter 9 of this book.)

In the following pages, we define family and discuss theoretical issues surrounding gender and family life. Then we provide an overview of the empirical literature to illustrate both change and stability over the past 30 years, focusing primarily on family and somewhat less on market work. Finally, we speculate about the diversity of future gendered family arrangements, and we provide a scenario of family life in America to suggest how paid and unpaid labor might be distributed in the year 2030.

THE ILLUSORY IDEAL FAMILY: THEN AND NOW

The changes in women's paid and unpaid labor over the past 30 years have been accompanied by a cultural struggle to redefine what it means to be engaged in "ideal" family life. Intertwined with this struggle has been a critique of the normative definition of an ideal family. This definition is intimately connected to sociocultural beliefs and practices related to gender, race, ethnicity, class, and sexual orientation. Traditionally, families have been conceived of as persons related by blood, marriage, or adoption living in the same household (Barrett & McIntosh, 1982). In the 1950s, this definition was exaggerated into an idealized image known as the nuclear family (Murdock, 1949) or Standard North American Family (Smith, 1993). This type of family, usually portrayed as white and middle class, consists of a breadwinner father, a homemaker mother, and children all living together. Though this image no longer has hegemonic hold over our collective view of the ideal family, it continues to influence cultural and research practices (Coontz, 1992). For example, the ideology of the Standard North American Family persists in shaping research and the collection of information by government agencies such as the U.S. Bureau of Census (Smith, 1993).

Feminists and other progressive family researchers, however, conceptualize families more broadly, focusing on the interdependence among family members rather than on a specific structural ideal (e.g., Scanzoni, Polonko, Teachman, & Thompson, 1989). This broader conceptualization reflects the reality of family life today and in the past. For us, *family* means persons who are bound by ties of marriage, blood, adoption, or commitment, legal or otherwise, who consider themselves a family. We do not restrict our definition of family to members who live in the same household, recognizing instead the complexity of household connections resulting from divorce and remarriage, cohabitation, and intergenerational relationships in adulthood. We also include nonheterosexual unions in our definition (Weston, 1991).

Though we strive for a broader conceptualization of family life, we recognize the limitations inherent in the practice of social research. For years, we and other family scientists have thought about families as if they were all white and also middle class. This practice is deplorable, given that the United States has always had a significant portion of families of color and far too many families in poorer and working classes. This diversity is even more prominent today. Fully 25% of the U.S. population—one in every four persons—is either Hispanic, African American, Asian American, Pacific Islander, American Indian, or some racial/ethnic combination other than non-Hispanic white (Harris & Sim, 2002). This proportion will continue to increase in the future.

Family scientists also have tended to minimize or problematize the diversity of structures within which family members struggle and prosper (Allen, 2001). This practice has become increasingly difficult to justify considering the diversity of family arrangements within the United States. For example, the model household today is not a nuclear family but a married couple without children present (U.S. Bureau of the Census, 2001). This change has occurred because younger married couples are delaying childbearing and older married couples are living together for longer periods of time after their children have left home—a factor that is influenced by an increasing life expectancy. There are also more single-parent households today than in the past, and mothers head most of them (U.S. Bureau of the Census, 2001). The numbers of these families have increased because of an accompanying increase in the rate of divorce and nonmarital childbearing. The relatively high divorce rate also has contributed to a large portion of remarried couples, many with children from previous and present unions (Coleman, Ganong, & Fine, 2000). Cohabitation before marriage is now common, especially for couples in which at least one partner was married before (Smock, 2000). Furthermore, gay and lesbian couples with and without children have also become more visible during this time (Patterson, 2000). Clearly, family life in the United States cannot be characterized by the nuclear family.

Finally, the definition of family is connected to our values concerning ideal family functioning and the proper work for women and men. Many people today, both in academic settings and in popular culture,

continue to idealize the image of the traditional nuclear family—one consisting of a breadwinner father and a homemaker mother. The persistence of this image has a profound influence on the social supports that are created for families. Because this ideology remains strong, a dearth of support exists for families that do not conform to the image—both in structure and in the gendered organization of paid and unpaid labor. In the next section, we discuss both mainstream thought related to women and men's participation in market and family work and challenges to that thinking. We describe ways that family researchers conceptualize the roles of men and women differently to show that, although researchers generally agree that family life has changed, they do not always agree on how to interpret these changes.

THEORETICAL OVERVIEW

Family scholars suggest that the work patterns of men and women have remained consistent since the rise of the Industrial Revolution and are intertwined with the ideology of domesticity (Ferree, 1991). This ideology is a gender system that (a) organizes market work around the ideal of an employee who works full time and overtime and takes little or no time off for childbearing and (b) marginalizes caregivers and those who engage in family work (Williams, 2000). The ideology of domesticity is rooted in the beliefs that men are "naturally" competitive and aggressive and best suited for work in the paid labor force, whereas women are "naturally" nurturing, cooperative, and caring and best suited for unpaid family work. These core ideas continue to structure market and family work in traditionally sex-segregated ways, especially for women with children. For example, though the wages of women who are not mothers have risen from 72% to 95% of men's wages, mothers' wages are only 75% of men's (Blau & Ehrenberg, 1997). As Williams (2000) pointed out, "Our economy is divided into mothers and others" (p. 2).

Within the scholarly study of families, the notion of domesticity took root in Talcott Parson's theory of structural-functionalism (Parsons, 1951; Parsons & Bales, 1955). Structural-functionalism states that adult family roles are divided into instrumental and expressive activities (Kingsbury & Scanzoni, 1993). According to Parsons, these activities are sex and gender segregated, evolving from biological predispositions and normative values. Husbands and fathers carry out instrumental activities such as providing financial resources for their families and protecting women and children from dangers in the outside world. Wives and mothers, in turn, engage in expressive activities. These activities include supporting husbands and nurturing children. From a structural-functionalist's perspective, women and men have inherently different family experiences because they are biologically and psychologically predisposed toward these differences.

Though structural-functionalism remains central to the field of family studies, alternative ideas have risen to challenge the theoretical underpinnings of the theory. For this chapter, we focus on feminist critiques of the ideology of domesticity in general and structural-functionalism in particular. Feminists reject the notion that there are two distinct spheres of life—private and public, expressive and instrumental—that are predetermined by men and women's differing biologies. Rather, feminists emphasize how unequal relationships between women and men are embedded in social processes related to power dynamics at all levels of social interaction. The gender perspective, a predominant theory used by feminist family scholars, "simultaneously emphasizes the symbolic and the structural, the ideological

and the material, the interactional and the institutional levels of analysis" (Ferree, 1991, p. 105). This view is particularly relevant for understanding families, as they are the primary sites in which gender is taught, learned, and transformed (Osmond & Thorne, 1993). Finally, the gender perspective highlights how family members actively negotiate meanings of gender in their daily interactions with one another (West & Zimmerman, 1991).

Implicit in a gender perspective is an acknowledgment of how race, class, and other social locations, in addition to gender, influence family relationships. Drawing insights from feminist theorists of color, feminist family researchers acknowledge the diversity among women, men, families, and work, incorporating race into the mainstream of their thinking rather than marginalizing minority families as special cultural cases (Baca Zinn, 1991; Dilworth-Anderson, Burton, & Johnson, 1993). This insight is applicable to families of lower socioeconomic classes as well. Family researchers tend to identify ideal family structures and processes within a middle-class context and to compare lower-class families to these ideals. For example, today's social scientists are emphasizing how marriage protects women and children from poverty, but minority married couples and their children are at a very high risk for poverty relative to white married couples (Lichter & Landale, 1995). Marriage clearly is not the answer to poverty for these couples. Feminist family scholars acknowledge class as a fundamental social structure that permeates all aspects of family life and results in different organizational and interactional patterns among families in different socioeconomic contexts (Lareau, 2002; Rubin, 1994). Rather than touting marriage as a cure for poverty, feminists focus on the intersections of gender, race, and class to highlight how low wages and poor educational opportunities are at the root of poverty, particularly for single-mother, minority households.

Differential access to resources and power exists not only between families but also within families. Thorne (1992) argued that the best way to analyze the social processes among family members is to examine the family's embedded structures of race, class, gender, generation, and sexuality. To illustrate within family social processes, think about a white, wealthy woman who does not work for pay but is held in high regard because of access to her husband's income. Should she and her husband divorce, her economic vulnerability and lower social status, relative to her husband's, will become more visible. In turn, both partners in an African American working-class couple are likely to have experienced racism and the frustration of receiving low wages, but only the wife is disadvantaged because of her gender. For example, African American women, relative to African American men, receive lower pay and are more responsible for providing the unpaid labor of child care and housework.

THE MORE FAMILY LIFE CHANGES

The Transformation of Women's Paid and Unpaid Work

As we stated earlier, one of the most significant changes in family life to occur is the unprecedented movement of women, particularly women with young children, into the paid labor force (Lichter, Anderson, & Hayward, 1995). Although women have always engaged in both reproductive and productive work, most women living in the middle of the 20th century did not engage in paid market work. In the 1950s, for example, only 16% of children had mothers who worked full time for wages outside the home. Fifty-nine percent of today's children, however, have mothers who are employed (Spain & Bianchi, 1996). The rate of maternal employment has increased steadily for all racial and ethnic groups. Women from different groups, however, do not participate in market work at the same rate. Black women (78.3%) are slightly more likely than white women (76.6%), Asian/Pacific Islander women (71.4%), and Hispanic women (65.8) to participate in the paid labor force (White & Rogers, 2000). The main point, however, is that women from all racial and ethnic groups are participating in the paid workforce at high levels, a finding that dispels the structural-functionalist belief that women are not well suited to participate in market work.

Women are not only increasing their participation in productive work but also decreasing their involvement in reproductive or family work. Family work, initially conceptualized by scholars as housework and child care, has come to describe many unpaid activities in which people engage on behalf of their families. Examples of family work include housework, childcare, kinkeeping, emotion work, volunteering, and caregiving.

Robinson and Godbey (1997) showed that women's time spent on housework declined substantially between 1965 and 1985, with employed women doing one third less housework than other women. Mothers also have reduced the time they spend in direct contact with their children (Demo, 1992). Rather than engage in housework and child care themselves, middle- and upper-middle class women are increasingly purchasing the services of others to cook and clean for them and to care for their young children while they are working for pay (Oropesa, 1993). Other women have lowered their standards of acceptable family work to engage in market work (Hochschild, 1997). Most women, however, struggle to participate in both market and family work (Garey,

1999). Clearly, the increasing participation of women in market work has transformed the organization of family life (Hochschild, 1989).

Women's lesser involvement in family work is partially attributable to their increased participation in market work and partially associated with other factors. A decrease in marriage and fertility rates and an increase in education are related to women's lesser participation in housework and child care. Cohabiting women, for example, do less housework than married women (Shelton & John, 1993a; South & Spitze, 1994). Cohabitation rates have increased and marriage rates have decreased over the last 30 years (Teachman, Tedrow, & Crowder, 2001). Mothers who have fewer children understandably do less than mothers with more children (Ferree, 1991; Shelton & John, 1993a). The overall birth-rate in the United States has declined in the last 30 years, particularly among white women (Casterline, Lee, & Foote, 1996). Finally, highly educated women do less family work than poorly educated women (Shelton & John, 1993a). Women are better educated today than they were 30 years ago (U.S. Bureau of the Census, 2001). More highly educated women are more likely to be employed in well-paying jobs and to be married to men with higher levels of education and income. These resources provide more highly educated women with the ability to hire other women to do family work.

Men's Response to Change

In response to women's changing work lives, men have increased slightly their participation in housework (Coltrane, 2000) and child rearing (Marsiglio, Amato, Day, & Lamb, 2000). Demo and Acock (1993), for example, using data from the National Survey of Families and Households, showed that husbands invested 9 hours per week in housework in the 1960s (excluding child care and other aspects of family work) and 13 hours per week in the late 1980s. Robinson and Godbey (1997) described a similar trend in men's housework participation. Their study, using national time-diary studies, found that men's contributions to routine housework increased from about 2 hours per week in 1965 to about 4 hours per week in 1985.

Though men are participating in family work at slightly higher rates than they did 30 years ago, men and women have reached gender parity neither in housework nor in child care (Coltrane, 2000). As we will see in the next section, much of family work remains the responsibility of women.

THE MORE FAMILY LIFE REMAINS THE SAME

The Persistence of Patriarchy in Family Work

Though women increasingly work for pay, they continue to be responsible for the unpaid and underrecognized work of maintaining homes and family relationships. Both men and women participate in unpaid family work, but women continue to do so to a greater extent and with more consistency than do men, regardless of age, race, ethnicity, or marital status (Walker, 1999). In fact, the average woman does two times more family work than the average man (Coltrane, 2000), despite the popular belief that men and women are sharing unpaid work. Even when couples are committed to egalitarian divisions of family work, women do more (Blaisure & Allen, 1995; Schwartz, 1994). The fact that women do a majority of family work—work that is unpaid and undervalued—serves to highlight the persistence of the patriarchal work structure within which women and men struggle for meaning and happiness.

The variability of women's participation in family work illustrates that this work is not in the nature of women but instead is shaped by the social and historical circumstances within which girls and women live. For example, as we stated earlier, white women in upper-income families are likely to purchase the services of other women— usually working-class women—to assist them with family work (Cohen, 1998; Oropesa, 1993). These middle- and upper-class women, then, coordinate and manage the work of other women (Leslie, Anderson, & Branson, 1991; Mederer, 1993). In comparison, working-class women, particularly those women who are not white, do greater amounts of routinized and undervalued work for both their employers and their families (Ferree, 1987; Jones, 1995). Family work has less to do with the essential nature of women and more to do with the resources women draw from to serve their interests.

Family work also has little to do with the essential nature of men. Men are fully capable of engaging in housework and child care (Blaisure & Allen, 1995; Coltrane, 2000; Schwartz, 1994), yet they do so to varying degrees, depending on their social circumstances. Generally, white men in upper-income families do less child care and housework relative to lower-income men and men of color (Coltrane, 2000). For example, African American fathers in middle-income, dual-earner families spend more time with their children than do white fathers (Ahmeduzzaman & Roopnarine, 1992). Men of color do more housework than white men (Shelton & John, 1993b). Men also do more housework when they are divorced or widowed (South & Spitze, 1994), when they perceive their wives to be co-providers (Perry-Jenkins & Crouter, 1990), and when their wives earn more than they do (Shelton & John, 1993a). Gay male couples too are more likely to share housework than heterosexual men who are cohabiting or married (Kurdek,

1993). Men's family work participation, like women's participation, is rooted, not in their essential natures, but in the sociohistorical circumstances in which they live and in the resources they can use to serve their interests.

In addition to understanding how women and men in various social groups experience family work, researchers working in the last half of the 20th century and the early 21st century have attempted to dissect the various components of family work and the qualities that characterize this work. Housework is the most frequently researched form of family work and includes tasks such as housecleaning, washing dishes, doing laundry, shopping, preparing meals, driving, gardening, and balancing household budgets (Walker, 1999). Ferree (1991) argued, however, that the definition of housework is amorphous because it "comes from imposing culturally shared gender categories on a historically shifting domain" (p. 111). In other words, what counts as housework changes depending on the time frame and culture being investigated.

Regardless of the changing nature of housework, present-day researchers continue to refine their operationalization of it. One way researchers have done this is by distinguishing between routine and discretionary tasks. Housework defined as "women's work" is more likely to be routine, and that defined as "men's work" is more likely to be discretionary, giving men more freedom and control over their housework (Blair & Lichter, 1991; Coltrane, 2000, Hochschild, 1989; Starrels, 1994). Twiggs, McQuillan, and Ferree (1999) showed that housework is segregated by sex much as occupations are segregated. These authors suggested that a hierarchy of household tasks exists, with dishwashing as the task men are most likely to do and preparing meals as the task they are least likely to do. They also argue that there is more than one *gendered threshold* husbands must cross to become high participators in housework (p. 722). For example, husbands who wash dishes need only normative support to do so. Stated another way, husbands will wash dishes when it is expected of them and when they and those around them think it is not unmanly to do so. Husbands who prepare meals, however, must have both normative support and practical circumstances to push them toward this household chore. Men who prepare meals are more likely to have wives who work more hours and contribute a higher proportion of family income than wives of husbands who do not prepare meals. .

Caregiving is another type of family work that remains highly gendered. Caregiving takes place across the life span and includes care given to children, dependent older people, and those who have short-term and long-term illnesses or disabilities. Caring for children, for example, is a caregiving activity that takes place relatively early in the life span and is done mainly by either mothers or mother substitutes. Similar to mothers of the past, present-day mothers provide most of the primary care for children of all ages, particularly children with intense needs (Traustadottir, 1991). Mothering gives women a sense of personal fulfillment and joy, as well as feelings of distress, depression, and anxiety (Oberman & Josselson, 1996). Contrary to the popular belief that working mothers are neglecting their children, empirical evidence suggests that employed and full-time mothers engage in the same types of child care activities and spend similar amounts of time in intense interaction with their children (Arendell, 2000).

Fathers also provide care for their children, but they spend less time and take less responsibility for them than mothers do (Asmussen & Larson, 1991). In 1988, LaRossa wrote that the culture of fatherhood had changed but the conduct of fathers had not. Though popular representations of fathers suggest that men are increasingly

involved in the day-to-day lives of their children, empirical evidence suggests only a small increase in the level of father involvement in two-parent households since the 1970s, in both proportionate and absolute terms (Pleck, 1997). Children today see their fathers as much less involved with them than their mothers are. This finding is particularly true for daughters (Asmussen & Larson, 1991; Starrels, 1994). These fathering patterns are similar to patterns that existed 30 years ago.

As with parenting, women and girls remain predominantly responsible for providing care to family members who are frail, are ill, or have long-term disabilities (Hooyman & Gonyea, 1995; Traustadottir, 1991). For example, daughters rather than sons are more likely to be responsible for providing care to their aging parents, particularly those with high needs (Stoller & Pugliesi, 1989). Though sons feel obligated to provide care for their parents (Finley, Roberts, & Banahan, 1988), they are more likely than daughters to be secondary care providers (Mathews & Rosner, 1988).

Finally, volunteering on behalf of children and other family members in organizations such as schools and churches is another type of family work in which mostly women engage. Women often see their volunteer work as an extension of their roles as wives and mothers (Wilson, 2000). Sometimes their volunteer work springs from a particular family challenge. For example, Traustadottir (1991) found that women who have children with disabilities extend their caring work to advocate for their own and other children in the larger community. The unpaid work of family advocacy is one way that women have been influential in changing the political climate of their local communities and the larger society (Pardo, 1990). Another example is the work of African American women who fought for civil rights for themselves and their families in the 1950s and 1960s (Jones, 1995). Similar to other types of unpaid family work, women's volunteering is often unrecognized and undervalued (Daniels, 1987; Margolis, 1979).

Unlike women, men are more likely to regard volunteering as complementary to their paid work (Wilson, 2000). Rather than engage in volunteer opportunities that involve helping others, men volunteer in organizations that benefit their paid employment and that support their leisure activities. Men gravitate more toward leadership positions in volunteer organizations and are more likely than women to volunteer in public and political groups (Wilson, 2000).

The Ideology of Domesticity Prevails in Market Work

Not only do women continue to be responsible for family work, but men also continue to be responsible for providing, though to a lesser degree than in the past. For example, the gap between men's rates and women's rates of labor force participation is far smaller today than it was 30 years ago (White & Rogers, 2000). Still, many men continue to feel a deep sense of commitment to the role of breadwinning and are reluctant to accept their wives as equal providers (Gerson, 1993; Hochschild, 1989). Today, masculinity, authority, and paid work are as inextricably intertwined as they were in the 1970s. The fact that men continue to earn higher wages than women (White & Rogers, 2000) supports men's primary participation in market work and rewards their resistance to doing family work. Women, however, tend to work in the secondary labor market. This market offers low wages and little job security but also offers women the flexibility to combine both family and market work (Wright, 1995).

Because many men do so little family work, their primary contribution to families is often financial. Empirical evidence suggests, for example, that some nonresidential fathers are involved with their children only through financial support (McLanahan & Sandefur, 1994). Regardless of family structure, fathers who provide economic resources improve their children's well-being and developmental outcomes (Acock & Demo, 1994). As historian Robert Griswold (1993) explained, "Despite men's differences, breadwinning has remained the great unifying element in fathers' lives. Its obligations bind men across the boundaries of color and class, and shape their sense of self, manhood, and gender" (p. 2).

Though men are more highly rewarded for their breadwinning than are women, both are constrained by our economic system. The organization of market work in the United States encourages at least one parent, usually a father, to become the primary breadwinner and another parent, usually the mother, to become a secondary breadwinner in combination with primary responsibility for family work (Hochschild, 1989). It is exceedingly difficult in our system for both parents to participate in the primary paid market while ensuring that all of their children's developmental needs are met (Hochschild, 1997). This is particularly true given that Americans so highly value primary care by mothers and do not encourage the development of institutions that would replace them as primary nurturers of their children (Garey, 1999; Hays, 1996). The practices of employers and the policies of our government also do not support the restructuring of the primary market to encourage parental care by both mothers and fathers. Rather, the same principles and forces that evolved during the rise of industrialization and the beginning of the ideology of domesticity continue to regulate today's market economy (Williams, 2000).

To be a primary breadwinner at the beginning of the 21st century, a worker must be able to participate in an economy that was founded on the principle that employees will be solely committed to wage work without obligations to engage in family work. This is true for blue- as well as white-collar workers. The current definition of an ideal worker is someone who works full time and overtime (Williams, 2000). Workers in elite jobs, for example, often must be able to work 50 to 70 hours a week. This is true for employees in manufacturing and other skilled trade positions as well. Ideal workers are also those employees who can move if the job requires it. For example, employees in research and management must be able to relocate when opportunities arise—to advance in a profession or even to get a job (Williams, 2000). Few women with children can meet the standards required of ideal workers, mainly because they do not have the social support men have. In other words, women do not have wives to help them meet the demands of their paid employment and raise their children. Similarly, few men feel free to diverge from the ideal worker norm because doing so could jeopardize the financial well-being of their families.

The problematic nature of the market structure and the accompanying ideology of domesticity are magnified in the high poverty rate of single-mother families, particularly those who are racial and ethnic minorities. Even though single-father and single-mother families are both at risk for poverty (partially because of having only one wage earner), single mothers are particularly vulnerable to poverty (Seccombe, 2000). One reason for this vulnerability is that single-mother families earn lower wages than single-father families. Single-mother families also are especially unlikely to be able to afford child care because they are among the poorest of the poor (Edin & Lein, 1997). Single women with children do not fit into the structure of domesticity because they cannot engage in market work unencumbered by family work and usually do not have the financial resources to purchase the services of other women to care for their children and to do their housework.

Similar to other single-mother families, divorced-mother families face many obstacles within the system of domesticity. Present-day divorce court judges, for example, operate under the assumption that men and women own their wages—a reasonable assumption except that most mothers are less involved than most fathers in wage work in order to raise children and manage households. Coinciding with the assumption of wage ownership is the fact that judges tend to ignore or minimize mothers' family work—both during marriage and after divorce—in ways that detrimentally affect women's awards of property, child support, and alimony (Williams, 2000). These patterns mean that divorced mothers raising children can expect to live below the standard of living available to them in marriage. Men, however, maintain ownership of their wages, benefit from having their children cared for, and often have a better standard of living than do women after divorce (Arendell, 1995).

Domesticity's Influence on Family Relationships

We end this section by considering how the ideology of domesticity shapes the quality of family relationships—encouraging women's connectedness and accepting men's relatively distant ties. Domesticity also makes it difficult for men and women to engage in egalitarian relationships, even when both partners are interested in equality for women.

Much of the research on gender and family relationships focuses on the discrepancy between wives' higher levels of participation in unpaid family work relative to husbands' and spouses' assessments that this arrangement is fair. Thompson (1991) postulated that women might do more family work, in part, because they value the positive relational outcomes that result from such work. Mothers may accept primary responsibility for child care, for example, because they believe that relationships with their children are important to nurture. Research supports the idea that caregiving and relationship quality are connected. Across the life course, fathers, who engage in relatively less child care than mothers, have less close ties with their children than mothers do (Aquilino, 1994; Rossi & Rossi, 1990; Silverstein & Bengtson, 1997). More broadly, when a woman is involved in any type of family relationship, the relationship is more likely to be described as close by both partners (Rossi & Rossi, 1990). This correlation coincides with the fact that women continue to feel responsible for family members' well-being and are more likely than men to adjust their schedules to accommodate others (Hochschild, 1989; Sanchez & Thomson, 1997; Shelton, 1992; Spain & Bianchi, 1996). Part of promoting connection, then, seems linked to the process of engaging in family work.

Hochschild (1989) showed how couples' negotiations about family work were fundamentally negotiations about care. When one partner, usually the husband, refused to do a fair share of family work, the other partner, usually the wife, felt less loved and valued. Within our patriarchal society, these couples were not negotiating for husbands' equal participation in family work. Wives, instead, wanted husbands to increase their participation in housework and child care to lessen wives' burdens of full-time paid employment and care for very young children. Most wives were willing to do more family work than their husbands.

Evidence suggests that husbands can make up for their lack of participation in family work by being emotionally supportive of their wives. Erickson (1993) showed that husbands' performance of emotion work was more important to their wives' marital well-being than was husbands' performance of housework and child care.

Though husbands' emotion work generally is more important to wives' marital well-being than performance of housework and child care, the unequal division of paid and unpaid work can have a detrimental influence on relationship quality (Schwartz, 1994), particularly if couples disagree on appropriate gender behavior (Hochschild, 1989). For example, Zvonkovic, Greaves, Schmiege, and Hall (1996) showed that couples' decisions about participation in paid and unpaid work were shaped by their gender beliefs and by the quality of their relationship. Positive relationship processes were associated with decisions that benefited wives' viewpoints on a minority of occasions. Negative relationship processes were correlated with wives' awareness of having less power in their relationships than their husbands. Ambivalent relationship processes were related to decisions benefiting husbands and to wives' desire for more support from their husbands. In these ambivalent relationships, an apparent consensual decision-making process was undermined by husbands' passive contention.

Zvonkovic et al. (1996) indicated that their findings were congruent with Komter's (1989) conceptualization of hidden power. Komter explored three types of power dynamics in marital relationships: manifest, latent, and invisible. Manifest power usually consists of husbands' negative responses to changes suggested by wives. In latent power dynamics, wives anticipate the needs of husbands and act in ways to minimize conflict. Finally, invisible power reflects the patriarchal social structure surrounding couples, resulting in power inequity between husbands and wives. Like the work and family decisions made by the couples in Zvonkovic et al.'s (1996) study, invisible power serves to justify and confirm the status quo.

Common conflict patterns between spouses in mostly white, middle-class married couples also are evidence of the unequal power distribution between men and women (Christensen & Heavy, 1990; Heavey, Layne, & Christensen, 1993). The pattern of wives demanding and husbands withdrawing during conflict occurs only during discussion of something wives want. Christensen and Heavey argued that men's favored position in society ensures that relationships are already structured as they wish, whereas women's weaker position encourages their desire for change. To avoid change sought by wives, husbands withdraw. This demand-withdraw pattern is harmful both to relationship quality and to marital stability (Heavey et al., 1993). (For a more detailed discussion on gendered marital negotiations, see Chapter 5 of this book.)

WHAT DOES THE FUTURE HOLD?

Throughout this chapter, we have explored how the system of domesticity—a gender system that organizes market work around the ideal of an employee who works full and overtime and takes little or no time off for childbearing and that marginalizes those who engage in family work—shaped family life in 1970 and continues to do so today. Even though domesticity exerts a powerful force on family life, women and men are purposeful in the ways they create their lives within this system. The most dramatic changes to take place have been women's increasing participation in market work and their decreasing participation in family work. The system of domesticity persists, however, and much about family life remains the same. Men continue to be responsible for providing, and women continue to be responsible for family work. This pattern has implications for family life generally and for family relationships specifically. Will the system of domesticity change in the future?

If the last 30 years are any indication of what families will be like in the future, then the next 30 years will probably consist of increasingly diverse family arrangements, both in the ways that families are structured and in the ways that women and men cooperate (or not) to accomplish family life. Earlier, we critiqued the structural-functionalist's family ideal (consisting of a breadwinner father and a homemaker mother) by illustrating the variety of ways women and men engage in paid and unpaid work and the diversity of family structures that operate in the United States. Our assertion has been that the organization of work and the structure of families have less to do with the essential, biological natures of women, men, and children and more to do with the resources people draw from to serve their interests. Resources are inequitably distributed in the United States, resulting in contradictory and diverse constructions of gender in families.

This process will remain constant in the future. For example, an increasingly disparate class system will mean that women with more financial means will have increasing opportunities to choose how to structure their paid and unpaid labor, whereas women with fewer financial resources will increasingly "have to work" to support themselves and their families. Wealthier, more highly educated women will be able to choose from a variety of cultural scripts, from creating traditional family structures in partnership with men to focusing singularly on their careers—and they will have the means to enact these scripts. Wealthier, better-educated men will have a similar opportunity to choose how committed to family life they would like to be and how enlightened they will become in terms of sharing all aspects of family life with women.

For most men and women, however, choice will play less of a role in their lives.

Most will have to work for pay, and couples, particularly those with children, will have to negotiate an acceptable sharing of family work. Spouses and partners will continue to interpret their gender arrangements as satisfactory or problematic, depending on their values. Significant sectors of the U.S. population continue to idealize the nuclear family and believe that men should have more authority than women. Many other people within our society remain ambivalent about men's and women's family roles. Still others are firmly committed to equality for women and to the creation of democratic family relationships. Because of this continuing diversity of views, no pervasive social or political will exists to challenge our system of domesticity.

In addition to the cultural lack of will, worker unions are relatively weak, and suspicion of government intervention is relatively high. Both of these mechanisms have been traditional vehicles for progressive change. We are not optimistic that our vision of equality will come to fruition because of this lack of organization and because our society remains unable to agree on the answers to these questions: (a) How should paid and unpaid work be organized? (b) Who should be responsible for engaging in both types of work? (c) What value should we place on "men's" and "women's" work? and (d) What role should society play in resolving these questions? In essence, the family values debate rages on.

Though we are not optimistic that gender relations will be transformed in the future, we remain steadfastly hopeful that they will be. We believe that one key to opening the door of progress will be to reevaluate the importance of family work or family care. We agree with Tronto (1993), who says,

> To recognize the value of care calls into question the structure of values in our society. Care is not a parochial concern of women, a type of secondary moral question, or the work of the least well off in society. Care is a central concern of human life. It is time that we began to change our political and social institutions to reflect this truth. (p. 180)

REFERENCES

Acock, A. C., & Demo, D. H. (1994). *Family diversity and well-being.* Newbury Park, CA: Sage.

Ahmeduzzaman, M., & Roopnarine, J. L. (1992). Sociodemographic factors, functioning style, social support, and fathers' involvement with preschoolers in African American families. *Journal of Marriage and the Family, 54,* 699–707.

Allen, K. R. (2001). A conscious and inclusive family studies. In R. M. Milardo (Ed.), *Understanding families into the new millennium: A decade in review* (pp. 38–51). Minneapolis, MN: National Council on Family Relations.

Aquilino, W. S. (1994). Impact of childhood family disruption on young adults' relationships with parents. *Journal of Marriage and the Family, 56,* 295–313.

Arendell, T. (1995). *Fathers and divorce.* Thousand Oaks, CA: Sage.

Asmussen, L., & Larson, R. (1991). The quality of family time among young adolescents in single-parent and married-parent families. *Journal of Marriage and the Family, 53,* 1021–1030.

Baca Zinn, M. (1991). Families, feminism, and race in America. In J. Lorber & S. A. Farrell (Eds.), *The social construction of gender* (pp. 119–134). Newbury Park, CA: Sage.

Barrett, M., & McIntosh, M. (1982). *The anti-social family*. London: Verso.

Blair, S. L., & Lichter, D. T. (1991). Measuring the division of household labor: Gender segregation of housework among American couples. *Journal of Family Issues, 12*, 91–113.

Blaisure, K. R., & Allen, K. R. (1995). Feminists and the ideology and practice of marital equality. *Journal of Marriage and the Family, 57*, 5–19.

Blau, F., & Ehrenberg, R. (Eds.). (1997). *Gender and family issues in the workplace*. New York: Sage.

Casterline, J., Lee, R., & Foote, K. (Eds.). (1996). *Fertility in the United States: New patterns, new theories 1996*. Washington, DC: Government Printing Office.

Christensen, A., & Heavey, C. L. (1990). Gender and social structure in the demand/withdraw pattern of marital conflict. *Journal of Personality and Social Psychology, 59*, 73–81.

Cohen, P. N. (1998). Replacing housework in the service economy: Gender, class, and race-ethnicity in service spending. *Gender and Society, 12*, 219–231.

Cohen, P. N., & Bianchi, S. M. (1999, December). Marriage, children, and women's employment: What do we know? *Monthly Labor Review*, 22–31.

Coleman, M., Ganong, L., & Fine, M. (2000). Reinvestigating remarriage: Another decade of progress. *Journal of Marriage and the Family, 62*, 1288–1307.

Coltrane, S. (2000). Research on household labor: Modeling and measuring the social embeddedness of routine family work. *Journal of Marriage and the Family, 62*, 1208–1233.

Coontz, S. (1992). *The way we never were: American families and the nostalgia trap*. New York: Basic Books.

Daniels, A. K. (1987). Invisible work. *Social Problems, 34*, 403–415.

Demo, D. H. (1992). Parent-child relations: Assessing recent changes. *Journal of Marriage and the Family, 54*, 104–117.

Demo, D. H., & Acock, A. C. (1993). Family diversity and the division of domestic labor: How much have things really changed? *Family Relations, 42*, 323–331.

Dilworth-Anderson, P., Burton, L. M., & Johnson, L. B. (1993). Reframing theories for understanding race, ethnicity, and families. In P. G. Boss, W. J. Doherty, R. LaRossa, W. R. Schumm, & S. Steinmetz (Eds.), *Sourcebook of family theories and methods: A contextual approach* (pp. 591–622). New York: Plenum.

Edin, K., & Lein, L. (1997). *Making ends meet: How single mothers survive welfare and low-wage work*. New York: Russell Sage Foundation.

Erickson, R. J. (1993). Reconceptualizing family work: The effect of emotion work on perceptions of marital quality. *Journal of Marriage and the Family, 55*, 888–900.

Ferree, M. M. (1987). She works hard for a living: Gender and class on the job. In B. B. Hess & M. M. Ferree (Eds.), *Analyzing gender: A handbook of social science research* (pp. 322–347). Newbury Park, CA: Sage.

Ferree, M. M. (1991). Beyond separate spheres: Feminism and family research. In A. Booth (Ed.), *Contemporary families: Looking forward, looking backward* (pp. 103–121). Minneapolis, MN: National Council on Family Relations.

Finley, N. J., Roberts, M. D., & Banahan, B. F., III. (1988). Motivators and inhibitors of attitudes of filial obligation toward aging parents. *Gerontologist, 28*, 73–78.

Garey, A. I. (1999). *Weaving work and motherhood*. Philadelphia: Temple University Press.

Gerson, K. (1993). *No man's land: Men's changing commitment to family and work*. New York: Basic Books.

Glass, J., & Estes, S. B. (1997). Employment and childcare. In T. Arendell (Ed.), *Contemporary parenting: Challenges and issues* (pp. 254–288). Thousand Oaks, CA: Sage.

Griswold, R. L. (1993). *Fatherhood in America: A history*. New York: Basic Books.

Harris, D. R., & Sim, J. J. (2002). Who is multiracial? Assessing the complexity of lived race. *American Sociological Review, 67,* 614–627.

Hays, S. (1996). *The cultural contradictions of motherhood*. New Haven, CT: Yale University Press.

Heavey, C. L., Layne, C., & Christensen, A. (1993). Gender and conflict structure in marital interaction: A replication and extension. *Journal of Consulting and Clinical Psychology, 61,* 16–27.

Hochschild, A. (1989). *The second shift: Working parents and the revolution at home*. New York: Viking.

Hochschild, A. R. (1997). *The time bind: When work becomes home and home becomes work*. New York: Holt.

Hooyman, N. R., & Gonyea, J. (1995). *Feminist perspectives on family care: Policies for gender justice*. Thousand Oaks, CA, Sage.

Jones, J. (1995). *Labor of love, labor of sorrow: Black women, work and the family, from slavery to the present*. New York: Vintage.

Kingsbury, N., & Scanzoni, J. (1993). Structural-functionalism. In P. G. Boss, W. J. Doherty, R. LaRossa, W. R. Schumm, & S. Steinmetz (Eds.), *Sourcebook of family theories and methods: A contextual approach* (pp. 195–217). New York: Plenum.

Komter, A. (1989). Hidden power in marriage. *Gender and Society, 3,* 187–216.

Kurdek, L. A. (1993). The allocation of household labor in homosexual and heterosexual cohabiting couples. *Journal of Social Issues, 49,* 127–139.

Lareau, A. (2002). Invisible inequality: Social class and childrearing in black families and white families. *American Sociological Review, 67,* 747–776.

LaRossa, R. (1988). Fatherhood and social change. *Family Relations, 37,* 451–457.

Leslie, L. A., Anderson, E. A., & Branson, M. P. (1991). Responsibility for children: The role of gender and employment. *Journal of Family Issues, 12,* 197–210.

Lichter, D. T., Anderson, R. N., & Hayward, M. D. (1995). Marriage markets and marital choice. *Journal of Family Issues, 16,* 412–431.

Lichter, D. T., & Landale, N. S. (1995). Parental work, family structure, and poverty among Latino children. *Journal of Marriage and the Family, 57,* 346–354.

Margolis, D. R. (1979). The invisible hands: Sex roles and the division of labor in two local political parties. *Social Problems, 26,* 314–324.

Marsiglio, W., Amato, P., Day, R. D., & Lamb, M. E. (2000). Scholarship on fatherhood in the 1990s and beyond. *Journal of Marriage and the Family, 62,* 1173–1191.

Mathews, S. H., & Rosner, T. T. (1988). Shared filial responsibility: The family as the primary caregiver. *Journal of Marriage and the Family, 50,* 185–195.

McLanahan, S., & Sandefur, G. (1994). *Growing up with a single parent: What hurts, what helps*. Cambridge, MA: Harvard University Press.

Mederer, H. J. (1993). Division of labor in two-earner homes: Task accomplishment versus household management as critical variables in perceptions about family work. *Journal of Marriage and the Family, 55,* 133–145.

Murdock, G. P. (1949). *Social structure*. New York: Macmillan.

Oberman, Y., & Josselson, R. (1996). Matrix of tensions: A model of mothering. *Psychology of Women Quarterly, 20,* 341–359.

Oropesa, R. S. (1993). Using the service economy to relieve the double burden: Female labor force participation and service purchases. *Journal of Family Issues, 14,* 438–473.

Osmond, M. W., & Thorne, B. (1993). Feminist theories: The social construction of gender in families and society. In P. G. Boss, W. J. Doherty, R. LaRossa, W. R. Schumm, & S. Steinmetz (Eds.), *Sourcebook of family theories and methods: A contextual approach* (pp. 591–622). New York: Plenum.

Pardo, M. (1990). Mexican American women grassroots community activists: "Mothers of east Los Angeles." *Frontiers, 11,* 1–7.

Parsons, T. (1951). *The social system.* New York: Free Press.

Parsons, T., & Bales, R. F. (1955). *Family socialization and interaction process.* Glencoe, IL: Free Press.

Patterson, C. J. (2000). Family relationships of lesbians and gay men. *Journal of Marriage and the Family, 62,* 1052–1069.

Perry-Jenkins, M., & Crouter, A. C. (1990). Men's provider-role attitudes. *Journal of Family Issues, 11,* 136–156.

Pleck, J. H. (1997). Paternal involvement: Levels, sources, and consequences. In M. E. Lamb (Ed.), *The role of the father in child development* (3rd ed., pp. 66–103, 325–332). New York: John Wiley.

Popenoe, D. (1993). American family decline, 1960–1990: A review and reappraisal. *Journal of Marriage and the Family, 55,* 527–555.

Robinson, J., & Godbey, G. (1997). *Time for life.* University Park: Pennsylvania State University Press.

Rossi, A. S., & Rossi, P. H. (1990). *Of human bonding: Parent-child relations across the life course.* New York: Aldine de Gruyter.

Rubin, L. (1994). *Families on the faultline: America's working class speaks about the family, the economy, race, and ethnicity.* New York: HarperCollins.

Sanchez, L., & Thomson, E. (1997). Women's power and the gendered division of domestic labor in the third-world. *Gender and Society, 7,* 434–459.

Scanzoni, J., Polonko, K., Teachman, J., & Thompson, L. (1989). *The sexual bond: Rethinking families and close relationships.* Newbury Park, CA: Sage.

Schwartz, P. (1994). *Peer marriage: How love between equals really works.* New York: Free Press.

Seccombe, K. (2000). Families in poverty in the 1990s: Trends, causes, consequences, and lessons learned. *Journal of Marriage and the Family, 62,* 1094–1113.

Shelton, B. A. (1992). *Women, men and time: Gender differences in paid work, housework and leisure.* New York: Greenwood.

Shelton, B. A., & John, D. (1993a). Does marital status make a difference? Housework among married and cohabiting men and women. *Journal of Family Issues, 14,* 401–420.

Shelton, B. A., & John, D. (1993b). Ethnicity, race, and difference: A comparison of white, black, and Hispanic men's household labor time. In J. C. Hood (Ed.), *Men, work, and family* (pp. 131–150). Newbury Park, CA: Sage.

Silverstein, M., & Bengtson, V. L. (1997). Intergenerational solidarity and the structure of adult child-parent relationships in American families. *American Journal of Sociology, 103,* 429–460.

Smith, D. E. (1993). The standard North American family: SNAF as an ideological code. *Journal of Family Issues, 14,* 50–65.

Smock, P. J. (2000). Cohabitation in the United States: An appraisal of research themes, findings, and implications. *Annual Review of Sociology, 26,* 1–20.

South, S. J., & Spitze, G. (1994). Housework in marital and nonmarital households, *American Sociological Review, 59,* 327–347.

Spain, D., & Bianchi, S. M. (1996). *Balancing act: Motherhood, marriage, and employment among American women.* New York: Sage.

Stacey, J. (1993). Good riddance to "The Family": A response to David Popenoe. *Journal of Marriage and the Family, 55,* 545–547.

Starrels, M. E. (1994). Husbands' involvement in female gender-typed household chores. *Sex Roles: A Journal of Research, 31,* 473–491.

Stoller, E. P., & Pugliesi, K. L. (1989). Other roles of caregivers: Competing responsibilities or supportive resources. *Journal of Gerontology: Social Sciences, 44,* S231–S238.

Teachman, J. D., Tedrow, L. M., & Crowder, K. D. (2001). The changing demography of America's families. In R. M. Milardo (Ed.), *Understanding families into the new millennium: A decade in review* (pp. 453–465). Minneapolis, MN: National Council on Family Relations.

Thompson, L. (1991). Family work: Women's sense of fairness. *Journal of Family Issues, 12,* 181–196.

Thorne, B. (1992). Feminism and the family: Two decades of thought. In B. Thorne & M. Yalom (Eds.), *Rethinking the family: Some feminist questions* (2nd ed.). Boston: Northeastern University Press.

Traustadottir, R. (1991). Mothers who care: Gender, disability, and family life. *Journal of Family Issues, 53,* 211–228.

Tronto, J. C. (1993). *Moral boundaries: A political argument for an ethic of care.* New York: Routledge.

Twiggs, J. E., McQuillan, J., & Ferree, M. M. (1999). Meaning and measurement: Reconceptualizing measures of the division of household labor. *Journal of Marriage and the Family, 61,* 712–724.

U.S. Bureau of the Census. (2001). *Statistical abstract of the United States: 2001.* Retrieved August 16, 2002, from www.census.gov/prod/www/abs/popula.html #popspec.

Walker, A. J. (1999). Gender and family relationships. In M. Sussman, S. K. Steinmetz, & G. W. Peterson (Eds.), *Handbook of marriage and the family* (2nd ed., pp. 439–474). New York: Plenum.

West, C., & Zimmerman, D. H. (1991). Doing gender. In J. Lorber & S. A. Farrell (Eds.), *The social construction of gender* (pp. 13–37). Newbury Park, CA: Sage.

Weston, K. (1991). Is "straight" to "gay" as "family" is to "no family"? In K. Weston, *Families we choose* (pp. 22–29). New York: Columbia University Press.

White, L., & Rogers, S. J. (2000). Economic circumstances and family outcomes: A review of the 1990s. *Journal of Marriage and the Family, 62,* 1035–1051.

Williams, J. (2000). *Unbending gender: Why family and work conflict and what to do about it.* New York: Oxford University Press.

Wilson, J. (2000). Volunteering. *Annual Review of Sociology, 26,* 215–240.

Wright, M. M. (1995). "I never did any fieldwork, but I milked an awful lot of cows!": Using rural women's experiences to reconceptualize models of work. *Gender and Society, 9,* 216–235.

Zvonkovic, A. M., Greaves, K. M., Schmiege, C. J., & Hall, L. (1996). The marital construction of gender through work and family decisions: A qualitative analysis. *Journal of Marriage and the Family, 58,* 91–100.

CHAPTER 11

Feminist Visions for Transforming Families
Desire and Equality Then and Now

Katherine R. Allen

Feminist visions for transforming families must be placed in social-historical context, consciously referencing the past, grounded in the present, and envisioning the future. In this chapter, I address topics that often run counter to prevailing assumptions about family development and change. The method I use to construct my argument is to rely upon my own structural and processual connections to the ideologies and activism I describe. I weave in stories from my private life to illustrate a key principle of feminism, that the personal is political. What occurs in private life is a reflection of power relations in society. The analytic strategy I employ in this chapter is to reveal the connection between the personal and political by using my own life as a bridge for the transfer of feminist insights into family studies. My aim is to invite others into the conscious, reflexive practice of applying feminist knowledge to one's own life and scholarship. I trust that others, in reading these ideas saturated with personal and political implications, will take the risk of incorporating their own resonances about private life and power relations. By inviting others into their own feminist journey from "silence to language to action" (Collins, 1990, p. 112), I show one way that we as a community of scholars can produce more realistic perspectives about the families we study (Allen, 2000).

DEFINING FEMINISM

Like a sandcastle built on the beach, my working definition of feminism reflects the historical moment in which it is posed. In

AUTHOR'S NOTE: An earlier version of this chapter was presented as the closing plenary at the Groves 2000 Conference on Marriage and the Family, Asheville, North Carolina, June 17, 2000. Many thanks to Marilyn Coleman, Larry Ganong, Stacey Floyd-Thomas, and an anonymous reviewer for their helpful comments on this chapter.

sharing this definition, I am aware of the elements that attempt to knock down my metaphoric sandcastle—to whisk it away with the daily flow of the tides or to flagrantly step on it as a mischievous child might do when no one is looking. Whatever the tide or the children do not level, the cleaning machines that rumble down the beach after dark surely will. Like sand fashioned into temporary shapes, feminism can never be encapsulated in a singular treatise; neither can it remain static after being printed on the page. In proposing a working definition of *feminism*, I take the risk of representing and misrepresenting in unique ways the ideas that fascinate me.

With these caveats in mind, I work toward an understanding of feminism in which I acknowledge the partiality of any definition. It is dangerous to speak seriously as a feminist scholar in a field in which feminist ideas continue to be marginalized (Thompson & Walker, 1995). Human perceptions and relationships are so fragile and tentative that the opportunities for misunderstanding are vast. The potential for connecting around the politicized inquiry associated with feminist family scholarship requires an inclusive, open mind and a patient, loving heart (Allen, 2000). The rewards for looking at family life from a feminist perspective include a deepening connection between how we live and what we study. Feminism is against the status quo. It is an activist endeavor with the goal of social change.

Feminism is a way of being in the world (ontology), a way of investigating and analyzing the world (methodology), and a theory or model of how we know what we know about the world (epistemology) (for variations on these analytic categories, see Cook & Fonow, 1986; Harding, 1987; Hawkesworth, 1989; Riger, 1998). Feminism is not just an idea or a theory; it is also a *praxis*, the term that Marx used to "distinguish between what one does and what one thinks and to distinguish

revolutionary practice from other types of activity" (Nielsen, 1990, p. 34). Praxis is "that continuous reflexive integration of thought, desire, and action" (Simon, 1992, p. 49). Nielsen (1990) further explained that praxis, originating with critical theory, is the active, reflective process that allows us to demystify and expose the real nature of the power relations that drive human interactions and transactions and motivate the desire for social change. Feminist praxis is a conscious, inclusive, and impassioned way of thinking about and operating in the world (Allen, 2000).

Feminism is a liberationist project emerging most recently from the civil rights movement for American blacks in the 1950s and 1960s and spawning the gay liberation movement in the 1970s. The women's liberation movement, or second-wave feminism, was ignited in the mid-1960s as more and more women started to speak about what they were enduring under capitalist patriarchy, topics that until the publication of Friedan's *The Feminine Mystique* (1963) were still taboo to either name or discuss (Brownmiller, 1999). The grassroots attempt to emancipate women from oppression, starting in consciousness-raising (CR) groups, grew into a multitude of liberationist efforts (Christensen, 1997). In its current manifestations, feminism is joined with other ideologies and practices embraced by those on the margins to seek justice for all people exploited by global patriarchal capitalism (see Agger, 1998; Alexander & Mohanty, 1997; Ebert, 1996; White, 1991). Combining theory and praxis, then, feminism is a conscious action with the goal of unsettling the normativity (e.g., status quo) that gives unearned privileges to an elite few and exploits the labor, life, and desire of multiple others (Collins, 1990; Lorde, 1984; McIntosh, 1995). This exploitation occurs in systematic ways through the structural and ideological mechanisms of racism, sexism, heterosexism, classism, ethnocentrism, ageism, able-bodyism, and colonialism.

Feminism shares with other critical theories and practices a challenge to the oppressive conditions that contribute to the individual's alienation from self, other, and society by unfairly harming some and irrationally privileging others (Agger, 1998). There are countless varieties of feminism and, as in any liberationist movement, many internal and external debates. For example, Brownmiller (1999) chronicled the birth, growth, and transformation of the women's movement, addressing key feminist issues for the 30 years following 1968, including abortion, rape, heterosexuality and lesbianism, racial injustice, sexual harassment, and pornography. Also, in a recent exchange in the premier journal for feminist scholarship, *Signs: Journal of Women in Culture and Society*, Walby (2001a, 2001b), Harding (2001), and Sprague (2001) debated current ideas about the role of science in feminist scholarship. Each day, each conversation, each published work brings a new way to pose a feminist perspective of knowing, being, and acting in the world.

There are many feminist theories (for various accounts, see Ebert, 1996; Herrmann & Stewart, 1994; Jaggar & Rothenberg, 1984; Rosser, 1992; Spender, 1983), including some of the following. Feminism has a liberal slant, wanting to secure equal rights and help women get their fair share of the economic and legal pie. Feminism has a radical slant, characterized by the admonition to "get your laws and your hands off my body." Feminism has a lesbian slant, in which women choose a woman-centered private life in congruence with their politics as well as their desire (Rich, 1980). Feminism has a cultural slant of valorizing and celebrating women's unique and, to some, superior ways of being in the world, as in "men have had the power for so long, and look at what a mess they've made of things." Feminism has

a multicultural slant, decentering what Morrison (1992) calls *whitethings* as the unquestioned authority on agency and social relations for all people, including people of color. Feminism has a critical slant, aimed at redistributing the means and ends of production so that "the hand that picks the grapes also gets to drink the wine."

LOCATING MYSELF IN FEMINISM

The feminisms from which I draw traverse all of these categories. As an educated, middle-class white woman who came of age and into a radical consciousness in the second wave of feminist activity in the United States, I have certain unearned privileges that to an extent tolerate and even indulge my challenge of male dominance. When I am seeking equity in work, pay, and legal rights, I am aligned with liberal feminism (Rosser, 1992). When I came to realize that the feelings I had for another woman were passionate love—what women in the 19th century called "the love that dared not speak its name" (Faderman, 1991)—I claimed a lesbian life, aligning myself with lesbian feminism. The merger of lesbianism and feminism is a cohort phenomenon initiated by women who came of age in the late 1960s and early 1970s (Faderman, 1991). I am a lesbian feminist, then, in the sense that I found in feminism congruence between my lived reality of desiring an end to embodied oppression and my liberationist epistemology. I abandoned heterosexual privilege and let my career slow down to pursue this love that would change my standpoint or the way I looked at the world. When I am critical of feminist ideologies and practices in and of themselves or questioning of my own lesbian standpoint, I am a postmodern feminist (Elam & Wiegman, 1995; Gagnier, 1990).

I am also a critical antiracist white feminist (Frankenberg, 1993), which brings me to the work that ignites my passion now, interrogating my own race and class privilege, opening myself to a feminist politics in which I seek to understand how my identity as a middle-class white woman is complicit in the oppression of others (Allen, 2000). Antiracist feminism, with ties to radical-critical theory (Osmond, 1987), gives me the tools to deconstruct the ways that I am marked by the privilege and power of white patriarchal wealth (Alexander & Mohanty, 1997; Collins, 1990; Ellsworth, 1997; McIntosh, 1995). My praxis is to uncover how I manipulate and employ privilege for my own gain so that I can consciously oppose any participation in racist, classist, or sexist action. I wish to use my knowledge of how unearned privilege wounds those without it to challenge and redirect my impulse to reach for the choicest piece of pie.

Looking through the lens of diverse feminist perspectives on methodology (Harding, 1998), when conducting research in family gerontology, I am a feminist empiricist (Allen, Blieszner, Roberto, Farnsworth, & Wilcox, 1999). When combining my identity politics as an antiracist lesbian feminist, I am drawing from feminist standpoint theory (e.g., Allen, 2000). When applying postmodern theory to feminist family science, as a reconstructionist of women's experiences in families (Baber & Allen, 1992), I am a feminist postmodernist. Feminists both critique and may incorporate any or all of these perspectives on science: empiricist, standpoint, and postmodern (Harding, 1987; Hawkesworth, 1989; Riger, 1998; Rosser, 1992).

Feminism is a worldview, but it is also a home base. It is a way of living in which I can struggle free from the alienating bonds of patriarchal expectations for a truncated life and envision and then become an authentic self even as I know that authenticity can never be fully realized (Sawhney, 1995). Feminism gives me a position from which to tell the truth, particularly to myself, even if it means speaking bitterness from my raised consciousness. Feminism gives me the courage to love those I desire with passion and without shame. Feminism is the place where my deepest connections are found. With an active feminist awareness, I can name my fears about the future, face my demons from the past, handle the assaults of an unforgiving world, and find joy in living through the process of becoming as fully conscious as my mind, heart, spirit, and body allow (see Krieger, 1996, for an elegant evocation of such a synthesis). This process, of course, has been called many things, from *conscientization* (Freire, 1970/1997), to *enlightenment* (Wilber, 1998), and even *salvation* or *serenity*. Feminists did not make it up, but at the same time, feminist scholars and activists have generated innovative ways to pursue the conscious desire for truth, justice, equality, integrity, and freedom in terms of exploring sexism (Morgan, 1970), materialism (Ebert, 1996), and racism (Christensen, 1997; Collins, 1990), among other manifestations of oppression. With this as background, I now illustrate feminist desire and equality in the past and present, constructing a sense of feminist history and its influence on family change.

LOVE BETWEEN EQUALS IN THE 19TH CENTURY

Consider the following passage describing the "the beautiful friendship of two ladies," and the time frame in which it was written:

In their youthful days, they took each other as companions for life, and this union, no less sacred to them than the tie of marriage, has subsisted, in uninterrupted harmony, for 40 years, during which they have shared each other's occupations and pleasures and works of charity while in health, and watched over each other tenderly in sickness. . . . They slept on the same pillow and had a common purse, and adopted each other's relations, and . . . . I would tell you of their dwelling, encircled with roses, ... and I would speak of the friendly attentions which their neighbors, people of kind hearts and simple manners, seem to take pleasure in bestowing upon them. (Faderman, 1991, p. 1)

This passage was published in an American newspaper in 1843 by William Cullen Bryant, describing a trip to Vermont, where he met these unmarried women (e.g., "maiden ladies") who lived together. In the 19th century, female same-sex love, or *romantic friendship*, was a respected social institution in America. At the height of the Industrial Revolution, the worlds of white middle-class men and women were highly segregated. It was during this time that contemporary gender roles took root. Men worked outside the home in the business world, and women of means withdrew from the world of commerce to the female world of love and ritual (Smith-Rosenberg, 1975).

Gender-segregated marriage was a radical departure from the corporate family unit common in Colonial America over the previous two centuries, where the homestead had been the center of life and survival (Hareven, 1991). In the 19th century, women were not yet full citizens. The U.S. Constitution enfranchised only one third of the population: white, landowning men. Women, native people, and people of color were excluded. Black males, in principle, gained the right to vote with the passage of the 15th Amendment in 1870, but in practice, the Black Codes and Jim Crow laws, particularly in the South, severely restricted full citizenship for those of African descent whose ancestors had been brought to this country by force (Bell, 1992; D'Emilio & Freedman, 1997). Women derived their rights through men; a woman had no sovereignty over her own body, children, or livelihood.

Perhaps because women were second-class citizens, their love for each other did not threaten the establishment. Women who loved other women were invisible (Faderman, 1981). There was no such thing as a lesbian until the late 19th century because women were not believed to be sexual. By the time the emerging discipline of modern sexology came into being, women who loved each other passionately were considered deviant and labeled as *female sexual inverts* (D'Emilio & Freedman, 1997; Gagnon & Parker, 1995).

By the 20th century, women who realized they were lesbian had little chance to lead an authentic life (Faderman, 1991). They were forced to deny, repress, or hide their feelings because being *out* had serious consequences. Some women did sacrifice what little freedom they had throughout the past century. Despite being labeled as *other*, they carved out a life economically, socially, and sexually independent of men, creating a lesbian subculture, most notably among working-class butch or femme women, that had never existed before love between women was defined as abnormal and unusual (Davis & Kennedy, 1986; Faderman, 1991). Their legacy for 21st-century women is that now some women find a lesbian identity viable, appropriate, and healthy (Baber & Allen, 1992). For some, it is a consciously chosen way of life.

In the 19th century, women of color experienced double and triple jeopardy in their struggle for full citizenship (Dill, 1988). The Chinese Exclusion Act of 1882 prohibited entry of Chinese women except as prostitutes or wives of merchants, teachers, and students. The bulk of Chinese immigrants were laborers, and their wives and daughters were not allowed to immigrate (Chow, 1998). By 1890, females constituted about 3% of the Chinese population in the United States. Most of these women had been sold to men in Hong Kong, who later forced them into prostitution. Chinese women were not permitted to enter this country until 1943, when the Chinese Exclusion Act of 1882 was repealed (Chow, 1998). Consider, as well, the following quote from an older black woman that reveals a profound understanding of female oppression in the context of race difference: "The black woman is the white man's mule and the white woman is his dog" (Collins, 1990, p. 106). One was forced to work much harder than the other, but both women were still the personal property of the master. Feminist historians have uncovered the reality of the constraints placed on women, retelling history from perspectives other than military and political events. They have uncovered ways that women of all backgrounds resisted and created their own lives in spite of the severe restrictions carved into law and everyday practice (Kerber & DeHart-Mathews, 1987).

FEMINIST EXPERIMENTS FOR RADICAL CHANGE IN THE 20TH CENTURY

After a 70-year struggle of organized activism on many fronts, women earned the right to vote in 1920 with the passage of the 19th Amendment. The next major historic milestone did not occur until half a century later, when another significant female cultural revolution was ignited. Feminist essayist Robin Morgan, editor of the classic 1970 text *Sisterhood Is Powerful,* called the New Left and its student members "the little boys movement" because its leaders were white middle-class young men who were challenging the hegemonic, militaristic, and capitalist values of their fathers. Yet few acknowledged their debts to the black civil rights movement. Fewer recognized how they were repeating the very patriarchal privilege of the establishment males that they were rebelling against by using women only as sex partners and servants.

Second-wave feminism arose out of women's dissatisfaction that they were often the invisible laborers in all the liberation movements in which they were involved. Male leaders and partners were not taking their quest for or right to emancipation seriously.

Women started rap groups, or CR groups, anywhere and everywhere—suburban kitchens, urban mental health centers, and church basements. I attended my first "speak out" in 1972 when I was a freshman at San Diego State University. I was alarmed by observing women who were speaking and acting with anger. I felt like I was witnessing something taboo, obscene, foreign, and wrong when I heard women speak their bitterness by naming and challenging the patriarchy that severely restricted their opportunities in life.

A year later, I transferred to the University of Connecticut and joined my first CR group. We were a collection of undergraduate and graduate students, faculty wives, women exploring their feelings for other women, and young mothers in turmoil over their seemingly isolated inability to be satisfied with the domestic monotony of their lives. I still have the mimeographed sheets of questions that were distributed in the CR group, which I reread periodically to remind myself that dialogue has always been a revolutionary self-help activity (Freire, 1970/1997). This early process of interrogating the social construction of gender steered me toward the qualitative methodologies I employ as a social scientist today.

We explored messages and expectations from childhood, puberty, and young adulthood. We addressed sex roles and perceptions of masculinity/femininity. We discussed what virginity meant to us and whether any of us still had it. We spent a lot of time discussing our bodies and self-image. We talked about sex, men, and men's bodies—our desire for them but our disappointment that men did not respond to us in the physical and emotional ways we wanted. We called ourselves *emotional lesbians* and wore buttons announcing "Together Women Together." Acknowledging that we felt more comfortable in female space but being too afraid to cross some imaginary line into an authentically embodied space, most of us were unable to transcend the rigid boundaries that heterosexism enforced on all of us from birth. We fought and challenged each other. It was in that context that I began to consciously practice the self-interrogation and rhetorical skills that I incorporate into my scholarship and teaching today.

As embarrassing as it is to tell, I take the risk to share the following story because only in our most vulnerable disclosures can we reveal the truth of how inauthenticity is internalized. Krieger (1991, 1996) explained that such theorized self-disclosure, in which one tells on oneself, is a particular window into the general phenomenon of structural oppression. One Tuesday night in 1975, I was in the midst of describing to my CR sisters how I no longer wanted to go out with a guy I was seeing because he was too nice. My friends pressed me for further information. Baffled by my own untheorized analysis of what was wrong with my partner, I mumbled something about his penis being too small. One of the older participants in the group—a woman in her late 40s who had raised five children, and whose husband, a psychology professor, had a reputation for sleeping with students—challenged the absurdity of what I was saying: "What do you mean, 'too nice'?" "What do you mean, 'too small'?" She attacked these parroted gendered messages that I had internalized— messages that I needed a real man, who was rough around the edges and well endowed underneath his clothes—to make me a woman. I broke into tears, I felt hatred for her, I shot back with something like "You are a pathetic wife who puts up with your husband's infidelity in the name of love," but

the truth is, she got to me. She broke through my denial, the distorted sexual script that had been spoonfed to me by my sexist culture. She held up a mirror so that I could confront the convoluted fundamentals of heterosexuality that were motivating my behavior and poisoning any potential partnership with a man.

That CR group endured for the 3 years I spent as an undergraduate at Connecticut. In all its messy confusion and gut-wrenching challenges, it got me through young adulthood and paved the way for deepening my feminist consciousness through reading political texts—a process that taught me how to theorize my experience. Faderman (1991) explained that out of this CR context, a new vision of equality emerged. In its purest form, it became the lesbian feminism of the 1970s and 1980s, before AIDS devastated the gay male community in the 1980s (Gagnon & Parker, 1995) and before the lesbian baby boom in the 1980s and 1990s (Patterson, 1994). Like the anomalous social arrangements of the 1950s, with the majority of women staying at home, men in the workforce, and the baby boom in full force (Coontz, 1992), lesbian feminism, as a political ideal, is historically situated—a product of the late-20th-century liberation movements.

Lesbian feminism began with a radical separatist impulse. Women who loved women defined themselves in opposition to patriarchy and in opposition to the reformers in the National Organization for Women who wanted lesbians purged from the white middle-class women's movement (Brownmiller, 1999). But separatism is a project that is doomed to failure, at least on a large scale, as many of the alternative communities (e.g., Shakers, Oneidans, Free Lovers) of the 1800s showed (D'Emilio & Freedman, 1997). Formed in reaction to male-dominated culture, separatism is fueled by negative energy to not do things, such as vote, interact with males, or support the patriarchy (Johnson, 1989). An "us versus them" mentality is responsible for the demise of many liberation movements and ideological feuds, such as the capitalists versus the communists, the men versus the women, the straight women versus the lesbians, the blacks versus the whites, the structural functionalists versus the symbolic interactionists, the Hatfields versus the McCoys. These binary oppositions make neat boxes to dump our confusing thoughts into, but all they produce are scapegoats, heartache, and further oppression (Lorde, 1984). The challenge is to be for something without necessarily being against some arbitrary other.

Today, feminist desires for equality no longer freeze on gender as the only category. Black women, Latina women, Asian American women, working-class women, lesbians, old women, and men who love women, among others, have demonstrated that an analysis of gender alone is not sufficient to resist and transform oppressive social structures and processes. We must interrogate the intersections among gender, race, class, and sexual orientation by examining issues in all of their complexity. Bernice Johnson Reagon, a scholar, performer, and activist who organized the African American women's vocal ensemble Sweet Honey in the Rock, is unapologetic about the need for all of us, regardless of race, class, gender, ethnicity, or sexual orientation, to acknowledge our debt to the blacks who started and sustained the civil rights movement and to correct our reluctance to recognize more than one form of oppression as primary (Christensen, 1997). Reagon (1983) uses her standpoint as a black woman as a starting point for any project and as grounds for reforming and redefining political expression:

> Black folks started it, Black folks did it, so everything you've done politically rests on the efforts of my people—that's my

arrogance! Yes, and it's the truth; it's my truth. You can take it or leave it, but that's the way I see it. So once we did what we did, then you've got women, you've got Chicanos, you've got the native Americans, and you've got homosexuals, and you got all of these people who also got sick of somebody being on their neck. And maybe if they come together, they can do something about it. And I claim all of you as coming from something that made me who I am. You can't tell me that you ain't in the Civil Rights movement. You are in the Civil Rights movement that we created that just rolled up to your door. But it could not stay the same, because if it was gonna stay the same it wouldn't have done you no good. (p. 362)

FEMINIST VISIONS FOR NOW AND INTO THE FUTURE

World Traveling

Feminist scholars have demonstrated how inaccurate it is to treat gender as a separate and singular analytic category (Christensen, 1997; Hawkesworth, 1997). Yet in the discipline of family studies, even talking about gender is a taboo subject in many quarters (see the critique by Thompson & Walker, 1995). The dominant discourse about gender roles is still protected and rarely questioned (for an elaboration of how privilege and oppression operate in the theory and science of family studies, see recent analyses by Allen, 2000; Marks, 2000; and Walker, 2000). But there is a progressive energy in family studies to acknowledge how the world is changing. Underscoring this energy is the spiritual ability to hold oneself responsible as a positive force for change (Allen, 2000). I desire social justice not just for myself and those I love but for anyone who is at risk. As we enter the 21st century, feminist theory is incorporating a renewed critique of the "exploitive relations of production and the unequal divisions of labor, property, power, and privilege these produce" (Ebert, 1996, p. xi) into the current postmodern trend in which a "localist genre of descriptive and immanent writing" (p. xii) prevails. Both social critique and cultural analysis are needed to enable a transformative feminism "of transnational equality for all people of the world" (p. xiii).

Feminist practice in family studies is active and ongoing, but much more work still needs to be done. We cannot just talk about how oppression has affected and made us into the women and men we are today. Feminist praxis is revolutionary. Thompson and Walker (1995) concluded that feminism has had a far greater impact on family pedagogy than on family research. Indeed, activist feminist teaching continues to inspire the discipline (for recent examples, see Allen, Floyd-Thomas, & Gillman, 2001; Baber & Murray, 2001; Fletcher & Russell, 2001). We can make greater progress in terms of how we envision and study families by incorporating feminist lessons into our work. Lugones (1990) proposed the metaphor of world traveling to apply the principle of the personal as political to our practice in coming to value and respect the humanity of others. She described how we can bridge the span between our own experiences and those of others, thereby challenging traditional assumptions about individuals, families, and societies:

> There are worlds we enter at our own risk, worlds that have agony, conquest, and arrogance as the main ingredients in their ethos. These are worlds that we enter out of necessity and which would be foolish to enter playfully. But there are worlds that we can travel to lovingly and traveling to them is part of loving at least some of their inhabitants. The reason why I think that travelling to someone's world is a way of identifying with them is because by traveling to their world we can understand what it is to be them and what it is to be ourselves in their eyes. Only when we have traveled to each other's worlds are we fully subjects to each other. (p. 401)

Building on Lugones's (1990) suggestion, we can adopt an attitude of careful curiosity toward the experiences of others (Thompson, 1995). What does it mean to travel to someone else's world? What can we gain by becoming "fully subjects to each other?" I offer a glimpse of this process in a story from my own life. I hope, like Hansel and Gretel in one of Grimm's fairy tales (Lang, 1969), that by leaving these stones, others can retrace their steps out of the forest of denial and into a place of renewed commitment to uncovering the realities of family life from the perspectives of those who live it.

Traveling to My Son's World My son, at 14, has just experienced his mother's second divorce. The first one occurred when his father and I parted company after a long and difficult decision-making process, concluding that our marriage was never going to work out as planned. Matt was 2 at the time, and although I retained physical custody, his father has remained an active part of his life. After this divorce, I entered a lesbian partnership with another woman, who assumed most of the primary caregiving for our chosen family. Eventually, we had a second child (born to her), whose father was my brother's life partner. Our family seemed complete, and we proudly professed to the world how well our chosen family was working. Open in our community, we enjoyed the lesbian poster family status we achieved, feeling protected and secure in how we presented ourselves to the world.

Then, the unfathomable happened, at least from my perspective. My former partner and I had just gotten a civil union in the state of Vermont, the first state in the United States to offer marriagelike benefits to gay and lesbian partners. We had also completed the legal work to add her last name onto Matt's name and to give me joint custody of our second child. It seemed that after 12 years in a committed partnership, we now had as many legal safeguards in place as possible. Yet soon after the civil union in Vermont, my partner found herself falling in love with another woman in our community, a divorced, heterosexual mother of two whose children also attended our children's school. In a matter of weeks, my partner confessed her newfound love and left our home and family to be with this woman and her children. She took our second child with her, leaving Matt and me behind.

Like most people who are left in marriage or other domestic partnerships, I experienced the abrupt ending of this relationship as a painful surprise (Chodron, 1997; Fisher & Alberti, 2000; Kingma, 2000; Murray, 1994). After all, we had just repeated our vows to love and care for each other for the rest of our lives. I was not prepared for her seemingly sudden change of heart, but after several months of denial, I had to admit to myself that she was gone. Almost overnight, the old definition of our family as headed by two lesbian mothers raising two young sons with several fathers in the picture was also over. I had to play catch-up to my former partner in terms of coming to terms with the fact that the family I had staked my identity on no longer existed. What's worse, we were unable to negotiate a new family relationship. The odd branches we had sprouted on the family tree (Stacey, 2000), of which I had once been so proud, had been chopped off, and my ex-partner no longer resembled the person I once cherished.

As self-absorption with my own pain subsided, I started to notice my son's reactions to this ordeal. He seemed happier now that there were only the two of us. I was unprepared for his point of view on the family breakup: Now he finally had me, his mom, all to himself. He said that although he felt abandoned by my ex-partner, our home was much more relaxed without her rules and without having to share me with his sibling.

It has taken me a while to face up to the fact that my son's definition of our family was not the same as mine. My writings about chosen family ties and the careful construction of a lesbian family disintegrated under his scrutiny. As I experienced this unitarily constructed definition of my family crumble, like those grains of sand in my metaphoric sandcastle, I learned some painful lessons that are already in the family studies literature but were not yet real to me. I had not yet lived through the crucible in which I felt the heat of their truth. My son was a major teacher of these lessons.

He was taking the breakup of my partnership and our chosen family in stride. He was sorry that I was so sad to be left by someone I trusted and loved, but from his point of view, life was far easier with only one doting parent in his home. Having had two mothers was fine, he said, when he was little, but now that he was about to enter high school, he asked me, with a slight smile, if I would start dating guys until he graduated. The things that mattered to him were not really what I thought would matter. He wanted to be reassured that his standard of living would not decrease, that I would get the emotional support I needed from friends and therapy to still be a strong person, that I would have more time to spend with him in the ways he wanted me available (e.g., at home, but not scrutinizing his activities too closely), and that I would continue to have my own life and not meddle in his. I thought he would be devastated by the loss of his other mother and his sibling, but to the contrary, he expressed relief.

In these conversations with and observations of my son, I saw that the person I was raising was thinking very differently than I. I saw that one loving and relatively well-functioning parent was enough for him to feel safe and secure. I witnessed something I had given lip service for years—that children need somebody to be intensely connected to them (Bronfenbrenner & Weiss, 1983). I saw that I needed to be as strong and healthy as I could and not give into my grief over being left because my primary responsibility was to raise this boy to adulthood. I saw that grief takes the course that all the self-help books say it does: at least 1 year to recover from the catastrophic exit of a life partner. I saw that despite the two divorces to which I had subjected my son, he was wise beyond his years and more loving toward me than I thought I deserved. Contrary to being the failure I felt I was in my own eyes, I was a capable and successful adult in his. He wanted me to know that nothing could take away his love for me and that I did not need a second adult in the home to cushion his transition to adulthood.

This experience has taught me the importance of social support, adequate economic resources, sobriety in thought and deed, and a deepening appreciation for a spiritual power beyond my own control. At midlife, I learned that although life can deal some devastating blows, it is possible to renew and rebuild. I could not have gained this perspective without traveling to my son's world or without the incredible support I received from friends in my private life and teachers in the books I read. A feminist vision for transforming families is one in which clear-sighted honesty for what is really going on takes precedence over the myths we tell ourselves of how things should function (Ruddick, 1989).

Traveling to Others' Worlds

In this chapter, I have activated my own experience to illustrate how feminist ideas can inform family scholarship because I am committed to the revolutionary project of social change. I want to see families taken seriously at all levels. To do that, we need clear-sighted vision, not cockeyed optimism or gloomy denial found in traditional family social science. Real life is the greatest teacher, and it is not surprising that some of the most profound and lasting insights have come from lived experience, as evident in the process by which Piaget's observations of his three children metamorphosed into an intellectual industry in the behavioral and social sciences.

To initiate one's own journey for a deeper consciousness about the families we study, I offer the following reflective inventory of questions. These questions are guides for making the personal-to-political connection, thereby facilitating the journey of discovering how what goes on in private life reflects what goes on in the world.

1. What is it about my personal experience that is unresolved? What do I not yet understand about myself? In what areas of my experience do I feel negative emotions (e.g., shame, doubt, guilt, and remorse)? In what areas of my experience do I feel positive emotions (peace, acceptance, joy, and happiness)? How are these emotions connected to my thoughts about families?

2. What are my motivations for doing this work? Who am I trying to impress? What would I rather be doing than working on this project? What do I hope to contribute to my own life and to family scholarship by pursuing this work?

3. What is my responsibility to the people whose lives I am studying? What do I owe them for giving me the opportunity to get inside their lives? What do I want to give back? What do I now understand about human existence (my own included) as a result of conducting this work? How can this work benefit the well-being of others?

Answering these questions makes it clear that the process of reflecting on one's life and writing down the responses without self-censorship can be the kind of liberatory experience feminism promises. By freeing the writer within (Goldberg, 1986), we can replace our distanced stance from the subjects of our study with a critical eye toward the private-public connection. Taking these steps brings us closer to the revolutionary feminist praxis I have described in this chapter. In these ways, we can travel from silence to language to action (Collins, 1990), learning to theorize private experience in the service of creating a more just world.

REFERENCES

Agger, B. (1998). *Critical social theories*. Boulder, CO: Westview.

Alexander, M. J., & Mohanty, C. T. (1997). Introduction: Genealogies, legacies, movements. In M. J. Alexander & C. T. Mohanty (Eds.), *Feminist genealogies, colonial legacies, democratic futures* (pp. xiii–xlii). New York: Routledge.

Allen, K. R. (2000). A conscious and inclusive family studies. *Journal of Marriage and the Family, 62*, 4–17.

Allen, K. R., Blieszner, R., Roberto, K. A., Farnsworth, E. B., & Wilcox, K. L. (1999). Older adults and their children: Family patterns of structural diversity. *Family Relations, 48*, 151–157.

Allen, K. R., Floyd-Thomas, S. M., & Gillman, L. (2001). Teaching to transform: From volatility to solidarity in an interdisciplinary family studies classroom. *Family Relations, 50*, 317–325.

Baber, K. M., & Allen, K. R. (1992). *Women and families: Feminist reconstructions*. New York: Guilford.

Baber, K. M., & Murray, C. I. (2001). A postmodern feminist approach to teaching human sexuality. *Family Relations, 50*, 23–33.

Bell, D. (1992). *Faces at the bottom of the well: The permanence of racism*. New York: Basic Books.

Bronfenbrenner, U., & Weiss, H. B. (1983). Beyond policies without people: An ecological perspective on child and family policy. In E. F. Zigler, S. L. Kagan, & E. Klugman (Eds.), *Children, families and government: Perspectives on American social policy* (pp. 393–414). New York: Cambridge University Press.

Brownmiller, S. (1999). *In our time: Memoir of a revolution*. New York: Delta.

Chodron, P. (1997). *When things fall apart: Heart advice for difficult times*. Boston: Shambhala.

Chow, E. N-L. (1998). Family, economy, and the state: A legacy of struggle for Chinese American women. In S. J. Ferguson (Ed.), *Shifting the center: Understanding contemporary families* (pp. 93–114). Mountain View, CA: Mayfield.

Christensen, K. (1997). "With whom do you believe your lot is cast?" White feminists and racism. *Signs: Journal of Women in Culture and Society, 22*, 617–648.

Collins, P. H. (1990). *Black feminist thought: Knowledge, consciousness, and the politics of empowerment*. New York: Unwin Hyman.

Cook, J. A., & Fonow, M. M. (1986). Knowledge and women's interests: Issues of epistemology and methodology in feminist sociological research. *Sociological Inquiry, 56*, 2–29.

Coontz, S. (1992). *The way we never were: American families and the nostalgia trap*. New York: Basic Books.

Davis, M., & Kennedy, E. L. (1986). Oral history and the study of sexuality in the lesbian community: Buffalo, New York, 1940–1960. *Feminist Studies, 12,* 7–26.

D'Emilio, J., & Freedman, E. B. (1997). *Intimate matters: A history of sexuality in America* (2nd ed.). Chicago: University of Chicago Press.

Dill, B. T. (1988). Our mothers' grief: Racial ethnic women and the maintenance of families. *Journal of Family History, 13,* 415–431.

Ebert, T. L. (1996). *Ludic feminism and after: Postmodernism, desire, and labor in late capitalism.* Ann Arbor: University of Michigan Press.

Elam, D., & Wiegman, R. (Eds.). (1995). *Feminism beside itself.* New York: Routledge.

Ellsworth, E. (1997). Double binds of whiteness. In M. Fine, L. Weis, L. C. Powell, & L. M. Wong (Eds.), *Off white: Readings on race, power, and society* (pp. 259–269). New York: Routledge.

Faderman, L. (1981). *Surpassing the love of men: Romantic friendship and love between women from the Renaissance to the present.* New York: William Morrow.

Faderman, L. (1991). *Odd girls and twilight lovers: A history of lesbian life in twentieth- century America.* New York: Penguin.

Fisher, B., & Alberti, R. (2000). *Rebuilding when your relationship ends* (3rd ed.). Atascadero, CA: Impact.

Fletcher, A. C., & Russell, S. T. (2001). Incorporating issues of sexual orientation in the classroom: Challenges and solutions. *Family Relations, 50,* 34–40.

Frankenberg, R. (1993). *White women, race matters: The social construction of whiteness.* Minneapolis, MN: University of Minnesota Press.

Freire, P. (1997). *Pedagogy of the oppressed* (Rev. ed.; M. B. Ramos, Trans.). New York: Continuum. (Original work published 1970)

Friedan, B. (1963). *The feminine mystique.* New York: Norton.

Gagnier, R. (1990). Feminist postmodernism: The end of feminism or the ends of theory? In D. L. Rhode (Ed.), *Theoretical perspectives on sexual difference* (pp. 21–30). New Haven, CT: Yale University Press.

Gagnon, J. H., & Parker, R. G. (1995). Conceiving sexuality. In R. G. Parker & J. H. Gagnon (Eds.), *Conceiving sexuality: Approaches to sex research in a postmodern world* (pp. 3–16). New York: Routledge.

Goldberg, N. (1986). *Writing down the bones: Freeing the writer within.* Boston: Shambhala.

Harding, S. (1987). Introduction: Is there a feminist method? In S. Harding (Ed.), *Feminism and methodology* (pp. 1–14). Bloomington, IN: Indiana University Press.

Harding, S. (1998). Subjectivity, experience, and knowledge: An epistemology from/for rainbow coalition politics. In M. F. Rogers (Ed.), *Contemporary feminist theory* (pp. 97–108). Boston: McGraw Hill.

Harding, S. (2001). Comment on Walby's "Against epistemological chasms: The science question in feminism revisited": Can democratic values and interests ever play a rationally justifiable role in the evaluation of scientific work? *Signs: Journal of Women in Culture and Society, 26,* 511–525.

Hareven, T. K. (1991). The history of the family and the complexity of social change. *American Historical Review, 96,* 95–124.

Hawkesworth, M. E. (1989). Knowers, knowing, known: Feminist theory and claims of truth. *Signs: Journal of Women in Culture and Society, 14,* 533–557.

Hawkesworth, M. (1997). Confounding gender. *Signs: Journal of Women in Culture and Society, 22,* 649–685.

Herrmann, A. C., & Stewart, A. J. (Eds.). (1994). *Theorizing feminism: Parallel trends in the humanities and social sciences.* Boulder, CO: Westview.

Jaggar, A. M., & Rothenberg, P. S. (1984). *Feminist frameworks: Alternative theoretical accounts of the relations between women and men* (2nd ed.). New York: McGraw-Hill.

Johnson, S. (1989). *Wildfire: Igniting the she/volution*. Albuquerque, NM: Wildfire.

Kerber, L. K., & DeHart-Mathews, J. (Eds.). (1987). *Women's America: Refocusing the past* (2nd ed.). New York: Oxford University Press.

Kingma, D. R. (2000). *Coming apart: Why relationships end and how to live through the ending of yours*. Berkeley, CA: Conari.

Krieger, S. (1991). *Social science and the self: Personal essays on an art form*. New Brunswick, NY: Rutgers University Press.

Krieger, S. (1996). *The family silver: Essays on relationships among women*. Berkeley: University of California Press.

Lang, A. (Ed.). (1969). *The blue fairy book*. New York: Airmont.

Lorde, A. (1984). *Sister outsider: Essays and speeches*. Freedom, CA: Crossing.

Lugones, M. (1990). Playfulness, "world"-travelling, and loving perception. In G. Anzaldua (Ed.), *Making face, making soul: Haciendo caras: Creative and critical perspectives by feminists of color* (pp. 390–402). San Francisco: Aunt Lute.

Marks, S. R. (2000). Teasing out the lessons of the 1960s: Family diversity and family privilege. *Journal of Marriage and the Family, 62,* 609–622.

McIntosh, P. (1995). White privilege and male privilege: A personal account of coming to see correspondences through work in women's studies. In M. L. Andersen & P. H. Collins (Eds.), *Race, class, and gender: An anthology* (2nd ed., pp. 76–87). Belmont, CA: Wadsworth.

Morgan, R. (Ed.). (1970). *Sisterhood is powerful*. New York: Random House.

Morrison, T. (1992). *Playing in the dark: Whiteness and the literary imagination*. New York: Vintage.

Murray, N. P. (1994). *Living beyond your losses: The healing journey through grief*. Ridgefield, CT: Morehouse.

Nielsen, J. M. (1990). Introduction. In J. M. Nielsen (Ed.), *Feminist research methods* (pp. 1–37). Boulder, CO: Westview.

Osmond, M. W. (1987). Radical-critical theories. In M. B. Sussman & S. K. Steinmetz (Eds.), *Handbook of marriage and the family* (pp. 103–124). New York: Plenum.

Patterson, C. J. (1994). Children of the lesbian baby boom: Behavioral adjustment, self-concepts, and sex-role identity. In B. Greene & G. Herek (Eds.), *Contemporary perspectives on lesbian and gay psychology: Theory, research and application* (pp. 156–175). Thousand Oaks, CA: Sage.

Reagon, B. J. (1983). Coalition politics: Turning the century. In B. Smith (Ed.), *Home girls: A black feminist anthology* (pp. 356–368). New York: Kitchen Table.

Rich, A. (1980). Compulsory heterosexuality and lesbian existence. *Signs: Journal of Women in Culture and Society, 5,* 631–660.

Riger, S. (1998). Epistemological debates, feminist voices: Science, social values, and the study of women. In D. L. Anselmi & A. L. Law (Eds.), *Questions of gender: Perspectives and paradoxes* (pp. 61–75). New York: McGraw-Hill.

Rosser, S. V. (1992). Are there feminist methodologies appropriate for the natural sciences and do they make a difference? *Women's Studies International Forum, 15,* 535–550.

Ruddick, S. (1989). *Maternal thinking: Toward a politics of peace*. Boston: Beacon.

Sawhney, S. (1995). Authenticity is such a drag! In D. Elam & R. Wiegman (Eds.), *Feminism beside itself* (pp. 197–215). New York: Routledge.

Simon, R. I. (1992). *Teaching against the grain: Texts for a pedagogy of possibility*. New York: Bergin & Garvey.

Smith-Rosenberg, C. (1975). The female world of love and ritual. *Signs: Journal of Women in Culture and Society, 1,* 1–29.

Spender, D. (Ed.). (1983). *Feminist theories: Three centuries of key women thinkers.* New York: Pantheon.

Sprague, J. (2001). Comment on Walby's "Against epistemological chasms: The science question in feminism revisited:" Structured knowledge and strategic methodology. *Signs: Journal of Women in Culture and Society, 26,* 527–536.

Stacey, J. (2000). The handbook's tail: Toward revels or a requiem for family diversity. In D. H. Demo, K. R. Allen, & M. A. Fine (Eds.), *Handbook of family diversity* (pp. 424–439). New York: Oxford University Press.

Thompson, L. (1995). Teaching about ethnic minority families using a pedagogy of care. *Family Relations, 44,* 129–135.

Thompson, L., & Walker, A. J. (1995). The place of feminism in family studies. *Journal of Marriage and the Family, 57,* 847–865.

Walby, S. (2001a). Against epistemological chasms: The science question in feminism revisited. *Signs: Journal of Women in Culture and Society, 26,* 485–509.

Walby, S. (2001b). Reply to Harding and Sprague. *Signs: Journal of Women in Culture and Society, 26,* 537–540.

Walker, A. J. (2000). Refracted knowledge: Viewing families through the prism of social science. *Journal of Marriage and the Family, 62,* 595–608.

White, S. (1991). *Political theory and postmodernism.* New York: Cambridge University Press.

Wilber, K. (1998). *The marriage of sense and soul: Integrating science and religion.* New York: Broadway.

Part IV

RAISING CHILDREN IN CONTEMPORARY FAMILIES

Encountering Oppositions
A Review of Scholarship About Motherhood

SUSAN WALZER

The experience of being a mother—no matter how one becomes one—is both an embodied and a social experience. It is an individual identity and a relationship. It is pleasure and pain. It is work and relief from work. It is a wholly unique experience and one that is patterned and predictable in some ways. Too often we think about motherhood as though it had to be one thing or another. One of the stories that I tell in this chapter is about how the dominant approaches in academic work about motherhood over the last three decades both reflect and criticize this tendency to compartmentalize mothers—a tendency related to the larger issue of gender.

As Ann Oakley (1979) has written: "There have always been mothers but motherhood was invented" (p. 17). From Oakley's sociological perspective, when we differentiate the biological fact that women produce babies from the less fixed social expectations for how women should care for children, becoming a mother is a confrontation with "the full reality of what it means to be a woman in our society" (p. 1). More than a physical passage, the transition into motherhood reveals the meanings and contradictions associated with being female in the context of particular relationships, institutional settings, and historical moments. On one hand, for example, mothers are perceived as naturally and ultimately responsible for the care of children. And on the other hand, it is assumed that mothers are mothering in a nuclear family, that they are not economically necessary to children, and that they, unlike fathers, must answer for their employment behavior.

The study of motherhood uncovers these kinds of intersections between cultural understandings and social arrangements—at

AUTHOR'S NOTE: I am grateful for the flexibility of Alex and Leah Walzer Koechlin and for the insight and help of Michael Ennis-McMillan, Glenna Spitze, Janet Walzer, and the editors and reviewers of this volume. Thank you also to Michelle Blocklin and Elizabeth Umbro for research assistance.

times revealing them and at other times reinforcing them. There is a voluminous assortment of literature about mothers with differing purposes. One body of work, for example, focuses on identifying social norms for mothers and the processes through which mothers negotiate these norms. This literature tends to be more qualitative, interpretive, and directed at generating theoretical perspectives on motherhood and mothering. Another body of work represents more positivistic attempts to document the determinants and effects of mothers' behavior through the use of surveys and other statistical methodologies (Arendell, 2000). My emphasis in this chapter is on the former, but I do not provide an exhaustive description of either of these academic approaches in this chapter. Rather, my goals are to describe some of the major themes and texts in scholarship on motherhood, to provide some historical context for how they have evolved, and to suggest some directions for work on motherhood in the future.

I use the words *academic* and *scholarship* in the broadest senses possible. Work on motherhood crosses many disciplines and also exists outside conventional academic contexts while employing academic methods. I chose in this chapter to focus on providing an overview of how the study of motherhood mirrors and is embedded in the massive shifts in behavior and beliefs related to gender since the 1970s, emphasizing some of the most highly cited and influential texts that define particular developments in thinking about motherhood. There is much that I leave out because of the quantity of work on motherhood as well as its connections to many other topics (see other chapters in this book and Arendell, 2000, Dixon, 1991, and Ross, 1995, for reviews of research about motherhood).

I begin the chapter with some historical background in which to situate analyses of motherhood and to understand the imagery

associated with it. The next sections deal with how scholars have described motherhood as a social institution and theorized about how institutionalized motherhood is reproduced. Because the issue of work is so implicated in dilemmas surrounding mothers, the following section addresses theoretical and empirical treatments of this issue. Throughout these sections, I share the struggle present in this scholarship to represent general contentions about motherhood while also recognizing that all mothers are not alike, in part because they do not live in the same social categories and circumstances. I conclude with a discussion of directions for future work.

HISTORICAL SHIFTS AND CULTURAL IMAGERY OF MOTHERHOOD

To understand how the work on motherhood in North America developed during and since the 1970s, it is useful to know something of what preceded it. The post-1960s work on which this chapter focuses emerged in the context of increases in mothers' labor force participation that seemed to conflict with a particular image of mothers as "always there" for their children. Thompson and Walker (1989) described this "enduring" image as follows: "Motherhood is a constant and exclusive responsibility. A mother is all-giving and all-powerful. Within the 'magic circle' of mother and child, the mother devotes herself to her child's needs and holds her child's fate in her hands" (p. 860).

These dominant cultural expectations that mothers will always be patient, available, and focused on their children are active in individual mothers' imaginations and reinforced in advice literature for parents (Hays, 1996; Walzer, 1998). They even make their way into public parody. In Roz Chast's cartoon of "bad mom cards," there is a picture of Gloria

B., who promised to take her daughter to the mall after school "*and then didn't.*" Suzie M. let her kid play 2 hours of Nintendo "*just to get him out of her hair*" and Deborah Z. has "never even *tried* to make Play-Doh from scratch" (Chast, 2001, p. 50).

The point that some analysts of motherhood make is that the imagery associated with "good" mothering is historically specific. During the 18th century, for example, motherhood was not particularly emphasized, and "child rearing was neither a discrete nor an exclusively female task. . . . [B]oth parents were simply advised to 'raise up' their children together" (Margolis, 1984, p. 12; see also Chapter 13 of this book). With the process of industrialization in the 19th century, there was a shift in norms for parents because of a new separation between reproductive and productive labor. As other productive activities moved out of households, a home economics movement emerged in which children became perceived as a project in themselves rather than as integrated participants in family work (Ehrenreich & English, 1978). Middle-class wives whose husbands were absent from the household in a new way were urged to devote themselves to parenting full time; the mother-child relationship was now viewed as central and exclusive (Margolis, 1984).

Skipping ahead to the middle of the 20th century, it was the image of a stay-at-home mother that appeared on the televisions of postwar 1950s families in shows like *Leave It to Beaver*. As Coontz (1992) noted, the prosperity of the postwar years affected family arrangements in ways that have been perceived as typical or "traditional" but were in fact anomalous (see also Cherlin, 1992). During the 1950s, and for the first time in 100 years, the ages at which people married and became mothers fell, fertility increased, and families were more insulated than ever before—encouraged to make domesticity a central part of their identities.

There was an underside to the insulation of nuclear families that Betty Friedan (1963) addressed in a widely read book called *The Feminine Mystique*. In this book, Friedan identified a malaise in well-educated, middle class mothers who were full-time homemakers. From her point of view, for women to have to choose between full-time homemaking and careers kept them from "growing to their full human capacities" (p. 364). Friedan's book was one catalyst in a social movement that was percolating among middle-class women in particular (see Umansky, 1996, for a discussion of the various strains of the second wave of the women's movement as well as the discourse associated with motherhood). Although it was not the first time that women had challenged their social positions—they had won the right to vote a few decades before—in this wave of collective activity, one of the areas of focus was women's participation in another part of the public world: the labor force.

The changes in attitudes that became visible during the late 1960s and early 1970s happened in the context of already existing shifts in the economy and in women's work behavior (Umansky, 1996). The proportion of women in the formal labor force had increased across racial-ethnic groups (Garey, 1999), but perhaps the most notable change occurred in the rates of employment of mothers, and mothers of young children in particular. Whereas less than 20% of married mothers of children under 6 were employed in 1960, by 1970, a third of them were (Chadwick & Heaton, 1999). In 1983, the Bureau of Labor Statistics reported that more than half of all mothers with children under the age of 6 were employed (Rubin, 1984). And by 1990, close to 60% of married women with children under 6 and 80% of married women with children aged 6 to 17 were employed (Chadwick & Heaton, 1999).

The sharp increase in the labor force participation of mothers sparked the questions that underlie an increasingly large and multidisciplinary collection of literature about motherhood. In 1974, for example, the *Journal of Marriage and the Family* devoted a whole issue to the question of mothers and employment, whereas there had been no such attention in the prior decade's review. But the vast changes in mothers' behavior generated even broader reflections about what it means to be a mother and how society influences definitions of motherhood. Academic work emerged that addressed what appeared to be the "unnatural" trend of mothers working outside their homes. "What are the consequences of maternal employment?" researchers asked. Another body of literature challenged the premise of this question, however, and suggested that the conflict perceived between work and motherhood was socially constructed.

MOTHERHOOD AS AN INSTITUTION

One of the slogans of the women's movement in the 1960s and 1970s was that the personal is political. It might be said that what is personal and political became academic as well. Before the 1970s, much academic research assumed that motherhood was intrinsically rewarding and not particularly problematic (Boulton, 1983). Many of the analyses of motherhood that emerged in the 1970s, however, were openly motivated by the researchers' own experiences of becoming mothers, their challenges in negotiating social expectations and judgments of mothers, and their identification with feminism as a conceptual framework with which to analyze and change motherhood.

A related theme that appeared then and continues now was the need to speak some form of "truth" about motherhood—to get past taboos, clichés, and highly idealized or critical images of mothers. Writing in 1999, for example, Susan Maushart described a conversation with her older sister, who had said to her: "I'm going to tell you this now, and I want you to remember it. . . . Everyone lies. Do you hear me? Everyone lies about what it's like to have a baby. Don't listen to them. Just watch me, and remember" (p. 11). The secret, Maushart and others argued, was that being a mother was not an easy experience. Ross (1995) wrote, for example, that "the love and care of children is, for everyone, an open invitation not only to unending hard work but also to trouble and sorrow, if not usually to tragedy. Telling the hard things about motherhood has usually been labeled gossip and been confined to women's private conversations on playgrounds, doorsteps, or telephones" (p. 398).

When scholars in the 1970s began to talk about the problems associated with being a mother, they focused on the social organization of motherhood as a role. Adrienne Rich's (1976) much-cited literary and historical analysis *Of Woman Born* differentiated between mothering as an experience and motherhood as a social institution. For Rich, the intimacies, gratifications, and thoughtfulness involved in mothering are embedded in a social environment that expects rather than credits mothers for choosing to behave as they do: "Institutionalized" motherhood, she wrote, demands of women "maternal 'instinct' rather than intelligence, selflessness rather than self-realization" (p. 42).

Another prominent voice in identifying and criticizing motherhood as an institution, Jessie Bernard (1974) argued that "assigning sole responsibility for child care to the mother, cutting her off from the easy help of others in an isolated household, requiring round-the-clock tender, loving care, and making such care her exclusive activity—is not only new and unique, but not even a good way for either women or for children"

(p. 9). Citing cross-cultural studies, Bernard noted the effects of heavy child care loads on maternal warmth toward children; in cultures with the heaviest loads, mothers are more erratic in expressing warmth toward children. Isolated mother-child households also tend to have higher rates of infliction of pain on children. In cultures where isolation is decreased, and grandmothers or other caretakers are present, "maternal instability" is decreased.

These cross-cultural findings resonate with more recent studies of maternal violence and stress in the United States. Mothers who handle rearing children by themselves tend to be more stressed than other mothers (Arendell, 2000). Demo (1992) cited research suggesting that rates of child abuse are "highest among women who normally spend the most time with their children—housewives with preschool children—and lowest among those assumed to spend the least time with their children—mothers with full-time jobs" (p. 301).

Aside from questioning the notion that the separation of reproductive and productive work is a healthy context for children, Bernard (1974) pointed out that in most parts of the world, "women have been, and still are, too valuable in their productive capacity to be spared for the exclusive care of children" (p. 7). Her identification of cultural differences was implicitly a rebuttal of the notion that biology determines the gender-differentiated arrangements of the nuclear family. As Hays (1996) pointed out, even though women have the capacity to grow babies and perhaps "some animal instinct" to ensure their offspring's survival, "this makes up only a minuscule portion of what is understood as socially appropriate mothering" (p. 14). Nature also does not explain the mothering of women such as adoptive or stepmothers who are not biologically connected to their children (Woollett & Marshall, 2001). Hrdy (1999) noted that

"there is probably no mammal in which maternal commitment does not emerge piecemeal and chronically sensitive to external cues. Nurturing has to be teased out, reinforced, maintained" (p. 174). But if nurturing itself needs to be nurtured and is not instinctually induced, what explains the ways that mothers mother?

THEORETICAL APPROACHES TO THE REPRODUCTION OF MOTHERING

Intergenerational Transmission of Mothering

Analyses of motherhood in the 1970s pointed to its social organization as a form of oppression of women in patriarchal society, suggesting that power imbalances between women and men result from women's being tied to child care (Umansky, 1996). With this analysis, the riddle became: Why do women do it? And one of the answers, argued influentially by Nancy Chodorow (1978), was: because their mothers did.

In her book, *The Reproduction of Mothering*, Chodorow (1978) attempted to explain the tendency for women rather than men to care for children by examining how mothers reproduce themselves in their daughters. Her argument, grounded in psychoanalytic theory, was that women's exclusive investment in mothering, within the context of a sexual division of labor, reproduces in daughters a new generation of women who will be overly involved in mothering as a sole and insufficient source of self-esteem and personal accomplishment. Because mothers are denied outlets in the public sphere and are isolated from relationships with other adults, Chodorow suggested, they overinvest and overwhelm their children. Girls identify with their mothers, and boys must disidentify with their mothers to achieve their appropriate gender roles;

boys therefore devalue caretaking behavior, which they associate with femaleness.

Chodorow's theory has been criticized for leaving out other variables that influence the dynamics of male dominance and female devaluation that she rooted in mothering (see Boyd, 1989; Lorber, Coser, Rossi, & Chodorow, 1981; Johnson, 1988). She countered, however (in Lorber et al., 1981), that alternative arguments focus on how mothers are *forced* into primary caretaking roles but do not explain why mothers *want* these roles. For Chodorow, that enigma is explained by women's internalization of their mothers' gender identities.

Maternal Practice and Maternal Thinking

Whereas Chodorow's aim was to explain women's voluntary oppression as mothers, some of the work that emerged in the 1980s was more affirming of motherhood (Ross, 1995), suggesting that maternal practice and thinking hold the potential to decrease oppression. Sara Ruddick's work is widely cited as an affirmation of the potential power in motherhood because she argued that the behavior of mothers generates a quality of thinking that provides nothing less than a blueprint for human caring and peace in the world (Umansky, 1996). Ruddick (1983) wrote that when mothers respond to the needs of children—preserve their lives, foster their growth, and shape them into social acceptability—they acquire a conceptual scheme in which there is "a unity of reflection, judgment, and emotion" (p. 214). She referred to this unity as "maternal thinking" and argued that it can benefit the public realm, "to make the preservation and growth of *all* children a work of public conscience and legislation" (p. 226).

Ruddick did not suggest that this way of thinking is biologically innate in mothers or even socialized; rather, she saw it as an outgrowth of their day-to-day experience of mothering, which at its best reflects a desire to sustain and facilitate life. Children demand care; and mothers, in ways that may vary for them as individuals, respond. Ruddick's themes echo in some more recent work on mothering as a caring practice potentially redemptive of society (McMahon, 1995) or at least as representing a kind of opposition to relationships based on the competitive pursuit of one's own interests. Hays (1996) argued, for example, that women are primary caregivers not only because they have less power than men but because their mothering represents an alternative to the paradigm of self-interest that dominates society.

Mothering as an Enactment of Cultural Contradictions and Gender

Whereas Ruddick suggested that maternal thinking comes out of maternal behavior, another approach looks at how mothers' thinking about their children's needs is influenced by dominant ideologies about socially appropriate motherhood—ideologies that make their way into the practice and interaction of parents. One of the cultural artifacts that has been analyzed in this kind of work is advice literature for parents. Ehrenreich and English (1978) noted, for example, that the change in ideology about motherhood that occurred in the 19th century was part of a general orientation toward making a science of the domestic world. Male child-rearing experts emerging in the context of the home economics movement perpetuated the notion that mothering was an "all-engulfing" activity, while also suggesting that mothers were at great risk of doing it wrong.

With the increase of mothers in the paid labor force, Margolis (1984) suggested, experts began to speak of a more important role for fathers and to find an absence of negative effects on children from mothers' involvement in paid work. Dr. Spock, for example, deleted his discussion of "The Working Mother" from the "Special Problems" section of his 1976 edition of *Baby and Child Care*, including instead a new chapter on "The Changing Family." But not all of the changes were what they seemed, as Hays (1996) pointed out in a content analysis of best-selling child experts Drs. Spock, Brazelton, and Leach (see also Marshall, 1991). Advice literature still contains an implicit ideology of "intensive mothering," a style of child rearing that requires much time, energy, and money from individual mothers. Expert advice has changed more in form than in content, Hays argued: For example, Spock undermines gender-neutral language when he suggests that "the 'parent' buy 'a new dress' or go to the 'beauty parlor' if child-rearing is giving (him or) her the blues" (p. 55). Other forms of advice literature, including breast-feeding guides, reinforce the sense that mothers are essential to babies in a way that fathers are not and that there are negative effects for babies and mothers in spending too much time apart (Blum, 1999; Walzer, 1998).

McMahon (1995) noted that dominant representations of woman's character "so tie women to caring, and in particular to caring for their own children, that it becomes unthinkable for a woman not to act in a responsible way toward her child—to be an irresponsible mother" (p. 159). More than that, however, McMahon suggested that women are not merely victims of cultural ideology. Rather, they change as a result of becoming mothers in ways that produce in them a gendered experience of their identities. A woman does not simply become a parent; she becomes a mother and "makes decisions about motherhood on the basis of her conception of who she is, rather than in terms of conformity to social roles" (p. 21). Mothers' changed identities represent a

moral transformation, McMahon argued, and one that has a meaning different from that which is ascribed to fathers.

In the "doing gender" perspective of West and Zimmerman (1987), gender is accomplished in the context of social interactions. Men and women create gender by behaving in the ways that socially defined men and women are supposed to behave or by being accountable to social expectations even if their behavior diverges from them. This perspective has been applied to the interactions of men and women who become parents together—the ways that they "do" parenthood reflecting accountability to gender-differentiated expectations for mothers and fathers (Walzer, 1998). This can be stressful for mothers in particular because the standards to which they hold themselves feel unattainable and contradictory. Some mothers in qualitative interviews speak of feeling judged negatively by other people regardless of whether they are at home with their children or employed. Although their male partners can easily exceed ambiguous social models for being a good father, these mothers describe feeling as if they can only do worse (Hays, 1996; Walzer, 1998).

Within the context of the expert assertion of the primacy of the mother-child bond, there is much room for mothers to question what they are doing and to wonder about the proper balance between too little and too much mothering. Glenn (1994) suggested that ideology of motherhood revolves around both idealization and blame, around the glorification of mothers' selflessness and condemnation of their influence: "Mothers are romanticized as life-giving, self-sacrificing, and forgiving, and demonized as smothering, overly involved, and destructive" (p. 11). Mothers are held ultimately responsible for children, but not necessarily with any authority.

The academic work about how gendered cultural imagery influences women's approaches to mothering has largely been qualitative and, like much of the theoretical work in motherhood, untested on large populations (Arendell, 2000). There is no doubt, however, that among heterosexual couples, mothers do a disproportionate amount of child care (Coltrane, 1996). Qualitative studies of "shared" parenting arrangements between women and men reflect that mothers remain ultimately responsible for parenting arrangements even in couples who claim to evenly split the work of parenting (Coltrane, 1996; Deutsch, 1999; Ehrensaft, 1990). It is this enduring norm that some mothers report as the biggest downside to being a mother (McMahon, 1995) and that underlies tensions surrounding mothers and employment.

MOTHERS AND WORK

The amount of empirical research that has been generated about mothers and employment throughout the last three decades illustrates the importance of norms about paid work to dominant conceptions of motherhood. Spitze's (1988) review of research literature investigating possible effects of women's employment on children described a change from relatively negative assessments before the 1970s to more benign assessments after this period, but the vast number of studies focused on this question is an indication of the unresolved role of work in social definitions of motherhood.

Ideology and Maternal Employment

Some researchers argue that mothers' involvement in both reproductive and productive work is receiving greater societal recognition and that more and more mothers experience their involvement in financially supporting their children as part of their

parental role (e.g., Nock, 1987). Garey (1999) suggested, in contrast, that we continue to analyze mothering and working from a model of opposition, constructing mothers as being more oriented toward either family or work. This may, in part, be because of the dominant perception that mothers are employed in managerial and professional positions—an assumption underlying some past research that cast mothers as either oriented toward having a career or not (Ferree, 1987; Garey, 1999). When the experiences of working-class women are brought into the study of maternal employment, the existence in mothers of both economic and domestic identities becomes apparent: "Working-class women, unlike more affluent women, are not offered the financial incentives to deny or minimize the experience of contradiction and so to express an unqualified preference for either paid work or housework" (Ferree, 1987, p. 298).

Garey (1999) proposed the metaphor of "weaving" work and family to replace the dominant cultural notion that women choose between them, yet mothering continues to be perceived as somehow incompatible with wage work (Thompson & Walker, 1989). Writing in 1992, Moen suggested that although Americans are increasingly comfortable with married women's employment, they are still not necessarily comfortable about the employment of mothers of young children. Ten or so years later, the question of whether women in high-status positions (such as tenured professorships) can "have it all" is very much alive (Cohen, 2002).

Lewis (1991) argued that the experiences of both motherhood and employment are affected by the notion that the ideal for both is full-time, exclusive attention. The current counterpart to the ideology of the stay-at-home mother is the supermom who makes no "concessions" to motherhood "while doing all the things 'good mothers' are expected to do" (p. 197). Hays (1996) suggested that the coexistence of the traditional mom and the supermom reflects a serious cultural ambivalence about how mothers should behave; and mothers in both groups respond by returning to the ideology of intensive mothering. "Bad mom cards" do not address whether a mother is employed or not—only that she waits until the next day to retrieve her daughter's stuffed bear from the grocery store (Chast, 2001).

Against this ideological backdrop is the lingering question examined quite frequently over the last three decades: Why is it that new mothers are or are not employed? The opposition model of motherhood and employment is revealed in research that seeks to find the determinants of new mothers' work statuses and related well-being in their personality characteristics, sex role attitudes, and career orientations. Questioning why a parent is employed assumes a nuclear family context and does not seem to pertain to new fathers, although as it turns out, the greatest impetus for mothers appears to be that which is assumed for fathers: financial need (Volling & Belsky, 1993). Mothers who contribute more to the total family income tend to return to work more quickly (Sanchez & Thomson, 1997; Wenk & Garrett, 1992), as do those who receive maternity benefits (Coltrane, 1996) and perceive more rewards on their jobs (Desai & Waite, 1991).

Work as a Lens on Differences Between Mothers

Framing the question as why some mothers choose work does not necessarily get at the larger context in which mothers negotiate employment (Walzer, 1997), including differences in their social locations and relationship statuses. Recent scholarship has emerged that looks at mothering from more particular standpoints rather than as a general experience (see, e.g., Collins, 1994).

When we bring race into the discussion, for example, we see the bias in treating employed mothers as a new category. Collins (1987) pointed out that African American women "have long integrated their activities as economic providers into their mothering relationships" (p. 5). In fact, the maternal roles of racial ethnic women have largely been ignored in favor of their roles as workers (Glenn, 1987).

Hays (1996) noted that native-born white mothers of the dominant classes are most likely to be able "to have the cultural and economic resources as well as the time to define and engage in the form of mothering that is considered proper" (p. 164). Dominant notions about what is "proper" for mothers may differ depending on their social locations. Most mothers are not supposed to be wage workers, yet poor, single mothers should be, even though having a job does not guarantee living above the poverty line (Arendell, 2000).

Currently one third of births in the United States are to unmarried women. This is an increase from one in 10 in 1970 and from one in five in 1980, and the rates are expected to continue to rise (Arendell, 2000). About 30% of nonmarital births are to women less than 20 years old (Seltzer, 2000). Mothers who become mothers outside institutionalized expectations are mothering "against the odds" (see analyses in Coll, Surrey, & Weingarten, 1998). This may be most starkly expressed in a comparison of poverty rates between female-headed households with children present (31.6%) and married-couple families with children (5.2%) (Arendell, 2000). The feminization of poverty is in large part created by the negative consequences for single mothers of the opposition approach to family and work. According to Pearce (1990),

> In concrete terms, as long as we accept the denigration of women who take care of dependent children as "dependent," and as

long as the welfare problem is termed one of "dependency," then the policy choices are constrained to a set of equally impossible choices for a single mother. She must choose between limiting her paid employment to devote more time to her children or limiting her time with her children in order to take more time for paid employment. Either choice perpetuates her poverty, both of income and of life. (p. 275)

Mothers as Disenfranchised Workers

In the dominant imagery of motherhood, it is not necessarily enough to be a woman who nurtures children to have one's motherhood validated. Mothers who fall outside biological nuclear families and heterosexual relationships may find their motherhood contested and devalued. Barbara Katz Rothman (1989) wrote a book called *Recreating Motherhood* after hearing debate about a surrogate mother who did not want to give up the baby to whom she had given birth. What Rothman felt was crystallized in this mother's loss of the baby to the wealthier couple who had contracted her surrogacy was the commodification and denigration of motherhood—its "use as cheap labor, in the service not only of men, but also of women of higher status" (p. 24). This is another lens on women as workers—the notion of women as containers for fetuses, producing babies as a job, under contract.

Rothman argued that pregnancy should be perceived as both a physical and social relationship between a mother and her fetus—the implication being that the fetus "is part of its mother's body as long as it is in her body" (p. 258). For Rothman, the mother who grows the baby is the mother until she decides not to be. As Ragoné (1994) pointed out, however, surrogacy raises even greater dilemmas in defining motherhood because it creates potentially three "categories" of mothers:

(1) the biological mother, the woman who contributes the ovum (the woman whom we have traditionally assumed to be the "real mother"); (2) the gestational mother, the woman who gestates the embryo but bears no genetic relationship to the child; and (3) the social mother, the woman who nurtures the child. (p. 111)

When becoming a mother is taken out of the culturally expected family context, new questions surface about who and what invents motherhood. I suspect that the use of reproductive technology as well as the increasing disassociation of baby making from nuclear families and marital relationships will revive scholarly debate about the role of biology in defining motherhood and family in general. In fact, the most recent decade review of research in the *Journal of Marriage and the Family* had its first article about biosocial perspectives (Booth, Carver, & Granger, 2000). And whereas scholars in the 1970s cautioned against biologically based arguments as justifications for mothers' primary responsibility for children, some analysts in the 1990s invoke women's bodily connections to children to enhance mothers' positions.

Hrdy (1999), for example, used an evolutionary perspective to support the naturalness of women's interweaving of work and mothering. Taking a long-term view, she argued, supports the recognition that primate mothers for "most of human existence, and for millions of years before that" have combined productive lives and reproduction (p. 109). The difficulty lies not in the link between maternity and ambition but in the greater compartmentalization of productive and reproductive work and in a scarcity of people to help mothers with the care of children. "Acknowledging infant needs does not necessarily enslave mothers," Hrdy suggested (p. 494). But it remains to be seen whether the return of biology to scholarly discourse will challenge or reinforce women's experiences in the institutions of work and motherhood.

FUTURE DIRECTIONS FOR SCHOLARSHIP ON MOTHERHOOD

This chapter illustrates that the evolution of knowledge about motherhood is more of a circular process than a linear one. The questions underlying much research about mothers are asked and answered and asked again. Who defines motherhood and how? What are the implications for mothers and their children of the social environments in which mothering is embedded? What are the meanings, experiences, and consequences of the work that mothers do?

We need to continue efforts to convey the multidimensionality of motherhood—to bridge the oppositions that have shaped mothers and study of them: biological and social, domestic and public, love and work. We need to continue working to integrate analysis of the rich individual narratives of mothering with the sweeping, systematic social structuring of motherhood. To quote Terry Arendell (2000),

> [W]e need more attention to the lives of particular mothers—to mothers' own voices—and to the lives and voices of diverse groups of mothers. . . . At the same time, we need to study the influences on mothers' activities and experiences of various political, economic, and other social arrangements and developments. We need work that connects mothers' personal beliefs and choices with their social situations. (p. 1202)

Although some academic work about motherhood combines theoretical conceptualizations and empirical examination, there continue to be gaps between interpretive and positivistic approaches (Arendell, 2000). Qualitative studies are able to ground

theoretical narratives in data, but we need research that tests the findings and contentions of qualitative studies with larger samples in ways that generate new qualitative studies. We need research that seeks to validate some of the theoretical arguments we take for granted, particularly about differences between mothers.

Race is theorized to affect mothers' standpoints, for example, but there are similarities across race that surface in empirical research about transitions into parenthood. In one study, African American and white spouses appear to experience similar decreases in marital quality and similar increases in conflict, although there may be differences in how the conflict is expressed (Crohan, 1996). The imagery of good mothering to which women are accountable appears to override social location differences, while at the same time some groups of mothers have greater potential to realize the ideal of intensive mothering than others (Hays, 1996). We need more research that gets at these kinds of nuances and does not position mothers as entirely the same or different by virtue of their class, race, or ethnicity.

At the same time, we also need to recognize other kinds of diversity that may affect women's experiences of motherhood, including the forms that their families and life courses take. Some female-headed households begin with single mothers; others become so as a result of divorce or death; still others evolve into new forms when mothers are joined by partners. The fluidity of maternal practice becomes visible when we examine mothers' living arrangements and life transitions.

The compartmentalizing of motherhood leads to research that isolates women's experiences from the interactions and institutions in which their views of themselves as mothers are created. One study concludes, for example, that mothers who are too conflicted or are not conflicted enough about holding jobs may have lower-quality interactions with their babies, yet the roles of mothers' partners, workplace expectations, babies' temperaments, and other situational variables are not necessarily addressed in identifying the sources of mothers' conflict. This kind of analysis harks back to the early-20th-century expert literature condemning both rejecting and overprotective mothers. How much conflict is just right? What is a mother to do?

We will understand more about mothers by focusing less exclusively on them and more on their social contexts and relationships. Hertz and Ferguson (1995) pointed out that doing paid work carries with it the consequence that women who have grown up believing that mothers are irreplaceable must find a way of "replacing" themselves during the hours that they are at their jobs. This issue has generated a vast array of research attempting to ascertain the consequences for children of nonmaternal child care (Scarr, Phillips, & McCartney, 1989), yet research about maternal employment has not generally intersected with research about nonmaternal child care, even though both are focused on child outcomes (Perry-Jenkins, Repetti, & Crouter, 2000).

Children are the people with whom mothers do their mothering, yet the agency of children is relatively unexamined (Thorne, 1987; Woollett & Marshall, 2001). How do children's ages, identities, and temperaments shape what mothers do and feel? How does ideology related to children and childhood affect the experiences of mothers? What are the relationships *between* mothers and children like, and how do the relationships between children affect the experiences of mothers?

Though on some level it is frequently assumed that all mothers have partners, on another level mothers are often studied as if none of them do (Walzer, 1995). This reinforces a sense of maternal practice as automatic and fixed. We need more studies that

reveal how mothers negotiate partnership and motherhood—studies that treat women's own relationships as a salient context for understanding their approaches to mothering. Qualitative work on lesbian couples suggests, for example, that differentiation in parenting roles is not an inevitable outcome of a mother's biological connection to a baby (Reimann, 1997).

Coltrane's review of research about fathering in Chapter 13 of this book is instructive in revealing the presence of gender-differentiated approaches to parenthood in heterosexual couples. Many studies ask what makes fathers "involved" with their children, yet it would be surprising to see research addressing this question in relation to mothers. We need more work that examines how social definitions of fatherhood affect expectations for mothers. Mothers may be implicated in explaining fathers' approaches to parenthood (Walzer, 1995), but we have relatively less analysis of the impact that interactions with fathers have on the shape of mothers' mothering. Given the recent surge of research about fathering and how men think about fatherhood (Marsiglio & Hutchinson, 2002), there is good potential for synthesis in this area.

Finally, we can certainly use more applied research that contributes to improving the well-being of mothers and children as well as to policy debates about what is best for them. The scholarship of motherhood reviewed in this chapter has mattered to women. We can expect for texts to be created that mothers, as well as people who work with and make decisions about mothers, will read. Scholars of motherhood should take advantage of this opportunity by producing studies that point toward ways of bridging the oppositions in women's lives.

Just as the scholars of 30 years ago found themselves in a changing world, we are living in a social environment in which there are vast economic and social shifts. For us, new forms of domestic and international violence make it ever more difficult to fulfill the promise of maternal practice. Now, as then, it may be tempting to cling to the idea that mothers alone can make everything all right for children. But now, as then, we have to acknowledge that mothers do not mother in a social vacuum. There is all the more reason to examine the variety and fullness and potential in the ways that we mother and know about motherhood.

REFERENCES

Arendell, T. (2000). Conceiving and investigating motherhood: The decade's scholarship. *Journal of Marriage and the Family, 62*, 1192–1207.

Bernard, J. (1974). *The future of motherhood*. New York: Dial.

Blum, L. M. (1999). *At the breast: Ideologies of breastfeeding and motherhood in the contemporary United States*. Boston: Beacon.

Booth, A., Carver, K., & Granger, D. A. (2000). Biosocial perspectives on the family. *Journal of Marriage and the Family, 62*, 1018–1034.

Boulton, M. G. (1983). *On being a mother*. New York: Tavistock.

Boyd, C. J. (1989). Mothers and daughters: A discussion of theory and research. *Journal of Marriage and the Family, 51*, 291–301.

Chadwick, B. A., & Heaton, T. B. (1999). *Statistical handbook on the American Family* (2nd ed.). Phoenix, AZ: Oryx.

Chast, R. (2001). Bad mom cards. In R. Mankoff (Ed.), *The New Yorker book of kids cartoons* (p. 50). Princeton, NJ: Bloomberg.

Cherlin, A. J. (1992). *Marriage, divorce, remarriage*. Cambridge, MA: Harvard University Press.

Chodorow, N. (1978). *The reproduction of mothering: Psychoanalysis and the sociology of gender*. Berkeley: University of California Press.

Cohen, H. (2002, August 4). The baby bias. *New York Times*, p. 4A.

Coll, C. G., Surrey, J. L., & Weingarten, K. (1998). *Mothering against the odds: Diverse voices of contemporary mothers*. New York: Guilford.

Collins, P. H. (1987). The meaning of motherhood in black culture and black mother/daughter relationships. *Sage, 4*, 3–10.

Collins, P. H. (1994). Shifting the center: Race, class, and feminist theorizing about motherhood. In E. N. Glenn, G. Chang, & L. R. Forcey (Eds.), *Mothering: Ideology, experience, and agency* (pp. 45–65). New York: Routledge.

Coltrane, S. (1996). *Family man: Fatherhood, housework, and gender equity*. New York: Oxford University Press.

Coontz, S. (1992). *The way we never were: American families and the nostalgia trap*. New York: Basic Books.

Crohan, S. E. (1996). Marital quality and conflict across the transition to parenthood in African American and white couples. *Journal of Marriage and the Family, 58*, 933–944.

Demo, D. H. (1992). Parent-child relations: Assessing recent changes. In A. S. Skolnick & J. H. Skolnick (Eds.), *Family in transition* (8th ed., pp. 294–314). Boston: Allyn & Bacon.

Desai, S., & Waite, L. (1991). Women's employment during pregnancy and after the first birth: Occupational characteristics and work commitment. *American Sociological Review, 56*, 551–566.

Deutsch, F. M. (1999). *Halving it all: How equally shared parenting works.* Cambridge, MA: Harvard University Press.

Dixon, P. (1991). *Mothers and mothering: An annotated feminist bibliography.* New York: Garland.

Ehrenreich, B., & English, D. (1978). *For her own good.* Garden City, NY: Anchor.

Ehrensaft, D. (1990). *Parenting together: Men and women sharing the care of their children.* Urbana: University of Illinois Press.

Ferree, M. M. (1987). Family and job for working-class women: Gender and class systems seen from below. In N. Gerstel & H. E. Gross (Eds.), *Families and work* (pp. 289–301). Philadelphia: Temple University Press.

Friedan, B. (1963). *The feminine mystique.* New York: Norton.

Garey, A. I. (1999). *Weaving work and motherhood.* Philadelphia: Temple University Press.

Glenn, E. N. (1987). Gender and the family. In B. B. Hess & M. M. Ferree (Eds.), *Analyzing gender: A handbook of social science research,* (pp. 348–380). Beverly Hills, CA: Sage.

Glenn, E. N. (1994). Social constructions of mothering: A thematic overview. In E. N. Glenn, G. Chang, & L. R. Forcey (Eds.), *Mothering: Ideology, experience, and agency* (pp. 1–29). New York: Routledge.

Hays, S. (1996). *The cultural contradictions of motherhood.* New Haven, CT: Yale University Press.

Hertz, R., & Ferguson, F. I. T. (1995). Childcare choices and constraints in the United States: Social class, race, and the influence of family views. *Journal of Comparative Family Studies, 26,* 249–280.

Hrdy, S. B. (1999). *Mother nature: A history of mothers, infants, and natural selection.* New York: Pantheon.

Johnson, M. M. (1988). *Strong mothers, weak wives: The search for gender equality.* Berkeley: University of California Press.

Lewis, S. (1991). Motherhood and employment: The impact of social and organizational values. In A. Phoenix, A. Woollett, & E. Lloyd (Eds.), *Motherhood: Meanings, practices, and ideologies* (pp. 195–215). Newbury Park, CA: Sage.

Lorber, J., Coser, R. L., Rossi, A. S., & Chodorow, N. (1981). On *The Reproduction of Mothering:* A methodological debate. *Signs, 6,* 482–514.

Margolis, M. L. (1984). *Mothers and such.* Berkeley: University of California Press.

Marshall, H. (1991). The social construction of motherhood: An analysis of childcare and parenting manuals. In A. Phoenix, A. Woollett, & E. Lloyd (Eds.), *Motherhood: Meanings, practices, and ideologies* (pp. 66–85). Newbury Park, CA: Sage.

Marsiglio, W., & Hutchinson, S. (2002). *Sex, men, and babies: Stories of awareness and responsibility.* New York: New York University Press.

Maushart, S. (1999). *The mask of motherhood: How becoming a mother changes everything and why we pretend it doesn't.* New York: Penguin.

McMahon, M. (1995). *Engendering motherhood: Identity and self-transformation in women's lives.* New York: Guilford.

Moen, P. (1992). *Women's two roles: A contemporary dilemma.* New York: Auburn House.

Nock, S. L. (1987). The symbolic meaning of childbearing. *Journal of Family Issues, 8,* 373–393.

Oakley, A. (1979). *Becoming a mother.* New York: Schocken

Pearce, D. (1990). Welfare is not *for* women: Why the war on poverty cannot conquer the feminization of poverty. In L. Gordon (Ed.), *Women, the state and welfare* (pp. 265–279). Madison: University of Wisconsin Press.

Perry-Jenkins, M., Repetti, R. L., & Crouter, A. (2000). Work and family in the 1990s. *Journal of Marriage and the Family, 62,* 981–998.

Ragoné, H. (1994). *Surrogate motherhood: Conception in the heart.* Boulder, CO: Westview.

Reimann, R. (1997). Does biology matter? Lesbian couples' transitions to parenthood and their division of labor. *Qualitative Sociology, 20,* 153–185.

Rich, A. (1976). *Of woman born.* New York: Norton.

Ross, E. (1995). New thoughts on "the oldest vocation": Mothers and motherhood in recent feminist scholarship. *Signs, 20,* 397–413.

Rothman, B. K. (1989). *Recreating motherhood.* New York: Norton.

Rubin, N. (1984). *The mother mirror: How a generation of women is changing motherhood in America.* New York: G. P. Putnam's Sons.

Ruddick, S. (1983). Maternal thinking. In J. Trebilcot (Ed.), *Mothering: Essays in feminist theory* (pp. 213–230). Savage, MD: Rowman & Littlefield.

Sanchez, L., & Thomson, E. (1997). Becoming mothers and fathers: Parenthood, gender, and the division of labor. *Gender and Society, 11,* 747–772.

Scarr, S., Phillips, D., & McCartney, K. (1989). Working mothers and their families. In A. S. Skolnick & J. H. Skolnick (Eds.), *Family in transition* (8th ed., pp. 411–427). Boston: Allyn & Bacon.

Seltzer, J. A. (2000). Families formed outside of marriage. *Journal of Marriage and the Family, 62,* 1247–1268.

Spitze, G. (1988). Women's employment and family relations. *Journal of Marriage and the Family, 50,* 595–618.

Thompson, L., & Walker, A. J. (1989). Women and men in marriage, work, and parenthood. *Journal of Marriage and the Family, 51,* 845–871.

Thorne, B. (1987). Re-visioning women and social change: Where are the children? *Gender and Society, 1,* 85–109.

Umansky, L. (1996). *Motherhood reconceived: Feminism and the legacies of the sixties.* New York: New York University Press.

Volling, B. L., & Belsky, J. (1993). Parent, infant, and contextual characteristics related to maternal employment decisions in the first year of infancy. *Family Relations, 42,* 4–12.

Walzer, S. (1995). *Gender and transitions into parenthood.* Unpublished doctoral dissertation, State University of New York, Albany.

Walzer, S. (1997). Contextualizing the employment decisions of new mothers. *Qualitative Sociology, 20,* 211–227.

Walzer, S. (1998). *Thinking about the baby.* Philadelphia: Temple University Press.

Wenk, D., & Garrett, P. (1992). Having a baby: Some predictions of maternal employment around childbirth. *Gender and Society, 6,* 49–65.

West, C., & Zimmerman, D. H. (1987). Doing gender. *Gender and Society, 1,* 125–151.

Woollett, A., & Marshall, H. (2001). Motherhood and mothering. In R. K. Unger (Ed.), *Handbook of the psychology of women and gender* (pp. 170–182). New York: John Wiley.

CHAPTER 13

Fathering
Paradoxes, Contradictions, and Dilemmas

Scott Coltrane

The beginning of the 21st century offers a paradox for American fathers: Media images, political rhetoric, and psychological studies affirm the importance of fathers to children at the same time that men are becoming less likely to live with their offspring. Although the average married father spends more time interacting with his children than in past decades, marriage rates have fallen, and half of all marriages are predicted to end in divorce. Additionally, the proportion of births to unmarried mothers has increased dramatically for all race and ethnic groups, and single-mother households have become commonplace. These contradictory tendencies—more father-child interaction in two-parent families but fewer two-parent families in the population—have encouraged new research on fathers and spawned debates about how essential fathers are to families and normal child development (Blankenhorn, 1995; Silverstein & Auerbach, 1999).

Scholars attribute the current paradox in fathering to various economic and social trends. Whereas most men in the 20th century were sole breadwinners, contemporary fathers' wages can rarely support a middle-class standard of living for an entire family. The weakening of the good-provider model, coupled with trends in fertility, marriage, divorce, and custody, has resulted in the average man spending fewer years living with children (Eggebeen, 2002). Simultaneously, however, men rank marriage and children among their most precious

AUTHOR'S NOTE: This chapter incorporates some material from a November 21, 2002, National Council on Family Relations (NCFR) Annual Conference Special Session, "Future Prospects for Increasing Father Involvement in Child Rearing and Household Activities," reprinted as "The Paradox of Fatherhood: Predicting the Future of Men's Family Involvement" in *Vision 2003* (Minneapolis, MN: National Council on Family Relations/Allen). I thank Marilyn Coleman, Lawrence Ganong, Joseph Pleck, Carl Auerbach, and two anonymous reviewers for valuable feedback on an earlier draft of this chapter.

goals, single-father households have increased, and fathers in two-parent households are spending more time with co-resident children than at any time since data on fathers were collected (Pleck & Masciadrelli, 2003). Although married fathers report that they value their families over their jobs, they spend significantly more time in paid work and less time in family work than married mothers, with most men continuing to serve as helpers to their wives, especially for housework and child maintenance activities (Coltrane, 2000). Personal, political, religious, and popular discourses about fathers reveal similar ambivalence about men's family involvements, with ideals ranging from stern patriarchs to nurturing daddies, and public portrayals frequently at odds with the actual behavior of average American fathers (LaRossa, 1997). We can understand these contradictions by recognizing that fatherhood has gained symbolic importance just as men's family participation has become more voluntary, tenuous, and conflicted (Griswold, 1993; Kimmel, 1996).

In this chapter, I summarize how fathering practices have varied across cultures and through history; highlight how different social, economic, and political contexts have produced different types of father involvement; review how social scientists have measured father involvement; and examine findings about causes and consequences of father involvement. I end with a short analysis of debates over family policy and offer tentative predictions about the future of fathering in America.

CROSS-CULTURAL VARIATION

Fatherhood defines a biological and social relationship between a male parent and his offspring. *To father* means to impregnate a woman and beget a child, thus describing a kinship connection that facilitates the intergenerational transfer of wealth and authority (at least in patrilineal descent systems such as ours). Fatherhood also reflects ideals about the rights, duties, and activities of men in families and in society and generalizes to other social and symbolic relationships, as when Christians refer to "God the Father," Catholics call priests "Father," and Americans label George Washington "the Father" of the country. Fatherhood thus reflects a normative set of social practices and expectations that are institutionalized within religion, politics, law, and culture. Social theories have employed the concept of *social fatherhood* to explain how the institution of fatherhood links a particular child to a particular man (whether father or uncle) in order to secure a place for that child in the social structure (Coltrane & Collins, 2001).

Fathering (in contrast to *fatherhood*) refers more directly to what men do with and for children. Although folk beliefs suggest that fathering entail behaviors fixed by reproductive biology, humans must learn how to parent. In every culture and historical period, men's parenting has been shaped by social and economic forces. Although women have been the primary caretakers of young children in all cultures, fathers' participation in child rearing has varied from virtually no direct involvement to active participation in all aspects of children's routine care. Except for breastfeeding and the earliest care of infants, there are no cross-cultural universals in the tasks that mothers and fathers perform (Johnson, 1988). In some societies, the social worlds of fathers and mothers were so separate that they rarely had contact and seldom performed the same tasks; in other societies, men participated in tasks like infant care, and women participated in tasks like hunting (Coltrane, 1988; Sanday, 1981).

Drawing on worldwide cross-cultural comparisons, scholars have identified two general patterns of fathers' family involvement, one intimate and the other aloof. In the intimate pattern, men eat and sleep with their wives and children, talk with them during evening meals, attend births, and participate actively in infant care. In the aloof pattern, men often eat and sleep apart from women, spend their leisure time in the company of other men, stay away during births, and seldom help with child care (Whiting & Whiting, 1975). Societies with involved fathers are more likely than societies with aloof fathers to be peaceful, to afford women a role in community decision making, to have intimate husband-wife relationships, to feature more gender equality in the society, and to include nurturing deities of both sexes in their religions. Aloof-father societies are more likely to have religious systems with stern male gods, social institutions that exclude women from community decision making, marriage systems in which husbands demand deference from wives, and public rituals that focus on men's competitive displays of masculinity (Coltrane, 1988, 1996; Sanday, 1981).

Research on fathering among indigenous peoples such as the African Aka suggests why involved fathering and gender egalitarianism are associated (Hewlett, 1991). Anthropologists such as Hewlett have drawn on Chodorow's (1974) work to suggest that when fathers are active in infant care, boys develop an intimate knowledge of masculinity, which makes them less likely to devalue the feminine, whereas when fathers are rarely around, boys lack a clear sense of masculinity and construct their identities in opposition to things feminine by devaluing and criticizing women (Hewlett, 2000). In reviews of data on father involvement over the past 120,000 years, Hewlett concluded that fathers contribute to their children in many ways, with the relative importance of different contributions varying dramatically; that different ecologies and modes of production have a substantial impact on the contributions of fathers to their children; and that fathers' roles today are relatively unique in human history (Hewlett, 1991, 2000).

HISTORICAL VARIATION

Historical studies have focused on practices in Europe, chronicling and emphasizing men's public lives: work, political exploits, literary accomplishments, scientific discoveries, and heroic battles. This emphasis shows how various economic, political, and legal practices have structured privileges and obligations within and beyond families. For example, the historical concept of family in the West is derived from the Latin *famulus,* meaning servant, and the Roman *familia,* meaning the man's domestic property. Linking institutional arrangements with linguistic forms tells us something important about men's relationships to families. Recent historical studies have focused more directly on men's ideal and actual behaviors in families, thereby documenting complexity and diversity in past fathering practices (e.g., Griswold, 1993; Kimmel, 1996; LaRossa, 1997; Mintz, 1998; Pleck & Pleck, 1997).

Before these studies, many scholars erroneously assumed that changes in fatherhood were linear and progressive (Coltrane & Parke, 1998). For example, early family history emphasized that peasant families were extended and governed by stern patriarchs, whereas market societies produced nuclear families, companionate marriages, and involved fathers. In fact, historical patterns of fathering have responded to a complex array of social and economic forces, varying considerably across regions, time periods, and ethnic or cultural groups. Although it is useful to identify how men's work and production have shaped their public and private statuses, actual family relations have been diverse, and fatherhood ideals have followed different trajectories in different regions of the same country (Griswold, 1993; Mintz, 1998; Pleck & Pleck, 1997).

The economy of the 17th and 18th centuries in Europe and America was based on agriculture and productive family households. For families that owned farms or small artisan shops, their place of work was also their home. Slaves, indentured servants, and others were expected to work on family estates in return for food, a place to live, and sometimes other rewards. In this pattern of household or family-based production, men, women, and children worked together. Regional variations could be large, and fathers and mothers often did different types of work, but many tasks required for subsistence and family survival were interchangeable, and both mothers and fathers took responsibility for child care and training (Coltrane & Galt, 2000).

Because most men's work as farmers, artisans, and tradesmen occurred in the family household, fathers were a visible presence in their children's lives. Child rearing was a bmore collective enterprise than it is today, with family behaviors and attitudes ruled primarily by duty and obligation. Men introduced sons to farming or craft work within the household economy, oversaw the work of others, and were responsible for maintaining harmonious household relations. The preindustrial home was a system of control as well as a center of production, and both functions reinforced the father's authority (Griswold, 1993). Though mothers provided most direct care for infants and young children, men tended to be active in the training and tutoring of children. Because they were moral teachers and family heads, fathers were thought to have greater responsibility for and influence on children than mothers and were also generally held responsible for how the children acted outside the home (Pleck & Pleck, 1997).

Because the sentimental individualism of the modern era had not yet blossomed, emotional involvement with children in the Western world during the 17th and early 18th centuries was more limited than today. Prevailing images of children also were different from modern ideas about their innocence and purity. Religious teachings stressed the corrupt nature and evil dispositions of children, and fathers were admonished to demand strict obedience and use swift physical punishment to cleanse children of their sinful ways. Puritan fathers justified their extensive involvement in children's lives because women were seen as unfit to be disciplinarians, moral guides, or intellectual teachers. Griswold (1997) pointed out, however, that stern unaffectionate fathering, though not confined to Puritans, was not representative of all of the population. In fact, most American fathers attempted to shape and guide their children's characters, not break them or beat the devil out of them. As more privileged 18th-century fathers gained enough affluence to have some leisure time, many were affectionate with their children and delighted in playing with them (Griswold, 1997).

As market economies replaced home-based production in the 19th and 20th centuries, the middle-class father's position as household head and master and moral instructor of his children was slowly transformed. Men increasingly sought employment outside the home, and their direct contact with family members declined. As the wage labor economy developed, men's occupational achievement outside the household took on stronger moral overtones. Men came to be seen as fulfilling their family and civic duty, not by teaching and interacting with their children as before, but by supporting the family financially. The middle-class home, previously the site of production, consumption, and virtually everything else in life, became a nurturing, child-centered haven set apart from the impersonal world of work, politics, and other public pursuits.

The separate-spheres ideal became a defining feature of the late 19th and early 20th centuries (Bernard, 1981; Coltrane & Galt, 2000; Kimmel, 1996).

The ideal that paid work was only for men and that only women were suited to care for family members remained an unattainable myth rather than an everyday reality for most families. Many working-class fathers were not able to earn the family wage assumed by the separate-spheres ideal, and a majority of African American, Latino, Asian American, and other immigrant men could not fulfill the good-provider role that the cultural ideal implied. Women in these families either had to work for wages, participate in production at home, or find other ways to make ends meet. Although the emerging romantic ideal held that women should be sensitive and pure keepers of the home on a full-time basis, the reality was that women in less advantaged households had no choice but to simultaneously be workers and mothers. In fact, many working-class and ethnic minority women had to leave their homes and children to take care of other people's children and houses (Dill, 1988). Even during the heyday of separate spheres (in the early 20th century), minority women, young single women, widows, and married women whose husbands could not support them worked for wages.

As noted above, attempts to understand the history of fatherhood have often painted a simple before-and-after picture: *Before* the Industrial Revolution, families were rural and extended, and patriarchal fathers were stern moralists; *after* the Industrial Revolution, families were urban and nuclear, and wage-earning fathers became companionate husbands, distant breadwinners, and occasional playmates to their children. This before-and-after picture captures something important about general shifts in work and family life, but its simple assumption of unidirectional linear change and its

binary conceptualization contrasting men's patriarchal roles in the past with egalitarian roles in the present is misleading (Coontz, 1992). Stage models of family history have ignored the substantial regional and race/ethnic differences that encouraged different family patterns (Pleck & Pleck, 1997). For example, as most of the United States was undergoing industrialization, large pockets remained relatively untouched by it. The experience of white planters in the antebellum South was both like and unlike that of men in the commercial and industrial North (Griswold, 1993). Another major drawback of early historical studies is the tendency to overgeneralize for the entire society on the basis of the experience of the white middle class. Even during the heyday of separate spheres at the turn of the 20th century, minority and immigrant men were unlikely to be able to support a family. Race and class differences also intersect with regional differences: Not only did southern fathering practices differ from northern ones, but slave fathers and freedmen in the South had much different experiences than either group of white men (Griswold, 1993; McDaniel, 1994).

THE EMERGENCE OF MODERN FATHERING

Throughout the 20th century, calls for greater paternal involvement coexisted with the physical presence, but relative emotional and functional absence, of fathers (LaRossa, 1997). Nevertheless, some fathers have always reported high levels of involvement with their children. By the 1930s, even though mothers bore most of the responsibility for care of homes and families, three out of four American fathers said they regularly read magazine articles about child care, and nearly as many men as women were members of the PTA (Kimmel, 1996). Increases in women's labor force participation during the

1940s briefly challenged the ideal of separate family and work roles, but in the postwar era, high rates of marriage and low rates of employment reinforced the ideology of separate spheres for men and women. The ideal father at midcentury was seen as a good provider who "set a good table, provided a decent home, paid the mortgage, bought the shoes, and kept his children warmly clothed" (Bernard, 1981, pp. 3-4). As they had during the earlier Victorian era, middle-class women were expected to be consumed and fulfilled by wifely and motherly duties. With Ozzie and Harriet–style families as the 1950s model, women married earlier and had more children than any group of American women before them. Rapid expansion of the U.S. economy fueled a phenomenal growth of suburbs, and the consumer culture from that era idolized domestic life on radio and television. Isolated in suburban houses, many mothers now had almost sole responsibility for raising children, aided by occasional reference to expert guides from pediatricians and child psychologists (Hays, 1996). Fathers of the 1950s were also told to get involved with child care—but not *too* involved (Kimmel, 1996). The separate spheres of white middle-class men and women were thus maintained, though experts deemed them permeable enough for men to participate regularly as a helper to the mother (Coltrane & Galt, 2000; Hays, 1996).

During the mid–20th century, separate-spheres ideology and the popularity of Freud's ideas about mother-infant bonding led to widespread acceptance of concepts like *maternal deprivation,* and few researchers asked who besides mothers took care of children, although some researchers began to focus on *father absence* during the baby boom era (roughly 1946–64). Empirical studies and social theories valued the symbolic significance of fathers' breadwinning, discipline, and masculine role modeling, even though few studies controlled for social class or measured what fathers actually did with children. Studies including fathers found that they were more likely than mothers to engage in rough and tumble play and to give more attention to sons than daughters (Parke, 1996; Pleck, 1997). In general, research showed that child care was an ongoing and taken-for-granted task for mothers but a novel and fun distraction for fathers (Thompson & Walker, 1989).

Compared to the wholesome but distant good-provider fathers pictured on television programs like *Ozzie and Harriet* and *Father Knows Best* in the 1950s, a new father ideal gained prominence in the 1980s (Griswold, 1993). According to Furstenberg (1988), "[T]elevision, magazines, and movies herald the coming of the modern father—the nurturant, caring, and emotionally attuned parent. . . . Today's father is at least as adept at changing diapers as changing tires" (p. 193). No longer limited to being protectors and providers, fathers were pictured on television and in magazines as intimately involved in family life. Fatherhood proponents focused on the potential of the new ideals and practices (Biller, 1976), but researchers in the 1980s reported that many fathers resisted assuming responsibility for daily housework or child care (Thompson & Walker, 1989). Some researchers claimed that popular images far exceeded men's actual behaviors (LaRossa, 1988), and others suggested that men, on the whole, were less committed to families than they had been in the past (Ehrenreich, 1984). In the 1990s, researchers also began to examine how the modern ideal of the new father carried hidden messages about class and race, with some suggesting that the image of the sensitive and involved father was a new class/ethnic icon because it set middle-class fathers apart from working-class and ethnic minority fathers, who presented a more masculine image (Messner, 1993). Others suggested that the sensitive or androgynous parenting styles of new fathers might lead to gender identity confusion in sons (Blankenhorn, 1995).

MEASURING FATHER INVOLVEMENT

Before the 1980s, the rare researchers who included fathers focused on simple distinctions between father-present and father-absent families, finding that children from families with co-resident fathers generally fared better, on average, than those without co-resident fathers. Although the structural aspects of fatherhood (marriage, paternity, co-residence) sometimes correlate with various child and family outcomes, most researchers now agree that what fathers do with and for children is more important than co-residence or legal relationship to the mother and recommend that dichotomous measures (e.g., father presence/absence) be replaced by more nuanced ones.

The most influential refinement in fathering measurement was offered by Lamb, Pleck, Charnov, and Levine (1987), who suggested three components: (a) interaction, the father's direct contact with his child through caregiving and shared activities; (b) availability (or accessibility), a related concept concerning the father's potential availability for interaction, by virtue of being accessible to the child (whether or not direct interaction is occurring); and (c) responsibility, the role the father takes in ascertaining that the child is taken care of and in arranging for resources to be available for the child. Within each of these categories, two further distinctions should be made. First, it is critical to distinguish the amount from the quality of involvement: Both are important to child development and parental well-being (Parke, 1996). Second, absolute as well as relative (in relation to partner) indices of involvement are

independent and may affect children and adults in different ways (Pleck, 1997).

A recent tabulation of father involvement assessment in 15 large social science family data sets showed that all but one measured About half measured the fathers' "communication" or "emotional support," only a few measured "thought processes" (e.g., worrying, dreaming) or "planning" (e.g., birthdays, vacations, friend visits), and none measured "sharing interests" (e.g., providing for instruction, reading together) or "child maintenance" (e.g., cleaning or cooking for the child) (Federal Interagency Forum, 1998, pp. 144, 400; Palkovitz, 1997, pp. 209–210). Structural availability is thus the most common fathering indicator, with various routine parent-child interactions and support activities sometimes assessed, and with fathers' planning and responsibility rarely measured. In addition, many studies collect fathering data from just one reporter, even though self-reports of fathers' involvement tend to be higher than mothers' reports of fathers' involvement, especially for nonresident fathers (Coley & Morris, 2002; Smock & Manning, 1997).

LEVELS AND PREDICTORS OF FATHERS' INVOLVEMENT

Research on fathering in two-parent households shows a noticeable and statistically significant increase in men's parenting involvement, both in absolute terms and in relation to mothers. Simultaneously, however, average levels of fathers' interaction with, availability to, and responsibility for children lag well behind those of mothers (Marsiglio, Amato, Day, & Lamb, 2000; Parke, 1996; Pleck & Masciadrelli, 2003). Measurement strategies vary, with time-use diaries generally producing the most accurate estimates of fathers' interaction and availability. On average, in the 1960s to early-1980s, fathers interacted with their children about a third as much as mothers and were available about half as much as mothers (Lamb et al., 1987). During the mid-1980s to early-1990s, the average co-resident father interacted about two fifths as much as mothers and was available to his children almost two thirds as much (Pleck, 1997). In the late 1990s, he was available to his children about three fourths as much as mothers, interacting on weekdays about two thirds as often, but over four fifths as much on weekends (Pleck & Masciadrelli, 2003; Yueng, Sandberg, Davis-Kean, & Hofferth, 2001). In an estimated 20% of two-parent families, men are now about as involved as mothers interacting with and being available to their children. At the same time, in most families, fathers and mothers share much less of the responsibility for the planning, scheduling, emotional management, housework, and other maintenance activities associated with raising children (Deutsch, 1999; Hochschild, 1989; see also Chapter 10 of this book).

Researchers have begun to isolate the effects of income, race/ethnicity, education, family structure, marriage, employment, work schedules, and other factors on father involvement, though results are often incomplete or contradictory. For example, the relation between socioeconomic status and father involvement is complex. Income is often found to be positively correlated with father involvement among various ethnic groups (Fagan, 1998; Parke, 1996). Relative income contributions by wives are also associated with higher proportionate levels of father involvement in housework and child care (Coltrane, 2000; Yeung et al., 2001), though some studies still find that financially dependent husbands do less domestic work than others (Brines, 1994). Wealthier men do little routine family work, but the amount their wives do varies dramatically, with higher-earning wives more likely to purchase domestic services (e.g., child care, house cleaning, laundry) (Cohen, 1998; Oropesa, 1993).

Although most contemporary studies of fathering have been based on white, middle-class, two-parent families, we are beginning to get a more complete picture about similarities and differences across family types. When financial stability is hard to achieve, fathers only minimally involved with their children may nevertheless see themselves as "good fathers" because they work hard to provide financially. Because of inequities in the labor market, men of color are disproportionately likely to face difficulties being adequate providers (Bowman & Sanders, 1998; Hamer & Marchioro, 2002). Comparisons between white, African American, and Latino fathers suggest similar levels of involvement with infants and similar styles of engagement with young children (e.g., proportionately more play and less caretaking than mothers; Coltrane, Parke, & Adams, 2001; Toth & Xu, 1999). Contrary to cultural stereotypes, some research also shows that Latino fathers are more likely than their European American counterparts to spend time in shared activities with children, to perform housework and personal care, and to engage in monitoring and supervising children's activities (Coltrane et al., 2001; Toth & Xu, 1999; Yeung et al., 2001). Results for African American fathers in two-parent households are mixed, with most reporting levels of father-child interaction comparable to other race/ethnic groups, and several studies finding that black men do more housework than white men, net of other predictors (Ahmeduzzaman & Roopnarine, 1992; Broman, 1991; Hossain & Roopnarine, 1993; John & Shelton, 1997), and that nonresident black fathers contribute more to children than nonresident white fathers (Wilson, Tolson, Hinton, & Kiernan, 1990). Studies of African American and Latino fathers reveal a wide range of behaviors across families, depending on employment, income, education, gender and religious ideology, family structure, marital status, age of children, immigration status, neighborhood context, cultural traditions, and presence of extended or fictive kin, and a similar pattern of association between social contextual variables and levels and styles of paternal participation (Auerbach, Silverstein, & Zizi, 1997; Cabrera, Tamis-LeMonda, Bradley, Hofferth, & Lamb, 2000; Hossain & Roopnarine, 1993; Hunter & Davis, 1994; Padgett, 1997; Pleck & Steuve, 2001; Silverstein, 2002).

Fathers tend to spend more time with young children than they do with older children and adolescents, probably because younger children require more attention and care, even though many men feel more comfortable interacting with older children. Most research finds that a father's availability (as determined by work hours) is a strong predictor of his involvement in child care. When mothers of preschool children are employed, a father's time availability predicts whether he will serve as a primary caregiver (Brayfield, 1995; Casper & O'Connell, 1998). Fathers and mothers with nonoverlapping work shifts are the most likely to share child care (Presser, 1995). When mothers of school-aged children are employed more hours, their husbands tend to do a greater portion of the child care and housework, and fathers tend to be more involved to the extent that they view their wives' career prospects more positively (Pleck, 1997). For instance, Brewster (2000) found that fathers in the late 1980s and 1990s were likely to use nonworking discretionary hours for child care, whereas in the late 1970s and early 1980s they tended to use those hours for other activities.

As demonstrated in comprehensive reviews (Pleck, 1997; Pleck & Masciadrelli, 2003), father involvement is multiply determined, with no single factor responsible for the different types of involvement. In addition, studies often report contradictory effects of factors like income, education, age, family size, and birth timing. One of the most consistent findings is that men are more involved with sons than with daughters (Harris, Furstenberg, & Marmer, 1998; Harris & Morgan, 1991; Marsiglio, 1991; McBride, Schoppe, & Rane, 2002), especially with older children (Pleck, 1997). However, some recent studies have found no differences in father involvement by sex of child (Fagan, 1998; Hofferth, 2003), leading Pleck and Masciadrelli (2003) to suggest that fathers' preference for sons may be weakening. Some researchers also find that if fathers get involved during pregnancy or early infancy they tend to sustain that involvement later in children's lives (Coltrane, 1996; Parke, 1996).

Lamb, Pleck, and colleagues suggested that fathers, to become actively involved, required four facilitating factors: (a) motivation, (b) skills and self-confidence, (c) social approval, and (d) institutional support (Lamb et al., 1987; see also Pleck, 1997). Many studies find that fathers are more involved and show more warmth if they believe in gender equality (Cabrera et al., 2000; Hofferth, 1998), though others find no significant association (Marsiglio, 1991; Pleck, 1997). Others find that fathers get more involved when they have a strong fatherhood identity or actively embrace the father role (Beitel & Parke, 1998; Hawkins, Christiansen, Sargent, & Hill, 1993; Pasley, Ihinger-Tallman, & Buehler, 1993; Rane & McBride, 2000; Snarey, 1993). In general, fathers feel more competent as parents when they are more involved with their children, though it is difficult to say whether this competence is a precursor or a result of active fathering (Beitel & Parke, 1998; McHale & Huston, 1984). Evidence suggesting that competence leads to involvement comes from interventions designed to develop fathers' parenting skills (e.g., Cowan &

Cowan, 2000; McBride, 1990). In terms of social support, fathers tend to be more involved when the children's mothers facilitate it, when the mothers had positive relationships with their own fathers when they were children (Allen & Hawkins, 1999; Cowan & Cowan, 2000; McBride & Mills, 1993; Parke, 1996), and when kin and other community members support father involvement (Pleck, 1997). Finally, institutional supports can include factors such as fewer work hours and more flexible work schedules (Pleck, 1993).

Another approach to identifying predictors of father involvement is based on a process model of parenting (Belsky, 1984; McBride et al., 2002). This framework suggests that fathering is shaped by three categories of influence: (a) characteristics of the father (e.g., personality, attitudes toward child rearing), (b) characteristics of the child (e.g., temperament, age, gender), and (c) contextual sources of stress and support (e.g., marital relationships, social support networks, occupational experiences). Many of these facilitating influences overlap with factors in the Lamb and Pleck model, but this approach also includes consideration of things like child temperament and parental stress. Emergent findings suggest that child temperament or other characteristics may have a larger influence on father-child involvement than mother-child involvement, probably because fathering is seen as more discretionary than mothering (Cabrera et al., 2000; McBride et al., 2002).

The nature of the marital relationship is also associated with paternal involvement, though causality is sometimes difficult to assess. Some find that greater marital satisfaction leads to greater father involvement (Parke, 1996), and others suggest that higher levels of men's relative contributions to child care lead to women's greater marital satisfaction (Brennan, Barnett, & Gareis, 2001; Ozer, Barnett, Brennan, & Sperling, 1998).

In addition, satisfaction with men's levels of family involvement appears to be strongly related to mothers' and fathers' gender ideals and expectations. We cannot simply assume that more father involvement is better for all families. As the emerging gatekeeping literature (e.g., Allen & Hawkins, 1999; Beitel & Parke, 1998) attests, too much involvement by fathers can be interpreted as interference rather than helpfulness. In general, if family members want a father to be more involved, his participation has positive effects on family functioning. If family members feel that fathers should not change diapers or do laundry, then such practices can cause stress (Coltrane, 1996).

THE POTENTIAL INFLUENCE OF FATHERS

As scholars pay more attention to fathers, they are beginning to understand what influence their involvement might have on child development. Most researchers find that father-child relationships are influential for children's future life chances (Federal Interagency Forum, 1998; Parke, 1996; Pleck & Masciadrelli, 2003). The focus of this research tends to be on the positive aspects of fathers' involvement, though it should be noted that because men are more likely than women to abuse children or to use inappropriate parenting techniques, increased male involvement can lead to increased risk and negative outcomes for children, particularly if the father figure does not have a long-term relationship with the mother (Finkelhor, Hotaling, Lewis, & Smith, 1990; Margolin, 1992; National Research Council, 1993; Radhakrishna, Bou-Saada, Hunter, Catellier, & Kotch, 2001).

Many researchers continue to focus on fathers' economic contributions to children and report that fathers' resources improve children's life chances. Longitudinal research shows that children from one-parent households (usually mother headed) are at greater risk for negative adult outcomes (e.g., lower educational and occupational achievement, earlier childbirth, school dropout, health problems, behavioral difficulties) than those from two-parent families (Marsiglio et al., 2000; McLanahan & Sandefur, 1994). Although comparisons between children of divorced parents and those from first-marriage families show more problems in the former group, differences between the two are generally small across various outcome measures and do not necessarily isolate the influence of divorce or of father involvement (Crockett, Eggebeen, & Hawkins, 1993; Furstenberg & Harris, 1993; Seltzer, 1994). For children with nonresident fathers, the amount of fathers' earnings (especially the amount that is actually transferred to children) is a significant predictor of children's well-being, including school grades and behavior problems (Amato & Gilbreth, 1999; McLanahan, Seltzer, Hanson, & Thomson, 1994; Marsiglio et al., 2000). Because the great majority of children from single-parent homes turn out to be happy, healthy, and productive adults, debates continue about how such large-group comparisons should be made and how we should interpret their results in terms of fathers' economic or social contributions (Amato, 2000; Coltrane & Adams, in press).

Earlier reviews suggested that the level of father involvement has a smaller direct effect on infant attachment than the quality or style of father interaction, though time spent parenting is also related to competence (Lamb et al., 1987; Marsiglio et al., 2000). Preschool children with fathers who perform 40% or more of the within-family child care show more cognitive competence, more internal locus of control, more empathy, and less gender stereotyping than preschool children with less involved fathers (Lamb et al., 1987; Pleck, 1997). Adolescents with involved fathers are more likely to have positive developmental outcomes such as self-control, self esteem, life skills, and social competence, provided that the father is not authoritarian or overly controlling (Mosley & Thomson, 1995; Pleck & Masciadrelli, 2003). Studies examining differences between the presence of biological fathers versus other father figures suggest that it is the quality of the father-child relationship rather than biological relationship that enhances the cognitive and emotional development of children (Dubowitz et al., 2001; Hofferth & Anderson, 2003; Silverstein & Auerbach, 1999). Reports of greater father involvement when children were growing up have also been associated with positive aspects of adult children's educational attainment, relationship quality, and career success (Amato & Booth, 1997; Harris et al., 1998; Nock, 1998; Snarey, 1993). Because of methodological inadequacies in previous studies such as not controlling for maternal involvement, most scholars recommend more carefully controlled studies using random samples and multirater longitudinal designs, as well as advocating caution in interpreting associations between fathering and positive child outcomes (Amato & Rivera, 1999; Parke, 1996; Pleck & Masciadrelli, 2003). It will take some time to isolate the specific influence of fathers as against the influence of mothers and other social-contextual factors such as income, education, schools, neighborhoods, communities, kin networks, and cultural ideals.

We do know that when fathers share child care and housework with their wives, employed mothers escape total responsibility for family work, evaluate the division of labor as more fair, are less depressed, and enjoy higher levels of marital satisfaction (Brennan et al., 2001; Coltrane 2000; Deutsch, 1999). When men care for young children on a regular basis, they emphasize verbal interaction, notice and use more subtle cues, and treat sons and daughters similarly, rather than focusing on play, giving orders, and sex-typing children (Coltrane, 1996, 1998; Parke, 1996). These styles of father involvement have been found to encourage less gender stereotyping among young adults and to encourage independence in daughters and emotional sensitivity in sons. Most researchers agree that these are worthy goals that could contribute to reducing sexism, promoting gender equity, and curbing violence against women (but see Blankenhorn, 1995).

DEMOGRAPHIC CONTEXTS FOR FATHER INVOLVEMENT

As Furstenberg (1988) first noted, conflicting images of fathers are common in popular culture, with nurturing, involved "good dads" contrasted with "bad dads" who do not marry the mother of their children or who move out and fail to pay child support. Recent research suggests that both types of fathers are on the rise and that the demographic contexts for fatherhood have changed significantly over the past few decades. In many industrialized countries, at the same time that some fathers are taking a more active role in their children's lives, growing numbers of men rarely see their children and do not support them financially. In the United States, for example, single-parent households are increasing, with only about half of U.S. children eligible for child support from nonresident parents via court order and only about half of those receiving the full amount (Scoon-Rogers, 1999). Both trends in fatherhood—toward more direct involvement and toward less contact and financial support—are responses to the same underlying social developments, including women's rising labor force participation and the increasingly optional nature of marriage.

Marriage rates have fallen in the past few decades, with people waiting longer to get married and increasingly living together without marrying. Women are having fewer children than they did just a few decades ago, waiting longer to have them, and not necessarily marrying before they give birth (Eggebeen, 2002; Seltzer, 2000). One of three births in the United States is to an unmarried woman, a rate that is three times higher than it was in the 1960s, with rates for African American women highest, followed by Latinas, and then non-Hispanic whites (National Center for Health Statistics, 2000). It is often assumed that nonmarital births produce fatherless children, but recent studies show that most of the increase in nonmarital childbearing from the 1980s to the 1990s is accounted for by the increase in the number of cohabiting women getting pregnant and carrying the baby to term without getting married. Historically, if an unmarried woman became pregnant, she would marry to legitimate the birth. Today, only a minority of women do so.

In addition, an increasingly large number of American fathers live apart from their children because of separation or divorce. Because most divorcing men do not seek (or are not awarded) child custody following divorce, the number of divorced men who are uninvolved fathers has risen (Eggebeen, 2002; Furstenberg & Cherlin, 1991), although recent research shows that the actual involvement of fathers with children after divorce varies enormously, sometimes without regard to official postdivorce court orders (Braver, 1998; Hetherington & Stanley-Hagan, 1999; McLanahan & Sandefur, 1994; Seltzer, 1998). The number of men with joint physical (residential) custody has grown, though joint legal (decision-making) custody is still a more common postdivorce parenting arrangement (Maccoby & Mnookin, 1992; Seltzer, 1998). And although single father-households have increased in recent years, single-mother households continue to outpace them five to one. Demographers suggest that because of all these trends, younger cohorts will be less likely to experience sustained involved fathering than the generations that immediately preceded them (Eggebeen, 2002).

Marriage and the traditional assumption of fatherhood have become more fragile, in part because an increasing number of men face financial difficulties. Although men continue to earn about 30% higher wages than women, their real wages (adjusted for inflation) have declined since the early 1970s, whereas women's have increased (Bernstein & Mishel, 1997). As the U.S. economy has shifted from heavy reliance on domestic manufacturing to global interdependence within an information and service economy, working-class men's prospects of earning a family wage have declined. At the same time, women's labor force participation has risen steadily, with future growth in the economy predicted in the areas where women are traditionally concentrated (e.g., service, information, health care, part-time work). The historical significance of this shift cannot be overestimated. For most of the 19th and 20th centuries, American women's life chances were determined by their marriage decisions. Unable to own property, vote, or be legally independent in most states, daughters were dependent on fathers and wives were dependent on their husbands for economic survival. Such dependencies shaped family relations and produced fatherhood ideals and practices predicated on male family headship. As women and mothers have gained independence by entering the labor force in record numbers, it is not surprising that older ideals about marriage to a man legitimating childbearing have been challenged.

GENDER AND THE POLITICS OF FATHERHOOD

In the 1990s, popular books and articles revived a research and policy focus that had been popular in the 1960s: father absence. For example, Popenoe (1996) suggested that drug and alcohol abuse, juvenile delinquency, teenage pregnancy, violent crime, and child poverty were the result of fatherlessness and that American society was in decline because it had abandoned traditional marriage and child-rearing patterns. Such claims about father absence often rely on evolutionary psychology and sociobiology and define fathers as categorically different from mothers (Blankenhorn, 1995; Popenoe, 1996). Even some proponents of nurturing fathers warn men against trying to act too much like mothers (Pruett, 1993). Following this reasoning, some argue for gender-differentiated parenting measurement strategies: "[T]he roles of father and mother are different and complementary rather than interchangeable and thus the standards for evaluating the role performance of fathers and mothers should be different" (Day & Mackey, 1989, p. 402). Some label the use of measures developed on mothers to study fathers and the practice of comparing fathers' and mothers' parenting as the *deficit model* (Doherty, 1991) or the *role inadequacy perspective* (Hawkins & Dollahite, 1997).

Because parenting is a learned behavior for both men and women, most social scientists focus on the societal conditions that create gender differences in parenting or find proximate social causes of paternal investment that outweigh assumed biological causes (e.g., Hofferth & Anderson, 2003). Nevertheless, questioning taken-for-granted cultural ideals about families can cause controversy. When Silverstein and Auerbach (1999) challenged assertions about essential differences between fathers and mothers in an *American Psychologist* article entitled "Deconstructing the Essential Father," they received widespread public and academic criticism. Their scholarly article (based on a review of research findings) was ridiculed as "silliness" and "junk science" by Wade Horn (1999; formerly of the National Fatherhood Initiative and now Assistant Secretary in the U.S. Department of Health and Human Services), and the U.S. House of Representatives debated whether to pass a resolution condemning the article (Silverstein, 2002). Clearly, debates about fathers, marriage, and family values carry symbolic meanings that transcend scientific findings. The contentious political and scholarly debates about fathers that emerged in the 1990s appear to be framed by an older political dichotomy: Conservatives tend to focus on biological parenting differences and stress the importance of male headship and breadwinning, respect for authority, and moral leadership (Blankenhorn, 1995; Popenoe, 1996), whereas liberals tend to focus on similarities between mothers and fathers and stress the importance of employment, social services, and possibilities for more equal marital relations (Coontz, 1992; Silverstein & Auerbach, 1999; Stacey, 1996).

A full analysis of contemporary family values debates is beyond the scope of this chapter, but elsewhere I analyze marriage and fatherhood movements using data and theories about political opportunities, resource mobilization, and the moral framing of social issues (Coltrane, 2001; Coltrane & Adams, 2003; see also Gavanas, 2002). In general, cultural tensions in the larger society are mirrored in policy proposals and academic debates about the appropriate roles of fathers and the importance of marriage. One cannot adjudicate among various scholarly approaches to fathering without acknowledging gendered interests and understanding the political economy of expert knowledge production. Recent policies and programs promoting marriage and fatherhood using faith-based organizations are designed to advance a particular vision of fatherhood. Whether they will benefit the majority of American mothers and children is a question that cannot be resolved without more sophisticated research with controls for mothers' parenting and various other economic and social-contextual issues (Marsiglio et al., 2000; Marsiglio & Pleck, in press).

PROSPECTS FOR THE FUTURE

The forces that are driving changes in fathers' involvement in families are likely to continue. In two-parent households (both married and cohabiting), men share more family work if their female partners are employed more hours, earn more money, and have more education. All three of these trends in women's attainment are likely to continue for the foreseeable future. Similarly, fathers share more family work when they are employed fewer hours and their wives earn a greater portion of the family income. Labor market and economic trends for these variables are also expected to continue for several decades. Couples also share more when they believe that family work should be shared and that men and women should have equal rights. According to national opinion polls, although the country has become slightly more conservative about marriage and divorce than it was in the 1970s and 1980s, the belief in gender equality continues to gain acceptance among both men and women. In addition, American women are waiting longer, on average, to marry and give birth, and they are having fewer children—additional factors sometimes associated with more sharing of housework and child care. Thus, I predict that increasing economic parity and more equal gender relations will allow women to buy out of some domestic obligations and/or recruit their partners to do more. Middle- and upper-class wives and mothers will rely on working-class and immigrant women to provide domestic services (nannies, housekeepers, child care workers, fast food employees, etc.), thereby reducing their own hours of family labor but simultaneously perpetuating race, class, and gender hierarchies in the labor market and in the society. Some fathers in dual-earner households will increase their contributions to family work, whereas others will perform a greater proportion of housework and child care by virtue of their wives' doing less. Other men will remain marginal to family life because they do not stay connected to the mothers of their children, do not hold jobs allowing them to support their children, or do not seek custody or make regular child support payments. These two ideal types—of involved and marginalized fathers—are likely to continue to coexist in the popular culture and in actual practice.

The context in which American couples negotiate fathering has definitely changed. The future is likely to bring more demands on fathers to be active parents if they want to stay involved with the mothers of their children. For fathers to assume more responsibility for active parenting, it may be necessary to change cultural assumptions that men are entitled to domestic services and that women are inherently predisposed to provide them. Further changes in fathering are likely to be driven by women's increasing independence and earning power. Ironically, women's enhanced economic position also makes them able to form families and raise children without the father's being present. In the future, men will be even less able to rely on their superior earning power and the institution of fatherhood to maintain their connection to families and children. Increasingly, they will need to adopt different fathering styles to meet specific family circumstances and to commit to doing things men have not been accustomed to doing. Some men will be able to maintain their economic and emotional commitments to their children, whereas others will not. Some men will participate in all aspects of child rearing, whereas others will hardly see their children. Unless living wages and adequate social supports are developed for all fathers (as well as for mothers and children), we can expect that the paradoxes, contradictions, and dilemmas associated with fathering described in this chapter will continue for the foreseeable future.

REFERENCES

Ahmeduzzaman, M., & Roopnarine, J. L. (1992). Sociodemographic factors, functioning style, social support, and fathers' involvement with preschoolers in African American intact families. *Journal of Marriage and the Family, 54,* 699–707.

Allen, S. M., & Hawkins, A. J. (1999). Maternal gatekeeping. *Journal of Marriage and the Family, 61,* 199–212.

Amato, P. (2000). Diversity within single-parent families. In D. H. Demo, K. R. Allen, & M. A. Fine (Eds.), *Handbook of family diversity* (pp. 149–172). New York: Oxford University Press.

Amato, P., & Booth, A. (1997). *A generation at risk: Growing up in an era of family upheaval.* Cambridge, MA: Harvard University Press.

Amato, P., & Gilbreth, J. (1999). Nonresident fathers and children's well-being: A meta-analysis. *Journal of Marriage and the Family, 61,* 557–573.

Amato, P., & Rivera, F. (1999). Paternal involvement and children's behavior problems. *Journal of Marriage and the Family, 61,* 375–384.

Auerbach, C., Silverstein, L., & Zizi, M. (1997). The evolving structure of fatherhood. *Journal of African American Men, 2,* 59–85.

Beitel, A. H., & Parke, R. D. (1998). Paternal involvement in infancy: The role of maternal and paternal attitudes. *Journal of Family Psychology, 12,* 268–288.

Belsky, J. (1984). The determinants of parenting. *Child Development, 55,* 83–96.

Bernard, J. (1981). The good provider role: Its rise and fall. *American Psychologist, 36,* 1–12.

Bernstein, J., & Mishel, L. (1997). Has wage inequality stopped growing? *Monthly Labor Review, 120,* 3–17.

Biller, H. B. (1976). The father and personality development. In M. E. Lamb (Ed.), *The role of the father in child development.* New York: John Wiley.

Blankenhorn, D. (1995). *Fatherless America.* New York: Basic Books.

Bowman, P. J., & Sanders, R. (1998). Unmarried African American fathers. *Journal of Comparative Family Studies, 29,* 39–56.

Braver, S. L. (1998). *Divorced dads.* New York: Jeremy Tarcher/Putnam.

Brayfield, A. (1995). Juggling jobs and kids. *Journal of Marriage and the Family, 57,* 321–332.

Brennan, R. T., Barnett, R. C., & Gareis, K. C. (2001). When she earns more than he does: A longitudinal study of dual-earner couples. *Journal of Marriage and Family, 63,* 168–182.

Brewster, K. L. (2000, March). *Contextualizing change in fathers' participation in child care.* Paper presented at the Alfred P. Sloan Foundation and Business and Professional Women's Foundation Conference, "Work and Family: Expanding the Horizons," San Francisco.

Brines, J. (1994). Economic dependency, gender, and the division of labor at home. *American Journal of Sociology, 100,* 652–688.

Broman, L. L. (1991). Gender, work, family roles, and psychological well-being of blacks. *Journal of Marriage and the Family, 53,* 509–520.

Cabrera, N., Tamis-LeMonda, C., Bradley, R., Hofferth, S., & Lamb, M. (2000). Fatherhood in the 21st century. *Child Development, 71,* 127–136.

Casper, L. M., & O'Connell, M. (1998). Work, income, the economy, and married fathers as childcare providers. *Demography, 35,* 243–250.

Chodorow, N. (1974). Family structure and feminine personality. In M. Z. Rosaldo & L. Lamphere (Eds.), *Woman, culture and society* (pp. 43–66). Palo Alto, CA: Stanford University Press.

Cohen, P. N. (1998). Replacing housework in the service economy: Gender, class, and race-ethnicity in service spending. *Gender and Society, 12,* 219–231.

Coley, R. L., & Morris, J. E. (2002). Comparing father and mother reports of father involvement among low-income minority families. *Journal of Marriage and Family, 64,* 982–997.

Coltrane, S. (1988). Father-child relationships and the status of women. *American Journal of Sociology, 93,* 1060–1095.

Coltrane, S. (1996). *Family man.* New York: Oxford University Press.

Coltrane, S. (1998). *Gender and families.* Newbury Park, CA: Pine Forge /Alta Mira.

Coltrane, S. (2000). Research on household labor. *Journal of Marriage and the Family, 62,* 1209–1233.

Coltrane, S. (2001). Marketing the marriage "solution." *Sociological Perspectives, 44,* 387–422.

Coltrane, S., & Adams, M. (2003). The social construction of the divorce "problem": Morality, child victims, and the politics of gender. *Family Relations, 52,* 21–30.

Coltrane, S., & Collins, R. (2001). *Sociology of marriage and the family* (5th ed.). Belmont, CA: Wadsworth/Thomson Learning.

Coltrane, S., & Galt, J. (2000). The history of men's caring. In M. H. Meyer (Ed.), *Care work: Gender, labor, and welfare states* (pp. 15–36). New York: Routledge.

Coltrane, S., & Parke, R. D. (1998). *Reinventing fatherhood: Toward an historical understanding of continuity and change in men's family lives* (WP 98–12A). Philadelphia: National Center on Fathers and Families.

Coltrane, S., Parke, R. D., & Adams, M. (2001, April). *Shared parenting in Mexican-American and European-American families.* Paper presented at the biennial meeting of the Society for Research in Child Development, Minneapolis, MN.

Coontz, S. (1992). *The way we never were.* New York: Basic Books.

Cowan, C. P., & Cowan, P. A. (2000). *When partners become parents.* Mahwah, NJ: Lawrence Erlbaum.

Crockett, L. J., Eggebeen, D. J., & Hawkins, A. J. (1993). Fathers' presence and young children's behavioral and cognitive adjustment. *Journal of Family Issues, 14,* 355–377.

Day, R. D., & Mackey, W. C. (1989). An alternate standard for evaluating American fathers. *Journal of Family Issues, 10,* 401–408.

Deutsch, F. (1999). *Halving it all.* Cambridge, MA: Harvard University Press.

Dill, B. T. (1988). Our mother's grief: Racial ethnic women and the maintenance of families. *Journal of Family History, 13,* 415–431.

Doherty, W. J. (1991). Beyond reactivity and the deficit model of manhood. *Journal of Marital and Family Therapy, 17,* 29–32.

Dubowitz, H., Black, M. M., Cox, C. E., Kerr, M. A., Litrownik, A. J., Radhakrishna, A., et al. (2001). Father involvement and children's functioning at age 6 years: A multisite study. *Child Maltreatment, 6,* 300–309.

Eggebeen, D. (2002). The changing course of fatherhood. *Journal of Family Issues, 23,* 486–506.

Ehrenreich, B. (1984). *The hearts of men.* Garden City, NY: Anchor Press/Doubleday.

Fagan, J. A. (1998). Correlates of low-income African American and Puerto Rican fathers' involvement with their children. *Journal of Black Psychology, 3,* 351–367.

Federal Interagency Forum on Child and Family Statistics. (1998). Report of the Working Group on Conceptualizing Male Parenting (Marsiglio, Day, Evans, Lamb, Braver, & Peters). In *Nurturing fatherhood* (pp. 101–174). Washington, DC: Government Printing Office.

Finkelhor, D., Hotaling, G., Lewis, I., & Smith, C. (1990). Sexual abuse in a national survey of adult men and women. *Child Abuse and Neglect, 14,* 19–28.

Furstenberg, F. F. (1988). Good dads—bad dads. In A. Cherlin (Ed.), *The changing American family and public policy* (pp. 193–218). Washington, DC: Urban Institute Press.

Furstenberg, F. F., & Cherlin, A. (1991). *Divided families.* Cambridge, MA: Harvard University Press.

Furstenberg, F. F., & Harris, K. (1993). When and why fathers matter. In R. Lerman & T. Ooms (Eds.), *Young unwed fathers* (pp. 150–176). Philadelphia: Temple University Press.

Gavanas, A. (2002). The fatherhood responsibility movement. In B. Hobson (Ed.), *Making men into fathers* (pp. 213–242). New York: Cambridge University Press.

Griswold, R. L. (1993). *Fatherhood in America: A history.* New York: Basic Books.

Griswold, R. L. (1997). Generative fathering: A historical perspective. In A. J. Hawkins & D. Dollahite (Eds.), *Generative fathering* (pp. 71–86). Thousand Oaks, CA: Sage.

Hamer, J., & Marchioro, K. (2002). Becoming custodial dads: Exploring parenting among low-income and working-class African American fathers. *Journal of Marriage and Family, 64,* 116–129.

Harris, K. H., Furstenberg, F. F., & Marmer, J. K. (1998). Paternal involvement with adolescents in intact families. *Demography, 35,* 201–216.

Harris, K. H., & Morgan, S. P. (1991). Fathers, sons and daughters: Differential paternal involvement in parenting. *Journal of Marriage and the Family, 53,* 531–544.

Hawkins, A. J., Christiansen, S. L., Sargent, K. P., & Hill, E. J. (1993). Rethinking fathers' involvement in child care. *Journal of Family Issues, 14,* 531–549.

Hawkins, A. J., & Dollahite, D. C. (1997). Beyond the role-inadequacy perspective of fathering. In A. J. Hawkins & D. C. Dollahite (Eds.), *Generative fathering: Beyond deficit perspectives* (pp. 3–16). Thousand Oaks, CA: Sage.

Hays, S. (1996). *The cultural contradictions of motherhood.* New Haven, CT: Yale University Press.

Hetherington, E. M., & Stanley-Hagan, M. M. (1999). Stepfamilies. In M. E. Lamb (Ed.), *Parenting and child development in "nontraditional" families* (pp. 137–159). Mahwah, NJ: Lawrence Erlbaum.

Hewlett, B. S. (1991). *The nature and context of Aka pygmy paternal infant care.* Ann Arbor: University of Michigan Press.

Hewlett, B. S. (2000). Culture, history, and sex: Anthropological contributions to conceptualizing father involvement. *Marriage and Family Review, 29,* 59–73.

Hochschild, A. R. (1989). *The second shift.* New York: Viking.

Hofferth, S. L. (1998). *Healthy environments, healthy children: Children in families.* Ann Arbor: Institute for Social Research, University of Michigan.

Hofferth, S. L. (2003). Race/ethnic differences in father involvement in two-parent families: Culture, context, or economy. *Journal of Family Issues, 24,* 185–216.

Hofferth, S. L., & Anderson, K. G. (2003). Are all dads equal? Biology versus marriage as a basis for paternal investment. *Journal of Marriage and Family, 65,* 213–232.

Horn, W. (1999). Lunacy 101: Questioning the need for fathers. Retrieved April 29, 2003, from the Smart Marriages Web site: http://listarchives.his.com/smart-marriages/smartmarriages.9907/msg00011.html.

Hossain, Z., & Roopnarine, J. L. (1993). Division of household labor and child care in dual-earner African-American families with infants. *Sex Roles, 29,* 571–583.

Hunter, A. G., & Davis, J. E. (1994). Hidden voices of black men: The meaning, structure, and complexity of manhood. *Journal of Black Studies, 25,* 20–40.

John, D., & Shelton, B. A. (1997). The production of gender among black and white women and men: The case of household labor. *Sex Roles, 36,* 171–193.

Johnson, M. (1988). *Strong mothers, weak wives.* Berkeley: University of California Press.

Kimmel, M. (1996). *Manhood in America: A cultural history.* New York: Free Press.

Lamb, M. E., Pleck, J., Charnov, E., & Levine, J. (1987). A biosocial perspective on parental behavior and involvement. In J. B. Lancaster, J. Altman, & A. Rossi (Eds.), *Parenting across the lifespan* (pp. 11–42). New York: Academic Press.

LaRossa, R. (1988). Fatherhood and social change. *Family Relations, 37,* 451–457.

LaRossa, R. (1997). *The modernization of fatherhood: A social and political history.* Chicago: University of Chicago Press.

Maccoby, E., & Mnookin, R. (1992). *Dividing the child.* Cambridge, MA: Harvard University Press.

Margolin, L. (1992). Child abuse by mother's boyfriends. *Child Abuse and Neglect, 16,* 541–551.

Marsiglio, W. (1991). Paternal engagement activities with minor children. *Journal of Marriage and the Family, 53,* 973–986.

Marsiglio, W., Amato, P., Day, R. D., & Lamb, M. E. (2000). Scholarship on fatherhood in the 1990s and beyond. *Journal of Marriage and the Family, 62,* 1173–1191.

Marsiglio, W., & Pleck, J. H. (In press). Fatherhood and masculinities. In R. W. Connell, J. Hearn, & M. Kimmel (Eds.), *The handbook of studies on men and masculinities.* Thousand Oaks, CA: Sage.

McBride, B. A. (1990). The effects of a parent education/play group program on father involvement on child rearing. *Family Relations, 39,* 250–256.

McBride, B. A., & Mills, G. (1993). A comparison of mother and father involvement with their preschool age children. *Early Childhood Research Quarterly, 8,* 457–477.

McBride, B. A., Schoppe, S., & Rane, T. (2002). Child characteristics, parenting stress, and parental involvement: Fathers versus mothers. *Journal of Marriage and Family, 64,* 998–1011.

McDaniel, A. (1994). Historical racial differences in living arrangements of children. *Journal of Family History, 19,* 57–77.

McHale, S. M., & Huston, T. L. (1984). Men and women as parents: Sex role orientations, employment, and parental roles with infants. *Child Development, 55,* 1349–1361.

McLanahan, S., & Sandefur, G. (1994). *Growing up with a single parent: What hurts, what helps.* Cambridge, MA: Harvard University Press.

McLanahan, S., Seltzer, J., Hanson, T., & Thomson, E. (1994). Child support enforcement and child well-being. In I. Garfinkel, S. S. McLanahan, & P. K. Robins (Eds.), *Child support and child well-being* (pp. 285–316). Washington, DC: Urban Institute.

Messner, M. (1993). "Changing men" and feminist politics in the U.S. *Theory and Society, 22,* 723–737.

Mintz, S. (1998). From patriarchy to androgyny and other myths. In A. Booth & A. C. Crouter (Eds.), *Men in families* (pp. 3–30). Mahwah, NJ: Lawrence Erlbaum.

Mosley, J., & Thomson, E. (1994). Fathering behavior and child outcomes. In W. Marsiglio (Ed.), *Fatherhood* (pp. 148–165). Thousand Oaks, CA: Sage.

National Center for Health Statistics. (2000, January). Nonmarital birth rates, 1940–1999. Retrieved on April 29, 2003 from the Centers for Disease Control and Prevention Web site: www.cdc.gov/nchs/data/nvsr/nvsr48.

National Research Council. (1993). *Understanding child abuse and neglect.* Washington, DC: National Academy Press.

Nock, S. (1998). *Marriage in men's lives.* New York: Oxford University Press.

Oropesa, R. S. (1993). Using the service economy to relieve the double burden: Female labor force participation and service purchases. *Journal of Family Issues, 14,* 438–473.

Ozer, E. M., Barnett, R. C., Brennan, R. T., & Sperling, J. (1998). Does childcare involvement increase or decrease distress among dual-earner couples? *Women's Health: Research on Gender, Behavior, and Policy, 4,* 285–311.

Padgett, D. L. (1997). The contribution of support networks to household labor in African American families. *Journal of Family Issues, 18,* 227–250.

Palkovitz, R. (1997). Reconstructing "involvement." In A. Hawkins & D. Dollahite (Eds.), *Generative fathering* (pp. 200–216). Thousand Oaks, CA: Sage.

Parke, R. D. (1996). *Fatherhood.* Cambridge, MA: Harvard University Press.

Pasley, K., Ihinger-Tallman, M, & Buehler, C. (1993). Developing a middle-range theory of father involvement postdivorce. *Journal of Family Issues, 14,* 550–576.

Pleck, E. H., & Pleck, J. H. (1997). Fatherhood ideals in the United States: Historical dimensions. In M. E. Lamb (Ed.), *The role of the father in child development* (3rd ed., pp. 33–48). New York: John Wiley.

Pleck, J. H. (1993). Are "family-supportive" employer policies relevant to men? In J. C. Hood (Ed.), *Men, work, and family* (pp. 217–237). Newbury Park, CA: Sage.

Pleck, J. H. (1997). Paternal involvement: Levels, sources, and consequences. In M. E. Lamb (Ed.), *The role of the father in child development* (3rd ed., pp. 66–103). New York: John Wiley.

Pleck, J. H., & Masciadrelli, B. P. (2003). Paternal involvement: Levels, sources, and consequences. In M. E. Lamb (Ed.), *The role of the father in child development* (4th ed.). New York: John Wiley.

Pleck, J. H., & Steuve, J. L. (2001). Time and paternal involvement. In K. Daly (Ed.), *Minding the time in family experience* (pp. 205–226). Oxford, UK: Elsevier.

Popenoe, D. (1996). *Life without father: Compelling new evidence that fatherhood and marriage are indispensable for the good of children and society.* New York: Free Press.

Presser, H. B. (1995). Job, family, and gender. *Demography, 32,* 577–598.

Pruett, K. D. (1993). The paternal presence. *Families in Society, 74,* 46–50.

Radhakrishna, A., Bou-Saada, I. E., Hunter, W. M., Catellier, D. J., & Kotch, J. B. (2001). Are father surrogates a risk factor for child maltreatment? *Child Maltreatment, 6,* 281–289.

Rane, T. R., & McBride, B. A. (2000). Identity theory as a guide to understanding father's involvement with their children. *Journal of Family Issues, 21,* 347–366.

Sanday, P. R. (1981). *Female power and male dominance.* New York: Cambridge University Press.

Scoon-Rogers, L. (1999). *Child support for custodial mothers and fathers* (Current Population Reports, P60-196). Washington, DC: U.S. Bureau of the Census.

Seltzer, J. A. (1994). Consequences of marital dissolution for children. *Annual Review of Sociology, 20,* 235–266.

Seltzer, J. A. (1998). Father by law: Effects of joint legal custody on nonresident fathers' involvement with children. *Demography, 35,* 135–146.

Seltzer, J. A. (2000). Families formed outside of marriage. *Journal of Marriage and the Family, 62,* 1247–1268.

Silverstein, L. B. (2002). Fathers and families. In J. McHale & W. Grolnick (Eds.), *Retrospect and prospect in the psychological study of fathers* (35–64). Mahwah, NJ: Lawrence Erlbaum.

Silverstein, L. B., & Auerbach, C. F. (1999). Deconstructing the essential father. *American Psychologist, 54,* 397–407.

Smock, P., & Manning, W. (1997). Nonresident parents' characteristics and child support. *Journal of Marriage and the Family, 59,* 798–808.

Snarey, J. (1993). *How fathers care for the next generation.* Cambridge, MA: Harvard University Press.

Stacey, J. (1996). *In the name of the family.* Boston: Beacon.

Thompson, L., & Walker, A. J. (1989). Gender in families: Women and men in marriage, work, and parenthood. *Journal of Marriage and the Family, 51,* 845–871.

Toth, J. F., & Xu, X. (1999). Ethnic and cultural diversity in fathers' involvement: A racial/ethnic comparison of African American, Hispanic, and white fathers. *Youth and Society, 31,* 76–99.

Whiting, J., & Whiting, B. (1975). Aloofness and intimacy of husbands and wives. *Ethos, 3,* 183–207.

Wilson, M. N., Tolson, T. F. J., Hinton, I. D., & Kiernan, M. (1990). Flexibility and sharing of childcare duties in black families. *Sex Roles, 22,* 409–425.

Yueng, W. J., Sandberg, J. F., Davis-Kean, P. E., & Hofferth, S. L. (2001). Children's time with fathers in intact families. *Journal of Marriage and Family, 63,* 136–154.

CHAPTER 14

Pathogenic-Conflict Families and Children

What We Know, What We Need to Know

W. GLENN CLINGEMPEEL AND
EULALEE BRAND-CLINGEMPEEL

Disagreements among family members, including interparental conflicts, are ubiquitous features of family life and occur in well-functioning families (Cummings & Davies, 1994). However, a substantial body of empirical research has demonstrated that interparental conflicts exhibiting specific properties (e.g., severe, prolonged, focusing on child-rearing issues) and under specific circumstances (e.g., witnessed by children) may have a myriad of pathogenic effects on children, including a greater likelihood of internalizing and externalizing behaviors, insecure attachments, problematic sibling and peer relationships, and sustained academic difficulties (Cummings & Davies, 1994; Grych & Fincham, 1990; Katz & Gottman, 1996).

This chapter characterizes families whose interparental conflicts have negative effects on children/adolescents as *pathogenic-conflict families,* but given its limited scope,

it will not focus on parent-child conflicts or child maltreatment separate from the influence of destructive interparental conflicts. The chapter has two major goals: first, to outline *what we know*, or the most robust findings, pertaining to the effects of interparental conflict/violence on children; and second, to elucidate *what we need to know* in three domains of inquiry: (a) cultural variations in interparental conflict and its sequalae; (b) comorbidity of spousal violence and physical child abuse; and (c) the impact of multilevel and reciprocal-influence processes on interparental conflict and its effects.

PATHOGENIC-CONFLICT FAMILIES AND CHILDREN: WHAT WE KNOW

The effects of interparental conflict on children depend in part upon properties of the conflicts; children's cognitive appraisals, emotions, and reactions to interparental disputes; and the extent to which couple conflicts "spill over" into parent-child, sibling, and peer relationships (Cummings & Davies, 1994; Grych & Fincham, 1990). Summaries of our knowledge in these areas are given below.

Properties of Conflicts

Continuum of Severity

Exposure to more frequent and intense episodes of interparental conflict results in greater emotional distress, psychopathology, and health problems in children (Cummings & Davies, 1994; Gottman & Katz, 1989). The more frequent and severe the conflicts, the greater is the risk that children will be adversely affected (Cummings & Davies, 1994; Grych & Fincham, 1990). Physical violence appears to have pernicious effects over and above high-intensity verbal conflicts (Cummings & Davies, 1994); and the use of potentially lethal weapons in interparental disputes (i.e., knives, guns) has greater negative effects than physical violence not involving lethal weapons (Jouriles et al., 1998).

Topic of Conflict

Conflicts focusing on parental differences on child rearing are more likely to have negative effects than conflicts focusing on other issues (Belsky & Hsieh, 1998). Children may be exposed more often to conflicts that involve them and may also be more likely to form maladaptive appraisals (e.g., self-blame attributions) of child-rearing disputes. Interparental hostilities over child rearing are more likely to engender both loyalty conflicts and cross-generation alliances—two family processes linked to maladaptive child outcomes (Buchanan, Maccoby, & Dornbush, 1991; Mann, Borduin, Henggeler, & Blaske, 1990).

Conflict Exposure

Interparental conflicts that occur in the presence of children are likely to have more negative effects than those not observed by children (Davies & Cummings, 1994; Davis, Hops, Alpert, & Sheeber, 1998). Direct observation triggers negative affect and emotional insecurity (Davies & Cummings, 1994). The failure to shield children from unproductive parental disputes may reflect ineffective parenting and inadequate boundaries around marital or couple subsystems (Davis et al., 1998). Repeated exposure to interparental conflict sensitizes children to later conflicts, producing greater emotional reactivity, emotion-focused (e.g., attempts to escape or avoid conflict) and/or problem-focused (e.g., interventions designed to interrupt conflict) coping, and pessimistic expectations about the future status of the interparental relationship (Davies & Cummings, 1998; Davies & Forman, 2002). In the long run, this sensitization process increases children's vulnerability to disturbances in psychological functioning.

Resolution Status

The manner in which conflicts are managed differentiates well-functioning and poorly functioning families better than the mere presence of conflicts (Cummings & Davies, 1994). Parents who resolve low-intensity conflicts successfully via negotiation and positive communication may have few negative effects, and may even have positive effects, on children (Grych, 1998). Children may acquire the expectation that conflicts with significant others can be successfully resolved. Alternatively, high-intensity conflicts that remain unresolved may inculcate children with the relationship message that conflict resolution in relationships is unlikely and thus may portend negatively for children's future close relationships.

Children's Appraisals and Reactions to Conflict

A Cognitive-Contextual Model: Children's Appraisals

In a seminal article, Grych and Fincham (1990) proposed a cognitive-contextual framework assigning children's appraisals of interparental disputes a significant role as mediators of the effects of interadult hostilities on children. According to this proposal, interparental conflict usually engenders both primary and secondary processing of conflict parameters. Initially, a child engages in *primary processing,* in which affective reactions varying in intensity signal perceived negativity and the level of threat to his or her personal well-being. If a threshold of negativity/threat is exceeded, the child engages in *secondary processing,* in which he or she evaluates three questions: Why is the conflict occurring (causal attributions)? Who is responsible for the conflict (responsibility attributions)? Does the child have adequate skills for coping with the conflict (efficacy attributions/expectations)? Properties of the specific conflicts, conflict histories, and characteristics of the child (e.g., age, temperament, coping skills) influence the specific appraisals. Certain types of attributions, including self-blame and inability to cope, are more likely to engender psychopathology than less threatening attributions (e.g., temporary causes of conflict, ability to cope effectively).

Aggressogenic Cognitions

Children exposed to severe interparental conflicts may acquire aggressogenic cognitions, or beliefs that support aggression as normative and a legitimate response to provocation. Aggressogenic cognitions have been found to mediate the relations between interparental conflict and children's aggressive behavior at school (Marcus, Lindahl, & Malik, 2001). They also may shape children's processing of social information, leading them to interpret benign behaviors of others as provocations warranting aggression. Parents' use of aggressive conflict resolution strategies (as opposed to withdraw or discuss/negotiate approaches) have been shown to increase children's proclivities to use aggression to cope with interpersonal disputes with peers (Dadds, Atkinson, Turner, Blums, & Lendich, 1999), and aggressogenic cognitions are mechanisms that may account for the linkage between parental and child tactics in confronting interpersonal conflict scenarios.

Specific Emotions Hypothesis

Elaborating upon the cognitive-contextual model (Grych & Fincham, 1990), Crockenberg and her colleagues (Crockenberg & Forgays, 1996; Crockenberg & Langrock, 2001) proposed a specific emotions model in which interparental conflict elicits specific negative emotions (anger, sadness, and fear) that vary depending upon both the goals that are threatened (e.g., to be loved and protected, to be able do things over which parents have control) and children's estimations of the likelihood that goal attainment will be reinstated. Maternal and paternal marital aggressiveness are proposed to have different effects, with the behavior of the same-gendered parent having greater influence on children's emotions and behaviors. Certain emotions are presumed to correlate with specific behavioral symptoms (e.g., fear with internalizing symptoms, anger with externalizing symptoms).

In a recent study, Crockenberg and Langrock (2001) found strongest support for the specific emotions model as applied to fathers' marital aggression and the behavior of their sons. For boys, fathers' marital hostility had a differential effect on behavior depending on the emotion elicited. Boys who reported fear engaged in internalizing behavior, and boys who reported anger engaged in externalizing behavior. Moreover, fathers' marital aggression elicited greater negative emotions for both boys and girls. Certain features of fathers' aggression (e.g., they may yell louder) may trigger more negative emotions, and paternal hostility also may signal a greater threat to goal attainment (e.g., angry fathers may be more likely to leave the home). For girls, anger, sadness, and fear increased with rising levels of fathers' hostility.

Emotional Security Hypothesis

According to the emotional security hypothesis (Davies & Cummings, 1994, 1998), children are motivated to achieve emotional security that is threatened by sustained, high-intensity interparental conflicts. In an effort to cope with the insecurity triggered by these disputes, children may activate three interrelated processes: (a) emotional reactivity with prolonged emotional distress, (b) regulation of conflict exposure by involvement in and/or avoidance of conflict, and (c) pessimistic expectations about the meaning of the conflicts for the future welfare of the self and family. These strategies may imbue children with a transient perception of control that is adaptive during the conflict itself but is maladaptive in the long run. Exposure to destructive histories of interparental conflict sensitizes children to respond with elevated levels of these processes in response to subsequent conflicts, which, in turn, ultimately lead to adjustment problems and psychopathology. Moreover, sensitization has been shown to mediate associations between interparental conflict and children's adjustment problems (Davies & Cummings, 1998; Davies, Myers, Cummings, & Heindel, 1999).

Children may vary substantially in the extent to which interparental conflict activates each of the three processes. For example, Davies and Forman (2002) found three distinct profiles: (a) secure children, who showed well-regulated concern and positive representations of interparental relationships; (b) insecure-preoccupied children, who both overtly and subjectively (i.e., in self-reports) evinced elevated levels of emotional distress, involvement in or avoidance of conflict, and pessimistic representations of interparental relationships; and (c) insecure-dismissing children, who displayed overt signs of heightened levels of the three component processes but self-reported low levels of subjective distress. Both profiles of insecure children reported higher levels of interparental conflict and more adjustment problems than did secure children. Preoccupied children exhibited the highest levels of internalizing symptoms, and dismissing children evidenced the highest levels of externalizing symptoms.

Children's Responses to Conflict

Children may exhibit a variety of reactions to ongoing interparental conflict, including aggression, peacekeeping efforts, and withdrawal; and the types of reactions may influence the trajectory of interparental disputes (e.g., whether they escalate or de-escalate) and the psychological functioning of children. Aggression toward one or both parents—a common response among adolescents of both genders—may increase the severity of the couple's conflict and elevate the probability that the children will behave aggressively in other contexts (Davis et al., 1998). Aggressive responding toward a parent during severe interparental disputes may also increase the likelihood of physical child abuse (Appel & Holden, 1998).

Spillover Into Other Relationships

Spillover Into Parenting

Negative moods and emotions generated by interparental conflict may spill over, or transfer, to parenting behaviors, resulting in parents' exhibiting greater hostility and less warmth toward children (Almeida, Wethington, & Chandler, 1999). A substantial body of evidence has found support for spillover effects (Almeida et al., 1999; see Erel & Burman, 1995, for a review). At high levels of marital discord, positive parent-child relationships may be difficult to achieve (Erel & Burman, 1995). Marital conflict assessed prenatally has predicted severe physical punishment of children at 2 and 5 years following the child's birth (Kanoy, Ulka-Steiner, Cox, & Burchinal, 2003). Moreover, consistent with a parenting-as-mediator hypothesis (Katz & Gottman, 1996), several studies have found that interparental conflict exerts negative effects on children via adverse effects on parent-child relationships (Gonzales, Pitts, Hill, & Roosa, 2000; Maughan & Cicchetti, 2002).

Interparental conflict also may have a differential impact upon mothers' and fathers' parenting. Several studies have found that the father-child relationship may be especially vulnerable to disturbances associated with marital disputes (Katz & Gottman, 1996; Kelly, 2000). At least two studies have found that fathers' hostile or rejecting parenting mediated the link between interparental conflict and children's problematic peer relationships (Katz & Gottman, 1996; Stocker & Youngblade, 1999).

Frosch and Magelsdorf (2001) hypothesized that the quality of parenting in the face of marital conflict may operate as a moderator, rather than mediator, of preschool children's behavior problems. Consistent with their hypothesis, warm/supportive parenting buffered, or reduced, the negative effects of marital conflict on young children; whereas hostile/intrusive parenting exacerbated the negative effects of couple disputes. The authors speculated that parenting behaviors may assume a mediator role over time as the 3-year-olds in their study experience more destructive interparental conflicts.

Spillover Into Co-Parenting

Interparental conflicts may also adversely affect the quality of the co-parental relationship. Co-parenting measures the extent to which parents cooperate as a team or undermine each other on child-rearing issues (McHale, 1997). Co-parenting is conceptually distinct from both the marital and the parent-child relationship (Margolin, Gordis, & John, 2001). Parents in distressed marriages, motivated by mutual desires to protect their children, may collaborate successfully on parenting issues despite hostility toward each other. Likewise, parents may have good behavior management skills and positive relationships with their children, but they may exhibit poor co-parenting by disparaging or undermining each other's child rearing.

The early research on co-parenting focused on parents' ability to cooperate with each other after divorce (Maccoby, Depner, & Mnookin, 1991), but more recent studies have examined co-parenting in two-parent families. For example, in newly formed stepfamilies, the presence of co-parental problems between former spouses was the most robust predictor of increases in adolescents' externalizing behavior over time (Anderson, Hetherington, & Clingempeel, 1999). In first-marriage families, the available empirical evidence suggests that negative co-parenting may mediate the link between marital conflict and disturbances in parent-child relations and children's adjustment (Floyd, Gilliom, & Costigan, 1998; Margolin et al., 2001).

Negative co-parenting may involve both triangulation and differential parenting mechanisms. Triangulation, or parental attempts to involve children in their disputes, may engender negative effects due to youngsters' feeling caught between parents with whom they want to preserve positive relationships (Belsky & Hsieh, 1998; Buchanan et al., 1991). Similarly, differential parenting, or parents' favoritism to one sibling over another, may be used to form or maintain coalitions with children that undermine or exclude the other parent. Differential parenting has been associated with negative sibling relationships and children's adjustment problems and has been shown to contribute uniquely to children's developmental outcomes beyond the effects of absolute levels of parental affection/control (Brody, Stoneman, & Burke, 1987; Singer & Weinstein, 2000).

Spillover Into Other Subsystems

Destructive interparental conflict has been associated with negative effects on sibling relationships (Brody et al., 1987; Stocker & Youngblade, 1999), the larger family system (Greene & Anderson, 1999), and peer relationships (Gottman & Katz, 1989; Stocker & Youngblade, 1999). Moreover, parental hostility toward children has been found to mediate the adverse effects of marital conflict on sibling and peer relationships, with only fathers' hostility accounting for the negative effects of marital conflict on peer relationships (Stocker & Youngblade, 1999).

In a rare observational study of negative reciprocity in tetradic relationships (two caregivers and two children), Greene and Anderson (1999) found that, in comparison with families of nonconflictual marriages and girls, families with conflictual marriages and boys consistently exhibited greater negative reciprocity, or contingent negativity across more conversational turns without de-escalation. Girls were more likely to engage in behaviors that defused hostile interparental exchanges (e.g., peacekeeping efforts); whereas boys more often behaved aggressively, resulting in longer sequences of contingent negative reciprocity.

PATHOGENIC-CONFLICT FAMILIES AND CHILDREN: WHAT WE NEED TO KNOW

Despite substantial progress, there are still significant gaps in our understanding of the diverse processes through which interparental disputes exert their effects on children. A comprehensive discussion of these gaps is beyond the scope of this chapter. Consequently, we limit our discussion in the forthcoming section to "what we need to know" in three domains of inquiry: cultural and ethnic variations in interparental conflict effects; comorbidity of interparental violence and physical child abuse; and the impact of multilevel reciprocal-influence processes on interparental conflict and its effects.

Interparental Conflict: Cultural and Ethnic/Racial Variations

Few researchers have focused on cultural/ethnic/racial variations in the effects of interparental conflicts on children. In this section, we examine how cultural variations in global belief systems, level of exposure to violence, norms regarding child socialization and emotional expressiveness, and religious practices may alter the properties of interparental conflicts, their mechanisms of influence (i.e., spillover effects), and children's outcomes. Problems in defining culture/ethnicity/race are also discussed.

Individualism-Collectivism: Influence on Conflict Properties

Cultures vary on the global belief systems of *individualism* (emphasizing independence, autonomy, and uniqueness) and *collectivism* (emphasizing interdependence, obligations to family and the larger group, and self in relation to others), with substantial data indicating that North Americans are more individualistic than people from other parts of the world (Oyserman, Coon, & Kemmelmeier, 2002). To the extent that cultural norms emphasize harmony over independence, promote loyalty to family over personal gratification, and discourage conflict and anger, couples may engage in fewer and less severe conflicts, may be more adept at de-escalating disputes and resolving them via negotiation, may be more successful at encapsulating conflicts from children, and may cooperate better as co-parents despite animosity toward each other.

Couples in more collectivistic cultures also may experience less frequent and intense hostilities over child rearing and less parent-child conflict due to norms emphasizing family harmony and children's obedience to parents. Korean youngsters, for example, view *controlling* parents as promoting the family's welfare rather than suppressing their personal autonomy (Miller, 2002). Increased parental control is associated with greater perceived parental warmth among Korean populations but greater perceived parental hostility among European Americans (Rohner & Pettengill, 1985).

Cultural Violence: Influence on Conflict Properties

Cultures vary in the extent to which they expose individuals to violence and tolerate aggression as a solution to interpersonal problems; and these differences may be reflected in levels of interparental conflict and family aggression. Some scholars argue that the United States is a culture of violence (Straus, Gelles, & Steinmetz, 1980), and empirical evidence regarding the contributions of observing frequent media violence to subsequent aggression is compelling (Huesmann, 1999). Parents in different cultures may react differently to children's aggressive acts, with responses ranging from explanations why aggression is inappropriate, to physical discipline, to ignoring or even

reinforcing hostile behaviors (Segall, Dasen, Berry, & Poortinga, 1990). Different conflict resolution styles among couples may emerge in response to cultural forces. The level of violence exposure in the larger sociocultural context may influence the extent to which marital partners use attack, withdraw, or compromise/discuss strategies in response to inevitable disagreements, and their choice of strategies may in turn affect children's conflict resolution strategies.

Cultural Variations in Conflict Reactions

Culture plays an important role in determining both the emotional significance of events and socially prescribed ways to communicate and act on such events (Cole & Tamang, 1998). However, little is known about how children from different cultural and racial/ethnic groups vary in their reactions to interparental conflict. Comparing two cultures of Nepali children, Cole and Tamang (1998) found that Tamang children who were ostensibly influenced by Buddhist teachings encouraging the avoidance of anger and other strong emotions were less likely to report feeling negative emotions in response to parental conflict/violence than Chhetri-Brahmin children who were not exposed to these teachings.

Cultural norms of some Asian, Indian, and West African countries discourage expression of negative emotions though tolerating disclosures of physical distress (Miller, 2002). The expression of anger may be more tolerated in cultures that emphasize the self as unique and independent (and entitled to certain rights) than in cultures that emphasize an interdependent self expected to sacrifice personal gain for the collective good (Cole & Tamang, 1998). The tendency toward passivity and behavioral inhibition (i.e., shyness) found in some Asian cultures may reduce the likelihood of overt responses to parental conflicts (Rubin, 1998). Children's aggressive responses may be less likely in collectivistic cultures that emphasize obedience to authority and compliance with family rules. Among the Japanese, disturbances in self-esteem associated with interparental conflict may involve a diminution in culturally healthy episodes of self-criticism rather than a disruption in the optimism/self-confidence underlying the self-esteem construct in European American cultures (Kitayama, 2002). Disruptions in the attachment process stemming from interparental conflict may have different manifestations among Korean mothers and their young children than are typically found in European American parent-child relationships (Rothbaum, Weisz, Pott, Miyake, & Morelli, 2000).

Children's emotional security in more collectivistic cultures may be distributed among more adults, and thus conflicts between biological parents may be less threatening to their personal well-being. Consequently, in comparison with European American families (which grant almost exclusive responsibility for child rearing to biological parents), children living in cultures that promote involvement of multiple caregivers in child rearing may have higher thresholds for triggering security-preserving processes in the face of severe interparental conflicts. Moreover, the relationships among the three component processes outlined in the emotional security model (Davies & Cummings, 1994) may vary across cultures.

Cultural variations in manifestations of distress at both the individual and the relationship levels suggest that widely used measures of interparental conflict, parent-child relationships, and children's mental health based largely on European American samples may need to be recalibrated for different cultures and ethnic/racial groups in both the United States and other countries. The burgeoning diversity paradigm may require not only new ways of thinking about old constructs but completely new constructs capturing variations in family relationships currently not tapped by well-established measures (Fiske, 2002).

Cultural Variations in Spillover Effects

The extent to which spillover effects vary across cultures and ethnic/racial groups is an understudied area of inquiry and a matter of debate among family scholars. More collectivistic cultures emphasizing interdependence over independence may exhibit more spillover from interparental conflict to disruptions in parenting and sibling relationships due to the greater permeability of boundaries and interdependence of intrafamilial subsystems in these cultures (Rothbaum, Morelli, Pott, & Liu-Constant, 2000).

Moreover, for collectivistic cultures that discourage discord, conflict may be interpreted more negatively by family members and thus have greater adverse effects on multiple family subsystems (Marin & Marin, 1991). Alternatively, families from more collectivistic cultures, including Hispanic and African American families, may be buffered at least to some extent against spillover effects because of greater support from extended kin and multiple caregiver support systems (Ruiz, Roosa, & Gonzales, 2002). Thus, when spillover effects do disrupt parenting practices, the effects on children may be less negative than in European American families because more adults are involved in the child-rearing process (Ruiz et al., 2002). Moreover, families with more collectivistic orientations may be less likely to exhibit spillover because of incentives to maintain strong parent-child bonds in the face of adversity. However, at least one well-designed study (Gonzales et al., 2000) found that African American and Latino families were not immune to spillover mechanisms, as interparental conflict had adverse effects on parenting behaviors that in turn were related to children's internalizing/externalizing symptoms.

Understanding Cultural Variation: The Definition Problem

Research on cultural variations in the effects of interparental conflict and related mechanisms of influence has been hampered by the absence of clear definitions of culture/ethnicity (Jensen & Hoagwood, 1997). Cultural, racial, and ethnic groups are not static, independent entities that cause behavioral variation in individuals and family members (Kitayama, 2002); rather, they involve dynamic processes, including sociocultural practices, meanings, social institutions, and daily activities, that in turn may lead to variations in individual functioning. Studies comparing cultures presumed to differ on individualism-collectivism measures often have not measured directly the extent to which parental behaviors adhere to the socialization practices consistent with these global cultural belief systems. For example, studies of Asian populations often fail to measure parental attempts to promote interdependence, group harmony, behavioral inhibition, and respect for authority.

The extant research has relied too often upon transethnic, binary labels (e.g., African American, Hispanic, Asian) that obfuscate the moderating effects of national origin, level of acculturation, ethnic identification, personal and family immigration history, and religious beliefs and practices (Jensen & Hoagwood, 1997). For example, the frequency and severity of interparental conflicts may vary within specific minority families depending upon the level of acculturation or the extent to which behaviors of immigrant groups have changed toward the host culture as a result of exposure to its values, norms, and social institutions (Santisteban,

Muir-Malcolm, Mitrani, & Szapocznik, 2002). Intergenerational differences on the degree of acculturation may result in interparental and parent-child conflicts. Adolescents' rejection of the ethnic values of the culture of origin that remain important to their parents is an example of this problem (Santisteban et al., 2002). For collectivistic cultures, high acculturation within families may relate to more frequent and severe conflicts, whereas low acculturation may forecast less frequent and intense conflicts. Failure to assess the potential moderating effects of level of acculturation may obscure important sources of variation within cultural groups (Conteras, Lopez, Rivera-Mosquera, Raymond-Smith, & Rothstein, 1999).

Religion as a Cultural Variable

Future studies of cultural influences on the effects of interparental conflict on children will need to go beyond global belief systems and examine the impact of specific social institutions, including religious rituals and beliefs. Conducting a meta-analysis of 94 studies of religion and family relations, Mahoney, Pargament, Tarakeshwar, and Swank (2001) reported that greater parental religiousness was linked to less marital conflict/violence, more effectiveness at resolving marital disputes, better co-parental relationships, more consistent parenting practices, greater use of corporal punishment, and less psychopathology. Moreover, in a well-designed longitudinal study of two-parent African American families, Brody, Stoneman, and Flor (1996) demonstrated that parental religiosity had positive effects on children's psychological adjustment via the mediating influence of less conflictual and higher-quality marital, parent-child, and family relations.

However, most studies in the meta-analysis used community samples rather than maritally aggressive couples, relied solely on self-report measures tapping global constructs, and obtained data from single informants rather than multiple sources. Thus, generalizability of the findings is limited. Furthermore, the processes by which specific religious practices and beliefs influence interparental conflict and its effect on children remain an underresearched and fruitful area for scientific inquiry in the 21st century (see Chapter 24 of this book).

Comorbidity of Spousal Violence and Physical Child Abuse

Until the 1990s, research on marital violence was segregated from research on physical child abuse, and little attention was paid to co-occurrences of violence in couple and parent-child subsystems. Although extensive research has documented that marital and parental physical aggression are independently linked to greater child psychopathology (see Slep & O'Leary, 2001), our knowledge of comorbid family violence is limited in three areas: (a) the extent of co-occurrence; (b) the nature of comorbid effects (e.g., additive, interactive, mediational, or synergistic); and (c) the individual and family-level processes leading to comorbid violence within families.

Extent of Co-Occurrence

Children who live in maritally violent homes may be at greater risk for physical child abuse. The base rate of co-occurrence among families referred to shelters for battered women or child protective services agencies for physical child abuse has been estimated at 40% (Appel & Holden, 1998). Two thirds of a sample of 232 clinic-referred adolescents who were exposed to marital aggression in the past year also experienced parental aggression (Mahoney, Donnelly, Boxer, & Lewis, 2003). The base rate of

co-occurrence found in representative community samples has been estimated at 6% (Appel & Holden, 1998).

On the basis of a review of 31 studies that examined the co-occurrences of spousal violence and child abuse, Appel and Holden (1998) concluded that there is an inadequate database to evaluate the extent of co-occurrence in the United States. Significant impediments include reliance on a single informant, widely disparate definitions of marital violence and child abuse, and the absence of data from couples of different cultural and ethnic backgrounds. Most information regarding co-occurrence comes from battered women's shelters. Few studies have collected data regarding child abuse incidents and related this information to marital violence. Longitudinal studies using more representative samples would be especially informative.

Nature of Comorbid Effects

Few studies have examined the interactive and unique effects of co-occurring marital violence and physical abuse of children. With regard to possible multiplicative effects, the results are mixed, with some studies finding that children exposed to both types of family violence experience greater psychological problems but others failing to replicate this finding (see Slep & O'Leary, 2001). With regard to unique effects (i.e., the effects of violence in one subsystem after controlling for the impact of violence in the other), there is empirical evidence that the negative effects of marital violence on children are accounted for by parental aggression against children (Mahoney et al., 2003; Maughan & Cicchetti, 2002). Less is known about the circumstances in which the links between parental aggression toward children and psychopathology are attributable to marital violence. Interestingly, Mahoney et al. (2003) obtained different results depending upon the informant. On the basis of mothers' reports, marital aggression was not related to adolescents' adjustment beyond disruptions in parenting. However, from adolescents' perspectives, marital aggression was related to emotional and behavioral disturbances beyond the effects of hostile parenting behaviors.

Pathways of Influence

Appel and Holden (1998) proposed five contrasting models of the directionality of abusive relationships in families with co-occurring spousal and physical child abuse: (a) the *single-perpetrator model*, in which one parent operates as the sole source of violence and abuses both the spouse and child, who are passive recipients; (b) the *sequential-perpetrator model*, in which the victim of marital abuse is the perpetrator of child maltreatment; (c) the *dual-perpetrator model*, in which only one spouse is abusive toward the other but both parents abuse the child; (d) the *marital violence model*, in which both husband and wife are perpetrators of marital abuse and one or both parents abuse the child; and (e) the *family dysfunction model*, in which reciprocal aversive interactions between parents and children leading to violence are superimposed upon the bidirectional cycle of violence between husband and wife.

Various theories, including social learning, social-cognitive, developmental-ecological, family systems, and behavior genetics, may explain these contrasting pathways of influence (Appel & Holden, 1998), but to date, few studies have explicitly contrasted the models and associated theoretical explanations. In a noteworthy exception, Mahoney et al. (2003) examined the interplay of severe marital and parental aggression and adolescents' psychopathology among a sample of clinic-referred youth. They tested two hypotheses embedded within Appel and Holden's (1998) *dual-perpetrator* and *marital violence* models. According to the *parent aggressor* hypothesis, parents who direct aggression toward their partner are more likely to aggress against their offspring. According to the *parent victim* hypothesis, parents who are victims of marital violence are more likely to physically abuse their adolescents. Consistent with the *parent victim* pathway, both mothers and fathers who were targets of physical violence from partners were more likely to direct severe physical aggression toward their adolescents, even after the researchers controlled for level of marital aggression. Support for the *parent aggressor* pathway was obtained for fathers but not mothers. Fathers who hit their partners were more likely to direct physical aggression toward their adolescents, even after the researchers controlled for whether the men had been victims of marital aggression by wives.

Although data on base rates of the pathways-of-influence models are unavailable, there is some evidence for reciprocal-influence processes consistent with both the marital violence and family dysfunction models. Bidirectional aggression is the most common pattern in marital violence (see Capaldi & Owen, 2001); aggression toward a parent during interparental disputes may be the most common response, at least among adolescents (Davis et al., 1998), and may increase the probability of physical child abuse (Appel & Holden, 1998). Although Mahoney et al. (2003) did not examine the *family dysfunction* model, their data showed that about half of families corresponded to the *marital violence* model, in which both parents use physical aggression in the marriage and at least one parent directs severe physical aggression toward the adolescent. A very small number of their families fit with either of the two unidirectional models, *sole-perpetrator* or *sequential-perpetrator*. However, multiple models may apply depending upon the family, and families may progress through different models over time (Appel & Holden, 1998).

Understanding Comorbid Violence: The Definition Problem

A fundamental task for researchers attempting to achieve greater understanding of comorbid family violence will be to achieve consensus on definitions, methods, and measures for assessing marital violence and physical child abuse. There is empirical support for distinguishing between the degree of severity in defining and measuring marital violence (Lawrence & Bradbury, 2001) and child abuse (Emery & Laumann-Billings, 1998), with more severe acts in both cases linked to more deleterious outcomes. Couples who engage in severe aggressive acts at the early stages of marriage are more likely to exhibit subsequent marital discord than those who engage in moderately aggressive acts (Lawrence & Bradbury, 2001). In addition, the physical and psychological impact and degree of injury resulting from aggressive behaviors as well as the type of aggressive acts should be taken into account in diagnosing marital abuse. Similar aggressive acts may have dramatically different consequences. Questionnaire measures used to classify physically abusive marital behavior typically have relied solely upon the occurrence of aggression as the diagnostic criterion for abuse, with little attention to impact and injury (Heyman, Feldbau-Kohn, Ehrensaft, Langhinrichsen-Rohling, & O'Leary, 2001).

There is no scientifically accepted consensus on what constitutes child maltreatment, including physical child abuse (Appel & Holden, 1998; Emery & Laumann-Billings, 1998). In Appel and Holden's (1998) review, 15 different measures and/or definitions of physical abuse were used across 31 studies. Physical aggression toward children varies along multidimensional continua, including the type of

behavior, intent of the perpetrator, context in which the behavior occurs, level of coercion, and community norms. The question of what is the cutoff point demarcating abuse and nonabuse and why this point is chosen rather than another is a value-laden and thorny issue. For many parents in the United States, spanking, including the use of switches and belts, is normative (Kanoy et al., 2003; Mahoney et al., 2001) and not physical child abuse, as it would be defined in some widely used measures. Distinguishing between violent and nonviolent forms of child maltreatment may have both pragmatic and scientific advantages (Emery & Laumann-Billings, 1998), but the intrusion of values and cutoff points will remain problematic.

Multilevel and Reciprocal-Influence Processes

Multilevel Conceptualizations

Children exposed to destructive interparental conflicts may exhibit substantial variability in outcomes due largely to the highly idiosyncratic interplay of protective and risk factors operating at different levels of analysis within the families' social ecology (e.g., genetic, biological, intrapsychic, family relationships, peer group and school experiences, neighborhoods, communities, ethnicity, race, social institutions, culture). However, few studies of pathogenic-conflict families have used research designs and strategies that simultaneously assess constructs at multiple levels of analysis using multiple methods and longitudinal designs (Cicchetti & Dawson, 2002).

Multilevel research strategies may elucidate moderator effects of risk and protective factors within the broader social ecology that may attenuate or potentiate the adverse effects of interparental conflict on children. A pileup of stressors in the neighborhood and community (e.g., poverty, violence, discrimination) may increase the frequency and severity of interparental conflicts and, when conflicts occur, may also exacerbate their negative effects on children. Murray, Brown, Brody, Cutrona, and Simons (2001) found that African American mothers who perceived high levels of racism in comparison with those who perceived low levels responded to a pileup of other stressors with greater psychological distress, which in turn was linked to more pervasive disturbances in relationships with intimate partners and children. Adding risk factors to destructive interparental conflict histories may have additive, multiplicative, or exponential effects on children's negative outcomes.

Little is known about possible protective factors that may buffer the negative effects of interparental conflicts. Although several studies have found that positive parent-child relationships may reduce the adverse effects of interparental conflict (Frosch & Magelsdorf, 2001; Katz & Gottman, 1997), researchers have given relatively little attention to protective factors in extrafamilial social environments (e.g., peer group and academic settings) or at other levels of analysis (e.g., neighborhood, community). In an exception, high levels of positive peer relationships were found to reduce the negative effects of violent marital conflict and harsh discipline on children's externalizing behavior (Criss, Pettit, Bates, Dodge, & Lapp, 2002). Academic achievement and concomitant positive relationships with teachers and school personnel consistently emerge as factors promoting resilient outcomes in high-risk children (Masten & Coatsworth, 1998), but few studies have examined children's cognitive competence and characteristics of the school environment as possible protective factors that may reduce specifically the adverse effects of interparental conflicts and violence on children.

Interparental Conflict: Reciprocal-Influence Processes

Most studies of the effects of interparental conflict on children have focused on unidirectional models. Extensive research has documented that interparental conflict has direct negative effects on children's adjustment as well as indirect adverse effects via the mediating influences of disruptions in parent-child and co-parental relationships. However, plausible bidirectional or reciprocal-influence processes rarely have been studied. Children's psychiatric symptoms (e.g., externalizing behavior) may engender interparental conflict and physical child abuse (Appel & Holden, 1998). Problematic parent-child relationships including harsh punishment and abuse may trigger interparental disputes escalating to marital violence (Belsky & Hsieh, 1998). The bidirectional models proposed by Appel and Holden (1998) to account for co-occurrences of interparental violence and physical child abuse (e.g., negative reciprocity between parents and/or parents and children may escalate to violence) have received relatively little research attention. Children's conflict with siblings and peers may aggravate parents, leading to more hostility in parent-child and marital relationships (Stocker & Youngblade, 1999).

The relative strength of effects of bidirectional pathways may vary depending upon family structure and stage of the family life cycle. For example, in the Hetherington and Clingempeel (1992) longitudinal study of remarriage, interdependencies of marital conflict, parent-child relationship problems, and adolescents' externalizing behavior differed for newly formed stepfamilies (custodial mothers remarried 4–26 months) and well-established first-marriage families (biological parents married 9–15 years). In first-marriage families, the data strongly supported the pathway from marital negativity to problematic parenting to adolescent externalizing behaviors. In contrast, in stepfamilies, the results indicated a pathway from adolescent externalizing behaviors to negative parenting/stepparenting to marital conflict. Thus, in first-marriage families, marital conflict was the driving force, whereas in stepfamilies, adolescent-driven effects were prominent. Reciprocal-influence processes also may vary within and across cultural/ethnic/racial groups, but so far this topic has received little research attention.

CONCLUSION

Family researchers have amassed an impressive body of knowledge regarding the effects of interparental conflict on children. Many features of Grych and Fincham's (1990) cognitive-contextual model have received empirical support, and refinements of their seminal framework, including the specific emotions model (see Crockenberg & Langrock, 2001), the emotional security hypothesis (Davies & Cummings, 1994; Davies, Harold, Goeke-Morey, & Cummings, 2002) and documentation of spillover and parenting-as-mediator effects (Erel & Burman, 1995; Maughan & Cicchetti, 2002), have enhanced our understanding of pathogenic-conflict families. However, many questions in the three domains of "what we need to know" discussed in this chapter remain unanswered. Twenty-first-century family scholars who address these questions will confront substantial theoretical, methodological, and data analytic challenges; but a greater understanding and appreciation of human diversity in all its forms will be the valuable fruits of their labor.

REFERENCES

Almeida, D. M., Wethington, E., & Chandler, A. L. (1999). The transmissions of tensions between marital dyads and parent-child dyads. *Journal of Marriage and the Family, 61*, 49–61.

Anderson, E. R., Hetherington, E. M., & Clingempeel, W. G. (1999). The dynamics of parental remarriage: Adolescent, parent, and sibling influences. In E. M. Hetherington (Ed.), *Coping with divorce, single parenting, and remarriage: A risk and resiliency perspective.* Mahwah, NJ: Lawrence Erlbaum.

Appel, A. E., & Holden, G. W. (1998). The co-occurrence of spouse and physical child abuse: A review and appraisal. *Journal of Family Psychology, 12*, 578–599.

Belsky, J., & Hsieh, K.-H. (1998). Patterns of marital change during the early childhood years: Parent personality, coparenting, and division of labor correlates. *Journal of Family Psychology, 12*, 511–528.

Brody, G. H., Stoneman, Z., & Burke, M. (1987). Family system and individual child correlates of sibling behavior. *American Journal of Orthopsychiatry, 57*, 561–569.

Brody, G. H., Stoneman, Z., & Flor, D. (1996). Parental religiosity, family processes, and youth competence in rural, two-parent African American families. *Developmental Psychology, 32*, 696–706.

Buchanan, C. M., Maccoby, E. E., & Dornbush, S. M. (1991). Caught between parents: Adolescents' experiences in divorced homes. *Child Development, 62*, 1008–1029.

Capaldi, D. M., & Owen, L. D. (2001). Physical aggression in a community sample of at-risk young couples: Gender comparisons for high frequency, injury, and fear. *Journal of Family Psychology, 15*, 425–440.

Cicchetti, D., & Dawson, G. (2002). Editorial: Multiple levels of analysis. *Development and Psychopathology, 14,* 417–420.

Cole, P. M., & Tamang, B. L. (1998). Nepali children's ideas about emotional displays in hypothetical challenges. *Developmental Psychology, 34,* 640–646.

Conteras, J. M., Lopez, I. R., Rivera-Mosquera, E. T., Raymond-Smith, L., & Rothstein, K. (1999). Social support and adjustment among Puerto Rican adolescent mothers: The moderating effect of acculturation. *Journal of Family Psychology, 13,* 228–243.

Criss, M. M., Pettit, G. S., Bates, J. E., Dodge, K. A., & Lapp, A. L. (2002). Family adversity, positive peer relationships, and children's externalizing behavior: A longitudinal perspective on risk and resilience. *Child Development, 73,* 1220–1237.

Crockenberg, S., & Forgays, D. (1996). The role of emotion in children's understanding and emotional reactions to marital conflict. *Merrill-Palmer Quarterly, 42,* 22–47.

Crockenberg, S., & Langrock, A. (2001). The role of specific emotions in children's responses to interparental conflict: A test of the model. *Journal of Family Psychology, 15,* 163–182.

Cummings, E. M., & Davies, P. T. (1994). *Children and marital conflict: The impact of family dispute and resolution.* New York: Guilford.

Dadds, M. R., Atkinson, E., Turner, C., Blums, G. J., & Lendich, B. (1999). Family conflict and child adjustment: Evidence for a cognitive-contextual model of intergenerational transmission. *Journal of Family Psychology, 13,* 194–208.

Davies, P. T., & Cummings, E. M. (1994). Marital conflict and child adjustment: An emotional security hypothesis. *Psychological Bulletin, 116,* 387–411.

Davies, P. T., & Cummings, E. M. (1998). Exploring children's emotional security as a mediator of the link between marital relations and children's adjustment. *Child Development, 69,* 124–139.

Davies, P. T., & Forman, E. M. (2002). Children's patterns of preserving emotional security in the interparental subsystem. *Child Development, 73,* 1880–1903.

Davies, P. T., Harold, G. T., Goeke-Morey, M. C., & Cummings, E. M. (2002). Children's emotional security and interparental conflict. *Monographs of the Society for Research in Child Development, 67*(3), Serial No. 270.

Davies, P. T., Myers, R. L., Cummings, E. M., & Heindel, S. (1999). Adult conflict history and children's subsequent responses to conflict: An experimental test. *Journal of Family Psychology, 13,* 475–483.

Davis, B. T., Hops, H., Alpert, A., & Sheeber, L. (1998). Child responses to parental conflict and their effect on adjustment: A study of triadic relations. *Journal of Family Psychology, 12,* 163–177.

Emery, R. E., & Laumann-Billings, L. (1998). An overview of the nature, causes consequences of abusive family relationships: Toward differentiating maltreatment and violence. *American Psychologist, 53,* 121–135.

Erel, O., & Burman, B. (1995). Interrelatedness of marital relations and parent-child relations: A meta-analytic review. *Psychological Bulletin, 118,* 108–132.

Fiske, A. P. (2002). Using individualism and collectivism to compare cultures: A critique of the validity and measurement of constructs. Comments on Oyserman et al. (2002). *Psychological Bulletin, 128,* 78–88.

Floyd, F. J., Gilliom, L. A., & Costigan, C. L. (1998). Marriage and the parenting alliance: Longitudinal prediction of change in parenting perceptions and behaviors. *Child Development, 69,* 1461–1479.

Frosch, C. A., & Magelsdorf, S. C. (2001). Marital behavior, parenting behaviors, and multiple reports of preschoolers' behavior problems: Mediation or moderation? *Developmental Psychology, 37,* 502–519.

Gonzales, N. A., Pitts, S. C., Hill, N. E., & Roosa, M. W. (2000). Mediational model of the impact of interparental conflict on child adjustment in a multiethnic, low-income sample. *Journal of Family Psychology, 14,* 365–379.

Gottman, J. M., & Katz, L. F. (1989). Effects of marital discord on young children's peer interactions and health. *Developmental Psychology, 25,* 373–381.

Greene, S. M., & Anderson, E. R. (1999). Observed negativity in large family systems: Incidents and reactions. *Journal of Family Psychology, 13,* 372–392.

Grych, J. H. (1998). Children's appraisals of interparental conflict: Situational and contextual influences. *Journal of Family Psychology, 12,* 437–453.

Grych, J. H., & Fincham, F. (1990). Marital conflict and children's adjustment: A cognitive-contextual framework. *Psychological Bulletin, 108,* 267–290.

Hetherington, E. M., & Clingempeel, W. G. (1992). Coping with marital transitions: A family systems perspective. *Monographs of the Society for Research in Child Development, 57*(2-3), Serial No. 227.

Heyman, R. E., Feldbau-Kohn, S. R., Ehrensaft, M. K., Langhinrichsen-Rohling, J., & O'Leary, K. D. (2001). Can questionnaire reports correctly classify relationship distress and partner physical abuse? *Journal of Family Psychology, 15,* 334–346.

Huesmann, L. R. (1999). The effects of childhood aggression and exposure to media violence on adult behaviors, attitudes, and mood: Evidence from a 15-year cross-national study. *Aggressive Behavior, 25,* 18–29.

Jensen, P. S., & Hoagwood, K. (1997). Developmental psychopathology and the notion of culture: Introduction to the special issue on "Cultural influences on the assessment and psychopathology of children and adolescents." *Applied Developmental Science, 1,* 108–112.

Jouriles, E. N., McDonald, R., Norwood, W. D., Ware, H. S., Spiller, L. C., & Swank, P. R. (1998). Knives, guns, and interparental violence: Relations with child behavior problems. *Journal of Family Psychology, 12,* 178–194.

Kanoy, K., Ulka-Steiner, B., Cox, M., & Burchinal, M. (2003). Marital relationship and individual psychological characteristics that predict physical punishment of children. *Journal of Family Psychology, 17,* 20–28.

Katz, L. F., & Gottman, J. M. (1996). Spillover effects of marital conflict: In search of parenting and co-parenting mechanisms. In J. P. McHale & P. A. Cowan (Eds.), *Understanding how family-level dynamics affect children's development: Studies of two-parent families* (pp. 57–76). San Francisco: Jossey-Bass.

Katz, L. F., & Gottman, J. M. (1997). Buffering children from marital conflict and dissolution. *Journal of Clinical Child Psychology, 26,* 157–171.

Kelly, J. (2000). Children's adjustment in conflicted marriage and divorce: A decade review of research. *Journal of the American Academy of Child and Adolescent Psychiatry, 39,* 963–973.

Kitayama, S. (2002). Culture and psychological processes: Toward a system view of culture. Comment on Oyserman et al. (2002). *Psychological Bulletin, 128,* 89–96.

Lawrence, E., & Bradbury, T. N. (2001). Physical aggression and marital dysfunction: A longitudinal analysis. *Journal of Family Psychology, 15,* 135–154.

Maccoby, E. E., Depner, C. E., & Mnookin, R. H. (1991). Co-parenting in the second year after divorce. In J. Folberg (Ed.), *Joint custody and shared parenting* (2nd ed., pp. 132–152). New York: Guilford.

Mahoney, A., Donnelly, W. O., Boxer, P., & Lewis, J. (2003). Marital and severe parent-to-adolescent physical aggression in clinic-referred families: Mother and adolescent reports on co-occurrence and links to child behavior problems. *Journal of Family Psychology, 17,* 3–19.

Mahoney, A., Pargament, K. I., Tarakeshwar, N., & Swank, A. B. (2001). Religion in the home in the 1980's and 1990's: A meta-analysis review and conceptual analysis of the links between religion, marriage, and parenting. *Journal of Family Psychology, 15,* 559–596.

Mann, B. J., Borduin, C. M., Henggeler, S. W., & Blaske, D. M. (1990). An investigation of systemic conceptualizations of parent-child coalitions and symptom change. *Journal of Consulting and Clinical Psychology, 58,* 336–344.

Marcus, E. M., Lindahl, K. M., & Malik, N. M. (2001). Interparental conflict, children's social cognitions and child aggression: A test of a mediational model. *Journal of Family Psychology, 15,* 315–333.

Margolin, G., Gordis, E. B., & John, R. S. (2001). Coparenting: A link between marital conflict and parenting in two-parent families. *Journal of Family Psychology, 15,* 3–21.

Marin, G., & Marin, B. V. (1991). *Research with Hispanic populations.* Newbury Park, CA: Sage.

Masten, A. S., & Coatsworth, J. D. (1998). The development of competence in favorable and unfavorable environments: Lessons from research on successful children. *American Psychologist, 53,* 205–220.

Maughan, A., & Cicchetti, D. (2002). Impact of child maltreatment and interadult violence on children's emotion regulation abilities and socioemotional adjustment. *Child Development, 78,* 1525–1542.

McHale, J. P. (1997). Overt and covert coparenting processes in the family. *Family Process, 36,* 183–201.

Miller, J. G. (2002). Bringing culture to basic psychological theory: Beyond individualism and collectivism: Comment on Oyserman et. al (2002). *Psychological Bulletin, 128,* 97–109.

Murray, V. M., Brown, P. A., Brody, G. H., Cutrona, C. E., & Simons, R. L. (2001). Racial discrimination as a moderator of the links among stress, maternal psychological functioning, and family relationships. *Journal of Marriage and Family, 63,* 915–926.

Oyserman, D., Coon, H. M., & Kemmelmeier, M. (2002). Rethinking individualism and collectivism: Evaluation of theoretical assumptions and meta-analysis. *Psychological Bulletin, 128,* 3–72.

Rohner, R., & Pettengill, S. (1985). Perceived parental acceptance-rejection and parental control among Korean adolescents. *Child Development, 56,* 524–528.

Rothbaum, F., Morelli, G., Pott, M., & Liu-Constant, Y. (2000). Immigrant-Chinese and Euro-American parents' physical closeness with young children: Themes of family relatedness. *Journal of Family Psychology, 14,* 334–348.

Rothbaum, F., Weisz, J., Pott, M., Miyake, K., & Morelli, G. (2000). Attachment and culture: Security in the United States and Japan. *American Psychologist, 55,* 1093–1104.

Rubin, K. H. (1998). Social and emotional development from a cultural perspective. *Developmental Psychology, 34,* 611–615.

Ruiz, S. Y., Roosa, M. W., & Gonzales, N. A. (2002). Predictors of self-esteem for Mexican American and European American youth: A reexamination of the influence of parenting. *Journal of Family Psychology, 16,* 70–80.

Santisteban, D. A., Muir-Malcolm, J. A., Mitrani, V. B., & Szapocznik, J. (2002). Integrating the study of ethnic culture and family psychology intervention science. In H. A. Liddle, D. A. Santisteban, R. F. Levant, & J. A. Bray (Eds.), *Family psychology: Science-based interventions* (pp. 331–351). Washington, DC: American Psychological Association.

Segall, M. H., Dasen, P. R., Berry, J. W., & Poortinga, Y. H. (1990). *Human behavior in global perspective.* New York: Pergamon.

Singer, A. T. B., & Weinstein, R. S. (2000). Differential parental treatment predicts achievement and self-perceptions in two cultural contexts. *Journal of Family Psychology, 14,* 491–509.

Slep, A. M., & O'Leary, S. G. (2001). Examining partner and child abuse: Are we ready for a more integrated approach to family violence? *Clinical Child and Family Psychology Review, 4,* 87–107.

Stocker, C. M., & Youngblade, L. (1999). Marital conflict and parental hostility: Links with children's sibling and peer relationships. *Journal of Family Psychology, 13,* 475–483.

Straus, M. A., Gelles, R. J., & Steinmetz, S. K. (1980). *Behind closed doors: Violence in the American family.* New York: Anchor.

Part V

CHANGING FAMILY STRUCTURES

Divorce in Social and Historical Context

Changing Scientific Perspectives on Children and Marital Dissolution

PAUL R. AMATO

One of the goals of science—social science as well as natural science—is to formulate principles and explanations that apply to a wide range of phenomena, irrespective of time and place. Many theorists, for example, assume that the basic principles of children's learning (reward, punishment, identification, modeling, internalization of social rules) are applicable across cultures and historical periods. According to this view, the basic processes that underlie child socialization are the same, irrespective of whether children grow up in an urban area in the United States in the 21st century, a Puritan colony in New England in the 17th century, or an extended family in India in the 19th century.

Although the attempt to discover general principles of social behavior is a useful goal,

social scientists can never be free entirely of historical and cultural context, for two reasons. First, many of the phenomena of interest to social scientists change over time. This statement applies to divorce, which changed from a relatively uncommon form of behavior at the beginning of the 20th century to a relatively common form of behavior by the end of the 20th century. Second, social scientists are influenced by the worldviews of the particular eras in which they are trained and conduct their research. As I show below, the demand for divorce among married couples, the laws regulating divorce, and public attitudes toward divorce shaped the views and research agendas of family scholars during the 20th century.

The purpose of this chapter is to summarize social scientific research about divorce within a social and historical context. This purpose is best achieved by dividing U.S. history into three periods: (a) 1900 to 1960, a time when most family scholars believed that divorce harmed children and that the increasing rate of divorce was a serious social problem; (b) the 1960s through the 1980s, a time when many family scholars viewed children as resilient and redefined divorce as a transition consistent with the goals of resolving destructive marital relationships and maximizing personal happiness; and (c) the 1990s to the present, a time when family scholars moved toward a more complex synthesis of earlier perspectives. These three periods can be distinguished not only in terms of scientific views about divorce but also in terms of the frequency of divorce, the legal regulation of divorce, and public attitudes toward divorce. Although researchers have studied the causes as well as the consequences of marital disruption, I focus most of my discussion in this chapter on research dealing with the effects of divorce on children.

DIVORCE AS A SOCIAL PROBLEM: 1900–1960

The Divorce Rate

Data on divorce in the United States are available from 1860 to the present. A useful way to track the frequency of divorce over time is to calculate the refined divorce rate, which is the number of divorces in a given year per every 1,000 married women. The divorce rate increased from about 2 in 1865 to about 4 in 1900. Divorce continued to increase during the early part of the 20th century, reaching about 8 in 1940. The divorce rate spiked sharply upward during World War II (the first half of the 1940s). After the war, the divorce rate declined, and by the end of the 1950s, it was back to where it had

been 20 years earlier. Despite the postwar decline in divorce, marital dissolution became increasingly common in American society during the second half of 19th century and the first half of the 20th century.

During this time, divorce rates also responded (involving short-term increases and decreases) to specific events and changing social circumstances. The divorce rate stabilized during the Great Depression of the 1930s, a time when many couples could not afford to divorce. The surge in divorces during World War II indicates that wartime marriages were not very stable, partly because military service separated many husbands and wives for long periods. The 1950s, in contrast, represented a relatively "profamily" period in U.S. history. In addition to the declining divorce rate, the marriage rate was high, and fertility increased dramatically (the baby boom). Several forces came together to create the stable, two-parent, child-oriented family of the 1950s: a strong economy, real increases in men's wages, veterans taking advantage of the G.I. Bill to obtain university educations, the growth of home construction in the suburbs, and a desire on the part of many people to move beyond the tumultuous war years and to concentrate on home and family life. (See Cherlin, 1992, for a detailed discussion.)

The Legal Regulation of Divorce

During the 19th century and throughout most of the 20th century, divorces were granted only when one spouse demonstrated to the court's satisfaction that the other spouse was "guilty" of violating the marriage contract. Although divorce laws varied from state to state, grounds for divorce often included infidelity, physical or mental cruelty, and abandonment. Under this system, the "innocent" spouse often received a better deal than the guilty spouse with respect to the division of marital property, alimony, and child custody. In other words, the law "punished" the spouse who was guilty of undermining the marriage (Katz, 1994).

Note that this system did not allow for the possibility that two spouses simply might be unhappy with their marriage and wish to go their separate ways. Instead, by making it difficult to divorce, and by requiring one spouse to accept responsibility for violating the marriage contract, the law affirmed its commitment to the norm of marital permanence. Despite the difficulty and cost of proving fault in court, however, demand for divorce increased throughout this period. To accommodate this growing demand, the courts gradually broadened the grounds for marital dissolution, and an increasing proportion of divorces were granted on the relatively vague grounds of "mental cruelty" (Emery, 1988).

Public Attitudes Toward Divorce

Historically, Americans have disapproved of divorce. Few attitudes surveys were conducted before the 1960s. Nevertheless, most religions have discouraged divorce, and Americans are a religious people. The Catholic Church explicitly forbids marital dissolution, although an annulment is possible if couples can demonstrate that reasonable expectations for marriage were not met (for example, the marriage was not consummated). Mainline Protestant denominations, along with Judaism, allow divorce but believe that it should avoided if at all possible. Because many people viewed divorce as a form of deviance (or a sin), divorced individuals were, to a certain extent, stigmatized—although the stigma was stronger for women than for men (Kitson, 1992). Before the 1960s, divorce was a campaign liability, even for a man. Adlai Stevenson (who was divorced in 1949) served as the Democratic Party's candidate for president in 1952. During the campaign, Dwight Eisenhower

(the Republican Party candidate) raised Stevenson's divorce as a campaign issue— an issue that resonated strongly among women voters (Rothstein, 2002). Partly for this reason, Stevenson lost the election.

Social Scientific Views of Divorce

Like the general public, early family scholars took a dim view of divorce. Developmental theories of the time, such as Freudian theory, assumed that children needed to grow up with two parents to develop normally. For this reason, most social scientists in the first half of the 20th century saw the rising level of marital disruption as a serious social problem. Sociologists, in particular, were concerned that one of the fundamental institutions of society—the family—was being undermined. In the 1920s and 1930s, social scientists published books with titles such as *The Marriage Crisis* (Groves, 1928), *Family Disorganization* (Mowrer, 1927), and *Marriage at the Crossroads* (Stekel, 1931). Curiously, few studies focused on children, presumably because the idea that divorce was bad for children seemed self-evident. Instead, researchers focused primarily on factors that promoted or eroded marital happiness (e.g., Burgess & Cottrell, 1939; Terman, 1938).

Ernest Burgess was one of the most influential of these early family scholars (Burgess & Cottrell, 1939; Burgess & Locke, 1945). Burgess argued that the increasing rate of divorce reflected a transformation in the nature of marriage: That is, marriage was changing from a formal social institution to a private arrangement based on companionship. By *institution*, Burgess meant a fundamental unit of social organization—a formal status regulated by social norms, public opinion, law, and religion. According to Burgess, the industrialization and urbanization of the United States were weakening the institutional basis of marriage. As parents, religion, community expectations, and patriarchal traditions exerted less control over individuals, marriages were based increasingly on the mutual affection and individual preferences of spouses. Burgess referred to the new model (and ideal) of marriage as *companionate marriage.*

Companionate marriages are held together, not by bonds of social obligation, but by ties of love, friendship, and common interest. And unlike institutional marriage, companionate marriage allows for an ample degree of self-expression and personal development. Burgess further argued that in an urbanized society in which interaction takes place largely within the context of impersonal, secondary relationships, companionate marriage becomes the most important source of social and emotional support in people's lives. Because companionate marriage was central to people's well-being, and because institutional barriers to divorce were becoming weaker, an increasing number of spouses were electing to leave unsatisfactory marriages to find happiness with alternative partners.

The notion that marriage should be based on mutual affection, sexual attraction, and equality began to gain public acceptance during the first few decades of the 20th century. Psychologists, educators, and social service providers applied these ideas in their professional practice, and it was in this context that marital counseling emerged as a discipline, with its goal being to help couples achieve emotional closeness and sexual satisfaction through improved communication and conflict management. By the 1950s, the great majority of Americans, irrespective of social class, accepted the companionate model of marriage as the cultural ideal (Mintz & Kellogg, 1989). Although Burgess believed that the ascendance of companionate marriage was responsible for the increase in divorce, he also believed that the divorce rate would decline once society adjusted to this new arrangement. In particular, he (and others) believed that a combination of public education and marital counseling—based on emerging social scientific information about marriage—would help couples to achieve stable and happy marriages in the new era. Burgess and his colleagues did not foresee the massive increase in marital disruption that was shortly to occur.

THE DIVORCE REVOLUTION: 1960 THROUGH THE 1980S

The Divorce Rate

After declining for more than a decade, the divorce rate increased sharply during the 1960s and 1970s. The divorce rate reached a peak in 1980, then declined modestly. Currently, the rate of divorce is about 20, which means that about 2% of all marriages end in divorce every year $[(20/1,000) \times 100]$. Although the 2% figure may seem low, it is based on a single year. By applying duration-specific probabilities of divorce across all the years of marriage, it is possible to project the percentage of marriages that will end in divorce. Using this method, demographers estimate that about one half of first marriages, and about 60% of second marriages, will end in divorce (Cherlin, 1992). These figures represent a historically high level of marital disruption in the United States. In comparison, about one eighth of all marriages ended in divorce in 1900, and about one fourth of all marriages ended in divorce in the 1950s (Preston & McDonald, 1979).

The Legal Regulation of Divorce

During the first half of the 20th century, all U.S. states granted divorces under a fault regime. In 1953, Oklahoma became the first state to allow no-fault divorce (Vlosky & Monroe, 2002). Although fault-based divorces still were possible, spouses could dissolve marriages even if neither spouse had committed a serious marital offense. In these cases, "incompatibility" became the grounds for divorce. Several other states added no-fault options during the next decade, including Alaska in 1963 and New York in 1967 (Vlosky & Monroe, 2002).

The most dramatic change in divorce law occurred in California in 1969. In that year, the California legislature threw out fault-based divorce entirely and replaced it with no-fault divorce. Under the new legislation, only one ground for divorce existed: the marriage was "irretrievably broken" due to "irreconcilable differences" (Glendon, 1989). Moreover, courts in California granted divorces even if one spouse wanted the divorce and the other did not—a system known as unilateral no-fault divorce. The assumption underlying unilateral no-fault divorce is that it takes two committed spouses to form a marriage; if one spouse no longer wishes to remain in the relationship, then the marriage is not viable.

Other states quickly followed California's lead, and by the mid-1980s, no-fault divorce existed in all 50 states. Most states adopted versions of unilateral no-fault divorce. Other states introduced no-fault divorce but only by mutual consent. In Pennsylvania, for example, if one spouse wants a divorce and the other does not, then a no-fault divorce can be obtained only after the spouses are separated for 2 years. Otherwise, the spouse who wants the divorce must prove fault (Schwartz, 1999). Although some states require mutual consent, and although many states have retained fault-based divorce alongside no-fault divorce by mutual consent, most divorces in the United States today take place under unilateral no-fault divorce regimes (Katz, 1994).

States introduced no-fault divorce for several reasons. First, it was widely known that many couples who wished to dissolve their marriages colluded to fabricate grounds for divorce. The recognition that many couples were making a mockery of the law was one factor leading to the reformation of divorce law (Katz, 1994). In addition, legal scholars increasingly accepted the proposition that spouses had a legal right to end their marriages if they were incompatible, had fallen out of love, or were no longer happy living together (Glendon, 1989). Finally, fault-based divorce is an inherently adversarial procedure. Legislators believed that no-fault divorce would lessen the level of animosity between former spouses and hence make it easier for them to cooperate in raising their children following marital dissolution (Glendon, 1989; Katz, 1994).

Some scholars believe that the liberalization of divorce laws stimulated further demand for divorce (e.g., Parkman, 2000). Other scholars disagree with this claim (Glenn, 1999). Even if legal changes encouraged more couples to divorce, however, this effect probably was modest. Changes in the law, as well as changes in divorce rates, were primarily reflections of the broad shift from institutional marriage to companionate marriage, as described earlier (Burgess & Cottrell, 1939; Burgess & Locke, 1945).

Public Attitudes Toward Divorce

Public attitudes toward divorce became more liberal during the 1960s and 1970s. For example, between 1965 and 1976, the percentage of respondents who felt that divorce laws were "too strict" increased (Cherlin, 1992). In another study, the percentage of women who *disagreed* with the statement "When there are children in the family, parents should stay together even if they don't get along" increased from 51 in 1962 to 80 in 1977 (Thornton & Young-DeMarco, 2001). As noted earlier, Adlai Stevenson's divorce was a major campaign issue in the 1952 presidential election. In contrast, Ronald Reagan ran successfully for president in 1980, and his opponent, Jimmy Carter, did not raise Reagan's divorce as a campaign issue (Rothstein, 2002). Indeed, Reagan ran on a profamily platform, despite his history of troubled relationships with his adult children. By the end of the 1970s, the great majority of Americans viewed divorce as an unfortunate but common event, and the stigma of divorce, although still present, was considerably weaker than in earlier eras.

The growing acceptance of divorce was consistent with a larger cultural shift that occurred during the 1960s and 1970s. According to Furstenberg and Cherlin (1991, Chap. 6), people's expectations for personal happiness from marriage increased throughout the 20th century. With personal fulfillment becoming the main criterion by which people judged their marriages, spouses tended to seek divorces when they became unhappy with their relationships, even if the marriage did not include serious problems such as abuse. Moreover, rather than condemning the decision to divorce, friends and family members tended to support spouses who left unsatisfying marriages. This shift in people's views, and the corresponding decrease in social pressure to stay married, is consistent with Burgess's notion of the decline of institutional marriage and the rise of companionate marriage, as described earlier. (Also see Bellah, Madsen, Sullivan, Swidler, & Tipton, 1985.)

Social Scientific Research on Children and Divorce

During the 1960s and 1970s, research on the effects of divorce on children proliferated. Congruent with popular opinion, most family scholars in the 1960s assumed that children who grew up without two biological parents in the household were prone to a variety of emotional, behavioral, and academic problems. Studies conducted in the 1960s and early 1970s appeared to support this assumption. Research indicated that children from single-parent households were substantially overrepresented in samples of juvenile delinquents (Glueck & Glueck, 1962) and children with behavioral or emotional disorders (McDermott, 1970).

In 1971, psychologists Judith Wallerstein and Joan Kelly began an influential longitudinal study of 60 families and 131 children (ages 3 to 18). Wallerstein and Kelly published a variety of academic papers during the 1970s that described these families, and they later summarized their results in a widely read book (Wallerstein & Kelly, 1980). According to the authors, 5 years after divorce, one third of children were adjusting well and had good relationships with both parents. Another group of children (more than one third of the sample) were clinically depressed, were doing poorly in school, had difficulty maintaining friendships, experienced chronic problems such as sleep disturbances, and continued to hope for the reconciliation of their parents. A second book published at the end of the 1980s was based on a 10-year follow-up of the sample (Wallerstein & Blakeslee, 1989). In this book, Wallerstein claimed that children with divorced parents often developed into troubled youth who were prone to psychological distress and anxious about forming relationships. As she stated, "Almost half of the children entered adulthood as worried, underachieving, self-deprecating, and sometimes angry young men and women" (p. 299). Although not all children were affected negatively, this study confirmed many people's fear that divorce was a serious risk factor for long-term child maladjustment.

Although early research supported the belief that divorce was intrinsically bad for children, other studies in the 1970s challenged this dominant view. For example, Mavis Hetherington and her colleagues (Hetherington, 1979; Hetherington, Cox, & Cox, 1982) studied 144 preschool children, half from recently divorced families and half from nondivorced families. During the first year of the study, children with divorced parents exhibited more behavioral and emotional problems than did children with continuously married parents. Two years after divorce, however, most children with divorced parents no longer exhibited an elevated number of problems, although a few problems lingered for boys. Contrary to Wallerstein's findings, Hetherington's research suggested that most problems associated with marital disruption improve once family members have time to adjust to their new circumstances. (It is difficult to compare the Hetherington and Wallerstein studies directly. Compared with Hetherington, Wallerstein used a broader age range of children, did not have a comparison group of married-couple families, and used a qualitative rather than quantitative approach.)

During the 1970s and 1980s, an increasing number of family scholars began to question the assumption that divorce inevitably harms children. In an influential review of the literature, Herzog and Sudia (1973) argued that single-parent households (usually headed by single mothers) tend to be poor and that children from poor families are especially likely to drop out of school or become delinquent. Therefore, many of the problems exhibited by children in single-parent families may be due to poverty rather than parental absence. Subsequent studies provided support for this conclusion. For example, in a national study, Guidobaldi, Cleminshaw, Perry, and McLaughlin (1983) found that without controls for income, children in divorced families scored significantly lower than children in nondivorced families on 27 out of 34 outcomes. Controlling for income, however, reduced the number of significant differences to 13, which suggested that income accounted for most of the differences between children with divorced and continuously married parents.

In another widely cited review, Robert Emery (1982) pointed out that marital conflict among continuously married parents has negative effects on children comparable to those attributed to parental divorce. Given that marital conflict precedes divorce, it is plausible that much of the apparent "effect" of divorce on children is due to interparental discord rather than parental absence. This view was consistent with research showing that children with continuously married, discordant parents have as many—or more—problems than children with divorced parents (Long, 1986). Also consistent with this explanation were studies showing that children's well-being is negatively related to the level of conflict between parents following divorce (Guidobaldi, Perry, & Nastasi, 1987; Kurdek & Berg, 1983).

Using meta-analytic techniques, Amato and Keith (1991) summarized 92 studies of children and divorce that had been published between 1953 and the end of the 1980s. Their meta-analysis confirmed that children with divorced parents, compared to children with continuously married parents, scored lower (on average) on measures of academic achievement, conduct, psychological well-being, self-esteem, and social competence. However, the effect sizes in this literature were small rather than large, with the median effect size being 0.14 of a standard deviation. An effect size of this magnitude indicates a substantial degree of overlap between children with divorced and continuously married parents, with many children in the former group doing well and many children in the latter group doing poorly. The meta-analysis also found that effect sizes tended to be smaller in more recent studies, which suggested that the effects of divorce were becoming weaker over time.

By the late 1970s and the 1980s, many family scholars had adopted the position that research on divorce had relied too heavily on a *family deficit perspective* (Demo & Acock,

1988; Marotz-Baden, Adams, Buech, Munro, & Munro, 1979). According to these critics, the deficit perspective inaccurately assumed that any departure from the nuclear family is deviant and therefore deleterious to children's well-being. Although existing research suggested that children with divorced parents are at risk for a variety of problems, most of these studies were weak methodologically, the differences between children with divorced and continuously married parents were small in magnitude, and most—perhaps all—of these differences could be accounted for by factors such as low income and interparental discord before and after divorce.

In contrast to the deficit perspective, these scholars advocated a framework that I refer to as a *family pluralism perspective*. This new perspective assumed that family structure has few intrinsic consequences (negative or positive) for children's well-being and that children can develop successfully in a variety of family forms. Even if divorce created problems for children in the past, these negative effects have declined because society no longer harshly stigmatizes children with single parents. And although divorce may be a stressful experience, most children are resilient (rather than vulnerable) and are capable of adjusting well after a period of time. According to advocates of this new perspective, family processes (such as the level of marital conflict and the closeness of parent-child relationships) are more important than family structure in understanding children's development and adjustment. Consequently, rather than "privilege" the traditional two-parent family and stigmatize divorced parents and their children, advocates of family pluralism emphasized the strengths of all types of families.

The perspective of family pluralism, by breaking with the notion that single-parent families have uniformly harmful effects on children, provided a good fit with the historical era—an era in which half of all first marriages ended in divorce, the general public had become tolerant of divorce (including divorces involving children), and the legal system had made it easier for couples to dissolve their marriages. Family pluralism acknowledged that divorce was a necessary safety valve for individuals in marriages marked by violence, substance abuse, and destructive behavior. Moreover, the pluralism perspective suggested that it was neither necessary nor desirable to sacrifice personal happiness for the sake of an unsatisfying marriage. According to this perspective, the provision of developmentally appropriate levels of warmth and supervision by competent, well-adjusted, and happy parents was the key to children's well-being. Consequently, children were likely to be better off—rather than worse off—when unhappily married parents divorced to find greater happiness elsewhere.

THE EMERGENCE OF A MIDDLE GROUND: 1990 TO THE PRESENT

The Divorce Rate

After reaching a peak in the early 1980s, the divorce rate began to decline. At first, it was not clear whether this change represented a temporary fluctuation or the beginning of a long-term trend. However, the decline in divorce persisted throughout the 1980s and well into the 1990s, albeit modestly.

The Legal Regulation of Divorce

During the 1990s, the Marriage Movement—a loosely aligned group of academics, social scientists, religious leaders, legislators, family therapists, and members of the public—emerged in the United States. This movement was diverse politically, with liberal as well as conservative elements. What connected these individuals was a concern that the institution of marriage in the United States had become weaker, with detrimental consequences for children, adults, and society in general. (See Blankenhorn, Bayme, & Elshtain, 1990; Council on Families in America, 1995; Ooms, 2002; Parke & Ooms, 2002, for varied perspectives on the Marriage Movement.)

Some conservative members of this groups adopted the goal of divorce law reform and attempted to lower the frequency of marital dissolution by placing restrictions on unilateral no-fault divorce. During the 1990s, legislators in nearly a dozen states introduced bills that would require the consent of both spouses for a no-fault divorce if they had dependent children. Fault-based divorce would be available without mutual consent in cases of abuse, desertion, or adultery. Other bills attempted to lengthen the waiting period before divorce or to require marital counseling (with the goal of attempting a reconciliation) before divorce. Despite attracting a good deal of media attention, none of these bills was passed in any state (Crouch, 2002).

Divorce law reformers were more successful with the introduction of covenant marriage in three states. Louisiana was the first state to introduce this legislation in 1997, followed by Arizona and Arkansas. Under this system, couples choose between two types of marriage: a standard marriage or a covenant marriage. To obtain a covenant marriage, couples must attend premarital education classes and promise to seek marital counseling to preserve the marriage if problems arise later. Unilateral no-fault divorce is not an option for ending a covenant marriage. To terminate a covenant marriage, one spouse must prove fault, although a couple also can obtain a divorce after a 2-year separation. (For a detailed description of covenant marriage in Louisiana, see Thompson & Wyatt, 1999). Although proponents of covenant marriage see it as a way to strengthen marriage and lower the divorce rate, only a small percentage of couples in Louisiana have chosen covenant marriages (Sanchez, Nock, Wright, Pardee, & Ionescu, 2001).

The impact of the divorce law reform movement has been modest, but other legislative efforts to strengthen marriage (rather than restrict access to divorce) have met with more success. Although it was not widely recognized at the time, the 1996 federal welfare reform legislation referred to promoting marriage and encouraging the formation and maintenance of two-parent families as explicit policy goals (Ooms, 2002). Since that time, several state governments have enacted legislation and programs to strengthen marriage and reduce divorce. For example, Oklahoma provides publicly funded premarital education classes to a wide range of couples, including poor, unmarried parents. Florida decreased the fee for a marriage license, along with the waiting period between obtaining a license and getting married, for couples who have taken a premarital education course. Florida also requires all high school students to take a course on marriage skills. In Arizona, Florida, and Utah, couples are given marriage materials (booklets or videos) that include information on how to build strong marriages, the effects of divorce on children, and available community resources. (See Parke & Ooms, 2002, for details on these policies.) Studies to assess the effectiveness of these interventions, however, have not been conducted.

Public Attitudes Toward Divorce

Contrary to trends in the 1960s and 1970s, American's attitudes toward divorce were less positive at the end of the 20th century. Two national surveys, one carried out in 1980 (Booth, Johnson, White, & Edwards, 1981) and the other carried out in 2000 (Amato, Johnson, Booth, & Rogers,

2003), provide the latest information on this issue. These two independent samples each involved about 2,000 married individuals. Agreement with the statement "Couples are able to get divorced too easily today" increased from 33% in 1980 to 47% in 2000. Correspondingly, agreement with the statement "The personal happiness of an individual is more important than putting up with a bad marriage" declined from 74% in 1980 to 64% in 2000. Overall, a scale based on these and other items (scored to reflect support for the norm of lifelong marriage) increased by more than one third of a standard deviation during this 20-year period. This strengthening of attitudes in support of lifelong marriage was apparent for wives as well as husbands.

Despite this shift in attitudes, it would be a mistake to assume that the American public is against divorce. Instead, people appear to be deeply ambivalent. For example, in the 2000 survey (Amato et al., 2003), only a minority of people (17%) agreed with the statement "It's okay for people to get married thinking that if it does not work out, they can always get a divorce." But at the same time, as noted earlier, the majority of people believe that personal happiness is more important than remaining in an unhappy marriage. Similarly, a poll by Time Magazine in 2000 found that 66% of people believed that children are better off after "a divorce in which the parents are more happy" than in "an unhappy marriage in which parents stay together mainly for the kids." At the same time, however, 64% of people believed that children always or frequently are harmed when parents get divorced (Kirn, 2000).

Social Scientific Research on Children and Divorce

During the last decade of the 20th century, research on divorce became considerably more sophisticated. Compared with studies in prior decades, studies conducted in the 1990s were more likely to rely on large, randomly selected samples; to employ control variables to decrease the likelihood of observing spurious associations; to use psychometrically sound measures; and to include multiple indicators of child outcomes (see Amato, 2001, for a review). These methodological improvements were made possible partly by the public release of large, federally funded, longitudinal studies of families, such as the National Survey of Families and Households, the National Longitudinal Survey of Youth (Mother and Child Supplement), and the National Adolescent Health Study. The availability of these data sets made it possible for researchers to employ multiple respondents and multiple waves of data and to design studies in which children are assessed before as well as after parental divorce. (Although some large data sets, such as the National Survey of Children, were collected as early as the 1970s, this was the exception rather than the rule.) The widespread use of new statistical methods, such as structural equation modeling, pooled time-series analysis, growth curve analysis, and hierarchical linear modeling, complemented the availability of more complex and sophisticated data.

The scholarly literature on divorce since 1990 parallels, in certain respects, the increasing concern with marital stability—along with an increase in ambivalence—among policy makers and the general public. Some scholars argued, on the basis of research conducted mainly in the late 1980s and 1990s, that married individuals are healthier and happier than single individuals (see Waite, 1995, for a review). Similarly, scholars argued that children are better off in two-parent families than in divorced families (Popenoe, 1996; Wallerstein, Lewis, & Blakeslee, 2001). Other scholars contested this claim, arguing that research continues to reflect an unwarranted, ideologically driven bias in favor of marriage and traditional nuclear families (Coontz, 1992; Demo, 1992; Stacey, 1996). This debate became one of the central (and most interesting) features of family studies in the 1990s.

In the midst of this debate, a growing body of evidence suggested that the deficit perspective and the family pluralism perspective both represented simplified, one-sided accentuations of reality (Cherlin, 1999). One of the central assumptions of the pluralism perspective is that the negative effects of marital disruption on children are only temporary. Contrary to this assumption, however, studies since 1990 have demonstrated that parental divorce is associated with a variety of problems for adult offspring, including chronic psychological distress (Cherlin, Chase-Lansdale, & McRae, 1998), low socioeconomic attainment (McLanahan & Sandefur, 1994), seeing one's own marriage end in divorce (Bumpass, Martin, & Sweet, 1991), and having weak ties with parents (Amato & Booth, 1997). A second assumption is that the apparent "effects" of divorce are due to unmeasured variables, such as poverty or the disturbed family relationships that precede divorce. However, research in the 1990s demonstrated that the links between parental divorce and child problems persist even after parents' social class, parents' marital happiness, parents' personality characteristics, parents' attitudes and religiosity, and genetic factors are controlled for. Although it is possible that some as yet unmeasured factor is responsible for parental divorce as well as problems among children, most family scholars now agree that divorce has at least some negative implications for children (see Amato, 2000, for a review). A third assumption is that the effects of divorce on children have become weaker (or even nonexistent) as divorce has become more frequent. This assumption was called into question by a recent meta-analysis, which

indicated that the estimated effects of divorce on children were stronger (rather than weaker) in the 1990s than in the 1980s (Amato, 2001). Although the explanation for this increase is unclear, this finding indicates that the gap in well-being between children with divorced and continuously married parents is not likely to go away soon.

Now consider the family deficit perspective. The central assumption of this perspective is that deviations from the nuclear family result in serious problems for the great majority of children. Contrary to this assumption, however, the problems associated with divorce do not appear to be shared by all—or even most—children. For example, Hetherington (Hetherington & Kelly, 2002), in summarizing nearly 30 years of results from her longitudinal studies, estimated that 20% to 25% of children with divorced parents reach adulthood with significant problems in psychological or social functioning, compared with about 10% of children with continuously married parents. Similarly, Amato (in press) estimated that parental divorce leads about 10% of offspring to have lower levels of psychological well-being in adulthood than they would have had if their parents had remained married. These results suggest that although marital disruption results in long-term problems for a significant minority of children, it does not condemn the majority of children to a lifetime of misery.

Given the limitations of these two perspectives, most studies published in the 1990s have focused not on whether divorce is harmful for children but on the mechanisms through which divorce affects children, as well as the circumstances under which divorce can have harmful, neutral, or positive consequences for children. A large number of studies have shown that divorce affects children through a few key mechanisms: (a) The stress of divorce tends to disrupt the quality of parenting from custodial parents; (b) living in a single-parent household often undermines the quality of relations with noncustodial parents; (c) divorce typically is followed by a decline in household income; (d) divorce tends to exacerbate conflict between parents, causing many children to feel "caught in the middle" between warring parents; and (e) divorce frequently is followed by other stressful events for children, such as moving, parental remarriage (which children often oppose), and additional parental divorces. Other studies show that protective factors (such as social support from peers, close relationships with grandparents and other involved adults, active coping styles on the part of children, and the availability of therapeutic interventions) can buffer the negative effects of divorce (see Amato, 2000, for a review).

The delineation of these mechanisms helps us to understand why the consequences of divorce vary from one child to the next. For example, when divorce is followed by inept parenting on the part of the custodial parent, a loss of contact with the noncustodial parent, a substantial decline in household income, additional conflict between parents, and a period of residential instability, then divorce is likely to have harmful effects on children. In contrast, when divorce is followed by authoritative parenting on the part of the custodial parent, a close relationship with the noncustodial parent, little or no decline in household income, a cooperative relationship between parents, and few additional stressful transitions, then divorce is likely to have minimal effects on children. When divorce is followed by a mix of these circumstances, then divorce is likely to have mixed effects on children as well.

Another line of research is pertinent to this issue. A series of studies have shown that when parents exhibit high levels of chronic, overt conflict (frequent loud arguments, expressions of hostility, and violence), children are better off, in the long run, if parents

divorce rather than remain married. If parents exhibit relatively little overt conflict, however, then children are better off if parents remain married, even if parents are dissatisfied with the relationship (Booth & Amato, 2001; Hanson, 1999; Jekielek, 1998). These studies are of interest because they reveal conditions under which divorce is a better alternative for children than remaining in a two-parent family. Using longitudinal data, Amato (2002) estimated that about 40% of marriages that end in divorce fit this pattern.

Overall, research in 1990 led to a growing consensus among family scholars—a consensus that represents a middle ground between those who view divorce as being a catastrophic event (the deficit perspective) and those who view divorce as a relatively benign, transitory event (the pluralism perspective). This emerging perspective—which I refer to as a *contingency perspective*—sees divorce as a stressor and a risk factor for subsequent academic, behavioral, emotional, and social problems. However, depending on family circumstances before and after divorce, and depending on the presence of a variety of protective factors in children's environments, divorce may be harmful or benign to children (Amato, 2000). Moreover, research in the 1990s consistently demonstrated that children do best when they grow up with two happily *and* continuously married parents (Amato & Booth, 1997; Cherlin, 1999; Hetherington & Kelly, 2002). Consequently, it is necessary to take into account family structure (divorce) as well as family process (the quality of family relationships) to understand children's long-term development and well-being. In this sense, the contingency perspective of the 1990s represented a synthesis of the earlier deficit and pluralism perspectives.

Proponents of this new perspective value the benefits of marriage and are wary of the risks associated with divorce, but they also recognize that some marriages are harmful and some divorces are beneficial. This perspective is congruent with social trends in the 1990s—a decade in which divorce rates declined modestly, policy interventions attempted to improve marital quality and stability, and public attitudes became increasingly supportive of the norm of lifelong marriage (but also continued to value the freedom to leave troubled marriages). The dissemination of research findings on the value of strong marriages for children and adults may have influenced public attitudes toward divorce and helped to propel legislative changes to support marriage. At the same time, the growing respect for marriage and the declining status of divorce in the popular culture and in political circles made it easier for family scholars to combine ideas from the deficit and pluralism models into a new synthesis.

FUTURE TRENDS

During the 20th century, the frequency of divorce, the legal regulation of divorce, the public's view of divorce, and social scientific conclusions about divorce changed in ways that were consistent and mutually reinforcing. Before the 1960s, divorce was relatively uncommon, laws in every state made it difficult to divorce, and the general public disapproved of divorce. Correspondingly, most social scientists believed that divorce was harmful to children, and they viewed the increase in divorce as a serious problem. During the 1960s, 1970s, and 1980s, the divorce rate increased dramatically, the legal system made divorce easier to obtain, and the general public became more accepting of divorce. These changes created a context within which family scholars could move beyond the limitations of the deficit model and see marital dissolution in a more favorable light. In the 1990s, the divorce rate

declined, state governments enacted programs to strengthen marriage, and support for the norm of lifelong marriage increased among the public. Correspondingly, research in the 1990s repeatedly demonstrated that divorce can be harmful under some circumstances and that children develop best when they grow up with two continuously and happily married parents. It is difficult to predict the next stage of social change, but it seems likely that the present period will continue for some time, as social scientists, legislators, the media, and the general public continue to sort out the roles of marriage and divorce in the American family system.

Where is research on children and divorce headed? Two improvements seem likely. First, future research will become more sophisticated methodologically. The growing availability of national, longitudinal studies of children and families, innovations in statistical modeling, and the development of new measurement techniques will provide a clearer understanding of how marital dissolution affects children over the life course. Second, future research will become more sophisticated theoretically. Most scholars now recognize that asking whether divorce harms of helps children is too simple a question. Instead, future research will make progress in delineating the mechanisms through which divorce affects children and in specifying the conditions under which marital disruption has varied consequences for children. Moreover, an increasing percentage of children are born outside marriage—mainly to parents who are either cohabiting or in romantic relationships. Because most of these parents are poor, and because these parents are at high risk for relationship dissolution, researchers refer to these unions as "fragile families" (McLanahan, Garfinkel, Reichman, & Teitler, 2002). Yet we know little about how these informal family arrangements affect children. In keeping with new demographic realities, future researchers will need to broaden their conceptual and operational definitions of "two-parent families" and "divorce" if they are to understand how these trends are shaping children's lives.

In conclusion, social research does not take place in a cultural and historical vacuum. Instead, family scholarship both shapes and is shaped by events and processes in the larger society. This conclusion does not mean that social research is incapable of generating objective, factual knowledge. Indeed, family research has provided a great deal of useful information about the circumstances under which divorce disadvantages children. Instead, this conclusion indicates that family scholars draw on current worldviews to challenge, refine, and synthesize the knowledge and perspectives of the past. Social scientific information about families should be seen, not as something independent of culture and history, but as part of our culture and history.

REFERENCES

Amato, P. R. (2000). Consequences of divorce for adults and children. *Journal of Marriage and the Family, 62,* 1269–1287.

Amato, P. R. (2001). Children of divorce in the 1990s: An update of the Amato and Keith (1991) meta-analysis. *Journal of Family Psychology, 15,* 355–370.

Amato, P. R. (2002). Good enough marriages: Parental discord, divorce, and children's well-being. *Virginia Journal of Social Policy and the Law, 9,* 71–94.

Amato, P. R. (In press). Resolving divergent perspectives: Judith Wallerstein, quantitative family research, and children of divorce. *Family Relations.*

Amato, P. R., & Booth, A. (1997). *A generation at risk: Growing up in an era of family upheaval.* Cambridge, MA: Harvard University Press.

Amato, P. R., Johnson, D., Booth, A., & Rogers, S. J. (2003). Continuity and change in marriage between 1980 and 2000. *Journal of Marriage and Family, 65,* 1–22.

Amato, P. R., & Keith, B. (1991). Consequences of parental divorce for children's well-being: A meta-analysis. *Psychological Bulletin, 110,* 26–46.

Bellah, R. N., Madsen, R., Sullivan, W. M., Swidler, A., & Tipton, S. M. (1985). *Habits of the heart: Individualism and commitment in American life.* New York: Harper & Row.

Blankenhorn, D., Bayme, S., & Elshtain, J. B. (Eds.). (1990). *Rebuilding the nest: A new commitment to the American family.* Milwaukee, WI: Family Service Association.

Booth, A., & Amato, P. R. (2001). Parental predivorce relations and offspring postdivorce well-being. *Journal of Marriage and Family, 63,* 197–212.

Booth, A., Johnson, D. R., White, L. K., & Edwards, J. (1981). *Female labor force participation and marital instability: Methodology report.* Lincoln: University of Nebraska-Lincoln, Bureau of Sociological Research.

Bumpass, L. L, Martin, T. C., & Sweet, J. A. (1991). The impact of family background and early marital factors on marital disruption. *Journal of Family Issues, 12,* 22–42.

Burgess, E. W., & Cottrell, L. S. (1939). *Predicting success or failure in marriage.* New York: Prentice Hall.

Burgess, E. W., & Locke, H. J. (1945). *The family: From institution to companionship.* New York: American Book.

Cherlin, A. J. (1992). *Marriage, divorce, remarriage.* Cambridge, MA: Harvard University Press.

Cherlin, A. J. (1999). Going to extremes: Family structure, children's well-being, and social science. *Demography, 36*, 421–428.

Cherlin, A. J., Chase-Lansdale, P. L., & McRae, C. (1998). Effects of divorce on mental health throughout the life course. *American Sociological Review 63*, 239–249.

Coontz, S. (1992). *The way we never were: American families and the nostalgia trap*. New York: Basic Books.

Council on Families in America. (1995). *Marriage in America: A report to the nation*. New York: Institute for American Values.

Crouch, J. (2002). Divorce reform page: Laws and legislation. Retrieved from the Crouch & Crouch Web site: http://patriot.net/~crouch/divorce.html.

Demo, D. H. (1992). Parent-child relations: Assessing recent changes. *Journal of Marriage and the Family, 54*, 104–117.

Demo, D. H., & Acock, A. C. (1988). The impact of divorce on children. *Journal of Marriage and the Family, 50*, 619–648.

Emery, R. (1982). Interparental conflict and the children of discord and divorce. *Psychological Bulletin, 92*, 310–330.

Emery, R. (1988). *Marriage, divorce, and children's adjustment*. Thousand Oaks, CA: Sage.

Furstenberg, F. F., & Cherlin, A. J. (1991). *Divided families: What happens to children when parents part*. Cambridge, MA: Harvard University Press.

Glendon, M. A. (1989). *The transformation of family law: State, law, and family in the United States and western Europe*. Chicago: University of Chicago Press.

Glenn, N. D. (1999). Further discussion of the effects of no-fault divorce on divorce rates. *Journal of Marriage and the Family, 61*, 800–802.

Glueck, S., & Glueck, E. (1962). *Family environment and delinquency*. Boston: Houghton Mifflin.

Groves, E. R. (1928). *The marriage crisis*. New York: Longman, Green.

Guidobaldi, J., Cleminshaw, H. K., Perry, J. D., & McLaughlin, C. S. (1983). The impact of parental divorce on children: Report of the Nationwide NASP study. *School Psychology Review, 12*, 300–323.

Guidobaldi, J., Perry, J. D., & Nastasi, B. K. (1987). Growing up in a divorced family: Initial and long-term perspectives on children's adjustment. In S. Oskamp (Ed.), *Applied social psychology annual: Vol. 7. Family processes and problems* (pp. 202–237). Newbury Park, CA: Sage.

Hanson, T. L. (1999). Does parental conflict explain why divorce is negatively associated with child welfare? *Social Forces, 77*, 1283–1316.

Heaton, T. B. (2002). Factors contributing to increasing marital stability in the U.S. *Journal of Family Issues, 23*, 392–409.

Herzog, E., & Sudia, C. E. (1973). Children in fatherless families. In B. Caldwell & H. N. Ricciuti (Eds.), *Review of child development research* (Vol. 3, pp. 141–232). Chicago: University of Chicago Press.

Hetherington, E. M. (1979). Divorce: A child's perspective. *American Psychologist, 34*, 851–858.

Hetherington, E. M., Cox, M., & Cox, R. (1982). Effects of divorce on parents and children. In M. Lamb (Ed.), *Nontraditional families* (pp. 233–288). Hillsdale, NJ: Lawrence Erlbaum.

Hetherington, E. M., & Kelly, J. (2002). *For better or worse: Divorce reconsidered*. New York: Norton.

Jekielek, S. M. (1998). Parental conflict, marital disruption and children's emotional well-being. *Social Forces, 76*, 905–935.

Katz, S. N. (1994). Historical perspective and current trends in the legal process of divorce. *Future of Children, 4*, 44–62.

Kirn, W. (2000, September 25). Should you stay together for the kids? *Time Magazine, 156*, 75–82.

Kitson, G. C. (1992). *Portrait of divorce: Adjustment to marital breakdown.* New York: Guilford.

Kurdek, L. A. & Berg, B. (1983). Correlates of children's adjustment to their parents' divorce. In L. A. Kurdek (Ed.), *Children and divorce* (pp. 47–60). San Francisco: Jossey-Bass.

Long, B. (1986). Parental discord vs. family structure: Effects of divorce on the self-esteem of daughters. *Journal of Youth and Adolescence, 15,* 19–27.

Marotz-Baden, R., Adams, G. R., Buech, N., Munro, B., & Munro, G. (1979, January). Family form or family process? Reconsidering the deficit family model approach. *Family Coordinator,* pp. 5–14.

McDermott, J. F. (1970). Divorce and its psychiatric sequelae in children. *Archives of General Psychiatry, 23,* 421–427.

McLanahan, S., Garfinkel, I., Reichman, N. E., & Teitler, J. O. (2002). Unwed parents or fragile families? Implications for welfare and child support policy. In L. L. Wu & B. Wolfe (Eds.), *Out of wedlock: Causes and consequences of non-marital fertility* (pp. 202–228). New York: Russell Sage.

McLanahan, S., & Sandefur, F. (1994). *Growing up in a single-parent family: What helps, what hurts.* Cambridge, MA: Harvard University Press.

Mintz, S., & Kellogg, S. (1989). *Domestic revolutions: A social history of American family life.* New York: Free Press.

Mowrer, E. R. (1927). *Family disorganization.* Chicago: University of Chicago Press.

Ooms, T. (2002, August). *Marriage and government: Strange bedfellows?* (Policy Brief, Couples and Marriage Series, No. 1). Washington, DC: Center for Law and Social Policy.

Parke, M., & Ooms, T. (2002, October). *More than a dating service? State activities designed to strengthen and promote marriage* (Policy Brief, Couples and Marriage Series, No. 2). Washington, DC: Center for Law and Social Policy.

Parkman, A. M. (2000). *Good intentions gone awry: No-fault divorce and the American family.* Lanham, MD: Rowman & Littlefield.

Popenoe, D. (1996). *Life without father: Compelling new evidence that fatherhood and marriage are indispensable for the good of children and society.* New York: Martin Kessler.

Preston, S. H., & McDonald, J. (1979). The incidence of divorce within cohorts of American marriages contracted since the Civil War. *Demography, 16,* 1–25.

Rothstein, B. (2002, April 10). Marital strife: Do the voters really care? *The Hill.* Retrieved July 8, 2003, from www.hillnews.com/041002/marital.aspx.

Sanchez, L., Nock, S. L., Wright, J .D., Pardee, J. W., & Ionescu, M. (2001). The implementation of covenant marriage in Louisiana. *Virginia Journal of Social Policy and the Law, 23,* 192–223.

Schwartz, L. A. (1999). Divorce options [Pennsylvania]. Retrieved July 8, 2003, from the DivorceNet Web site: www.divorcenet.com/pa/pa-art15.html.

Stacey, J. (1996). *In the name of the family: Rethinking family values in the postmodern age.* Boston: Beacon.

Stekel, W. (1931). *Marriage at the crossroads.* New York: W. Godwin.

Terman, L. M. (1938). *Psychological factors in marital happiness.* New York: McGraw-Hill.

Thompson, R. A., & Wyatt, J. M. (1999). Values, policy, and research on divorce. In R. A. Thompson & P. R. Amato (Eds.), *The postdivorce family: Children, parenting, and society* (pp. 191–232). Thousand Oaks, CA: Sage.

Thornton, A., & Young-DeMarco, L. (2001). Four decades of trends in attitudes toward family issues in the United States: The 1960s through the 1990s. *Journal of Marriage and Family, 63,* 1009–1037.

Vlosky, D. A., & Monroe, P. A. (2002). The effective dates of no-fault divorce laws in the 50 states. *Family Relations, 51,* 317–324.

Waite, L. J. (1995). Does marriage matter? *Demography, 32,* 483–507.

Wallerstein, J. S., & Blakeslee, S. (1989). *Second chances: Men, women, and children a decade after divorce.* New York: Ticknor & Fields.

Wallerstein, J. S., & Kelly, J. B. (1980). *Surviving the breakup: How children and parents cope with divorce.* New York: Basic Books.

Wallerstein, J. S., Lewis, J. M., & Blakeslee, S. (2001). *The unexpected legacy of divorce: A 25 year landmark study.* New York: Hyperion.

CHAPTER 16

Single-Parent Families
Risks, Resilience, and Change

MICHELE T. MARTIN, ROBERT E.
EMERY, AND TARA S. PERIS

T he past 40 years have witnessed profound changes in the structure of American families. Single-parent families in particular have proliferated due to dramatic increases in divorce (see Chapter 15 of this book), nonmarital childbearing, and cohabitation (see Chapter 4 of this book), sparking vigorous debate about the consequences these family structures may have for children. Despite myriad efforts to understand this phenomenon, both from a policy standpoint and from a psychological perspective, findings have been largely inconsistent (Demo & Cox, 2000; Lipman, Boyle, Dooley, & Offord, 2002). In this chapter, we review key findings regarding outcomes for children raised in single-parent families, calling attention to their subtle but psychologically important responses. We then consider several factors that may contribute to these outcomes and discuss methodological and theoretical issues inherent to work in this area as well as how they might be addressed in future research.

CHANGES IN AMERICAN FAMILIES

Interest in single-parent families and their influence on children stems both from the increased occurrence of these households and from evidence that youth in these homes may be exposed to numerous environmental stressors that place them at risk for subsequent poor outcomes. Indeed, single-parent homes headed by women account for approximately 18% of all American families, with nearly half of these households living below the poverty level (Federal Interagency Forum on Child and Family Statistics (FIFCFS, 2000; see also Chapter 27 of this book). Further, these trends are evident cross-culturally, with nearly half of all white children and two thirds of black children likely to live in single-parent households at some point in their childhoods (Teachman, Tedrow, & Crowder, 2000). In the context of these staggering statistics, however, an equally important issue pertains to the mechanisms by which single-parent households emerge. In this section, we briefly consider demographic changes in divorce, nonmarital childbearing, and cohabitation as important contributing factors.

The prevalence of divorce is well documented, with over 40% of children born in married households expected to experience their parents' divorce (Schoen & Standish, 2000). Further, about one third of all births in the United States occur outside marriage, including 25.7% of all births to white mothers, 40.9% of births to Hispanic mothers, and 69.8% of births to African American mothers in 1996 (Ventura, Peters, Martin, & Maurer, 1997). In addition, although rates of teen pregnancy have declined somewhat in recent years, they nearly quadrupled between the 1960s and the early 1990s (Hogan, Sun, & Cornwell, 2000), thereby serving (in many cases) to create a generation of single-parent households. Similarly, rates of cohabitation have increased dramatically, with 25% to 50% of nonmarital childbirths involving children born to cohabiting parents (see Chapter 4 of this book). Although research on these families is just beginning to emerge, preliminary evidence suggests that they may be more fragile (Manning & Smock, 2002) and thus more likely to result in single-parent households. Collectively, these rapid shifts in family structure have converged to produce an increasing number of single-parent families.

The proliferation of one-parent households has in turn generated heated and often polemical debate about the consequences these family environments may hold fo children. Specifically, although some researchers raise strong concerns about the well-being of children in single-parent families (e.g., Popenoe, 1993; Wallerstein, Lewis, & Blakeslee, 2002), others argue vehemently in support of children's adaptability to changing families (e.g., Demo, 1993). In this chapter, we take the position that the best evidence does not suggest that the truth lies in between these two extremes. Rather, the best research implies the need for a more nuanced approach to understanding the consequences of divorce and nonmarital childbearing for children. As we have argued elsewhere, we must at once recognize that (a) children in single-parent families face many challenging economic and family stressors; (b) despite the stress, the great majority of these children demonstrate considerable psychological resilience; (c) even many resilient children report painful feelings and memories about their growing-up experiences; and (d) many of the putative effects of single-parent families are, in fact, partially attributable to nonrandom selection, including selection influenced by correlated genetic factors (Emery, 1999; Emery, Waldron, Kitzmann, & Aaron, 1999; Laumann-Billings & Emery, 2000). As the literature on single-parent families is vast, our focus here is on the overarching pattern of findings that has emerged in the past 30 years. Further, because the great majority of children—over 80%—live with their single mothers, and because research in this area refers largely to female-headed households (Emery, 1998), we focus primarily on single-mother families. Finally, as the death of a parent may carry its own unique risks for child well-being, we use the term *single-parent family* to refer to situations in which both parents are living but only one remains in the home.

THE FUNCTIONING AND WELL-BEING OF CHILDREN FROM SINGLE-PARENT FAMILIES

The risks that accrue to children in single-parent homes are well documented (Ackerman, D'Eramo, Umylny, Schultz, & Izard, 2001; Lipman et al., 2002). Indeed, much of the research on single-parent households has focused on the link between single-parent families and poor outcomes for children, indicating that children in these households may experience an array of problematic behaviors. In the following section, we summarize findings pertaining to child behavior problems in both the internalizing and externalizing spectra, outcomes related to academic competence, and teen pregnancy. Further, as there is evidence that the risks associated with life in a single-parent home may persist into adulthood, we extend this discussion to include outcomes related to mental health and relationship stability in adulthood. Critically, we note that most children are psychologically resilient, as documented by the absence of any of these difficulties. At the same time, however, we suggest that the absence of a psychological disorder is not the same as the absence of psychological distress, and we use this distinction as a springboard to elaborate upon methodological issues related to the assessment of child well-being.

Externalizing and Internalizing Behavior Problems

Of all of children's psychological problems, parents' marital status is most consistently and strongly associated with an increased risk for externalizing behavior (Amato & Keith, 1991b; Emery, 1982; Patterson, De Baryshe, & Ramsey, 1989). This pattern of findings, although often more pronounced for boys than for girls (Ackerman et al., 2001; Hetherington & Stanley-Hagan, 1999), has emerged cross-culturally and in studies employing a range of methodological designs. For example, in their intensive, multimethod study of a nonclinic sample of 4- to 6-year-olds, Hetherington, Cox, and Cox (1978) found that children from divorced families were disobedient, aggressive, demanding, and lacking in self-control compared to children in married-parent families. Findings such as these have also been replicated in large national studies conducted in both

Britain and the United States and have been shown to persist into adolescence (Mott, Kowaleski-Jones, & Menaghan, 1997; Peterson & Zill, 1986). Moreover, they are not limited to studies of divorce but have been repeatedly borne out in research more broadly examining the impact of single-parent families on child well-being (Ackerman et al., 2001).

Research is much more equivocal in establishing single-parent status as a risk factor for children's internalizing problems, such as depression, anxiety, and low self-esteem (Amato & Keith, 1991b). For example, a recent study found no difference in children's depression between single-parent and two-parent families after family process variables were controlled (Lansford, Ceballo, Abbey, & Stewart, 2001). Hypothesized impairments in self-concept also have been studied, but differences typically are small in magnitude and not statistically significant (Amato & Keith, 1991b; Barber & Eccles, 1992). A similarly inconsistent pattern exists with regard to the link between family structure and child anxiety disorders (Dunn, O'Connor, & Levy, 2002; Tweed, Schoenbach, George, & Blazer, 1989).

Academic Competence

Divorce and single parenthood are associated with worse performance on a variety of academic measures (Kurdek, Fine, & Sinclair, 1995; McLanahan & Sandefur, 1994; Zill, 1995). However, one methodological difficulty in this area has been that of distinguishing among different domains of academic outcome, with differing results emerging with regard to (a) standardized test scores, (b) grades and related indicators of performance in school, (c) various measures of misconduct in school, and (d) school completion and educational attainment.

Family structure differences on standardized test scores and school grades, although often statistically significant, are typically quite small in magnitude and may diminish when confounding environmental stressors (e.g., poverty) are carefully controlled (Zimiles & Lee, 1991). More substantial differences commonly are found on indices of misbehavior in school. In fact, one direct comparison of the three categories of school outcomes found effect sizes ranging from 0.10 to 0.20 standard deviation units for standardized test scores, 0.15 to 0.28 standard deviation units for GPA, and 0.20 to 0.36 standard deviation units for misbehavior (Zill, 1995). However, the largest and most meaningful differences associated with family status relate to school completion and educational attainment (Amato & Keith, 1991a). Numerous studies have documented that children from single-parent households are about twice as likely to drop out of school as children from married families across national samples, ethnic groups, and divorced versus never-married families and with socioeconomic status controlled for (McLanahan & Sandefur, 1994).

Teen Pregnancy

Although there is considerable support for the link between single-parent family status and teen pregnancy (Davis & Friel, 2001), the most compelling findings in this area come from work by McLanahan and Sandefur (1994). Specifically, their work analyzed data from five different national surveys and found that single parenthood was linked with a significant and substantial increased risk of teen pregnancy. Risk was slightly higher for children from never-married versus divorced families, but nevertheless children from divorced families were about twice as likely as children from married families to have a teen childbirth.

Children's Resilience

Although research has often focused on psychological problems, most children who experience living in a single-parent family do *not* get pregnant, drop out of school, or require treatment from a mental health professional. For example, Zill, Morrison, and Coiro (1993) found that twice as many 12- to 16-year-old children from divorced as married families received psychological counseling in their national sample of children: 21% versus 11%. However, this means that 79% of 12- to 16-year-old children from divorced families (versus 89% from married families) had coped with their parents' divorce without receiving psychological help. Similar results emerge when one computes the inverse of risk in other prominent studies (e.g., McLanahan & Sandefur, 1994). Such evidence is an important reminder that most children are resilient in coping. Thus, it seems clear that the majority of children from single-parent families proceed along a relatively healthy child development trajectory as measured by key indicators of their academic, social, and psychological adjustment.

Psychological Distress or Pain

It is important to stress, however, that resilience is not the same as invulnerability; rather, resilience implies that children may bounce back from the stress of living in a single-parent family. In many cases, children may experience psychological difficulties that do not meet clinical criteria but are problematic nonetheless. For example, marital transitions can lead to difficult feelings and worries among children, even when these feelings are not severe enough to warrant a clinical diagnosis. Kurdek and Berg (1987) reported that, among a sample of children whose parents had been separated an average of 17 months, more than 40% agreed that "I can make my parents unhappy with each other by what I say or do." Similarly, Laumann-Billings and Emery (2000) found that many of 99 well-functioning, resilient young adults from divorced families still reported painful feelings. For example, 49% said that they worried about big events like graduations or weddings when both of their parents would be there; 48% felt that they had a harder childhood than most other people; 44% said that their parents' divorce still caused struggles for them; and 28% wondered if their father even loved them. Feelings of responsibility, guilt, and painful memories are psychologically important and can be difficult for children to cope with even if they do not lead to depression. In fact, we suspect that the high levels of pain may help to account for some of the different conclusions about the consequences of single parenting reached by clinicians and researchers. Researchers focus on children's resilience, namely the absence of psychological problems found among most children from divorced and single-parent families (despite the increased risk). Clinicians note the emotional struggles often reported even by resilient children who have coped successfully with stress. Although little work to date has examined subclinical distress as it specifically relates to single-parent family status, we contend that this is an important area for future research and one that might be well suited to addressing previous patterns of inconsistent findings with regard to child outcome (e.g., internalizing behaviors).

Social Competence

Relatively little research has focused on the adaptive skills of children from single-parent families. Growing up in a single-parent family may disrupt the development of prosocial skills, or the converse may be true. For some children, divorce may promote positive development such as a greater sense of personal responsibility, self-esteem, and more gender-neutral attitudes and aspirations (Barber & Eccles, 1992). In this regard, Robert Weiss (1979) has suggested that divorce makes children grow up a little faster. Because of increased family demands, as well as changes in the family's authority structure, children in single-parent families may have to assume responsibilities at an earlier age than their peers. This may cause them to become precociously competent in social and practical matters (Barber & Eccles, 1992; Weiss, 1979).

A study of a nonclinic sample of children living in two-parent families is suggestive in this regard (Block, Block, & Morrison, 1981). In this longitudinal study, a measure of parental agreement over child-rearing practices completed when children were 3 years old predicted lower levels of aggression in school among boys at ages 3, 4, and 7, but agreement tended to be associated with *higher* levels of externalizing among girls. In fact, higher levels of *disagreement* predicted some *increases* in social competence among the girls but not among boys (e.g., empathic relatedness, resourcefulness, protectiveness of others). When parents fight, girls may be more likely to respond to the stress with increased prosocial behavior, whereas boys may be more likely to respond with increased aggression and noncompliance.

Although intuitively appealing, such an interpretation is speculative. Despite some astute observation, the increased social competence assertion has yet to be adequately documented (Barber & Eccles, 1992). Moreover, if increased maturity is found among children whose parents have divorced, it is not clear whether this is a desirable outcome. The words *increased maturity* have favorable connotations, but demands for early competence may deprive children of the opportunity to engage in activities that have less immediate benefit but serve them well in the long run. Although the issue of increased or perhaps exaggerated social competence is still open to question, one issue seems increasingly clear. Asking children to perform more adult instrumental duties may not hinder their healthy development. However, children who take on adult emotional responsibilities, in particular attempting to meet their parents' psychological needs, are more prone to depression during early adult life (Martin, 1995).

Adult Mental Health and Relationship Stability

A considerable body of research has linked growing up in a single-parent family with differences in adult psychological functioning. Studies using large, national samples have found a relationship between growing up in a single-parent family (due to death, divorce, or parents who never married) and depression in adulthood (Amato, 1991; Furstenberg & Teitler, 1994). Similarly, recent twin studies have found that parental loss (due to separation or death) is associated with increased risk for alcohol dependence and major depression in adulthood (Kendeler, Sheth, Gardner, & Prescott, 2002). On the whole, however, research tends to indicate that single-parent family status is more strongly related to social functioning in adulthood than to psychological disorders per se. In particular, research has linked living in a single-parent family with later differences in the quality of young adult romantic relationships. This link with premature or problematic intimate relationships is of growing interest as the children of the divorce boom cohort come of age. Interest is propelled by consistent evidence that children from divorced families are more likely to divorce themselves compared to adults who grew up in married families (Amato, 1996; Bumpass, Martin, & Sweet, 1991). Estimates vary across studies and ethnic groups (weaker transmission effects sometimes are reported for blacks: e.g., Haurin, 1992), but the increase is substantively important, typically ranging from a 25% to 50% increase in divorce risk. Although much

of the work in this area to date has focused on children of divorce, we suggest that growing up with only one parent (regardless of the reason) may have substantial implications for adult functioning in romantic relationships, and we underscore the need for further examination of the long-term consequences of being reared in a single-parent household.

FUNCTIONING IN SINGLE-PARENT FAMILIES

Although child adjustment has been more widely examined, research has increasingly focused on patterns of family interaction in single-parent households and on how these families may differ in their functioning from two-parent families. This line of research has faced the formidable challenge of untangling the effects of single-parent family status from the effects of the numerous other risk factors with which it is associated. From a methodological standpoint, careful examination of how these subtle, complex family dynamics mediate the link between family structure and child outcome will be essential in testing hypotheses about the specific influence of single-parent family status. Moreover, we note that many of these family stressors are important to children's well-being in their own right (e.g., economic hardship), regardless of their relationship to family structure or mental health measures.

Economic Strain

One of the most robust and striking differences between single-parent and dual-parent families is that single-parent families are more likely to be economically disadvantaged. Single-parent family status is strongly associated with poverty in the United States, nonmarital childbirth more so than divorce. In 2001, 28.6% of female-headed single-parent homes and 13% of male-headed single-parent households fell below the poverty level (U.S. Bureau of the Census, 2002). Further, single-parent family status explains a substantial proportion of racial differences in poverty. In 1995, for example, 43.2% of black children versus 16.6% of white children were living in poverty; much of the difference was attributable to the greater prevalence of single parenthood among blacks than whites. Among black children who lived with two parents, 14.8% fell below poverty cutoffs versus 61.6% who lived with a single mother. The comparable figures for white children were 9.9% for two parents and 44.2% for single mothers (U.S. Bureau of the Census, 1996).

Although both single mothers and fathers are more likely to experience financial strain than their counterparts in first-marriage households, on the whole, single mothers tend to fare worse in this regard. Hilton, Desrochers, and Devall (2001) reported that single fathers had better resources than single mothers, who tended to be less educated, maintain lower-status employment, and have fewer financial and social resources. In addition, economic strain may be particularly pronounced for teenage mothers, who have fewer social and economic supports and are at greater risk for psychological problems (Moffitt, 2002).

Economic hardship is a multifaceted stressor, and there is much to suggest that financial strain may negatively affect parents' psychological well-being, in turn undermining effective parenting (Mistry, Vandewater, Huston, & McLoyd, 2002). Recent work in this area has focused on the interplay between economic hardship, parental emotional distress, and parenting skills, suggesting that these family dynamics may mediate the effect of economic strain on child development (Conger et al., 2002). As each of these family process variables has been independently linked to poor child outcomes, an important task for future research is to address further patterns of bidirectional influence among these parental variables as well as their collective influence on child adjustment.

However, it is important to recognize that financial difficulties may also exert direct effects on children by causing them to have to move into marginal housing, lose contact with friends, attend inadequate schools, cope with their parents' worries about money, and face various threats to their physical safety, experiences that are taxing in their own right. Thus, economic strains have a substantial direct impact on children's adjustment, regardless of the family context in which they occur (Conger, Reuter, & Conger, 2000). In particular, financial hardship has been linked to a host of poor child outcomes, including behavioral and academic difficulty as well as cognitive and physical impairment (McLoyd, 1998). Moreover, adding statistical controls for income reduces differences between the adjustment of children in married and single-parent families by about half for academic measures like school attainment and by a lesser amount for internalizing and externalizing problems (Duncan & Brooks-Gunn, 1997; McLanahan, 2000; McLanahan & Sandefur, 1994).

Task Strain and Parenting

Single mothers report higher levels of life stress compared to women in two-parent homes and may often feel that they have to fulfill both parental roles to their children. In addition, they often have sole responsibility for all household tasks, while simultaneously juggling work and family demands (Heath & Orthner, 1999). These multiple roles can lead to considerable task strain. Examination of this parenting stress and how it is managed is particularly important in light of recent research indicating that parenting variables mediate the link between economic hardship and child well-being (Mistry et al., 2002), as well as other research indicating that family process variables may mediate the effects of family structure on child well-being (Lansford et al., 2001).

Men and women who are residential parents commonly experience strain in fulfilling tasks traditionally assumed by the opposite-gender parent (Chase-Lansdale & Hetherington, 1990; Luepnitz, 1982). In addition, they may have less time alone, which is often beneficial in buffering the transmission of negative emotion from parent to child (Larson & Gillman, 1999). As single parents are likely to be under more stress, this may affect how much energy, time, and focus they can direct toward parenting, including tasks of both affection and discipline. Moreover, their experience of negative emotion may serve to undermine their ability to parent effectively.

Hetherington's research (Hetherington, 1989; Hetherington, Cox, & Cox, 1982) has provided convincing evidence that single mothers demonstrate poorer parenting skills after marital separation than married mothers. They make fewer maturity demands, communicate less well, show less affection, and are less consistent and less effective in controlling their children. Boys in particular receive less positive feedback and more negative sanctions than daughters. These findings are critical, given research suggesting that the quality of parenting may account for much of the effect of family structure on child outcome (Amato & Fowler, 2002; Martinez & Forgatch, 2002), as well as findings indicating that ineffective parenting in single-parent homes is likely to persist and exacerbate over time (Loeber et al., 2000).

Affection and discipline, the two key domains of parenting, must be carefully negotiated in single-parent families (Emery, 1992, 1994; Emery & Tuer, 1993). Although increased closeness and affection often is a goal, some seemingly close relationships can be problematic. Some children in single-parent families assume inappropriate practical and perhaps emotional responsibilities (Hetherington & Kelly, 2000). One particular concern is that some seemingly close mother-child relationships may be a response to the parent's needs, not the child's. Teenagers are less well adjusted when they worry about and feel a need to take care of their parents (Buchanan, Maccoby, & Dornbusch, 1996). Emotional parentification also can be a special concern for younger children who appear to be well adjusted and responsible but who are judged as overburdened by clinicians (Byng-Hall, 2002; Johnston, 1990).

Family processes in father-headed single-parent households have not been studied often or in much detail, but many of the concerns of single mothers are surely shared by single fathers. Residential single fathers have fewer financial problems, but they struggle more with new parental and household responsibilities. Both male and female adolescents report feeling somewhat closer emotionally to their residential single mothers than their residential single fathers, although they report similar levels of parental control (Buchanan et al., 1996). Interestingly, authoritative parenting is associated with better child adjustment in father-residence families, but the relation is stronger in mother-residence families (Buchanan et al., 1996). These findings may be attributable either to selection factors or to difficulties in residential fathering. In either case, it appears that, on average, residential fathers have a few more problems with parenting than residential mothers.

Contact With Nonresidential Parent

Unfortunately, researchers consistently report a low amount of contact between nonresidential fathers and their children, on average (McLanahan & Carlson, 2002). In one of the more recent surveys, for example, approximately one third of divorced fathers saw their children only once or not at all in the past year. About 4 out of 10 fathers saw their children a few times a year up to three times a month, while about 25% saw them once a week or more (Seltzer, 1991). Contact is higher shortly after a marital separation, but it declines with time. In contrast to fathers, nonresidential mothers maintain somewhat greater contact with their children (Stewart, 1999). In one national survey, 30% of nonresidential mothers saw their children once a week or more (versus 25% of nonresidential fathers), and 42% of mothers (versus 55% of fathers) saw their children less than once a month to not at all (Zill, 1988). Furthermore, nonresidential mother-child contact may actually increase, not decrease, over time (Buchanan et al., 1996).

In general, research points to a reluctance of fathers to assume the single-parent role (Hamer & Marchioro, 2002), and thus the vast majority of studies in this area focus on nonresidential fathers. These fathers often have been described as Disneyland dads, and evidence does indicate that visiting fathers place less emphasis on discipline, chores, and schoolwork than fathers in two-parent families (Furstenberg & Nord, 1985). Visits normalize considerably over time, but divorced fathers continue to be less restrictive than married fathers (Hetherington et al., 1982). Compared to married fathers, adolescents rate divorced fathers as less involved, less democratic, and less consistent (Simons & Beaman, 1996). Further, recent evidence suggests that engaging in leisure activities with nonresident fathers as a form of parental involvement is not associated with increased child well-being (Stewart, 2003), underscoring the need for more substantive paternal involvement in children's lives.

Research on nonresident mothers remains scant and has produced relatively inconsistent findings. For example, there is evidence to suggest that children living with their fathers following paternal remarriage experience greater disruption in the mother-child relationship than children who live with their mothers following maternal remarriage (Aquilino, 1994). However, other studies suggest that children may have an easier time preserving the mother-child relationship than the father-child relationship (Clarke-Stewart & Hayward, 1996). In addition, recent work indicates that nonresident mothers and fathers may be similar in terms of how they interact with their children, with both parents more inclined to participate in leisure activities versus school and disciplinary activities (Stewart, 1999).

Is the quantity of contact or the quality of the nonresidential parent-child relationship associated with difficulties or enhancements in children's social, psychological, or academic functioning? A fair amount of research has been conducted on this topic in recent years, but the answer appears to be more complicated than the question. For example, one synopsis of the literature found 17 studies where better child adjustment was related to more father contact, 6 studies where better adjustment was associated with less contact, and 9 studies reporting no relation (Amato & Rezac, 1994).

The most likely explanation for the conflicting results is that a number of variables moderate the association between contact with the nonresidential parent and children's psychological adjustment. One likely moderator is the definition of frequent contact. In one widely cited study, the most frequent of four levels of contact included fathers who saw their children 25 times a year or more, an average of about 2 days per month (Furstenberg, Morgan, & Allison, 1987). Much more frequent contact, perhaps up to the level of joint physical custody, might be necessary to observe benefits in children's adjustment. Second, the consistency of visitation is another likely moderator, as inconsistent contact and missed visits may actually be harmful to children (Healy, Malley, & Stewart, 1990). Third, the quality of the nonresidential parent-child relationship is probably more important than the quantity of contact, as other research suggests (Barber, 1994; Clarke-Stewart & Hayward, 1996; Simons, Whitbeck, Beaman, & Conger, 1994). Fourth, and perhaps most important, frequent contact may be beneficial to children when interparental conflict is low but harmful when conflict is high (due to children's increased exposure to the conflict). Some research also supports this possibility (Amato & Rezac, 1994; Healy, Malley, & Stewart, 1990). Other research suggests that parental conflict is a better predictor of child well-being than is marital status (Demo & Acock, 1996; Vandewater & Lansford, 1998).

Creative Coping

Single-parent families have often found creative solutions in dealing with challenges of living. A frequent adaptation is the reliance on extended family networks, or kinship, to provide both practical and emotional support. George and Dickerson (1995) noted that sharing child care responsibilities among adult kin other than biological parents in African American families is a practice that can be traced to traditional African communities. Other extrafamilial resources that may provide support include day care personnel, teachers, and friends. Santrock and Warshak (1979) found that the amount of contact with adult caretakers outside the family (the noncustodial parent, babysitters, relatives, day care personnel) was positively related to a child's functioning following parental divorce. The quality of the contact would appear to be particularly important (Jenkins & Smith, 1990).

Coping with single parenthood when it is due to divorce or an ended cohabiting relationship often takes several years to achieve (Morrison & Cherlin, 1995). Feelings of success in adapting to single parenthood are linked with a number of qualities, such as relinquishing anger at the noncustodial parent; developing informal support networks, including professional counseling before problems get out of hand; relating to children without relying on them for emotional support; and attaining a sense of confidence and pride in managing one's family.

Marital Transitions

Single-parent families frequently undergo one or more marital or cohabiting transitions. These can take the form of legal marriages or, more often, cohabiting relationships. The remarriages or repartnerings are often temporary. In one national survey, 37% of children with a remarried parent later experienced a second divorce (Furstenberg, Peterson, Nord, & Zill, 1983).

Remarried families have fewer fixed assets, such as owning a home, than do first-marriage families (Thomson, 1994), but following remarriage single mothers regain disposable incomes comparable to their always-married counterparts (Duncan & Hoffman, 1985). Remarriage thus solves many financial problems created by divorce, and some have viewed it as a similar solution to other problems of divorced families. However, a growing body of research clearly indicates that remarriage is not a simple reconstitution of the two-parent family but is instead yet another difficult transition for biological parents, stepparents, and children (Booth & Dunn, 1994; Hetherington & Clingempeel, 1992).

On average, the combined benefits and costs of remarriage seem to about cancel each other out in terms of children's mental health. Children in remarried families exhibit about the same levels of psychological problems as do children living with single, divorced parents (Amato, 1994; Zill, 1988). As with divorce, however, there are considerable individual differences in children's adjustment to remarriage. Future research, especially prospective studies beginning before cohabitation, will be important in helping to untangle the impact of remarriage or repartnering on children.

Parents' Mental Health

Parents experiencing mental health problems are more likely to be single, and studies of adult mental health invariably find a link between marital status and psychopathology. Married or remarried adults have fewer mental health problems than single or divorced adults. In fact, marital status has been found to be a better predictor of adult mental health than age, race, socioeconomic status, or childhood experience (e.g., Gove, Hughes, & Styles, 1983).

Once again, however, the question arises as to whether the adult mental health problems are consequences of divorce or whether the parental problems predate and perhaps precipitate the divorce. The mental health problems that have been implicated most are depression, antisocial behavior, major mental illness such as schizophrenia or bipolar disorder, and personality disorders. Of these difficulties, depression has received the most attention. However, questions of cause and effect are basic in considering the relation between depression and divorce. Although a marital separation is likely to trigger or exacerbate grieving (Emery, 1994), it is not clear whether syndromal depression is better viewed as a consequence or a cause of marital discord and divorce (Fincham, Beach, Harold, & Osborne, 1997; Gotlib & McCabe, 1990). If adult depression causes divorce, depression is unlikely to (directly) explain adverse psychological adjustment among children from divorced families.

Even if parental depression is a consequence of divorce, research suggests that

parental conflict or marital status (Downey & Coyne, 1990; Emery, Weintraub, & Neale, 1982) or inadequate parenting (Simons & Johnson, 1996) is likely to mediate much of the link between parental depression and children's adjustment. Larson and Gillman (1999) found that negative emotions such as anxiety and anger are transmitted from single mothers to their adolescent children. Finally, it is obvious, though commonly overlooked, that genetic factors may contribute both to parental depression and to children's psychological problems, with divorce serving as an exacerbating or spurious variable.

ETHNICITY

Surely the most significant oversight in research on children and divorce is the relative absence of empirical research on the unique experiences of ethnic minorities. Research on national samples, which contain large number of minorities, generally has failed to find differences in the adjustment of white and black children from married versus divorced (or never-married or remarried) families (Fine, McKenry, Donnelly, & Voydanoff, 1992; McLanahan & Sandefur, 1994). One study, however, found that family structure was unrelated to psychosocial outcomes among African American adolescents (Salem, Zimmerman, & Notaro, 1998). Instead, their functioning was linked to living in a supportive, positive, and controlled family environment. Still, research examining different processes in ethnic minority families is sorely needed (McLoyd & Smith, 2002). For example, it has been suggested that extended family support buffers single African American mothers and their children from many of the strains of parenting alone (Wilson, 1989). However, some research with national samples suggests that kin support is neither widely available nor clearly beneficial to the adjustment of African American children (Jayakody, Chatters, & Taylor, 1993; McLanahan & Sandefur, 1994). Such negative evidence is far from conclusive, especially given the complexity and fluidity of the living arrangements of African American children (Dunifon & Kowaleski-Jones, 2002). Rather, it suggests that researchers need a better understanding of the experience of divorce among African Americans and other ethnic minorities before conceptual models of the consequences for children can be adequately tested.

METHODOLOGICAL AND THEORETICAL ISSUES

Although single-parent households are beginning to receive increased empirical scrutiny, salient methodological and conceptual issues remain (see Demo & Cox, 2000, for review). First, much of the work in this area to date has been largely atheoretical. For the most part, such research has worked from the premise that children in two-parent households benefit from ongoing exposure to both same-sex and opposite-sex role models and that transitions from one family structure to another (i.e., divorce/separation) are sources of stress and anxiety for children (Demo & Cox, 2000). However, theoretical models of how family structure per se affects child adjustment have yet to be specified. As with the literature on divorce, which has frequently indicated that family factors associated with marital disruption (e.g., marital conflict, family cohesiveness) may account for much of the link between divorce and poor child outcome, it is critical to consider relevant correlates of single-parent family status (many of which have been discussed above) that may serve to mediate its effects.

Closely related to this issue is the need for more dynamic analyses of familial interaction. By and large, studies of family structure have been somewhat static methodologically, relying on cross-sectional reports of marital status at a single time point and thus neglecting the complex patterns of interaction that unfold over time (Schrag, Peris, & Emery, 2003). Though instructive, this approach undermines the importance of continuity that may be provided by other caregivers in the home environment (e.g., siblings, grandparents) and fails to consider how the developmental timing of changes in family structure may influence child adjustment. Further, such research often groups children on the basis of two-parent versus single-parent family status alone, a choice that masks critical differences in family resources, education, and child adjustment within each of these groups. Again, we underscore the need for longitudinal examination of family processes associated with single-parent households and for careful consideration of potential mediator and moderator variables in examining links between family structure and child outcomes. Having considered the literature in this area, we turn now to a discussion of how these points might be integrated into future research.

FUTURE DIRECTIONS

Careful Measurement of Outcome

Different sampling and measurement strategies may differentially influence the conclusions of clinical and empirical experts. Clinicians commonly emphasize the negative consequences of divorce reported by children in therapy (e.g., Kalter, 1990; Wallerstein & Blakeslee, 1989), but clinicians can overlook the similar struggles faced by children from married families, the resilience of those not in treatment, or, indeed, the strengths of their own clients. In contrast, demographers often highlight the small differences found between children from divorced and married families in large, representative samples (e.g., Allison & Furstenberg, 1989), but they run the risk of inappropriately accepting the null hypothesis of no differences, a particular problem for large surveys with limited measurement. Finally, some controversy about the consequences of divorce can be traced to the political agendas not only of politicians but also of family scholars (see Amato, 1993, and replies; Popenoe, 1993, and replies).

Many of psychologists' empirical measures of children's psychological health are not especially sensitive to the subtleties of emotional experience. These measures often assess a global, concrete outcome, such as a parent's ratings of a child's behavior problems or the number of years in school a child completes. Clearly, parent-rated behavior problems and level of educational attainment are important indices of children's well-being. At the same time, the measures used in empirical research commonly assess children from the outside in: that is, from the perspective of adults. These objective measures may miss many of the concerns that are of emotional importance to children themselves, even among children who cope well on the outside despite their inner concerns.

Future studies should continue to work toward increased methodological sophistication. For example, conducting observational ratings of parenting behaviors may more accurately represent what the child experiences in terms of parenting than the parent's self-report of his or her parenting behaviors. Researchers should examine the quality of relationships rather than simply assessing family structure variables or the quantity of contact (Demo, Fine, & Ganong, 2000). In addition, future studies should continue to examine more specific interactional variables that may be mediators for the effects of living in single-parent families on children's adjustment.

Cohort Effects

As there have been such dramatic shifts in the numbers of children living in single-parent families, researchers should specifically examine cohort effects. Living in a single-parent family in this decade is likely to be a different experience than it was in the 1960s. Cohort effects may reflect decreasing social stigma and a decreasing sense of being different from other children. These changes may reduce negative impacts on children's functioning.

Behavior Genetics

Behavior genetics is a newly emerging field that is likely to contribute greatly to our understanding of human behavior. Genetically controlled personality characteristics may in part explain how growing up in a single-parent family is linked to certain outcomes. For example, people who graduate from high school or college have lower divorce rates than those who complete only part of either educational experience, suggesting that a personality characteristic may be linked both with completing school and remaining married (U.S. Bureau of the Census, 1992). Genetic influences contribute to divorce (McGue & Lykken, 1992), and intergenerational continuities can be explained as well by genes as by environments. Opponents of the genetic view can rightly argue that genes cannot account for cohort or cross-cultural differences in divorce rates. However, this argument does not preclude a genetic explanation. The normative threshold for single parenthood may be determined by (shifting) cultural standards, but individual differences—who becomes a single parent, given a set threshold—may be determined by one, probably several, genetically mediated personality characteristics and psychological disorders. Because of this important possibility, and the growing body of research indicating that gene-environment correlations do explain many putative environmental effects, it is essential that researchers use genetically informed designs in future studies of single parenting and of family influences more generally.

CONCLUSION

Research indicates that living in a single-parent family increases the risk for a number of negative outcomes for children. On average, children fare better in a two-parent family than in a single-parent family. At the same time, the great majority of children living in divorced and single-parent families function well despite the expected stress and sources of distress. Thus, it is important to recognize both the struggles and the strengths of single-parent families. We should be particularly cautious about labeling single parenthood as inevitably bad, lest we similarly label those segments of our society where single-parent families not only are common but represent a part of normative family life for the majority of children.

REFERENCES

Ackerman, B. P., D'Eramo, K. S., Umylny, L., Schultz, D., & Izard, C. E. (2001). Family structure and the externalizing behavior of children from economically disadvantaged families. *Journal of Family Psychology, 15,* 288–300.

Allison, P. D., & Furstenberg, F. F. (1989). How marital dissolution affects children: Variations by age and sex. *Developmental Psychology, 25,* 540–549.

Amato, P. R. (1991). Parental absence during childhood and depression in later life. *Sociological Quarterly, 32,* 543–556.

Amato, P. R. (1993). Children's adjustment to divorce: Theories, hypotheses, and empirical support. *Journal of Marriage and the Family, 55,* 23–38.

Amato, P. R. (1994). Father-child relations, mother-child relations, and offspring psychological well-being in early adulthood. *Journal of Marriage and the Family, 56,* 1031–1042.

Amato, P. R. (1996). Explaining the intergenerational transmission of divorce. *Journal of Marriage and the Family, 58,* 628–640.

Amato, P. R., & Fowler, F. (2002). Parenting practices, child adjustment, and family diversity. *Journal of Marriage and Family, 64,* 703–716.

Amato, P. R., & Keith, B. (1991a). Parental divorce and adult well-being: A meta-analysis. *Journal of Marriage and the Family, 53,* 43–58.

Amato, P. R., & Keith, B. (1991b). Parental divorce and the well-being of children: A meta-analysis. *Psychological Bulletin, 110,* 26–46.

Amato, P. R., & Rezac, S. J. (1994). Contact with nonresidential parents, interparental conflict, and children's behavior. *Journal of Family Issues, 15,* 191–207.

Aquilino, W. S. (1994). Impact of childhood family disruption on young adults' relationships with parents. *Journal of Marriage and the Family, 56,* 295–313.

Barber, B. L. (1994). Support and advice from married and divorced fathers: Linkages to adolescent adjustment. *Family Relations, 43,* 433–438.

Barber, B. L., & Eccles, J. S. (1992). Long-term influence of divorce and single parenting on adolescent family- and work-related values, behavior, and aspirations. *Psychological Bulletin, 111,* 108–126.

Block, J. H., Block, J., & Morrison, A. (1981). Parental agreement-disagreement on child-rearing orientations and gender-related personality correlates in children. *Child Development, 52,* 965–974.

Booth, A., & Dunn, J. (Eds.). (1994). Stepfamilies: Who benefits? Who does not? Hillsdale, NJ: Lawrence Erlbaum.

Buchanan, C. M., Maccoby, E. E., & Dornbusch, S. M. (1996). *Adolescents after divorce.* Cambridge, MA: Harvard University Press.

Bumpass, L. L., Martin, T. C., & Sweet, J. A. (1991). The impact of family background and early marital factors on marital disruption. *Journal of Family Issues, 12,* 22–42.

Byng-Hall, J. (2002). Relieving parentified children's burdens in families with insecure attachment patterns. *Family Process, 3,* 375–388.

Chase-Lansdale, P., & Hetherington, E. M. (1990). The impact of divorce on life-span development: Short and longterm effects. In P. B. Baltes, D. L. Featherman, & R. M. Lerner (Eds.), *Life-span development and behavior* (Vol. 10, pp. 107–151). Hillsdale, NJ: Lawrence Erlbaum.

Clarke-Stewart, K., & Hayward, C. (1996). Advantages of father custody and contact for the psychological well-being of school-age children. *Journal of Applied Developmental Psychology, 17,* 239–270.

Conger, K. J., Reuter, M. A., & Conger, R. D. (2000). The role of economic pressure in the lives of parents and their adolescents: The family stress model. In L. J. Crockett & R. K. Silbereisen (Eds.), *Negotiating adolescence in times of social change* (pp. 201–22?). New York: Cambridge University Press.

Conger, R. D., Wallace, L. E., Sun, Y., Simons, R. L., McLoyd, V. C., & Brody, G. H. (2002). Economic pressure in African American families: A replication and extension of the family stress model. *Developmental Psychology, 38,* 179–193.

Davis, E. C, & Friel, L. V. (2001). Adolescent sexuality: Disentangling the effects of family structure and family context. *Journal of Marriage and Family, 63,* 669–681.

Demo, D. H. (1993). The relentless search for effects of divorce: Forging new trails or tumbling down the beaten path? *Journal of Marriage and the Family, 55,* 42–45.

Demo, D. H., & Acock, A. C. (1996). Family structure, family process, and adolescent well-being. *Journal of Research on Adolescence, 6,* 457–488.

Demo, D. H., & Cox, M. J. (2000). Families with young children: A review of research in the 1990s. *Journal of Marriage and the Family, 62,* 876–896.

Demo, D., Fine, M., & Ganong, L. (2000). Divorce as a family stressor. In P. C. McKenry & S. J. Price (Eds.), *Families and change: Coping with stressful events and transitions* (2nd ed., pp. 279–302). Thousand Oaks, CA: Sage.

Downey, G., & Coyne, J. C. (1990). Children of depressed parents: An integrative review. *Psychological Bulletin, 108,* 50–76.

Duncan, G. J., & Brooks-Gunn, J. (1997). The effects of poverty on children. *Future of Children, 7,* 55–71.

Duncan, G. J., & Hoffman, S. D. (1985). Economic consequences of marital instability. In M. David & T. Smeeding (Eds.), *Horizontal equity, uncertainty and well-being* (pp. 427–469). Chicago: University of Chicago Press.

Dunifon, R., & Kowaleski-Jones, L. (2002). Who's in the house? Race differences in cohabitation, single parenthood, and child development. *Child Development, 73,* 1249–1264.

Dunn, J., O'Connor, T. G., & Levy, I. (2002). Out of the picture: A study of family drawings by children from step-, single-parent and non-step families. *Journal of Clinical Child and Adolescent Psychology, 31,* 505–512.

Emery, R. E. (1982). Interparental conflict and the children of discord and divorce. *Psychological Bulletin, 92,* 310–330.

Emery, R. E. (1992). Family conflicts and their developmental implications: A conceptual analysis of meanings for the structure of relationships. In C. U. Shantz & W. W. Hartup (Eds.), *Conflict in child and adolescent development* (pp. 270–298). New York: Cambridge University Press.

Emery, R. E. (1994). *Renegotiating family relationships: Divorce, child custody, and mediation.* New York: Guilford.

Emery, R. E. (1998). *Marriage, divorce, and children's adjustment.* Thousand Oaks, CA: Sage.

Emery, R. E. (1999). *Marriage, divorce, and children's adjustment* (2nd ed.). Thousand Oaks, CA: Sage.

Emery, R. E., & Tuer, M. (1993). Parenting and the marital relationship. In T. Luster & L. Okagi (Eds.), *Parenting: An ecological perspective* (pp. 121–148). Hillsdale, NJ: Lawrence Erlbaum.

Emery, R. E., Waldron, M., Kitzmann, K. M., & Aaron, J. (1999). Delinquent behavior, future divorce or nonmarital childbearing, and externalizing behavior among offspring: A 14-year prospective study. *Journal of Family Psychology, 13,* 568–579.

Emery, R. E., Weintraub, S., & Neale, J. M. (1982). Effects of marital discord on the school behavior of children with schizophrenic, affectively disordered, and normal parents. *Journal of Abnormal Child Psychology, 10,* 215–228.

Federal Interagency Forum on Child and Family Statistics. (2000). *America's children: Key national indicators of well-being, 2000.* Washington, DC: Government Printing Office.

Fincham, F. D., Beach, S. R., Harold, G. T., & Osborne, L. N. (1997). Marital satisfaction and depression: Different causal relationships for men and women? *Psychological Science, 8,* 351–357.

Fine, M. A., McKenry, P. C., Donnelly, B. W., & Voydanoff, P. (1992). Perceived adjustment of parents and children: Variations by family structure, race, and gender. *Journal of Marriage and the Family, 54,* 118–127.

Furstenberg, F. F., Morgan, S. P., & Allison, P. D. (1987). Paternal participation and children's well-being after marital dissolution. *American Sociological Review, 52,* 695–701.

Furstenberg, F. F., & Nord, C. W. (1985). Parenting apart: Patterns of child rearing after marital disruption. *Journal of Marriage and the Family, 47,* 893–904.

Furstenberg, F. F., Peterson, J. L., Nord, C. W., & Zill, N. (1983). The life course of children of divorce: Marital disruption and parental contact. *American Sociological Review, 48,* 656–668.

Furstenberg, F. F., & Teitler, J. O. (1994). Reconsidering the effects of marital disruption: What happens to children of divorce in early adulthood? *Journal of Family Issues, 15,* 173–190.

George, S. M., & Dickerson, B. J. (1995). The role of the grandmother in poor single-mother families and households. In B. J. Dickerson (Ed.), *African American single mothers: Understanding their lives and families.* Thousand Oaks, CA: Sage.

Gotlib, I. H., & McCabe, S. B. (1990). Marriage and psychopathology. In F. Fincham & T. Bradbury (Eds.), *The psychology of marriage* (pp. 226–257). New York: Guilford.

Gove, W. R., Hughes, M., & Styles, C. B. (1983). Does marriage have positive effects on the psychological well-being of the individual? *Journal of Health and Social Behavior, 24,* 122–132.

Hamer, J., & Marchioro, K. (2002). Becoming custodial dads: Exploring parenting among low-income and working-class African American fathers. *Journal of Marriage and Family, 64,* 116–129.

Haurin, R. J. (1992). Patterns of childhood residence and the relationship to young adult outcomes. *Journal of Marriage and the Family, 54,* 846–860.

Healy, J. M., Jr., Malley, J. E., & Stewart, A. J. (1990). Children and their fathers after parental separation. *American Journal of Orthopsychiatry, 60,* 531–543.

Heath, D. T., & Orthner, D. K. (1999). Stress and adaptation among male and female single parents. *Journal of Family Issues, 20,* 557–588.

Hetherington, E. M. (1989). Coping with family transitions: Winners, losers, and survivors. *Child Development, 60,* 1–14.

Hetherington, E. M., & Clingempeel, W. G. (1992). Coping with marital transitions: A family systems perspective. *Monographs of the Society for Research in Child Development, 57,* 1–242.

Hetherington, E. M., Cox, M., & Cox, R. (1978). The aftermath of divorce. In J. H. Stevens & M. Matthews (Eds.), *Mother-child, father-child relations* (pp. 110–155). Washington, DC: National Association for the Education of Young Children.

Hetherington, E. M., Cox, M., & Cox, R. (1982). Effects of divorce on parents and children. In M. Lamb (Ed.), *Nontraditional families* (pp. 233–288). Hillsdale, NJ: Lawrence Erlbaum.

Hetherington, E. M., & Kelly, J. (2000). *For better or for worse: Divorce reconsidered.* New York: Norton.

Hetherington, E. M., & Stanley-Hagan, M. (1999). The adjustment of children with divorced parents: A risk and resiliency perspective. *Child Psychology and Psychiatry and Allied Disciplines, 40,* 129–140.

Hilton, J. M., Desrochers, S., & Devall, E. L. (2001). Comparison of role demands, relationships, and child functioning in single-mother, single father, and intact families. *Journal of Divorce & Remarriage, 35,* 29–56.

Hogan, D. P., Sun, R., & Cornwell, G. T. (2000). Sexual and fertility behaviors of American females aged 15-19 years: 1985, 1990, and 1995. *American Journal of Public Health, 90,* 1421–4125.

Jayakody, R., Chatters, L. M., & Taylor, R. J. (1993). Family support to single and married African American mothers: The provision of financial, emotional, and child care assistance. *Journal of Marriage and the Family, 55,* 261–276.

Jenkins, J. M., & Smith, M. A. (1990). Factors protecting children living in disharmonious homes. *Journal of the American Academy of Child and Adolescent Psychiatry, 29,* 60–69.

Johnston, J. R. (1990). Role diffusion and role reversal: Structural variations in divorced families and children's functioning. *Family Relations, 15,* 493–509.

Kalter, N. (1990). *Growing up with divorce.* New York: Free Press.

Kendeler, K. S., Sheth, K., Gardner, C. O., & Prescott, C. (2002). Childhood parental loss and risk for first-onset of major depression and alcohol dependence: The time-decay of risk and sex differences. *Psychological Medicine, 32,* 1187–1194.

Kurdek, L. A., & Berg, B. (1987). Children's beliefs about parental divorce scale: Psychometric characteristics and concurrent validity. *Journal of Consulting and Clinical Psychology, 55,* 712–718.

Kurdek, L. A., Fine, M. A., & Sinclair, R. J. (1995). The relation between parenting transitions and adjustment in young adolescents. *Journal of Early Adolescence, 14,* 412–432.

Lansford, J. E., Ceballo, R., Abbey, A., & Stewart, A. J. (2001). Does family structure matter? A comparison of adoptive, two-parent biological, single-mother, stepfather, and stepmother households. *Journal of Marriage and Family, 63,* 840–852.

Larson, R. W., & Gillman, S. (1999). Transmission of emotions in the daily interactions of single-mother families. *Journal of Marriage and the Family, 61,* 21–38.

Laumann-Billings, L., & Emery, R. E. (2000). Distress among young adults from divorced families. *Journal of Family Psychology, 14,* 671–687.

Lipman, E. L., Boyle, M. H., Dooley, M. D., & Offord, D. R. (2002). Child well-being in single-mother families. *Journal of the American Academy of Child and Adolescent Psychiatry, 41,* 75–82.

Loeber, R., Drinkwater, M., Yin, Y., Anderson, S. J., Schmidt, L. C., & Crawford, A. (2000). Stability of family interaction from ages 6 to 18. *Journal of Abnormal Child Psychology, 28,* 353–369.

Luepnitz, D. A. (1982). *Child custody: A study of families after divorce.* Lexington, MA: Lexington.

Manning, W. D., & Smock, P. J. (2002). First comes cohabitation then comes marriage? A research note. *Journal of Family Issues, 23,* 1065–1087.

Martin, M. (1995). *Parentification in divorced families.* Unpublished doctoral dissertation, University of Virginia.

Martinez, C. R., & Forgatch, M. S. (2002). Adjusting to change: Linking family structure transitions with parenting and boys' adjustment. *Journal of Family Psychology, 16,* 107–117.

McGue, M., & Lykken, D. T. (1992). Genetic influence on risk of divorce. *Psychological Science, 3,* 368–373.

McLanahan, S. (2000). Family, state, and child well-being. *Annual Review of Sociology, 26,* 703–706.

McLanahan, S., & Carlson, M. J. (2002). Welfare reform, fertility, and father involvement. *Future of Children, 12,* 147–165.

McLanahan, S., & Sandefur, G. (1994). *Growing up with a single parent: What hurts, what helps.* Cambridge, MA: Harvard University Press.

McLoyd, V. C. (1998). Socioeconomic disadvantage and child development. *American Psychologist, 53,* 185–204.

McLoyd, V. C., & Smith, J. (2002). Physical discipline and behavior problems in African American, European American, and Hispanic children: Emotional support as a moderator. *Journal of Marriage and Family, 64,* 40–53.

Mistry, R. S., Vandewater, E. A., Huston, A. C., & McLoyd, V. C. (2002). Economic well-being and children's social adjustment: The role of family process in an ethnically diverse low-income sample. *Child Development, 73,* 935–951.

Moffitt, T. E. (2002). Teen-aged mothers in contemporary Britain. *Journal of Child Psychology and Psychiatry and Allied Disciplines, 43,* 727–742.

Morrison, D. R., & Cherlin, A. J. (1995). The divorce process and young children's well-being: A prospective analysis. *Journal of Marriage and the Family, 57,* 800–812.

Mott, F. L., Kowaleski-Jones, L., & Menaghan, E. G. (1997). Paternal absence and child behavior: Does a child's gender make a difference? *Journal of Marriage and the Family, 59,* 103–118.

Patterson, G. R., De Baryshe, B. D., & Ramsey, E. (1989). A developmental perspective on antisocial behavior. *American Psychologist, 44,* 329–335.

Peterson, J. L., & Zill, N. (1986). Marital disruption, parent-child relationships, and behavior problems in children. *Journal of Marriage and the Family, 48,* 295–307.

Popenoe, D. (1993). American family decline, 1960–1990: A review and appraisal. *Journal of Marriage and the Family, 55,* 527–542.

Salem, D. A., Zimmerman, M. A., & Notaro, P. C. (1998). Effects of family structure, family process, and father involvement on psychosocial outcomes among African American adolescents. *Family Relations, 47,* 331–341.

Santrock, J. W., & Warshak, R. A. (1979). Father custody and social development in boys and girls. *Journal of Social Issues, 35,* 112–125.

Schoen, R., & Standish, N. (2000, April). *The footprints of cohabitation: Results from marital status life tables for the U.S., 1995.* Paper presented at the Population Research Institute, Pennsylvania State University, University Park.

Schrag, R. D. A., Peris, T. S., & Emery, R. E. (2003). Understanding children's responses to marital conflict: A family systems model. In F. Jacobs, D. Wertlieb, & R. M. Lerner (Eds.), *Handbook of applied developmental science* (Vol. 2, pp. 39–65). Thousand Oaks, CA: Sage.

Seltzer, J. A. (1991). Relationships between fathers and children who live apart: The father's role after separation. *Journal of Marriage and the Family, 53,* 79–101.

Simons, R. L., & Beaman, J. (1996). Father's parenting. In R. L. Simons (Ed.), *Understanding differences between divorced and intact families* (pp. 95–103). Thousand Oaks, CA: Sage.

Simons, R. L., & Johnson, C. (1996). Mother's parenting. In R. L. Simons (Ed.), *Understanding differences between divorced and intact families* (pp. 81–93). Thousand Oaks, CA: Sage.

Simons, R. L., Whitbeck, L. B., Beaman, J., & Conger, R. D. (1994). The impact of mothers' parenting, involvement by nonresidential fathers, and parental conflict on the adjustment of adolescent children. *Journal of Marriage and the Family, 56,* 356–374.

Stewart, S. D. (1999). Disneyland dads, Disneyland moms? How nonresident parents spend time with absent children. *Journal of Family Issues, 20,* 539–556.

Stewart, S. D. (2003). Nonresident parenting and adolescent adjustment: The quality of nonresident father-child interaction. *Journal of Family Issues, 24,* 217–244.

Teachman, J. D., Tedrow, L. M., & Crowder, K. D. (2000). The changing demography of America's families. *Journal of Marriage and the Family, 62,* 1234–1247.

Thomson, E. (1994). "'Setting' and 'Development' from a Demographic Point of View." In A. Booth & J. F. Dunn (Eds.), *Step-families: Who benefits? Who does not?* Hillsdale, NJ: Lawrence Erlbaum.

Tweed, J. L., Schoenbach, V. J., George, L. K., & Blazer, D. G. (1989). The effects of childhood parental death and divorce on six-month history of anxiety disorders. *British Journal of Psychiatry, 154,* 823–828.

U.S. Bureau of the Census. (1992). *Marriage, divorce, and remarriage in the 1990's* (Current Population Reports, Series P23-180). Washington, DC: Government Printing Office.

U.S. Bureau of the Census. (1996). *Marital status and living arrangements: March 1994* (Current Population Reports, Series P20-484). Washington, DC: Government Printing Office.

U.S. Bureau of the Census. (2002). *Poverty in the United States, 2001.* Washington, DC: Government Printing Office.

Vandewater, E. A., & Lansford, J. E. (1998). Influences of family structure and parental conflict on children's well-being. *Family Relations, 47,* 323–330.

Ventura, S. J., Peters, K. D., Martin, J. A., & Maurer, J. D. (1997). *Births and deaths: United States, 1996* (Monthly Vital Statistics Report, 46[1], Suppl. 2). Hyattsville, MD: National Center for Health Statistics.

Wallerstein, J. S., & Blakeslee, S. (1989). *Second chances.* New York: Ticknor & Fields.

Wallerstein, J., Lewis, J., & Blakeslee, S. (2002). The unexpected legacy of divorce: A 25 year landmark study. *Journal of the American Academy of Child and Adolescent Psychiatry, 41,* 359–360.

Weiss, R. S. (1979). *Going it alone.* New York: Basic Books.

Wilson, M. N. (1989). Child development in the context of the black extended family. *American Psychologist, 44,* 380–385.

Zill, N. (1988). Behavior, achievement, and health problems among children in stepfamilies: Findings from a national survey of child health. In E. M. Hetherington & J. D. Arasteh (Eds.), *Impact of divorce, single parenting, and stepparenting on children* (pp. 325–368). Hillsdale, NJ: Lawrence Erlbaum.

Zill, N. (1995). National surveys as data resources for public policy research on poor children. In P. L. Chase-Lansdale & J. Brooks-Gunn (Eds.), *Escape from poverty: What makes a difference for children?* (pp. 272–290). New York: Cambridge University Press.

Zill, N., Morrison, D. R., & Coiro, M. J. (1993). Long-term effects of parental divorce on parent-child relationships, adjustment, and achievement in young adulthood. *Journal of Family Psychology, 7,* 91–103.

Zimiles, H., & Lee, V. E. (1991). Adolescent family structure and educational progress. *Developmental Psychology, 27,* 314–320.

CHAPTER 17

Britain's Changing Families

GRAHAM ALLAN, SHEILA HAWKER, AND GRAHAM CROW

In this chapter, we explore the ways in which family relationships and domestic circumstances have been changing in Britain over recent years. The intention is to provide some, albeit limited, basis for comparison with the other chapters in this book, which focus principally on North America. The chapter starts by discussing the recent radical transformations in household and family demography in Britain, highlighting the diversity there now is in "family" pathways. As well as considering the growth of new family forms resulting from increasing rates of divorce and lone parenthood, it examines how routes into partnership have been altering over the last generation as cohabitation has become more prominent.

The chapter then considers why these changes have arisen, drawing on theoretical accounts of the growth of individualization within the transition to late modernity. These accounts highlight the changes that have taken place in gender relationships, especially the comparatively greater freedoms open to

women as a result of social, economic, and technological innovation. The emergence of modified patterns of dependency between partners has in their turn fostered new understandings of the character of commitment within partnerships. In particular, the idea of partnership commitment as lifelong and irrevocable ceases to carry the moral force it once did.

In turn, the new understandings of commitment in normal partnerships have had considerable implications for the routine organization of other "family" relationships. The last part of the chapter explores some of these ramifications, suggesting that the increased diversity in aspects of partnership formation and dissolution has rendered family practices (Morgan, 1996), as well as family boundaries, more complex and negotiable. Building on a study of stepfamily kinship, the chapter concludes by arguing that in common usage the idea of family is becoming increasingly "fuzzy," with aspects of "family as kinship" and "family as

AUTHORS' NOTE: We are grateful for the support of the Economic and Social Research Council (Grant No. R000237504) in financing the research on which this chapter is based.

household" overlying emergent patterns of family solidarity and commitment.

DEMOGRAPHIC SHIFTS

Throughout much of the 20th century, trends in family and household composition in Britain and many other European countries followed a relatively predictable trajectory. Changes occurred, but they did so in ways that, outside wartime, were generally consistent. Thus, in Britain between 1900 and 1970, for example, the rate of marriage for single women increased systematically from 45 per 1,000 unmarried women to 60 per 1,000; age at first marriage declined from 25.4 to 23.2 for men and from 24.0 to 21.3 for women; divorce rates remained relatively low; the number of children born within the average marriage declined from approximately four to less than two; and relatively few children were brought up by lone parents (Coleman, 2000; Marriage and Divorce Statistics, 1990). Similarly, there was a degree of consistency in the demographic changes occurring in other European countries, though the specifics of the changes differed depending in part on religious and welfare policies.

In sociological rather than demographic terms, two features characterized the period. First, there was a consistency in the routine family pathways or "careers" that were constructed. In this sense, it was a highly conventional period—in family terms, most people's experiences followed a broadly similar route. Most married, had and raised children, and then lived as a couple until one or the other spouse died. Second, and very much linked to this first point, there was a clear moral and empirical connection between sex, marriage, and childbearing (Kiernan, Land, & Lewis, 1998). Indeed, the relationship between these three elements served as the cornerstone of what constituted "family life."

What was understood as their inherent connection symbolized and framed the ordering of "proper" family organization.

In the last part of the 20th century, these patterns, so rooted in what "family" was previously taken to be, began to change, raising a host of intriguing conceptual and theoretical issues for analysts and policy makers concerned with understanding contemporary patterns of family life (Jensen, 1998; Schoenmaeckers & Lodewijckx, 1999). As in the United States, a common model of family experience could no longer be assumed (Murphy & Wang, 1999). Where there had previously been predictability, now there was increasing diversity, so that what had been taken for granted could no longer be assumed. Importantly too, the diverse patterns that were emerging could not be explained as a consequence of subcultural behavior associated with distinct groups, whether defined religiously, ethnically, or economically. Instead a sea change was occurring throughout society, though influencing patterns of sexual and familial behavior in different ways for different groups (see, e.g., Berrington, 1994).

The first and most obvious change concerned divorce rates. With only slight exaggeration, divorce remained morally charged and comparatively rare throughout most of western Europe until the last quarter of the 20th century, at least outside Scandinavia. Marriage was defined as a lifelong institution that conferred social, economic, and legal rights on individuals but that in return committed them—again socially, economically, and legally—to one another. In this sense, marriage was quite highly institutionalized, with spouses' responsibilities and obligations to each other being governed by relatively rigid rules, sanctioned through religious and social codes, that informed appropriate behavior. Gradually this changed, so that rather than being defined popularly within an institutional framework, marriage came to be seen as an essentially negotiated partnership given special legal recognition and privilege. In Britain, this shift from what Farber (1973) termed a "natural-family" paradigm to a "legal-family" one, was captured quite explicitly in the 1967 Divorce Reform Act. Before this legislation, divorce was available only if one of the spouses could demonstrate that the other had broken the marriage contract through adultery, desertion, or unreasonable behavior. Legally, the quality of the marital tie was of no consequence. In contrast, the 1967 legislation placed prime emphasis on relationship quality, emphasizing "irretrievable breakdown" of the marriage as the key criterion for divorce. Adultery, desertion, and unreasonable behavior were still to be used as indicators of such breakdown, but so too was a period spent living apart, effectively making divorce a matter of individual or joint choice.

The result of these changes in legislation—and social climate—has been a very significant rise in divorce rates. The numbers of divorces in England and Wales increased from a little over 6,000 in 1938 to more than 45,000 in 1968. Between 1968 and 1998, they increased further to over 145,000 a year, an increase in the crude divorce rate from 3.7 per 1,000 marriages to over 12.9 per 1,000 marriages (Marriage and Divorce Statistics, 1990; Marriage, Divorce and Adoption Statistics, 2000). Although the British divorce rate is among the highest in Europe, increases are also evident in other countries (Coleman & Chandola, 1999). Thus, the divorce rate between 1970 and 1990 trebled in France and Holland and doubled in Belgium (Goode, 1993). It has been estimated that throughout northern Europe approximately one in three marriages will currently end in divorce (Prinz, 1995). The divorce rates in predominantly Roman Catholic countries are less but are nonetheless rising.

One of the consequences of rising rates of marital separation and divorce has been a growth in lone-parent households. In Britain, the numbers of such households increased from 570,000 in 1971 to 1.6 million in 1996 (Haskey, 1998). Importantly, this rise was not just a consequence of divorce; it reflects a much broader change in social and moral constructions of appropriate reproductive behavior and the interests of children. Thus, as well as marital breakdown leading to increasing numbers of lone-parent households, there has been a particularly marked rise in the number of unmarried (though not necessarily unpartnered) mothers. In 1976, some 54,000 children were born out of wedlock (9.2% of all births); by 1998, this had increased to over 240,000 (37.8% of all births) (Birth Statistics, 1978, 1999).

Although these figures clearly indicate that social understandings of the relationship between marriage and childbirth have altered, they are part of a broader transformation in "marital" behavior. Throughout Europe, there has been a noticeable decline in the popularity of marriage (Jensen, 1998; Pinnelli, 1995). In part, this is a result of later marriage (Kuijsten & Strohmeier, 1997)—in England and Wales, mean age at first marriage increased from 22.4 to 27.0 for women and from 24.4 to 28.9 for men between 1970 and 1998 (Marriage and Divorce Statistics, 1990; Marriage, Divorce and Adoption Statistics, 2000)—but it is also a consequence of more people choosing not to get married. Thus, again using England and Wales as an example, only 87% of women and 80% of men aged 40 had ever been married in 1998, compared to 95% and 91% in 1975.

Equally significant has been the very rapid rise in cohabitation as a form of partnership. Initially most common in Britain among those who had been divorced (as well as gay couples), it has over the last 20 years become an entirely normal and routine mode of living for many people (Haskey, 1999; see also Manting, 1996). Although still opposed by some ethnic and religious groups, the stigma—both personal and, importantly, institutional—once attached to "living in sin" has almost entirely disappeared. In other European countries with stronger Catholic traditions, the change may not have been quite so rapid, but it is nonetheless developing in the same direction (Kiernan, 1999b). In Britain, a period of cohabitation has become the dominant form of engagement among couples planning to marry. More recently, and in line with the decline in rates of marriage, increasing numbers of couples are choosing informal cohabitation rather than legal marriage as the most appropriate mode of constructing their relationship, even after the birth of children (Berrington, 2001; Ermisch & Francesconi, 2000).

Interestingly, the more couples there are who choose cohabitation rather than marriage as the appropriate form of partnership for them, the more pressure there is for legal recognition to be given to cohabitation as a mode of commitment. As with gay couples, issues concerning property distribution on separation, pension entitlements, and inheritance rights need legal resolution, thereby requiring formal regulation, the absence of which was initially part of the attraction of cohabitation for many. In turn, the growth of cohabitation as an alternative to marriage influences changing cultural understandings of marriage. In particular, the perception of cohabitation as a lifestyle choice rather than a relationship premised on legal contract effectively fosters the view that marriage is also a lifestyle choice, a perception that consequently fuels the belief that marriage too should be sustained only for as long as it provides satisfaction. Clearly, both marriage and (longer-term) cohabitation involve the couple in forms of mutual emotional and material commitments that are often complex to dissolve (Jamieson, 1998; Smart & Neale, 1999). It is interesting here that as cohabitation becomes more established, so marriage and (longer-term) cohabitation appear to be moving toward one another as forms of relationship, both being a lifestyle choice with no guarantee of permanence and both requiring regulation for the protection of individual rights.

Paralleling some of these changes, there has also been a significant increase in stepfamilies, though precise estimates of the trends in this are more difficult to obtain, partly because of definitional problems over what really counts as a stepfamily. As with lone parenthood, the issue is whether the definition of *stepfamily* is taken as having a "household" or "family" frame. Thus, Haskey (1994) estimated that approximately one in eight children lived in a household with a stepparent for some period of time. But in addition, many others living in lone-parent households will be involved to differing degrees in stepfamily ties as a result of their nonresidential parent's new partnership. Furthermore, some children will have had "serial" stepparents as a result of their parents' various partnerships, though it would appear rare for children to continue to have active relationships with their parents' ex-partners. As modes of cohabitation become more common, and with increasing legal and social encouragement for the continuation of parent-child involvement after separation, what constitutes stepparenthood becomes increasingly complex. Certainly, stepparenthood can no longer be understood as replacement parenting in any simple manner.

Various other changes have also been occurring in the demographic fashioning of the familial/domestic realm. There is, for example, a greater incidence, and a greater acceptance, of gay households and families. The extent to which this has occurred varies both within and across the countries of western Europe, but the trend overall is one of more openness and tolerance, even though many gay individuals and couples continue to experience stigma and abuse in their personal lives. There has also been an increase in the number of single-person households, partly as a result of divorce and widowhood, but also as a consequence of choice (Hall, Ogden, & Hill, 1999). Similarly, more young people than previously now live for shorter or longer periods in shared housing (Kenyon, 2002). So too there has been an increase in the number of couples "living apart together"—couples who are committed to one another but who live separately, usually for some period each week (Lesthaeghe, 1995). Though often a result of employment constraints, for some it is a decision aimed at sustaining a degree of independence while still recognizing a shared commitment. Such patterns seem most common among the middle class in northern European countries, especially Scandinavia, but given the changes already occurring in other countries, they are likely to become a more common experience throughout Europe.

Another level of diversity in family patterns has been added by the increasing levels of migration into European societies from countries and regions with quite distinct religious and ethnic traditions. The migration process, which often involves some family members moving a considerable time before others, can itself generate disrupted family and household patterns (Ballard, 1994). More importantly in the longer run, the movement of people with different cultural and religious traditions into the countries of western Europe has further diversified the modes of family and household organization that are seen as morally appropriate. Though forms of adaptation can modify later generations' commitment to "traditional" ways, nonetheless the maintenance of familial standards, whether these concern sexual relationships outside marriage, partner selection, care of elderly people, common residence, or the breadth of kinship solidarities, is often of major concern in defining and protecting a valued cultural heritage and affirming the moral standing of those involved.

What all these developments represent is a far greater degree of diversity in family and domestic arrangements than existed throughout most of the 20th century. And as a result, notions like "family" and "household" can now no longer be understood in as simple a manner as they once were. The whole question of "Who is a family member?" now raises substantial issues that were of minor consequence two generations ago. For example, when does a cohabiting partner become a member of your family, and when does he or she become a member of your children's, your parents', or your siblings' families? Does this happen when the two of you marry, or has the rise in, and legitimacy of, cohabitation altered this? When does a stepfamily become socially recognized as such? Is this a household determination (i.e., a matter decided by domestic living arrangements), or is it a family matter (i.e., one based upon notions of a common kinship)? With increasing separation and divorce, complicated further by repartnering, it is evident that many parents and children have different "families" in ways that did not arise at all frequently two generations ago. So too, the term *household* contains a range of elements that makes it necessary to recognize the permeability of household boundaries rather than assume that membership can be categorized in an unproblematic way. Indeed, people may be thought of as members of different households for different activities or alternatively may be members—or partial members—of households for some periods of the day or week but not others (Allan & Crow, 2001; Morgan, 1996).

ACCOUNTING FOR CHANGE

Why have these transformations in the domestic and family realm occurred? Socially and economically, why has the relationship between sex, marriage, and childbearing altered to this degree? How is the greater diversity emergent in family and household patterns to be explained? One of the more influential lines of theorizing here focuses on the process of individualization within late modernity. Associated in particular with the writings of Beck (1992, 1997) and Giddens (1991, 1992), this approach is concerned with the ways in which developments within industrial and commercial economies have altered the character of the dependencies in which people are embedded. For example, the shifting requirements of a global economy, the increased involvement of women with children in paid labor, the growth of a somewhat "degendered" citizenship, and the greater control of reproductive behavior have all contributed to women's experiencing fewer economic and social constraints than previously. In particular, the nature of their dependency on men as partners and husbands has altered in ways that have had profound impacts on patterns of couple, family, and household solidarities.

In his work with Beck-Gernsheim (Beck & Beck-Gernsheim, 1995), Beck holds that because of increased labor market participation, together with control over fertility, women are less economically dependent on men than previously. With alternative sources of income—state benefits as well as employment—and increasing opportunities for social participation, women are less trapped in the traditional domestic division of labor than previous generations were. As a consequence, marriage and the standard nuclear model of family structure and domestic organization become less a matter of routine, constrained practice and more a matter of lifestyle choice. From this viewpoint, contemporary social and economic organization allows women to be increasingly active in constructing and negotiating their personal lives, their partnership commitments, and the forms of domestic organization in

which they are involved. Though gender differentials clearly continue to be of consequence, women have a degree of choice over these matters that was largely absent for their grandmothers, if not their mothers.

In a somewhat similar vein, Giddens (1992) has argued that there has been a growth in "pure relationships" based upon "confluent love." Unlike romantic love, which is understood to involve a "once and for always" commitment associated with traditional marriage, confluent love is far more contingent, being rooted more firmly in the continuing emotional satisfactions and pleasures that the relationship provides. Like Beck, Giddens sees this new form of commitment as emerging from shifts in women's dependencies on men, which in turn relate to broader economic, social, and technological change. In particular, he highlights the pervasive labor market restructuring of the late 20th century, the growth of women's control over reproduction, and increased rights of citizenship. Whereas in earlier periods the division of labor inside and outside the home made women highly dependent on their husbands—with marriage representing both a form of "protection" and a site of oppression—under contemporary conditions the structural framing of partnership has shifted.

As a result, a new mode of "pure" relationship emerges, sustained less by economic constraint or social convention but more by choice and intrinsic satisfaction. In this regard, these relationships are highly expressive, in theory negotiated and structured to suit each individual's needs and desires as they develop. Most importantly, they embody a different "relational morality" to that dominant in earlier eras, with the individual being prioritized more evidently. These relationships are not expected to continue if, for whatever reason, they cease to deliver the satisfactions desired by one or both partners. Though there is a sense that established relationships should not be jettisoned too readily, equally there is little value placed in staying in relationships that have "broken down" and now provide little or no intrinsic satisfaction. From the pure relationship/confluent love perspective, the individual is free—and morally right—to leave a relationship that is no longer rewarding. It is better to seek a different relationship or live alone than to stay bound or trapped in one that has become moribund.

Thus, it can be argued, processes of individualization have had a significant impact on sexual and domestic partnerships (see also Lesthaeghe, 1995; Schoenmaeckers & Lodewijckx, 1999). Certainly, whether or not credence is given to the detailed theorizing of writers like Giddens and Beck, especially concerning gender equality in the expression and practice of intimacy (see Jamieson, 1999, for a powerful critique of Giddens's claims), the types of demographic transformation outlined earlier in this chapter appear compatible with the idea that new forms of sexual, domestic, and familial commitment are developing. There can be little doubt that people now experience greater freedom and choice over the construction of their personal worlds and are less willing than in the past to tolerate the continuation of what have become unsatisfactory relationships, whether based on marriage or cohabitation. To this degree, there is a higher level of reflexivity about these relationships and a stronger sense that they should be intrinsically rewarding. Culturally too, there is more tolerance of diversity in personal life and less acceptance of a single normative model as inherently better than others, although some still believe strongly that personal life should be governed by particular religious injunctions. For many, however, these issues are seen as matters of lifestyle choice rather than moral imperative. Indeed, as states adapt policies in recognition of increased cohabitation, as births outside marriage become "legitimated" socially, and as the stigma of divorce disappears, so "traditional" ways, including marriage itself, lose their moral force. That is, what were once matters requiring public regulation become transformed into private issues.

COMMITMENT: PARTNERSHIPS AND FAMILIES

In these regards, there is a resonance between Giddens's analysis of shifts in understandings of intimacy and contemporary partnership behavior. Commitment is no longer organized in the standard ways it was—dating, followed by engagement, followed by marriage. Cohabitation now enters into this process at different stages for different couples, effectively rendering the construction of commitment less formal (Manting, 1996). Noticeably, cohabitation lacks the ritual and ceremony that mark the way engagement and marriage are celebrated. Indeed, the beginning of cohabitation is often private and sometimes gradual, occurring without much social reporting or recognition unless it overlaps with an announcement of engagement. For some couples, the start of cohabitation signifies a long-term commitment. Like engagement, this represents for them a relationship that they hope and expect to last, ideally for the rest of their lives. For other couples, however, cohabitation does not represent this in any real sense. It is defined as a relationship for now, one to be enjoyed and valued but not seen as necessarily signifying a long-term future commitment.

However, whatever the sense of commitment at the beginning of a long-term relationship, it is clear that increasingly promises about the future are being interpreted as desires, hopes, ambitions, and aims but not—and this is the crucial change—as inevitably binding in the way they were in earlier periods. In other words, younger couples are recognizing the potential instability of the unions they are forming. There is a recognition that no matter what they feel and believe now, circumstances change. There can be no certainty that their dreams will come to fruition. Precisely because the relationship they are constructing is predominantly founded on issues of continuing self-fulfillment, happiness, and mutual reward, there can be no guarantee as to its future. Happiness and self-fulfillment are not issues that are understood as being simply a matter of will. They are states that are emergent within the relationship, dependent on its quality. Moreover, it is not just new couples who are generating these understandings of partnership. These cultural shifts infuse longer-term relationships too, reframing the way they are understood and the tolerances individuals have for different levels of dissatisfaction (Allan & Harrison, 2002).

Though understandings of partnership commitment have been altering, the breaking up of established relationships is still usually problematic. There may be more acceptance of it as a solution to relationship problems, but it nonetheless frequently generates major difficulties for those involved—emotional, practical, social, economic, and legal. Of course, the extent to which this happens depends on the nature of the relationship. Those that were always defined as short term, and in which there was relatively little shared investment, are more easy to end without recrimination or rancor. But other ties, established over time, involving shared property, imagined futures, and a deep emotional commitment, are rarely ended without disharmony, pain, and friction, sometimes over a prolonged period. Such difficulties are clearly exacerbated when children, especially dependent children, are involved. Separation and divorce remain traumatic for most people, usually involving a powerful sense of loss. What this indicates is that although the character of partnership commitment has altered with

individualization and associated structural changes, the development of commitment continues to tie people together socially and materially, as well as emotionally.

In other words, when people form partnerships they become enmeshed and embedded in modes of living that are inevitably constraining. At times, it appears that Giddens sees confluent love as able to escape such enmeshment. All that matters is each individual's self-fulfillment and emotional satisfaction. Clearly, though, over time relationships come to involve far more than this, so that ending them involves processes of "dis-embedding" and "de-meshing" lives that have, to a degree, become "as one" (Jamieson, 1998). Research into what might be termed the "domestic economy" of long-term cohabitation is sparse throughout Europe, but analyses of separation processes are notably absent (Haskey, 1999). However, there is little reason to think that for those who have cohabited longer term the issues involved are radically different from those faced by married couples separating. Indeed, some issues may be made more complex through the absence of a legal framework regulating the separation. However, this is an area about which we have very little knowledge.

Though it can be recognized that the nature of partnership commitment has been altering, what about other forms of family commitment and, in particular, the commitment between parents and children? Have individualization and similar macro-level processes also influenced the solidarities evident between parents and children? More specifically, has the rise in marital and other partnership separation influenced the character of these ties? The picture here is complex and diverse, though some underlying patterns are evident. Many analysts have pointed to the changes in childhood experience over the 20th century (Qvortrup, Bardy, Sgritta, & Wintersberger, 1994). Ideologically and practically, parents appear to be focusing more attention than previously, and for longer periods, on the well-being of their children. More concern is expressed about their emotional development, their educational achievement, and the quality of their childhood experiences than at any time in the past. They are seen as needing nurturing in ways that would have been highly questionable even two generations ago, representing a clear shift in the balance between "spoiling" and "caring." This is apparent in the growth of markets for different goods and services catering for children and adolescents. Moreover, in Britain and other European countries, there is now greater diversity in youth transitions than there was previously. As with family course, whereas for much of the 20th century there tended to be uniformity in the pathways people took to adulthood, though allowing for class and gender differences, recently this transition has become far more variable (Wallace & Kovatcheva, 1998).

Yet although it can be argued that dependent children have become an increasingly significant project for parents both culturally and economically, at the same time demographic trends make this problematic for growing numbers of parents (Ribbens McCarthy, Edwards, & Gillies, 2000). In particular, nonresidential biological parents, predominantly fathers, frequently need to construct relationships with their children that do not mesh well with cultural ideals. Indeed, in the past in Britain, credence was given to the idea that children were best served by the same "clean break" that applied to divorce resolution. In other words, the tendency, especially if children were young at the time of parental separation, was for many of these fathers to play little effective part in their children's lives. Despite the growth of research on lone-parent families, estimates of paternal contact are problematic, partly because of sampling difficulties and partly because of problems of measuring

adequately what concepts like effective contact really mean (Bradshaw & Millar, 1991; Bradshaw, Stimson, Skinner, & Wilson, 1999a, 1999b). However, recent social and legal changes in Britain and other European countries are likely to have had a significant impact on these issues. In Britain, for example, the 1991 Child Support Act introduced a consistent, though highly complex, framework for calculating the financial obligations of nonresidential biological parents. Although not regulated in this way, behind this legislation lay a recognition that, socially as well as financially, biological parenting should, in principle, continue even after the marriage/partner relationship ends (Smart, 1999). Clearly, such policy initiatives both reflect and inform contemporary cultural understandings of postseparation parenting. Exactly how much they have altered the quality (and quantity) of nonresidential parenting is difficult to know. This is another area where more research is badly needed, though for Britain some evidence of change is reported in recent studies by Bradshaw et al. (1999a, 1999b).

The growth of "repartnering" and the formation of residential and nonresidential stepfamilies further complicates these issues. One consequence of the shifts in cultural and policy constructions of nonresidential parenting is that the symbolic and physical boundaries around both one-parent and stepfamily households become more permeable. As the emphasis on continued parental involvement is realized, and as variants of a co-parenting model develop, parents are encouraged to sustain a relationship despite no longer living together or wanting each other involved in their lives. As Smart and Neale (1999) have shown in their study of parenting following separation in England, this often creates a degree of tension between the parents that is less liable to occur under the "clean break" model. In the case of stepfamilies, it also often diversifies the modes of

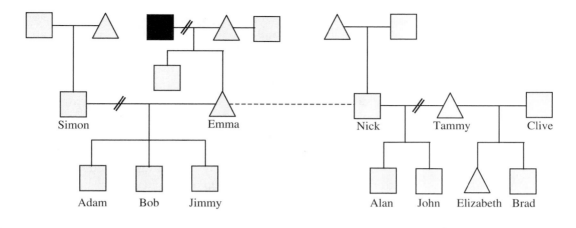

Figure 17.1 Stepfamily Kinship, a Case Illustration

SOURCE: Allan, Crow, & Harker (1999).

"parenting," and especially "fathering," that children experience. As a result, too, many children are now incorporated into more complex kinship networks than previous generations were, with implications for the ways in which concepts like family and kinship are understood.

FAMILY AND KINSHIP

Thus, although analysts like Beck and Beck-Gernsheim (1995) may be right in pointing to the ways individualization has encouraged demographic heterogeneity and diversified the lifestyle options available to people, the destabilization of traditional family and household patterns has an impact on the construction of kinship networks and what people understand their family to be. Importantly too, it generates greater diversity than previously in the family networks of people who belong to the "same" family. This is most easy to see in the case of step-families, but it applies to other new family formations too. Consider as an example the case illustration in Figure 17.1, taken from a

recent study of stepfamily kinship (Allan, Crow, & Hawker, 1999). In this, Emma has been cohabiting with Nick for 3 years. She was previously married to Simon, with whom she had three children, Adam, Bob, and Jimmy, who now live with her and Nick. Nick was also married previously and has two children from that partnership, Alan and John, who spend alternate weeks with Nick and Emma and with his ex-wife Tammy and her new partner, Clive. Tammy and Clive also have two children of their own, Elizabeth and Brad.

At issue here is how the various members of this network construct their family and how this differs depending on their location within the network in ways that are much more diverse than in family networks where there has been no marital disruption. So, for example, the family relationships of Alan and John include sibling ties with Elizabeth and Brad, though Elizabeth and Brad are not part of Emma's or Nick's family any more than Adam, Bob, and Jimmy are part of Tammy's or Clive's family. Whether Alan and John are part of Adam's, Bob's, or Jimmy's family is moot and depends on the distinctions those involved make between "household" and "family" and, in the longer run, on what happens to the partnership between Emma and Nick. Similarly, the overlap between Emma's family network and Nick's family network is less strong than would be the case if they were in a long-lasting marriage. Moreover, the recognized family relationships of Emma's, Nick's, Tammy's, and Simon's parents are complicated by the presence of stepgrandchildren as well as the complex domestic circumstances of their biological grandchildren.

Within this context, analyses of the "negotiation" of kinship relationships (Finch, 1989; Finch & Mason, 1993) becomes particularly interesting. The essential premise of this theoretical perspective is that kinship solidarities are not normatively determined but are negotiated in a variety of ways over time within networks of family relationships. Sometimes these negotiations are overt, but more frequently they are implicit and emergent. Either way, they shape the ways in which responsibilities, solidarities, and connections are constructed. In "traditional" families, negotiations around these issues certainly occurred, but the calculation of family membership was more straightforward, even allowing for complexities about, say, which in-laws were really "family" and where lateral extension of "family" ended (e.g., under what circumstances second cousins would be recognized as family). With new modes of family, the spheres around which negotiation occurs become broader, but, as importantly, the degree to which "family" frames the negotiation of solidarity and responsibility within these "family-relevant" relationships itself becomes part of their negotiation.

So, for example, how is "fatherhood" negotiated in "families" where there are two or more fathers—a nonresidential biological father, a (nonresidential) ex-stepfather, and a current stepfather, say? How is "stepgrandparenthood" negotiated? Who is considered family under what circumstances and with what consequences? In recent years, researchers have attempted to resolve some of these issues by making clear-cut analytical distinctions. In particular, as family and domestic complexity have increased, it has become more important than ever to distinguish between family and household, the one involving a set of kinship relations and the other a set of relationships based on a common, or linked, domestic economy. Yet although this distinction is extremely useful for many issues, not least in analyzing household patterns where no claim is based upon notions of family connection, in other regards it misrepresents the reality it is trying to clarify. That is, in everyday constructions the overlay between the notions of "family," "home," "household," and "domestic" is marked. To some degree, each makes sense only within the contexts of the boundaries of the others. Thus, "family" is not the same as "home," but to share a domestic economy in a household in which other relationships are premised upon "family connections" rather than "nonfamily" ones renders those relationships within it in which "family connection" is moot more rather than less familylike.

As family patterns become more diverse and complex, the parameters around the notion of family become more "fuzzy" (Simpson, 1998). Moreover, such fuzziness cannot be resolved by analytically tighter definitions of what family "really" is and what it is not. The point about the changes occurring is that family actually *is* becoming more fuzzy—in Bauman's (2000) terms, more "liquid" and less "solid." As Morgan (1996, 1999) has developed, there are a range of "family practices" that involve different senses, different constellations, and different involvements of "family." Increasingly, because family relationships need to be understood as process, as flux, rather than as an established, given structure, the process of negotiation around family practices comes to the fore, although of course such negotiation is itself structured by past family practices and negotiated outcomes. To draw on Giddens's expression, there is a greater "contingency" than was apparent in the past around family relationships in general. In part, this is based on the reduced certainty informing the construction of couple relationships, but it is more than just this. It is a broader potentiality for the demography or configuration of "family" to alter in ways that are not predictable. Events lead to the reconstitution of the complex of household, family, and, consequently, kinship in a manner that is not understood as part of a foreseeable narrative in the same way that constructions around the "nuclear family" were in the past.

Of course, many couples remain together; some family networks are relatively stable in this regard. But increasingly people's sense of family is less certain, more contingent than it was. Changes in partnership formation and dissolution are central to this precisely because of their impact outside the couple on family networks and family practices. Movements out of partnerships into lone and nonresidential parenthood and into new partnerships across family or kinship networks capture the potential there now is for flux and reconfiguration in "family" relationships. One lay response to this has been a differentiation of what "family" really is, with an emphasis on blood as the defining criteria. For example, distinctions are often made in stepfamilies between "real" family and other family. People speak of their "real" father or "real" siblings in contrast to a stepfather or stepsiblings, who are not defined as family in this sense. Arguably, such notions of family and kinship being "in essence" about "blood" will become more prominent. As we have seen, this, after all, is the message behind ideas that parents retain parental responsibilities even when they no longer live with their child(ren). Yet as noted, such blood ties are by no means always sustained following separation. Some fathers, in particular, have little involvement in their children's lives, and the fathers' kin may also have little involvement. Other relationships, however defined, do enter the family realm and become involved in family practices, especially when co-residence is involved. Thus, residential stepparents over time come to embody aspects of parenting, and co-resident stepsiblings aspects of siblinghood. So too, stepgrandparents may act like grandparents, at least to those stepgrandchildren residing with their (adult) child. However, as our own research into stepfamily kinship demonstrated, these relationships are often understood to be highly contingent on the continuation of the intermediary partnership. If and when the partnership ends, then so most typically do the step-kin ties that it engendered. In other words, the sense of family commitment that develops in these step-kin relationships is distinct because of this underlying contingency from the more enduring commitment normatively expected of blood kinship (Allan et al., 1999).

CONCLUSION

It is evident that major changes have been occurring to family patterns in Britain and other western European countries over the last 30 years, changes that were not predicted at the time, despite the research interest there was then (as now) in family life. The roots of these changes are structural; they lie in the transformations in the social and economic order occurring in late modernity. More specifically, though, the changes constitute new understandings of the relationship between sex, marriage, and childbearing. Throughout Europe, as elsewhere, there has been a dissociation between what might be termed relationship-based sexual activity and marriage. Equally, there has been a weakening of the association between marriage and childbearing, with Britain standing out for its high levels of "unpartnered" births (Kiernan, 1999a). Although there are differences in detail, broadly similar shifts can be discerned in patterns of partnership formation and dissolution in many European countries.

Such demographic trends are congruent with an increase in individualism and the (relatively) reduced economic and social dependence of women on men as husbands. Certainly in Britain, there has been a highly significant change in people's "family careers." The uniformity evident for much of the 20th century has been replaced by increased diversity, especially with regard to partnership formation and dissolution. Clearly, these changes alter the experience of "family" that individuals have, whether these individuals are directly or indirectly involved. Thus, as the nature of relationship commitment among adults has been shifting, so more people construct forms of serial commitment, and so more children experience diverse forms of parenting. In turn, however, these changes affect cultural constructions of what family is. Whereas once this could be taken for granted as (largely) unproblematic at a lay level, this is no longer

so. The boundaries between "family" and "nonfamily" are less tightly constructed.

In turn, though there is a clear distinction to be made between "family" and "household," for many people the realms of family practices have become more blurred. For many, the whole complex of family/household activities now crosses household boundaries, but equally it incorporates into "family" people whose status as family members is less securely based. At times, the response to this is to tighten definitions of family and fall back onto notions of blood connection. Here, ideas of "real" family come to the fore, supported in part by cultural understandings of genetic "certainty" resulting from new scientific developments. However, at a day-to-day level, more diverse and complex forms of solidarity (and antagonism) develop between people who have familial involvement with one another. Stepfamilies provide classic illustrations of the working out of these matters, but so too the rise in cohabitation as a form of adult commitment, together with shifts in marriage and divorce, has altered the ways in which family relationships are negotiated. Analyzing how these changing family-relevant processes are constituted over time should ensure the vibrancy of British and European family research well into the future.

REFERENCES

Allan, G., & Crow, G. (2001). *Families, households and society*. London: Palgrave.

Allan, G., Crow, G., & Hawker, S. (1999). *Step-families and the construction of kinship*. Unpublished report to Economic and Social Research Council, University of Southampton.

Allan, G., & Harrison, K. (2002). Marital affairs. In R. Goodwin & D. Cramer (Eds.), *Inappropriate relationships* (pp. 45–63). Mahwah, NJ: Lawrence Erlbaum.

Ballard, R. (Ed.). (1994). *Desh Pardesh: The South Asian presence in Britain*. London: Hurst.

Bauman, Z. (2000). *Liquid modernity*. Cambridge, UK: Polity.

Beck, U. (1992). *Risk society*. Newbury Park, CA: Sage.

Beck, U. (1997). *The reinvention of politics*. Cambridge, UK: Polity.

Beck, U., & Beck-Gernsheim E. (1995). *The normal chaos of love*. Cambridge, UK: Polity.

Berrington, A. (1994). Marriage and family formation among the white and ethnic-minority populations in Britain. *Ethnic and Racial Studies, 17*, 517–546.

Berrington, A. (2001). Entry into parenthood and the outcome of cohabiting partnerships in Britain. *Journal of Marriage and Family, 63*, 80–96.

Birth Statistics. (1978). *Birth statistics 1976* (OPCS, Series FM1, No. 3). London: HMSO.

Birth Statistics. (1999). *Birth statistics 1998* (ONS, Series FM1, No. 27). London: Stationery Office.

Bradshaw, J., & Millar, J. (1991). *Lone parent families in the UK* (Department of Health and Social Security Research Report No. 6). London: HMSO.

Bradshaw, J., Stimson, C., Skinner, C., & Williams, J. (1999a). *Absent fathers?* London: Routledge.

Bradshaw, J., Stimson, C., Skinner, C., & Williams, J. (1999b). Non-resident fathers in Britain. In S. McRae (Ed.), *Changing Britain: Families and households in the 1990s* (pp. 404–426). New York: Oxford University Press.

Coleman, D. (2000). Population and family. In A. H. Halsey & J. Webb (Eds.), *Twentieth century British social trends* (pp. 27–93). New York: Macmillan.

Coleman, D., & Chandola, T. (1999). Britain's place in Europe's population. In S. McRae (Ed.), *Changing Britain: Families and households in the 1990s* (pp. 37–67). New York: Oxford University Press.

Ermisch, J., & Francesconi, M. (2000). Patterns of family and household formation. In R. Berthoud & J. Gershuny (Eds.), *Seven years in the lives of British families* (pp. 21–44). Bristol, UK: Policy.

Farber, B. (1973). *Family and kinship in modern society*. Glenview, IL: Scott, Foresman.

Finch, J. (1989). *Family obligations and social change*. Cambridge, UK: Polity.

Finch, J., & Mason, J. (1993). *Negotiating family responsibilities*. London: Routledge.

Giddens, A. (1991). *Modernity and self-identity*. Cambridge, UK: Polity.

Giddens, A. (1992). *The transformation of intimacy*. Cambridge, UK: Polity.

Goode, W. J. (1993). *World changes in divorce patterns*. New Haven, CT: Yale University Press.

Hall, R., Ogden, P., & Hill, C. (1999). Living alone: Evidence from England and Wales and France for the last two decades. In S. McRae (Ed.), *Changing Britain: Families and households in the 1990s* (pp. 265–296). New York: Oxford University Press.

Haskey, J. (1994). Stepfamilies and stepchildren in Great Britain. *Population Trends, 76*, 17–28.

Haskey, J. (1998). One-parent families and their dependent children in Great Britain. *Population Trends, 91*, 5–14.

Haskey, J. (1999). Cohabitational and marital histories of adults in Great Britain. *Population Trends, 96*, 13–24.

Jamieson, L. (1998). *Intimacy*. Cambridge, UK: Polity.

Jamieson, L. (1999). Intimacy transformed? A critical look at the "pure relationship." *Sociology, 33*, 477–494.

Jensen, A. M. (1998). Partnership and parenthood in contemporary Europe. *European Journal of Population, 14*, 89–99.

Kenyon, E. (2002). Young adults' household formation: Individualization, identity and home. In G. Allan & G. Jones (Eds.), *Social relations and the life course* (pp. 103–119). Basingstoke, UK: Palgrave.

Kiernan, K. (1999a). Childbearing outside marriage in western Europe. *Population Trends*, *98*, 11–20.

Kiernan, K. (1999b). Cohabitation in western Europe. *Population Trends*, *96*, 25–32.

Kiernan, K., Land, H., & Lewis, J. (1998). *Lone motherhood in twentieth century Britain*. New York: Oxford University Press.

Kuijsten, A., & Strohmeier, K. (1997). Ten countries in Europe: An overview. In F. X. Kaufman, A. Kuijsten, H. J. Schulze, & K. Strohmeier (Eds.), *Family life and family policies in Europe* (pp. 394–423). Oxford, UK: Clarendon.

Lesthaeghe, R. (1995). The second demographic transition in western countries: An interpretation. In K. Mason & A. M. Jensen (Eds.), *Gender and family change in industrialized countries* (pp. 17–62). Oxford, UK: Clarendon.

Manting, D. (1996). The changing meaning of marriage and cohabitation. *European Journal of Sociology*, *12*, 53–65.

Marriage and Divorce Statistics. (1990). *Marriage and divorce statistics 1837–1883* (OPCS, Series FM2, No. 16). London: HMSO.

Marriage, Divorce and Adoption Statistics. (2000). *Marriage, divorce and adoption statistics* (ONS, Series FM2, No. 26). London: Stationery Office.

Morgan, D. (1996). *Family connections*. Cambridge, UK: Polity.

Morgan, D. (1999). Risk and family practices: Accounting for change and fluidity in family life. In E. B. Silva & C. Smart (Eds.), *The new family?* (pp. 13–30). Thousand Oaks, CA: Sage.

Murphy, M., & Wang, D. (1999). Forecasting British families into the twenty-first century. In S. McRae (Ed.), *Changing Britain: Families and households in the 1990s* (pp. 100–137). New York: Oxford University Press.

Pinnelli, A. (1995). Women's condition, low fertility, and emerging union patterns in Europe. In K. Mason & A. M. Jensen (Eds.), *Gender and family change in industrialized countries* (pp. 82–101). Oxford, UK: Clarendon.

Prinz, C. (1995). *Cohabiting, married, or single*. Aldershot, UK: Avebury.

Qvortrup, J., Bardy, M., Sgritta, G., & Wintersberger, H. (Eds.). (1994). *Childhood matters: Social theory, practice and politics*. Aldershot, UK: Avebury.

Ribbens McCarthy, J., Edwards, R., & Gillies, V. (2000). Moral tales of the child and the adult. *Sociology*, *34*, 785–803.

Schoenmaeckers, R., & Lodewijckx, E. (1999). Demographic behaviour in Europe. *European Journal of Population*, *15*, 207–240.

Simpson, B. (1998). *Changing families*. Oxford, UK: Berg.

Smart, C. (1999). The "new" parenthood: Fathers and mothers after divorce. In E. B. Silva & C. Smart (Eds.), *The new family?* (pp. 100–114). Thousand Oaks, CA: Sage.

Smart, C., & Neale, B. (1999). *Family fragments?* Cambridge, UK: Polity.

Wallace, C., & Kovatcheva, S. (1998). *Youth in society: The construction and deconstruction of youth in East and West Europe*. New York: Macmillan.

CHAPTER 18

Stepfamilies
Changes and Challenges

KAY PASLEY AND BRAD S. MOOREFIELD

Given the changing social, legal, and economic contexts (Arnup, 1999), it is not surprising that the heterogeneity of the American family has become more visible. This diversity is evident in increases in the numbers of people that have experienced divorce, remarriage, and cohabitation since the 1970s (Teachman, 2000), and academic discourse about this diversity has followed these trends.

One outcome of the increased diversity is greater attention given to the study of stepfamilies. Historically, stepfamilies were most often formed following the death of a parent; now they usually follow parental divorce. In addition, stepfamilies are more broadly defined than in the past, reflecting their greater diversity. Stepfamilies are now recognized as consisting of any biological or adoptive parent (heterosexual, gay, or lesbian) with a child from a prior relationship who elects to marry or to cohabit (the latter have been called nonlegal stepfamilies; Bumpass, Raley, & Sweet, 1995).

In this chapter, we briefly summarize the literature, noting insights gleaned especially from research since the new millennium. We identify conceptual, methodological, and empirical topics that need to be examined more completely, and we offer suggestions for addressing them.

Remarriage and stepfamilies were the focus of few research efforts before 1970. In fact, beyond two articles addressing the incidence of these marital transitions (Glick & Norton, 1971; Troll, 1971), few studies were published on stepparents in these early years. The body of knowledge regarding stepfamilies has grown immensely since then. By 1980, stepfamilies had received some attention by researchers, as evident in decade reviews on nontraditional family forms (Macklin, 1980) in the *Journal of Marriage and the Family (JMF)* that included stepfamilies. In another *JMF* review, stepfamilies were classified as noninstitutions, and terms like *reconstituted, blended,* and *binuclear families* were used to describe them (Price-Bonham & Balswick, 1980). By 1990, there were well over 200 scholarly publications from which to draw in a *JMF* decade review, justifying an entire article addressing research on remarriage and stepfamilies (Coleman & Ganong, 1990). However, the 1990s were seen as "a period of enormous productivity in the study of remarriage and stepfamilies" (Coleman, Ganong, & Fine, 2000, p. 1288), and the resulting review was derived from the examination of over 850 publications. Thus, an increasing number of studies are contributing to the knowledge base on stepfamilies. (For a comprehensive bibliography of the empirical literature on stepfamilies, visit the Stepfamily Association of America Web site at www.saafamilies. org.)

DEMOGRAPHIC TRENDS

The *Population Profile of the United States: 2000* (U.S. Bureau of the Census, 2002), weighting the 1996 Survey of Income and Program Participation (SIPP) data by population controls based on the decennial census, reported that 17% of all children in the United States under the age of 18 lived in a remarried stepfamily household and another 5% lived with a parent and the parent's cohabiting partner. Because these figures exclude nonresident stepfamilies, our best guess is that legal and nonlegal resident and nonresident stepfamilies compose about 30% of the households containing children under 18 years of age. These are estimates because the National Center for Health Statistics suspended collection of detailed information on marriage, divorce, and remarriage in 1996, making it is impossible to identify accurately the number and characteristics of remarriages and stepfamilies. Further, recent estimates, based on national surveys completed before the 2000 decennial census, contain inconsistencies because data were gathered retrospectively or because different comparison groups were used in various reports (e.g., data from both men and women or from women of certain age ranges). In addition, the number of children

residing with a biological parent and stepparent cannot be determined from many of the reports from the U.S. Bureau of the Census. Data typically are reported on whether children are living with two adults, but the relationship of the adults to the children in the household is not known.

Kreider and Fields (2002), reporting findings from a nationally representative sample of men and women ages 15 years and older in 1996 from the SIPP data, estimated that about 50% of all first marriages ended in divorce (50% for men regardless of age group, and 44–52% for women depending on the referenced age group). Further, 54% of men and 60% of women had been married once, about 13% of both men and women had been married twice, and about 3% of both genders had been married three or more times. The median duration of first marriages that ended in divorce was 7.8 years, time from first separation to divorce was 0.8 years, median time between divorce and remarriage was 3 years, and duration of remarriages that ended in divorce was 7.3 years for men and 6.8 years for women. These results are similar to data from earlier periods (e.g., Norton & Moorman, 1987), with two notable exceptions: In the more recent data, individuals were spending about 1 year longer between divorce and remarriage, and remarried couples that had divorced remained together longer than the median of 4.5 years reported earlier (Norton & Miller, 1993).

Recent reports from the National Survey of Family Growth showed that black women experienced the highest rate of relationship disruption and were the least likely to remarry; they also were more likely to end a second marriage (Bramlett & Mosher, 2002). Social class indicators—lower median family income, male unemployment, poverty, and receipt of welfare— also are associated with instability in remarriage for women, as is the presence of children (Bumpass,

Sweet, & Martin, 1990; Furstenberg & Cherlin, 1991; Wilson & Clarke, 1992).

RESEARCH ON REMARRIAGE AND STEPFAMILY ADJUSTMENT

Before the 1970s, mentions of the quality of remarriages or stepfamily adjustment were rare. By 1980, there were several studies with conflicting results regarding whether individuals in remarriages were more or less happy than those in first marriages (e.g., Glenn & Weaver, 1977; Renne, 1971; White, 1979). During the 1980s, the few researchers that focused on marital processes or stepfamily functioning (Coleman & Ganong, 1990) generally found few differences in marital satisfaction (e.g., Vemer, Coleman, Ganong, & Cooper, 1989) and well-being (e.g., Nock, 1981; Weingarten, 1980) between individuals in remarriages and first marriages.

Stepfamilies were noted to be less cohesive and less effective problem solvers than nuclear families, but most were not in the clinical range for these behaviors (e.g., Anderson & White, 1986; Bray, 1988; Peek, Bell, Waldren, & Sorell, 1988). Most studies in the 1980s were between-group designs that ignored stepfamily complexity, continuing a deficit-model approach and upholding the nuclear family as the ideal family structure.

By the 1990s, there was an increased focus on marital dynamics, quality, and stability among remarriage researchers (Coleman et al., 2000). Studies using larger samples as well as qualitative designs increased in number. Cohabitation before remarriage was found to be a common part of courtship, but research was lacking on decision-making processes regarding cohabitation and the effects of cohabitation on stepfamily life (Coleman et al., 2000). Few researchers examined the processes and mechanisms for building satisfying remarriages or for disrupting these relationships. However, researchers

in the last decade of the 20th century showed more interest in remarriage dynamics than they had in earlier periods. They reported that decision making was perceived to be shared between spouses (e.g., Crosbie-Burnett & Giles-Sims, 1991; Pyke & Coltrane, 1996); that remarried couples expressed criticism, anger, and irritation more openly than first-married couples (Bray & Kelly, 1998; Hetherington, 1993); that men conceded more during marital conflicts than they did in their first marriages (Hobart, 1991); and that women had more power in financial decisions in remarriage than they had in their first marriages (e.g., Burgoyne & Morrison, 1997). Moreover, consensus-building behaviors were found to be important to stepfamily adjustment (Bray, Berger, & Boethel, 1994; Ganong & Coleman, 1994b), and expecting the remarriage and stepfamily to operate like a first-marriage family could be problematic (Bray & Kelly, 1998).

Research examining gay and lesbian stepfamilies expanded somewhat in recent years. These studies were characterized by use of qualitative methods and small samples (Lynch, 2000). The presence of a child was associated with increased relationship satisfaction and intimacy for lesbian couples (Koepke & Hare, 1992), and stepfamily satisfaction was associated with gay stepfathers' feeling included and experiencing fewer problems with children's movement between households (Crosbie-Burnett & Helmbrecht, 1993).

STEPPARENTING

Early authors identified the major problem areas for stepparents as children, finances, and the ambiguity surrounding stepparenting (e.g., Bohannon, 1970; Duberman, 1975; Messinger, 1976). Most stepparenting studies have focused on stepfather families. Interestingly, an early study (Goldstein, 1974) suggested that being a stepmother was less difficult than being a stepfather—a conclusion that has not received much support since then (e.g., Bray, 1988; MacDonald & DeMaris, 1996).

In general, a common conclusion from research in the 1980s and 1990s is that being a stepparent is more difficult than raising one's own children, especially when the stepparent is a stepmother (e.g., MacDonald & DeMaris, 1996). Variations in role expectations and behaviors present problems for stepparents in deciding what their roles are or should be in the lives of stepchildren, especially early in remarriage (Bray & Kelly, 1998; Hetherington & Kelly, 2002), but typically there is couple consensus that involvement should increase over time and that stepparents should and do assume more parental responsibilities (Bray & Berger, 1993; Ganong & Coleman, 1994a). This pattern is characteristic also of gay- and lesbian-headed stepfamilies; however, Lynch (2000) found homosexual stepparents to be more flexible in adopting parenting roles than heterosexual stepfamilies.

Stepparents are provided greater latitude than biological parents in what is perceived as acceptable behavior. For example, stepfathers are expected to assume less responsibility for the care and control of stepchildren than are fathers (e.g., Fine, 1995; Hetherington & Kelly, 2002). However, if greater latitude is not coupled with realistic expectations, then stepparenting is difficult (Bray & Kelly, 1998).

Researchers have shown interest in identifying factors that affect stepparenting (e.g., age and sex of the child and sex of the stepparent). Stepparents have more conflicts with adolescent stepchildren than with younger stepchildren (Bray & Kelly, 1998; Golish & Caughlin, 2002; Hetherington & Kelly, 2002; MacDonald & DeMaris, 1996). Adolescents react negatively to attempts by stepparents to limit or control their behavior (Bray & Kelly, 1998; Golish & Caughlin, 2002;

Hetherington & Kelly, 2002), even when the stepparent uses strategies characteristic of an authoritative parenting style (e.g., warmth, control). Parenting a stepdaughter is more challenging than parenting a stepson, as relationships between stepparents and stepdaughters are characterized by more conflict and negative interactions than are relationships between stepparents and stepsons (e.g., Hetherington & Clingempeel, 1992). In one of the few observational studies, Vuchinich, Hetherington, Vuchinich, and Clingempeel (1991) found that stepdaughters avoided conflicts and other interactions with stepfathers; however, when stepfathers initiated conflict, stepdaughters' oppositional responses persisted. Such extended conflicts are consistent with reports in earlier studies of hostile, resentful withdrawal by stepdaughters (e.g., Bray, 1988; Hetherington, 1989).

When the stepparent is a resident stepmother, conflict and negativity are exacerbated (Bray, 1988; MacDonald & DeMaris, 1996). In part, this may stem from implicit expectations associated with women's family roles and the structural complexity of stepmother families (Dunn, Davies, O'Connor, & Sturgess, 2000). For example, as stepmothers take on an inequitable share of family work, as they believe they should (Ceglian & Gardner, 2000; Orchard & Solberg, 1999), their relationships with stepchildren suffer (Ceglian & Gardner, 2000; Fine, Donnelly, & Voydanoff, 1991).

Stepfathers typically develop more positive relationships with stepchildren than stepmothers do, especially with stepsons over time. This may be because they make fewer attempts to monitor or control stepchildren's behaviors early in remarriage (Bray & Kelly, 1998). Hetherington (1993) noted that stepfathers control their own negative feelings better than biological fathers do, and they attempt to establish a relationship with their stepchildren by self-disclosing and searching for common interests and experiences—all in the face of aversive behavior from their stepchildren. There is no evidence that these strategies are used by stepmothers or, if used, are successful.

Recently, researchers have examined linkages among relationships *within* the family. For example, MacDonald and DeMaris (2002) found (a) that when the quality of the mother-child relationship was good, the stepfather-stepchild relationship benefited; and (b) that conflict between the biological parents was related negatively to the quality of the stepfather-stepchild relationship. Other researchers reported that mother-child relationship quality was related to the quality of the mother's relationship with her partner and that the termination of that partnership was associated with poorer parenting quality (Thomson, Mosley, Hanson, & McLanahan, 2001).

We think that extant research findings do not adequately explain why stepparent-stepchild relationships are so challenging. Speculations offered by researchers suggest that stepparents' problems stem from stepchildren's perception that they are being treated differently than biological children (Clingempeel, Coylar, & Hetherington, 1994; Ganong & Coleman, 1994a). Findings indicate that (a) stepparents communicate more poorly with stepchildren than with their own children, (b) stepparents feel less warmth toward stepchildren and vice versa, (c) stepparents express fewer positive feelings and make fewer positive comments to stepchildren, and (d) stepparents provide less support and monitoring of stepchildren (Bray et al., 1994; Ganong & Coleman, 1994b; MacDonald & DeMaris, 1996; Mekos, Hetherington, & Reiss, 1996; Thomson, McLanahan, & Curtis, 1991). Poor communication, lack of warmth, fewer positive expressions, and less support and monitoring may combine to foster children's feeling more disconnected and more resistant to change (parental remarriage) and agents of change (stepparents). It also has been

suggested that part of this differential treatment results from the competition that occurs between stepparents and stepchildren as they vie for attention from the biological parents (Saint-Jacques, 1995). However, these speculations imply a unidirectional effect (i.e., stepparent behaviors affect children) rather than bidirectional effects (i.e., stepparents and stepchildren mutually influence each other's behavior). Golish and Caughlin (2002) reported that adolescent stepchildren communicated infrequently with stepparents and avoided confiding in them as a means of reducing potential conflict, suggesting that stepchildren's behavior plays a role in interactions with stepparents. Braithwaite, Olson, Golish, Soukup, and Turman (2001) found that failure to set boundaries and establish trust in the stepparent-stepchild relationship was associated with increased conflict, loss of hope, and lack of cohesion. Studies exploring bidirectional interactions (e.g., Vuchinich et al., 1991) are needed, especially addressing changes over time.

Studies are also needed that examine intergenerational relationships between older remarried parents, stepparents, and adult stepchildren. Although there have been some studies of intergenerational relationships (e.g., Ganong & Coleman, 1999; Spitze & Logan, 1992; Marks, 1995), particularly of transfers of resources (e.g., economic, informal care; Goldscheider, Thornton, & Li-Shou, 2001), more research is needed on stepfamilies across the life course.

RESEARCH ON CHILD OUTCOMES

There has been tremendous growth in the number of studies in which the effects of remarriages and stepfamilies on children have been examined. Coleman and Ganong (1990) suggested that two paradigms, a problem-oriented perspective and a normative-adaptive perspective, characterized this research, with the former receiving the greatest attention. Typically, problem-oriented studies included between-group comparisons of psychological (e.g., self-esteem) and behavioral problems in children residing in stepfamily households, nuclear family households, and single-parent-headed households. Normative-adaptive studies tended to examine children's outcomes and stepfamily processes like emotional closeness and conflict. By 2000, over one third of the studies "dealt with the effects on children of living with a remarried or cohabiting stepparent" (Coleman et al., 2000, p. 1292), and many used data from national, longitudinal studies (e.g., National Survey of Families and Households). Typical outcome measures included multiple indicators of academic performance, internalizing behaviors, and externalizing behaviors. The results of a meta-analysis (Amato, 1994) indicated that differences in children's outcomes by family structure were small and that most stepchildren did not have psychological and behavior difficulties or school-related problems. Since the review by Coleman et al. (2000), researchers continue to report mixed findings regarding stepchildren's outcomes: In some studies, there are no differences between stepchildren and other children (e.g., Ackerman, D'Eramo, Umylny, Schultz, & Izard, 2001); in other studies, stepchildren are at a deficit (e.g., Aquilino & Supple, 2001; Wills, Sandy, Yaeger, & Shinar, 2001); and in other studies, differences disappear when demographic controls are included (e.g., Hoffman, 2002).

A good deal is known about factors associated with children's outcomes, such as demographic and other characteristics of children and their parents that predate the remarriage (Amato & Booth, 1996; Simons & Associates, 1996). Findings also show that multiple transitions and marital conflict are related to poor adjustment for stepchildren (Hanson & McLanahan, 1996; Kurdek, Fine, & Sinclair, 1995). However, few researchers have examined causal linkages among various factors and stepchildren's outcomes (e.g., Buchanan, Maccoby, & Dornbusch, 1996).

Some studies have provided information on factors that may protect stepchildren from poor outcomes. Coughlin and Vuchinich (1996) found in a prospective study that good family problem solving protected boys in stepfamilies from increased risk for delinquency but that problem solving did not offer the same positive effect for children in two-parent nuclear families or single-mother families. Other research suggests that stepparents may buffer the negative outcomes of divorce on children through improving their economic status (McLanahan & Sandefur, 1994). Still other research (Bray & Kelly, 1998; Hetherington & Clingempeel, 1992) showed that a stepparent who assumes the role of monitor (e.g., camp counselor) is less likely to exacerbate child-related problems than are stepparents who quickly attempt to take control and to initiate many changes in household rules and routines. Parents' and stepparents' use of authoritative parenting involving warmth, high monitoring, low coerciveness, firm but responsive control and demands, and expectations for mature behavior has been associated with less externalizing and internalizing behavior and greater social and academic competence in children (Hetherington, 1993; Hetherington & Kelly, 2002).

It would be difficult to accurately predict which children resided in stepfamilies and which resided in first-marriage families on the basis of behavioral outcomes (e.g., academic achievement, aggression, anxiety, depression, delinquent acts). However, this is not to suggest that children in stepfamilies are problem free. Findings from nationally representative samples in both the United States and Britain suggest that about 20% of stepchildren are at risk for negative outcomes—somewhat more than children living with both biological parents (Cherlin et al., 1991). This represents a sizable portion of children and deserves attention and concern (Bray, 1999).

FUTURE RESEARCH

Demographic Needs

We think it is essential that demographers and other researchers keep stepfamilies' structural complexities at the forefront of new data collection efforts. A primary concern with available demographic data is that the number of stepfamilies is underestimated. Stepfamilies often are omitted from demographic studies when residential stepchildren are older than 18 and when stepchildren reside elsewhere (i.e., with their other parent, a grandparent, on their own). In addition, stepfamilies headed by cohabiting adults often are designated as single-parent families. The lack of accurate stepfamily demographic data makes it difficult for researchers to determine the representativeness of local samples. If researchers are to successfully study the complexity of stepfamilies, reliable demographic information is needed.

Remarriage and Stepfamily Interaction Research

In additional to the need for demographic information, we think that studies are needed that identify stepfamily processes and strategies related to making effective decisions, resolving problems, and effectively negotiating solutions, particularly involving issues related to children. Searching for similarities and differences in processes among varied stepfamily structures and within different cultural contexts is an essential activity. Some questions worthy of study include:

- Are there common strategies used in making decisions and resolving problems in stepfamilies? Do strategies vary in different structural variations of stepfamilies?
- How does the remarried stepfamily process differ from that in cohabiting stepfamilies and first-marriage families?
- How does the intersection of socioeconomic status and race affect stepfamily processes?
- What influence, if any, do interactions from previous relationships have on remarriages?
- What factors contribute to remarital adjustment?
- How does the intersection of gender and parental status affect remarriage? How does this intersection affect the way in which conflict is resolved and finances are managed?

Although some researchers suggest that the greater instability of remarriages may be due in part to spouses' personality characteristics, this has not been examined thoroughly (see Coleman et al., 2000, for a discussion). Important for future efforts are studies that tease out the nature, level, and processes through which personality characteristics interact with demographic characteristics and marital interaction patterns to explain marital interaction and stability. Because scholars often examine few explanatory variables (e.g., either personality characteristics or demographic characteristics), testing more comprehensive models of the etiology and outcomes of marital interaction is needed. Only by doing so will we understand developmental pathways and conditions that affect these pathways (e.g., redivorce).

Between-group designs can be used to address potential differences between first marriages and remarriages. For example, it would be worthwhile to identify the threshold under which the balance between exchanges of negative messages (e.g., criticism) and positive messages (e.g., concession;

Gottman, 1994) is disrupted by husbands' willingness to concede to wives during arguments (Hobart, 1991) and prompts movement toward marital dissatisfaction and instability.

There is limited research on the effects of multiple relationship transitions beyond those that are legal marriages. Future researchers need to examine the complexity of relationship transitions because many individuals experience multiple relationships between marriages, and others elect not to marry at all but experience a succession of cohabiting relationships.

Intersecting Systems and Stepfamily Research

Few scholars have addressed the ways in which various systems (e.g., family, work, school) affect remarriages and stepfamilies. Presser (2000), a notable exception, found that nonstandard work schedules (e.g., working evenings, nights, or rotating schedules and weekends) increased marital instability only for those with children and that remarried women married 5 or more years were more likely to divorce. Although this study represents an effort to connect work and stepfamilies, future research could address how nonstandard work schedules affect different types of stepfamilies, how stepfamilies are affected when only one or both partners have nonstandard work schedules, and the influence of competent child care on work-stepfamily intersections. Research on the intersections of work, income, and race should also be undertaken with stepfamilies to provide insight into work-stepfamily linkages.

Another systemic link of importance is between current and prior family relationships. For example, a recent study showed that for women in stepfamilies, economic obligations to stepchildren, jealousy of husbands'

former wives, and lack of support from friends and family were associated with less marital happiness, more thoughts of divorce, and regrets regarding marriage (Knox & Zusman, 2001). Although there are some studies regarding co-parenting after divorce (e.g., Stewart, 1999), little is known about co-parenting relationships after remarriage (Buehler & Ryan, 1994). For instance, there is no research on how co-parenting following remarriage affects children who reside in stepfamily households compared to those who live elsewhere and visit stepfamily households.

There is even less knowledge about the intersection between stepfamilies and extended kin, such as grandparents, aunts, and cousins. Although there have been are a few recent studies about extended kin relationships (e.g., Mills, Wakeman, & Fea, 2001), these studies have not shed much light on the dynamics of such relationships or their effects on stepfamily members. The dearth of information on these relationships might suggest that stepfamilies reside in isolation or are immune to the effects of relationships with extended family members; stepfamily researchers' pragmatic decisions to limit data collection to household residents prevents scholars from exploring these relationships.

Child Outcome Research and Stepfamilies

We agree with other scholars who contend that stepfamily researchers persist in focusing on negative outcomes for stepchildren (see Chapter 15 of this book; Bray, 1999; Coleman et al., 2000). Moreover, most researchers focus on statistical significance and fail to address the magnitude of effects. Bray (1999) argued that many of the statistically significant differences between children from different family structures, including stepfamilies, are due to developmental changes rather than deficits resulting from residing in a particular family structure. We question the value of continuing to ask about differences in child outcomes by family structure unless there are greater attempts to employ conceptual models that address the processes and mechanisms by which certain outcomes result. In place of exploring between-group differences, greater attention must be directed toward making within-group comparisons in which the diversity of developmental pathways experienced by stepchildren and stepfamilies and the conditions that enhance or inhibit certain outcomes are examined.

Theoretical and Methodological Needs

Researchers have long called for the use of theories (e.g., systems, life course, exchange, and stress; Price-Bonham & Balswick, 1980) and for increased theory-building efforts in the study of stepfamilies (Coleman & Ganong, 1990). Some of these calls have been heeded. For example, Robila and Taylor (2001) noted that many studies on stepparent-adolescent relationships explicitly relied on theory (most often systems theory) to frame their studies. There has been greater use of life course theory (e.g., Vartanian & McNamara, 2002; Wilmoth & Koso, 2002) to examine stepfamilies, with a focus on multiple trajectories and social contexts. More use of social exchange and other economic theories has occurred (e.g., Elman & London, 2002; Sweeney, 2002). Since the 1990s, in particular, the use of qualitative approaches, such as phenomenology and grounded theory (e.g., Arnaut, Fromme, Stoll, & Felker, 2000), has increased.

Because family structure alone provides little, if any, explanatory power (e.g., Biblarz & Gottainer, 2000), inductive theory-building efforts have increased (e.g., Braithwaite et al., 2001; Lansford, Ceballo, & Stewart, 2001; Kim, Hetherington, & Reiss, 1999). The development and testing of inductive models, especially in concert with observational methods, have potential to provide insight into stepfamily dynamics.

Measures used to assess remarriage and stepfamily dynamics continue to be instruments that were designed and validated on first-marriage families. Thus, there is a need for the development of reliable and valid measures that are developed to assess the unique aspects of stepfamilies.

Further, few researchers have used mixed-methods design in studying remarriages and stepfamilies. The use of mixed-methods designs, observational methods, and sequential analyses would better inform us about the patterns of interaction that serve stepfamilies well.

Over the last several years, there has been an increased reliance on secondary analyses of data sets drawn from nationally representative samples (e.g., National Education Longitudinal Study [NELS]:88; the National Survey of Families and Households [NSFH], SIPP). For researchers, this means working within the confines of existing questions and measures that often were not created to study stepfamilies. Although these data provide fertile grounds for scholars to pursue valuable research questions, reliance on these data limits the ability to understand stepfamily processes.

Ultimately, research that provides insight into stepfamily processes is helpful to prevention and intervention efforts that can best serve stepfamilies in the future. We challenge researchers to continue to identify and discuss the application of their findings to the real-life needs of stepfamilies. Only then will research contribute to the improving the quality of life in these complex families.

REFERENCES

Ackerman, B. P., D'Eramo, K. S., Umylny, L., Schultz, D., & Izard, C. E. (2001). Family structure and the externalizing behavior of children from economically disadvantaged families. *Journal of Family Psychology, 15*, 288–300.

Amato, P. R. (1994). The implication of research findings on children in stepfamilies. In A. Booth & L. Dunn (Eds.), *Stepfamilies: Who benefits? Who does not?* (pp. 81–87). Hillsdale, NJ: Lawrence Erlbaum.

Amato, P. R., & Booth, A. (1996). A prospective study of divorce and parent-child relationships. *Journal of Marriage and the Family, 58*, 356–365.

Anderson, J. Z., & White, G. D. (1986). Dysfunctional intact families and stepfamilies. *Family Process, 25*, 407–422.

Aquilino, W., & Supple, A. (2001). Long-term effects of parenting practices during adolescence on well-being outcomes in young adults. *Journal of Family Issues, 22*, 289–308.

Arnaut, G., Fromme, D., Stoll, B., & Felker, J. (2000). A qualitative analysis of stepfamilies: The biological parent. *Journal of Divorce and Remarriage, 33*(3/4), 111–128.

Arnup, K. (1999). Out of this world: The social and legal context of gay and lesbian families. *Journal of Gay and Lesbian Social Services, 10*, 1–25.

Biblarz, T., & Gottainer, G. (2000). Family structure and children's success: A comparison of widowed and divorced single-mother families. *Journal of Marriage and the Family, 62*, 533–548.

Bohannon, P. (1970). Divorce chains, households of remarriage, and multiple divorcers. In P. Bohannon (Ed.), *Divorce and after* (pp. 113–123). New York: Doubleday.

Braithwaite, D., Olson, L., Golish, T., Soukup, C., & Turman, P. (2001). "Becoming a family": Developmental process represented in blended family discourse. *Journal of Applied Communication Research, 29*, 221–247.

Bramlett, M. D., & Mosher, W. D. (2002). *Cohabitation, marriage, divorce, and remarriage in the United States* (Vital Health Statistics, 23[22], DHHS Publication No. [PHS] 2002-1998). Hyattsville, MD: U.S. Department of Health and Human Services.

Bray, J. H. (1988). Children's development during early remarriage. In E. M. Hetherington & J. Arasteh (Eds.), *The impact of divorce, single-parenting and step-parenting on children* (pp. 279–298). Hillsdale, NJ: Lawrence Erlbaum.

Bray, J. H. (1999). From marriage to remarriage and beyond: Findings from the Developmental Issues in Stepfamilies Research Project. In E. M. Hetherington (Ed.), *Coping with divorce, single parenting and remarriage: A risk and resiliency approach* (pp. 253–271). Mahwah, NJ: Lawrence Erlbaum.

Bray, J. H., & Berger, S. H. (1993). Developmental issues in stepfamilies research project: Family relations and parent-child interactions. *Journal of Family Psychology, 7*, 3–8.

Bray, J. H., Berger, S. H., & Boethel, C. L. (1994). Role integration and marital adjustment in stepfamilies. In K. Pasley & M. Ihinger-Tallman (Eds.), *Stepparenting: Issues in theory, research, and practice* (pp. 69–86). Westport, CT: Greenwood.

Bray, J. H., & Kelly, J. (1998). *Stepfamilies.* New York: Broadway.

Buchanan, C. M., Maccoby, E. E., & Dornbusch, S. M. (1996). *Adolescents after divorce.* Cambridge, MA: Harvard University Press.

Buehler, C., & Ryan, C. (1994). Former spouse relations and noncustodial father involvement during marital and family transitions: A closer look at remarriage following divorce. In K. Pasley & M. Ihinger-Tallman (Ed.), *Stepparenting: Issues in theory, research, and practice* (pp. 127–150). Westport, CT: Greenwood.

Bumpass, L. L., Raley, R. K., & Sweet, J. (1995). The changing character of stepfamilies: Implications of cohabitation and nonmarital childbearing. *Demography, 32,* 425–436.

Bumpass, L. L., Sweet, J. A., & Martin, T. C. (1990). Changing patterns of remarriage. *Journal of Marriage and the Family, 52,* 747–756.

Burgoyne, C. B., & Morrison, V. (1997). Money in remarriage: Keeping things simple and separate. *Sociological Review, 45,* 363–395.

Ceglian, C. P., & Gardner, S. (2000). Attachment style and the "wicked stepmother" spiral. *Journal of Divorce and Remarriage, 34*(1–2), 111–129.

Cherlin, A. J., Furstenberg, F. F., Jr., Chase-Lansdale, P. L., Kiernan, K., Robins, P., Morrison, D., & Teitler, J. (1991). Longitudinal studies of effects of divorce on children in Great Britain and the United States. *Science, 252,* 1345–1460.

Clingempeel, W. G., Coylar, J. J., & Hetherington, E. M. (1994). Toward a cognitive dissonance conceptualization of stepchildren and biological children loyalty conflicts: A construct validity study. In K. Pasley & M. Ihinger-Tallman (Eds.), *Stepparenting* (pp. 151–174). Westport, CT: Greenwood.

Coleman, M., & Ganong, L. (1990). Remarriage and stepfamily research in the 80s: New interest in an old family form. *Journal of Marriage and the Family, 52,* 925–940.

Coleman, M., Ganong, L., & Fine, M. A. (2000). Reinvestigating remarriage: Another decade of progress. *Journal of Marriage and the Family, 62,* 1288–1307.

Coughlin, C., & Vuchinich, S. (1996). Family experience in preadolescence and the development of male delinquency. *Journal of Marriage and the Family, 58,* 491–501.

Crosbie-Burnett, M., & Giles-Sims, J. (1991). Marital power in stepfather families: A test of normative resource theory. *Journal of Family Psychology, 4,* 484–496.

Crosbie-Burnett, M., & Helmbrecht, L. (1993). A descriptive empirical study of gay male stepfamilies. *Family Relations, 42,* 256–263.

Duberman, L. (1975). *The reconstituted family.* Chicago: Nelson-Hall.

Dunn, J., Davies, L. C., O'Connor, T. G., & Sturgess, W. (2000). Parents' and partners' life course and family experiences: Links with parent-child relationships in different family settings. *Journal of Child Psychology and Psychiatry, 41,* 955–968.

Elman, C., & London, A. S. (2002). Sociohistorical and demographic perspectives on U.S. remarriage in 1910. *Social Science History, 26,* 199–241.

Fine, M. A. (1995). The clarity and content of the stepparent role: A review of the literature. *Journal of Divorce and Remarriage, 24*(1/2), 19–34.

Fine, M., Donnelly, B. W., & Voydanoff, P. (1991). The relation cognitions and maternal satisfaction in stepfather families. *Family Perspective, 25,* 19–26.

Furstenberg, F. F., Jr., & Cherlin, A. (1991). *Divided families.* Cambridge, MA: Harvard University Press

Ganong, L., & Coleman, M. (1994a). Adolescent stepchild-stepparent relationships: Changes over time. In K. Pasley & M. Ihinger-Tallman (Eds.), *Stepfamilies* (pp. 87–104). Westport, CT: Greenwood.

Ganong, L., & Coleman, M. (1994b). *Remarried family relationships.* Thousand Oaks, CA: Sage.

Ganong, L., & Coleman, M. (1999). *Changing family responsibilities.* Mahwah, NJ: Lawrence Erlbaum.

Glenn, N. D., & Weaver, C. N. (1977). The marital happiness of remarried divorced persons. *Journal of Marriage and the Family, 39,* 331–337.

Glick, P. C., & Norton, A. J. (1971). Frequency, duration, and probability of marriage and divorce. *Journal of Marriage and the Family, 33,* 307–317.

Goldscheider, F., Thornton, A., & Li-Shou, Y. (2001). Helping out the kids: Expectations about parental support in young adulthood. *Journal of Marriage and Family, 63,* 727–740.

Goldstein, H. S. (1974). Reconstituted families: The second marriage and its children. *Psychiatric Quarterly, 48,* 433–440.

Golish, D. T., & Caughlin, J. P. (2002). Life satisfaction in teenage boys: The moderating role of father involvement and bullying. *Aggressive Behavior, 28,* 126–133.

Gottman, J. M. (1994). *What predicts divorce.* Hillsdale, NJ: Lawrence Erlbaum.

Hanson, T. L., & McLanahan, S. S. (1996). Double jeopardy: Parental conflict and stepfamily outcomes for children. *Journal of Marriage and the Family, 58,* 141–154.

Hetherington, E. M. (1989). Coping with family transitions: Winners, losers, and survivors. *Child Development, 60,* 1–14.

Hetherington, E. M. (1993). An overview of the Virginia Longitudinal Study of Divorce and Remarriage with a focus on early adolescence. *Journal of Family Psychology, 7,* 39–96.

Hetherington, E. M., & Clingempeel, W. (1992). Coping with marital transitions: A family systems perspective. *Monographs of the Society for Research in Child Development, 1–2, 54.*

Hetherington, E. M., & Kelly, J. (2002). *For better or worse.* New York: Norton.

Hobart, C. (1991). Conflict in remarriage. *Journal of Divorce and Remarriage, 15*(3–4), 69–86.

Hoffman, P. (2002). The community context of family structure and adolescent drug use. *Journal of Marriage and Family, 64,* 314–330.

Kim, J. E., Hetherington, E. M., & Reiss, D. (1999). Associations among family relationships, antisocial peers, and adolescents' externalizing behaviors: Gender and family type differences. *Child Development, 70,* 1209–1230.

Knox, D., & Zusman, M. E. (2001). Marrying a man with "baggage": Implications for second wives. *Journal of Divorce and Remarriage, 35*(3/4), 67–79.

Koepke, L., & Hare, J. (1992). Relationship quality in a sample of lesbian couples with children and child-free lesbian couples. *Family Relations, 41,* 224–230.

Kreider, R. M., & Fields, J. M. (2002). *Number, timing, and duration of marriage and divorces: 1996* (Current Population Reports, P70-80). Washington, DC: U.S. Bureau of the Census.

Kurdek, L., Fine, M., & Sinclair, R. (1995). School adjustment in sixth graders: Parenting transitions, family climate, and peer norm effects. *Child Development, 66,* 430–445.

Lansford, J., Ceballo, R., & Stewart, A. (2001). Does family structure matter? A comparison of adoptive, two-parent biological, single-mother, and stepmother households. *Journal of Marriage and Family, 63,* 840–854.

Lynch, J. M. (2000). Considerations of family structure and gender composition: The lesbian and gay stepfamily. *Journal of Homosexuality, 40*(2), 81–95.

MacDonald, W. L., & DeMaris, A. (1996). The effects of stepparent's gender and new biological children. *Journal of Family Issues, 17,* 5–25.

MacDonald, W. L., & DeMaris, A. (2002). Stepfather-stepchild relationship quality: The stepfather's demand for conformity and the biological father's involvement. *Journal of Family Issues, 23,* 121–137.

Macklin, E. D. (1980). Nontraditional family forms: A decade of research. *Journal of Marriage and the Family, 52,* 905–922.

Marks, N. F. (1995). Midlife marital status differences in social support relationships with adult children and psychological well-being. *Journal of Family Issues, 16,* 5–28.

McLanahan, S. S., & Sandefur, G. (1994). *Growing up with a single parent.* Cambridge, MA: Harvard University Press.

Mekos, D., Hetherington, E. M., & Reiss, D. (1996). Sibling differences in problem behavior and parental treatment in nondivorced and remarried families. *Child Development, 67,* 2148–2165.

Messinger, L. (1976). Remarriage between divorced people: A proposal for preparation for remarriage. *Journal of Marriage and Family Counseling, 2,* 193–200.

Mills, T. L, Wakeman, M. A., & Fea, C. B. (2001). Adult grandchildren's perceptions of emotional closeness and consensus with their maternal and paternal grandparents. *Journal of Family Issues, 22,* 427–456.

Nock, S. (1981). Family life-cycle transitions: Longitudinal effects on family members. *Journal of Marriage and the Family, 43,* 703–713.

Norton, A. J., & Miller, L. F. (1993). *Marriage divorce and remarriage in the 1990's* (Current Population Reports, Series P-23, No. 180). Washington, DC: Government Printing Office.

Norton, A. J., & Moorman, J. E. (1987). Current trends in marriage and divorce among American women. *Journal of Marriage and the Family, 49,* 3–14.

Orchard, A. L., & Solberg, K. B. (1999). Expectations of the stepmother role. *Journal of Divorce and Remarriage, 31*(1/2), 107–123.

Peek, C., Bell, N., Waldren, T., & Sorell, G. (1988). Patterns of functioning in families of remarried and first-married couples. *Journal of Marriage and the Family, 50,* 699–708.

Presser, H. B. (2000). Nonstandard work schedules and marital instability. *Journal of Marriage and the Family, 62,* 93–110.

Price-Bonham, S., & Balswick, J. O. (1980). The noninstitutions: Divorce, desertion, and remarriage. *Journal of Marriage and the Family, 52,* 959–972.

Pyke, K., & Coltrane, S. (1996). Entitlement, obligation, and gratitude in family work. *Journal of Family Issues, 17,* 60–82.

Renne, K. S. (1971). Health and marital experience in an urban population. *Journal of Marriage and the Family, 33,* 338–350.

Robila, M., & Taylor, A. (2001). The recent use of theory within stepparent and adolescent relationship research. *Journal of Divorce and Remarriage, 35*(3/4), 81–92.

Saint-Jacques, M. (1995). Role strain prediction in stepfamilies. *Journal of Divorce and Remarriage, 24*(2), 51–72.

Simons, R., & Associates. (Eds.). (1996). *Understanding differences between divorced and intact families.* Thousand Oaks, CA: Sage.

Spitze, G., & Logan, J. R. (1992). Helping as a component of parent-adult child relationships. *Research on Aging, 14,* 291–312.

Stewart, S. (1999). Disneyland dads, Disneyland moms? How nonresident parents spend time with absent children. *Journal of Family Issues, 20,* 539–556.

Sweeney, M. (2002). Remarriage and the nature of divorce: Does it matter which spouse choose to leave? *Journal of Family Issues, 23,* 410–440.

Teachman, J. (2000). The changing demography of America's families. *Journal of Marriage and the Family, 62,* 1234–1246.

Thomson, E., McLanahan, S. S., & Curtis, R. B. (1991). Family structure, gender, and parental socialization. *Journal of Marriage and the Family, 51,* 368–378.

Thomson, E., Mosely, J., Hanson, T. L., & McLanahan, S. S. (2001). Remarriage, cohabitation, and changes in mothering behavior. *Journal of Marriage and Family, 63,* 370–380.

Troll, L. (1971). The family of later life: A decade review. *Journal of Marriage and the Family, 33,* 263–290.

U.S. Bureau of the Census. (2002). Population profile of the United States 2000: From birth to 17: The living arrangements of children, 2000. Retrieved December 9, 2001, from www.census.gov/population/www/pop-profile/profile2000.html.

Vartanian, T., & McNamara, J. (2002). Older women in poverty: The impact of midlife factors. *Journal of Marriage and Family, 64,* 532–548.

Vemer, E., Coleman, M., Ganong, L. H., & Cooper, H. (1989). Marital satisfaction in remarriage: A meta-analysis. *Journal of Marriage and the Family, 51,* 713–725.

Vuchinich, S., Hetherington, E. M., Vuchinich, R., & Clingempeel, W. G. (1991). Parent-child interaction and gender differences in early adolescents' adaptation to stepfamilies. *Developmental Psychology, 27,* 618–626.

Weingarten, H. R. (1980). Remarriage and well-being: National survey evidence of social and psychological effects. *Journal of Family Issues, 1,* 533–559.

White, L. (1979). Sex differentials in the effects of remarriage on global happiness. *Journal of Marriage and the Family, 41,* 869–876.

Wilmoth, J., & Koso, G. (2002). Does marital history matter? Marital status and wealth outcomes among preretirement adults. *Journal of Marriage and Family, 64,* 254–268.

Wills, T., Sandy, J., Yaeger, A., & Shinar, O. (2001). Family risk factors and adolescent substance use: Moderation effects for temporal dimensions. *Developmental Psychology, 37,* 283–297.

Wilson, B. F., & Clarke, S. C. (1992). Remarriages: A demographic profile. *Journal of Family Issues, 13,* 123–131.

Part VI

RACE AND ETHNICITY IN CONTEMPORARY FAMILIES

Continuing Research on Latino Families
El Pasado y el Futuro

Linda Citlali Halgunseth

Recently, Latinos have become the largest minority group in the United States. At 35.3 million in 2000, they make up 13% of the total U.S. population (U.S. Bureau of the Census, 2003). Latinos are also the fastest growing minority group in the United States. Seventy percent of the Latino population is estimated to be younger than 40 years old; if current fertility and immigration rates continue for this relatively youthful population, demographers project that one of every four Americans will be Latino by the year 2050 (U.S. Bureau of the Census, 2001).

Given the increasing number of Latinos, it is not surprising that the amount of research on Latino families has enlarged greatly over the last three decades. In this chapter, we will examine patterns of similarities among and differences between Latino families, describe the theories and research methods that have been applied in this field of study and evaluate their effectiveness in generating new knowledge about Latino families, offer suggestions for future policy and research, and envisage future trends for Latino families.

NOMENCLATURE

Over the last 30 years, a variety of ethnic labels have been assigned to what are now referred to as Latino families. The terms *Latin Americans* and *Spanish* were often used interchangeably until approximately 1980 when the term *Hispanic* then began to dominate in the literature. *Hispanic* literally means "of Spain" but is used to describe people of Spanish-speaking heritage. In the late 1980s, young Mexican Americans coined the term *Chicano* as a name for those who are of Mexican descent but who were born in the United States. This term was the first instance of defiance in that it was self-created and was intended to represent opposition to a power structure. However, some Mexican Americans considered the term offensive, and it soon faded from the literature (Fox, 2002).

Currently, *Latino* is the nomenclature most frequently used in the scholarly literature. This term (a) includes people from all countries in Latin America as well as parts of the Caribbean that have Latin-based languages but may not necessarily speak Spanish, such as parts of Brazil (Fox, 2002; Harwood, Leyendecker, Carlson, Asencio, & Miller, 2002); (b) disconnects the term from Spain, a country that is still not forgiven for its colonial past; and (c) disorients non-Latinos who have over time developed assumptions or generalizations regarding the Hispanic population (Fox, 2002). Most Latinos prefer to be identified by their specific ethnic background (e.g., Mexican, Colombian, Cuban).

In this chapter, I refer to specific ethnic groups (e.g., Cubans) when they have been identified by researchers. The terms *Latino* and *Hispanic* are used when specific ethnic group membership is unclear or when the information can be generalized.

HETEROGENEITY AMONG LATINO FAMILIES

Latino families come from approximately 20 countries, each containing its own history, culture, and reasons for emigration. In 2000, the largest percentage (66.1%) claimed Mexican heritage, followed by Puerto Rican (9%) and Cuban (4%). In addition, Dominicans (2.2%), Salvadorans (1.9%), Guatemalans (1.1%), Hondurans (0.6%), Colombians (1.3%), Ecuadorians (0.7%), and some countries in the Caribbean are represented by the broad term *Latino* or *Hispanic* (U.S. Bureau of the Census, 2001).

Reasons for emigration or residence in the United States vary for Latino families from different countries. For example, after the Mexican-American War in 1848, a large portion of Mexico was annexed and many Latinos in the Southwest region were "acquired" as U.S. citizens. Later, during World War II, Mexicans were actively recruited to fill jobs left by American soldiers. This initiative, the Bracero Program, lasted over 20 years. The program allowed

for the importation of 4 million workers (400,000 a year) and their families (Becerra, 1998).

After the Spanish-American War in 1917, Puerto Ricans became U.S. citizens. Puerto Rican and Mexican migration generally was and continues to be caused by economic hardships and better economic opportunities in the United States (Becerra, 1998; Sánchez-Ayéndez, 1998). This is in contrast to the immigration patterns of Cuban families. Fleeing political oppression in 1959, members of the elite classes of Cuba came to the United States for safety. Three distinct waves of Cuban migration have occurred since then (Harwood et al., 2002; Sánchez-Ayéndez, 1998). Central and South American immigrants have come to the United States for various reasons. Some are educated professionals who came for employment opportunities, and others immigrated because of war in their home countries (Harwood et al., 2002).

Although 62% of Latinos were born in the United States and are U.S. citizens (U.S. Bureau of the Census, 1993), researchers have differentiated between four generations because the immigration of many Latinos was relatively recent. The first or *immigrant generation* represents Latinos who migrated to the United States after the age of 12. Children under the age of 12 who migrated with their families are referred to as the *1.5 generation*. *Second-generation* Latinos are individuals who were born in the United States but whose parents were not. *Third-generation* Latinos were born in the United States, as were their parents, but their grandparents were born elsewhere (Harwood et al., 2002; Rumbaut, 2001). It is not uncommon for first-generation Latinas to carry their father's last name, even after they marry. Therefore, many first-and second-generation Latino children may share the same last name with their fathers but not with their mothers.

RESEARCH METHODS AND CONCEPTUAL FRAMEWORKS

Acknowledgment of Latino families as flexible units that adjust and adapt to their ever-changing environments has increased over the last three decades in the literature. The social adaptation framework has contributed to this improvement. Issues that are pertinent to Latinos, such as family structure, gender roles, and employment, are examined from the perspective that Latino families, like most families, are dynamic (not static) units that can and do accommodate themselves to the socioeconomic context (Vega, 1990).

A social adaptation framework has been useful in conceptualizing change in Latino families as a result of socioeconomic conditions; however, this orientation has not been useful in conceptualizing factors related to cultural changes (Buriel & DeMent, 1997; Zambrana, 1995). From a cultural perspective, two processes have been often used to explain Latino family functioning: *assimilation* and *acculturation*.

Assimilation

Assimilation is the adoption of the majority culture's norms and standards while rejecting those of one's own ethnic group. This most frequently used framework suggests a unidirectional process of sociocultural change and stems from the cultural-mismatch theory, which argues that the cultural practices and values between the home and school environment must be consistent in order for children to succeed (see Bernal, Saenz, & Knight, 1995). Cultural-mismatch theory and the assimilation framework imply superiority of the host culture. Cultural-mismatch theory was allegedly supported by findings that school performance was lower for minority children who spoke a foreign language than for minorities with English-language backgrounds (Steinberg, Blinde, &

Chan, 1984), but it fails to explain why first-generation children have been found to have higher academic success than their later-generation peers (Bernal et al., 1995).

In the past, minority families were strongly encouraged by U.S. society to assimilate in order to be accepted. In fact, the American dream of career success, economic prosperity, and a comfortable lifestyle was often associated with the rejection of one's native culture in order to be a part of the dominant culture. However, for many people, full assimilation is impossible to achieve. Some members of Latino families never become fully accepted into society due to their physical characteristics (e.g., skin color) or because they speak with an accent. These individuals feel marginalized and estranged (Steinberg, 1999; Suárez-Orozco & Suárez-Orozco, 1995).

Family relations are affected when individuals in a Latino family differ in their views about assimilation. For example, Latino children who think they must not identify themselves with Latino culture so that they can become successful in society often experience more detached and strained relationships with their less assimilated parents and siblings (Suárez-Orozco & Suárez-Orozco, 1995). Family strains typically consist of conflicting values or the inability to communicate verbally due to language barriers.

Acculturation

Unlike assimilation, acculturation does not imply relinquishing native culture and values; it merely signifies the adoption of values from the host culture. Since the 1980s, acculturation, the process of learning, borrowing, or adopting elements from other ethnic groups, has been studied extensively from various theoretical perspectives (Berry, 1980; Padilla, 1980). Previously, acculturation was evaluated using simple models that assumed there were two polar extremes, strong ethnic identification and strong mainstream identification (Keefe & Padilla, 1987; Phinney, 1990). The traditional view that acculturation was a unidimensional process (Marina, 1979) has been rejected by most scholars because acculturation is based on the dynamic between the environment and personal choice, and unidimensional processes do not include factors that reflect a complex multicultural society like the United States (Garza & Gallegos, 1995).

Acculturation is usually operationalized as (a) the ability to speak English, (b) acceptance of and promotion of American ideals, or (c) generational status (Buriel, 1993; Rumbaut, 2001). Other ways to assess acculturation exist but are infrequently used, such as the Cultural Information Scale (CIS; Saldaña, 1988, 1995), which is based on both demographic variables (e.g., language preference, generational status, bilingual fluency) and psychological items (e.g., ethnic loyalty, cultural celebrations, ethnicity of close friends and dating partners).

In recent years, researchers have developed more complex acculturation models. For instance, Rueschenberg and Buriel's (1995) acculturation model takes a family systems perspective to categorize families into three groups: *unacculturated* (all family members were born in Mexico, parents are monolingual Spanish speaking and have immigrated within the past 5 years), *moderately acculturated* (parents were born in Mexico, parents resided in the United States at least 10 years, children were born in the United States, parents were monolingual Spanish speaking or Spanish dominant, and children have English-speaking ability), and *acculturated* (both parents and children were born in the United States, and both have a bilingual or English-speaking preference). Their findings suggest that acculturation influences familial practices outside but not inside the home.

Research over the past two decades has found acculturation to be more of a risk factor than a protective factor for Latino families. There is evidence that Latinos who are less acculturated are in better health, have lower rates of delinquency, and less psychological distress and that they score higher on achievement tests than Latinos who are more acculturated (Anderson & Wood, 1997; Buriel, Calzada, & Vasquez, 1982; Burnam, Hough, Karno, Escobar, & Telles, 1987; Rumbaut, 2001). In addition, Rumbaut (2001) found that youth who were not fluent in the language of their immigrant parents exhibited higher parental conflict, higher feelings of embarrassment over their parents' culture, and lower family cohesion than youth who were fluent in the parental language.

In an attempt to explain the negative association between acculturation and family well-being, Rumbaut (2001) argued that acculturation should be conceptualized as a dynamic process in which both parents and children need to be considered. The acculturation process is influenced by contextual factors (e.g., school, peers, and society); however, the pace of acculturation may differ between Latino parents and children. Three modes of acculturation were identified in the study: consonant, dissonant, and selective. In *consonant* acculturation, the learning process and gradual abandonment of the home language and culture occur at roughly the same pace for immigrant parents and their children. This situation is most common when the parents have levels of education sufficient to accompany and monitor the acculturation of their children. *Dissonant* acculturation occurs when there is a discrepancy in acculturation pace between immigrant parents and their children. This often occurs among immigrant families. Under these circumstances, linguistic and other gaps develop between parents and children that can exacerbate intergenerational conflicts or cause children to feel embarrassed rather than proud of their parents as the children try to fit in with their American peers. This can lead to role reversals if children prematurely assume adult roles (Rumbaut, 2001). In *selective* acculturation, there is a relative lack of intergenerational conflict, children have co-ethnic friends, and second-generation Latinos are fluently bilingual. Geographical factors, such as residence in a Latino enclave or neighborhood or proximity to Latin American countries such as Mexico, facilitate this type of acculturation.

Rates of acculturation may depend on patterns of residence (Harwood et al., 2002). Geographic locations with the highest concentration of Latinos are more likely to develop ethnic enclaves, areas where cultural preservation predominates (Harwood et al., 2002). The states with the highest concentration of Latinos are New Mexico (38.2% of total population), California (25.8%), Texas (25.5%), and Arizona (18.8%) (U.S. Bureau of the Census, 1993). Both positive and negative circumstances can arise when Latino families reside in an ethnic enclave. If the family has a weak association with the dominant culture and a strong association with its own ethnic group, then the family may not adopt elements from the dominant culture, instead emphasizing the preservation of its ethnic heritage (Steinberg, 1999). Some families choose to separate themselves from the dominant society in response to past experiences of prejudice and discrimination. Strong cultural preservation in families is quite beneficial in developing self-esteem and ethnic identity in Latino children; however, it is not without cost. Latino children who perform well academically or who succeed in an institution that is considered mainstream are often ridiculed by peers (e.g., called coconuts) and feel guilty or uneasy (Suárez-Orozco & Suárez-Orozco, 1995). Thus, the original ethnic culture not only is preserved in some areas but has transformed

into a counterculture (Suárez-Orozco & Suárez-Orozco, 1995).

Bicultural Models

Families who choose to maintain the values of their native culture as they adopt values from the host culture are characterized as bicultural. Abalos (1986) conceptualized biculturalism as the synthesis of two cultures out of which arises "a third enriched reality that was not there before" (p. 94). Szapocznik, Kurtines, and Fernandez (1980) argued that to minimize the detrimental effects of adaptation to a new culture, individuals living in bicultural communities must become bicultural themselves. Becoming bicultural involves learning to communicate and negotiate skills in two different cultural contexts, each with a separate set of rules. Szapocznik and colleagues encouraged bicultural youths to be aware of the differences between cultures and to develop flexibility in order to implement different survival skills according to cultural contexts. In both bicultural and acculturative models, the transmission of culture across generations is individual and dynamic. It depends on factors such as available social networks and individual and family demographic variables (Portes & Rumbaut, 2001).

Szapocznik and Kurtines (1980) typed Latino families on two dimensions: acculturation, defined as a linear process of adapting to the host culture; and biculturalism, the ability to relinquish or retain characteristics of the culture of origin. On the basis of these dimensions, a Latino child could be seen as (a) *high cultural involvement and bicultural* (an active bicultural child); (b) *high cultural involvement and monocultural* (a child who is fully involved in only one culture); (c) *marginal and monocultural* (marginalized child who is more involved in the Latino culture); and (d) *marginal and bicultural* (marginalized child who is equally involved or uninvolved in both cultures). Students who had high cultural involvement and were bicultural were perceived by their teachers to be better adjusted than children of the other three groups.

Ramírez (1983) defined biculturalism as the simultaneous adoption of the language, values, and social competencies of two cultures. Using data from previous research, he delineated four bicultural/multicultural identities. First, the *synthesized multicultural* identity is held by a person who has a positive attitude toward Mexican American and mainstream culture. This person is able to function in Mexican American, mainstream, and other cultures with ease. Second, the *functional bicultural/mainstream* orientation refers to a person who has positive attitudes toward both Anglo and Mexican American cultures but a greater acceptance of and comfort in the Anglo cultural setting. Third, the *functional bicultural/Latino* orientation characterizes a person who is like the functional bicultural/mainstream person but has a stronger commitment to the Mexican American culture. Fourth, the *monocultural* identity describes a person who is more comfortable with the Mexican American culture and has a strong commitment to it only.

Assimilation of mainstream cultural values and behaviors is uncharacteristic of many recent Mexican immigrants (Buriel & DeMent, 1997). Instead, an intermediate bicultural adaptation that incorporates aspects of the home culture with the mainstream culture occurs. Therefore, families may change more by adding new cultural competencies to their ethnic competencies, thereby becoming bicultural, than by assimilating (i.e., replacing their existing cultural values and behaviors). This bicultural adaptation represents the sociocultural change that distinguishes many recent Latino immigrant families from the European immigrants who preceded them.

Ethnic Socialization

Latino parents can facilitate their children's development of biculturalism with ethnic socialization, the process through which parents teach their children about their ethnic identity and about the special experiences they may encounter in the broader society, given their ethnic background (Thornton, Chatters, Taylor, & Allen, 1990). Ethnic socialization is strongly predictive of ethnic identity achievement in adolescents (Quintana, Castañeda-English, & Ybarra, 1999; Umaña-Taylor & Fine, 2001). Ethnic identity achievement, in turn, is related to higher self-esteem, self-efficacy, and proactive styles of coping with discrimination (Phinney & Chavira, 1995; Umaña-Taylor, Diversi, & Fine, 2002).

Trends in Latino Family Values and Processes

Across ethnic groups and generations, Latino families share several values that stem from a collectivistic orientation to the world (i.e., a view that focuses on the betterment of a group rather than promoting self-interest or individualism). Sacrificing for the common good, maintaining harmonious relationships with close others, and believing that group membership is a central aspect to one's identity are core components of a collectivistic orientation (Hofstede, 1980). Over the last 20 years, the collectivist model has frequently been applied to the study of Latinos (Oyserman, Coon, & Kemmelmeier, 2002). In their meta-analysis, Oyserman and colleagues found that European Americans rated lower than Latinos on collectivism, but no significant differences were found between them with regard to individualism.

Traditions practiced in many Latino families, including collectivistic behaviors, are influenced by Catholicism (57% of

Latinos are Catholic; City University of New York, 2001). For example, close friends of the family may be asked to be god-parents or *padrinos* (from the word *padres,* "parents"). *Padrinos* are often assigned at a child's baptism and are considered another set of parents to Latino children. A Latino child's father and godfather refer to each other as *compadres* (co-fathers), and a Latino child's mother and godmother refer to each other as *comadres* (co-mothers) (Vidal, 1988).

In addition, the Latino value of *familism* (i.e., all members strongly identify with their respective family units and feel a deep sense of family loyalty) stems from a collectivistic orientation. Latino parents implement many strategies to instill the importance of family in their children. Latino children are often expected to contribute by performing work roles within the family such as household chores, baby-sitting, transporting other family members by car, or helping their parents at their place of employment. Additionally, the emphasis on interdependence among Latino family members ensures that familism is main-tained. Latino parents may also foster feel-ings of familism by limiting the amount of contact their children have with others out-side their immediate family environment (e.g., peers) and insisting that their children spend time with the family (Moore, 1991). Parental control over the extrafamilial behaviors of children is much more com-mon for Latinos than for European Americans (Bulcroft, Carmody, & Bulcroft, 1996). Because independence in the U.S. culture is valued both within the family and across other social institutions, European American parents can rely on indirect soci-etal assistance in the teaching of individual-istic values. Thus, European American parents tend to use less direct controls over the extrafamilial behaviors of their children than Latino parents (Bulcroft et al., 1996).

Parenting

In addition to the emphasis on familism, Latino parenting is noted to be nurturing and permissive in early childhood. Escovar and Lazarus (1982) found that Latino families displayed closer mother-child relationships and more open verbal and physical expres-sion of parental affection than European American families. Latino parents also have a relaxed attitude toward individual behav-ior such as the attainment of early skills and achievement of developmental milestones (Zuniga, 1992). In addition, Latino children are socialized to reciprocate acts of kindness to individuals inside and outside the home (Leyendecker & Lamb, 1999).

The Latino parenting style fosters interde-pendence and relational learning, whereas the European American parenting style empha-sizes independence and self-initiated learning. A major parenting strategy used by Latino parents in teaching their children is *model-ing.* This differs from the commonly used European American teaching technique of *inquiry and praise* (Brice, 2002; Zuniga, 1992). For example, if a child is learning how to set a table, a Latino parent will teach the child through parental demonstration, whereas a European American parent will inquire (e.g., "Where do you think the glass goes?") and then provide praise (e.g., "Very good. You did that all by yourself!"). Latino families with more than one child differ slightly in their mode of teaching in that parents assign older siblings the tasks of teaching and being social-izing agents for their younger siblings (Valdés, 1996). The teaching and support that Latino siblings provide resembles the support given to European American children by their mothers (Volk, 1999).

To maintain harmonious familial and nonfamilial relationships, Latino parents often endorse interpersonal skills (i.e., warm, individualized attention and responsiveness) that can take the form of both verbal and nonverbal communication. These skills of *interpersonal relatedness* include interacting with others so that they will enjoy the child's company, find him or her pleasant, and feel mutually respected. In addition, these skills are believed to maintain harmonious familial and nonfamilial relationships, a goal of many Latino families. Latino parents often focus on regulating their children's affective states by directly dealing with their children's emotional expressions (Maccoby, 1984). Positive emotional expressions are generally reinforced, and negative emotions such as anger and aggression are punished. For example, verbal arguments among siblings are quickly discouraged and are quite distressing to Latino parents (Goodman & Beman, 1971). In addition, Latino parents closely monitor nonverbal cues (i.e., body language). During parent-child communication, Latino parents reinforce positive body language (i.e., gestures and facial expressions that show respect) in children and admonish body language that they consider disrespectful (e.g., crossing arms, rolling eyes) (Zuniga, 1992).

The Latino family context fosters the acquisition of acute field-dependent skills in children (i.e., they become sensitized to the nonverbal communication cues and responses of others; Ramirez & Price-Williams, 1974), and children strive for non-conflicting interactions (Zuniga, 1992). In cross-cultural studies, Latino children were found to have more passive coping styles, to be more respectful to and dependent on authority, to have a greater need for affiliation, and to be more cooperative and group oriented than African American and European American children (Diaz-Guerrero, 1975; Holtzman, Diaz-Guerrero, & Schwartz, 1975; Kagan & Madsen, 1971; Rotheram-Borus & Phinney, 1990; Sanders, Scholz, & Kagan, 1976). Children belonging to cultures that emphasize family loyalty, achievement for the family, and respect for parents score higher on field dependency

scores than children from cultures that encourage questioning of convention and an individual identity (Berry, 1966; Cohen, 1969; Dershowitz, 1971; Martinez & Norman, 1984; Ramirez & Price-Williams, 1974; Rand, 1971).

Another Latino child-rearing value is *personalism,* an inner quality that emphasizes the inner importance (i.e., self-confidence), dignity, and respect of an individual (Ramirez & Price-Williams, 1974; Sánchez-Ayéndez, 1998). It includes an orientation to treating others with respect and dignity. Parents choose parenting strategies that contribute to their children's becoming *bien educado* (i.e., well educated). In the Latino culture, *bien educado,* in referring to a child, implies not only school education or intelligence but also qualities of being *tranquilo* (i.e., calm), *obediente* (i.e., obedient), and *respetuoso* (i.e., courteous to others, especially adults). Calling a child *mal educado* (i.e., not educated) is considered a terrible insult to his or her parents because it implies that they have not provided him or her with the education valued by Latino families (Zuniga, 1992). Harwood and Miller (1991) contrasted Puerto Rican and European American mothers' descriptions of a "secure child." European American mothers liked how the securely attached child displayed self-confidence and independence, whereas the Puerto Rican mothers complimented the securely attached child's demeanor, obedience, and quality of relatedness.

Latino parenting strategies attempt to inculcate personalism in their children. Latino parents require children to speak and behave with absolute respect to their elders. The slightest form of disobedience and disrespect is negatively reinforced or punished and is directly acknowledged as being disrespectful or disobedient. Thus, Latino children quickly learn the importance of these two qualities, and this endures in them well beyond childhood. Also, children are encouraged to be calm in their play (i.e., low noise level) so not to disturb others. In addition, the work roles that are required of adolescents are believed to instill a strong sense of responsibility and obedience. Finally, living a dignified lifestyle in the Latino culture promotes a self-purity theme that is reinforced by religious ideology. As a result, parenting strategies that highlight the protection of girls and restriction of their freedom are often found in Latino families (Sánchez-Ayéndez, 1998; Zuniga, 1992).

A Caution

Even though there are similarities in Latino values and practices, it is incorrect to assume that all Latino families adhere to the same goals and standards. Latino families adapt or change depending on the context. For example, a common characteristic of collectivism is that members of a group are concerned with conforming to external standards (e.g., appropriate manners, attire, customs). However, Okagaki and Sternberg (1991) found that level of acculturation influenced preferences of Latino parents: Immigrant Latinas preferred a child who followed rules, whereas Latinas born in the United States favored autonomous behavior.

In addition, the teaching strategy of modeling may change according to levels of maternal education or acculturation. In general, Mexican American, Puerto Rican, and Dominican Republic mothers used more modeling, visual cues, and directives during a teaching task than European American mothers (Laosa, 1980; Planos, 1993; Vargas, 1991); however, Planos (1993) found that more acculturated Puerto Rican and Dominican Republic mothers used more "inquiry and praise" techniques than less acculturated counterparts. Laosa (1980) also found that Mexican American mothers with higher levels of education and income used teaching strategies characterized by "praise

and inquiry" and that those with lower education used more modeling.

Furthermore, Buriel (1993) detected parenting differences across three generations of Latino parents. First- and second-generation Latino children experienced a parenting style that enforced early self-reliance (e.g., performing work roles at an early age), adherence to family rules, and emphasis on productive use of time. Parents also tended to reinforce their children depending on the outcome of the child's performance (success or failure), and they used techniques such as modeling to teach their children. Third-generation (highly acculturated) Latino children characterized their parents as emphasizing support and caring. These parents used a teaching style similar to that of the school systems that they had experienced: They reinforced children more on the basis of effort than on whether they completed the task successfully. Third-generation parents may emphasize different parenting strategies for three reasons: (a) Due to acculturation, these parents have acquired a European American parenting style that emphasizes support and less restriction on their children as they explore their environment; (b) these parents have experienced prolonged exposure to lower societal expectations for minorities, which has attenuated their expectation of child success; or (c) through personal experiences, these parents are aware that Latino children receive less praise, support, or acceptance from school teachers (U.S. Commission on Civil Rights, 1973), even when they answer correctly (Buriel, 1993), and they consequently seek to compensate with a more supportive parenting style.

Finally, the field dependency skills of Latino children are suspected to decrease with acculturation. Ramirez and Price-Williams (1974) found that children from a community in Mexico that most identified with traditional Mexican values were more field dependent in cognitive style than children from less traditional communities that are located closer to the U.S. border. Therefore, parenting was not the sole influence on children's cognition. Children, as well as parents, are influenced by and will adapt to their environments (Ramirez & Price-Williams, 1974; Vega, 1990).

Acculturation and Child Outcomes

The environment and levels of acculturation may influence parents and children; however, a review of the literature suggests that this change may not always be for the better. Among three generations, first-generation children exhibited lower rates of delinquency (Buriel et al., 1982), showed less psychological distress (Burnam et al., 1987), and performed better on achievement tests (Nielsen & Fernandez, 1981) than their later-generation peers. This may be explained by the parenting strategies that first-generation Latinos experience, which emphasize obedience and respect to authority, or it could be due to the fact that the home environment (e.g., Spanish-speaking parents and parenting strategies that emphasize traditional Latino values) may covertly enhance a strong ethnic identity in Mexican American children (Umaña-Taylor & Fine, 2002), which has been associated with many developmental benefits (Chavira & Phinney, 1991; Phinney, 1989). Therefore, information that higher levels of acculturation do not necessarily lead to better child outcomes has existed for over 20 years. Despite such information, however, mainstream institutions such as school systems commonly endorse English immersion programs to accelerate the acculturation process.

Changes in Latino Family Structure and Processes

The notion of Latino families as large units living in nuclear households is a myth that continues, despite changes in family structure. Between 1960 and 1980, the average size of Latino households decreased while the rate of marital disruption increased (Vega, 1990). Female-headed households are not uncommon among Latino groups (Angel & Tienda, 1982). In the 1980s, mainland Puerto Ricans had the highest fertility rates, were the most likely to have female-headed households with children, and had the lowest family income of any Latino group (Moore & Pachon, 1985). The rates of Puerto Rican female-headed households are twice as high than for Mexican American and Cuban American women, and Puerto Rican families have the highest poverty rate (30%) (McLoyd, Cauce, Takeuchi, & Wilson, 2000; U.S. Bureau of the Census, 1999).

In the 1990s, Latinas (with the exception of Cubanas) were less likely to be married, more likely to be single heads of households, and more likely to have children at younger ages outside marriage (McLoyd et al., 2000). Migration has had far-reaching consequences for Latino family formation and family structure. Social, economic, and cultural stressors involved in immigration are possible reasons for increases in separation, divorce, and single-mother households (Bean & Tienda, 1987; Frisbie, Opitz, & Kelly, 1985; Muschkin & Myers, 1989). Maternal education has also been proposed as a contributing factor to marital disruptions (Cortés, 1995). Educational attainment was inversely related to marital stability among Mexican American and Cuban American households; however, for Puerto Rican families, educational attainment increases marital stability (Frisbie, 1986).

Male-Female Relationships in Families

The literature on Latino families often includes reference to the concept of machismo, which has characterized Latin American men for decades. Machismo is a system of behavioral traits marked by exaggerated masculinity (e.g., aggressiveness, courage, domination of women, and sexual conquests). It is commonly believed that because Latinos have the dominant role in a marital relationship and Latinas have the subordinate role of housekeeper and child-bearer, Latin American parents prepare their sons to be macho or independent and their daughters to be subservient.

These stereotypes have their roots in the 1500s, when Spanish conquerors set out to find gold and the Fountain of Youth. In countries such as Mexico, Peru, and Puerto Rico, the Spanish forced the natives to adopt their language and religion, and they also exploited the native women, forcing them to have sex and treating them like slaves. The native women's children by the Spanish conquerors were called *mestizos* (i.e., half-Indian and half-Spanish). Because they grew up in an environment where their father had power and their mother was equivalent to a slave, the *mestizos* (i.e., both sons and daughters) learned that males were dominant and females were subordinate. As generations passed, Latin American men and women continued to fulfill those roles set by their ancestors (Penalosa, 1968).

The concept of machismo was predominant in the literature until the early 1980s, when researchers on Latino families realized the danger of relying on monocausal explanations for family dynamics (Vega, 1990; Ybarra, 1982). The social adaptation framework became useful for conceptualizing the influence of social context on gender roles in Latino families rather than assuming that these were static and that Latinos families functioned in a vacuum (Ybarra, 1982). Hence, Latino families began to be portrayed as adaptive to their social environments so that gender role expectations would change as socioeconomic conditions required (Vega, 1990).

Despite some traditional descriptions (Bird & Canino, 1982; Gonzalez, 1982), the bulk of the literature on gender roles in Latino families rests upon the concept that socioeconomic conditions are met by flexible and adaptive Latino families who do what it takes to survive in their environment (Griswold del Castillo, 1984). For example, the availability of employment has been found to be the most important determinant of whether Mexican American and Puerto Rican women work outside the home (Moore & Pachon, 1985; Zinn, 1982). In another study, researchers reported that immigrant Mexican American women actively sought employment because they believed that their labor was required for family survival (Kelly & Garcia, 1989). As more Latinas entered the workforce, attained higher levels of education, and adopted North American ideals, more equal divisions in household labor also emerged (Cromwell & Ruiz, 1979; Rodríguez, 1999; Zinn, 1982). This pattern was especially evident in the 1980s, when the number of women who accompanied their husbands in migrating to the United States increased (Passel & Woodrow, 1984). External employment contributed to greater personal autonomy for Latinas; the consequences of this for families were related to whether this occurred in the context of socioeconomic marginality (Kelly & Garcia, 1989).

Latina mothers are revered; they are considered to be the heart of the family and enjoy lifelong reverence from their children (Brice, 2002; Rodríguez, 1999). Family decision making is either a joint process or primarily the job of the mother (Vega, 1990). Even though fathers are made to feel that they rule the home, Latina mothers are described as the ones with the actual power (Brice, 2002; Rodríguez, 1999). In addition, Latino fathers are more involved in child rearing than in the past, especially with regard to nurturing (López & Hamilton, 1997).

How Effective Has Latino Family Scholarship Been?

Over the last 30 years, the steady growth rate of Latinos has continually motivated family researchers to learn more about this heterogeneous population. In the 1980s, researchers began to implement a social adaptation framework (Vega, 1990). Instead of relying on cultural stereotypes and myths, researchers started to realize that Latino families, like all families, are flexible units that change in response to cultural influences and challenging social situations. As a result, events such as immigration and internal migration became factors of consideration in the study of Latino families and family structure. Review of census data revealed evidence of similarities with regard to family structure between Latino and non-Latino families (Bean & Tienda, 1987; Griswold del Castillo, 1984). One consistent theme continued to appear in the literature, however: The importance and prevalence of the cultural value of *familism* seemed to be a feature more typical for Latino families than for non-Latino families (Harwood et al., 2002; Vega, 1990).

Research on Latino families in the 1990s continued to focus on the effects of social context. The process of acculturation from the perspective of family members became of interest (Suárez-Orozco & Suárez-Orozco, 1995). Acculturation models were refined, and the influences of acculturation were more commonly considered in studies of Latino families (Anderson & Wood, 1997; Bernal et al., 1995; Buriel, 1993; Rueschenberg & Buriel, 1995; Saldaña, 1995). Unfortunately, researchers seemed to be interested in acculturation only in relation to mainstream normative standards (Buriel & DeMent, 1997; Steinberg, 1999). Such comparisons maintained the assumption of unidirectional assimilation by immigrant groups.

Recent research on Latino families has improved in many areas. Rumbaut's (2001) finding that the pace of acculturation differs across family members has furthered our understanding of dynamics in multigenerational Latino families. In addition, researchers are beginning to examine individual nationalities within the Latino population (Umaña-Taylor & Fine, 2001), without stereotyping or overgeneralizing findings across ethnic groups. However, more research that attempts to replicate these findings is needed.

There have been improvements over the last 30 years in the scholarship of Latino families. Whether these new findings and conceptualizations have influenced the practices of mainstream institutions toward Latino families is less clear. Unless the scholarship improves the lives of Latino families, it is difficult to say whether it truly has been effective.

IMPLICATIONS FOR FUTURE RESEARCH, PRACTICE, AND POLICY

In the last decade, few Latino family scholars have focused their research on the diversity among Latino families. Even though similarities in family values and parenting practices exist, within-group variation also exists in areas such as family size, values, and family functioning. Homogenizing Latino families leads to results that do not accurately reflect all Latino ethnic groups and may reinforce hostility toward researchers if individuals feel invisible or inaccurately represented. To achieve a richer and more accurate understanding of Latino families and their diversity, current research methods need improvement. The characteristics of samples (e.g., ethnic group membership, generational status, and acculturation characteristics) should be reported in all studies (Treviño,

1988). To avoid misrepresentation, Latino ethnic groups that are generally smaller should be oversampled (e.g., Colombians, Ecuadorians). Longitudinal designs as opposed to cross-sectional research would best reveal the influence of processes such as acculturation and immigration (Vega, 1990). Researchers need to devise culturally appropriate measures and conceptual frameworks that apply to all ethnic groups and generations of immigrants that constitute the U.S. Latino population. Last, ethnically sensitive measures developed from observing Latino families are needed, and convergent reliability on current instruments such as acculturation scales should be assessed (Vega, 1990).

Empirical research on Latino parenting and parent-child relations needs more attention. Most of what we understand of Latino parenting is based on conjecture rather than empirical research (Vega, 1990). Rather than apply measures to Latino families that were previously normed on European American samples, researchers should conduct observational studies like those by Baumrind (1971) to identify parenting styles that are indigenous to Latino families. An emic approach, such as conducting qualitative interviews, could also serve as the basis for the development of future assessments of parenting styles and typologies that are relevant to this population. Currently, research literature explains certain parenting patterns, but it does not detail which parental strategies are effective for Latino families. Further, how parenting strategies differ across country of origin or change across generations is also an unexplored area.

Research is needed in the area of ethnic versus racial socialization strategies. In addition to generational status and country of origin, the Latino population is diverse in skin color. Is it necessary for Latino parents to implement racial socialization strategies (e.g., "Brown Pride"), or should ethnic socialization be the cornerstone for Latino parenting?

Is racial and/or ethnic socialization related to generational status? Generally, research on racial socialization has been restricted to African American families and has demonstrated many developmental benefits for African American children (McAdoo, 2002).

Last, policy needs to be directed by empirical research findings on Latino families. An examination of findings from current research on acculturation and cultural identity implicates the need for educational and medical institutions to create culturally sensitive environments in which Latinos, especially immigrant Latinos, feel comfortable accessing resources. Programs such as transitional bilingualism, English as a second language, and the incorporation of institutional interpreters would promote the educational success and health of the Latino population, which would inevitably benefit U.S. society.

FUTURE TRENDS FOR LATINO FAMILIES

A review of past and current research illuminates the various processes that Latino families experience as they adapt to U.S. society. Understanding these processes allows scholars to envisage future trends for Latino families and inform mainstream institutions. This will be particularly important as the Latino population continues to grow at rapid rates (U.S. Bureau of the Census, 2001).

The projected growth of Latino immigrants will inevitably influence the socialization processes of all Latino families. The prevalence of Latino family values and practices will become more apparent in the United States as immigrant parents attempt to socialize their children to become respectful and contributing members to their families and society. The pressure to assimilate to mainstream European American values and practices will continue to exist for all generations of Latino families. However, an increased prevalence of Latino customs will allow second- and third-generation Latino parents to maintain connection with their cultural heritage as they negotiate the values and practices that they choose to implement in their bicultural lives and families.

In turn, Latino children will continue to face challenges as they try to navigate their bicultural worlds. Some Latino children may choose to assimilate and replace their ancestors' values and language for those more characteristic of mainstream society, whereas other Latino children will try to balance and incorporate both cultures into their identity. Children who decide to reject the cultural values and practices of their parents may experience more feelings of guilt, uneasiness, or strained relations with their parents than Latino children who explore both dimensions of their cultural identity (Rumbaut, 2001; Suárez-Orozco & Suárez-Orozco, 1995). Therefore, it is important that Latino family members as well as parent educators understand the importance of ethnic socialization and the benefits for Latino children to develop a healthy bicultural identity and sense of self.

Cultural myths and stereotypes are not easily dispelled, despite the increased sensitivity in the literature. Latino families will continue to be misunderstood and misrepresented by mainstream society members who rely on dated, nonempirical research for information. In addition, Latino family members will continue to experience frustration and obstacles as they attempt to work with mainstream organizations that persist in relating to Latino families using a deficit perspective or an assimilation framework. Last, communication between non-English-speaking Latino family members and English-speaking-only federal, state, and city workers will continue to be strained, especially as the Latino population continues to grow rapidly.

As the number of Latino families increase, however, it is possible that mainstream institutions will eventually realize the necessity of meeting the needs of non-English-speaking family members. Family professionals and medical practitioners may meet the increase demand of their clients with bilingual and bicultural resources for Latino families. In trying to curtail the dropout rate, school officials may begin to incorporate bilingual programs and services for Latino children and parents. In their need to turn a profit, commercial businesses may begin to target Latino families as consumers of goods and services by advertising and developing products specifically for this population.

In conclusion, Latino families, non-Latino families, U.S. society, and mainstream institutions will be influenced by the rapid growth rate of Latinos. Certain projections can be made as Latinos continue to represent larger percentages of the population; however, how well current research on Latino families is communicated and incorporated into mainstream practice will be the best indicator for how Latino families will fare in the future.

REFERENCES

Abalos, D. (1986). *Latinos in the United States*. Notre Dame, IN: University of Notre Dame Press.

Anderson, L. M., & Wood, D. L. (1997). Maternal acculturation and childhood immunization levels among children in Latino families in Los Angeles. *American Journal of Public Health, 87,* 2018–2022.

Angel, R., & Tienda, M. (1982). Determinants of extended household structure: Cultural pattern or economic need? *American Journal of Sociology, 6,* 1360–1383.

Baumrind, D. (1971). Current patterns of parental authority. *Developmental Psychology Monograph, 4,* 1–103.

Bean, F., & Tienda, M. (1987). *The Hispanic population of the United States.* New York: Russell Sage Foundation.

Becerra, R. (1998). The Mexican-American family. In C. H. Mindel, R. W. Habenstein, & R. Wright, Jr. (Eds.), *Ethnic families in America* (pp. 153–198). Englewood Cliffs, NJ: Prentice Hall.

Bernal, M. E., Saenz, D., & Knight, G. P. (1995). Ethnic identity and adaptation of Mexican American youths in school settings. In A. M. Padilla (Ed.), *Hispanic psychology: Critical issues in theory and research* (pp. 71–89). Thousand Oaks, CA: Sage.

Berry, J. W. (1966). Temne and Eskimo perceptual skills. *International Journal of Psychology, 1,* 207–229.

Berry, J. W. (1980). Acculturation as varieties of adaptation. In A. M. Padilla (Ed.), *Acculturation theories, models and some new findings* (pp. 9–26). Boulder, CO: Westview.

Bird, H., & Canino, G. (1982). The Puerto Rican family: Cultural factors and family intervention strategies. *Journal of the American Academy of Psychoanalysis, 10,* 257–268.

Brice, A. (2002). *The Hispanic child.* Boston: Allyn & Bacon.

Bulcroft, R. A., Carmody, D. C., & Bulcroft, J. S. (1996). Patterns of parental independence giving to adolescents: Variations by race, age, and gender of child. *Journal of Marriage and the Family, 58,* 866–883.

Buriel, R. (1993). Acculturation, respect for cultural differences and biculturalism among three generations of Mexican American and Euro American school children. *Journal of Genetic Psychology, 4,* 531–543.

Buriel, R., Calzada, S., & Vasquez, R. (1982). The relationship of traditional Mexican American cultures to adjustment and delinquency among three generations of Mexican American male adolescents. *Hispanic Journal of Behavioral Sciences, 4,* 41–55.

Buriel, R., & DeMent, T. (1997). Immigration and sociocultural changes in Mexican, Chinese, and Vietnamese American families. In A. Booth, A. C. Crouter, & N. Landale (Eds.), *Immigration and the family research and policy on U.S. immigrants* (pp. 165–200). Mahwah, NJ: Lawrence Erlbaum.

Burnam, M., Hough, R., Karno, M., Escobar, J., & Telles, C. (1987). Acculturation and lifetime prevalence of psychiatric disorders among Mexican Americans in Los Angeles. *Journal of Health and Social Behavior, 28,* 89–102.

Chavira, V., & Phinney, J. S. (1991). Adolescents' ethnic identity, self-esteem, and strategies for dealing with ethnicity and minority status. *Hispanic Journal of Behavioral Sciences, 13,* 226–227.

City University of New York. (2001). American Religious Identification Survey (ARIS). Religion and identity: Hispanics and Jews. Retrieved July 11, 2003, from www.gc.cuny.edu/studies/religion_identity.htm.

Cohen, R. A. (1969). Conceptual styles, culture conflict and nonverbal tests of intelligence. *American Anthropologist, 71,* 828–856.

Cortés, D. E. (1995). Variations in familism in two generations of Puerto Ricans. *Hispanic Journal of Behavioral Sciences, 17,* 249–255.

Cromwell, R., & Ruiz, R. (1979). The myth of macho dominance in decision-making within Mexican and Mexican American families. *Hispanic Journal of Behavioral Sciences, 1,* 355–373.

Dershowitz, A. (1971). Jewish subcultural patterns and psychological differentiation. *International Journal of Psychology, 6*, 223–231.

Diaz-Guerrero, R. (1975). *Psychology of the Mexican.* Austin: University of Texas Press.

Escovar, P., & Lazarus, P. (1982). Cross-cultural child-rearing practices: Implications for school psychology. *School Psychology International, 3*, 143–148.

Frisbie, W. (1986). Variation in patterns of marital instability among Hispanics. *Journal of Marriage and the Family, 48*, 99–102.

Frisbie, W., Opitz, W., & Kelly, W. (1985). Marital instability trends among Mexican Americans as compared to blacks and Anglos: New evidence. *Social Science Quarterly, 66*, 587–601.

Fox, G. (2002). *Hispanic nation: Culture, politics, and the constructing of identity.* Tucson: University of Arizona Press.

Garza, R. T., & Gallegos, P. I. (1995). Environmental influences and personal choice: A humanistic perspective on acculturation. In A. M. Padilla (Ed.), *Hispanic psychology* (pp. 3–14). Thousand Oaks, CA: Sage.

Gonzalez, A. (1982). Sex roles of the traditional Mexican family. *Journal of Cross-Cultural Psychology, 13*, 330–339.

Goodman, M., & Beman, A. (1971). Child's-eye-views of life in an urban barrio. In N. Wagner & M. Haug (Eds.), *Chicanos: Social and psychological perspectives* (pp. 109–122). St. Louis: C. V. Mosby.

Griswold del Castillo, R. (1984). *La familia.* Notre Dame, IN: University of Notre Dame Press.

Harwood, R., Leyendecker, B., Carlson, V., Asencio, M., & Miller, A. (2002). Parenting among Latino families in the U.S. In M. H. Bornstein (Ed.), *Handbook of parenting: Vol. 4. Social conditions and applied parenting* (pp. 21–46). Mahwah, NJ: Lawrence Erlbaum.

Harwood, R. L., & Miller, J. G. (1991). Perceptions of attachment behavior: A comparison of Anglo and Puerto Rican mothers. *Merrill-Palmer Quarterly, 37*, 583–599.

Hofstede, G. (1980). *Culture's consequences.* Beverly Hills, CA: Sage.

Holtzman, W. H., Diaz-Guerrero, R., & Schwartz, J. D. (1975). *Personality development in two cultures.* Austin: University of Texas Press.

Kagan, S., & Madsen, M. C. (1971). Cooperation and competition of Mexican, Mexican-American children and Anglo-American children of two ages under four instructional sets. *Developmental Psychology, 5*, 32–39.

Keefe, S., & Padilla, A. (1987). *Mexican American ethnicity.* Albuquerque: University of New Mexico Press.

Kelly, P., & Garcia, A. (1989). Power surrendered, power restored: The politics of home and work among Hispanic women in southern California and Southern Florida. In L. Tilly & P. Guerin (Eds.), *Women and politics in America.* New York: Russell Sage Foundation.

Laosa, L. M. (1980). Maternal teaching strategies in Chicano and Anglo-American families: The influence of culture and education on maternal behavior. *Child Development, 51*, 759–765.

Leyendecker, B., & Lamb, M. (1999). Latino families. In M. Lamb (Eds.), *Parenting in "non traditional" families* (pp. 247–262). Mahwah, NJ: Lawrence Erlbaum.

López, L., & Hamilton, M. (1997). Comparison of the role of Mexican-American and Euro-American family members in the socialization of children. *Psychological Reports, 80*, 283–288.

Maccoby, E. (1984). Socialization and developmental change. *Child Development, 55*, 317–328.

Marina, D. (1979). The Cuban immigrant family: What changes and what stays the same. In J. Szapocznik & M. C. Herrera (Eds.), *Cuban Americans.* Washington, DC: National Coalition of Hispanic Health and Human Services Organizations (COSSMHO).

Martinez, R., & Norman, R. (1984). Effects of acculturation on field independence among Chicano children. *Hispanic Journal of Behavioral Sciences, 6,* 113–126.

McAdoo, H. (2002). *Black children.* Thousand Oaks, CA: Sage.

McLoyd, V. C., Cauce, A., Takeuchi, D., & Wilson, L. (2000). Marital processes and parental socialization in families of color: A decade of review of research. *Journal of Marriage and the Family, 62,* 1070–1094.

Moore, J. W. (1991). *Going down to the barrio.* Philadelphia: Temple University Press.

Moore, J., & Pachon, H. (1985). *Hispanics in the United States.* Englewood Cliffs, NJ: Prentice Hall.

Muschkin, C., & Myers, G. (1989). Migration and household family structure: Puerto Ricans in the United States. *International Migration Review, 23,* 495–501.

Nielsen, F., & Fernandez, R. M. (1981). *Hispanic students in American high schools: Background characteristics and achievement.* Washington, DC: National Center for Education Statistics.

Okagaki, L., & Sternberg, R. (1991). Cultural and parental influences on cognitive development. In L. Okagaki and R. Sternberg (Eds.), *Directors of development: Influences on the development of children's thinking. (pp. 101–120).* Hillsdale, NJ: Lawrence Erlbaum.

Oyserman, D., Coon, H., & Kemmelmeier, M. (2002). Rethinking individualism and collectivism: Evaluation of theoretical assumptions and meta-analyses. *Psychological Bulletin, 128,* 3–72.

Padilla, A. M. (1980). *Acculturation.* Boulder, CO: Westview.

Passel, J., & Woodrow, K. (1984). Geographic distribution of undocumented aliens counted in the 1980 census by state. *International Migration Review, 18,* 642–671.

Penalosa, F. (1968). Mexican family roles. *Journal of Marriage and the Family, 30,* 680–689.

Phinney, J. S. (1989). Stages of ethnic identity development in minority group adolescents. *Journal of Early Adolescence, 9,* 34–49.

Phinney, J. S. (1990). Ethnic identity in adolescents and adults: Review of research. *Psychological Bulletin, 108,* 499–514.

Phinney, J. S., & Chavira, V. (1995). Parental ethnic socialization and adolescent coping with problems related to ethnicity. *Journal of Research on Adolescence, 5,* 31–53.

Planos, R. (1993). *Correlates of maternal teaching behaviors in low income Dominican and Puerto Rican mothers.* Unpublished doctoral dissertation, Fordham University, Bronx, NY.

Portes, A., & Rumbaut, R. (2001). *Legacies: The story of the immigrant second generation.* Los Angeles: University of California Press and Russell Sage Foundation.

Quintana, S. S., Castañeda-English, P., & Ybarra, V. (1999). Role of perspective-taking abilities and ethnic socialization in development of adolescent ethnic identity. *Journal of Research on Adolescence, 9,* 161–184.

Ramírez, M. (1983). *Psychology of the Americas mestizo perspective on personality and mental health.* New York: Pergamon.

Ramirez, M., & Price-Williams, D. (1974). Cognitive styles in children: Two Mexican communities. *Interamerican Journal of Psychology, 8,* 93–101.

Rand, Y. (1971). *Styles cognitifs et personnalité dans une situation de rencontre interculturelle: Etude comparative et analytique.* Unpublished doctoral dissertation, Sorbonne.

Rodríguez, G. (1999). *Raising nuestros niños.* New York: Fireside.

Rotheram-Borus, M., & Phinney, J. (1990). Patterns of social expectations among black and Mexican-American children. *Child Development, 61,* 542–556.

Rueschenberg, E., & Buriel, R. (1995). Mexican American family functioning and acculturation: A family systems perspective. In A. M. Padilla (Ed.), *Hispanic psychology* (pp. 15–42). Thousand Oaks, CA: Sage.

Rumbaut, R. (2001). Acculturation, discrimination, and ethnic identity among children of immigrants. Retrieved March 1, 2003, from the Kennedy School of Government Web site: www.ksg.harvard.edu/inequality/seminar/papers/Rumbaut1.pdf.

Saldaña, D. H. (1988). *Acculturation and stress: Latino students at a predominantly Anglo university.* Unpublished doctoral dissertation, University of California, Los Angeles.

Saldaña, D. (1995). Acculturative stress: Minority status and distress. In A. M. Padilla (Ed.) *Hispanic psychology* (pp. 71–89). Thousand Oaks, CA: Sage.

Sánchez-Ayéndez, M. (1998). The Puerto Rican family. In C. H. Mindel, R. W. Habenstein, & R. Wright, Jr. (Eds.), *Ethnic families in America* (pp. 199–222). Englewood Cliffs, NJ: Prentice Hall.

Sanders, M., Scholz, J., & Kagan, S. (1976). Three social motives and field-dependence in Anglo-American and Mexican-American children. *Journal of Cross-Cultural Psychology, 7,* 451–461.

Steinberg, L. (1999). *Adolescence.* Boston: McGraw-Hill College.

Steinberg, L., Blinde, P., & Chan, K. (1984). Dropping out among language minority youth. *Review of Educational Research, 54*(1), 113–132.

Suárez-Orozco, C., & Suárez-Orozco, M. (1995). *Transformations: Migration, family life, and achievement motivation among Latino adolescents.* Stanford, CA: Stanford University Press.

Szapocznick, J., & Kurtines, W. (1980). Acculturation, biculturalism and adjustment among Cuban Americans. In A. M. Padilla (Ed.), *Acculturation theories, models, and some new findings* (pp. 139–159). Boulder, CO: Westview.

Szapocznick, J., Kurtines, W., & Fernandez, T. (1980). Bicultural involvement and adjustment in Hispanic-American youths. *International Journal of Intercultural Relations, 4,* 353–365.

Thornton, M., Chatters, L., Taylor, R., & Allen, W. (1990). Sociodemographic and environmental correlates of racial socialization by black parents. *Child Development, 61,* 401–410.

Treviño, F. M. (1988). Uniform minimum data sets: in search of demographic comparability. *American Journal of Public Health, 78,* 126–127.

Umaña-Taylor, A. J., Diversi, M., & Fine, M. A. (2002). Ethnic identity and self-esteem of Latino adolescents: Distinctions among the Latino populations. *Journal of Adolescent Research, 17,* 303–327.

Umaña-Taylor, A. J., & Fine, M. A. (2001). Methodological implications of grouping Latino adolescents into one collective ethnic group. *Hispanic Journal of Behavioral Sciences, 23,* 347–362.

Umaña-Taylor, A. J., & Fine, M. A. (2002). *Examining a model of ethnic identity among Mexican-origin adolescents.* Manuscript submitted for publication.

U.S. Bureau of the Census. (1993). *Hispanic Americans today* (Current Populations Reports, P23-183). Washington, DC: Government Printing Office.

U.S. Bureau of the Census. (1999). *Hispanic Americans* (Current Population Reports, P20-513). Washington, DC: U.S. Department of Commerce.

U.S. Bureau of the Census. (2001, May). *The Hispanic population* (Census 2000 Brief). Washington, DC: U.S. Department of Commerce, Economics and Statistics Administration.

U.S. Bureau of the Census. (2003, January). Table US-EST2001-ASRO-04: National population estimates—characteristics [News release]. Retrieved March 1, 2003, from http://eire.census.gov/popest/data/national/asro.php.

U.S. Commission on Civil Rights. (1973). Teachers and students: Report V. Mexican American education study. In *Differences in teacher interaction with Mexican American and Anglo students.* Washington, DC: Government Printing Office.

Valdés, G. (1996). *Con respeto.* New York: Teachers College.

Vargas, M. (1991). *Predictors of maternal teaching strategies in Puerto Rican mothers.* Unpublished doctoral dissertation, Fordham University, Bronx, NY.

Vega, W. A. (1990). Hispanic families in the 1980's: A decade of research. *Journal of Marriage and the Family, 52,* 1015–1024.

Vidal, C. (1988). Godparenting among Hispanic Americans. *Child Welfare, 67,* 453–459.

Volk, D. (1999). "The teaching and the employment and being together. . . .": Sibling teaching in the family of a Puerto Rican kindergartner. *Early Childhood Research Quarterly, 14*(1), 5–34.

Ybarra, L. (1982). When wives work: The impact on the Mexican American family. *Journal of Marriage and the Family, 44,* 169–178.

Zambrana, R. (1995). *Understanding Latino families.* Thousand Oaks, CA: Sage.

Zinn, M. (1982). Mexican American men and masculinity. *Journal of Ethnic Studies, 10,* 29–44.

Zuniga, M. (1992). Families with Latino roots. In E. Lynch & M. Hanson (Eds.), *Developing cross-cultural competence* (pp. 151–179). Baltimore, MD: Brookes.

CHAPTER 20

Diversity in African American Families
Trends and Projections

M. BELINDA TUCKER, SASKIA K.
SUBRAMANIAN, AND ANGELA D. JAMES

T hroughout their history in the Western Hemisphere, African Americans have displayed great diversity in the form and function of family units. Due to both the cultural heterogeneity that characterized people who represented many different ethnic groupings and the varied conditions under which Africans lived in the New World, the establishment and development of domestic units necessarily took many paths. As we have argued previously, this background may be a factor in the dramatic changes that have characterized African American family formation over the past 30 years (Tucker & Mitchell-Kernan, 1995a). That is, the experience of enslavement, racial discrimination, and severe economic deprivation fostered an adaptive flexibility that may have been the basis for their

responses to the more recently experienced array of challenging conditions. In some respects, African American family diversity foretold many of the changes that would eventually be manifest in the U.S. population as a whole. Though the causes of specific trends in family formation may differ among U.S. subpopulations, it seems clear that today no specific family type can be considered characteristic of any one group. Increased diversity in the form of domestic units may be the hallmark of African American family life.

The purpose of this chapter is threefold: (a) to describe what has happened to African American families and domestic units over the last 30 years, (b) to discuss whether and how new scholarship has helped professionals and families adapt to any changes that might have occurred, and (c) to offer predictions about

AUTHORS' NOTE: This research was supported by two grants from the National Institute of Mental Health: research grant no. RO1 MH 47434 to Tucker and Claudia Mitchell-Kernan and Independent Scientist Award no. KO2 MH 01278 to Tucker. We greatefully acknowledge the assistance of Ana Johnson in the preparation of this paper.

the course of African American family and domestic development over the next several decades. With these goals in mind, however, we must emphasize that in our view, the construct of family is evolving and dynamic—both in terms of societal definitions and as experienced by individuals over time. This discussion therefore focuses on family as a lived, sometimes irregular, experience rather than an idealized and fixed representation.

AFRICAN AMERICAN FAMILY FORMATION AND MAINTENANCE IN THE LATE 20TH CENTURY

There have been numerous examinations of late-20th-century trends in African domestic arrangements (see Bennett, Bloom, & Craig, 1989, 1992; Cherlin, 1981; Espenshade, 1985; Hernandez, 1993; Hill, 1993; Mare & Winship, 1991; Rodgers & Thornton, 1985; Taylor, Chatters, Tucker, & Lewis, 1990; Taylor, Tucker, Chatters, & Jayakody, 1997; Tucker, 2000a; Tucker & Mitchell-Kernan, 1995b; Wilson, 1987). Conclusions about the nature, magnitude, and meanings of trends vary, reflecting differences in temporal boundaries, comparative intent, and ideological orientation (Tucker, 2000a). That is, comparisons anchored in the 1950s, a fairly aberrant period characterized by high rates of marriage, marital stability, and the growth of nuclear families, rather than earlier or later periods would reveal more dramatic behavioral shifts. This suggests that to understand certain family trends, a broader historical perspective is required. Just as importantly, however, recent changes in African American family formation must be considered within the context of the remarkable stability characteristic of previous generations (Franklin, 1997). In the discussion that follows, we refer to more detailed analyses of the key structural changes that have distinguished African American families

in the latter half of the 20th century (Tucker, 2000a; Tucker & Mitchell-Kernan, 1995a). Major trends in African American domestic life can be examined in terms of several broad domains: marriage and divorce, family and household composition, childbearing behavior and child-rearing arrangements, the economic support of families, and racial characteristics of families.

AFRICAN AMERICAN FAMILY TRENDS SINCE THE 1970S

Marriage and Divorce

There has been a decline in marital prevalence among African Americans, reflecting greater marital delay, a greater tendency for some to never marry, and higher divorce rates (see Tucker, 2000a). Between 1970 and 2000, the percentage of African Americans who had ever married declined from 64% to 55% among men and from 72% to 58% among women (U.S. Bureau of the Census, 2003). During the same time period, those who were currently married declined from 57% to 39% for men and from 54% to 31% among women. During the 1980s, it had appeared that the rate of decline in marriage was slowing, but new figures show a major swing away from marriage among blacks during the 1990s, especially among women as the percentage currently married declined by a full 10%. For the first time in recent history, the percentage of never-married women (42%) and men (45%) exceeded the percentage currently married (U.S. Bureau of the Census, 2001b).

Reflecting a larger societal trend, between 1970 and 1990, the African American divorce ratio (number of divorced persons per 1,000 married persons) more than tripled from 104 to 358 (Tucker & Mitchell-Kernan, 1995b). Though divorce rates leveled off during the 1990s, the Bureau of the

Census's 1996 Panel of the Survey of Income and Program Participation (SIPP) revealed that half of ever-married black women were divorced from their first husbands, compared to 40% of white and 24% of Asian/Pacific Islander women (Kreider & Fields, 2002). Amato and Keith (1991) projected that three quarters of African American children born to married parents would experience their parents' divorce before reaching the age of 16. (Unfortunately, the primary source of national data on marriage and divorce, the National Center for Health Statistics [NCHS], stopped collecting detailed information on marriage and divorce in 1996.)

These trends were most pronounced among the young. For example, although marriage is unlikely before the age of 24, in the year 2000 75% of black women aged 45 to 49 and over 90% of those over 60 had been married. Marriage is also normative among older African American men, with about 75% of those in their 40s and 85% of those in their early 50s having married at least once (U.S. Bureau of the Census, 2001b).

As the population of African-descended persons in the United States becomes more ethnically diverse through immigration by blacks from several nations, family domestic patterns are seen to vary along these cultural lines. For example, Nigerians and persons from the Dutch West Indies have a greater tendency to marry, and Dutch West Indians and Cape Verdeans are more likely to divorce (Tucker, 2000a).

Family and Household Composition

As both consequence and corollary of changing marital behavior, there has been a fundamental shift in the proportional representation of various family and household types and in the visibility of family arrangements that were once rare. For example, in 1970, black married couples with children made up nearly 25% of households; in 2000, that figure had dropped to less than 17% of households. Households headed by women, with no male present, have increased substantially. In 30 years, the proportion of households containing individuals living alone increased from 15% to 27% (which is 9.4% of the total population), and by 2000, fully half (49.2%) of households maintained by persons aged 15 to 64 did not include children (U.S. Bureau of the Census, 1973, 2001b, 2002a, 2002c).

Approximately 8% of the black population is age 65 and over (U.S. Bureau of the Census, 2001a). Older blacks are far more likely to live alone than those who are younger and are more likely to live alone than older persons of other races: 45% of black householders aged 65 and over and 30% of the total older population live alone (U.S. Bureau of the Census, 2002a, 2003). This is due partly to spousal loss, which (based on 1993 data) was also greater than for other races for both men (23%) and women (56%) (U.S. Bureau of the Census, 1999b). At the same time, however, older blacks are also twice as likely as whites to live in households with three or more persons in what are likely to be both extended and child-rearing family situations (U.S. Bureau of the Census, 2002a).

On the whole, these data paint a picture of an African American population that appears in some respects to be less communal over time, with more persons living alone, fewer children, and less marriage. Sudarkasa (1997) cited this disaggregation of households as the most significant change in black family organization over the last 30 years. Paralleling these trends is the societywide increased visibility of two household types that were in earlier times relatively rare: increased nonmarital cohabitation among persons of the opposite sex and greater numbers of same-sex couples sharing domiciles.

Nonmarital Cohabitation

In 2000, approximately 11% of African American women and men in heterosexual couples sharing a domicile were not married (Fields & Casper, 2001)—a percentage that is probably underestimated, according to the Bureau of the Census. Though cohabiting relationships are generally less enduring than marriages, this is especially true for African Americans. Recent data from the National Survey of Family Growth showed that black women were more likely than other groups to experience disruption of cohabiting relationships and were less likely to make the transition from such relationships into marriage (Bramlett & Mosher, 2002).

Same-Sex Couples

Census data on race for same-sex couples are problematic because they are classified on the basis of the race of the main householder. Yet African Americans make up 10.8% of all same-sex couples (U.S. Bureau of the Census, 2003). Though the total number accounts for less than 2% of all couples containing an African American, this figure is quite likely an underestimate due to a hesitancy to report such relationships.

Childbearing Behavior and Living Arrangements of Children

One area in which there has been tremendous change over the last several decades is the circumstances surrounding the birth and rearing of African American children. The decline in marriage among African Americans has been accompanied by a shift in the proportion of children born to and/or reared by married parents. Overall birth rates of black women (without respect to marital status) have declined by nearly half over the last four decades, from 31.9 per 1,000 women in

1960 to 17.6 in 2000 (Martin, Hamilton, Ventura, Menacker, & Park, 2002; Ventura, Martin, Curtin, Menacker, & Hamilton, 2001). In 1996, births among African American teenagers reached the lowest point ever recorded—54.7 births per 1,000 women (Ventura, Curtin, & Matthews, 1998).

Children's living arrangements have undergone similar change. In 1970, nearly 60% of children lived with both parents; by 2000, only 38% lived with both a mother and a father (U.S. Bureau of the Census, 2001c). Although this figure has been stable since 1990, national estimates from the SIPP data set richly portray the increasingly complex living arrangements of children societywide, even within two-parent homes. In 1996, just over 20% of African American children under 18 lived in stepfamilies, composed of various combinations of stepparents, stepsiblings, half-siblings, and other relatives (Fields, 2001). Moreover, if national trends apply equally to blacks, a significant proportion of African American children are living under the care of lesbian, gay, bisexual, or transsexual parents (Kearl, 2002).

Perhaps the living situation that has received most attention in recent times is that of the grandparent—even great-grandparent—(most often a woman) as custodian (Minkler & Roe, 1993; Ruiz, 2000; Taylor et al., 1997; U.S. Bureau of the Census, 1999a). The number of children overall with custodial grandparents has nearly doubled since 1970, from 3% to 5.6%, with such households significantly more likely to be black, in the South, in central cities, and poor (Casper & Bryson, 1998).

Family Type and Poverty

Though the details are beyond the scope of this chapter, changes in living arrangements of children have been accompanied by increased child poverty (Tucker, 2000a).

In 1999, although just over 9% of black two-parent families with children were impoverished, 42% of single-mother families had incomes below poverty levels, and 25% of single fathers were poor (U.S. Bureau of the Census, 2002b). Besides reflecting the greater economic difficulties of single women, who quite likely have few educational resources, such a difference is indicative of the increasingly selective nature of married black couples, which are more likely than ever to involve professional men and women. To the extent that family type is strongly associated with income, the changes in family organization observed for African Americans since 1970 are accompanied by significant economic correlates. Among blacks, married-couple families have incomes that come closest to white income levels.

An earlier review of 1997 Current Population Survey (CPS) data also showed that among both black and white couples two thirds relied on two or more salaries (Tucker, 2000a). However, because black wives' incomes are much closer to those of their husbands, black middle-class status is more dependent on the labor force participation of women. In 75% of households maintained by single black women, there was at least one wage earner, thus belying the image of welfare dependency (Tucker, 2000a). This was well before the new federal workfare regulations were instituted. Older blacks, however, are less able to work and less likely to have retirement funds or savings; consequently, they are much more likely to be impoverished than same-age persons of other races. According to the 2001 Current Population Survey, nearly 17% of black men aged 65 and over and 26% of black women lived below the poverty level—which is about 3 and 2.5 times, respectively, the level of poverty among elderly whites (U.S. Bureau of Labor Statistics & U.S. Bureau of the Census, 2002).

Multiethnic and Multiracial Families

Though still proportionately small as a total percentage of households containing black members, the number of persons who are in multiracial/ethnic households or families, or are multiracial/ethnic themselves, is steadily increasing. In the 1970 census, 0.7% of all marriages involved persons of at least two different races; by 1980, such marriages represented 2% of the total (U.S. Bureau of the Census, 1998), and unmarried partners were twice as likely to be of different races than married partners (Fields & Casper, 2001). Interracial marriages were still about three times more likely to involve African American men than women. However, data from our surveys indicated that over half of single black women have dated someone of another race and that many now express a willingness to outmarry (Taylor, Tucker, & Mitchell-Kernan, 2003; Tucker & Mitchell-Kernan, 1995a).

The racial makeup of homes has changed in other ways. In 1990, 6.3% of children in households in which at least one parent was black were reported to be of a race different from that of at least one of their parents, triple the percentage observed for whites (U.S. Bureau of the Census, 1998).

Summary

African American families have undergone significant structural changes and diversification over the last three decades. Factors believed to be driving these trends (e.g., economic changes, societal value shifts, demographic shifts) are discussed elsewhere (e.g., Billingsley, 1992; Franklin, 1997; Tucker, 2000a; Wilson, 1996). Although we did not explore these potentially causal factors, it seems clear to us that many of the structural changes are adaptive attempts to maintain family units in the face of adversity. These particular changes, though, convey greater salience for certain research topics. The next section assesses the meaningfulness of such research for individual actions and professional support.

THE ROLE OF SCHOLARSHIP IN SOCIETY'S ADJUSTMENT TO FAMILY DIVERSITY

Although arguably a key aim of family research is to inform the public and advance professional support for families, it is not entirely clear that this objective has been met. First, whether and how the general public, and African Americans in particular, gain access to the results of research remains a question. As more universities and scientific organizations maintain media relations units, reports on the products of academe appear rather regularly in conventional news outlets and even the popular media. In addition, the proliferation of Web sites on family life has further helped to distill (and in some cases distort) scholarly findings. However, compared to other racial groups in the United States, African Americans have limited computer and Internet access (National Telecommunications and Information Administration, 2002). Even when the general public gains access to data reports, understanding the nuanced results of complex, often equivocal, research may be beyond the means of most nonscientists. In this section, we will discuss several of the main lines of scholarship relevant to African American family trends and the extent to which findings in these areas are constructive in broadening public knowledge. A particularly problematic area of study has been the attempt to discern whether certain types of family arrangements are beneficial or harmful to children. Research has focused on several dimensions of parenthood that in recent years have become more pervasive among African Americans, including divorce, father

absence, working mothers, and child- or marriage-free households.

Divorce

Emblematic of the conflict that permeates this area of research is a 1997 article in the *Nation* in which family historian Stephanie Coontz traced the public frenzy surrounding the publication of Judith Wallerstein's two-decade study of the outcomes of 131 children of divorced parents in Marin County, California (Wallerstein & Blakeslee, 1989). Wallerstein reported high rates of long-term psychological distress and, in a later follow-up, drug and alcohol abuse as well in children whose parents had divorced (Wallerstein, Lewis, & Blakeslee, 2000). Despite the decidedly skewed sample in terms of income and initial family functioning, the media embraced these findings with over 200 articles and opinion pieces, popularizing the notion that divorce had tremendous long-term impacts on children (Coontz, 1997). Less publicly visible were other studies with more representative samples that reached different conclusions, demonstrating far weaker effect sizes and the transitory nature of some negative effects (Amato & Keith, 1991; Hetherington & Kelly, 2002; Stewart, Copeland, Chester, Malley, & Barenbaum, 1997; also see Chapter 15 of this book).

The more limited studies on African Americans seem to portray a more negative picture, however, based largely on the more economically precarious circumstances of many blacks. Furstenberg (1990) has noted that because women compared to men suffer more economically after divorce (due to unequal physical custody of children, low or absent child support/alimony, and disparate earning capacity), the impact is even greater for African American women, who are "especially vulnerable to all these sources of poverty" (p. 387). He cited census data showing that both separated and divorced black women were more likely to be poor than their white counterparts. Though white women were likely to marry again, thereby enjoying some economic gain, African American women were further disadvantaged in this regard by a diminished pool of available and financially able mates.

Clearly, our understanding of the effects of divorce on African American children and families is far from complete, which compromises the utility of the work for public use. One area that remains relatively unexplored is how extended kinship networks in African American communities may mediate the potentially negative effects on children of parental separations.

Black Fathers

Much scholarly research has considered the effects of father absence on households and children. As noted earlier, African American children are likely to live in homes without two parents and without biological fathers or stepfathers. The economic issues noted above are central (Lerman, 2002), and the lack of child support from fathers contributes to the impoverishment of single-mother families. Sorensen and Zibman (2000), who conducted one of the few studies specifically addressing the issue of poor fathers and barriers to the provision of support for their children, noted that only 35% of children (of all races and income levels) with a nonresident father receive formal child support payments and that following separation children are 70% more likely to be poor than their fathers. Yet one third of nonresidential fathers who do not pay formal child support are poor themselves and, as is characteristic of impoverished persons in this society more generally, are more likely to be black or Latino.

Sorensen and Zibman (2001) further observed that despite facing similar employment barriers (e.g., limited education and work experience), poor fathers typically have less access than poor women to most work support programs. The economic coping of poor noncustodial fathers, however, is little explored or understood, and relatively little research has focused specifically on African American fathers and black fatherhood. This is due in part to widespread undercounting of this population by national surveys and the census (which tends to miss men who are not in stabile domiciles and often does not report data on institutionalized fathers or those in group settings such as the military). Hairston (1998) pointed out that incarcerated fathers (who are overrepresented by African Americans; U.S. Department of Justice, 2002) are most marginalized and that the structural conditions of prison life and visitation make maintaining contact and negotiating a viable parenting role nearly impossible.

The research focus has been primarily on the effect of single parenthood on child outcomes. Less noted has been evidence that black fathers (custodial or noncustodial) may be as engaged or even more engaged with children than white fathers. Although Isaacs and Leon (1988) found that African American fathers living outside the household saw their children less frequently than did white fathers, later studies countered this view. Mott (1994), using data from the National Longitudinal Survey of Youth, found that despite differences in father residency across race, noncustodial black fathers were more likely than whites to be regular visitors of their children. Ahmeduzzaman and Roopnarine (1992) determined that although African American men in intact family settings spent less time than female partners in primary child care activities (like men in general in this society), they were accessible and involved with their children.

Cochran's (1997) decade review of literature on African American fathers discussed the overuse of two models to understand father involvement: the deficit paradigm (in which behaviors and values diverging from a white middle-class standard are framed as aberrant and lacking) and the matriarchy model (in which black women are assumed to be serving as household heads because of the inability of African American men to fulfill this role). Although citing empirical advances enjoyed by adopting more Afrocentric and ecological approaches, she called for more qualitative work that captures the experience of black fathers and more longitudinal studies. Studies of black fathers have also focused disproportionately on absence among economically disadvantaged fathers, as opposed to the contributions of black fathers with greater economic means who do reside with their children. Adams and Nelson (2001) suggested that until scholars develop models that include the positive dimensions of African American males and their parenting patterns, our understanding of the values and norms of this sector of society will be incomplete.

Researchers on the whole suggest that father presence and involvement contributes to positive outcomes for children. And, given societal gender economic inequality, a father's economic contributions are key to children's economic well-being. However, in many African American communities, men are simply less available and less economically viable. The women in those communities, with few economic resources themselves, have limited options. The findings of research on the consequences of father absence have little meaning in this context, where the socioemotional benefits of motherhood would be compelling. The research, however, accentuates the need to further explore the documented role of the wider support system in the survival and maintenance of African American families (Stack, 1974; Taylor et al., 1990).

Working Mothers

The effect on children of nonparental child care is a matter of great concern to parents, policy makers, and scholars alike. Well over half of all children between the ages of birth and 6 years (and not in kindergarten) spend time in child care; of these children, over half are looked after by a nonrelative in a home or in a center-based program (Childtrends Databank, 2002). This issue may have even greater significance for African American families, given that black children are more likely to be in a nonparental child care setting: 75% of black non-Hispanic children receive such care, as compared to 62% of white children and 47% of Hispanic children (Childtrends Databank, 2002). We simply do not know whether these kinds of arrangements are better or worse than parental care. Though research on this subject has been fairly extensive, the results are not without controversy and are ultimately far from conclusive (Aughinbaugh & Gittleman, 2003; Harvey, 1999; Hoffman, 1998; Waldfogel, Han, & Brooks-Gunn, 2002).

Some intriguing recent data, however, may have particular relevance for African American families. Harvey (1999) reported findings from the National Longitudinal Survey of Youth indicating that early maternal employment is not consistently related to children's development and that employment has positive effects for single mothers and low-income families. She suggested that in situations of great economic deprivation, the positive effects of maternal employment may stem from the benefits of increased family income.

Child- and/or Marriage-Free Households

Generally, research on the family has focused on family presence, not the lack thereof. Yet a significant proportion of the population foregoes marriage and/or children and is largely overlooked by scholars. This is an especially critical issue for African American women, among whom the numbers who do not have children and/or are single continue to grow. Crouse (1999) observed that the number of married women overall is at the lowest level in over 100 years. The NCHS (2002, Table 4, p. 85) showed that over 25% of women in their early 30s have not given birth (compared to 12% in 1970). Sixteen percent of women in their 40s are without children. (It is difficult to distinguish between those who are childless by choice or by circumstance; see Chapter 7 of this book.) In recent years, organizations have formed locally and on the Internet for childless/child-free couples (www.nokidding.net) and singles (www.unmarried.org). The extent to which African Americans are involved in such movements is unknown.

Conventional wisdom dictates that children are a natural outcome and necessary addition to a marriage/family. However, social scientists have long observed a negative association between the presence of children and marital quality (Belsky, 1990; Somers, 1993; Waite & Lillard, 1991), though more recent research suggests that this phenomenon may be more complex and variable than previously realized (Bradbury, Fincham, & Beach, 2000). Our data from the Survey of Families and Relationships for 21 cities across the nation showed that having even one child is associated with decreased marital happiness (Tucker, in press). Conversely, Waite and Gallagher (2000) have detailed a series of highly controversial findings that being married is related to greater financial, social, and health (mental and physical) benefits. Studies of African Americans tend to confirm these results (Broman, 1988; Chatters, 1988; Zollar & Williams, 1987). Yet analyses of our data show that when the availability of social and socioeconomic resources is controlled for, African American women who have never married are not more psychologically distressed than those who are married, widowed, or in cohabiting nonmarital relationships (Tucker, in press).

Whether marriage is beneficial or not, singlehood is on the rise among African Americans, yet it is rarely explored in scholarly work. Further, there is little differentiation between those who elect not to marry and those who are less able to do so due to barriers such as limited mate availability, disabilities, or geographic isolation. Similarly, though infertility is studied, we know little about African American persons who are childless by choice or because of sociostructural constraints (limited access to partners).

Summary

Overall, there is little question that parents and professionals dealing with families rely on information disseminated by researchers. However, it is not clear how helpful scholars have been to these groups, given the equivocal nature of most results and given the limited accessibility to accurate and complete reports of research findings. Additionally, because many of the studies mentioned above either largely ignore or overutilize race (and confound it with socioeconomic status) as a variable, their usefulness to African Americans and support professionals is severely limited.

LOOKING TOWARD THE FUTURE

In many ways, African Americans are leading the revolution in family life in the United States. Although not unique to African American families, declines and delays in marriage, increases in the proportion of single-parent families, and many other recent family changes have all been more extreme.

However, amidst the significant changes that have occurred in black family life in the last several decades, there is also significant continuity. For example, although African Americans have led most indicators of family change, they have not led in propensity to live alone as opposed to living in family households. Changes in single-parent households can be seen as a result of both the increased separation of marriage and childbearing and the constancy in the propensity of women to bear children at younger ages. So it should be acknowledged that most recent changes in family life are rooted in shifting marriage patterns rather than in diminishing family related values or commitments.

The Future of Marriage

Reflecting on the continuities as well as the discontinuities of family behavior among African Americans, we are willing to make several predictions about the future directions of African American families. First, we feel confident that despite low levels of marriage, the institution of marriage will continue to be highly valued and sought after. We base this expectation on a number of indicators. First, marriage is still favored by religious institutions, which appear to be regaining membership as well as dominance in black communities in recent years. Further, most surveys reveal that the great majority of young adults, African American and white, expect to marry even as they express high levels of acceptance of singlehood (East, 1998; Sweet & Bumpass, 1992). Despite relatively large racial differences in marital behavior, blacks are only slightly less likely than whites to want and expect to get married (East, 1998; Sweet & Bumpass, 1992). Indeed, Tucker (2000b) found that when age, education, and income were controlled for, African Americans were no less likely to expect to marry than whites.

Whether these marital expectations will translate into marriage, however, remains to be seen.

Divorce

We expect that present divorce rates will continue to decline among African Americans. We base this prediction on several contemporary marriage patterns. First, the increasing prevalence of single, never-married adults suggests that there may be substantial selection into marriage. Individuals who are perhaps ill suited to marriage but who in times past married because of social pressure to do so may now be more likely to remain unmarried. Further, people marrying today may be less motivated to do so by transitory sexual or romantic attraction and more motivated by longer-term considerations of lifestyle and personal compatibility, which enhance the likelihood of marital stability. The conservative trend toward covenant marriage and other explicitly promarriage policies may act to discourage those in unhappy marriages from divorcing.

Women and Work

Women's labor market participation and success have increasingly made them more attractive as potential marriage partners. However, viewing economic considerations as important and actually combining work and family roles and responsibilities are very different matters. Although most people have the notion that black women have continuously and universally participated in the labor force, this perception is rooted in the previous dramatic differences between black and white women. Our own analysis of data from the Current Population Surveys shows that in March 1971, 48% of married black women and 36% of white women worked outside the home; by March 2000, that figure had risen to just over 60% for black women and 57% for white women. So although in 1970 black women were considerably more likely than married white women to work, in 2000 the difference was negligible. Given the general rise in women's labor force participation, as well as the long-standing presence of black women in the labor force, we predict the continuing importance of labor force participation of both marital partners among African Americans. Increasingly, middle-class economic standing for either black or white families is accomplished only by virtue of two incomes. Home ownership, private schools, and a host of other middle-class "necessities" require substantial economic resources Moreover, given the insecurities associated with employment today, a second income serves as a buffer when one partner faces job separation.

We want to add a caveat to this prediction, though, by noting two divergent trends. Recent convergence of white and black married women's labor force participation is due both to dramatic increases in white women's labor market participation and to a slight decline in black married women's labor force participation. Recent, though small, declines in black married women's labor force participation, along with rising numbers of families who home-school their children (Bauman, 2001), suggest a trend of family conservatism among African Americans. Families who are able to subsist on a single income may increasingly consider unattractive the difficulty of combining two careers with family life. That said, we predict that the engine of economic necessity and female economic importance in the global, postmodern economy will necessitate ever-increasing shifts in gender roles and familial expectations among African Americans.

The continuing labor force participation of black women may lead to several other cultural changes. First, we expect that the added economic value of two partners will act to shore up the worth, though perhaps not the stability, of African American marriages, which are subject to a number of economic, social, and physical strains. According to marriage theorists, women's employment could affect the formation of marriage in two very different ways. On the one hand, it could decrease the motivation to marry, as it provides an economic alternative for women (Becker, 1981). On the other hand, it could increase the opportunity to marry by having a positive effect on the ability of young couples to set up independent households (Oppenheimer, 1988, 1994). Of course, women's labor force participation, particularly in high-salaried occupations, may merely affect the timing of marriage. Increasing the amount of time women spend obtaining training and academic credentials could consequently delay marriage for them (Oppenheimer, 1988, 1994). The continuing value of married women's labor suggests several cultural changes. For instance, obtaining high-quality child care and arranging flexible work schedules will be of increasing significance as social problems.

Another trend we anticipate in the next several decades also has to do with the labor force participation of married women. In 1996, one third of married black women made more money than their spouses (Freeman, 2000). Given current gender imbalances in college and university enrollments, which are particularly pronounced among African Americans, we expect that it may become increasingly common for black women to have higher incomes than their spouses. Although such changes may be difficult to negotiate in the short run, and marital conflict may result, in the long run there may well be an expanded definition of appropriate gender role behavior.

Conceptualizations of women and appropriate female behavior have changed dramatically over the last half-century (Buss, Shackelford, Kirkpatrick, & Larsen, 2001; Thornton & Young-DeMarco, 2001). Not so long ago, men valued women's domestic qualities as important mate selection criteria. By contrast, men today rarely rank domestic qualities as particularly important. Although there are signs of significant shifts, conceptualizations of men's gender role and family responsibility have not changed nearly as fast as women's have. Our perhaps optimistic prediction is that household power and housework will become more equitably shared and that married African American men and women will lead this trend. We also predict that these struggles over equity and power sharing may lead to more concerted efforts to redefine men's roles and gender role expectations more generally.

Expansion of Family Roles and Responsibilities: Big Mama and the Beloved Aunt

We also envisage the increasing importance and prominence of expanded family ties. As people live longer, and if marriages continue to be somewhat fragile and increasingly rare, a wider range of kinship ties will become progressively more central to everyday family life. A range of family members outside the co-resident household may be available to perform family functions. For example, our research team notes the presence and importance of a beloved aunt in many African American families, usually a single and child-free woman who has a particularly close and influential role in the lives of young people. Similarly, male role models for many young men are their mother's

brothers rather than their biological fathers. We expect that as the population of never-married and child-free individuals increases so will the presence of this special beloved aunt/beloved uncle relationship. Another family trend is the increasingly important family roles and responsibilities of grandparents. Grandparents have already become a significant resource for many families, as evidenced by the dramatic increase in the numbers of grandparents serving as primary guardians for their children's offspring. Melvin Wilson (1984) and Flaherty, Factreau, and Garver (1987) have elucidated the critical role of African American grandparents in caregiving, instruction, and management. Though Burton and colleagues (Burton & Bengtson, 1985; Burton & Dilworth-Anderson, 1991) and Minkler and Roe (1993) cautioned that the context of grandparent involvement has changed, with both younger entry into grandparenthood and more parental incapacitation (e.g., substance abuse, criminal justice involvement), grandparent providers are now under much greater stress. For this reason, we believe that people will increasingly take advantage of a wider range of family members, as well as community members, to offset the uncertainties of marriage and family life. At base, we believe that the family as an institution is adaptive and highly responsive to changing demands and needs. As such, our predictions spring from the expectation that African American families will continue to exhibit flexibility in the face of modern and postmodern exigencies.

REFERENCES

Adams, V. H., III, & Nelson, J. (2001). Hope, happiness, and African American fathers: Changes between 1980 and 1992. *African American Research Perspectives, 7,* 148–156.

Ahmeduzzaman, M., & Roopnarine, J. L. (1992). Sociodemographic factors, functioning style, social support, and fathers' involvement with preschoolers in African-American families. *Journal of Marriage and the Family, 54,* 699–707.

Amato, P., & Keith, B. (1991). Parental divorce and the well-being of children. *Psychological Bulletin, 110*, 26–46.

Aughinbaugh, A., & Gittleman, M. (2003). *Maternal employment and adolescent risky behavior* (U.S. Bureau of Labor Statistics, Working Paper 366). Washington, DC: U.S. Department of Labor.

Bauman, K. J. (2001). *Home schooling in the United States: Trends and characteristics* (Working Paper Series No. 53). Washington, DC: U.S. Bureau of the Census. Retrieved July 11, 2003, from www.census.gov/population/www/documentation/twps0053.html.

Becker, G. S. (1981). *A treatise on the family*. Cambridge, MA: Harvard University Press.

Belsky, J. (1990). Children and marriage. In F. D. Fincham & T. Bradbury (Eds.), *The psychology of marriage* (pp. 172–200). New York: Guilford.

Bennett, N. G., Bloom, D. E., & Craig, P. H. (1989). The divergence of black and white marriage patterns. *American Journal of Sociology, 95*, 692–722.

Bennett, N. G., Bloom, D. E., & Craig, P. H. (1992). American marriage patterns in transition. In S. J. South & S. E. Tolnay (Eds.), *The changing American family: Sociological and demographic perspectives*. Boulder: CO: Westview.

Billingsley, A. (1992). *Climbing Jacob's ladder: The enduring legacy of African-American families*. New York: Simon & Schuster.

Bradbury, T. N., Fincham, F. D., & Beach, S. R. H. (2000). Research on the nature and determinants of marital satisfaction: A decade in review. *Journal of Marriage and the Family, 62*, 964–998.

Bramlett, M. D., & Mosher, W. D. (2002). *Cohabitation, marriage, divorce, and remarriage in the United States: Data from the National Survey of Family Growth*. (Vital and Health Statistics, Series 23 [22]). Hyattsville, MD: Department of Health and Human Services, Centers for Disease Control and Prevention.

Broman, C. (1988). Satisfaction among blacks: The significance of marriage and parenthood. *Journal of Marriage and the Family, 50*, 45–51.

Burton, L. M., & Bengtson, V. L. (1985). Black grandmothers: Issues of timing and continuity of roles. In V. L. Bengtson & J. F. Robertson (Eds.), *Grandparenthood* (pp. 61–77). Beverly Hills, CA: Sage.

Burton, L. M., & Dilworth-Anderson, P. (1991). The intergenerational roles of black Americans. *Marriage and Family Review, 16*, 311–330.

Buss, D., Shackelford, T. K., Kirkpatrick, L., & Larsen, R. J. (2001). A half century of mate preferences: The cultural evolution of values. *Journal of Marriage and Family, 63*, 491–503.

Casper, L. M., & Bryson, K. R. (1998). *Coresident grandparents and their grandchildren: Grandparent-maintained families* (Population Division Working Paper Series No. 26). Washington, DC: U.S. Bureau of the Census.

Chatters, L. M. (1988). Subjective well-being evaluations among older black Americans. *Psychology and Aging, 3*, 184–190.

Cherlin, A. J. (1981). *Marriage, divorce, remarriage*. Cambridge, MA: Harvard University Press.

Childtrends Databank. (2002). Child care. Retrieved September 20, 2002, from www.childtrendsdatabank.org/socemo/early/21ChildCare.htm.

Cochran, D. (1997, July-August). African American fathers: A decade review of the literature. *Families in Society: The Journal of Contemporary Human Services, 78*, 340–350.

Coontz, S. (1997). Divorcing reality. *Nation, 265*, 16, 21–25.

Crouse, J. S. (Ed.). (1999). The state of marriage in 20th century America: Implications for the next millennium. Retrieved September 20, 2002, from http://beverlylahayeinstitute.org/events/1999-10_marriage/20-america.shtml.

East, P. L. (1998). Racial and ethnic differences in girls' sexual, marital, and birth expectations. *Journal of Marriage and the Family, 60*, 150–162.

Espenshade, T. J. (1985). Marriage trends in America: Estimates, implications, and underlying causes. *Population and Development Review, 11*, 193–245.

Fields, J. (2001). *Living arrangements of children: 1996* (Household Economic Studies. No. P70-74). Washington, DC: U.S. Bureau of the Census. Retrieved from www.census.gov/population/www/socdemo/child/la-child.html.

Fields, J., & Casper, L. (2001). *America's families and living arrangements 2000: Population characteristics* (Current Population Reports, No. P20-537). Washington, DC: U.S. Bureau of the Census. Retrieved July 11, 2003, from www.census.gov/prod/ 2001pubs/p20-537.pdf.

Flaherty, M. J., Facteau, L., & Garver, P. (1987). Grandmother functions in multigenerational families: An exploratory study of black adolescent mothers and their infants. *Maternal Child Nursing Journal, 60*, 61–73.

Franklin, D. (1997). *Ensuring inequality: The structural transformation of the African American family.* New York: Oxford University Press.

Freeman, R. B. (2000). The feminization of work in the USA: A new era for (man)kind. In S. S. Gustafsson & D. E. Meulders (Eds.), *Gender and the labour market: Econometric evidence of obstacles to achieving gender equality.* New York: St. Martin's Press.

Furstenberg, F. F., Jr. (1990). Divorce and the American family. *Annual Review of Sociology, 16*, 379–403.

Hairston, C. F. (1998). The forgotten parent: Understanding the forces that influence incarcerated fathers' relationships with their children. *Child Welfare, 77*, 617–639.

Harvey, E. (1999). Short-term and long-term effects of early parental employment on children of the National Longitudinal Survey of Youth. *Developmental Psychology, 35*, 2, 445–459.

Hernandez, D. J. (1993). *America's children: Resources from family, government and the economy.* New York: Russell Sage Foundation.

Hetherington, E. M., & Kelly, J. (2002). *For better or for worse: Divorce reconsidered.* New York: Norton.

Hill, R. B. (1993). *Research on African American families: A holistic perspective.* Boston: University of Massachusetts, William Monroe Trotter Institute.

Hoffman, L. W. (1998). The effects of the mother's employment status on the family and the child. *CEIC Review, 7*(1). Retrieved July 11, 2003, from Temple University Web site: www.temple.edu/lss/htmlpublications/ceicreviews/ceic7-1.htm#hoffman.

Isaacs, M., & Leon, G. (1988). Race, marital dissolution and visitation: An examination of adaptive family strategies. *Journal of Divorce, 11*(2), 17–31.

Kearl, M. C. (2002). Singlehood and alternative family forms. Retrieved September 20, 2002, from the Trinity University Web site: www.trinity.edu/~mkearl/fam-alts.html.

Kreider, R. M., & Fields, J. M. (2002). *Number, timing, and duration of marriages and divorces: 1996* (Current Population Reports, P70-80). Washington, DC: U.S. Bureau of the Census.

Lerman, R. I. (2002). *How do marriage, cohabitation, and single parenthood affect the material hardships of families with children?* Report prepared for the U.S. Department of Health and Human Services Office of the Assistant Secretary for Planning and Evaluation. Washington, DC: Urban Institute and American University.

Mare, R. D., & Winship, C. (1991). Socioeconomic change and the decline of marriage for blacks and whites. In C. Jencks & P. Peterson (Eds.), *The urban underclass* (pp. 175–202). Washington, DC: Brookings Institution.

Martin, J. A., Hamilton, B. E., Ventura, S. J., Menacker, F., & Park, M. P. (2002). *Births: Final data for 2000. Table 13: Total number of births, rates (birth, fertility, and total fertility), and percent of births with selected demographic characteristics, by detailed race of mother and place of birth of mother: United States, 2000* (National Vital Statistics Reports, 50[5]). Washington, DC: U.S. Bureau of the Census

Minkler, M., & Roe, K. M. (1993). *Grandmothers as caregivers: Raising children of the crack cocaine epidemic.* Newbury Park, CA: Sage.

Mott, F. L. (1994). Sons, daughters and fathers' absence: Differentials in father-leaving probabilities and in-home environments. *Journal of Family Issues, 15,* 97–128.

National Center for Health Statistics. (2002). *Health, United States, 2002: With chartbook on trends in the health of Americans.* Hyattsville, MD: Author.

National Telecommunications and Information Administration. (2002). *A nation online: How Americans are expanding their use of the Internet.* Washington, DC: U.S. Department of Commerce.

Oppenheimer, V. K. (1988). A theory of marriage and timing. *American Journal of Sociology, 94,* 563–591.

Oppenheimer, V. K. (1994). Women's rising employment and the future of the family in industrial societies. *Population and Development Review, 20,* 293–342.

Rodgers, W. L., & Thornton, A. (1985). Changing patterns of first marriage in the United States. *Demography, 22,* 265–279.

Ruiz, D. S. (2000). Guardians and caretakers: African American grandmothers as primary caregivers in intergenerational families. *African American Research Perspectives, 6*(1), 1–12.

Somers, M. D. (1993). A comparison of voluntarily childfree adults and parents. *Journal of Marriage and the Family, 55,* 643–650.

Sorensen, E., & Zibman, C. (2000). A look at poor dads who don't pay child support. Retrieved July 11, 2003, from the Urban Institute Web site: www.urban.org/UploadedPDF/discussion00-07.pdf.

Sorensen, E., & Zibman, C. (2001). *Poor dads who don't pay child support: Deadbeats or disadvantaged?* (New Federalism: National Survey of America's Families Series, No. B-30). Washington, DC: Urban Institute.

Stack, C. (1974). *All our kin: Strategies for survival in a black community.* New York: Harper & Row.

Stewart, A. J., Copeland, A. P., Chester, N. L., Malley, J. E., & Barenbaum, N. B. (1997). *Separating together: How divorce transforms families.* New York: Guilford.

Sudarkasa, N. (1997). African American families and family values. In H. P. McAdoo (Ed.). *Black families* (3rd ed., pp. 9–40). Thousand Oaks, CA: Sage.

Sweet, J. A., & Bumpass, L. L. (1992). Young adults' views of marriage, cohabitation, and family. In S. South (Ed.), *The changing American family: Sociological and demographic perspectives* (pp. 143–170). Boulder, CO: Westview.

Taylor, P. L., Tucker, M. B., & Mitchell-Kernan, C. (2003). *"I do" but to whom: Attitudes toward intermarriage.* Unpublished manuscript.

Taylor, R. J., Chatters, L. M., Tucker, M. B., & Lewis, E. (1990). Developments in research on black families: A decade review. *Journal of Marriage and the Family, 52,* 993–1014.

Taylor, R. J., Tucker, M. B., Chatters, L. M., & Jayakody, R. (1997). Recent demographic trends in African American family structure. In R. J. Taylor & L. Chatters (Eds.), *Family life in black America* (pp. 14–62). Thousand Oaks, CA: Sage.

Thornton, A., & Young-DeMarco, L. (2001). Four decades of trends in attitudes toward family issues in the United States: The 1960's through the 1990's. *Journal of Marriage and Family, 63,* 1009–1037.

Tucker, M. B. (2000a). Considerations in the development of family policy for African Americans. In J. S. Jackson (Ed.), *New directions: African Americans in a diversifying nation* (pp. 162–206). Washington, DC: National Policy Association.

Tucker, M. B. (2000b). Marital values and expectations in context: Results from a 21 city survey. In L. Waite, C. Bacharach, M. Hindin, E. Thomson, & A. Thornton (Eds.), *The ties that bind: Perspectives on marriage and cohabitation* (pp. 166–187). New York: Aldine de Gruyter.

Tucker, M. B. (In press). Intimate relationships and psychological well-being. In D. R. Brown & V. M. Keith (Eds.), *In and out of our right minds*. New York: Columbia University Press.

Tucker, M. B., & Mitchell-Kernan, C. (1995a). Interracial dating and marriage in southern California. *Journal of Social and Personal Relationships, 12*, 341–361.

Tucker, M. B., & Mitchell-Kernan, C. (1995b). Trends in African American family formation: A theoretical and statistical overview. In M. B. Tucker & C. Mitchell-Kernan (Eds.), *The decline in marriage among African Americans: Causes, consequences and policy implications.* New York: Russell Sage Foundation.

U.S. Bureau of the Census. (1973). *U.S. census of the population: 1970. Subject reports. Family composition. Final report PC(2)-4A. Table 3: Households by type, size, and number of related children under 18 years old, and race and age of head: 1970.* Washington, DC: Government Printing Office.

U.S. Bureau of the Census. (1998, June 10). Table 4. Race of child by race of householder and of spouse or partner: 1990. Retrieved July 11, 2003, from www.census.gov/population/socdemo/race/interractab4.txt.

U.S. Bureau of the Census. (1999a, January 7). Table CH-3. Living arrangements of black children under 18 years old: 1960 to present. Retrieved July 11, 2003, from www.census.gov/population/www/socdemo/hh-fam.html.

U.S. Bureau of the Census. (1999b, January 7). Table MS-1. Marital status of the population 15 years old and older by sex and race: 1950 to present. Retrieved July 11, 2003, from www.census.gov/population/socdemo/hh-fam/tabMS-1.xls.

U.S. Bureau of the Census. (2001a, June 1). Table 1. Population by age, sex, race and Hispanic origin: March 2000. Retrieved July 11, 2003, from www.census.gov/population/www/socdemo/age/ppl-147.html.

U.S. Bureau of the Census. (2001b, June 29). Table A1. Marital status of people 15 years and over, by age, sex, personal earnings, race, and Hispanic origin: March 2000. Retrieved July 11, 2003, from www.census.gov/population/socdemo/ hh-fam/cps2002/tabA1-whnh.pdf.

U.S. Bureau of the Census. (2001c, June 29). Table CH-3. Living arrangements of black children under 18 years old: 1960 to present. Retrieved July 11, 2003, from www.census.gov/population/socdemo/hh-fam/tabCH-3.

U.S. Bureau of the Census. (2002a). Table P146B. Households by age of householder by household type (including living alone) by presence of own children under 18 years (black or African American alone householder). From Census 2000 Summary File 3—Sample Data. Retrieved July 13, 2003, from http://factfinder.census.gov.

U.S. Bureau of the Census. (2002b). Table P160B. Poverty status in 1999 of families by family type by presence of related children under 18 years of age of related children (black or African American alone householder). From Census 2003 Summary File 3—Sample Data. Retrieved July 13, 2003, from http://factfinder.census.gov.

U.S. Bureau of the Census. (2002c). Table PCT14. Unmarried partner households by sex of partners. Summary File 1. Retrieved July 11, 2003, from http://factfinder.census.gov.

U.S. Bureau of the Census. (2003, June 12). Table MS-1. Marital status of the population 15 years old and over, by sex and race: 1950 to present. Retrieved July 11, 2003, from www.census.gov population/www/socdemo/hh-fam.html.

U.S. Bureau of Labor Statistics & U.S. Bureau of the Census. (2002). Table 1. Age, sex, household relationship, race and Hispanic origin: Poverty status of people by selected characteristics in 2001. Current Population Survey: March supplement. Retrieved July 11, 2003, from http://ferret.bls.census.gov/macro/032002/pov/new01_001.htm.

U.S. Department of Justice. (2002). Correctional populations in the United States, 1998: A BJA Internet report (NCJ 192929). Retrieved July 11, 2003, from www.ojp.usdoj.gov/bjs/pub/pdf/cpus9808.pdf.

Ventura, S. J., Curtin, S. C., & Matthews, T. J. (1998). *Teenage births in the United States: National and state trends, 1990–1996.* Hyattsville, MD: National Center for Health Statistics.

Ventura, S. J., Martin, J. A., Curtin, S. C., Menacker, F., & Hamilton, B. R. (2001, April 17). *Births: Final data for 1999. Table 1. Live births, birth rates, and fertility rates, by race: United States, specified years 1940–55 and each year, 1960–99* (National Vital Statistics Report, 49[1]). Washington, DC: U.S. Bureau of the Census.

Waite, L. J., & Gallagher, M. (2000). *The case for marriage: Why married people are happier, healthier, and better off financially.* New York: Doubleday.

Waite, L. J., & Lillard, L. A. (1991). Children and marital disruption. *American Journal of Sociology, 96,* 930–953.

Waldfogel, J., Wen-Jui, H., & Brooks-Gunn, J. (2002). The effects of early maternal employment on child cognitive development. *Demography 39,* 369–392.

Wallerstein, J. S., & Blakeslee, S. (1989). *Second chances: Men, women and children a decade after divorce.* New York: Tichnor & Fields.

Wallerstein, J. S., Lewis, J. M., & Blakeslee, S. (2000). *The unexpected legacy of divorce: A 25 year landmark study.* New York: Hyperion.

Wilson, M. N. (1984). Mothers' and grandparents' perceptions of parental behavior in three-generation black families. *Child Development, 55,* 1333–1339.

Wilson, W. J. (1987). *The truly disadvantaged.* Chicago: University of Chicago Press.

Wilson, W. J. (1996). *When work disappears: The world of the new urban poor.* New York: Knopf.

Zollar, A. C., & Williams, J. S. (1987). The contribution of marriage to the life satisfaction of black adults. *Journal of Marriage and the Family, 49,* 87–92.

Asian American Families

Diverse History, Contemporary Trends, and the Future

Masako Ishii-Kuntz

Asian Americans are diverse in culture, socioeconomic status, immigration history, and generations. They represent over 28 subgroups; some immigrated to the United States in the late 19th century and early 20th century, whereas other more recent immigrants or refugees arrived after the 1965 Immigration Reform Act (Ishii-Kuntz, 2000). Although Asian Americans share commonalities—ethnic origins in Asia, similar physical appearance, cultural values—they are not a monolithic group. This chapter focuses on diverse Asian American family experiences over the last three decades and is divided into four parts: (a) demographic characteristics and changes of Asian Americans and their families, (b) theoretical approaches and major research findings on Asian American families, (c) contributions of Asian American family scholarship, and (d) a discussion of future Asian American families.

DEMOGRAPHIC CHANGES

Widespread immigration began in 1852, when large numbers of Chinese laborers came to California to work in mining and railroad construction. The history of these immigrants is tainted by numerous "institutionalized racial discrimination of public policies" (Takaki, 1989, p. 14), including the Chinese Exclusion Act of 1882 and the National Origins Act of 1924, both enacted to curtail Chinese and Japanese immigration. The internment of Japanese Americans during World War II also exemplifies discriminatory treatment of Asian Americans. The period since the 1965 immigration reform has been significant due to the large influx of Asian immigrants. The 1965 reform increased numbers of Asian immigrants, who were extremely underrepresented compared to European immigrants, and also changed the characteristics of Asian American immigration from male laborers to those who were middle class, educated, and urbanized. Most importantly, unlike pre-1965, Asian immigrants arrived in the United States as family units rather than as individuals.

According to data from the U.S. Bureau of the Census (2000), the most notable post-1965 change was the rapid population growth of Asian Americans, from less than 1.5 million in 1970 to 11.9 million in 2000. Today, Asian Americans constitute about 4.2% of the total U.S. population; by the year 2060, they are projected to constitute approximately 10% of the population.

The largest Asian ethnic group in 1970 was Japanese (about 41% of the Asian American population). However, Chinese, Filipinos, and Asian Indians emerged as the first-, second-, and third-largest Asian ethnic groups in 2000 (U.S. Bureau of the Census, 2002b). Asian-born residents in the United States made up 26% of the country's foreign-born population in 2000 (U.S. Bureau of the Census, 2002c); about 60% to 70 % speak their native languages at home (U.S. Bureau of the Census, 2000).

Although increasing, the median age of Asian Americans is about 2.6 years younger than that of the total population (U.S. Bureau of the Census, 2002a). Higher fertility rates among recent immigrants (especially Vietnamese) and lower proportions of elderly contribute to the youthfulness of the Asian American population.

In 1999, 80% of Asian American families were maintained by married couples (U.S. Bureau of the Census, 1999); 10% were female-headed households, and 7% were families maintained by men with no spouses. Hmong had the largest average family size with 6.6 persons, and Japanese the smallest with 3.1 persons (U.S. Bureau of the Census, 1999). The median household income of Asian Americans has been consistently higher than that of non-Hispanic whites, perhaps because among Asian Americans more

family members are in the labor force than among their white counterparts (U.S. Bureau of the Census, 1999) or because they are concentrated in metropolitan areas (about 94%), where average incomes are likely to be higher than in rural areas. Over half live in large cities in the West (U.S. Bureau of the Census, 2002a).

Despite higher incomes than white families, the rate of poverty among Asian Americans (10.2%) is also slightly higher than that of whites (9.9%) (U.S. Bureau of the Census, 2001). Hmong had the highest poverty rate (63.6%), followed by Cambodians (42.6%) and Laotians (34.7%) (U.S. Bureau of the Census, 1999). These figures suggest substantial income divergences among Asian American subgroups.

In summary, demographic characteristics of Asian Americans over the last three decades have shown considerable population growth, a dramatic increase of foreign-born Asian Americans, and a slight increase in the median age. However, household size and the proportion of married couples, dual-worker families, and female householders have remained relatively stable. Finally, there is significant variation in demographic characteristics among subgroups of Asian Americans, with recent immigrants reporting smaller incomes, larger household size, younger ages, and higher poverty rates than more established Asian Americans.

ASIAN AMERICAN FAMILIES

In contrast to the large body of literature on white, black, and Hispanic American families, research on Asian American families has been minimal (Fong, 1998). This may have been due to the relatively small numbers of Asian Americans and/or their problem-free image, derived in part from economic and educational success stories of Asian Americans reported in the media (e.g., Mathews, 1987;

William, 1984), low divorce rates, and seemingly strong family commitment. Empirical work focusing on economic and educational achievement has reinforced this problem-free image of Asian Americans (e.g., Hirschman & Wong, 1984; Sowell, 1981).

Popular, recurrent explanations for Asian American economic and educational success and strong family bonds have been cultural. Culturally based explanations dominated Asian American scholarship in the 1960s and 1970s. For example, Kitano (1969) found that Japanese American assimilation and/or success could be attributed to Japanese values that were compatible, if not similar, to those of middle-class white Americans, such as diligence, punctuality, self-discipline, and high achievement motivation. Caudill and DeVos (1956) argued that because Japanese and American middle-class cultures share the values of politeness, respect for authority, diligence, and emphasis on personal achievement, the Japanese adapted to the U.S. way of life more quickly than other immigrant groups. The implication of the cultural approach is that immigrants' assimilation can be achieved by adopting mainstream cultural values and that if the cultural values of the immigrants' home country are compatible to those of white Americans, it will be easier for them to assimilate into American society. This approach also implies that lack of success among other ethnic minority groups can be attributed to weak cultural values (Glenn & Yap, 1994). Thus, the cultural approach used in early Asian American scholarship is a deficit model: Deviations from the Anglo norm in terms of family structures and values are seen as maladaptive rather than adaptive responses to structural forces.

Although the value compatibility thesis may make intuitive sense, it has not always received theoretical and empirical support. Osako (1976) argued that some American middle-class values, particularly concerning kinship relationships, differ significantly from traditional Japanese practice and norms. Japanese families emphasize solidarity, dependence, obedience, and inequality between sexes, values that differ greatly from U.S. kinship values. Sue and Sue (1971) argued that traditional Asian cultural values strongly conflicted with U.S. middle-class values, making assimilation difficult for some, particularly those who adhered to traditional Asian values and who identified with Asian culture to the exclusion of the dominant society.

The cultural argument also has been challenged by contemporary social scientists for its circular reasoning (Liberson, 1980). According to Liberson, "The argument then frequently involves using the behavioral attribute one is trying to explain as the indicator of the normative or value difference one is trying to use as the explanation" (p. 8). The cultural argument also ignores that Chinese and Japanese immigrants differ cross-sectionally between places of origin and across historical periods (Nee & Wong, 1985). Further, although there is considerable overlap in traditional values among different Asian groups, subgroup values are not identical. Filipinos are more likely to be Catholic, Koreans are most often Protestants, and large numbers of Southeast Asians are Buddhists. This religious diversity suggests that one set of cultural values cannot be used to explain behaviors, expectations, and attitudes of all Asian Americans.

After the late 1960s, Asian American scholars began questioning the validity of cultural theories and offered alternative explanations that focused on the role of external structural conditions affecting Asian American families and immigrants' economic adaptation. For example, Nee and Wong (1985) found the formation of household production units to be an important factor in Asian American social and economic mobility. Profit generated from household production units such as small businesses, unlike that generated under labor contracts, directly benefited families and provided stable environments for socializing and educating an upwardly mobile second generation. Kibria (1993) took the structural approach in suggesting that the increase in Vietnamese women's control over economic and social resources and the concomitant decline in Vietnamese men's earning power and social status contributed to a shift in relative power from men to women. A variation of the structural approach is a critical perspective that takes into account the constraints imposed on Asian American families in terms of legal, political, and institutional structures. For example, in her study of first- and second-generation domestic workers, Glenn (1986) found that although all Japanese American family members struggled together against external forces like racism, at the same time, Japanese American women were subjugated by being placed at the bottom of family hierarchy.

Immigration policies also played an important role in the structural approach. In the early 20th century, male laborers could not bring their families to the United States, but entrepreneurs could. Therefore, laborers became small family business entrepreneurs so their families could immigrate. These immigration policies played an important role in creating household production units, which were related to family stability among Asian Americans. Also important in shaping family structure among Asian Americans was the 1965 immigration reform, which limited each country to 20,000 immigrants but exempted parents, spouses, and children of immigrants from the quotas. This means that relatively recent immigrant groups have stronger family ties. They also are more likely to be economically successful because post-1965 immigration policies give priority to successful professionals. Immigrants now represent educated high achievers from the country of origin.

In summary, early studies on Asian American families heavily relied on the cultural theory to explain how Asian cultural values affected the educational and occupational achievement of Asian American children. However, unlike cultural theory, structural and critical perspectives allow us to examine internal family conflicts and diverse relationships across Asian American subgroups. Given the diversity among Asian subgroups, the most fruitful approach to study their families is perhaps the model that combines both cultural and structural components.

Parenting and Socialization

Studies focusing on how parents contribute to Asian American children's educational achievement (e.g., Julian, McKenry, & McKelvey, 1994; see also Chao & Tseng, 2002, for a summary) have found that Asian American parents' academic expectations for their children are higher than those of other parents (Peng & Wright, 1994), as is their emphasis on self-control and academic achievement (Julian et al., 1994). Although Chao (1994) found that immigrant Chinese mothers practice authoritarian parenting more than European American mothers, they do not adhere to the strict parental authority and control of European American mothers who practice authoritarian parenting. Chinese mothers also love their children in order to foster close and enduring parent-child relationships; European American mothers love their children to foster children's self-esteem (Chao, 1995). Chao and Tseng (2002) summarized that "both groups of mothers stressed the same value, but Chinese mothers were motivated toward relational goals, and European American mothers were motivated toward individual goals" (p. 68). These studies point out the need to interpret authoritarian parenting within cultural contexts.

The effects of family socialization and parenting on ethnic identity of Asian American children have also been studied. Parental pressure to preserve ethnic culture affects the Chinese immigrant children's ethnic identity, but factors such as birth order, sibling size, language ability, age, and gender do not (Cheng & Kuo, 2000). Nagata (1993) found that second- and third-generation Japanese American parents who deemphasized their ethnic heritage increased ethnic identity among their children more than did parents who emphasized family histories.

Immigration experiences alter parent-child relationships. For example, Kibria (1993) found that immigration had eroded parental power and authority of Vietnamese refugee families over children. Many parents felt the U.S. cultural environment undermined their efforts to educate and socialize their children with appropriate ethnic values and cultural norms. This may also be because immigrant children assist their non-English-speaking parents by playing the role of language and cultural brokers. They often acculturate and learn to speak English more quickly than their parents, so that their parents end up relying on them to interpret or translate (Tse, 1995, 1996), and they assist their parents in daily cross-cultural transactions such as making medical appointments and dealing with schools and the legal system (Chao, 2002). Findings are mixed as to whether children's language acculturation has a negative effect on communication and cohesion for immigrant families (Tseng & Fulgini, 2000) or no effect (Chao, 2002). Adolescents with East Asian and Filipino backgrounds who conversed with their parents in different languages felt more emotionally distant from them than did youths who shared the same language with their parents; parents and adolescents who mutually communicated in the native language reported the highest levels of cohesion.

In summary, researchers that focused on parenting styles and attitudes reported that cultural values play an important role in Asian American parenting and socialization practices. Because of the emphasis on interdependence in Asian American families, parenting styles used by white families need to be reinterpreted and modified by researchers when examining Asian American parenting. Also, language plays an important role in assessing immigrant children's roles in the family and parent-child relationship quality.

Interracial Marriages

A relatively large number of studies on Asian American interracial marriage (marriage between two people of difference races) that were conducted in the 1980s and early 1990s (e.g., Shinagawa & Pang, 1990) examined factors affecting the high rate of Asian-white interracial marriages. Kitano, Yeung, Chai, and Hatanaka (1984) found that 49.9%, 30.2%, and 19.2% of Japanese, Chinese, and Korean Americans in Los Angeles married outside their own group. Women were much more likely to outmarry than men, and interracial marriages were more prevalent among well-educated and professional Asian Americans (Lee & Yamanaka, 1990).

Three reasons offered for high rates of Asian American interracial marriage are individual choice, the need to assimilate (Sung, 1990), and hypergamy theory (Shinagawa & Pang, 1990). The individual-choice explanation is that Asian American interracial marriage is a matter of individual preference: Asian Americans meet, fall in love, and decide to marry someone outside their race (Tseng, McDermott, & Maretzki, 1977). However, the problem with this explanation is that it fails to explain the lower rates of interracial marriages for other ethnic minority groups. For example, if interracial marriages are solely based on individual choice, why is there such a low rate of interracial marriages for other minorities, such as African Americans?

The second perspective is the need for assimilation. According to this view, inter-marriage or marital assimilation is a positive sign of acceptance by the larger society (Sung, 1990). Problems with this approach are twofold. First, this view is strongly embedded within the assimilation-as-a-healthy outcome framework for minority populations. By analogy, it means that ethnic minority individuals who are not interra-cially married are not assimilated into society. This model also fails to explain why interracial marriages are not evenly dis-tributed across the entire Asian American populations (i.e., why they occur more fre-quently among more educated Asian Americans with higher incomes). It also does not account for the fact that more Asian American women than men outmarry.

The individual-choice and assimilation perspectives were challenged by Shinagawa and Pang (1990), who proposed hypergamy theory, which states that women are more likely to marry men of equal or higher social status and that men are more likely to marry women of lower social status. In the United States, about 33% of women with 4 or more years of college marry men with less educa-tion, and 50% of men with that same level of education marry less-educated women (Goldman, Westoff, & Hammerslough, 1984). However, Shinagawa and Pang (1990) argued that in a racially stratified society such as the United States, race is also an important factor contributing to social status. They con-cluded that the prevalence of interracial mar-riage between educated Asian American women and white men is a way for Asian American women to maximize their status (i.e., marrying the most advantaged individu-als with the highest racial position). They also projected that Asian American interethnic marriage will become more prevalent. Critics

of this view argue that Shinagawa and Pang's interpretation is based on statistical data that cannot accurately assess personal and subjec-tive topic such as reasons for marriage. Reflecting this criticism, Fong and Yung (1995) interviewed Asian American men and women and found that reasons for interracial marriage are complex and cannot be explained by one perspective. Many respon-dents gave both individual preference and the need to gain social status as reasons for choosing their partners. Motivations for interracial marriage among Asian Americans seem to be derived from a multitude of com-plex factors. Recent and projected increases in interethnic marriages are trends that need to be examined further.

Biracial and Multiracial Asian Americans

Given the prevalence in interracial mar-riages, the number of biracial or multiracial Asian Americans has increased. Information about numbers of mixed-heritage Asian Americans was not available until the 2000 census; previous census data did not include a racial category identifying people with mixed ethnic background. The 2000 census identified individuals as Asian with one or more other races as 0.6% of the U.S. popu-lation; approximately half identified them-selves as Asian and white. Japanese (31%) were most likely to report one or more other races, and Vietnamese (8.3%) were least likely to be in combination with one or more other races (U.S. Bureau of the Census, 2002a). Multiracial Asian Americans have geographical distributions similar to those of monoracial Asian Americans, with nearly half living in the western United States.

Racial identity is an important issue for biracial or multiracial Asian Americans (Fong, 1998). Few identify with only one part of their inheritance (Spickard, 1992), and many adopt situational ethnicity: They assume white or African American or Hispanic identity when they are among white or African American or Hispanic relatives and friends and take on mainly an Asian identity when among Asians (Mass, 1992).

Multiracial Asian Americans originally were believed to display lower self-esteem and poor social adjustment due to parental pathology, marital instability, and marginal belonging of children due to their ambiguous status (Root, 1998). However, several studies have found that some groups of multiracial Asians raised in the United States are well adjusted and have high self-esteem (Cauce et al., 1992; Johnson & Nagoshi, 1986). However, large differences exist among multiracial Asians. For example, multiracial Vietnamese Americans experienced more adjustment problems and reported lower self-esteem than multiracial Japanese Americans (Valverde, 1992). Many Vietnamese immigrants settled into areas with a large Vietnamese population where harsh and discriminatory attitudes toward multiracial Vietnamese American children are prevalent. Vietnamese American children are more likely to have problems if they are males, have African American fathers, and have unstable home environments (Felsman, Jonson, Leong, & Felsman, 1989).

In summary, most studies of mixed-heritage Asian Americans have examined multiracial Japanese and Vietnamese Americans. Ethnic identity and psychological adjustment are important issues for all multiracial Asian Americans. It is important to understand the ways in which race is performed and the ways in which this understanding is facilitated by family, community, and peers.

Kinship Network and Social Support

Asian American kinship research focused on historical analysis of kinship networks (Yanagisako, 1985), the nature of kinship relations (Johnson, 1977), social network patterns and social supports (Kim & McKenry, 1998), and the dynamics of kinship-based networks among newly arrived immigrants (Menjivar, 1997). Johnson (1977) explained the Japanese American kinship system as an obligatory rather than an optional system, using the concept of reciprocity within social exchange theory. According to exchange theory, the principle of give-and-take or reciprocity enables harmonious social relationships, and stability and maintenance are enhanced if there is mutual dependence and reciprocal interchange. In contrast, if there is no reciprocal exchange, relationships are likely to be terminated. Johnson found that the Japanese American kinship system emphasizes obligation to parents, reciprocity, and dependence, all part of Japanese values. However, her findings may not apply outside the Japanese American population, whose higher socioeconomic status and resources, as compared to those of other Asian Americans, may enable such mutual kinship support.

Yanagisako's (1985) comparison of Japanese American kinship to white middle-class Americans found that although household composition was similar, Japanese American family gatherings were much larger and genealogically more extended than those of the white middle class. Kinship support and network are more central to Asian American experience than to African American, white, or Hispanic experience (Kim & McKenry, 1998). Asian Americans also are more likely to spend social evenings with friends and relatives, more likely to be involved in personal hobby groups, and, along with whites, more likely to be involved in sports. Kim and McKenry speculated that these findings reflected the importance of the collective orientation in Asian American culture. However, they found more similarities than differences in social networks and social support among the four groups of Americans.

Social and kinship networks play an important role for Asian immigrants all through the migration process. For example, Menjivar (1997) found that the family support network was the most important factor in the transition of Vietnamese immigrants to the United States. However, consequences of heavy reliance on social and family networks for later adjustment have been questioned. For example, recently arrived Vietnamese who settle where there is a heavy concentration of Vietnamese can be provided with the assistance to make their transition easier (Gold, 1992). However, those who settle in areas with no ethnic enclave may find it difficult to find jobs and establish their family life. In summary, Asian American kinship systems and supportive networks are largely based on obligatory relationships, and for newly arrived immigrants, supportive family networks and an ethnic enclave play important roles in facilitating adjustment.

Household Labor and Gender Issues

Gender role expectations of women can vary widely on the basis of class of origin, current class, ethnic group of origin, and generation in the United States. For Asian American women, generational differences as a result of acculturation affect gender roles at home. Because one of the primary goals of the 1965 immigration reform was to facilitate family reunification, the numbers of Asian women immigrants have dramatically increased (Donato, 1992). Some Asian immigrant women had informal resources in their home country because they were the center of family affairs but did not possess more formal resources, such as economic capital, until they immigrated to the United States. In fact, labor force participation among Asian immigrant women surpasses that of native-born Asian American women (Espiritu, 1997). Kibria (1993) found that the most important difference between Vietnamese

women's experience in the United States and the experiences of modern, urban South Vietnamese women was that the relative economic resources of men and women had shifted, giving women more economic resources. That is, whereas many Vietnamese men encountered unemployment and low-wage jobs, women were successful in earning incomes in a wide variety of sectors, thereby creating a more gender-balanced family environment. This also was true for Chinese women (Glenn, 1983) and for Korean men and women in the United States (Min, 1995). Korean immigrant women usually work long hours in small businesses assisting their husbands, a central factor in the success of their businesses (Min, 1988). The necessity to work with their husbands gave Korean women more opportunities to negotiate work roles, and the interdependence between spouses contributed to more egalitarian gender relationships among Korean Americans. It can be concluded that Asian American women gain considerable power after immigrating to the United States, although Asian American men still enjoy overall advantages in incomes and occupational positions (Ong & Hee, 1993).

Although we know little about the division of household labor among Asian Americans, there are a few insightful studies (Johnson, 1998; Kibria, 1993; Min, 1995; Osako, 1980). Overall, Asian American women still bear most of the responsibilities for cooking, domestic tasks, and child rearing even in dual-earner families. Although Osako (1980) noted a tendency toward gender equality among second-generation Japanese Americans compared to their parents' generation, there still remained a fairly strict division of household labor among the second-generation couples. Although gender equality among Asian American couples has not been achieved, this pattern is not unique to this population. Numerous studies of other populations report that housework and child care are usually performed by women (Coltrane & Ishii-Kuntz, 1992; Ishii-Kuntz & Coltrane, 1992). What is unique to Asian American family experiences with respect to gender is the shift that has frequently occurred among immigrant families. Asian immigrant women have gained more power at home primarily because of their economic contributions.

Elderly Asian Americans and Intergenerational Relations

Although the experiences of Asian American elderly are wide-ranging and depend on their nativity, immigration experiences, residential arrangement, and the existence of supportive kinship and friendship networks, their relationships with their children have been viewed from a monolithic cultural perspective. Because filial piety, including a great respect for the elderly family members, has been a long admired tradition of Asians, it is generally considered that Asian American elderly are accorded authority and privilege over their junior members. Asian American adult children have been viewed as conforming to parental demands and expectations, feeling more obligated to their parents, providing more financial aid to their parents, and interacting more frequently with their parents than their white counterparts (Ishii-Kuntz, 1997; Osako, 1976). Perhaps due to this rosy picture, little research on intergenerational relationships among Asian Americans was conducted until the late 1980s, and most of it was on the Chinese and Japanese, reflecting the higher proportion of elderly in these populations compared to other Asian American subgroups. These studies focused primarily on the quality of relationships between elderly parents and their adult children, residential arrangements, and service needs (e.g., Kamo & Zhou, 1994; Phua, Kaufman, & Park, 2001). For example, Kamo and Zhou (1994) found that

older Chinese and Japanese American parents were more likely to live in three-generation households than their white counterparts and that many displayed their own cultural traditions of filial obligations. Recently, Pyke (2000) found that Korean and Vietnamese immigrant children considered filial piety an important value.

The living arrangements of elderly Asian Americans vary among subgroups. For example, elderly Japanese are more likely to live with their spouses only, as opposed to living with other family members, than are Chinese, Filipino, Korean, and Asian Indian Americans (Phua et al., 2001). The level of acculturation may be the main reason why Japanese American elderly are more likely than other Asian Americans to maintain independent households. They are more likely to be later generations of Americans than the other groups and thus more likely to be acculturated into mainstream culture. Immigrant Asian elderly in the United States constitute a distinct group of immigrants. First, immigration laws governing the immigration of elderly persons are different from those governing younger persons. That is, elderly immigrants are more likely to immigrate under the nonquota immediate-family preference category as parents of U.S. citizens. Second, elderly immigrants are more likely to immigrate to be with their families; younger immigrants are more likely to arrive for economic opportunities. Last, the older immigrants are at the time of their arrival, the more they are used to their native country's way of life and the greater difficulty they have in adjusting to the new environment.

Gays and Lesbians, and Their Families

Diversity with respect to sexual orientation among Asian Americans has been rather infrequently discussed by media, the general public, and Asian Americans. This does not mean that gay and lesbian Asian Americans are nonexistent. On the contrary, Asian American gays and lesbians have been active in social organizations and conferences on Asian American lesbian and gay experiences (Takagi, 1994). However, open discussion of Asian American gay and lesbian experiences did not take place until the 1990s (see Leong, 1996, for personal reflections by Asian American gays and lesbians). The year 1994 was particularly important, with the adoption of a resolution by the Japanese Americans Citizens League (JACL) supporting same-sex marriages and the publication of a special issue of *Amerasia Journal*, the leading scholarly journal in Asian American studies, focusing on Asian American gays, lesbians, and bisexuals. Although we are beginning to understand the diversity of sexual orientations and experiences in relation to identity among Asian Americans, knowledge about Asian American gay and lesbian families is still extremely limited. The most important personal issue surrounding Asian American gays and lesbians seems to be coming out to parents. Chan (1989) found only 9 out of 35 interviewees had told their parents about their sexual orientation. Chan concluded that, given the emphasis on conformity in many Asian American families, gay and lesbian adult children who do not conform to the traditional heterosexual roles may assume that their parents would be much less tolerant and more homophobic than parents of other groups. Chinese, Japanese, Filipino, Vietnamese, and Korean mothers and fathers with lesbian daughters and gay sons expressed a wide range of emotions and feelings when they discovered their children's sexual identities (Hom, 1994). One of the first reactions by parents is self-blame and sadness, with the realization that their long-term goals and plans for their children may never materialize. Not all the parents, however, had negative reactions to

their children's coming out (Ordona, 1994). Given that not all the coming out experiences among Asian American gays and lesbians are negative, it is important to better understand how Asian American families create and construct a new and different set of expectations when faced with their children's homosexuality.

Contribution of Asian American Family Scholarship

Overall, research on Asian American families over the last three decades contributes to our understanding of these families in two ways. First, scholarship since the 1970s has helped us better understand the complexity and diversity within Asian American families. Whereas studies in earlier decades mainly focused on more established Asians in the United States (e.g., Japanese, Chinese), more recent research has focused on the growing number of Asian immigrants and their children. We now know that considerable parenting and socialization diversity and complexity exists across Asian American subgroups, although there are important commonalities as well (e.g., emphasis on interdependence and education). The diversity, however, is mainly derived from experiences related to immigration. For instance, immigrant children who play a cultural- and language-brokering role for their parents are accorded more power within the family, and foreign-born Asian parents become more dependent on their children. We know that the rate of interracial marriage tends to be higher among more established Asian Americans (e.g., Japanese) compared to more recent Asian immigrants, and we know that later generations of Asian Americans (e.g., Japanese, Chinese) are more egalitarian than their parents and grandparents.

Findings from the studies reported here suggest that it is misleading to speak of the

Asian American experience as if all Asian Americans' experiences are similar. We know from past studies that Asians' experiences in the United States vary considerably depending on such factors as immigration history and family networks. Thus, professionals helping Asian American children and families may need to create programs that specifically cater to the needs of each Asian ethnic group.

Second, research over the past three decades helped us identify a variety of Asian American family issues. The relationship between Asian American educational and occupational achievement and family values was the main topic of investigation in the 1960s and the first half of the 1970s, and although it is still an important issue, Asian American family scholarship since the 1980s has largely moved beyond this topic to a variety of topics such as parenting, interracial marriages, biraciality/multiraciality, kinship networks, gender relations, and intergenerational relationships in Asian American families. These studies generated a wealth of knowledge that helped professionals identify different dimensions of Asian American family life. For example, we know that authoritarian parenting among Asian Americans needs to be redefined because the concept of authority does not have the same meaning for Asian Americans as for non-Hispanic whites. We also need to examine combined aspects of individual choice, assimilation needs, and hypergamy to explain the prevalence of interracial marriage among some groups of Asian Americans. Although biracial and multiracial Asian Americans are often faced with identity dilemmas, they are as socially adjusted as other U.S. ethnic groups. The obligation-based kinship and support networks of Asian Americans may not always characterize intergenerational relationships among Asian Americans. Additionally, although changes in gender relations in Asian American families have

been slow, more egalitarian relationships between husbands and wives have been emerging. Women's labor force participation seems to be an important prerequisite for this transition.

Finally, an area of study that is important for family professionals is Asian Americans' underutilization of public services, particularly mental health services (see Sue, 1993). Reasons for this may include (a) the lack of accessibility and availability of mental health services for Asian Americans; (b) Asian Americans' general unwillingness to use these services and cultural stigmatization of them; and (c) the need for culturally appropriate mental health services and culturally sensitive mental health professionals. Similar arguments can be made with respect to other services related to Asian American families and children.

FUTURE OF ASIAN AMERICAN FAMILIES

The Asian American population will continue to expand, with projections indicating that it will reach 20.2 million in the year 2020 (Ong & Hee, 1993). Much of this increase can be attributed to the continuing growth of the numbers of immigrants. For family scholars, this means that a monolithic picture of the Asian American family will no longer be sufficient. At the same time, cultural theory alone does not explain complex relationships within Asian American families. Because immigration is an important factor affecting Asian Americans, it is necessary to look into structural and historical conditions in addition to cultural components surrounding Asian American families. Further, although past studies often compared Asian Americans with whites and/or other ethnic minority groups, it may be fruitful to engage in comparisons among Asian subgroups due to their diverse experiences in the United States.

Considering the multiplicity of Asian American family experiences, I predict that our scholarship will be expanded to better understand (a) the conflict between immigrant parents and their Americanized children; (b) the adjustment and identity issues of biracial and multiracial Asian Americans; (c) the intersection of class, gender, and race among Asian Americans; (d) alternative lifestyles, including gay and lesbian parenting and families; and (e) the extent of domestic violence within Asian American families. Some additional intriguing questions include (a) the extent to which we can use Anglo-centered models and measures to study Asian American families; (b) similarities or differences among and between established and recent immigrant Asian American subgroups; (c) the impact of immigration on children, conjugal relations, and parent-child relations; (d) how major external forces (e.g., economics, policies, institutional barriers) and internal forces (e.g., conflict within the family) affect the psychological well-being of Asian American family members; and (e) the extent to which Asian American family experiences are influenced by the complexity of race, gender, and class in American society.

Also needed is a better understanding of the concept and the extent of Asian American pan-ethnicity. The American public often treats Asian Americans as a homogeneous, pan-ethnic group without recognizing differences among them. Asian American pan-ethnicity is largely a result of political and social, but not cultural, bonds. Espiritu (1992) suggested that at least three things must occur for Asian American pan-ethnicity to continue to survive: the development of pan-ethnic organizations, the existence of pan-ethnic entrepreneurs, and a perspective of individual pan-ethnicity. With the increasing need to protect their common interest in politics, education, social services, and other areas,

many Asian Americans may value the power created by such solidarity among Asian Americans. The increase in Asian American studies programs in many U.S. universities may also enhance the diverse experiences of Asian subgroups as well as the need for Asian American pan-ethnic solidarity.

Finally, the continued increase in Asian American population will have a significant impact on social institutions as well as attitudes among the U.S. public toward Asian Americans. First, the increase of Asian American families and their children will have significant effects on public schools, colleges and universities, private corporations and politics. There has already been evidence that Asian Americans have influenced admission policies in higher education. For instance, Takagi (1992) has described controversial college admission procedures in which the most selective universities and colleges in the United States have used quotas and ceilings to limit the enrollment of Asian Americans. Second, Americans will come to better understand and view more positively Asian American experiences. Like other visible minorities, Asian Americans face the danger of always being perceived within the narrow confines of stereotypes. However, research on Asian Americans and their experiences and the emphasis on multiculturalism in the larger society will contribute to positive change. In summary, although past scholarship on Asian American families has generated insightful findings, it is clear that we have only touched the surface of complex Asian Americans family relationships. Many research questions remain. It is hoped that findings from future research will significantly improve the lives of Asian Americans and encourage better understanding of them among other populations in the United States.

REFERENCES

Cauce, A. M., Hiraga, Y., Mason, C., Aguilar, T., Ordonez, N., & Gonzales, H. (1992). Between a rock and a hard place: Social adjustment of biracial youth. In M. P. P. Root (Ed.), *Racially mixed people in America* (pp. 207–222). Newbury Park, CA: Sage.

Caudill, W., & DeVos, G. (1956). Achievement, culture and personality: The case of Japanese Americans. *American Anthropologist, 58*, 1102–1126.

Chan, C. S. (1989). Issues of identity development among Asian-American lesbians and gay men. *Journal of Counseling and Development, 68*, 16–20.

Chao, R. (1994). Beyond parental control and authoritarian parenting style: Understanding Chinese parenting through the cultural notion of training. *Child Development, 65*, 1111–1119.

Chao, R. (1995). Chinese and European American cultural models of the self reflected in mothers' childrearing beliefs. *Ethos, 23*, 328–354.

Chao, R. (2002, April). *The role of children's linguistic brokering among immigrant Chinese and Mexican families.* Paper presented at the biennial meetings of the Society for Research in Child Development, Minneapolis, MN.

Chao, R., & Tseng, V. (2002). Parenting of Asians. In M. H. Bornstein (Ed.), *Handbook of parenting* (2nd ed., pp. 59–93). Mahwah, NJ: Lawrence Erlbaum.

Cheng, S. H., & Kuo, W. H. (2000). Family socialization of ethnic identity among Chinese American pre-adolescents. *Journal of Comparative Family Studies, 16*, 463–482.

Coltrane, S., & Ishii-Kuntz, M. (1992). Men's housework: A life course perspective. *Journal of Marriage and the Family, 54*, 43–57.

Donato, K. M. (1992). Understanding U.S. immigration: Why some countries send women and others send men. In D. Gabaccia (Ed.), *Seeking common ground* (pp. 159–184). Westport, CT: Greenwood.

Espiritu, Y. L. (1992). *Asian American panethnicity.* Philadelphia: Temple University Press.

Espiritu, Y. L. (1997). *Asian American women and men.* Thousand Oaks, CA: Sage.

Felsman, J. K., Johnson, M. C., Leong, F. T. L., & Felsman, I. C. (1989). Vietnamese Amerasians. Washington, DC: Department of Health and Human Services, Family Support Administration, Office of Refugee Resettlement.

Fong, C., & Yung, J. (1995). In search of the right spouse: Interracial marriage among Chinese and Japanese Americans. *Amerasia Journal, 21*, 77–98.

Fong, T. P. (1998). *The contemporary Asian American experience.* Upper Saddle River, NJ: Prentice Hall.

Glenn, E. N. (1983). Split household, small producer and dual wage earner: An analysis of Chinese-American family strategies. *Journal of Marriage and the Family, 45*, 35–46.

Glenn, E. N. (1986). *Issei, Nisei, war bride.* Philadelphia: Temple University Press.

Glenn, E. N., & Yap, S. G. H. (1994). Chinese American families. In R. L. Taylor (Ed.), *Minority families in the United States* (pp. 115–145). Englewood Cliffs, NJ: Prentice Hall.

Gold, S. J. (1992). *Refugee communities.* Newbury Park, CA: Sage.

Goldman, N, Westoff, C. F., & Hammerslough, C. (1984). Demography of the marriage market in the United States. *Population Index, 50*, 5–25.

Hirschman, C., & Wong, M. G. (1984). Socioeconomic gains of Asian Americans, blacks, and Hispanics: 1960–1976. *American Journal of Sociology, 90*, 584–607.

Hom, A. Y. (1994). Stories from the homefront: Perspectives of Asian American parents with lesbian daughters and gay sons. *Amerasia Journal, 20*, 19–32.

Ishii-Kuntz, M. (1997). Intergenerational relationship among Chinese, Japanese, and Korean Americans. *Family Relations, 46*, 23–32.

Ishii-Kuntz, M. (2000). Diversity within Asian American families. In D. H. Demo, K. R. Allen, & M. A. Fine (Eds.), *Handbook of family diversity* (pp. 274–292). New York: Oxford University Press.

Ishii-Kuntz, M., & Coltrane, S. (1992). Predicting the sharing of household labor: Are parenting and housework distinct? *Sociological Perspectives, 35,* 629–647.

Johnson, C. L. (1977). Interdependence, reciprocity and indebtedness: An analysis of Japanese American kinship relations. *Journal of Marriage and the Family, 39,* 351–363.

Johnson, P. J. (1998). Performance of household tasks by Vietnamese and Laotian refugees: Tradition and change. *Journal of Family Issues, 19,* 245–273.

Johnson, R., & Nagoshi, C. (1986). The adjustment of offspring of within group and interracial/intercultural marriages: A comparison of personality factor scores. *Journal of Marriage and the Family, 28,* 279–284.

Julian, T. W., McKenry, P. C., & McKelvey, M. W. (1994). Cultural variations in parenting perceptions of Caucasian, African-American, Hispanic and Asian-American parents. *Family Relations, 43,* 30–37.

Kamo, Y., & Zhou, M. (1994). Living arrangements of elderly Chinese and Japanese in the United States. *Journal of Marriage and the Family, 56,* 544–558.

Kibria, N. (1993). *Family tightrope.* Princeton, NJ: Princeton University Press.

Kim, H. K., & McKenry, P. C. (1998). Social networks and support: A comparison of African Americans, Asian Americans, Caucasians, and Hispanics. *Journal of Comparative Family Studies, 24,* 313–334.

Kitano, H. H. (1969). *Japanese Americans: The evolution of a subculture.* Englewood Cliffs, NJ: Prentice Hall.

Kitano, H. H., Yeung, W.-T., Chai, L., & Hatanaka, H. (1984). Asian-American interracial marriage. *Journal of Marriage and the Family, 46,* 179–190.

Lee, S. M., & Yamanaka, K. (1990). Patterns of Asian American intermarriage and marital assimilation. *Journal of Comparative Family Studies, 21,* 227–305.

Leong, R. (1996). *Asian American sexualities.* New York: Routledge.

Liberson, S. (1980). *A piece of the pie.* Berkeley: University of California Press.

Mass, A. I. (1992). Interracial Japanese Americans: The best of both worlds or the end the Japanese American community? In M. P. P. Root (Ed.), *Racially mixed people in America* (pp. 265–279). Newbury Park, CA: Sage.

Mathews, L. (1987, July 19). When being the best isn't good enough. *Los Angeles Times Magazine,* pp. 22–28.

Menjivar, C. (1997). Immigrant kinship networks: Vietnamese, Salvadoreans and Mexicans in comparative perspective. *Journal of Comparative Family Studies, 28,* 1–24.

Min, P. G. (1988). *Ethnic business enterprise: Korean small business in Atlanta.* Staten Island, NY: Center for Migration Studies.

Min, P. G. (1995). Korean Americans. In P. G. Min (Ed.), *Asian Americans* (pp. 199–231). Thousand Oaks, CA: Sage.

Nagata, D. (1993). *Legacy of silence.* New York: Plenum.

Nee, V., & Wong, H. Y. (1985). Asian American socioeconomic achievement: The strength of the family bond. *Sociological Perspectives, 28,* 281–306.

Ong, P., & Hee, S. J. (1993). The growth of the Asian Pacific American population: Twenty million in 2020. In Leadership Education for Asian Pacifics (Ed.), *The state of Asian Pacific America: Policy issues to the year 2020* (pp. 11–24). Los Angeles: Leadership Education for Asian Pacifics, Asian Pacific American Public Policy Institute and University of California at Los Angeles, Asian American Studies Center.

Ordona, T. (1994). In our own way. *Amerasia Journal, 20,* 137–147.

Osako, M. (1976). Intergenerational relations as an aspect of assimilation: The case of Japanese Americans. *Sociological Inquiry, 46,* 67–72.

Osako, M. M. (1980). *Aging, social isolation and kinship ties among Japanese Americans: Project for[the Administration on Aging.* Washington, DC: U.S. Administration on Aging.

Peng, S. S., & Wright, D. (1994). Explanation of academic achievement of Asian American students. *Journal of Educational Research, 87,* 346–352.

Phua, V. C., Kaufman, G., & Park, K. S. (2001). Strategic adjustments of elderly Asian Americans: Living arrangements and headship. *Journal of Comparative Family Studies, 23,* 263–281.

Pyke, K. (2000). "The normal American family" as an interpretive structure of family life among grown children of Korean and Vietnamese immigrants. *Journal of Marriage and the Family, 62,* 240–255.

Root, M. (1998). Multiracial Asian Americans. In L. Lee & N. Zane (Eds.), *Handbook of Asian American psychology* (pp. 261–287). Thousand Oaks, CA: Sage.

Shinagawa, L. H., & Pang, G. Y. (1990). Marriage patterns of Asian Americans in California, 1980. In S. Chan (Ed.), *Income and status differences between white and minority Americans* (pp. 225–282). Lewiston, NY: Edwin Mellon.

Sowell, T. (1981). *Ethnic America: A history.* New York: Basic Books.

Spickard, P. R. (1992). The illogic of American racial categories. In M. P. P. Root (Ed.), *Racially mixed people in America* (pp. 12–23). Newbury Park, CA: Sage.

Sue, S. (1993). The changing Asian American population: Mental health policy. In Leadership Education for Asian Pacifics (Ed.), *The state of Asian Pacific America: Policy issues to the year 2020* (pp. 79–94). Los Angeles: Leadership Education for Asian Pacifics, Asian Pacific American Public Policy Institute and University of California at Los Angeles, Asian American Studies Center.

Sue, S., & Sue, D. (1971). Chinese-American personality and mental health. *Amerasia Journal, 1,* 36–49.

Sung, B. L. (1990). *Chinese American intermarriage.* New York: Center for Migration Studies.

Takagi, D. Y. (1992). *The retreat from race.* New Brunswick, NJ: Rutgers University Press.

Takagi, D. Y. (1994). Maiden voyage: Excursion into sexuality and identity politics in Asian America. *Amerasia Journal, 20,* 1–17.

Takaki, R. (1989). *Strangers from a different shore.* New York: Penguin.

Tse, L. (1995). Language brokering among Latino adolescents: Prevalence, attitudes and school performance. *Hispanic Journal of Behavioral Sciences, 17,* 180–193.

Tse, L. (1996). Language brokering in linguistic minority communities: The case of Chinese- and Vietnamese-American students. *Bilingual Research Journal, 20,* 485–498.

Tseng, V., & Fulgini, A. J. (2000). Parent-adolescent language use and relationships among immigrant families with East Asian, Filipino and Latin American backgrounds. *Journal of Marriage and the Family, 62,* 465–476.

Tseng, W., McDermott, J., & Maretzki, T. (1977). *Adjustment in intercultural marriage.* Honolulu: University Press of Hawaii.

U.S. Bureau of the Census. (1999). *The Asian and Pacific Islander population in the United States: Population characteristics.* Washington, DC: Government Printing Office.

U.S. Bureau of the Census. (2000). *Current population survey.* Washington, DC: Government Printing Office.

U.S. Bureau of the Census. (2001). *Poverty in the United States: 2001.* Washington, DC: Government Printing Office.

U.S. Bureau of the Census. (2002a). *The Asian population: 2000* (Census 2000 Brief). Washington, DC: Government Printing Office.

U.S. Bureau of the Census. (2002b). *Census 2000: Chinese largest Asian group in the United States.* Washington, DC: Government Printing Office.

U.S. Bureau of the Census. (2002c). *A profile of the nation's foreign-born population from Asia (2000 update).* Washington, DC: U.S. Government Printing Office.

Valverde, K. L. C. (1992). From dust to gold: The Vietnamese American experience. In M. P. P. Root (Ed.), *Racially mixed people in America* (pp. 144–161). Newbury Park, CA: Sage.

William, D. (1984, April 23). A formula for success. *Newsweek,* pp. 77–78.

Yanagisako, S. J. (1985). *Transforming the past.* Stanford, CA: Stanford University Press.

CHAPTER 22

A "Seven-Generation" Approach to American Indian Families

Walter T. Kawamoto and Tamara C. Cheshire

My grandfather once told me a story about how our tribe would gather the very young to preteen children and take them to another camp without their parents. They were supervised by a few elders, who explained to them that they were there to learn a very important lesson. They were told that they would be away from their parents and the main camp for some time, representing the times when they would need to rely on and trust their extended family and other tribal members. The children were also informed that there would be limited food, representing the times when the tribe would have little food. To keep warm, all of the children stayed in the same tipi. Many of the younger children became frightened and homesick the first night. They relied on the older children for comfort. It didn't help much that the children were not fed that first evening. The next day, the elders came to the children with a small amount of food. They explained that the amount of food they had was very little, but that their families had worked hard in seeking out the buffalo and had given up the choicest of meats for their children, the buffalo tongue. The meat was cut into small cubes. There was not even enough meat to give each child one small cube. The elders explained that each child would be given the choice to either eat their fill or pass on the food. They were also told that there might not be any food to eat for the next few days and that by eating even one cube they would be taking food from the other children, their relatives. The elders lined up the children, the oldest to the youngest, and began to give each child a choice as to what he or she would do. The older children were instructed to look at the younger when they made their choice, and the younger children were instructed to look at the older when they made their choice. The reason was that the children needed to see how their action would affect other members of their tribe and ultimately the survival of their nation on through to the next seven generations. The older children decided that they would give up the food so that the younger ones could survive, and ultimately the tribe. The younger children also witnessed this self-sacrifice for the good of the tribe and knew that when their time came, they would also consider the next seven generations when making even individual decisions (originally told by Phil Lane, Sr., Lakota elder, to Tami Cheshire).

The term *seven generations* is relatively common among American Indians. There are several meanings of this term, some ancient and some contemporary. As in this story, *seven generations* can refer to individual decisions that affect the survival of the tribe into the next seven generations, implying an eternal responsibility. Although each person represents one generation, each one is the legacy of his or her great grandparents (three generations ago), and his or her actions have an impact on his or her great grandchildren (three generations to follow). Another ancient use of this phrase is the Ojibwa prophecy that it is the choice of each person whether the time of the seventh fire (generation) will be a time of great enlightenment or great suffering. Currently, the term *seven generations* refers to the Iroquois principle to consider the impact of major decisions on the next seven generations. The concept of *seven generations* has inspired the American Indian Institute and an organization called the Seven Generation Youth Society in Oklahoma that works with American Indians on justice issues ("Rally for Justice Held in Stilwell," 1994). It is with the philosophy of *seven generations* in mind, taught to us by an elder of the Confederated Tribes of Siletz, Oregon, that we look into the past and the present and suggest a few indicators of the future of American Indian family research.

RESEARCH ON AMERICAN INDIANS

The recent history of the study of American Indian families, regarded by many as the *self-determination period* (Garrett & Herring, 2001), is peppered with methodological challenges. There are not many studies of American Indian families, perhaps because most researchers interested in American Indians have had limited resources with which to work (Cheshire, 2001; Hennessy & John, 2002; Kawamoto, 2001b), and American Indians often are not identified as a separate ethnic group in national studies (Gruber, DiClemente, & Anderson, 2002).

Demographic Changes

Although the study of American Indians has gone through many changes over the last few decades, demographic characteristics of American Indian communities also have undergone change. For example, Parke and Buriel (2002) reported a dramatic increase in the census count of American Indians, from 345,000 in 1940 to 2,000,000 in 1990. Over the last several decades, American Indians have moved from rural to urban areas; most (as many as 78%) live in urban communities (Banks, 1991; Gruber et al., 2002; Parke & Buriel, 2002). This migration has been attributed to federal policies between 1953 and 1968 that forced American Indians to move from the reservations in search of jobs to support their families (Cheshire, 2001; Pevar, 1992). Although urban and reservation communities differ in many ways, American Indians, regardless of where they live, maintain complex connections with each other (Parke & Buriel, 2002).

Another demographic change has been a dramatic increase in life expectancy for American Indians over the last 40 years (Hennessy & John, 2002). Life expectancy has increased to 73.2 years, 3.3 years less than whites (Baldridge, 2001). However, American Indian communities are disproportionately younger than other communities, increasing the likelihood of youth-related risk behaviors (Wallace, Sleet, & James, 1997). Compared to white Americans, Indians are 4.6 times more likely to die of alcoholism, 4.2 times more likely to die of tuberculosis, 1.6 times more likely to die of diabetes, and 0.51 times more likely to die of pneumonia (Baldridge, 2001).

Another significant change has been in family structure. Reddy (1993) reported that the percentage of single-parent households was 50%, whereas Banks (1991) estimated that in 1980 the percentage of two-parent families was 70%.

Current Challenges

Adolescent Problems

Gruber et al. (2002) indicated that American Indian adolescents tended to have higher rates of antisocial behavior (violence, shoplifting, running away from home, and vandalism) and substance abuse (tobacco, alcohol, and marijuana) than European American and African American adolescents but not higher rates of sexual activity. The age of first sexual activity for American Indian adolescents was significantly older than for European American adolescents. Urbanization and contact with other ethnic groups have facilitated changes in attitudes (Sage, 1997) and behaviors, contributing to higher rates of antisocial activities for urban American Indian adolescents than for reservation-dwelling adolescents. This suggests that adolescents living off reservations experience higher rates of acculturation stress (Yates, 1987).

Identity and Cultural Transmission

Personal strength is derived from knowing oneself and one's culture: the bases for identity. Identity is strongly associated with family roles, relationships, and responsibilities; American Indian children are taught roles and obligations in the family and society mostly from their mothers. Children's views

of themselves as Indians and the positive or negative connotations associated with those views are due in part to their mothers' identities as Indians and in part to societal views of Indians. The American Indian mother's transmission of a positive sense of self to her child is extremely important, not only for the child as an individual who needs to overcome institutional and social oppression, but for the survival of the culture and ultimately the tribe (Rodgers, 2001; Wilson, 2002). Cultural identity in children is fostered and valued to preserve the culture and empower the next generation to fight the injustices of oppression (Cheshire, 2001). Urban American Indian mothers foster a strong sense of identity and pass on their culture to their children in many ways, such as encouraging observation and modeling (Garrett, 1996). Women's roles in American Indian families are complex; they are mothers and sources of cultural tradition to tribal leaders (Kawamoto & Cheshire, 1997; LaFromboise, Heyle, & Ozer, 1990).

Rodgers (2001) argued that traditional Indian family dynamics have been destroyed by premeditated assimilation strategies of European Americans, citing increased rates of domestic violence, suicide, drug and alcohol abuse and the loss of cultural identity and pride as examples of problems. However, American Indian parents are beginning to realize the impact of culture on their children and are "mending the hoop for the children of the future" (p. 1514).

According to Harjo (1993), American Indian parents are more likely to have children taken away than non-Indians. Government officials have repeatedly disrupted Indian families, knowing the damage they would inflict on family structure, parenting, and the maintenance of American Indian culture and hoping it would further assimilation. Such assimilation strategies began in the late 1800s and early 1900s with creation of the boarding school system (Szasz,

1996). Indian children were kidnapped and placed in federally sanctioned, church-operated boarding schools, where they endured "emotional, physical and sexual abuse" (Baldridge, 2001, p. 1521). When these children grew up, they were not able to teach traditional values or serve as cultural role models for their own children. In fact, many attempted to hide their Indian heritage because of their lack of positive Indian identity and because they did not want to see their children experience the same abuse they had endured. Many American Indian elders, products of the boarding schools, engaged in risk-taking behaviors that led to health dangers for themselves and their children (Beauvais, Oetting, Wolf, & Edwards, 1989; Blum, Harmon, Harrish, Berguisen, & Resnick, 1992; Gruber et al., 2002; McShane, 1988). Today, many boarding schools have been reclaimed by American Indian families; they are safe havens where Indian youth can be supported and can have access to tribal-specific and intertribal cultural traditions (Dinges & Duong-Tran, 1994; Kawamoto, 2001a).

Extended Family

Extended family members play significant roles in the survival of American Indian families. Elders, whether biologically related or created kin, are important to a child's care, upbringing, and development, contributing to family cohesiveness and stability (Rodgers, 2001). They help maintain cultural norms by serving as mentors and advisors who reinforce culturally specific roles and responsibilities (Baldridge, 2001). Out of respect for their commitment to communities and families, elders are cared for by adult women and other extended kin (Hennessy & John, 2002; John, 1988).

Federal policies to assimilate American Indians have changed the roles of family members. Once Indians were forced to relocate from reservations, they had little access to extended family support (Baldridge, 2001). To adapt, urban Indians created community organizations and formed their own pan-Indian, intertribal support groups. Indian families now have access to a larger group of elders from many different tribes who can help guide and advise them (Kawamoto & Cheshire, 1999). The newly developed community works to obtain resources to care for the elderly. To transmit and preserve culture, there must be adaptations. For instance, because urban American Indian families are more migratory than reservation families (Sage, 1997), American Indian elder Frank Merrill has identified pan-Indian urban events such as powwows as key opportunities for families to learn about their culture (Kawamoto & Cheshire, 1997).

Today, American Indian elders are dealing with a multitude of issues ranging from poverty to poor health and minimal access to services in both urban and reservation areas (Baldridge, 2001). Many elders are also experiencing abuse or neglect from informal caregivers (Baldridge & Brown, 1998). Although elders from reservations are asking for Abused Elderly Protection Teams (National Indian Council on Aging [NICOA] 1998 National Aging Conference, cited in Baldridge, 2001), elders often do not recognize abuse as a crime because it is a new phenomenon for American Indians. Brown (1989) found that elders who were victims of financial exploitation often refused to accept this as abuse because of the cultural value of sharing resources with other family members.

Recently, many elders have once again become primary caregivers and providers for their extended families (Baldridge, 2001). This is difficult because they often must try to find jobs to supplement their fixed retirement budget; they often go without medical services because they cannot afford them. In particular, American Indian women elders, who are more likely to be divorced or widowed, are at higher risk for economic hardship (John & Baldridge, 1996). Many American Indian families feel they have little control over issues related to elder care, but they seem to place more emphasis on the positive aspects of caregiving by accentuating acceptance and adaptation rather than dwelling on control (Strong, 1984).

Health

Today, instead of diseases brought by the Europeans, such as smallpox, measles, and influenza, or even modern diseases such as diabetes and asthma, behavioral health issues dominate mortality statistics for American Indians (Baldridge, 2001). The current leading causes of death for Indians 55 to 64 years old relate to lifestyle choices and behaviors such as alcoholism and poor diet (Baldridge, 2001; U.S. Department of Health and Human Services, 1997). Changes in mortality statistics have significant implications for elders, their families, and Indian public health care providers.

Alcoholism is an important behavior-related disease with historical connections, as American Indians have used alcohol to deal with post-traumatic stress unique to their communities (Kawamoto, 2001a). Alcoholism has led to problems such as fetal alcohol syndrome and child abuse (Dixon, 1989) and many other concerns such as homicide and suicide (Wallace et al., 1997).

To address alcoholism and other behavioral issues, helping professionals must be cognizant of at least three key characteristics of American Indian families: cultural identity, sense of humor, and attitudes about seeking help (Garrett & Herring, 2001). Humor serves many purposes beyond relaxing tense situations, improving the atmosphere, and reaffirming a sense of connectedness and humility (Garrett & Garrett, 1994). Humor provides a positive

way of coping with stress, which is critical because few traditional American Indians seek counseling, and many perceive counseling as a threat to the maintenance of cultural values (LaFromboise, 1988).

Although treaty rights included provisions for a government-run Indian health care system, "Indian Health Service budgets are discretionary, and must be reauthorized every year by Congress. The result is a pattern of chronically insufficient funding, resulting in the Indian Health Service being unable to meet . . . immediate . . . care needs" (Baldridge, 2001, p. 1523). The Indian health care delivery system does not provide a geriatric focus; it offers no individual case management; and it has not, over five decades, created an infrastructure for long-term care (Baldridge, 2001). The burden of long-term care is heavy: tribal values emphasize familial obligations and interdependence (Red Horse, 1980), so family members often undertake demanding tasks caring for and preventing the institutional placement of older relatives (Manson, 1989).

Aside from substance abuse, diabetes is the disease that has had the greatest impact on Indian families. The Indian Health Service Diabetes Program reports that more than 20% of Indian elders have this disease, and in some communities, more than half of the residents over 50 suffer from diabetes (Baldridge, 2001), a rate four times the national average. Some Arizona reservations have the highest rates of diabetes in the world. Diabetes has a cultural as well as a medical impact on American Indian family life. When we were in an Indian student group at Oregon State University, we were among several who were running behind with preparations for a university powwow. Everything was running late, including the meal that is usually given to the elders, the dancers, and others. One of the elders chastised the group for getting the food ready late because many of the elders had diabetes and needed to take their medicine with food. Feeding the elders first at an event was no longer just an issue of cultural tradition; it was also a matter of medical necessity.

As a way of dealing with contemporary mental health issues, programs that focus on a wellness model inspired by ancient traditions have been developed. The wellness model is a "holistic integrated approach to health and well-being" (Rodgers, 2001, p. 1513). It encompasses four components, physical, mental, emotional, and spiritual wellness (Cross, 1998), called the "Circle of Life" or the "Four Winds/Directions of Life" (Garrett & Garrett, 1996). Within the last 12 years, this movement has acquired thousands of followers. In fact, Indian communities have had wellness gatherings, and conferences as well as most powwows are now drug and alcohol free. According to Rodgers (2001), "[T]he wellness model has helped many native people become healthy, assisted in empowering them, and diminished a sense of hopelessness while utilizing a lifestyle model that is culturally significant" (p. 1514). Such wellness programs reflect a desire to integrate numerous relevant contemporary Western systems with aboriginal systems (Angus, 1999).

One of the principal distinctions between urban and reservation American Indians is that tribal sovereignty has had a more significant role on reservation communities. For American Indian nations, sovereignty is the power of self-determination, considered to be the supreme power from which other powers are derived (Pevar, 1992). Contemporary attempts to create more efficient tribal government structures have affected elders' roles on many reservations Baldridge, 2001). Once the principal determinants of tribal policy and the center of power, elders' influences may have begun to fade, although efforts to strengthen traditions in urban settings suggest otherwise (Cheshire, 2001).

UNIFYING/DISTINCTIVE TRADITIONS

In this last section, we focus on a few specific ancient traditions that are being reinterpreted as unifying pan-Indian and/or distinctive tribal nation principles for modern Indian families. These common worldviews are essential to a sense of *Indianness* (Garrett & Garrett, 1994).

Parke and Buriel (2002) identified the pan-Indian tradition of respect for elders. Although male elders are very active in families (Kawamoto & Cheshire, 1997), female elders are especially responsible for the oral tradition of storytelling, which is recognized as a key component of survival and is often referred to as passing down memories (Wilson, 2002). History-based stories are especially important, as evidenced by the frequency of their use. Storytelling has other impacts as well. For example, stories help define roles of responsibility in extended families (Wilson, 2002).

Although the traditions of respect for elders and storytelling are widespread among American Indians, the ways in which storytelling are enacted are distinct from one group to the next. For many reservation-based communities, stories help maintain connection to land and place (Wilson, 2002). Also, the way in which storytelling happens can differ. For example, some communities regard a talent for storytelling as an innate gift, whereas Dakota tradition holds that the oral tradition is an acquired skill (Wilson, 2002). Many communities feature trickster stories in their oral tradition, but the trickster takes different forms (Goble, 1988; Wilson, 2002).

Another pan-Indian principle is identifying with the group. Although Parke and Buriel (2002) focused on tribal identification, we suggest it can also be a regional/intertribal identification, as exemplified in the contemporary intertribal confederations in Oregon (Kawamoto, 2001b) and in urban intertribal communities in Sacramento, California. This sociocentric nature is cited in numerous other studies (Baines, 1992; Hennessy & John, 2002). Connected to it is the pan-Indian principle of cooperation and partnership within the group and family (Parke & Buriel, 2002; Red Horse, 1980). Group identification and cooperation also have served to create a sense of interregional or intertribal competition. Traditionally, families socialized younger family members with the values of interdependency and caregiving, although dependence was not valued more than independence (Hennessy & John, 2002).

FUTURE TRENDS

Many of the methodological frustrations experienced historically in the study of American Indian families are being addressed today, which bodes well for the future of the field. One frustration has been the lack of valid, reliable instruments designed for use with American Indian families. One example of an instrument that has recently been developed is the Native American Cultural Involvement and Detachment Anxiety Questionnaire (CIDAQ), an instrument designed to measure American Indians' culturally related anxiety. It has been tested in a variety of American Indian communities and in depth with Navajos. This instrument measures involvement within the American Indian community, economic stress, and interaction with non-Indians (McNeil, Porter, Zvolensky, Chaney, & Kee, 2000).

The trend of designing projects for American Indian families, often by Indian scholars, also has influenced practitioners. A *Four Circles* strategy in which the interconnected elements of a family are addressed has been developed (Manson, Walker, & Kivlahan, 1987); it is supported by research indicating that when American Indian families participate in treatment, members are better able to deal with depression, gang involvement, and substance abuse (Whitbeck, Hoyt, Chen, & Stubben, 2002), and chances for academic success increase (Whitbeck, Hoyt, Stubben, & LaFromboise, 2001).

Another concern has been the focus of most family scholars on nuclear families, ignoring extended families. Some researchers have attempted to include extended family members in studies (Baines, 1992; Cheshire, 2001; Hennessy & John, 2002; Lamarine, 1998). The future of family counseling looks promising, as clinicians become aware of the need to respect the role of extended families (Garrett & Herring, 2001).

This has been a brief overview of the current status of American Indian family scholarship. We take satisfaction in knowing that there is much more available and much more to come.

REFERENCES

Angus, D. O. (1999). Thinking about our children. *Saskatchewan Sage, 3*(6), 5.

Baines, D. R. (1992). Issues in cultural sensitivity: Examples from the Indian peoples. In D. M. Becker, D. R. Hill, J. S. Jackson, D. M. Levine, F. A. Stillman, & S. M. Weiss (Eds.), *Health behavior research in minority populations: Access, design, and implementation* (pp. 230-233). Washington, DC: Public Health Service.

Baldridge, D. (2001). Indian elders: Family traditions in crisis. *American Behavioral Scientist, 44,* 1515–1527.

Baldridge, D., & Brown, A. (1998). *An American Indian elder abuse monograph.* Center of Child Abuse and Neglect. Norman: University of Oklahoma Press.

Banks, J. A. (1991). *Teaching strategies for ethnic studies* (5th ed.). Boston: Allyn & Bacon.

Beauvais, F., Oetting, E. R., Wolf, W., & Edwards, R. W. (1989). American Indian youth and drugs, 1976–87: A continuing problem. *American Journal of Public Health, 79,* 634–636.

Blum, R. W., Harmon, B., Harrish, L., Berguisen, L., & Resnick, M.D. (1992). American Indian-Alaska native youth. *Journal of the American Medical Association, 267,* 1637–1644.

Brown, A. (1989). A survey on elder abuse at one Native American tribe. *Journal of Elder Abuse and Neglect, 1,* 17–38.

Cheshire, T. C. (2001). Cultural transmission in urban American Indian families. *American Behavioral Scientist, 44,* 1528–1535.

Cross, T. L. (1998). Understanding family resiliency from a relational world view. In H. I. McCubbin, E. A. Thompson, A. I. Thompson, & J. E. Fromer (Eds.), *Resiliency in Native American and immigrant families* (pp. 143–157). Thousand Oaks, CA: Sage.

Dinges, N. G., & Duong-Tran, Q. (1994). Suicide ideation and suicide attempt among American Indian and Alaska Native boarding school adolescents. *American Indian and Alaska Native Mental Health Research Monograph Series, 4,* 167–188.

Dixon, J. K. (1989). *Group treatment for Native American women survivors of child sexual abuse.* New York: Harper & Row.

Garrett, J. T., & Garrett, M. T. (1994). The path of good medicine: Understanding and counseling Native Americans. *Journal of Multicultural Counseling and Development, 22,* 134–144.

Garrett, J. T., & Garrett, M. T. (1996). *Medicine of the Cherokee.* Santa Fe, NM: Bear.

Garrett, M. T. (1996). Reflection by the riverside: The traditional education of Native American children. *Journal of Humanistic Education and Development, 35,* 13–28.

Garrett, M. T., & Herring, R. D. (2001). Honoring the power of relation: Counseling native adults. *Journal for Humanistic Counseling, Education and Development, 40,* 39–161.

Goble, P. (1988). *Iktomi and the boulder.* New York: Orchard.

Gruber, E., DiClemente, R. J., & Anderson, M. M. (2002). Risk-taking behavior among American Indian, black, and white adolescents. In N. V. Benokraitis (Ed.), *Contemporary ethnic families in the United States* (pp. 263–268). Upper Saddle River, NJ: Pearson Education.

Harjo, S. S. (1993). The American Indian experience. In H. P. Mcadoo (Ed.), *Family ethnicity* (pp. 199–207). Newbury Park, CA: Sage.

Hennessy, C. H., & John, R. (2002). Elder care in Pueblo Indian families. In N. V. Benokraitis (Ed.), *Contemporary ethnic families in the United States* (pp. 368–377). Upper Saddle River, NJ: Pearson Education.

John, R. (1988). The Native American family. In C. H. Mindel, R. Habenstein, & R. Wright (Eds.), *Ethnic families in America* (3rd ed., pp. 325–363). New York: Elsevier.

John, R., & Baldridge, D. (1996). *The NICOA report.* Washington, DC: National Indian Policy Center.

Kawamoto, W. T. (2001a). Community mental health and family social issues in sociohistorical context: The confederated tribes of Coos Lower, Umpqua, and Siuslaw Indians. *American Behavioral Scientist, 44,* 1482–1491.

Kawamoto, W. T. (2001b). Introduction: Looking deeper into the lives of American Indian families. *American Behavioral Scientist, 44,* 1445–1446.

Kawamoto, W. T., & Cheshire, T. C. (1997). American Indian families. In M. K. DeGenova (Ed.), *Families in a cultural context* (pp. 15–34). Mountain View, CA: Mayfield.

Kawamoto, W. T., & Cheshire, T. C. (1999). Contemporary issues in the urban American Indian family. In H. P. McAdoo (Ed.), *Family ethnicity* (pp. 94–104). Thousand Oaks, CA: Sage.

LaFromboise, T. D. (1988). American Indian mental health policy. *American Psychologist, 43,* 388–397.

LaFromboise, T. D., Heyle, A., & Ozer, E. (1990) Changing and diverse roles of women in American Indian cultures. *Sex Roles, 22,* 455–476.

Lamarine, R. J. (1998). Alcohol abuse among Native Americans. *Journal of Community Health, 13,* 143–155.

Manson, S. M. (1989). Long-term care in American Indian communities: Issues in planning and research. *Gerontologist, 29,* 38–44.

Manson, S. M., Walker, R. D., & Kivlahan, D. R. (1987). Psychiatric assessment and treatment of American Indians and Alaska Natives. *Hospital and Community Psychiatry, 38,* 5–173.

McNeil, D. W., Porter, C. A., Zvolensky, M. J., Chaney, J. M., & Kee, M. (2000). Assessment of culturally related anxiety in American Indians and Alaska natives. *Behavior Therapy, 31,* 301–325.

McShane, B. (1988). An analysis of mental health research with American Indian youth. *Journal of Adolescence, 11,* 87–116.

Parke, R. D., & Buriel, R. (2002). Socialization concerns in African, American Indian, Asian American, and Latino families. In N. Benokraitis (Ed.), *Contemporary ethnic families in the United States* (pp. 18–29). Upper Saddle River, NJ: Pearson.

Pevar, S. L. (1992). *The rights of Indians and tribes* (2nd ed.). Carbondale: Southern Illinois University Press.

Rally for justice held in Stilwell. (1994, May 31). *Cherokee Observer, 2*(5), 1.

Red Horse, J. (1980). American Indian elders: Unifiers of Indian families. *Social Casework, 61,* 490–493.

Reddy, M. (1993). *Statistical record of native North Americans.* Detroit: Gale Research.

Rodgers, B. (2001). A path of healing and wellness for native families. *American Behavioral Scientist, 44,* 1512–1514.

Sage, G. P. (1997). Counseling American Indian adults. In C. C. Lee (Ed.), *Multicultural issues in counseling* (2nd ed., pp. 33–52). Alexandria, VA: American Counseling Association.

Strong, C. (1984). Stress and caring for elderly relatives: Interpretations and coping strategies in an American Indian and white sample. *Gerontologist, 24,* 251–256.

Szasz, M. C. (1996) Educational policy. In M. B. Davis (Ed.), *Native America in the 20th century* (pp. 182–183). New York: Garland Reference Library of Social Science.

U.S. Department of Health and Human Services. (1997). Trends in Indian health. Retrieved February 10, 2003, from www.ihs.gov/PublicInfo/publications/trends97/trends97.asp.

Wallace, L., Sleet, D., & James, S. (1997). Injuries and the ten leading causes of death for Native Americans in the U.S.: Opportunities for prevention. *IHS Primary Care Provider, 22,* 140–145.

Whitbeck, L., Hoyt, D. R, Chen, X., & Stubben, J. D. (2002). Predictors of gang involvement among American Indian adolescents. *Journal of Gang Research, 10,* 11–26.

Whitbeck, L., Hoyt, D. R., Stubben, J. D., & LaFromboise, T. (2001). Traditional culture and academic success among American Indian children in the upper Midwest. *Journal of American Indian Education, 40,* 48–60.

Wilson, A. C. (2002). Grandmother to granddaughter: Learning to be a Dakota woman. In N. V. Benokraitis (Ed.), *Contemporary ethnic families in the United States* (pp. 49–54). Upper Saddle River, NJ: Prentice Hall.

Yates, A. (1987). Current status and future directions of research on the American Indian child. *American Journal of Psychology, 144,* 1135–1142.

CHAPTER 23

Muslim Families in the United States

Bahira Sherif-Trask

Recent social and political events have triggered a growing curiosity in the United States about the lives and beliefs of Muslim American families. This interest can be attributed to several factors: world events that have brought issues occurring in the Islamic world to the foreground, the rapid growth of Islam among African Americans, and a recent large influx of Muslim immigrants from the Middle East, North Africa, Sub-Saharan Africa, Pakistan, India, and Southeast Asia. Despite this interest and concern about the global role of Islam, there is relatively little research or public knowledge about Muslims and their families in the United States. In the Western context, Islam and Muslims are often viewed from a monolithic perspective. In fact, although Islam is characterized by a common underlying belief system, there is a great deal of variation in its actualization. This diversity is also reflected in the beliefs and traditions of adherents to Islam in the United States. This chapter seeks to elucidate some of the basic tenets of Islam with respect to family life and to highlight aspects of contemporary research that illustrate the diversity that is characteristic of Muslim families in the United States.

DEMOGRAPHICS

Although Islam is one of the youngest religions in the world (its inception dates to 622 A.D), it is, globally, the fastest growing religion, with currently approximately 1.3 billion adherents worldwide. Estimating an exact figure for the number of Muslims in the United States is complicated by the fact that the census does not require religious information as part of its surveys. Thus, estimates for the number of Muslims in the United States range from approximately 3 million (Smith, 2002) to 4 to 6 million (Stone, 1991; *World Almanac,* 1998). The question about ancestry in the 2000 census shows that 0.7 percent of the population claimed to have origins in countries with a majority Muslim population (Smith, 2002, p. 413). Crude estimates from census and Immigration and Naturalization Service figures indicate that the Muslim population ranges between 1,456,000 to 3,397,000, or 0.5% to 1.2% of the total population when the American-born Muslim population is included (Smith, 2002, p. 414). Most of these statistics rely on percentages derived from data on national origin, language use, and mosque association and how these are linked to religious affiliation. These are, however, such tenuous linkages that it is uncertain which estimates of the Muslim population are reliable (Smith, 2002).

American Muslims can be roughly divided into several groups: immigrants who came from Asia, Africa, Iran and the Middle East; African Americans; and converts from other groups found in the United States (Cooper, 1993). From 1924 to 1975, Muslim immigrants from the Middle East and North Africa outnumbered all those from other parts of the world. More recently, Muslim immigrants have come primarily from western Asia, specifically Iran, Pakistan, and India (Walbridge, 1999). In the last several years, there has also been a very small increase in the number of immigrant Muslims from eastern Europe (Smith, 2002). Recent immigrants tend to be highly educated professionals, independent business people, or factory workers.

According to estimates, nearly half of all Muslim Americans are African Americans who have converted to Islam. The other half are almost entirely immigrants, except for a few converts to Islam from various other cultural groups (Cooper, 1993; Stone, 1991). Immigrant Muslims live primarily in major metropolitan areas that have historically drawn new arrivals. These include some of the largest cities in the United States (e.g., New York, Los Angeles, Chicago). The largest numbers of mosques and prayer halls are found in California, New York, Michigan, Illinois, and Pennsylvania (Nimer, 2002). The fewest Muslim immigrants are located in the Southeast and Northwest regions of the country, with the exceptions of southern Florida and the Seattle area. The largest concentration of African American Muslims is in Illinois (Stone, 1991).

The majority of immigrant Arab, African, and Asian Muslims subscribe primarily to Sunni (or orthodox) Islam, while those from Iran, Bahrain, and Oman tend to be Shi'ites. Some immigrant Muslims are also adherents of less familiar sects such as the Alawis or Zaidis. African American Muslims include Sunnis, members of the Nation of Islam, and members of other smaller denominations.

Historically, interaction between immigrant Muslims and African American Muslims has been limited. Language skills, historical factors, racial issues, and vastly different cultural traditions form major barriers between these groups. Furthermore, unlike immigrants, many African Americans are converts. To observe their new religion, they tend to alter every aspect of their lives. They usually adopt Muslim names, styles of dress (particularly, among women, veiling), and a consciously projected Islamic image. For many converts, their new religious identity may take precedence over their former ethnic/racial identity. In contrast, many Muslim immigrants work harder to maintain their ethnic than their religious identities, while trying to assimilate into American culture (Kolars, 1994).

American Muslims are distinguished by different levels of education, types of occupations, arrival time in the United States, adherence to religious beliefs, and desire to assimilate in society. The diversity among Muslim Americans has contributed to a lack of feeling of solidarity or group identity. This also makes it difficult to generalize about American Muslim families, for this is equivalent to trying to find commonalities among all Christian families in the United States. It is possible, however, to explicate some of the basic beliefs in Islam with respect to family issues and to examine the current state of scholarship on Muslim Americans in the United States. Religious principles constitute only *one* arena from which individuals actively and selectively draw their beliefs. These beliefs are negotiated within sociohistorical contexts and may vary over time, not just among specific groups, but also among individuals themselves.

ISLAMIC PRINCIPLES

Islam provides a foundation for understanding the religious beliefs and practices of Muslim families (Al-Hali & Khan, 1993). Islam is a monotheistic religion based on the belief that there is one God and that this is the same God that Christians and Jews believe in. *Islam* is an Arabic word meaning "submission to the will of God." A Muslim is anyone who follows the religion of Islam.

Muslims regard the Old and New Testaments as revelations that came from God (Allah). With respect to morals and human behavior, Islam, Judaism, and Christianity are virtually identical. A primary difference is that Islam does not accept the Christian concept of the Trinity or Jesus Christ as the Son of God. Instead, Jesus is regarded as a prophet who was then followed by Muhammad, the last prophet. Furthermore, there are two major strands of Islam, Sunni Islam and Shi'a Islam, their distinction resulting from a crisis of succession after the death of Muhammad.

Islam has a somewhat less formal structure than the other monotheistic religions (Cooper, 1993). The imam of a mosque is perceived as a teacher rather than a leader or mediator, and every individual is thought to have a direct relationship to God. Another distinctive feature of Islam is the five pillars of faith. In addition to worshipping Allah, a practicing Muslim must pray five times a day, practice the yearly fast from sunrise to sunset during the month of Ramadan, contribute to the poor, and make a pilgrimage to Mecca at least once in his or her lifetime. Furthermore, every Muslim is expected to be moderate, and he or she may not drink alcohol, eat pork, or gamble. Due to the visible, daily nature of these practices, Islam is often perceived as more ritualized than other religions (El-Amin, 1991).

ISLAMIC TEACHINGS ON FAMILY

Both the Qur'an and the *hadith*s (the collection of sayings and teaching of the Prophet Mohammad) deal with issues relating to the regulation of mate selection, marriage, children, divorce, authority, inheritance, and family rights and responsibilities. Of the legal injunctions in the Qur'an, about a third relate to marriage and the family (Nasir, 1990). To understand some of the principles underlying Islamic beliefs with respect to family, it is instructive to look at some Islamic teachings on gender, marriage, parent-child relationships, and divorce.

Gender Roles

Many Islamic religious injunctions deal specifically with the relationship between men and women in families. These are often regarded by Muslims as the basis for *legitimizing* gender roles. Islamic teachings stress the equality of all people before God. Nonetheless, interpretations vary considerably, particularly with respect to women's roles.

A fundamental Islamic belief is the distinct difference between male and female in terms of their personalities, social roles, and functions. References to women and their appropriate behavior are scattered throughout the Qur'an and the hadiths, and their meanings and interpretation have been a source of controversy since the earliest days of Islam. Various Qur'anic passages focus specifically on women's unique nature, place in society, and role within the general congregation of believers. Innate differences between the sexes are not perceived in terms of a dichotomy of superior and inferior but as complementary (Macleod, 1991). However, underlying Islamic ideological formulations with respect to gender is the belief that women must remain in their place for political and social harmony to prevail. Practices such as veiling and distinct male and female activities, both in and outside the family, often reinforce this gender dichotomy. If women do not adhere to this moral order, then society runs the risk of degenerating into *fitna* (temptation or, more importantly, rebellion, social dissension, or disorder). A saying of the Prophet Muhammad is that there is no fitna more harmful to men than women. Women are potentially so powerful that they are required to submit to their husbands, segregate themselves from men to whom they are not immediately related, and restrain themselves lest the pattern of gender relations at the core of a properly ordered society be overturned.

Even though the Qur'an is the central source of Islamic beliefs with respect to gender roles, there is considerable controversy about the meaning of passages and their implications for the status of women (Fernea & Bezirgan, 1977). Contemporary scholarship illustrates that, rather than determining attitudes about women, parts of the Qur'an are used at certain times to legitimate particular acts or sets of conditions with respect to women (Marcus, 1992; Mernissi, 1987). This selective use is part of the way in which gender hierarchies and sexuality are negotiated and enforced. It does not explain gender roles; instead, it is part of a constant process of gender role negotiation. Muslim feminist writers have gone to great lengths to illustrate that gender asymmetry and the status of women cannot be attributed to Islam. Instead, beliefs and practices with respect to women and men's roles are part of a complicated interwoven set of social traditions, religions, and ever-changing political and economic conditions (Chatty & Rabo, 1997). Recent research has highlighted that the teachings of the Prophet Muhammad

specified protections and rights for women that were radical departures from the existing culture. These included limitations on polygyny, inheritance and property rights for women, and marriage contracts and maintenance in cases of divorce and child custody (Baron, 1994). These studies highlight that gender constructions are always embedded in sociohistorical contexts. What it means to be a Muslim male or female is shaped not only by Islamic traditions and beliefs but also by the social environment in which these concepts are negotiated and the personal characteristics of the individual.

Significance of Marriage

Marriage is a central aspect of the lives of all Muslim men and women. Every Muslim is expected to marry, and marriage is governed by a complex set of legal rules. A Muslim family is established on the concept of a contractual exchange that legally commences with a marriage contract and its consummation. Every school of Islamic law perceives marriage as a contract, the main function of which is to make sexual relations between a man and a woman licit (Nasir, 1990). Several conditions make a Muslim marriage valid: consent of the bride and her legal guardian, two witnesses, and payment of a dower, or *mahr*. The mahr, depending on custom, can range from gifts of a coin to large sums of money or valuables. The signing of the contract entitles the bride to the mahr, a suitable home, maintenance (i.e., food, clothes, gifts), and a partial inheritance from the husband. According to Islamic law, women are not required to share in the costs and expenditures of their spouses or their male relatives. They are not expected or required to work outside the home. In return for financial investment, husbands acquire authority as the head of the family and access to the sexual and reproductive abilities of their wives (Mir-Hosseini, 1993).

Once an Islamic marriage becomes valid through the signing of the marital contract, it is the duty of the husband to provide for his wife under three conditions: She also signs the contract; she puts herself under her husband's authority and allows him free access to her; and she obeys him for the duration of the marriage. This division of gender roles in the family is often legitimated by the following quote from the Qur'an:

> Men are in charge of women, because Allah hath made the one of them to excel the other, and because they spend of their property [for support of women]. So good women are the obedient, guarding in secret that which Allah hath guarded. As for those from whom ye fear rebellion, admonish them and banish them to beds apart, and scourge them. Lo! Allah is ever High Exalted, Great. (4:34; Pickthall, 1994, p. 80)

Beyond its legal components, marriage also has a religious dimension and is invested with many ethical injunctions. Any sexual contact outside marriage is considered adultery and is subject to punishment. Islam also condemns and discourages celibacy. Muslim jurists have gone so far as to elevate marriage to the level of a religious duty. The Qur'an supports this notion with the phrase "And marry such of you as are solitary and the pious of your slaves and maid servants" (24:32), which is commonly interpreted as advocating marriage to fulfill religious requirements. An often-quoted hadith states that the prayer of a married man is equal to 70 prayers of a single man.

The significance of the Islamic ideals of marriage inherent in the Qur'an and the *shari'a* (legal interpretations) is that they provide a primary frame of reference for legitimizing the actions of individuals and validating certain power relations within the family. Ideologies are, however, not static. They are forged, negotiated, and re-expressed in connection with other social, economic, and historical factors. These ideals provide one *potential* area from which individuals draw their beliefs, which they negotiate within their social and cultural environment.

Parent-Child Relationships

The Qur'an and the *sunna* (practices) are extremely concerned with motherhood, fatherhood, and the protection of children from the moment of conception until the age of maturity. Besides the Qur'an, many significant Islamic texts indicate the primary importance of children and their well-being in the family unit. This emphasis can be attributed to several factors. Children are believed to strengthen the marital tie, they continue the family line by carrying their father's name, they provide for their parents in old age, and they are partial inheritors of their parents' estate.

The legal aspects of Islam deal with the socioeconomic conditions of children, both within the family and in the event of divorce or death of the parents (Schacht, 1964). Islamic law states that every Muslim infant is entitled to *hadana*, which loosely translates into the fulfillment of physical and emotional needs. This includes, besides care and protection, socialization and education. The child is entitled to love, attention, and devotion to all its needs.

According to religious law, responsibilities of parents to children and of children to parents parallel rights and obligations established through marriage, notwithstanding specific social contexts. An examination of the Islamic religious and legal ideals of the relationship between children and parents reveals a strong emphasis on the guardianship of the individual throughout the various stages of his or her life. The shari'a reflects the highly protective attitude of the Qur'an toward minors and aged parents. Specifically, the primary legal relationship centers on adequate maintenance of dependent children and parents. Islamic tenets stress parents' responsibility, which begins at conception, for the economic and social welfare of children. This parental responsibility is enforceable under Islamic law (Fluehr-Lobban, 1987). Reciprocally, it is the responsibility of children to take care of their aged parents, both financially and socially: "And that ye show kindness to parents. If one of them or both of them attain old age with thee, say not 'fie' unto them nor repulse them, but speak unto them a gracious word" (Qur'an, 17:23). It is important to note the reciprocal rights and obligations of *both* parents and children.

Divorce

Divorce is treated as a serious matter both in the Qur'an and hadiths and in Islamic law. Several *suras* (passages) (2:225–232; 65:1–7) deal in detail with divorce, and an often recited hadith states that "[n]o permissible thing is more detested by Allah than divorce." Divorce implicates men and women differently in the legal domain. According to Islamic law, a Muslim husband has the unilateral right to divorce his wife without having to justify his actions before any legal body or any witnesses. A wife, however, to initiate a divorce, must place her claim before a shari'a court and argue her case on the basis of certain legal precepts. Legally, the most concrete factor that prevents divorce is the portion of the mahr that becomes owed to the wife upon the dissolution of the marriage (Nasir, 1990). Women who stipulate a mahr in their marriage contracts will use it primarily as a bargaining tool, should their husband threaten to divorce them. Thus, the mahr acts as a deterrent to divorce and may give a woman some financial security and bargaining power.

Besides the mahr, the *'idda* also acts as a restraint to divorce. The *'idda* is the period between separation of the couple and the final termination of marriage, and it carries with it certain obligations and rights for both spouses. These include a temporary legal restraint from remarrying, sexual abstinence for a woman, the mutual entitlement to inheritance, and the maintenance and lodging of the wife, who must wait three menstrual cycles before the divorce is final (Qur'an, 2:228). According to Islamic law, a divorce cannot be finalized until the 'idda requirement is completed. In the case of a pregnant woman, the 'idda continues until her child is born (Qur'an, 65:6). The reasons for observing the 'idda are threefold: (a) to ascertain the possibility of a pregnancy and, if necessary, to establish the paternity of the child; (b) to provide the husband with an opportunity to return to his wife if the divorce is revocable; and (c) to enable a widow to mourn her deceased husband (Nasir, 1990). The stress in the Qur'an and Islamic law on the 'idda illustrates the Islamic emphasis on ensuring the well-being of the unborn child. Again, this points to the religious emphasis on creating a family and ensuring that the woman and her children have a form of social protection.

Islamic Family Structure

An examination of the specific Islamic rulings that deal with marriage and the maintenance of the wife, the child, and elderly parents reveals a concern with a social group that can be characterized as a nuclear family. Throughout the Qur'an, even though the Arabic terminology is inconsistent, the relations within the nuclear family are primary, and the concept of the extended family (three generations or more within the same household) is only secondary (Lecerf, 1956). This is further emphasized by the Qur'anic conception that believers should enjoy the pleasures of paradise as a family: that is, as the conjugal couple together with their children and parents (Qur'an, 13:23; 40:8; 52:21). Furthermore, all of the religious provisions concerning wifely maintenance, divorce, and the economic and social well-being of children and parents indicate the supreme importance in Islam of the sustenance and stabilization of the family unit. These provisions also point to the importance attributed to the protection of the individual and the necessity of ensuring this protection through the stability of the family.

RESEARCH ON MUSLIM AMERICAN FAMILIES

Trends in Contemporary Research

Researchers have focused on several distinct areas with respect to Muslim American families, but many aspects of these families have not been explored. Muslim American families, therefore, provide a venue for the further development of theories, frameworks, and empirical studies that can assist family scholars in developing a greater understanding of culturally diverse families.

The "Muslim Family" Defined as a Religious Institution

Some studies on Muslim families focus specifically on the Islamic family as a religious institution. These works have become almost exclusively the focus of Muslim researchers bent on defending their faith against perceived Western imperialistic threats to their social order. These works do not acknowledge religious variation or interpretation. Instead, they deal with Islam as a unified body of dogma that is not linked with popular practice (Abd al Ati, 1977; Barakat, 1985; Disuqi, 1996). These religiously oriented works have fallen prey to the orientalist truism that Islam is about

texts rather than people (Said, 1978). Until recently, they tended to ignore the dynamic relationship between individuals, social processes, and ideologies. Even so, there is evidence in these studies that far from being uniform, Muslim families vary in size, in composition, and according to historical and social circumstances.

Overviews of Muslim American Families

Several recent compilations on family ethnicity and diversity (McAdoo, 1999; McGoldrick, Giordano, & Pearce, 1996) included overviews of the current state of understanding about Muslim families. These works, whose purpose was to provide general information, focused either on the Arab family (Abudabbeh, 1996) or on aspects of Muslim families (Carolan, 1999; Sherif, 1999). For the most part, they were not based on ethnographic or other social scientific data; instead, they outlined basic principles that can be applied to contemporary understandings of Muslim families. Although these types of works may provide insight into Muslim families, they run the risk of promoting stereotypes by not adequately addressing the diversity that belies categorical designations. The few other overview studies on Muslim American families (Aswad & Bilge, 1996; Haddad, 1991; Waugh, McIrvin, Abu-Laban, & Qureshi, 1991) are rarely used or cited in family studies research. Although these particular works focus specifically on Muslim families in the United States, their interdisciplinary orientation (anthropology and religion) has aroused only marginal interest in the field.

Muslim American Families as Mental Health and Social Services Clients

Recently, the greatest proliferation of research on and about Muslim American families has taken place in the mental health domain. Several articles have sought to address the needs of Muslims and to provide specific recommendations for providing culturally relevant service delivery. The authors of most of these primarily qualitative studies have attempted to understand mental health issues and appropriate forms of care for American Muslims (Abudabbeh & Nydell, 1993; Carolan, Bagherinia, Juhari, Himelright, & Mouton-Sanders, 2000; Erickson & al-Timimi, 2001; Faragallah, Schumm, & Webb, 1997; Jackson, 1997; Lawrence & Rozmus, 2001; Nobles & Sciarra, 2000). These works, which focus primarily on Arab Muslims, highlight the importance of understanding family issues in providing services. They attempt to negate stereotypes that Muslim families are more patriarchal than other types of families by providing multiple examples of how women's roles can vary both before and after marriage (Carolan et al., 2000; Erickson & al-Timimi, 2001). Issues such as veiling as a symbolic statement and not as a symbol of subjugation are also highlighted (Erickson & al-Timimi, 2001). These studies indicate that, as with many other groups in the United States, the importance of extended family for providing social and emotional support remains at least a sought-after ideal, even if not actualized in practice.

Gender Issues in Muslim American Families

Several recent works have highlighted issues specifically facing Muslim women in the United States. They deal with topics such as domestic violence (Ayyub, 2000), religiosity and veiling (Bartkowski & Read, 2003), wife abuse and polygamy (Hassouneh-Phillips, 2001), gender roles and egalitarianism (Juhari, 1998), female role identity (Abu-Ali & Reisen, 1999), and discrimination against African American Muslim women (Byng, 1998). These studies indicate

that religion is only one aspect of identity formation among young Muslim women. Varying constructions of appropriate gender roles, as they are defined not only in the home but also in the wider society, play a crucial role in the lives of both unmarried and married women. These works indicate that among American Muslims the strict gender hierarchy commonly portrayed in the media and scholarly literature is often not followed. It is common for women to work outside the home and contribute to the family income. This phenomenon is congruent with changes in the Middle East and Asia, where it is increasingly common for women to secure and maintain external employment. Such economic involvement does not support the traditional Islamic model of distinct marital spheres. Instead, among many American Muslims a more egalitarian model of shared economic responsibilities and household obligations is becoming the norm. Furthermore, as Carolan et al. (2000) pointed out, for many individuals gender equity may be defined as respect rather than complete equality in the Western sense. Other issues faced by some Muslim American families are young women's rebelliousness regarding issues of modest dress and veiling. Although the return to veiling in many parts of the Islamic world has taken the form of a cultural symbolic statement for young women, some young Muslim American women fear that it will target them for harassment and discrimination. This creates unique problems for Muslim families trying to maintain their religious identity in the United States.

Many research trends with respect to Muslim American families are comparable to those regarding other culturally diverse groups in the United States. A distinguishing feature of Muslim Americans, however, is their extreme heterogeneity, which creates unique research obstacles as well as opportunities.

Theoretical and Methodological Issues

In the field of family studies, research on Muslim families in the United States has been sporadic at best. This paucity of research on Muslim American families can be attributed to a myriad of issues. One contributing factor pertains to the lack of culturally sensitive frameworks for studying ethnically diverse families in general (Dilworth-Anderson, Burton, & Johnson, 1993). This problem is compounded because Muslim American families elude research categories that often classify individuals along racial or ethnic lines. Their voices are thus not represented when family diversity issues are addressed. In addition, designating individuals purely by religion can be deceptive. Labels such as *Christian, Muslim,* or *Jewish* do not address degree of belief, measures of religiosity, or the relationship between belief and practice (Waugh et al., 1991). Further, determining whether a family is Muslim, or for that matter Christian, Jewish, or any other religious category, can be ambiguous if family members are not part of a formal community such as a mosque, neighborhood, or association. And with respect to Muslim Americans, national origin cannot be equated with religious affiliation, beliefs, race, or ethnicity. For example, many immigrants from the Middle East, particularly before 1975, were Christians and not Muslims. More recently, a large group of Middle Eastern immigrants to the United States has been from Iran. Many of these Iranian immigrants, though designated as Muslim, are highly secular and identify themselves by their cultural and not their religious backgrounds (Walbridge, 1999).

Definitional Issues With Respect to Family

The paucity of studies on American Muslim families is part of a larger problem that is reflected in the overall field of research on Islamic marriage and family formation. Until very recently, definitional issues hampered studies of all Muslim families, both in the United States and abroad. Although recognition of family diversity is now an integral aspect of research on more mainstream families, many studies of Muslim families assumed that the terms *Arab family, Islamic family,* and *Middle Eastern family* were interchangeable (Barakat, 1985; McGoldrick et al., 1996). This family was primarily described in opposition to its Western counterpart: It was purported that the institution of the Muslim family had not undergone the significant structural transformations that are associated with the rise of capitalism in the West and that it had not been the object of modernization that promoted individualism at the expense of family control (Tucker, 1993). These static conceptualizations of Islamic families abroad were applied to understandings of Muslim families in the United States. This has led to a certain degree of stereotyping, particularly with respect to gender issues in Muslim families. In one sense, Muslim families, both in the United States and abroad, are now understood to face the same globalizing challenges, constraints, and opportunities as other families with respect to issues of gender roles, marital stability, and parenting. In another sense, Muslim families must deal with the unique dilemma of being characterized and frequently stereotyped as adherents of a religion that is falsely thought to be, in the popular consciousness, particularly prescriptive with respect to women and men's roles, both in the family and in the larger society.

Defining Muslim Communities

The complexity of Muslim American communities is another barrier to studies on Muslim American families. There exists a wealth of diversity between and within

Muslim communities. For example, there are older Muslim communities in the United States that are composed of Arab immigrants, and there are Muslim neighborhoods that are composed of African Americans who have converted to Islam (Haddad & Smith, 1994). Clearly delineating specific Muslim communities is complicated by the fact that until the mid-1970s, immigrant Muslims and African American practitioners had very little contact with each other. As part of its policy, the Nation of Islam (NOI) excluded nonblacks, and for their part, immigrants perceived NOI followers as un-Islamic (Kelley, 1994). In the 1970s, as more African Americans converted to orthodox Islam, some joined largely immigrant religious communities. Nevertheless, the relationship between these groups has not improved due to widely varying experiences and concerns.

Demographics

Another complicating factor with respect to researching American Muslim families is demographics. Only a relatively small number of American Muslims live in recognized Muslim communities. Most Muslims are spread out over metropolitan areas and tend to congregate more by ethnicity or national origin than by religious affiliation. Lack of common experiences also divides communities. Third- and fourth-generation Muslim families may know little of the immigrant experience and may practice a version of Islam that is dissimilar to that of their parents or their country/community of origin. These factors do not allow researchers to easily identify where and how to identify Muslim American families.

The study of Muslim families shares a problem with other culturally diverse families that are not easily accessible to researchers. Linguistic, religious, and cultural barriers make social scientific studies of Muslim Americans by non-Muslims particularly difficult. Minority populations in the United States have long been suspicious of outside researchers, and Muslim Americans are no exception. In the contemporary context, where some Muslim Americans feel stereotyped and discriminated against, these suspicions may, in some communities, become even more heightened (Walbridge, 1999).

Future Theoretical Research Directions

Currently, understandings about the dynamics of culturally diverse families, in general, are limited at best (Allen, 2000; Andersen & Collins, 1995; Bacca-Zinn, 2000; Dilworth-Anderson et al., 1993; Thompson, 1995; Thorne, 1997). This problem is exacerbated in research on amorphous groups such as Muslim Americans. A common approach is to portray culturally diverse groups by a series of descriptive characteristics. This is neither an accurate nor a fruitful approach to explaining intragroup or intergroup variability, and it can lead to stereotyping or worse. By choosing to designate families by a label, be it religious, racial, or ethnic, we run the risk of implying that this is the main determinant of identification for these individuals and their families.

Ecological/Systems Approaches

Although Muslim American families are among the most diverse groups today in the United States, the study of their experiences is constrained due to the inadequacy of frameworks that are unable to capture their heterogeneity. Muslim American families, like all culturally diverse families, need to be studied as the product of complex interactions between various social subsystems operating outside the ethnic cultures. These interrelated systems include not only the individual and environment but also a myriad of situational, temporal, cultural, and societal influences. Class, family composition, regional differences, and gender relations all affect Muslim American families. By applying an ecological/systems approach to the study of issues relevant to these families, we may be able to better determine the extent to which religious beliefs, cultural traditions, and external and internal familial factors play a role in their lives.

Feminist Perspectives

Feminist perspectives also offer potential frameworks for the deconstructive analysis of Muslim American families. In-depth qualitative studies of specific issues such as marital relationships or the role of working Muslim immigrant women could provide further insight into specific group dynamics with respect to power and privilege.

Although it is now understood that gender roles and expectations differ significantly between families of varied traditions and cultures, we do not know to what extent there may be variables that bind groups together. We do not know, for example, the extent to which regional variations, class, and education play a role in the types of interpretations of appropriate gender roles among Muslim women. Developing a well-articulated analysis of gender among different groups of Muslim American women would allow for a clearer insight into family relationships, power relations, and family dynamics.

Symbolic Interactionism

A symbolic interactionist framework allows researchers to understand the experiences of Muslim American families from their vantage point. By incorporating a perspective that group experiences are always the product of social constructs, researchers move away from a static perspective on the role of Islam in individuals' lives. From this perspective, it is possible to debate "when and under what circumstances does Islamic law direct [individuals' lives], and when and under what conditions does it reflect [individuals' actions]?" (Mir-Hosseini, 1993, p. 14).

Life Course Analysis

Life course analysis provides another important venue for understanding the experiences of both immigrant and African American Muslims. By focusing on the intertwined nature of individual trajectories within kinship networks in the context of time, culture, and social change, this framework offers the conceptual flexibility to address a variety of family forms in diverse environments (Dilworth-Anderson et al., 1993). Given the particularly diverse nature of Muslim Americans, this perspective has the potential for the development of culturally relevant constructs of family and family experiences.

These theoretical frameworks provide a foundation for capturing the intertwined, complex nature of Muslim American families. These families do not live in a vacuum but are instead part of the larger American and world landscape. Theoretical approaches that incorporate concepts of agency and systemic change are best used to assist in interpreting the relationship between religious values and ideals and people's actual lives in a constantly shifting environment.

Future Empirical Research Directions

The study of Muslim American families provides a useful venue for theoretical and empirical contributions not only about these families but also about the study of group complexity and family experiences in general. As globalizing influences are felt in all parts of the world, taken-for-granted assumptions about families and approaches to studying them are increasingly being questioned. Thus, researchers need to employ new paradigms in their studies and formulate new types of questions about the subject matter. As a discipline, family studies also needs to reinvestigate its multidisciplinary roots in an effort to build on what we know and what we still need to learn. This may be best accomplished by reconceptualizing the focus of study in less traditional terms and incorporating innovative collaborative approaches.

Interdisciplinary Collaborations

Interdisciplinary comparative studies between religious groups could provide one potential area for exploration. *Muslim* is a religious designation, and Muslim families' experiences should thus be compared to those of other such groups, such as Christian, Jewish, or Mormon families. Comparisons between Muslim and American, white, or ethnic families are misleading because the latter designate geographic and/or racial affiliations instead of religious connections. Cross-disciplinary research, specifically in conjunction with anthropology, history, and religious studies, could lend insight into the complexity of understanding the dynamic relationship between religion and social groups.

The Immigration Experience

Comparisons of aspects of the immigration experience are another crucial area of study. All immigrants share the experience of uprooting themselves from one culture and trying to establish themselves in a new one. The extent to which religious beliefs play a role in those experiences has not been widely pursued. Do strong religious beliefs and identification perhaps facilitate this transition? With respect to Muslim Americans, the literature takes a negative slant on this topic, adhering to the view that Muslims face prejudice due to their religion (Abudabbeh & Nydell, 1993;

Erickson & al-Timimi, 2001; Jackson, 1997). But given the heterogeneity of Muslims and their patterns of regional settlement, this may not always be the case. Furthermore, immigration research draws attention to the international aspect of these families. Many different ethnic groups maintain strong ties with friends, relatives, and colleagues from their country of origin. This creates a flow of movement of people, information, and ideological orientations. Studies of Muslim immigrant families' experiences could provide insight into global influences on family structures and relations by highlighting the different experiences within families associated with the adaptation to new environments.

Socialization of Children

The socialization of children with respect to their religious, gender, and linguistic identities provides another venue for better understanding Muslim families. Although currently some studies are looking at the acculturation of young Muslim women (Byng, 1998; Abu-Ali & Reisen, 1999), the discussion of gender with respect to the development of boys has been completely ignored. Also, the many issues raised with respect to immigrant parent-child relations provide multiple opportunities for research.

Muslim Fatherhood

The lack of research on Muslim men also extends to the issue of fatherhood and Islam. Although there is acknowledgment that parenthood is an important aspect of religious ideals, there are no empirical studies on the relationship between Islamic values of parenting and men. Particularly given the recent emphasis on fatherhood initiatives, examining the relationship between men, Islam, and fatherhood in African American Muslims may provide valuable insights.

Interfaith Marriages

Another long-neglected area of study is interfaith marriages with respect to Muslims. According to religious law, Muslim women must marry within the faith, whereas Muslim men may marry outside the faith. Research that examines the extent of influence of varying religious ideals in the broader context of civil marriage in the United States may give us more insight into the dynamics of religiously heterogeneous marriages.

CONCLUSION

Muslim American families provide a rich new area of exploration for family scholars interested in issues of diversity, gender, religion, and group identity. The heterogeneity of Muslim Americans provides an opportunity for the testing and application of new theoretical and empirical research approaches. On the one hand, this group is characterized by its adherence to Islam. On the other, Muslim Americans include devout believers and practitioners as well as secular individuals with no visible ties to the religion. This provides both a barrier and an opportunity for researchers grappling with capturing the social complexity of families. Research on Muslim American families illustrates that with respect to family life, most are dealing with issues that are in many ways similar to those faced by others in the United States. Families struggle with issues concerning gender roles and the division of labor, the raising of children, caretaking of the elderly, immigration-related concerns, and many other topics. A specific difference is that one area of definition for many Muslim American families is their negotiation of religious concepts derived from the teachings of the Qur'an. The significance of the Islamic ideals with respect to family lies not in the extent to which they reflect actual practice but in the frame of reference they provide for legitimizing individual actions. These ideals validate certain power relations in the family but are not unchanging. They are forged, negotiated, and re-expressed in connection with other social, economic, and historical factors. This dynamic relationship between religion and families needs to be explored through the conscious application of frameworks such as ecological systems theory or symbolic interactionism and may in fact lead to new theoretical designs that more concisely capture complex phenomena. In an increasingly global world, static theoretical frameworks do not allow us to fully understand how families perceive themselves and their issues or how they are adapting to the stresses and challenges around them.

Currently, the study of culturally diverse families needs to be invigorated through the application of more explicit theoretical approaches, the development of culturally sensitive frameworks, and a wider, more imaginative range of topics to be studied. The study of Muslim American families provides family scholars with the chance to pursue truly innovative research that will further the field of family diversity as well as family studies as a whole.

REFERENCES

Abd al Ati, H. (1977). *The family structure in Islam*. Indianapolis, IN: American Trust.

Abu-Ali, A., & Reisen, C. (1999). Gender role identity among adolescent Muslim girls living in the U.S. *Current Psychology, 18*, 185–192.

Abudabbeh, N. (1996). Arab families. In M. McGoldrick, J. Giordano, & J. K. Pearce (Eds.), *Ethnicity and family therapy* (2nd ed., pp. 333–346). New York: Guilford.

Abudabbeh, N., & Nydell, M. K. (1993). Transcultural counseling and Arab Americans. In J. McFadden (Ed.), *Transcultural counseling* (pp. 261–284). Alexandria, VA: American Counseling Association.

Al-Hali, T., & Khan, M. (1993). *Interpretation of the meanings of the noble Quar'an in the English language.* Kingdom of Saudi Arabia: Maktaba Dar-us-Salam.

Allen, K. (2000). A conscious and inclusive family studies. *Journal of Marriage and the Family, 62,* 4–5.

Andersen, M., & Collins, P. (1995). *Race, class, and gender.* New York: Wadsworth.

Aswad, B., & Bilge, B. (1996). *Family and gender among American Muslims.* Philadelphia: Temple University Press.

Ayyub, R. (2000). Domestic violence in the South Asian Muslim immigrant population in the United States. *Journal of Social Distress and the Homeless, 9,* 327–248.

Bacca-Zinn, M. (2000). Feminism and family studies for a new century. *Annals of the American Academy of Political and Social Science, 571,* 42–57.

Barakat, H. (1985). The Arab family and the challenge of social transformation. In E. Fernea (Ed.), *Women and the family in the Middle East* (pp. 27–48). Austin: University of Texas Press.

Baron, B. (1994). *The women's awakening.* New Haven, CT: Yale University Press.

Bartkowski, J., & Read, J. (2003). Veiled submission: Gender, power and identity among evangelical and Muslim women in the United States. *Qualitative Sociology, 26,* 71–92.

Byng, M. (1998). Mediating discrimination: Resisting oppression among African-American Muslim women. *Social Problems, 45,* 473–489.

Carolan, M. (1999). Contemporary Muslim women and the family. In H. McAdoo (Ed.), *Family ethnicity* (pp. 213–221). Thousand Oaks, CA: Sage.

Carolan, M., Bagherinia, G., Juhari, R., Himelright, J., & Mouton-Sanders, M. (2000). Contemporary Muslim families: Research and practice. *Contemporary Family Therapy, 22,* 67–79.

Chatty, D., & Rabo, A. (1997). *Organizing women.* New York: Berg.

Cooper, M. H. (1993). Muslims in America. *National Law Journal, 17,* 363–367.

Dilworth-Anderson, P., Burton, L., & Johnson, L. (1993). Reframing theories for understanding race, ethnicity and families. In P. Boss, W. Dougherty, R. La Rossa, W. Schumm, & S. Steinmetz (Eds.), *Sourcebook of family theories and methods* (pp. 627–665). New York: Plenum.

Disuqi, R. (1996). Family values in Islam. In S. Roylance (Ed.), *The traditional family in peril* (pp. 33–42). South Jordan, UT: United Families International.

El-Amin, M. M. (1991). *Family roots.* Chicago: International Ummah Foundation.

Erickson, C. D., & al-Timimi, N. R. (2001). Providing mental health services to Arab Americans: Recommendations and considerations. *Cultural Diversity and Ethnic Minority Psychology, 7,* 308–327.

Faragallah, M., Schumm, W., & Webb, F. (1997). Acculturation of Arab-American immigrants: An exploratory study. *Journal of Contemporary Family Studies, 28,* 182–203.

Fernea, E., & Bezirgan, B. (1977). *Middle Eastern Muslim women speak.* Austin: University of Texas Press.

Fluehr-Lobban, C. (1987). *Islamic law and society in the Sudan.* London: Frank Cass.

Haddad, Y. (1991). *The Muslims of America.* New York: Oxford University Press.

Haddad, Y., & Smith, J. (1994). *Muslim communities in North America.* Albany: SUNY Press.

Hassouneh-Phillips, D. (2001). Polygamy and wife abuse: A qualitative study of Muslim women in America. *Health Care for Women International, 22,* 735–748.

Jackson, M. (1997). Counseling Arab Americans. In C. Lee (Ed.), *Multicultural issues in counseling* (2nd ed., pp. 333–349). Alexandria, VA: American Counseling Association.

Juhari, R. (1998). Marital quality as a function of gender-role egalitarianism among the Malay-Muslim student couples in the Midwest region of the United States. *Dissertation Abstracts International, 58,* 4754B.

Kelley, R. (1994). Muslims in Los Angeles. In Y. Haddad & J. Smith (Eds.), *Muslim communities in North America* (pp. 135–167). Albany: SUNY Press.

Kolars, C. (1994). Masjid ul-Mutkabir: The portrait of an African American orthodox Muslim community. In Y. Haddad (Ed.), *The Muslims of America* (pp. 475–499). New York: Oxford University Press.

Lawrence, P., & Rozmus, C. (2001). Culturally sensitive care of the Muslim patient. *Journal of Transcultural Nursing, 12,* 228–233.

Lecerf, J. (1956). Note sur la famille dans le monde arabe et islamique. *Arabica, 3,* 31–60.

Macleod, A. (1991). *Accommodating protest.* New York: Columbia University Press.

Marcus, J. (1992). *A world of difference.* London: Zed.

McAdoo, H. (1999). *Family ethnicity.* Thousand Oaks, CA: Sage.

McGoldrick, M., Giordano, J., & Pearce, J. (1996). *Ethnicity and family therapy.* New York: Guilford.

Mernissi, F. (1987). *Beyond the veil: Male-female dynamics in modern Muslim society.* Bloomington: Indiana University Press.

Mir-Hosseini, Z. (1993). *Marriage on trial: A study of Islamic family law.* London: I. B. Tauris.

Nasir, J. (1990). *The Islamic law of personal status.* London: Graham & Trotman.

Nimer, M. (2002). Muslims in American public life. In Y. Haddad (Ed.), *Muslims in the West: From sojourners to citizens* (pp. 169–186). New York: Oxford University Press.

Nobles, A., & Sciarra, D. (2000). Cultural determinants in the treatment of Arab Americans: A primer for mainstream therapists. *American Journal of Orthopsychiatry, 70,* 182–191.

Pickthall, M. (Trans.). (1994). *The glorious Qur'an.* Des Plaines, IL: Library of Islam.

Said, E. (1978). *Orientalism.* New York: Pantheon.

Schacht, J. (1964). *An introduction to Islamic law.* Oxford, UK: Clarendon.

Sherif, B. (1999). Islamic family ideals. In H. McAdoo (Ed.), *Family ethnicity* (pp. 203–212). Thousand Oaks, CA: Sage.

Smith, T. (2002). The polls-review. The Muslim population of the United States: The methodology of estimates. *Public Opinion Quarterly, 66,* 404–414.

Stone, C. (1991). Estimate of Muslims in America. In Y. Haddad (Ed.), *The Muslims of America* (pp. 25–36). New York: Oxford University Press.

Thompson, L. (1995). Teaching about ethnic minority families using a pedagogy of care. *Family Relations, 44,* 129–135.

Thorne, B. (1997). *Feminist sociology.* New Brunswick, NJ: Rutgers University Press.

Tucker, J. (1993). An introduction. In J. Tucker (Ed.), *Arab women* (pp. vii–xvii). Bloomington: Indiana University Press.

Walbridge, L. (1999). Middle Easterners and North Africans. In E. Barkan (Ed.), *A nation of peoples* (pp. 391–410). Westport, CT: Greenwood.

Waugh, E., McIrvin, S., Abu-Laban, B., & Qureshi, R. (Eds.). (1991). *Muslim families in North America.* Edmonton, Canada: University of Alberta Press.

World almanac and book of facts. (1998). Mahwah, NJ: World Almanac Books.

Part VII

FAMILIES IN SOCIETY

Families and Religious Beliefs, Practices, and Communities

Linkages in a Diverse and Dynamic Cultural Context

DAVID C. DOLLAHITE, LOREN D. MARKS,
AND MICHAEL A. GOODMAN

Families are sacred and central to major world religions, and all world religions include beliefs and practices that influence families (Eliade, 1993; Houseknecht & Pankhurst, 2000; Madsen, Lawrence, & Christiansen, 2000). The United States may be the most religious and religiously diverse nation in terms of voluntary participation in religious institutions (Eck, 2001; Melton, 2003; Stark & Finke, 2000). Ninety-five percent of all married couples and parents in America report a religious affiliation (Mahoney, Pargament, Tarakeshwar, & Swank, 2001), about 90% desire religious training for their children (Gallup & Castelli, 1989), over half say they attend religious services at least monthly (Heaton & Pratt,

1990), and 60% say religion is "important" or "very important" to them (McCullough, Hoyt, Larson, Koenig, & Thoresen, 2000); only 2% say they do not believe in God (Sherkat & Ellison, 1999). Even given the tendency of U.S. survey respondents to exaggerate their religious participation, religious beliefs and activities continue to be reported as an important part of American family life (Christiano, 2000).

As Pankhurst and Houseknecht (2000) stated, "[R]eligion and family may be primordial institutions, but they are also dynamic and 'modern' institutions" (p. 28). The latter half of the 20th century in the United States was characterized by remarkable growth in both religious and family diversity owing

AUTHORS' NOTE: We are indebted to Howard Bahr, Lili Anderson, Bruce Chadwick, Tom Draper, Tim Heaton, and four anonymous reviewers for their helpful feedback on a previous draft.

to changes in religious expression, increasing numbers of immigrants with non-Jewish and non-Christian religious affiliations, and changes in family structure. There now is tremendous diversity in North America in how individuals and families experience and express spiritual beliefs and practices, with as much diversity within major faith groups as between them (Eck, 2001). Linder (2003) has listed 216 major Christian denominations, and Melton (2003) has documented over 2,600 distinct faith communities in the United States and Canada (70% are Christian). Increases in religious diversity continue at a rapid pace; indeed, religious diversity may be greater than other types of diversity (Eck, 2001; Melton, 2003). Moreover, Americans have always been dynamic in their religious identities and degrees of adherence, as manifested in high levels of intergenerational and personal changes in orthodoxy and activity within faith communities and high levels of conversions from one faith community to another. Scholars have only begun to capture this religious diversity in relation to marriage and family life.

According to the 2000 U.S. census, there is widespread variation in how family households are structured (U.S. Bureau of the Census, 2001). Recent important changes in families include higher proportions of individuals not marrying or marrying later, increased numbers of couples cohabiting, higher rates of divorce and remarriage, increased age at birth of first child, more adult children living with parents, and married couples having more years together after children are raised. As several chapters in this book illustrate, scholars disagree as to whether the changes in marriage and family life generally have been a boon or bane to individuals, families, and societies (see also Browning, Miller-McLemore, Couture, Lyon, & Franklin, 1997).

Increased family diversity probably is associated with increased religious diversity.

For example, parental divorce is positively associated with increased likelihood that children will change their religious identity through either conversion or apostasy (Lawton & Bures, 2001). The growing diversity in families complicates analyses of the connections between religiosity and family life. This is especially true if one attempts to address whether and how a specific aspect of religiosity helps or harms family relationships. Evidence from history, recent events, and social science research confirms that religion can be a potent force for good or ill; both positive *and* negative relationship outcomes may derive from religious factors.

In this chapter, we focus on aspects of religiosity that seem to be related to marital and parent-child relationships. Although we recognize the limits of knowledge grounded only in empirical research, we think that a careful review of research on religiosity and family offers insights for future work. We first briefly discuss the history and current status of the social scientific study of the religiosity-family linkage, along with some critical methodological and theoretical issues relevant to the religiosity-family interface. We review empirical work done in the United States during the last two decades, highlighting what we consider to be some of the best studies. Throughout this chapter, we address the difficult yet important issue of the ways in which religiosity seems to benefit or harm marriages and families. We conclude with suggestions for future scholarship and predictions about the future of family-religion interaction.

SOCIAL SCIENTIFIC STUDY OF THE RELIGIOSITY-FAMILY LINKAGE

The religiosity-family linkage has received relatively little attention from social scientists when compared to other aspects of personal and social life (Pankhurst & Houseknecht,

2000). Many social scientists have been skeptical of the viability and even the desirability of research on religiosity and have treated personal and familial religious beliefs and practices as nonissues (Sherkat & Ellison, 1999).

In recent years, however, there has been an increase in both the quantity and the quality of empirical research linking religiosity and families, due in part to a growing acknowledgment that "even from an atheistic or agnostic position, it is important to understand what motivates and energizes a large portion of the world's population" (Pankhurst & Houseknecht, 2000, p. 9). There was some sustained attention by family scholars to religion in the 1980s (see Bahr & Chadwick, 1985; D'Antonio & Aldous, 1983; Marciano, 1987; Thomas, 1988; Thomas & Cornwall, 1990; Thornton, 1985), and in the later 1990s and early 2000s special issues on religion and family life were published in a number of scholarly journals: *Journal of Family Psychology* (Vol. 15, No. 4), *Journal of Family Psychotherapy* (Vol. 13, Nos. 3/4), *Journal of Men's Studies* (Vol. 7, No. 1), and *Review of Religious Research* (Vol. 43, No. 3). Despite the increased international scholarly and popular interest in religion, however, there was no article on religion and family in the 2000 decade review issue (Vol. 62, No. 4) of the *Journal of Marriage and the Family*, probably the most influential scholarly journal dealing with marriage and family issues.

Critical Issues in the Family-Religiosity Literature

Many studies examining the linkages between personal, marital, and familial life indicate correlations between religiosity and various beneficial outcomes (Koenig, McCullough, & Larson, 2001; Mahoney et al., 2001), but there is also evidence linking religiosity and negative outcomes, although such studies are relatively rare. Apparently a blend of positive and negative family outcomes is associated with religious involvement, depending on the type of involvement, family structure, and other contextual factors (e.g., Ellison & Levin, 1998; Pargament, Smith, Koenig, & Perez, 1998).

Dimensions of Religiosity

Religiosity is complex and multifaceted and has been conceptualized and measured in many ways (Hill & Hood, 1999). Marks and Dollahite (2001) described religiosity as a three-dimensional construct composed of (a) *religious beliefs* (personal, internal beliefs, framings, meanings, perspectives), (b) *religious practices* (outward, observable expressions of faith such as prayer, scripture study, rituals, traditions, or less overtly sacred practices or abstinence that is religiously grounded), and (c) *religious communities* (support, involvement, and relationships grounded in a congregation or less formal religious group). Past research has too frequently examined only one of these dimensions at a time, thereby failing to capture the complex interaction of religious beliefs, practices, and communities in family life. We emphasize here that religiosity is multidimensional and that generalization across dimensions is risky, although some of the studies considered below engage in it.

Types of Religiosity

Religious denomination is an important consideration, although generally less potent than it is presumed to be and was formerly. Faith communities differ dramatically in the degree of familism and the extent to which their practices affect families. There are also important differences between orthodox or traditional bodies and their more progressive or liberal counterparts. Extreme levels of belief, commitment, and behavior differ dramatically from lower or moderate levels in their consequences for families. Faith communities include highly individualistic spiritualities (e.g., New Age), more institutional forms (e.g., mainstream Protestantism), and highly familistic faiths (e.g., Mormonism), and teachings and expectations of family life differ among them. In addition to variants between individualistic and familistic types of faith, Arterburn and Felton (2001) identified several hazardous religious beliefs and practices that they characterized as abuses of religion or *toxic faith*, the antithesis of healthy faith. It is essential to index not just religiosity but type of religiosity.

Types of Family

It is also important to specify the types of families being considered. For example, on the basis of doctrine presented in Jewish, Christian, and Muslim religious texts, gay and lesbian couples are less likely to find congenial homes in most conservative and moderate faith communities than elsewhere (Gordis, 1991), although there have been shifts in recent history (Francoeur, 1983). Some types of families seem to draw more benefits from religious involvement than others. For example, a study of depression in unmarried adolescent mothers found that (a) young single mothers with no particular faith reported the lowest levels of depression, (b) the tension between religious values and unmarried pregnancy was stressful for young women who reported a significant religious orientation, and (c) "even greater distress [was] experienced by young women who lived in an unmarried relationship while at the same time taking part in religious activities" (Sorenson, Grindstaff, & Turner, 1995, p. 80). In comparison, religiosity was not related to depression among married, religiously active teen mothers.

Moving from structure to race, a growing number of studies suggest that faith communities are especially important to black families (McAdoo, 1995). Black churches tend to be more supportive of single-parent families than white churches, but even in black churches divorced and separated women receive less social support than do widows (Taylor & Chatters, 1988). A key challenge for most American churches in the 21st century will be to find a balance between supporting the standard of marriage-based families that is idealized in most American churches and addressing the pluralistic family realities that confront them.

Types of Scholarship

Scholars differ widely in the questions they ask, the approaches they employ, the motivations for their research, and the degree to which they are aware of and articulate their biases and agenda in their work. In the past, family and religious scholars with sociological training have dominated empirical work on religiosity-family linkages, but recently more psychologically oriented scholars have entered this domain (Holden, 2001; Parke, 2001). Sociologists tend to view both religion and family as social institutions, and their approach is more demographic (or distal) in nature (e.g., key variables are denomination, homogamy, church attendance) than the approaches emphasizing intrapersonal and interpersonal processes (proximal variables) that are favored by psychologists. Psychologists are also more likely to foster pragmatic intervention in churches or social service agencies.

In a society that values diversity, scholars should be aware of diversity in religiosity, family type, method, outcomes, and scholarly agenda. When all the permutations of the foregoing possibilities are considered, two implications arise: (a) Scholars should be as clear as possible with themselves and their readers on the issues mentioned above, and (b) they should present their work within contexts and their results as tentative.

Religiosity and Family Relationships

Religiosity and Marriage

Marital Satisfaction. Several reviews have reported that religious involvement is associated with greater marital happiness, adjustment, commitment, and lower risk of conflict (Bahr & Chadwick, 1985; Mahoney et al., 1999; Sherkat & Ellison, 1999). A few such studies will be briefly reviewed. First, in a study of Seventh-Day Adventists, family worship was related to marital satisfaction (Dudley & Kosinski, 1990). Two recent studies employed innovative conceptual and methodological approaches to religiosity and marital satisfaction. Mahoney et al. (1999) found that couples who reported higher levels of sanctification of their marriage (considered their marriage to be sacred) had greater levels of marital functioning in various domains. In a study of 120 predominantly Christian (51% Catholic, 34% Protestant) couples, Fiese and Tomcho (2001) found that two proximal variables (meaning of holiday religious rituals, practice of rituals) were significantly related to marital satisfaction, whereas a more distal variable (importance of religion to the family) had little association with satisfaction. All three of these studies indicated positive correlations between some religious practices (dimensions of religiosity) and marital satisfaction among samples of married, predominantly white couples (types of families). However, the strengths of the correlation varied across denominations and sects (types of religiosity).

In a recent longitudinal study, Sullivan (2001) found that although couples that were more religious were less likely to seek divorce and more likely to seek help for their marriage, religiosity seemed to promote marital satisfaction only for couples in which the husbands had relatively greater mental health than other husbands; both husbands and wives in religious couples with a more reactive, negative husband were less satisfied. Another longitudinal study (Booth, Johnson, Branaman, & Sica, 1995) of a national data set over a 12-year period reported a positive association between marital satisfaction and religiosity, with increased religiosity related to heightened satisfaction. This study suggests that family factors influence religious involvement, indicating a bidirectional relationship between families and religiosity (see also Palkovitz, 2002). Finally, religious involvement (as opposed to nominal religious homogamy) has been found to be related to marital satisfaction, consistent with Masters and Bergin's (1992) observation that it "seems important that one actually behaves in synchrony with one's religious values in order for there to be beneficial . . . consequences" (p. 228) (see also Pankhurst & Houseknecht, 2000).

Certain types of religiosity also have been connected with greater support for gender inequality (Bartkowski, 1997, 2001), which could contribute to lower satisfaction, at least for wives. However, several researchers have found that many women in conservative faith communities report that they prefer traditional gender roles and relationships, that some choose such a life with full knowledge and experience with alternatives, and that they find meaning and fulfillment in this lifestyle (Griffith, 1997; Kaufman, 1993; Stacey, 1990). Other women may leave such religious communities to seek less gendered alternatives.

Some researchers have reported a relation between religiosity and higher acceptance of spousal abuse (Hathaway-Clark, 1980), especially in conservative religious communities.

In contrast, more recent studies report no relationship between conservative Protestantism and domestic violence (Ellison & Anderson, 2001; Ellison, Bartkowski, & Anderson, 1999), and Cunradi, Caetano, and Schafer (2002) found that rates of male-female intimate violence "were highest among those in Liberal groups and lowest among those in Fundamentalist groups" (p. 149).

A final point regarding religiosity and domestic violence is that an estimated 65% to 80% of all domestic abuse is related to alcohol abuse (Gallagher, 1987). Many studies report an inverse relation between religiosity and alcohol and illicit drug use and abuse (Cunradi et al., 2002; Koenig et al., 2001). Thus, through its impact on alcohol and drug abuse, religiosity may decrease domestic abuse in some contexts. However, the generalization that religiosity helps prevent abuse is not without empirical opposition. For example, a notable counterexample is presented by Hathaway-Clark (1980), who found that battered women are often highly religious and concluded that religious beliefs frequently contributed to the ongoing victimization of these women (see also Arterburn & Felton, 2001). In sum, in connection with domestic violence, religiosity apparently may serve as either a risk factor or a protective factor.

Marital Stability. Meta-analytic research indicates that there is a relation between religiosity and commitment to marriage (Mahoney et al., 2001). Religious practice seems especially significant as a predictor of marital stability. Mahoney et al. (2001) found that the relation between church attendance and marital stability remained after a wide range of variables were controlled for; they concluded that couples who attended church regularly had a divorce rate of 44% compared to 60% for nonattenders. Call and Heaton (1997) reported that various aspects of couple religiosity were related to marital stability, with meeting attendance being the best predictor. A qualifying note is that these researchers studied attendance *together*; there was evidence that attending different congregations might foster marital instability.

From a subset of the National Survey of Families and Households (NSFH) data set, Lehrer and Chiswick (1993) found that those who had classified themselves as not religious had the lowest marital stability, whereas Latter-day Saints (Mormons) and those with "other religions" (most of which were Eastern religions such as Islam and Buddhism) had the highest rates of marital stability. Same-faith marriages were much more stable than interfaith marriages (Bahr, 1981), and interfaith marriages were more stable than marriages between nonreligious persons (Lehrer & Chiswick, 1993). The amount of agreement on Jewish issues among same-faith Jewish and interfaith Jewish-Christian marriages was a more powerful predictor of marital conflict and stability than the type of marriage (Chinitz & Brown, 2001).

In a qualitative study of 15 couples married for 30 years or more, Robinson (1994) reported four ways that religiosity seemed to help stabilize marriages: (a) moral guidance, (b) social support, (c) emotional support, and (d) spiritual support. Noticeably absent from Robinson's list was an aversion to divorce, held by many faiths, and the possibility that this faith-based aversion to divorce might preserve marriages that were abusive or irredeemably unhealthy.

Wilson and Musick (1996), using a subset of NSFH data, found that those with higher religiosity viewed themselves as more dependent on their marriages than those of lower religiosity. This was especially true of respondents from more conservative denominations. This feeling of greater dependence may be one reason why marriages between highly religious persons consistently appear to be more stable than marriages between nonreligious persons.

Communication and Conflict Resolution Through Prayer and Forgiveness. Couples who share the same strong religious faith might have greater marital satisfaction because they have fewer major issues over which to disagree. Another hypothesis is that they rely on similar conflict resolution strategies. Two studies (Brody, Stoneman, Flor, & McCrary, 1994; Mahoney et al., 1999) indicated that religiosity may be related to marital satisfaction and stability because religious couples are more likely to employ effective communication and conflict resolution skills, perhaps due to religious emphasis on prayer and forgiveness.

A study of Protestants and Catholics (Gruner, 1985) found that the association of marital satisfaction with prayer was highest in Pentecostal and evangelical groups. Scripture reading also was related to marital satisfaction, but only among members of Pentecostal and evangelical groups. Prayer is one of the variables often measured as a dichotomy. This variable can be studied more appropriately as an ordinal or continuous variable. Qualitative differences in prayer also deserve consideration. For example, Poloma and Pendleton (1991) identified four types of prayer: colloquial, petitional, ritual, and meditative. They found that two types of prayer, colloquial and meditative, were correlated with general well-being but that petitional and ritualistic prayers were not. Butler and colleagues have shown that prayer helps religious couples resolve their conflicts in a variety of ways (Butler, Gardner, & Bird, 1998; Butler & Harper, 1994; Butler, Stout, & Gardner, 2002) and is used as a conflict resolution ritual that serves as a spiritual self-intervention strategy (Butler et al., 2002).

Another important religion-family link is the emphasis on forgiveness in many faith communities. Since the mid-1980s, a burgeoning clinical literature has documented the benefits of relational forgiveness in a variety of personal and family issues, including couple and intergenerational relationships (Hope, 1987; Worthington & DiBlasio, 1990). There is evidence that religious teachings have a significant influence on relational forgiveness (Aponte, 1998; Benson, 1992; McCullough & Worthington, 1994; Sells & Hargrave, 1998). The links between prayer and forgiveness in couples and families certainly deserve further exploration.

Sexuality. The influence of religious *beliefs* regarding sexuality has been documented by Cochran and Beeghley (1991), who examined the effect of religiosity on attitudes toward nonmarital sexuality across several U.S. religions (e.g., Jewish, Catholic, Baptist), based on data collected between 1972 and 1989, and found less tolerance of extramarital relations and homosexuality in more proscriptive religions. However, Sherkat (2002) found that "gay men have high rates of religious participation, while lesbians and bisexuals have significantly lower rates of participation [and] nonheterosexuals are more likely to become apostates when compared to female heterosexuals, but no more so than are heterosexual men" (p. 313).

In connection with *practice*, religiosity has been consistently associated with lower premarital sexual activity (see Batson, Schoenrade, & Ventis, 1993). Early studies linked strict religious upbringing with sexual dysfunction (Masters & Johnson, 1970) and greater sex guilt among married persons (Peterson, 1964), illustrating potential complexities inherent in the religiosity-and-sexuality connection. Runkel (1998) similarly argued that permanent anxiety, guilt, and tension regarding sexuality are prominent in religion and further posited an especial enmity of sexuality in Christianity generally and Catholicism specifically. Although a tension clearly exists between certain types of religiosity and sexuality, some research indicates that the main effort of even conservative churches is to *channel* sexual expression into the confines of marriage rather than to promote sexual asceticism or guilt. For example, Kennedy and Whitlock (1997) surveyed 31 pastors of conservative evangelical denominations and found that although these pastors held conservative moral principles they affirmed and promoted sexuality within marriage. According to these pastors, religion and sexuality were fully compatible in the marital relationship. And Laumann, Gagnon, Michael, and Michaels (1994) found that evangelical/fundamentalists had the highest reports of sexual satisfaction.

Finally, case study research by Simpson and Ramberg (1992) indicated that religious beliefs were among the (positive or negative) factors that determined whether sexually dysfunctional persons sought sex therapy. These researchers also found that therapists who were sensitive to patients' religious beliefs improved the likelihood of successful treatment.

Conclusions: Religiosity and Marriage. Although religiosity has repeatedly been associated positively with both marital satisfaction and marital stability, researchers have not adequately explained these findings. It may be that high levels of reported religiosity and marital satisfaction are artifacts of widely perceived social desirability of religiosity and marital satisfaction in America. If so, cross-cultural studies in countries where religiosity is not the social norm (e.g., Sweden) would be illuminating. We agree with Mahoney et al. (2001) that a better understanding of the marriage-religiosity linkage may be derived from increased emphasis on the relationship between well-measured proximal variables (e.g., religious beliefs about the marriage, joint religious activities) than from a continued focus on global indicators of more distal variables (e.g., denominational homogamy, church attendance).

Religiosity and Parent-Child Relationships

Recent empirical studies report positive connections between religiosity and parent functioning (Brody et al., 1994; Brody, Stoneman, & Flor, 1996; Chadwick & Top, 1993; Gunnoe, Hetherington, & Reiss, 1999), parental warmth (Bartkowski & Wilcox, 2000; Wilcox, 1998), and family-centeredness (Christiano, 2000). Parental religiosity has also been associated with various desirable child outcomes, such as fewer behavior problems, less alcohol and drug use, less antisocial behavior, and less depression (Mahoney et al., 2001).

However, the religiosity-parenting relationship is complex. Ellison (1994) theorized that congregational involvement might compound some family stressors because of the emphasis placed on family harmony. Consistent with this idea, Strawbridge, Shema, Cohen, Roberts, and Kaplan (1998) found that "[o]rganizational religiosity buffered the associations between all of the non-family stressors (financial problems, neighborhood problems, fair or poor health, disability, and chronic illness) and depression. [However], exacerbating effects were indicated for three of the [five] family stressors (abuse, marital problems, and caregiving)" (p. 123) and that for "non-family stressors, religiosity appears to buffer associations with depression, whereas for family stressors it appears to exacerbate associations with depression. Clearly, the relationships . . . are complex" (p. 124).

With this complexity in mind, we address four different issues relating to religiosity and parent-child relationships: (a) religiosity and fertility, (b) religiosity and responsible fathering, (c) religiosity and mothering, and (d) religiosity and authoritarian parenting.

Fertility. Certain religious denominations (and the more orthodox couples within them) are more likely to have stronger pronatalist views than others. In 1964, Westoff, Potter, and Sagi found that religious affiliation had "the strongest [influence] of all major social issues on fertility" (p. 133), with Catholics exhibiting higher fertility than Protestants, and Protestants higher fertility than Jews. At present, however, denominational differences in fertility are minimal and tend to be associated more with ethnicity than religion, with the exceptions that Jews have lower fertility than other religious groups and that the fertility rates of fundamentalist Christians, Latino Catholics, and Latter-day Saints are markedly above U.S. norms (Christiano, 2000; Mosher, Williams, & Johnson, 1992; Wilson, Parnell, & Pagnini, 1997). Christiano (2000) has noted that conservative Christians and Latter-day Saints are characterized by "a strongly 'pronatalist' ideology and a tightly knit system of social bonds that make acting on that belief less burdensome for married couples than it might otherwise be" (p. 57). It might be hypothesized that a decrease in either pronatalist teaching or social support in child rearing would be likely to result in fertility declines among these groups.

Fathers. Recent interest in responsible fathering has prompted some research on the religiosity-fathering linkage. In one study, father religiosity predicted marital and family cohesion and fewer child behavioral and emotional problems (Brody et al., 1996). In a three-generation study of father-child relationships, Snarey (1993) found that father-child church attendance provided significant "social-emotional child-rearing support" for fathers (p. 315). In another study, religious fathers scored higher than others on a measure of generativity (father involvement) and commitment toward their children (Christiansen & Palkovitz, 1998). Wilcox (2002), using NSFH longitudinal data, found

a positive relation between religiosity and father involvement. The positive associations in the religiosity-fathering literature have not yet been explained systematically.

An emerging body of qualitative research based on in-depth interviews with fathers has provided some answers to questions about religiosity and fathering. Evangelical Christian fathers reported that faith provided the spiritual motivation for them to be involved in parenting (Latshaw, 1998). Palkovitz (2002) reported that the birth or presence of children prompted personal religious introspection and/or religious involvement for some fathers, illustrating the bidirectional influences of family and religiosity variables (see also Palkovitz, Marks, Appleby, & Holmes, 2003). Religious belief and practice seem to be particularly helpful in encouraging responsible and meaningful involvement among fathers who are adapting to the death or disability of a child (Dollahite, 2003; Marks & Dollahite, 2001).

Mothers. Although studies often find differences in the ways that religiosity is linked to marital and family variables for men and women (e.g., Fiese & Tomcho, 2001), there is relatively little empirical research specifically addressing mothering and religion. Among the relevant research findings is that mothers are more likely than fathers to seek social support and are therefore likely to benefit more from faith community involvement (Koenig et al., 2001).

Although qualitative work on the religiosity-fathering connection is beginning to illuminate some of the processes underlying religiosity effects, parallel data illuminating the processes at work in connection with mothers are badly needed (for a notable exception, see Kaufman, 1993). The religiosity-mothering connection is particularly important because the influence of religiosity appears to be greater for mothers than fathers (see

Strawbridge, Cohen, Shema, & Kaplan, 1997), although in some instances this influence is negative (Bridges & Spilka, 1992).

Parenting Style. Studies of African Americans in the rural South found religiosity positively correlated with positive parent-child relationships and co-caregiver support and negatively correlated with co-caregiver conflict and inconsistent, scolding parenting (Brody et al., 1994, 1996). Possible intervening mechanisms by which religiosity might contribute to such outcomes included heightened self-perception, attentional processes, attributional processes, and social support.

Most research shows that compared to authoritative parenting, authoritarian parenting is associated with less desirable outcomes in children (Hart, Newell, & Olsen, 2003). It has also been posited that religious parents, especially conservative Protestant parents, may be more authoritarian than others in their parenting style because corporal punishment and obedience are advocated by some influential religious leaders (Ellison, Bartkowski & Segal, 1996a, 1996b).

Some empirical research also supports an extrinsic religiosity-authoritarianism linkage (Altemeyer & Hunsberger, 1992). Batson et al. (1993) noted that 11 of 14 studies found a negative relationship between religiosity and open-mindedness and flexibility. Theological conservatism and orthodoxy have also been associated with authoritarianism (Black, 1985; Lupfer, Hopkinson, & Kelley, 1988). Some scholars have argued that closed-mindedness, self-righteousness, prejudice, and authoritarianism are associated with fundamentalist religions and further suggest that the beliefs correlated with these outcomes in such "religions were inherited by high RWAs [right-wing authoritarians] from their parents almost as certainly as the color of their eyes" (Altemeyer & Hunsberger, 1992, p. 127). More recent research indicates that Christian orthodoxy is inversely correlated with

prejudice but positively correlated with authoritarian attitudes (Laythe, Finkle, Bringle, & Kirkpatrick, 2002). Other research suggests that religiosity is negatively related to authoritarian parenting and positively related to authoritative parenting (Gunnoe et al., 1999; Wilcox, 1998). Flor and Knapp (2001) found that dyadic and bidirectional discussion between parents and their adolescent children (an authoritative parenting style) was significantly and positively associated with their children's religious behavior and with the importance children attached to religion. Thus, one of the outcomes that many religious parents would find desirable (children who voluntarily accept and practice religion) is associated with an authoritative parenting style.

Summary of Research Findings on Religiosity and Family Life

How do religious beliefs, practices, and communities affect families? The short answer is: It depends. In connection with the dimension of *religious beliefs*, Musick (2000) stated that the relationship is complex because "on one hand, religion serves as an integrative component which boosts levels of life satisfaction. . . . On the other, certain religious beliefs [i.e., a vindictive and punishing God] are associated with lower life satisfaction" (p. 282).

Complexity also exists for the dimension of *religious practices*. The literature reviewed manifests strong correlations between marital satisfaction and prayer and scripture study for certain types of religions and families, as well as a number of other beneficial psychological and relational outcomes. Even so, rigidity or dogmatism in religious practice has been correlated with outcomes such as prejudice, intolerance, and authoritarianism. Additionally, though family worship has been linked with both marital and family satisfaction, it seems that compulsory family worship may be more detrimental to well-being and satisfaction than no family worship at all (Lee, Rice, & Gillespie, 1997).

In connection with the dimension of *religious community*, it seems that degree of involvement, not merely type of denominational affiliation, is correlated with higher marital stability, higher marital satisfaction, and several beneficial outcomes for the parent-child relationship. Research shows that faith communities that have higher levels of tension with the broader culture and that tend to ask *more* of adherents tend to be more successful in attracting and retaining members (Stark & Finke, 2000). On the other hand, Ellison and Levin (1998) indicated that some faith communities may be "greedy institutions" that demand time, energy, money, and other resources, "potentially at high costs to families" (p. 713). Even so, many seem willing to meet these costs because in the last several decades membership in low-tension communities (e.g., mainstream Protestantism) has significantly declined whereas membership in some higher-tension faith communities (evangelical Christianity, Mormonism) has steadily risen (Melton, 2003; Stark & Finke, 2000). A further complication is that although religious communities seem to buffer many forms of nonfamily stress, they may also exacerbate stress surrounding family challenges that do not mesh with the congregational ideals (e.g., divorce or out-of-wedlock pregnancy).

In conclusion, though we cannot summarily state that "religiosity" is either good or bad for families, the preponderance of studies point to a positive relationship between religiosity and salutary outcomes in marriage and family relationships. More specifically, it appears that many couples and families are strengthened by their religious beliefs, practices, and communities. On the other hand, there is some evidence that certain types of religious beliefs and practices seem to have harmful consequences for families. We reiterate that the type of religion, the dimension of religiosity (belief, practice, or community), and the type of family must all be considered in assessing the religiosity-family connection with appropriate empirical, conceptual, and contextual sensitivity.

Limitations and Weaknesses of Extant Research

Typically, when religious beliefs and practices have been included as variables in research on families, they have been conceptualized and measured without much sophistication (Mahoney et al., 2001; Thomas & Cornwall, 1990). Although the following limitations apply to much family-religiosity research, several of them are also manifest in social science research generally.

Limitation 1: Lack of Theory on the Religiosity-Family Linkage

In contemporary social science, methodological rigor is fairly common, but accompanying theoretical excellence is more rare. Mahoney et al. (2001), in a review of the literature on religion and family life, stated that lack of conceptual clarity is a significant problem. Likewise, Sullivan (2001) noted that "perhaps the largest impediment to a more complete understanding of how religiosity affects marital functioning is that many studies have been exploratory in nature or empirically-driven rather than theory-driven" (p. 611). Further progress is unlikely until there is more coherent conceptualization of religiosity within family contexts. Currently, relevant findings are more or less loosely connected, but there is no coherent, organized conceptual framework to integrate them. With relatively few exceptions, researchers continue to corroborate previous findings or find correlations but offer few grounded explanations of the religiosity-family interface. Snarey and Dollahite (2001) argued that there is an urgent need for better use of theory, including good middle-range theories that address the complex relationships between familial and religious processes and perhaps even an overarching theory that links religiosity and family. Such contributions would facilitate needed explanations. Of course, exceptions exist. Recent notable conceptual work includes Mahoney and her colleagues (Mahoney et al., 1999, 2001; Mahoney, Pargament, Murray-Swank, & Murray-Swank, 2003) on links between marriage, parenting, and religiosity; Sullivan (2001) on religiosity and marriage; Fiese and Tomcho (2001) on religious practices and marital satisfaction; Carr and van Leeuwen (1996) on religion and feminism in a family context; Flor and Knapp (2001) on the intergenerational transmission of religiosity; Butler et al. (1998, 2002) on prayer and marital conflict resolution; Garland (2002) on faith development in families; Bartkowski (1997, 2001) on evangelical gender roles; and Wilcox (1998) on parenting style.

Limitation 2:
Research Design Restrictions

Most research on the religiosity-family connection is cross-sectional or correlational, making questions regarding direction of influence and causation difficult to determine. An increased emphasis on longitudinal as well as qualitative studies could significantly increase our understanding (Mahoney et al., 2001).

Limitation 3:
Scant Sampling of Family Diversity

The literature on religiosity is limited in its treatment of family diversity, mostly working from samples of white, two-parent, marriage-based families, a family form that has declined over the past 50 years (Amato, 2000). There is substantive work on religiosity in African American families (e.g., Brody et al., 1994; McAdoo, 1995; Taylor & Chatters, 1988), but other American racial minorities, including Asians and Hispanics, are rarely represented (for notable exceptions, see Levin, Markides, & Ray, 1996; Zhou & Bankston, 1998). Significant increases in the number of single-parent families, stepfamilies, and families with gay and lesbian parents have not been followed by corresponding increases in the scale of religiosity-family research in such contexts.

Limitation 4: Sampling of Few Religions

One of the most conspicuous weaknesses in the literature is the lack of research on non-Christian religions and family life (Satlow, 1998; Sherif, 1999). Research on Jewish families (Brodbar-Nemzer, 1988; Chinitz & Brown, 2001) rarely appears in mainstream social science journals, and there is even less empirical data on Muslim families, despite their numerical importance (about one in five inhabitants of the earth) (see Chapter 23 of this book). There is also a paucity of research on the impact of "Eastern religions" (e.g., Hinduism, Shintoism, Buddhism) on family life. Moreover, the literature on non-Christian religiosity and family life is generally descriptive rather than empirical (Schlossberger & Hecker, 1998). The over-representation of studies on the dominant cultural-religious groups inhibits learning about "the complex ways that faith and family life interact among those whose beliefs and practices differ from the dominant or mainstream faith traditions" (Snarey & Dollahite, 2001, p. 649). A recent exception to this tendency is the collection of studies on religiosity and family life in various cultures and subcultures found in Houseknecht and Pankhurst (2000).

RECOMMENDATIONS FOR FUTURE SCHOLARSHIP: EXPLORING DYNAMIC DIVERSITY

Given the complexities inherent in this domain of inquiry and the continuing trends toward religious and familial diversity, what should scholarship on the religiosity-family connection in a postmodern context look like? What are the most compelling questions to ask? What are the best methods to address these questions? What are the most relevant contexts and most important populations that should be studied?

More Research on Families From Diverse Faiths

First, we need more creative scholarship on families from a much wider variety of religious perspectives. With over 800 non-Christian primary religious bodies (denominations) and tens of thousands of non-Christian congregations or groups in the United States, there are abundant possibilities (Melton, 2003).

More Prejudice-Free Studies of Highly Religious Families

Highly religious families are themselves a diverse type of family and also are likely to be disproportionately present among racially, ethnically, and culturally diverse families. However, Stark and Finke (2000) asserted that "today most social scientists continue to display a substantial bias against those who take their religion very seriously ('fundamentalist' being a deadly epithet)" (p. 14). An example of such bias is much scholarly discourse about gender roles in conservative or orthodox Jewish, Christian, and Muslim families. Ironically, perhaps some of the best and most balanced research with such families has been done by scholars with liberal and feminist orientations (see Bartkowski, 2001; Griffith, 1997; Kaufman, 1993; Stacey, 1990). Such efforts to avoid bias against highly religious families facilitate efforts to understand the family-religion linkage among those for whom religion is the center of life and who therefore often have the richest linkages between their faith and their family life.

More Detailed Comparative Research

Researchers in large-scale studies tend to ask more broad, superficial questions to many people of varied backgrounds, and most qualitative researchers tend to ask more detailed, in-depth questions to fewer people of homogeneous groups. Relatively few studies provide in-depth comparative exploration of the same issues across diverse families. Thus, one important strategy is to do intensive studies while employing quantitative measures and qualitative interviews with members of multiple faith communities, using the same questions and methods. This will provide important comparative data that move research beyond the more global, superficial studies of the past. There also is a need for replications of existing work across different ethnic and religious communities.

More Focus on the Paradoxes of Religiosity

There are many important and interesting paradoxes in the domain of religion and family life that deserve special attention: (a) Religion is a unifying force for many couples and families but a divisive force in others; (b) religiosity is both a conservative and a transformative force in relationships; (c) there are both mundane and transcendental aspects to religious life, and both of these affect families in meaningful ways; (d) a strong religious identity both unites a family with other adherents and separates them from members of other faiths or nonbelievers;

(e) religion both excites and calms passions within families; (f) strong religious commitments have important binding *and* liberating features to them; and (g) faith has both highly private and highly public aspects, and both are relevant to family life. Such paradoxes merit sustained exploration because careful attention to paradox may provide telling insights on the religion-family interface.

More Excellent Qualitative Research

Creative and rigorous qualitative research is needed in a number of areas. Some key correlations between religious involvement and family life are well enough established that efforts might be profitably spent on research aimed at interpretation and application. Though the correlations have mounted, the field still has few empirically documented explanations. Although the mantra "correlation does not prove causation" is certainly true, it is possible to simply ask people straight out whether and how *they* believe their religious beliefs, practice, and communities influence their marriage and family life and to ask them to examine critically their own impressions of these matters.

Focus on Adaptive and Maladaptive Aspects of Religiosity

The challenge to simultaneously and systematically assess both adaptive and maladaptive influences of religious involvement at individual, marital/couple, and familial levels should be a central aim of future scholarship (Mahoney et al., 2001; Pargament, 1997). There must be greater attention to (a) the direction(s) of established relationships, (b) the processes involved in the linkage, and (c) the meanings inherent in the multidimensional expressions of religiosity for families and their members. Americans have a tendency toward spiritual and religious eclecticism, a long history of pragmatic

progressivism, and a growing emphasis on enhancing physical, emotional, and relational well-being. These tendencies, coupled with the currently diverse and dynamic nature of religiosity and family life, suggest that there may be many people for whom exploration of the contexts in which religiosity helps or hinders family well-being has critical applied as well as academic relevance. Thus, we suggest that scholars seriously consider the potential benefits involved in more systematic exploration of aspects of religious belief, practice, and community that are most likely to encourage or inhibit healthy and happy relationships among family members.

Scholars exploring the effectiveness of family therapy, for example, try to discover what types of therapeutic interventions, under what kinds of conditions, and with what kinds of families, are most likely to promote improved functioning or prevent dysfunction. Viewing religious faith as a physical or mental health intervention would be distasteful and offensive to many religious people. However, this type of thinking may help scholars move beyond simplistic attacks or defenses of religion and its relationship to family life that have too often characterized past discourse (Thomas & Sommerfeldt, 1984). For example, it is unlikely that there is a linear relationship between religiosity and family outcomes, but it is likely that both great benefits and great problems are associated with high levels of some types of religiosity. More careful and creative theory and methodology may help us to better understand how much, what type, and what dimensions of religiosity are likely to improve family relationships.

Does Religiosity Provide Transcendent Benefits?

Evidence suggests that a meaningful relationship with God can positively influence relationships with family members. Yet some may argue that religion offers merely psychological and social benefits not qualitatively or quantitatively different from those provided by nonreligious beliefs and communities. Because religion addresses transcendent questions and aims to put people in touch with transcendent realities, a fair question is: Does religiosity provide transcendent "added value" beyond the merely psychological benefits of a coherent value system and beyond the merely social benefits of a supportive community? Dollahite (2003) argued that one of the major conceptual and empirical challenges of the future will be to explore this question of whether and how religiosity transcends other (secular) belief systems or support groups. In a society like the United States, with its extensive number and variety of nonreligious philosophies, voluntary associations, and practices oriented toward mental and physical health and relationship enhancement, it should be possible to design studies that explore differential effects on family relationships of comparable secular and religious beliefs, practices, and communities.

In brief, in the future, the most fruitful scholarly work on the links between religiosity and couple and family relationships will probably be done by scholars who (a) give careful attention to diverse families from a variety of faith communities in a diversity of contexts and cultures, (b) employ diverse methodologies to explore these linkages creatively, (c) explicitly attend to their own biases and agendas, and (d) ask people about the varieties of ways their religious beliefs, practices, and communities help and hinder their efforts to have satisfying family relationships.

CONTEMPLATING THE FUTURE

In connection with the "contemplating the future" theme of this book, we now make some general predictions regarding the future of religiosity and families. The once widely held secularization thesis that religion would be abolished in modern societies by science and reason has been largely disproved and discarded (Stark & Bainbridge, 1996; Stark & Finke, 2000). In retrospect, the oft-predicted trend toward a linear increase in societal secularization was both simplistic and dogmatic; indeed, few social trends are truly unilateral. With this in mind, we posit three simultaneous yet divergent trends in connection with American religiosity and family life for the next 30 years.

First, we predict that both atheism and secular humanism will steadily increase, although at a fraction of the rate once predicted by secularization-thesis proponents. A key reason for this prediction rests in the increasing percentage of the population who obtain a secularized university education and, more specifically, the dramatic rise in university-educated women. American women have historically been more religious than American men (Koenig et al., 2001) and also have been more likely to teach religion to their children. It is likely that this secular conversion will be most prevalent among nominally versus actively religious individuals. Clearly, a secular conversion, like a religious conversion, can influence multiple generations.

Second, on the basis of the prevalence of expressive individualism and the rise of the self-help movement in America (Bellah, Madsen, Sullivan, Swindler, & Tipton, 1985) as well as cynicism regarding organized religion, we predict a continuing increase in "religions of one" and New Age and congregation-free spirituality. Because Americans prize their time, money, and energies so highly, formal religious communities will probably have to (a) deliver high returns, rewards, and compensators or (b) lower the "costs" to their members if they are to compete in the market with the low-cost, low-commitment options that congregation-free spirituality offers (Stark & Finke, 2000).

This trend away from congregational involvement may also influence families in many ways, including the loss of social support systems, communal opportunities to serve, and close and consistent interaction with persons from across the life course.

Third, we predict that certain high-tension familistic faiths whose doctrines are markedly different from those of the dominant secular culture will continue to grow. Although the handful of rapidly growing high-tension faiths, most notably Islam, certain strains of evangelical Christianity, and Mormonism, differ in doctrines and practices, they share a decided family-centeredness (Stark & Finke, 2000). Thus, there probably will be more families of a unique and diverse type: the strongly familistic, highly religious family. In sum, the increase in individualistic spirituality, secular humanism, and high-tension familistic faith will all continue, with each of the expressions of belief, practice, and community influencing families in various ways.

Religion will remain a visible force in contemporary American family life, but because of growing complexity and diversity the religiosity-family connection will need to be more carefully examined to be understood. The linkage between religiosity and families will continue to be a compelling, valuable, and relevant domain of social science scholarship and promises to become even more interesting in the future.

REFERENCES

Altemeyer, B., & Hunsberger, B. (1992). Authoritarianism, religious fundamentalism, quest, and prejudice. *International Journal for the Psychology of Religion, 2,* 113–133.

Amato, P. (2000). The consequences of divorce for adults and children. *Journal of Marriage and the Family, 62,* 1269–1287.

Aponte, H. J. (1998). Love, the spiritual wellspring of forgiveness: An example of spirituality in therapy. *Journal of Family Therapy, 20,* 37–58.

Arterburn, S., & Felton, J. (2001). *Toxic faith.* Colorado Springs, CO: Waterbrook.

Bahr, H. M. (1981). Religious intermarriage and divorce in Utah and the mountain states. *Journal for the Scientific Study of Religion, 20,* 251–261.

Bahr, H. M., & Chadwick, B. A. (1985). Religion and family in Middletown, USA. *Journal of Marriage and the Family, 47,* 407–414.

Bartkowski, J. (1997). Debating patriarchy: Discursive disputes over spousal authority among evangelical family commentators. *Journal for the Scientific Study of Religion, 36,* 393–410.

Bartkowski, J. (2001). *Remaking the godly marriage.* New Brunswick, NJ: Rutgers University Press.

Bartkowski, J. P., & Wilcox, W. B. (2000). Conservative Protestant child discipline: The case of parental yelling. *Social Forces, 79,* 265–290.

Batson, C., Schoenrade, P., & Ventis, W. L. (1993). *Religion and the individual.* New York: Oxford University Press.

Bellah, R. N., Madsen, R. Sullivan, W. M., Swindler, A., & Tipton, S. M. (1985). *Habits of the heart.* Berkeley: University of California Press.

Benson, C. K. (1992). Forgiveness and the psychotherapeutic process. *Journal of Psychology and Christianity, 11,* 76–81.

Black, A. W. (1985). The impact of theological orientation and of breadth of perspective on church members' attitudes and behaviors: Roof, Moll, and Kaill revisited. *Journal for the Scientific Study of Religion, 24,* 87–100.

Booth, A., Johnson, D. R., Branaman, A., & Sica, A. (1995). Belief and behavior: Does religion matter in today's marriage? *Journal of Marriage and the Family, 57,* 661–671.

Bridges, R. A., & Spilka, B. (1992). Religion and the mental health of women. In J. F. Schumaker (Ed.), *Religion and mental health* (pp. 43–53). New York: Oxford University Press.

Brodbar-Nemzer, J. Y. (1988). The contemporary American Jewish family. In D. L. Thomas (Ed.), *The religion and family connection: Social science perspectives* (pp. 66–87). Provo, UT: Brigham Young University, Religious Studies Center.

Brody, G. H., Stoneman, Z., & Flor, D. (1996). Parental religiosity, family processes, and youth competence in rural, two-parent African American families. *Developmental Psychology, 32,* 696–706.

Brody, G. H., Stoneman, Z., Flor, D., & McCrary, C. (1994). Religion's role in organizing family relationships: Family process in rural, two parent, African-American families. *Journal of Marriage and the Family, 56,* 878–888.

Browning, D. S., Miller-McLemore, B. J., Couture, P. D., Lyon, K. B., & Franklin, R. M. (1997). *From culture wars to common ground.* Louisville, KY: Westminster John Knox.

Butler, M. H., Gardner, B. C., & Bird, M. H. (1998). Not just a time-out: Change dynamics of prayer for religious couples in conflict situations. *Family Process, 37,* 451–478.

Butler, M. H., & Harper, J. M. (1994). The divine triangle: Deity in the marital system of religious couples. *Family Process, 33,* 277–286.

Butler, M. H., Stout, J. A., & Gardner, B. C. (2002). Prayer as a conflict resolution ritual: clinical implications of religious couple's report of relationship softening, healing perspective, and change responsibility. *American Journal of Family Therapy, 30,* 19–37.

Call, V. A., & Heaton T. B. (1997). Religious influence on marital stability. *Journal for the Scientific Study of Religion, 36,* 382–392.

Carr, A., & van Leeuwen, M. S. (1996). *Religion, feminism, and the family.* Louisville, KY: Westminster John Knox.

Chadwick, B. A., & Top, B. L. (1993). Religiosity and delinquency among LDS adolescents. *Journal for the Scientific Study of Religion, 32,* 51–67.

Chinitz, J. G., & Brown, R. A. (2001). Religious homogamy, marital conflict, and stability in same-faith and interfaith Jewish marriages. *Journal for the Scientific Study of Religion, 40,* 723–733.

Christiano, K. (2000). Religion and the family in modern American culture. In S. Houseknecht & J. Pankhurst (Eds.), *Family, religion, and social change in diverse societies* (pp. 43–78). New York: Oxford University Press.

Christiansen, S. L., & Palkovitz, R. (1998). Exploring Erikson's psychosocial theory of development: Generativity and its relationship to paternal identity, intimacy, and involvement in childcare. *Journal of Men's Studies, 7,* 133–156.

Cochran, J. K., & Beeghley, L. (1991). The influence of religion on attitudes toward nonmarital sexuality: A preliminary assessment of reference group theory. *Journal for the Scientific Study of Religion, 30*(1), 45–62.

Cunradi, C. B., Caetano, R., & Schafer, J. (2002). Religious affiliation, denominational homogamy, and intimate partner violence among U.S. couples. *Journal for the Scientific Study of Religion, 41,* 139–151.

D'Antonio, W. V., & Aldous, J. (1983). *Families and religions.* Beverly Hills, CA: Sage.

Dollahite, D. C. (2003). Fathering for eternity: Generative spirituality in Latter-day Saint fathers of children with special needs. *Review of Religious Research, 44,* 339–351.

Dudley, M. G., & Kosinski, F. A., Jr. (1990). Religiosity and marital satisfaction: A research note. *Review of Religious Research, 32,* 78–86.

Eck, D. L. (2001). *A new religious America.* San Francisco: HarperCollins.

Eliade, M. (1993). Domestic observances. In M Eliade (Ed.), *The Encyclopedia of Religion* (Vol. 5, pp. 400–417). New York: Macmillan.

Ellison, C. G. (1994). Religion, the life stress paradigm, and the study of depression. In J. S. Levin (Ed.), *Religion in aging and health.* Thousand Oaks, CA: Sage.

Ellison, C. G., & Anderson, K. L. (2001). Religious involvement and domestic violence among U.S. couples. *Journal for the Scientific Study of Religion, 40,* 269–286.

Ellison, C. G., Bartkowski, J. P., & Anderson, K. L. (1999). Are there religious variations in domestic violence? *Journal of Family Issues, 20,* 87–113.

Ellison, C. G., Bartkowski, J. P., & Segal, M. L. (1996a). Conservative Protestantism and the parental use of corporal punishment. *Social Forces, 74,* 1003–1028.

Ellison, C. G., Bartkowski, J. P., & Segal, M. L. (1996b). Do conservative Protestant parents spank more often? Further evidence from the National Survey of Families and Households. *Social Science Quarterly, 77,* 663–673.

Ellison, C. G., & Levin, J. S. (1998). The religion-health connection: Evidence, theory, and future directions. *Health Education and Behavior, 25(6),* 700–720.

Fiese, B. H., & Tomcho, T. J. (2001). Finding meaning in religious practices: The relation between religious holiday rituals and marital satisfaction. *Journal of Family Psychology, 15,* 597–609.

Flor, D. L., & Knapp, N. F. (2001). Transmission and transaction: Predicting adolescents' internalization of parental religious values. *Journal of Family Psychology, 15,* 627–645.

Francoeur, R. T. (1983). Religious reactions to alternative lifestyles. In E. D. Macklin & R. H. Rubin (Eds.), *Contemporary families and alternative lifestyles.* Thousand Oaks, CA: Sage.

Gallagher, B. (1987). *The sociology of mental illness* (2nd ed.). Upper Saddle River, NJ: Prentice Hall.

Gallup, G., Jr., & Castelli, J. (1989). *The people's religion.* New York: Macmillan.

Garland, D. R. (2002). Faith narratives of congregants and their families. *Review of Religious Research, 44,* 68–92.

Gordis, R. (1991). Homosexuality is not on a par with heterosexual relations. In R. T. Francoeur (Ed.), *Taking sides* (pp. 45–52). Guilford, CT: Duskin.

Griffith, R. M. (1997). *God's daughters.* Berkeley: University of California Press.

Gruner, L. (1985). The correlation of private, religious devotional practices and marital adjustment. *Journal of Comparative Family Studies, 16,* 47–59.

Gunnoe, M. L., Hetherington, E. M., & Reiss, D. (1999). Parental religiosity, parenting style, and adolescent social responsibility. *Journal of Early Adolescence, 19,* 199–225.

Hart, C. H., Newell, L. D., & Olsen, S. F. (2003). Parenting skills and social-communicative competence in childhood. In J. O. Greene & B. R. Burleson (Eds.), *Handbook of communication and social interaction skills* (pp. 753–800). Mahwah, NJ: Lawrence Erlbaum.

Hathaway-Clark, C. (1980, April). *Multidimensional locus of control in battered women.* Paper presented at the Convention of the Rocky Mountain Psychological Association, Tucson, AZ.

Heaton, T. B., & Pratt, E. L. (1990). The effects of religious homogamy on marital satisfaction and stability. *Journal of Family Issues, 11,* 191–207.

Hill, P. C., & Hood, R. W., Jr. (Ed.). (1999). *Measures of religiosity*. Birmingham, AL: Religious Education.

Holden, G. W. (2001). Psychology, religion, and the family: It's time for a revival. *Journal of Family Psychology, 15*, 657–662.

Hope, D. (1987). The healing paradox of forgiveness. *Psychotherapy, 24*, 240–244.

Houseknecht, S. K., & Pankhurst, J. G. (Eds.). (2000). *Family, religion, and social change in diverse societies*. New York: Oxford University Press.

Kaufman, D. R. (1993). *Rachel's daughters*. New Brunswick, NJ: Rutgers University Press.

Kennedy, P., & Whitlock, M. L. (1997). Therapeutic implications of conservative clergy views on sexuality: An empirical analysis. *Journal of Sex and Marital Therapy, 23*(2), 140–153.

Koenig, H. G., McCullough, M. E., & Larson, D. B. (Eds.). (2001). *Handbook of religion and health*. New York: Oxford University Press.

Latshaw, J. S. (1998). The centrality of faith in fathers' role construction: The faithful father and the axis mundi paradigm. *Journal of Men s Studies, 7*, 53–70.

Laumann, E. O., Gagnon, J. H., Michael, R. T., & Michaels, S. (1994). *The social organization of sexuality: Sex practices in the United States*. Chicago: University of Chicago Press.

Lawton, L. E., & Bures, R. (2001). Parental divorce and the "switching" of religious identity. *Journal for the Scientific Study of Religion, 40*, 99–111.

Laythe, B., Finkle, D. G., Bringle, R. G., & Kirkpatrick, L. A. (2002). Religious fundamentalism as a predictor of prejudice: A two-component model. *Journal for the Scientific Study of Religion, 41*, 623–635.

Lee, J. W., Rice, G. T., & Gillespie, V. B. (1997). Family worship patterns and their correlation with adolescent behavior and beliefs. *Journal for the Scientific Study of Religion, 36*, 372–381.

Lehrer, E. L., & Chiswick, C.U. (1993). Religion as a determinant of marital stability. *Demography, 30*, 385–403.

Levin, J. S., Markides, K. S., & Ray, L. A. (1996). Religious attendance and psychological well-being in Mexican Americans: A panel analysis of three-generations data. *Gerontologist, 36*, 454–463.

Linder, E. W. (Ed.). (2003). *The yearbook of American and Canadian churches* (71st ed.). New York: National Council of Churches in the USA.

Lupfer, M. B., Hopkinson, P. L., & Kelley, P. (1988). An exploration of the attributional styles of Christian fundamentalists and of authoritarians. *Journal for the Scientific Study of Religion, 27*, 389–398.

Madsen, T. G., Lawrence, K., & Christiansen, S. L. (2000). The centrality of family across world faiths. In D. C. Dollahite (Ed.), *Strengthening our families* (pp. 370–381). Salt Lake City, UT: Bookcraft.

Mahoney, A., Pargament, K. I., Jewell, T., Swank, A.B., Scott, E., Emery, E., et al. (1999). Marriage and the spiritual realm: The role of proximal and distal religious constructs in marital functioning. *Journal of Family Psychology, 13*, 321–338.

Mahoney, A., Pargament, K. I., Murray-Swank, A., & Murray-Swank, N. (2003). Religion and the sanctification of family relationships. *Review of Religious Research, 44*, 220–236.

Mahoney, A., Pargament, K. I., Tarakeshwar, N., & Swank, A. B. (2001). Religion in the home in the 1980s and 90s: A meta-analytic review and conceptual analyses of links between religion, marriage and parenting. *Journal of Family Psychology, 15*, 559–596.

Marciano, T. D. (1987). Families and religions. In M. B. Sussman & S. K. Steinmetz (Eds.), *Handbook of marriage and the family* (pp. 285–316). New York: Plenum.

Marks, L. D., & Dollahite, D. C. (2001). Religion, relationships, and responsible fathering in Latter-day Saint families of children with special needs. *Journal of Social and Personal Relationships, 18,* 625–650.

Masters, K. S., & Bergin, A. E. (1992). Religious orientation and mental health. In J. F. Schumaker (Ed.), *Religion and mental health* (pp. 221–232). New York: Oxford University Press.

Masters, W. H., & Johnson, V. (1970). *Human sexual inadequacy.* Boston: Little, Brown.

McAdoo, H. P. (1995). Stress levels, family help patterns, and religiosity in middle- and working-class African American single mothers. *Journal of Black Psychology, 21,* 424–449.

McCullough, M. E., Hoyt, W. T., Larson, D. B., Koenig, H. G., & Thoresen, C. E. (2000). Religious involvement and mortality: A meta-analytic review. *Health Psychology, 19,* 211–222.

McCullough, M., & Worthington, E. (1994). Encouraging clients to forgive people who have hurt them: Review, critique, and research prospectus. *Journal of Psychology and Theology, 22,* 3–20.

Melton, J. G. (2003). *Encyclopedia of American religions* (7th ed.). Farmington Hill, MI: Gale.

Mosher, W. D., Williams, L. B., & Johnson, D. P. (1992). Religion and fertility in the United States: New patterns. *Demography, 29,* 199–214.

Musick, M. A. (2000). Theodicy and life satisfaction among Black and White Americans. *Sociology of Religion, 61,* 267–287.

Palkovitz, R. (2002). *Involved fathering and men's adult development.* Hillsdale, NJ: Lawrence Erlbaum.

Palkovitz, R., Marks, L. D., Appleby, D. W., & Holmes, E. K. (2003). Parenting and adult development: Contexts, processes and products of intergenerational relationships. In L. Kucynski (Ed.), *The handbook of dynamics in parent-child relationships* (pp. 307–323). Thousand Oaks, CA: Sage.

Pankhurst, J. G., & Houseknecht, S. K. (2000). Introduction: The religion–family linkage and social change: A neglected area of study. In S. K. Houseknecht & J. G. Pankhurst (Eds.), *Family, religion, and social change in diverse societies* (pp. 1–40). New York: Oxford University Press.

Pargament, K. I. (1997). *The psychology of religion and coping.* New York: Guilford.

Pargament, K. I., Smith, B., Koenig, H., & Perez, L. (1998). Patterns of positive and negative religious coping with major life stressors. *Journal for the Scientific Study of Religion, 37,* 711–725.

Parke, R. D. (2001). Introduction to the special section on families and religion: A call for a recommitment by researchers, practitioners, and policymakers. *Journal of Family Psychology, 15,* 555–558.

Peterson, J. A. (1964). *Education for marriage* (2nd ed.). New York: Scribner's.

Poloma, M. M., & Pendleton, B. F. (1991). The effects of prayer and prayer experiences on measures of general well-being. *Journal of Psychology and Theology, 19,* 71–83.

Robinson, L. C. (1994). Religious orientation in enduring marriage: An exploratory study. *Review of Religious Research, 35,* 207–218.

Runkel, G. (1998). Sexual morality of Christianity. *Journal of Sex and Marital Therapy, 24,* 103–122.

Satlow, M. L. (1998). One who loves his wife like himself: Love in rabbinic marriage. *Journal of Jewish Studies, 49,* 67–86.

Schlossberger, E. S., & Hecker, L. L. (1998). Reflections of Jewishness and its implications for family therapy. *American Journal of Family Therapy, 26,* 129–146.

Sells, J. N., & Hargrave, T. D. (1998). Forgiveness: A review of the theoretical and empirical literature. *Journal of Marital and Family Therapy, 20,* 21–36.

Sherif, B. (1999). The prayer of a married man is equal to seventy prayers of a single man. *Journal of Family Issues, 20,* 617–632.

Sherkat, D. E. (2002). Sexuality and religious commitment in the United States: An empirical examination. *Journal for the Scientific Study of Religion, 41,* 313–323.

Sherkat, D., & Ellison, C. G. (1999). Recent developments and current controversies in the sociology of religion. *Annual Review of Sociology, 25,* 363–394.

Simpson, W. S., & Ramberg, J. A. (1992). The influence of religion on sexuality: Implications for sex therapy. *Bulletin of the Menninger Clinic, 56,* 511–523.

Snarey, J. (1993). *How fathers care for the next generation.* Cambridge, MA: Harvard University Press.

Snarey, J. R., & Dollahite, D. C. (2001). Varieties of religion-family linkages. *Journal of Family Psychology, 15,* 646–651.

Sorenson, A. M., Grindstaff, C. F., & Turner, R. J. (1995). Religious involvement among unmarried adolescent mothers: A source of emotional support? *Sociology of Religion, 56,* 71–81.

Stacey, J. (1990). *Brave new families.* New York: Basic Books.

Stark, R., & Bainbridge, W. S. (1996). *A theory of religion.* New Brunswick, NJ: Rutgers University Press.

Stark, R., & Finke, R. (2000). *Acts of faith.* Berkeley: University of California Press.

Strawbridge, W. J., Cohen, R., Shema, S., & Kaplan, G. (1997). Frequent attendance at religious services and mortality over 28 years. *American Journal of Public Health, 87,* 957–961.

Strawbridge, W. J., Shema, S. J., Cohen, R. D., Roberts, R. E., & Kaplan, G. A. (1998). Religiosity buffers effects of some stressors on depression but exacerbates others. *Journal of Gerontology, 53B*(3), S118–S126.

Sullivan, K. T. (2001). Understanding the relationship between religiosity and marriage: An investigation of the immediate and longitudinal effect of religiosity on newlywed couples. *Journal of Family Psychology, 15,* 610–626.

Taylor, R. J., & Chatters, L. M. (1988). Church members as a source of informal social support. *Review of Religious Research, 30,* 193–202.

Thomas, D. (Ed.). (1988). *The religion and family connection: Social science perspectives* (Specialized Monograph Series No. 3). Provo, UT: Brigham Young University, Religious Studies Center.

Thomas, D. L., & Cornwall, M. (1990). Religion and family in the 1980s: Discovery and development. *Journal of Marriage and the Family, 52,* 983–992.

Thomas, D. L., & Sommerfeldt, V. (1984). Religion, family, and the social sciences: A time for dialogue. *Family Perspective, 18,* 117–125.

Thornton, A. (1985). Reciprocal influences of family and religion in a changing world. *Journal of Marriage and the Family, 47,* 381–394.

U.S. Bureau of the Census. (2001). *Statistical abstract of the United States: 2001* (121st ed.). Washington, DC: Government Printing Office.

Westoff, C. F., Potter, R. G., & Sagi, P. C. (1964). Some selected findings of the Princeton Fertility Study: 1963. *Demography, 1,* 130–135.

Wilcox, W. B. (1998). Conservative Protestant childrearing: Authoritarian or authoritative? *American Sociological Review, 63,* 796–809.

Wilcox, W. B. (2002). Religion, convention, and parental involvement. *Journal of Marriage and Family, 64,* 780–792.

Wilson, J., & Musick, M. (1996). Religion and marital dependence. *Journal for the Scientific Study of Religion, 35,* 30–40.

Wilson, J., Parnell, A. M., & Pagnini, D. L. (1997). Religious fundamentalism and family behavior. *Research in the Social Scientific Study of Religion, 8,* 163–191.

Worthington, E. L., & DiBlasio, F. A. (1990). Promoting mutual forgiveness within the fractured relationship. *Psychotherapy, 27,* 219–223.

Zhou, M., & Bankston, C. L. (1998). *Growing up American.* New York: Russell Sage.

CHAPTER 25

Family Law for Changing Families in the New Millennium

MARY ANN MASON, MARK A. FINE,
AND SARAH CARNOCHAN

Marriage and family have historically played an important role in U.S. society. According to one judge in a 1939 divorce case, "[O]ne of the foundation pillars of our government is the sanctity of the marriage relation and the influences of the home life, where the holy bond of wedlock is looked upon with profound reverence and respect, and where the marriage vows are sedulously observed" (*Fania v. Fania,* 1939, p. 373). Marriage remains a cherished institution; 93% of Americans rate a happy marriage as one of their most important life goals (Gallagher & Waite, 2000). However, Americans are marrying less often and for shorter periods (Nagourney, 2000). In the last part of the 20th century, family law has focused on redefining the legal institution of marriage and, at the same time, recognizing other family and child-rearing forms.

Although there is not a consensual definition, for the purposes of this chapter, family law is defined as the branch of law that addresses issues pertaining to romantically involved partners (e.g., marriage, divorce, domestic partnerships) and children (e.g., child custody following divorce, assisted reproduction, adoption). Changes in family law have typically lagged behind societal changes; the law struggles to come to terms with new social realities (e.g., domestic partnerships, unwed fathers, and alternative reproduction) by either incorporating or reacting against those changes. However, in some instances, such as no-fault divorce statutes, changes in the law have served to facilitate social change. Finally, some family issues of great social importance are virtually neglected in family law—most strikingly, the role of stepparents.

Most issues in family law are decided state by state. Therefore, wide variations exist among states in fundamental issues, such as the division of property following divorce.

AUTHORS' NOTE: The authors acknowledge the assistance of Nicole Zayac with this chapter.

Nonetheless, it is possible to recognize trends that cross all, or most, state lines. Although several federal laws have had substantial impacts, family law remains solidly within states' jurisdiction.

Another part of the revolution in family law is the role played by the social sciences. Both legal rhetoric and judicial reasoning have been greatly influenced in some parts of family law by professionals in mental health and related social science disciplines. Judges often refer to research in their opinions regarding the best interests of the child, and mental health experts are routinely called upon in familial disputes. Still, the application of the social sciences is uneven and uncertain, and there are many areas in which research is routinely ignored or manipulated.

TRENDS IN FAMILY LAW

Marriage

Though marriage remains a central cultural paradigm, substantial changes have occurred in marriage as a legal institution over the past 30 years. During most of U.S. history, a married couple was regarded as having a single legal identity. Although married women made significant progress in the 19th century in obtaining the right to own and manage their own property through the passage of property legislation, women were still largely considered dependents of their husbands. Husbands were responsible for their families' financial well-being, and women who worked were eligible for lesser benefits than their male counterparts on the basis of the assumption that they were not the household's primary wage earner. Prenuptial agreements were not honored by the courts, and the obligations at divorce differed for men and women—only women could receive alimony. Debts incurred by women were their husbands' responsibility, but women had no corresponding responsibility for their husbands' debts (Regan, 1999). Moreover, there was no tort liability between spouses, spouses could not testify against one another in court, and police were hesitant to intervene in cases of domestic violence. For example, in *Ennis v. Donovan* (1960), a Maryland court held that "a married woman had no common-law right to sue her husband for injuries suffered by her as the result of his negligence, and, the Legislature has not yet seen fit to grant her such a right" (p. 543). Despite changes in women's position throughout the last century, the rhetoric of a unitary spousal identity—"husband and wife as 'a single person, represented by the husband.'"—remained in judicial discourse into the 1970s (*Lewis v. Lewis*, 1976).

In the last three decades of the 20th century, this paradigm of dependence shifted toward a partnership model in which marriage is more like a contractual relationship between two individuals. Under the new model, a husband and wife are considered equal partners contracting in a marriage, and both retain an independent legal existence. The current law relating to marriage views "the marital relationship as one constituted by personal choice, the natural character of which is rooted in the desire of individuals to seek happiness through intimate association with another" (Regan, 1999, p. 652). With this shift, the nature of marriage has undergone a fundamental alteration. Spouses now hold mutual rights and responsibilities with respect to one another (*Queen's Medical Center v. Kagawa*, 1998). The presumption that the husband is the breadwinner and the wife the homemaker has been replaced with the partnership concept. Spouses are now perceived as creating their own marital roles. This perception led courts to uphold and enforce the validity of prenuptial agreements upon divorce (*McHugh v. McHugh*, 1980). Under the partnership model, these agreements presumably do not weaken marriage by making divorce more desirable; they secure the rights of the individuals entering marriage against future disputes. Support obligations and responsibility for a spouse's debts are now placed equally on men and women, and contributions that women outside the workforce make to the family are gaining recognition.

The push for equal treatment between men and women in marriage, and ultimately in divorce and child custody, was driven primarily by the movement to obtain equal rights for women (Mason, 1988). In addition to the recognition of the contributions that women make to a marriage, this feminist attentiveness has resulted in an increasing awareness that women often suffer when there are marital problems. As a result, law enforcement and the courts are now more likely to intervene when there are problems within a marriage. Domestic violence and marital rape are given more attention, and men and women now have the right to decide whether they will testify against their spouses in federal court (*Trammel v. United States*, 1980). Moreover, tort liability between spouses now exists in most states, albeit at a higher standard than between legal strangers (*Lewis v. Lewis*, 1976). These changes reflect recognition that legal institutions have a role to play in enforcing the rights and responsibilities created by marriage, while also respecting the independent identity of each spouse.

Changes in reproductive laws also have affected the spousal relationship. U.S. Supreme Court decisions such as *Roe v. Wade* (1973) have given women more reproductive choices and have empowered them to make those choices independent of their husbands. Though married women could take few actions fully independent of their husbands under the dependent marriage model, under the partnership model women can make important reproductive decisions (e.g., to have an abortion) independently, even

against their husbands' objections. This change reflects the increasing recognition of each spouse's independent identity and rights within marriage.

Divorce

The shift to a partnership model of marriage was accompanied by a change in how the partnership could be dissolved. The last 30 years ushered in what has been termed a divorce revolution. Drastic changes in divorce law rendered divorce a unilateral decision not based on fault. This made divorce far easier to obtain and in most states created a fundamentally different framework for the distribution of property and the allocation of support following divorce. Following the lead of California's revolutionary Family Law Act of 1969, all states by 1985 offered some form of no-fault divorce (Krause, 1986). In some states, one party had only to complain that the marriage had reached a point of "irretrievable breakdown" with no requirement of proof; in other states, "incompatibility" or "irreconcilable differences" had to be demonstrated if one party objected, but if one partner chose to live separately for a period of time, that was also seen as proof of marital breakdown. There are debates about how much changes in divorce law contributed to rising divorce rates; some claim the rise was an extension of earlier increases that were temporarily reversed in the 1950s. Regardless of the reasons for the increase, demographic trends clearly reveal that the divorce rate doubled between 1966 and 1976. By the 1980s, it was predicted that half of all marriages would end in divorce (Cherlin, 1992).

The basic assumption underlying the changes in divorce and custody law was that men and women should be treated equally before the law. This was a sharp departure from the beliefs in the era of dependent marriage and fault-based divorce. Family law had then perhaps favored women (and children) by making divorce hard to obtain and by allowing extended support for wives and children after divorce, in the belief that wives were less able to take care of themselves economically than were husbands. A maternal presumption in custody, established by the early 20th century, also favored mothers, reflecting beliefs that they were more nurturing than fathers.

The assumption that men and women should be treated equally had serious consequences for the distribution of property and for alimony. Traditionally, unless the woman was at fault, alimony, or spousal support, was routinely granted for life in most states, but collection and enforcement rates were low. As divorce law changed to reflect the equality of partners, the concept of alimony came under negative scrutiny. The Uniform Marriage and Divorce Act of 2002 (UMDA) moved that alimony only be used when the spouse could not take care of herself and that fault in the divorce should not be a consideration. Fault also was deemed an inappropriate consideration in determining property division. UMDA did, however, pursue a substantial change, allowing women to have a claim to the equitable distribution of property in common-law states where the person who held title, typically the husband, was usually granted the property.

Only women with children still had the expectation of support, through child support, and even here the amounts were generally low and the majority not collected. In 1975, the Federal Office of Child Support Enforcement was created, with state agency counterparts, to increase child support collection. Subsequently, the Family Support Act of 1988 set stricter standards for state child support enforcement, resulting in increased enforcement among the Aid to Families with Dependent Children (AFDC) population. States are also now required to maintain federal locator services and to enforce sister states' judgments. The Child Support Recovery Act of 1992 criminalized a parent's failure to pay court-ordered child support when the parent and child live in different states. Despite these and other federal efforts to improve compliance with and enforcement of child support orders, the rate of collection remains low in most states (Mason, 2000).

The shift toward easy-to-obtain divorce has not gone unchallenged. One aspect of the backlash against it is the recent passage of "covenant marriage" statutes (Louisiana Act 1380, 1977; Ariz. Rev. Stat. Ann. § 25-901-906 [West, 1998]). These laws allow couples to enter into a marriage that can be ended only on statutorily specified grounds. Proponents argue that covenant marriage increases respect for marriage as an institution and will reduce the divorce rate. Supporters of covenant marriage also believe "that no-fault divorce is responsible for the high divorce rate and for other societal problems that are correlated with divorce and single-parent homes" (Pearson, 1999, p. 633). Opponents claim that these statutes are both too restrictive (they may trap an individual in a bad marriage) and not restrictive enough (they are voluntarily entered and may be invalidated with the consent of both spouses). At their strongest, statutory covenant marriages eliminate only one aspect of the no-fault divorce statutes: In the absence of wrongdoing, one spouse in a covenant marriage cannot unilaterally demand and be granted a divorce (Wardle, 1999).

Child Custody

Whereas in previous eras child custody issues ordinarily involved orphans or children of parents who could not care for them, in the modern era the majority of child custody matters are the product of divorce. Although under the jurisdiction of courts, most child custody determinations are made by the parties rather than by a judge at trial (Mason, 1994). In the wake of radical divorce reforms, the number of child custody cases has greatly increased, and the substantive rules that the courts use to determine custody have shifted drastically. This shift has followed and reflected the new emphasis on egalitarian marriage.

"The simple fact of being a mother does not, by itself, indicate a capacity or willingness to render a quality of care different from that which the father can provide" (*State ex rel. Watts v. Watts*, 1973). With this statement, a New York court challenged nearly a century of a judicial presumption in favor of mothers. Not all courts were as outspoken in reducing the importance of mothers; nevertheless, the presumption that the interest of a child of tender years is best served in the custody of the mother was legally abolished or demoted to a "factor to be considered" in nearly all states between 1960 and 1990. By 1982, only seven states gave mothers a custody preference over fathers for children of tender years (Atkinson, 1984). Rather, most states mandate that custody decisions be based on a consideration of the "best interests of the child," a standard that is far less clear and specific than the maternal preference standard. In an attempt to address this ambiguity, state legislatures drafted statutes to direct judges left with the task of applying the elusive "best interests" standard. Most legislatures also suggested joint custody as an alternative to awarding custody to one parent, giving fathers as much time with children as mothers, and thereby avoiding the problem of having to choose between legally equal parents. Some states adopted a primary caretaker preference, providing custody to the parent who spent the most time with the child (Mason, 1994).

California led the way in custody initiatives, as it had in no-fault divorce, by introducing a preference for joint legal custody in 1980. By 1988, 36 states had followed California's lead. Legislatures, and sometimes courts, produced several variations on the joint custody theme. Joint physical custody dictated that parents should share their time with the child as equally as possible. Joint legal custody, on the other hand, allowed a more traditional sole custody arrangement with visitation for the noncustodial parent. Both parents retained equal input into decisions affecting the child, such as choosing medical treatment and schools. By the end of the century, joint legal and physical custody was the preference in most states (Mason, 2000).

Remarriage and Stepfamilies

Because most partners who divorce eventually remarry, the dramatic increase in divorce resulted in a steep rise in the number of stepfamilies (Seltzer, 1994). Although changes in law and practice relating to marriage and divorce have led to more stepfamilies, little has changed with respect to the legal status of stepparents. Stepparents who do not adopt their stepchildren remain in an ambiguous role with no legal identity (Mahoney, 1994). Their rights and duties toward their stepchildren are largely undefined, and, when they are defined, a consistent understanding of their role in the family is not reflected (Mason, 1998). The American Law Institute (2000) addressed some of the legal issues surrounding stepfamilies by defining de facto parents and parents by estoppel (i.e., individuals who are considered parents because they have presented themselves as parents and because it would be inequitable for them to later deny that role) and allowing them to petition for custody of children at divorce. Many stepparents would meet the requirements of these rules. However, even this measure is limited in its applicability because it only indirectly defines stepparent rights and responsibilities to stepchildren during marriage. For example, stepparents are often unable to consent to medical treatment or sign a school permission slip for their stepchildren (*State v. Miranda*, 1997). Generally, stepparents do not have a legal obligation to support their stepchildren, and those who take on such an obligation by acting in loco parentis (i.e., "in the place of the parent") do so voluntarily and may end their obligation unilaterally at any time (*Niesen v. Niesen*, 1968). Nonetheless, some federal and state welfare programs take a stepparent's income into account when determining a child's eligibility, whereas others do not.

Stepchildren face legal obstacles in most states that prevent them from filing wrongful death suits on behalf of their stepparents or inheriting when a stepparent dies intestate (i.e., without a will) (*Champagne v. Mcdermott, Inc.*, 1992). Despite the confusion that this ambiguity may cause for families, courts and legislatures have been hesitant to address the problem and define a legal role for stepparents. Thus, the changes that are occurring in the law relating to stepparent relationships come slowly and indirectly through changes designed to benefit others. For example, some stepparents are having success in obtaining visitation with their stepchildren following divorce. To a large extent, this success results from states' general third-party visitation statutes, which allow stepparents (and others) to petition for visitation when there is disruption in the family but do not create for stepparents the presumptive right to visitation that exists for biological parents.

Unwed Fathers

Through much of the 20th century, unwed fathers were largely invisible in family law. In the last 25 to 30 years, however, as the number of children born to unmarried parents has risen (McLanahan & Sandefur, 1994), substantial changes have occurred

with regard to the legal consequences of "illegitimacy" and the paternity, custody, and child support rights and obligations of unwed fathers. It is difficult to determine the precise number of unwed fathers: They are frequently not listed on birth certificates and, when not involved in the child's life, do not come into contact with the agencies that maintain data on families (Blank, 1997). However, the increase in unwed mothers over the last 30 years has clearly been accompanied by an increase in the number of unwed fathers. A number of high-profile cases have involved unmarried fathers seeking custody of their children, but these fathers as a group do not play a consistent parenting role for their children. Lerman (1993) estimated the number of unwed fathers who were not supporting their children at 1.6 million. Still, the rights and obligations of unwed fathers are increasingly recognized and enforced.

Beginning in the late 1960s, courts and state legislatures began offering rights and protections to "illegitimate" children comparable to those of "legitimate" children (Sugarman, 1998). As the rights of illegitimate children began to be recognized, so did the rights and obligations of their fathers. Under the Uniform Parentage Act, based upon common-law tradition and adopted in numerous states, the husband of the child's mother is presumed to be the father. Historically, this presumption has barred an unwed father from claiming paternity in order to preserve intact families, protect the child, and ensure child support. The U.S. Supreme Court affirmed this presumption as recently as 1989, ruling that the biological unwed father's interest did not outweigh the state's interest in preserving an intact family (*Michael H. v. Gerald D.*, 1989). However, numerous state courts and legislatures have overridden the presumption, granting unwed fathers the right to claim paternity even when the mother is married to someone else. For example, the California Supreme Court has granted an unwed father the right to establish paternity, arguing that the child was conceived before the mother married (Mason, 2000).

With the increasing recognition of an unwed father's right to claim paternity, courts and legislatures have begun to recognize rights in custody disputes and cases in which the mother has decided to relinquish the child for adoption. In *Stanley v. Illinois* (1971), the U.S. Supreme Court first recognized the custodial rights of an unwed father, ruling that an unwed father who had acted as a parent was entitled to a fitness hearing after the mother's death, before the children were made wards of the court. However, the custody rights of an unwed father are not automatic. In subsequent decisions, the U.S. Supreme Court has ruled that the biological link of an unwed father may be insufficient to confer rights and has required that he act as a father and participate in child rearing (*Caban v. Mohammed*, 1979; *Lehr v. Robertson*, 1983). State courts, however, have granted unmarried fathers rights comparable to those of married fathers (Mason, 2000).

Recently, in *In re Nicholas H.* (2002), the California Supreme Court allowed an unwed, nonbiological father to claim paternity, giving weight to the established paternal relationship between the man and the child. The court held that the statutory presumption that a man who "receives a child into his home and openly holds the child out as his own" has a claim to paternity was not negated by the fact that the presumed father was not the biological father.

Finally, as the number of children living in single-parent households has increased, policy initiatives in the last quarter-century have focused on enforcing child support obligations. In 1985, only about 13% of never-married mothers reported receiving support from the fathers of their children (Lerman,

1993). In 1975, the Federal Office of Child Support Enforcement was created, with state agency counterparts, to increase child support collection. Subsequently, the Family Support Act of 1988 set stricter standards for state child support enforcement, resulting in increased enforcement among the AFDC population. Despite enforcement efforts, the frequency and amount of child support awards and payments remain low (Mason, 2000). However, welfare reform, with time-limited benefits for parents to receive aid, has made the enforcement of child support a critical issue. As pressure grows to collect child support from both unmarried and formerly married fathers, remaining legal distinctions between them are likely to disappear.

Third-Party Visitation

Unwed fathers are not the only group that has won increased protection of their interests in maintaining a relationship with a child. As a result of the loosening hold of marriage, any number of adults, related and unrelated, are raising children with little or no legal backing. State legislatures and a number of courts have begun to recognize the roles of these multiple parties by expanding visitation rights to individuals other than parents. Third-party visitation statutes have been enacted in all states, granting a right to petition for visitation to certain categories of petitioners that may include stepparents, grandparents (upon the death or divorce of their child), unmarried parents, or, in the broadest conception, any interested party (Elrod, Spector, & Atkinson, 1999). These statutes usually grant such rights because of family disruption, although some statutes are broadly worded to allow third-party visitation petitions any time.

Third-party visitation statutes have been challenged on constitutional grounds in a number of states with varied results. The state of Washington enacted one of the broadest statutes, allowing any person to petition for visitation at any time and authorizing courts to grant visitation on a showing of best interest. In *Troxel v. Granville* (2000), one of the few examples of U.S. Supreme Court intervention in a visitation dispute, the mother and unmarried father had two children before the father died. The paternal grandparents sought more extensive visitation than the mother desired and prevailed in the trial court. The state Supreme Court overruled the lower court, holding that the statute unconstitutionally infringed upon parents' fundamental right to raise their children. The U.S. Supreme Court upheld this decision on the grounds that the statute was too broad and gave no weight to the parents' judgment regarding the children's best interest (for a recent case that looked to the *Troxel* decision, see *Wickham v. Burne*, 2002). The court refrained from deciding whether all third-party statutes require a showing of harm or potential harm if visitation is not awarded as a condition of granting visitation.

In contrast, a number of state courts have upheld third-party visitation statutes against constitutional challenges. For example, in *West v. West* (1998), the appellate court ruled that the Illinois statute did not violate the "long-recognized constitutionally protected interest of parents to raise their children without undue State influence" and affirmed the state's interest in maintaining relationships found to be in the child's best interest. In *Williams v. Williams* (1998), the court upheld Virginia's law, interpreting it to require a finding of harm if visitation is not granted. In a contrary holding, the Georgia Supreme Court found the state's grandparent visitation statute to be unconstitutional on the grounds that it did not clearly promote the welfare of the child and did not require a showing of harm (*Brooks v. Parkerson*, 1995). It is likely that the decisions affirming third-party visitation statutes will stand (*Troxel v. Granville*, 2000).

Nontraditional Partnerships

While the number of single-parent households has increased, in a trend that has been well documented and has received considerable attention from policy makers and researchers, there has been a simultaneous increase in nontraditional or nonmarital partnerships, including cohabitation, same-sex marriage, and domestic partnerships. These nontraditional relationship forms raise legal issues relating to property division and support obligations following termination of the relationship, access to the legal benefits conferred on spouses, and parental rights issues such as custody, visitation, and second-parent adoption (i.e., the partner who is the nonbiological parent adopts the child).

Perhaps the most well-known case dealing with the rights of cohabiting partners is *Marvin v. Marvin* (1976), in which the California Supreme Court allowed the woman to sue her male partner on contractual grounds for compensation following termination of the relationship. The court held that when there is an explicit or implied contract between mutually assenting individuals in a nonmarital relationship, a court may use principles of equity to divide property at the termination of the relationship. Such a reading of a cohabitation relationship reflects a partnership rather than a dependency model. Subsequent decisions in other states have been more restrictive, however, requiring proof of a contract of cohabitation and refusing to enforce agreements based upon sexual obligations or promises. Recently, a Massachusetts court upheld the validity of a written cohabitation agreement (*Wilcox v. Trautz*, 1998). But although a contractually based right to compensation may be recognized by the courts, cohabitation does not entitle participants to other benefits of marriage, such as social security benefits (Katz, 1999).

The issue of same-sex marriage has been far more controversial than the rights of cohabiting heterosexual couples. In the early 1970s, several cases challenging state marriage laws were rejected (Chambers & Polikoff, 1999). In the early 1990s, the issue gained national prominence when the Hawaiian Supreme Court set forth a presumption that the legislative ban on same-sex marriage violated the state's constitutional provision granting equal protection and barring sex-based discrimination (*Baehr v. Lewin*, 1993). Legislative responses to the decision have been almost uniformly negative. Hawaii passed a constitutional amendment allowing the legislature to limit marriage to heterosexual couples, 29 states had enacted laws barring recognition of same-sex marriage by mid-1999, and the U.S. Congress enacted the Defense of Marriage Act, declaring that states have the right to refuse recognition to same-sex marriages from other states and defining marriage as heterosexual for the purposes of federal law (Chambers & Polikoff, 1999).

Most recently, Vermont passed a civil union statute, taking effect in July 2000, which grants to partners in civil unions, including same-sex partners, the benefits and responsibilities afforded to married couples under state laws (15 Ver. Stat. Ann. § 1201). The legislature acted in response to the Vermont Supreme Court's decision in *Baker v. State of Vermont* (1999), holding that the state is constitutionally required to extend to same-sex couples the benefits and protections afforded to married couples, through inclusion either in the marriage laws or in an equivalent statutory alternative. The Vermont Supreme Court dismissed a challenge to the civil union statute in *Brady v. Dean* (2001); however, it remains to be seen how these unions will be treated by other states or by federal law (Bonauto, 2000). The Vermont civil union statute provides more benefits than the domestic partnership laws, which permit unmarried partners to register their relationships and/or

provide benefits to partners of employees of the city, county, or state enacting the law. Numerous cities and counties have enacted such laws, and, by 1999, Hawaii, New York, Oregon, and Vermont provided partner benefits to employees.

In contrast to the flurry of legislative activity relating to same-sex marriage and domestic partnership, states have for the most part declined to enact statutes regulating the rights of gay and lesbian parents in custody and visitation disputes, leaving the courts to develop the law in this area. Since the first cases arose in the 1970s, courts have ruled both for and against gay and lesbian parents in determining the best interests of the child but have more frequently denied gay and lesbian parents custody of their children. As recently as the late 1990s, state supreme court decisions in the South and Midwest have restricted visitation rights or transferred custody away from a gay or lesbian parent (*Marlow v. Marlow*, 1998; *Pulliam v. Smith*, 1998). Some state legislatures have chosen to act in the area of adoption or foster parenting by gay men or lesbians. The first example was Florida, where a law prohibiting adoption by lesbians and gay men was enacted in 1977 (Fla. Stat. Ann. § 63.042[3], West 1985 and Supp. 1995). The Florida statute was upheld by the U.S. District Court (*Lofton v. Kearney*, 2001). However, in numerous other states, gay men and lesbians have been allowed to adopt, in second-parent adoptions (Chambers & Polikoff, 1999).

Assisted Reproduction

The National Center for Health Statistics (NCHS) reported in 1995 that 6.1 million women between the ages of 15 and 44 experienced an impaired ability to have children; the number of infertile married couples was estimated at 2.1 million. NCHS (1995) further estimated that 9 million women had used infertility services by 1995. The development of medical technologies enabling infertile women and couples to bear children has presented legal and ethical challenges. Perhaps because of the rapidity of the developments, or perhaps due to the complexity of the relationships established by these new techniques, adequate legal and ethical structures or systems to guide participants in assisted reproduction have not been developed. As use of these technologies becomes more prevalent, courts and legislatures will be increasingly pressured to respond. This is already beginning; the National Conference of Commissioners on Uniform State Laws' 1998 Draft Revision of the Uniform Parentage Act includes provisions relating to assisted reproduction. These revisions are in discussion, and it may be years before the project is complete and states can consider adopting it.

Infertility treatment may include relatively uncontroversial procedures such as artificial insemination with a husband's sperm or ovarian stimulation to enhance the chances of conception. Other methods (e.g., *in vitro* fertilization, ovum donation) raise complex legal issues by introducing additional parties contributing genetic material or biological support to the reproductive process or by creating unprecedented decision-making options at each stage of the process. The involvement of a third party in a couple's efforts to create a family is not itself a new event. Donor sperm conception has long been available, as it does not require advanced medical intervention. Similarly, traditional surrogacy, in which a woman agrees to conceive and bear a child for a couple, using the man's sperm, has also been historically available. The increasing range of treatment options, however, creates pressure for the law to respond.

Although the law is underdeveloped in the area of assisted reproduction, we can identify several issues that may require legal resolution. First, the standard in vitro fertilization process using the sperm and eggs of a couple seeking to conceive creates pre-embryos that exist outside of the uterus and can be frozen for an undetermined period. Consequently, disputes over the custody and control of the pre-embryos may arise between the partners, as in *Davis v. Davis* (1992), where the Tennessee Supreme Court ruled that both spouses had a right regarding procreation but that the father's desire not to procreate outweighed the mother's interest in donating the embryos. Second, with ovum donation, the donor may also claim an interest in decisions about the pregnancy, the embryos, or a child born of the process. Finally, with gestational and traditional surrogacy, disputes over decisions regarding pregnancy, embryos, or children may develop among the individuals intending to act as parents, the donors of genetic material, and the surrogate carrying the fetus. In the case of *In the Matter of Baby M.* (1988), the court held that the surrogacy contract was void because it was contrary to public policy. Treating the case as a custody dispute between the biological surrogate mother and the biological father, the court granted custody to the father, with limited visits for the surrogate mother. Claims by donors and surrogates challenge the law to address the interests of parties outside the marital or partnership relationship.

Legislation governing disputes between participants in assisted reproduction is rare, so the courts are playing the most significant role. Judges are relying on varying legal concepts, including property law, contract law, child custody law, and constitutional law (Triber, 1998). The novel concept of intent to parent was articulated in a California Court of Appeals case; the court ruled that individuals who intend to and act to create a child through assisted reproduction technology become legally responsible for the resulting child, even where there is no genetic relationship to the child (*In re Marriage of Buzzanca*, 1998).

Adoption

Although adoption is not a new phenomenon in family law, three trends merit attention: transracial, intercountry, and open adoptions. Intercountry and transracial adoptions are criticized on the grounds that parents whose racial, ethnic, or cultural identity differs from that of their children cannot provide an essential element of parenting in a society where racial and ethnic discrimination exists. Open adoption gives rise to a different controversy: the potential conflict between adopted children who seek information about and possible contact with birth parents and birth parents who may want to maintain anonymity.

The issue of transracial adoption arises primarily in the adoption of children in the foster care system whose parents' rights have been terminated by the state. In 1999, the U.S. Department of Health and Human Services estimated that there were 117,000 children in the foster care system seeking adoption (Mosher & Bachrach, 1996). Of these, 51% were African American, 32% were white, and 11% were Hispanic. The groups most likely to adopt include childless women, women with fecundity impairments, white women, and women with higher levels of income and education. The number of transracial adoptions is unknown, but estimates range from 1% to 11% of all children in foster care (Avery & Mont, 1994; Stolley, 1993). With the majority of foster children ready for adoption being African American, and with white women seeking to adopt more frequently, transracial adoption deserves greater attention.

The federal government has enacted legislation to facilitate transracial adoption in the foster care system. The Howard Metzenbaum Multiethnic Placement Act of 1994 had the stated purpose of preventing discrimination in placement decisions on the basis of race, color, or national origin. In 1996, another federal law repealed and replaced the Multiethnic Placement Act with stronger provisions barring the use of race as a criterion in decisions about foster care or adoption placements (42 U.S.C.S. § 1996b). For those who question "whether white adoptive parents can raise Black children to be well-adjusted productive adults with a positive sense of racial identity," the federal government's promotion of transracial adoption is problematic (Perry, 1999, p. 470). Others may view the federal government's response to the increasing number of African American children awaiting placement as consistent with a broader trend toward interracial marriage and partnerships (U.S. Bureau of the Census, 1999).

Intercountry adoption also raises the question of parental competency when the parents' and the child's race, ethnicity, or culture differ. Over the last 10 years or so, the number of children adopted in the United States from other countries has more than doubled, from 8,102 in 1989 to 20,099 in 2002 (U.S. Department of State, 2002). On October 6, 2000, President Clinton signed the Intercountry Adoption Act, ratifying the Hague Adoption Convention, which is designed to encourage intercountry adoption (U.S. Department of State, 2000).

Open adoption, in which adopted children are provided with information about and, in some cases, the choice to contact birth parents, is another example of society's recognition that families can include more parties than two spouses and their biological children. Even though adopted children may desire information about or a relationship with their birth parents, birth parents may want anonymity. Adoption laws changed from relatively open records to sealed records by the mid-1960s (Cahn & Singer, 1999). In the 1970s, adoptees began challenging sealed adoption records, seeking access to birth certificates through the courts. Rejected by the courts, adoptees pursued legislative remedies with success. Most states now provide nonidentifying information about birth parents and have established procedures for contact when there is mutual consent. The first state laws making original birth records fully accessible passed in 1999, with efforts underway in other states. The Oregon statute was challenged, but the U.S. Supreme Court denied a motion that would have barred it from going into effect (Roseman, 2000).

SOCIAL SCIENCE AND FAMILY LAW

Social scientists have increasingly played a role in legal processes pertaining to families (Mason, 1994), although this increase has been sporadic. This is partly because the relation between social science and law is complex and because many factors must be considered in formulating policy, not just the results of social science research. There is debate about the extent to which social science research has influenced family policy decisions (Bogenschneider, 2000). One reason for the limited influence of social science is that many of the shifts in family law (e.g., divorce reform, third-party visitation rights) were initiated by social forces rather than by research findings. Actually, social science has had more of a role in assessing the consequences of these changes (e.g., child custody decisions after divorce) than in initiating them.

Roles of Social Scientists in the Legal Process

Social scientists' influence on law is often traced to the beginning of the 1900s, when empirical research gradually overtook the reliance on "natural" or "divine" law as informers of legal decision making (Mason, 1994). However, it was not until the last third of the 20th century that social science researchers had an explicit and substantial effect on legal processes in at least three ways: (a) informing public policy and legal reform, (b) developing interventions that were integrated into legal processes, and (c) serving as expert witnesses in court. Because the law tends to be more involved when families are undergoing transitions (e.g., divorce, adoption), the influence of social scientists has been greatest during these periods of change.

Informing Public Policy and Law

In the 1970s, social science theories became particularly influential in child custody after divorce (Mason, 1994). In fact, *theories* have had perhaps as great an impact as research. For example, one of the influential early social scientific works was written by Goldstein, Freud, and Solnit (1973), who introduced the notion of the "psychological parent" as the individual with whom the child is most closely attached and, by extension, the individual who should have complete (and possibly exclusive) custody rights. Although this was a concept rooted in attachment theory rather than in systematic empirical study, Goldstein et al. (1973) presented it as if it were empirically supported. Despite the lack of support, the notion of the psychological parent was frequently used by courts to choose which parent should be granted custody following divorce and/or to defeat a joint custody arrangement (Mason, 1994). It was also influential in justifying gender-neutral child custody decisions after divorce because the psychological parent could be either parent (Mason, 2000).

As findings accumulated, social science *research* was increasingly influential in court decisions. For example, research on the potential benefits of joint custody (Johnston, Kline, & Tschann, 1989) was used to justify policies that made joint custody the preferred custodial arrangement, and research on the well-being of children raised by gay and lesbian couples has informed court decisions regarding adoption rights for gay and lesbian couples (Patterson, 2000).

Research-Informed Interventions

Social scientists have also influenced legal processes affecting families when social science interventions have become part of court proceedings. Two examples are mediation and parent education programs for divorcing parents. Divorce mediation attempts to help spouses negotiate divorce settlements in nonadversarial ways and has become popular, even mandated, in many jurisdictions. The elimination of fault-based divorce laws and a growing sense that the adversarial process leads to long-term negative outcomes contributed to the growth in mediation (Mason, 1994). There is evidence that mediation leads to positive outcomes, including lower relitigation rates, greater compliance with mediated agreements, and high rates of satisfaction with the process (Emery, 1995). But mediation is not without critics. For example, feminists have argued that mediation favors men because men have more power than women and because mediation is based on the assumption that fault should be left out of the process, which advantages men who may have oppressed their wives (e.g., spousal abuse) and/or have benefited from support provided by their wives in their careers (Emery, 1995; Mason, 1994).

Parenting education programs attempt to enable divorcing parents to more effectively help their children cope with the stressful divorce process. Even before the accumulation of data supporting their efficacy, these programs were mandated in almost half of the counties in the United States (Blaisure & Geasler, 1999).

Social Scientists as Expert Witnesses

Social scientists have become more frequent fixtures in legal proceedings as expert witnesses. Although there have been changes in standards used to determine if expert testimony is admissible, the most common one states that, to be admissible, evidence must be based on peer-accepted scientific methods and that the scientific evidence must be directly applicable to the issues in the specific trial (Siegel, 2000).

Social scientists as expert witnesses have probably had their greatest influence in the child custody determination process. As the best-interests-of-the-child criterion replaced maternal preference child custody laws, mental health professionals were called upon to provide evaluations regarding the parent with whom the child should reside. Further, because judges had more discretion than they did under maternal preference laws, they were more likely to call on experts to assist them in their decision making (Mason, 1994).

Limits of Social Science's Influence on the Legal Process

Several factors have contributed to the slow, gradual, and limited influence of social science on legal processes.

Legal Professionals' Not Understanding Social Science Research

Courts, lawyers, and policy makers are not typically sophisticated consumers of social scientific research. They may not understand the limitations of research and may misinterpret the meaning of research findings. Consequently, social scientists must be careful to clarify the limitations of and the appropriate uses of their research and to educate legal and policy experts.

Legal Professionals' Doubts About Social Science Research

Many legal professionals question the validity of social science research. Fueling the skepticism are disagreements among social scientists regarding certain issues (e.g., fathers' importance to children's development, the custody situations in which children fare best), the likelihood that two experts can reach diametrically opposing conclusions regarding the same case, and the tendency among some social scientists to prematurely advance a position in legal venues before it has support in the social scientific community. For example, parental alienation syndrome, which involves a child's becoming estranged from a parent, has recently been used in custody hearings (Warshak, 2000). Although there is abundant research suggesting that children can experience deterioration in the quality of their relationships with parents after divorce, there is no compelling evidence to justify elevating this phenomenon to a *syndrome*. Social scientists who advance untested syndromes and disorders magnify underlying doubts about the integrity of social science research, at least partly because premature pronouncements in court settings inevitably are accompanied by critics of unsupported claims.

Expectations of Clear Findings

Policy makers, lawyers, and judges often take what has been described as a positivist approach to research, in that they expect it to provide clear, unambiguous, and objective answers to questions. However, social science research does not typically lead to unambiguous and unqualified findings. To some extent, social science and the law have opposing foundations. Most social scientists now adopt some variant of a postpositivist approach, which includes the premises that research is not objective and value free, that knowledge is not absolute but is context dependent (i.e., the context in which research is conducted and in which participants live affects findings in known and unknown ways), and that the views of researchers and other outsiders may differ from those of study participants. Thus, there is tension between the legal professionals' desire for absolute and clear answers and most social scientists' disinclination to provide such answers. This tension, and others, has led some to argue that social scientists should limit their involvement in legal proceedings, claiming that social scientific theories and research are sufficiently imprecise that experts, for example, could not accurately determine which parent would best serve the interests of the child (Weithorn & Grisso, 1987).

Research results can be selectively reviewed to advance political or ideological positions. For example, differing value stances affect how researchers (and others) interpret research on the effects of divorce on children and parents (Fine & Demo, 2000). Occasionally, research is misinterpreted to support a particular policy preference (Fine & Fine, 1994). For example, findings suggesting that children's well-being was greater when they were in their mothers' custody than when they were in mandatory joint custody arrangements (Johnston et al., 1989) were misleadingly used to justify the claim that joint custody, whether mandatory or voluntary, was inferior to sole custody for children.

Distinguishing Between Theory and Data

Many legal professionals justify their arguments and decisions by using social science theoretical constructs that make intuitive sense to them. However, many concepts lack empirical evidence and thus can easily be challenged. For example, the claim that children will fare better with their psychological parent can be challenged by the competing claim that children will fare better living with two caring parents actively involved in their lives. Thus, legal reliance on theories to the exclusion of empirical research often contributes to criticisms that social science is soft, inconclusive, and ideological.

Differing Units of Interest

Social science research is generally designed to make generalizations about groups (albeit within the specific contexts in which they live) and tends to place less emphasis on exceptions (some qualitative research is an exception to this). Although policy makers need to base their decisions on soundly derived *group* generalizations, judges need to make decisions in *individual* cases. No matter how well any piece of research has been done or how sound its conclusions are, generalizations do not necessarily fit any specific individual. Therefore, research is necessarily limited in its ability to inform courts.

Differing Time Tables

Social science research takes time to complete. However, there are instances when policy makers and the court cannot afford to wait to make decisions regarding legislation and, perhaps more importantly, individual cases. Thus, decisions need to be made with or without sound research, and social scientists may be tempted to convey greater confidence in preliminary findings or the efficacy of interventions than is warranted.

LOOKING TO THE FUTURE

It is possible to develop optimistic hypotheses about family law in the new millennium.

With regard to marriage, divorce, and nontraditional relationship forms, it seems clear that the partnership model will continue to prevail over the earlier dependence model. The underlying economic and social changes relating to the role of women in society are not likely to be reversed. Alternative relationships, such as those between same-sex couples, will slowly receive recognition as society strives to create structures that support stable relationships in which children can thrive. However, resistance to nontraditional families and relationships will continue to generate legislative responses such as the Defense of Marriage Act and covenant marriage statutes. Child custody laws and laws relating to unwed fathers will continue to promote fathers' parenting role, motivated in part by a desire to impose financial responsibility for child support. Similarly, nonparents will continue to gain access to children with whom they have close relationships, and laws will still struggle to mediate varying interests in stepfamilies.

The legal ambivalence toward gay or lesbian parents should gradually fade if evidence of their children's well-being continues to accumulate. For families created through assisted reproduction technology and for stepfamilies, the courts and legislatures will continue to struggle with the interests of multiple parties. Recent reforms favoring transracial adoption may not endure: The pendulum could swing back in favor of same-race placements as Americans continue to struggle with race relations and racism. However, intercountry adoption seems unlikely to disappear. Individual countries may limit adoptions or make the adoption process more difficult, but economic pressures are likely to prevail.

FUTURE INVOLVEMENT OF SOCIAL SCIENCE IN THE LAW

As in the past century, shifts in family law are likely to be driven by demographic and social changes. Nevertheless, it is likely that social scientists will continue to influence legal processes. The factors that contributed to the increasing role of social science—such as more judicial flexibility, greater legitimacy of social science research, greater likelihood of courts requiring intervention programs, and more need for expert testimony —are likely to continue to expand social scientists' roles in legal proceedings. We support the use of social science research to inform and guide the development of the law. To maximize the extent to which research affects the process of legal reform, social scientists need to appropriately qualify and explain their findings so that professionals not trained in research methods can understand their work. Social scientists may need to educate legal professionals regarding the limits of research and the difficulties inherent in drawing generalizations that apply across contexts. However, it is unlikely that the role of social science will dramatically increase in the next century.

In which areas of family law are social scientists likely to make their greatest contributions? Divorce, remarriage, adoption, and, in general, issues surrounding parenting and parent-child relationships will be in the forefront of social science contributions. For example, issues such as how children's time will be allocated among divorced parents and the effect of parenting plans will be of great interest. In addition, as technologies change how families are formed (e.g., surrogate childbearing), social science research may be helpful in working through the delicate issues related to the roles, rights, and responsibilities of the multiple parties involved in these family processes. Overall, in the future, we can expect a continuing revolution in family law as the ways in which families are formed and maintained continue to evolve. We can also expect that both law and social science will be seriously challenged to keep up with the changes.

REFERENCES

American Law Institute. (2000). *Principles of the law of family dissolution: Analysis and recommendations* (Tentative Draft No. 4). Philadelphia: Author.

Atkinson, J. (1984). Criteria for deciding custody in the trial and appellate courts. *Family Law Quarterly, 18*, 11–32.

Avery, R. J., & Mont, D. M. (1994). *Special needs adoption in New York State: Final report on adoptive parent survey* (DHHS Contract No. 90CW1012). Washington, DC: U.S. Department of Health and Human Services.

Baehr v. Lewin, 852 P.2d 44 (Haw. Sup. Ct. 1993).

Baker v. State of Vermont, 744 A.2d 864 (Ver. Sup. Ct. 1999).

Blaisure, K., & Geasler, M. (1999, July). *Divorce education across the U.S.* Paper presented at the Coalition for Marriage, Family and Couples Education Conference, Washington, DC.

Blank, R. M. (1997). *It takes a nation.* New York: Russell Sage Foundation.

Bogenschneider, K. (2000). Has family policy come of age? A decade review of the state of U.S. family policy in the 1990s. *Journal of Marriage and the Family, 62*, 1136–1159.

Bonauto, M. (2000). Civil union update. Retrieved November 2001 from the Web site of Gay and Lesbian Advocates and Defenders: www.glad.org.

Brady v. Dean, No. 2000-547 (Ver. Sup. Ct. 2001).

Brooks v. Parkerson, 454 S.E.2d 769 (Geor. Sup. Ct. 1995).

Caban v. Mohammed, 441 U.S. 380 (1979).

Cahn, N., & Singer, J. (1999). Adoption, identity, and the Constitution: The case for opening closed records. *University of Pennsylvania Journal of Constitutional Law, 2,* 150–194.

Chambers, D. L., & Polikoff, N. D. (1999). Family law and gay and lesbian family issues in the twentieth century. *Family Law Quarterly, 33,* 523–542.

Champagne v. Mcdermott, Inc., No. 91-1221, 1992 U.S. Dist. LEXIS 7359 (E.D. La. 1992).

Cherlin, A. (1992). *Marriage, divorce, remarriage.* Cambridge, MA: Harvard University Press.

Child Support Recovery Act of 1992, 18 U.S.C. § 228.

Davis v. Davis, 842 S.W. 2d 588 (Tenn. Sup. Ct. 1992).

Defense of Marriage Act, Pub. L. No. 104-199, 110 Stat. 2419, adding 1 U.S.C.S. § 7 and 28 U.S.C.S. § 1738C and amending tables of sections preceding 1 U.S.C.S. § 1 and 28 U.S.C.S. § 1731.

Elrod, L. D., Spector, R. G., & Atkinson, J. (1999). A review of the year in family law: Children's issues dominate. *Family Law Quarterly, 32,* 661–717.

Emery, R. E. (1995). Divorce mediation: Negotiating agreements and renegotiating relationships. *Family Relations, 44,* 377–383.

Ennis v. Donovan, 161 A.2d 698 (Mar. Ct. App. 1960).

Family Law Act of 1969 (Calif. Stats. 1969, ch. 1608).

Family Support Act of 1988, Pub. L. No. 100-485, Title I, Subtitle A, § 104(b), Subtitle B, § 111(c), Subtitle C, § 123(a), (d), 102 Stat. 2348, 2349, 2352.

Fania v. Fania, 133 S.W.2d 654 (Ark. Sup. Ct. 1939).

Fine, M. A., & Demo, D. (2000). Divorce: Societal ill or normative transition? In R. Milardo & S. Duck (Eds.), *Families as relationships* (pp. 135–156). Chichester, UK: John Wiley.

Fine, M. A., & Fine, D. R. (1994). An examination and evaluation of recent changes in divorce laws in five Western countries: The critical role of values. *Journal of Marriage and the Family, 56,* 249–263.

Gallagher, M., & Waite, L. (2000). *The case for marriage.* New York: Doubleday.

Goldstein, J., Freud, A., & Solnit, A. (1973). *Beyond the best interests of the child.* New York: Free Press.

Howard Metzenbaum Multiethnic Placement Adoption Act, 42 U.S.C. § 5115(a) (1994).

In re Marriage of Buzzanca, 72 Cal.Rptr.2d 280 (Cal. Ct. App. 1998).

In re Nicholas H., 2002 Cal. Lexis 3774 (2002).

In the Matter of Baby M., 537 A.2d 1227 (N.J. Sup. Ct. 1988).

Intercountry Adoption Act, 106 Pub. L. No. 279, 114 Stat. 825 (2000).

Johnston, J., Kline, M., & Tschann, J. (1989). Ongoing postdivorce conflict: Effects on children of joint custody and frequent access. *American Journal of Orthopsychiatry, 59,* 576–592.

Katz, S. N. (1999). Establishing the family and family-like relationships: Emerging models for alternatives to marriage. *Family Law Quarterly, 33,* 663–675.

Krause, H. (1986). *Family law* (2nd ed.). St. Paul, MN: West.

Lehr v. Robertson, 463 U.S. 248 (1983).

Lerman, R. L. (1993). A national profile of young unwed fathers. In R. L. Lerman & T. J. Ooms (Eds.), *Young unwed fathers* (pp. 35–39). Philadelphia: Temple University Press.

Lewis v. Lewis, 351 N.E.2d 526 (Mass. Sup. Ct. 1976).

Lofton v. Kearney, No. 99-10058 (S.D. Fla. 2001).

Louisiana Act 1380 (1977), amending La. Civ. Code Arts. 102 & 103, and La. Rev. Stat. § 9:234, 9:245, and adding § 9:224(C), and § 9:225(A)(3), §§ 9:272–9:275, and §§ 9:307–9:309.

Mahoney, M. (1994). *Stepfamilies and the law*. Ann Arbor: University of Michigan Press.

Marlow v. Marlow, 702 N.E.2d 733 (Ind. Ct. App. 1998).

Marvin v. Marvin, 557 P.2d 106 (Cal. Sup. Ct. 1976).

Mason, M. A. (1988). *The equality trap*. New York: Simon & Schuster.

Mason, M. A. (1994). *From father's property to children's rights*. New York: Columbia University Press.

Mason, M. A. (1998). The modern American stepfamily: Problems and possibilities. In M. A. Mason, A. Skolnick, & S. D. Sugarman (Eds.), *All our families* (pp. 95–116). New York: Oxford University Press.

Mason, M. A. (2000). *The custody wars*. New York: Basic Books.

McHugh v. McHugh, 436 A.2d 8 (Conn. Sup. Ct. 1980).

McLanahan, S., & Sandefur, G. (1994). *Growing up with a single parent*. Cambridge, MA: Harvard University Press.

Michael H. v. Gerald D., 491 U.S. 110 (1989).

Mosher, W. D., & Bachrach, C. A. (1996). Understanding U.S. fertility: Continuity and change in the National Survey of Family Growth, 1988–1995. *Family Planning Perspectives, 28*(1). Retrieved January 17, 2003, from the Alan Guttmacher Institute Web site: www.agi-usa.org/pubs/journals/2800496. html.

Nagourney, E. (2000, February 15). Study finds families bypassing marriage. *New York Times*, p. F8.

National Center for Health Statistics. (1995). Fertility/infertility. Retrieved January 17, 2003, from www.cdc.gov/nchs/fastats/fertile.htm.

Niesen v. Niesen, 157 N. W.2d 660 (Wis. Sup. Ct. 1968).

Patterson, C. J. (2000). Family relationships of lesbians and gay men. *Journal of Marriage and the Family, 62*, 1052–1069.

Pearson, J. (1999). Domestic and international legal framework of family law: Court services: Meeting the needs of twenty-first century families. *Family Law Quarterly, 33*, 617–635.

Perry, T. L. (1999). Race matters: change, choice, and family law at the millennium. *Family Law Quarterly, 33*, 461–474.

Pulliam v. Smith, 501 S.E.2d 898 (N.C. Sup. Ct. 1998).

Queen's Medical Center v. Kagawa, 967 P.2d 686 (Haw. Ct. App. 1998).

Regan, M. C., Jr. (1999). Establishing the family and family-like relationships: Marriage at the millennium. *Family Law Quarterly, 33*, 647–662.

Roe v. Wade, 410 U.S. 959 (1973).

Roseman, E. (2000, Fall). OPEN 2000: Are you ready for open records? *Resolve of Northern California Quarterly Newsletter*, p. 6.

Roth v. Weston, No. 16565 (Conn. Sup. Ct. 2002).

Seltzer, J. (1994). Intergenerational ties in adulthood and childhood experience. In A. Booth & J. Dunn (Eds.), *Stepfamilies* (pp. 89–96). Hillsdale, NJ: Lawrence Erlbaum.

Siegel, A. J. (2000). Note: Setting limits on judicial scientific, technical, and other specialized fact-finding in the new millennium. *Cornell Law Review, 86*, 167.

Stanley v. Illinois, 405 U.S. 645 (1971).

State ex rel. Watts v. Watts, 350 N.Y.S.2d. 285 (N.Y. Fam. Crt. 1973).

State v. Miranda, 715 A.2d 650 (Conn. Sup. Ct. 1997).

Stolley, K. S. (1993). Statistics in adoption in the United States. *Future of American Children, Adoption, 3*(1), 26–42. Retrieved January 17, 2003, from ftp://futureof American children.org/usr_doc/vol3no1ART2.PDF.

Sugarman, S. (1998). Single-parent families. In M. A. Mason, A. Skolnick, & S. Sugarman (Eds.), *All our families* (pp. 13–38). New York: Oxford University Press.

Trammel v. United States, 445 U.S. 40 (1980).

Triber, G. A. (1998). Growing pains: Disputes surrounding human reproductive interests stretch the boundaries of traditional legal concepts. *Seton Hall Legislative Journal, 23*, 103–140.

Troxel v. Granville, 530 U.S. 57 (2000).

Uniform Marriage and Divorce Act. (2002). For Missouri, V.A.M.S. §§ 452.300 to 452.416.

Uniform Parentage Act. (2000). Retrieved July 31, 2003, from www.law.upenn.edu bll/ulc/upa/final2002.htm.

U.S. Bureau of the Census. (1999). *Interracial married couples: 1960 to present.* Retrieved January 17, 2003, from www.census.gov/population/socdemo/ms-la/tabms-3.txt.

U.S. Department of State. (2000). Hague convention on intercountry adoptions. Retrieved July 17, 2003, from www.travel.state.gov/adoption_info_sheet.html.

U.S. Department of State. (2002). Immigrant visas issued to orphans coming to the U.S. Retrieved January 17, 2003, from www.travel.state.gov/orphan_numbers.html.

Wardle, L. D. (1999). Reorganizing the family: Divorce reform at the turn of the millennium: Certainties and possibilities. *Family Law Quarterly, 33*, 783–800.

Warshak, R. A. (2000). Remarriage as a trigger of parental alienation syndrome. *American Journal of Family Therapy, 28*, 229–241.

Weithorn, L. A., & Grisso, T. (1987). Psychological evaluations in divorce custody: Problems, principles, and procedures. In L. Weithorn (Ed.), *Psychology and child custody determinations: Knowledge, roles, and expertise* (pp. 157–181). Lincoln: University of Nebraska Press.

West v. West, 689 N.E.2d 1215 (Ill. Crt. App. 1998).

Wickham v. Byrne, No. 92048 (Ill. Sup. Ct. 2002).

Wilcox v. Trautz, 693 N.E.2d 141 (Mass. Crt. App. 1998).

Williams v. Williams, 501 S.E.2d 417 (Vir. Sup. Ct. 1998).

CHAPTER 26

Building Enduring Family Policies in the 21st Century

The Past as Prologue?

KAREN BOGENSCHNEIDER AND TOM CORBETT

T hough it is not always recognized, public policy discourse in the United States has always had a family tilt: an underlying, often unexpressed premise that families are the basic building block in society, to be relied upon, protected, and nurtured. The American colonies imported the Elizabethan Poor Laws as the framework for a system in which the extended family was the fundamental societal unit responsible for impoverished individuals. The local town became the responsible jurisdiction only if the family failed in its primary role. Even then, town leaders would try to find and often provide financial support to other families in the community willing to care for the indigent.

It is one thing, however, to intuitively accept the importance of families to a strong and vital society. It is quite another to consciously and systematically place families at the center of the policy process. To do so, we must shift the nature of discourse from appreciating families to prioritizing them as worthy of study, investment, and political action. Families need to be viewed as an area of study that deserves federal support and encouragement, a specific population to be assessed as an indicator of societal health, and an explicit object of and criterion for evaluating the impact of policies and programs.

The field of family policy is young in terms of both intellectual inquiry and policy formation centered on the family concept. According to Kamerman and Kahn (1978), the field of family policy was formally conceived in the 1970s, during the Senate's landmark hearings on American families. Acceptance of family policy as a field made little headway in the 1980s, in part because of divisive ideological debates that surfaced during the controversial 1980 White House Conference on Families. Despite these birth pains, family policy evolved into a legitimate field of empirical and theoretical inquiry during the 1990s (Bogenschneider, 2000, 2002; Ooms, 1995).

The 1990s began with the question of legitimacy: Are families a legitimate focus of policy attention and public investments, or are families a private matter? When the decade drew to a close, this question appeared to have been answered by the policy initiatives, political judgments, and priorities of the American people. Across the political spectrum, with important exceptions, a consensus emerged that government had a legitimate role in nurturing and protecting well-functioning families and that the private sector also had responsibilities.

During the 1990s, federal policy makers enacted an impressive range of innovative policies regarding adoption, child abuse, child care, child support, domestic violence, education, family leave, family preservation, family poverty, same-sex marriage, and welfare reform (Bogenschneider, 2000, 2002). Over two thirds (34) of the states funded programs for preschoolers, and about half funded programs for infants and toddlers (24) and parents (25) (Knitzer & Page, 1998). In addition, policies increasingly were examined in terms of their potential effects on family formation and stability—the marriage penalties built into certain tax policies (e.g., the earned income tax credit) being one example. Federal and state expenditures on child care tripled, direct cash benefits to families doubled, and family services saw a 50% increase (Kamerman & Kahn, 2001). In public opinion polls, these family policy initiatives and laws reflected the values and priorities of the American people. When asked how much government could be doing to help them, 47% of parents said that government *could do a great deal* to help them, and another 37% said that government *could do something to help them* (Hewlett & West, 1998).

The 1990s also saw an impressive number of private philanthropic commitments, some influencing the choice of issues for government actions and others exploring whether government actions achieved their family-focused goals. For example, the Edna McConnell Clark Foundation's commitment to family preservation (e.g., cautioning against the too-easy removal of children from families in which abuse or neglect is suspected or substantiated) subsequently was reflected in many state and federal policies (T. Ooms, personal communication, October 16, 1999).

Although no single formal decision was made, it was apparent that families had emerged as a legitimate focus of government policy in the 1990s. The shift was remarkable. A generation before, President Richard Nixon had vetoed a federal child care bill as an unwarranted governmental intrusion into a family concern. Child care now has become the largest single expenditure under the federal cash assistance program, Temporary Assistance for Needy Families. Thirty years ago, the role of government in collecting child support was minimal; child support was deemed a private matter between the parties involved. Now both Democrats and Republicans readily agree to expansions of the public role in ensuring that child support is collected when children do not reside with both parents.

The question remains: Is this palpable shift toward a focus on the family permanent or merely a passing policy fad? Political observers claim that interest in family policy issues is now at its highest peak in 20 years (Hutchins, 1998; Ooms, 1990). Yet despite this popularity, the term *family policy* is still not widely used by policy makers, journalists, or the public. Moreover, few academics are actively engaged in the field in the sense that they explicitly structure their research agendas around family policy (Ooms, 2002). In fact, a review of the history of family policy from the early 20th century to the present warns against undue optimism. Historically, interest in family policy has ebbed and flowed; periods of interest and investment in family matters have been followed by periods of benign neglect. Families have often drawn considerable political attention, but arguably they have failed to secure a sustained niche in American public policy.

In this chapter, we examine three major efforts over the past century to establish family policy in the public arena and ask whether the themes and cycles of the past will dictate the future. Can analysis and understanding of the roots of American social policy inform political debate and shape a more enduring set of family policies in the 21st century? Like Robert Cairns, we believe that we are as much "determined by history as we are makers of it," (quoted in Parke, 2003). The past may not be prologue. We are not necessarily doomed to repeated, short-term waves of interest in family policy, particularly if we can carefully draw insights from the history of family policies that might help us shape the direction and dissemination of our research, the design of our policies, and the operation of our institutions. To begin this look back in time, we clarify what we mean by the terms *family policy* and *family*.

DEFINITIONS OF FAMILY POLICY AND FAMILY

This chapter defines *family policy* as the development, enactment, and implementation of laws, rules, codes, or judicial decisions in the public or private sector that address four family functions: (a) family creation (marriage and divorce, childbearing and adoption, the provision of foster care), (b) economic support, (c) child rearing, and (d) caregiving (e.g., provision of assistance to the ill, frail, and elderly) (see Bogenschneider, 2000, 2002; Consortium of Family Organizations, 1990; Ooms, 1990). Families also provide members with love and transmit cultural and religious values, but these intimate functions matter to social policy only when they interfere with the four main family functions (Ooms, 1990). This chapter does not address policies that fall outside this explicit definition, although we fully recognize that a wide range of issues may benefit from a family perspective in policy making that analyzes the consequences of any policy or program for its effect on family well-being.

In our work with policy makers, we seldom receive requests to define what we mean by *family*, which leads us to believe that the definition of family need not be a barrier to achieving progress as a field. In fact, we believe that no single definition of family may be possible. Existing definitions of family might be categorized in two ways: (a) structural definitions that specify family membership according to certain characteristics such as blood relationship, legal ties, or residence; and (b) functional definitions that specify behaviors that family members perform, such as sharing economic resources and caring for the young, elderly, sick, and disabled (see Bogenschneider, 2002; Moen & Schorr, 1987). Either a structural or a functional definition can be written to reinforce the intent of a specific program or policy (Eshleman, 1991). For example, if the issue were child support, a structural definition would require financial support only from those people related to the child by blood, marriage, or adoption, whereas a functional definition would require support from any committed caregiver. If the issue were care for the elderly, structuralists would provide benefits only to those who had legal responsibility for the dependent, whereas functionalists would include any close companion who provided care. When considered in the context of specific legislation, structural definitions seem more appropriate for some goals and functional definitions for others. We believe that definitions will vary over time, across jurisdictions, and in different political contexts.

Precedent exists for the lack of a single, preferred definition of *family*. No legal definition of family appears in the U.S. Constitution, the federal statutes or regulations (Ooms, 1998), or most state statutes (Bogenschneider, Young, Melli, & Fleming, 1993). Defining the family is not a matter that can be answered by research. Instead, it is a question of values and priorities—the types of decisions that policy makers are elected to make. For some, leaving the matter to policy makers may seem unsettling. Yet given the multiple goals of policies, it may be impossible to settle on a single definition that will suit all purposes, and a protracted debate over language and definition may impede progress toward more useful and pragmatic policy initiatives. Rather, it may be more prudent and productive to define families in ways that reinforce the intent of a specific policy or program (Moen & Schorr, 1987).

Whatever definition is used, the term *family* makes an important conceptual distinction by moving our attention beyond the individual to relationships among two or more persons tied together by blood, legal bonds, or the performance of family functions such as caregiving and economic support. This is a critical distinction that is too often overlooked in policy circles. For example, any children's or women's policy is often incorrectly equated with family policy, even when the target of interest is an individual, not a family relationship or family unit.

Using this distinction, we selected three examples that illustrate how family policies have waxed and waned over the century. Embedded in these scenarios are some of the origins of contemporary family policy: the activism of middle-class women between 1890 and 1920, the child- and family-saving movement from 1900 to 1930, and the Social Security Amendments of 1939. We extract from these examples six themes that may be instructive in designing more enduring family policies in the future.

THE ORIGINS OF FAMILY POLICY IN WOMEN'S ADVOCACY, 1890–1920

The rapid industrialization, massive immigration, and urbanization of America in the 1880s and 1890s were accompanied by social conditions such as unemployment, low wages, homelessness, and poverty. A relatively unregulated workplace led to high rates of injuries and death (Sklar, 1993); and unhealthy living conditions, particularly in urban settings, contributed to high mortality rates among infants and children (Lindenmeyer, 1997). In 1890, 9% of children lived with one parent, and most of these single parents were widowed mothers (Gordon, 1994). Single mothers who lost a breadwinning husband were typically thrust into dire economic need (Skocpol, 1997). In the first decade of the 1900s, when a living wage was $8 per week, single mothers could earn about $2 to $4 per week. To earn enough to afford food and housing, children without fathers were more than six times more likely to be pressed into the workforce (33%) as children with fathers (6%). The impulse of early reformers was to separate highly vulnerable children from their impoverished families and place them in what they considered more suitable family situations or institutions. In fact, the primary reason for institutionalizing children, in one Massachusetts study, was the inability of mothers to support them. By the end of the 19th century, single mothers and their children were perceived to be a social problem of such magnitude that they needed public attention (Gordon, 1994).

To an extent unparalleled anywhere else in the world, government's response to the problems of working-class mothers and children was shaped by American women reformers, particularly middle-class women. The agenda of these women activists extended beyond motherhood to the workplace. Nowhere else in the world did protective labor legislation focus so directly on women, and nowhere else were women so involved in its enactment. The success of these women's groups in restructuring America's social and political priorities at the local, state, and federal levels can be attributed to their success in mobilizing grassroots, class-bridging coalitions that lobbied for benefits for working-class mothers and children—many of whom were unable to lobby on their own behalf (Sklar, 1993).

By 1890, about 56,000 women were pursuing a college education, and in lieu of graduate school many leaders of the social reform movement chose to live and work in settlement homes in working-class immigrant neighborhoods. These settings provided a venue for collecting data and experimenting with the design and implementation of welfare programs and policies (Koven & Michel, 1993; Sklar, 1993). This knowledge and skill was subsequently put to use in the nation's women's clubs (Sklar, 1993). In the last quarter of the 19th century, literally hundreds of local women's organizations formed national associations (Koven & Michel, 1993), including the Congress of Mothers, the Daughters of the American Revolution, the National American Woman Suffrage Association, the National Council of Catholic Women, the National Consumers' League, the National Council of Jewish Women, the National Women's Trade Union League, and the Young Women's Christian Association (Sklar, 1993).

The most important woman's organization, the Woman's Christian Temperance Union (WTCU), was formed in 1875 as an umbrella organization with 39 departments, 25 of which did not deal with temperance. In Chicago, the WTCU maintained two nurseries, an industrial school, a mission, a medical dispensary, and a lodging house for men. In 1890, the General Federation of Women's Clubs pulled together a vast number of local networks that addressed a range of topics. For example, in 1893, the federation resolved that each club should appoint a standing committee to inquire into the labor conditions of women and children and another committee to investigate state labor laws. By 1919, the General Federation of Women's Clubs represented an impressive grassroots network of 800,000 women (Sklar, 1993).

During the peak of American industrialization between 1900 and 1920, these middle-class women's organizations worked in collaboration with male professionals to pass an array of social policies to protect current and future mothers and their children that men had been unable to enact on their own—campaigns for compulsory education, protective labor legislation for women, and child labor (Sklar, 1993). Most of these campaigns were family policy in the truest sense because they focused, not only on the child or the woman, but on the state's interest in preserving the family (Gordon, 1994) and on the parents', usually the mother's, responsibility for the child. The most important of the issues they addressed were compulsory school attendance (passed by every state by 1918), mothers' pensions to support impoverished widows (enacted by 44 states), limits to the hours that women wage earners could work (46 states), and minimum wages for women workers (15 states). Curiously, during the same time period in which these laws were passed to protect women and mothers, proposed benefits and regulations for male workers often were defeated (Skocpol, 1995). Later, these policies for women workers were extended to wage-earning men and non-wage-earning women and children (Sklar, 1993).

These Progressive-minded women activists challenged the rigid determinism of Social Darwinism by working to change the social conditions in which families operated (Gordon, 1994). Experts contributed to these early reform campaigns with studies and reports that exposed social problems

(Smith, 1991). For example, the Bureau of Labor Statistics published 19 volumes on their investigation of the predicaments faced by many women and child wage earners (Lindenmeyer, 1997). In addition, the writing of Samuel McCune Lindsay and G. Stanley Hall in the early 1900s helped establish childhood and adolescence as unique periods of development that deserved special attention.

Quite remarkably, this political activism at the turn of the century occurred at a time when a woman's sphere of influence was almost universally accepted as the home and a ·full two decades before women had the right to vote. The lexicon of these early reformers helped legitimize women's involvement in policy making by domesticating politics. For example, in the words of Frances Willard, "[G]overnment was only housekeeping on the broadest scale," and according to Ellen Swallow Richards, women could move into the larger world and "clean it up, as if it were no more than a dirty house" (both cited in Stage, 1997, pp. 28, 30). Historians have noted, however, that this movement was not entirely altruistic in that it created new jobs and positions of power for women and tended to advance white, middle-class notions of women and child rearing. It operated primarily in the North and mostly separately from the activism of black women (Sklar, 1993).

The commitment of these women's organizations to grassroots organization and social reform waned in the 1920s. Professions like home economics and social work lost their spirit of systemic social change and focused more on skill building, individual pathologies, and therapeutic treatment modalities. This narrowing of professional mission reflected larger societal trends—a shift toward greater individualism following World War I; the Hoover era's emphasis on individuals, standards, and profitability; a backlash against women's reform efforts outside the home; the end of the Progressive Era; and the rise of Frederick Taylor's scientific management theories (Stage, 1997).

THE ORIGINS OF FAMILY POLICY AS "CHILD AND FAMILY SAVING," 1900–1930

Children slowly became more prominent as a distinct population of social policy interest over the last half of the 19th century. Theodore Roosevelt, U.S. president from 1901 to 1909, poured over turn-of-the-century census data, which he thought signaled family decline. Between 1890 and 1910, the number of Americans who divorced tripled. Between 1880 and 1920, the U.S. birthrate fell by over 30%. Because immigration rates were high, this led to concerns, particularly in some geographic regions, over the decline in the proportion of native stock. In 1918, the infant mortality rate was double that of western Europe, 80% of pregnant mothers did not receive prenatal care, and 23,000 mothers died in childbirth (Carlson, 2002a). Given these trends, Trattner (1999) noted that a focus on children and family once again became paramount to many social reformers of the time:

> The fate of the world is determined by the influences which prevail with the child from birth to 7 years of age. . . . All the problems go back to the child—corrupt politics, dishonesty and greed in commerce, war, anarchism, drunkenness, incompetence. (p. 109)

The establishment of the Children's Bureau is often regarded as the first political victory in a series of family- and child-saving policies. In the words of Florence Kelley, feminist social reformer and a founder of Hull House in 1903, "If the government can have a department to take such a interest in the cotton crop, why can't it have a bureau to look after the nation's child crop?" (Carlson 2002a, p. 15). The U.S. Children's Bureau was established 9 years later with support from a number of women's associations. Julia Lathrop, its first director, was also the first woman to head a federal agency, albeit one with a small budget of $25,640 and a staff of only 15. To advance the bureau's agenda, Lathrop mobilized thousands of volunteers in Settlement Houses and women's clubs (Carlson, 2002a).

Building on the Progressive Era's faith in research and education, the Children's Bureau organized a grassroots movement to save babies through better mothering and family life (Ladd-Taylor, 1993). The Children's Bureau published books, organized 50,000 girls in 44 cities into Little Mother Leagues, elevated Mother's Day to a national holiday, and spearheaded a National Baby Week. In 1917, with war looming on the horizon, Lathrop helped develop an innovative compensation plan designed to maintain decent living standards for families. Half of the wages of soldiers and sailors were paid directly to their wives and children, and a family allowance was provided on a sliding scale of up to $50 per month for families with four or more children. Death and disability benefits were also provided for widows and children (Carlson, 2002b). Perhaps the greatest accomplishment of the Children's Bureau was the passage of the 1921 Sheppard-Towner Act.

> The American Medical Association fiercely opposed the bill as "German paternalism" and "sob stuff." However, women's organizations . . . actively sought its passage, forming "one of the strongest lobbies that has ever been seen in Washington." When a powerful Congressman blocked the measure in a House Committee, Florence Kelley appeared before its members and compared Congress to King Herod and the slaughter of the innocents, asking: "Why does Congress wish women and children to die?" (quoted in Carlson, 2002a, p. 17)

The Democratic, Socialist, Prohibition, and Farmer-Labor Parties endorsed the act, as did Republican presidential candidate, Warren Harding. The Sheppard-Towner Act won an easy victory, in part, because Congress was nervous about facing newly enfranchised women voters for the first time (Ladd-Taylor, 1993).

Eventually 45 of 48 states participated in the program (Carlson, 2002a). During its 7 years of operation, the bureau distributed 22 million pieces of literature, held 183,000 health conferences, established 3,000 prenatal centers, and visited 3 million homes. By 1929, the bureau estimated that its child-rearing information had benefited half of U.S. babies. Moreover, the Children's Bureau was the federal leader in statistics, providing most Depression Era poverty data and serving as a primary consultant for the establishment of the Bureau of Labor Standards. Job applicants to the Children's Bureau had to be able to design a study of a major social problem and create a table from raw statistical data (Gordon, 1992).

Yet even though the Sheppard-Towner program remained broadly popular with American women and retained most of its political support from women's groups, it was vigorously opposed by the male physicians and bureaucrats who had come to dominate children's health policy (Ladd-Taylor, 1993). Congress never made the program permanent, and it was unable to secure access to stable funding, as Social Security had done via the trust fund. The program was killed through legislative maneuvers in 1929.

THE ORIGINS OF FAMILY POLICY IN THE SOCIAL SECURITY AMENDMENTS OF 1939

Franklin D. Roosevelt assumed the presidency in the midst of an economic depression that followed closely on the heels of the stock market crash of 1929. In March 1933, one third of the U.S. labor force was out of work. Between 1928 and 1932, when Hoover was president, rates of birth and marriage each declined about 20%. These work and family trends led to starkly different interpretations by the two prominent ideologies of the time: the Hoover technocrats and the American Maternalists of the 1920s.

In 1930, Herbert Hoover appointed a number of distinguished social scientists, referred to as Hoover technocrats, to the President's Research Committee on Social Trends. According to their report, released in 1933, falling birthrates were evidence of the failing of the family, particularly the housewife, who arguably could contribute more by entering the labor force. The report claimed that most family functions—care of the elderly, child care, cooking, education, health care, laundering, religious acts, and sewing—could be better and more efficiently carried out by experts in corporate, state, or charitable bodies that were organized according to industry guidelines. As summarized by Carlson (2002b):

> The frail nature of the family meant that "schools, nurseries or other agencies" would need to enroll a "larger proportion of the very young children in the future" so as "to conserve childhood in the midst of rapidly shifting conditions of family life." Only "society" has the new expertise needed to grapple with "developing the personality of its children." . . . Concern should no longer focus on family strength. . . . Instead, attention should be on "the individualization of the members of the family." (p. 4)

These views, which were endorsed by business leaders, were perceived as an attack on family life by the Maternalists—a motherhood movement with roots dating back to the Settlement House movement. Maternalists believed that the ideal family—the breadwinning father, mother at home, and their children—was being threatened by industrialization. The cornerstone of the Maternalists' policy agenda was a family wage—a living wage for the father so that the mother could stay home to raise the children (Carlson, 2002b). This Maternalist defense of the value of women's traditional labor against the forces of industrialization undergirded the New Deal domestic policies of the Roosevelt administration and continues to shape the American welfare state to this day.

The New Deal has been criticized by feminists as creating female dependency through patriarchal policies, a debate that extends beyond the purposes of this chapter. The New Deal did come to reflect the Maternalist perspective on social policy—a perspective consistent with views of the family that were widely accepted at the time. When asked in a 1936 Gallup poll if wives should work when their husbands had jobs, a resounding 82% said no, leading George Gallup to contend that this issue was one that voters were "about as solidly united as on any subject imaginable—including sin and hay fever" (quoted in Carlson, 2002b, p. 6). Even unmarried women reformers of the day, Gordon (1992) noted, "did not . . . contradict the prevailing premises that children and women needed breadwinner husbands, that children needed full-time mothers, that women should choose between family and career" (p. 34).

We will consider here how these Maternalist views of the family shaped only one New Deal policy, the Social Security Act of 1935, which is considered the foundation of U.S. public social programs to this day and the origin of one of the country's most effective antipoverty policies. In the original act, Old Age pensions were funded by contributions to individual accounts. With overwhelming political support, the Social Security Act was amended in 1939 to add survivor and dependent benefits.

Old Age pensions were thus transformed from a program for an individual worker to a social insurance program for the entire family unit. Widowed mothers received 75% of the pension their husbands would have received, as long as they did not remarry or earn more than $15 per month. Surviving children received half of the benefit their fathers would have received. An aged woman who had been married for at least 5 years and was not divorced was eligible for 50% of the pension her husband would have received, whether or not she herself had a work history. Thus, the 1939 Social Security Amendments established the American welfare system on the family wage, marriage, and a nonemployed mother at home. Those who deviated from these family norms through divorce, deliberate childlessness, illegitimacy, or maternal employment incurred financial penalties (see Carlson, 2002b).

The New Deal is one example of how an individualistic society appears to justify social programs by explicitly acknowledging recipients' service to the nation—for example, rewarding mothers for bearing and rearing children. The legislation was based on the premise that mothers deserved to be honorably supported if a breadwinning husband was not available (Skocpol, 1995). In the words of Molly Dewson, who served on the Social Security Board:

> [When] you begin to help the family to attain some security you are at the same time beginning to erect a National structure for the same purpose. Through the well-being of the family, we create the well-being of The Nation. Through our constructive contributions to the one, we help the other to flourish. (quoted in Carlson, 2002b, p. 10)

Experts played a new, more active role in the design of the New Deal. Roosevelt attracted hordes of intellectuals to Washington by establishing various advisory and planning agencies, including his legendary Brain Trust.

He also reorganized the Executive Office in the late 1930s in ways that ensured that his successors would have access to intellectual resources. By 1938, when most of the New Deal programs were in place, more than 7,800 social scientists were working in the federal government.

IMPLICATIONS FOR BUILDING ENDURING FAMILY POLICIES

Over time, demographics (concerns about family decline), economics (the Great Depression), intellectual fads (Social Darwinism), and advocacy (particularly by women's organizations) played key roles in how social policy and family issues were framed and deliberated. National policy in the United States has always been cyclical in character. For example, it has cycled between individual and structural explanations for social problems, whether policy should be protective of or mainstream women and children, and whether government policies should be proactive or remedies of last resort. Political pushes to strengthen families and use them as instruments of social change have often been followed by periods of neglect when the family was viewed as the exclusive province of the principals themselves. Consequently, it proved challenging to sustain the promise of an activist family policy perspective over the course of the 20th century.

Some challenges to a sustained family policy perspective may well persist. Yet we think that family professionals must deconstruct the repeated rise and fall of family policies over the past century to identify circumstances that hold the promise of bringing family policy into the mainstream of social policy debate so that it has a status commensurate with that of economic policy or poverty policy. Indeed, the similarities between the development of poverty policy and family policy as legitimate fields of study are illuminating.

As a distinct area of inquiry, poverty research and analysis is typically dated back to the early 1960s, when a definition of poverty was developed at the Social Security Administration and public policy was directed to this societal challenge by President Johnson's declaration of the War on Poverty. By the late 1960s, one litmus test for policy proposals was "What does it do for the poor?" Although concern for the poor can be traced back to the emergence of civilization itself, and although poverty research, as we now know it, was being practiced as early as the late 19th century, the pace and sophistication of research did not pick up until a distinct field of inquiry developed. Today, our understanding of poverty is immeasurably more advanced and nuanced than it was 40 years ago.

Family policy is in much the same condition that poverty policy was in the 1960s. There is a good deal of it going on, but ways of distilling and translating the work to shape and inform policy have yet to be fully exploited. We still need a generally accepted definition of the concept. We need a policy arena that continues to accept families as a legitimate subject of public discourse. This will require more than wishful thinking and good intentions. We need to reflect on the history of family policy and learn from the past how to fashion a better future. In this final section, we offer six precepts on which family professionals can build so that family policy may be more firmly established as a field and an enduring set of family policies can be constructed for the new century.

Family Policies Move Forward When Legitimated by Relevant Research and Theory

One impetus for the development and enactment of family policy in the past was clear data that family structure was changing in deleterious ways, some evidence that family integrity was being compromised, and a theoretical rationale for understanding the consequences of these changes for society. For example, family policies were enacted early in the 20th century when Progressive reformers were able to document trends that high numbers of women were dying in childbirth, infant mortality rates far exceeded those of other industrialized nations, and incidences of child labor were escalating. Child labor reformers were able to justify their advocacy, in part, by drawing on theories that conceptualized childhood and adolescence as distinct periods of development that warranted special protections. New Deal legislation emerged when one third of Americans were unemployed, with obvious repercussions for family stability and well-being.

What this means for today's family professional is that good data can help policy makers determine whether social action is needed, either by identifying problems or by refuting contentions that problems exist (Bogenschneider, 2002). Moynihan's (1941) claim, stated more than 60 years ago, that data may be more important for family policy than for other aspects of social policy still holds true: "Family matters, in other words, are not a subject for which there is a well-established alarm system that alerts the larger society to dangers as they arise. Something truly alarming has to happen" (pp. xii–xiii).

Moynihan's words capture an important, often misunderstood, element of policy making—that data are more apt to evoke public interest and a political response when they point out potential risks or a pending crisis. Rightly or wrongly, policy makers tend to deal with outliers, such as child-abusing parents, crime-committing youth, or students that need special education. Data are more apt to be policy relevant when they spotlight risks to the individual and, perhaps more importantly, the prevalence of these risks in the population (Scott, Mason, & Chapman, 1999). For example, the increased risk of mental retardation is similar for individuals born premature or postmature (88% and 81% respectively). Yet premature births have a greater impact on society than postmature births because they are five times more common. If problems are known to pose substantial risk to a significant segment of the population, research findings can stimulate public outrage and catapult issues onto the political agenda.

For family policy purposes, however, research also needs to move beyond examination of the risks to and outcomes for the individual—a focus that is so pervasive in our culture and in our research methods that it almost goes unnoticed. There is no better illustration of this bias than the effort in the 1990s to develop social indicators of societal well-being. Several federal executive agencies, with substantial input from the academic community, supported a concerted effort to identify key indicators by which to assess how well we were doing as a society and to help guide and shape future policy development and social investments.

Looking back, it is curious that there was so little debate about the underlying basis for organizing the social indicator initiative. By default, the organizing principle ended up being children, not the families in which the children resided. Arguably, the major intellectual work to come out of this effort was titled *Indicators of Children's Well-Being*, even though many of the indicators discussed were based on the family concept (Hauser, Brown, & Prosser, 1997). Moreover, a 1997 Executive Order established the Federal Interagency Forum on Child and Family Statistics to publish a set of national statistics from 18 federal agencies on the health of families. The resulting annual publication conspicuously left the word *family* out of the title: *Trends in the Well-Being of America's Children and Youth* (Westat, 2000).

This omission may be attributable, in part, to the individualistic focus of data collection. Employment statistics make no distinction between an unemployed father of nine, a teenager looking for a part-time job, and a senior citizen supplementing pension and Social Security incomes (Moynihan, 1986). When researchers document the increasing number of Americans working long hours, are they careful to point out whether these long hours occur in families raising children and whether one or both parents are working overtime? Only when data analysts, program designers and evaluators deliberately examine the family's role in social problems will results emerge like those in recent interventions to prevent youth crime and substance use—that interventions are cost effective only when they emphasize training of parents and avoid bringing together high-risk youth, no matter how skillfully (Dishion, McCord, & Poulin, 1999). Collecting family data, developing family theory, and designing family programs is no simple task, according to Ooms (2002): "Families are not easy units of analysis; they are complex, dynamic, messy, ever-changing systems. A family orientation requires us to think about individuals and families in a comprehensive way and to design holistic responses for meeting their needs" (p. xiii).

The Family Perspective Is Influential When Relevant Research and Theory Are Communicated to Policy Makers

For example, Theodore Roosevelt, who has been called the first American president to philosophically describe the importance of family life to the nation, was influenced to a large extent by census data that, he believed, spelled out a crisis in family life (Carlson, 2001). The Children's Bureau was a pioneer in collecting quantitative data about the need for and effectiveness of its programs and in translating the numbers for public consumption. Moreover, a number of family policies were triggered, in part, by the Bureau of Labor Statistics' investigations of the predicaments faced by women and child wage earners. Conversely, research and theory can also impede progress, as evidenced by the efficiency-based tenets of Taylor's scientific management theory and the individualistic, industry-driven recommendations of Hoover's panel of social science technocrats. Extrapolating from the past, social scientists can no longer trust that good research and theory will somehow find their way into the policy-making process (Rist, 1994). We need to devote as much energy and as many resources to developing practices and procedures for disseminating rigorous analysis into the policy-making process as we have devoted to generating high-quality research and publishing it in the leading journals. A three-pronged approach is needed: (a) directing more attention to the science of translation and to ways that information can be packaged to meet policy makers' unique information needs, (b) encouraging a family impact perspective in policy making, whereby policy makers consider the effects of policies on families as well as the potential benefit of taking the role of families into account, and (c) taking systematic steps inside the academy to encourage and reward efforts to connect research to policy making outside the academy.

We are familiar with two promising models: the Family Impact Seminars and the Welfare Peer Assistance Network (WELPAN). The Family Impact Seminars are a series of seminars, briefing reports, newsletters, and discussion sessions that provide state policy makers with nonpartisan, solution-oriented information on current issues that affect families, like child care, juvenile crime, and welfare reform (see Bogenschneider, 2002; Bogenschneider, Olson, Linney, & Mills,

2000). Policy makers report that the seminars have increased their knowledge of research on family issues in ways that are useful in decision making and that have shaped the development and enactment of public policies. What's more, we have been able to substantiate that, because of the legislators' participation in the seminars, they are more apt to see the practical value of research and to consider how pending legislation affects families.

WELPAN regularly brings together state-level welfare officials for discussion about common problems and solutions and for exchange of views with researchers and policy makers (see Corbett et al., 1998). From this dialogue have emerged some common solutions to shared problems as well as new insights that might not have been apparent without the dialogue. For example, in several reports, WELPAN members have identified and supported a shift in the direction of welfare policies toward family promotion and stability purposes (WELPAN, 2002).

Family Policies Move Forward When Policy Makers and the Public Support Structural Rather Than Individual Explanations for Social Problems

Throughout the nation's history, we have wavered between structural and individual explanations for social problems. The examples in this chapter suggest that family policies were more likely to have been enacted when more comprehensive structural explanations for social problems were in vogue. For example, it was hard to blame the high rates of infant mortality on individuals when they affected the rich and poor alike. The death of male breadwinners was difficult to attribute to individual choice and behavior. When one third of the nation's workers were unemployed, it was hard to imagine that so many were unwilling or unable to work.

Whether political candidates use individual or structural explanation does not always depend on their political party or the constituency they represent (Ross & Staines, 1972). For example, the Sheppard-Towner Act was passed when Republican Warren Harding was elected president, and the New Deal was enacted when Democrat Franklin Roosevelt assumed the presidency. Structural explanations for social problems seemed more apt to emerge during political campaigns and at the time of a change in administration. Challenges for political office tend to have a vested interest in structural or systemic explanations of social problems that point out the inadequacies of the current officeholders. In contrast, it is typically more politically expedient for incumbents to defend the system by arguing that their administration has contributed to a good quality of life with few problems. Any problems that are difficult to deny are attributed, not to the administration, but rather to the actions of certain individuals or groups.

Beyond political considerations, research can often bring about change by determining whether social problems are driven more by structural or individual factors. For example, at the turn of the century, data collected in the Settlement Houses demonstrated the feasibility of government intervention on behalf of families. Public opinion polls in the 1930s demonstrated widespread support for the family focus of the New Deal legislation. Historically, debates about particular public policies have been linked, not only to public perceptions about *what* government should do, but also to beliefs about *how* effective government intervention can be (Skocpol, 1995). Thus, research is policy relevant when it identifies the success of prior programs or policies that address family factors, the receptivity of the public

or affected organizations to family-oriented political responses (Rist, 1994), and the probable consequences of familistic versus individualistic policy interventions (see Dishion et al., 1999).

Family Policy Moves Forward When There Is a Broad Interdisciplinary Focus on Families

Between 1900 and 1920, female middle-class activists adopted a comprehensive agenda that included compulsory education, child labor, and protective labor legislation for women. The Sheppard-Towner Law of 1921 encompassed activities ranging from parent education and home visits to prenatal centers and health conferences. By including the terms *survivor* and *dependent*, the 1939 Social Security Amendments explicitly transformed the American welfare state from a system that focused narrowly on the individual to one that incorporated the individual's most important context, the family.

By its very nature, a family focus leads policy makers toward an integrative perspective. How do diverse policies and systems interact with complex family dynamics to affect families? One recent example is the refocusing of welfare policy on behavior and community rather than on merely handing out checks. This has prompted many policy analysts to think more broadly rather than merely zeroing in on specific problems and service strategies; we now think about how families function overall rather than focus on specific issues such as lack of child care or Food Stamps. What does it take to change fundamental behaviors such as work, fertility, parenting, or family formation? Focusing on the family with its complex set of individual needs and relationships pushes thinking outside the box where the interactions among issues and systems become more apparent. A family focus demands a sophisticated, cross-disciplinary approach to policy challenges.

But think for a moment about how we typically organize our policy and analytic spheres. The policy world is structured into what we might call program and system arenas. Narrowly targeted programs have separate funding streams and program requirements. Legislative committees are organized and segregated around relatively narrow jurisdictions, and most executive departments are equally specialized. Similarly, the academic world is divided into disciplines and subdisciplines; synthesis and interdisciplinary work remain the exception. The field of evaluation is expert driven and dominated by experimental methods, which are most powerful for examining narrowly defined programs and policies. In a time of shrinking portfolios, the philanthropic community is targeting its resources to increasingly narrow and specific priorities.

If family policy is to become more than kissing babies (Jacobs & Davies, 1994), we must restructure how we organize our policy and intellectual worlds—break down program arenas, reorganize legislatures and executive agency expertise, transform academic reward systems, make some fundamental changes in how we evaluate policies, and encourage funding priorities to move toward a more holistic emphasis on the family system. A real focus on family policy also demands rethinking how we train professionals and how our institutions do business. Ooms (2002) has aptly asked:

> Why are there only a handful of family policy courses taught in family life departments and social work schools, and even fewer in public policy schools? When increasing numbers of policy researchers in the major think tanks are working on specific family issues, why are there no units within these institutions established to encourage and pursue family policy as an organizing theme? Why are there still

no groups within government agencies dedicated to examining the impact of their policies on families? (p. xii)

Family Policy Moves Forward When There Are Formal Structures in Place

The Children's Bureau and Roosevelt's Brain Trust are prime examples of formal policy structures. Over 50 years ago, the Council of Economic Advisers and the Joint Economic Committee were established to help the nation set and reach its economic goals. No such entity exists with sole responsibility for families. This is unfortunate given that leaders today, according to Smith (1991), are far more dependent on their immediate counselors and bureaucratic experts. Such a council could give the family visibility, access to the key levers of power, a forum around which to bring together diverse and separate public entities working on relevant family issues, a locus for integrating policy- and family-relevant research, and a central agenda-setting body for developing a plan of action and assigning responsibility. Would a Council on Families have any real power and influence, or would it be a small cog in a big bureaucracy? A Council on Families could wield power, according to Moynihan (1986), who argued that the 1946 Employment Act, which established the Council of Economic Advisers, may have been more important than any jobs bill:

> The mere declaration of policy was an event; it marked acceptance of a social responsibility. . . . The point was not what answers were provided, but what questions were posed. . . . It would be enough for a national family policy to declare that the American government would be formulated and administered with this object in mind; and finally that the President, or some person designated by him, would report to the Congress on the condition of

the American family in all its many facets. (pp. 10–11)

Family Policy Moves Forward When There Is Broad-Based Citizen Activism

In the early years of the Progressive Era, "social policy—formerly the province of women's voluntary work—became public policy" (Barker, quoted in Stage, 1997, p. 18). Women's advocacy for labor legislation between 1890 and 1920 helped establish the constitutionality of government interventions on behalf of working families (Sklar, 1993). Julia Lathrop's success in the political arena can be attributed to the endorsements that she solicited from liberal and conservative organizations like the General Federation of Women's Clubs and the National Congress of Mothers, which later became the Parent Teacher Association (Skocpol, 1995, 1997). According to Skocpol (1995), successful U.S. social programs tend to emerge from partnerships between government and voluntary organizations, typically those organized at the local, state, and national levels. Considerable leverage can be exerted by organizations that can coordinate concerted political pressure across legislative districts.

In the United States, most organizations that include families in their advocacy promote an agenda with a particular political cast. Is it Pollyannaish to think that liberal and conservative advocacy groups would ever join forces for the ultimate good of the whole family unit? Could advocates from any political persuasion rally around a fundamental first step—encouraging policy makers to routinely ask, "How would this policy or program affect families?" Family issues, because of their fundamental importance, have a unique capacity to generate unexpected alliances that mirror the inherent give and take of family life (Bogenschneider, 2002).

CONCLUSION

Families have always played an important role in public policy deliberations in the United States, but one that has not always been explicit and fully acknowledged. Family-centered policy making has enjoyed periods of robust support followed by years of benign neglect. The reasons for our ambivalence toward families in public policy probably can be inferred. Children are politically safe; they do not bear responsibility for their circumstances, at least during their early years. In contrast, the adult members of families are held responsible and sometimes judged harshly. This line of reasoning tends to draw our attention to selected individual targets, leading to fractured and disconnected policies that fail to appreciate the all-important interactions among family members. This individualistic focus has also undercut political support for family policies because of voters' apprehension that programs for children are merely disguised welfare programs (Skocpol, 1995).

If we want the current period of interest in the family and its primary role in ensuring social well-being to endure, we should look to earlier periods in which activist social policies drew upon the family as both a focus of attention and a source of inspiration. The vacillation between family policy feast and famine of the past may not be prologue if we draw upon these lessons from earlier periods of the nation's history as guidelines for the future. Professionals can build more enduring family policies in the 21st century by conducting research that is more policy and family relevant and communicating its findings to policy makers in ways that will entice them to be more research sensitive. Professionals can conduct studies, design theories, and develop programs that deliberately include structural and family factors and encourage political participation, especially when such factors are in vogue. Family professionals can encourage a broad, interdisciplinary focus on families through top-down approaches like developing formal structures to elevate the status of families in policy making and by bottom-up approaches that encourage broad-based citizen support and activism.

It takes only a moment's reflection to realize that policy makers do not have a choice about whether to affect family life; they already do through their action and also their inaction. This chapter identifies several steps that professionals can take to elicit policy decisions that are more informed, deliberate, and self-conscious about their impact on families. We believe that the potential exists to build a set of family policies in the 21st century that are more explicit, expected, and enduring.

REFERENCES

Bogenschneider, K. (2000). Has family policy come of age? A decade review of the state of U.S. family policy in the 1990s. *Journal of Marriage and the Family, 62,* 1136–1159.

Bogenschneider, K. (2002). *Taking family policy seriously.* Mahwah, NJ: Lawrence Erlbaum.

Bogenschneider, K., Olson, J. R., Linney, K. D., & Mills, J. (2000). Connecting research and policymaking: Implications for theory and practice from the Family Impact Seminars. *Family Relations, 49,* 327–339.

Bogenschneider, K., Young, R., Melli, M., & Fleming, M. (1993). *Building policies that put families first.* Madison: University of Wisconsin-Madison, Center for Excellence in Family Studies.

Carlson, A. (2001). Theodore Roosevelt's new politics of the American family. *Family in America, 15*(10), 1–8.

Carlson, A. (2002a). Hyphenates, hausfraus, and baby-saving: The peculiar legacy of German-America. *Family in America, 16*(1/2), 1–20.

Carlson, A. (2002b). "Sanctif[ying] the traditional family": The New Deal and national solidarity. *Family in America, 16*(5), 1–12.

Consortium of Family Organizations. (1990). *Family policy report* (Vol. 1, No. 1). Washington, DC: Author.

Corbett, T., Burkett-Simms, C., Crandall, L., Howard, D., Le, N., Powers, P., et al. (1998). *The Midwest Welfare Peer Assistance Network* (Rev. ed.). Madison: University of Wisconsin, Institute for Research on Poverty.

Dishion, T. J., McCord, J., & Poulin, F. (1999). When interventions harm: Peer groups and problem behavior. *American Psychologist, 54,* 755–764.

Eshleman, R. (1991). *The family: An introduction.* Boston: Allyn & Bacon.

Gordon, L. (1992). Social insurance and public assistance: The influence of gender in welfare thought in the United States, 1890–1935. *American Historical Review, 97,* 19–54.

Gordon, L. (1994). *Pitied but not entitled.* New York: Free Press.

Hauser, R. M., Brown, B. V., & Prosser, W. R. (1997) *Indicators of children's well-being.* New York: Russell Sage.

Hewlett, S. A., & West, C. (1998). *The war against parents.* New York: Houghton Mifflin.

Hutchins, J. (1998). *Coming together for children and families.* Washington, DC: Family Impact Seminar.

Jacobs, F. H., & Davies, M. W. (1994). On the eve of a new millennium. In F. H. Jacobs & M. W. Davies (Eds.), *More than kissing babies?* (pp. 277–298). Westport, CT: Auburn House.

Kamerman, S. B., & Kahn, A. J. (1978). Families and the idea of family policy. In S. B. Kamerman & A. J. Kahn (Eds.), *Family policy* (pp. 1–16). New York: Columbia University Press.

Kamerman, S. B., & Kahn, A. J. (2001). Child and family policies in an era of social policy retrenchment and restructuring. In T. Smeeding & K. Vleminckx (Eds.), *Child well-being, child poverty and child policy in modern nations* (pp. 501–525). Bristol, UK: Policy Press.

Knitzer, J., & Page, S. (1998). *Map and track: State initiatives for young children and families, 1998 edition.* New York: Columbia University School of Public Health, National Center for Children in Poverty.

Koven, S., & Michel, S. (1993). *Mothers of a new world.* New York: Routledge.

Ladd-Taylor, M. (1993). "My work came out of agony and grief": Mothers and the making of the Sheppard-Towner Act. In S. Koven & S. Michel (Eds.), *Mothers of a new world* (pp. 321–342). New York: Routledge.

Lindenmeyer, K. (1997). *A right to childhood.* Urbana: University of Illinois Press.

Moen, P., & Schorr, A. L. (1987). Families and social policy. In M. B. Sussman & S. K. Steinmetz (Eds.), *Handbook of marriage and the family* (pp. 795–813). New York: Plenum.

Moynihan, D. P. (1941). Foreword to the paperback edition. In *Nation and family.* Cambridge, MA: MIT Press.

Moynihan, D. P. (1986). *Family and nation.* New York: Harcourt Brace Jovanovich.

Ooms, T. (1990). Families and government: Implementing a family perspective in public policy. *Social Thought, 16,* 61–78.

Ooms, T. (1995, October). *Taking families seriously: Family impact analysis as an essential policy tool.* Paper presented at the Expert Meeting on Family Impact, University of Leuven, Leuven, Belgium.

Ooms, T. (1998). *Towards more perfect unions: Putting marriage on the public agenda.* Washington, DC: Family Impact Seminar.

Ooms, T. (2002). Foreword. In K. Bogenschneider, *Taking family policy seriously.* Mahwah, NJ: Lawrence Erlbaum.

Parke, R. D. (2002, April). *SCRD at 70: Progress and promise.* Invited address presented at the biennial meeting of the Society for Research on Child Development, Tampa, FL.

Rist, R. C. (1994). Qualitative program evaluation: Practice and promise. In N. Denzin & Y. Lincoln (Eds.), *Handbook of qualitative research* (pp. 545–558). Thousand Oaks, CA: Sage.

Ross, R., & Staines, G. L. (1972). The politics of analyzing social problems. *Social Problems, 20,* 18–40.

Scott, K, G., Mason, C. A., & Chapman, D. A. (1999). The use of epidemiological methodology as a means of influencing public policy. *Child Development, 70,* 1263–1272.

Sklar, K. K. (1993). The historical foundations of women's power in the creation of the American welfare state, 1840–1930. In S. Koven & S. Michel (Eds.), *Mothers of a new world* (pp. 321–342). New York: Routledge.

Skocpol, T. (1995). *Social policy in the United States.* Princeton, NJ: Princeton University Press.

Skocpol, T. (1997). A partnership with American families. In S. B. Greenberg & T. Skocpol (Eds.), *The new majority* (pp. 104–129). New Haven, CT: Yale University Press.

Smith, J. A. (1991). *The idea brokers*. New York: Free Press.

Stage, S. (1997). Ellen Richards and the social significance of the home economics movement. In S. Stage & V. B. Vincenti (Eds.), *Rethinking home economics* (pp. 17–33). Ithaca, NY: Cornell University Press.

Trattner, W. I. (1999). *Poor law to welfare state*. New York: Free Press.

Welfare Peer Assistance Network. (2002). Welfare then, welfare now: Expenditures in some midwestern states. *Focus* (University of Wisconsin-Madison, Institute for Research on Poverty), 22(1), pp. 11–14.

Westat. (2000). Trends in the well-being of America's children and youth. Retrieved April 6, 2003, from the U.S. Department of Health and Human Services Web site: http://aspe.hhs.gov/hsp/00trends.

CHAPTER 27

The Disturbing Paradox of Poverty in American Families
What We Have Learned Over the Past Four Decades

MARK R. RANK

The issue of poverty within America's families has been both paradoxical and troubling—a paradox in that impoverishment occurs in the context of American prosperity; troubling because of the detrimental outcomes associated with poverty. This juxtaposition provided much of the moral justification behind President Lyndon Johnson's declared War on Poverty, when he announced, in his 1965 Inaugural Address:

> In a land of great wealth, families must not live in hopeless poverty. In a land rich in harvest, children just must not go hungry. In a land of healing miracles, neighbors must not suffer and die unattended. In a great land of learning and scholars, young people must be taught to read and write.

Although the War on Poverty attempted to raise the moral and policy consciousness of the nation, it also set in motion the beginnings of our modern-day research understanding into American poverty. In fact, it was only with the onset of the War on Poverty that the United States began to measure poverty on an official basis, while at the same time initiating a series of policy and academic analyses funded out of the newly created Office of Economic Opportunity. These studies, along with many others that followed, have greatly informed us as to the nature and character of American poverty.

This chapter takes stock of what we have learned from the research community during the past four decades. The review is divided into five substantive areas: (a) the scope and dynamics of American poverty; (b) factors associated with poverty; (c) the effects and consequences of impoverishment; (d) policy strategies for assisting poor families; and (e) needed future research directions.

THE SCOPE AND DYNAMICS OF POVERTY

It was not until 1964 that the United States had an official measure of poverty. The task

469

of devising such a standard fell to Mollie Orshansky, an economist in the Social Security Administration (see Orshansky, 1965). Orshansky's basic methodology has remained intact to this day and represent the most common measure of poverty found in governmental reporting and academic research. Poverty was operationalized as the lack of a specific level of income necessary to purchase a basic basket of goods and services allowing for a minimally decent level of existence (for an extended discussion on the measurement of poverty, see Brady, 2003; Glennerster, 2002; Institute for Research on Poverty, 1998; National Research Council, 1995; U.S. Bureau of the Census, 1999).

Total household income is thus the measuring stick to determine whether individuals and families fall below the poverty line. Households under specific income levels are considered poor. To account for the factor of inflation, the poverty thresholds are adjusted each year in accordance with consumer price index changes. The level itself also varies depending on household size. For example, in 2001, a household of one was considered poor if its income fell below $9,039; for a household of two, the level was $11,569; for a household of three, $14,128; for a household of four, $18,104; and so on (U.S. Bureau of the Census, 2002b).

Cross-Sectional Rates

Each year, a representative sample of approximately 50,000 to 60,000 U.S. households is included in the U.S. Bureau of the Census's Current Population Survey. One of its purposes is to gather information regarding individual and household income. From these data, analysts estimate the scope of poverty in the United States and track changes in the official poverty rate.

In 1959, the U.S. poverty rate stood at 22.4% (U.S. Bureau of the Census, 2002b; although the measure was created in 1964, it

was backdated to 1959). During the 1960s, the rate fell sharply, such that by 1973 it had reached a low of 11.1%. Since 1973, the poverty rate has fluctuated between 11% and 15%. It has tended to rise during periods of economic recession (early 1980s, early 1990s) and has fallen during periods of economic expansion (middle to later 1980s, middle to later 1990s).

The poverty rate in 2001 stood at 11.7%, which represented 32.9 million Americans (U.S. Bureau of the Census, 2002b). The percentage of the population falling into poverty or near poverty (125% of the poverty line) was 16.1% (or 45.3 million Americans), whereas 4.8% of the population, representing 13.4 million Americans, experienced extreme poverty (falling below 50% of the poverty line).

Longitudinal Dynamics

Beginning in the 1970s, researchers have increasingly sought to uncover the longitudinal dynamics of poverty. These studies have used several nationally representative panel data sets, including the Panel Study of Income Dynamics (PSID), the National Longitudinal Survey of Youth (NLSY), and the Survey of Income and Program Participation (SIPP). Results from these longitudinal analyses have shed considerable light on the patterns of U.S. poverty. Several broad conclusions can be drawn from this body of work.

First, most spells of poverty are fairly short. The typical pattern is that households are impoverished for 1 or 2 years and then manage to get above the poverty line (Bane & Ellwood, 1986; Blank, 1997; Duncan, 1984; Walker, 1994). They may stay there for a period of time, only to experience an additional fall into poverty at some point (Stevens, 1999). Because their economic distance above the poverty threshold is often narrow, a detrimental economic event such as the loss of a job or the breakup of a family can easily throw a family back below the poverty line (Duncan et al., 1995).

In contrast, a much smaller number of households experience chronic poverty for years at a time. Typically, they have characteristics that put them at a severe disadvantage vis-à-vis the labor market (e.g., individuals with serious work disabilities, female-headed families with large numbers of children, racial minorities living in inner-city areas). Their prospects for getting out of poverty for any significant period of time are severely diminished (Devine & Wright, 1993).

And of course, some individuals and households fall in between these two ends of the spectrum. For example, Blank (1997) relied upon the Panel Study of Income Dynamics (PSID) data to calculate the occurrence of poverty over a 13-year span. She found that during the period of 1979 to 1991 one third of Americans experienced a spell of poverty. However, of those who fell below the poverty line, one half were poor for 3 years or less, one third were in poverty for between 4 and 9 years, and 14.6% fell below the poverty line for 10 of the 13 years (4.5% of the poor fell below the poverty line for each of the 13 years).

Finally, research into the dynamics of poverty has also shown that many households will reexperience poverty in the future. Using annual estimates of poverty from the PSID data, Stevens (1994) calculated that of all persons who had managed to get themselves above the poverty line, over half would return to poverty within 5 years.

The picture of poverty drawn from this body of research is thus characterized by fluidity. Individuals and households tend to weave their way in and out of poverty, depending upon the occurrence or nonoccurrence of particular detrimental events (e.g., job loss, family disruption, ill health). Similar findings have been obtained with respect to the longitudinal patterns of welfare use (Bane & Ellwood, 1994; Blank, 1997; Duncan, 1984; Rank, 1985, 1994a).

Comparative Studies

A third body of research examining the scope and dynamics of poverty has focused on how U.S. rates of poverty contrast with those of other countries, specifically, other industrialized nations. Several problems have made such comparisons difficult. First and foremost has been the lack of analogous data sets large enough to allow for such an analysis. Fortunately, this obstacle has been partially overcome with the Luxembourg Income Study (LIS). Initiated in the 1980s, the LIS contains income and demographic information on households in 25 different nations from 1967 to the present. Variables have been standardized across 70 data sets, allowing researchers to conduct cross-national analyses regarding poverty and income inequality.

Impoverishment in the United States exceeds that of all similar countries. Smeeding, Rainwater, and Burtless (2001) compared the rates of poverty among 18 developed nations, using two relative measures of poverty along with an absolute measure. All three measures showed a similar pattern. For example, by defining poverty as the percentage of persons living with incomes below 50% of the median income, the authors found that the U.S. rate of 17.8% was substantially above those found in the other 17 nations. Italy was next at 13.9%, followed by the United Kingdom, Canada, and Spain, with the Scandinavian and Benelux countries falling near the bottom. The overall average for the 18 nations was 8.6%. Similar findings were found for children and the elderly. What is startling about these results is that the United States is also the wealthiest nation in the world.

This paradox is revealed in additional LIS analyses of how well children and adults from middle and upper incomes do. Not surprisingly, the United States has the highest standards of living at these points in the income distribution scale. The conclusion to be drawn from these divergent patterns regarding American children is stated by Rainwater and Smeeding (1995):

> In other words, while the United States has a higher real level of income than most of our comparison countries it is the high and middle income children who reap the benefits (and much more the former than the latter). Low income American children suffer in both absolute and relative terms. The average low income child in the other 17 countries is at least one-third better off than is the average low-income American child. (p. 9)

Two reasons stand out as to why Americans at the lower end of the economic distribution do so badly when compared to their counterparts in other countries. First, the social safety net in the United States is considerably weaker than in other Western industrialized countries. Second, the United States is plagued by relatively low wages at the bottom of the income distribution scale when compared to other developed countries (Smeeding, 1997; Smeeding et al., 2001). These factors contribute to both the relative and absolute depths of poverty in the United States as compared with other industrialized nations (for additional work, see Oyen, Miller, & Samad, 1996; United Nations Development Programme, 2000, 2003).

Life Course Risk

A final approach for assessing the scope of American poverty has been to analyze poverty as a life course event. Specifically, how likely is it that an American will experience poverty during his or her lifetime? Some of the earliest social scientific work on poverty attempted to place it within a life course framework. Seebohm Rowntree's

(1901) description of 11,560 working-class families in the English city of York was pioneering in developing this approach. Likewise, Robert Hunter, in his book *Poverty* (1904), attempted to locate impoverishment within the context of the life course.

Despite these early writings, examining poverty as a potential life course event has been largely overlooked in the research community. The work of Rank and Hirschl has recently employed this approach. Relying upon the PSID, they have constructed a series of life tables estimating the likelihood of poverty across the American life course.

Their results indicate that between the ages of 20 and 85, two thirds of Americans will experience at least 1 year of impoverishment (Rank & Hirschl, 1999c). The odds of encountering poverty across adulthood are significantly raised for African Americans and those with lower levels of education (Rank & Hirschl, 2001c). Those who experience poverty do so for generally 1 or 2 consecutive years. However, once an individual experiences poverty, he or she is quite likely to encounter poverty again (Rank & Hirschl, 2001b). Similar patterns have been found regarding the use of welfare across the life course (Rank & Hirschl, 2002).

Rank and Hirschl's analyses (1999a, 1999b) also indicate that poverty is prevalent during the periods of childhood and old age. Between the ages of 1 and 17, 34% of American children will have spent at least 1 year below the poverty line, and 40% will have experienced poverty or near poverty (125% of the poverty line). Similarly, 40% of the elderly will encounter at least 1 year of poverty between the ages of 60 and 90, while 48% will encounter poverty at the 125% level.

For the majority of Americans, it would appear that the question is not if they will encounter poverty but rather when. The experience of poverty can thus be viewed within the wider context of the life course as a normative American event. Rank and Hirschl (2001a) argued that understanding poverty from such a perspective entails a fundamental shift in the perception and meaning of poverty (for further work applying a life course perspective to poverty, see Leisering & Leibfried, 1999).

FACTORS ASSOCIATED WITH POVERTY

A second area of research has examined the factors and causes underlying poverty. As O'Connor (2001) noted, the thrust of this research has shifted from an examination into industrial capitalism as a fundamental cause of poverty at the turn of the century to a highly technical analysis of the demographic and behavioral characteristics of the poor (particularly welfare recipients) by the end of the 20th century. One of the reasons for this shift has been the growing importance of survey research, which has become the dominant methodological tool in the social sciences. Such an approach lends itself to an empirical analysis of individual characteristics rather than the structural conditions underlying poverty. For example, race and gender are often treated as demographic attributes to be controlled for within multivariate models rather than as dimensions of social and economic stratification in their own right (O'Connor, 2001).

Individual Factors

Attitudes

The notion of poverty resulting from individual character flaws goes back hundreds of years. Survey research confirms that a majority of Americans continue to believe that this is a very important reason for the existence of poverty (Feagin, 1975; Gans, 1995; Gilens, 1999; Kluegel & Smith, 1986;

Smith & Stone, 1989; Wolfe, 1998). In particular, the argument has been that the poor lack the correct attitudes, motivation, or morals to get ahead (Schwartz, 2000).

Researchers who have examined the attitudes of the poor have found little evidence for this position (Dunbar, 1988; Duncan, 1984; Edwards, Plotnick, & Klawitter, 2001; Goodwin, 1972, 1983; Rank, 1994a, 1994b; Seccombe, 1999). Contrary to popular opinion, the poor tend to amplify and reiterate mainstream American values such as the importance of hard work, personal responsibility, and a dislike of the welfare system. Although poverty is accompanied by increasing levels of stress and frustration (discussed later, in the section "The Effects and Consequences of Poverty"), the vast majority of the poor express a set of core attitudes and motivations similar to those found in middle-class America (Lichter & Crowley, 2002).

Welfare

A variation of the above perspective has been that individual attitudes and behaviors have been negatively altered as a result of public assistance: specifically, that various welfare programs have created work and marriage disincentives, which in turn have encouraged dependency upon the government, along with counterproductive behaviors such as teenage pregnancy and marital disruption, and that these behaviors have then trapped individuals and families into a cycle of poverty. This position also goes back hundreds of years (Tocqueville, 1983) and has been articulated more recently by Charles Murray in his book *Losing Ground* (1984; in addition, see Mead, 1986; Olasky, 1992).

Extensive research has been conducted over the past 30 years into the effects of welfare programs upon individual and family behavior. The vast majority of this research indicates that although the welfare system (specifically AFDC) has had a minor impact upon work incentives and several areas of family formation (e.g., marital dissolution), in general the overall effect have been quite small in terms of altering individual and family behavior and/or fostering dependency and consequently poverty (Bane & Jargowsky, 1988; Blank, 1997; Moffitt, 1992; Rank, 1989; Rank & Cheng, 1995). As Bane and Ellwood (1994) noted, "Although theories about welfare effects . . . are forcefully argued, existing evidence is quite limited. In the case of welfare, the bulk of evidence to date has shown only small effects" (p. 120).

One reason for this has been that the amount of income and/or in-kind assistance available from the U.S. welfare system has been historically quite small (particularly in comparison to that provided in other industrialized countries). Furthermore, the 1996 welfare reform changes have resulted in a system that is even less generous. In short, the argument that poverty has been created and exasperated by the generosity of the U.S. welfare system has found little empirical support from the research community.

Human Capital

The importance of human capital in affecting earnings (and consequently the risk of poverty) has been studied extensively within the labor economics and social stratification literatures. The argument is that individuals acquiring greater human capital will be in greater demand in the marketplace (Becker, 1964). As a result, they will be able to pursue more lucrative careers resulting in higher-paying and relatively stable jobs. Those lacking in human capital are not able to compete as effectively in the labor market and therefore must settle for unstable, low-wage work.

The effect of human capital upon the risk of poverty has been shown to be substantial (Schiller, 2004). In particular, greater levels of education, skills, and training are strongly associated with higher levels of earnings. Conversely, those lacking in marketable job skills and education are at a much greater risk of experiencing poverty.

In addition, several other individual and family characteristics have been shown to be important factors in increasing or decreasing the risk of poverty. These include race, gender, work disability, family structure, number of children, residence, and age. All of these can be conceptualized as affecting the ability to interact with and take advantage of opportunities in the labor market. Specifically, poverty rates tend to be higher for minorities, women, those with work disabilities, single-parent families, households with large numbers of children, families in economically depressed areas such as inner cities or remote rural locations, and younger adults (U.S. Bureau of the Census, 2002b).

Cultural and Neighborhood Factors

A second level of analysis has addressed the importance of cultural and neighborhood factors in maintaining poverty. The focus is on the residential environment and its influence in shaping the way in which families cope and adjust to that environment.

Culture of Poverty

The culture-of-poverty framework arose from the ethnographic work of Oscar Lewis. His study *Five Families* (1959) examined lower-class Mexican family life, and a later work, *La Vida* (1966b), focused on Puerto Rican families residing in slum communities in both New York City and Puerto Rico. Lewis argued that chronic conditions of high unemployment and underemployment, coupled with little opportunity for upward mobility, had led to a culture of poverty within approximately 20% of the U.S. poor population. Such a culture was most likely to arise in economically depressed and isolated areas such as Appalachia or urban inner cities. This culture provided individuals and families with a means for coping with their impoverished situations. Traits included a present-time orientation, stronger networks of kinship ties, and an unwillingness to delay gratification. As Lewis (1966a) wrote, "It is both an adaptation and a reaction of the poor to their marginal position in a class-stratified, highly individuated capitalistic society. . . . Once the culture of poverty has come into existence it tends to perpetuate itself" (p. 22). Such a culture enabled families to cope and adapt to their environment, but it also made it more difficult for them to eventually break out of poverty.

The culture-of-poverty thesis exerted a significant impact on social policy in the 1960s. Policy initiatives and programs arising out of the War on Poverty, such as the Moynihan Report, Head Start, and community action, were all influenced by the concept of a culture of poverty. However, empirical verification of the theory failed to materialize, and the culture-of-poverty thesis fell out of favor by the early 1970s. It was not until the work of William Julius Wilson that the concept was seriously revisited.

Social Isolation

Wilson (1987, 1996) sought to provide a framework for understanding the increasing social problems and poverty found in the inner city over the past 30 years. In particular, his concern was with the underclass, or "the truly disadvantaged." Wilson argued that many of the problems found in the inner city of today are the result of neighborhoods' becoming more socially isolated from mainstream behavior while at the same time experiencing a greater concentration of deviant behavior. These two trends have arisen as a result of the loss of decent-paying jobs, along with the migration of the black middle and working class out of the inner city.

The effect of social isolation and the concentration of deviant behavior have led to the rise of what Wilson referred to as a *ghetto-specific culture*. This culture includes the acceptance of behaviors such as out-of-wedlock births, welfare dependency, and crime, which in turn have made escaping from poverty more difficult. Yet Wilson argued that the ultimate solution to inner-city poverty must lie in providing decent economic opportunities within these neighborhoods. When opportunities are provided, the current ghetto-specific culture and its counterproductive behaviors will quickly fade.

The work of Elijah Anderson (1990, 1999) has explored the role of culture and social isolation in helping to explain inner-city poverty and its accompanying social problems. Anderson's ethnographies have provided in-depth qualitative material that has generally been consistent with Wilson's overall thesis (for a review of the line of research focusing on social isolation, culture, and inner cities, see Small & Newman, 2001).

Residential Segregation

A third neighborhood factor posited as critical for understanding the causes of poverty within the urban black family has been that of racial residential segregation. Douglas Massey has been at the forefront of this research. This body of work has demonstrated that residential segregation on the basis of race is widespread, leading to deteriorating economic and social conditions within such neighborhoods. As Massey and Denton write in *American Apartheid* (1993):

> Deleterious neighborhood conditions are built into the structure of the black community. They occur because segregation concentrates poverty to build a set of mutually reinforcing and self-feeding spirals of decline into black neighborhoods. When

economic dislocations deprive a segregated group of employment and increase its rate of poverty, socioeconomic deprivation inevitably becomes more concentrated in neighborhoods where that group lives. . . . Segregation is the missing link in prior attempts to understand the plight of the urban poor. (pp. 2-3)

Residential segregation restricts the opportunities available to urban black families through social isolation and increasing levels of deprivation. These, in turn, ensure high levels of poverty and widespread social disorganization (in addition, see Jargowsky, 1997; Yinger, 1995).

Structural Factors

Structural factors represent a third conceptual level for understanding poverty within American families. Rather than looking to the individual or neighborhood, the emphasis is upon the economic, political, and/or social structure as the source of poverty.

Economic Structure

The argument developed by Karl Marx and Friedrich Engels (1968) during the middle 19th century and continuing through the more recent class analysis literature (Wright, 1994) has been that poverty is a direct result of the capitalist economic structure. Businesses are profit driven yet at the same time constrained by the laws of competition. To abide by both of these imperatives, businesses keep labor costs as low as possible by paying workers substandard wages while continually seeking out labor-saving devices, such as automation, and sending jobs overseas. This results in significant economic vulnerability for a segment of the population that Marx and Engels referred to as the *industrial reserve army*. As a result of their vulnerable position in the economy, these individuals and families are often at the edge of poverty.

A second economic perspective to explain poverty among American families has been that of the dual labor market. This argument rests on the assumption that there are two distinctly different labor markets operating in the American economy, the primary and secondary labor markets. In the primary market, jobs are characterized by stability, relatively high wages, and good working conditions. Jobs in the secondary labor market are more likely to have poor working conditions, marked by instability and low wages. Individuals with less marketable skills, education, and characteristics often find themselves working in the secondary labor market. As Hodson and Kaufman (1982) noted, "[O]nce workers enter the secondary market, they acquire unstable work histories" (p. 730). Employers in the primary labor market then use these histories as evidence that the workers are inadequate and thus block them from moving into the primary market (Doeringer & Piore, 1975). Such individuals will likely remain in secondary jobs during their adult working careers, resulting in an elevated risk of poverty throughout their lives.

Empirical work into these areas has been relatively sparse but has generally confirmed the existence of the above dynamics. As Beeghley (2000) summarized, "[T]he structure of the economy insures that millions of people will be poor no matter how hard they work, no matter what their skills, no matter how much they try. This fact exists independently of their individual efforts" (p. 252).

Social and Political Structure

Beginning with Davis and Moore's (1945) functional theory of social stratification and continuing through the work of Gans (1972, 1995), an argument has been made that poverty serves a number of economic, social, and political functions for society in general and for the middle and affluent classes in particular. As a result, poverty is conceptualized as a vital component of the social structure. For example, the existence of the poor ensures that there will be a labor pool to work at undesirable but necessary jobs (e.g., fast food, janitorial work). In addition, such jobs pay low wages, thereby keeping the costs of these services down for the rest of society. From this perspective, poverty is the result of a system of social stratification that guarantees that a certain percentage of the population will be economically unstable.

In a somewhat similar fashion, the role of racial and gender discrimination can be understood. Substantial research has shown that economic, social, and political discrimination remains prevalent in American society, largely to the benefit of the white male population (Feagin, 2000). Such discrimination has disproportionately affected the life chances of racial minorities and women, resulting in higher rates of poverty among these groups. Likewise, the concept of social exclusion has been used particularly in a European context to understand the existence of poverty (Barnes et al., 2002; Bhalla & Lapeyre, 1999; Sen, 1992, 1999).

A social policy factor that has been examined to explain American poverty has been the weakness of its social safety net. Contrary to the popular rhetoric of vast amounts of tax dollars being spent on public assistance (as argued earlier in the section "Welfare"), the American welfare state can more accurately be described as minimal when compared to the expansive support provided by other industrial countries (Esping-Andersen, 1990). In addition, the United States has failed to offer the type of universal coverage for child care, medical insurance, or child allowances that most other developed countries routinely provide. The result is that social policies aimed at economically vulnerable populations in Europe

and Canada substantially reduce the extent of poverty, whereas American social policy only minimally protects families from poverty (Ritakallio, 2001).

Structural Vulnerability

An approach that bridges the empirical importance of human capital, with the significance of structural forces, has been my concept of structural vulnerability (Rank, 1994a, 2000, 2004). This approach recognizes that human capital is associated with who loses in the economic game (and hence is more likely to experience poverty) but that structural factors predominately ensure that there will be losers in the first place. Those who experience poverty are likely to have characteristics that put them and their families at a disadvantage in terms of competing in the economy (e.g., lower education, fewer skills, single-parent families, minorities in inner cities, younger adults). However, given the lack of enough decent-paying jobs for everyone (along with many other structural factors restricting economic opportunities), a certain percentage of the population will experience economic vulnerability regardless of what their characteristics are. Consequently, although a lack of human capital and its accompanying vulnerability lead to an understanding of who the losers of the economic game are likely to be, the more structural components of our economic, social, and political systems explain why there are losers in the first place.

An analogy illustrates this concept. Imagine a game of musical chairs in which there are 10 players but only eight chairs. On one hand, individual success or failure in the game will depend upon the skill and luck of each player. Those who are less agile or less well placed when the music stops are likely to lose. These are appropriately cited as the reasons that a particular individual has lost the game. On the other hand, given that there are only eight chairs available, two players are bound to lose regardless of their individual characteristics. Even if all the players were suddenly to double their speed and agility, there would still be two losers. From this broader context, the characteristics of the individual players are no longer important in terms of understanding that the structure of the game ensures that someone will lose.

The structural vulnerability perspective thus recognizes the importance of human capital characteristics in influencing the risk of individual poverty but places the existence of such poverty within the broader context of the wider social and economic environment. Thus the causes of poverty will shift depending on whether one chooses to analyze the losers of the game or the game itself (for further detail, see Rank, 2003, 2004; Rank, Yoon, & Hirschl, in press).

THE EFFECTS AND CONSEQUENCES OF POVERTY

A third major stream of research has analyzed the effect of poverty on individuals and families. The damaging effects of American poverty were documented over 100 years ago in Jacob Riis's landmark book, *How the Other Half Lives* (1890/1972), which detailed the impoverished conditions of tenement families in an area known as "the Bend" in New York City. More recently, the 1962 publication of Michael Harrington's book *The Other America* raised the nation's consciousness regarding the human pain associated with poverty. Since the early 1960s, an enormous amount of research has examined both the costs and consequences of American poverty.

Individual Effects

One of the most consistent findings in epidemiology has been that the quality of an individual's health is negatively affected by lower socioeconomic status, particularly impoverishment (Kawachi & Kennedy, 2002; Kawachi, Kennedy, & Wilkinson, 1999; Smith, 1999). Poverty is associated with a host of health risks, including elevated rates of heart disease, diabetes, hypertension, cancer, infant mortality, mental illness, undernutrition, lead poisoning, asthma, and dental problems (Lichter & Crowley, 2002; Sherman, 1994; Williams & Collins, 1995). The result is a death rate for the poverty stricken that is approximately three times higher than that for the affluent between the ages of 25 and 64 (Pappas, Queen, Hadden, & Fisher, 1993). As Leidenfrost (1993) noted, "Health disparities between the poor and those with higher incomes are almost universal for all dimensions of health" (p. 1).

These effects are particularly profound with regard to children (Seccombe, 2000). Poor infants and young children are much more likely to have lower levels of physical and mental growth (as measured in a variety of ways) than their nonpoor counterparts (Duncan & Brooks-Gunn, 1997). Both the duration and depth of poverty intensify these effects (McLeod & Shanahan, 1993; Smith, Brooks-Gunn, & Klebanov, 1997). The result is that poverty can have long-lasting physical and mental consequences as children become adults.

In a similar fashion, research has demonstrated that poverty negatively affects the acquisition of human capital. Various analyses have indicated that differences in parental economic and social class result in significant differences in resources and opportunities for children (Corcoran, 1995, 2001; McMurrer & Sawhill, 1998). For example, the quality and quantity of education that a child receives is strongly influenced by the level of parental income. Children in poverty are more likely to receive an inferior education, which then affects their ability as adults to compete effectively in the labor market

(Duncan, Yeung, Brooks-Gunn, & Smith, 1998).

Family Effects

The likelihood of marriage is substantially reduced among the poverty stricken (Cheal, 1996). This is because individuals contemplating marriage are seeking, or often desire to be, an economically secure partner (Becker, 1981). Poverty undermines the availability of such partners. Hence, individuals in these situations are more likely to forego marriage.

Most recent and well known within this vein of research has been the work of Wilson (1987, 1996). As noted earlier, his analyses have addressed the increasing problems found within the inner city among African Americans and the reasons why such problems appear to have worsened over the past three decades. According to Wilson, a critical factor in understanding the falling rate of marriage within the inner-city population has been the economic restructuring that has resulted in the movement of capital and job opportunities out of central-city areas.

Women at lower income and educational levels also tend to have children at earlier ages and are more likely to bear children out of wedlock (Maynard, 1997). For example, the fertility rate per 1,000 unmarried women aged 18 to 24 is 300.9 for those with 0 to 8 years of education, 123.5 for those with 12 years of education, and 23.7 for those with 13 to 15 years of education (National Center for Health Statistics, 1997).

Several ethnographic studies over the past four decades have indicated that those in poverty are more likely to use a larger network of kinship than the nonpoor to exchange resources and services. This extended network has served as a coping mechanism for dealing with the uncertainties and hardships of poverty (e.g., Edin & Lein, 1997; Harvey, 1993; Kwong, 2001; Lewis,

1966a; Stack, 1974). For example, Carol Stack (1974) found in her study of a poor, black community called The Flats that it was virtually impossible for families to cover their various expenses and needs completely on their own. Consequently, a system of collective sharing arose within The Flats as an adaptive strategy to survive the daily uncertainties and depravation of poverty. As Stack wrote:

> In the final months of my life in The Flats, I learned that poverty creates a necessity for this exchange of goods and services. The needs of families living at bare subsistence are so large compared to their average daily income that it is impossible for families to provide independently for fixed expenses and daily needs. Lacking any surplus of funds, they are forced to use most of their resources for major monthly bills: rent, utilities, and foods. After a family pays these bills they are penniless. (p. 29)

This system of exchange encompassed a wide network of kin and friends. Only through such a collective response were families able to get through the daily trials and tribulations of long term poverty.

Likewise, in Harvey's (1993) study of a white, displaced farming population that had located in a community called Potter Addition, a similar process of mutual sharing and obligation developed across a wide network of kin. Family and kin members could be counted on to help in various situations, just as they themselves would be counted on for mutual assistance by others.

Research has consistently found that poverty and lower income are associated with greater levels of marital stress, dissatisfaction, and dissolution (U.S. Bureau of the Census, 1992; Vosler, 1996; Voydanoff, 1990; White & Rogers, 2000). In essence, poverty and low income act to amplify the daily stress found in everyday life and its relationships. Married couples in poverty face mounting economic stress that subsequently lowers their levels of marital happiness and well-being (Conger, Ge, & Lorenz, 1994; Shirk, Bennett, & Aber, 1999). This in turn increases the likelihood that couples will attempt to resolve such dissatisfaction through separation and/or divorce.

Largely as a result of the aforementioned stresses and economic strains, lower socioeconomic status is associated with higher levels of domestic violence (Gelles, 1993; Moore, 1997; Sedlak & Broadhurst, 1996; Straus, Gelles, & Steinmetz, 1980). This is particularly true in understanding men's violence against their wives (Anderson, 1997).

In addition to the direct effects upon the family, research has also examined the effect that high rates of neighborhood poverty have on the viability of the community, which in turn influences the viability of the family (Brooks-Gunn, Duncan, & Aber, 1997; Burton & Jarrett, 2000). Major research areas have included the relationship between neighborhood poverty and elevated rates of crime (Sampson, Raudenbush, & Earls, 1997), neighborhood poverty and declining social capital (Putnam, 2000), and neighborhood poverty and the increasing risk of environmental hazards (Bullard, 1990). All of these have been shown to have a detrimental impact on the health and functioning of low-income families residing in impoverished neighborhoods.

AMELIORATING POVERTY

At the heart of the policy analysis community is the question of how best to help American families below the poverty line. A number of programs have been proposed and implemented during the past 40 years. Three of the more influential approaches for economically assisting low-income families are discussed next. Each has been gaining in political importance over the past decade, carries a bipartisan appeal, and has been supported with empirical research.

Earned Income Tax Credit

During the past 25 years, the American economy has increasingly produced larger numbers of jobs that are low paying, part time, and/or lacking in benefits (Bartik, 2001; Ellwood, 2000). Studies analyzing the percentage of the U.S. workforce falling into the low-wage sector of the economy have shown that a much higher percentage of Americans (25 percent of all full-time workers) are employed in low-wage jobs compared with an average of 12.9 percent for workers in other industrialized countries (Smeeding et al., 2001).

The Earned Income Tax Credit (EITC) represents a social and economic policy that partially offsets this pattern. The EITC was enacted in 1975 and underwent a significant expansion during the 1990s. It currently represents the largest cash antipoverty program in the United States. The program is designed to provide a refundable tax credit to low-income workers, with the vast majority going to families with children. For example, a parent with two children, employed at $8 an hour, would receive an additional $3.20 an hour from the government through the EITC. The program thus provides a significant supplement to low earners. In 2002, more than 19 million households received EITC tax credits averaging $1,700 (Schiller, 2004).

The EITC appeals to both liberals and conservatives. As Danziger and Gottschalk (1995) wrote, "It has retained bipartisan support because of a number of its features: it assists only those who work; it helps two-parent as well as single parent families; it raises the employee's take-home pay without increasing the employer's labor costs" (p. 158). In addition, it has helped to offset the above mentioned trend since the early 1970s of declining real wages among low-skilled workers.

According to Schiller (2004), approximately 2 million more individuals would have fallen below the poverty line without the EITC program. For families remaining in poverty, the EITC has helped to reduce the distance between their household income and the poverty line. It has also enabled families to purchase particular resources that can improve their economic and social mobility (e.g., pay tuition, purchase a car, and change residence), as well as helping to meet daily expenses (Smeeding, Phillips, & O'Connor, 2000).

Child Support

Child support and its enforcement has become an increasing American concern. Beginning with the work of Weitzman (1985), the economic impact of divorce and single parenthood upon women and their children has been extensively documented (McLanahan & Sandefur, 1994). This body of work has demonstrated that newly created female-headed families with children are at a significant risk of poverty. One of the reasons for this is that mothers often fail to receive their court-ordered child support payments. For example, in 1999, 45.9% of mothers received the full amount of court-ordered child support payments, 28.7% received only partial payment, and 25.4% received no payment. Of the $29.5 billion that was due in child support payments in 1997, $17.6 billion were actually received (U.S. Bureau of the Census, 2002a).

From the mid 1970s onward, a series of changes in federal laws have attempted to make child support enforcement more effective (Institute for Research on Poverty, 2000). This was particularly true of the 1996 welfare reform changes. States are required to operate a child support program that meets federal mandates (e.g., expanded efforts in income withholding, paternity establishment, enforcement of orders, and use of central registries). Failing to do so disqualifies a state from block grant monies

under the Temporary Assistance for Needy Families program (TANF). Although these initiatives are at a beginning stage, evidence suggests that there has been an increase in the amount of child support received by divorced and never-married mothers (Sorenson & Halpern, 1999).

Several researchers have noted the importance of extending these policies beyond child support enforcement. For example, Garfinkel (1992) has argued that the present system should be strengthened into a child support assurance program that would provide far greater protection for mothers and their children. Such a system would contain three key elements. First, the noncustodial parent would pay a set percentage of his or her income for child support. Second, the support payments would be automatically withheld from the nonresident parent's paycheck in the same manner as Social Security payments. Third, a minimum benefit would be assured. If nonresident parents were not making enough income to meet this benefit level, the government would make up the difference. Garfinkel (1998) argued that such a system would significantly reduce poverty among mothers and their children. Various simulations have resulted in a range of poverty reductions resulting from such a system.

Asset Development

Building the assets of low-income families is another innovative step toward economically assisting impoverished families. This approach has been developed and brought into the policy arena by Michael Sherraden (1991, 2000, 2001). Sherraden (1991) argued that government policy should provide incentives and resources that would allow low-income families to build their economic assets, much as it does for middle- and upper-class families (e.g., home mortgage tax deductions, lowered capital gains tax). His assertion was that "asset accumulation and investment, rather than income and consumption, are the keys to leaving poverty" (p. 294). Thus, government policies should attempt to facilitate the building of individuals' and families' resources through the process of asset accumulation.

To accomplish this, Sherraden formulated the concept of Individual Development Accounts (IDAs), which allow poor individuals and families to participate in matched savings accounts, with the match being at least one to one and often much higher. Accumulated assets in these accounts can then be used for a broad array of development purposes that are intended to strengthen a family's economic position. As Sherraden (2000) noted,

> IDAs have been introduced as a matched saving strategy to show that the poor can accumulate assets if they, like the middle and upper classes, have incentives and opportunities. IDAs are special saving accounts, started as early as birth, with savings matched for the poor, to be used for education, job training, home ownership, small business, or other development purposes. IDAs can have multiple sources of matching deposits, including governments, corporations, foundations, community groups, and individual donors. (p. 161)

The 1996 federal welfare reform legislation included a provision allowing states to use part of their block grant money to establish and fund IDAs. Presidents Clinton and Bush have demonstrated strong support for the concept, and 44 states have some form of IDA policy. The concept is also gaining ground in countries such as Canada, Taiwan, and the United Kingdom. Early evidence from a large demonstration project in the United States indicates that IDAs enable poor families to save and accumulate assets (Schreiner et al., 2002).

FUTURE RESEARCH DIRECTIONS

In looking back over the past 40 years, much has been learned regarding poverty and its effect on American families. This body of research has greatly facilitated our understanding of the dynamics related to impoverishment. Yet at same time, much of our understanding remains cursory. Perhaps this is to be expected given that the dominant analytical and methodological approach over this period of time has been multivariate modeling of survey data. When applied to describing the occurrence and timing of events, this approach is appropriate and revealing. When applied to understanding the meaning and processes behind these events, it often comes up short.

Future research must strive to lift our understanding to a more insightful level. I suggest three avenues to facilitate this. The first is methodological. Social realities, including family poverty, are nuanced and complex. Research methods should reflect this complexity through a range of approaches (e.g., in-depth interviewing, experimentation, focus groups, panel surveys, participant observation, and life histories). Relying on a single methodology reveals a mere slice of reality. It is time to greatly expand our methodological imagination.

In addition to using a wider array of methodologies, researchers should strive to incorporate multiple methods into their research designs. Such designs have numerous advantages over single-method approaches (Rank, 1992). For example, researchers might construct a research design that contained a large-scale survey but also incorporated in-depth interviewing of a selected subsample and participant observation. Such triangulation holds the promise of a more nuanced and deeper meaning of poverty and how it influences families.

A second avenue for enhancing our knowledge is through a deeper conceptual and theoretical understanding of poverty. The heavy reliance upon survey research has resulted in an inordinate amount of attention focused on the association of individual and household characteristics with the risk of poverty. Yet this largely overlooks an equally important dynamic. That is, although American social scientists have addressed who loses out at the economic game, they have largely ignored the question of why there are losers in the first place.

There is thus a need for future theoretical and analytical work to more thoroughly examine the structural components of poverty. Such work would help close a gap in the knowledge base as to why so many American families find themselves below the poverty line. In addition, such work could be further enhanced by exploring the relationships between the structural causes of poverty, the influence of neighborhoods, and the role of individual factors.

Finally, a third avenue for enriching the field is enhancing our ability to articulate the importance of poverty to the wider American society (Rank, 2004). This involves framing our research in different ways. Rather than focusing simply upon poor families, we also need to consider the relevancy of such conditions for America at large. As O'Connor (2001) wrote:

> The single most important challenge for poverty knowledge in the post-welfare era is to put poverty on the national agenda as a legitimate public policy concern: not in the narrow sense of income deprivation, but as part of the larger problem of the steady and rapid growth of economic, political, and social inequality. (p. 292)

Many other grounds could be explored as well. These might include arguments based on economic costs, social justice, or the responsibilities of citizenship. Understanding and articulating these connections is critical in establishing that American poverty is indeed a cause for concern. Without such an understanding, efforts to reduce or alleviate poverty will continue to fall on too many deaf ears. The ultimate challenge and reward ahead lies in reawakening our collective conscience to the disturbing paradox of poverty within America's families.

REFERENCES

Anderson, E. (1990). *Streetwise: Race, class, and change in an urban community.* Chicago: University of Chicago Press.

Anderson, E. (1999). *Code of the street: Decency, violence, and the moral life of the inner city.* New York: Norton.

Anderson, K. L. (1997). Gender, status and domestic violence: An integration of feminist and family violence approaches. *Journal of Marriage and the Family, 59,* 655–669.

Bane, M. J., & Ellwood, D. T. (1986). Slipping into and out of poverty: The dynamics of spells. *Journal of Human Resources, 21,* 1–23.

Bane, M. J., & Ellwood, D. T. (1994). *Welfare realities: From rhetoric to reform.* Cambridge, MA: Harvard University Press.

Bane, M. J., & Jargowsky, P. A. (1988). The links between government policy and family structure: What matters and what doesn't. In A. J. Cherlin (Ed.), *The changing American family and public policy* (pp. 219–261). Washington, DC: Urban Institute Press.

Barnes, M., Heady, C., Middleton, S., Papdopoulos, F., Room, G., & Tsakloglou, P. (2002). *Poverty and social exclusion in Europe.* Cheltenham, UK: Edward Elgar.

Bartik, T. J. (2001). *Jobs for the poor: Can labor demand policies help?* New York: Russell Sage.

Becker, G. S. (1964). *Human capital.* New York: Columbia University Press.

Becker, G. S. (1981). *A treatise on the family.* Cambridge, MA: Harvard University Press.

Beeghley, L. (2000). *The structure of social stratification in the United States.* Boston: Allyn & Bacon.

Bhalla, A. S., & Lapeyre, F. (1999). *Poverty and exclusion in a global world.* New York: St. Martin's.

Blank, R. M. (1997). *It takes a nation: A new agenda for fighting poverty.* Princeton, NJ: Princeton University Press.

Brady, D. (2003). Rethinking the sociological measurement of poverty. *Social Forces, 81,* 715–752.

Brooks-Gunn, J., Duncan, G. J., & Aber, J. L. (1997). *Neighborhood poverty: Vol. 1. Context and consequences for children.* New York: Russell Sage.

Bullard, R. D. (1990). *Dumping in Dixie: Race, class, and environmental quality.* Boulder, CO: Westview.

Burton, L. M., & Jarrett, R. L. (2000). In the mix, yet on the margins: The place of families in urban neighborhood and child development research. *Journal of Marriage and the Family, 62,* 1114–1135.

Cheal, D. (1996). *New poverty: Families in postmodern society.* Westport, CN: Greenwood.

Conger, R. D., Ge, X. J., & Lorenz, F. O. (1994). Economic stress and marital relations. In R. D. Conger & G. H. Elder, Jr. (Eds.), *Families in troubled times: Adapting to change in rural America* (pp. 187–203). New York: Aldine de Gruyter.

Corcoran, M. (1995). Rags to rags: Poverty and mobility in the United States. *Annual Review of Sociology, 21,* 237–267.

Corcoran, M. (2001). Mobility, persistence and the consequences of poverty for children: Child and adult outcomes. In S. H. Danziger & R. H. Haveman (Eds.), *Understanding poverty* (pp. 127–161). Cambridge, MA: Harvard University Press.

Danziger, S., & Gottschalk, P. (1995). *America unequal.* New York: Russell Sage.

Davis, K., & Moore, W. (1945). Some principles of stratification. *American Sociological Review, 7,* 242–249.

Devine, J. A., & Wright, J. D. (1993). *The greatest of evils: Urban poverty and the American underclass.* New York: Aldine de Gruyter.

Doeringer, P. B., & Piore, M. J. (1975). Unemployment and the "dual labor market." *Public Interest, 38,* 67–79.

Dunbar, L. (1988). *The common interest: How our social-welfare policies don't work, and what we can do about them.* New York: Pantheon.

Duncan, G. J. (1984). *Years of poverty, years of plenty: The changing economic fortunes of American workers and families.* Ann Arbor, MI: Institute for Social Research.

Duncan, G. J., & Brooks-Gunn, J. (1997). *Consequences of growing up poor.* New York: Russell Sage.

Duncan, G. J., Gustafsson, B., Hauser, R., Schmaus, G., Jenkins, S., Messinger, H., et al. (1995). Poverty and social-assistance dynamics in the United States, Canada, and Europe. In K. McFate, R. Lawson, & W. J. Wilson (Eds.), *Poverty, inequality and the future of social policy: Western states in the new world order* (pp. 67–108). New York: Russell Sage.

Duncan, G. J., Yeung, W. J., Brooks-Gunn, J., & Smith, J. R. (1998). How much does childhood poverty affect the life chances of children? *American Sociological Review, 63,* 406–423.

Edin, K., & Lein, L. (1997). *Making ends meet: How single mothers survive welfare and low-wage work.* New York: Russell Sage.

Edwards, M. E., Plotnick, R., & Klawitter, M. (2001). Do attitudes and personality characteristics affect socioeconomic outcomes? The case of welfare use by young women. *Social Science Quarterly, 82,* 827–843.

Ellwood, D. T. (2000). Winners and losers in America: Taking the measure of the new economic realities. In D. T. Ellwood, R. M. Blank, J. Blasi, D. Kruse, W. A. Niskanen, & K. Lynn-Dyson (Eds.), *A working nation: Workers, work, and government in the new economy* (pp. 1–41). New York: Russell Sage.

Esping-Andersen, G. (1990). *The three worlds of welfare capitalism.* Princeton, NJ: Princeton University Press.

Feagin, J. R. (1975). *Subordinating the poor: Welfare and American beliefs.* Englewood Cliffs, NJ: Prentice Hall.

Feagin, J. R. (2000). *Racist America: Roots, current realities, and future reparations.* New York: Routledge.

Gans, H. J. (1972). Positive functions of poverty. *American Journal of Sociology, 78,* 275–289.

Gans, H. J. (1995). *The war against the poor: The underclass and antipoverty policy.* New York: Basic Books.

Garfinkel, I. (1992). *Assuring child support: An extension of social security.* New York: Russell Sage.

Garkinkel, I. (1998). *Fathers under fire: The revolution in child support enforcement.* New York: Russell Sage.

Gelles, R. J. (1993). Poverty and violence towards children. *American Behavioral Scientist, 35,* 258–274.

Gilens, M. (1999). *Why Americans hate welfare: Race, media, and the politics of antipoverty policy.* Chicago: University of Chicago Press.

Glennerster, H. (2002). United States poverty studies and poverty measurement: The past twenty-five years. *Social Service Review, 76,* 83–107.

Goodwin. L. (1972). *Do the poor want to work? A social-psychological study of work orientations.* Washington, DC: Brookings Institution.

Goodwin. L. (1983). *Causes and cures of welfare: New evidence on the social psychology of the poor.* Lexington, MA: Lexington.

Harrington, M. (1962). *The other America: Poverty in the United States.* New York: Macmillan.

Harvey, D. L. (1993). *Potter addition: Poverty, family, and kinship in a heartland community.* New York: Aldine de Gruyter.

Hodson, R., & Kaufman, R. L. (1982). Economic dualism: A critical review. *American Sociological Review, 47,* 727–739.

Hunter, R. (1904). *Poverty: Social conscience in the Progressive Era.* New York: Macmillan.

Institute for Research on Poverty. (1998). Revising the poverty measure. *Focus, 19,* 1–55.

Institute for Research on Poverty. (2000). Child support enforcement policy and low-income families. *Focus, 21,* 1–86.

Jargowsky, P. A. (1997). *Poverty and place: Ghettos, barrios, and the American city.* New York: Russell Sage.

Johnson, L. B. (1965). Inaugural address. Retrieved July 2003 from the Web site of the Lyndon Baines Johnson Library and Museum, National Archives and Records Administration, www.lbjlib.utexas.edu.

Kawachi, I., & Kennedy, B. P. (2002). *The health of nations: Why inequality is harmful to your health.* New York: New Press.

Kawachi, I., Kennedy, B. P., & Wilkinson, R. G. (1999). *The society and population health reader: Income inequality and health.* New York: New Press.

Kluegel, J. R., & Smith, E. R. (1986). *Beliefs about inequality: Americans' views of what is and what ought to be.* New York: Aldine de Gruyter.

Kwong, P. (2001). Poverty despite family ties. In J. Goode & J. Maskovsky (Eds.), *The new poverty studies: The ethnography of power, politics, and impoverished people in the United States* (pp. 57–78). New York: New York University Press.

Leidenfrost, N. B. (1993). *An examination of the impact of poverty on health.* Report prepared for the Extension Service, U.S. Department of Agriculture. Washington, DC: U.S. Department of Agriculture.

Leisering, L., & Leibfried, S. (1999). *Time and poverty in Western welfare states: United Germany in perspective.* New York: Cambridge University Press.

Lewis, O. (1959). *Five families: Mexican case studies in the culture of poverty.* New York: Basic Books.

Lewis, O. (1966a). The culture of poverty. *Scientific American, 215,* 19–25.

Lewis, O. (1966b). *La Vida: A Puerto Rican family in the culture of poverty.* New York: Random House.

Lichter, D. T., & Crowley, M. L. (2002). Poverty in America: Beyond welfare reform. *Population Bulletin, 57,* 1–36.

Marx, K., & Engels, F. (1968). *Selected works.* New York: International Publishers.

Massey, D. S., & Denton, N. A. (1993). *American apartheid: Segregation and the making of the underclass.* Cambridge MA: Harvard University Press.

Maynard, R. A. (1997). *Kids having kids: Economic costs and social consequences of teen pregnancy.* Washington, DC: Urban Institute Press.

McLanahan, S., & Sandefur, G. (1994). *Growing up with a single parent: What hurts, what helps.* Cambridge, MA: Harvard University Press.

McLeod, J. D., & Shanahan, M. J. (1993). Poverty, parenting, and children's mental health. *American Sociological Review, 58,* 351–366.

McMurrer, D. P., & Sawhill, I. V. (1998). *Getting ahead: Economic and social mobility in America.* Washington, DC: Urban Institute Press.

Mead, L. (1986). *Beyond entitlement: The social obligations of citizenship.* New York: Free Press.

Moffitt, R. (1992). Incentive effects of the U.S. welfare system: A review. *Journal of Economic Literature, 30,* 1–61.

Moore, A. M. (1997). Intimate violence: Does socioeconomic status matter? In A. P. Cardarelli (Ed.), *Violence between intimate partners: Patterns, causes, and effects* (pp. 90–103). Boston: Allyn & Bacon.

Murray, C. (1984). *Losing ground: American social policy, 1950–1980.* New York: Basic Books.

National Center for Health Statistics. (1997). Birth and fertility rates by educational attainment: United States, 1994. *Monthly Vital Statistics Report, 45*(10S).

National Research Council. (1995). *Measuring poverty: A new approach.* Washington, DC: National Academy Press.

O'Connor, A. (2001). *Poverty knowledge: Social science, social policy, and the poor in twentieth-century U.S. history.* Princeton, NJ: Princeton University Press.

Olasky, M. (1992). *The tragedy of American compassion.* Washington, DC: Regnery.

Orshansky, M. (1965, January). Counting the poor: Another look at the poverty profile. *Social Security Bulletin, 28,* 3–29.

Oyen, E., Miller, S. M., & Samad, S. A. (1996). *Poverty: A global review.* Oslo: Scandinavian University Press.

Pappas, G., Queen, S., Hadden, W., & Fisher, G. (1993). The increasing disparity in mortality between socioeconomic groups in the United States, 1960 and 1986. *New England Journal of Medicine, 329,* 103–115.

Putnam, R. (2000). *Bowling alone: The collapse and revival of American community*. New York: Simon & Schuster.

Rainwater, L., & Smeeding, T. M. (1995). *Doing poorly: The real income of American children in a comparative perspective* (Luxembourg Income Study Working Paper Series No. 127). Syracuse, NY: Syracuse University, Maxwell School of Citizenship and Public Affairs.

Rank, M. R. (1985). Exiting from welfare: A life-table analysis. *Social Service Review, 59*, 358–376.

Rank, M. R. (1989). Fertility among women on welfare: Incidence and determinants. *American Sociological Review, 54*, 296–304.

Rank, M. R. (1992). The blending of qualitative and quantitative methods in understanding childbearing among welfare recipients. In J. F. Gilgun, K. Daly, & G. Handel (Eds.), *Qualitative methods in family research* (pp. 281–300). Newbury Park, CA: Sage.

Rank, M. R. (1994a). *Living on the edge: The realities of welfare in America*. New York: Columbia University Press.

Rank, M. R. (1994b). A view from the inside out: Recipients' perceptions of welfare. *Journal of Sociology and Social Welfare, 21*, 27–47.

Rank, M. R. (2000). Poverty and economic hardship in families. In D. H. Demo, K. R. Allen, & M. A. Fine (Eds.), *Handbook of family diversity* (pp. 293–315). New York: Oxford University Press.

Rank, M. R. (2003). As American as apple pie: Poverty and welfare. *Contexts, 2*.

Rank, M. R. (2004). *One nation, underprivileged: Why American poverty affects us all*. New York: Oxford University Press.

Rank, M. R., & Cheng, L. C. (1995). Welfare use across generations: How important are the ties that bind? *Journal of Marriage and the Family, 57*, 673–684.

Rank, M. R., & Hirschl, T. A. (1999a). The economic risk of childhood in America: Estimating the probability of poverty across the formative years. *Journal of Marriage and the Family, 61*, 1058–1067.

Rank, M. R., & Hirschl, T. A. (1999b). Estimating the proportion of Americans ever experiencing poverty during their elderly years. *Journal of Gerontology: Social Sciences, 54B*, S184–S193.

Rank, M. R., & Hirschl, T. A. (1999c). The likelihood of poverty across the American adult lifespan. *Social Work, 44*, 201–216.

Rank, M. R., & Hirschl, T. A. (2001a). The measurement of long term risks across the life course. *Social Science Quarterly, 82*, 680–686.

Rank, M. R., & Hirschl, T. A. (2001b). The occurrence of poverty across the life cycle: Evidence from the PSID. *Journal of Policy Analysis and Management, 20*, 737–755.

Rank, M. R., & Hirschl, T. A. (2001c). Rags or riches? Estimating the probabilities of poverty and affluence across the adult American life span. *Social Science Quarterly, 82*, 651–669.

Rank, M. R., & Hirschl, T. A. (2002). Welfare use as a life course event: Toward a new understanding of the U.S. safety net. *Social Work, 47*, 237–248.

Rank, M. R., Yoon, H. S., & Hirschl, T. A. (in press). American poverty as a structural failure: Evidence and arguments. *Journal of Sociology and Social Work*.

Riis, J. (1972). *How the other half lives: Studies among the tenements of New York*. Williamson, MA: Corner House. (Original work published 1890)

Ritakallio, V. M. (2001). *Trends of poverty and income inequality in cross-national comparison*. (Luxembourg Income Study Working Paper No. 272). Syracuse, NY: Maxwell School of Citizenship and Public Affairs.

Rowntree, B. S. (1901). *Poverty: A study of town life*. London: Thomas Nelson & Sons.

Sampson, R. J., Raudenbush, S. W., & Earls, F. (1997). Neighborhoods and violent crime: A multilevel study of collective efficacy. *Science, 277,* 918–924.

Schiller, B. R. (2004). *The economics of poverty and discrimination.* Englewood Cliffs, NJ: Prentice Hall.

Schreiner, M., Clancy, M., Johnson, L., & Sherraden, M. (2002). *Savings performance in the American dream demonstration: A national demonstration of Individual Development Accounts.* St. Louis, MO: Washington University, Center for Social Development.

Schwartz, J. (2000). *Fighting poverty with virtue: Moral reform and America's urban poor, 1825–2000.* Bloomington, IN: Indiana University Press.

Seccombe, K. (1999). *So you think I drive a Cadillac? Welfare recipients' perspectives on the system and its reform.* Needham Heights, MA: Allyn & Bacon.

Seccombe, K. (2000). Families in poverty in the 1990s: Trends, causes, consequences, and lessons learned. *Journal of Marriage and the Family, 62,* 1094–1113.

Sedlak, A. J., & Broadhurst, D. D. (1996). *Third national incidence study of child abuse and neglect: Final report.* Washington, DC: U.S. Department of Health and Human Services.

Sen, A. (1992). *Inequality reexamined.* New York: Russell Sage.

Sen, A. (1999). *Development as freedom.* New York: Alfred A. Knopf.

Sherman, A. (1994). *Wasting America's future: The Children's Defense Fund report on the costs of child poverty.* Boston: Beacon Press.

Sherraden, M. (1991). *Assets and the poor: A new American welfare policy.* Armonk, NY: Sharpe.

Sherraden, M. (2000). From research to policy: Lessons from Individual Development Accounts. *Journal of Consumer Affairs, 34,* 159–181.

Sherraden, M. (2001). Asset building policy and programs for the poor. In T. Shapiro & E. Wolff (Eds.), *Benefits and mechanisms for spreading asset ownership in the United States* (pp. 302–323). New York: Russell Sage.

Shirk, M., Bennett, N. G., & Aber, J. L. (1999). *Lives on the line: American families and the struggle to make ends meet.* Boulder, CO: Westview.

Small, M. L., & Newman, K. (2001). Urban poverty after *The Truly Disadvantaged:* The rediscovery of the family, the neighborhood, and culture. *Annual Review of Sociology, 27,* 23–45.

Smeeding, T. A. (1997). *Financial poverty in developed countries: The evidence from LIS. Final report to the United Nations Development Programme.* (Luxembourg Income Study Working Paper Series No. 155). Syracuse, NY: Maxwell School of Citizenship and Public Affairs.

Smeeding, T. A., Phillips, K. R., & O'Connor, M. (2000). The EITC: Expectation, knowledge, use, and economic and social mobility. *National Tax Journal, 53,* 1187–1209.

Smeeding, T. A., Rainwater, L., & Burtless, G. (2001). U.S. poverty in a cross-national context. In S. H. Danziger & R. H. Havemen (Eds.), *Understanding poverty* (pp. 162–189). Cambridge, MA: Harvard University Press.

Smith, J. P. (1999). Healthy bodies and thick wallets: The dual relation between health and economic status. *Journal of Economic Perspectives, 13,* 145–166.

Smith, J. R., Brooks-Gunn, J., & Klebanov, P. K. (1997). Consequences of living in poverty for young children's cognitive and verbal ability and early school achievement. In G. J. Duncan & J. Brooks-Gunn (Eds.), *Consequences of growing up poor* (pp. 132–189). New York: Russell Sage.

Smith, K. B., & Stone, L. H. (1989). Rags, riches, and bootstraps: Beliefs about the causes of wealth and poverty. *Sociological Quarterly, 30,* 93–107.

Sorenson, E., & Halpern, A. (1999). Child support enforcement is working better than we think. In Urban Institute (Ed.), *New federalism: Issues and options for states* (Series A-31). Washington, DC: Urban Institute.

Stack, C. B. (1974). *All our kin*. New York: Harper.

Stevens, A. H. (1994). The dynamics of poverty spells: Updating Bane and Ellwood. *American Economic Review, 84,* 34–37.

Stevens, A. H. (1999). Climbing out of poverty, falling back in: Measuring the persistence of poverty over multiple spells. *The Journal of Human Resources, 34,* 557–588.

Straus, M. A., Gelles, R. J., & Steinmetz, S. K. (1980). *Behind closed doors: Violence in the American family*. Garden City, NY: Anchor.

Tocqueville, A. D. (1983). Memoir on pauperism. *Public Interest, 70,* 102–120.

United Nations Development Programme. (2000). *UNDP poverty report 2000: Overcoming human poverty*. New York: United Nations Publications.

United Nations Development Programme. (2003). *Human development report 2003*. New York: Oxford University Press.

U.S. Bureau of the Census. (1992). *Studies in household and family formation* (Current Population Reports, Series P23-179). Washington, DC: Government Printing Office.

U.S. Bureau of the Census. (1999). *Experimental poverty measures: 1990 to 1997* (Current Population Reports, Series P60-205). Washington, DC: Government Printing Office.

U.S. Bureau of the Census (2002a). *Custodial mothers and fathers and their child support* (Current Population Reports, Series P60-217). Washington, DC: Government Printing Office.

U.S. Bureau of the Census. (2002b). *Poverty in the United States: 2001* (Current Population Reports, Series P60-219). Washington, DC: Government Printing Office.

Vosler, N. (1996). *New approaches to family practice: Confronting economic stress*. Thousand Oaks, CA: Sage.

Voydanoff, P. (1990). Economic distress and family relations: A review of the eighties. *Journal of Marriage and the Family, 52,* 1099–1115.

Walker, R. (1994). *Poverty dynamics: Issues and examples*. Brookfield, VT: Avebury.

Weitzman, L. J. (1985). *The divorce revolution: The unexpected social and economic consequences for women and children in America*. New York: Free Press.

White, L., & Rogers, S. J. (2000). Economic circumstances and family outcomes: A review of the 1990s. *Journal of Marriage and the Family, 62,* 1035–1051.

Williams, D. R., & Collins, C. (1995). U.S. socioeconomic and racial differences in health: Patterns and explanations. *Annual Review of Sociology, 21,* 349–386.

Wilson, W. J. (1987). *The truly disadvantaged: The inner city, the underclass, and public policy*. Chicago: University of Chicago Press.

Wilson, W. J. (1996). *When work disappears: The world of the new urban poor*. New York: Knopf.

Wolfe, A. (1998). *One nation, after all*. New York: Viking.

Wright, E. O. (1994). *Interrogating inequality: Essays on class analysis, socialism and Marxism*. London: Verso.

Yinger, J. (1995). *Closed doors, opportunities lost: The continuing costs of housing discrimination*. New York: Russell Sage.

Part VIII

TECHNOLOGY AND CONTEMPORARY FAMILIES

Brave New Families

Modern Health Technologies and Family Creation

DIANNE M. BARTELS

Health care technologies can extend life, decrease disability, and expand reproductive options. With technical assistance, members of families can often survive life-threatening illnesses. Infants can survive when born at increasingly earlier stages of gestation. Couples experiencing infertility can have biologically related children.

Families faced with decisions to use or to bypass these technologies are likely to encounter profound psychosocial and ethical challenges (McDaniel, Hepworth, & Doherty, 1992). In these deliberations, families consider not only survival but also the quality of life that will be possible following technological intervention. Nowhere are these challenges more evident than in making choices about the use of reproductive and genetic technologies. These health care interventions can change family structure, family functioning, and even how we define family (Bartels, 2002).

In this chapter, I will describe the role of reproductive technologies and genetic testing in family creation. I will address available data on how people make decisions about using technologies and how these methods of family creation have affected children, families, and family relationships. Finally, I will discuss theoretical underpinnings and research strategies that have been, and could be, used to expand our knowledge about these modern-day families.

The Nashes are one family that faced a series of technologically related health decisions to aid in the survival of one child while creating another. Their situation exemplifies the power of new technologies and the possibilities they afford. Molly Nash was born with Fanconi's anemia (FA), a rare genetic disorder that affects all bone marrow elements, resulting in anemia. Without treatment, the person with FA will develop a life-threatening leukemia (Online Mendelian Inheritance in Man, 2000). The Nash family became the subject of national media attention when the parents chose to have another child using reproductive technologies and genetic testing. They requested that embryos be tested before implantation in the mother's uterus so that one could be selected that would not be affected with FA. Additionally, they asked their physician to test the embryos in order to select one that could be a stem cell donor for Molly. Their hope was that by transplanting stem cells from the umbilical cord of their next child, they could ameliorate the progression of Molly's illness. The Nashes' second child was born healthy as a result of these interventions, and his stem cells were used for a bone marrow transplant procedure for Molly.

The Nashes' situation is quite rare in that they used reproductive technology (in vitro fertilization [IVF]), genetic diagnosis, and bone marrow transplantation in an effort to have one healthy child and to offer treatment to another. More typically, couples use reproductive technologies and genetic testing to enhance fertility and to increase the likelihood that they will have a healthy child.

CREATING FAMILIES USING REPRODUCTIVE AND GENETIC TECHNOLOGIES

Reproductive Technologies

Childbearing and child rearing are inherent parts of family development and in many cases are inherent parts of one's personal identity. Because this is so, the inability to have children has been described as both an individual and a family crisis (Hammer Burns & Covington, 1998). Societies have created a myriad of approaches to addressing the crisis of infertility. These approaches have included changes in social relationships (e.g., divorce, adoptions) as well as spiritual and medical interventions (Rosenblatt et al., 1973). Today, couples experiencing infertility will most likely turn to the health care system in their quest for answers. IVF is the primary remedy used to address infertility problems.

IVF is a medical intervention that has helped thousands of couples annually to have biologically related children (Society for Assisted Reproductive Technology & American Society of Reproductive Medicine, 2002). First successfully used in the birth of Louise Brown in 1972 (Edwards, 1980), the procedure involves combining an egg and a sperm in a laboratory dish, then implanting developing embryos into the womb (Strong & DeVault, 1992). Donor eggs (ova) and donor sperm can also be used to increase the likelihood of becoming pregnant.

For women who cannot conceive or who cannot carry a pregnancy, there is an option of contracting with another woman to carry the pregnancy in her womb until birth. The surrogate mother (also called a gestational carrier) may donate her eggs, or she may carry a fetus that is a product of the contracting couple's egg and sperm. Couples initiating these relationships assume that the surrogate mother will relinquish parental rights at birth so they can adopt the child (Bartels, 1990). With all of these options available, children could potentially have two social (adoptive) parents who raised them, two other biological parents (an egg donor and a sperm donor), and a surrogate mother involved in their creation.

The possibility for human cloning may be the most controversial issue on the reproductive technology horizon. Cloning involves replacing the female genetic material of an unfertilized egg with a nucleus from a different cell. Thus, the genetic material in the nucleus will be identical to that of the donor, essentially creating a twin born at another time (Gurdon & Colman, 1999). Cloning, unlike other reproductive technologies, has been the focus of much legislative oversight and restriction.

The availability of reproductive techniques has fundamentally changed the ways families are created (Golombok, MacCallum, & Goodman, 2001). People who in the past might have remained childless or sought other alternatives like adoption (e.g., single adults, gay and lesbian couples) are now able to have biologically related children (Fasouliotis & Schenker, 1999). Success in cloning would eliminate the need for a sperm donor in the reproductive process. These reproductive techniques, in combination with testing to predict genetic traits, can also determine the structure and membership of entire families.

Genetic Research and Family Creation

During the 1950s, genetic researchers developed techniques that made it possible to detect prenatal chromosomal abnormalities associated with medical problems ranging from malformation and retardation to infertility and reproductive failure (Thompson & Thompson, 1986). In the United States today, pregnant women over 35 years of age are routinely advised by their physicians to have prenatal testing to detect potential chromosomal problems like Down's syndrome because the risk increases with the age of the mother. Family members concerned about passing on familial genetic conditions to their children can also use prenatal testing to see if a fetus is affected.

In seeking genetic and reproductive technologies, most expectant parents hope for a perfect baby—one with maximum health and minimum defects (Hammer Burns, 1999). Although most people receive reassurance that a chromosome problem is not present, when testing reveals there is a problem, couples may face a decision about whether to continue or to terminate the pregnancy. A decision to terminate appears to have psychological consequences similar to having a miscarriage, including grief, loss, sadness, and depression (Hammer Burns & LeRoy, 1998). Preimplantation genetic diagnosis (PGD), as used in the Nash case, allows detection and selection of healthy embryos before implantation. Some couples prefer

this option because it avoids the need to consider terminating pregnancy.

Advances in molecular biology, especially the discovery of recombinant DNA techniques during the 1970s, have further increased medicine's ability to analyze human hereditary material. In hopes that genetic research will lead to treatments and preventive strategies for common as well as rare genetic disorders, both the private and public sectors have invested heavily to develop genetic technologies. The success of these efforts means that we can now identify many genetic conditions before symptoms arise (Center for Bioethics, 1999). Genetic prediction will become a major tool for health care management (Collins, 1999). Physicians will use genetic tests to predict future health conditions and will make treatment plans based on identified genetic susceptibilities (Doukas, 1993). These predictive abilities will expand the range of medical problems that can be detected prenatally as well.

The combination of reproductive technologies and genetic tests creates powerful tools to enhance abilities to have healthy children and even to save children's lives. Many questions have been raised about the impact of these technologies on families, and some questions have been answered. The following section describes what we have learned about families' use of reproductive and genetic technologies in family creation.

STUDIES ADDRESSING FAMILY RESPONSES TO REPRODUCTIVE AND GENETIC TECHNOLOGIES

Family scholars and health professionals have taken a variety of approaches to exploring the impact of technologies, including (a) describing how people make decisions about whether to have prenatal testing or to use reproductive technologies, (b) describing outcomes of reproductive technologies in terms of children's health and family relationships, and (c) addressing genetic and reproductive technologies in the context of the health care system and the broader society.

Making Decisions About Reproductive Technology and Genetic Testing

Potential parents might decide to have no children, to have biological children, to adopt, to request prenatal testing, to use reproductive technologies, or to pursue a combination of alternatives in the process of creating their families. Initial studies focused on outcomes following prenatal genetic testing and on factors that related to decisions about whether to have testing.

Rational choice models have been used to describe factors that influence decisions about using prenatal testing and/or reproductive planning in the face of genetic risks. Those who come for prenatal testing are often white, upper-middle-class, and highly educated couples (Burke & Kolker, 1993). Couples who have a child with a genetic problem also may be likely to pursue testing to ascertain their genetic risk for having another child with problems. Couples who have no children may accept a risk of genetic disease rather than remain childless (Evers-Kiebooms, Denayerr, & Van Den Berghe, 1990). In one study, the birth of a child with cystic fibrosis had a major influence on reproductive planning (Evers-Kiebooms et al., 1990). For these parents, the risk of recurrence played the most important role in postponing or deciding against further progeny.

Rates of pregnancy termination following nearly 26,000 amniocenteses (prenatal genetic tests) increased with the severity of the health effects of the chromosome problem (Vincent, Edwards, Young, & Nachtigal, 1991). However, when Frets et al. (1990) interviewed couples with a history of genetic problems 2 or 3 years after genetic counseling,

they found that 70% of couples opted to have children despite the risk. They surmised that the couple's interpretation of risk, rather than actual risk, and their desire to have children were the paramount factors influencing reproductive planning. People who had a child, sibling, or spouse affected with a genetic condition also described guilt feelings as they considered their options. This was more true of people who had a sibling with a genetic condition than of those who had an affected child (Frets et al., 1990).

Couples who have experienced infertility may be ambivalent about genetic testing. The potential for a genetic diagnosis may be seen as further evidence of flaw or failure that could precipitate feelings of shame, embarrassment, guilt, deficiency, and inadequacy (Hammer Burns & LeRoy, 1998).

Parents who decided to continue a pregnancy in the face of a prenatal genetic diagnosis indicated that they did not actively decide; rather, a decision was made in a more subtle process that occurred over time. Factors that influenced the final outcome included religious and personal beliefs, past experiences, and uncertainty about outcomes with a specific diagnosis. These parents said they needed informational and emotional support from family, friends, and health professionals; a lack of emotional support from parents and grandparents was particularly troubling during this time (Redlinger-Grosse, Bernhart, Berg, Muenke, & Biesecker, 2002).

Couples asked about their *process* for making decisions about continuing or terminating a pregnancy indicated that rather than using logical models to make decisions, they created scenarios to help limit uncertainty and to decide. They imagined various future scenarios with a disabled child, then asked themselves whether they could cope or manage (Lippman-Hand & Fraser, 1979). These scenarios were influenced by prenatal history and whether they already had a healthy child, as well as consideration of what they had experienced as a person or relative of a person with a genetic condition, what the early death of a child might mean to them, and how others outside family might react to their situation. Other factors (e.g., religion and career commitments) also influenced reproductive decisions. Ultimately, these decisions centered on profound social meanings and imagined social consequences rather than on biomedical data or abstract principles (Beeson & Golbus, 1985).

As the U.S. population diversifies, investigators looking at systemic influences have found substantial variation of opinion about prenatal screening and diagnostic testing. Western-culture couples are more likely to see genetic testing as providing hope and promise, and they may be more sensitive to social criticism for foregoing testing than are couples from non-Western cultures (Hammer Burns & LeRoy, 1998). Mexican American women, who refuse prenatal testing at high rates, do so because of their general attitude toward doctors, medicine, and prenatal care, as well as their personal assessment of risk and uncertainty (Browner, Preloran, & Cox, 1999). In a culturally diverse group of women, factors influencing their views included available resources, feelings about a child with Down's syndrome, moral beliefs, family and social influences, perceptions of one's own health, the difficulty of becoming pregnant, and willingness to put a fetus at elevated miscarriage risk (Moyer et al., 1999). These findings suggest that policies for recommending testing should go beyond medical indications and must be more sensitive to how ethnic minority clients make choices.

In summary, these investigations have identified a broad range of factors influencing prenatal decisions and have shown that rational choice models cannot capture the entirety of reproductive decision making. Researchers have generally not addressed

decision situations in the context of the family, the health care system, and the broader society, although health care practitioners' beliefs and values also are likely to influence whether clients accept or decline testing (Anderson, 1999). Post hoc interviewers appear to have presumed that couples' voices were united throughout the decision-making process, although health care professionals have reported major couple disagreements in the context of making these decisions (McCarthy Veach, Bartels, & LeRoy, 2001).

The studies just described addressed prenatal planning and testing in situations that focused on whether the risk of genetic health problems would be avoided by not having children. In the late 1990s, investigators began to look at the outcomes of assisted reproductive techniques that had been used both to enhance fertility and, in some circumstances, to avoid transmitting genetic conditions.

Impact of Assisted Reproduction on Children

Research efforts to address the effects of reproductive techniques focused on whether the infants, children, and adolescents conceived using reproductive technologies varied from those who were naturally conceived. These studies addressed concerns about the unintended effects of new technologies and growing unease about potentially negative consequences for children. Some concerns related to residual effects of distress related to infertility and its treatment (Golombok, MacCallum, Goodman, & Rutter, 2002). Other researchers worried that parents who had had difficulty conceiving might be overprotective and emotionally overinvested in their children (Montgomery et al., 1999). Overall, these studies focused on the early years of development and found no deleterious effects for children conceived using reproductive technologies. A study of infant attachment at 12 months postpartum showed "predominantly secure attachments" and no significant differences in interaction during play between children conceived through the use of technologies and children whose parents did not use them (Gibson, Ungerer, McMahon, Leslie, & Saunders, 2000, p. 1015). Behavioral observations of mother-child interactions and self-rated questionnaires also found no significant differences related to means of conception in children 24 to 30 months old (Colpin, Demyttenaere, & Vandemeulebroecke, 1995). Children ages 6 to 10 years performed equally well in school (Olivennes et al., 1997), and children at age 12 who had been born after donor insemination were well adjusted in terms of social and emotional development when compared with adopted and normally conceived children (Golombok et al., 2002). Additionally, Montgomery et al. (1999) reported normal psychological development and no adverse effects in school-age children who had been conceived by IVF when compared to control groups. Similar findings were true for IVF-conceived adolescents (Golombok et al., 2001). Finally, a meta-analysis found no significant differences in terms of emotions, behavior, self-esteem, or children's perception of family relationships between children conceived with reproductive assistance and children of parents who had not used technology (Hahn, 2001).

Impact on Family Relationships

One outcome of IVF is an increased rate of multiple births. One preliminary study suggested that parents who had twins following IVF experienced more stress than those who had naturally conceived twins (Cook, Bradley, & Golombok, 1998) but that the stress did not affect parenting or child behaviors. Overall, a lack of genetic relationships does not lead to difficulties in the parent-child relationship. In fact, greater psychological

well-being has been found among mothers and fathers where there is no genetic link between mother and child (Golombok, Murray, Brinsden, & Abdallah, 1999).

Regarding specifically families who used donor insemination, the only things that distinguished them from others were mothers who exhibited greater expressive warmth and fathers who were less involved in discipline than in families where the social father was the biological father (Golombok et al., 2002). Conclusions from an examination of literature from 1980 to 1995 were similar; the quality of parent-child relations was better with the donor insemination group than in naturally conceived families (Brewaeys, 1996). Similar conclusions were derived from a meta-analysis of the literature from 1980 to 2000; mothers of children born with artificial reproductive technologies reported less parenting stress and more positive mother-child and father-child relationships than was true of mothers of naturally conceived children (Hahn, 2001).

All of these studies of children and parent-child relationships suggest that parents who embark on creating children using reproductive technologies can be optimistic about the likely outcomes (Hahn, 2001). Overall, reproductive technologies are not more likely to lead to problems in terms of child health outcomes, co-parenting, or parent-child relationships. However, because these technologies are so new, we do not yet have empirical evidence of how adults who were born using reproductive technologies were influenced.

It should be noted that European scholars have conducted most research on reproductive outcomes, and similar data about U.S. children and their family relationships are not available. The reasons for this are not clear. We might speculate that it relates to reproductive autonomy and donor confidentiality, which are highly prized in the United States. U.S. legislators have taken a much more "hands off" position and been less supportive financially to reproductive technology researchers than in Canada and the United Kingdom, where federal commissions have long provided oversight and support of new reproductive technologies. There is much to learn about U.S. families using reproductive technologies, and approaches examining whole family systems, rather than just children, parent-child, and couple relationships, need to be undertaken. For instance, one may wonder about the responses of other children in the family, about family communication and relationships over time, and about families in other societal contexts.

Families in the Health Care and Societal Context

Most decisions about whether and how to use reproductive and genetic technologies occur in the context of the health care system, yet few studies have addressed the experiences of families in that context. In one study, clinicians described families who experienced distress, including feelings of blame, shame, guilt, and responsibility for passing on a genetic condition to a child and concluded that one partner may blame the other for being the carrier who passed on a condition to a child. In some instances, couples divorced following a disagreement about whether to have prenatal testing or whether to terminate a pregnancy (Bartels, 2002). Clinicians also expressed concern about family secrets that could prevent a child from knowing about his or her genetic heritage. These secrets included revelations of false paternity (i.e., the social father not being the biological father) and parents who chose not to tell their children about genetic problems that could affect them. Professionals believed that children ought to have data that might be relevant for their own health care and for making reproductive decisions.

Clinicians were most concerned about requests from parents who wished to select traits in their future children. These requests might be to select an embryo that could be a bone marrow donor, as in the Nash case, but more troubling for clinicians were requests for sex selection or decisions to terminate a pregnancy for a condition that did not involve a threat to the future child's health (Bartels, 2002; McCarthy Veach et al., 2001).

Concern has been registered about "tentative pregnancies" and about a "technology of quality control" that turns the process of having children into a production process where only certain products are acceptable (Katz Rothman, 1993, p. viii). Although supposedly giving women more freedom of choice, these technologies may, in the long run, constrain choices by societal insistence on prenatal testing. Children could come to be seen as *products of conception*, with abortion as an integral part of using the new technology (Katz Rothman, 1993). Clinicians who interacted with families were also concerned about societal judgments of parents who make difficult reproductive decisions (Bartels, 2002).

Like any new technology, new reproductive technologies raise controversial psychosocial and ethical concerns. For example, people who do not believe in abortion would repudiate all genetic testing and reproductive interventions that destroy embryos. Disability advocates have expressed concern about the availability of prenatal testing that provide parents with a choice about whether to have a child with disabilities, and some believe that offering this choice will lead to greater intolerance of existing people with disabilities (Asch, 1999).

An additional concern relates to resource allocation and disparities in who has access to new technologies. In 1992, IVF costs averaged $60,000 to $114,000 for young couples and $800,000 for older couples (Hahn, 2001). Most of these procedures were not covered by insurance, leaving many people unable to afford them. This disparity raises many policy questions that need to be addressed in the context of families, the health care system, and broader society.

Nondisclosure to Children

Another expressed concern is that many parents do not plan to disclose means of conception to their children (Bartels, 2002; Brewaeys, 1996; Golombok et al., 2002; Oliviennes et al., 1997; McWhinnie, 2001). This could be problematic for children in view of the expectation that health care in the future will be premised on genetic data (Collins, 1999; Doukas, 1993). To benefit from genetically based health care, a person needs to know his or her biological makeup. Children who are not told about the involvement of egg or sperm donors in their conception will make inaccurate assumptions about their health history and genetic risks. Unlike adopted children, who now are generally told about their origins, these children could be surprised to find out as teens or adults about their donor conceptions (Golombok, 1999). Children might discover information about their conception from genetic test information or from more routine tests like blood typing, or they could figure it out in a biology class where they learn about patterns of genetic inheritance. Furthermore, without reliable information about their family history, they cannot make predictions about whether they might pass on genetic disorders to their children. Most parents who withhold information about conception from their children indicate that they told other friends or relatives about their attempts to solve problems of infertility (McWhinnie, 2001). Such disclosures increase the chances that children will learn from other people who know about the parent's use of reproductive technologies.

Only a few investigators have directly addressed the issue of nondisclosure. Brewaeys (2001) described three reasons parents gave for withholding this information: (a) concern for the well-being of the child, who could feel confused or insecure with this knowledge, (b) a desire to protect the social father, for fear the child might feel less attached if the lack of a genetic relationship were known, and (c) uncertainty about what information to share or when to talk about it. Other reasons for withholding information included social stigma related to infertility or to the use of reproductive technologies, as well as attempts to preserve family harmony and to protect the feelings of the infertile husband (Landau, 1998). Unlike adoption, which is a well-known, accepted practice, use of reproductive technologies, especially gamete (egg and sperm) donation, is more controversial (Brewaeys, 1996). Parents who disclosed the use of biological donors did so because of their understanding of negative effects on adopted children who found out later in life. Deciding to share this information did not solve all of their problems, however. Concerns remained about what to tell their children about the sperm donor when they were teens or adults, given that anonymity precludes obtaining genetic information (Brewaeys, 2001).

Data about opinions of adults who were born following gamete donation have come from people participating in support groups or communicating with one another via Internet chat lines (McWhinnie, 2001). A look at these exchanges revealed that people who learned about their origin later in life wished they had been told much earlier. Their feelings of anger and resentment were similar to those of adults who had been adopted and had not been told. They also wanted information about their donor's appearance, education, interests, and personality. These concerns, however, were unlikely to be resolved. Unlike adoption, records of gamete donation are not generally available to families, nor are they kept for later availability (McWhinnie, 2001). Policies for donations were designed to protect the anonymity of the donor and the privacy of infertile adults (McWhinnie, 2001). However, there is growing consensus that adult children should have access to the identity of their genetic parents (Caulfield, 2002; Eichler, 1996). What that information would mean to children has yet to be determined.

HOW HAVE TECHNOLOGIES CHANGED FAMILIES?

The introduction of new reproductive technologies in the 20th century constituted a fundamental change in the way in which families can be created (Golombok et al., 2001). Technologies make it possible to have healthy children and even to save lives. Eligibility to have children is no longer limited primarily by biological parameters. Edwards (1991) discussed how the advent of medical technologies, especially genetic and reproductive technologies, created a need to reconsider the prevailing model of the family—nuclear family with heterosexual parents and gender-specific roles (Gates & Lackey, 2000). Clearly, static definitions of family are much too narrow to encompass the range of relationships and structures that make up what we are coming to know of families in this age of advancing technologies.

Family scholars have suggested some of the likely effects of these technologies on families. First, family relationships and family structure will become more complicated as family creation is mediated by technologies (Edwards, 1991). Families who have genetic testing may face moral decisions that revolve around individual rights versus collective responsibility. Specifically, families will need to address (a) decisions about secrecy, confidentiality, and disclosure; (b) feelings of despair and hope; (c) life cycle choices; and (d) family roles and relationships (Taswell, 1999).

With expanding reproductive options, we will need much more analysis to begin to understand what these technologies mean to families. We might learn by applying what we already know about families facing similar challenges in other contexts. Weil (2000), a family therapist, has reminded us that although genetic and reproductive sciences create new options, these options will be applied to human experiences that are age old. "The science is contemporary, but the hopes, fears, and anxieties surrounding genetic disorders and birth defects remain, in many respects, unchanged" (p. vii).

SUMMARY OF WHERE WE HAVE BEEN

A focus on reproductive decisions has identified a number of issues of consequence for families, therapists, and researchers. Family scholars and therapists have previously addressed many of the issues—family decision making and handling of grief, guilt, and family secrets—in other contexts. That knowledge could be incorporated into approaches for family counseling about genetic testing and reproductive decision making. We have some knowledge about factors that influence who uses reproductive technologies and why. We are just beginning to listen to women's voices, to recognize diversity, and to look at the contexts in which both decisions and technologies occur. We have yet to listen to the voices of potential fathers or other family members who would also be affected by reproductive decisions. Reproductive technologies and genetic tests have solved many problems for people wishing to have children. The last 20 years of investigation indicate that parents planning to use reproductive technologies can be reassured that there are no devastating health effects or major disruptions in parent-child and parent-parent relationships (Hahn, 2001). Findings have suggested that children's psychological adjustment may be less influenced by family structure than by warm, supportive relationships (Fasouliotis & Schenker, 1999).

We have much more to learn about genetic and reproductive health care. We have not yet looked at families who use these interventions as systems acting together or in the context of other systems (e.g., health care, schools, broader society). We know that health professionals have identified a number of challenges that families face in the health care context. However, we do not know what families would say about themselves in terms of psychosocial and ethical challenges that they encounter in the health care system or in other societal systems in which they participate. Studies have been driven by questions of interest to researchers; families have not generally been involved in developing research questions and/or research methods.

Reproductive and genetic technologies have expanded the need to explore definitions of families that are not dependent on biological relationships. Families and users of medical technologies, generally, are increasingly diverse, yet most outcome studies have described families headed by two middle-class, heterosexual parents (Hahn, 2001). More attention could be paid to the relative influences of family structure and family relationships by including other families (i.e., single parents, gay and lesbian couples) and by including more racial and ethnic diversity in samples (Golombok, 1999; Hahn, 2001). Perhaps most striking is the disconnection between medical and family researchers. Family scholars have suggested a number of issues that could be examined, although research thus far has focused primarily on medical decisions and health outcomes.

WHAT MIGHT THE FUTURE HOLD?

One thing about which we can be certain is that family forms and options for creating

them will continue to evolve and to bring new challenges for family scholars and practitioners. Embryo adoption will offer new possibilities to infertile people seeking to have children. Artificial wombs might give women the option to forego pregnancy, and human cloning could eliminate the need for gamete donors (Weaver, Umana-Taylor, Hans, & Malia, 2001). A growing understanding of the role of genetics in common diseases may create options for in utero treatment of genetic diseases or for preselection of embryos that will not be affected by them.

Lessons from family scholars in past decades can add depth and breadth to future investigations. To explicitly state the theoretical assumptions that guide research would provide focus and could link findings to other family data. In the research reviewed here, research questions were usually explicitly stated, whereas theoretical underpinnings were less explicit. As new technologies raise new questions, new theoretical approaches may be needed.

More collaboration among family science and health sciences practitioners and scholars could address a number of concerns that have been raised. For instance, adoption studies could potentially tell us a lot about families who are not biologically related and could predict outcomes of disclosure related to gamete donation or gestational carriers (surrogate mothers). Adoption scholars have found that many of the concerns initially raised about openness in adoptions were unfounded. As a result, adoption practices have become increasingly open. Not only do parents disclose relationships to their adopted children, but many families have arrangements where the biological mother continues a relationship with the child after adoption (Grotevant & McRoy, 1998). Looking at family processes rather than family structures could help us to look at strengths and resources rather than potential deficits and threats. Indeed, one might learn about parenting skills from parents who have been intentional about having children and who have spent time, money, and effort in creating these technologically mediated families (Weaver et al., 2001).

Most importantly, we will want to avoid judging what is normal from what is typical and assuming that what differs from the norm is pathological. In past decades, we have witnessed much anxiety over diverse families (e.g., single-parent families, stepfamilies, gay and lesbian families, ethnically diverse families), yet a focus on family functioning has revealed unique strengths in these families (Walsh, 1993). Families created using genetic and reproductive technologies can be seen as an additional type of diversity with similar challenges and resources.

REFERENCES

Anderson, G. (1999). Nondirectiveness in prenatal genetics: Patients read between the lines. *Nursing Ethics, 6,* 126–136.

Asch, A. (1999). Prenatal diagnosis and selective abortion: A challenge to practice and policy. *American Journal of Public Health, 89,* 1649–1657.

Bartels, D. M. (1990). Surrogacy arrangements: An overview. In D. M. Bartels, R. Priester, D. E. Vawter, & A. L. Caplan (Eds.), *Beyond Baby M* (pp. 173–182). Clifton, NJ: Humana.

Bartels, D. M. (2002). Genetics in health care: Ethical challenges in interactions of family systems and health system. *Dissertation Abstracts International #AAT3031959, 62,* 5426.

Beeson, D., & Golbus, M. S. (1985). Decision making: Whether or not to have prenatal diagnosis and abortion for X-linked conditions. *American Journal of Medical Genetics, 20,* 107–114.

Brewaeys, A. (1996). Donor insemination, the impact on family and child development. *Journal of Psychosomatic Obstetrics and Gynaecology, 17,* 1–13.

Brewaeys, A. (2001). Review: Parent-child relationships and child development in donor insemination families. *Human Reproduction Update, 7,* 38–46.

Browner, C. H., Preloran, H. M., & Cox, S. J. (1999). Ethnicity, bioethics, and prenatal diagnosis: The amniocentesis decisions of Mexican-origin women and their partners. *American Journal of Public Health, 89,* 1658–1666.

Burke, M., & Kolker, A. (1993). Clients undergoing chorionic villus sampling versus amniocentesis: Contrasting attitudes toward pregnancy. *Health Care for Women International, 14,* 193–200.

Caulfield, T. (2002). A shifting concept of family? *Nature Reviews/Genetics, 3,* 823.

Center for Bioethics, University of Minnesota. (1999). *New frontiers in genetic testing.* St. Paul: Author.

Collins, F. S. (1999). Shattuck lecture: Medical and societal consequences of the Human Genome Project. *New England Journal of Medicine, 341,* 28–37.

Colpin, H., Demyttenaere, K., & Vandemeulebroecke, L. (1995). New reproductive technology and the family: The parent-child relationship following *in vitro* fertilization. *Journal of Child Psychology and Psychiatry and Allied Disciplines, 36,* 1429–1441.

Cook, R., Bradley, S., & Golombok, S. (1998). A preliminary study of parental stress and child behavior in families with twins conceived by *in vitro* fertilization. *Human Reproduction, 13,* 3244–3246.

Doukas, D. J. (1993). The family in medical decision-making. *Hastings Center Report, 23,* 6–13.

Edwards, J. N. (1991). New conceptions: Biosocial innovations and the family. *Journal of Marriage and the Family, 53,* 349–360.

Edwards, R. G. (1980). *Conception in the human female.* London: Academic Press.

Eichler, M. (1996). The construction of technologically-mediated families. *Journal of Comparative Family Studies, 27,* 281–308.

Evers-Kiebooms, G., Denayerr, L., & Van Den Berghe, H. (1990). A child with cystic fibrosis II: Subsequent family planning decisions, reproduction and use of prenatal diagnosis. *Clinical Genetics, 37,* 207–215.

Fasouliotis, S. J., & Schenker, J.G. (1999). Social aspects in assisted reproduction. *Human Reproduction Update, 5,* 26–39.

Frets, G. P., Duinvenvoorden, H. G., Verhage, F., Niermeijer, M. F., Vande Berge, S. M., & Galjaard, H. (1990). Factors influencing the reproductive decisions after genetic counseling. *American Journal of Medical Genetics, 35,* 503–509.

Gates, M. F., & Lackey, N. R. (2000). The researcher experience in health care research with families. In S. Diemert & M. F. Gates (Eds.), *The researcher experience in qualitative research* (pp. 22–30). Thousand Oaks, CA: Sage.

Gibson, F. L., Ungerer, J. A., McMahon, C. A., Leslie, G. I., & Saunders, D. M. (2000). The mother-child relationship following *in vitro* fertilization (IVF): Infant attachment, responsivity, and maternal sensitivity. *Journal of Child Psychology and Psychiatry and Allied Disciplines, 41,* 1015–1023.

Golombok, S. (1999). New family forms: Children raised in solo mother families, lesbian mother families, and in families created by assisted reproduction. In L. Balter & C. S. Tamis-LeMonda (Eds.), *Child psychology* (pp. 429–446). Philadelphia: Psychology Press/Taylor & Francis.

Golombok, S., MacCallum, F., & Goodman, E. (2001). The "test-tube" generation: Parent-child relationships and the psychological well-being of *in vitro* fertilization children at adolescence. *Child Development, 72,* 599–608.

Golombok, S., MacCallum, F., Goodman, E., & Rutter, M. (2002). Families with children conceived by donor insemination: A follow-up at age twelve. *Child Development, 72,* 952–968.

Golombok, S., Murray, C., Brinsden, P., & Abdallah, H. (1999). Social versus biological parenting: Family functioning and the socioemotional development of children conceived by egg or sperm donation. *Journal of Child Psychology and Psychiatry, 40,* 519–527.

Grotevant, H., & McRoy, R. G. (1998). *Openness in adoption.* Newbury Park, CA: Sage.

Gurdon, J. B., & Colman, A. (1999). The future of cloning. *Nature, 402,* 743–746.

Hahn, C. S. (2001). Review: Psychosocial well-being of parents and their children born after assisted reproduction. *Journal of Pediatric Psychology, 26,* 525–538.

Hammer Burns, L. (1999). Genetics and infertility: Psychosocial issues in reproductive counseling. *Families, Systems and Health, 17,* 87–110.

Hammer Burns, L., & Covington, S. N. (1998). Psychology of infertility. In L. Hammer Burns & S. N. Covington (Eds.), *Infertility counseling* (pp. 3–25). New York: Parthenon.

Hammer Burns, L., & LeRoy, B. S. (1998). Genetic counseling and the infertile patient. In L. Hammer Burns & S. N. Covington (Eds.), *Infertility counseling* (pp. 199–225). New York: Parthenon.

Katz Rothman, B. (1993). *The tentative pregnancy.* New York: Norton.

Landau, R. (1998). Secrecy, anonymity, and deception in donor insemination: A genetic, psycho-social, and ethical critique. *Social Work in Health Care, 28,* 75–89.

Lippman-Hand, A., & Fraser, F. C. (1979). Genetic counseling: Parents' responses to uncertainty. *Birth Defects Original Article Series, 15*(5C), 325–339.

McCarthy Veach, P., Bartels, D. M., & LeRoy, B. S. (2001). Ethical and professional challenges posed by patients with genetic concerns: A report of focus group discussions with genetic counselors, physicians, and nurses. *Journal of Genetic Counseling, 10*, 97–119.

McDaniel, S., Hepworth, J., & Doherty, W. J. (1992). *Medical family therapy.* New York: Basic Books.

McWhinnie, A. (2001). Gamete donation and anonymity: Should offspring from donated gametes continued to be denied knowledge of their origins and antecedents? *Human Reproduction, 16*, 807–817.

Montgomery, T. R., Aiello, F., Adelman, R. D., Waslyshyn, N., Andrews, M. C., Brazelton, T. B., Jones, G. S., & Jones, W. H. (1999). The psychological status at school age of children conceived by *in vitro* fertilization. *Human Reproduction 14*, 2162–2165.

Moyer, A., Brown, B., Gates, E., Daniels, M., Brown, H. D., & Kuppermann, M. (1999). Decisions about prenatal testing for chromosomal disorders: Perceptions of a diverse group of pregnant women. *Journal of Women's Health and Gender-Based Medicine, 8*, 521–531.

Olivennes, F., Kerbrat, V., Rufat, P., Blanchet, V., Fanchin, R., & Frydman, R. (1997). Follow-up of a cohort of 422 children aged 6 to 13 years conceived by *in vitro* fertilization. *Fertility and Sterility, 67*, 284–289.

Online Mendelian Inheritance in Man. (2000). McKusick-Nathans Institute for Genetic Medicine, Johns Hopkins University (Baltimore, MD) and National Center for Biotechnology Information, National Library of Medicine (Bethesda, MD). Retrieved April 25, 2003, from www.ncbi.nlm.nih.gov/omim.

Redlinger-Grosse, K., Bernhart, B. A., Berg, K., Muenke, M., & Biesecker, B. B. (2002). The decision to continue: The experiences and needs of parents who receive a prenatal diagnosis of holoprosencephaly. *American Journal of Medical Genetics 112*, 369–378.

Rolland, J. S. (1999). Commentary: Families and genetic fate: A millennial challenge. *Families, Systems and Health, 17*, 123–132.

Rosenblatt, P. C., Peterson, P., Portner, J., Cleveland, M., Mykkanen, A., Foster, R., et al. (1973). A cross-cultural study of responses to childlessness. *Behavior Science Notes, 8*, 221–231.

Society for Assisted Reproductive Technology & American Society of Reproductive Medicine. (2002). Assisted reproductive technology in the United States: 1999 results generated from the American Society for Reproductive Medicine/Society for Assisted Reproductive Technology registry. *Fertility and Sterility, 78*, 918–931.

Strong, B., & DeVault, C. (1992). *The marriage and family experience.* St. Paul, MN: West.

Taswell, H. F. (1999). Predictive genetic testing: A story of one family. *Families, Systems and Health, 17*, 217–231.

Thompson, J., & Thompson, M. (1986). *Genetics in medicine* (4th ed.). Philadelphia: J. B. Saunders.

Vincent, V. A., Edwards, J. G., Young, R. S., & Nachtigal, M. (1991). Pregnancy termination because of chromosomal abnormalities: A study of 25,950 amniocenteses in the southeast. *Southern Medical Journal, 84*, 10.

Walsh, F. (1993). *Normal family processes* (2nd ed.). New York: Guilford.

Weaver, S. E., Umana-Taylor, A. J., Hans, J. D., & Malia, S. (2001). Challenges family scholars may face in studying family diversity: A focus on Latino families, stepfamilies, and reproductive technologies. *Journal of Family Issues, 22*, 922–939.

Weil, J. (2000). *Psychosocial genetic counseling.* New York: Oxford University Press.

CHAPTER 29

Understanding the Effects of the Internet on Family Life

ROBERT HUGHES, JR., AND JASON D. HANS

" [T] he American family during the past 25 years has entered a new world of rapid change," (p. 415) wrote Ernest Burgess in 1928 as he reflected on the introduction into society of technologies such as the automobile, motion pictures, radios, airplanes, and telephones. A review of any decade of the 20th century would include the introduction of an array of technological developments, including radio, television, videocassette recorders (VCRs), microwave ovens, air conditioners, refrigerators, personal computers, and the Internet.

Less than two decades ago, computers were primarily used in science, engineering, and business, and the Internet was the province of the military. Yet in 2001, 57% of all households had a computer, and 51% had direct access to the Internet (National Telecommunications and Information Administration [NTIA], 2002). Social critics and technologists have been active in discussing the implications of these changes for individuals, families, work, and society. There are those who see computers and the Internet as a positive force that will foster greater communication and better access to education, promote global understanding, and make the world a better place to live (Rheingold, 1993). Some also believe that the Internet will lead to better social relationships because people will be freed from the constraints of time and place (Katz & Aspden, 1997). Other critics suggest that computer technology will impoverish relationships, isolate family members from each other, and distance families from the outside world (Stoll, 1995).

A quick look at the history of technological developments in the past century reveals that at each introduction of a new technological device there have been similar arguments. Fischer (1992), who traced the introduction of the automobile and telephone in the early part of the 20th century, found numerous accounts that parallel the current debates. For example, notes from a 1926 Knights of Columbus committee meeting called to discuss whether modern inventions help or hurt character and health included the following questions: "Does the telephone make men more active or more lazy?" "Does the telephone break up home life and the old practice of visiting friends?" "How can a man be master of the auto instead of it being his master?" (quoted in Fischer, 1992, p. 1). In contrast, in 1916 AT&T issued a public relations announcement noting that "the telephone is essentially democratic, it carries the voice of the child and the grown-up with equal speed and directness. . . . [I]t is not only the implement of the individual, but it fulfills the needs of all the people" (quoted in Fischer, 1992, p. 2).

Family scientists also have entered into these discussions, sometimes with empirical data, sometimes as polemists. The Lynds, in their studies of Middletown during the 1920s, argued that the automobile liberated young people to attend movies and road-houses, thus leading to promiscuity and undermining the family (Lynd & Lynd, 1929). Ogburn and Nimkoff (1955) asserted that the machines of the Industrial Revolution determined the character and nature of families at the beginning of the 20th century. In contrast, Burgess (1928) cautioned against the view that families are shaped solely by environmental factors: "Only through research can the necessary basis of fact be found for any practical program to meet the problems of the changing American family" (p. 415).

In keeping with the advice of Burgess (1928), we examine research on the effects of computers and the Internet on families to bring about a better understanding of how this technology influences family life. We begin with an overview of the extent to which computers and the Internet have become part of the landscape of family life. To provide perspective, we also consider information about other communication technologies. Then we look at five questions regarding the effects of computers and the Internet on families: (a) How has the Internet affected romantic relationships? (b) How has the Internet affected family relationships? (c) How does the Internet affect family ties to social networks? (d) How is the intersection of work and family altered by the Internet? and (e) How can the Internet be used to help families?

THE INFORMATION TECHNOLOGY CONTEXT

Much has been made of the rapid introduction of computers and the Internet into the private realm of family life. However, this is just the latest wave of information technology to become commonplace in households. The older technologies—radios, telephones, and televisions—are in well over 90% of U.S. households, and although the proportion of households with these devices has remained steady over the last three decades, an increasing number have multiple radios and televisions (Newburger, 1999).

The prevalence of personal computers and Internet use in the home has grown rapidly in recent years, but ownership of computers and access to the Internet vary on the basis of income, education, household composition, and ethnicity. Low-income and single-parent households and households headed by individuals with little education are far less likely to have Internet access in their homes than affluent, two-parent households composed of adults with more years of formal education (NTIA, 2002). However, the growth rate in Internet access is much greater among the former, leading to a gradual diminishing of the gap. Ethnic differences follow a similar pattern. Asians (60.4%) and whites (59.9%) are more likely to use the Internet than blacks

(24.7%) or Hispanics (20.1%), but between 2000 and 2001 Internet use grew the most rapidly among blacks and Hispanics. Personal computers and the Internet may eventually become commonplace in families across a broader spectrum of socioeconomic and racial strata, but for now, there are large differences in who has in-home computer capabilities and who does not.

HOW HAS THE INTERNET AFFECTED ROMANTIC RELATIONSHIPS?

Dating and Intimacy

Although interactive Internet applications (e.g., electronic mail, newsgroups, chat rooms) were first developed in the early 1970s, the role personal computers played in romantic relations went largely unnoticed until the number of Internet users mushroomed in the mid-1990s. Early on, there was a stigma attached to seeking and finding love online, but the number of people engaging in online dating has grown rapidly. Jupiter Research reported that in 2002, 16.3 million people visited online dating sites; there are now more paying subscribers to online dating services than any other content area on the Internet (cited in O'Connell, 2003).

Models have been hypothesized to explain the lure of online romantic/sexual relationships, such as Cooper's (1998) Triple-A Engine (Access, Affordability, Anonymity) and Young's (1999) ACE Model of Cybersexual Addiction (Anonymity, Convenience, Escape). Although empirical validation of these models is needed, early research has demonstrated that certain types of people prefer Internet-facilitated courtship. For example, those who are socially anxious or lonely are more likely to form intimate relationships via the Internet (McKenna, Green, & Gleason, 2002), and shy individuals are able to overcome many relationship-initiation barriers (Scharlott & Christ, 1995). It is likely that other barriers to relationship formation (e.g., proximity, social class, some physical traits) also become less important at the outset of computer-mediated relationships (Cooper & Sportolari, 1997; McKenna at al., 2002), although participants in a study on attitudes toward online relationships indicated discomfort with meeting potential partners online when their physical appearance is not known (Donn & Sherman, 2002).

There is evidence that online relationship development is different from traditional courting. Online romantic relationships have much higher levels of self-disclosure and intimacy early in the relationship (Clark, 1998; Gerlander & Takala, 1997). McKenna et al. (2002) found that the stability of online relationships over a 2-year period compared favorably to that of traditional relationships. If an online interaction is going well, the relationship often evolves into a conventional face-to-face relationship (McKenna et al., 2002; Parks & Roberts, 1998), or at least occasional contacts for those who are geographically distant. Concern has been expressed because one can easily deceive another in computer-mediated relationships (Cooper & Sportolari, 1997), a concern that is especially pertinent for relationships that have not resulted in face-to-face meetings. However, due to the relative anonymity and discreetness of e-mail, many lies (e.g., marital status) may still be quite easily maintained even when meetings occur.

Researchers studying courtship behavior vis-à-vis technology should examine how online dating differs from traditional courtship behavior and whether mate selection criteria differ in online relationships versus face-to-face relationships. An interesting line of research would be to monitor how the characteristics of people who use online services and the reasons and meanings they attribute to their use change over time as online dating finds greater acceptance among the general population. The role of cellular phones, instant messaging, and other emerging communication technologies in the development and maintenance of early relationships also should be investigated.

Extramarital Relationships

Infidelity has usually been defined as sexual relationships outside marriage; however, the emergence of computer-mediated relationships and virtual sex has raised new questions about boundaries of intimacy (Merkle & Richardson, 2000). Anecdotal evidence suggests that many people know of a friend, family member, or acquaintance whose face-to-face romantic relationship was threatened by an online relationship. Thus, intimate online relationships, even if not physical, may become common sources of tension in existing face-to-face romantic relationships (Young, Griffin-Shelley, Cooper, O'Mara, & Buchanan, 2000). Indeed, Schneider (2000) found that among 94 respondents whose marital relationships were seriously and adversely affected by a partner's cybersex activities, more than 60% indicated that the online relationship never progressed beyond computer-mediated interaction. Clearly, research is needed that investigates the changing boundaries of intimacy brought about by computer-mediated interaction.

HOW HAS THE INTERNET AFFECTED FAMILY RELATIONSHIPS?

Most researchers have focused on broad descriptions of trends in the use of the Internet, such as time spent using computers and the Internet (Howard, Raine, & Jones, 2001) and the ways in which children and adults use these technologies (Orleans & Laney, 2000). Few researchers have examined the ways in which the Internet has altered family functioning.

One area of speculation is whether computer technology strengthens or damages relationships among family members. One of the earliest studies on the role of the Internet in family life (Kraut, Mukophadyay, Szczypula, Kiesler, & Scherlis, 2000) monitored a group of parents and their teenagers over their first 1 to 2 years of Internet use. Parents and adolescents used the Internet more often to interact (e.g., sending and receiving e-mail) with non–household members than to seek information or entertainment. They also spent less time communicating in the household with family members than they did before gaining Internet access. These results give credibility to the fears that Internet use damages family relationships; however, a follow-up study 2 to 3 years later found that these initial declines in family communication did not persist (Kraut et al., 1998).

In one of the few observational studies about computers and family relationships, Orleans and Laney (2000) observed 32 children between the ages of 8 and 17 on at least three occasions each for an hour or more while they did computer work on their own or with others at home. Children and their parents seldom talked to each other while the children were using the computer. Generally, children used the computers independently and were more likely to talk with siblings or peers for help regarding computer problems than they were to ask their parents. About 65% of the time that the children were online, they sent and received e-mail, visited chat rooms, and played interactive games. Boys and girls used the computers in different ways:

> The girls were more likely to be serious about using the computer. They were more focused on using the computer for particular purposes, and their demeanor while using [the computer] was more somber than the boys. The boys seemed more likely to view the computer as a multipurpose toy

that was itself fun to use and integrated it into their social lives. (Orleans & Laney, 2000, p. 67)

Another area of interest to family scientists has been the ways in which parents manage the use of technology. There is a long history of increasing parental awareness of media content through labeling systems (e.g., parental advisory warning labels) and developing various parental control devices for technologies. Family scientists are in the early stages of understanding parental regulation of children's use of the Internet, in terms of both managing family boundaries and dealing with dangerous situations. There are numerous technological attempts (e.g., filtering software) to address these issues, but there is little understanding about how parents actually regulate the Internet and what types of technological tools, if any, work.

Livingstone (2002) found that only 6% of parents were concerned about their children's use of computers and the Internet. Parents were far more concerned about illegal drugs (51%), crime (39%), and educational standards (38%). These data suggest that when viewed in the context of other hazards children face, parents perceive that there are more serious threats to children's wellbeing than their children's computer and Internet use. However, 50% of the parents in Livingstone's (2002) study reported having rules about children's use of the Internet. In contrast, children reported about half as many restrictions as their parents. The inconsistency between reports of parents and of their children points to a need for a better understanding of computers and Internet use in family contexts on a day-to-day basis. This may require observational and longitudinal data in addition to self-reports by children and parents.

The contextual nature of parents' Internet concerns compared with their concerns about other aspects of life illustrates the importance of studying the Internet in context to provide a more complete understanding of how the technology fits with other aspects of family life. When the Internet is studied in isolation, it is easy to misunderstand how it fits with other aspects of family life and to distort its significance and influence. These studies provide a glimpse into the variety of ways that computers and the Internet may affect relationships in families. Whether they have a positive or negative impact on family interactions is a complicated question that requires more research and the consideration of how other household technologies, such as cell phones, video games, and television, foster or hinder family communication, conflict, and socialization.

Another important question related to the Internet concerns aggressive behavior. There is much research about the contribution of television and video games to aggressive behavior in children and adults (e.g., Johnson, Cohen, Smailes, Kasen, & Brook, 2002). The Internet not only provides additional opportunities for family members to be exposed to violent images and activities but makes it possible to be in contact with people who are engaged with violent material and activities. Given the level of violence in the world, understanding how family members are affected by these potentially harmful opportunities is critical.

Another important direction for research is to focus, not on computer technology itself, but rather on computer technology in the context of family issues such as intergenerational relationships, postdivorce relationships, social network processes, and work. For example, the Internet may provide new ways for older family members to communicate with distant family members, and there are many unanswered questions regarding ways this technology may serve as a bridge for homebound elderly. Similarly, using the Internet to maintain relationships with nonresidential children or parents would have quite different effects than participating in online games for recreation. The Internet can become an important way for family members to stay connected after divorce.

As communication technologies evolve (e.g., as wireless connections become more commonplace), it will be important to consider the ways that families incorporate these opportunities. Specific uses of computers and the Internet in the home, such as doing office work, maintaining geographically distant relationships, participating in family life education, or engaging in virtual sex, may play an important role in understanding modern family environments and should be studied. Researchers should begin to explore questions such as "With whom are family members communicating?" "What is being communicated?" "What role does computer-mediated conversation play in the overall communication in families?" and "How does computer-mediated communication differ from other forms of communication?"

HOW DOES THE INTERNET AFFECT FAMILY TIES TO SOCIAL NETWORKS?

Another early concern regarding the Internet was that people would abandon face-to-face relationships and live their lives online. In an analysis of the decline of involvement in community and other social activities, Putnam (2000) asserted that this decline was due in part to television and that the Internet would contribute to further loss of social ties.

An early study reporting on new Internet users seemed to confirm the idea that the Internet could lead to withdrawal from social involvements (Kraut et al., 1998). New users who spent more time on the Internet reported less social involvement with both geographically close and distant friends. However, over the next 2 to 3 years, social support and interaction with close and distant network members returned to pre-Internet levels. This study took place when Internet technology was newer and people were less familiar with it than they are now. Thus, participants may have withdrawn from social ties because of the novelty of this new technology and the time needed to master it. Few members of their social network would have had access to the Internet, so they would have been less able to use it to maintain existing social ties than current Internet users would be. In a second study with a new sample, Kraut et al. (2002) added more control variables and a wider range of social network measures. In this study, they found that Internet use was related to *increases* in the number of close and distant social contacts and face-to-face communication with family and friends, indicating that the Internet had a positive impact on development and maintenance of social networks.

Other investigators have begun to provide evidence that the Internet may help maintain social ties. Among home Internet users, 96.6% of women and 93.6% of men reported using the Internet to communicate with friends and family (NTIA, 2000). In fact, the primary reason why people send and receive e-mail messages is to maintain interpersonal relationships (Stafford, Kline, & Dimmick, 1999). Almost twice as many people reported interpersonal reasons for using e-mail (42%) as those who reported using e-mail for business (25%) or information (23%). About 60% of Internet users reported that they communicated more with family and friends now that they had e-mail access (Howard et al., 2001). Franzen (2000) found that, over time, e-mail had a positive effect on the maintenance of social ties. Nearly half of online seniors were persuaded to get Internet access by family members, and a majority reported that the Internet enhanced communication with family members (Fox et al., 2001).

In a unique study of social networks, Hampton and Wellman (2000) surveyed a neighborhood in which all the residents had free access to a high-speed Internet connection. The wired residents recognized almost three times as many neighbors, talked with nearly twice as many, and had been invited or had invited, one and a half times as many neighbors into their homes as had residents of a nearby neighborhood that was not wired. The authors suggested that rather than replacing face-to-face ties, computer-mediated ties supported and strengthened neighborhood social ties by providing new opportunities for social relationships and engagement in community. In a large study of Internet users, Wellman, Haase, Witte, and Hampton (2001) found that online activity supplemented rather than replaced or diminished offline social contacts. Overall, these findings suggest that the Internet has positive effects on family members' ability to maintain real-world social ties outside the immediate family.

HOW IS THE INTERSECTION OF WORK AND FAMILY ALTERED BY THE INTERNET?

For over 100 years, forecasters have predicted that technology will eliminate the constraints of geographical proximity between home and work. In 1893, a writer forecasted that by 1993 work would take place within homes via the telephone (as cited in Fischer, 1992). In 1980, Toffler introduced the idea of the "electronic cottage" and predicted that downtowns would "stand empty, reduced to use as ghostly warehouses or converted to living space" (p. 221). The decreasing cost of computer technology coupled with the increasing cost of office space has led to additional predictions about the ways in which technology will alter family-work balance (Piskurich, 1996).

A recent review of telework, defined as work performed at an offsite location and most typically within one's home, suggests that many of the forecasts of changing work environments are unlikely to occur (Ellison, 1999). Although there are many optimistic reports about telework, findings from a recent U.S. Bureau of Labor Statistics (2002) report indicated that only about 15% of employees work at home at least 1 day per week. Taken at face value, telecommuting sounds like a solution to work-family strain, child care, and numerous other family dilemmas. However, studies of telecommuting suggest that there may be significant limitations to overcome with regard to working at home.

In one survey, although 88% of workers preferred telecommuting, only 11% were doing it (Mokhtarian & Salomon, 1996). The constraints against telecommuting have little to do with technology but rather are related to supervisor unwillingness, concern about lack of visibility to management, household distractions, and a lack of self-discipline to do the work (Mokhtarian, Bagley, & Salomon, 1998). Women with children in particular are more likely to cite household distractions as a constraint when compared to women without children.

Reflecting on studies of the impact of technology on work, Kraut (1987) commented, "Office structure has remained virtually unchanged since the late 19th century, despite . . . major changes in office technology" (p. 130). He suggested that predictors of changes in work as the result of technology have often failed to understand the importance of socializing as a source of worker satisfaction and the importance of co-workers in conducting many work assignments.

Another hypothesis about the effect of technology on work and family life is that the availability of computers and the Internet at home leads to more people taking work home from the office. Surprisingly, the trend has been in the opposite direction. Between 1991 and 1997, there was a modest decline (from 12.2 million to 11.1 million) in the number of workers taking work home (U.S. Bureau of Labor Statistics, 1998).

Although there may not be dramatic changes in the work-family relationship due to computers and the Internet, there have been subtle shifts. Hill and his colleagues (Hill, Hawkins, Ferris, & Weitzman, 2001; Hill, Hawkins, & Miller, 1996) have chronicled the implementation of flextime and flexplace in the IBM Corporation and reports by employees on work-family balance. In one study, workers assigned to virtual offices reported no better ability to balance work and family (Hill et al., 1996); however, recent findings indicate that workers report being better able to achieve work-life balance when they have more flexibility, either flextime or flexplace (Hill et al., 2001). Additionally, some surveys of family members suggest that the boundary between work and home is blurring: About 10% of Internet users who have access only on the job do something unrelated to work almost daily; about 66% report some use of the Internet for home-related activities while at work (Howard et al., 2001). Likewise, almost 25% of Internet users with access only at home report doing something for work at home. These data indicate that work-related tasks are performed in some homes and that some personal tasks are completed in the workplace but that the effects of technology on work and family life appear to be subtle.

Most of the literature that has explored work-family connections has focused on changes in the ways that families balance work and family as the result of "family-friendly" workplace policies such as flextime scheduling and telecommuting. This focus may overlook the more subtle ways in which Internet connections both at work and at home may blur the boundaries between work and family. Analysis of these subtle shifts is important for understanding the ways in which technology may be altering families' management of work and family tasks.

HOW CAN THE INTERNET BE USED TO HELP FAMILIES?

The Internet has been used to create new ways of providing peer support, family life education, and family therapy. For example, there are numerous news groups online devoted to family issues such as divorce, death, or children with special needs. Additionally, family life educators and family therapists have begun to create online opportunities to provide help to families. It is important to understand more about the effectiveness of these activities.

Peer Support

Peer support through news groups was one of the first Internet developments. There are groups devoted to a wide range of family issues. Some groups have small readerships, and some have thousands of participants. Participants in these self-help activities find them beneficial (King & Moreggi, 1998). Online groups may be especially important to individuals whose face-to-face social relationships are inadequate or for groups that feel stigmatized, such as parents of special-needs children (King & Moreggi, 1998). Several studies have examined these issues.

Miller and Gergen (1998) concluded, from a content analysis of helping strategies offered on one self-help site, that the help provided differed from change strategies used by trained family therapists. They speculated that although participants may feel like they are getting help through these online groups, the help may not be as effective as that provided by skilled therapists.

Those in online groups, unlike those in face-to-face groups, can participate in three ways: reading messages, posting messages to the group, or sending private e-mail to selected group members (Mickelson, 1997). Different patterns of social support are evident in these three styles of interacting.

Mickelson found that although merely reading newsgroup messages was not related to any of the social support behaviors, posting public messages was related to fears of rejection, and private e-mail requests were related to lack of perceived support from spouses. Thus, the Internet may provide an alternative source of social relationships for those who have difficulty developing social ties face to face. Similarly, Cummings, Sproull, and Kiesler (2002) found that members of an online hearing-loss support group were more likely to participate if they lacked real-world social support. Additionally, these researchers found that in online support groups, unlike face-to-face groups, friends and family members can also participate, and participants whose real-world social network participated reported benefiting the most from online help. Cummings and his colleagues concluded that the paths through which social support may benefit individuals may differ in online support groups as opposed to face-to-face groups. It would be important to examine whether the paths found in a hearing-loss group would be similar to those found in family-issue support groups, such as groups related to divorce, single parenting, new parents, or stepfamilies. This function may be especially important for individuals whose face-to-face social relationships among friends and family are inadequate or for groups that feel stigmatized.

Family Life Education and Family Therapy

Family life educators and family therapists have begun to explore the ways in which the Internet can be used to help individuals and families. It has been suggested that the Internet provides a valuable medium through which to teach families (Hughes, Ebata, & Dollahite, 1999) and that the Web may be especially suitable for reaching fathers (Grant, Hawkins, & Dollahite, 2001) because

Web-based methods are more instrumental, thereby tending to be a better fit for men's learning style. Most of the work in this area has been limited to descriptions of models used for Web site delivery of family life information (Elliott, 1999; Smith, 1999). Hughes (2001) described a preliminary model for collecting process and outcome evaluation data regarding Web site delivery, but there is little information about the overall effectiveness of Web-based family life education. To advance this line of content delivery, family life educators will need to describe their online teaching models and assess the effectiveness of these approaches.

Online family therapy poses many of the challenges of family life education, with added concerns about ethics and hazards of these techniques. More has been written about the promise of online therapeutic approaches (e.g., Jencius & Sager, 2001) than about their effectiveness. For example, Jedlicka and Jennings (2001) described their clinical experiences in treating married couples through e-mail, provided insight into their techniques, and shared their clinical judgments about effectiveness, but they did not make comparisons to other treatment approaches.

The ethics of online family therapy remain an important consideration. Until there is evidence that the exclusive use of e-mail, chat rooms, and virtual therapy is effective, online therapy cannot be considered an ethically viable substitute for empirically validated approaches.

For professionals in family life education and family therapy, both programmatic efforts in refining models of providing education and therapy online and evaluation efforts are needed. Researchers have collected information about the general public's efforts to find health and financial information online, but there has been no similar study regarding information related to family life. This may be one of the first ways to understand how people are seeking family information online and what types of help they are seeking. Researchers could also examine whether peer support on the Internet is useful. Online news groups that focus on family issues deserve to be studied in more detail, with attention to who participates and what difference it makes.

DIRECTIONS FOR THEORY AND RESEARCH

It is easy when looking at technology to find historical predictions that were mistaken, but these mistaken predictions about the use and impact of technology should serve as a caution. They suggest that we are unlikely in the short run to understand the implications of new technologies and that these technological changes deserve study. We were surprised by the lack of study of personal computers in relation to family life. Little has been published since a 1985 issue of *Marriage and Family Review* devoted to personal computers and the family. The advent of the Internet has sparked new interest in the role of computers and the Internet in family life, but how should family scientists address issues of technology in general in family life?

Theoretical Issues

In general, family scientists have little to say about the ways in which the physical environment affects families. Family theories are silent about the ways in which technologies for food preparation (e.g., microwave ovens, dishwashers), communication (e.g., telephone, faxes, the Internet), and recreation (e.g., VCRs, televisions, gaming devices) affect family life. Even ecological theories (e.g., Bronfenbrenner, 1986) offer little guidance about families' technological context and focus primarily on their social ecology. The lack of discussion of these issues makes it difficult to distinguish between important and trivial questions.

The sociology of technology provides some overarching perspective on how to consider the effects of computers on social life. Fischer (1992) described two general approaches to considering the effects of technology on social life. One is a deterministic approach that treats technology as an external force. The other assumes that technology embodies cultural values that shape history. Fischer argued that both of these approaches are problematic because they fail to take into account the ways in which people actively shape the use and influence of technology. For example, it was not inevitable that telephones would be used primarily as private two-way communication devices; early in their development, they were used as a broadcast medium, much as televisions are now used. Thus, the telephone did not determine how people used it; rather, people's use of the telephone shaped how it influenced them. Fischer suggests a social constructivist approach to studying the impact of technology on social life. Research guided by this perspective would examine the ways in which computers get used and the meanings attached to those uses. Researchers should focus their attention on the ways in which the Internet is used in the context of family life. For example, family scientists will obtain a better understanding of the role of the Internet in courtship by studying both online and offline romantic behaviors rather than focusing only on the online behaviors in the absence of broader social interactions.

Methodological Issues

The ways in which the Internet in family life has been studied are limited and problematic. In general, most reports about the use of computers are based on large-scale studies using self-report, cross-sectional data from one household member. The range of methods used to study the Internet and families needs to be broader. For example, qualitative studies are needed to provide a richer description of the families, processes, and context surrounding Internet use. Innovative approaches to collecting quantitative data are also necessary.

Although self-report methods are good ways to document the existence of a computer in the household and connections to the Internet, it is not clear that one member of a family can give an accurate picture of the family's computer use. There is ample evidence that people are unable to provide accurate reports about how much time they spend doing various activities unless that information is collected through time-diary methods. For example, Kraut et al. (2002) compared self-reports of Internet time use to actual Internet logs and obtained correlation coefficients in the range of .42 to .55, well below a level usually acceptable for reliability. This discrepancy may be a fruitful area of inquiry in itself but also suggests that researchers will need to incorporate a variety of data collection methods (e.g., observations, time diaries, automated computer logs) to fully understand Internet use in the family.

Most studies are simple social address comparisons that compare groups based on family type, social class, or educational background. To understand the outcomes of family processes, it is necessary to go beyond social address comparisons to consider models that include personal characteristics (e.g., net-savvy parents), various family processes (e.g., parents who report spending time involved in children's activities), and specific social contexts (e.g., home, child care) (Bronfenbrenner, 1986). Process-context models or person-process-context models will provide a richer understanding of how individuals and families are affected by the Internet and through what processes and in what settings this occurs. However, it is likely that the Internet affects families in complex ways because it is a psychological, social, play, and consumer space open to a wide range of positive and negative activities. Kraut et al. (2002) provided a good example of this: They reported that introverts became lonelier and extroverts became less lonely the more they used the Internet. The wide variation in family interaction styles and circumstances suggests that the effects of the Internet may vary greatly depending on family communication styles and other behaviors. Studies of television use in families may provide some initial hypotheses about family interaction and Internet use. For example, children in high-conflict households are more likely to watch television than children in low-conflict households (Morgan, Alexander, Shanahan, & Harris, 1990). A similar pattern of Internet use also may occur. Thus, it seems unlikely that this medium will be understood without looking more closely at the specifics of what people are doing.

Additionally, researchers need to consider longitudinal designs that take into consideration ways in which families change and adapt to technological changes. It is likely that patterns of interaction with home computers and the Internet change over time on the basis of a number of factors, such as age of children and computer proficiency.

The Internet presents researchers with new methods of data collection that may be appealing to those who study computer technology (e.g., savvy computer and Internet users). Online data collection via e-mail or the Internet can save time and reduce error through automated data entry. Dynamic generation of response options and skip patterns invisible to respondents can allow for complex and personalized survey designs, and printing and postage costs can be avoided. An important disadvantage is that variations in computer hardware and software may result in respondents' experiencing the same survey in different ways (e.g., based on software used, monitor size and resolution), although a skilled programmer and careful planning can minimize (but not eliminate) this problem. Another concern is that representative samples of the general population cannot yet be achieved online due to the socioeconomic bias in Internet users, but samples of specific populations, such as those that are likely to be sought when studying computers and the Internet, can be obtained. Finally, some initial guidelines for online survey design have been outlined (see Dillman, 2000), but reliability, validity, and ethical issues of online data collection need further investigation.

CONCLUSION

The major conclusion from this review is that for the most part family scientists are not engaged in exploring the role of computer technology in family life. Much of the debate about the effects of computers on families has been left to social commentators who often have limited access to empirical data or to technologists who predict use on the basis of the capacity of computers. Past approaches to studying technology and families that have assumed that people are passively affected by technology are problematic. It is essential that we develop conceptual models about families in context and study the ways in which families adapt to technological developments.

REFERENCES

Bronfenbrenner, U. (1986). Ecology of the family as a context for human development: Research perspectives. *Developmental Psychology, 22,* 723–742.

Burgess, E. W. (1928). The changing American family. *Religious Education, 23,* 408–415.

Clark, L. S. (1998). Dating on the Net: Teens and the rise of "pure" relationships. In S. G. Jones (Ed.), *Cybersociety 2.0: Revisiting computer-mediated communication and community* (pp. 159–183). Thousand Oaks, CA: Sage.

Cooper, A. (1998). Sexuality on the Internet: Surfing into the new millennium. *CyberPsychology and Behavior, 1,* 181–187.

Cooper, A., & Sportolari, L. (1997). Romance in cyberspace: Understanding online attraction. *Journal of Sex Education and Therapy, 22,* 7–14.

Cummings, J. N., Sproull, L., & Kiesler, S. B. (2002). Beyond hearing: Where real-world and online support meet. *Group Dynamics: Theory, Research, and Practice, 6,* 78–88.

Dillman, D. A. (2000). *Mail and Internet surveys: The tailored design method.* New York: John Wiley.

Donn, J. E., & Sherman, R. C. (2002). Attitudes and practices regarding the formation of romantic relationships on the Internet. *CyberPsychology and Behavior, 5,* 107–123.

Elliott, M. (1999). Classifying family life education on the World Wide Web. *Family Relations, 48,* 7–13.

Ellison, N. B. (1999). Social impacts: New perspectives on telework. *Social Science Computer Review, 17,* 338–356.

Fischer, C. S. (1992). *America calling.* Berkeley: University of California Press.

Fox, S., Rainie, L., Larsen, E., Horrigan, J., Lenhart, A., Spooner, T., et al. (2001). Wired seniors: A fervent few, inspired by family ties. Washington, DC: Pew Internet & American Life Project. Retrieved March 30, 2003, from www.pewinternet.org/reports/pdfs/PIP_Wired_Seniors_Report.pdf.

Franzen, A. (2000). Does the Internet make us lonely? *European Sociological Review, 16,* 427–438.

Gerlander, M., & Takala, E. (1997). Relating electronically: Interpersonality in the Net. *Nordicom Review, 18,* 77–81.

Grant, T. R., Hawkins, A. J., & Dollahite, D. C. (2001). Web-based education and support for fathers: Remote but promising. In J. Fagan & A. J. Hawkins (Eds.), *Clinical and educational interventions for fathers* (pp. 143–170). New York: Haworth.

Hampton, K. N., & Wellman, B. (2000). Examining community in the digital neighborhood: Early results from Canada's wired suburb. In T. Ishida & K. Isbister (Eds.), *Digital cities: Technologies, experiences, and future perspectives* (pp. 194–208). New York: Springer-Verlag.

Hill, E. J., Hawkins, A. J., Ferris, M., & Weitzman, M. (2001). Finding an extra day a week: The positive influence of perceived job flexibility on work and family life balance. *Family Relations, 50,* 49–58.

Hill, E. J., Hawkins, A. J., & Miller, B. C. (1996). Work and family in the virtual office: Perceived influences of mobile telework. *Family Relations, 45,* 293–301.

Howard, P. E. N., Raine, L., & Jones, S. (2001). Days and nights on the Internet: The impact of a diffusing technology. *American Behavioral Scientist, 45,* 383–404.

Hughes, R., Jr. (2001). A process evaluation of a website for family life educators. *Family Relations, 50,* 164–170.

Hughes, R., Jr., Ebata, A., & Dollahite, D. C. (1999). Family life in the information age. *Family Relations, 48,* 5–6.

Jedlicka, D., & Jennings, G. (2001). Marital therapy on the Internet. *Journal of Technology in Counseling, 2,* 1. Retrieved March 30, 2003, from http://jtc.colstate.edu/vol2_1/Marital.htm

Jencius, M., & Sager, D. E. (2001). The practice of marriage and family counseling in cyberspace. *Family Journal, 9,* 295–301.

Johnson, J. G., Cohen, P., Smailes, E. M., Kasen, S., & Brook, J. S. (2002). Television viewing and aggressive behavior during adolescence and adulthood. *Science, 295,* 2468–2471.

Katz, J. E., & Aspden, P. (1997). A nation of strangers. *Communications of the ACM, 40(12),* 81–86.

King, S. A., & Moreggi, D. (1998). Internet therapy and self-help groups: The pros and cons. In J. Gackenbach (Ed.), *Psychology and the Internet: Intrapersonal, interpersonal, and transpersonal implications* (pp. 77–109). San Diego: Academic Press.

Kraut, R. E. (1987). Predicting the use of technology: The case of telework. In R. E. Kraut (Ed.), *Technology and the transformation of white-collar work* (p. 113–133). Hillsdale, NJ: Lawrence Erlbaum.

Kraut, R., Kiesler, S., Boneva, B., Cummings, J., Helgeson, V., & Crawford, A. (2002). Internet paradox revisited. *Journal of Social Issues, 58,* 49–74.

Kraut, R., Mukophadyay, T., Szczypula, J., Kiesler, S., & Scherlis, B. (2000). Information and communication: Alternative uses of the Internet in households. *Information Systems Research, 10,* 287–303.

Kraut, R., Patterson, M, Lundmark, V., Kiesler, S., Mukophadyay, T., & Scherlis, W. (1998). Internet paradox: A social technology that reduces social involvement and psychological well-being. *American Psychologist, 53,* 1017–1031.

Livingstone, S. (2002). *Young people and new media.* Thousand Oaks, CA: Sage.

Lynd, R. S., & Lynd, H. M. (1929). *Middletown*. New York: Harcourt Brace Jovanovich.

McKenna, K. Y. A., Green, A. S., & Cleason, M. E. J. (2002). Relationship formation on the Internet: What's the big attraction? *Journal of Social Issues, 58*, 9–31.

Merkle, E. R., & Richardson, R. A. (2000). Digital dating and virtual relating: Conceptualizing computer mediated romantic relationships. *Family Relations, 49*, 187–192.

Mickelson, K. D. (1997). Seeking social support: Parents in electronic support groups. In S. Kiesler (Ed.), *Culture of the Internet* (pp. 157–178). Mahwah, NJ: Lawrence Erlbaum.

Miller, J. K., & Gergen, K. J. (1998). Life on the line: The therapeutic potentials of computer-mediated conversation. *Journal of Marital and Family Therapy, 24*, 189–202.

Mokhtarian, P. C., Bagley, M. N., & Salomon, I. (1998). The impact of gender, occupation, and presence of children on telecommuting motivations and constraints. *Journal for the American Society for Information Science, 49*, 1115–1134.

Mokhtarian, P. C., & Salomon, I. (1996). Modeling the choice of telecommuting 2: A case of the preferred impossible alternative. *Environment and Planning, 28*, 1859–1876.

Morgan, M., Alexander, A., Shanahan, J., & Harris, C. (1990). Adolescents, VCRs, and the family environment. *Communication Research, 10*, 175–194.

National Telecommunications and Information Administration. (2000). Falling through the Net: Toward digital inclusion. Retrieved March 30, 2003, from www.ntia.doc.gov/ntiahome/fttn00/contents00.html

National Telecommunications and Information Administration. (2002). A nation online: How Americans are expanding their use of the Internet. Retrieved March 30, 2003, from www.ntia.doc.gov/ntiahome/dn.

Newburger, E. C. (1999). *Computer use in the United States* (Current Population Reports, Series P20, No. 522). Washington, DC: U.S. Bureau of the Census. Retrieved March 30, 2003, from www.census.gov/prod/99pubs/p20-522.pdf.

O'Connell, P. L. (2003, February 13). Love clicks. *New York Times*. Retrieved February 21, 2003, from www.nytimes.com.

Ogburn, W. F., & Nimkoff, M. F. (1955). *Technology and the changing family*. Boston: Houghton Mifflin.

Orleans, M., & Laney, M. C. (2000). Children's computer use in the home: Isolation or sociation? *Social Science Computer Review, 18*, 56–72.

Parks, M. R., & Roberts, L. D. (1998). "Making MOOsic": The development of personal relationships on line and a comparison to their off-line counterparts. *Journal of Social and Personal Relationships, 15*, 517–537.

Piskurich, G. M. (1996, February). Making telecommuting work. *Training and Development, 50*, 20–27.

Putnam, R. D. (2000). *Bowling alone*. New York: Simon & Schuster.

Rheingold, H. (1993). *The virtual community: Homesteading on the electronic frontier*. Reading, MA: Addison Wesley.

Scharlott, B. W., & Christ, W. G. (1995). Overcoming relationship-initiation barriers: The impact of a computer-dating system on sex role, shyness, and appearance inhibitions. *Computers in Human Behavior, 11*, 191–204.

Schneider, J. P. (2000). Effects of cybersex addiction on the family: Results of a survey. *Sexual Addiction and Compulsivity, 7*, 31–58.

Smith, C. A. (1999). Family life pathfinders on the new electronic frontier. *Family Relations, 48*, 31–34.

Stafford, L., Kline, S. L., & Dimmick, J. (1999). Home e-mail: Relational maintenance and gratification opportunities. *Journal of Broadcasting and Electronic Media, 43*, 659–669.

Stoll, C. (1995). *Silicon snake oil*. New York: Doubleday.

Toffler, A. (1980). *The third wave*. New York: William Morrow.

U.S. Bureau of Labor Statistics. (1998). *Work at home in 1997*. Retrieved March 30, 2003, from http://stats.bls.gov/news.release/homey.nr0.htm.

U.S. Bureau of Labor Statistics. (2002). Work at home in 2001. Retrieved March 30, 2003, from www.bls.gov/news.release/homey.toc.htm.

Wellman, B., Haase, A. Q., Witte, J., & Hampton, K. (2001). Does the Internet increase, decrease, or supplement social capital? *American Behavioral Scientist, 45,* 436–455.

Young, K. S. (1999). Cybersexual addiction. Retrieved March 30, 2003, from www.netaddiction.com/cybersexual_addiction.htm.

Young, K. S., Griffin-Shelley, E., Cooper, A., O'Mara, J., & Buchanan, J. (2000). Online infidelity: A new dimension in couple relationships with implications for evaluation and treatment. *Sexual Addiction and Compulsivity, 7,* 59–74.

Part IX

WORKING WITH CONTEMPORARY FAMILIES

Family Therapy's Response to Family Diversity
Looking Back, Looking Forward

Leigh A. Leslie and Goldie Morton

The profession of marriage and family therapy has faced a rapidly changing environment in the last several decades. The changes have been far-flung and include medical advances, legislative and regulatory modifications to established ways of practicing, and a virtual revolution in technology. Yet the most significant change has been the nature of families themselves. In this chapter, we examine how marriage and family therapy has responded to the increasing diversity of families. In addition, we consider recent developments in marriage and family therapy and how these developments may affect the profession's future responses to diverse families.

Although marriage and family therapy is an international profession, we focus here on the United States. We do this because (a) the rate and nature of change in families has varied throughout the world, (b) the profession's response to these changes has been somewhat culturally bound, and (c) both the demographic data and the scholarly journals most accessible to us are from the United States.

CHANGING FAMILY PATTERNS

Two primary sources of change in families have influenced marriage and family therapy in the past 30 years. The first has been the dramatic shift in patterns of family formation and organization (Cherlin, 1992). What were once thought of as alternative family forms have now become commonplace. The second change has been in the area of shifting power balances both in families and in the society at large.

Family Formation and Organization

The U.S. Bureau of the Census identifies two basic types of households, family and nonfamily. A family household is composed of at least two persons related by birth, marriage, or adoption. A nonfamily household is either a person living alone or people living together who are not related by blood or marriage (Rawlings, 1995).

Nonfamily Households

Families have traditionally accounted for a large majority of all households, but according to the U.S. Bureau of the Census, their proportion of the total is significantly lower now than in the past. In 1998, there were 31.6 million nonfamily households as compared to 11.9 million in 1970 (Casper & Bryson, 1998). During this 28-year period, the proportion of all households that were nonfamily households climbed from 19% to 31%. Although the majority (83%) of nonfamily households consist of one person, part of this increase is due to growth in cohabiting heterosexual adults and gay and lesbian partnerships.

The rapid increases in cohabitation and the bearing of children by cohabiting couples at the end of the 20th century have dramatically altered family life in the United States (Bumpass & Hsien-Hen, 2000). Although cohabitation was once rare, a majority of young men and women of marriageable age today will spend some time in a cohabiting relationship, and about 40% of all children will spend some time in a cohabiting family before age 16 (Bumpass & Hsien-Hen, 2000). Whether such consensual unions are temporary arrangements that will lead to marriage or are alternatives to marriage, cohabitation results in households that differ from the once traditional two-parent, first-marriage family.

Absent or difficult to ascertain from past census statistics is information on households composed of gay and lesbian partners, a group that would appear as a nonfamily household. However, in both the 1990 and 2000 censuses, individuals for the first time had the option of identifying themselves as unmarried partners (U.S. Bureau of the

Census, 2001). Reporting increases in this 10-year period for the state data released so far range from 200% to 700% (Cohn, 2001). Black, Gates, Sanders, and Taylor (1999) published one of the first reports on the demographics of the gay and lesbian population in the United States and based their information on the General Social Survey, the National Health and Social Life Survey, and the 1990 census. Although the authors were unable to determine the number of gay or lesbian couple households, they gleaned a sample of 6,800 such households; about 60% of these were composed of gay male couples, and 40% were lesbian couples. Children were present in about 22% of partnered lesbian households and 5% of partnered gay male households, compared to 59% of married-partner households.

Family Households

Not only nonfamily households but also family households have changed in the past 30 years. Although married-couple families continue to represent the majority of family households, postponement of marriage, increases in the divorce rate, and increases in nonmarital births have created a rise in single-parent households, most often headed by women. The divorce rate in the United States increased by almost half from 1970 to 1980, growing from a rate of 3.5 of every 1,000 people in the total population in 1970 to a peak of 5.2 in 1980 (National Center for Health Statistics, 2000). Although the rate has decreased slightly since the high of the early 1980s, it is still estimated that about half of all marriages will end in divorce, the highest rate of all developed countries (Cherlin, 1999).

By 1994, about 35% of all first births occurred outside marriage, up from 17% in 1969. Similarly, one in every three births during the 12-month period preceding the June 1998 Current Population Survey occurred to unmarried mothers (Bacchu & O'Connell, 2000; U.S. Bureau of the Census, 1999).

Given the increase in divorce and non-marital childbearing, it is not surprising that in 1997, single-parent families accounted for 28% of all families, an increase of 138% since 1970. Single women headed 23% of all families, and single men headed 5% (Casper & Bryson, 1998). No data are available to suggest what percentage of these single-parent homes were headed by unpartnered gay men or lesbians. About 19.8 million, or 27.7%, of all children younger than 18 lived with one parent in 1998. For almost 56% of children living in single-parent families, no other adults were present in the household (Casper & Bryson, 1998).

Shifting Power Balances

The second transformation affecting family therapy has been the result of social movements. The past several decades have seen an increase in specific populations asking for recognition and appreciation. Most notably, women, racial-ethnic minorities, and gays, lesbians, and bisexuals have demanded that their life experiences no longer be hidden from view by a public discourse that uses the perspective of white heterosexual males as the standard. The growth of feminist thought and societal critiques coupled with the movement of increasing numbers of women into the labor force as sole or joint breadwinners have led women to seek parity with men in a vast array of social institutions, not the least of which is the family. Emboldened by their burgeoning numbers and, in some areas, growing financial and political strength, racial and ethnic families have challenged assumptions of normative family behavior as the behavior shown primarily by white middle-class families. Racial-ethnic families have increasingly demanded that the variations in structure, interaction, and values in their families

be appreciated instead of pathologized. Gays and lesbians have demanded an end to discriminatory practices and laws that limit their life options in education, work, and family life.

Certainly, marriage and family therapy has not been alone in being affected by the increasing prominence and power of these groups in social and political arenas. These movements have truly been calls to realign the way we think and act as a nation. But their relevance for marriage and family therapy is great because so many of the calls for recognition have been about interpersonal relationships, the core focus of marriage and family therapy.

FAMILY THERAPY'S RESPONSE TO CHANGING FAMILY PATTERNS

Although the proof of family therapy's responsiveness to changes in families is what happens in the privacy of thousands of therapy sessions across the country, such evidence is difficult to access and calculate. Much easier to access is the research and clinical writing that family therapists generate. Therefore, we examine trends in the professional and scholarly publications of marriage and family therapy in recent decades to examine the field's acknowledgment of and attempts to address the growing diversity of families. We examine the clinical literature in two ways: (a) a count of articles in family therapy journals addressing these issues and (b) an overview of the substantive issues considered in the literature.

Prevalence of Articles on Diverse and Changing Families

First, we examine the number of clinical and empirical articles addressing diverse families that have been published in the last 30 years in the two leading family therapy journals, *Journal of Marital and Family Therapy* and *Family Process*. Although these are not the only journals that publish clinical articles on marriage and family therapy, they are the major journals that make the publication of such work their primary focus. The *Journal of Feminist Family Therapy* (*JFFT*) is also devoted to publishing articles on family therapy, but it has a more limited audience. Its mission is to apply a feminist perspective to the field of family therapy and treatment issues, particularly for women and other devalued groups. Therefore, the majority, if not all, of *JFFT*'s articles focus on changing family patterns and diverse families. Thus, including this journal in our count could distort the perception of how widely diverse families are being addressed in the mainstream family therapy journals. We acknowledge that journal articles do not totally reflect how the field is addressing an issue. Recent decades have witnessed a growth in both chapters and books about diverse families. The late 1980s marked a peak in the publication of books addressing issues of gender, race, and ethnicity in family therapy. The deluge of books in this decade included the groundbreaking *Ethnicity and Family Therapy* (McGoldrick, Pearce, & Giordano, 1982), *Black Families in Therapy* (Boyd-Franklin, 1989), *The Invisible Web: Gender Patterns in Family Relationships* (Walters, Carter, Papp, & Silverstein, 1988), *The Family Interpreted: Feminist Theory in Clinical Practice* (Luepnitz, 1988), and *Women in Families: A Framework for Family Therapy* (McGoldrick, Anderson, & Walsh, 1989). Although these books have significantly influenced the dialogue in family therapy, we believe that journal articles best reflect how widely a topic is integrated into the discourse and thinking of a field.

It is clear that the two dominant family therapy journals have increasingly addressed gender, race, ethnicity, and diverse family forms. Of the 1,850 articles published in these journals between 1970 and 2000, 208 articles, or 11.2%, were devoted to family diversity. Of those 208 articles, 15.4% were published in the 1970s, 29.8% were published in the 1980s, and 54.8% were published in the 1990s and early 2000s (for this analysis, articles published in 2000 were included in the 1990s count).

The topic receiving the most attention was gender: 86 (41.3%) of the articles focused on gender issues in treatment or training. Only 7 gender articles were published in the 1970s; 19 (22.1%) were published in the 1980s; and the majority, 40 (69.8%), appeared in the 1990s.

Race, ethnicity, and culture, as a group, was the second most frequently considered in the literature, with a total of 62, or 29.8% of the articles. Seven (11.2%) of these articles were published in the 1970s, 17 (27.4%) in the 1980s, and 38 (61.3%) in the 1990s.

The third most frequently addressed topic was divorce, with 23 (11.1%) articles. But for divorce, unlike gender and race, the trend in the literature showed equally low rates in the 1970s and 1990s, with a larger representation in the 1980s. In both the 1970s and 1990s, 6 articles pertaining to divorce were published, whereas 11 articles were published in the 1980s.

Despite the number of articles pertaining to divorce, few ($n = 7$) mentioned remarriage and/or stepfamilies. The majority of the remarriage/stepfamily articles ($n = 4$) were published in the 1980s, with 2 articles appearing in the 1970s and only 1 published in the 1990s. Even more striking, in the 30-year period under consideration, only 3 articles in these two major clinical journals specifically addressed clinical issues with single-parent families. This omission is noteworthy given the increase in the number of these families during the same time period. One would expect a concomitant increase in the number of single-parent families seen in clinical practices during this period. Although it might be assumed that articles on divorce articles also addressed single-parent family issues, our review indicated that this would not be a safe assumption. Only 12 of the 23 divorce articles addressed issues in single-parent families. However, much of the increase in single-parent families was the result of nonmarital births, not divorce. Single-parent families headed by an unmarried parent basically were ignored in these clinical journals.

The final area addressed in these clinical journals was sexual orientation. Fifteen (7.2%) of the articles pertained to gay, lesbian, and bisexual issues. Of these, 12 were published in the 1990s, with 5 articles appearing in one special issue focusing on sexual orientation.

Cohabitation was conspicuously absent from the clinical and empirical literature in the these family therapy journals. None of the 1,850 articles reviewed addressed this growing family form.

In conclusion, although the field has increased its attention to some issues of family diversity and changing family patterns, the treatment has not been uniform across family types. Changes emanating from shifting gender and race power balances in families and in society at large have received the most attention. Changes in family organization or structure have received much less attention.

Substantive Overview of Literature on Diverse and Changing Families

In addition to examining the volume of the clinical literature on working with diverse families, it is worthwhile to consider the focus of this literature. Although a comprehensive review of family therapy literature is beyond the scope of this chapter, major trends and themes can be identified. As a review by Leslie (1995) pointed out, the field of marital and family therapy as traditionally practiced has been oppressive to certain family members or types of families by (a) not taking into consideration the effect of the broader social context on family dynamics, (b) ignoring power differences both in and outside the family, and (c) working from an assumption of one superior family form. Rather than reexamine these criticisms, we explore how the family therapy literature has responded to or incorporated them.

Gender

Efforts to incorporate knowledge on diverse families into treatment have varied on the basis of the type of diversity in question. Gender has received the most comprehensive treatment. The body of work generated in the last few decades has focused on the role of gender in specific clinical problems, examined gender as a process variable in therapy, advanced feminist adaptations of family therapy models and specific techniques for addressing gender issues in therapy, and offered training guidelines for developing gender-sensitive therapists.

Much of the literature on gender has focused on gender-sensitive ways to address specific problems, such as substance abuse (Nelson, McCollum, Wetcher, Trepper, & Lewis, 1996) or eating disorders (Olson, 1995; Romney, 1995). However, the clinical problem that has received the most attention is wife abuse. Bograd (1984) was one of the first to challenge family therapy's conceptualization of interdependence in relationships in which women were abused. She has since become one of many voices challenging the implicit values in family therapy that can dismiss or endanger women who are being abused by continuing a commitment to working with the couple (Bograd, 1992; Dell, 1989; Goldner, Penn, Sheinberg, & Walker, 1990; Serra, 1993). Responding to these challenges, the past decade has seen increasing attention to specific therapeutic approaches to working with abused women and their abusive partners. These approaches recognize the vulnerability of the abused partner in therapy, hold the abuser accountable, and work to alter the problematic beliefs and values sustaining abuse (Almeida & Bograd, 1991; Avis, 1992; Jory, Anderson, & Greer, 1997; O'Leary, Curely, Rosenbaum, & Clarke, 1985; O'Leary, Vivian, & Malone, 1992).

Another major focus has been on gender as a process variable in family therapy. For example, Newberry, Alexander, and Turner (1991) examined how the gender combination of therapist and clients affects the course and style of therapy and of therapist-client interaction. Similarly, Shields and McDaniel (1992) delineated differences in the experience of male and female therapists in initial sessions. Focusing on the couple, researchers examined the dislocation of women's experience in family therapy (Almeida, 1998) and gender dilemmas and myths in the construction of marital bargains (Knudson-Martin & Mahoney, 1996).

Also offered in the last decade were feminist revisions of extant family therapy models, including Bowen family systems theory (Knudson-Martin, 1994) and narrative therapy (Gosling & Zangari, 1996; Prouty & Bermundez, 1999). Likewise, there was a significant increase in articles on clinical tools, techniques, and strategies for addressing gender issues in therapy. For example, gender questions and gender mantras were presented as techniques for breaking impasses in therapy related to gendered beliefs (Sheinberg & Penn, 1991), and "gendergrams" were used to illuminate intergenerational patterns of gender dynamics in families (White & Tyson-Rawson, 1995). A feminist family therapy scale was developed to assess the degree to which family therapists conceptualize the process of family therapy from a feminist perspective (Black & Piercy, 1991), and a "power equity guide" was offered as a training, research, and therapeutic tool that provides guidance for addressing gender and power differentials in the practice of family therapy (Haddock, Zimmerman, & MacPhee, 2000).

In addition, gender as an important variable in the training process for clinicians was addressed. This work began in the mid-1980s, when Wheeler, Avis, Miller, and Chaney (1985) first called into question the methods and models used to trained family therapists. Avis (1989) then laid out a framework for integrating gender into training curricula. Subsequent work built on this foundation, focusing on the implications of a gender perspective for the professional development of therapists (Roberts, 1991) and the basic tenets of feminist-based family therapy training (Leslie & Clossick, 1992).

Finally, beginning in the late 1980s with the special issue of *JMFT*, the effect of gender on men in families and in therapy has increasingly been explored. For example, the ties between men's early experiences in families and the roles and behaviors they assume as adults were explicated (Napier, 1989; Pittman, 1989). Subsequent work discussed the origin of the role of fathers (Kraemer, 1991), men in couples therapy (Neal & Slobodnik, 1991), the influence of absent fathers, and the role of family therapists in working with families with an absent father (Schnitzer, 1993). Deinhart and Avis (1994) provided a beginning formulation of a gender-sensitive approach to working with men in family therapy that promotes mutual responsibility, develops perceptual and conceptual skills regarding gender, and challenges stereotypical behaviors and attitudes. Real (1995) offered a map for fathers in parenting their sons in ways that challenge the problematic legacies of masculinity.

Race/Ethnicity/Culture

The majority of journal-based literature incorporating race, culture, and ethnicity throughout the latter decades of the 20th century focused on culturally sensitive therapy with specific groups. For example, Stein (1978) explored the systemic relationships among culture, family dynamics, personality development, and child-rearing patterns among multigeneration Slovak Americans. Other scholars wrote about the unique dynamics and cultural values of specific groups of families, offering treatment recommendations for practitioners. Among the racial and ethnic families examined were African American (Bagarozzi, 1980; Watts-Jones, 1997), Chinese (Jung, 1984), Asian American (Berg & Jaya, 1993), first-generation Filipino American (Cimmarusti, 1996), and Muslim (Daneshpour, 1998).

In addition, empirical and clinical articles from the 1990s offered general guidelines and techniques for understanding families and working with them in a culturally competent manner. Hardy and Laszloffy (1995) offered a cultural genogram as an effective training tool to promote cultural awareness and sensitivity for family therapists in training. Similarly, Preli and Bernard (1993) emphasized the importance of making multiculturalism relevant for majority-culture graduate students, especially with respect to students' own identity. Kogan (1996) suggested that presenting problems are best understood by examining the intersection of clients' culture and societal power. As a clear applications of this principle, Baker (1999) noted the importance of cultural sensitivity and therapist self-awareness when working with mandatory clients. Parke (2000) discussed cultural variations in families and the implication of those variations for assessments, clinical processes, and policies. Specifically, Parke called for using a strengths perspective to understand cultural variations in families rather than the previously used deficit model.

Divorce, Remarriage, and Single Parenthood

The major focus of the divorce literature was on facilitating postdivorce adjustment with family members (Dreyfus, 1979; Goldman & Coane, 1977). For example, Barnes (1999) discussed the short-term effects of divorce on children, described the transitions that accompany divorce and family reordering, and suggested clinical interventions to promote long-term connections between parents and children. Buehler, Betz, Ryan, Legg, and Trotter (1992) offered practitioners program suggestions for separated and divorced parents, with special attention to support networks, parenting skills, and conflict management skills.

A second major focus of this work has been on postdivorce custody arrangements. For example, Everett and Volgy (1983) discussed the role of family assessment in child custody disputes, Isaacs (1988) looked at the visitation schedule as it pertained to child adjustment, and Rothberg (1983) explored joint custody as a means for promoting parents' involvement in their children's lives as well as freedom for themselves. Whiteside (1998) discussed the parental alliance following divorce, suggesting the need for parental cooperation and co-parenting behavior and the implications of this behavior for children. A third focus of this work was on divorce prevention (Bray & Jouriles, 1995) and helping couples make decisions throughout the separation and divorce process (Oz, 1994).

The limited literature on remarriages was directed toward practitioner awareness of the unique issues in remarried families. For example, Walker and Messinger (1979) analyzed remarriage from the perspective of family boundaries and roles, suggesting some solutions to problems confronting family members. Whiteside (1982) explored remarriage from a family development process, and Sager, Walker, Brown, Crohn, and

Rodstein (1981) looked at ways to improve the functioning of the family system after remarriage. Pasley and colleagues provided clinical applications for working with spouses in the stepparent role in remarriage (Pasley, Dollahite, & Ihinger-Tallman, 1993) and emphasized the need for specialized training in working with remarried families (Pasley, Rhoden, Visher, & Visher, 1996).

Sexual Orientation

Gay, lesbian, and bisexual issues are largely ignored by family therapy clinicians, and highly relevant information is often marginalized in specialized publications (Clark & Serovich, 1997). The work that does exist spans a range of topics, from working with gay, lesbian, or bisexual couples, to working with families of gay, lesbian, or bisexual individuals, to issues of training, practice, and supervision. For example, Roth (1985) discussed the significance of individual issues, female socialization, and the social context as it affects women in lesbian relationships. A recurrent theme in work published in *JFFT* was the challenge of mothering for lesbians (Muzio, 1995; Shore, 1996). Beeler and DiProva (1999) focused on the disclosure of homosexuality through the utilization of family members' narrative themes. Bepko and Johnson (2000) offered perspectives for the contemporary family therapist and specifically suggested that working with gay and lesbian couples requires a sensitivity to the internal stresses and to the external, sociocultural, and familial sources of stress on the couple.

In summary, the clinical literature generated on diverse families called for acceptance and recognition. The increasing attention given to theoretical discussions, treatment models, and training guidelines has been premised on the assumption that marriage and family therapists need to become more cognizant of the variations in how families both choose and are constrained to live their lives. Furthermore, it is assumed that clinicians need to work with these families in nonjudgmental ways that validate their clients' experiences. Family therapy has struggled with this challenge, and many would argue that the field has achieved more success in responding to some groups than to others. Nevertheless, the call to accept family variation has become a major voice in the discourse in family therapy.

Recent Developments

As the field of marriage and family therapy has moved toward greater acceptance and responsiveness to the diversity of families in the United States, new voices have risen recently to question the influence of some of these changes. Concerns about the effects of increased tolerance have come both from professional marriage and family therapists (Doherty, 1999; Ooms, 1998), and from nonclinical social scientists (McLanahan & Booth, 1991) and the public (Blankenhorn, 1995). Just as family therapy's shift toward acceptance and responsiveness to diverse family forms was motivated by many political factors outside the profession itself, so too the questions and criticism countering this shift are in part an outgrowth of larger political factors. Any consideration of marriage and family therapy's future responsiveness to diverse families must examine the concerns now being voiced.

The criticism seem to fall into two categories. First, some family scholars and practitioners have raised concerns that mental health professionals, including family therapists, are insensitive to the moral obligations of family and community life and are putting the needs and desires of adult family members above the needs of children (Doherty, 1995). These concerns began to surface with the accumulation of data suggesting more negative financial academic, and interpersonal outcomes for children whose parents divorced than for children raised in two-parent families (Amato & Booth, 1997). Data on children with never-married mothers, cohabiting parents, and remarried parents also have fueled these complaints (McLanahan & Sandefur, 1994). However, these data and their interpretation are controversial: Most children in single-parent and stepparent households do not show negative outcomes (Amato & Booth, 1997), and there are empirically based arguments that family structures do not have uniform effects on children (Booth & Amato, 2001). The purpose here is not to summarize or weigh in on that debate but to examine its impact on marriage and family therapy: A movement within the family field supports the view that children often suffer when raised in homes other than with their two biological parents.

A second criticism is that in accepting different family forms, the field has traveled down a slippery slope to promoting no family form over others, to becoming anti-marriage, to suggesting that all forms of adult relationships offer equal life satisfaction (Doherty, 1999; Glenn, 1997). Critics contend that research indicates that marriage enhances psychological and financial well-being for children and for adults compared to other living arrangements (Waite & Gallagher, 2000).

Spokespersons for these two perspectives have most recently coalesced in what is called the Marriage Movement (2000). This is a "grass-roots movement to strengthen marriage" (p. 1) made up of professionals who have "come together to enlarge and energize this emerging effort to renew the marriage vow and the marriage vision ... [and to] turn the tide on marriage and reduce divorce and unmarried childbearing" (p. 3). This group is actively advocating changes in many social institutions, and its members have

specific recommendations for marriage and family therapy. At a general level, they want the field of marriage and family therapy to not be "marriage neutral." Specifically, they encourage therapists to focus on the interests of the family as a unit versus the interests of the individual family members. Therapists are asked to seriously consider the needs of children, who are often the absent voices in marital therapy, as well as those of the adults. Part of this task is recognizing the commitments and moral responsibility inherent in the roles of spouse and parent (Doherty, 1995; Marriage Movement, 2000). Outgrowths of this movement in marriage and family therapy include the Coalition for Marriage, Family, and Couples Education, which has offered the annual Smart Marriages Conference since 1997; a growing marriage education movement; and the development of systematic treatment models to reduce divorce and strengthen marriage (Markham, Stanley, & Blumberg, 1996; Weiner-Davis, 1993).

FUTURE DIRECTIONS IN MARRIAGE AND FAMILY THERAPY'S APPROACH TO DIVERSITY

The challenge posed by the Marriage Movement to the field of marriage and family therapy is significant. The tension between calls for continued and increased acceptance of diverse family forms and calls to promote marriage as the superior family form is obvious. As a field, marriage and family therapy has always valued relationships and been involved in helping people improve and enhance those relationships. Furthermore, recognizing that most people desire and enter into heterosexual marriage, the profession has mainly focused on improving these marriages. Yet the field has moved to a position of greater acceptance of alternative lifestyles. The potential conflict for marriage and family therapy led the American Association for Marriage and Family Therapy to devote a plenary session at the 2000 conference to a panel discussion entitled "Till Death Do Us Part? Family Therapy and the Marriage Movement."

The challenge for marriage and family therapy as a profession is to wrestle with the question of whether the two perspectives can coexist in the field. Can the field respect and support the life choices people while also maintaining that one choice is better than others? Is there a way to help those who choose heterosexual marriage have the most satisfying relationships possible while working equally hard to make alternative relationships satisfying, even if one does not see these alternative arrangements as desirable? Is there a place for morality and responsibility to one's family and community obligations that is not premised on heterosexual marriage? The Statement of Principles generated by members of the Marriage Movement (2000) gives recognition to this challenge and acknowledges that the movement may be subject to charges of being regressive and biased with regard to race and gender. In response, the document clearly states that the movement does not want to undermine progress that has been made toward gender equity in marriage, stigmatize single parents, or discredit ethnic minority families who may more frequently have nonmarital households.

Nevertheless, what is not said in the Statement of Principles (Marriage Movement, 2000) concerns many advocates of family diversity. The only example given of gender issues in marriage is domestic violence, accompanied by a recognition that not all marriages should be saved. There seems to be no acknowledgment of the gender implications of putting the family's needs before the needs of the individual adults. Feminists have long contended that if this is the prevailing thought, it will be women who are most likely to sacrifice their needs for the good of the family (Boss & Thorne, 1989; Walters et al., 1988). Furthermore, although the statement expresses an intention to not stigmatize single parents, there is no acknowledgment that emphasizing the superiority of marriage implicitly suggests a negative evaluation of parents and partners who are not married. As recent research has shown (Schultz, 1999), emphasizing the superiority of marriage can negatively affect the way marriage and family therapists evaluate divorced clients. Finally, the document is silent on gay and lesbian partnerships or unions. The marriages being promoted are clearly heterosexual marriages.

Ultimately, marriage and family therapy's struggle is society's struggle. Recent legislative and political battles in Vermont over same-sex unions and the Defense of Marriage Act are only two of the many examples attesting that our country is embroiled in a debate over whether to value all relationships or give preference to some. Marriage and family therapy will certainly continue to be one front on which that debate is carried out. At this point, however, it is too early to predict the short- and long-term effects of contrasting approaches to this issue on the therapeutic treatment offered to all types of families in this country.

REFERENCES

Almeida, R. V. (1998). The dislocation of women's experience in family therapy. *Journal of Feminist Family Therapy, 10,* 1–22.

Almeida, R. V., & Bograd, M. (1991). Sponsorship: Holding men accountable for domestic violence. *Journal of Feminist Family Therapy, 2,* 243–259.

Amato, P., & Booth, A. (1997). *A generation at risk: Growing up in an era of family upheaval.* Cambridge, MA: Harvard University Press.

Avis, J. M. (1989). Integrating gender into the family therapy curriculum. *Journal of Feminist Family Therapy, 1,* 3–26.

Avis, J. M. (1992). Where are all the family therapists? Abuse and violence within families and family therapy's response. *Journal of Marital and Family Therapy, 18,* 225–232.

Bacchu, A., & O'Connell, M. (2000). *The fertility of American women, June 1998* (Current Population Report, P20-526). Washington, DC: U.S. Bureau of the Census.

Bagarozzi, D. A. (1980). Family therapy and the black middle class: A neglected area of study. *Journal of Marital and Family Therapy, 6,* 159–173.

Baker, K. A. (1999). The importance of cultural sensitivity and therapist self-awareness when working with mandatory clients. *Family Process, 38,* 55–67.

Barnes, G. G. (1999). Divorce transitions: Identifying risk and promoting resilience for children and their parental relationships. *Journal of Marital and Family Therapy, 25,* 425–441.

Beeler, J., & DiProva, V. (1999). Family adjustment following disclosure of homosexuality by a member: Themes discerned in narrative accounts. *Journal of Marital and Family Therapy, 25,* 443–460.

Bepko, C., & Johnson, T. (2000). Gay and lesbian couples in therapy: Perspectives for the contemporary family therapist. *Journal of Marital and Family Therapy, 26,* 409–419.

Berg, I. K., & Jaya, J. (1993). Different and same: Family therapy with Asian-American families. *Journal of Marital and Family Therapy, 19,* 31–38.

Black, D., Gates, G., Sanders, S., & Taylor, L. (1999). *Demographics of the gay and lesbian population in the United States: Evidence from available systematic data sources.* (Working Paper No. 12). Syracuse, NY: Center for Policy Research.

Black, L., & Piercy, F. P. (1991). A feminist family therapy scale. *Journal of Marital and Family Therapy, 17,* 111–120.

Blankenhorne, D. (1995). *Fatherless America: Confronting our most urgent social problem.* New York: Basic Books.

Bograd, M. (1984). Family systems approaches to wife battering: A feminist critique. *American Journal of Orthopsychiatry, 54,* 558–568.

Bograd, M. (1992). Values in conflict: Challenges to family therapists' thinking. *Journal of Marital and Family Therapy, 18,* 245–256.

Booth, A., & Amato, P. (2001). Parental predivorce relations and offspring postdivorce well-being. *Journal of Marriage and Family, 63,* 197–212.

Boss, P., & Thorne, B. (1989). Family sociology and family therapy: A feminist linkage. In M. McGoldrick, C. M. Anderson, & F. Walsh (Eds.), *Women in families: A framework for family therapy* (pp. 78–96). New York: Norton.

Boyd-Franklin, N. (1989). *Black families in therapy: A multisystems approach.* New York: Guilford.

Bray, J. H., & Jouriles, E. N. (1995). Treatment of marital conflict and prevention of divorce. *Journal of Marital and Family Therapy, 21,* 461–473.

Buehler, C., Betz, P., Ryan, C. M., Legg, B. H., & Trotter, B. B. (1992). Description and evaluation of the orientation for divorcing parents: Implications for post-divorce prevention programs. *Family Relations, 41,* 154–162.

Bumpass, L., & Hsien-Hen, L. (2000). Cohabitation: How the families of U.S. children are changing. *Focus, 21,* 5–8.

Casper, L. M., & Bryson, K. (1998). *Household and family characteristics: March 1998 update* (Current Population Reports). Washington, DC: U.S. Bureau of the Census.

Cherlin, A. J. (1992). *Marriage, divorce, remarriage.* Cambridge, MA: Harvard University Press.

Cherlin, A. J. (1999). *Public and private families: An introduction* (2nd ed.). New York: McGraw-Hill.

Cimmarusti, R. A. (1996). Exploring aspects of Filipino-American families. *Journal of Marital and Family Therapy, 22,* 205–218.

Clark, W. M., & Serovich, J. M. (1997). Twenty years and still in the dark: Content analysis of articles pertaining to gay, lesbian, and bisexual issues in marriage and family therapy journals. *Journal of Marital and Family Therapy, 23,* 239–254.

Cohn, D. (2001, June 19). Census shows big increase in gay households. *Washington Post,* p. 1.

Daneshpour, M. (1998). Muslim families and family therapy. *Journal of Marriage and the Family, 24,* 355–368.

Deinhart, A., & Avis, J. M. (1994). Working with men in family therapy: An exploratory study. *Journal of Marital and Family Therapy, 20,* 397–417.

Dell, P. (1989). Violence and the systemic view: The problem of power. *Family Process, 28,* 1–14.

Doherty, W. J. (1995). *Soul searching: Why psychotherapy must promote moral responsibility.* New York: Basic Books.

Doherty, W. J. (1999). How therapy can be hazardous to your mental health. Paper presented at the annual conference of the Coalition for Marriage, Family, and Couples Education. Retrieved July 22, 2003, from www.smartmarriages.org.

Dreyfus, E. A. (1979). Counseling the divorced father. *Journal of Marital and Family Therapy, 5,* 79–87.

Everett, C. A., & Volgy, S. S. (1983). Family assessment in child custody disputes. *Journal of Marital and Family Therapy, 9,* 343–353.

Glenn, N. (1997). A critique of twenty family and marriage and the family textbooks. *Family Relations, 47,* 197–208.

Goldman, J., & Coane, J. (1977). Family therapy after the divorce: Developing a strategy. *Family Process, 16,* 357–362.

Goldner, V., Penn, P., Sheinberg, M., & Walker, G. (1990). Love and violence: Gender paradoxes in volatile attachments. *Family Process, 29,* 343–364.

Gosling, A. L., & Zangari, M. (1996). Feminist family therapy and the narrative approach: Dovetailing two frameworks. *Journal of Feminist Family Therapy, 8,* 47–65.

Haddock, S. A., Zimmerman, T. S., & MacPhee, D. (2000). The power equity guide: Attending to gender in family therapy. *Journal of Marital and Family Therapy, 26,* 153–170.

Hardy, K. V., & Laszloffy, T. A. (1995). The cultural genogram: Key to training culturally competent family therapists. *Journal of Marital and Family Therapy, 21,* 227–237.

Isaacs, M. B. (1988). The visitation schedule and child adjustment: A three year study. *Family Process, 27,* 251–256.

Jory, B., Anderson, D., & Greer, C. (1997). Intimate justice: Confronting issues of accountability, respect, and freedom in treatment for abuse and violence. *Journal of Marital and Family Therapy, 23,* 399–419.

Jung, M. (1984). Structural family therapy: Its application to Chinese families. *Family Process, 23,* 365–374.

Knudson-Martin, C. (1994). The female voice: Applications to Bowen's family systems theory. *Journal of Marital and Family Therapy, 20,* 35–46.

Knudson-Martin, C., & Mahoney, A. (1996). Gender dilemmas and myths in the construction of marital bargains: Issues for marital therapy. *Family Process, 35,* 137–153.

Kogan, S. M. (1996). Clinical praxis: Examining culture and power in family therapy. *Journal of Feminist Family Therapy, 8,* 25–44.

Kraemer, S. (1991). The origins of fatherhood: An ancient family process. *Family Process, 30*, 377–392.

Leslie, L. A. (1995). Family therapy's evolving treatment of gender, ethnicity, and sexual orientation. *Family Relations, 44*, 359–367.

Leslie, L. A., & Clossick, M. L. (1992). Changing set: Teaching family therapy from a feminist perspective. *Family Relations, 41*, 256–263.

Luepnitz, D. A. (1988). *The family interpreted: Feminist theory in clinical practice.* New York: Basic Books.

Markham, H., Stanley, S., & Blumberg, S. (1996). *Fighting for your marriage.* San Francisco: Jossey-Bass.

Marriage Movement. (2000). A statement of principles. Retrieved July 22, 2003, from www.marriagemovement.org/html/report.html.

McGoldrick, M., Anderson, C. M., & Walsh, F. (Eds.). (1989). *Women in families: A framework for family therapy.* New York: Norton.

McGoldrick, M., Pearce, J., & Giordano, J. (Eds.). (1982). *Ethnicity and family therapy.* New York: Guilford.

McLanahan, S., & Booth, K. (1991). Mother-only families: Problems, prospects, and politics. In A. Booth (Ed.), *Contemporary families: Looking forward, looking back* (pp. 405–428). Minneapolis: National Council on Family Relations.

McLanahan, S., & Sandefur, G. (1994). *Growing up with a single parent: What hurts, what helps.* Cambridge, MA: Harvard University Press.

Muzio, C. (1995). Lesbians choosing children: Creating families, creating narrative. *Journal of Feminist Family Therapy, 7*, 33–45.

Napier, A. (1989). Heroism, men and marriage. *Journal of Marital and Family Therapy, 17*, 9–16.

National Center for Health Statistics. (2000). *Marriages and Divorce: 1970–1998* (Vital Statistics of the United States, Monthly Vital Statistics Report, No. 146). Washington, DC: U.S. Department of Health and Human Services.

Neal, J. H., & Slobodnik, A. J. (1991). Reclaiming men's experience in couples therapy. *Journal of Feminist Family Therapy, 2*, 101–122.

Nelson, T. S., McCollum, E. E., Wetcher, J. L., Trepper, T. S., & Lewis, R. A. (1996). Therapy with women substance abusers: A systemic couples approach. *Journal of Feminist Family Therapy, 8*, 5–27.

Newberry, A. M., Alexander, J. F., & Turner, C. W. (1991). Gender as a process variable in family therapy. *Journal of Family Psychology, 5*, 145–157.

O'Leary, K. D., Curely, A., Rosenbaum, A., & Clarke, C. (1985). Assertion training for abused wives: A potentially hazardous treatment. *Journal of Marital and Family Therapy, 11*, 319–322.

O'Leary, K. D., Vivian, D., & Malone, J. (1992). Assessment of physical aggression against women in marriage: The need for multimodal assessment. *Behavioral Assessment, 14*, 5–14.

Olson, M. E. (1995). Conversation and writing: A collaborative approach to bulimia. *Journal of Feminist Family Therapy, 6*, 21–44.

Ooms, T. (1998). *Towards more perfect unions: Putting marriage on the public agenda.* Washington, DC: Family Impact Seminar.

Oz, S. (1994). Decision making in divorce therapy: Cost-cost comparisons. *Journal of Marital and Family Therapy, 20*, 77–81.

Parke, R. (2000). Beyond white and middle class: Cultural variations in families. Assessments, processes, and policies. *Journal of Family Psychology, 14*, 331–333.

Pasley, K., Dollahite, D. C., & Ihinger-Tallman, M. (1993). Bridging the gap: Clinical applications of research findings on the spouse and stepparent roles in remarriage. *Family Relations, 42*, 315–322.

Pasley, K., Rhoden, L., Visher, E. B., & Visher, J. S. (1996). Successful stepfamily therapy: Clients' perspectives. *Journal of Marital and Family Therapy, 22*, 343–367.

Pittman, F. (1989). The secret passions of men. *Journal of Marital and Family Therapy, 17*, 17–24.

Preli, R., & Bernard, J. M. (1993). Making multiculturalism relevant for majority culture graduate students. *Journal of Marital and Family Therapy, 19*, 5–16.

Prouty, A., & Bermundez, J. (1999). Experiencing multiconsciousness: A feminist model for therapy. *Journal of Feminist Family Therapy, 11*, 19–39.

Rawlings, S. W. (1995). *Single parents and their children.* (Current Populations Reports, Series P 23, 162). Washington, DC: U.S. Bureau of the Census.

Real, T. (1995). Fathering our sons: Refathering ourselves: Some thoughts on transforming masculine legacies. *Journal of Feminist Family Therapy, 7*, 27–43.

Roberts, J. M. (1991). Sugar and spice, toads and mice: Gender issues in family therapy training. *Journal of Marital and Family Therapy, 17*, 121–132.

Romney, P. (1995). The struggle for connection and individuation in anorexia and bulimia. *Journal of Feminist Family Therapy, 6*, 45–62.

Roth, S. (1985). Psychotherapy with lesbian couples: Individual issues, female socialization, and the social context. *Journal of Marital and Family Therapy, 11*, 273–286.

Rothberg, B. (1983). Joint custody: Parental problems and satisfactions. *Family Process, 22*, 43–52.

Sager, C., Walker, E., Brown, H., Crohn, H., & Rodstein, E. (1981). Improving functioning of the remarried family system. *Journal of Marital and Family Therapy, 7*, 3–10.

Schnitzer, P. K. (1993). Tales of the absent father: Applying the story metaphor in family therapy. *Family Process, 32*, 441–458.

Schultz, C. (1999). *Family therapy trainee perception of divorced mothers: A test of bias in informational recall.* Unpublished master's thesis, University of Maryland.

Serra, P. (1993). Physical violence in the couple relationship: A contribution toward the analysis of the context. *Family Process, 32*, 21–33.

Sheinberg, M., & Penn, P. (1991). Gender dilemmas, gender questions, and the gender mantra. *Journal of Marital and Family Therapy, 17*, 33–44.

Shields, C. G., & McDaniel, S. H. (1992). Process differences between male and female therapists in a first family interview. *Journal of Marital and Family Therapy, 18*, 143–151.

Shore, E. A. (1996). What kind of lesbian is a mother? *Journal of Feminist Family Therapy, 8*, 45–62.

Stein, H. F. (1978). Slovak American swaddling ethos: Homeostasis for family dynamics and cultural continuity. *Family Process, 17*, 31–46.

U.S. Bureau of the Census. (1999). *Motherhood: The fertility of American women, 1998* (Current Population Reports). Washington, DC: U.S. Bureau of the Census.

U.S. Bureau of the Census. (2001). Unmarried-partner households by sex of partners. Retrieved July 22, 2003, from http://factfinder.census.gov/servlet/DTTable.

Waite, L. J., & Gallagher, M. (2000). *The case for marriage: Why married people are happier, healthier, and better-off financially.* New York: Doubleday.

Walker, K., & Messinger, L. (1979). Remarriage after divorce: Dissolution and reconstruction of family boundaries. *Family Process, 18*, 185–192.

Walters, M., Carter, B., Papp, P., & Silverstein, O. (Eds.). (1988). *The invisible web: Gender patterns in family relationships.* New York: Guilford.

Watts-Jones, D. (1997). Toward an African American genogram. *Family Process, 36*, 375–383.

Weiner-Davis, M. (1993). *Divorce busting: A step-by-step approach to making your marriage loving again.* New York: Fireside.

Wheeler, D., Avis, J. M., Miller, L. A., & Chaney, S. (1985). Rethinking family therapy training and supervision: A feminist model. *Journal of Psychotherapy and the Family, 1,* 53–71.

White, M. B., & Tyson-Rawson, K. J. (1995). Assessing the dynamics of gender in couples and families: The gendergram. *Family Relations, 44,* 253–260.

Whiteside, M. F. (1982). Remarriage: A family development process. *Journal of Marital and Family Therapy, 8,* 59–68.

Whiteside, M. F. (1998). The parental alliance following divorce: An overview. *Journal of Marital and Family Therapy, 24,* 3–24.

CHAPTER 31

Contemporary Family Life Education
Thirty Years of Challenge and Progress

DEBORAH B. GENTRY

Gladly have we learned and taught.

—Adaptation of line 310 of Chaucer's *Canterbury Tales*

Numerous scholars have traced the long history of family life education in the United States (e.g., Arcus, 1995; Darling, 1987; Powell & Cassidy, 2001). In this chapter, I will focus on the last 30 years and the coming decades. My aim is to answer the following questions: What has happened to family life education and teaching about families in the last 30 years? Has the scholarship of family life teaching and learning during this time period helped professionals and families adapt to change? What could and should happen in the realm of family life education and teaching about contemporary family life in the first decade or two of the new millennium? I will address family life education in both academic and lay communities.

To fully understand and appreciate what happened to family life education and teaching about families, it is beneficial to have some basic knowledge about the 1960s. Chilman (1983) recalled the early years of the 1960s as ones of social protest in pursuit of the "utopian dreams of liberty, justice, and peace for all" (p. 16). Also evidenced were attitudes and behaviors that some have described as narcissistic, selfish, indulgent, and impulsive (Chilman, 1983). Amidst efforts to build a "great society" were newspaper headlines reporting race riots; pronouncements that the family was irrelevant; rising divorce rates; declining marriage and birth rates; increasing births outside marriage; increasing nonmarital intercourse; an inflationary economy; declining rates of poverty, with real income rising for most families; and a rebirth of the women's movement. Incidents of domestic violence, child neglect, incest, rape, school violence, and dirty politics also came to light with greater frequency (Chilman, 1983).

Lewis-Rowley, Brasher, Moss, Duncan, and Stiles (1993) placed the 1960s within a 40-year period of entrenchment for family life education. By *entrenchment*, these scholars meant "solid establishment." Post–World War II economic growth and well-being enabled increased public and private funding for social reform, therapeutic services, and educational programs, resulting in an explosion of printed information about marriage and family issues. Family professionals with generalist backgrounds were in demand, though they were increasingly dependent upon specialists for research to inform the applied programs they designed and delivered (Lewis-Rowley et al., 1993).

FAMILY LIFE EDUCATION: DEFINITION AND PURPOSE

Although there was general consensus regarding the rationale for and purpose of family life education during the 1970s, there was little agreement about what it comprised. Family life education was perceived to be needed primarily for preventing societal and family problems but also for solving problems and developing individual and family strengths (Arcus, Schvaneveldt, & Moss, 1993). The facilitation of constructive and fulfilling personal and family life was paramount.

Though efforts to define family life education had previously been undertaken, new and noteworthy definitions appeared in the literature in the 1970s (see Arcus et al., 1993, pp. 5–6). Some definitions sought to objectively describe the enterprise; others subjectively prescribed how family life education should be done (Soltis, 1978).

In 1981, *Family Relations* devoted an issue to various facets of family life education. Contributing authors provided perspectives on the why, what, where, who, how, and how well of this budding profession. For example, Fisher and Kerckhoff (1981) called for renewed efforts to better articulate family life education. Scholars heeded this call in various ways (see Arcus et al., 1993, pp. 5–6).

More recently, the National Council on Family Relations (NCFR) promoted the following definition: "preventive and educational activities including program development, implementation, evaluation, teaching, training, and research related to individual and family well-being" (Bredehoft, 2001, p. 134). Arcus et al. (1993) outlined operational principles of family life education:

A. Is relevant to individuals and families throughout the lifespan,

B. Should be based on the needs of individuals and families,

C. Is a multidisciplinary area of study and multiprofessional in its practice,

D. Programs are offered in many different settings,

E. Takes an educational rather than a therapeutic approach,

F. Should present and respect differing family values, and

G. Requires qualified practitioners in order to successfully realize its goals as a profession (p. 20)

SUBSTANCE AND CONTEXT: ISSUES OF CONTENT, SETTING, PROVIDERS, AND AUDIENCE

Content

One means of understanding the substantive nature of the last 30 years of family life education is to examine the content of textbooks, journals, and curricular plans and frameworks during that time. Such content analysis reveals information to which family life educators in training and practice were probably exposed.

Textbooks

Rodman (1970) concluded from an analysis of family life textbooks available in the 1960s that the content was noncontroversial, was overly simplistic and contrived, and evidenced little appreciation of diversity. He recommended that textbook authors incorporate more scholarly material; illustrate concepts with real-life case studies; introduce more cross-cultural material; demonstrate variations within societies more; pointedly criticize ethnocentrism and prejudice; acknowledge that family life involves solving difficult problems; and include controversial issues of contemporary living. Although textbooks published during the next three decades evidenced some advancement along the lines suggested by Rodman, room for improvement continued to exist.

During the 1980s, most family texts ignored gay and lesbian families and provided only minor coverage of class issues; African American, Hispanic American, Asian American, and other racially and ethnically diverse families; and family violence (Mann, Grimes, Kemp, & Jenkins, 1997). Those that included black families did so only minimally and primarily from a perspective that regarded them as culturally deviant or culturally equivalent to white families (Bryant & Coleman, 1988). Authors were encouraged to expand coverage of black families from a cultural variant perspective (Bryant & Coleman, 1988). Coverage of other topics was found lacking as well. For example, textbook information on stepfamilies was scant, drawing on limited, outdated empirical studies or on clinical work and popular self-help sources, and based on a subtle deficit-family perspective (Nolan, Coleman, & Ganong, 1984). Also limited

were perspectives used to discuss topics such as dual-career marriages, child care/nurturing approaches, childlessness, homosexuality, family violence, and divorce (Meyer & Rosenblatt, 1987). Greater use of feminist perspectives and frameworks was recommended (Meyer & Rosenblatt, 1987). Glenn (1997) cited deficiencies ranging from presenting negative images of marriage to being overly adult centered, demonstrating unbalanced coverage of controversial issues, and evidencing flawed scholarship and wasted space. Glenn's viewpoint prompted criticism and debate (see *Family Relations*, 46[3] and 46[1] for commentaries and rebuttal).

Journals

During the last 30 years, journals featured numerous articles on the design, delivery, and evaluation of family life education programs. Among the most noteworthy early contributors was the *Family Coordinator* (now *Family Relations*), sponsored by the NCFR. Family life education articles in the *Family Coordinator* during the 1970s focused primarily on topics taught, such as sexuality education, parent education, and premarital and/or marital education and enrichment (Darling, 1987). As can be seen in Table 31.1, an analysis of *Family Relations* articles published in the 1980s and 1990s, topics similar to those published in the 1970s continued to dominate, though Macklin (1981) had earlier advocated expanded coverage of alternative family forms and lifestyles in the design of family life education programs. However, Harriman (1986) demonstrated that prescribing what *should* be done does not easily translate to what *is* done. Her questioning of home economics family life educators about the teaching of emerging family life concepts indicated that overall, these educators viewed traditional concepts (e.g., interpersonal relationships, child development, resource

Table 31.1 Family Life Education: Two Decades of Varying Interests

	1980–1984	1985–1989	1990–1994	1995–1999	Total	(%)
Research-teaching linkage	1	0	0	0	1	(0)
Conceptual framework(s)	1	1	3	0	5	(2.8)
Feminism	0	1	1	0	2	(1.1)
Marriage enrichment/ remarriage enrichment	9	3	5	4	21	(11.8)
Parent education, including teen	14	10	4	9	37	(20.8)
Sex education	13	6	2	2	23	(12.9)
Gender	1	0	0	0	1	(.6)
Communication in relationships	1	0	0	0	1	(.6)
Alternative lifestyles	1	0	0	0	1	(.6)
Multiculturalism/diversity	0	0	2	1	3	(1.7)
Families with special-needs members	0	0	1	0	1	(.6)
Work/dual-earner relationships	0	1	1	0	2	(1.1)
Health	0	0	1	0	1	(.6)
Resilience/strengths	0	1	0	0	1	(.6)
Family stress/crises	1	6	2	0	9	(5.1)
Divorce	0	0	0	2	2	(1.1)
Later-life families	1	0	2	0	3	(1.7)
Values education/ethics	2	1	0	0	3	(1.7)
Public policy	1	0	1	0	2	(1.1)
Profession/identity/ definition/rationale	3	0	4	2	9	(5.1)
Educator preparation	1	0	1	1	3	(1.7)
Students/learners	1	0	0	0	1	(.6)
Learning environment	1	0	0	0	1	(.6)
Context/setting	8	1	2	0	11	(6.2)
Textbook contents	0	2	3	5	10	(5.6)
Teaching methods	1	3	2	5	11	(6.2)
Teaching materials/ resources/texts	3	4	0	0	7	(3.9)
Media/TV/Internet	1	0	0	3	4	(2.2)
Assessment/evaluation	1	1	1	0	3	(1.7)
Total	65	40	37	34	176	

management) as more important to teach than emerging concepts (e.g., divorce and remarriage, conflict, violence, changing sex roles). Harriman concluded that curriculum materials and texts gave disproportionate attention to traditional concepts, which reinforced their importance, and she advocated that authors expand their coverage of emerging concepts. Curriculum developers also were urged to incorporate feminist frameworks, especially those that emphasized cultural context; to be responsive to the vulnerable; to celebrate diversity; to respect learners' experiences and insights; and to suggest strategies for empowerment (Walker, Martin, & Thompson, 1988).

*Curricular Frameworks
and Theoretical Underpinnings*

The *Framework for Life-Span Family Life Education,* published in 1987 by the NCFR, identified seven topic areas (families in society; internal dynamics of families; human growth and development; human sexuality; interpersonal relationships; family resource management; parent education and guidance; family law and public policy; and ethics) and three processes (i.e., communicating, decision making, and problem solving) relevant to three life span categories (i.e., childhood, adolescence, and adulthood). The framework emanated from efforts undertaken to establish the Certified Family Life Educator (CFLE) designation (Bredehoft, 2001). As a result of user feedback and continued review of the literature, the need for revision of the framework became increasingly apparent, and in 1997, it was (a) expanded to include the later-adulthood age group, (b) adjusted to more closely parallel the categories in the College and University Curriculum Guidelines developed by the NCFR in 1984, (c) expanded to more pointedly include a system/ecosystem perspective, and (d) given a richer, more culturally diverse perspective for interpreting family life content (Bredehoft, 2001; NCFR, 1997).

Although the system/ecosystem perspective has been of considerable influence, other theoretical frameworks have also guided the design, delivery, and evaluation of instructional programs during the last 30 years (Allen & Baber, 1992; Hughes, 1994; Powell & Cassidy, 2001; Schvaneveldt & Young, 1992). In subtle and more deliberate ways, parent education programs have evidenced numerous theoretical underpinnings. Developmental, behavioral, humanistic, cognitive-developmental, social learning, Adlerian, and psychoanalytic theories have had considerable impact (Brock, Oertwein, &

Coufal, 1993; Powell & Cassidy, 2001). For example, the widely taught Systematic Training for Effective Parenting (STEP) program is primarily Adlerian based. General developmental, as well as moral developmental, and social learning theories have served to guide the design of sexuality education programs (Engel, Saracino, & Bergen, 1993; Powell & Cassidy, 2001). Both separately and in combination, social exchange, systems, social learning, developmental, cognitive, and humanistic theories have influenced educational programs related to marriage and intimate relationships (Powell & Cassidy, 2001; Stahmann & Salts, 1993). For example, Guerney's Relationship Enhancement (RE) program is rooted in both humanistic/Rogerian and social learning theories (Powell & Cassidy, 2001), and the Couple Communication Program developed by Miller, Nunnally, and Wackman (1975) is systems based (Powell & Cassidy, 2001). More recently, structural, feminist, and historical perspectives have had an impact on couple and marriage education programs as well (Allen & Baber, 1992; Schvaneveldt & Young, 1992).

Programs

The number of educational programs related to human sexuality, parenting, and couple relationships and marriage increased during the last three decades. As a result of their wide use, publicity, and documentation, these nonacademic/community programs are worth noting: Teen Outreach Program (TOP), as cited by Engel et al. (1993); Zero Adolescent Pregnancy (ZAP), as cited by Powell and Cassidy (2001); Gordon's (1975) Parent Effectiveness Training (PET); Dinkmeyer and McKay's (1976) STEP program; Miller et al.'s (1975) Couple Communication; Mace and Mace's (1976) Association for Couples in

Marriage Enrichment (ACME); Guerney's (1977) Relationship Enhancement (RE); Markman, Stanley, and Blumberg's (1994) Prevention and Relationship Enhancement Program (PREP), and the National and/or Worldwide Marriage Encounter programs (Hof & Miller, 1980). Though programs of this nature have been predominant, educational programs pertaining to other aspects of family life have been offered as well. For example, programs emphasizing rebuilding after divorce, stepfamily life, later-life family dynamics, coping with stress and loss, balancing work and family, and managing financial resources have been provided.

The growth of family life education, specifically parent education, is well illustrated by the explosion of divorce education programs for parents in the last decade. Such programs are court connected as well as offered by private entities. Geasler and Blaisure (1998) analyzed materials associated with 37 different divorce education programs used by the courts of 541 counties in the United States in 1994. A year later, the Association of Family and Conciliation Courts (1995) documented 99 divorce education programs of varying design offered across the country. McKenry, Clark, and Stone (1999) estimated that there were over 500 such programs for divorcing parents nationwide, and the numbers continue to grow. Relatively few of these programs have been systematically evaluated, but on the basis of the evaluation studies that have been done, effectiveness is enhanced when the design and delivery of programs are rooted in clearly articulated theory and emphasize active learning of communication and other interpersonal skills (Geasler & Blaisure, 1998; McKenry et al., 1999). As some divorce education programs are designed to include the children of divorcing parents (Gentry, 1997), more research regarding the benefits and cautions of such programs is needed.

Settings, Providers, and Audiences

During the 1970s, family life education was delivered predominantly by middle-class persons of European descent to other middle-class persons of European descent. Although family life education programs had previously been designed by women for women, especially homemakers and mothers, those who designed and delivered instruction during the 1970s were of both genders. This gender mix was also true of their audiences: primarily adolescents, young adults, or middle-aged people. Although participants in family life education were more diverse than ever before, there was room for improvement (Arcus, 1995).

Primarily prepared in disciplines such as sociology, home economics, psychology, social work, and education, professional family life educators delivered their instruction in a variety of community settings in addition to traditional classrooms—junior high, senior high, or college. The first Ph.D. program in family life education had been established by Ernest R. Groves in 1962 at Columbia University in New York, and undergraduate and graduate programs focusing on family studies and family life education proliferated in universities and colleges through the 1970s (Czaplewski & Jorgensen, 1993). Family professionals associated with the U.S. Cooperative Extension Service were key providers of community-based family life education (Rasmussen, 1989), and paraprofessionals and trained laypersons also served as family life educators. Self-help approaches were popular as well. Expansion of formal and informal family life education continued throughout the 1980s.

Family life education preparation was expanded during the 1990s to include health/ nursing and theology. The demographic characteristics, personal experiences, lifestyles, and family patterns of family life educators and the learners that participated in their educational programs also became more diverse (Allen & Crosbie-Burnett, 1992). The challenge was to design and deliver instruction that honored and respected diversity. Audiences incorporated previously neglected or underserved persons such as fathers, ethnic families, and families whose members had special needs. Instructional settings that had been commonplace continued to be used (Arcus et al., 1993; Powell & Cassidy, 2001), but family life educators also took their programs to other settings: the workplace, military bases, and prisons (Arcus, 1995; Lewis-Rowley et al., 1993; Powell & Cassidy, 2001).

As the new millennium approached, family life education was available in most settings for persons of nearly every age and background. Formal instruction continued in public and private classrooms; in 1991, 121 academic units in colleges and universities in the United States and Canada offered family-related programs of study (Touliatos & Lindholm, 1991), and by 2002, the number had grown to 235 (Hans, 2002). Family life educators in informal settings increasingly targeted new audiences such as immigrant families, grandparents fulfilling parental roles, singles, gay and lesbian families, and families coping with the aftermath of divorce, alcoholism and drug abuse problems, and violence (Arcus, 1995; Smith & Ingoldsby, 1992). Most of these learners voluntarily attended family life education offerings, though some came as a result of court orders. For example, parents were often court-ordered to attend parenting classes in order to maintain or regain custody of their children (Powell & Cassidy, 2001).

PROFESSIONALIZATION AND ISSUES OF ENSURING COMPETENCE

During the 1980s, issues of professionalization and certification for family life

educators became the concern of organizations such as the NCFR, the American Home Economics Association (now known as the American Association of Family and Consumer Sciences), the American Association for Marriage and Family Therapy (AAMFT), the American Association for Sex Educators, Counselors, and Therapists (AASECT), the American Association for Counseling and Development (AACD), and the National Association of Social Workers (ACSW) (Czaplewski & Jorgensen, 1993). Family life educators also dealt with the ramifications of continued politicization of family issues throughout the 1980s. As had been the case in previous decades, there were those who were sure that the family was a fragile entity on the brink of extinction; others were equally confident in its spongelike or chameleonlike abilities to absorb and adapt to challenge and change with considerable resiliency (Vincent, as cited in Berardo, 1980).

Efforts to fully professionalize the field of family life education continued through the 1990s. In 1995, the Family Science Section of the NCFR approved *Ethical Principles and Guidelines* (1995) for use. The CFLE designation continued to be sought by professionals and their prospective employers, and undergraduate family science programs could now seek certification through the NCFR as well. Individual states began requiring licensure or certification to practice family life education within settings associated with the government, and the NCFR began working to have the criteria for the CFLE designation incorporated into state licensing qualifications (Powell & Cassidy, 2001).

Continuing professional development has been an expectation for family life educators who sought and then wished to maintain certification designations. To help meet these expectations, the Family Science Association in collaboration with the NCFR began sponsoring annual Teaching Family Science Conferences in the late 1980s.

INSTRUCTIONAL DESIGN AND DELIVERY

Design

Many family life educators' philosophy during the 1970s included a belief that "knowledge acquired through empirical research is considered to be applicable to all individuals who share common characteristics. [Further,] professionals can then distribute these understandings to others with the expectation that once people have acquired this knowledge, life change will follow. In essence, scientific knowledge is perceived as capable of controlling and shaping human action" (Morgaine, 1992, p. 13). Keeping the primary goal of bringing about significant change in learners' patterns of behavior, family life educators would next formulate specific objectives and corresponding learning activities. The teaching-learning relationship was characterized by words such as *transfer, shape,* and *mold*; learners were likened to vessels to be filled or clay to be molded and shaped (Tiberius, 2002). Finally, educators evaluated the success of their instruction by documenting that the change sought in the learners had indeed occurred. Although this model continues to have its adherents, it has been criticized for failing to address many aspects of human motivation, readiness, and uniqueness as well as people's abilities to make meaning and engage in critical insight (Fay, 1977; Thomas, Schvaneveldt, & Young, 1993).

In the late 1980s, Thomas (cited in Arcus, 1995, pp. 341–342; Czaplewski & Jorgensen, 1993, pp. 55–59) provided family life educators in both academic and nonacademic domains with helpful theoretical insights into the processes of education. Thomas applied three paradigms to the enterprise of designing and delivering educator preparation programs that were equally applicable to organizing and presenting family life education programs to lay audiences. The teaching-learning process in the *behavoristic paradigm* is characterized as structured, formal, and relatively rigid, with an emphasis on content mastery, whether of knowledge or skills. A learner is analogous to a passive consumer. The *personalistic paradigm* has its roots in humanistic psychology and phenomenology. The teaching-learning process is unstructured, with two-way transmission of information and insight. Teacher and learner are equally engaged in the pursuit of personal growth and self-actualization as they attempt to make sense of the content being considered. Within the *inquiry-oriented paradigm*, both teacher and learner are expected to "draw upon cognitive and affective resources to reflect critically upon life situations and current social conditions [in an effort] to help foster a social reality that is conducive to the personal development and well-being of the members of a society" (Czaplewski & Jorgensen, 1993, p. 58). Although Thomas (1989) identified examples of family life education programs that illustrated each paradigm, the most common perspective regarding the teaching-learning enterprise during the 1980s was likely to be an eclectic one evidencing a blend of two or more of these paradigms (Czaplewski & Jorgensen, 1993).

In the 1990s, Morgaine (1992) challenged family life educators to undergo a paradigmatic shift in thought and action. Though acknowledging that *instrumental/technical* approaches to instruction that centered on imparting empirical findings and demonstrating skills had their place, she warned of their excessive use. She urged educators to employ *interpretive* and *critical/emancipatory* approaches with greater frequency, especially as they demonstrated respect for learners' life experiences and the insights and meanings gained from them. Critical/emancipatory approaches prompted learners to examine discrepancies that existed between ideals and realities, reveal underlying assumptions, and dispel myths. Critical thinking assignments, problem-based learning activities, and the experiential and service learning opportunities afforded students in the 1990s gave evidence that many instructional designers were heeding Morgaine's advice (Sandifer-Stech & Gerhardt, 2001; Vuchinich, 1999).

Delivery

Family life education has been delivered in three modes: (a) mass instruction, (b) group instruction—optimally small group, and (c) individualized instruction (Arcus & Thomas, 1993; Darling, 1987; Somerville, 1972). Information has been disseminated to the masses in multiple ways, including books, pamphlets, magazines, newspapers, films, radio, television, and lectures by experts. The well-known parent education and relationship/marriage education programs have used the group mode, and individualized instruction has most frequently occurred in conjunction with counseling or caseworker services.

Although family life education occurred in each of these formats before the 1980s, the work of Harman and Brim (1980) facilitated better understanding of various modes of instructional delivery to lay audiences. Books, magazines, newspapers, pamphlets, radio, television, and films continued to be popular means of reaching the masses, but some family life educators, and especially Cooperative Extension Service educators (Rasmussen, 1989), began using newsletters, particularly those packaged as a series (Arcus, 1995). Family life educators also became more aware of the varied learning styles and preferences of their audiences and the impact these could have on the methods used to deliver instruction. Thus, there were increasing opportunities for research investigating which modes and means were most effective with which audiences and

why (Gregorc, Kolb, & Sternberg, cited in Powell & Cassidy, 2001).

The number and types of technological advances in communication and instruction exploded throughout the 1990s. Electronic innovations facilitated information dissemination in creative ways not before imagined. Early in the decade, family life educators began using audiotape, video, and computer-based instruction as modes of instruction (DeGenova & Buchanan, 1997; Fitzpatrick, Smith, & Williamson, 1992; Gentry, 1991). By the close of the decade, instructors and learners were becoming adept with the capabilities of distance education and the Internet (Day & Baugher, 1999; Klein, 1999).

ACCOUNTABILITY AND IMPACT

Evaluation has not been a program focus of family life education until relatively recently. Only 8% of family life education articles published in the *Family Coordinator* during the 1970s focused on program evaluation (Darling, 1987). For the most part, evaluative studies were limited in number, scope, and rigor. Although professional journals other than *Family Relations* may have featured family life education articles that were evaluative, Table 31.1 provides evidence of the lack of attention to program evaluation. Small (1990) identified a number of likely reasons for this. First, although funding for family life education was often dependent upon a master plan that included program evaluation, the budget was seldom generous enough to allow high-quality assessment. Second, even when adequate funds were available, program staff often did not have the expertise or time to implement rigorous evaluation strategies. Nonetheless, in 1981, the Joint Committee on Standards for Educational Evaluation (formed 6 years earlier by the American Education Research Association,

American Psychological Association, and National Council on Measurement in Education) published the *Standards for Evaluation of Educational Programs, Projects, and Materials*. Four standards for evaluation research put forward in that publication continue to be advocated today: utility, feasibility, propriety, and accuracy (Evaluation Center, 2003). Providing further direction for family life educators, Jacobs (1988) suggested that evaluations of instructional programs be conducted in five tierlike stages: preimplementation, accountability, program clarification, progress toward objectives, and program impact. A primary assumption of Jacobs's approach is that family programs have a life cycle and that different evaluation tasks are appropriate at different points in the cycle. Scholars have noted various strengths of the approach, including use of needs assessments as well as both formative and summative evaluation practices. Emphasis on maintaining fidelity, or strict adherence to elements of original program design, during program implementation has been identified as a limitation (Thomas et al., 1993).

Giblin, Sprenkle, and Sheehan (1985) conducted a meta-analysis of studies evaluating premarital, marital, and family enrichment programs and found that, overall, enrichment programs yielded positive outcomes for the predominantly middle-class, moderately educated, white audiences that attended them. Greater impact was found when programs were longer and included experiential learning activities as well as behavioral rehearsal processes. Departing from traditional quantitative methods, particularly surveys and experiments, a few scholars undertook noteworthy evaluation studies using qualitative methods. For example, Travers and colleagues (cited in Nauta & Hewett, 1988) conducted an ethnographic study of the Child and Family Resources Program (CFRP), and the Adolescent Parents Project involved observation and interviews (Miller, 1988). Evaluation research in marriage and family enrichment advanced the use of longitudinal methods. Markman, Floyd, Stanley, and Storaasli (1988) investigated the effectiveness of a relationship education program over time and found that although some positive effects dissipated over time, long-term benefits occurred.

Demands for accountability continue to rise. Funding agencies increasingly seek evidence of tangible outcomes of family life education programs. In an effort to guide program design, delivery, and evaluation, United Way of America affiliates across the nation have advocated the use of logic models that require deliberate thought to intended program inputs (resources), activities (strategies and techniques), outputs (products), outcomes (benefits and changes), and outcome indicators (measurable evidence of achieved outcomes). Logic models have helped program directors identify key components to track over time in order to demonstrate effectiveness (Powell & Cassidy, 2001; United Way of America, 1996).

The greatest attention among evaluative studies has been given to group parent education programs, although there is little evidence that any given parent education program is significantly more effective than another (Brock et al., 1993). Most offerings appear beneficial, though in differing ways. For example, a summary by the American Guidance Service (cited in Brock et al., 1993, p. 98) of 51 generally well-designed and well-implemented studies of the STEP program noted positive changes in parent-child interaction, parental attitudes, child behaviors, and parent perceptions of child behaviors. When both parents attended educational sessions, greater improvement in family climate resulted.

Several studies provided findings that were both reassuring and controversial for those designing and delivering marriage and relationship instruction. Stanley, Markman, St. Peters, and Leber (1995) reported generally positive outcomes for participants in the Prevention and Relationship Enhancement Program (PREP) over time, although they acknowledged certain limitations. However, as a result of longitudinal research of newlyweds, major changes in the practice of marital therapy and education have been recommended (Gottman, Coan, Carrere, & Swanson, 1998). Gottman et al. called for the abandonment of interventions that taught and promoted active listening, such as PREP. Lively discussion and debate (Cole & Cole, 1999; Stanley, Bradbury, & Markman, 2000) regarding these recommendations have ensued.

THE FUTURE: ENHANCING THE PROFESSION, PRACTICE, AND SCHOLARSHIP

In multiple and varied ways, individuals and families have been positively affected by advancements in family life education over the past several decades. Family life educators in training, as well as new and experienced practitioners, their employers, and their clients, have benefited from efforts to professionalize the field. The enterprise as a whole is on more solid ground as a result of increased consensus regarding definition, rationale, essential content, operating principles, and ethical codes of conduct. Instructional designs and their means of delivery have become more varied, innovative, and learner focused. Those who provide instruction as well as those who partake in it have more diverse backgrounds and experiences. Settings for educational programs have become more varied and less traditional as well.

In general, calls for improvement issued in the 1970s and early 1980s have been addressed. For example, family life textbook authors responded to earlier criticisms, and resource materials for lay audiences have improved, as have approaches to program evaluation. Written materials have increasingly (a) attended to controversial and sensitive topics; (b) acknowledged the growing diversity among families and society; (c) incorporated fewer illustrations that were stereotypical, simplistic, or contrived; (d) applied family strength and resiliency models rather than family deficit models to nontraditional family forms; and (e) used a variety of theoretical approaches to better describe the dynamics of family functioning. Similarly, family life education program evaluations are conducted with greater frequency and rigor. As a result, family life education has become more accessible, relevant, and effective for more individuals and families than ever before. Recommendations for family life education during the next few years tend to fall into one of three categories: furthering the profession, furthering practice, or furthering scholarship.

The momentum toward professionalization is still strong and should continue to be emphasized. Currently, there are 1,285 active CFLEs and 72 university programs approved to train them (Goddard, Gilliland, & Goddard, 2003). The movement toward self-regulation and quality control through certification and/or licensure must continue to be pursued. Efforts to enhance employers' and the general public's acceptance of the expertise of those who practice the profession must be undertaken. As recommended over a decade ago, new and better ways to market the profession and its practitioners should be identified and adopted (Cassidy, 2002; Czaplewski & Jorgensen, 1993). How has the CFLE program benefited those educators who have become certified? Have there been discernable benefits accruing to the participants in family life programs led by CFLEs? How has the certification program influenced educator preparation programs? These questions, originally posed by Arcus (1995, p. 343), have yet to be answered.

Ethics, family law, and public policy have been among the most challenging of the content areas of the *Framework for Life-Span Family Life Education* to address (D. Cassidy, personal communication, March 31, 2003; L. L. Eiklenborg, personal communication, March 31, 2003). The work of Adams, Dollahite, Gilbert, and Keim (2001) regarding innovative ways to teach about ethical principles and guidelines and the work of Henderson and Martin (2002) related to teaching family law provide an excellent foundation for future investigation and application. Another work to build upon is Bogenschneider's (2002) book featuring case studies that demonstrate roles family professionals can play in the policy arena, two different approaches for operationalizing these roles (education and advocacy), and multiple strategies for influencing policy makers in ways that strengthen and support families.

Past research has given the most attention to materials and resources used for group instruction; evaluation of educational materials for the masses has been of limited scope. Hughes and Hans note in Chapter 29 of this book that only a few decades ago computers were primarily used in technical fields and that a decade ago Internet use was the province of the military. Yet computers now exist in the majority of households, and about half of all households have access to the Internet. Professional and lay audiences alike can benefit from scholarly efforts to investigate what and how well information about family life is disseminated via the Internet. Hughes (2001) outlined a useful process for evaluating educational Web sites, which, unlike professional journals, are not peer reviewed.

The increasing diversity of families is well documented in this book. The ramifications of this phenomenon are many and complex. In light of the inevitability of further societal change, scholar-educators must continue to investigate which programs work best for which people, under what conditions, and why. To ensure adequate rigor for their program evaluation studies, Kirby (1997) recommended that researchers aim for a sufficient number of program participants and then randomly assign them to experimental and control groups, conduct long-term follow-up, apply appropriate statistical analyses, use independent evaluators, conduct replications, and report both positive and negative results. Rich insights about effectiveness are also likely to surface when quantitative and qualitative methods of data collection are combined (Patton, 1980). Matthews and Hudson's (2001) recent efforts to formulate guidelines for evaluating parent training programs provide direction and guidance to researchers involved in other areas of family life education as well.

The literature on the scholarship of teaching and learning has been steadily growing since Boyer (1990) first introduced the concept over a decade ago. Richlin (2001) and others have made attempts to distinguish between such terms as *scholarship of teaching, scholarly teaching, excellence in teaching,* and *expert teacher.* Though the goal is perhaps impossible to achieve, it can be hoped that every family life educator will engage in scholarly teaching. To do so means that one is deliberate and well informed when undertaking the design, delivery, and evaluation of instruction. Family life educators must make more concerted efforts to take advantage of relevant scholarly advances (Arcus, 1995). Their ability to do so would be facilitated if authors of scholarly works routinely incorporated implications for family life education into their writings.

In addition to conducting high-quality program evaluations, there are other means by which family life educators can engage in the scholarship of teaching and learning in the years ahead. Such scholarship entails a public account of some or all of the following aspects of teaching—vision, design, interaction, outcomes, and analysis—in a manner that can be peer reviewed and used by members of one's professional community (Kreber, 2001). Basing their work on Mezirow's (1991) theory of transformative learning, Kreber and Cranton (2000) offered family life educators guidance for any endeavors in the scholarship of teaching and learning that they may undertake. They encourage educators to systematically engage in premise reflection related to curricular knowledge. In doing so, they should seek answers to the question: Why do I teach this way? Similarly, they prompt teachers to partake in process reflection related to pedagogical knowledge. For this, they must consider

the question: How can I best foster student learning? Finally, Kreber and Cranton urged instructors to engage in content reflection regarding instructional knowledge. The question they must address during such reflection is: What action(s) do I take in teaching? Though their model was formulated with a higher-education context in mind, it appears applicable for other traditional and nontraditional contexts as well. Family life educators can and should be active participants in the scholarship of teaching and learning movement.

Family life education has a proud history. Empirical and anecdotal evidence demonstrates its positive impact on individuals and families. Although challenges persist, the future of the profession holds considerable promise.

REFERENCES

Adams, R. A., Dollahite, D. C., Gilbert, K. R., & Keim, R. E. (2001). The development and teaching of the Ethical Principles and Guidelines for family scientists. *Family Relations, 50*, 41–48.

Allen, K. R., & Baber, K. M. (1992). Starting a revolution in family life education: A feminist vision. *Family Relations, 41*, 378–384.

Allen, K. R., & Crosbie-Burnett, M. (1992). Innovative ways and controversial issues in teaching about families: A special collection on family pedagogy. *Family Relations, 41*, 9–11.

Arcus, M. E. (1995). Advances in family life education: Past, present, and future. *Family Relations, 44*, 336–344.

Arcus, M. E., Schvaneveldt, J. D., & Moss, J. J. (1993). The nature of family life education. In M. E. Arcus, J. D. Schvaneveldt, & J. J. Moss (Eds.), *Handbook of family life education* (Vol. 1, pp. 1–25). Newbury Park, CA: Sage.

Arcus, M. E., & Thomas, J. (1993). The nature and practice of family life education. In M. E. Arcus, J. D. Schvaneveldt, & J. J. Moss (Eds.), *Handbook of family life education* (Vol. 2, pp. 1–32). Newbury Park, CA: Sage.

Association of Family and Conciliation Courts. (1995). *Parent education program profiles.* Madison, WI: Author.

Berardo, F. M. (1980). Decade preview: Some trends and directions for family research and theory in the 1980s. *Journal of Marriage and the Family, 42*, 723–728.

Bogenschneider, K. (2002). *Family policy matters: How policymaking affects families and what professionals can do.* Mahwah, NJ: Lawrence Erlbaum.

Boyer, E. L. (1990). *Scholarship reconsidered: Priorities of the professoriate.* Princeton, NJ: Carnegie Foundation for the Advancement of Teaching.

Bredehoft, D. J. (2001). The framework for life span family life education revisited and revised. *Family Journal, 9*, 134–139.

Brock, G. W., Oertwein, M., & Coufal, J. D. (1993). Parent education: Theory, research, and practice. In M. E. Arcus, J. D. Schvaneveldt, & J. J. Moss (Eds.), *Handbook of family life education* (Vol. 2, pp. 87–114). Newbury Park, CA: Sage.

Bryant, Z. L., & Coleman, M. (1988). The black family as portrayed in introductory marriage and family textbooks. *Family Relations, 37*, 255–259.

Cassidy, D. (2002). How NCFR members assess the CFLE program. *National Council on Family Relations Report, 47*(3), 6–8.

Chilman, C. S. (1983). Prologue: The 1970s and American families: A comitragedy. In E. D. Macklin & R. H. Rubin (Eds.), *Contemporary families and alternative lifestyles: Handbook on research and theory*. Beverly Hills, CA: Sage.

Cole, C. L., & Cole, A. L. (1999). Marriage enrichment and prevention really works: Interpersonal competence training to maintain and enhance relationships. *Family Relations, 48*, 273–275.

Czaplewski, M. J., & Jorgensen, S. R. (1993). The professionalization of family life education. In M. E. Arcus, J. D. Schvaneveldt, & J. J. Moss (Eds.), *Handbook of family life education* (Vol. 1, pp. 51–75). Newbury Park, CA: Sage.

Darling, C. A. (1987). Family life education. In M. B. Sussman & S. K. Steinmetz (Eds.), *Handbook of marriage and family* (pp. 815–833). New York: Plenum.

Day, R. D., & Baugher, S. L. (1999). Distance education and the changing nature of university life. *Family Science Review, 12*, 154–160.

DeGenova, M. K., & Buchanan, T. (1997). Family insights through literature and film: Teaching strategy revisited. *Family Science Review, 10*, 220–232.

Dinkmeyer, D., & McKay, G. (1976). *Systematic training for effective parenting: Parent's handbook*. Circle Pines, MN: American Guidance Service.

Engel, J. W., Saracino, M., & Bergen, M. B. (1993). Sexuality education. In M. E. Arcus, J. D. Schvaneveldt, & J. J. Moss (Eds.), *Handbook of family life education* (Vol. 2, pp. 62–86). Newbury Park, CA: Sage.

Evaluation Center. (2003). Program evaluation standards. Retrieved March 24, 2003, from www.wmich.edu/evalctr/jc.

Fay, B. (1977). How people change themselves: The relationship between critical theory and its audience. In T. Ball (Ed.), *Political theory and praxis: New perspectives* (pp. 200–233). Minneapolis: University of Minnesota Press.

Fisher, B. L., & Kerckhoff, R. K. (1981). Family life education: Generating cohesion out of chaos. *Family Relations, 30*, 505–511.

Fitzpatrick, J. A., Smith, T. A., & Williamson, S. A. (1992). Educating extension agents: An evaluation of method and development of a remarried family education program. *Family Relations, 41*, 70–73.

Geasler, M. J., & Blaisure, K. R. (1998). A review of divorce education program materials. *Family Relations, 47*, 167–175.

Gentry, D. B. (1991). Using computer-aided interactive video (CAIV) for family science instruction. *Family Science Review, 4*, 21–30.

Gentry, D. B. (1997). Including children in divorce mediation and education: Potential benefits and cautions. *Families in Society, 78*, 307–315.

Giblin, P., Sprenkle, D. H., & Sheehan, R. (1985). Enrichment outcome research: A meta-analysis of premarital, marital, and family interventions. *Journal of Marital and Family Therapy, 11*, 257–271.

Glenn, N. D. (1997). A critique of twenty family and marriage and family textbooks. *Family Relations, 46*, 197–208.

Goddard, W., Gilliland, T., & Goddard, N. C. (2003). *NCFR fact sheet. Assuring the future: Family life education*. Minneapolis, MN: National Council on Family Relations.

Gordon, T. (1975). *Parent effectiveness training*. Bergenfield, NJ: Penguin.

Gottman, J. M., Coan, J., Carrere, S., & Swanson, C. (1998). Predicting marital happiness and stability from newlywed interactions. *Journal of Marriage and the Family, 60,* 5–22.

Guerney, B. G., Jr. (1977). *Relationship enhancement: Skill training programs for therapy, problem prevention, and enrichment*. San Francisco: Jossey-Bass.

Hans, J. (2002). *Graduate and undergraduate study in marriage and family: A guide to bachelor's, master's, and doctoral programs in the United States and Canada*. Columbia, MO: Family Scholar.

Harman, D., & Brim, O. G., Jr. (1980). *Learning to be parents: Principles, programs, and methods*. Beverly Hills, CA: Sage.

Harriman, L. C. (1986). Teaching traditional vs. emerging concepts in family life education. *Family Relations, 35,* 581–586.

Henderson, T. L., & Martin, K. J. (2002). Cooperative learning as one approach to teaching family law. *Family Relations, 51,* 351–360.

Hof, L., & Miller, W. R. (1980). Marriage enrichment. *Marriage and Family Review, 3,* 1–27.

Hughes, R. (1994). A framework for developing family life education programs. *Family Relations, 43,* 74–80.

Hughes, R. (2001). A process evaluation of a website for family life educators. *Family Relations, 50,* 164–170.

Jacobs, F. H. (1988). The five-tiered approach to evaluation: Contexts and implementation. In H. B. Weiss & F. H. Jacobs (Eds.), *Evaluating family programs* (pp. 37–68). New York: Aldine de Gruyter.

Joint Committee on Standards for Educational Evaluation. (1981). *Standards for evaluation of educational programs, projects, and materials*. New York: McGraw-Hill.

Kirby, D. (1997). *No easy answers: Research findings on programs to reduce teen pregnancy (summary)*. Washington, DC: National Campaign to Prevent Teen Pregnancy.

Klein, R. C. A. (1999). Ways of knowing in the virtual classroom: Experiences with an Internet course on couple conflict and violence. *Family Science Review, 12,* 194–204.

Kreber, C. (2001). Conceptualizing the scholarship of teaching and identifying unresolved issues. In C. Kreber (Ed.), *Scholarship revisited: Perspectives on the scholarship of teaching* (New Directions for Teaching and Learning, No. 86, pp. 1–18). San Francisco: Jossey-Bass.

Kreber, C., & Cranton, P. A. (2000). Exploring the scholarship of teaching. *Journal of Higher Education, 71,* 476–495.

Lewis-Rowley, M., Brasher, R. E., Moss, J. J., Duncan, S. F., & Stiles, R. J. (1993). The evolution of education for family life. In M. E. Arcus, J. D. Schvaneveldt, & J. J. Moss (Eds.), *Handbook of family life education* (Vol. 1, pp. 26–50). Newbury Park, CA: Sage.

Mace, D. R., & Mace, V. (1976). Marriage enrichment: A preventive group approach for couples. In D. H. L. Olson (Ed.), *Treating relationships* (pp. 321–338). Lake Mills, IA: Graphic Publishing.

Macklin, E. D. (1981). Educating for choice: Implications of alternatives in lifestyles for family life education. *Family Relations, 30,* 567–577.

Mann, S. A., Grimes, M. D., Kemp, A. A., & Jenkins, P. J. (1997). Paradigm shifts in family sociology? Evidence from three decades of family textbooks. *Journal of Family Issues, 18,* 315–349.

Markman, H., Floyd, F. J., Stanley, S., & Storaasli, R. D. (1988). Prevention of marital distress: A longitudinal investigation. *Journal of Consulting and Clinical Psychology, 56,* 210–217.

Markman, H. J., Stanley, S. M., & Blumberg, S. L. (1994). *Fighting for your marriage: Positive steps for a loving and lasting relationship*. San Francisco: Jossey-Bass.

Matthews, J. M., & Hudson, A. M. (2001). Guidelines for evaluating parent training programs. *Family Relations, 50*, 77–86.

McKenry, P. C., Clark, K. A., & Stone, G. (1999). Evaluation of a parent education program for divorcing parents. *Family Relations, 48*, 129–137.

Meyer, C. J., & Rosenblatt, P. C. (1987). Feminist analysis of family textbooks. *Journal of Family Issues, 8*, 247–252.

Mezirow, J. (1991). *Transformative dimensions of adult learning*. San Francisco: Jossey-Bass.

Miller, S. H. (1988). The Child Welfare League of America's Adolescent Parents Project. In H. B. Weiss & F. H. Jacobs (Eds.), *Evaluating family programs* (pp. 371–388). New York: Aldine de Gruyter.

Miller, S. L., Nunnally, E. W., & Wackman, D. B. (1975). *Alive and aware*. Minneapolis, MN: Interpersonal Communication Programs.

Morgaine, C. A. (1992). Alternative paradigms for helping families change themselves. *Family Relations, 41*, 12–17.

National Council on Family Relations. (1984). *Standards and criteria for the certification of family life educators, college/university curriculum guidelines, and content guidelines for family life education: A framework for planning programs over the lifespan*. Minneapolis, MN: Author.

National Council on Family Relations. (1987). *Framework for life-span family life education* [Poster]. Minneapolis, MN: Author.

National Council on Family Relations. (1995). *Ethical principles and guidelines*. Minneapolis, MN: Author.

National Council on Family Relations. (1997). *Framework for life-span family life education* [Poster] (Rev. ed.). Minneapolis, MN: Author.

Nauta, M. J., & Hewett, K. (1988). Studying complexity: The case of the Child and Family Resource Program. In H. B. Weiss & F. H. Jacobs (Eds.), *Evaluating family programs* (pp. 389–405). New York: Aldine de Gruyter.

Nolan, J., Coleman, M., & Ganong, L. (1984). The presentation of stepfamilies in marriage and family textbooks. *Family Relations, 33*, 559–566.

Patton, M. Q. (1980). *Qualitative evaluation methods*. Beverly Hills, CA: Sage.

Powell, L., & Cassidy, D. (2001). *Family life education: An introduction*. Mountain View, CA: Mayfield.

Rasmussen, W. D. (1989). *Taking the university to the people: Seventy-five years of Cooperative Extension*. Ames: Iowa State University Press.

Richlin, L. (2001). Scholarly teaching and the scholarship of teaching. In C. Kreber (Ed.), *Scholarship revisited: Perspectives on the scholarship of teaching* (New Directions for Teaching and Learning, No. 86, pp. 57–68). San Francisco: Jossey-Bass.

Rodman, H. (1970). *Teaching about families*. Cambridge, MA: Howard A. Doyle.

Sandifer-Stech, D. M., & Gerhardt, C. E. (2001). Real world roles: Problem-based learning in undergraduate family studies courses. *Journal of Teaching in Marriage and Family, 1*, 1–17.

Schvaneveldt, J. D., & Young, M. H. (1992). Strengthening families: New horizons in family life education. *Family Relations, 41*, 385–389.

Small, S. A. (1990). Some issues regarding the evaluation of family life education programs. *Family Relations, 39*, 132–135.

Smith, S., & Ingoldsby, B. (1992). Multicultural family studies: Educating students for diversity. *Family Relations, 41*, 25–30.

Soltis, J. F. (1978). *An introduction to the analysis of educational concepts* (2nd ed.). Reading, MA: Addison-Wesley.

Somerville, R. M. (1972). *Introduction to family life and sex education*. Englewood Cliffs, NJ: Prentice Hall.

Stahmann, R. F., & Salts, C. J. (1993). Educating for marriage and intimate relationships. In M. E. Arcus, J. D. Schvaneveldt, & J. J. Moss (Eds.), *Handbook of family life education* (Vol. 2, pp. 33–61). Newbury Park, CA: Sage.

Stanley, S. M., Bradbury, T. N., & Markman, H. J. (2000). Structural flaws in the bridge from basic research on marriage to interventions for couples. *Journal of Marriage and the Family, 62,* 256–264.

Stanley, S. M., Markman, H. J., St. Peters, M., & Leber, D. (1995). Strengthening marriages and preventing divorce: New directions in prevention research. *Family Relations, 44,* 392–401.

Thomas, J. (1989). *Alternative paradigms of teacher education and the preparation of family life educators: Using theory to guide practice*. Unpublished manuscript, University of British Columbia.

Thomas, J., Schvaneveldt, J. D., & Young, M. H. (1993). Programs in family life education: Development, implementation, and evaluation. In M. E. Arcus, J. D. Schvaneveldt, & J. J. Moss (Eds.), *Handbook of family life education* (Vol. 1, pp. 106–130). Newbury Park, CA: Sage.

Tiberius, R. G. (2002). A brief history of educational development: Implications for teachers and developers. In D. Lieberman & C. Wehlberg (Eds.), *To improve the academy: Resources for faculty, instructional, and organizational development* (pp. 20–37). Bolton, MA: Anker.

Touliatos, J., & Lindholm, B. W. (1991). Graduate study in marriage and the family. *Family Science Review, 4,* 165–176.

United Way of America. (1996). *Measuring program outcomes: A practical approach*. Alexandria, VA: Author.

Vuchinich, S. (1999). *Problem solving in families: Research and practice*. Thousand Oaks, CA: Sage.

Walker, A. J., Martin, S. S. K., & Thompson, L. (1988). Feminist programs for families. *Family Relations, 37,* 17–22.

Name Index

Aaron, J., 283
Abalos, D., 337
Abbey, A., 284, 289
Abd al Ati, H., 400
Abdallah, H., 498
Aber, J. L., 480
Abshoff, K., 122, 123
Abu-Ali, A., 401, 405
Abudabbeh, N., 400, 401, 405
Abu-Laban, B., 400, 402
Ackerman, B. P., 283, 284, 322
Ackley, K. A., 161
Acock, A. C., 10, 12, 180, 183, 271-272, 291
Acs, G., 65-66
Adams, G., 163
Adams, G. R., 272
Adams, M., 231, 234, 237
Adams, R. A., 549
Adams, V. H., III, 359
Adelman, R. D., 497, 498
Agger, B., 193, 194
Aguilar, T., 375
Ahmeduzzaman, M., 181, 231, 358
Ahrons, C., 87
Aiello, F., 497, 498
Alberti, R., 201
Aldous, J., 413
Alexander, A., 516
Alexander, B. B., 127
Alexander, J. C., 7
Alexander, J. F., 528
Alexander, M. J., 193, 195
Alford-Cooper, F., 138, 139
Al-Hali, T., 396
Allan, G., 306, 309, 311, 313
Allen, K., 403
Allen, K. R., 23, 145, 146, 177, 180, 181, 192,
        193, 195, 196, 199, 200, 542, 544
Allen, S. M., 233

Allen, W., 338
Allison, P. D., 290, 294
Almeida, D. M., 248
Almeida, R. V., 528
Alpert, A., 245, 247, 254
Altemeyer, B., 420
al-Timimi, N. R., 401, 405
Amato, P. R., 156, 180, 230, 234, 237,
        271, 273-274, 275, 284, 285, 287, 289,
        290, 291, 292, 294, 322, 354, 357,
        422, 531
Anapol, D., 31
Andersen, M., 403
Anderson, C. M., 526
Anderson, D., 528
Anderson, E., 475
Anderson, E. A., 181
Anderson, E. R., 248, 249
Anderson, G., 497
Anderson, J. Z., 319
Anderson, K. G., 64, 65, 234, 236
Anderson, K. L., 416, 480
Anderson, L. M., 336, 344
Anderson, M. L., 164
Anderson, M. M., 386, 387, 388
Anderson, R. N., 179
Anderson, S. J., 289
Andersson, G., 126
Andrews, M. C., 497, 498
Angel, R., 158, 342
Angus, D. O., 390
Aponte, H. J., 417
Appel, A. E., 247, 253, 254-255, 256
Appleby, D. W., 419
Aquilino, W. S., 67, 185, 290, 322
Arbuckle, N. W., 142
Archibald, A. A., 97
Arcus, M. E., 538, 539, 543, 544, 545,
        546, 549

Arendell, T., 182, 184, 210, 213, 216, 217, 219
Armistead, L., 97
Arnaut, G., 325
Arnup, K., 317
Arterburn, S., 414, 416
Asch, A., 499
Asencio, M., 334, 337, 344
Ashby, L., 41, 42
Asmussen, L., 182
Aspden, P., 506
Astone, N. M., 121
Aswad, B., 400
Atkinson, E., 246
Atkinson, J., 436, 438
Auerbach, C. F., 224, 232, 234, 236-237
Aughinbaugh, A., 359
Auriat, N., 69
Avery, R. J., 442
Avis, J. M., 528
Axinn, W. G., 58, 67, 122
Ayyub, R., 401

Baack, D. W., 96, 109
Babchuck, N., 141, 145, 147
Baber, K. M., 195, 196, 200, 542
Baca Zinn, M., 178
Bacca-Zinn, M., 403
Bacchu, A., 525
Bachrach, C. A., 442
Bacu, A., 117
Bagarozzi, D. A., 529
Bagherinia, G., 401
Bagley, M. N., 512
Bahr, H. M., 413, 415, 416
Bailey, J. M., 98
Bainbridge, W. S., 425
Baines, D. R., 391
Bakeman, R., 97
Baker, K. A., 529
Baldridge, D., 386, 387, 388, 389, 390
Bales, R. F., 178
Ballard, R., 306
Balsam, K. F., 99, 100, 106, 107
Balswick, J. O., 317, 325
Banahan, B. F., III, 182
Bane, M. J., 470, 471, 474
Banks, J. A., 387
Bankston, C. L., 422
Barakat, H., 400, 402
Barber, B. L., 284, 286, 291
Bardwick, J. M., 119
Bardy, M., 309
Barenbaum, N. B., 357
Barer, B. M., 128

Barling, J., 158
Barnes, G. G., 529
Barnes, H., 126
Barnes, M., 477
Barnes, R. O., 144
Barnet, H. S., 127
Barnett, R. C., 157, 158, 159, 160,
    166-167, 233, 234
Baron, B., 397
Barrett, M., 176
Bartell, G., 27-28
Bartels, D. M., 493, 494, 497, 499, 500
Bartik, T. J., 480
Bartkowski, J. P., 401, 415, 416, 418, 420,
    422, 423
Baruch, G. K., 158, 160
Bates, J. E., 256
Batson, C., 417, 420
Baugher, S. L., 546
Bauman, K. J., 63, 362
Bauman, Z., 312
Baumrind, D., 345
Bayme, S., 273
Beach, S. R. H., 292, 360
Beaman, J., 290, 291
Bean, F., 342, 344
Bearman, K. J., 65
Beauvais, F., 388
Becerra, R., 334
Beck, U., 129, 307, 311
Becker, G. S., 362, 474, 479
Becker, P. E., 168
Beck-Gernsheim, E., 129, 307, 311
Beeghley, L., 417, 476
Beeler, J., 530
Beeson, D., 497
Beitel, A. H., 232, 233
Bell, D., 17, 196
Bell, N., 319
Bellah, R. N., 270, 425
Belsky, J., 217, 233, 245, 249, 256, 360
Beman, A., 340
Bengston, V. L., 185, 363
Bennett, N. G., 353, 480
Benson, C. K., 417
Bepko, C., 530
Berardo, F., 141
Berardo, F. M., 544
Berg, B., 271, 285
Berg, I. K., 529
Berg, K., 496
Bergen, M. B., 542
Berger, M., 143
Berger, R. M., 146, 147

Berger, S. H., 319, 320, 321
Bergin, A. E., 415
Berguisen, L., 388
Bermundez, J., 528
Bernal, M. E., 335, 344
Bernard, J., 212-213, 228, 229
Bernard, J. M., 529
Bernhart, B. A., 496
Bernstein, J., 236
Berrington, A., 303, 305
Berrol, S. C., 47
Berry, B. J. L., 31-32
Berry, J. W., 250, 335, 340
Betz, P., 529
Bezirgan, B., 397
Bhalla, A. S., 477
Bian, Y., 160
Bianchi, S. M., 59, 60-61, 63, 137, 146,
    155, 174, 179, 185
Biblarz, A., 30
Biblarz, D. N., 30
Biblarz, T. J., 106, 325
Biener, L., 158
Biernat, M., 159
Biesecker, B. B., 496
Bilge, B., 400
Biller, H. B., 229
Billingsley, A., 9, 356
Bird, G., 158
Bird, H., 343
Bird, M. H., 417, 422
Black, A. W., 420
Black, D., 59, 524
Black, L., 528
Black, L. W., 90
Black, M. M., 234
Blackwell, D. L., 60
Blair, J., 107
Blair, S. L., 160, 181
Blaisure, K. R., 180, 181, 444, 543
Blake, J., 116
Blakeslee, S., xii, 270, 274, 283, 293, 357
Blanchard, R., 98
Blancher, V., 498, 500
Blank, R. M., 437, 470, 471, 474
Blankenhorn, D., 224, 230, 235, 236, 237,
    273, 530
Blaske, D. M., 245
Blau, F., 178
Blau, P., 83, 88
Blazer, D. G., 284
Blee, K., 161
Blieszner, R., 195
Blinde, P., 335

Block, J., 286
Block, J. H., 286
Bloom, D. E., 118, 120, 353
Blosfeld, H. P., 121
Bluhm, H. P., 140
Blum, L. M., 90, 215
Blum, R., 97
Blum, R. W., 388
Blumberg, S., 531
Blumberg, S. L., 543
Blumenthal, S., 7
Blums, G. J., 246
Blumstein, P., 58, 63, 68, 99, 100, 101, 103,
    104, 106, 108
Boethel, C. L., 319, 321
Bogenschneider, K., 443, 451, 452, 453,
    454, 460, 462, 465, 549
Bograd, M., 527, 528
Bograd, R., 140
Bohannon, P., 319
Bonauto, M., 440
Boneva, B., 511, 516
Booth, A., 59, 218, 234, 273-274, 275,
    291, 322, 415, 531
Booth, K., 530
Borduin, C. M., 245
Boss, P., 532
Boulton, M. G., 212
Bou-Saada, I. E., 233
Bowen, G. L., 98, 99
Bowman, P. J., 231
Boxer, A. M., 146, 147
Boxer, P., 253, 254
Boyd, C. J., 214
Boyd, R., 142
Boyd-Franklin, N., 90, 526
Boyer, E. L., 549
Boyle, M. H., 282, 283
Bradbury, T. N., 104, 108, 255, 360, 548
Bradford, J., 99
Bradley, R., 232, 233
Bradley, S., 498
Bradley, S. J., 98
Bradshaw, J., 310
Brady, D., 470
Braithwaite, D., 321, 325
Bramlett, M. D., 59, 60, 79, 86-87, 318, 355
Branaman, A., 415
Branson, M. P., 181
Brasher, R. E., 539, 544
Braver, S. L., 235
Bray, J. H., 319, 320, 321, 322, 323, 324, 529
Brayfield, A., 232
Brazelton, T. B., 497, 498

Bredehoft, D. J., 539, 542
Breedlove, J., 27
Breedlove, W., 27
Breena, M. B., 127
Brennan, R. T., 159, 166-167, 233, 234
Brenzel, B. M., 42
Brewaeys, A., 107, 498, 500
Brewster, K. L., 232
Brice, A., 339, 343
Bridges, R. A., 420
Bried, E., 30
Brien, M. J., 57, 70
Brim, O. G., Jr., 546
Brines, J., 63, 231
Bringle, R. G., 420
Brinsden, P., 498
Broadhurst, D. D., 480
Brock, G. W., 542, 547
Brodbar-Nemzer, J. Y., 422
Brody, G. H., 249, 252, 256, 288, 417, 418,
    419, 420, 422
Broman, C. L., 164-165, 360
Broman, L. L., 231
Bronfenbrenner, U., 84, 85, 156, 157, 163,
    165, 202, 515, 516
Brook, J. S., 510
Brooks, R. C., 101
Brooks-Gunn, J., 288, 359, 478, 479, 480
Brown, A., 388
Brown, B., 497
Brown, B. V., 461
Brown, H., 529-530
Brown, H. D., 497
Brown, P. A., 256
Brown, R. A., 416, 422
Brown, S. L., 58, 64, 65
Browner, C. H., 497
Browning, D. S., 412
Brownmiller, S., 193, 194, 198
Brubaker, T., 138, 139
Bruer, J., 12
Bryant, A. S., 99, 100, 106
Bryant, Z. L., 540
Bryson, K. R., 355, 524, 525
Buchanan, C. M., 245, 249, 289, 290, 322
Buchanan, J., 509
Buchanan, T., 546
Buchmann, M., 138
Buck, P., 127
Buckley, W., 7
Buech, N., 272
Buehler, C., 158, 232, 324, 529
Bulbeck, C., 123
Bulcroft, J. S., 339

Bulcroft, K. A., 140, 141, 143, 147
Bulcroft, R. A., 143, 147, 339
Bullard, R. D., 480
Bumpass, L. L., 57, 58, 59, 60, 61-62, 64, 66,
    68, 69, 79, 125, 142, 148, 275, 287, 317,
    318-319, 361, 524
Bumpass, M. F., 159, 162
Burchinal, M., 245, 248
Bures, R., 412
Burgess, E. W., 267, 269, 506, 507
Burgoyne, C. B., 319
Buriel, R., 335, 336, 338, 341, 342, 344, 386,
    390, 391
Burke, M., 249, 496
Burke, P., 146
Burkett-Simms, C., 462
Burkhauser, R. V., 141
Burks, V., 140
Burman, B., 104, 248, 257
Burnam, M., 336, 342
Burns, T., 82
Burt, M. R., 144
Burt, R., 16
Burtless, G., 471, 472, 480
Burton, L. M., 178, 363, 402, 403, 404, 480
Buss, D. M., 119, 362
Butler, A. C., 97
Butler, J. S., 141
Butler, M. H., 417, 422
Buunk, B. P., 9, 23, 96, 104, 109
Byng, M., 401, 405
Byng-Hall, J., 289

Cabrera, N., 90, 232, 233
Caetano, R., 416
Cahn, N., 442
Call, V., 69
Call, V. A., 416
Callan, V. J., 126
Calvert, K. L. F., 38, 40
Calzada, S., 336, 342
Campbell, L. D., 128
Campbell, R., 85
Canino, G., 343
Cantor, M. H., 127
Capaldi, D. M., 106, 254
Capizzano, J., 163
Carey, R. G., 141
Carlson, A., 456, 457, 458, 459, 461
Carlson, M. J., 64, 289
Carlson, V., 334, 337, 344
Carmody, D. C., 339
Carolan, M., 401
Carr, A., 422

Carrer, S., 126
Carrere, S., 548
Carrington, C., 104, 110
Carstensen, L. L., 139
Carter, B., 526, 532
Carter, E. B., 8
Carver, K., 218
Case, A., 64
Case, D., 30
Caserta, M. S., 142
Casler, L., 29
Casper, L. M., 58, 59, 60-61, 63, 67, 69, 232, 355, 356, 524, 525
Cassidy, D., 538, 542, 544, 546, 547, 548
Castañeda-English, P., 338
Castelli, J., 411
Casterline, J., 180
Castillo, R. J., 84
Catellier, D. J., 233
Cauce, A., 91, 342
Cauce, A. M., 165, 375
Caudill, W., 371
Caughlin, J. P., 99, 320, 321
Caulfield, T., 501
Cazenave, N. A., 9
Ceballo, R., 284, 289, 325
Ceglian, C. P., 320
Chadwick, B. A., 211, 413, 415, 418
Chai, L., 373
Chambers, D. L., 440
Chan, C. S., 378
Chan, K., 335
Chan, R. W., 101
Chandler, A. L., 248
Chandola, T., 304
Chandra, P. S., 127
Chaney, J. M., 391
Chao, R., 372, 373
Chapman, D. A., 461
Charnov, E., 230, 231, 232, 234
Chase-Lansdale, P. L., 275, 289, 323
Chast, R., 211, 217
Chatters, L. M., 293, 338, 353, 355, 359, 360, 414, 422
Chatty, D., 397
Chaturvedi, S. K., 127
Chavira, V., 338, 342
Cheal, D., 479
Chen, D., 30
Chen, F. F., 96
Chen, R., 118, 120
Chen, X., 391
Cheng, L. C., 474
Cheng, S. H., 373

Cherlin, A. J., 32, 58, 60, 63, 79, 86, 148, 211, 235, 266, 268, 269, 270, 275, 276, 291, 319, 323, 353, 434, 523, 524
Chesire, T. C., 386, 387, 388, 390, 391
Chester, N. L., 357
Chetra, H., 127
Chevan, A., 148
Chilman, C., 4, 9, 10
Chilman, C. S., 539
Chinitz, J. G., 416, 422
Chiswick, C. U., 416
Chodorow, N., 213, 214, 226
Chodron, P., 201
Choi, N. G., 128
Choi, N. K., 145, 146
Chow, E. N. L., 196, 197
Christ, W. G., 508
Christensen, A., 186
Christensen, K., 193, 195, 199
Christiano, K., 411, 418, 419
Christiansen, S. L., 232, 411, 419
Chudacoff, H. P., 37, 46, 47
Cicchetti, D., 248, 253, 255, 257
Cimmarusti, R. A., 529
Citro, C. F., 63
Clancy, M., 482
Clark, K. A., 543
Clark, L. S., 508
Clark, R. L., 65-66
Clark, W. M., 530
Clarkberg, M., 60, 63
Clarke, C., 528
Clarke, L., 69
Clarke, S. C., 319
Clarke-Stewart, K., 290, 291
Clawson, D., 10
Cleason, M. E. J., 508
Clement, P., 40, 41
Cleminshaw, H. K., 271
Cleveland, M., 494
Clingempeel, W. G., 248, 256, 291, 320, 321, 322
Clossick, M. L., 528
Cloud, J., 31
Clunis, D. M., 101, 102-103
Coan, J., 548
Coane, J., 529
Coatsworth, J. D., 256
Cochran, D., 358-359
Cochran, J. K., 417
Cochran, S. D., 101, 104, 107
Cogswell, B., 6, 10
Cohen, E. L., 161
Cohen, H., 216

Cohen, P., 510
Cohen, P. H., 67, 69
Cohen, P. N., 155, 174, 181, 231
Cohen, R. A., 340
Cohen, R. D., 418, 420
Cohler, B. J., 147
Cohn, D., 524
Coiro, M. J., 285
Cole, A. L., 548
Cole, C. L., 548
Cole, P. M., 250
Coleman, D., 303, 304
Coleman, J. S., 15, 16, 17
Coleman, M., 125, 177, 318, 319, 320,
    321, 322, 323, 324, 325, 540
Coleman, R., 6
Coley, R. L., 230
Coll, C. G., 163, 217
Collins, C., 478
Collins, F. S., 495, 500
Collins, P., 403
Collins, P. H., 192, 193, 195, 197, 203, 217
Collins, R., 225
Colman, A., 494
Colpin, H., 498
Coltrane, S., 160, 180, 181, 216, 217, 225,
    226, 227, 228, 229, 231, 232, 233,
    234, 235, 237, 319, 377
Conger, K. J., 288
Conger, R. D., 161, 288, 291, 480
Connidis, I. A., 124, 127, 128
Constantine, J. M., 26, 28
Constantine, L., 26, 28
Conteras, I. M., 252
Cook, J. A., 193
Cook, K., 16, 83
Cook, R., 498
Cooksey, E. C., 64, 161
Coon, H. M., 250, 338
Cooney, T. M., 142, 143
Coontz, S., 167, 176, 198, 211, 228,
    237, 275, 357
Cooper, A., 508, 509
Cooper, H., 319
Cooper, M. H., 395, 396
Copeland, A. P., 357
Corbett, T., 462
Corcoran, M., 478
Cornwall, M., 413, 421
Cornwell, G. T., 283
Corsaro, W. A., 12
Cortés, D. E., 342
Coser, R. L., 214
Costa, P. T., 143, 144

Costigan, C. L., 248
Cott, N. F., 40
Cottrell, L. S., 267, 269
Coufal, J. D., 542, 547
Coughlin, C., 322
Couture, P. D., 412
Coveney, P., 39
Covington, S. N., 494
Cowan, C. P., 11, 232-233
Cowan, P. A., 11, 232-233
Cox, C. E., 234
Cox, F., 9
Cox, M., 245, 248, 270-271, 284, 289, 290
Cox, M. J., 282, 293
Cox, R., 270-271, 284, 289, 290
Cox, S., 9
Cox, S. J., 497
Coylar, J. J., 321
Coyle, A. T., 127
Coyne, J. C., 292
Craig, P. H., 64, 353
Crandall, L., 462
Cranton, P. A., 550
Cravens, H., 44
Crawford, A., 289, 511, 516
Criss, M. M., 256
Crockenberg, S., 246, 257
Crockett, L. J., 234
Crohan, S. E., 126, 219
Crohn, H., 529-530
Cromwell, R., 343
Crosbie-Burnett, M., 98, 99, 319, 544
Cross, T. L., 390
Crouch, J., 273
Crouse, J. S., 360
Crouter, A. C., 59, 156, 157, 159, 161,
    162, 165-166, 167, 181, 220
Crow, G., 306, 311, 313
Crowder, K. D., 180, 282
Crowley, M. L., 473, 478
Cuber, J. D., 8, 11
Cummings, E. M., 244, 245, 247, 251, 257
Cummings, J., 511, 516
Cummings, J. N., 514
Cunradi, C. B., 416
Curely, A., 528
Curtin, R. B., 64, 321
Curtin, S. C., 355
Cutrona, C. E., 256
Czaplewski, M. J., 543, 544, 545, 548

Dadds, M. R., 246
D'Amico, C., 169
Daneshpour, M., 529

Daniels, A. K., 183
Daniels, M., 497
Daniels-Mohring, D., 143
D'Antonio, W. V., 413
Danziger, S., 480
Darling, C. A., 538, 540, 546
Dasen, P. R., 250
D'Augelli, A. R., 98
Davidson, K. J., 32
Davies, L., 128
Davies, L. C., 320
Davies, M. W., 464
Davies, P. T., 244, 245, 247, 251, 257
Davis, B. T., 245, 247, 254
Davis, E. C., 285
Davis, J. E., 232
Davis, K., 116, 476
Davis, M., 196
Davis-Kean, P. E., 231
Dawson, G., 255
Day, R. D., 156, 180, 230, 234, 236, 237, 546
De Baryshe, B. D., 284
Deenen, A., 147
DeFrain, J., 32
DeGenova, M. K., 546
DeHart, J., 7, 10
DeHart-Mathews, J., 197
Deinhart, A., 528
de Jong Gierveld, J., 67, 70
DeLamater, J. D., 158, 159, 160
DeLeire, T., 63
Dell, P., 527
DeLora, J. R., 28
DeLora, J. S., 28
DeMaris, A., 320, 321
DeMent, T., 335, 338, 344
Demian,, 99, 100, 106
D'Emilio, J., 196, 198
Demo, D. H., 10, 12, 23, 179, 180, 183, 213, 271-272, 275, 282, 283, 291, 293, 294, 445
Demos, J., 38
Demyttenaere, K., 498
Denayerr, L., 496
Denfield, D., 28
Denton, N. A., 475-476
Depner, C. E., 248
D'Eramo, K. S., 283, 284, 322
Dershowitz, A., 340
Desai, S., 217
Desrochers, S., 288
Deussen, T., 90
Deutsch, F., 155, 168, 216, 231, 234
Devall, E. L., 288

DeVault, C., 494
Devine, J. A., 471
DeVos, G., 371
deVries, B., 142
Diamant, A. L., 103, 107
Diamond, L. M., 97
Diaz-Guerrero, R., 340
DiBlasio, F. A., 417
Dickerson, B. J., 291
Dickert-Conlin, S., 69
DiClemente, R. J., 386, 387, 388
Diemer, M. A., 104
Dijkstra, P., 96, 109
Di Leonardo, M., 141
Dill, B. T., 196, 228
Dillman, D. A., 517
Dilworth-Anderson, P., 178, 363, 402, 403, 404
Dimmick, J., 511
Dinges, N. G., 388
Dinkmeyer, D., 542
DiProva, V., 530
Dishion, T. J., 461, 463
Disuqi, R., 400
Diversi, M., 338
Dixon, J. K., 30, 389
Dixon, P., 210
Dizard, J. E., 6, 14
Dodge, K. A., 256
Doeringer, P. B., 476
Doherty, W. J., 7, 236, 493, 530, 531
Dollahite, D. C., 236, 413, 419, 422, 425, 514, 530, 549
Donato, K. M., 376
Donn, J. E., 508
Donnelly, B. W., 292, 320
Donnelly, W. O., 253, 254
Dooley, M. D., 282, 283
Dorfman, R., 146
Dornbusch, S. M., 245, 249, 289, 290, 322
Doukas, D. J., 495, 500
Douvan, E., 90, 91
Dowling-Guyer, S., 125
Downey, G., 292
Dreyfus, E. A., 529
Drinkwater, M., 289
Dube, E. M., 96
Duberman, L., 29, 319
Dubowitz, H., 234
Duck, S. W., 84
Duckworth, J., 30
Dudley, M. G., 415
Duff, R. W., 142, 145
Duffer, A. P., 68

Duinvenvoorden, H. G., 496
Dunbar, L., 473
Duncan, G. J., 142, 288, 291, 470, 471, 473, 478, 479, 480
Duncan, S. F., 539, 544
Dunifon, R., 66, 293
Dunn, J., 284, 291, 320
Duong-Tran, Q., 388

Earls, F., 480
East, P. L., 361
Easterlin, R. A., 116
Ebata, A., 514
Ebert, T. L., 193, 194, 195, 200
Eccles, J. S., 284, 286
Eck, D. L., 411, 412
Edelmann, R. J., 119
Edin, K., 62, 71, 184, 479
Edwards, B., 16
Edwards, J., 273-274
Edwards, J. G., 496
Edwards, J. N., 501
Edwards, M. E., 473
Edwards, R., 310
Edwards, R. G., 494
Edwards, R. W., 388
Eggebeen, D. J., 224, 234, 235, 236
Ehrenberg, R., 178
Ehrenreich, B., 211, 214, 229
Ehrensaft, D., 216
Ehrensaft, M. K., 255
Ehrhardt, A. A., 98
Eichler, M., 501
Ekeh, P., 16
Elam, D., 194
El-Amin, M. M., 396
Elder, G. H., Jr., 161
Eliade, M., 411
Elliott, M., 514
Ellis, A., 28
Ellison, C. G., 411, 413, 415, 416, 418, 420, 421
Ellison, N. B., 512
Ellsworth, E., 195
Ellwood, D. T., 470, 471, 474, 480
Elman, C., 325
Elrod, L. D., 438
Elshtain, J. B., 273
Emerson, R., 81, 83
Emery, E., 415, 417, 422
Emery, R. E., 255, 267, 271, 283, 284, 285, 289, 292, 293, 444
Engel, J. W., 542
Engels, F., 476

English, D., 211, 214
Erel, O., 104, 248, 257
Erickson, C. D., 401, 405
Ermisch, J., 305
Escobar, J., 336, 342
Escovar, P., 339
Eshleman, R., 453
Espenshade, T. J., 353
Esping-Andersen, G., 477
Espiritu, Y. L., 376, 380
Estes, S. B., 174
Everett, C. A., 529
Evers-Kiebooms, G., 496

Facteau, L., 363
Faderman, L., 194, 196, 198
Fagan, J. A., 231, 232
Falkner, A., 99, 107
Fanchin, R., 498, 500
Faragallah, M., 401
Farber, B., 304
Faris, E., 16
Farnsworth, E. B., 195
Fasouliotis, S. J., 495, 502
Fay, B., 545
Fea, C. B., 324
Feagin, J. R., 473, 477
Feldbau-Kohn, S. R., 255
Felker, J., 325
Felsman, I. C., 375
Felsman, J. K., 375
Felton, J., 414, 416
Ferguson, A., 122
Ferguson, F. I. T., 220
Fernandez, R. M., 342
Fernandez, T., 337
Fernea, E., 397
Ferree, M. M., 105, 158, 160, 164, 177, 178, 180, 181, 216
Ferris, M., 513
Fethke, C., 143
Fields, J., 121, 355, 356
Fields, J. M., 318, 354
Fiese, B. H., 415, 419, 422
Finch, J., 312
Fincham, F., 244, 245, 246, 257
Fincham, F. D., 292, 360
Fine, D. R., 445
Fine, M. A., 23, 177, 284, 292, 294, 318, 319, 320, 322, 323, 324, 338, 342, 344, 445
Finke, R., 411, 421, 423, 425, 426
Finkel, E. J., 108, 110
Finkelhor, D., 233
Finkle, D. G., 420

Finley, N. J., 182
Fischer, C. S., 506, 507, 512, 515
Fisher, B., 201
Fisher, B. L., 539
Fisher, G., 478
Fiske, A. P., 251
Fitzpatrick, J. A., 546
Flaherty, M. J., 363
Fleming, M., 454
Fletcher, A. C., 200
Flor, D. L., 252, 417, 418, 419, 420, 422
Floyd, F. J., 97, 248, 547
Floyd-Thomas, S. M., 200
Fluehr-Lobban, C., 399
Foa, E. B., 81
Foa, U. G., 81
Foley, M. W., 16
Folk, K., 160-161, 164
Fong, C., 374
Fong, T. P., 370, 374
Fonow, M. M., 193
Foote, K., 180
Forgatch, M. S., 289
Forgays, D., 246
Forman, E. M., 245, 247
Foster, E. M., 71
Foster, R., 494
Foster, T. L., 98, 99
Fowler, F., 289
Fox, G., 333, 334
Fox, G. L., 105
Fox, S., 511
Francesconi, M., 305
Francoeur, A. K., 29
Francoeur, R. T., 29, 414
Frankenberg, R., 194-195
Franklin, A. J., 90
Franklin, D., 353, 356
Franklin, R. M., 412
Franzen, A., 511
Fraser, F. C., 496
Freedman, E. B., 196, 198
Freedman, V. A., 128
Freeman, R. B., 362
Freire, P., 195, 197
Frets, G. P., 496
Freud, A., 443
Frideres, J., 126
Friedan, B., 193, 211
Friedman, D., 121
Friedman, M., 17
Friel, L. V., 285
Friend, R. A., 109, 146, 147
Frisbie, W., 342

Fromme, D., 325
Frosch, C. A., 256
Frydman, R., 498, 500
Fujimoto, T., 158
Fulgini, A. J., 373
Furstenberg, F. F., 12, 229, 232, 234, 235, 270, 287, 290, 291, 294, 319, 323, 357

Gadlin, H., 6, 14
Gagnier, R., 194
Gagnon, J. H., 67, 96, 196, 198, 418
Gaines, S. O., 104
Galambos, N. L., 158, 159
Galatzer-Levy, R., 147
Galjaard, H., 496
Gallagher, B., 416
Gallagher, M., 10, 12, 33, 87, 360, 432, 531
Gallagher, S. K., 158
Gallegos, P. I., 336
Gallup, G., Jr., 411
Galt, J., 227, 228, 229
Gander, A. M., 142
Ganong, L. H., 125, 177, 294, 318, 319, 320, 321, 322, 323, 324, 325, 540
Gans, H. J., 473, 476
Garber, J., 99, 107
Garcia, A., 343
Gardner, B. C., 417, 422
Gardner, C. O., 287
Gardner, S., 320
Gareis, K. C., 233, 234
Garey, A. I., 179-180, 183, 211, 216
Garfinkel, I., 277, 481
Garland, D. R., 422
Garrett, J. T., 389, 390
Garrett, M. T., 386, 387, 389, 390, 391
Garrett, P., 217
Garver, P., 363
Garza, R. T., 336
Gates, E., 497
Gates, G., 59, 524
Gates, M. F., 501
Gaudet, D. S., 143
Gavanas, A., 237
Ge, X. J., 480
Geary, D. C., 119
Geasler, M. J., 444, 543
Gebhard, P. H., 96
Gelles, R. J., 250, 480
Gentry, D. B., 543, 546
Gentry, M., 140
George, L. K., 284
George, S. M., 291
Gergen, K. J., 513

Gerhardt, C. E., 546
Gerlander, M., 508
Gerson, K., 183
Gerstel, N., 158, 167
Getis, V., 44
Gibbs, J., 141
Giblin, P., 547
Gibson, F. L., 498
Giddens, A., 7, 8, 17, 307
Gijs, L., 147
Gilbert, J. B., 50
Gilbert, K. R., 549
Gilbreth, J., 234
Gilens, M., 473
Giles-Sims, J., 319
Gillespie, R., 117, 119, 122, 123
Gillespie, V. B., 421
Gillies, V., 310
Gilliland, T., 548
Gilliom, L. A., 248
Gillis, J. R., 39
Gillman, L., 200
Gillman, S., 289, 292
Gilmartin, B., 29-30, 31
Giordano, J., 400, 402, 526
Gittleman, M., 359
Glass, J., 158, 174
Glassner, B., 7
Glendon, M. A., 269
Glenn, E. N., 215, 217, 371, 372, 376
Glenn, N., 531
Glenn, N. D., 126, 269, 319, 540
Glennerster, H., 470
Glick, P. C., 59, 60, 67, 317
Glueck, E., 270
Glueck, S., 270
Goble, P., 390
Godbey, G., 179, 180
Goddard, N. C., 548
Goddard, W., 548
Godwin, D., 11, 18
Goeke-Morey, M. C., 257
Golbus, M. S., 497
Gold, S. J., 376
Goldberg, N., 203
Goldman, J., 529
Goldman, N., 142, 144, 145, 374
Goldner, V., 527
Goldscheider, F., 122, 321
Goldsmith, J., 87
Goldstein, A., 10
Goldstein, H. S., 319-320
Goldstein, J., 443
Goldstein, J. R., 57, 71

Golish, D. T., 320, 321
Golish, T., 321, 325
Golombok, S., 107, 119, 494, 497, 498, 500, 501, 502
Gongla, P., 10, 12
Gonyea, J., 182
Gonzales, H., 375
Gonzales, N. A., 248, 251-252
Gonzalez, A., 343
Gonzalez, R., 110
Goode, W. J., 6, 304
Goodman, C., 138, 139
Goodman, E., 494, 497, 498, 500, 501
Goodman, M., 127, 340
Goodwin, L., 473
Goodwin, R., 85
Gordis, E. B., 248
Gordis, R., 414
Gordon, L., 43, 454, 455, 457, 458
Gordon, M., 28
Gordon, T., 542
Gosling, A. L., 528
Gotlib, I. H., 292
Gottainer, G., 325
Gottman, J. M., 91, 108, 126, 139, 244, 245, 248, 249, 256, 324, 548
Gottschalk, P., 480
Goudy, W., 165
Gould, T., 30-31, 32
Gove, W. R., 292
Goyette, K., 60
Graber, J. A., 97
Graebner, W., 45
Granger, D. A., 218
Grant, T. R., 514
Gray, J., 106
Greaves, K. M., 185
Green, A. S., 508
Green, G. D., 101, 102-103
Green, R., 106
Greenberger, E., 161
Greene, B., 109
Greene, S. M., 249
Greenfield, S., 96
Greenwood, D. J., 15
Greer, C., 528
Gregg, C. H., 140
Greven, P. J., 39
Griffin, D., 110
Griffin-Shelley, E., 509
Griffith, R. M., 415, 423
Grimes, M. D., 540
Grimm-Thomas, K., 161
Grindstaff, C. F., 414

Grisso, T., 445
Griswold, R. L., 183, 225, 226, 227, 228, 229
Griswold del Castillo, R., 343, 344
Gross, A. E., 142
Gross, H., 30
Gross, M., 30
Grossbard-Schechtman, S., 121
Grotevant, H., 502
Groves, E. R., 267
Gruber, E., 386, 387, 388
Gruen, R. S., 98
Gruner, L., 417
Grych, J. H., 244, 245, 246, 257
Guarnaccia, P. J., 158
Guelzow, M., 158
Guerney, B. G., Jr., 542, 543
Guidobaldi, J., 271
Gunn, S. P., 30
Gunnoe, M. L., 418, 420
Gupta, G., 9
Gupta, S., 62, 63
Gurdon, J. B., 494
Gustafsson, B., 471

Haas, S. M., 104
Haase, A. Q., 512
Haddad, Y., 400, 403
Hadden, W., 478
Haddock, S. A., 528
Hahn, C. S., 498, 499, 501, 502
Hairston, C. F., 358
Hajnal, J., 60
Hall, L., 185
Hall, R., 306
Halpern, A., 481
Hamer, J., 231, 290
Hamilton, B. E., 62, 355
Hamilton, B. R., 355
Hamilton, M., 343
Hammer Burns, L., 494, 495, 496, 497
Hammerslough, C., 374
Hammond, R. J., 143
Hampton, K. N., 511-512
Handel, G., 6
Hannon, P. A., 108, 110
Hans, J., 544
Hans, J. D., 502, 503
Hanson, T. L., 64-66, 234, 276, 321, 322
Hansson, R., 142
Hao, L., 66
Hardin, L., 146
Harding, S., 193, 194, 195
Hardy, K. V., 529
Hare, J., 319

Hareven, T. K., 196
Hargrave, T. D., 417
Harjo, S. S., 387
Harkness, S., 84
Harman, D., 546
Harmon, B., 388
Harold, G. T., 257, 292
Harper, J. M., 417
Harriman, L. C., 540
Harrington, M., 478
Harris, C., 516
Harris, D. R., 177
Harris, J., 12
Harris, K. H., 232, 234
Harris, L., 97
Harrish, L., 388
Harrison, K., 309
Hart, C. H., 420
Hart, H. H., 28
Harvey, D. L., 479
Harvey, E., 156, 359
Harwood, R., 334, 337, 340, 344
Hasell, M. J., 15
Haskey, J., 304, 305, 309
Hassouneh-Phillips, D., 401
Hastings, C., 9
Hatala, M. N., 96, 109
Hatanaka, H., 373
Hatch, L. R., 141
Hatchett, S., 90, 91
Hathaway-Clark, C., 415, 416
Haurin, R. J., 287
Hauser, R. M., 461, 471
Hawes, J. M., 45, 48
Hawkesworth, M. E., 193, 199
Hawkins, A. J., 232, 233, 234, 236, 513, 514
Hays, S., 183, 210, 213, 214, 215, 217, 219, 229
Hayward, C., 290, 291
Hayward, M. D., 128, 179
Head, M. R., 162
Heady, C., 477
Healy, J. M., Jr., 291
Heard, A., 30
Heath, D. T., 288
Heaton, T. B., 117, 119, 120, 121, 122, 211, 411, 416
Heavey, C. L., 186
Hechter, M., 121
Hecker, L. L., 422
Heclo, H., 14
Hee, S. J., 376, 379
Heindel, S., 247
Heinemann, G. D., 141

Helgeson, V., 511, 516
Helmbrecht, L., 319
Henderson, M. C., 104
Henderson, T. L., 549
Henggeler, S. W., 245
Hennessy, C. H., 386, 388, 391
Hepworth, J., 493
Herbst, J. H., 143, 144
Herek, G. M., 99
Hernandez, D. J., 353
Herring, R. D., 386, 389, 391
Herrmann, A. C., 194
Hertz, R., 220
Herzog, A. R., 143
Herzog, E., 271
Hetherington, E. M., xii, 235, 248, 256,
     270-271, 275, 276, 284, 289, 290, 291,
     319, 320, 321, 322, 325, 357, 418, 420
Hewett, K., 547
Hewitt, C., 96
Hewitt, E. C., 158, 159, 160
Hewlett, B. S., 226
Hewlett, S. A., 452
Heyle, A., 387
Heyman, R. E., 255
Heywood, C., 36
Hill, C., 306
Hill, E. J., 232, 513
Hill, N. E., 248, 251-252
Hill, P. C., 413
Hill, R. B., 353
Hilton, J. M., 288
Himelright, J., 401
Himmelfarb, S., 142
Hindin, M., 59
Hinton, I. D., 231
Hiraga, Y., 375
Hird, M., 122, 123
Hirschl, T. A., 472, 473, 478
Hirschman, C., 371
Hoagwood, K., 252
Hobart, C., 319, 324
Hochschild, A. R., 155, 160, 162, 179,
     180, 181, 183, 185, 231
Hodson, R., 476
Hof, L., 543
Hofferth, S. L., 64, 163, 231, 232, 233,
     234, 236
Hoffman, L. W., 116, 359
Hoffman, M. L., 116
Hoffman, P., 322
Hoffman, S. D., 71, 142, 291
Hofstede, G., 84, 338
Hogan, D. P., 283

Holden, G. W., 247, 253, 254-255, 256, 414
Holden, K. C., 141
Holland, K., 119, 120, 121, 122
Holloran, P. C., 42
Holmes, E. K., 419
Holt, J. C., 48
Holt, M. I., 42
Holtzman, W. H., 340
Hom, A. Y., 378
Homans, G. C., 83, 88
Hong, L. K., 142, 145
Hood, R. W., Jr., 413
Hooyman, N. R., 182
Hope, D., 417
Hopkinson, P. L., 420
Hops, H., 245, 247, 254
Horn, W., 237
Horowitz, J. L., 98
Horrigan, J., 511
Hossain, Z., 231, 232
Hostetler, A. J., 147
Hotaling, G., 233
Hotvedt, M. E., 106
Hough, R., 336, 342
Houseknecht, S. K., 116, 117, 120, 121,
     123, 125, 411, 412-413, 415, 422
Houser, S., 69
Howard, D., 462
Howard, P. E. N., 509, 511, 513
Howe, L. K., 28-29
Hoyt, D. R., 391
Hoyt, W. T., 411
Hrdy, S. B., 213, 218
Hsieh, K. H., 245, 249, 256
Hsien-Hen, L., 524
Hu, Y., 142, 144, 145
Huber, J., 160
Hudson, A. M., 549
Huesmann, L. R., 250
Hughes, M., 292
Hughes, R., 542, 549
Hughes, R., Jr., 514
Hui, C. H., 84
Hume, C. S., 98
Hunsberger, B., 420
Hunter, A. G., 232
Hunter, R., 472
Hunter, W. M., 233
Huston, A. C., 288-289
Huston, T. L., 104, 109, 110, 232
Hutchins, J., 452
Hutchinson, S., 220
Hyde, J. S., 158, 159, 160
Hyman, H. H., 143

Ihinger-Tallman, M., 232, 530
Illick, J., 36
Ingersoll-Dayton, B., 85
Ingoldsby, B., 544
Ionescu, M., 273
Ireland, M. S., 125
Isaac, M. K., 127
Isaacs, M., 358
Isaacs, M. B., 529
Isenberg, D. Y., 119
Ishii-Kuntz, M., 369, 377
Izard, C. E., 283, 284, 322

Jackson, D. D., 87
Jackson, M., 401, 405
Jacobs, F. H., 464, 547
Jacobson, C. K., 117, 119, 120, 121, 122
Jaenichen, U., 121
Jaggar, A. M., 194
James, S., 386, 389
Jamieson, L., 305, 308, 309
Jargowsky, P. A., 474, 476
Jarrett, R. L., 480
Jaya, J., 529
Jayakody, R., 90, 293, 353, 355
Jedlicka, D., 514
Jekielek, S. M., 161, 276
Jencius, M., 514
Jenkins, J. M., 291
Jenkins, P., 49
Jenkins, P. J., 540
Jenkins, S., 471
Jenks, R. J., 28, 30
Jennings, G., 514
Jensen, A. M., 303, 304
Jensen, P. S., 252
Jewell, T., 415, 417, 422
Jobe, T., 58, 69
John, D., 63, 161, 180, 181, 231
John, R., 386, 388, 389, 391
John, R. S., 248
Johnson, C., 292
Johnson, C. L., 128, 375
Johnson, D. P., 419
Johnson, D. R., 273-274, 415
Johnson, J. G., 510
Johnson, L., 482
Johnson, L. B., 178, 402, 403, 404
Johnson, Lyndon Baines, 469
Johnson, M. C., 375
Johnson, M. M., 214, 225
Johnson, M. P., 160
Johnson, P. J., 376
Johnson, R., 375

Johnson, S., 199
Johnson, T., 530
Johnson, V., 137, 417
Johnston, J., 443, 445
Johnston, J. R., 289
Jones, G. S., 497, 498
Jones, I., 65
Jones, J., 181, 183
Jones, K. W., 44
Jones, S., 509, 511, 513
Jones, W. H., 497, 498
Jorgensen, S. R., 543, 544, 545, 548
Jory, B., 528
Josselson, R., 182
Jouriles, E. N., 245, 529
Joyner, K., 63
Judy, R. W., 169
Juhari, R., 401
Julian, T. W., 372
Jung, M., 529
Jurich, A., 9

Kagan, J., 12
Kagan, S., 340
Kahn, A. J., 451, 452
Kalil, A., 63
Kalmijn, M., 60
Kalter, N., 293
Kamerman, S. B., 451, 452
Kamo, Y., 161, 377
Kanazawa, S., 121
Kanoy, K., 245, 248
Kanter, R. M., 31
Kaplan, G. A., 418, 420
Kaplan, H., 65
Karanik, T., 146
Karney, B. R., 104, 108
Karno, M., 336, 342
Kasen, S., 510
Kashy, D. A., 104, 110
Kassel, V., 28
Katz, J. E., 506
Katz, L. F., 244, 245, 248, 249, 256
Katz, S. N., 267, 269, 439
Katz Rothman, B., 499
Kaufman, D. R., 415, 419, 423
Kaufman, G., 120, 377
Kaufman, R. L., 476
Kawachi, I., 478
Kawamoto, W. T., 386, 387, 388, 389, 390
Kearl, M. C., 355
Kee, M., 391
Keefe, N., 163
Keefe, S., 336

Keim, R. E., 549
Keith, B., 271, 284, 285, 354, 357
Kelley, H., 80, 82, 83, 89
Kelley, P., 420
Kelley, R., 403
Kellogg, S., 39, 268
Kelly, J., xii, 248, 275, 276, 289, 319,
    320, 322, 357
Kelly, J. B., 270
Kelly, J. E., 68
Kelly, J. J., 146, 147
Kelly, P., 343
Kelly, W., 342
Kemmelmeier, M., 250, 338
Kemp, A. A., 540
Kendeler, K. S., 287
Kennedy, B. P., 478
Kennedy, E. L., 196
Kennedy, P., 418
Kenney, C. T., 57, 63, 71
Kenny, D. A., 104, 110
Kenrick, D. T., 96
Kenyon, E., 306
Kerber, L. K., 197
Kerbrat, V., 498, 500
Kerckhoff, R. K., 539
Kerr, M. A., 234
Kessler, R., 158
Kessler, R. C., 142, 144
Kett, J. F., 37, 45, 46, 47
Khan, M., 396
Kibria, N., 372, 373, 376
Kiernan, K. E., 59, 121, 122, 303,
    305, 314, 323
Kiernan, M., 231
Kiesler, S., 509, 511, 516
Kiesler, S. B., 514
Kim, H. K., 375
Kim, J. E., 325
Kimmel, D. C., 141
Kimmel, M., 225, 226, 228, 229
Kimond, M. F., 142
King, S. A., 513
Kingma, D. R., 201
Kingsbury, N., 7, 178
Kinnunen, U., 165
Kinsey, A., 137
Kinsey, A. C., 96
Kinsey, S. H., 68
Kirby, D., 549
Kirkpatrick, L., 362
Kirkpatrick, L. A., 420
Kirn, W., 274
Kitano, H. H., 371, 373

Kitayama, S., 251, 252
Kitson, G. C., 143, 267
Kitzmann, K. M., 283
Kivlahan, D. R., 391
Klawitter, M., 473
Klebanov, P. K., 478
Klein, D. M., 121
Klein, R. C. A., 546
Kline, M., 443, 445
Kline, S. L., 511
Klinkenberg, D., 107
Kluegel, J. R., 473
Knapp, N. F., 420, 422
Knight, G. P., 335, 344
Knitzer, J., 452
Knox, D., 324
Knudson-Martin, C., 528
Koball, E., 158
Koenig, H. G., 411, 413, 416, 419, 425
Koepke, L., 319
Kogan, S. M., 529
Kohn, M. L., 157
Kolars, C., 395
Kolker, A., 496
Kollock, P., 108
Komarovsky, M., 164
Komter, A., 185
Koropeckyj-Cox, T., 128
Kosinski, F. A., Jr., 415
Koso, G., 325
Kotch, J. B., 233
Kovatcheva, S., 310
Koven, S., 455
Kowaleski-Jones, L., 66, 284, 293
Kraemer, S., 528
Krause, H., 434
Kraut, R. E., 509, 511, 512, 516
Kreber, C., 550
Kreider, R. M., 318, 354
Krieger, S., 195, 198
Krishnan, V., 119, 120, 121, 122
Kumashiro, M., 108, 110
Kuo, W. H., 373
Kuppermann, M., 497
Kurdek, L. A., 99, 101, 102, 103, 104,
    105-106, 107, 108, 109, 110, 181, 271,
    284, 285, 322
Kurokawa, T., 85
Kurtines, W., 337
Kwong, P., 479

Lackey, G., 17
Lackey, N. R., 501
Ladd-Taylor, M., 457

LaFromboise, T. D., 387, 389, 391
Laird, J., 100
Lamarine, R. J., 391
LaMastro, V., 125
Lamb, K., 65-66
Lamb, M., 339
Lamb, M. E., 180, 230, 231, 232,
    233, 234, 237
Lambert, S. J., 167
Lampman, C., 125
Lancaster, J. B., 65
Land, H., 303
Landale, N. S., 63, 64, 178
Landau, R., 500
Laney, M. C., 509, 510
Lang, A., 200
Lang, E., 159
Langabeer, K. A., 97
Langhinrichsen-Rohling, J., 255
Langrock, A., 246, 257
Lansford, J. E., 284, 289, 291, 325
Laosa, L. M., 341
Lapeyre, F., 477
Lapp, A. L., 256
Lareau, A., 178
LaRossa, R., 182, 225, 226, 228, 229
Larsen, A., 126
Larsen, E., 31, 32, 511
Larsen, R. J., 362
Larson, D. B., 411, 413, 416, 419, 425
Larson, R., 182
Larson, R. W., 289, 292
Laszloffy, T. A., 529
Latshaw, J. S., 419
Laumann, E. O., 67, 96, 418
Laumann-Billings, L., 255, 283, 285
Lawrence, E., 255
Lawrence, K., 411
Lawrence, P., 401
Lawson, D. M., 126
Lawton, L. E., 412
Layne, C., 186
Laythe, B., 420
Lazarus, P., 339
Le, N., 462
Leasure, J. W., 121
Leber, D., 548
Lecerf, J., 399
Lederer, W. J., 87
Lee, G. R., 138, 139, 141, 142
Lee, J. W., 421
Lee, R., 180
Lee, S. M., 373
Lee, V. E., 285

Leffler, A., 164
Legg, B. H., 529
Lehrer, E., 121
Lehrer, E. L., 416
Leibfried, S., 473
Leidenfrost, N. B., 478
Lein, L., 184, 479
Leisering, L., 473
Lendich, B., 246
Lenhart, A., 511
Leon, G., 358
Leong, F. T. L., 375
Leong, R., 378
Leridon, H., 70
Lerman, R. I., 358
Lerman, R. L., 437, 438
LeRoy, B. S., 495, 496, 497, 499
Leslie, G. I., 498
Leslie, L. A., 181, 527, 528
Lesthaeghe, R., 62, 306, 308
Letherby, G., 117
Levenson, R. W., 108, 139
Lever, J., 103, 107
Levin, J. S., 413, 421, 422
Levine, D., 8
Levine, J., 230, 231, 232, 234
Levinger, G., 83
Levi-Strauss, C., 16
Levitt, E. E., 30
Levy, B., 39
Levy, I., 284
Lewis, E., 353, 359
Lewis, I., 233
Lewis, J., 253, 254, 283, 303
Lewis, J. M., 274, 357
Lewis, O., 474, 475, 479
Lewis, R. A., 527
Lewis, S., 216
Lewis-Rowley, M., 539, 544
Leyendecker, B., 334, 337, 339, 344
Libby, R. W., 29
Liberson, S., 371
Lichter, D. T., 60, 63-64, 178, 179,
    181, 473, 478
Lieberman, B. E., 127
Liefbroer, A. C., 67, 70
Lillard, L. A., 57, 70, 122, 126, 360
Lim, N., 60
Lin, I. L., 64
Lin, N., 16
Lindahl, K. M., 246
Lindenmeyer, K., 43, 44, 454, 456
Linder, E. W., 412
Lindholm, B. W., 544

Linney, K. D., 451, 452, 453, 462
Lipman, E. L., 282, 283
Lippman-Hand, A., 496
Li-Shou, Y., 321
Litrownik, A. J., 234
Litwak, E., 127
Liu-Constant, Y., 251
Livi, S., 32
Livingstone, S., 510
Llabre, M. M., 127
Locke, H. J., 267, 269
Lodewijckx, E., 303, 308
Loeber, R., 289
Logan, J. R., 321
London, A. S., 325
London, J., 164
Long, B., 271
Loosley, E., 6
Lopez, I. R., 252
López, L., 343
Lorber, J., 214
Lorde, A., 193, 199
Lorenz, F. O., 165, 480
Loulan, J., 103
Lu, H. H., 57, 59, 60, 61-62, 66
Luborsky, M., 127
Luepnitz, D. A., 289, 526
Lugones, M., 200
Lund, D. A., 140, 142
Lundmark, V., 509, 511
Lunneborg, P., 124, 125
Lupfer, M. B., 420
Lupri, E., 126
Luschen, K., 161
Lykken, D. T., 294
Lynch, J. M., 106, 319, 320
Lynd, H. M., 507
Lynd, R. S., 507
Lyon, K. B., 412

MacCallum, F., 494, 497, 498, 500, 501
Maccoby, E. E., 235, 245, 248, 249, 289,
    290, 322, 340
MacDermid, S. M., 162, 167
MacDonald, W. L., 320, 321
Mace, D. R., 542-543
Mace, V., 542-543
MacEwen, K. E., 158
Mackey, R. A., 104
Mackey, W. C., 236
Macklin, E. D., ix, x, xi, 10, 13, 27,
    57, 59, 317, 540
Macleod, A., 396
Macleod, D. I., 43, 45, 46, 47

Macoby, E., 162
MacPhee, D., 528
Madsen, M. C., 340
Madsen, R., 270, 425
Madsen, T. G., 411
Magelsdorf, S. C., 256
Maguen, S., 97
Maguire, M. C., 159, 167
Mahoney, A., 252, 253, 254, 255, 411, 413,
    415, 416, 417, 418, 421, 422, 424, 528
Mahoney, M., 436
Maines, D., 7
Majumdar, D., 57
Males, M. A., 50
Malia, S., 502, 503
Malik, N. M., 246
Malley, J. E., 291, 357
Malone, J., 528
Mandel, J. B., 106
Manke, B., 165-166
Mann, B. J., 245
Mann, S. A., 540
Mannetti, L., 104, 110
Manning, W. D., 57, 58, 59, 60, 63-64,
    65-66, 70, 230, 283
Manson, S. M., 389, 391
Manting, D., 58, 304, 308
Mapes, D., 125
Marchioro, K., 231, 290
Marciano, T. D., 6, 8, 9, 413
Marcus, E. M., 246
Marcus, J., 397
Mare, R. D., 71, 353
Maretzki, T., 373
Margolin, G., 248
Margolin, L., 233
Margolis, D. R., 183
Margolis, M. L., 211, 214-215
Marin, B. V., 251
Marin, G., 251
Marina, D., 336
Markham, H., 531, 548
Markides, K. S., 422
Markman, H., 543, 547
Marks, L. D., 413, 419
Marks, N. F., 321
Marks, S. R., 199
Marmer, J. K., 232, 234
Marotz-Baden, R., 272
Marshall, H., 213, 215, 220
Marshall, N. L., 157, 159, 163, 166-167
Marshall, V. W., 128
Marsiglio, W., 16, 156, 180, 220,
    230, 232, 234, 237

Martin, C., 137
Martin, C. E., 96
Martin, J., 162
Martin, J. A., 62, 283, 355
Martin, K. J., 549
Martin, M., 287
Martin, S. S. K., 541
Martin, T. C., 142, 275, 287, 318-319
Martinez, C. R., 289
Martinez, R., 340
Martin-Mathews, A., 127
Marx, F., 163
Marx, K., 476
Masciadrelli, B. P., 225, 230, 231,
    232, 233, 234
Mason, C., 375
Mason, C. A., 461
Mason, J., 312
Mason, M. A., 434, 435, 436, 438, 443, 444
Mass, A. I., 375
Massey, D. S., 475-476
Masten, A. S., 256
Masters, K. S., 415
Masters, W. H., 137, 417
Mathews, L., 370-371
Mathews, R., 127
Mathews, S. H., 182
Matthews, D., 7, 10
Matthews, J. M., 549
Matthews, T. J., 355
Mattison, A. M., 100-101, 102, 103, 107
Maughan, A., 248, 253, 257
Mauno, S., 165
Maurer, J. D., 283
Maushart, S., 212
Maxwell, J. W., 143
May, E., 120, 122, 123
Maynard, R. A., 479
Mays, V. M., 104, 107
Mazur, R., 29
McAdoo, H. P., 345, 400, 414, 422
McBride, B. A., 232, 233
McBride, T. D., 144
McCabe, S. B., 292
McCarthy Veach, P., 497, 499
McCartney, K., 158, 163, 220
McCollum, E. E., 527
McCord, J., 461, 463
McCrae, R. R., 143, 144
McCrary, C., 417, 418, 420, 422
McCubbin, H., 126
McCullough, M. E., 411, 413, 416,
    417, 419, 425
McDaniel, A., 228

McDaniel, S., 493
McDaniel, S. H., 528
McDermott, J., 373
McDermott, J. F., 270
McDonald, E., 125
McDonald, G. W., 80, 82, 83, 85
McDonald, J., 268
McDonald, R., 245
McGoldrick, M., 400, 402, 526
McGonagle, K., 167
McGue, M., 294
McHale, J. P., 248
McHale, S. M., 159, 161, 162, 232
McHenry, P. C., 292
McIntosh, M., 176
McIntosh, P., 193, 195
McIrvin, S., 400, 402
McKay, G., 542
McKelvey, M. W., 372
McKenna, K. Y. A., 508
McKenry, P. C., 372, 375, 543
McLanahan, S. S., 64-66, 126, 144, 183, 234,
    235, 275, 277, 284, 285, 288, 289, 292,
    293, 321, 322, 437, 481, 530, 531
McLaughlin, C. S., 271
McLaughlin, S. D., 121
McLeod, J. D., 478
McLloyd, V., 91
McLoyd, V. C., 161, 165, 288-289, 292, 342
McMahon, C. A., 498
McMahon, M., 214, 215, 216
McMullen, P. A., 142
McMullin, J. A., 124, 127, 128
McMurrer, D. P., 478
McNally, J., 70
McNamara, J., 325
McNeil, D. W., 391
McQuillan, J., 181
McRae, C., 275
McRoy, R. G., 502
McShane, B., 388
McWhinnie, A., 500, 501
McWhirter, D. P., 100-101, 102, 103, 107
Mead, L., 473
Mead, M., 5, 9, 14, 15
Mederer, H. J., 181
Mekos, D., 321
Melli, M., 454
Melton, J. G., 411, 412, 421, 423
Menacker, F., 62, 355
Menaghan, E. G., 157, 161, 162, 165, 284
Menjivar, C., 375, 376
Merkle, E. R., 509
Mernissi, F., 397

Messinger, H., 471
Messinger, L., 319, 529
Messner, M., 229
Meyer, C. J., 540
Meyer, J. A., 144
Meyer-Bahlburg, H. F. L., 98
Mezirow, J., 550
Miall, C. E., 125
Michael, R. T., 60, 63, 67, 87-88, 96, 418
Michaels, S., 67, 96, 418
Michel, S., 455
Mickelson, K. D., 513-514
Micklin, M., 121
Middleton, S., 477
Millar, J., 310
Miller, A., 334, 337, 344
Miller, B. C., 513
Miller, E., 8
Miller, J. G., 250, 340
Miller, J. K., 513
Miller, L. F., 318
Miller, N. B., 143
Miller, S. H., 547
Miller, S. L., 542
Miller, S. M., 472
Miller, W. B., 125
Miller, W. R., 543
Miller-McLemore, B. J., 412
Mills, G., 233
Mills, J., 451, 452, 453, 462
Mills, T. L., 324
Min, P. G., 376
Minkler, M., 355, 363
Mintz, S., 39, 226, 227, 268
Mir-Hosseini, Z., 397, 404
Mirowsky, J., 160
Mishel, L., 236
Mistry, R. S., 288-289
Mitchell-Kernan, C., 89, 90-91, 352, 353, 356
Mitrani, V. B., 252
Miyake, K., 251
Mnookin, R. H., 235, 248
Moen, P., 168, 216, 453, 454
Moffitt, R., 474
Moffitt, R. M., 63
Moffitt, T. E., 288
Mohanty, C. T., 193, 195
Mokhtarian, P. C., 512
Monach, J. H., 127
Monroe, P. A., 268, 269
Mont, D. M., 442
Montgomery, T. R., 497, 498
Moore, A. M., 480

Moore, J. W., 339, 342, 343
Moore, N. B., 32
Moore, W., 476
Moorman, J. E., 318
Moreggi, D., 513
Morell, C., 122, 123, 127
Morelli, G., 251
Morgaine, C. A., 545
Morgan, D., 302, 306, 312
Morgan, E. S., 38
Morgan, M., 516
Morgan, R., 195, 197
Morgan, S. P., 117-118, 120, 232, 290
Morris, J. E., 230
Morris, J. F., 99, 100, 106, 107
Morrison, A., 286
Morrison, D. R., 63-64, 285, 291, 323
Morrison, T., 194
Morrison, V., 319
Morten, L., 15
Mortimer, J. T., 164
Mosely, J., 321
Mosher, W. D., 59, 60, 68, 79, 86-87, 118, 318, 355, 419, 442
Mosley, J., 64-65, 234
Moss, J. J., 539, 544
Mott, F. L., 284, 358
Mouton-Sanders, M., 401
Mowrer, E. R., 267
Moyer, A., 497
Moynihan, D. P., 460, 461, 464
Mudd, E., 8, 12
Mueller, K. A., 125
Muenke, M., 496
Muir-Malcolm, J. A., 252
Mukophadyay, T., 509, 511
Muller, C., 163
Muller, G. O., 143
Munro, B., 272
Munro, G., 272
Murdock, G. P., 32, 176
Murphy, M., 303
Murr, A., 32
Murray, C., 473, 498
Murray, C. I., 98, 99, 200
Murray, N. P., 201
Murray, V. M., 256
Murray-Swank, A., 422
Murray-Swank, N., 422
Murrell, S. A., 142
Murry, V. M., 105
Murstein, B., 30
Muschkin, C., 342
Musick, M. A., 416, 420

Muxen, M., 126
Muzio, C., 530
Myers, E., 29
Myers, G., 342
Myers, R. L., 247
Myers, S., 119, 120, 121, 122
Mykkanen, A., 494

Nachtigal, M., 496
Nagata, D., 373
Nagel, S. K., 161
Nagoshi, C., 375
Nagourney, E., 432
Napier, A., 528
Nasaw, D., 41, 47
Nasir, J., 396, 397, 399
Nason, E. M., 116
Nastasi, B. K., 271
Nathanson, C. A., 121
Nauta, M. J., 547
Neal, J. H., 528
Neale, B., 305, 310
Neale, J. M., 292
Nee, V., 371
Nelson, J., 359
Nelson, S., 65-66
Nelson, T. S., 527
Neugarten, B. L., 136
Neuwalder, H. F., 98
Newberry, A. M., 528
Newburger, E. C., 507
Newcomb, M. D., 98
Newell, L. D., 420
Newman, J., 30
Newman, K., 475
Nichols, W. C., 121
Nielsen, F., 342
Nielsen, J. M., 193
Niermeijer, M. F., 496
Nimer, M., 395
Nimkoff, M. F., 507
Nisbet, R. A., 5
Nobles, A., 401
Nock, S. L., 58, 63, 67, 119, 216, 234, 273, 319
Nolan, J., 540
Nord, C. W., 290, 291
Norman, R., 340
Norton, A. J., 60, 67, 317, 318
Norwood, W. D., 245
Notarius, C. I., 91
Notaro, P. C., 292
Nunnally, E., 9
Nunnally, E. W., 542

Nydell, M. K., 401, 405
Nye, F. I., 81, 82

Oakley, A., 209
Oberman, Y., 182
O'Brien, B. A., 104
O'Bryant, S. L., 142, 144
O'Connell, M., 117, 232, 525
O'Connell, P. L., 508
O'Connor, A., 473, 483
O'Connor, M., 140, 147, 481
O'Connor, S., 42
O'Connor, T. G., 165, 284, 320
Odem, M. E., 47
Oertwein, M., 542, 547
Oetting, E. R., 388
Offord, D. R., 282, 283
Ogburn, W. F., 507
Ogden, P., 306
Okagaki, L., 341
Olasky, M., 473
O'Leary, K. D., 255, 528
O'Leary, S. G., 253
Olivennes, F., 498, 500
Olsen, S. F., 420
Olson, D., 6, 126
Olson, D. H., 32
Olson, J. R., 451, 452, 453, 462
Olson, L., 321, 325
Olson, M. E., 527
O'Mara, J., 509
O'Neil, R., 161
O'Neill, G., 25, 28, 59
O'Neill, N., 25, 28
Ong, P., 376, 379
Ooms, T., 92, 273, 451, 452, 453, 454, 461, 464, 530
Opitz, W., 342
Oppenheimer, V. K., 60, 61, 362
Orchard, A. L., 320
Ordona, T., 378
Ordonez, N., 375
Orleans, M., 509, 510
Oropesa, R. S., 59, 60, 64, 179, 181, 231
Orshansky, M., 470
Orthner, D. K., 288
Ory, M. G., 119
Osako, M. M., 371, 376, 377
Osborne, L. N., 292
Osmond, M. W., 178, 195
Oswald, R. F., 99, 108
Otto, H., 4, 5-6
Otto, H. A., 28
Owen, L. D., 254

Oyen, E., 472
Oyserman, D., 250, 338
Oz, S., 529
Ozer, E., 387
Ozer, E. M., 233

Pace-Nichols, M. A., 121
Pachon, H., 342, 343
Paden, S. L., 158
Padgett, D. L., 232
Padilla, A., 335, 336
Page, S., 452
Pagnini, D. L., 419
Pahl, R., 16
Palkovitz, R., 230, 415, 419
Pang, G. Y., 373, 374
Pankhurst, J. G., 411, 412-413, 415, 422
Papdopoulos, F., 477
Papp, P., 526, 532
Pappas, G., 478
Parcel, T. L., 157, 161, 162, 165
Pardee, J. W., 273
Pardo, M., 182
Pargament, K. I., 252, 255, 411, 413, 415, 416,
    417, 418, 421, 422, 424
Park, K. S., 377
Park, M. M., 62
Park, M. P., 355
Parke, M., 92, 273
Parke, R. D., 226, 229, 230, 231, 232, 233,
    234, 235, 386, 390, 391, 414, 453, 529
Parker, R. G., 196, 198
Parkman, A. M., 269
Parks, M. R., 508
Parmenter, R., 96, 109
Parnell, A. M., 419
Parsons, T., 3, 8, 178
Pasley, K., 232, 530
Passel, J., 343
Pasta, D. J., 125
Patterson, C. J., 101, 106, 108, 109, 177,
    198, 444
Patterson, G. R., 106, 284
Patterson, M., 509, 511
Patterson, O., 90
Patton, M. Q., 549
Peabody, S. A., 30
Pearce, D., 217-218
Pearce, J., 400, 402, 526
Pearson, J., 435
Peck, K., 87
Peek, C., 319
Peiss, K. L., 47
Penalosa, F., 343

Pendleton, B. F., 417
Peng, S. S., 372
Penn, P., 527, 528
Peplau, L. A., 96, 98, 101, 103, 104, 107, 110
Perez, L., 413
Peris, T. S., 293
Perry, J. D., 271
Perry, T. L., 442
Perry-Jenkins, M., 156, 157, 160-161,
    162, 164, 181, 220
Peters, H. E., 69
Peters, K. D., 283
Peterson, G., 23
Peterson, J. A., 417
Peterson, J. L., 284, 291
Peterson, P., 494
Petit, G. S., 256
Pettengill, S., 250
Pevar, S. L., 386, 390
Phifer, J. F., 142
Phillips, D., 158, 220
Phillips, J. A., 60
Phillips, K. R., 481
Phinney, J. S., 336, 338, 340, 342
Phoenix, A., 122
Phua, V. C., 377
Pickthall, M., 398
Piercy, F. P., 528
Pierro, A., 104, 110
Pinderhughes, E. B., 90
Pinnelli, A., 304
Pinsoff, W. M., 87, 89
Piore, M. J., 476
Piskurich, G. M., 512
Pittman, F., 528
Pitts, J. R., 8, 11
Pitts, S. C., 248, 251-252
Planos, R., 341
Platt, A. M., 41
Pleck, E. H., 43, 226, 227, 228
Pleck, J. H., 157, 159, 160, 166-167, 182, 225,
    226, 227, 228, 229, 230, 231, 232, 233,
    234, 237
Plotnick, R., 473
Polikoff, N. D., 440
Pollard, M. S., 127, 128
Poloma, M. M., 116, 417
Polonko, K., 11, 176
Pomeroy, W., 137
Ponjaert, I., 107
Pooringa, Y. H., 250
Popenoe, D., 4, 6, 7, 10, 11, 12, 87, 175, 236,
    237, 274, 283, 294
Popenoe, P., 116, 118-119

Porter, C. A., 391
Portes, A., 16, 337
Portner, J., 494
Poston, D. L., 120
Pott, M., 251
Potter, R. G., 419
Poulin, F., 461, 463
Powell, L., 538, 542, 544, 546, 547
Powers, P., 462
Pratt, E. L., 411
Pratt, W., 118
Preli, R., 529
Preloran, H. M., 497
Prescott, C., 287
Prescott, H. M., 43
Presser, H. B., 162-163, 232, 324
Preston, S. H., 268
Price-Bonham, S., 317, 325
Price-Williams, D., 340, 341, 342
Prinz, C., 304
Prosser, W. R., 461
Prouty, A., 528
Pruett, K. D., 236
Pugliesi, K. L., 182
Putnam, R., 17, 480
Putnam, R. D., 511
Putney, C., 46
Pyke, K., 319, 377

Quam, J. K., 147
Queen, S., 478
Quintana, S. S., 338
Qureshi, R., 400, 402
Qvortrup, J., 309

Rabo, A., 397
Raboy, B., 101
Radhakrishna, A., 233, 234
Ragoné, H., 218
Rainie, L., 509, 511, 513
Rainwater, L., 6, 471, 472, 480
Raley, R. K., 60, 61, 62, 317
Ramberg, J. A., 418
Ramey, J., 29
Ramírez, M., 338, 340, 341, 342
Rampage, C., 92
Ramsey, E., 284
Rand, Y., 340
Rane, T., 232, 233
Ranjit, N., 69
Rank, M. R., 471, 472, 473, 474, 477,
    482, 483
Raphael, J., 146
Rasmussen, W. D., 543, 546

Ratcliff, K. S., 160
Raudenbush, S. W., 159, 166-167, 480
Raughman, R., 69
Raval, H., 127
Rawlings, S. W., 524
Ray, L. A., 422
Raymo, J., 60
Raymond-Smith, L., 252
Rayner, R., 30
Read, J., 401
Reagon, B. J., 199
Real, T., 528
Reddy, M., 387
Red Horse, J., 389, 391
Redlinger-Grosse, K., 496
Regan, M. C., Jr., 433
Reichman, N. E., 277
Reimann, R., 220
Reinier, J. S., 40
Reisen, C., 401, 405
Reiss, D., 321, 325, 418, 420
Remafedi, G., 97
Rendall, M. S., 69
Renne, K. S., 319
Repetti, R. L., 156, 157, 162, 220
Resnick, M., 97
Resnick, M. D., 388
Reuter, M. A., 288
Revelle, R., 63
Rezac, S. J., 290, 291
Rheingold, H., 506
Rhoden, L., 530
Ribbens McCarthy, J., 310
Rice, G. T., 421
Rich, A., 194, 212
Richardson, J. H., 30
Richardson, R. A., 509
Richlin, L., 549
Riger, S., 193, 195
Riis, J., 478
Rimmer, R. H., 26
Rist, R. C., 462, 463
Ritakallio, V. M., 477
Ritualo, A., 63-64
Rivera, F., 234
Rivera-Mosquera, E. T., 252
Rivers, I., 98
Rivers, R. M., 16, 17
Roberto, K. A., 195
Roberts, J. M., 528
Roberts, L. D., 508
Roberts, M. D., 182
Roberts, R. E., 418
Robila, M., 325

Robins, P., 323
Robinson, J., 179, 180
Robinson, L. C., 416
Rodgers, B., 387, 388, 390
Rodgers, W. L., 353
Rodman, H., 83, 540
Rodríguez, G., 343
Rodstein, E., 529-530
Roe, K. M., 355, 363
Rogers, S. J., 158, 159, 179, 183, 273-274, 479
Rohner, R., 250
Romney, P., 527
Room, G., 477
Roopnarine, J. L., 181, 231, 232, 358
Roosa, M. W., 248, 251-252
Root, M., 375
Rorabaugh, W. J., 39
Rose, S., 107
Roseman, E., 443
Rosen, L. R., 98
Rosenbaum, A., 528
Rosenblatt, P. C., 494, 540
Rosner, T. T., 182
Ross, C. E., 160
Ross, D., 46
Ross, E., 210, 212, 214
Ross, R., 463
Rosser, S. V., 194, 195
Rossi, A. S., 185, 214
Rossi, P. H., 185
Roth, M., 30
Roth, S., 530
Rothbaum, F., 251
Rothblum, E. D., 99, 100, 106, 107
Rothenberg, P. S., 194
Rotheram-Borus, M., 340
Rotheram-Borus, M. J., 97
Rothman, B. K., 218
Rothstein, B., 267, 270
Rothstein, K., 252
Rouse, L., 23
Rovi, S., 117, 118, 119, 120, 121-122
Rowland, D., 128
Rowntree, B. S., 472
Roy, D., 24, 28
Roy, R., 24, 28
Rozmus, C., 401
Rubin, K. H., 251
Rubin, L., 178
Rubin, L. B., 164
Rubin, N., 211
Rubin, R. H., ix, x, xi, 10, 13, 26, 27
Rubinstein, R. L., 127, 145, 146
Ruddick, S., 202, 214

Rueschenberg, E., 336, 344
Rufat, P., 498, 500
Ruh, J., 163
Ruiz, D. S., 355
Ruiz, R., 343
Ruiz, S. Y., 251
Rumbaut, R., 334, 336, 337, 344, 346
Runkel, G., 417
Rusbult, C. E., 108, 110
Russell, S. T., 97, 98, 200
Rutter, M., 165, 497, 498, 500
Ryan, C., 99, 324
Ryan, C. M., 529
Ryan, M. P., 40

Sabatelli, R. M., 80, 81, 82, 83, 85
Saenz, D., 335, 344
Saenz, R., 165
Sage, G. P., 387, 388
Sager, C., 529-530
Sager, D. E., 514
Sagi, P. C., 419
Said, E., 400
Saint-Jacques, M., 321
Saito, M., 85
Saldaña, D. H., 336, 344
Salem, D. A., 292
Salomon, I., 512
Salts, C. J., 542
Saman, S. A., 472
Sampson, R. J., 480
Sanchez, L., 185, 217, 273
Sánchez-Ayendez, M., 334, 340, 341
Sanday, P. R., 225, 226
Sandberg, J. F., 163, 231
Sandefur, F., 275
Sandefur, G., 183, 234, 235, 284, 285, 288, 292, 293, 322, 437, 481, 531
Sanders, M., 340
Sanders, R., 231
Sanders, S., 59, 524
Sandifer-Stech, D. M., 546
Sandy, J., 322
Santisteban, D. A., 252
Santrock, J. W., 291
Saracino, M., 542
Sargent, K. P., 232
Sassler, S., 58, 69, 70
Satlow, M. L., 422
Saunders, D. M., 498
Savin-Williams, R. C., 97, 98, 99
Sawhill, I. V., 478
Sawhney, S., 195
Sayer, L. C., 58

Scanzoni, J., 7, 9, 11, 15, 16, 17, 18, 83, 176, 178
Scarisbrick-Hauser, A., 145, 146
Scarr, S., 158, 220
Schacht, J., 398
Schafer, J., 416
Scharlott, B. W., 508
Schenker, J. G., 495, 502
Scherlis, B., 509
Scherlis, W., 509, 511
Schiller, B. R., 474, 480-481
Schlesinger, B., 119
Schlesinger, R., 119
Schlossberger, E. S., 422
Schmaus, G., 471
Schmidt, L. C., 289
Schmiege, C. J., 185
Schmitt, J. P., 103
Schneider, E. C., 42
Schneider, J. P., 509
Schnitzer, P. K., 528
Schoen, R., 60, 121, 138, 141, 283
Schoenbach, V. J., 284
Schoenmaeckers, R., 303, 308
Schoenrade, P., 417, 420
Scholz, J., 340
Schooler, C., 157
Schoppe, S., 232, 233
Schor, J. B., 144, 162
Schorr, A. L., 453, 454
Schrag, R. D. A., 293
Schreiner, M., 482
Schreurs, K. M. G., 104
Schultz, D., 283, 284, 322
Schumm, W., 401
Schuster, M. A., 103, 107
Schvaneveldt, J. D., 539, 542, 544, 545, 547
Schwartz, J., 473
Schwartz, J. D., 340
Schwartz, L. A., 269
Schwartz, P., 58, 63, 68, 99, 100, 101, 103, 104, 106, 108, 180, 181, 185
Schwartz, S., 84
Sciarra, D., 401
Scoon-Rogers, L., 235
Scott, E., 415, 417, 422
Scott, J. P., 139
Scott, K. G., 461
Sears, H. A., 158, 159
Seccombe, K., 119, 121, 141, 142, 184, 473, 478
Sedlak, A. J., 480
Seeley, J. R., 6
Segal, M. L., 420

Segall, M. H., 250
Seif, H., 97, 98
Sells, J. N., 417
Seltzer, J. A., 58, 59, 63, 64, 217, 234, 235, 290, 436
Selznick, P., 8
Sen, A., 477
Serovich, J. M., 530
Sgritta, G., 309
Shackelford, T. K., 362
Shaffer, S. K., 142
Shanahan, J., 516
Shanahan, M. J., 478
Shapiro, A. F., 126
Sheeber, L., 245, 247, 254
Sheehan, R., 547
Shehan, C. L., 80, 82, 83, 138, 139
Sheinberg, M., 527, 528
Shelton, B. A., 63, 161, 180, 181, 185, 231
Shema, S. J., 418, 420
Sherif, B., 400, 422
Sherkat, D. E., 411, 413, 415, 417
Sherman, A., 478
Sherman, R. C., 508
Sherraden, M., 481-482
Sheth, K., 287
Shields, C. G., 528
Shinagawa, L. H., 373, 374
Shinar, O., 322
Shirk, M., 480
Shore, E. A., 530
Shulman, A. D., 140
Sica, A., 415
Siegel, A. J., 444
Siegler, I. C., 143, 144
Silverstein, E., 146
Silverstein, L. B., 224, 232, 234, 236-237
Silverstein, M., 141, 185
Silverstein, O., 526, 532
Sim, J. J., 177
Sim, R. A., 6
Simmons, T., 59
Simon, R. I., 193
Simons, R., 322
Simons, R. L., 127, 161, 256, 288, 290, 291, 292
Simpson, B., 312
Simpson, W. S., 418
Sinclair, R., 322
Sinclair, R. J., 284
Singer, A. T. B., 249
Singer, J., 442
Skinner, C., 310
Sklar, K. K., 454, 455, 456, 465

Skocpol, T., 454, 455, 459, 463, 465
Skolnick, A., 10, 12
Slade, P., 127
Sleet, D., 386, 389
Slep, A. M., 253
Slobodnik, A. J., 528
Smailes, E. M., 510
Small, M. L., 475
Small, S. A., 546
Smart, C., 305, 310
Smeeding, T. A., 471, 472, 480, 481
Smerglia, V. L., 143
Smith, B., 413
Smith, C., 233
Smith, C. A., 514
Smith, D. E., 176
Smith, E. R., 473
Smith, J., 292, 403
Smith, J. A., 456, 464
Smith, J. P., 478
Smith, J. R., 29, 478, 479
Smith, K. B., 473
Smith, K. R., 141, 144
Smith, L., 106
Smith, L. G., 29
Smith, M. A., 291
Smith, S., 544
Smith, T., 394, 395
Smith, T. A., 546
Smith, W. L., 31, 33
Smith-Rosenberg, C., 196
Smock, P. J., 57, 58, 59, 60, 62, 70, 177, 230, 283
Snarey, J., 232, 234
Snarey, J. R., 419, 422
Solberg, K. B., 320
Solnit, A., 443
Soltis, J. F., 539
Somers, M. D., 126, 360
Somerville, R. M., 546
Sommerfeldt, V., 424
Sorell, G., 319
Sorensen, A., 144
Sorensen, E., 358
Sorenson, A. M., 414
Sorenson, E., 481
Soukup, C., 321, 325
South, S. J., 63, 180, 181
Sowell, T., 371
Spain, D., 137, 146, 179, 185
Spalding, L. R., 103, 110
Spanier, G. B., 59
Spector, R. G., 438
Spender, D., 194

Sperling, J., 233
Spickard, P. R., 374
Spilka, B., 140, 420
Spiller, L. C., 245
Spitze, G., 63, 160, 180, 181, 216, 321
Spooner, T., 511
Sportolari, L., 508
Sprague, J., 194
Sprenkle, D. H., 547
Sproull, L., 514
St. Peters, M., 548
Stacey, J., 11, 106, 175, 201, 237, 275, 415, 423
Stack, C., 359
Stack, C. B., 479
Stafford, L., 104, 511
Stage, S., 456, 465
Stahmann, R. F., 542
Staines, G. L., 463
Standish, N., 283
Stanley, S., 531, 543, 547, 548
Stanley-Hagan, M. M., 235, 284
Stansell, C., 41
Stark, R., 411, 421, 423, 425, 426
Starr, B., 137
Starrels, M. E., 181, 182
Stayton, W. R., 32
Steil, J. M., 158
Stein, H. F., 529
Steinberg, L., 335, 337, 344
Steiner, G., 4
Steinmetz, S., 23
Steinmetz, S. K., 250, 480
Stekel, W., 267
Sternberg, R., 341
Steuve, J. L., 232
Stevens, A. H., 470, 471
Stewart, A. J., 194, 284, 289, 291, 325, 357
Stewart, S., 324
Stewart, S. D., 290
Stiles, R. J., 539, 544
Stimson, C., 310
Stocker, C. M., 248, 249, 256
Stoll, B., 325
Stoll, C., 506
Stoller, E. P., 182
Stoller, F. H., 17
Stolley, K. S., 442
Stolzenberg, R. M., 63
Stone, C., 394, 395
Stone, G., 543
Stone, L., 3
Stone, L. H., 473

Stoneman, Z., 249, 252, 417, 418, 419, 420, 422
Storaasli, R. D., 547
Storrs, L. R. Y., 45
Stout, J. A., 417, 422
Straus, M. A., 250, 480
Straw, L. B., 144
Strawbridge, W. J., 418, 420
Strohmeier, K., 304
Strong, B., 494
Strong, C., 389
Stubben, J. D., 391
Stull, D. E., 145, 146
Sturgess, W., 320
Styles, C. B., 292
Suárez-Orozco, C., 335, 337, 344, 346
Suárez-Orozco, M., 335, 337, 344, 346
Sudarkasa, N., 354
Sudarshan, C. Y., 127
Sudia, C. E., 271
Sue, D., 371
Sue, S., 371, 379
Sugarman, S., 437
Sugarman, S. D., 12
Sullivan, K. T., 415, 421, 422
Sullivan, W. M., 270, 425
Sun, R., 283
Sun, Y., 288
Sung, B. L., 373, 374
Super, C. M., 84
Supple, A., 322
Surrey, J. L., 217
Sussman, M. B., ix, x, xi, 4, 6, 10, 23, 29, 30, 57
Sutton, J., 42
Sutton, P. D., 62
Swank, A. B., 252, 255, 411, 413, 415, 416, 417, 418, 421, 422, 424
Swank, P. R., 245
Swanson, C., 108, 548
Swanson, K., 108
Sweeney, M., 325
Sweeney, M. M., 60
Sweet, J. A., 58, 59, 60, 61, 64, 67, 69, 79, 142, 148, 275, 287, 317, 318-319, 361
Swidler, A., 270
Swindler, A., 425
Szapocznik, J., 252, 337
Szasz, M. C., 387-388
Szczypula, J., 509
Szinovacz, M., 11

Tacheuchi, D., 91
Takagi, D. Y., 378, 380

Takaki, R., 369
Takala, E., 508
Takeuchi, D., 165, 342
Tamang, B. L., 250
Tamis-LeMonda, C., 232, 233
Tarakeshwar, N., 252, 255, 411, 413, 416, 418, 421, 422, 424
Targ, D. B., 167
Taris, T., 119, 122
Taswell, H. F., 501
Taubin, S., 8, 12
Taylor, A., 325
Taylor, K. M., 117, 119, 120, 121, 122
Taylor, L., 59, 524
Taylor, P. L., 356
Taylor, R. J., 293, 338, 353, 355, 359, 414, 422
Teachman, J. D., 11, 71, 176, 180, 282, 317
Tedrow, L. M., 180, 282
Teitler, J. O., 277, 287, 323
Telles, C., 336, 342
Terman, L. M., 267
Tevlin, J., 32
Thelen, M., 96
Thibaut, J., 80, 82, 83, 89
Thomas, D. L., 413, 421, 424
Thomas, J., 545, 546, 547
Thompson, E. H., 10, 12
Thompson, J., 495
Thompson, L., 11, 160, 164, 176, 184-185, 193, 199, 200, 210, 216, 229, 403, 541
Thompson, M., 495
Thompson, R. A., 273
Thomson, E., 59, 64-66, 117, 125, 185, 217, 234, 291, 321
Thoresen, C. E., 411
Thorne, B., 166, 178, 179, 220, 403, 532
Thornton, A., 57, 58, 59, 60, 62, 67, 71, 118, 122, 269, 321, 353, 362, 413
Thornton, M., 338
Thurlow, C., 98
Tiberius, R. G., 545
Tickamyer, A., 161
Tienda, M., 342, 344
Tiffin, S., 43, 44
Tipton, S. M., 270, 425
Tocqueville, A. D., 473
Toffler, A., 512
Tolson, T. F. J., 231
Tomcho, T. J., 415, 419, 422
Tomes, N., 122
Top, B. L., 418
Toth, J. F., 162, 231
Touliatos, J., 544

Trattner, W. I., 45
Traustadottir, R., 182
Treas, J., 63, 137
Trepper, T. S., 527
Treviño, F. M., 344-345
Triandis, H. C., 84
Triber, G. A., 441
Troll, L., 128, 317
Trompenaars, F., 84
Tronto, J. C., 187
Trotter, B. B., 529
Truong, N. L., 97, 98
Trussell, J., 118, 120
Tryban, G. M., 139
Tsakloglou, P., 477
Tschann, J., 443, 445
Tse, L., 373
Tseng, V., 372, 373
Tseng, W., 373
Tucker, J., 402
Tucker, M. B., 89, 90-91, 352, 353, 354,
    356, 359, 360, 361
Tuer, M., 289
Turman, P., 321, 325
Turner, C., 246
Turner, C. W., 528
Turner, R. J., 414
Tweed, J. L., 284
Twiggs, J. E., 181
Tyson, R., 108

Udry, J. R., 65
Uhlenberg, P., 86, 138, 142, 143
Ulbrich, P. M., 127
Ulka-Steiner, B., 245, 248
Umaña-Taylor, A. J., 338, 342, 344, 502, 503
Umansky, L., 211, 213, 214
Umberson, D., 142, 144
Umylny, L., 283, 284, 322
Ungerer, J. A., 498

Valdés, G., 339
Valverde, K. L. C., 375
Vande Berge, S. M., 496
Vandemeulebroecke, L., 498
Van Den Berghe, H., 496
Vandewater, E. A., 288-289, 291
van Driel, B., 9, 23
Vangelisti, A. L., 99
Van Hall, E. V., 107
van Leeuwen, M. S., 422
Vann, F. H., 98
van Naerssen, L. X., 147
Vargas, M., 341

Vargus, B., 7
Vartanian, T., 325
Vasquez, R., 336, 342
Veevers, J. E., 116, 117, 122, 124, 125
Vega, W. A., 335, 343, 344, 345
Vemer, E., 319
Ventis, W. L., 417, 420
Ventura, S. J., 62, 283, 355
Verhage, F., 496
Veridiano, N. P., 98
Veroff, J., 90, 91
Verropoulou, G., 69
Vidal, C., 339
Villeneuve-Gokalp, C., 70
Vincent, V. A., 496
Visher, E. B., 530
Visher, J. S., 530
Vivian, D., 528
Vlosky, D. A., 268, 269
Volgy, S. S., 529
Volk, D., 339
Volling, B. L., 217
Vosler, N., 479
Voydanoff, P., 158, 292, 320, 479
Vuchinich, R., 320, 321
Vuchinich, S., 320, 321, 322, 546

Wackman, D. B., 542
Wade, A., 138, 140, 145
Waite, L. J., 10, 12, 33, 57, 59, 63, 70, 122,
    126, 217, 274, 360, 432, 531
Wakeman, M. A., 324
Walbridge, L., 395, 402, 403
Walby, S., 194
Waldfogel, J., 359
Waldren, T., 319
Waldron, M., 283
Walker, A. J., 160, 164, 180, 181, 193, 199,
    200, 210, 216, 229, 541
Walker, E., 529-530
Walker, G., 527
Walker, K., 529
Walker, R., 470
Walker, R. D., 391
Wallace, C., 310
Wallace, L., 386, 389
Wallace, L. E., 288
Wallerstein, J. S., xii, 270, 274, 283, 293, 357
Walsh, F., 503, 526
Walter, C. A., 122
Walters, K., 146
Walters, M., 526, 532
Walzer, S., 210, 215, 217, 220
Wang, D., 303

Wardell, B. P., 96
Wardle, L. D., 435
Ware, H. S., 245
Warshak, R. A., 291, 445
Waslyshyn, N., 497, 498
Wasser, S. K., 119
Watts-Jones, D., 529
Waugh, E., 400, 402
Weaver, C. N., 319
Weaver, S. E., 502, 503
Webb, F., 401
Webster, P. S., 143
Weil, J., 501
Weiner, M., 137
Weiner-Davis, M., 531
Weingarten, H. R., 319
Weingarten, K., 217
Weinick, R. M., 60, 138, 141
Weinstein, R. S., 249
Weintraub, S., 292
Weiss, H. B., 202
Weiss, R. S., 286
Weisz, J., 251
Weithorn, L. A., 445
Weitzman, L. J., 481
Weitzman, M., 513
Wellman, B., 511-512
Wenger, G., 128
Wen-Jui, H., 359
Wenk, D., 217
West, C., 178, 215, 452
Westat,, 461
Westoff, C. F., 374, 419
Weston, K., 176
Wetcher, J. L., 527
Wethington, E., 158, 248
Whitbeck, L. B., 161, 291, 391
White, G. D., 319
White, J. M., 121, 122
White, L., 66, 179, 183, 319, 479
White, L. K., 273-274
White, S., 193
Whitehurst, R. N., 29, 30
Whitford, G. S., 147
Whiting, B., 226
Whiting, J., 226
Whitlock, M. L., 418
Wickrama, K. A. S., 161
Wiegman, R., 194
Wilber, K., 195
Wilcox, K. L., 195
Wilcox, W. B., 418, 419, 420, 422
Wilkie, J. R., 160
Wilkinson, R. G., 478

Willetts, M. C., 141, 142
William, D., 371
Williams, D. R., 478
Williams, J., 177, 178, 183, 184, 310
Williams, J. S., 360
Williams, L. B., 419
Williams, N., 165
Williamson, S. A., 546
Willis, R. J., 60
Wills, T., 322
Wilmoth, J., 325
Wilson, A. C., 387, 390
Wilson, B. F., 319
Wilson, J., 182, 183, 416, 419
Wilson, L., 91, 165, 342
Wilson, M., 126
Wilson, M. N., 231, 292, 363
Wilson, P., 16
Wilson, T. J. B., 29
Wilson, W. J., 353, 356, 475, 479
Wineberg, H., 126
Winkler, A. E., 63
Winship, C., 353
Wintersberger, H., 309
Witte, J., 512
Wolf, W., 388
Wolfe, A., 473
Wong, H. Y., 371
Wong, M. G., 371
Wood, D. L., 336, 344
Wood, J., 162
Woodrow, K., 343
Woollett, A., 122, 213, 220
Worobey, J. L., 158
Worthington, E., 417
Worthington, E. L., 417
Wortman, C. B., 142, 144, 159
Wright, C. L., 143
Wright, D., 372
Wright, E. O., 476
Wright, J. D., 273, 471
Wright, M. M., 183
Wu, Z., 127, 128
Wyatt, J. M., 273

Xie, G., 66
Xie, Y., 60
Xu, W., 164
Xu, X., 162, 231

Yaeger, A., 322
Yamanaka, K., 373
Yanagisako, S. J., 375
Yap, S. G. H., 371

Yates, A., 387
Ybarra, L., 164, 343
Ybarra, V., 338
Yeung, W. J., 479
Yeung, W. T., 373
Yin, Y., 289
Yinger, J., 476
Yoder, J. D., 125
Yoon, H. S., 478
Yoshimoto, D., 108
Young, K. S., 508, 509
Young, M. H., 542, 545, 547
Young, R., 454
Young, R. S., 496
Young, Y. J., 121
Youngblade, L., 248, 249, 256
Young-DeMarco, L., 57, 62, 71, 118, 269, 362
Yueng, W. J., 231
Yung, J., 374

Zablocki, B., 6
Zabol, M., 30-31, 32

Zagorsky, J. L., 66
Zambrana, R., 335
Zangari, M., 528
Zedlewski, S. R., 144
Zelizer, V. A. R., 47
Zhang, Z., 128
Zhou, M., 377, 422
Zibman, C., 358
Zick, C. D., 141, 144
Zill, N., 284, 285, 290, 291, 292
Zimiles, H., 285
Zimmerman, D. H., 178, 215
Zimmerman, M. A., 292
Zimmerman, T. S., 528
Zinn, M., 343
Zizi, M., 232
Zollar, A. C., 360
Zucker, K. J., 98
Zuniga, M., 339, 340, 341
Zuo, J., 160
Zusman, M. E., 324
Zvolensky, M. J., 391
Zvonkovic, A. M., 185

Subject Index

Acculturation:
    American Indians, 387
    Asian Americans, 373, 376
    Latinos/Hispanics, 335-338, 341,
        342, 344-345
ACE Model of Cybersexual Addiction, 508
Action research methodology, 15-18
Activism:
    family life education, 538-539
    family policy, 454-456, 465, 466
    lesbian feminism, 192, 193-194,
        197-199, 200
    marriage, 272-273, 531-532
    motherhood, 211, 212
Adolescence (Hall), 46
Adolescent Parents Project, 547
Adoption:
    disclosure, 502
    embryo adoption, 502
    family law, 442-444
Adultery, 29, 509
African American families:
    absent-father focus, 359
    birth rates, 355
    Cape Verdeans, 354
    childcare, 362
    child development, 357-360
    childlessness, 120, 128, 359-360, 363
    child living arrangements, 355
    child protection, 41
    cohabitation, 60, 355, 359-360
    cultural heterogeneity, 352, 354, 356
    Current Population Survey (CPS), 356,
        361-362
    deficit-model perspective, 358-359
    deviant families, 8-9
    diversity of, 8-9, 352, 357-360
    divorce, 353-354, 357-358, 361
    dual-earner families, 161, 162, 164-165

Dutch West Indians, 354
ecological theory, 359
economics, 355-356, 357-358, 359,
    360, 361-362
education, 358, 362
employment, 358, 359, 361-363
family life education, 540
family networks, 355, 358, 359, 363
family policy, 361
family structure transformation, 356-357
family therapy, 526, 529
family values, 361
fathering, 228, 231-232, 235, 358-359
future trends, 360-363
gay/lesbian couples, 355
gender differences, 353, 356, 358, 361,
    362, 363
gendered family relations, 176-177,
    179, 181, 182-183
gender roles, 362-363
household composition, 354-355
intergenerational relations, 355, 363
Internet accessibility, 357, 507-508
interracial marriage, 356
lesbian feminism, 196, 197, 199
marital relations, 360
marriage, 353, 354, 356, 360, 361
marriage variations, 89-91
maternal employment, 359, 361-363
matriarchy model, 358-359
motherhood, 217, 219
Muslim, 394, 395, 403, 405
National Center for Health Statistics
    (NCHS), 354
National Longitudinal Survey of Youth
    (NLSY), 358, 359
National Survey of Family Growth
    (NSFG), 355
Nigerians, 354

pathogenic-conflict families, 251-252, 256
poverty, 355-356, 472, 475, 476, 479
power dynamics, 363
racial/ethnic differences, 353-354, 355, 356, 357-358, 359, 361-362
religiosity, 414, 420, 422
research accessibility, 357, 358, 360
research agenda, 353, 358, 359
research limitations, 357-360
research overview, 352-353
research review, 353
singlehood, 354, 361, 363
single-parent families, 282, 288, 291, 292-293, 354, 356, 358, 361
socioeconomic status, 356, 358-359, 362
stepfamilies, 318, 355
Survey of Income and Program Participation (SIPP), 353-354, 355
teen pregnancy, 355
transracial adoption, 442
U.S. Bureau of the Census, 353-354, 355
Age differences:
    childlessness, 119, 127-128
    cohabitation, 59, 60-61
    older-adult relationships, 140, 142, 143, 144
AIDS:
    alternative lifestyles impact, 23-24, 32
    gay/lesbian adolescents, 98
    gay/lesbian couples, 109, 147
Aid to Families with Dependent Children (AFDC), 435, 438, 473-474
Alaska, 269
Alternate families, 4-7
    acceptance of, 9-11
Alternative Life Styles, 32
Alternative lifestyles:
    adultery, 29
    AIDS impact, 23-24, 32
    American Psychological Association meeting (1967), 28
    androgyny, 25
    bigamy, 24
    child development, 25
    childlessness, 116
    communes, 23, 24-25, 27-32
    defined, 23, 24-25, 27, 31
    family policy, 26
    family research, 23-27, 32-33
    family therapy, 32, 531-532
    freedom ideology, 24
    gay/lesbian couples, 23, 24
    gender roles, 28
    group marriage, 23, 25, 26, 27-31
    group sex, 28

Groves Conference on Marriage and the Family (1971), 24, 27, 29
Groves Conference on Marriage and the Family (1972), 25, 27
Groves Conference on Marriage and the Family (1981), 27
Groves Conference on Marriage and the Family (2000), 27
health professionals, 32
Institute for 21st Century Relationships, 31
Internet impact, 31
marital roles, 25
marriage ideology, 25
Minnesota Multiphasic Personality Inventory (MMPI), 30
monogamy obsolescence, 24
New Horizon, 32
open marriage, 25, 28
polyamory, 31
polygamy, 32-33
polygyny, 28
public attitudes, 25, 26-27
research agenda, 32-33
research overview, 24
research paucity, 23-24, 27, 32
research publications, 24, 25, 26, 27-31, 32
safe sex, 32
swinging, 23, 24, 27-31
University of Maryland conference (1975), 26, 27
America Law Institute, 436
American Apartheid (Massey & Denton), 475-476
American Association for Counseling and Development (AACD), 544
American Association for Marriage and Family Therapy (AAMFT), 532, 544
American Association for Sex Educators, Counselors, and Therapists (AASECT), 544
American Association of Family and Consumer Sciences, 544
American Couples study, 68-69
American Indian families:
    Abused Elderly Protection Teams, 388
    acculturation, 387
    adolescents, 387
    assimilation, 387-388
    boarding school system, 387-388
    child development, 387-391
    Circle of Life, 390
    Confederated Tribes (Oregon), 386, 390-391
    Cultural Involvement and Detachment Anxiety Questionnaire (CIDAQ), 391
    cultural transmission, 386-387

Dakota, 390
demographics, 386-387
diabetes, 389-390
divorce, 388-389
economics, 388-389
education, 387-388
elderly, 388-390
family networks, 385-386, 388-389, 391
family policy, 387-388
family research, 386-390
family structure, 387
Four Circles, 391
gendered family relations, 176-177
health, 386-387, 388, 389-390
humor, 389
identity development, 387, 388, 390-391
Indian Health Service, 389
Iroquois, 386
life expectancy, 386
maternal identity, 387
mental health, 390
modeling strategy, 387
Navajo, 391
oral tradition, 390
population data, 386
poverty, 388
racial/ethnic differences, 386-387
research agenda, 391
research methodology, 386, 391
reservations, 386, 387, 388, 390
respect, 388, 390
responsibility, 387, 388
role identification, 387, 388, 390
self-determination period, 386
seven generations philosophy, 385-386
Seven Generation Youth Society
    (Oklahoma), 386
single-parent households, 387
socialization, 391
substance abuse, 386-387, 388, 389, 391
tribal identification, 390-391
tribal sovereignty, 390
wellness model, 390
American Indian Institute, 386
American Maternalists, 458
American Psychological Association, 28
American Psychologist, 236-237
Androgyny, 25
Arizona:
    covenant marriage, 273
    divorce barriers, 92
    Latino/Hispanic population, 337
    premarital education, 273
Arkansas, 273

Asian American families:
    acculturation, 373, 376
    Asian Indians, 370, 377
    assimilation, 371, 373, 374
    Cambodians, 370
    childcare, 375-376
    child development, 371, 373, 375, 377, 378
    Chinese, 369, 370, 371, 373, 376, 377,
        378, 529
    Chinese Exclusion Act (1882), 196-197, 369
    cohabitation, 60
    critical perspective, 372
    cultural heterogeneity, 374-375, 378-380
    cultural theory, 371, 372
    cultural values, 371, 372, 373
    deficit-model perspective, 371
    demographics, 369-370, 379, 380
    diversity of, 369, 371, 378-380
    divorce, 370-371
    domestic labor division, 376
    economics, 370, 371-372, 376-377
    education, 371-372, 374, 379, 380
    elderly, 377
    employment, 370, 371-372, 376, 379, 380
    family life education, 540
    family networks, 375-376, 379, 380
    family relations, 372-373, 377-380
    family structure, 371-372
    family therapy, 529
    family values, 371, 372-373
    fathering, 228
    Filipino, 370, 371, 373, 377, 378, 529
    first-generation, 372
    future trends, 379-380
    gay/lesbian couples, 377-378, 380
    gender differences, 373, 374
    gendered family relations, 176-177
    gender roles, 376-377
    Hmong, 370
    household production units, 371-372
    hypergamy theory, 373
    identity development, 373, 374-375,
        378-380
    immigration, 369-370, 371, 372, 373,
        375, 376, 377, 378, 379, 380
    Immigration Reform Act (1965), 369, 376
    intergenerational relations, 377
    Internet accessibility, 507-508
    internment camps, 369
    interracial marriage, 373-374, 379
    Japanese, 369, 370, 371, 373, 374,
        375, 376, 377, 378
    Japanese Americans Citizens League
        (JACL), 378

Koreans, 250, 251, 371, 373, 376, 377, 378
language, 373, 378
Laotians, 370
lesbian feminism, 196-197
marriage, 370, 373-374
mental health services, 379
National Origins Act (1924), 369
parenting style, 372-373, 378
pathogenic-conflict families, 250-251, 252
population data, 370, 379
poverty, 370
power dynamics, 372, 376, 377
racial/ethnic differences, 370, 371,
    373-374, 375, 379
regional differences, 370
religiosity, 371, 422
research agenda, 379-380
research contribution, 378-379
research overview, 369
second-generation, 372, 373, 376
single-parent households, 370
situational ethnicity, 374-375
social exchange theory, 375
socialization, 371-372, 373, 378
social networks, 375-376, 379
socioeconomic status, 374
structural perspective, 371-372
third-generation, 373
U.S. Bureau of the Census, 370
value compatibility theory, 371
Vietnamese, 372, 373, 374, 375, 376, 377, 378
Assimilation:
    American Indians, 387-388
    Asian Americans, 371, 373, 374
    Latinos/Hispanics, 335, 338, 345-346
    Muslim Americans, 395
Association for Couples in Marriage
Enrichment (ACME), 542-543
Association of Family and Conciliation
    Courts, 543

Baby and Child Care (Spock), 215
Baby farming, 43
Baehr v. *Lewin* (1993), 440
Baker v. *State of Vermont* (2001), 440
Behavior genetics, 294-295
Best-interest standard, 42, 436, 441, 444, 445
Beyond Monogamy (Smith & Smith), 29
Bicultural families, 337-338, 346
Bigamy, 24
Bilingualism, 346
Binuclear families, 317
Black Families in Therapy (Boyd-Franklin), 526
Blended families, 317

*Board of Education of Independent School
    District No. 92 of Pottawatomie
    County* v. *Earls* (2002), 49
Brady v. *Dean* (2001), 440
Brain Trust, 459, 464
Brooks v. *Parkerson* (1995), 439
Bush, George, 482

Caban v. *Mohammed* (1979), 438
California:
    American Indian confederations, 390-391
    Chinese labor, 369
    divorce research, 357
    Family Law Act (1969), 434
    Latino/Hispanic population, 337
    no-fault divorce, 269, 434, 436
    parental leave, 167
    unwed fathers, 437-438
Canada:
    family life education, 544
    poverty, 471, 477, 482
    reproductive technology, 498-499
Carey v. *Population Services International*
    (1977), 48
Carter, Jimmy, 269-270
Center for the Study of Innovative Lifestyles, 26
Certified Family Life Educator (CFLE),
    542, 544, 548-549
Champagne v. *Mcdermott, Inc.* (1992), 437
Child and Family Resources Program
    (CFRP), 547
Childcare:
    dual-earner families, 163
    family policy, 452
    fathering, 225, 231, 232, 234, 237
    gendered family relations, 174, 179, 180,
        181, 183, 184, 185
    racial/ethnic differences, 343, 362, 375-376
    single-parent families, 291
Child custody:
    family law, 435-436, 440, 441,
        443-444, 445-446
    family therapy, 529
Child development:
    alternative lifestyles impact, 25
    childhood transformation, 44-45, 46
    cohabitation impact, 57-58, 63-66, 71-72
    divorce impact, 267, 270-272,
        274-278, 309, 310
    dual-earner families, 156, 157, 161-163
    family law impact, 443-446
    family policy impact, 456-457, 458,
        460-461, 463
    family therapy, 530-531

fathering impact, 224, 226, 229-230, 233-235
gay/lesbian parenting, 106-107, 109
gendered family relations, 183
Great Britain, 309-310
household diversity impact, 11-12, 16-18
Internet impact, 510
lesbian feminism, 200-202
motherhood, 220
poverty impact, 478-480
religiosity impact, 418, 419-421, 423-425
reproduction technology, 497-502
single-parent families, 283-287, 288-289, 290-295
stepfamilies, 321-323, 324-325
See also Pathogenic-conflict families; *specific race/ethnicity*
Childhood transformation:
    active agent role, 47-48
    adolescence, 36-37, 38, 39-41, 44, 45-51
    baby farming, 43
    best-interest standard, 42
    child development, 44-45, 46
    childhood characteristics, 36, 37-38, 39-41, 45-47, 50-51
    child protection, 41-45
    child-saving agencies, 41-42, 43
    contemporary, 50-51
    demographics, 37, 38-39, 40, 41, 45, 48
    economic changes, 37, 38-39, 40-41, 42, 43-44, 45, 46-47
    education system, 40, 41, 42, 43, 45, 46-48, 49, 50, 51
    18th century, 39-40
    Fair Labor Standards Act (1937), 44, 45
    family policy, 48-51
    gender differences, 40, 41-42, 49, 50
    Head Start, 44
    health, 43
    infancy characteristics, 36, 37-38, 42-43
    juvenile justice system, 44
    legal precedents, 42
    legal rights, 45, 46-47, 48-50
    linguistic descriptions, 36-37
    little adults, 37, 50-51
    middle-class universalization, 45-47
    moral panics, 49-50
    mothers' pension law, 43-44
    New York Society for the Prevention of Cruelty to Children (1874), 41
    19th century, 39-43
    parens patriae doctrine, 42
    Progressive Era, 43-44, 48
    public attitudes, 37-47, 48-51
    Puritans, 37-38

Quakers, 39
racial/ethnic differences, 40, 41, 42, 43-44, 47, 50
regional differences, 38-39, 40-41, 42, 43, 47
religiosity, 38, 41, 46
semidependence stage, 38, 45
17th century, 37-39
sexual behavior, 40, 42, 46, 48-49, 51
Sheppard-Towner Act (1921), 44
social/cultural construction, 36
Social Security Act (1935), 44
socioeconomic status, 39-47, 48
stages, 36-37, 38, 45, 46, 50
Supreme Court rulings, 48-49
U.S. Children's Bureau (1912), 43
White House Conference on Children (1909), 43
youth, 36-37, 38
Childlessness:
    active-deciders, 123-124
    age differences, 119, 127-128
    alternative lifestyles, 116
    biological/evolutionary theory, 118-119, 128
    child-free terminology, 123, 129
    consequences, 126-128
    cultural norms theory, 119-120, 128
    decision-making process, 124-125
    defined, 117, 123
    demographics, 116, 117-118
    economic impact, 119, 120, 121
    eugenic advantage theory, 118-119
    experience of, 125-126
    feminism impact, 116, 122-123, 129
    future trends, 129-130
    gender differences, 119, 120, 124, 128
    gender roles, 120, 122-123, 124, 125-126, 129-130
    identity transformation, 122-123, 125-126, 129-130
    infertility, 116, 117, 118, 119, 125-126, 127, 128-129
    intentional, 117, 118, 119, 120, 121, 122, 123-126, 127, 129
    later-life consequences, 127-128
    life course theory, 121-122, 127, 128
    marriage impact, 126-127
    motivations for, 116, 123-124, 128
    parental investment theory, 119
    passive-deciders, 123-124
    prevalence rates, 117-118
    racial/ethnic differences, 120, 128, 359-360, 363

rate projection models, 118
rational choice theory, 120-121, 128
regional differences, 118, 120
religiosity, 120
reproduction suppression theory, 119
research agenda, 129
research conclusions, 128-130
research overview, 116
research theory, 118-123
sexual behavior, 124, 125, 127
social exchange theory, 121, 127-128
social stigma, 116, 123, 125-126, 128
socioeconomic status, 121
Child protection, 41-45
Children's rights. *See* Family law
Child-saving, 41-42, 43, 456-457
Child Support Act (1991) (Great Britain), 310
Child Support Recovery Act (1992), 435
Chinese Exclusion Act (1882), 196-197, 369
Circle of Life, 390
Clinton, Bill, 482
Cluster analysis, 166
Coalition for Marriage, Family, and Couples
     Education, 531
Cohabitation:
   age differences, 59, 60-61
   American Couples study, 68-69
   as courtship stage, 58, 61
   as marriage alternative, 58, 61
   childbearing impact, 61-62
   child development, 57-58, 63-66, 71-72
   Cohabitation and Marriage Study, 70
   couple lifestyle, 62-64
   Current Population Survey (CPS),
     67, 68
   defined, 58-59, 71
   demographics, 59-61, 67-68
   economic impact, 59, 60, 62, 63-64, 71
   education impact, 59, 60, 61, 63-64
   family law, 439-440
   family relations, 66-67
   family therapy, 524, 527
   Fragile Families and Child Wellbeing
     Study, 66, 70
   gendered family relations, 177, 180
   gender roles, 62, 63
   Great Britain, 304-305, 308-309, 312
   income pooling, 63-64
   Intergenerational Panel Study of Parents
     and Children, 69
   National Longitudinal Study of Adolescent
     Health, 65, 66
   National Longitudinal Survey of the High
     School Class of 1972, 69

National Longitudinal Survey of Youth
     (NLSY), 66
National Survey Families and Households
     (NSFH), 65, 66, 67-68, 69
National Survey of America's Families
     (NSAF), 65
National Survey of Family Growth (NSFG),
     68, 69
older-adult relationships, 72, 140-141,
     147-148
persons of the opposite sex sharing living
     quarters (POSSLQ), 67
prevalence rates, 57, 59, 60, 67, 283
racial/ethnic differences, 60, 355,
     359-360
religiosity, 60
research agenda, 71-72
research improvements, 67-71
research limitations, 66
research methodology, 70-71
research overview, 58
social network influence, 66-67
stepfamilies, 319
survey data, 65-70
Survey of Income and Program
     Participation (SIPP), 69
U.S. Bureau of the Census, 67, 68
Welfare, Children and Families Study, 70
See also Gay/lesbian couples
Cohabitation and Marriage Study, 70
College and University Curriculum
     Guidelines (NCFR), 542
Communes, 23, 24-25, 27-32
Communities Directory (Fellowship for
     Intentional Community), 31
Companionate marriage, 268, 270
Companionate Marriage, The (Lindsey), 29
Comparative research, 423, 471-472
Conflict resolution:
   dual-earner families, 167-169
   gay/lesbian couples, 108
   pathogenic-conflict families, 245, 250
   religiosity, 417
Confluent love theory, 307-308, 309
Conscientization, 195
Consonant acculturation, 336
*Contemporary Families and Alternative
     Lifestyles* (Macklin & Rubin), x, 27
Contingency perspective, 276-277, 313
Co-parenting model, 310-311
Couple Communication, 542-543
Covenant marriage, 273, 361, 435
Cultural contradiction theory, 214-216
Cultural Information Scale (CIS), 336

Cultural Involvement and Detachment Anxiety Questionnaire (CIDAQ), 391
Cultural-mismatch theory, 335
Cultural norms theory, 119-120, 128
Cultural scripts, 4, 7-8, 10-13, 14, 15
Culture-of-poverty framework, 474-475
Current Population Survey (CPS), 67, 68, 356, 361-362, 470, 524-525

Davis v. *Davis* (1992), 441
Decision-making process:
    childlessness, 124-125
    reproduction technology, 496-497, 500-501
    stepfamilies, 319, 323
Defense of Marriage Act, 440, 446, 532
Deficit-model perspective:
    divorce, 271-272, 275-277
    fathering, 236
    racial/ethnic differences, 358-359, 371
    stepfamilies, 319, 324-325
Dependent marriage model, 434-435
Determinism, 515
Developmental theory, 267
Deviant families, 8-9
Differentiation, 8
Dissonant acculturation, 336-337
Divorce:
    barriers to, 83, 92-93
    child development impact, 267, 270-272, 274-278, 309, 310, 357-358
    contingency perspective, 276-277
    covenant marriage, 273
    deficit-model perspective, 271-272, 275-277
    developmental theory, 267
    family law, 434-435, 436, 444
    family life education, 543
    family pluralism perspective, 272, 275-277
    family therapy, 524-525, 526-527, 529
    fathering impact, 224, 234, 235
    fragile families, 277
    future trends, 277
    gendered family relations, 175, 177, 179, 181, 184
    Great Britain, 303, 304, 309, 310
    historical/cultural context, 265-266
    incompatibility, 269, 434
    institutionalized marriage, 267-268, 270, 272-273
    irreconcilable differences, 269, 434
    legal regulation (1900-1960), 266-267
    legal regulation (1960-1990), 268-269
    legal regulation (1990-present), 272-273
    Marriage Movement, 272-273
    mental cruelty, 267
    meta-analysis, 271
    National Adolescent Health Study, 274
    National Longitudinal Survey of Youth (Mother and Child Supplement), 274
    National Survey of Children, 274
    National Survey of Families and Households (NSFH), 274
    no-fault divorce, 268-269, 273, 434, 436, 444
    older-adult relationships, 138, 140, 142-145
    political agendas, 267, 269-270, 294
    premarital education, 273
    prevalence rates, 79, 86-88, 91, 92, 283, 434
    prevalence rates (1900-1960), 266
    prevalence rates (1960-1990), 268
    prevalence rates (1990-present), 272
    public attitudes (1900-1960), 267
    public attitudes (1960-1990), 269-270
    public attitudes (1990-present), 273-274
    racial/ethnic differences, 342, 353-354, 357-358, 361, 370-371, 388-389, 399, 400
    religiosity, 267, 412, 414, 415, 416
    research agenda, 277-278
    research convergence (1990-present), 272-277
    research methodology, 277
    research overview, 265-266
    research theory, 277
    revolution period (1960-1990), 268-272
    social problem (1900-1960), 266-268
    social science research, 265-266
    social science research (1900-1960), 267-268
    social science research (1960-1990), 270-272
    social science research (1990-present), 274-277
    social stigma, 270
    socioeconomic status, 271
Divorce Reform Act (1967) (Great Britain), 304
Doing gender perspective, 215
Domestic labor division:
    dual-earner families, 160, 161, 164, 165, 168
    fathering, 225, 232, 234, 237
    gay/lesbian couples, 101
    older-adult relationships, 138, 144
    racial/ethnic differences, 343, 376, 401
    See also Gendered family relations
Domestic violence:
    family law, 434
    family therapy, 527-528, 532
    poverty impact, 480
    religiosity, 415-416, 418

Dual-earner families:
  adolescents, 167
  career-limitation strategy, 168
  child development, 156, 157, 161-163
  cluster analysis, 166
  conflict resolution, 167-169
  cutting-back strategy, 168
  demographics, 155
  diversity of, 165-167
  domestic labor division, 160, 161, 164,
     165, 168
  ecological theory, 157, 163-165
  equal-sharer strategy, 168
  experimental research, 167-168
  Family and Medical Leave Act (FMLA), 167
  family defined, 166
  family policy strategies, 167
  family process context, 157, 162, 165,
     167-168, 169
  family relations, 156-157, 161-163,
     164-165, 166, 167, 168
  family strategies, 168
  gay/lesbian couples, 157
  gender differences, 156, 158, 159, 160,
     161, 162, 164-165, 168
  gender roles, 160, 161, 164, 165, 168
  hierarchical linear modeling (HLM), 159,
     166-167
  historical context, 155
  life course theory, 167
  marital relations, 157, 159-161, 166,
     167, 168
  maternal employment theory, 156, 157,
     158, 159, 160, 162, 164
  mental health, 157, 158-159, 160, 161,
     164-165, 166, 167, 168
  multiple-roles theory, 157, 164-165
  National Institute of Child Health and
     Human Development (NICHD), 163
  nonparental childcare, 163
  occupational stress theory, 157,
     158-159, 162, 165
  one-job/one-career strategy, 168
  Panel Study of Income Dynamics
     (PSID), 163
  prevalence rates, 155
  racial/ethnic differences, 157, 161, 162,
     163-165, 168
  research agenda, 159, 161-162, 163-169
  research methodology, 165-167
  research overview, 156
  research review, 156, 157-163
  scarcity hypotheses, 159
  sexual behavior, 159

  shift work, 162-163
  social address model, 156, 165
  social networks, 168
  social role theory, 165
  socioeconomic status, 157, 158,
     163-165, 167, 168
  trading-off strategy, 168
  U.S. Bureau of Labor Statistics, 155
  work defined, 166
  workplace strategies, 167-168
  work socialization theory, 157,
     158-160, 161-163, 164, 165,
     166, 167-168
Dual-perpetrator model, 254

Earned Income Tax Credit (EITC), 480-481
Ecological theory:
  dual-earner families, 157, 163-165
  household diversity, 4, 13-14
  Internet, 515
  racial/ethnic differences, 359, 403-404
  See also Marriage variations
Economics:
  childhood transformation, 37, 38-39,
     40-41, 42, 43-44, 45, 46-47
  childlessness impact, 119, 120, 121
  cohabitation, 59, 60, 62, 63-64, 71
  family life education, 546
  family policy, 454-455, 456, 457-460,
     462-463, 464-465
  fathering impact, 224, 231-232,
     233-235, 236, 237-238
  gay/lesbian couples, 101
  Great Britain, 309, 310, 312
  older-adult relationships, 137, 139,
     141, 142-143, 144, 146, 147
  reproduction technology, 499-500
  single-parent families, 282, 287-288
  stepfamilies, 319
  See also Poverty; Socioeconomic status;
     specific race/ethnicity
Education:
  childhood transformation, 40, 41, 42,
     43, 45, 46-48, 49, 50, 51
  cohabitation influence, 59, 60, 61, 63-64
  family policy, 455
  fathering impact, 231-232, 237
  gendered family relations, 174,
     178-179, 180, 186
  Internet impact, 507
  older-adult relationships, 137, 138, 146
  poverty impact, 472, 478-479
  racial/ethnic differences, 334, 340, 341,
     342, 343, 358, 362, 387-388, 395

single-parent families, 284-285, 288
   See also specific race/ethnicity
Eisenhower, Dwight, 267
Elderly:
   American Indians, 388-390
   Asian Americans, 377
   Internet impact, 510, 511
   Muslim Americans, 398-399, 400
   See also Intergenerational relations;
      Older-adult relationships
Elizabethan Poor Laws, 451
Emotional lesbians, 198
Emotional security hypothesis, 247, 251
Empirical research, 404-406, 412, 413,
   419, 476
Employment:
   family policy, 454-456, 457, 458, 459,
      460, 461, 462-463, 465
   Great Britain, 307
   Internet impact, 512-513
   older-adult relationships, 137, 138,
      139-140, 142, 144, 146
   racial/ethnic differences, 334, 343, 358,
      359, 361-363, 395, 401
   See also Dual-earner families; Gendered
      family relations; Motherhood
Employment Act (1946), 464-465
Ennis v. *Donovan* (1960), 433
Equal Rights Amendment (1972), 7
Esquire, 30
Ethical Principles and Guidelines
   (NCFR), 544
Ethnicity and Family Therapy (McGoldrick
   et al.), 526
Eugenic advantage theory, 118-119
Evolutionary theory, 118-119, 128, 218-219
Experimental research, 167-168
Expert testimony, 444, 447
Exploring Intimate Life Styles (Murstein), 30

Fair Labor Standards Act (1937), 44, 45
Families and Communes (Smith), 31
Family and Medical Leave Act (FMLA), 167
Family Coordinator, 29, 540, 546
Family decline perspective, 175
Family Disorganization (Mowrer), 267
Family dysfunction model, 254
Family Impact Seminars, 462
Family in Search of a Future, The (Otto), 28
Family Interpreted, The (Luepnitz), 526
Family law:
   adoption, 442-444
   assisted reproduction, 440-441, 446
   best-interest standard, 436, 441, 444, 445

child custody, 435-436, 440, 441,
   443-444, 445-446
child development impact, 443-446
children's rights, 45, 46-47, 48-50
cohabitation, 439-440
covenant marriage, 435
defined, 432
dependent marriage model, 434-435
divorce, 434-435, 436, 444
domestic violence, 434
expert testimony, 444, 447
feminism, 434, 444
future trends, 446
gay/lesbian couples, 439-440, 443-444, 446
gender differences, 433-435, 436,
   437-438, 444
marriage, 433-434, 439-440
no-fault divorce, 434, 436, 444
nontraditional partnerships, 439-440
partnership model, 433-434
power dynamics, 444
remarriage, 436-437
research agenda, 446-447
research comprehension, 444
research expectations, 445
research influence, 443-444
research-informed interventions, 444
research limitations, 444-446
research role, 443
research theory/data distinction, 445-446
research time tables, 446
research units, 446
research validity, 445
social science research, 443-447
state jurisdiction, 433
state variation, 432-433
stepfamilies, 432, 436-437, 446
Supreme Court rulings, 48-49, 432, 433,
   434, 436-437, 438, 439, 440, 441
third-party visitation, 438-439
trends, 433-443
unwed fathers, 437-438, 446
See also Family policy; *specific*
   law/court case
Family Law Act (1969), 434
Family life education:
   accuracy standard, 547
   activism (1960s), 538-539
   Adolescent Parents Project, 547
   Association for Couples in Marriage
      Enrichment (ACME), 542-543
   Association of Family and Conciliation
      Courts, 543
   audiences (1960s), 543

audiences (1970s), 543
audiences (1990s), 543-544
behavioristic paradigm, 545
Certified Family Life Educator (CFLE),
    542, 544, 548-549
Child and Family Resources
    Program (CFRP), 547
College and University Curriculum
    Guidelines (NCFR), 542
Couple Communication, 542-543
critical/emancipatory approach, 545-546
curricular frameworks, 542
defined, 539
divorce, 543
entrenchment period (1960s), 539
family diversity, 549
feasibility standard, 547
feminism, 541, 542
funding, 546
future trends, 548-550
gay/lesbian couples, 540
group instruction, 546, 547
individualized instruction, 546
inquiry-oriented paradigm, 545
instructional delivery (1970s), 546
instructional delivery (1980s), 546
instructional delivery (1990s), 546
instructional design (1970s), 545
instructional design (1980s), 545
instructional design (1990s), 545-546
instrumental/technical approach,
    545-546
Internet impact, 514-515, 549
interpretive approach, 545
Joint Committee on Standards for
Educational Evaluation, 546-547
journals, 539, 540-541, 546
logic models, 547
mass instruction, 546
National Council on Family Relations
    (NCFR), 539, 540, 542, 544, 549
National/Worldwide Marriage Encounter,
    542-543
operational principles, 539
Parent Effectiveness Training (PET),
    542-543
personalistic paradigm, 545
political agendas, 538-539
Prevention and Relationship Enhancement
    Program (PREP), 542-543, 548
professionalization development, 548-549
professionalization (1980s), 544
professionalization (1990s), 544
professional organizations, 544

program evaluation development,
    547-548, 549-550
program evaluation (1970s), 546
program evaluation (1980s), 546-547
program evaluation (1990s), 547-548
programs, 542-543
propriety standard, 547
providers (1960s), 543
providers (1970s), 543
providers (1990s), 543-544
purpose (1970s), 539
purpose (1980s), 539
racial/ethnic differences, 540
reflexive research, 550
Relationship Enhancement (RE), 542-543
research methodology, 547-548
research overview, 538
research publication development,
    548, 549
research publications (1960s), 540
research publications (1970s), 540,
    546-547
research publications (1980s), 539,
    540-541, 542
research publications (1990s), 540-541, 544
research theory, 542, 550
research topics (1960s), 540
research topics (1970s), 540
research topics (1980s), 540-541, 542
research topics (1990s), 540-541
settings (1960s), 543
settings (1970s), 543
settings (1990s), 544
social exchange theory, 542
social learning theory, 542
socioeconomic status, 540
standards, 546-547
Systematic Training for Effective Parenting
    (STEP), 542-543, 547
system/ecosystem perspective, 542
Teaching Family Science Conference, 544
Teen Outreach Program (TOP), 542-543
textbooks, 540, 541, 548, 549
transformative learning theory, 550
U.S. Cooperative Extension Service,
    543, 546
utility standard, 547
Zero Adolescent Pregnancy (ZAP),
    542-543
Family networks:
    Great Britain, 311-313
    Internet impact, 510, 511
    poverty, 479
    stepfamilies, 311-312, 324

See also Intergenerational relations; Social networks; *specific race/ethnicity*
Family pluralism perspective, 272, 275-277
Family policy:
 alternative lifestyles, 26
 American Maternalists, 458
 Brain Trust, 459, 464
 childcare, 452
 child development impact, 456-457, 458, 460-461, 463
 child/family saving (1900-1930), 456-457
 childhood transformation, 48-51
 citizen activism, 465, 466
 defined, 453
 demographics (1880-1920), 456
 dual-earner families, 167
 economics, 454-455, 456, 457-460, 462-463, 464-465
 education, 455
 Elizabethan Poor Laws, 451
 employment, 454-456, 457, 458, 459, 460, 461, 462-463, 465
 Employment Act (1946), 464-465
 family defined, 453-454
 Family Impact Seminars, 462
 fathering, 237
 formal conception (1970s), 451
 formal policy structures, 464
 gender differences, 455
 gendered family relations, 187
 General Federation of Women's Clubs, 455, 465
 Great Britain, 304, 308, 310
 Great Depression, 457-458, 459
 historical context, 452-453, 454-459, 460, 461-463, 464-465
 Hoover technocrats, 458, 462
 household diversity, 10, 13-15, 18-19
 Indicators of Children's Well-Being, 461
 individualism ideology, 456, 458, 462, 465
 interdisciplinary research, 463-464
 Internet, 513
 intervention legitimacy (1990s), 452
 labor law, 454-456
 National Congress of Mothers, 465
 New Deal, 458-459, 463
 Old Age pensions, 459
 Parent Teacher Association (PTA), 465
 patriarchal ideology, 458-459
 philanthropic community, 452, 464
 political agendas, 451, 452, 455-459, 460, 461-462, 463, 464-465, 469

 poverty, 457, 459-460, 469, 475, 477, 480-481, 482
 President's Research Committee on Social Trends (1933), 458
 Progressive Era, 455-456, 457, 460, 465
 racial/ethnic differences, 361, 387-388
 reproduction technology, 499-501
 research communication, 461-462
 research conclusions, 465-466
 research methodology, 461
 research overview, 453
 research relevancy, 460-462
 research theory, 460-462
 scientific management theory, 456, 462
 Settlement Houses, 457, 463
 Sheppard-Towner Act (1921), 457, 463
 single-parent families, 454
 Social Darwinism, 456, 459
 Social Security Act (1935), 458
 Social Security Amendments (1939), 457-459, 463
 socioeconomic status, 454-456
 structural social problems, 462-463
 sustainability strategies, 459-466
 Temporary Assistance for Needy Families (TANF), 452
 Trends in the Well-Being of America's Children and Youth, 461
 U.S. Bureau of Labor Standards, 457
 U.S. Bureau of Labor Statistics, 456, 462
 U.S. Children's Bureau (1912), 456-457, 461-462, 464
 voting rights, 456, 457
 Welfare Peer Assistance Network (WELPAN), 462
 White House Conference on Families (1980), 451
 Woman's Christian Temperance Union (WCTU), 455
 women's activism (1890-1920), 454-456, 465
 women's organizations, 455, 456, 459
 See also Family law; *specific policy*
Family process:
 dual-earner families, 157, 162, 165, 167-168, 169
 family therapy, 529-530
 Great Britain, 312-313
 racial/ethnic differences, 338-344
 reproduction technology, 502-503
 stepfamilies, 323-324
Family Relations, 29, 539, 540, 546
Family relations:
 cohabitation impact, 66-67

gay/lesbian adolescents, 98, 99
Great Britain, 311-313
Internet impact, 506, 509-515
older-adult relationships, 140, 141-142,
    143-144, 145, 146, 147
religiosity impact, 415-421
reproduction technology, 498-499,
    501-502
See also Dual-earner families; Gendered
    family relations; specific race/ethnicity
Family Science Association, 544
Family Support Act (1988), 435, 438
Family therapy:
    alternative lifestyles, 32, 531-532
    American Association for Marriage and
Family Therapy, 532
    child custody, 529
    child development impact, 530-531
    Coalition for Marriage, Family, and
        Couples Education, 531
    cohabitation, 524, 527
    culturally-sensitive approach, 528-529
    Current Population Survey (CPS), 524-525
    divorce, 524-525, 526-527, 529
    domestic violence, 527-528, 532
    family diversity response, 523, 525-532
    family formation, 523-524
    family households, 523, 524-525
    family organization, 523-524
    family process context, 529-530
    family transformation, 523-525
    fathering, 528
    feminism, 525, 526, 527, 528, 532
    future trends, 531-532
    gay/lesbian couples, 524, 525, 527,
        530, 532
    gender differences, 525, 526, 527-528, 532
    gender roles, 528
    General Social Survey, 524
    intergenerational relations, 528
    Internet impact, 513, 514-515
    marriage, 530-532
    Marriage Movement, 531-532
    narrative therapy, 528
    National Health and Social Life Survey, 524
    nonfamily households, 523-524
    nonmarital childbirth, 524-525
    political agendas, 530
    power dynamics, 525, 528, 529
    professionalization, 528
    racial/ethnic differences, 525, 526,
        528-529, 532
    remarriage, 526, 529-530
    research developments, 530-531

    research focus, 526-530
    research limitations, 530-531
    research publications, 525-527, 528, 530
    single-parent families, 524-525, 526-527,
        529, 530, 532
    Smart Marriages Conference, 531
    stepfamilies, 529-530, 531
    strengths approach, 529
    systems theory, 528
    U.S. Bureau of the Census, 523-524
Family values:
    African Americans, 361
    Asian Americans, 371, 372-373
    fathering, 236-237
    gendered family relations, 175
    Latinos/Hispanics, 338-342, 346
Fania v. Fania (1939), 432
Father absence, 229, 236
Fathering:
    adolescents, 234
    aloof-father societies, 225-226
    availability measure, 230-232
    childcare, 225, 231, 232, 234, 237
    child development impact, 224, 226,
        229-230, 233-235
    child-identity development, 226, 229-230
    contradictions, 224-225
    cross-cultural variation, 225-227
    deficit-model perspective, 236
    defined, 225
    demographics, 235-236
    divorce impact, 224, 234, 235
    domestic labor division, 225, 232, 234, 237
    economic impact, 224, 231-232, 233-235,
        236, 237-238
    education impact, 231-232, 237
    18th century, 227
    European culture, 226-227
    family policy, 237
    family therapy, 528
    family value, 224-225
    family values, 236-237
    father absence, 229, 236
    fatherhood defined, 225
    future trends, 237-238
    gender politics, 236-237
    gender roles, 228, 233, 236-237
    gender stereotyping, 234-235
    historical variation, 226-228
    infants, 234
    influence potential, 233-235
    institutionalized, 226
    interaction measure, 230-232
    intimate-father societies, 225-226

involvement levels, 230-233
involvement measurement, 230
involvement predictors, 232-233
marital relations, 233
marriage value, 236-237
maternal deprivation, 229
modern ideal, 228-230
19th century, 227-228
nuclear family, 228
parenting process model, 233
patriarchal ideology, 228
preschool children, 234
Puritans, 227
racial/ethnic differences, 228, 229, 231-232,
    235, 358-359, 405
regional differences, 228
religiosity, 227, 231-232, 419
research agenda, 220
research methodology, 234
research overview, 225
responsibility measure, 230-232
role inadequacy perspective, 236
17th century, 227
single-parent families, 224-225,
    233-234, 235
social fatherhood, 225
socioeconomic status, 227-228, 229,
    231-232, 237-238
sons/daughters, 232, 234-235
to-father defined, 225
20th century, 227-229
unwed-father rights, 437-438, 446
younger/older children, 232
Federal Office of Child Support Enforcement,
    435, 438
Fellowship for Intentional Community, 31
Female sexual inverts, 196
Feminine Mystique, The (Friedan), 193, 211
Feminism:
    childlessness impact, 116, 122-123, 129
    family law, 434, 444
    family life education, 541, 542
    family therapy, 525, 526, 527, 528, 532
    gendered family relations, 176, 178-179
    household diversity, 4, 5, 6, 7, 9-10
    marriage impact, 79, 92
    racial/ethnic differences, 193-195, 196-197,
        199, 397, 404
    See also Lesbian feminism
Feminist praxis, 193, 200, 203
Fictive kin, 17
Five Families (Lewis), 474
Florida, 92, 273, 440
Four Circles, 391

Fragile families, 277, 283
Fragile Families and Child Wellbeing Study,
    66, 70
*Framework for Life-Span Family Life
    Education* (NCFR), 542, 549
Freedom ideology, 4, 5-6, 9-10, 14, 24
Functionalism:
    gendered family relations, 178, 179, 186
    household diversity, 7-9, 11-12
Future of the Family, The (Howe), 28-29

Gay/lesbian adolescents:
    AIDS, 98
    coming out process, 97-98, 99
    family relations, 98, 99
    General Social Survey, 97
    identity antecedents, 98-99
    identity stability, 99
    population data, 97
    public attitudes, 97
    research agenda, 98-99
    social-cognitive behavioral model, 98
Gay/lesbian couples:
    AIDS, 109, 147
    alternative lifestyles, 23, 24
    child development impact, 106-107, 109
    cohabitation prevalence, 99-100
    commitment construction, 107-108
    conflict, 101-102
    conflict resolution, 108
    couple diversity, 109-110
    Defense of Marriage Act, 440, 446, 532
    domestic labor division, 101
    dual-earner families, 157
    ethnography, 100-103
    family law, 102, 439-440, 443-444, 446
    family life education, 540
    family therapy, 524, 525, 527, 530, 532
    finances, 101
    first contact, 100-101
    gay/lesbian differences, 105-106
    gendered family relations, 176, 177, 181
    gender roles, 107
    Great Britain, 305-306
    heterosexual contrast, 103-105, 107-108
    homosexuality defined, 96
    National Health and Social Life Survey, 96
    older-adult relationships, 146-147
    partner identification, 100
    population data, 96, 99
    power dynamics, 108
    previous relationships, 100
    racial/ethnic differences, 355, 377-378, 380
    relationship rituals, 101

relationship stages, 102-103
religiosity, 414, 422
reproduction technology, 494-495
research agenda, 107-110
research methodology, 110
research overview, 96-97
research sampling, 107
research theory, 110
residence, 101
sexual behavior, 103, 107, 108-109
social networks, 102
social stigma, 96, 305
stepfamilies, 319, 320
U.S. Bureau of the Census, 99
See also Lesbian feminism
Gender differences:
    childhood transformation, 40, 41-42, 49, 50
    dual-earner families, 156, 158, 159, 160,
        161, 162, 164-165, 168
    family law, 433-435, 436, 437-438, 444
    family policy, 455
    family therapy, 525, 526, 527-528, 532
    Internet, 509-510, 511
    older-adult relationships, 138, 139-140,
        141-142, 143, 144, 145, 147
    pathogenic-conflict families, 246-247, 249
    poverty, 477
    religiosity, 415, 419-420
    single-parent families, 286, 287-288, 289-290
    stepfamilies, 318, 319-321
    See also specific race/ethnicity
Gendered family relations:
    birthrate impact, 180
    child development impact, 183
    cohabitation impact, 177, 180
    divorce impact, 175, 177, 179, 181, 184
    domesticity ideology, 177-178
    domesticity ideology/employment, 181,
        183-184
    domesticity ideology/family relations,
        184-186
    domesticity/patriarchal ideology,
        180-183, 185
    education impact, 174, 178-179, 180, 186
    family decline perspective, 175
    family defined, 176-177
    family diversity, 176-177
    family-member care, 176
    family policy impact, 187
    family structure diversity, 177, 186
    family values debate, 175
    female caregiving, 182, 185
    female childcare, 174, 179, 180, 181,
        184, 185

female domesticity transformation,
    174-175, 179-180
female employment transformation,
    174-175, 179-180, 183, 186
female housework, 174, 179, 180, 181, 185
female volunteer work, 182-183
female wages, 177-178, 179, 181, 183, 184
feminism, 176, 178-179
future trends, 177, 186-187
gay/lesbian couples, 176, 177, 181
gendered threshold, 181-182
gender theory, 178-179
housework defined, 181
ideal family illusion, 176-177, 186, 187
invisible power, 185
latent power, 185
male caregiving, 182, 185
male childcare, 174, 180, 181, 183, 185
male domesticity transformation, 174, 180
male employment transformation, 183
male housework, 174, 180, 181-182, 185
male volunteer work, 182
male wages, 177-178, 179, 183, 184
manifest power, 185
marital emotion work, 185
marital relations, 185-186
maternal employment theory, 175
National Survey of Families and Households
    (NSFH), 180
nuclear family, 176, 177, 187
one-job/one-caregiver policy, 175
poverty, 178-179, 184
power dynamics, 175, 179, 185-186
racial/ethnic differences, 174, 176-177,
    178-179, 181, 182-183, 184, 186
research agenda, 175, 187
research overview, 175-176
single-parent families, 177, 178-179, 184
socioeconomic status, 174, 178-179, 181,
    184, 186
Standard North American Family, 176
structural-functionalism, 178, 179, 186
U.S. Bureau of the Census, 176
workplace strategies, 175
Gendered threshold, 181-182
Gender politics, 236-237
Gender roles:
    alternative lifestyles, 28
    childlessness, 120, 122-123, 124, 125-126,
        129-130
    cohabitation, 62, 63
    dual-earner families, 160, 161, 164,
        165, 168
    family therapy, 528

fathering, 228, 233, 236-237
gay/lesbian couples, 107
lesbian feminism, 196, 197-198, 199
marriage variations, 84-85
motherhood, 213-215, 217, 220
older-adult relationships, 138, 141, 144
religiosity, 415
Gender socialization theory, 141-142, 147
Gender theory, 178-179
General Federation of Women's Clubs,
    455, 465
Generalized reciprocity, 16-17, 375
General Social Survey, 97, 524
Gentlemen's Quarterly, 30
Georgia, 439
Gerry, Elbridge, 41
Ghetto-specific culture, 475
Glamour, 30
Goss v. *Lopez* (1975), 49
Great Britain:
    child development impact, 309-310
    child protection, 41
    Child Support Act (1991), 310
    cohabitation, 304-305, 308-309, 312
    cohabitation domestic economy, 309, 312
    confluent love theory, 307-308, 309
    contingency perspective, 313
    co-parenting model, 310-311
    demographics, 303-306, 310, 311, 314
    divorce impact, 309, 310
    divorce rates, 303, 304
    Divorce Reform Act (1967), 304
    family defined, 306, 312, 313, 314
    family diversity, 303, 306-307, 308, 311
    family economics, 309, 310, 312
    family networks, 311-313
    family pathway transformation, 303, 308
    family policy, 304, 308, 310
    family process context, 312-313
    family transformation accountability,
        306-308
    female employment, 307
    female reproduction control, 307
    gay/lesbian couples, 305-306
    household defined, 306, 312, 314
    individualism ideology, 307-308, 311, 314
    institutionalized marriage, 303-304
    kinship negotiations, 312-313
    legal-family framework, 303-304, 305,
        308, 309
    marriage defined, 303-304
    marriage rates, 303
    nonmarital birthrate, 303, 304
    poverty, 471, 482

racial/ethnic differences, 306
relationship commitment, 305, 306, 308-311
religiosity, 304, 305, 306, 308
reproduction technology, 498-499
research agenda, 310
research conclusions, 313-314
research overview, 302-303
single-parent families, 303, 304,
    305-306, 310
stepfamilies, 305, 310-312, 314
stepfamily defined, 305
stepfamily kinship, 311-312
Great Depression, 457-458, 459
Group marriage, 23, 25, 26, 27-31
Group Marriage (Constantine &
    Constantine), 26
Group sex, 28
Group Sex (Bartell), 27-28
Groves, Ernest R., 543
Groves Conference on Marriage and the
    Family:
    feminism, x
    formation (1934), ix
    1971 theme, x, 4-5, 6, 24, 27, 29
    1972 theme, 25, 27
    1973 theme, 13
    1981 theme, x, 10, 27
    objectives, ix-x
    research publications, x, 27, 29
    research topics, x, xi, 4, 24-26, 27
    research transformation, xi-xii
    2000 theme, x, 27

Hall, G. Stanley, 46, 456
Harding, Warren, 457, 463
Harrad Experiment, The (Rimmer), 26
Hawaii, 440
Hazelwood School District v. *Kuhlmeier*
    (1988), 49
Head Start, 44
Health:
    childhood transformation, 43
    older-adult relationships, 142, 143-144,
        145, 146, 147
    racial/ethnic differences, 386-387, 388,
        389-390
    See also Mental health
Health services, 32, 379, 389, 400-401
Hierarchical linear modeling (HLM), 159,
    166-167
Hispanic Americans. *See* Latino
    families
Homosexuality. *See* Gay/lesbian adolescents;
    Gay/lesbian couples

Honest Sex (Roy & Roy), 24
Hoover, Herbert, 458
Hoover technocrats, 458, 462
Hot and Cool Sex (Francoeur & Francoeur), 29
Household diversity:
    action research methodology, 15-18
    alternate families, 4-7
    alternate family acceptance, 9-11
    child development, 11-12, 16-18
    cultural scripts, 4, 7-8, 10-13, 14, 15
    deviant families, 8-9
    differentiation, 8
    diversity defined, 4, 13-15
    ecological diversity, 4, 13-14
    Equal Rights Amendment (1972), 7
    external risks, 8
    family policy, 10, 13-15, 18-19
    feminism, 4, 5, 6, 7, 9-10
    fictive kin, 17
    freedom ideology, 4, 5-6, 9-10, 14
    functionalism, 7-9, 11-12
    generalized reciprocity, 16-17
    Groves Conference on Marriage and the
        Family (1971), 4-5, 6
    Groves Conference on Marriage and the
        Family (1973), 13
    Groves Conference on Marriage and the
        Family (1981), 10
    healthy family objective, 5-6, 12, 13-18
    infant determinism, 12
    intimate networks, 17
    mainstream society, 10-11
    marital roles, 3, 6, 7, 11, 18, 19
    marriage culture, 13-14
    marriage ideology, 10-11, 13-14, 18-19
    National Survey of Families and Households
        (NSFH), 12
    neostandard family, 11-14, 15-16, 18
    new action theory, 7
    New Right ideology, 9-10, 19
    process theory, 7
    professional advocacy, 4-6, 7, 9-10
    public household, 17
    research conclusions, 18-19
    research overview, 4
    research theory, 7-9
    single-parent families, 10-11, 18-19
    social capital networks, 14-19
    social constructivism, 7-9, 10-11
    social responsibility, 5, 9-10
    standard family critique, 5-6
    standard family isolation, 3-4, 5
    standard family structure, 3-4, 5, 6, 8-9,
        10-13, 19

    structuration theory, 7
    symbolic interactionism, 7
    variant families, 9-11, 12-18
    Welfare Reform Act (1996), 10
    See also specific race/ethnicity
Howard Metzenbaum Multiethnic Placement
    Act (1994), 442
How the Other Half Lives (Riis), 478
Hull House (1903), 456
Hypergamy theory, 373

Identity development:
    childless couples, 122-123, 125-126,
        129-130
    fathering impact, 226, 229-230
    gay/lesbian adolescents, 98-99
    lesbian feminist, 194-195
    See also specific race/ethnicity
Illinois, 438
Immigration:
    Asian Americans, 369-370, 371, 372, 373,
        375, 376, 377, 378, 379, 380
    Latinos/Hispanics, 334, 335, 341,
        342, 346
    Muslim Americans, 394, 395, 402, 403,
        404, 405
    See also Acculturation; Assimilation
Immigration and Naturalization Service (INS),
    394-395
Immigration Reform Act (1965), 369, 376
Indian Health Service, 389
Indicators of Children's Well-Being, 461
Individual Development Accounts (IDAs), 482
Individualism-collectivism:
    marriage variations, 84-85
    pathogenic-conflict families, 249-251, 252
    racial/ethnic differences, 338-339, 341
Individualism ideology:
    family policy, 456, 458, 462, 465
    Great Britain, 307-308, 311, 314
Industrial reserve army, 476
Infant determinism, 12
In re Gault (1967), 48
In re Marriage of Buzzanca (1998), 441
In re Nicholas H. (2002), 438
Institute for 21st Century Relationships, 31
Institutionalization:
    fathering, 226
    marriage, 267-268, 270, 272-273, 303-304
    motherhood, 212-213, 217
    religiosity, 400, 414
Interdisciplinary research, 400, 405, 463-464
Intergenerational Panel Study of Parents and
    Children, 69

Intergenerational relations:
    family therapy, 528
    Internet impact, 510
    pathogenic-conflict families, 252
    racial/ethnic differences, 336-337, 341, 344,
        345-346, 355, 363, 377
    stepfamilies, 321
Intergenerational transmission theory, 213-214
Internet:
    accessibility, 357
    ACE Model of Cybersexual Addiction, 508
    aggression facilitation, 510
    alternative lifestyles, 31
    child development impact, 510
    data collection, 516-517
    determinism, 515
    ecological theory, 515
    education impact, 507
    elderly impact, 510, 511
    employment-family balance, 512-513
    employment flextime/flexplace policy, 513
    extramarital relationships, 509
    family assistance, 513-515
    family life education, 514-515, 549
    family network impact, 510, 511
    family policy, 513
    family relations impact, 506, 509-515
    family therapy, 513, 514-515
    gender differences, 509-510, 511
    intergenerational relations impact, 510
    Jupiter Research, 508
    longitudinal research, 516
    parental regulation, 510
    peer support, 513-514
    process-context model, 516
    racial/ethnic differences, 357, 507-508
    research agenda, 509, 510, 511, 514-517
    research conclusions, 517
    research design, 517
    research methodology, 515-517
    research overview, 507
    research sampling, 517
    research theory, 515
    romantic relationships, 508-509
    self-report methodology, 515-516
    single-parent families, 507
    social address model, 516
    social constructivism, 515
    social ecology theory, 515
    social network impact, 511-512, 513-514
    socioeconomic status, 507, 508
    special-needs support, 513
    technology history, 506-507
    technology prevalence, 507-508
    telecommuting, 512-513
    Triple-A Engine model, 508
    U.S. Bureau of Labor Statistics, 512
    user characteristics, 508-509
In the Matter of Baby M. (1988), 441
Intimate Friendships (Ramey), 29
Intimate Life Styles (DeLora & DeLora), 28
Invisible Web, The (Walters et al.), 526
Is Marriage Necessary? (Casler), 29
Italy, 471

Johnson, Lyndon B., 460, 469
Joint Committee on Standards for Educational
    Evaluation, 546-547
Journal of Alternative Relationships, 31
Journal of Family and Economic Issues, 32
Journal of Family Issues, x
Journal of Family Psychology, 413
Journal of Family Psychotherapy, 413
Journal of Feminist Family Therapy, 526, 530
Journal of Marital and Family Therapy,
    525-526, 528
Journal of Marriage and the Family, x, 212,
    218, 317-318, 413
Journal of Men's Studies, 413
Journal of Sex Research, 25
Jupiter Research, 508
Juvenile justice system, 44

Kansas City Studies of Adult Life, 136
Kelley, Florence, 456-457

Lathrop, Julia, 457, 465
Latino families:
    acculturated family, 336
    acculturation, 335-337, 341, 342, 344-345
    acculturation defined, 335, 337
    assimilation, 335, 338, 345-346
    assimilation defined, 335
    bicultural/acculturated identities, 337-338
    bicultural families, 337-338, 346
    biculturalism defined, 337, 338
    bicultural/multicultural identities, 338
    bilingualism, 346
    Bracero Program, 334
    Carribean, 334
    Chicano defined, 333
    childcare, 343
    child development, 335, 336-338, 339-342
    cohabitation, 60
    Colombians, 334
    consonant acculturation, 336
    Cubans, 334, 342
    Cultural Information Scale (CIS), 336

cultural-mismatch theory, 335
dissonant acculturation, 336-337
divorce, 342
domestic labor division, 343
Dominicans, 334, 341
dual-earner families, 161, 162, 165
economics, 334, 342
Ecuadorians, 334
education, 334, 340, 341, 342, 343
employment, 334, 343
familism, 339, 344
family heterogeneity, 334
family life education, 540
family process context, 338-344
family relations, 335, 336-337, 338-342
family structure, 342-343, 344
family values, 338-342, 346
fathering, 228, 231-232, 235
field-dependent skills, 340, 341-342
first-generation, 334, 335, 341, 342
future trends, 345-346
gender differences, 343
gendered family relations, 176-177
gender roles, 342-343
Guatemalans, 334
Hispanic defined, 333, 334
historical context, 334
Hondurans, 334
immigration, 334, 335, 341, 342, 346
individualism-collectivism, 338-339, 341
intergenerational relations, 336-337, 341,
    344, 345-346
Internet accessibility, 507-508
interpersonal relatedness, 339-340
Latin American defined, 333
Latino defined, 333-334
machismo, 342-343
marital relations, 342-343
Mexican-American War (1848), 334
Mexicans, 334, 338, 341-342, 343
migration patterns, 334, 335, 341, 342,
    345-346
modeling strategy, 339, 341
moderately acculturated family, 336
nomenclature, 333-334
obedience, 340, 342
1.5 generation, 334
parenting style, 339-342, 345
pathogenic-conflict families, 251-252
personalism, 340-341
population data, 333, 337, 345, 346
poverty, 342, 474-475
Puerto Ricans, 334, 341, 342, 343
religiosity, 338-339, 341, 422

research agenda, 344-345
research effectiveness, 344
research methodology, 335, 344-345
research overview, 333
respect, 340, 342
Salvadorans, 334
second-generation, 334, 341, 346
selective acculturation, 336, 337
single-parent families, 342
social adaptation framework, 335
socialization, 338, 345-346
socioeconomic status, 343
Spanish-American War (1917), 334
Spanish defined, 333
third-generation, 334, 341, 346
transracial adoption, 442
unacculturated family, 336
World War II, 334
La Vida (Lewis), 474
Lehr v. *Robertson* (1983), 438
Lesbian feminism:
    activism, 192, 193-194, 197-199, 200
    antiracist feminism, 194-195
    child development, 200-202
    Chinese Exclusion Act (1882), 196-197
    conscientization, 195
    consciousness-raising groups, 197-198
    emotional lesbians, 198
    family perspective, 200-202
    female sexual inverts, 196
    feminism defined, 192-194
    feminist practice, 200
    feminist praxis, 193, 200, 203
    feminist theory, 193-194, 199-200
    gender roles, 196, 197-198, 199
    liberal feminism, 194
    National Organization for Women
        (NOW), 198
    19th century, 195-197
    postmodern feminism, 194, 195
    power dynamics, 192, 193-195,
        196-200
    racial/ethnic discrimination, 193-195,
        196-197, 199
    radical-critical theory, 195
    reflexive research, 192, 193, 194-195,
        197-198, 202-203
    relationships, 195-196, 200-202
    research methodology, 195
    research overview, 192
    romantic friendships, 196
    self-identity, 194-195
    separatism, 198-199
    sexual behavior, 196, 197-198

socioeconomic status, 193-195, 196
structural oppression, 198
20th century, 197-199
voting rights, 196
world traveling, 199-203
Lewis v. *Lewis* (1976), 433, 434
Life course theory:
    childlessness, 121-122, 127, 128
    dual-earner families, 167
    Muslim Americans, 404
    older-adult relationships, 137-138, 148
    poverty, 472-473
    stepfamilies, 325
Lifestyles, 32
Lindsay, Samuel McCune, 456
Lofton v. *Kearney* (2001), 440
Logic models, 547
Longitudinal research, 65, 66, 69, 274, 325,
    358, 359, 470-471, 516
Losing Ground (Murray), 473
Louisiana, 273
Luxembourg Income Study (LIS), 471-472

Mademoiselle, 30
Mainstream society, 10-11
Marital relations:
    dual-earner families, 157, 159-161, 166,
        167, 168
    fathering, 233
    gendered family relations, 185-186
    poverty impact, 479-480
    racial/ethnic differences, 342-343, 360,
        399-400
    religiosity impact, 415-416, 417-418
    stepfamilies, 319, 321, 322, 323-324
Marital roles, 3, 6, 7, 11, 18, 19, 25
Marital violence model, 254
Marlow v. *Marlow* (1998), 440
Marriage:
    childlessness impact, 126-127
    companionate marriage, 268, 270
    covenant marriage, 273
    culture of, 13-14
    family law, 433-434, 439-440
    family therapy, 530-532
    fathering value, 236-237
    Great Britain, 303-304
    ideology, 10-11, 13-14, 18-19, 25
    institutionalization, 267-268, 270, 272-273,
        303-304
    interfaith, 406, 416
    Internet impact, 509
    interracial, 356, 373-374, 379
    poverty impact, 479-480

racial/ethnic differences, 353, 354, 356, 360,
    361, 370, 373-374, 397-398, 406
religiosity impact, 406, 412, 415-418
Marriage and Alternatives (Libby &
    Whitehurst), 29-30
Marriage and Family Review, 30, 515
Marriage and Its Alternatives (Duberman), 29
Marriage at the Crossroads (Stekel), 267
Marriage Crisis, The (Groves), 267
Marriage (Hart), 28
Marriage Movement, 272-273, 531-532
Marriage Preparation and Preservation Act
    (1988) (Florida), 92
Marriage variations:
    between cohorts, 80
    cognitive orientations, 82
    cohabitation, 79
    comparison level (CL), 82
    comparison level of alternatives (CLalt),
        82-83
    cultural value orientations, 84-85, 88
    divorce barriers, 83, 92-93
    divorce rates, 79, 86-88, 91, 92
    ecological/exchange framework, 80, 81*f,*
        84-86, 87-88, 89-92
    exosystem influences, 85-86
    feminism impact, 79, 92
    gender roles, 84-85
    hierarchy versus egalitarianism, 84-85, 88
    historical/cultural context, 83-84
    individualism-collectivism, 84-85
    marriage expectations, 88-89
    nonvoluntary relationships, 83
    normative exchange orientations, 85, 93
    power dynamics, 83-84, 88-89, 90-91
    racial/ethnic differences, 84-85, 89-91
    relationship attractiveness, 80-82
    relationship dependence, 82-84
    relationship structure, 80, 82*f,* 89
    research agenda, 91-93
    single-parent families, 79
    social exchange theory, 80-83
    within cohorts, 79-80
    See also Older-adult relationships
Marvin v. *Marvin* (1976), 439
Maryland, 92
Maternal deprivation, 229
Matriarchy model, 358-359
McHugh v. *McHugh* (1980), 433
Mental health:
    dual-earner families, 157, 158-159, 160,
        161, 164-165, 166, 167, 168
    racial/ethnic differences, 379, 390,
        400-401

religiosity impact, 414, 418
single-parent families, 287, 292
Mexican-American War (1848), 334
Michael H. v. Gerald D. (1989), 437
Middle Age and Aging (Neugarten), 136
Minnesota, 92
Minnesota Multiphasic Personality
    Inventory (MMPI), 30
Modeling strategy, 339, 341, 387
Monogamy, 24
Moral panics, 49-50
Motherhood:
    activism, 211, 212
    advice literature, 214-215
    child development, 220
    compartmentalization, 209, 219-220
    cross-cultural research, 213
    cultural contradiction theory, 214-216
    cultural imagery, 210-212, 215-216
    diversity of, 219
    doing gender perspective, 215
    18th century, 211
    evolutionary theory, 218-219
    gender roles, 213-215, 217, 220
    historical context, 210-212
    institutionalized, 212-213, 217
    intergenerational transmission theory,
        213-214
    maternal employment disenfranchisement,
        218-219
    maternal employment diversity, 217-218
    maternal employment ideology, 216-217
    maternal employment transformation,
        211-212, 214-215
    maternal practice/thinking theory, 214
    19th century, 211, 214
    poverty, 217-218
    power dynamics, 213-214
    racial/ethnic differences, 217, 219
    religiosity impact, 419-420
    research agenda, 219-221
    research overview, 210
    research review, 210, 211, 212-219
    research theory, 213-216, 219
    single-parent families, 217-218, 219
    social constructivism, 209
    socioeconomic status, 216, 217, 219
    20th century, 211
    U.S. Bureau of Labor Statistics, 211
Mothers' pension law, 43-44
MTV, 31
Multiple-roles theory, 157, 164-165
Muslim American families:
    African American, 394, 395, 403, 405

Arab family, 402
as religious institution, 400
assimilation, 395
child development, 398-400, 405
demographics, 392-396, 403
diversity of, 394, 395, 400, 401,
    402-404, 406
divorce, 399, 400
domestic labor division, 401
ecological theory, 403-404
economics, 397, 398, 399, 400, 401
education, 395
elderly, 398-399, 400
empirical research, 404-406
employment, 395, 401
family defined, 402
family-member care, 399, 400
family networks, 399, 401
family relations, 398-399
family research, 400-402
family structure, 399-400, 402
family therapy, 529
fathering, 405
feminism, 397, 404
gender differences, 397-398, 399, 401, 405
gender roles, 396-398, 401, 402, 404, 405
hadiths, 396, 399
health services, 400-401
historical context, 395-396
identity development, 395, 401
immigration, 394, 395, 402, 403, 404, 405
Immigration and Naturalization Service
    (INS), 394-395
interdisciplinary research, 400, 405
interfaith marriages, 406
Islamic family, 402
Islamic principles, 396
Islamic teachings, 396-400
life course theory, 404
marital relations, 399-400
marriage, 397-398, 406
mental health, 400-401
Middle Eastern family, 402
Muslim community defined, 402-403
Muslim defined, 405
Nation of Islam (NOI), 395, 403
nuclear family, 399-400
population data, 394-395
power dynamics, 397, 399, 404, 406
Qur'an, 396-397, 398-400, 406
regional differences, 394, 395, 405
religious categories, 395, 396, 402, 405
research agenda, 403-406
research conclusions, 406

research methodology, 402-403
research theory, 402, 403-404
responsibility, 398-400, 401
sexual behavior, 397, 398, 399-400
Shi'ites, 395
socialization, 405
socioeconomic status, 398
stereotypes, 400, 401, 402, 403
Sunni (orthodox), 395, 396, 403
symbolic interactionism, 404
systems theory, 403-404
veiling, 395, 397, 401

Narrative therapy, 528
Nation, 357
National Adolescent Health Study, 274
National Association of Social Workers
    (NASW), 544
National Center for Health Statistics (NCHS),
    318, 354, 440-441
National Congress of Mothers, 465
National Council on Family Relations (NCFR),
    539, 540, 542, 544, 549
National Education Longitudinal Study
    (NELS), 325
National Health and Social Life Survey, 96, 524
National Institute of Child Health and Human
    Development (NICHD), 163
National Longitudinal Study of Adolescent
    Health, 65, 66
National Longitudinal Survey of the High
    School Class of 1972, 69
National Longitudinal Survey of Youth
    (Mother and Child Supplement), 274
National Longitudinal Survey of Youth
    (NLSY), 66, 358, 359, 470
National Organization for Women
    (NOW), 198
National Survey of America's Families
    (NSAF), 65
National Survey of Children, 274
National Survey of Families and Households
    (NSFH), 12, 65, 66, 67-68, 69, 180, 274,
    322, 325, 416
National Survey of Family Growth (NSFG),
    68, 69, 318, 355
National/Worldwide Marriage Encounter,
    542-543
Native Americans. *See* American Indian families
Neostandard family, 11-14, 15-16, 18
New action theory, 7
New Deal, 458-459, 463
New Horizon, 32
New Intimacy, The (Mazur), 29

New Mexico, 337
New Right ideology, 9-10, 19
Newsweek, 32
New York, 269, 436, 543
New York, New York, 30
New York Society for the Prevention of Cruelty
    to Children (1874), 41
New York Times Magazine, 30
Niesen v. *Niesen* (1968), 437
Nixon, Richard, 452
Non-Traditional Family Forms in the 1970's
    (Sussman), x
Nonvoluntary relationships, 83
North American Swing Club Association, 30
Nuclear family:
    fathering, 228
    gendered family relations, 176, 177, 187
    racial/ethnic differences, 399-400
    stepfamilies, 319

Occupational stress theory, 157, 158-159,
    162, 165
Office of Economic Opportunity, 469
Of Woman Born (Rich), 212
Oklahoma:
    divorce barriers, 92
    no-fault divorce, 268
    premarital education, 273
    Seven Generation Youth Society, 386
Old Age pensions, 459
Older-adult relationships:
    age differences, 140, 142, 143, 144
    cohabitation, 72, 140-141, 147-148
    demographics, 137-138
    divorce impact, 138, 140, 142-145
    domestic labor division, 138, 144
    economic impact, 137, 139, 141, 142-143,
        144, 146, 147
    education impact, 137, 138, 146
    employment impact, 137, 138, 139-140,
        142, 144, 146
    family relations, 140, 141-142, 143-144,
        145, 146, 147
    future trends, 138, 139-141, 142, 143, 144
        146, 147-148, 149
    gay/lesbian couples, 146-147
    gender differences, 138, 139-140, 141-142,
        143, 144, 145, 147
    gender roles, 138, 141, 144
    gender socialization theory, 141-142, 147
    health issues, 142, 143-144, 145, 146, 147
    Kansas City Studies of Adult Life, 136
    life course theory, 137-138, 148
    life expectancy, 137

long-term marriage, 138-140
marriage variations, 138-248
never-married adults, 145-146
prevalence rates, 137, 138
public attitudes, 137
remarriage, 140
research agenda, 148-149
research methodology, 148-149
research overview, 136, 137
research review, 136-137
retirement impact, 138, 139-140
sexual behavior, 137, 147-148
social networks, 141-142, 143-146, 147
social stigma, 146, 147
stereotypes, 137, 146
widowhood impact, 138, 140, 141-142
Open marriage, 25, 28
Open Marriage (O'Neill & O'Neill), 25, 28
Oregon, 386, 390-391, 443
Orshansky, Mollie, 469-470
Other America, The (Harrington), 478

Panel Study of Income Dynamics (PSID), 163,
470, 471, 472
Parens patriae doctrine, 42
Parent aggressor hypothesis, 254
Parental investment theory, 119
Parent Effectiveness Training (PET), 542-543
Parenting process model, 233
Parenting style:
racial/ethnic differences, 339-342, 345,
372, 378
religiosity impact, 420
stepfamilies, 322
Parent Teacher Association (PTA), 465
Parent victim hypothesis, 254
Partnership model, 433-434
Pathogenic-conflict families:
aggressogenic cognitions, 246
child appraisal, 246
child maltreatment defined, 255
child reaction, 246-247, 250-251
comorbidity, 253-255
comorbidity effects, 253-254
comorbidity extent, 253
conflict exposure, 245, 250
conflict properties, 245
conflict resolution, 245, 250
conflict topic, 245
co-parenting spillover, 248-249
cultural variation, 249-253
culture defined, 252
defined, 244
dual-perpetrator model, 254

emotional security hypothesis, 247, 251
ethnicity defined, 252
family dysfunction model, 254
gender differences, 246-247, 249
individualism-collectivism, 249-251, 252
intergenerational differences, 252
marital violence model, 254
multilevel conceptualizations, 255-256
parent aggressor hypothesis, 254
parental control, 250
parenting behavior spillover, 247-248
parent victim hypothesis, 254
pathway-of-influence models, 254-255
peer spillover, 249
primary conflict processing, 246
racial/ethnic differences, 249-252, 256
reciprocal-influence processes, 254, 256-257
religiosity, 250, 252-253
research agenda, 249-257
research conclusions, 257
research overview, 244
research terminology, 252, 255
secondary conflict processing, 246
sequential-perpetrator model, 254
severity continuum, 245
severity measures, 255
sibling spillover, 249
single-perpetrator model, 254
specific emotions model, 246-247
spillover effects, 247-249, 251-252
violence tolerance, 250
Patriarchal ideology:
family policy, 458-459
fathering, 228
gendered family relations, 180-183, 185
Pennsylvania, 269
Persons of the opposite sex sharing living
quarters (POSSLQ), 67
Planned Parenthood Association v. *Matheson*
(1983), 48-49
Political agendas:
divorce, 267, 269-270, 294
family life education, 538-539
family policy, 451, 452, 455-459, 460, 461
462, 463, 464-465, 469
family therapy, 530
gender politics, 236-237
poverty, 469, 480, 482
reproduction technology, 498-499
Polyamory, 31
Polyamory (Anapol), 31
Polyamory Society, 31
Polygamy, 32-33
Polygyny, 28

Population Profile of the United States: 2000
    (U.S. Census Bureau), 318
Poverty:
    amelioration strategies, 480-482
    asset development, 481-482
    attitude causation, 473
    causation factors, 473-478
    child development impact, 478-480
    child support enforcement, 481
    comparative research, 471-472
    cultural/neighborhood causation, 474-476
    culture-of-poverty framework, 474-475
    Current Population Survey (CPS), 470
    domestic violence impact, 480
    dual labor market, 476
    dynamics, 469-473
    Earned Income Tax Credit (EITC), 480-481
    economic structure causation, 476
    education impact, 472, 478-479
    empirical research, 476
    family effects, 479-480
    family networks, 479
    family policy, 457, 459-460, 469, 475, 477,
        480-481, 482
    gender differences, 477
    gendered family relations, 178-179, 184
    ghetto-specific culture, 475
    health impact, 478
    human capital causation, 474
    individual causation, 473-474
    Individual Development Accounts
        (IDAs), 482
    individual effects, 478-479
    industrial reserve army, 476
    life course theory, 472-473
    longitudinal dynamics, 470-471
    Luxembourg Income Study (LIS), 471-472
    marital relations, 479-480
    marriage impact, 479-480
    measurement, 469-470
    motherhood, 217-218
    National Longitudinal Survey of Youth
        (NLSY), 470
    Office of Economic Opportunity, 469
    Panel Study of Income Dynamics (PSID),
        470, 471, 472
    political agendas, 469, 480, 482
    poverty rate, 470
    racial/ethnic differences, 342, 355-356, 370,
        472, 474-475, 476, 477, 479
    racial/ethnic discrimination, 477
    research agenda, 482-483
    research communication, 483
    research design, 482

    research methodology, 473, 482
    research relevancy, 483
    research theory, 483
    residential segregation causation, 475-476
    scope, 469-473
    single-parent families, 282, 287-288
    social isolation causation, 475
    social/political structure causation, 476-477
    socioeconomic status, 476-477, 478, 480
    structural causation, 476-478
    structural vulnerability causation, 477-478
    Survey of Income and Program Participation
        (SIPP), 470
    Temporary Assistance for Needy Families
        (TANF), 481
    War on Poverty, 460, 469, 475
    welfare causation, 473-474
Poverty (Hunter), 472
Power dynamics:
    family law, 444
    family therapy, 525, 528, 529
    gay/lesbian couples, 108
    gendered family relations, 175, 179,
        185-186
    invisible power, 185
    latent power, 185
    lesbian feminism, 192, 193-195, 196-200
    manifest power, 185
    marriage variations, 83-84, 88-89, 90-91
    motherhood, 213-214
    racial/ethnic differences, 363, 372, 376, 377,
        397, 399, 404, 406
    stepfamilies, 319
President's Research Committee on Social
    Trends (1933), 458
Prevention and Relationship Enhancement
    Program (PREP), 542-543, 548
Primary conflict processing, 246
Process-context model, 516
Process theory, 7
Progressive Era, 43-44, 48, 455-456, 457,
    460, 465
Proposition 31 (Rimmer), 26
Public attitudes:
    alternative lifestyles, 25, 26-27
    childhood transformation, 37-47,
        48-51
    divorce, 267, 269-270, 273-274
    gay/lesbian adolescents, 97
    older-adult relationships, 137
Public household, 17
Public policy. *See* Family law; Family policy
Pulliam v. *Smith* (1998), 440
Puritans, 37-38, 227

Quakers, 39
Queen's Medical Center v. *Kagawa* (1998), 433

Racial/ethnic differences:
    childcare, 343, 362, 375-376
    childhood transformation, 40, 41, 42,
        43-44, 47, 50
    childlessness, 120, 128
    cohabitation, 60
    deficit-model perspective, 358-359, 371
    divorce, 342, 353-354, 357-358, 361,
        370-371, 388-389, 399, 400
    domestic labor division, 343, 376, 401
    dual-earner families, 157, 161, 162,
        163-165, 168
    ecological theory, 359, 403-404
    education, 334, 340, 341, 342, 343, 358,
        362, 387-388, 395
    employment, 334, 343, 358, 359,
        361-363, 395, 401
    family life education, 540
    family policy, 361, 387-388
    family process context, 338-344
    family therapy, 525, 526, 528-529, 532
    fathering, 228, 229, 231-232, 235
    feminism, 193-195, 196-197, 199, 397, 404
    gay/lesbian couples, 355, 377-378, 380
    gendered family relations, 174, 176-177,
        178-179, 181, 182-183, 184, 186
    Great Britain, 306
    health, 386-387, 388, 389-390
    individualism-collectivism, 338-339, 341
    intergenerational relations, 336-337, 341,
        344, 345-346, 355, 363, 377
    Internet, 357, 507-508
    marital relations, 342-343, 360, 399-400
    marriage, 353, 354, 356, 360, 361, 370,
        373-374, 397-398, 406
    marriage variations, 84-85, 89-91
    mental health, 379, 390, 400-401
    motherhood, 217, 219
    nuclear family, 399-400
    parenting style, 339-342, 345, 372, 378
    pathogenic-conflict families, 249-252, 256
    poverty, 342, 355-356, 370, 472, 474-475,
        476, 477, 479
    power dynamics, 363, 372, 376, 377, 397,
        399, 404, 406
    religiosity, 338-339, 341, 371, 414,
        420, 422
    reproduction technology, 497
    sexual behavior, 387, 397, 398, 399-400
    single-parent families, 282, 288, 291, 292-293
    social exchange theory, 375
    social networks, 375-376, 379
    socioeconomic status, 343, 356, 358-359,
        362, 374
    stepfamilies, 318
    See also specific race/ethnicity
Racial/ethnic discrimination, 193-195,
    196-197, 199, 477
Radical-critical theory, 195
Rational choice theory, 120-121, 128, 496, 497
Reagan, Ronald, 269-270
Reconstituted families, 317
Recreating Motherhood (Rothman), 218
Reflexive research:
    family life education, 550
    lesbian feminism, 192, 193, 194-195,
        197-198, 202-203
Regional differences:
    Asian Americans, 370
    childhood transformation, 38-39, 40-41, 42,
        43, 47
    childlessness, 118, 120
    fathering, 228
    Muslim Americans, 394, 395, 405
Relationship Enhancement (RE), 542-543
Religiosity:
    adaptive influences, 424
    affiliation, 411-412, 414, 415, 416,
        417-419, 420, 421, 422, 423
    child development impact, 418, 419-421,
        423-425
    childhood transformation, 38, 41, 46
    childlessness, 120
    cohabitation impact, 60
    comparative research, 423
    conflict resolution, 417
    dimensions, 413, 415
    diversity of, 411-412, 422, 423-426
    divorce, 267, 412, 414, 415, 416
    domestic violence, 415-416, 418
    empirical research, 412, 413, 419
    faith communities, 413-414, 417, 419
    family diversity impact, 411-412, 422,
        423, 425-426
    family linkage research, 412-422
    family relations impact, 415-421
    family type, 414
    fathering, 227, 231-232, 419
    fertility, 418-419
    forgiveness, 417
    future trends, 425-426
    gay/lesbian couples, 414, 422
    gender differences, 415, 419-420
    gender roles, 415
    Great Britain, 304, 305, 306, 308

growth predictions, 425-426
highly religious families, 423
individualistic forms, 414
institutional forms, 414
interfaith marriage, 406, 416
maladaptive influences, 424
marital relations, 415-416, 417-418
marriage impact, 406, 412, 415-418
mental health impact, 414, 418
motherhood, 419-420
National Survey of Families and Households
    (NSFH), 416
paradox focus, 423-424
parenting style, 420
pathogenic-conflict families, 250, 252-253
prayer, 417
qualitative research, 424
racial/ethnic differences, 338-339, 341, 371,
    414, 420, 422
religious beliefs, 413, 417, 420
religious communities, 413, 421
religious practices, 413, 417-418, 420-421
research agenda, 423-425
research design, 422
research diversity, 414-415
research limitations, 421-422
research methodology, 415, 421
research overview, 412
research publications, 413, 422
research sampling, 422
research theory, 421-422
sexual behavior, 417-418
substance abuse, 416, 418
toxic faith, 414
transcendent benefits, 424-425
types, 413-414, 415, 417
U.S. Bureau of the Census, 412
value of, 411
    See also Muslim American families
Remarriage:
    family law, 436-437
    family therapy, 526, 529-530
    older-adult relationships, 140
    single-parent families, 291-292
    See also Stepfamilies
Renovating Marriage (Whitehurst), 29
Reproduction of Mothering (Chodorow), 213
Reproduction suppression theory, 119
Reproduction technology:
    artificial wombs, 502
    child development impact, 497-502
    child nondisclosure, 500-501, 502
    cloning, 494-495, 502
    decision-making process, 496-497, 500-501

donor insemination, 494-495, 498
economics, 499-500
embryo adoption, 502
ethics, 499, 501
family diversity, 503
family impact, 495-502
family law, 440-441, 446, 494
family policy, 499-501
family process context, 502-503
family relations impact, 498-499, 501-502
Fanconi's anemia (FA), 493-494
future trends, 502-503
gamete donation, 500-501, 502
gay/lesbian couples, 494-495
genetic counseling, 496
genetic prediction, 495
genetic research, 495
genetic testing, 496-497
health system experience, 499-501
in vitro fertilization (IVF), 494, 498, 499
molecular biology, 495
political agendas, 498-499
preimplantation genetic diagnosis
    (PGD), 495
racial/ethnic differences, 497
rational choice model, 496, 497
research agenda, 502-503
research history, 501-502
research overview, 493
research theory, 502
socioeconomic status, 496
surrogate mother, 494
tentative pregnancies, 499
Review of Religious Research, 413
Roe v. *Wade* (1973), 434
Rolling Stone, 30
Romantic friendships, 196
Roosevelt, Franklin D., 457-458, 459,
    463, 464
Roosevelt, Theodore, 456, 461

Safe sex, 32
Scandinavia, 471
Scarcity hypotheses, 159
Scientific management theory, 456, 462
Secondary conflict processing, 246
Selective acculturation, 336, 337
Separatism, 198-199
Sequential-perpetrator model, 254
Settlement Houses, 457, 463
Seven generations philosophy, 385-386
Seven Generation Youth Society
    (Oklahoma), 386
Sex in the 90's (MTV), 31

Sexual behavior:
  childhood transformation, 40, 42, 46,
      48-49, 51
  childlessness, 124, 125, 127
  dual-earner families, 159
  gay/lesbian couples, 103, 107, 108-109
  lesbian feminism, 196, 197-198
  older-adult relationships, 137, 147-148
  racial/ethnic differences, 387, 397, 398,
      399-400
  religiosity, 417-418
  safe sex, 32
Sexual orientation. See Gay/lesbian adolescents;
    Gay/lesbian couples
Sheppard-Towner Act (1921), 44, 457, 463
Signs, 194
Single-parent families:
  adulthood mental health impact, 287
  adulthood relationship impact, 287
  behavior genetics, 294-295
  behavior impact, 284, 288
  childcare, 291
  child development impact, 283-287,
      288-289, 290-295
  cohabitation prevalence, 283
  cohort effects, 294
  creative coping, 291
  defined, 283
  demographics, 283
  divorce prevalence, 283
  economic functioning, 282, 287-288
  economic strain impact, 288
  education impact, 284-285, 288
  family policy, 454
  family therapy, 524-525, 526-527, 529,
      530, 532
  family transformation, 282-283
  fathering, 224-225, 233-234, 235
  fragile families, 283
  functioning capability, 287-292
  gender differences, 286, 287-288,
      289-290
  gendered family relations, 177,
      178-179, 184
  Great Britain, 303, 304, 305-306, 310
  household diversity, 10-11, 18-19
  increased maturity effect, 286-287
  Internet impact, 507
  motherhood, 217-218, 219
  nonmarital childbirth, 283
  nonresidential-parent contact, 289-291
  parental affection, 289
  parental control, 289
  parental discipline, 289, 290

  parental mental health, 292
  parental stress, 288-289
  poverty, 282, 287-288
  psychological impact, 285-286, 294
  racial/ethnic differences, 282, 288, 291,
      292-293, 342, 354, 356, 358, 361,
      370, 387
  remarriage impact, 291-292
  research agenda, 292, 293-295
  research conclusions, 295
  research measurement, 293-294
  research methodology, 284, 293, 294
  research overview, 282
  research sampling, 293-294
  research theory, 293
  resilience effect, 285
  social competence impact, 286-287
  social networks, 291, 292-293
  task strain impact, 288-289
  teen pregnancy causation, 283
  teen pregnancy impact, 285
Single-perpetrator model, 254
Sisterhood is Powerful (Morgan), 197
Situational ethnicity, 374-375
Slovak American families, 529
Smart Marriages Conference, 531
Social adaptation framework, 335
Social address model, 156, 165, 516
Social capital networks, 14-19
Social class. See Socioeconomic status
Social constructivism, 7-9, 10-11, 36, 209, 515
Social Darwinism, 456, 459
Social ecology theory, 515
Social exchange theory:
  childlessness, 121, 127-128
  family life education, 542
  racial/ethnic differences, 375
  stepfamilies, 325
  See also Marriage variations
Social fatherhood, 225
Socialization:
  gender socialization theory, 141-142, 147
  work socialization theory, 157, 158-160,
      161-163, 164, 165, 166, 167-168
  See also specific race/ethnicity
Social learning theory, 542
Social movements. See Activism
Social networks:
  cohabitation, 66-67
  dual-earner families, 168
  fictive kin, 17
  gay/lesbian couples, 102
  Internet impact, 511-512, 513-514
  intimate networks, 17

older-adult relationships, 141-142, 143-146, 147
    racial/ethnic differences, 375-376, 379
    single-parent families, 291, 292-293
    social capital networks, 14-19
    See also Family networks
Social policy. *See* Family law; Family policy
Social responsibility, 5, 9-10
Social role theory, 165
Social Security Act (1935), 44, 458
Social Security Amendments (1939), 457-459, 463
Social stigma:
    childlessness, 116, 123, 125-126, 128
    divorce, 270
    gay/lesbian couples, 96, 305
    older-adult relationships, 146, 147
Socioeconomic status:
    childhood transformation, 39-47, 48
    childlessness, 121
    divorce, 271
    dual-earner families, 157, 158, 163-165, 167, 168
    family life education, 540
    family policy, 454-456
    fathering impact, 227-228, 229, 231-232, 237-238
    gendered family relations, 174, 178-179, 181, 184, 186
    Internet impact, 507, 508
    lesbian feminism, 193-195, 196
    motherhood, 216, 217, 219
    poverty, 476-477, 478, 480
    racial/ethnic differences, 343, 356, 358-359, 362, 374
    reproduction technology, 496
    stepfamilies, 318
Spain, 471
Spanish-American War (1917), 334
Specific emotions model, 246-247
Standard family:
    critiques, 5-6
    isolation of, 3-4, 5
    structure, 3-4, 5, 6, 8-9, 10-13, 19
Standards for Evaluation of Educational Programs, Projects, and Materials, 546-547
Stanley v. *Illinois* (1971), 438
State ex rel. Watts v. *Watts* (1973), 436
State v. *Miranda* (1997), 436-437
Stepfamilies:
    binuclear families, 317
    blended families, 317
    child development impact, 321-323, 324-325
    cohabitation, 319

    decision-making process, 319, 323
    deficit-model perspective, 319, 324-325
    defined, 305, 317
    demographics, 318-319, 323
    diversity of, 317
    economics, 319
    family law, 432, 436-437, 446
    family networks, 311-312, 324
    family process context, 323-324
    family research, 319-321
    family therapy, 529-530, 531
    gay/lesbian couples, 319, 320
    gender differences, 318, 319-321
    Great Britain, 305, 310-312, 314
    intergenerational relations, 321
    life course theory, 325
    marital relations, 319, 321, 322, 323-324
    National Center for Health Statistics (NCHS), 318
    National Education Longitudinal Study (NELS), 325
    National Survey of Families and Households (NSFH), 322, 325
    National Survey of Family Growth (NSFG), 318
    normative-adaptive perspective, 321-322
    nuclear family ideal, 319
    parental control, 320
    parental role, 320, 322
    parenting style, 322
    power dynamics, 319
    prior-family relations, 324
    problem-oriented perspective, 321-322
    racial/ethnic differences, 318, 355
    reconstituted families, 317
    remarriage adjustment research, 319
    research agenda, 321, 323-325
    research methodology, 325
    research overview, 317
    research publications, 317-318
    research theory, 325
    social exchange theory, 325
    socioeconomic status, 318
    stepsons/stepdaughters, 320
    subsystem intersection, 324
    Survey of Income and Program Participation (SIPP), 318, 325
    U.S. Bureau of the Census, 318
    younger/older children, 320, 321
Stepfamily Association of America, 318
Stereotypes:
    gender, 234-235
    Muslim Americans, 400, 401, 402, 403
    older-adult relationships, 137, 146

Stevenson, Adlai, 267, 269
Strengths approach, 529
Structural-functionalism, 178, 179, 186
Structuration theory, 7
Substance abuse:
    American Indians, 386-387, 388, 389, 391
    religiosity impact, 416, 418
Supreme Court rulings:
    children's rights, 48-49
    family law, 432, 433, 434, 436-437, 438,
        439, 440, 441
Survey of Income and Program Participation
    (SIPP), 69, 318, 325, 353-354, 355, 470
Swinging, 23, 24, 27-31
Symbolic interactionism, 7, 404
Systematic Training for Effective Parenting
    (STEP), 542-543, 547
Systems theory, 403-404, 528
    system/ecosystem perspective, 542

Taiwan, 482
Teaching Family Science Conference, 544
Teen Outreach Program (TOP), 542-543
Telecommuting, 512-513
Temporary Assistance for Needy Families
    (TANF), 452, 481
Texas, 337
Third-party visitation, 438-439
Time, 31
Tinker v. *Des Moines School District* (1969),
    48, 49
Title IX, Educational Amendments (1972), 49
Title X, Public Health Service Act (1970), 49
Title XIX, Social Security Act (1965), 49
Toxic faith, 414
Trammel v. *United States* (1980), 434
Transformative learning theory, 550
*Trends in the Well-Being of America's Children
    and Youth*, 461
Triple-A Engine model, 508
Troxel v. *Granville* (2000), 439

Uniform Marriage and Divorce Act (2002), 435
Uniform Parentage Act, 437
    Draft Revision (1998), 441

United States v. *Sokolow* (1988), 49
University of Maryland conference (1975),
    26, 27
U.S. Bureau of Labor Standards, 457
U.S. Bureau of Labor Statistics, 155, 211,
    456, 462, 512
U.S. Bureau of the Census, 67, 68, 99, 176,
    318, 353-354, 355, 356, 370, 412,
    523-524
U.S. Children's Bureau (1912), 43, 456-457,
    461-462, 464
U.S. Cooperative Extension Service, 543, 546
U.S. Department of Health and Human
    Services, 442
Utah, 92, 273

Value compatibility theory, 371
Variant families, 9-11, 12-18
Vermont, 440, 532
Voting rights, 196, 456, 457

War on Poverty, 460, 469, 475
Washington, 438-439
Welfare, Children and Families Study, 70
Welfare Peer Assistance Network
    (WELPAN), 462
Welfare Reform Act (1996), 10
Wellness model, 390
West v. *West* (1998), 439
White House Conference on Children
    (1909), 43
White House Conference on Families
    (1980), 451
Wickham v. *Burne* (2002), 439
Wilcox v. *Trautz* (1998), 439
Williams v. *Williams* (1998), 439
Woman's Christian Temperance Union
    (WCTU), 455
Women in Families (McGoldrick et al.), 526
Work socialization theory, 157, 158-160, 161
    163, 164, 165, 166, 167-168
World War II, 334, 369

Zero Adolescent Pregnancy (ZAP), 542-543

About the Editors

Marilyn Coleman is a Professor of Human Development and Family Studies at the University of Missouri. **Lawrence Ganong** is a Professor of Nursing and Human Development and Family Studies at the University of Missouri. Together, they have coauthored over 130 articles and book chapters as well as four books, including *Stepfamily Relationships* (2004), *Changing Families, Changing Responsibilities* (1999), *Remarried Family Relationships* (1994), and *Bibliotherapy With Stepchildren* (1988). They are the editors of *Points and Counterpoints: Controversial Relationship and Family Issues in the 21st Century* (2003). They have conducted research on stepfamilies for 25 years. Recent work has focused on family responsibilities following divorce and remarriage and the development of stepparent-stepchild relationships. Dr. Coleman was Editor of the *Journal of Marriage and the Family* from 1992 to 1995 and Associate Editor of the *Home Economics Research Journal* from 1987 to 1990. Dr. Ganong was Associate Editor of the *Journal of Social and Personal Relationships* from 2000 to 2003.

About the Contributors

Graham Allan is Professor of Social Relations at Keele University. His research mainly focuses on aspects of informal social relationships. He is particularly interested in the sociology of friendship, family and domestic life, kinship, and community and has written widely on these subjects. His current research includes projects on stepfamily kinship and on marital affairs.

Katherine R. Allen, PhD, is Professor of Family Studies in the Department of Human Development at Virginia Polytechnic Institute and State University. She coordinates the Human Development Masters Program and is an Affiliate of the Center for Gerontology and an Adjunct Professor in Women's Studies. With an interest in family diversity over the life course, qualitative research methods, feminist pedagogy, and social justice work in the family field, she is currently investigating adult sibling ties, life histories of older gay men and lesbians, and the retention of women and people of color in educational environments. Her books include *Handbook of Family Diversity,* coedited with David Demo and Mark Fine (2000); *Women and Families: Feminist Reconstructions,* coauthored with Kristine Baber (1992); and *Single Women/Family Ties: Life Histories of Older Women* (Sage, 1989). She is also a member of the senior editorial team for the new *Sourcebook of Family Theory and Methods.*

Paul R. Amato received his PhD in social psychology from James Cook University in Australia, and he is currently a Professor of Sociology, Demography, and Family Studies at Pennsylvania State University. He was a researcher with the Australian Institute of Family Studies in the 1980s and was a Fulbright Fellow in India in 1992. His research focuses primarily on marital quality and the causes and consequences of divorce. During the last 20 years, he has published four books and over 100 book chapters and journal articles. In 1994, 2000, and 2002, he received the Reuben Hill Award from the National Council on Family Relations for the best article published in the previous year to combine research and theory on the family.

Dianne M. Bartels is the Associate Director of the University of Minnesota Center for Bioethics. She obtained her master's degree in psychosocial nursing from the University of Washington and her PhD in family social science from the University of Minnesota. Her research interests focus on ethics in genetic health care and in end-of-life care.

Karen Bogenschneider is a Professor of Human Development and Family Studies at the University of Wisconsin–Madison and a Family Policy Specialist in University Extension. She is Director of the Wisconsin Family Impact Seminars and Executive Director of the Policy Institute for Family Impact Seminars, which provides technical assistance to 12 sites conducting seminars in their state capitals. She is author of *Family Policy Matters: How Policymaking Affects Families and What Professionals Can Do*. She has published extensively in research and applied journals on competent parenting of adolescents and on strategies for connecting research to policy and practice. She was named one of the outstanding Extension Specialists in the country and was recognized by the National Council of Family Relations for her contributions to their policy efforts.

Eulalee Brand-Clingempeel, PhD, is Founder and Director of the Family Psychology Institute and a licensed clinical psychologist in independent practice in Florence, South Carolina, a position she has held for over 13 years. She has published numerous articles focusing on family processes and children's outcomes in stepfather and stepmother families. She also has published in the area of cognitive-behavioral interventions for depression, with an emphasis on adaptations for elderly populations. She previously served on the faculty of Pennsylvania State University at Harrisburg and is a past president of the Philadelphia Chapter of the Stepfamily Association of America.

Richard Bulcroft is an Associate Professor of Sociology at Western Washington University and Program Chair for the Theory Construction and Research Methodology Workshop at the National Council of Family Relations meetings in 2004. He has conducted extensive research on a variety of aspects of marriage and family life, including the effects of infant feeding practices on the transition to parenthood. He is currently examining the broader effects of modernity on romantic relationships, marriage, and family formation.

Sarah Carnochan is a doctoral student in social welfare at the University of California, Berkeley. She received her JD from the University of California at Berkeley in 1988 and practiced housing law. She is the coauthor with Chester Hartman of *City for Sale: The Transformation of San Francisco* (2002), examining urban development in San Francisco. Current research interests include the intersections between the legal and social welfare systems and the effects of welfare policy and programs on low-income families.

Tamara C. Cheshire, MA, is Adjunct Faculty in the Department of Anthropology at Sacramento City College. She is Lakota, and her interests lie in American Indian education, American Indian families, and tribal sovereignty issues. She currently teaches courses in Native American studies.

W. Glenn Clingempeel, PhD, is an Associate Professor of Psychology at the University of North Carolina–Fayetteville. He achieved national recognition in the 1980s for his research on family relationships and child outcomes in different structural types of stepfamilies. His collaboration with Dr. E. Mavis Hetherington on the Longitudinal Study of Remarriage (LSR) culminated in a 1992 *Monograph of the Society for Research in Child Development* that remains one of the most widely cited studies of the effects of divorce and remarriage on children. His recent research focuses on risk and protective mechanisms in children's adaptive and maladaptive responses to adverse family processes and events. He has served on the faculties of Temple University and Pennsylvania State University at Harrisburg.

Scott Coltrane is Professor of Sociology at the University of California, Riverside (UCR), and Associate Director of the UCR Center for Family Studies. He is recipient of the UCR Distinguished Teaching Award and Past President of the Pacific Sociological Association. His research focuses on the relationships among fatherhood, motherhood, marriage, parenting, domestic labor, and popular culture. His most recent National Institutes of Health–funded research projects investigate the impact of economic stress on family functioning and the meaning of fatherhood and stepfatherhood in Mexican American and European American families. He is the author of over 70 scholarly publications. He is the editor of *Families and Society* (2004), coauthor of *Sociology of Marriage and the Family* (2001), and author of *Gender and Families* (1998) and *Family Man* (1996).

Teresa M. Cooney is Associate Professor and Chair of the Department of Human Development and Family Studies at the University of Missouri–Columbia. She holds a doctorate in human development and family studies with a minor in demography from Pennsylvania State University and completed a postdoctoral fellowship in demography of families and aging at the University of North Carolina–Chapel Hill. Her research has focused primarily on family demography and gerontology, with particular attention devoted to how sociodemographic changes, such as increased divorce rates and the rise in custodial grandparenting, have affected family relationships among adults.

Tom Corbett has emeritus status at the University of Wisconsin–Madison and remains an active affiliate with the Institute for Research on Poverty, where, until recently, he served as Associate Director. He has long studied trends in welfare reform and social programs that affect the well-being of vulnerable families, along with methods for assessing their effectiveness. Recently, he served on a National Academy of Sciences panel examining methods for evaluating contemporary welfare reform initiatives. He has worked on welfare reform issues at all levels of government, including a year as senior policy advisor at the U.S. Department of Health and Human Services. He continues to work with a number of states through networks of senior state welfare officials in the Midwest and on the West Coast and on issues of program and systems integration to deliver better services to challenged families.

Graham Crow is Reader in Sociology at the University of Southampton, where he has worked since 1983. He is the author or coauthor of four books and editor or coeditor of four more, on various subjects relating to families, households, communities, and social theory. He has also coedited the electronic journal *Sociological Research Online*. He is currently writing a book on modes of sociological argument and working on a project exploring the issue of informed consent in the research process.

David C. Dollahite, PhD, is Professor of Family Life at Brigham Young University, where he teaches classes on religion and family life. His research focuses on the linkages between religion and marriage and family among Jewish, Christian, Muslim, and Mormon families with adolescent children and on faith and fathering among fathers of children with special needs.

Kathleen Dunne is a community development coordinator for the Alzheimer's Association Mid-Missouri Chapter, where she provides education, training, and support services for individuals with dementia and their family and professional caregivers. She received her master's in human development and family studies in 2000 from the University of Missouri. Her thesis research focused on the factors that influence the quality of interpersonal relationships between nursing home residents and staff.

Robert E. Emery is Professor of Psychology and Director of the Center for Children, Families, and the Law at the University of Virginia. His research interests include families, family conflict, divorce, and associated legal issues.

Mark A. Fine is a Professor in the Department of Human Development and Family Studies at the University of Missouri–Columbia. He was Editor of *Family Relations* from 1993 to 1996 and is currently Editor of the *Journal of Social and Personal Relationships*. His research interests lie in the areas of family transitions, such as divorce and remarriage; early intervention program evaluation; social cognition; and relationship stability. He is coeditor, along with David Demo and Katherine Allen, of the *Handbook of Family Diversity*, published in 2000.

Deborah B. Gentry, EdD, CFLE, CFCS, is Professor of Family and Consumer Sciences and Associate Dean of the College of Applied Science and Technology at Illinois State University–Normal. An experienced educator and scholar of teaching and learning, she has presented and published on the scholarship of teaching and learning, family life education, and family conflict. She is the current editor of the *Journal of Teaching in Marriage and Family: Innovations in Family Science Education*. She has been a recipient of the Marvin Sussman Award, sponsored by the Groves Conference on Marriage and Family.

Michael A. Goodman, MS, is a doctoral student in marriage, family, and human development at Brigham Young University, with an emphasis on religion and family life. He has been a religious educator for 14 years.

Linda Citlali Halgunseth received her BA in psychology and Spanish at the University of Texas at Austin and her MS at the University of Missouri–Columbia.

Currently, she is a doctoral student in the Department of Human Development and Family Studies at the University of Missouri–Columbia. Her research has focused on parenting styles and child socialization among Latino families, and she has coauthored two chapters that have focused on child-rearing goals and parent-child interactions among Latino families. In the community, she coordinates bilingual after-school homework assistance programs for Latino children and parent-teacher organizations for Latino parents.

Jason D. Hans is a doctoral student in the Department of Human Development and Family Studies at the University of Missouri. His professional interests include divorce and stepfamilies, especially as they relate to family law, technology, and international families. Several of his articles have appeared in some of the top journals in family science, including *Family Relations* and the *Journal of Family Issues*. A former McNair Scholar, he has received numerous awards and honors, including recognition as the most outstanding graduate instructor at the University of Missouri. In 2002, he was awarded the National Council on Family Relations Outstanding Student Award in recognition of his high potential for contribution to the field of family studies.

Sheila Hawker, PhD, is a Senior Health Researcher at the University of Southampton. Her main research interests are formal and informal support networks and emotional labor. Recent projects have focused on elderly patients' discharge from the hospital and coping with outpatient chemotherapy. She is currently engaged on a project exploring the provision of palliative care for elderly people in U.K. community hospitals.

Robert Hughes, Jr., PhD, is Professor and Head of the Department of Human and Community Development at the University of Illinois at Urbana–Champaign. He has also held faculty appointments at The Ohio State University and the University of Missouri–Columbia. With the development of the World Wide Web, he became interested in the development of Web-based family life education models and e-learning professional development strategies for human service providers. He conducted his first e-mail-based course in 1995. Recently, he was one of the lead designers in the development of http://missourifamilies.org, a family life education Web site for family members.

Masako Ishii-Kuntz is Associate Professor of Sociology at the University of California, Riverside. Her current research examines Japanese advocacy groups for shared parenting between mothers and fathers. Her collaborative project also examines the impact of transnational family arrangements on Asian children who have been sent by their parents to live in the United States in order to attend school. Her comparative research on Asian American families and fatherhood in Japan and the United States has appeared in the *Journal of Marriage and the Family, Family Relations, Journal of Family Issues, Sociological Perspectives*, and other journals, and she has contributed a number of book chapters. She is currently completing a book on Japanese corporate fathers who are actively involved in child care and housework.

Angela D. James is currently an Assistant Professor of Sociology at the University of Southern California. She is also a Research Scientist at the University of California, Los Angeles, Center for Culture and Health in the Neuropsychiatric Institute. Her current research is focused on understanding changes and continuities in black marriage and family patterns, as well as on issues surrounding urban inequality. She has written articles examining a range of topics, including changing patterns of home ownership among blacks, occupational patterns among women, the impact of economic restructuring on marriage, mate availability and the impact of marital status on psychological well-being, racial classification, assortative patterns of marriage among African Americans, and interracial marriage.

Walter T. Kawamoto, PhD, CFLE, was the 1998–2000 Secretary/Treasurer/ Webmaster of the Ethnic Minority Section of the National Council on Family Relations. His graduate work included a study sponsored by the National Institute of Mental Health and conducted with the assistance of the Confederated Tribes of Siletz Indians of Oregon. He launched a course focusing on indigenous families in the spring of 2001. He was also a member of the American Indian–Alaska Native Head Start Research and Outcomes Assessment Consultant Panel.

Lawrence A. Kurdek is Professor of Psychology at Wright State University, Dayton, Ohio. He has conducted one of the few longitudinal studies on gay and lesbian couples. He has published over 100 scholarly publications and is currently a member of the Editorial Board for *Developmental Psychology, Journal of Marriage and Family, Journal of Family Psychology,* and *Personal Relationships.*

Leigh A. Leslie is an Associate Professor of Family Studies and Marriage and Family Therapy in the Department of Family Studies at the University of Maryland. Her research focuses on social support, gender issues in families, and interracial families. She has published over 30 articles and chapters and serves on the editorial boards of numerous scholarly journals.

Loren D. Marks, PhD, is an Assistant Professor of Family, Child, and Consumer Sciences in the School of Human Ecology at Louisiana State University. He has conducted extensive qualitative research with Christian, Jewish, and Muslim families examining the interface between religious beliefs, practices, and community and family relationships. He is currently studying the importance of religion in African American families.

Michele T. Martin completed her undergraduate studies at Michigan State University and a PhD in psychology at the University of Virginia. She is a clinical psychologist in private practice who frequently teaches at Wesleyan College in Macon, Georgia.

Mary Ann Mason, PhD, JD, is a Professor of Social Welfare and Dean of the Graduate Division at the University of California, Berkeley. She publishes and lectures nationally on child and family law, the history of the American family and of childhood, and public policy issues related to child custody, children's rights, and stepfamilies. Currently, she is directing a major research project on the impact of family formation on the career paths of academic women and men, titled "Do Babies Matter?"

Lori A. McGraw is a Research Associate in the Department of Human Development and Family Sciences at Oregon State University. She is the recipient of the 2002 Outstanding Contribution to Feminist Scholarship Award and was recognized as a top 20 finalist for the 2001 Rosabeth Moss Kanter Award for Excellence in Work-Family Research. Her research focuses on how larger social hierarchies shape women's unpaid family labor and their family relationships.

Steven Mintz is John and Rebecca Moores Professor of History at the University of Houston and Director of the American Cultures Program. An authority on the history of the family, he is currently completing a history of children and youth in America from the Revolution to the present. His books include *Domestic Revolutions: A Social History of American Family Life,* with Susan Kellogg.

Brad S. Moorefield is a doctoral student in the Department of Human Development and Family Studies at the University of North Carolina at Greensboro. His research interests include family diversity, financial management in remarried women, and couple identity, especially in gay and lesbian couples.

Goldie Morton has a master's degree in marriage and family therapy and is a doctoral candidate in family studies at the University of Maryland, with a focus on program development for children and families, as well as research on at-risk youth, specifically juvenile female offenders. She has spent the past 3 years as Coordinator and Clinician of a grant-funded elementary school-based program that provided individual and group counseling to at-risk children and their families. Currently, she serves as the Clinical Director at a Youth Service Bureau in southern Maryland.

Kay Pasley, EdD, is Professor of Human Development and Family Studies at the University of North Carolina at Greensboro. She has conducted a number of research studies on marital processes in families of divorce and remarriage. Since 1992, her research has also examined fathering identity and the conditions (e.g., co-parenting conflict) that affect the link between fathering identity and father involvement, including nonresident fathers. She has published three books, numerous book chapters, and over 50 research articles. She currently serves as Editor of *Family Relations,* published by the National Council on Family Relations.

Tara S. Peris is a doctoral student in clinical psychology at the University of Virginia. She received her BA from the University of California, Los Angeles, in 1997. Her research interests center on family conflict and related policy issues. She is particularly interested in how hostile and enmeshed family dynamics shape the course of child psychopathology.

Maureen Perry-Jenkins is an Associate Professor of Psychology at the University of Massachusetts Amherst and Past Director of the University of Massachusetts Center for the Family. She received her doctorate in human development and family studies from Pennsylvania State University. She has numerous publications in *Journal of Family Issues, Journal of Marriage and Family,* and *Journal of Family and Economic Issues* that explore work and family issues for working-class families. Her current research involves a 10-year, longitudinal study funded by the National Institute of Mental Health that examines the transition to parenthood and transition back to paid employment for working-class couples and for African American and European American single mothers. She is exploring how these multiple transitions are related to family members' well-being and relationships and what risk and resilience factors differentially shape how well family members cope.

Mark R. Rank is the Hadley Professor of Social Welfare in the George Warren Brown School of Social Work at Washington University, St. Louis, Missouri. His research has addressed various topics dealing with poverty, social welfare, and families. His recent work has estimated the probabilities of experiencing poverty across the American life course. In addition, he has been developing a new conceptual approach for understanding the nature and causes of American poverty.

Karen Ripoll is a doctoral student in the School of Family Studies at the University of Connecticut. She is originally from Colombia, South America. She holds a degree in psychology and a master's degree in education from universities in Colombia and a master's degree in marriage and family therapy from Syracuse University. Her research focuses on how family-of-origin experiences influence the cognitive orientations that adults bring to their intimate partnerships.

Roger H. Rubin, PhD, is Associate Professor of Family Studies and Acting Department Chair at the University of Maryland, College Park. He has published in the areas of interpersonal lifestyles, human sexuality, family policy, and African American family life. His research interests include how penal and religious policies affect the family. He has served as President of the Groves Conference on Marriage and Families, Vice-President for Public Policy of the National Council on Family Relations, and Public Member, Commission on Supervision, American Association for Marriage and Family Therapy. Currently, he is examining the relationships between diagnosed schizophrenics and their families.

Ronald M. Sabatelli is a Professor in the School of Family Studies at the University of Connecticut. He teaches courses dealing with family patterns of interaction and functioning and the patterns of adjustment and satisfaction found within adult intimate partnerships. His current research focuses primarily on how family-of-origin experiences influence the structure and experience of parenthood and adult intimate partnerships.

John Scanzoni is Professor of Sociology at the University of Florida. He has published widely in the realm of households (families, marriages, and relationships). He has been particularly interested in the consequences of shifts in broad societal trends (economic, political, gender, community) on the internal patterns and processes of households. His approach to diversity is to treat it as an opportunity for households of varied compositions to build mutually reinforcing linkages. His latest book is *Designing Families: The Search for Self and Community in the Information Age* (Pine Forge/Sage, 2000).

Judith A. Seltzer, Professor of Sociology at the University of California at Los Angeles, studies kinship institutions that are in flux, such as marriage and cohabitation in the contemporary United States, or divorced and nonmarital families, in which family membership and co-residence do not coincide. Her research also explores the effects of social policies on U.S. families, including child support, nonresident fathers' involvement with children, and joint legal custody.

Bahira Sherif-Trask is an Associate Professor of Individual and Family Studies at the University of Delaware. Her research focuses on work-family-gender issues, intergenerational relations, and culturally diverse families. She has conducted anthropological research in Germany, Austria, Egypt, Turkey, and the United States.

Saskia K. Subramanian is an Assistant Research Sociologist at the University of California, Los Angeles, Center for Culture and Health in the Neuropsychiatric Institute. She has participated in a variety of family studies, including an investigation of the effect of child abuse prevention programs on high-risk populations, an evaluation of community-based projects designed to stem unplanned teen pregnancy, and the 21-city Study of Families and Relationships. She has taught at UCLA, the University of Pennsylvania, St. Joseph's University, and Mt. St. Mary's College.

Jay Teachman is Professor and Chair of the Department of Sociology at Western Washington University. He is a Fellow of the National Council of Family Relations and received the Reuben Hill Award in 1982 for his research on childlessness. Currently, he is engaged in a long-term study of the effects of childhood living arrangements on early adult outcomes.

M. Belinda Tucker is a Professor of Psychiatry and Behavioral Sciences at the University of California, Los Angeles, and a member of the Center for Culture and Health in the Neuropsychiatric Institute. Tucker directed the 21-city Survey of Families and Relationships in 1995 and 2002 and co-directed the landmark National Survey of Black Americans in 1979. She has written extensively on changing patterns of family formation and personal relationships, including *The Decline of Marriage Among African Americans* (1995). She also serves on the Family Research Consortium's national faculty.

Elizabeth Turner is a graduate student in clinical psychology at the University of Massachusetts Amherst. Her research interests include (a) the relationship between marital quality and aspects of infant and child development and (b) early sibling relationships.

Alexis J. Walker holds the Jo Anne Leonard Petersen Chair in Gerontology and Family Studies at Oregon State University, where she is Professor of Human

Development and Family Sciences. Her research is focused on the influence of gender and generation on family relationships. She is the author of more than three dozen scholarly publications and is a Fellow of both the Gerontological Society of America and the National Council on Family Relations. She is the editor of *Journal of Marriage and Family*.

Susan Walzer is Associate Professor of Sociology and Chair of the Department of Sociology, Anthropology, and Social Work at Skidmore College and was formerly a clinician. Her research and teaching interests include the sociology of families and gender as well as social psychology. She is the author of *Thinking About the Baby: Gender and Transitions Into Parenthood* (1998) as well as a number of articles about family changes and interactions.